# Principles Corporate Finance

RICHARD **BREALEY**

STEWART **MYERS**

GRAHAM **PARTINGTON**

DAVID **ROBINSON**

*The McGraw-Hill Companies, Inc.*

Sydney  New York  San Francisco  Auckland
Bangkok  Bogotá  Caracas  Hong Kong
Kuala Lumpur  Lisbon  London  Madrid
Mexico City  Milan  New Delhi  San Juan
Seoul  Singapore  Taipei  Toronto

# McGraw·Hill Australia

### A Division of The McGraw·Hill Companies

**National Library of Australia Cataloguing-in-Publication data:**

Principles of corporate finance.

1st Australian ed.
Includes index.
ISBN 0 074 70107 X.

1. Corporations—Finance. I. Brealey, Richard A.

658.15

Published in Australia by
**McGraw-Hill Book Company Australia Pty Limited**
**4 Barcoo Street, Roseville NSW 2069, Australia**
Acquisitions Editor: Karolina Kocalevski
Production Supervisor: Joanna Munnelly
Editor: Caroline Hunter, Burrumundi Partnership
Designer: Vivien Valk
Typesetter: Post Pre-Press Group
Proofreader: Tim Learner
Indexer: Puddingburn Publishing Services
Printed by Everbest Printing Co. LTD.

# brief contents

# contents

# preface

This book describes the theory and practice of corporate finance. We hardly need to explain why financial managers should master the practical aspect of their job, but a word on the role of theory may be helpful.

Managers learn from experience how to cope with routine problems. But the best managers are also able to respond rationally to change. To do this you need more than time-honoured rules of thumb; you must understand why companies and financial managers behave the way they do. In other words, you need a theory of corporate finance.

Does that sound intimidating? It shouldn't. Good theory helps you understand what is going on in the world around you. It helps you ask the right questions when times change and new problems must be analysed. It also tells you what things you do not need to worry about.

Throughout the book we show how to use financial theory to solve practical problems and also to illuminate the facts and institutional material that students of corporate finance must absorb.

Of course, the theory presented in this book is not perfect and complete—no theory is. There are some famous controversies in which financial economists cannot agree on what firms ought to do. We have not glossed over these controversies. We set out the main arguments for each side and tell you where we stand.

There are also a few cases where theory indicates that the practical rules of thumb employed by today's managers are leading to poor decisions. Where financial managers appear to be making mistakes, we say so, while admitting that there may be hidden reasons for their actions. In brief, we have tried to be fair but to pull no punches.

Once understood, good theory is common sense. Therefore, we have tried to present it at a commonsense level. We have avoided abstract proofs and heavy mathematics. However, parts of the book may require a significant intellectual effort for those unused to economic reasoning. We have marked the most difficult sections with asterisks, and suggest that you skim these sections on the first reading.

# A word about learning aids

There are no ironclad prerequisites for reading this book except algebra and the English language. An elementary knowledge of accounting, statistics and microeconomics is helpful, however.

Each chapter of the book closes with a summary, an annotated list of suggestions for further reading, a review quiz and some more challenging questions and problems. Answers to the quiz questions may be found on the publisher's Web site at *http://www.mcgraw-hill.com.au/mhhe/fin/brealey/homepage*, along with present value tables and a glossary.

A student Web page is being prepared to accompany this book. This Web page will contain additional illustrations, problems and other useful material. McGraw-Hill will also make available a computer software package that uses Excel templates to undertake a variety of financial calculations. These programs can be used to solve a variety of practical finance problems; alternatively, they can be used as a learning aid so that you can work through problems one step at a time.

For teachers who are using the book there is a Web page, an Instructor's Manual, a Test Bank with multiple choice and true/false questions, and a set of PowerPoint slides.

We should mention two matters of style now to prevent confusion later. First, you will notice that the most important financial terms are set in bold-face type the first time they appear. Definitions for such terms appear in the glossary. Second, most algebraic symbols representing dollar values are set in capital letters. Other symbols are lower case letters. Thus, the symbol for a dividend payment is DIV; the symbol for a percentage rate of return is $r$. We hope this will make our algebra easier to follow.

# Significant changes in the Australian edition

Reflecting the differences between the Australian and American capital markets and tax regimes, many chapters have been substantially rewritten. The effects of Australian regulatory, legal and tax systems are integrated throughout the book. Extensive use is made of Australian examples, data and terminology. But we have avoided xenophobic replacement of all non-Australian examples. The first criteria in choice of examples has been how well the example illustrates the point under discussion, and whether it is backed up by further reading, preferably in an academic journal. Overseas examples have also been retained because finance is an international discipline. Surveys by the authors have shown that this international dimension is valued by a majority of students, and particularly appeals to overseas students. Reference to Australian finance research has also been added throughout the text.

As well as Australianisation, there are some extensions to the original Brealey and Myers textbook. The cash flow identity is introduced in Chapter 1 as a means to integrate dividend, investment and financing decisions. More extensive coverage of the mathematics of finance and different approaches to DCF valuation can now be found in Chapter 3 and in an appendix to Chapter 4. Chapter 6 now stresses the consistency principle, alerts students to the need to consider imputation credits in project evaluation, and suggests one way this can be handled. The chapter also suggests an alternative to the traditional equivalent annual cost calculations.

The CML, SML and a proof of the CAPM are included in Chapter 8, and the discussion and references are updated to reflect more recent challenges to the CAPM. The use of MVA and EVA as performance measures are introduced in Chapters 10 and 12.

Recent changes in Australian corporate law regarding venture capital, the issuance of equity and debt securities, and corporate governance requirements, have been incorporated throughout Chapters 14 and 15. Chapters 16 to 19 contain extensive discussions of the effects of the imputation tax system on dividend policy, debt policy and investment evaluation. Options and other derivative securities are discussed in Chapters 20, 21, 22 and 25, and include applications involving derivatives traded at both the Australian Options Market and the Sydney Futures Exchange.

Australian debt markets differ from many other world debt markets in both the type and maturity of debt securities on issue. Such differences are explored in Chapters 23, 24, 26 and 32. Australian examples include securitised debt instruments, factoring, infrastructure bonds, and legal and taxation issues associated with financial leases. In Chapter 27, students are taken through the analysis of financial reports using an example from the major Australian company Brambles Industries Ltd. Chapter 34 highlights trading activity in the Australian dollar, and transaction, economic and translation exposures confronted by Australian firms trading internationally.

# Acknowledgments

We have a long list of people to thank for their assistance and helpful criticism of earlier editions or drafts of this edition: George Aragon (Boston College), W. Brian Barrett (University of Miami), Zvi Bodie (Boston University), Cynthia J. Campbell (Washington University, St. Louis), Ian Cooper (London Business School), Jerome L. Duncan, Jr. (Memphis State University), Frank Fabozzi (Massachusetts Institute of Technology), Alan E. Grunewald (Michigan State University), Manak C. Gupta (Temple University), Delvin D. Hawley (University of Mississippi), Leo Herzel (Mayer, Brown & Platt), Costas Kaplanis (Salomon Brothers), Evi Kaplanis (London Business School), William Kistler (Long Island University), Arnold Langs (California State University, Hayward), Dennis E. Logue (Dartmouth College), Thomas E. McCue (Duquesne University), William A. McCullough (University of Florida), John A. MacDonald (State University of New York, Albany), Saman Majd (Salomon Brothers), Surendra Mansinghka (San Francisco State University), Roger Mesznik (Baruch College), Lisa Meulbroek (MIT), Patrick Regan (BEA Associates), Scott Richard (Goldman Sachs), Richard Ruback (Harvard Business School), Bruce L. Rubin (Old Dominion University), Richard Shepro (Mayer, Brown & Platt), Bernard Shinkel (Wayne State University), Gordon Sick (University of Alberta), Lakshme Shyam Sunder (Dartmouth College), Richard J. Sweeney (Claremont McKenna College), Steven Thomas (MIT), Michael Whinihan (Ohio State University) and Thomas S. Zorn (University of Nebraska, Lincoln).

In relation to the Australian edition, particular thanks are due to: Mark Freeman, Max Stevenson and V. T. Alaganar (University of Technology Sydney), Marie Kanios (Datastream), Rex Zeeman and Kymberlee Simpson (University of Southern Queensland), Kevin Davis and Kim Sawyer (University of Melbourne), Joan Berkery-Coleman (Colonial Ltd) and Peter O'Reilly (ANZ Investment Bank).

We are also grateful to the following reviewers: Hamish Anderson (Massey University), Peter Andrews (UNSW), Susan Campbell (RMIT), Alex Clarke (University of Western Australia), Eileen Dunkley (James Cook University, Cairns Campus), Colin Dolley (Edith Cowan University), Alex Fino (University of Sydney), Terry Hallahan (RMIT), Lyndon Lyons (Griffith University, Nathan Campus), Peter Mayall (Curtin University of Technology), Jack Nightingale (Deakin University, Burwood Campus), John Polichronis (Queensland University of Technology, Gardens Point Campus), Andrew Prevost (Massey University), James A. Reiss (La Trobe University, Bundoora Campus), Graeme Robson (Sharyn Long Chartered Accountants), Julia Sawicki (University of Queensland), Rodney Sweet (Edith Cowan University), Subhrendu Rah (Curtin University of Technology), Russell Vinning (Deakin

University, Burwood Campus), Peter Wheelan (Queensland University of Technology, Gardens Point Campus), Brett Wheldon (University of Western Sydney, Hawkesbury Campus) and Ivan Woods (Melbourne Business School, University of Melbourne)

We extend special thanks to the editors and production staff at McGraw-Hill, particularly Julie McNab, Karolina Kocalevski, Jo Munnelly and Caroline Hunter.

This list is almost surely incomplete. We know how much we owe to our colleagues at the London Business School, MIT's Sloan School of Management, the UTS School of Finance and Economics and both the Faculty of Commerce at The University of Southern Queensland and The University of Melbourne Department of Accounting and Finance. In many cases, the ideas that appear in this book are as much theirs as ours.

Finally, we record the thanks due to our wives, Diana, Maureen, Gwenda and Carmel, who have been long suffering as we worked on 'the book'. The Australian authors also want to thank their children, Rhiannon, Christopher and Matthew, for their understanding when their dads were 'busy'.

*Richard A. Brealey*
*Stewart C. Myers*
*Graham H. Partington*
*David M. Robinson*

**How the book was made**     The Australian edition began when one of the authors was on sabbatical at the University of Wales (Bangor). He worked in a room with leadlight windows and a flagstone floor in an old, but charming, stone tower.

In a tower of ancient sandstone
With antique flagstones laid
Leadlighted gloom suffused the room
And so the book was made.

# part 1

## VALUE

# chapter 1

# WHY FINANCE MATTERS

This book is about financial decisions by corporations. We should start by saying what these decisions are and why they are important. The tasks of the financial manager boil down to decisions about spending money and decisions about raising money.

To carry on business a modern company needs an almost endless variety of real assets. Many of them are tangible assets, such as machinery, factories and offices; others are intangible, such as technical expertise, quality of management and workforce, trademarks and patents. All of them, unfortunately, need to be paid for. To obtain the necessary money the company sells pieces of paper called **financial assets** or securities. These pieces of paper have value because they are claims on the company's real assets. Financial assets include not only shares but also bonds, bank loans, lease obligations, and so on.

The financial manager faces two basic problems. First, how much should the company invest and what specific assets should the company invest in? Second, how should the cash required for investment be raised? The answer to the first question is the company's **investment**, or **capital budgeting, decision**. The answer to the second is its **financing decision**. Once the company is operating a third question arises: How much cash should be distributed to shareholders? The answer to this question is the company's **dividend decision**. The task of the financial manager is to seek answers to these questions that will make the company's shareholders as well off as possible.

Success is usually judged by value. Shareholders are made better off by any decision that increases the value of their stake in the company. Thus, you might say that a good investment decision is one that results in the purchase of a real asset that is worth more than it costs—an asset that makes a net contribution to value. The secret of success in financial management is to increase value. That is a simple statement, but not a very helpful one. It is like advising an investor in the share market to 'buy low, sell high'. The problem is how to do it.

There may be a few activities in which one can read a textbook and then 'do it', but financial management is not one of them. That is why finance is worth studying. Who wants to work in a field where there is no room for experience, creativity, judgement and a pinch of luck? Although this book cannot supply these items, it does present the concepts and information on which good financial decisions are based.

It is often tempting to skip the introductory chapter, particularly if you have studied finance before. Rather than giving in to this temptation, we strongly suggest that you read the section on how investment, financing and dividend decisions are linked.

## 1.1 The role of the financial manager

The financial manager stands between the company's operations and financial markets, where the company's securities are traded. These financial markets can be broadly divided into capital markets—where long-term finance is raised—and money markets—where short-term finance is raised. The financial manager's role is shown in Figure 1.1, which traces the flow of cash from investors to the company and back to investors again. The flow starts when securities are issued to raise cash (arrow 1 in the figure). The cash is used to purchase real assets used in the company's operations (arrow 2). (You can think of the company's operations as a bundle of real assets.) Later, if the company does well, the real assets generate cash inflows that more than repay the initial investment (arrow 3). Finally, the cash is either reinvested (arrow 4a) or returned to the

**figure 1.1** _____

Flow of cash between financial markets and the firm's operations. Key: (1) Cash raised by selling financial assets to investors; (2) cash invested in the firm's operations and used to purchase real assets; (3) cash generated by the firm's operations; (4a) cash reinvested; (4b) cash returned to investors; (5) tax payments to the government.

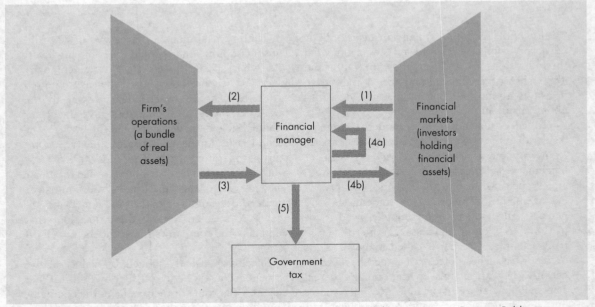

_Source_: Adapted from S. C. Myers (ed.), _Modern Developments in Financial Management_, Praeger Publications, New York, Fig. 1, p. 5.

investors who purchased the original security issue (arrow 4b). Of course, the choice between arrows 4a and 4b is not a completely free one. For example, if a bank lends the company money at stage 1, the bank has to be repaid this money plus interest at stage 4b. Some of the money also leaks out of this system in the form of tax payments to government (arrow 5). Financial managers spend considerable time working out ways to minimise leakage down arrow 5.

# How investment, financing and dividend decisions are linked

As suggested by Figure 1.1, investment, financing and dividend decisions are linked by the flow of cash through the business. This relationship can be expressed in the cash flow identity, which can be written as:

$$\text{Uses of cash} = \text{sources of cash}$$

The main uses of cash are payments for new investments and payment of dividends. The main sources of cash are a positive net cash flow from the company's operating activities, increased borrowings and occasionally a share issue. In this case the cash flow identity can be written as:

$$\frac{\text{Increase in}}{\text{investment}} + \text{dividends} = \frac{\text{cash from}}{\text{operations}} + \frac{\text{increase}}{\text{in debt}} + \frac{\text{proceeds of}}{\text{equity issues}}$$

We should note that although the above relationship is usual, there are other possibilities. Companies sometimes reduce their investment by selling off assets. This reduction in investment is then a source of cash to the business. After the 1987 share market crash many Australian companies embarked on debt reduction programs. Paying off debt represented a use of cash to those companies. Also, companies may experience a negative cash flow from operations, particularly during the start-up phase of a major project. Of course, this is only a temporary phenomenon; companies that are never expected to generate positive operating cash flows soon cease to exist! However, let us not get bogged down in detail, but instead turn our attention to the major lessons that we can learn from the cash flow identity.

The cash flow identity shows that there are four major financial decisions potentially under management's control.[1] These are the investment decision, the dividend decision, the decision on debt levels and the decision on new equity issues. The latter two decisions constitute the financing decision. Note that the level of cash flow from operations is not directly under management's control. Among other factors, cash flow from operations depends on competition in the market for the company's products.

Although management can apparently make decisions in four areas, their freedom of choice is really restricted to a maximum of three out of those four areas. To see why, consider the following example. A company has a net operating cash flow of $50 million. Management decides to make a $45 million investment, pay dividends of $30 million, raise an additional $10 million of debt and make no share issue. As shown below, this is not feasible. There is a $15 million shortfall.

$$\frac{\text{Investment}}{\$45M} + \frac{\text{dividend}}{\$30M} = \frac{\text{operating cash flow}}{\$50M} + \frac{\text{debt increase}}{\$10M} + \frac{\text{equity issue}}{\$0M}$$

$$\$75M > \$60M$$

---

[1] Earlier we mentioned three main financial decisions: the investment, financing and dividend decisions. We now have four decisions to make because we have subdivided the financing decision into the decision to issue debt and the decision to issue shares.

Management must either reduce the planned investment and/or dividends, raise more debt or make a share issue. The question is which? In practice management will usually increase the quantity of debt issued, in this case from $10 million to $25 million. Thus, management is able to make three decisions independently of each other—in this example, the level of investment, the level of dividends and the level of share issues, but this leaves no choice in regard to the fourth decision. The quantity of debt issued is determined as a residual.

Although the use of debt to balance the cash flow identity is a common practice, this will not always be the case. An important task of the financial manager therefore is to determine an order of importance for the four financial decision areas, determining which decisions will be taken independently and which will be residual. An important message of this book is that the investment decision is invariably the critical decision and should usually take priority over the other decisions.

The cash flow identity also highlights the close linkage between the financing decision and the dividend decision. If a firm has a policy of paying low dividends this will reduce the need for external financing. Conversely, higher dividends can be financed from cash raised by debt issues or share issues.[2]

## Understanding value and capital markets

Figure 1.1 shows that the financial manager has to deal with capital markets as well as the company's operations. Therefore, the financial manager must understand how capital markets work.

The financing decision always reflects some theory about capital markets. For example, suppose a company has chosen to finance a major expansion program by issuing corporate bonds. The financial manager must have considered the terms of the issue and concluded that it was fairly priced. That requires a theory of how corporate debt is priced. The financial manager must also have asked whether the company's shareholders would be made better off or worse off by the extra debt standing between them and the company's real assets. That requires a theory of how corporate borrowing affects the value of the company's shares.

The investment decision cannot be separated from capital markets either. A company which acts in its shareholders' interest should accept those investments which increase the value of their stake in the company. But that requires a theory of how ordinary shares (also called common stocks in the United States) are valued.

Understanding how capital markets work amounts to understanding how financial assets are valued. This is a subject on which there has been remarkable progress over the past 30 years. New theories have been developed to explain the prices of bonds and shares. When put to the test, these theories have worked quite well. We therefore devote a large part of this book to explaining these ideas and their implications.

Financial managers in Australia should be particularly aware of the importance of international capital markets. As a relatively small economy with substantial natural resources to develop, and a shortfall in domestic savings, Australia has traditionally been an importer of capital. Australian companies raise billions of dollars in overseas capital markets and foreign investors make large investments in the Australian capital market. Because of this Australian financial managers have to be aware of changes in international interest rates and changes in the exchange rate for the Australian dollar. These changes can affect the cost of funds in both overseas and domestic markets. The viability of investments is also affected. Changes in exchange rates can make or break natural resource projects because of effects on the project's expenses and revenue.

Financial managers also need to be aware that many securities trade infrequently in the Australian capital market. For example, if you buy company debentures when they are first issued and later decide to sell them, you will find that the resale is not easy to accomplish.[3]

---

2   Dividends cannot be financed without limit. There is a legal requirement that total dividends paid may not usually exceed the total of the current accounting profit plus any credit balance in the retained profit account.

3   Some pundits suggest that an active corporate bond market will develop over the next decade. We shall have to wait and see.

Similarly, some shares in the smaller companies listed on the Australian Stock Exchange (ASX) may not trade for weeks, or in some cases months, at a time. This thin trading has some important consequences. In this book we exhort you to trust market prices, but we do not mean you to do so if you are looking at stale prices associated with thinly traded assets. If the prices do not represent recent trades, then all information using that price data, such as dividend yields, earnings yields and market indices, should be interpreted with caution. Standard methods for pricing shares, bonds and other assets may not work so well if they are subject to thin trading.

## Time and uncertainty

The financial manager cannot avoid coping with time and uncertainty. Companies often have the opportunity to invest in assets that cannot pay their way in the short run and which expose the firm and its shareholders to considerable risk. The investment, if undertaken, may have to be financed by debt that cannot be fully repaid for many years. The firm cannot walk away from such choices—someone has to decide whether the opportunity is worth more than it costs and whether the additional debt burden can be safely borne. The decision boils down to answering two questions. Does the return offered by the investment compensate for the wait you endure until the cash flows back in? And does that return also compensate for the risk you bear while you are waiting?

## Financial objectives in complex organisations

Most of the time we assume that the financial manager acts to increase the value of the shareholders' investment in the firm. But thousands of people are involved in a large company. Each attends to his or her personal interests as well as to the shareholders'.

Think of the company's net revenue as a pie that is divided among a number of claimants. These include the management and the workforce, as well as the lenders and shareholders who have put up the money to establish and maintain the business. The government is a claimant too, since it gets to tax the profits of the enterprise. Suppliers and customers also have a stake in the business and may have claims on revenue. Customers, for example, expect warranties to be honoured and may require after-sales service for products they have purchased.

Of course, the objectives of these different parties do not always coincide and conflicts of interest can arise. These conflicts are often labelled agency problems. This is because one person— the principal—has to entrust an interest or asset to another person—the agent—who acts on his/her behalf. Shareholders, for example, have to entrust their cash to the company's managers.

All the company's claimants are bound together in a complex web of contracts and understandings. For example, when banks lend money to the company, they insist on a formal contract stating the rate of interest and the repayment dates, perhaps placing restrictions on dividends or additional borrowing and so on. However, you cannot devise written rules to cover every possible future event. So the written contracts are supplemented by understandings. For example, managers understand that in return for a fat salary they are expected to work hard and not to snaffle part of the pie for unwarranted personal luxuries.

What enforces this understanding? Is it realistic to expect financial managers always to act on behalf of the shareholders? The shareholders cannot spend their lives watching through binoculars to check that managers are not shirking.

A closer look reveals institutional arrangements that help align managers' and shareholders' interests. Here are three examples:

1. Managers are subject to the scrutiny of specialists. Their actions are monitored by the board of directors. Managers are also reviewed by banks, which keep an eagle eye on the progress of firms receiving their loans. Companies' financial performance is also closely monitored by a small army of financial analysts working in stockbroking firms and financial institutions.

2. Managers are spurred on by incentive schemes, such as share options, which pay off big if shareholders gain but are valueless if they do not.
3. Finally, shirkers are likely to find that they are ousted by more energetic managers. This competition may arise within the company, but poorly performing companies are also more likely to be taken over. That sort of takeover typically brings in a fresh management team.

We do not want to leave the impression that corporate life is a series of squabbles. It is not, because practical corporate finance has evolved to reconcile personal and corporate interests—to keep everyone working together to increase the value of the whole pie, not merely the size of each person's slice.

Nevertheless, the financial manager must stay alert to potential problems caused by conflicts of interest. We, too, have to think about potential conflicts in order to fully understand, for example, why takeovers occur, why lending contracts restrict dividend payouts, or why companies sometimes prefer to issue debt that investors can convert to shares.

## Understanding the value of information

Information is an unusual commodity. In financial markets, the right information can be worth millions—but only if other investors do not have the same information at the same time. To paraphrase Oscar Wilde, nearly all great private fortunes are built upon private information. The fortunes of some well-known merchant banks were founded on the early use of superior information technology. Carrier pigeons were used to bring the first news of Wellington's victory over Napoleon at the battle of Waterloo. This is reputed to have been the source of large trading profits in the market for British government bonds. Nowadays, as soon as important financial information leaks out, it travels instantly along various electronic pathways to major financial centres such as New York and London and to other smaller financial centres such as Sydney, Melbourne and Auckland.

Companies spend considerable time and money providing information to investors. If they did not do so, investors' suspicions would be aroused; they would have to try to collect the information for themselves; and they would not be willing to pay as much for the company's shares.

Words are cheap. Should investors trust the information given out by companies? Sometimes the information is certified by a firm of accountants or investment bankers, who put their reputation on the line when they endorse a company's report. Sometimes managers send a message of confidence by 'putting their money where their mouth is'. For example, you will find it easier to raise money for a new business if you can show the bank that you are investing a large fraction of your own net worth in the venture.

Many financial decisions take on extra importance because they signal information to investors. For example, the decision to reduce the cash dividends paid out to shareholders usually signals trouble for the company. The share price may fall sharply when the dividend cut is announced, not because of the dividend cut per se, but because the cut brings bad tidings for the future.

## 1.2 Who is the financial manager?

In this book we will use the term *financial manager* to refer to anyone responsible for a significant corporate investment or financing decision. Except in the smallest firms, no *single* person is responsible for all the decisions discussed in this book. Responsibility is dispersed throughout the company. Top management, of course, is continuously involved in financial decisions, but many others are also involved. For example, the engineer who designs a new production facility is involved. The design determines the kind of real asset the company will hold. The advertising manager and the marketing manager also make investment decisions, such as initiating a major advertising campaign. The campaign is an investment in an intangible asset that will pay off in future sales and earnings.

Nevertheless, there are managers who specialise in finance. The **corporate treasurer** is usually the person most directly responsible for obtaining financing, managing the company's cash account and arranging foreign currency transactions. The treasurer typically has responsibility for establishing and maintaining a good corporate relationship with suppliers of finance, such as banks and other financial institutions. The treasurer also makes sure that the company meets its obligations to those investors holding the company's securities, for example paying interest when it is due. In some companies, financial risk management is an important task for the treasurer. This involves protecting the company from the adverse effects of interest rate and exchange rate changes. Typical responsibilities of the treasurer are listed in the left-hand column of Table 1.1.

**table 1.1**

Some typical responsibilities of the treasurer and controller

| Treasurer | Controller |
|---|---|
| Banking relationships | Accounting |
| Cash management | Preparation of financial statements |
| Obtaining finance | Internal auditing |
| Dividend disbursement | Payroll |
| Financial risk management | Preparing budgets |
| Foreign currency transactions | Taxes |

*Note: This table is not an exhaustive list of tasks treasurers and controllers may undertake.*

In larger corporations you are likely to find both a treasurer and chief accountant or **controller**. The right-hand column of Table 1.1 lists the typical controller's responsibilities. Notice that there is a conceptual difference between the two jobs. The treasurer's function is primarily custodial—he or she obtains and manages the company's capital. By contrast, the controller's function is primarily one of inspecting to see that the money is used efficiently. The controller manages budgeting, accounting and auditing. In smaller firms the treasurer and controller's tasks may be undertaken by one individual.

The largest firms usually appoint a **chief financial officer** (**CFO**) to oversee both the treasurer and the controller's work. The CFO is deeply involved in financial policy making and corporate planning. Often he or she will have general managerial responsibilities beyond strictly financial issues.

Major capital investment projects are so closely tied to plans for product development, production and marketing that managers from these areas are inevitably drawn into planning and analysing the projects. If the firm has staff members specialising in corporate planning, they are naturally involved in capital budgeting too. Usually the treasurer, controller or CFO is responsible for organising and supervising the capital budgeting process.

Because of the importance of many financial issues, ultimate decisions often rest by law or by custom with the board of directors.[4] For example, only the board has the legal power to recommend a dividend or to sanction a public issue of securities. Boards usually delegate decision-making authority for small- or medium-sized investment outlays, but the authority to approve large investments is almost never delegated.

---

4   Often the firm's chief financial officer is also a member of its board of directors.

## 1.3 Topics covered in this book

This book covers investment decisions first, then financing decisions including the dividend decision, and finally a series of topics in which investment and financing decisions interact and cannot be made separately.

In Parts One, Two and Three we look at different aspects of the investment decision. The first is the problem of how to value assets, the second is the link between risk and value, and the third is the management of the investment process. Our discussion of these topics occupies Chapters 2 through to 12.

Eleven chapters devoted to the simple problem of 'finding real assets that are worth more than they cost' may seem excessive, but that problem is not so simple in practice. We will require a theory of how long-lived, risky assets are valued and that requirement will lead us to basic questions about capital markets. For example:

▮  How are corporate bonds and shares valued in capital markets?
▮  What risks are borne by investors in corporate securities? How can these risks be measured?
▮  What compensation do investors demand for bearing risk?
▮  What rate of return can investors in ordinary shares reasonably expect to receive?

Intelligent capital budgeting and financing decisions require answers to these and other questions about how capital markets work.

Financing decisions occupy Parts Four to Seven. We begin in Chapter 13 with another basic question about capital markets: Do security prices reflect the fair value of the underlying assets? This question is crucially important because the financial manager must know whether securities can be issued at a fair price. The remaining chapters in Part Four describe the kinds of securities corporations use to raise money and explain how and when they are issued.

Parts Five, Six and Seven continue the analysis of the financing decision, covering dividend policy, debt policy, risk management and the alternative forms of debt. Literally dozens of different financing instruments are described and analysed, including debentures, convertibles, leases, eurobonds, financial futures and many other exotic beasts. We also describe what happens when companies find themselves in financial distress because of poor operating performance, excessive borrowing, or both. Furthermore, we show how financing considerations sometimes affect capital budgeting decisions.

Part Eight covers financial planning. Decisions about investment, dividend policy, debt policy and other financial issues cannot be reached independently. They have to add up to a sensible overall financial plan for the firm, one that increases the value of the shareholders' investment yet still retains enough flexibility for the firm to avoid financial distress and to pursue unexpected new opportunities.

Part Nine is devoted to decisions about the firm's short-term assets and liabilities. There are separate chapters on three topics: channels for short-term borrowing or investment; management of liquid assets (cash and marketable securities); and management of accounts receivable (money lent by the firm to its customers).

Part Ten covers two important problems that require decisions about both investment and financing. First, we look at mergers and acquisitions, then we consider international financial management. All the financial problems of doing business at home are present overseas, but the international financial manager faces the additional complications created by multiple currencies, different tax systems and special regulations imposed by foreign institutions and governments.

Part Eleven is our conclusion. It also discusses some of the things that we *do not* know about finance. If you can be the first to solve any of these puzzles, you will be justifiably famous.

## 1.4 Summary

In Chapter 2 we will begin with the most basic concepts of asset valuation. However, let us first sum up the principal points made in this introductory chapter.

The overall task of financial management can be broken down into (1) the investment, or capital budgeting, decision, (2) the financing decision and (3) the dividend decision, which is closely related to the financing decision. In other words, the firm has to decide (1) how much to invest and what assets to invest in, (2) how to raise the necessary cash and (3) how much cash to distribute to shareholders as a dividend. These decisions are linked together by the cash flow identity. In making the decisions the objective is to increase the value of the shareholders' stake in the firm.

We pointed out three reasons why the financial manager has a challenging and interesting job:

▪ He or she acts as the intermediary between the firm and capital markets. Good financial managers must understand how capital markets work and how long-lived, risky assets are valued. They must also be aware of what is going on in international capital markets as well as in their own domestic market.

▪ Managers, shareholders and lenders would all like to see the value of the company increase. Each group would also like to grab a larger proportion of that value for itself. The financial manager has to be alert to conflicts of interest and must act to resolve them.

▪ The prices of shares and bonds depend on the information available to investors. The financial manager must pay attention to how investors will interpret the company's actions. He or she must tell the company's story convincingly to the capital markets and will often find that actions speak louder than words.

In small companies there is often only one financial executive. However, the larger corporation usually has both a treasurer and a controller. The treasurer's job is to obtain and manage the company's financing. By contrast, the controller's job is one of inspecting to see that the money is used correctly. In large companies there may also be a finance director, or financial vice-president, who acts as the firm's chief financial officer.

Of course, all managers, not just finance specialists, face financial problems. In this book we will use the term *financial manager* to refer to any person confronted with a corporate financing or investment decision.

### FURTHER READING

The classic paper that analyses the potential conflicts of interest between managers and owners is:

M. Jensen and W. Meckling, 'Theory of the Firm, Managerial Behaviour, Agency Costs and Ownership Structure', *Journal of Financial Economics*, pp. 306–460 (October 1976).

Below and in subsequent chapters you will find some quiz questions. You can use these questions to test your knowledge, and using the solutions given in the 'Answers to quizzes' section on the publisher's Web site at *http://www.mcgraw-hill.com.au/mhhe/fin/brealey/homepage.htm*, you can use the quizzes as worked examples of material covered in the chapters.

## QUIZ

**1.** Read the following passage: 'Companies usually buy (a) assets. These include both tangible assets such as (b) and intangible assets such as (c). The decision regarding which assets to buy is usually termed the (d) or (e) decision. The decision regarding how to raise the money is usually termed the (f) decision.' Now fit each of the following terms into the most appropriate space: *financing, real, investment, executive aeroplanes, capital budgeting, brand names.*

**2.** Which of the following statements more accurately describes the treasurer rather than the controller?
  a.  Likely to be the only financial executive in small firms.
  b.  Monitors capital expenditures to make sure that they are not misappropriated.
  c.  Responsible for investing the firm's spare cash.
  d.  Responsible for arranging any issue of ordinary shares.
  e.  Responsible for the company's tax affairs.

**3.** Which of the following are real assets, and which are financial?
  a.  A share.
  b.  A personal IOU.
  c.  A truck.
  d.  Undeveloped land.
  e.  The balance in the firm's cheque account.
  f.  An experienced and hardworking sales force.
  g.  A corporate bond.

## QUESTIONS AND PROBLEMS

**1.** Imagine that the year is 1815 and that you are a trader in British government consols (consolidated war loan—a perpetual security). It is the morning of Monday 19 June, the day after the battle of Waterloo. The British were the victors, but the battle was not decided until about nine in the evening. You believe that currently you are the only trader who knows the outcome of the battle. Would you be buying or selling consols? Explain your answer.

**2.** A company plans to invest $64 million, borrow $30 million, issue $50 million in shares and pay a $10 million dividend. Assume that the company has a net operating cash flow of $25 million. Also assume that the investment is profitable and that the company could issue the planned levels of debt and equity. Does the plan appear feasible? Is it sensible? What are the alternatives? How would you judge which alternative is best?

# chapter 2

# PRESENT VALUE AND THE OPPORTUNITY COST OF CAPITAL

Companies invest in a variety of real assets. These include tangible assets such as plant and machinery and intangible assets such as management contracts, patents and trademarks. The object of the investment, or capital budgeting, decision is to find real assets that are worth more than they cost. In this chapter we will show what this objective means in a country with extensive and well-functioning capital markets. At the same time we will take the first, most basic steps towards understanding how assets are valued. It turns out that if there is a good active market for an asset, its value is exactly the same as the market price.

There are a few cases in which it is not that difficult to estimate asset values. In real estate, for example, you can hire a professional valuer to do it for you. Suppose you own an apartment building. The odds are that your valuer's estimate of its value will be within a few per cent of what the building would actually sell for.[1] After all, there is continuous activity in the real estate market, and the valuer's stock-in-trade is knowledge of the prices at which similar properties have recently changed hands.

Thus, the problem of valuing real estate is simplified by the existence of an active market in which all kinds of properties are bought and sold. For many purposes no formal theory of value is needed. We can take the market's word for it.

But we have to go deeper than that. First, it is important to know how asset values are reached in an active market. Even if you can take the valuer's word for it, it is important to understand

---

[1] Needless to say, there are some kinds of properties that valuers find really difficult to value—for example, nobody knows the potential selling price of the Taj Mahal, the Opera House or Windsor Castle. If you own such a place, we congratulate you.

*why* that apartment building is worth say $250 000 and not a higher or lower figure. Second, the market for most corporate assets is pretty thin. Look in the advertisements in the *Australian Financial Review*: it is not often that you see a blast furnace for sale.

Companies are always searching for assets that are worth more to them than to others. That apartment block is worth more to you if you can manage it better than others can. But in that case, looking at the price of similar buildings will not tell you what your apartment block is worth under your management. You need to know how asset prices are determined. In other words, you need a theory of value.

We start to build that theory in this chapter. We will stick to the simplest problems and examples so that the basic ideas are made clear. Readers with a taste for more complication will find plenty to satisfy them in later chapters.

## 2.1 Introduction to present value

Later in this chapter we will prove why the concept of present value is useful. However, that concept will go down more easily if you first acquire an intuitive understanding of it.

Suppose your apartment block burns down, leaving you with a vacant lot worth $50 000 and a cheque for $200 000 from the fire insurance policy. You consider rebuilding, but your real estate adviser suggests putting up an office building instead. The construction cost would be $300 000, and there would also be the cost of the land, which might otherwise be sold for $50 000. On the other hand, your adviser foresees a shortage of office space and predicts that a year from now the new building would fetch $400 000 if you sold it. Thus you would be investing $350 000 now in the expectation of realising $400 000 a year hence.

The question is, how much is the expectation of $400 000 in a year hence worth today? Anyone with experience of a small child would know that the promise of an ice-cream tomorrow is a poor substitute for an ice-cream right now. In much the same way the expectation of $400 000 in a year's time is worth less than $400 000 today. This is true even if the investment is risk-free and you are sure to get the money. The value today of a cash flow to be received in the future is called the cash flow's **present value** (**PV**).

You should go ahead if the present value of the expected $400 000 payoff is greater than the investment of $350 000. Therefore, you need to ask yourself: What is the value *today* of $400 000 one year from now, and is that present value greater than $350 000?

### Calculating present value

The present value of $400 000 one year from now must be less than $400 000. After all, *a dollar today is worth more than a dollar tomorrow*. One reason is impatience to consume, as in our ice-cream example. Another reason is because the dollar today can be invested to start earning interest immediately. A dollar today being worth more than a dollar in the future is the first basic principle of finance.

Thus, the present value of a delayed payoff may be found by multiplying the expected payoff by a **discount factor** that is less than 1. (If the discount factor were more than 1, a dollar tomorrow would be worth *more* than a dollar today.) If $C_1$ denotes the expected payoff (cash flow) at time period 1 (one year hence), then

$$\text{Present value (PV)} = \text{discount factor} \times C_1$$

This discount factor is expressed as the reciprocal of 1 plus a *rate of return*:

$$\text{Discount factor} = \frac{1}{(1 + r)}$$

The rate of return, $r$, is the reward that investors demand for accepting delayed payment. This is called the **required return**.

Let us consider the real estate investment, assuming for the moment that the $400 000 pay-off is a sure thing. The office building is not the only way to obtain $400 000 one year from now. You could invest in Australian government securities maturing in a year. Suppose these securities yield 7 per cent interest. How much would you have to invest in them today in order to receive $400 000 at the end of the year? That question is easy. You would have to invest $400 000/1.07, which is $373 832. Therefore, at an interest rate of 7 per cent, the present value of $400 000 one year from now is $373 832.

Let us assume that, as soon as you have committed the land and begun construction on the building, you decide to sell your project. How much could you sell it for? That is another easy question. Since the property produces $400 000, investors would be willing to pay $373 832 for it. That is what it would cost them to get a $400 000 payoff from investing in government securities. Of course, you could always sell your property for less, but why sell for less than the market will bear? The $373 832 present value is the only feasible price that satisfies both buyer and seller. Therefore, the present value of the property is also its market price.

To calculate present value, we discount expected future payoffs by the rate of return offered by comparable investment alternatives. This is the required rate of return, but it is often referred to as the **discount rate, hurdle rate** or **opportunity cost of capital**. It is called the *opportunity cost* because it is the return forgone by investing in the project rather than investing in securities. In our example the opportunity cost was 7 per cent. Present value was obtained by dividing $400 000 by 1.07:

$$PV = \text{Discount factor} \times C_1 = \frac{1}{(1 + r)} \times C_1 = \frac{400\ 000}{1.07} = \$373\ 832$$

# Net present value

The building project is worth $373 832, but this does not mean that you are $373 832 better off. You committed $350 000, and therefore your **net present value** (NPV) is $23 832. Net present value is found by subtracting the required investment:

$$NPV = PV - \text{required investment} = 373\ 832 - 350\ 000 = \$23\ 832$$

In other words, your office development is worth more than it costs—it makes a *net* contribution to value. The formula for calculating NPV can be written as

$$NPV = C_0 + \frac{C_1}{(1 + r)}$$

Remember that $C_0$, the cash flow at time period 0 (i.e. today), will usually be a negative number. In other words, $C_0$ is usually an investment and therefore a cash *outflow*. In our example

$$C_0 = -\$350\ 000$$

# The meaning of NPV

Now let us look at the break up of the final cash flow if the building is sold at the end of the year:

| | |
|---|---|
| Cash received on sale of building | $400 000 |
| Less repayment of the initial investment | ($350 000) |
| Balance | $50 000 |
| Less servicing of investment ($350 000 @ 7%) | ($24 500) |
| Surplus cash | $25 500 |

The cash received is sufficient to repay the initial investment of $350 000, earn a return on that initial investment equal to the required return of 7 per cent and leave some surplus cash over. How much is that surplus cash worth today? That is easy:

$$\frac{25\ 500}{1.07} = \$23\ 832$$

It is no coincidence that we have just calculated the same number that we got in our net present value calculation. The net present value is the value today of the surplus cash that the project generates. What is more you can spend that net present value today. How? Borrow the net present value at an interest rate equal to the required return. In this case, borrow $23 832 at 7 per cent. How much do you repay at the end of the year?

$$(23\ 832\ +\ 23\ 832\ \times\ 7\%)\ =\ 23\ 832\ (1.07)\ =\ \$25\ 500$$
$$\text{loan}\ +\ \text{interest} \qquad\qquad\qquad\ =\ \text{repayment}$$

The surplus cash from the project is just sufficient to repay your borrowing plus interest.

So let us recap: A positive net present value for your project means that it is expected to repay your initial investment, earn the required return on that investment and generate surplus cash the present value of which you could spend today. Remember this. Although most people who have studied finance can do net present value calculations till the cows come home, many do not understand what the NPV numbers really mean.

## A comment on risk and present value

We made one unrealistic assumption in our discussion of the office development: Your real estate adviser cannot be *certain* about future values of office buildings. The $400 000 figure represents the best *forecast*, but it is not a sure thing. In your office development only the revenue is uncertain, but in other projects you may also have to face the problem that future costs are uncertain.

Therefore, our conclusion about how much investors would pay for the building is wrong. Since they could achieve $400 000 with certainty by buying $373 832 worth of Australian government securities, they would not buy your building for that amount. You would have to cut your asking price to attract investors' interest.

Here we can invoke a second basic financial principle: *A safe dollar is worth more than a risky one*. Most investors avoid risk when they can do so without sacrificing return. However, the concepts of present value and the opportunity cost of capital still make sense for risky investments. It is still proper to discount the *expected* payoff by the rate of return offered by a comparable investment. It is important for you to remember that we will usually be dealing with *expected* payoffs and the *expected* rates of return on other investments.

Not all investments are equally risky. The office development is riskier than a government security, but is probably less risky than drilling a wildcat oil well. Suppose you believe the project is as risky as investment in the share market and that you forecast a 12 per cent rate of return for share market investments. Then 12 per cent becomes the appropriate opportunity cost of capital. That is what you are giving up by not investing in comparable securities. You can now recompute NPV at 12 per cent:

$$\text{PV} = \frac{400\ 000}{1.12} = \$357\ 143$$

$$\text{NPV} = \text{PV} - 350\ 000 = \$7143$$

If other investors agree with your forecast of a $400 000 payoff and with your assessment of a 12 per cent opportunity cost of capital, then your property ought to be worth $357 143 once construction is under way. If you tried to sell it for more than that, there would be no takers, because the property would then offer an expected rate of return lower than the 12 per cent available in the share market. The office building still makes a net contribution to value, but it is much smaller than our earlier calculations indicated.

In Chapter 1 we said that the financial manager must be concerned with time and uncertainty and their effects on value. This is clearly so in our example. The $400 000 payoff would be worth exactly that if it could be realised instantaneously. If the office building is as risk-free as government securities, the one-year delay reduces value to $373 832. If the office building is as risky as investment in the share market, then uncertainty reduces value by a further $16 689 to $357 143.

Unfortunately, adjusting asset values for time and uncertainty is often more complicated than our example suggests. Therefore, we will take the two effects separately. For the most part, we will avoid the problem of risk in Chapters 2 to 6, either treating all payoffs as if they were known with certainty, or talking about expected cash flows and expected rates of return without worrying how risk is defined or measured. Then in Chapter 7 we will turn to the problem of understanding how capital markets cope with risk.

# Present values and rates of return

We have decided that construction of the office building is a smart thing to do, since it is worth more than it costs—it has a positive net present value. To calculate how much it is worth, we worked out how much we would have to pay to achieve the same income by investing directly in securities that have the same risk as the project. The project's present value is equal to its future income discounted at the rate of return offered by these equivalent risk securities.

We can re-express our criterion by saying that our property venture is worth undertaking because the return exceeds the cost of capital. The return on the capital invested is simply the profit as a proportion of the initial outlay:[2]

$$\text{Return} = \text{profit/investment} = \frac{(400\,000 - 350\,000)}{350\,000} = 14\%$$

The cost of capital for the investment, we remind you, is the return forgone by *not* investing in securities. In our present case, if the office building is about as risky as investing in the share market, the return forgone is 12 per cent. Since the 14 per cent return on the office building exceeds the 12 per cent cost, we should start digging the foundations of the building.

Here then we have two equivalent decision rules for capital investment:[3]

1. *Net present value rule*   Accept investments that have positive net present values.
2. *Rate-of-return rule*   Accept investments that offer rates of return in excess of their opportunity costs of capital.[4]

# Present values, rates of return and prices

We noted earlier that if buyers required a 12 per cent return and you sold the project today no one would pay more than $357 143 for it. Let us check that at that price the buyer's **expected rate of return** is 12 per cent:

$$\text{Expected return} = \frac{400\,000 - 357\,143}{357\,143} = 12\%$$

Notice that if a buyer invests in the project at a market price of $357 143 then:

$$\text{Expected return} = 12\% = \text{required return}$$

---

[2]   We use the terms profit and return rather loosely here, but we will refine these ideas later in the book.

[3]   You might check for yourself that these are equivalent rules. In other words, if the return 50 000/350 000 is greater than *r* then the net present value $-350\,000 + [400\,000/(1 + r)]$ *must* be greater than 0.

[4]   The two rules can conflict when there are cash flows in more than two periods. We address this problem in Chapter 5.

In general, prices for capital assets will tend to adjust to an equilibrium where the expected return is equal to the required return.

If the expected return exceeds the required return, buying pressure will push the price up and the expected return falls. Wouldn't you want to buy an asset if you expected to get a return greater than you required? At a selling price of $350 000 the office project yields 14 per cent: it would be selling too cheap. At $357 143 it yields 12 per cent: the price is just right. Conversely, if the expected return is less than the required return, selling pressure pushes the price down and the expected return rises.

At a price of $350 000 the office project has a positive net present value to the buyer. At a price of $357 143 the price equals the present value of the future cash flows—the NPV of buying the project is zero. In equilibrium then:

▌ Assets sell for their present value.
▌ The expected return is equal to the required return.[5]
▌ The NPV of an investment at the equilibrium price is zero.

In active security markets prices move quickly to this equilibrium. So if you are ever asked why share prices have gone up or down, you can reply immediately—expected or required returns have changed and prices have adjusted to the new equilibrium.[6]

## Two sources of confusion

Before moving on we need to alert you to a trap for new players. Sometimes writers refer to expected return when they really mean required return. Usually, they are assuming equilibrium. In which case expected and required returns are equal and it does not greatly matter which term they use. Sometimes people just talk about the rate of return, and you have to decide from the context whether they mean the expected rate of return or the required rate of return, or the rate of return that investors actually received (the realised return).[7] This can be confusing to the uninitiated, so watch out for it.

Here is another possible source of confusion. Let us suppose that office prices have fallen and you are likely to get only $385 000 if you build. The project is now offering only a 10 per cent return ((385 000 − 350 000)/350 000). With a 12 per cent required return the project's NPV is now negative.

Suppose a banker offers to finance your project. 'Your company is a fine safe company with few debts', she says. 'My bank will lend you the $350 000 you need for the office project at a rate of 8 per cent.' You might be tempted to think that your project has been rescued and that you should only require an 8 per cent return. If so, the project is once more above water with a PV at 8 per cent of 385 000/1.08 = $356 481 and NPV = 356 481 − 350 000 = $6481.

That cannot be right. First, the interest rate on the loan has nothing to do with the risk of the project: it reflects the good health of your existing business. Second, whether you take the loan or not, you still face the choice between the project which offers an expected return of only 10 per cent, or the equally risky investment in shares, which gives an expected return of 12 per cent. A financial manager who borrows at 8 per cent and invests at 10 per cent is not smart but stupid, when they could get 12 per cent in an equally risky investment. That is why the 12 per cent expected return in the share market is the opportunity cost of capital for the project.

---

5   We can get a handle on the required return (or opportunity cost of capital) from the expected return demanded by investors in shares or other securities that have the same risk as the project.

6   This will be a sufficiently intimidating answer to deter most questioners. In order to answer those that persist you will need to read more of this book. Alternatively, you may recommend that they buy it.

7   For risky assets the return investors get may differ from what they expected; for risk-free assets expected and realised returns are always equal.

# *2.2 Foundations of the net present value rule[8]

So far, our discussion of net present value has been rather casual. Increasing NPV *sounds* like a sensible objective for a company, but it is more than just a rule of thumb. We need to understand why the NPV rule makes sense and why we look to the bond and share markets to find the opportunity cost of capital.

**figure 2.1**
_____

Notice how borrowing and lending enlarge the individual's choice. By borrowing against future cash flow *F*, an individual can consume an extra *BD* today; by lending current cash flow *B*, the individual can consume an extra *FH* tomorrow.

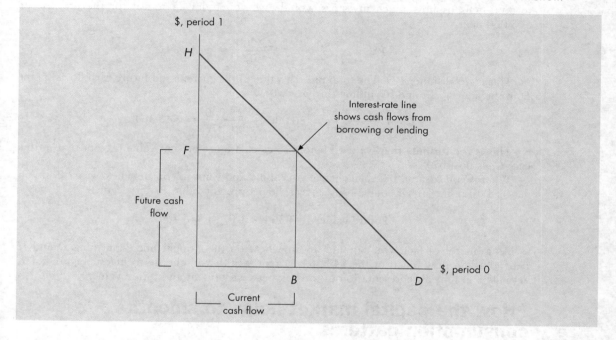

Figure 2.1 illustrates the problem of choosing between spending today and spending in the future. Assume that you have a cash inflow of *B* today and *F* in a year's time. Unless you have some way of storing or anticipating income, you will be compelled to consume it as it arrives. This could be inconvenient or worse, if the bulk of your cash flow is received next year, the result could be hunger now and gluttony later. This is where the capital market comes in. It allows the transfer of wealth across time, so that you can eat moderately both this year and next.

The capital market is simply a market where people trade between dollars today and dollars in the future. The downward-sloping line in Figure 2.1 represents the rate of exchange in the capital market between today's dollars and next year's dollars: its slope is $-(1 + r)$, where $r$ denotes the one-year rate of interest. The slope is negative because more consumption now means that less consumption is available in the future. For every \$1 you consume today you lose the opportunity to consume \$$(1 + r)$ in the future. By consuming nothing today and lending all your present cash flow, you could increase your *future* consumption by $(1 + r) \times B$ or *FH*. Alternatively, by borrowing against your future cash flow, you could increase your *present* consumption by $F/(1 + r)$ or *BD*.

_____

[8] Sections marked with an asterisk contain more difficult material and may be skipped on a first reading.

Let us put some numbers into our example. Suppose that your prospects are as follows:

$$\text{Cash on hand: } B = \$20\,000$$
$$\text{Cash to be received one year from now: } F = \$25\,000$$

If you do not want to consume anything today, you can invest \$20 000 in the capital market at, say, 7 per cent. The rate of exchange between dollars next year and dollars today is 1.07. The slope of the line in Figure 2.1 is −1.07. If you invest \$20 000 at 7 per cent, you will obtain \$20 000 × 1.07 = \$21 400. Of course, you also have \$25 000 coming in a year from now, so you will end up with \$46 400. This is point $H$ in the figure.

What if you want to cash in the \$25 000 future payment and spend everything today on some ephemeral frolic? You can do so by borrowing in the capital market. The present value formula tells us how much investors would give you today in return for the promise of \$25 000 next year:

$$PV = \frac{C_1}{(1+r)} = \frac{25\,000}{1.07} = \$23\,364$$

This is the distance $BD$. The total present value of the current and future cash flows (point $D$ in the figure) is found by adding this year's flow.

$$C_0 + \frac{C_1}{(1+r)} = 20\,000 + \frac{25\,000}{1.07} = \$43\,364$$

This is the formula that we used before to calculate net present value (except that in this case $C_0$ is positive).

What if you cash in, but then change your mind and want to consume next year? Can you get back to point $H$? Of course—just invest the net present value at 7 per cent.

$$\text{Future value} = 43\,364 \times 1.07 = \$46\,400$$

As a matter of fact, you can end up anywhere on the straight line connecting $D$ and $H$ depending on how much of the \$43 364 current wealth you choose to invest. Figure 2.1 is actually a graphical representation of the link between present and future value.

## *How the capital market helps to smooth consumption patterns

Few of us save all our current cash flow or borrow fully against our future cash flow. We try to achieve a balance between present and future consumption. But there is no reason to expect that the best balance for one person is the best for another.

Suppose, for example, that you have a prodigal disposition and favour present over future consumption. Your preferred pattern might be indicated by Figure 2.2: you choose to borrow $BC$ against future cash flow and consume $C$ today. Next year you are obliged to repay $EF$ and therefore can consume only $E$. By contrast, if you have a more miserly streak, you might prefer the policy shown in Figure 2.3: you consume $A$ today and lend the balance $AB$. In a year's time you receive a repayment of $FG$ and are therefore able to indulge in consumption of $G$.[9]

Both the miser and the prodigal *can* choose to spend cash only as it is received, but in these examples both prefer to do otherwise. By opening up borrowing and lending opportunities, the capital market removes the obligation to match consumption and cash flow.

---

[9] The exact balance between present and future consumption that each individual will choose depends on personal taste. Readers who are familiar with economic theory will recognise that the choice can be represented by superimposing an indifference map for each individual. The preferred combination is the point of tangency between the interest-rate line and the individual's indifference curve. In other words, each individual will borrow or lend until 1 plus the interest rate equals the marginal rate of time preference (i.e. the slope of the indifference curve).

**figure 2.2**

The prodigal chooses to borrow *BC* against tomorrow's cash flow, in order to consume *C* today and *E* tomorrow.

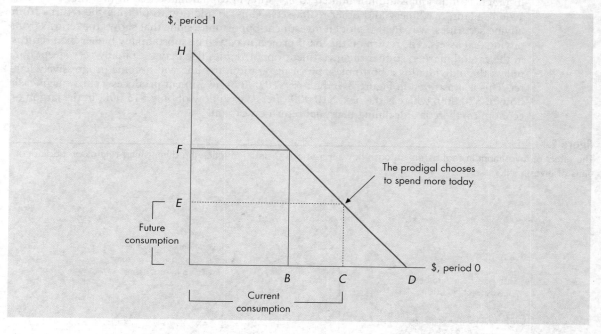

**figure 2.3**

The miser chooses to lend *AB*, in order to consume *A* today and *G* tomorrow.

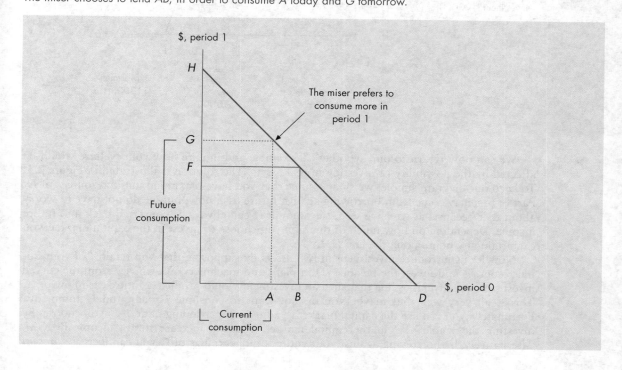

## *Now we introduce productive opportunities

In practice, individuals are not limited to investing in capital market securities: they may also acquire plant, machinery and other real assets. Thus, in addition to plotting the returns from buying securities, we can also plot an investment-opportunities line that shows the returns from buying real assets. The return on the 'best' project may well be substantially higher than returns in the capital market, so that the investment-opportunities line may be initially very steep. But, unless the individual is a bottomless pit of inspiration, the line will become progressively flatter. This is illustrated in Figure 2.4: the first $10 000 of investment produces a subsequent cash flow of $20 000, whereas the next $10 000 offers a cash flow of only $15 000. In the jargon of economics, there is a declining marginal return on capital.

**figure 2.4**

The effect of investment in real assets on cash flows in periods 0 and 1. Notice the diminishing returns on additional units of investment.

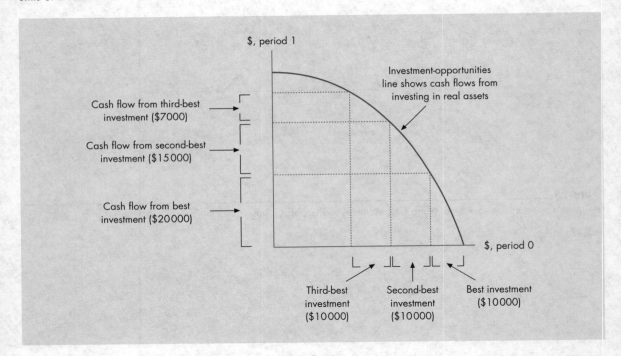

We can now return to our hypothetical example and inquire how your welfare would be affected by the possibility of investing in real assets. The solution is illustrated in Figure 2.5. To keep our diagram simple, we shall assume that you have maximum initial resources of D. Part of this may come from borrowing against future cash flow; but we do not have to worry about that because, as we have seen, the amount D can always be converted back into future income. Depending on how much of this sum you choose to invest in the capital market, you can attain any point along the line DH.

Now let us introduce investment in *real assets* by supposing that you retain J of your initial resources and invest the balance JD in plant and machinery. We can see from the curved investment-opportunities line that such an investment would produce a future cash flow of G. This is all very well, but maybe you do not want to consume J today and G tomorrow. Fortunately, you can use the capital market to adjust your spending pattern as you choose. By investing the whole of J in the capital market, you can increase future income by GM. Alternatively, by borrowing against your entire future earnings of G you can increase *present*

figure 2.5 _____

Both the prodigal and the miser have initial wealth of D. They are better off if they invest JD in real assets and then borrow or lend in the capital market. If they could invest *only* in the capital market, they would be obliged to choose a point along DH; if they could invest only in real assets, they would be obliged to choose a point along DL.

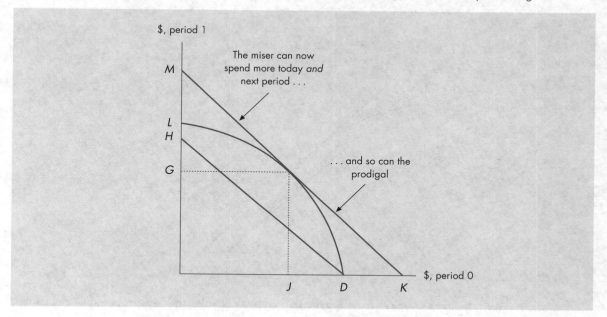

income by *JK*. In other words, by *both* investing *JD* in *real assets* and borrowing or lending in the capital market, you can obtain any point along the line *KM*. Regardless of whether you are a prodigal or a miser, you have more to spend either today or next year than if you invest *only* in the capital market (i.e. choose a point along the line *DH*). You also have more to spend either today or next year than if you invest *only* in real assets (i.e. choose a point along the curve *DL*).

Let us look more closely at the investment in *real assets*. The maximum sum that could be realised today from the investment's future cash flow is *JK*. *This is the investment's present value*. Its cost is *JD* and the difference between its present value and its cost is *DK*. *This is its net present value*. Net present value is the addition to your resources from investing in the *real assets*. It measures your increase in wealth. The amount *K* is the maximum consumption that you could enjoy today: it measures your current wealth. Without the investment your wealth is less: your maximum consumption is only *D*. The net present value of the investment *DK* therefore shows you how much your wealth will increase by taking on the investment.

Investing the amount *JD* is a smart move—it makes you better off. In fact, it is the smartest possible move. We can see why if we look at Figure 2.6. If you invest *JD* in real assets, the net present value is *DK*. If you invest, say, *ND* in real assets, the net present value declines to *DP*. In fact, investing either more or less than *JD* in real assets *must* reduce net present value.

Notice also that by investing *JD*, you have invested up to the point at which the investment-opportunities line just touches and has the same slope as the interest-rate line. Now the slope of the investment-opportunities line represents the return on the marginal investment, so that *JD* is the point at which the return on the marginal investment is exactly equal to the rate of interest. In other words, you will maximise your wealth if you invest in *real* assets until the marginal return on investment falls to the rate of interest. Having done that, you will borrow or lend in the capital market until you have achieved your desired balance between consumption today and consumption tomorrow.

**figure 2.6**

If the prodigal or the miser invested *ND* in real assets, the NPV of the investment would be only *DP*. The investor would have less to spend both today and tomorrow.

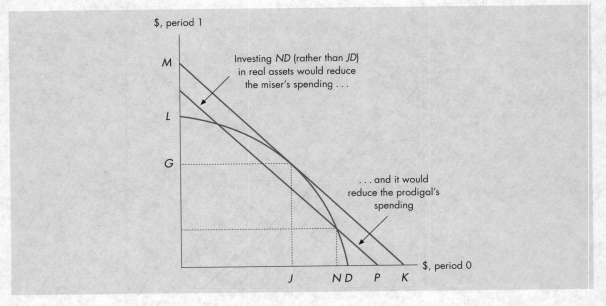

We now have a logical basis for the two equivalent rules that we proposed so casually at the end of Section 2.1. We can restate the rules as follows:

1.  *Net present value rule*   Invest so as to maximise the net present value of the investment. This is the difference between the discounted, or present, value of the future cash flows and the amount of the initial investment.
2.  *Rate-of-return rule*   Invest up to the point at which the marginal return on the investment is equal to the expected rate of return on equivalent investments in the capital market. This is the point of tangency between the interest-rate line and the investment-opportunities line.

## *A crucial assumption

In our examples, the miser and the prodigal placed an identical value on the firm's investment. They agreed because they faced identical borrowing and lending opportunities. Whenever firms discount cash flows at capital market rates, they are implicitly making some assumptions about their shareholders' opportunities to borrow and lend. Strictly speaking, they are assuming:

1.  There are no barriers preventing access to the capital market and no participant is sufficiently dominant as to have a significant effect on price.
2.  Access to the capital market is costless and there are no 'frictions' preventing the free trading of securities.
3.  Relevant information about the price and quality of each security is widely and freely available.
4.  There are no distorting taxes.

In sum, they are assuming a perfectly competitive capital market. In such a market mispricing will immediately be traded away, and all investors can achieve their desired pattern of consumption over time. Clearly this is at best an approximation, but it may not be too bad in some markets. For example, there are nearly 50 million shareholders in the United States. In

Australia, the number of individuals with shareholdings used to be only about one million. But, in recent years there have been several big share issues as a means of privatising government-owned organisations. The public has purchased shares in these floats in a big way, so the number of individuals owning shares in Australia has climbed sharply. However, the values of individual shareholdings are eclipsed by the value of institutional shareholdings, particularly shareholdings of superannuation funds. While there are some very large institutional share-holders such as AMP, no one institution dominates the share market. Rather, there is keen competition between institutions. That competition is likely to minimise the mispricing of shares, at least for actively-traded companies. However, remember our warning in Chapter 1 about the problem of thin trading in some areas of Australian capital markets.

In regard to frictions that may prevent trading, the costs of trading in securities are generally small, both in absolute terms and relative to the costs of trading in real assets such as office buildings and blast furnaces. With regard to availability of information, there are obviously cases in which investors have possessed privileged information. However, the mighty power of avarice, the Australian Securities and Investments Commission (ASIC) and the Australian Stock Exchange (ASX) ensure that potentially profitable information seldom remains for long the property of one individual.

Even though our conditions (1 to 4 above) are not fully satisfied, there is considerable evidence that security prices behave almost as if they were. This evidence is presented and discussed in Chapter 13.

You may protest that you have no opportunity to shift consumption back and forth like the miser and the prodigal. However, that is exactly what you do every time you make a bank deposit or take out a loan.

## *Imperfect capital markets

Suppose that we did not have such a well-functioning capital market. How would this damage our net present value rule?

As an example, Figure 2.7 shows what happens if the borrowing rate is substantially higher than the lending rate. This means that when you want to turn period 0 dollars into period 1 dollars (i.e. lend), you move *up* a relatively flat line; when you want to turn period 1 dollars into period 0 dollars (i.e. borrow), you move *down* a relatively steep line. You can see that would-be borrowers (who must move down the steep line) prefer the company to invest only *BD*. In contrast, would-be lenders (who must move *up* the relatively flat line) prefer the company to invest *AD*. In this case the two groups of shareholders want the manager to use different discount rates. The manager has no simple way to reconcile their differing objectives.

No one believes that the competitive market assumption is fully satisfied. Later in this book we will discuss several cases in which differences in taxation, transaction costs and other imperfections must be taken into account in financial decision making. However, we will also discuss research which indicates that, in general, capital markets function fairly well. That is one good reason for relying on net present value as a corporate objective. Another good reason is that net present value makes common sense; we will see that it gives obviously silly answers less frequently than its major competitors. But for now, having glimpsed the problems of imperfect markets, we shall, like an economist in a shipwreck, simply *assume* our life jacket and swim safely to shore.

## 2.3 A fundamental result

The net present value rule really dates back to the work of the great American economist Irving Fisher in 1930.[10] What was so exciting about Fisher's analysis was his discovery that

---

[10]  I. Fisher, *The Theory of Interest*, Augustus M. Kelley, Publishers, New York, 1965 (reprinted from the 1930 edition). Our graphical illustration closely follows the exposition in E. F. Fama and M. H. Miller, *The Theory of Finance*, Holt, Rinehart and Winston, New York, 1972.

**figure 2.7**
Here there are separate borrowing and lending rates. The steep line represents the interest rate for a borrower; the flatter line represents the rate for a lender. In this case the prodigal and the miser prefer different levels of capital investment.

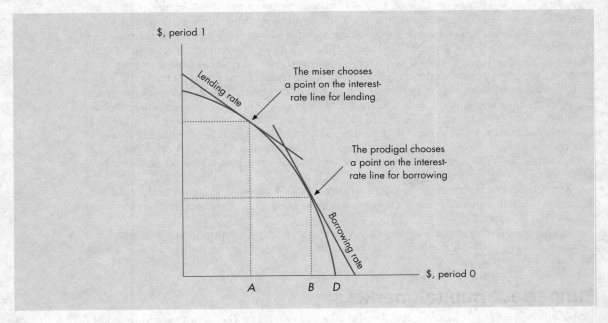

the capital investment criterion has nothing to do with the individual's preferences for current versus future consumption. The prodigal and the miser are unanimous in the amount that they want to invest in real assets. Because they have the same investment criterion, they can cooperate in the same enterprise and can safely delegate the operation of that enterprise to a professional manager. Managers do not need to know anything about the personal tastes of their shareholders and should not consult their own tastes. Their task is to maximise net present value. If they succeed, they can rest assured that they have acted in the best interests of their shareholders. Fisher's result is known as the separation theorem, because it shows how the investment decision can be separated from investors' consumption decisions.

Our justification of the net present value rule has been restricted to two periods and to certain cash flows. However, the rule also makes sense for cases in which the cash flows extend beyond the next period. The argument goes like this:

1. A financial manager should act in the interest of the firm's shareholders.
2. Each shareholder wants three things:
   a. To be as rich as possible, that is, to maximise current wealth.
   b. To transform that wealth into whatever time pattern of consumption he or she most desires.
   c. To choose the risk characteristics of that consumption plan.
3. But shareholders do not need the financial manager's help to reach the best time pattern of consumption. They can do that on their own, providing they have free access to competitive capital markets. They can also choose the risk characteristics of their consumption plan by investing in more or less risky securities.
4. How then can the financial manager help the firm's shareholders? By increasing the market value of each shareholder's stake in the firm. The way to do that is to seize all investment opportunities that have a positive net present value.

This gives us the fundamental condition for the successful operation of a capitalist economy. Separation of ownership and management is a practical necessity for large organisations. Many companies have hundreds of thousands of shareholders, no two with the same tastes, wealth or personal opportunities. There is no way for all the firm's owners to be actively involved in management: it would be like running Sydney through a series of town meetings for all its citizens. Therefore, authority has to be delegated. The remarkable thing is that managers of firms can all be given one simple instruction: maximise net present value.

## Other corporate goals

Managers sometimes speak about goals such as profit maximisation, and most investors would prefer to own a profitable company, rather than an unprofitable one. Taken literally, however, profit maximisation makes little sense as a corporate objective. Here are three reasons why:

1. Maximising profits leaves open the question of 'Which year's profits?' Shareholders might not want a manager to increase this year's profits at the expense of later years profits.
2. Profits may be increased by cutting dividends and investing the extra cash retained by the firm. As long as the return on investment is positive, say 1 per cent, profits will go up. This hardly seems likely to please shareholders.[11]
3. Different accountants may calculate profits in different ways, so whose measurement of profit do we maximise? It is worth remembering the firms like Bond Corporation and Girvan, who were reporting healthy profits not very long before their spectacular collapse.

Over the lifetime of the enterprise, total profit equals total net cash flow by definition. The trouble is that maximising that total profit does not allow for the timing of those cash flows or their risk. But you know what does— three letters ending in V!

**Do managers maximise NPV?**    Do real managers really follow the simple instruction: maximise net present value? Some idealists say that managers should not be obliged to act in the selfish interests of their shareholders. Some realists argue that, regardless of what managers ought to do, they in fact look after themselves.

Let us respond to the idealists first. A focus on value does not mean that managers must ride roughshod over the weak and helpless. Most of this book is devoted to financial policies that increase firm value, and we suggest that most of the time there is little conflict between doing well (maximising value) and doing good.[12]

We do not know how energetically managers seek to maximise net present value, but we are reminded of a survey of business people that inquired whether they attempted to maximise profits. They indignantly rejected the notion, protesting that they were responsible, God-fearing, and so on: their responsibilities went far beyond the narrow profit objective. But when the question was reformulated and they were asked whether they could increase profits by raising or lowering their selling price, they replied that neither policy would do so.[13] In other words, they were maximising profit. In a rather similar vein, we suspect that many managers do not have an explicit objective of maximising net present value and yet can think of no action that would do anything other than to reduce it.

Suppose, however, that we do believe that management should have these wider responsibilities. Management still must be able to analyse a decision from the shareholders' point of

---

11   Of course, they will be happy if the firm reinvests at more than their required rate of return, because then the investments will have a positive NPV.

12   We concede, however, that some corporate financial policies are directed to minimisation of tax. Some would argue that this is antisocial.

13   Cited in G. J. Stigler, *The Theory of Price*, 3rd ed., The Macmillan Company, New York, 1966.

view if it is to strike a proper balance between their interests and those of consumers, employees and society at large. The net present value calculation tells them how much a particular decision helps or hinders shareholders.

Of course, ethical issues arise in business as in other walks of life. And in business dealings managers do more than just observe the letter of the law and written contracts. They mostly play fair and follow ethical principles because they know it is in the general interest and also because it is good business practice. Many companies know that their most valuable asset is their reputation. In 1998, for example, there was a contamination threat to Sanitarium products. Sanitarium responded by withdrawing those products from supermarket shelves. This would have cost them dearly, possibly millions of dollars. Their reaction was an ethical one, but it was also consistent with maintaining their reputation. The potential cost of ignoring the threat was many times higher than taking the product off the shelves.

In many financial transactions, one party has more information than the other. This opens up plenty of opportunities for misrepresentation, sharp practice and outright fraud. But these cases are in the minority. Such illicit transactions are not usually pursed with the goal of shareholder wealth maximisation in mind.[14] Indeed, it seems that such transactions are often associated with financial difficulties. What is the reaction of honest financial firms? It is to build long-term relations with their clients and establish a reputation for fair dealing and integrity.

### Do managers look after their own interests?    Now, how about the realists who say that managers look after their own interests rather than those of their shareholders? We agree that managers do look to their own interests. But shareholders would not hand over their capital if they believed that their managers would dissipate it in luxury and leisure. What is it that prevents such dissipation—or at least keeps it down to acceptable proportions?[15]

First, compensation packages can be designed to align managers' and shareholders' interests. For example, top managers are usually given options to buy shares in the business: the options pay off only if the business does well. Second, managers who are successful in increasing shareholder wealth will find that they can move on to better jobs and higher salaries. Managers who ignore shareholder wealth may find their companies taken over by some other firm more concerned with profitability. After the takeover, they may also find themselves out on the street.

No compensation plan can ensure that managers always try to increase shareholders' wealth, but good managers know that it is in their long-run interest to demonstrate that shareholders' pockets are close to managers' hearts.

---

[14]  Indeed, they may result in destroying a large quantity of shareholder wealth. For example in 1991, the American finance house Salomon Brothers was involved in a scandal relating to bids for American Treasury bonds. Their price dropped by about one third, representing a $1.5 billion decline in the company's market value.

[15]  We discussed some of the mechanisms regulating management behaviour in Section 1.1 of Chapter 1.

## 2.4 Summary

In this chapter we have introduced the concept of present value as a way of valuing assets. Calculating present value is easy. Just discount future cash flow by an appropriate rate, *the required rate of return*, often called the *opportunity cost of capital* or *hurdle rate*.

$$PV = \frac{E[C_1]}{(1 + r)}$$

We use the expectation bracket $E[\ ]$ as a reminder that when you substitute into this formula you are substituting for an expected value.[16]

Net present value is calculated as present value plus any immediate cash flow.

$$NPV = C_0 + \frac{E[C_1]}{(1 + r)}$$

Remember that $C_0$ is usually negative, because the initial cash flow is usually payment for an investment.

The discount rate is determined by rates of return prevailing in capital markets. If the future cash flow is absolutely safe, then the discount rate is the interest rate on safe securities such as Australian government debt. If the size of the future cash flow is uncertain, then the expected cash flow should be discounted at the expected rate of return offered by equivalent risky securities. We will talk more about this in Chapter 7.

Cash flows are discounted for two simple reasons: first, because a dollar today is worth more than a dollar tomorrow and second, because a risky dollar is worth less than a safe one. Formulas for PV and NPV are numerical expressions of these ideas. We look to rates of return prevailing in capital markets to determine how much to discount for time and for risk. By calculating the present value of an asset, we are in effect estimating how much people will pay for it if they have the alternative of investing in the capital markets. The equilibrium price for the asset is its present value. Selling at that price, the asset's expected return equals the required return, and so the NPV of purchasing the asset is zero. If you want to make a positive NPV purchase you must either find an asset worth more in your hands than in hands of others, or find an asset that is underpriced. You are more likely to have success in this quest if you search in the market for real assets, rather than in securities markets.

The concept of net present value allows efficient separation of ownership and management of the corporation. A manager who invests only in assets with positive net present values serves the best interests of each one of the firm's owners—regardless of differences in their wealth and tastes. This is made possible by the existence of the capital market, which allows each shareholder to construct a personal investment plan that is custom-tailored to his or her own needs. For example, there is no need for the firm to arrange its investment policy to obtain a sequence of cash flows that matches shareholders' preferred time patterns of consumption. The shareholders can shift funds forward or back over time perfectly well on their own, provided they have free access to competitive capital markets. In fact, their plan for consumption over time is constrained by only two things: their personal wealth (or lack of it) and the interest rate at which they can borrow and lend. The financial manager cannot affect the interest rate but can increase shareholders' wealth. The way to do so is to invest in assets having positive net present values.

---

[16] We will not clutter up all our equations with the expectation bracket notation. After all $C_1$ is defined as an expected cash flow. But from time to time we will use the $E[\ ]$ notation when we think it useful to emphasise that we are dealing with expected values.

## FURTHER READING

The pioneering works on the net present value rule are:

I. Fisher, *The Theory of Interest*, Augustus M. Kelley, Publishers, New York, 1965 (reprinted from the 1930 edition).

J. Hirschleifer, 'On the Theory of Optimal Investment Decision', *Journal of Political Economy*, 66: 329–52 (August 1958).

For a more rigorous textbook treatment of the subject, we suggest:

E. F. Fama and M. H. Miller, *The Theory of Finance*, Holt, Rinehart and Winston, New York, 1972.

If you would like to dig deeper into the question of how managers may be motivated to maximise shareholders' wealth, we suggest:

M. C. Jensen and W. H. Meckling, 'Theory of the Firm: Managerial Behaviour, Agency Costs, and Ownership Structure', *Journal of Financial Economics*, 3: 305–60 (October 1976).

E. F. Fama, 'Agency Problems and the Theory of the Firm', *Journal of Political Economy*, 88: 288–307 (April 1980).

M. C. Jensen, 'The Modern Industrial Revolution, Exit, and the Failure of Internal Control Systems', *Journal of Applied Corporate Finance*, 6: 4–24 (Winter 1994).

## QUIZ

**\*1.** $C_0$ is the initial cash flow on an investment and $C_1$ is the cash flow at the end of one year. The symbol $r$ is the discount rate.
   a. Is $C_0$ usually positive or negative?
   b. What is the formula for the present value of the investment?
   c. What is the formula for the net present value?
   d. The symbol $r$ is often termed the *opportunity cost of capital*. Why?
   e. If the investment is risk-free, what is the appropriate measure of $r$?

**\*2.** If the present value of $150 paid at the end of one year is $130, what is the one-year discount factor? What is the discount rate?

**\*3.** Calculate the one-year discount factor $DF_1$ for discount rates of (a) 10 per cent, (b) 20 per cent and (c) 30 per cent.

**\*4.** A merchant pays $100 000 for a load of grain and is certain that it can be resold at the end of one year for $132 000.
   a. What is the return on this investment?
   b. If this return is *lower* than the rate of interest, does the investment have a positive or a negative net present value?
   c. If the rate of interest is 10 per cent, what is the present value of the investment?
   d. What is the net present value?

**5.** What is the net present value rule? What is the rate-of-return rule? Do the two rules give the same answer?

**\*6.** In Figure 2.8, the sloping line represents the opportunities for investment in the capital market and the solid curved line represents the opportunities for investment in plant and machinery. The company's only asset at present is $2.6 million in cash.

a. What is the interest rate?
b. How much should the company invest in plant?
c. How much will this investment be worth next year?
d. What is the average rate of return on the investment in plant?
e. What is the marginal rate of return?
f. What is the present value of this investment?
g. What is the net present value of this investment?
h. What is the total present value of the company?
i. How much will the individual consume today?
j. How much will he or she consume tomorrow?

**figure 2.8**

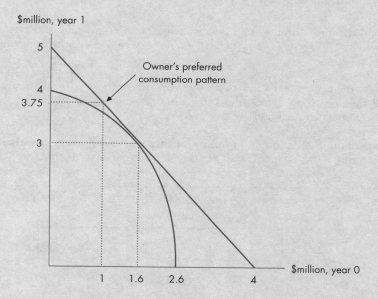

*7. We can imagine the financial manager doing several things on behalf of the firm's
shareholders. For example, the manager might:
a. Make shareholders as wealthy as possible by investing in real assets with
positive net present values.
b. Modify the firm's investment plan to help shareholders achieve a particular time
pattern of consumption.
c. Choose high- or low-risk assets to match shareholders' risk preferences.
d. Help balance shareholders' cheque books.
But in well-functioning capital markets, shareholders will vote for only one of these
goals. Which one? Why?

**8.** Which of the following conditions imply that an asset's price is in equilibrium?
a. Cost of capital = hurdle rate.
b. Expected return = required return.
c. Required return = hurdle rate.
d. Asset price = present value.
e. Hurdle rate = opportunity cost of capital.
f. NPV of asset purchase = zero.

# QUESTIONS AND PROBLEMS

**1.** In Section 2.1 we analysed the possible construction of an office building on a plot of land appraised as having a value of $50 000. We concluded that this investment had a positive NPV of $7143.

Suppose E. Coli Associates, the genetic engineers, offer to purchase the land for $60 000, $30 000 paid immediately and $30 000 after one year. Australian government securities maturing in one year yield 7 per cent.

a. Assume E. Coli is sure to pay the second $30 000 instalment. Should you take their offer or start on the office building? Explain.

b. Suppose you are *not* sure E. Coli will pay. You observe that other investors demand a 10 per cent return on their loans to E. Coli. Assume that the other investors have correctly assessed the risks that E. Coli will not be able to pay. Should you accept E. Coli's offer?

**2.** Write down the formulas for an investment's net present value and rate of return. Prove that NPV is positive *only* if the rate of return exceeds the opportunity cost of capital.

**3.** What is the net present value of a firm's investment in an Australian government bond yielding 15 per cent and maturing in one year? (*Hint*: What is the opportunity cost of capital? Ignore taxes.)

**4.** Calculate the NPV and rate of return for each of the following investments. The opportunity cost of capital is 20 per cent for all four investments.

| Investment | Initial cash flow, $C_0$ | Cash flow in year 1, $C_1$ |
|---|---|---|
| 1 | −10 000 | +20 000 |
| 2 | −5 000 | +12 000 |
| 3 | −5 000 | +5 500 |
| 4 | −2 000 | +5 000 |

a. Which investment is most valuable?

b. Suppose each investment would require use of the same parcel of land. Therefore, you can take only one. Which one? (*Hint*: What is the firm's objective? To earn a high rate of return? Or to increase firm value?)

**\*5.** Wildcat Explorations Ltd have just struck oil in Western Australia. Their share price jumps from $1 to $10.

a. Explain why the equilibrium price has changed.

b. Do you think the required rate of return for Wildcat will have changed?

c. Assume the required return does not change and is 20 per cent. Also assume that investors had believed there was no chance of an oil strike and expected that the company would wind up at the end of the year. How large a liquidating dividend had they expected? If the company is now to be sold to a multinational oil company at the end of the year, how much do investors expect to get per share?

d. Using your answers from Part (c), calculate the expected return before and after news of the oil strike.

e. Assume you got early news of the oil strike. What should you do, and what would be your expected return?

f. Calculate the NPV of investing $1000 in Wildcat immediately before the news of the oil strike, and calculate the NPV of a $1000 investment made immediately after the news.

**6.** There are two risky projects, B and C. B has the higher expected return, but both have the same NPV (zero).

a. Explain how this can be the case.

b. The company has 10 million dollars invested in government bonds yielding 7 per cent. Projects B and C are to be funded by selling these securities. The director of marketing claims that B and C *must* both be great projects since they both offer returns in excess of 7 per cent. Is he right?

c. Suppose instead that the 10 million dollars is all used up in a hostile takeover bid for United Technical Services. So before the company can take on B and C, it will have to borrow another 10 million at an interest rate of 8 per cent. The director of human resources argues that the cost of capital for both B and C is the 8 per cent borrowing rate. Is she right?

**7.** Redraw Figure 2.5 to scale to represent the following situation:
- A firm starts out with $10 million in cash.
- The rate of interest $r$ is 10 per cent.
- To maximise NPV the firm invests today $6 million in real assets ($C_0 = -6$ million). This leaves $4 million that can be paid out to the shareholders.
- The NPV of the investment is $2 million.

When you have finished, answer the following questions:

a. How much cash is the firm going to receive in year 1 from its investment?

b. What is the marginal return from the firm's investment?

c. What is the present value of the shareholders' investment after the firm has announced its investment plan?

d. Suppose shareholders want to spend $6 million today. How can they do this?

e. How much will they then have to spend next year? Show this on your drawing.

**8.** Re-sketch Figure 2.5 to show how the firm's investment plan should be affected by a decline in the interest rate. Mark the NPV of the revised investment plan. Show whether the miser or the prodigal would be better off.

**9.** Look again at Figure 2.5. Suppose the firm decides to invest *more* than JD in real assets. Redraw the interest-rate line to show the NPV of the revised investment plan. Show that both the miser *and* the prodigal are worse off.

**10.** The interest-rate line in our diagrams always has an absolute value for the slope greater than 1. Why?

**11.** 'The discount rate is the rate at which the company will be able to reinvest its cash flows.' Is that right? Discuss.

**\*12.** Respond to the following comment: 'It's all very well telling companies to maximise net present value, but "net present value" is just an abstract notion. What I tell my managers is that profits are what matters and it's profits that we're going to maximise.'

**13.** Respond to the following comment: 'It's no good just telling me to maximise my share price. I can easily take a short-term view and maximise today's price. What I would prefer is to keep it on a gently rising trend.'

**14.** Here is a harder question. It is sometimes argued that the net present value criterion is appropriate for corporations but not for governments. First, governments must consider the time preferences of the community as a whole rather than those of a few wealthy investors. Second, governments must have a longer horizon than individuals, for governments are the guardians of future generations. What do you think?

**15.** Give examples of potential conflicts of interest between managers and shareholders. Why do managers generally work hard to make the firm successful?

**16.** When a company's shares are widely held, it may not pay an individual shareholder to spend time monitoring the manager's performance and trying to replace poor management. Explain why. Do you think that a bank that has just made a large loan to the company is in a different position?

**17.** As you drive along a lonely stretch of Western Australia's coastline, you are overcome with a sudden desire for a hamburger. Fortunately, there are two hamburger outlets up ahead. One is owned by a national brand. The other appears to be owned by 'Joe'. Which outlet has the greater incentive to economise on their burgers by mixing in some minced goanna? Why? What lessons does your answer have for financial institutions?

**18.** Sometimes lawyers work on a contingency basis. They collect a percentage of their clients' settlement instead of receiving a fixed fee. Why might clients prefer this sort of arrangement? Would this sort of arrangement be more appropriate for clients that use lawyers regularly, or infrequently?

**19.** Discuss which of the following forms of compensation is most likely to align the interests of managers and shareholders:
   a. A fixed salary.
   b. A salary linked to company profits.
   c. A salary that is partly paid in the form of the company's shares.
   d. An option to buy the company's shares at an attractive price.

# chapter 3

# HOW TO CALCULATE PRESENT VALUES

In Chapter 2 we learned how to work out the value of an asset that produces cash exactly one year from now. But we did not explain how to value assets that produce cash two years from now or in several future years. That is the first thing that we must do in this chapter. We will then have a look at some shortcut methods for calculating present values and at some specialised present value formulas. We will also consider how inflation affects the purchasing power of future cash payments.

By then you will deserve some payoff for the mental investment you have made in learning about present values. Therefore, we will try out the concept on bonds. In Chapter 4 we will look at the valuation of ordinary shares, and after that we will tackle the firm's capital investment decisions at a practical level of detail.

## 3.1 Valuing long-lived assets

Do you remember how to calculate the present value (PV) of an asset that produces an expected cash flow ($C_1$) one year from now?

$$PV = DF_1 \times C_1 = \frac{C_1}{(1 + r_1)}$$

The discount factor for year 1 cash flows is $DF_1$, and $r_1$ is the opportunity cost of investing your money for one year. Suppose you will receive a certain cash inflow of $100 next year ($C_1 = 100$) and the rate of interest on one-year Commonwealth Treasury bonds is 7 per cent ($r_1 = 0.07$). Then present value equals

$$PV = \frac{C_1}{(1 + r_1)} = \frac{100}{(1.07)} = \$93.46$$

The present value of a cash flow 2 that you get two years hence can be written in a similar way as

$$PV = DF_2 \times C_2 = \frac{C_2}{(1 + r_2)^2}$$

$C_2$ is the year 2 cash flow, $DF_2$ is the discount factor for year 2 cash flows and $r_2$ is the annual rate of interest on money invested for two years. Continuing with our example, suppose you get a cash flow of $100 in year 2 ($C_2 = 100$). The rate of interest on two-year Commonwealth bonds is 7.7 per cent per year ($r_2 = 0.077$). This means that a dollar invested in two-year bonds will grow to $1.077^2 = \$1.16$ by the end of two years. The present value of your year 2 cash flow equals

$$PV = \frac{C_2}{(1 + r_2)^2} = \frac{100}{(1.077)^2} = \$86.21$$

## Valuing cash flows in several periods

One of the nice things about present values is that they are all expressed in current dollars—so that you can add them up. In other words, if you pool the cash flows $A$ and $B$, the present value of cash flow ($A + B$) combined is equal to the present value of cash flow $A$ plus the present value of cash flow $B$.

$$PV(A + B) = PV(A) + PV(B)$$

This happy result has important implications for investments that produce cash flows in several periods.

In the previous section we calculated the value of an asset that produces a cash flow of $C_1$ in year 1, and we calculated the value of another asset that produces a cash flow of $C_2$ in year 2. Following our additivity rule, we can write down the value of an asset that produces cash flows in both years. It is simply

$$PV = \frac{C_1}{(1 + r_1)} + \frac{C_2}{(1 + r_2)^2}$$

Returning to our example, but now assuming that we get $100 at the end of year 1 and year 2

$$PV = \frac{C_1}{(1 + r_1)} + \frac{C_2}{(1 + r_2)^2} = \frac{100}{(1.07)} + \frac{100}{(1.077)^2} = \$93.46 + \$86.21 = \$179.67$$

We can obviously continue in this way and find the present value of an extended stream of cash flows:

$$PV = \frac{C_1}{(1 + r_1)} + \frac{C_2}{(1 + r_2)^2} + \frac{C_3}{(1 + r_3)^3} + \ldots$$

This is called the **discounted cash flow** (or DCF) formula. A shorthand way to write it is

$$PV = \sum \frac{E[C_t]}{(1 + r_t)^t}$$

where $\sum$ refers to the sum of the series, and $E[C_t]$ is the *expected* cash flow in period $t$.

To find the *net* present value we add the (usually negative) initial cash flow, just as in the one period case:

$$\text{NPV} = C_0 + \text{PV} = C_0 + \sum \frac{E[C_t]}{(1 + r_t)^t}$$

Later you will discover how the present value calculations can be reversed to convert a present value to a future value (FV), or to convert a present value to a sequence of **equivalent annuity cash flows (EAC)**.[1]

# *Why the discount factor declines as futurity increases—and a digression on money machines

The discount factor $DF_t$ is always less than 1 and should get smaller the further into the future is period $t$. After all, if a dollar tomorrow is worth less than a dollar today, one might suspect that a dollar the day after tomorrow should be worth even less. In other words, the discount factor $DF_2$ should be less than the discount factor $DF_1$. But is this *necessarily* so, when there is a different interest rate $r_t$ for each period?

Suppose $r_1$ is 20 per cent and $r_2$ is 7 per cent. Then

$$DF_1 = \frac{1}{1.20} = 0.83$$

$$DF_2 = \frac{1}{(1.07)^2} = 0.87$$

In other words, a dollar received in two years is worth $0.87 today, while a dollar received in one year is worth only $0.83 today. Apparently the dollar received the day after tomorrow is *not* necessarily worth less than the dollar received tomorrow.

But there is something wrong with this example. Anyone who could borrow and lend at these interest rates could become a millionaire overnight. Let us see how such a 'money machine' would work. Suppose the first person to spot the opportunity is Hermione Kraft. Ms Kraft first lends $1000 for one year at 20 per cent. That is an attractive enough return, but she notices that there is a way to earn an *immediate* profit on her investment and be ready to play the game again. She reasons as follows. Next year she will have $1200 which can be reinvested for a further year. Although she does not know what interest rates will be at that time, she does know that she can always put the money in a cheque account and be sure of having $1200 at the end of year 2. Her next step therefore is to go to her bank and take a two-year loan for the present value of this $1200. At 7 per cent interest this present value is

$$\text{PV} = \frac{1200}{(1.07)^2} = \$1048$$

Thus Ms Kraft invests $1000, borrows back $1048 and walks away with a profit of $48. If that does not sound like very much, remember that the game can be played again immediately, this time with $1048. In fact, it would take Ms Kraft only 147 plays to become a millionaire (before taxes).[2]

Of course, this story is completely fanciful. Such an opportunity would not last long in capital markets like ours. Any bank that would allow you to lend for one year at 20 per cent and borrow for two years at 7 per cent per annum would soon be wiped out by a rush of small investors hoping to become millionaires and a rush of millionaires hoping to become billionaires. There are, however, two lessons to our story. The first is that a dollar tomorrow *cannot* be worth less than a dollar the day after tomorrow. In other words, the value of a dollar received at the end of one year ($DF_1$) must be greater than the value of a dollar received at the

---

[1]   In other books you may find EACs called equivalent annual costs or equivalent annual cash flows. These names all refer to the same idea.

[2]   That is, $1000 \times (1.04813)^{147} = \$1\,002\,000$.

end of two years (DF$_2$). There must be some extra gain[3] from lending for two periods rather than one: $(1 + r_2)^2$ must be greater than $(1 + r_1)$.

Our second lesson is a more general one and can be summed up by the precept 'There is no such thing as a money machine'.[4] In well-functioning capital markets, any potential money machine will be eliminated almost instantaneously by investors who try to take advantage of it. Therefore, beware of self-styled experts who offer you the chance to participate in a 'sure thing'.

Later in the book we will invoke the *absence* of money machines to prove several useful properties about security prices. That is, we will make statements like 'The prices of securities X and Y must be in the following relationship—otherwise there would be a money machine and capital markets would not be in equilibrium.'

# How present value tables help the lazy

In principle there can be a different interest rate for each future period. This relationship between the interest rate and the maturity of the cash flow is called the **term structure of interest rates**. We are going to look at term structure in Chapter 23, but for now we will finesse the issue by assuming that the term structure is 'flat'—in other words, the interest rate is the same regardless of the date of the cash flow. This means that we can replace the series of interest rates $r_1, r_2, \ldots, r_t$, etc with a single rate $r$ and that we can write the present value formula as

$$PV = \frac{C_1}{(1 + r)} + \frac{C_2}{(1 + r)^2} + \ldots$$

So far, all our examples can be worked out fairly easily by hand. Real problems are often much more complicated and require the use of an electronic calculator that is specifically programmed for present value calculations, or the use of present value tables. Here is an example that illustrates how such tables are used.

You have some bad news about your office building venture (the one described at the start of Chapter 2). The contractor says that construction will take two years instead of one and requests payment on the following schedule:

1. A $100 000 down payment now. (Note that the land, worth $50 000, must also be committed now.)
2. A $100 000 progress payment after one year.
3. A final payment of $100 000 when the building is ready for occupancy at the end of the second year.

Your real estate adviser maintains that despite the delay the building will still be worth $400 000 when completed.

All this yields a new set of cash flow forecasts:

| Period | $t = 0$ | $t = 1$ | $t = 2$ |
|---|---|---|---|
| Land | −50 000 | | |
| Construction | −100 000 | −100 000 | −100 000 |
| Payoff | | | +400 000 |
| Total | $C_0 = -150\,000$ | $C_1 = -100\,000$ | $C_2 = +300\,000$ |

---

3 The extra return for lending for two years rather than one is often referred to as a *forward rate of return*. Our rule says that the forward rate cannot be negative.

4 The technical term for money machine is **arbitrage**. There are no opportunities for arbitrage in well-functioning capital markets.

If the interest rate is 7 per cent, then NPV is

$$\text{NPV} = C_0 + \frac{C_1}{(1 + r)} + \frac{C_2}{(1 + r)^2} = -150\,000 - \frac{100\,000}{1.07} + \frac{300\,000}{(1.07)^2}$$

Table 3.1 shows how to set up the calculations and how to get the NPV. The discount factors can be found in Appendix Table 1. Look at the first two entries in the column headed 7 per cent. The top one is 0.935 and the second is 0.873. Thus you do not have to compute $1/1.07$ or $1/(1.07)^2$—you can pull the figures from the present value table. (Notice that the other entries in the 7 per cent column give discount factors out to 30 years and the other columns cover a range of discount rates from 1 to 30 per cent.)

Nowadays you can do this sort of calculation quite easily using a financial calculator. For students the calculator provides ease of calculation and often a sense of security. However, knowing which buttons to push is no substitute for understanding the calculations. Understanding is important for three reasons. First, it reduces the probability of errors, which in real business may cost millions of dollars. Second, there are discounted cash flow problems which are not accommodated by standard financial calculator functions. Your lecturer may put such a question in your exam. Third, you never know when your calculator is going to break down, but according to the corollary to Murphy's Law it will be at the most inconvenient time.

**table 3.1**
Present value worksheet

| Period | Discount factor | Cash flow | Present value |
|--------|-----------------|-----------|---------------|
| 0 | 1.0 | −150 000 | −150 000 |
| 1 | $1/(1.07) = 0.935$ | −100 000 | −93 500 |
| 2 | $1/(1.07)^2 = 0.873$ | +300 000 | +261 900 |
| | | | Total = NPV $18 400 |

Fortunately, the news about your office venture is not all bad. The contractor is now receiving a delayed payment: this means that the present value of the contractor's fee is less than before. This partly offsets the delay in the payoff. As Table 3.1 shows, the net present value is $18 400—not a substantial decrease from the $23 800 calculated in Chapter 2. Since the net present value is positive, you should still go ahead.

# 3.2 Looking for shortcuts—perpetuities and annuities

Sometimes there are shortcuts that make it very easy to calculate the present value of an asset that pays off in different periods. Let us look at some examples.

Among the securities that have been issued by the British government are so-called **perpetuities**. These are bonds such as the consols that were issued to finance the war against Napoleon. The government is under no obligation to repay the bond but offers a fixed income for each year into perpetuity. The rate of return on a perpetuity is equal to the promised annual payment divided by the present value:[5]

$$\text{Return} = \frac{\text{cash flow}}{\text{present value}}$$

$$r = \frac{C}{PV}$$

We can obviously twist this around and find the present value of a perpetuity given the discount rate $r$ and the cash payment C. For example, suppose that some worthy person wishes to endow a chair in finance at a business school. If the rate of interest is 10 per cent and if the aim is to provide $100 000 a year in perpetuity, the amount that must be set aside today is

$$\text{Present value of perpetuity} = \frac{C}{r} = \frac{100\ 000}{0.10} = \$1\ 000\ 000$$

## How to value growing perpetuities

Suppose now that our benefactor suddenly recollects that no allowance has been made for growth in salaries, which will probably average about 4 per cent a year. Therefore, instead of providing $100 000 a year in perpetuity, the benefactor must provide $100 000 in year 1, 1.04 × $100 000 in year 2, and so on. If we call the growth rate in salaries $g$, we can write down the present value of this stream of cash flows as follows:

$$PV = \frac{C_1}{(1 + r)} + \frac{C_2}{(1 + r)^2} + \frac{C_3}{(1 + r)^3} + \cdots$$

$$= \frac{C_1}{(1 + r)} + \frac{C_1(1 + g)}{(1 + r)^2} + \frac{C_1(1 + g)^2}{(1 + r)^3}$$

Fortunately, there is a simple formula for the sum of this geometric series.[6] If we assume that $r$ is greater than $g$, our clumsy-looking calculation simplifies to

$$\text{Present value of growing perepetuity} = \frac{C_1}{(r - g)}$$

Therefore, if our benefactor wants to provide perpetually an annual sum that keeps pace with the growth rate in salaries, the amount that must be set aside today is

$$PV = \frac{C_1}{(r - g)} = \frac{100\ 000}{0.10 - 0.04} = \$1\ 666\ 667$$

---

5   You can check this by writing down the present value formula
$PV = C/(1 + r) + C/(1 + r)^2 + C/(1 + r)^3 + \cdots$
Now let $C/(1 + r) = a$ and $1/(1 + r) = x$. Then we have
$PV = a(1 + x + x^2 + \cdots)$   (1)
Multiplying both sides by $x$, we have
$PVx = a(x + x^2 + \cdots)$   (2)
Subtracting (2) from (1) gives us
$PV(1-x) = a$
Therefore, substituting for $a$ and $x$,
$PV [1- 1/(1 + r)] = C/(1 + r)$
Multiplying both sides by $(1 + r)$ and rearranging gives
$r = C/PV$

6   We need to calculate the sum of an infinite geometric series $PV = a(1 + x + x^2 + \ldots)$ where $a = C_1/(1 + r)$ and $x = (1 + g)/(1 + r)$. In Footnote 5 we showed that the sum of such a series is $a/(1-x)$. Substituting for $a$ and $x$ in this formula we find that $PV = C_1/(r - g)$.

# How to value annuities

An **annuity** is an asset that pays a fixed sum each period for a specified number of periods. The equal-payment house mortgage or a hire purchase agreement are common examples of annuities.

Figure 3.1 illustrates a simple trick for valuing annuities. The first row represents a *perpetuity* that produces a cash flow of C in each year, *beginning in year* 1. It has a present value of

$$PV = \frac{C}{r}$$

The second row represents a second *perpetuity* that produces a cash flow of C in each year, *beginning in year t+1*. It *will* have a present value of C/r in year t and it therefore has a present value today of

$$PV = \frac{C}{r(1 + r)^t}$$

Both perpetuities provide a cash flow from year $t + 1$ onwards. The only difference between the two perpetuities is that the first one *also* provides a cash flow in each of the years 1 to t. In other words, the difference between the two perpetuities is an annuity of C for t years. The present value of this annuity therefore is the difference between the values of the two perpetuities

$$\text{Present value of annuity} = C\left[\frac{1}{r} - \frac{1}{r(1 + r)^t}\right]$$

The expression in brackets is the *present value annuity factor*, which is the present value at discount rate r of an annuity of $1 paid at the end of each of t periods.[7]

Suppose, for example, that our benefactor begins to vacillate and wonders what it would cost to endow the chair by providing $100 000 a year for only 20 years. The answer calculated from our formula is

$$PV = 100\,000\left[\frac{1}{0.10} - \frac{1}{0.10(1.10)^{20}}\right] = 100\,000 \times 8.514 = \$851\,400$$

Alternatively, we can simply look up the answer in the annuity table in the Appendix (Table 3). This table gives the present value of a dollar to be received in each of t periods. In our example $t = 20$ and the interest rate $r = 0.10$, and therefore we look at the twentieth number from the top in the 10 per cent column. It is 8.514. Multiply 8.514 by $100 000 and we have our answer, $851 400.

You should always be on the lookout for ways in which you can use these formulas to make life easier. For example, we sometimes need to calculate how much a series of annual payments earning a fixed annual interest would amass to by the end of t periods. We want the future value (FV) rather than the present value (PV). In this case it is easy to calculate the *present* value and then multiply it by $(1 + r)^t$ to find the future value.[8] Thus, suppose our

---

[7] Again we can work this out from first principles. We need to calculate the sum of the finite geometric series

$PV = a(1 + x + x^2 + \cdots + x^{t-1})$      (1)

where $a = C/(1 + r)$ and $x = 1/(1 + r)$. Multiplying both sides by x, we have

$PVx = a(x + x^2 + \cdots + x^t)$      (2)

Subtracting (2) from (1) gives us

$PV(1 - x) = a(1 - x^t)$

Therefore, substituting for a and x,

$PV[1 - 1/(1 + r)] = C[1/(1 + r) - 1/(1 + r)^{t+1}]$

Multiplying both sides by $(1 + r)$ and re-arranging gives

$PV = C[1/r - 1/r(1 + r)^t]$

[8] This trick also works for single cash flows. For example, suppose you receive a cash flow of C in year 6. If you invest this cash flow at an interest rate of r, you will have by year 10 an investment worth $C(1 + r)^4$. You can get the same answer by calculating the *present value* of the cash flow $PV = C/(1 + r)^6$ and then working out how much you would have by year 10 if you invested this sum today.

Future value $= PV(1 + r)^{10} = [C/(1 + r)^6](1 + r)^{10} = C(1 + r)^4$

**figure 3.1**

An annuity that makes payments in each of years 1 to $t$ is equal to the difference between the two perpetuities.

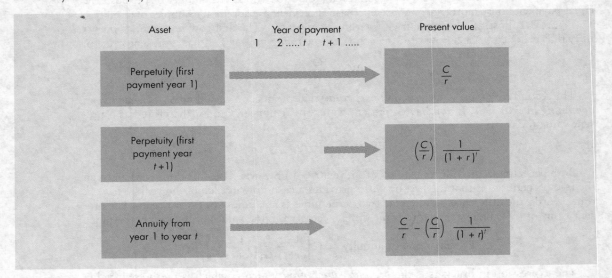

benefactor wished to know how much wealth the $100 000 per year would produce if it were invested each year instead of being given to those no-good academics. The answer would be

$$\text{Future value} = \text{PV} \times 1.10^{20} = \$851\,400 \times 6.727 = \$5.73 \text{ million}$$

How did we know that $1.10^{20}$ was 6.727? Easy, we just looked it up in Appendix Table 2. Some books will give you an extra table that combines the two calculations we just made. This extra table is the *future value annuity factor*, which gives you the accumulated value $t$ periods hence, at a discount rate $r$ of an annuity of $1 paid at the end of each of $t$ periods. The future value annuity factor is just the present value annuity factor multiplied by $(1 + r)^t$.

$$\text{Future value annuity factor} = \left[\frac{1}{r} - \frac{1}{r(1 + r)^t}\right] \times (1 + r)^t = \left[\frac{(1 + r)^t}{r} - \frac{1}{r}\right]$$

This works out to be 57.275 in the above example. Multiply this by $100 000 and we get back to $5.73 million.

As well as calculating future values from present values and vice versa, we can turn our annuity formulas around and calculate the equivalent annuity cash flow (EAC). We can do this for either a given present value or a given future value. Suppose that we know the present value and the interest rate, and we want to know the EAC for a 20-year cash flow. We simply write out the present value annuity formula. Then we solve for the cash flow $C$, which is the EAC value required. From the calculations we have just done, we know that a present value of $815 400 at an interest rate of 10 per cent is equivalent to a cash flow of $100 000 at the end of each year for 20 years, which is also equivalent to a future value of $5.73 million.

## Some other types of annuity

Now suppose our benefactor wants to start paying us $100 000 immediately. This type of annuity has a special name; it is called an *annuity due*. The other annuities that we looked at above are called *ordinary annuities*. Calculating the present value of the benefactor's new proposal is easy if he plans to provide for 21 payments. His proposal to provide us with $100 000 per annum for 20 years had a present value of $851 400, so if we get another $100 000 immediately we just add it on. The present value of the annuity due is $951 400. If the plan is to provide for only 20 payments, then we calculate the value of an ordinary annuity for 19 years and then add on the initial $100 000.

$$\text{PV annuity due} = \text{PV ordinary annuity for } (t - 1) \text{ payments} + \text{initial payment}$$

Our benefactor comes up with another plan. Can't this guy make up his mind? He still plans to provide sufficient funds immediately to finance $100 000 per year for 20 years, but now the payments do not start until the end of year 5. This is a deferred annuity. You already have all the techniques required to solve this one. So we will just show you the example.

$$\text{PV deferred annuity} = \frac{100\,000 \left[ \dfrac{1}{0.10} - \dfrac{1}{0.10(1 + 0.10)^{20}} \right]}{(1.1)^4} = \frac{851\,400}{(1.1)^4}$$

$$= \$581\,518$$

If this calculation puzzles you, see the section on page 49—'Some useful bits and pieces'.

## *How to value growing annuities

The cash flow for a growing annuity is just the same as in our earlier example for a growing perpetuity, except that the cash flows stop at time $t$.

$$\text{PV} = \frac{C_1}{(1 + r)} + \frac{C_1(1 + g)}{(1 + r)^2} + \frac{C_1(1 + g)^2}{(1 + r)^3} + \cdots + \frac{C_1(1 + g)^{t-1}}{(1 + r)^t}$$

Using the properties of a geometric progression this simplifies to[9]

$$\text{PV growing annuity} = C_1 \left[ \frac{1}{(r - g)} - \frac{(1 + g)^t}{(r - g)(1 + r)^t} \right]$$

So if our benefactor now proposes to allow for a 4 per cent increase in salary over 20 years, our calculation becomes

$$\text{PV} = 100\,000 \left[ \frac{1}{(0.10 - 0.04)} - \frac{(1 + 0.04)^{20}}{(0.10 - 0.04)(1 + 0.10)^{20}} \right]$$

$$= 100\,000\,(11.24) = \$1.124 \text{ million}$$

## 3.3 Compound interest and present values

There is an important distinction between **compound interest** and **simple interest**. When money is invested at compound interest, each interest payment is reinvested to earn more

---

[9]    We need to calculate the sum of an finite geometric series $\text{PV} = a(1 + x + x^2 + \cdots x^n)$ where $a = C_1/(1 + r)$ and $x = (1 + g)/(1 + r)$. In Footnote 6 we showed that for such a series

$$\text{PV}(1 - x) = a(1 - x^t)$$

Substituting for $a$ and $x$ in this formula and solving for PV we find

$$\text{PV} = \{[C_1/(1 + r)][1 - (1 + g)^t/(1 + r)^t]\}/[1 - (1 + g)(1 + r)]$$

This can be simplified to:

$$\text{PV} = C_1[1/(r - g) - (1 + g)^t/\{(r - g)(1 + r)^t\}]$$

As long as $r$ is greater than $g$, then as $t$ approaches infinity the last term of the equation approaches zero. So if the cash flow stream was infinite in duration we get our earlier equation for a growing perpetuity: $\text{PV} = C_1/(r - g)$.

interest in subsequent periods. In contrast, the opportunity to earn interest on interest is not provided by an investment that pays only simple interest. The formula for simple interest is

$$PV = \frac{C_t}{[1 + (t \times r)]}$$

Instead of raising $(1 + r)$ to a power of $t$, with simple interest we just multiply $r$ by $t$.

Table 3.2 compares the growth of $100 invested at compound versus simple interest. Notice that in the simple interest case, *the interest is paid only on the initial investment of $100*. Your wealth therefore increases by just $10 interest each year. In the compound interest case, you earn 10 per cent on your initial investment in the first year, which gives you a balance at the end of the year of $100 \times 1.10 = \$110$. Then in the second year you earn 10 per cent on this $110, which gives you a balance at the end of the second year of $100 \times 1.10^2 = \$121$.

**table 3.2**

Value of $100 invested at 10 per cent simple and compound interest

| | Simple interest | | | Compound interest | | | |
|---|---|---|---|---|---|---|---|
| Year | Starting balance | + Interest = | Ending balance | Starting balance | + | Interest | = Ending balance |
| 1 | 100 | + 10 = | 110 | 100 | + | 10 | = 110 |
| 2 | 110 | + 10 = | 120 | 110 | + | 11 | = 121 |
| 3 | 120 | + 10 = | 130 | 121 | + | 12.1 | = 133.1 |
| 4 | 130 | + 10 = | 140 | 133.1 | + | 13.3 | = 146.4 |
| 10 | 190 | + 10 = | 200 | 236 | + | 24 | = 259 |
| 20 | 290 | + 10 = | 300 | 612 | + | 61 | = 673 |
| 50 | 590 | + 10 = | 600 | 10 672 | + | 1 067 | = 11 739 |
| 100 | 1 090 | + 10 = | 1 100 | 1 252 783 | + | 125 278 | = 1 378 061 |
| 200 | 2 090 | + 10 = | 2 100 | 17 264 116 042 | + | 1 726 411 604 | = 18 990 527 646 |
| 215 | 2 240 | + 10 = | 2 250 | 72 116 497 132 | + | 7 211 649 713 | = 79 328 146 845 |

Table 3.2 shows that the difference between simple and compound interest is nil for a one-period investment, trivial for a two-period investment, but overwhelming for an investment of 20 years or more. A sum of $1 invested when the first fleet arrived in Australia and earning compound interest of 10 per cent a year would now be worth more than $370 million. Do you not wish your ancestors had shown rather more foresight? For the investment to have compounded at 10 per cent would have required a risky investment like shares. A compound interest rate for an investment in debt over this period might be 3 per cent. At that rate your ancestor's lack of foresight only cost you $454.

The two top lines in Figure 3.2 compare the results of investing $100 at 10 per cent simple interest and at 10 per cent compound interest. It looks as if the *rate of growth* is constant under simple interest and accelerates under compound interest. However, this is an optical illusion. The dollars of interest earned each year are growing but the *rate of growth* is the same as the interest rate. Under compound interest our wealth grows at a *constant rate*, 10 per cent in this example. Figure 3.3 is a more useful presentation. Here the numbers are plotted on a semilogarithmic scale. The constant compound growth rate shows up as straight lines, while the simple interest rate line curves down, showing that the growth rate is declining over time.

The bottom lines in Figures 3.2 and 3.3 show the discounted value (under compound interest) each year between now and year 10, of $100 to be received in year 10. Discounting takes us *down* the line, from future value to present value, and compounding takes us *back up* the line, from present value to future value.

**figure 3.2**

Compound interest versus simple interest. The top two ascending lines show the growth of $100 invested at simple and compound interest. The longer the funds are invested, the greater the advantage with compound interest. The bottom line shows that $38.55 must be invested now to obtain $100 after 10 periods. Conversely, the present value of $100 to be received after 10 years is $38.55.

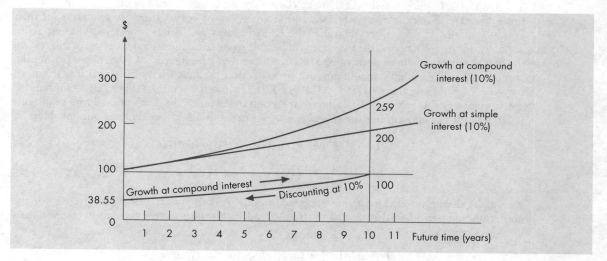

**figure 3.3**

The same story as Figure 3.2, except that the vertical scale is logarithmic. A constant compound rate of growth means a straight ascending line. This graph makes clear that the growth rate of funds invested at simple interest actually declines as time passes.

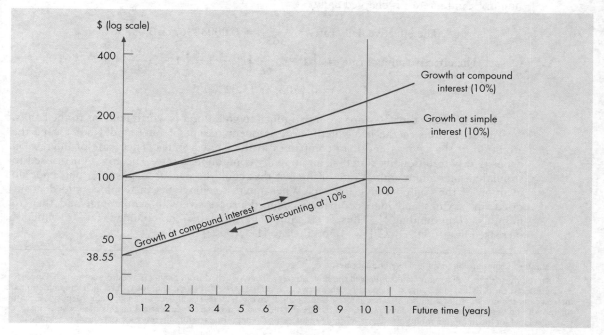

Problems in finance generally involve compound interest rather than simple interest, and therefore finance people will assume that you are talking about compound interest unless you specify otherwise. There is one exception and that is in the money market, where simple interest has traditionally been used. We discuss the valuation of money market securities using simple interest in Chapter 32.

## *A note on compounding intervals

So far we have implicitly assumed that each cash flow occurs at the end of the year. This is sometimes the case. For example, in France and Germany most corporations pay interest on their bonds annually. However, in Australia, the United States and Britain most pay interest semiannually. In these countries, the investor will be able to earn an additional six months interest on the first payment. So an investment of $100 in a bond that paid interest of 10 per cent per annum compounded semiannually would amount to $105 after the first six months, and by the end of the year it would amount to $1.05^2 \times 100 = \$110.25$. In other words, 10 per cent compounded semiannually is equivalent to 10.25 per cent compounded annually. The nominal rate of interest is 10 per cent per annum, but the *effective rate of interest* is 10.25 per cent per annum. Thus

$$(1 + \frac{0.10}{2})^2 = (1.05)^2 = (1 + 0.1025)$$

$$(1 + \frac{r}{2})^2 = (1 + r_{eff})^2 = (1 + R_{eff})$$

where $r$ is the nominal rate of interest per annum, $r_{eff}$ is the effective rate of interest for the compounding period, in this case *per half year*, and $R_{eff}$ is the effective rate of interest *per year*.

More generally

$$\left[1 + (\frac{r}{m})\right]^m = (1 + r_{eff})^m = (1 + R_{eff})$$

An investment of $1 at a rate of $r$ per annum compounded $m$ times a year amounts by the end of the year to $\$[1 + (r/m)]^m$, and the effective annually compounded rate of interest is $[1 + (r/m)]^m - 1$. Suppose your credit card has a nominal interest rate of 14 per cent per annum,[10] and interest is charged daily.

$$\text{The effective daily rate} = \frac{0.14}{365} = 0.0003836, \text{ or } 0.03836\%$$

$$\text{The effective annual rate} = \left[1 + (\frac{r}{m})\right]^m - 1 = \left[1 + (\frac{0.14}{365})\right]^{365} - 1$$

$$= 0.1502, \text{ or } 15.02\%$$

The extra 1 per cent may not seem that much to you, but it is worth millions to the banks. The attractions to the investor of more frequent receipt of interest did not escape the attention of the savings and loan companies in the United States. Their rate of interest on deposits was traditionally stated as an annually compounded rate. The government used to stipulate a maximum annual rate of interest that could be paid to depositors, but made no mention of the compounding interval. When interest ceilings began to pinch and deposits dried up, savings and loan companies changed progressively to semiannual and then to monthly compounding.[11] Thus, the equivalent annually compounded rate of interest increased first to $[1 + (r/2)]^2 - 1$ and then to $[1 + (r/12)]^{12} - 1$.

---

[10]   Annual interest rates are often quoted as nominal rates.

[11]   In Australia during the 1980s many banks followed the same strategy. They switched from paying interest on monthly balances to paying interest on daily balances. Investors could benefit in two ways. First, *provided* banks did not reduce their nominal annual interest rate, the investors got a higher effective interest rate. Second, investors with at call deposits might make deposits early in the month and withdraw the money before month end. Under the old system no interest was earned on this money since interest was calculated on the minimum monthly balance. With daily interest such deposits earn full interest each day they are in the bank.

Eventually, one company quoted a **continuously compounded rate**, so that payments were assumed to be spread evenly and continuously throughout the year. In terms of our formula, this is equivalent to letting $m$ approach infinity.[12] This might seem like a lot of calculations for our savings and loan companies. Fortunately, however, someone remembered high school algebra and pointed out that as $m$ approaches infinity $[1 + (r/m)]^m$ approaches $(2.718)^r$. The figure 2.718—or $e$, as it is called—is simply the base for natural logarithms.

The sum \$1 invested at a continuously compounded rate of $r$ will, therefore, grow to $e^r = (2.718)^r$ by the end of the first year. By the end of $t$ years it will grow to $e^{rt} = (2.718)^{rt}$. Appendix Table 4 is a table of values of $e^{rt}$. Let us practise using it.

## example 1

Suppose you invest \$1 at a continuously compounded rate of 10 per cent ($r = 0.10$) for one year ($t = 1$). The end of year value is simply $e^{0.10}$, which you can see from the second row of Appendix Table 4 is \$1.105. In other words, investing at 10 per cent a year *continuously* compounded is exactly the same as investing at 10.5 per cent a year *annually* compounded.

## example 2

Now suppose you invest \$1 at a continuously compounded rate of 11 per cent ($r = 0.11$) for one year ($t = 1$). The end-year value is now $e^{0.11}$, which you can see from the second row of Appendix Table 4 is \$1.116. In other words, investing at 11 per cent a year *continuously* compounded is exactly the same as investing at 11.6 per cent a year *annually* compounded.

## example 3

Finally, suppose you invest \$1 at a continuously compounded rate of 11 per cent ($r = 0.11$) for two years ($t = 2$). The final value of the investment is $e^{rt} = e^{0.22}$. You can see from the third row of Appendix Table 4 that $e^{0.22}$ is \$1.246.

There is a particular value to continuous compounding in capital budgeting, where it may often be more reasonable to assume that a cash flow is spread evenly over the year rather than arriving in one lump at the year's end. It is easy to adapt our previous formulas to handle this. For example, suppose that we wish to compute the present value of a perpetuity of $C$ dollars

---

[12] When we talk about *continuous* payments, we are pretending that money can be dispensed in a continuous stream like water out of a tap. One can never quite do this. For example, instead of paying out \$10 000 every year, our benefactor could pay out \$100 every eight hours or \$1 every 5.25 minutes or 1 cent every 31.17 seconds, but could not pay it out *continuously*. Financial managers *pretend* that payments are continuous rather than hourly, daily or weekly because (1) it simplifies the calculations and (2) it gives a *very* close approximation to the NPV of frequent payments.

a year. We already know that if the payment is made at the end of the year, we divide the payment by the *annually* compounded rate of $r$:

$$PV = \frac{C}{r}$$

If the same total payment is made in an even stream throughout the year, we use the same formula but substitute the *continuously* compounded rate. For example, suppose a perpetuity pays $10 continuously throughout the year and the annual interest rate is 11.6 per cent. In Example 2 above we saw that 11.6 per cent annually compounded was equivalent to 11 per cent continuously compounded. Therefore, the perpetuity is worth

$$PV = \frac{10}{0.11} = \$90.91$$

For any other continuous payments, we can always use our formula for valuing annuities. For instance, suppose that our philanthropist has thought more seriously and decided to found a home for elderly donkeys, which will cost $100 000 a year, starting immediately and spread evenly over 20 years. Previously we used the annually compounded rate of 10 per cent: now we must use the continuously compounded rate of $r = 9.53$ per cent ($e^{0.0953} = 1.10$). To cover such an expenditure, then, our philanthropist needs to set aside the following sum:[13]

$$PV = C\left[\frac{1}{r} - (\frac{1}{r} \times \frac{1}{e^{rt}})\right]$$
$$= 100\,000\left[\frac{1}{0.0953} - (\frac{1}{0.0953} \times \frac{1}{6.727})\right] = 100\,000 \times 8.932 = \$893\,200$$

Alternatively, we could have cut these calculations short by using Appendix Table 5. This shows that, if the annually compounded return is 10 per cent, then $1 a year spread over 20 years is worth $8.932.

If you look back at our earlier discussion of annuities, you will notice that the present value of $100 000 paid at the *end* of each of the 20 years was $851 406. Therefore, it costs the philanthropist about $41 800—or 5 per cent more to provide a continuous payment stream. Sometimes in finance we need only a ballpark estimate of present value. An error of 5 per cent in a present value calculation may be perfectly acceptable. In such cases it does not usually matter whether we assume that cash flows occur at the end of the year or in a continuous stream. At other times precision matters and we do need to worry about the exact frequency of the cash flows.

## *General annuities

Now that you know about effective rates of interest, we have one last trick to show you. In some cases the frequency with which annuity payments are made does not coincide with the compounding period. For example, payments may be made monthly, but interest may be compounded daily. Such annuities are called *general annuities*. In order to value such an annuity we must make the payment period and the interest period coincide. There are two ways that we can do this

---

13   Remember that an annuity is simply the difference between a perpetuity received today and a perpetuity received in year $t$. A continuous stream of $C$ dollars a year in perpetuity is worth $C/r$, where $r$ is the continuously compounded rate. Our annuity, then, is worth

$PV = C/r -$ present value of $C/r$ received in year $t$

Since $r$ is the continuously compounded rate, $C/r$ received in year $t$ is worth $(C/r) \times (1/e^{rt})$ today. Our annuity formula is therefore

$PV = C/r - [( C/r ) \times 1/e^{rt}]$

sometimes written as

$C/r (1 - e^{-rt})$

**1.** Convert the interest rate to the effective rate for the payment period.[14]
**2.** Convert the payments to EACs that correspond with the compounding period.

The first method is generally recommended, so let us try it. Suppose you plan to buy a car and finance it with a loan. You believe you can afford repayments of $100 per month. The bank will give you a three-year loan at an interest rate of 14 per cent per year compounded daily with payments monthly. What sort of car can you afford to buy? We assume that 'monthly' loan payments means a payment every four weeks (28 days), which totals 39 payments over the three years.[15] The effective interest rate per day is

$$\text{Effective } \textit{daily} \text{ rate} = 0.14/365 = 0.0003836, \text{ or } 0.03836\%$$

We convert this to an effective 'monthly' rate as

$$\text{Effective } \textit{'monthly'} \text{ rate} = (1 + 0.0003836)^{28} - 1 = 0.010796, \text{ or } 1.0796\%$$

To find out how much you can borrow we simply calculate the present value of an annuity for 39 payments at 1.0796 per cent interest per 'month'.

$$\text{PV loan} = 100\left[\frac{1}{0.010796} - \frac{1}{0.010796(1 + 0.010796)^{39}}\right] = 100[31.6928]$$
$$= \$3169.28$$

So you should start looking for a $3000 car.

The second approach requires us to convert our $100 per month to an equivalent annuity cash flow per day. We treat our $100 monthly payment as the future value of a 28-day annuity, with daily payments and a daily interest rate of 0.03836 per cent. Solving for the daily payment in the following equation gives us the daily EAC:

$$\$100 = \text{EAC}\left[\frac{1}{0.0003836} - \frac{1}{0.0003836(1 + 0.0003836)^{28}}\right]$$
$$\text{EAC} = \$3.553$$

Now we find the value of the loan that runs for 1092 days (39 × 28 days)

$$\text{PV loan} = 3.553\left[\frac{1}{0.0003836} - \frac{1}{0.0003836(1 + 0.0003836)^{1092}}\right]$$
$$= \$3169.28$$

# Some useful bits and pieces

The actuaries have developed a useful notation for annuity factors. You will probably come across this notation in books on financial mathematics, and you may also find it helpful in writing out problems.

- $A_{\overline{t}|r}$ stands for the present value annuity factor for a $t$ period annuity at a discount rate $r$.
- $S_{\overline{t}|r}$ stands for the future value annuity factor for a $t$ period annuity at a discount rate $r$.

---

[14] You may have noticed that we have already done this. When we costed the home for elderly donkeys we converted the annual interest rate to a continuous rate in order to match the cash flow.

[15] If monthly payments means payment on the same *date*, say the 20th of each month, then we have a problem. The periods between payments are not all the same. Therefore, it would not be strictly correct to use an annuity formula. We can ignore this and tolerate some error, which will usually be small. Alternatively, for an exact answer we can work out on what day each cash flow occurs and then discount each cash flow individually using the effective daily rate.

Another helpful technique for writing out discounting problems is the *time line*. We strongly recommend that you use this technique until you become familiar with discounted cash flow analysis. To demonstrate this technique we will use the philanthropist's deferred annuity proposal. The proposal was to set up a fund now which would provide $100 000 per year for 20 years, with the first payment starting at the end of year 5. This proposal is set up on a time line in Figure 3.4. Date 0 represents the present, which is also the beginning of year 1. Date 1 represents the end of year 1 and also the beginning of year 2, and so on to the end of year 24. The time line is constructed by writing in the first cash flow of $100 000 at the end of year 5 and continuing till we have entered 20 payments. As a consequence we discover that the last payment is at the end of year 24, not the end of year 25. Our next step is to calculate the present value of the annuity assuming we were at the *beginning* of year 5 (end of year 4). Applying the ordinary annuity formula to the cash flows gives us the required value, which we then discount for four years to give us the present value at date 0.

**figure 3.4**

Time line for the philanthropist's deferred annuity.

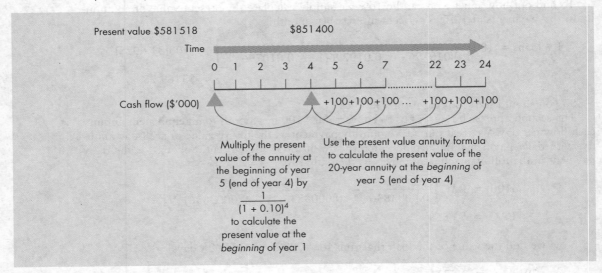

You now know how to solve a discounted cash flow calculation to obtain a present value, a future value or an EAC. Given the cash flows and either their present value or future value, it is also possible to solve for an unknown discount rate *r*. This is known as calculating the **internal rate of return (IRR)**, a concept we discuss more fully in Chapter 5. The calculation is easy for perpetuities and rather difficult for cash flows that vary over time. In the latter case the solution has to be obtained by trial and error—you keep trying discount rates till you find one that equates the calculated present value of the cash flows less the initial investment to zero. Fortunately, modern financial calculators are programmed to do all the hard work. To see how easy the calculation is for perpetuities, suppose a perpetuity offering $10 per year is purchased for $100. What is *r*? The answer is obviously 10 per cent per annum. Let us check:

$$\text{PV perpetuity} = \frac{C}{r}$$

$$\$100 = \frac{10}{0.10} = \text{purchase price}$$

So the PV at 10 per cent minus the initial investment (the $100 purchase price) is zero (i.e. the NPV is zero). The internal rate of return is therefore 10 per cent.

Finally, in Figure 3.5 we show you how all the discounting calculations fit together. We are almost ready to put our new found knowledge to work valuing bonds, but first we must briefly consider nominal and real interest rates.

**figure 3.5** _____

Different views of the same circle. The relationship between present values, future values and equivalent annuity cash flows.

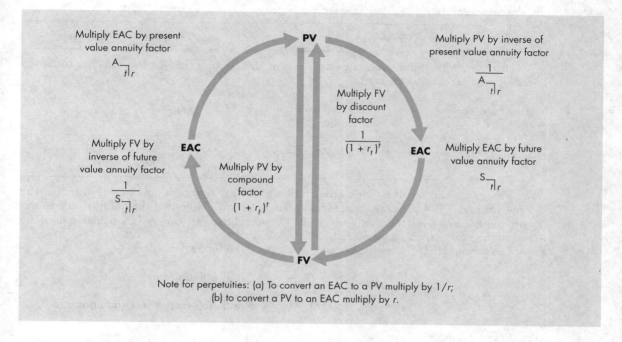

## 3.4 Nominal and real rates of interest

If you invest $1000 in a bank deposit offering an interest rate of 10 per cent, the bank promises to pay you $1100 at the end of the year. But it makes no promises about what the $1100 will buy. That will depend upon the rate of inflation over the year. If the price of goods and services increase by *more* than 10 per cent, you have lost ground in terms of the goods that you can buy.

Several indices are used to track inflation. The best known is the consumer price index (CPI), which measures the number of dollars that it takes to pay for a typical family's purchases. The change in the CPI from one period (usually a quarter or a year) to the next measures the rate of inflation. The Australian CPI has recorded annual increases for most of the second half of the twentieth century, and for much of the 1970s and 1980s inflation was running at 10 per cent or higher. As a consequence, interest rates reached very high levels in the 1980s with companies sometimes facing short-term interest rates in excess of 20 per cent. The inflationary beast appeared to have been tamed by the second half of the 1990s, with negative inflation recorded in some quarters during this period.

Economists sometimes talk about nominal dollars versus constant or real dollars. For example, the nominal cash flow from your one-year bank deposit is $1100. But if prices rise by say 6 per cent, then each dollar will buy you 6 per cent less goods next year than it does today. So at the end of the year $1100 will buy the same quantity of goods as 1100/1.06 = $1037.74 today. The nominal payoff on the deposit is $1100, but the *real* payoff is $1037.74. The real interest rate is 37.74/1000 = 3.774 per cent.

The general formula for converting nominal cash flows to real cash flows is

$$\text{Real cash flow} = \frac{\text{nominal cash flow}}{(1 + \text{inflation rate})}$$

When the bank quotes you a 10 per cent interest rate it is quoting you a nominal interest rate. The rate tells you how rapidly your money will grow:

| Invest current dollars | Receive period 1 dollars | Result |
| --- | --- | --- |
| $1000 ⟶ | $1100 | 10% *nominal* rate of return |

However, with an inflation rate of 6 per cent you are only 3.774 per cent better off at the end of the year than at the start:

| Invest current dollars | Expected real value of period 1 receipts | Result |
| --- | --- | --- |
| $1000 ⟶ | $1037.74 | Expected *real* rate of return is 3.774% |

Thus, we could say, 'The bank account offers a 10 per cent nominal rate of return' *or* 'The bank offers a 3.774 per cent *expected* real rate of return'. Note that the nominal rate is certain, but that the real rate is only expected. The actual real rate cannot be calculated until the end of the year arrives and the inflation rate is known.

The formula that relates the nominal interest rate to the real rate is:

$$1 + r_{\text{nominal}} = (1 + r_{\text{real}})(1 + \text{inflation rate})$$

$$= 1 + r_{\text{real}} + \text{inflation rate} + r_{\text{real}}(\text{inflation rate})$$

In our example

$$1.10 = (1.03774)(1.06)$$

## 3.5 Using present value formulas to value bonds

When governments borrow money, they often do so by issuing bonds. Companies can also issue bonds, but the corporate bond market in Australia is quite thin. A bond is simply a security that represents a long-term debt. If you own a bond, you are promised a fixed set of cash payoffs.[16] Each year until the bond matures, you get an interest payment and then at maturity you also get back the face value of the bond.[17]

Suppose that in July 1998 you invest in a 7.5 per cent 2005 Australian Treasury bond. Assume the bond's 7.5 per cent **coupon** rate is payable annually, and that it has a face value of $1000. This means that each year until 2005 you will receive an interest payment of 0.075 × 1000 = $75. The bond matures in July 2005: At that time, the Treasury pays you the final $75 interest, plus the $1000 face value. We will assume that you are buying the bond ex-interest.

---

16   As lenders to Bond Corporation and Qintex can tell you, with risky bonds there is some possibility that you may get less than you are promised.

17   The face value of the bond is known as the *principal*. Therefore, when the bond matures, the borrower pays you principal and the last interest payment.

This means that you will not get the current interest due for payment in July 1998. Assuming you hold the bond for the seven years to maturity, the cash flows from owning the bond are as follows:

| Year | 1999 | 2000 | 2001 | 2002 | 2003 | 2004 | 2005 |
|---|---|---|---|---|---|---|---|
| Cash flow ($) | 75 | 75 | 75 | 75 | 75 | 75 | 1075 |

What is the 1998 market value of this stream of cash flows? To determine that, we need to look at the return provided by similar securities. Commonwealth government Treasury bonds of similar maturity were *yielding* between 5.36 and 5.45 per cent. That is what investors were giving up when they bought the 7.5 per cent *coupon* Treasury bonds. The mid-point of the yield range is 5.41 per cent. Therefore, to value the 7.5 per cent bonds, we will discount the prospective stream of cash flows at 5.41 per cent.

$$PV = \sum_{t=1}^{7} \frac{E[C_t]}{(1 + r)^t}$$

$$= \frac{75}{(1 + r)} + \frac{75}{(1 + r)^2} + \frac{75}{(1 + r)^3} + \frac{75}{(1 + r)^4} + \frac{75}{(1 + r)^5} + \frac{75}{(1 + r)^6} + \frac{1075}{(1 + r)^7}$$

$$= \frac{75}{(1.0541)} + \frac{75}{(1.0541)^2} + \dots + \frac{1075}{(1.0541)^7}$$

$$= 1119.16$$

Notice that we assume that Australian Treasury bonds have negligible default risk and therefore the expected cash flow $E[C_t]$ is equal to the promised cash flow.

Bond prices can be expressed as a percentage of the face value. Thus, we can say that our 7.5 per cent Treasury bond is worth $1119.16, or 111.92 per cent of face value. We can also say that the bond sells at an 11.92 per cent *premium* over its face value. This is because the coupon rate it offers[18] (7.5 per cent) is higher than the required return in the market (5.41 per cent).

At a price of $1119.16 with a 7.5 per cent coupon, the bond offers an expected return of 5.41 per cent, which is exactly what investors require. The relation between the coupon rate and the market price is as follows:

| Coupon rate | Market price |
|---|---|
| Greater than required return | Greater than face value—bond sells at a **premium** |
| Equal to required return | Equal to face value |
| Less than required return | Less than face value—bond sells at a **discount** |

**A shortcut**    You may have noticed a shortcut way to value the Treasury bond. The bond is like a package of two investments. The first investment consists of seven annual coupon payments of $75 each, and the second investment consists of payment of the $1000 face value at maturity. Therefore, you can use the annuity formula to value the coupon payments and add on the value of the final payment.

$$\begin{aligned}
PV\ (bond) &= PV\ (\text{coupon payments}) + PV\ (\text{principal}) \\
&= (\text{coupon} \times \text{7-year annuity factor}) + (\text{final payment} \times \text{discount factor}) \\
&= 75 \times \left[ \frac{1}{0.0541} - \frac{1}{0.0541(1.0541)^7} \right] + \frac{1000}{1.0541^7} \\
&= \$427.60 + \$691.56 = \$1119.56
\end{aligned}$$

---

[18] You can think of the coupon rate as the expected return on the bond if it sold for a price equal to its face value.

Any bond can be valued as a package of an annuity (the coupon payments) and a single payment (the principal or face value).

You may have noticed a difference between the formula that we used to value the bonds and the *general* present value formula developed in Section 3.1. In the general formula we allowed for the fact that $r_1$, the rate of return offered by the capital market on one-year investments, may be different from $r_2$, the rate of return offered on two-year investments. Then we finessed this problem by assuming that $r_1$ is the same as $r_2$. In valuing the Treasury bond we again assume that investors use the same rate to discount cash flows occurring in different years. That may not matter as long as short-term rates are approximately the same as long-term rates. But often when we value bonds we should discount each cash flow at a different rate. There will be more about that in Chapter 23.

**Finding the bond yield**    In order to work out the expected return on the bond, we could have phrased our question about price the other way around: If the price of the bond is $1119.16, what return do investors expect? In that case, we need to find the value of $r$ that solves the following equation:

$$1119.16 = \frac{75}{(1 + r)} + \frac{75}{(1 + r)^2} + \frac{75}{(1 + r)^3} + \cdots \frac{1075}{(1 + r)^7}$$

The rate $r$ is often called the bond's **yield to maturity** or internal rate of return. In our case $r$ is 5.41 per cent. We are fortunate in that we already know that if you discount the cash flows at 5.41 per cent, you arrive at the bond's price of $1119.16. As we will see in Chapter 5, the only *general* procedure for calculating $r$ is trial and error. Fortunately, specially programmed electronic calculators can be used to calculate $r$, or you can use a book of bond tables that show values of $r$ for different coupon levels and different maturities.

## What happens to bond prices as interest rates change?

Interest rates fluctuate. It is not that long ago that Treasury bonds offered yields in excess of 10 per cent. So let us see how our 7.5 per cent coupon bond would be affected if yields (interest rates) jumped up to say 10 per cent. The new price would be:

$$PV = \frac{75}{(1 + 0.10)} + \frac{75}{(1 + 0.10)^2} + \frac{75}{(1 + 0.10)^3} + \frac{75}{(1 + 0.10)^4} + \frac{75}{(1 + 0.10)^5} +$$
$$\frac{75}{(1 + 0.10)^6} + \frac{1075}{(1 + 0.10)^7} = \$878.29$$

Not surprisingly, the higher the yield that investors demand, the less they will be prepared to pay for the bond, and vice versa.

Some bonds are more affected than others by changes in interest rates. A change may have a substantial effect on bond value when the cash flows on the bond last for many years. It will have a trivial effect if the bond matures tomorrow.

## Compounding intervals and bond prices

In calculating the value of 7.5 per cent Treasury bonds, we made two approximations. First, we assumed that interest payments occurred annually. In practice, most Australian bonds make coupon payments semiannually. Therefore, instead of receiving $75 every year, an investor holding 7.5 per cent bonds would receive $37.50 every *half* year. Second, yields in Australia are usually quoted as semiannual compound yields. Therefore, if the semiannual compound yield is 5.41 per cent, the yield over six months is 5.41/2 = 2.705 per cent.

Now we can recalculate the value of the 7.5 per cent Treasury bonds, recognising that there are 14 six-monthly coupon payments of $37.50 and a final payment of $1000.

$$PV = \frac{37.50}{(1 + 0.02705)} + \frac{37.50}{(1 + 0.02705)^2} + \frac{37.50}{(1 + 0.02705)^3} + \cdots + \frac{37.50}{(1 + 0.02705)^{13}}$$
$$+ \frac{1037.50}{(1 + 0.02705)^{14}} = \$1120.45$$

## 3.6 Summary

The difficult thing in any present value exercise is to set up the problem correctly, and time lines can be a great help here. Once you have done that, you must be able to do the calculations, but they are not that difficult. Now that you have worked through this chapter, all you should need is a little practice.

The basic present value formula for an asset that pays off in several periods is the following obvious extension of our 1-period formula:

$$PV = \frac{C_1}{(1 + r_1)} + \frac{C_2}{(1 + r_2)^2} + \frac{C_3}{(1 + r_3)^3} + \cdots$$

You can *always* work out *any* present value problem using this formula, but when the interest rates are the *same for each maturity* (note well this qualification) there may be some shortcuts that can reduce the tedium. We looked at three such cases. First, there was the case of an asset that pays C dollars a year in perpetuity. Its present value is simply

$$PV = \frac{C}{r}$$

Second, there was the case of an asset whose payments increase at a steady rate g in perpetuity. Its present value is

$$PV = \frac{C}{(r - g)}$$

Third, there was the case of an annuity that pays C dollars a year for t years. To find its present value we take the difference between the values of two perpetuities:

$$PV = C\left[\frac{1}{r} - \frac{1}{r(1 + r)^t}\right]$$

Other annuities considered were annuities due, deferred annuities, growing annuities and general annuities. We also introduced the concepts of the equivalent annuity cash flow (EAC) and the internal rate of return.

Our next step was to distinguish between simple and compound interest. At one end of the spectrum with no compounding periods we have simple interest and at the other end of the spectrum we have continuous compounding. We observed that compound interest calculations were standard practice, except in the money market. In discounting to calculate present values we assume compound interest.

Present value is the amount that we would have to invest now at compound interest r in order to produce the future cash flows $C_1$, $C_2$, etc. When someone offers to lend us a dollar at an annual rate of r, we should always check how frequently the interest is to be compounded so that we can work out the effective rate of interest. If the compounding interval is annual, we will have to repay $(1 + r)^t$ dollars; on the other hand, if the compounding is continuous, we will have to repay $2.718^{rt}$ (or, as it is usually expressed, $e^{rt}$) dollars. Very often in capital budgeting we are willing to assume that the cash flows occur at the end of each year, and therefore we discount them at an annually compounded rate of interest. Sometimes, however, it may be fairer to assume that they are spread evenly over the year: in this case we must make use of continuous compounding.

Present value tables will help us to perform many of these calculations. You have been introduced now to tables that show:

1. Present value of $1 received at the end of year $t$
2. Future value of $1 by the end of year $t$
3. Present value of $1 received at the end of each year until year $t$
4. Future value of $1 invested at a continuously compounded rate of interest
5. Present value of $1 received continuously for $t$ years when the annually compounded interest rate is $r$

It is important to distinguish between *nominal* cash flows (the actual number of dollars that you will receive) and *real* cash flows that are adjusted for inflation. An investment may promise a high nominal rate of interest, but if inflation is also high, the real interest rate may be very low or even negative.

Finally, we introduced in this chapter two very important ideas that we will come across several times again. The first is that you can add present values: If your formula for the present value of $(A + B)$ is not the same as your formula for the present value of $A$ plus the present value of $B$, you have made a mistake. The second is the notion that there is no such thing as a money machine: If you think you have found one, go back and check your calculations.

## FURTHER READING

The material in this chapter should cover all you need to know about the mathematics of discounting; but if you wish to dig deeper, there are a number of books on the subject. Try, for example:

H. Crapp and J. Marshall, *Money Market Maths*, Allen and Unwin, 1986.
D. M. Knox, P. Zima and R. L. Brown, *Mathematics of Finance*, 2nd ed., McGraw-Hill, Sydney, 1998.
J. Marshall, *Money Equals Maths*, Allen and Unwin, 1989.
M. Sherris, *Money and Capital Markets*, 2nd ed., Allen and Unwin, 1996.

## QUIZ

1. At an interest rate of 12 per cent, the six-year discount factor is 0.507. How many dollars is $0.507 worth in six years if invested at 12 per cent?

2. If the present value of $139 is $125, what is the discount factor?

3. If the eight-year discount factor is 0.285, what is the present value of $596 received in eight years?

4. If the cost of capital is 9 per cent, what is the present value of $374 paid in year 9?

5. A project produces the following cash flows:

   | Year | Flow |
   | --- | --- |
   | 1 | 432 |
   | 2 | 137 |
   | 3 | 797 |

   If the cost of capital is 15 per cent, what is the project's present value?

6. If you invest $100 at an interest rate of 15 per cent, how much will you have at the end of eight years?

**7.** An investment of $232 will produce $312.18 in two years. What is the annual interest rate?

**8.** An investment costs $1548 and pays $138 in perpetuity. If the interest rate is 9 per cent, what is the net present value?

**9.** It costs $2590 to insulate your home. Next year's fuel saving will be $220. If the interest rate is 12 per cent, what percentage growth rate in fuel prices is needed to justify insulation? Assume fuel prices will grow in perpetuity at the rate $g$.

**10.** An ordinary share will pay a cash dividend of $4 next year. After that, the dividends are expected to increase indefinitely at 4 per cent per year. If the discount rate is 14 per cent, what is the present value of the stream of dividend payments?

**11.** If you invest $502 at the end of each of the next nine years at an interest rate of 13 per cent, how much will you have at the end?

**12.** Harold Filbert is 30 years of age and his salary next year will be $20 000. Harold forecasts that his salary will increase at a steady rate of 5 per cent per annum until his retirement at age 60.
   a. If the discount rate is 8 per cent, what is the present value of these future salary payments?
   b. If Harold saves 5 per cent of his salary each year and invests these savings at an interest rate of 8 per cent, how much will he have saved by age 60?
   c. If Harold plans to spend these savings in even amounts over the subsequent 20 years, how much can he spend each year?

**13.** A factory costs $400 000. You reckon that it will produce an inflow after operating costs of $100 000 in year 1, $200 000 in year 2 and $300 000 in year 3. The opportunity cost of capital is 12 per cent. Draw up a worksheet like that shown in Table 3.1 and use tables to calculate the net present value.

**14.** Do not use tables for these questions. The interest rate is 10 per cent.
   a. What is the present value of an asset that pays $1 a year in perpetuity?
   b. The value of an asset that appreciates at 10 per cent per annum approximately doubles in seven years. What is the approximate present value of an asset that pays $1 a year in perpetuity beginning in year 8?
   c. What is the approximate present value of an asset that pays $1 a year for each of the next seven years?
   d. A piece of land produces an income that grows by 5 per cent per annum. If the first year's flow is $10 000, what is the value of the land?

**15.** Use the tables in the Appendix or your calculator for each of the following calculations:
   a. The cost of a new car is $10 000. If the interest rate is 5 per cent, how much would you have to set aside now to provide this sum in five years?
   b. You have to pay $12 000 a year in school fees at the end of each of the next six years. If the interest rate is 8 per cent, how much do you need to set aside today to cover these bills?
   c. You have invested $60 476 at 8 per cent. After paying the above school fees, how much would remain at the end of the six years?
   d. You have borrowed $1000 and in return have agreed to pay back $1762 in five years. What is the annually compounded rate of interest on the loan? What is the continuously compounded rate of interest?

# QUESTIONS AND PROBLEMS

1. Use the *discount factors* shown in Appendix Table 1 to calculate the present value of $100 received in:
   a. Year 10 (at a discount rate of 1 per cent).
   b. Year 10 (at a discount rate of 13 per cent).
   c. Year 15 (at a discount rate of 25 per cent).
   d. Each of years 1 to 3 (at a discount rate of 12 per cent).

2. Use the *annuity* factors shown in Appendix Table 3 to calculate the present value of $100 in each of:
   a. Years 1 to 20 (at a discount rate of 23 per cent).
   b. Years 1 to 5 (at a discount rate of 3 per cent).
   c. Years 3 to 12 (at a discount rate of 9 per cent).

3. a. If the one-year discount factor is 0.88, what is the one-year interest rate?
   b. If the two-year interest rate is 10.5 per cent, what is the two-year discount factor?
   c. Given these one- and two-year discount factors, calculate the two-year annuity factor.
   d. If the present value of $10 a year for three years is $24.49, what is the three-year annuity factor?
   e. From your answers to Parts (c) and (d), calculate the three-year discount factor.

4. A factory costs $800 000. You reckon that it will produce an inflow after operating costs of $170 000 a year for 10 years. If the opportunity cost of capital is 14 per cent, what is the net present value of the factory? What will the factory be worth at the end of five years?

5. Halcyon Lines is considering the purchase of a new bulk carrier for $8 million. The forecast revenues are $5 million a year and operating costs are $4 million. A major refit costing $2 million will be required after both the fifth and tenth years. After 15 years, the ship is expected to be sold for scrap at $1.5 million. If the discount rate is 8 per cent, what is the ship's NPV?

6. As the winner of a breakfast cereal competition, you can choose one of the following prizes:
   a. $100 000 now.
   b. $180 000 at the end of five years.
   c. $11 400 a year forever.
   d. $19 000 for each of 10 years.
   e. $6500 next year and increasing thereafter by 5 per cent a year forever.
   If the interest rate is 12 per cent, which is the most valuable prize?

7. Refer back to the story of Ms Kraft in Section 3.1.
   a. If the one-year interest rate were 25 per cent, how many plays would Ms Kraft require to become a millionaire? (*Hint*: You may find it easier to use a calculator and a little trial and error.)
   b. What does the story of Ms Kraft imply about the relationship between the one-year discount factor DF1, and the two-year discount factor DF2?

8. Siegfried Basset is 65 years of age and has a life expectancy of 12 years. He wishes to invest $20 000 in an annuity that will make a level payment at the end of each year until his death. If the interest rate is 8 per cent, what income can Mr Basset expect to receive each year?

**9.** Wise Owl and Pussy Cat are saving to buy a boat at the end of five years. If the boat costs $20 000 and they can earn 10 per cent a year on their savings, how much do they need to put aside at the end of years 1 to 5?

**10.** Kangaroo Autos is offering free credit on a new $10 000 car. You pay $1000 down and then $300 a month for the next 30 months. Turtle Motors next door does not offer free credit but will give you $1000 off the list price. If the rate of interest is 10 per cent a year, which company is offering the better deal?

**11.** Recalculate the net present value of the office building venture in Section 3.1 at interest rates of 5, 10 and 15 per cent. Plot the points on a graph with NPV on the vertical axis and the discount rates on the horizontal axis. At what discount rate (approximately) would the project have zero NPV? Check your answer.

**12. a.** How much will an investment of $100 be worth at the end of 10 years if invested at 15 per cent a year simple interest?
  **b.** How much will it be worth if invested at 15 per cent a year compound interest?
  **c.** How long will it take your investment to double its value at 15 per cent compound interest?

**13.** You own an oil pipeline that will generate a $2 million cash return over the coming year. The pipeline's operating costs are negligible and it is expected to last for a very long time. Unfortunately, the volume of oil shipped is declining and cash flows are expected to decline by 4 per cent per year. The discount rate is 10 per cent.
  **a.** What is the present value of the pipeline's cash flows if its cash flows are assumed to last forever?
  **b.** What is the present value of the cash flows if the pipeline is scrapped after 20 years?
  (*Hint*: For Part (b), start with your answer to Part (a), then subtract the present value of a declining perpetuity starting in year 21. Note that the forecast cash flow for year 21 will be much less than the cash flow for year 1.)

**\*14.** If the interest rate is 7 per cent, what is the value of the following three investments?
  **a.** An investment that offers you $100 a year in perpetuity with the payment at the end of each year.
  **b.** A similar investment with the payment at the beginning of each year.
  **c.** A similar investment with the payment spread evenly over each year.

**\*15.** Refer back to Section 3.2. If the rate of interest is 8 per cent rather than 10 per cent, how much would our benefactor need to set aside to provide each of the following?
  **a.** $100 000 at the end of each year in perpetuity.
  **b.** A perpetuity that pays $100 000 at the end of the first year and that grows at 4 per cent a year.
  **c.** $100 000 at the end of each year for 20 years.
  **d.** $100 000 a year spread evenly over 20 years.

**\*16.** For an investment of $1000 today, the Tiburon Finance Company is offering to pay you $1600 at the end of eight years. What is the annually compounded rate of interest? What is the continuously compounded rate of interest?

**\*17.** How much will you have at the end of 20 years if you invest $100 today at 15 per cent *annually* compounded? How much will you have if you invest at 15 per cent *continuously* compounded?

**\*18.** You have just read an advertisement stating, 'Pay us $100 a year for 10 years and we will pay you $100 a year thereafter in perpetuity.' If this is a fair deal, what is the rate of interest?

**\*19.** Which would you prefer?
a.  An investment paying interest of 12 per cent compounded annually.
b.  An investment paying interest of 11.7 per cent compounded semiannually.
c.  An investment paying 11.5 per cent compounded continuously.
Work out the value of each of these investments after 1, 5 and 20 years.

**\*20.** When calculating the value of growing perpetuities, we developed a shortcut formula. In order to do so we assumed that the growth rate $g$ was less than the discount rate $r$. Is this a reasonable assumption? (*Hint*: Consider what would happen to present value as $g$ gets close to $r$.)

**\*21.** You want to buy a house. Dragon Bank will give you a $100 000 loan for 20 years. They will charge you 5 per cent concessional interest for the first year, after which the loan reverts to their normal variable rate, which is currently 8.75 per cent. They will charge you a $600 application fee, plus when you make your loan enquiry you can have as much coffee as you can drink. The Public Bank will also give you a $100 000 loan for 20 years, but their concessional interest rate for the first year is 6.75 per cent, after which the loan reverts to their normal variable rate, which is also 8.75 per cent. However, there is no fee and no coffee. Both banks compound interest daily and you will make your loan payments fortnightly. What would your fortnightly loan payment be for each bank? Assuming you can drink $5 worth of coffee, which bank offers the best deal?

**\*22.** In this chapter we developed a present value formula for *growing* annuities using the properties of a geometric progression, and we developed a present value formula for *ordinary* annuities as the difference between two perpetuities. See if you can develop the formula for *growing* annuities as the difference between two *growing* perpetuities. (*Hint*: The second annuity makes its first payment of $C(1 + g)^t$ in year $t + 1$.)

**\*23.** You take out a $100 000 housing mortgage repayable over 20 years at an interest rate of 12 per cent per annum. Interest is compounded monthly and payments are made monthly.
a.  What are your monthly repayments?
b.  What is the total of your payments over the loan, and how much of that total is interest?
c.  At the end of five years how much would you still owe on the mortgage?
d.  How would your answer to Part (b) change if you made your payments once per year?

**\*24.** A friend who recently graduated with a law degree has married and just had a baby. She wants to provide sufficient funds for her daughter to go to law school at age 18. She therefore plans to set aside sufficient money to provide $50 000 on her daughter's eighteenth birthday and $25 000 each birthday thereafter for five years. Your friend approaches you for advice on how much money she will need to invest, in equal instalments, on each of her daughter's birthdays prior to age 18. The interest rate is 9 per cent. What is your answer?

**\*25.** Here are two useful rules of thumb. The Rule of 72 says that with discrete compounding the time it takes for an investment to double in value is roughly 72/(interest rate, in per cent). The Rule of 69 says that with continuous compounding the time that it takes to double is *exactly* 69.3/(interest rate, in per cent).

    a. If the annually compounded interest rate is 12 per cent, use the Rule of 72 to calculate roughly how long it takes before your money doubles. Now work it out exactly.

    b. Can you prove the Rule of 69?

**26.** In 1880 five aboriginal trackers were promised the equivalent of $100 for helping to capture the notorious outlaw Ned Kelly. In 1993 the granddaughters of two of the trackers claimed that this reward had not been paid. A senior politician stated that, if this were true, the government would be happy to pay the $100. However, the granddaughters also claimed that they were entitled to compound interest. How much was each entitled to if the interest rate was 5 per cent? What if it was 10 per cent?

**27.** A leasing contract calls for an immediate payment of $100 000 and nine subsequent $100 000 semiannual payments at six-month intervals. What is the present value of these payments if the *annual* discount rate is 8 per cent?

**28.** Use a spreadsheet program to construct your own set of annuity tables.

**29.** A famous winger just signed a $15 million contract providing $3 million a year for five years. A less famous mid-fielder signed a $14 million five-year contract providing $4 million now and $2 million for five years. Who is better paid? The interest rate is 10 per cent.

**30.** In August 1994 the *Wall Street Journal* reported that the winner of the Massachusetts State lottery prize had the misfortune to be both bankrupt and in prison for fraud. The prize was $9 420 713 to be paid in 19 equal annual instalments.[19] The Bankruptcy Court judge ruled that the prize should be sold off to the highest bidder and the proceeds used to pay off the creditors. If the interest rate was 8 per cent, how much would you have been prepared to bid for the prize? Enhance Reinsurance Company was reported to have offered $4.2 million. Use the Annuity Table 3 to find (approximately) the return that the company was looking for.

**31.** You estimate that by the time that you retire in 35 years, you will have accumulated savings of $2 million. If the interest rate is 8 per cent and you live 15 years after retirement, what annual level of expenditure will those savings support?

    Unfortunately, inflation will eat into the value of your retirement income. Assume a 4 per cent inflation rate and work out a spending program for your retirement that will allow you to maintain a level *real* expenditure during retirement.

**32.** An oil well now produces 100 000 barrels per year. The well will last forever, but production will decline by 4 per cent per year. Oil prices, however, will increase by

---

[19] There were 20 instalments but the winner had already received the first payment.

2 per cent per year. The discount rate is 8 per cent. What is the present value of the well's production?

**33.** An oil production platform in Bass Strait will operate for 15 or more years. At that time environmental regulations require dismantlement and removal. The current cost of this would be $10 million, but the cost is expected to increase by 5 per cent per year.
   a.  What is the present value of the future cost? Assume a discount rate of 11 per cent.
   b.  Suppose new regulations require the oil platform's owner to contribute an equal annual nominal amount to build up a trust fund sufficient to cover dismantlement and removal at year 15. The trust fund has to be invested in Australian Treasury bonds yielding 6.5 per cent. How much will the oil company have to put in each year?

**34.** You are considering the purchase of an apartment complex that will generate a net cash flow of $400 000 per year. You normally demand a 10 per cent rate of return on such investments. Future cash flows are expected to grow with inflation at 4 per cent per year. How much would you be willing to pay for the complex if it:
   a.  Will produce cash flows forever?
   b.  Will have to be torn down in 20 years? Assume that the site will be worth $5 million at that time net of demolition costs. (The $5 million includes 20 years inflation.)
Now calculate the real discount rate corresponding to the 10 per cent nominal rate. Redo the calculations for Parts (a) and (b) using real cash flows. (Your answers should not change.)

**35.** The following table shows national income per head in 1992 in a sample of OECD countries and recent rates of inflation:[20]

|  | Income per head (US$) | Annual inflation (%/year) |
| --- | --- | --- |
| France | 15 969 | 2.8 |
| Germany | 17 840 | 3.7 |
| Greece | 7 556 | 17.6 |
| Japan | 16 677 | 2.5 |
| Switzerland | 20 798 | 4.9 |
| Turkey | 3 560 | 68.0 |
| UK | 14 592 | 4.8 |
| USA | 20 360 | 3.6 |

If recent inflation rates persist in the future, what nominal income will be needed in each country in 2020 just to keep pace with inflation?

**36.** Vernal Pool, a self-employed herpetologist, wants to put aside a fixed fraction of her annual income as savings for retirement. Ms Pool is now 40 years old and makes $40 000 a year. She expects her income to increase by 2 percentage points over inflation (for example, 4 per cent inflation means a 6 per cent increase in

---

[20]  Income is measured in terms of equivalent purchasing power.

income). She wants to accumulate $500 000 in real terms to retire at age 70. What fraction of her income does she need to set aside? Assume her retirement funds are conservatively invested at an expected real rate of return of 5 per cent a year. Ignore taxes.

**37.** Calculate the real cash flows on a 6 per cent Australian Treasury bond assuming a five-year maturity, annual interest payments and an inflation rate of 5 per cent. Now show that by discounting the real cash flows at the real interest rate, you get the same PV as when you discount the nominal cash flows at the nominal interest rate.

**38.** Use a spreadsheet program to construct a set of bond tables that shows the present value of a bond given the coupon rate, maturity and yield to maturity. Assume that coupon payments are semiannual and yields are compounded semiannually. Use your bond tables to check the yields on a couple of Australian Treasury bonds quoted in the *Australian Financial Review*.

# chapter 4

# THE VALUE OF SHARES

We should warn you that being a financial expert has its occupational hazards. One is being cornered at cocktail parties by people who are eager to explain their system for making super profits by investing in shares. Fortunately, these bores go into temporary hibernation whenever the market goes down.

We may exaggerate the perils of the trade. The point is that there is no easy way to ensure superior investment performance. Later in the book we will show that changes in security prices are fundamentally unpredictable and that this result is a natural consequence of well-functioning capital markets. Therefore, in this chapter, when we propose to use the concept of present value to price shares and bonds, we are not promising you a key to investment success; we simply believe that the idea can help you to understand why some investments are priced higher than others.

Why should you care? If you want to know the value of the firm's shares, why cannot you look up the share price in the newspaper? Unfortunately, that is not always possible. For example, you may be the founder of a successful business. You currently own all the shares, but are thinking of 'going public' by selling off shares to other investors. You and your advisers need to estimate the price at which those shares can be sold. Or, suppose that Establishment Industries is proposing to sell its concatenator division to another company. It needs to figure out the value of this mini-firm.

There is also another, deeper reason why managers need to understand how shares are valued. We have stated that a firm, which acts in its shareholders' interest, should accept those investments that increase the value of their stake in the firm. But in order to do this, it is necessary to understand what determines the shares' value.

We start the chapter with a brief look at how shares are traded. Then we explain the basic principles of share valuation. We look at the fundamental difference between growth shares and income shares. We also look at the significance of earnings per share and price-earnings multiples. Finally, we discuss some of the special problems managers and investors encounter when they calculate the present values of entire businesses.

A word of caution before we proceed. Everybody knows that shares are risky and that some are more risky than others. Therefore, investors will not commit funds to shares unless the expected rates of return are commensurate with the risks. The present value formulas we have discussed so far can take account of the effects of risk on value, but we have not yet told you exactly *how* to do so. Recognise therefore that risk comes into the following discussion in a loose and intuitive way. A more careful treatment of risk starts in Chapter 7.

## 4.1 How ordinary shares are traded

Each public company listed on the Australian Stock Exchange (ASX) has millions, or hundreds of millions, of shares on issue. Listing rules set minimum requirements for the spread of ownership in companies traded on the ASX. A minimum of several hundred shareholders is required, but usually the number of shareholders will be many thousands.[1] These shareholders will include large investors owning millions of shares. Such investors include superannuation funds, financial institutions, companies owning shares in other companies and wealthy individuals. But there are also many individuals who hold small parcels of shares. If you own one millionth of the company's shares you have a claim on one millionth of its profits and one millionth of its net assets.

If a company such as BHP wishes to raise additional capital it may do so either by borrowing or by issuing new shares to investors. Sales of shares to raise new capital are said to occur in the **primary market**. But most trade in BHP shares consists of investors buying existing shares from each other and therefore does not raise new capital for the firm. This market for trading second-hand shares is known as the **secondary market**.

The principal secondary market for Australian companies is the ASX. In 1996 the ASX turnover was about $160 billion, roughly half the total value of shares listed. In contrast, additional capital raised from the issue of new shares was only of the order of $15 billion. The ASX is not large by world standards, and is dwarfed by the large markets of the United States, Japan and the United Kingdom.[2] Very large Australian companies like BHP often arrange to also be listed on overseas stock exchanges, such as the London and New York Stock Exchanges (NYSE).[3] This increases their opportunities to raise new capital.

Suppose you are the head trader of a superannuation fund that wishes to buy 100 000 shares in Boral. You contact your stockbroker, who will ask what price you are prepared to pay. She may discuss with you the level of trading activity, and current buying and selling offers in the market. She obtains this information from a display on her computer screen, which is connected into the ASX Stock Exchange Automated Trading System (SEATS). The broker will then enter into SEATS your bid price and the quantity of shares that you require. Other brokers on the system can then view your purchase bid. If there is already an offer to sell that matches your bid price, SEATS will automatically execute the trade. If there are insufficient shares to satisfy your order, it will be partially filled and the balance of the order will remain active on the system.

---

[1]   Shareholders may number hundreds of thousands for very large companies.

[2]   These latter markets account for roughly two-thirds of the world's equity stock market value, while Australia's contribution to total value is less than two per cent.

[3]   Strictly speaking, BHP shares are traded on the NYSE packaged up as BHP American Depository Receipts (ADRs).

You can follow the day's trading using an online data service such as Beacon, which will report prices and volumes for the trades that occur. Various Internet sites and telephone services also provide information on share prices. But many of you may still rely on the newspaper for your share price information. Here, for example, is how the *Australian Financial Review* recorded the day's trading in Boral for Thursday 23 July 1998:

| 52 week | | | Last | + | Quotes | | Dividend | | | Dividend | PE |
|---|---|---|---|---|---|---|---|---|---|---|---|
| High | Low | Company name | sale | or − | Buy | Sell | c per share | Cover | NTA | yield (%) | ratio |
| 4.48 | 2.71 | Boral | 3.04 | +3 | 3.01 | 3.04 | 15.00 f | 2.44 | 2.50 | 4.93 | 8.3 |

You can see that on this day the last trade in Boral's shares was at $3.01, a rise of three cents on the previous day's closing price. Since there are about 1.15 billion Boral shares on issue, investors were placing a total value on Boral of the order of $3.5 billion.

Buying shares is a risky occupation. You can see that by looking at the 52 week high and low for Boral's share price. An unfortunate investor who bought at the high of $4.48 and sold at a low of $2.71 would have lost nearly 40 per cent of the initial investment.

The *Financial Review* also provides other information about Boral's shares. Boral is paying an annual franked dividend of $0.15 per share, giving a dividend yield of 4.93 per cent.[4] The dividend is covered 2.44 times by earnings, and the shares are selling at a price above their net tangible asset (NTA) backing of $2.50. The ratio of share price to earnings (P/E ratio) is 8.3. We will explain shortly why investors pay attention to these figures.

# 4.2 How ordinary shares are valued

Think back to the last chapter where we described how to value future cash flows. The discounted cash flow (DCF) formula for the present value of a share is just the same as it is for the present value of any other asset. We just discount the cash flows from the share by the return that can be earned in the capital market on securities of comparable risk. Shareholders receive cash from the company in the form of a stream of dividends. So

$$PV(share) = PV(expected\ future\ dividends)$$

At first sight this statement may seem surprising. When investors buy shares, they usually expect to receive a dividend, but they also hope to make a capital gain. Why does our formula for present value say nothing about capital gains? As we now explain, there is no inconsistency.

## Today's price

The cash payoff to owners of ordinary shares comes in two forms: (1) cash dividends and (2) capital gains or losses. Usually investors expect to get some of each. So which should we discount when calculating prices? It turns out that we can either discount *all* future dividends, or we can discount the price at which we expect to sell the share plus the dividends we expect to receive before the sale.

Suppose that the current price of a share is $P_0$, that the *expected* price at the end of a year is $P_1$ and that the *expected* dividend per share is $DIV_1$. The return you require in order to invest in the share is $r$, sometimes known as the **market capitalisation rate**. If you invest, you will want to get back your initial investment $P_0$, plus earn a return on that investment of $rP_0$.

---

4    The dividend yield is the dividend divided by the share price.

The cash you expect to get back comes from the dividends and from selling the share. Therefore, you would be prepared to buy the share under the following condition:

$$\text{Cash invested } + \text{ cash return required } = \text{ cash you expect to receive}$$
$$P_0 + rP_0 = DIV_1 + P_1$$

Rearranging this equation

$$P_0 = \frac{DIV_1 + P_1}{(1 + r)}$$

The result should be no surprise. The equation says that the price today is the present value of the expected cash flow. You add the present value of dividend per share to the present value of the cash you expect to receive on selling the share.

Let us now see how our formula works. Consider the case of Fledgling Electronics. Investors expect a 50 cent cash dividend over the next year ($DIV_1 = 0.50$). They also expect the share to sell for \$11 a year hence ($P_1 = 11$).

$$P_0 = \frac{0.50 + 11}{(1 + r)}$$

But what is the required return $r$? If the expected return on securities in the same 'risk class' as Fledgling is 15 per cent, then $r$ is 15 per cent, and today's price for Fledgling should be \$10:

$$P_0 = \frac{0.50 + 11}{1.15} = \$10$$

At a price of \$10 the expected return on Fledgling shares is as follows

$$\text{Expected return} = \frac{DIV_1 + P_1 - P_0}{P_1} = \frac{0.50 + 11 - 10}{10} = 15\%$$

How do we know that \$10 is the right price? Because no other price could survive in competitive capital markets. What if $P_0$ was above \$10? Then Fledgling shares would offer an expected rate of return that was lower than other securities of equivalent risk. Investors would shift their capital to the other securities and in the process would force down the price of Fledgling shares. If $P_0$ were less than \$10 the process would reverse. Fledgling's shares would offer a higher rate of return than comparable securities. In that case, investors would rush to buy, forcing the price up to \$10.

The general conclusion is that at each point in time *all securities that are in an equivalent risk class are priced to offer the same expected return*. This is a condition for equilibrium in well-functioning capital markets. It is also common sense.

Equilibrium expected return = return on equivalent risk securities = required return = $r$

## But what determines next year's price?

We have managed to explain today's share price $P_0$ in terms of the dividend $DIV_1$ and the expected price next year $P_1$. Future share prices are not easy things to forecast directly. But think about what determines next year's price. If our price formula holds now, it ought to hold then as well:

$$P_1 = \frac{P_2 + DIV_2}{(1 + r)}$$

That is, a year from now investors will be looking forward to dividends in year 2 and the price at the end of year 2. Thus, we can forecast $P_1$ by forecasting $DIV_2$ and $P_2$ and we can express $P_0$ in terms of $DIV_1$, $DIV_2$ and $P_2$:

$$P_0 = \frac{DIV_1}{(1 + r)} + \frac{DIV_2 + P_2}{(1 + r)^2}$$

Take Fledgling Electronics. A plausible explanation why investors expect its share price to rise by the end of the first year is that they expect higher dividends and still more capital gains in the second year. For example, suppose that they are looking today for dividends of $0.55 in year 2 and a subsequent price of $12.10. That would imply a price at the end of year 1 of

$$P_1 = \frac{0.55 + 12.10}{1.15} = \$11$$

Today's price can then be computed either from our original formula

$$P_0 = \frac{0.50 + 11}{1.15} = \$10$$

or from our expanded formula

$$P_0 = \frac{DIV_1}{(1 + r)} + \frac{DIV_2 + P_2}{(1 + r)^2} = \frac{0.50}{1.15} + \frac{0.55 + 12.10}{(1.15)^2} = \$10$$

We have succeeded in relating today's price to the forecast dividends for two years ($DIV_1$ and $DIV_2$) plus the forecast price at the end of the *second* year ($P_2$). You will probably not be surprised to learn that we could go on to replace $P_2$ by $(DIV_3 + P_3)/(1 + r)$ and relate today's price to the forecast dividends for three years ($DIV_1$, $DIV_2$ and $DIV_3$) plus the forecast price at the end of the *third* year ($P_3$). In fact, we can look as far out into the future as we like, removing $P$s as we go. Let us call this final period $H$. This gives us a general share price formula

$$P_0 = \frac{DIV_1}{(1 + r)} + \frac{DIV_2}{(1 + r)^2} + \ldots + \frac{DIV_H + P_H}{(1 + r)^H}$$

$$= \sum_{t=1}^{H} \frac{E[DIV_t]}{(1 + r)^t} + \frac{E[P_H]}{(1 + r)^H}$$

The expression $\sum_{t=1}^{H}$ simply means the sum of the discounted dividends from year 1 to year $H$. The use of the expectation brackets $E[\ ]$ in the general share price formula is a reminder that when you substitute into this formula you are substituting for expected values. An obvious, but often neglected, point is that the price we have just calculated is an **ex-dividend price.** We are valuing the share without the current dividend since we did not include $DIV_0$ in our calculation. To calculate the **cum-dividend price** (the price with the current dividend) we simply add $DIV_0$ to the ex-dividend price.

Table 4.1 continues the Fledgling Electronics example for various time horizons, assuming that the dividends are expected to increase at a steady 10 per cent compound rate. The expected price $P_t$ increases at the same rate each year. Each line in the table represents an application of our general formula for a different value of $H$. Figure 4.1 provides a graphical representation of the table. Each column shows the present value of the dividends up to the time horizon and the present value of the price at the horizon. As the horizon recedes, the dividend stream accounts for an increasing proportion of present value, but the *total* present value of dividends plus terminal price always equals $10.

How far out could we look? In principle the horizon period $H$ could be infinitely distant. Ordinary shares do not expire of old age. Barring such corporate hazards as liquidation or takeover, they are immortal. As $H$ approaches infinity, the present value of the terminal price ought to approach zero, as it does in the final column of Figure 4.1. We can therefore forget about the terminal price entirely and express today's price as the present value of a perpetual stream of cash dividends. This is usually written as

$$P_0 = \sum_{t=1}^{\infty} \frac{E[DIV_t]}{(1 + r)^t}$$

where the sign $\infty$ is used to indicate infinity.

**table 4.1**

Applying the stock valuation formula to Fledgling Electronics

| | Expected future values | | | Present values | |
|---|---|---|---|---|---|
| Horizon period (H) | Dividend (DIV_t) | Price (P_t) | Cumulative Dividends | Future price | Total |
| 0 | — | 10 | — | 10 | 10 |
| 1 | 0.50 | 11 | 0.44 | 9.56 | 10 |
| 2 | 0.55 | 12.10 | 0.85 | 9.15 | 10 |
| 3 | 0.61 | 13.31 | 1.25 | 8.75 | 10 |
| 4 | 0.67 | 14.64 | 1.63 | 8.37 | 10 |
| | | | | | 10 |
| 10 | 1.18 | 25.94 | 3.59 | 6.41 | 10 |
| 20 | 3.06 | 67.28 | 5.89 | 4.11 | 10 |
| 50 | 53.36 | 1 173.91 | 8.92 | 1.08 | 10 |
| 100 | 6 263.92 | 137 806.12 | 9.88 | 0.12 | 10 |

*Notes:*
1. *Dividends are assumed to increase at 10 per cent per year compounded.*
2. *The discount rate is 15 per cent.*
3. *Figures are rounded to two decimal places.*

**figure 4.1**

As your horizon recedes the present value of the future price (shaded area) declines but the present value of the stream of dividends (unshaded area) increases. The total present value (future price and dividends) remains the same.

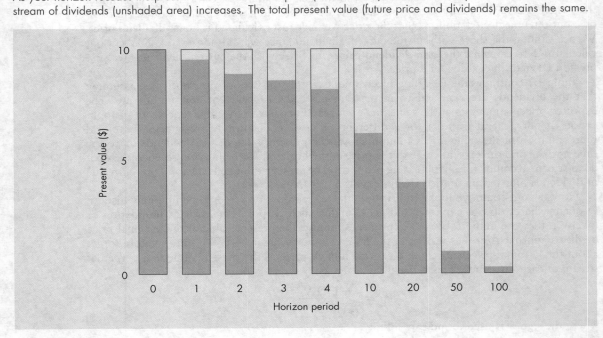

This discounted cash flow (DCF) formula for the present value of a share is just the same as it is for the present value of any other asset. We just discount the expected cash flows—in this case the expected dividend stream—by the return that can be earned in the capital market on securities of comparable risk. Some find the DCF formula implausible because it seems to ignore capital gains. But we know that the formula was *derived* from the assumption that price in any period is determined by expected dividends *and* capital gains over the next period.

Remembering our rule about adding present values, we might be tempted to conclude that the *total* value of a company's ordinary shares must be equal to the discounted stream of *all* future dividends paid by the company. But we need to be a little careful here. We must only include the dividends that will be paid on *existing* shares. The company may at some future date decide to sell more shares and holders of those shares will be entitled to their share of the subsequent dividend stream. The *total* value of a company's existing ordinary shares is therefore equal to the discounted value of that *portion* of the total dividend stream which will be paid to the shares outstanding today. It sounds obvious, but it is surprising how often people forget.

## 4.3 A simple way to estimate the capitalisation rate

In Chapter 3 we encountered some simplified versions of the basic present value formula. Let us see whether they offer any insights into share values. Suppose, for example, that we forecast a constant growth rate for a company's dividends. This does not preclude year-to-year deviations from the trend: it means only that *expected* dividends grow at a constant rate. Such an investment would be just another example of the growing perpetuity that we helped our fickle philanthropist to evaluate in the last chapter. To find its present value we must divide the next year's expected cash payment by the difference between the discount rate and the expected growth rate:

$$P_0 = \frac{E[DIV_1]}{r - E[g]}$$

This formula is often called the Gordon growth model, because it was popularised by the work of Myron Gordon. Remember that we can use this formula only when $g$, the anticipated growth rate, is less than $r$, the discount rate. As $g$ approaches $r$, the share price becomes infinite. Obviously, $r$ must be greater than $g$ if growth really is perpetual.

Our growing perpetuity formula explains $P_0$ in terms of next year's expected dividend $DIV_1$, the projected growth trend $g$ and the expected rate of return on other securities of comparable risk $r$. Alternatively, the formula can be used to obtain an estimate of $r$ from $DIV_1$, $P_0$ and $g$:

$$r = \frac{DIV_1}{P_0} + g$$

The market capitalisation rate equals the *expected dividend yield* ($DIV_1/P_0$) plus the expected rate of growth in dividends ($g$).

These two formulas are much easier to work with than the general statement that 'price equals the present value of expected future dividends'.[5] For instance, imagine that you are analysing BHP early in 1994 when its shares are selling for about $18.50 a share.[6] Dividend

---

[5]  These formulas were first developed in 1938 by Williams and were rediscovered by Gordon and Shapiro. See J. B. Williams, *The Theory of Investment Value,* Harvard University Press, Cambridge, Mass., 1938; and M. J. Gordon and E. Shapiro, 'Capital Equipment Analysis: The Required Rate of Profit', *Management Science*, 3:102–10 (October 1956).

[6]  You may wonder why we are not using a more recent price. The reason is that from a teaching point of view the numbers for this example work out particularly well.

payments for 1994 were forecast to be $0.43 a share. Now we can calculate the first half of our formula:

$$\text{Dividend yield} = \frac{\text{DIV}_1}{P_0} = \frac{0.43}{18.50} = 0.023, \text{ or } 2.3\%$$

This is a relatively low dividend yield and therefore investors expected growth in dividends. The question is how much? One line of reasoning starts with BHP's **payout ratio**, the ratio of dividends to earnings per share (EPS). This was about 45 per cent in the prior year. In other words, BHP was ploughing back into the business about 55 per cent of earnings per share:

$$\text{Ploughback ratio } (b) = 1 - \text{payout ratio} = 1 - \frac{\text{DIV}}{\text{EPS}} = 1 - 0.45 = 0.55$$

At that time, BHP's ratio of earnings per share to book equity per share[7] was about 14.5 per cent. This is its **return on equity** (ROE):

$$\text{Return on equity} = \text{ROE} = \frac{\text{EPS}}{\text{book equity per share}} = 0.145$$

The values we have estimated for ploughback and ROE are historic values. What we would really like to know are the prospective values $\text{DIV}_1/\text{EPS}_1$ and $\text{EPS}_1/\text{book equity per share}$. BHP was quite a stable company and it would not be too unreasonable to assume that the historic relationships continue to hold. Suppose we forecast that BHP will earn 14.5 per cent of book equity and reinvest 55 per cent of that return. Then book equity will increase by $0.55 \times 0.145 = 0.08$. Since we assumed that the return on equity and the payout ratio are constant, earnings and dividends per share will also increase by 8 per cent:

$$\text{Dividend growth rate} = g = \text{ploughback ratio} \times \text{ROE} = b \times \text{ROE} = 0.55 \times 0.145$$
$$= 0.08$$

Now you have your estimate of the market capitalisation rate (i.e. the rate of return that investors use to discount BHP's future dividends):

$$r = \frac{\text{DIV}_1}{P_0} + g = 0.023 + 0.08 = 0.103, \text{ or } 10.3\%$$

Unfortunately, the estimate appears too low. Early in 1994, 10-year government bonds offered a yield of 6.5 per cent. Our estimate of $r$ gives a risk premium for BHP of only 3.8 per cent over the government bond rate. This is too small.[8] Perhaps we should have used a higher value for expected ROE in our calculation. At the beginning of 1994 the economy appeared to be accelerating out of recession and corporate ROE looked set to rise sharply.

In early 1994 financial analysts were predicting a growth rate for BHP's earnings of 15.0 per cent for 1994 and 16.6 per cent for 1995.[9] The corresponding predictions for dividend growth rates were 6.0 per cent and 7.8 per cent. Notice how the growth in dividends lags the growth in earnings.[10] If BHP sustained a 16.6 per cent earnings growth, then dividend growth would eventually catch up, rising to 16.6 per cent. However, it is doubtful that 16.6 per cent is a perpetually sustainable rate of profit growth. So we expect the long-run earnings growth rate to fall below 16.6 per cent, but we also expect the dividend growth rate to

---

7    By book equity per share we mean net assets per share as reported in the company financial statements.

8    After you have read Chapter 7 you will be in a better position to judge appropriate market capitalisation rates and appropriate risk premia.

9    A useful source of this sort of data is *The BARCEP Report (Barclays Australasia Consensus Earnings Profile)* produced monthly by Barclays.

10    We explain why in Chapter 16.

rise above 7.8 per cent. Perhaps they will meet in the middle. In which case $g$ is expected to be[11]

$$g = \frac{16.6\% + 7.8\%}{2} = 12.2\%$$

Our revised estimate of $r$ is

$$r = \frac{DIV_1}{P_0} + g = 0.023 + 0.122 = 0.145, \text{ or } 14.5\%$$

The risk premium over the government bond rate is now 8 per cent, which seems a more likely figure. Clearly, an accurate estimate of $g$ is critical in using the constant growth formula. Equally clearly, there are dangers in making forecasts by simply extrapolating from the history of a company.

## Some warnings about constant-growth formulas

The simple constant-growth DCF formula is an extremely useful rule of thumb, but no more than that. Naïve trust in the formulas has led many financial analysts to silly conclusions.

First, remember the difficulty of estimating $r$ by analysis of one share only. Try to use a large sample of equivalent-risk securities. Even that may not work, but at least it gives the analyst a fighting chance, because the inevitable errors in estimating $r$ for a single security tend to balance out across a broad sample.

Second, resist the temptation to apply the formula to firms having high current rates of growth.[12] Such growth can rarely be sustained indefinitely, but the constant-growth DCF formula assumes it can. This erroneous assumption leads to an overestimate of $r$.

Consider Growth-Tech Ltd, a firm with $DIV_1 = \$0.50$ and $P_0 = \$50$. That firm has ploughed back 80 per cent of earnings and has had a return on equity of 25 per cent. This means that *in the past*

Dividend growth rate = ploughback ratio × ROE = 0.80 × 0.25 = 0.20

The temptation is to assume that the future long-term growth rate ($g$) also equals 0.20. This would imply

$$r = \frac{0.50}{50.00} + 0.20 = 0.21$$

But this is silly. No firm can continue growing at 20 per cent per year forever, except possibly under extreme inflationary conditions. Eventually, profitability will fall and the firm will respond by investing less.

In real life the return on investment will decline *gradually* over time, but for simplicity let us assume it suddenly drops to 16 per cent at year 3 and the firm responds by ploughing back only 50 per cent of earnings. Then $g$ drops to 0.50(0.16) = 0.08.

Table 4.2 shows what is going on. Growth-Tech starts year 1 with assets of $10.00. It earns $2.50, pays out 50 cents as dividends and ploughs back $2. Thus it starts year 2 with $10 + 2 = $12. After another year at the same ROE and payout it starts year 3 with equity of $14.40. However, ROE drops to 0.16 and the firm earns only $2.30. Dividends go up to $1.15, because the payout ratio increases, but the firm has only $1.15 to plough back. Therefore, subsequent growth in earnings and dividends drops to 8 per cent.

---

[11]　If you think this procedure appears ad hoc, you are right. There are no mechanical rules for forecasting the future.

[12]　There are also dangers in using simple growth models in times of inflation. See M. Lally, 'The Gordon-Shapiro Dividend Growth Formula and Inflation', *Accounting and Finance*, **28**: 45–51 (November 1998).

**table 4.2**

Forecasted earnings and dividends for Growth-Tech. Note the changes in year 3: ROE and earnings drop, but payout ratio increases, causing a big jump in dividends. However, subsequent growth in earnings and dividends falls to 8 per cent per year. Note that the increase in equity equals the earnings not paid out as dividends.

|  | Year 1 | Year 2 | Year 3 | Year 4 |
|---|---|---|---|---|
| Book equity | 10.00 | 12.00 | 14.40 | 15.55 |
| Earnings per share (EPS) | 2.50 | 3.00 | 2.30 | 2.49 |
| Return on equity (ROE) | 0.25 | 0.25 | 0.16 | 0.16 |
| Payout ratio | 0.20 | 0.20 | 0.50 | 0.50 |
| Dividends per share (DIV) | 0.50 | 0.60 | 1.15 | 1.24 |
| Growth rate of dividends | — | 0.20 | 0.92 | 0.08 |

Now we can use our general DCF formula to find the capitalisation rate $r$:

$$P_0 = \frac{DIV_1}{(1 + r)} + \frac{DIV_2}{(1 + r)^2} + \frac{DIV_3 + P_3}{(1 + r)^3}$$

Investors in year 3 will view Growth-Tech as offering 8 per cent per year dividend growth. We will apply the constant-growth formula:

$$P_3 = \frac{DIV_4}{r - 0.08}$$

$$P_0 = \frac{DIV_1}{(1 + r)} + \frac{DIV_2}{(1 + r)^2} + \frac{DIV_3}{(1 + r)^3} + \frac{1}{(1 + r)^3}\left[\frac{DIV_4}{r - 0.08}\right]$$

$$= \frac{0.50}{(1 + r)} + \frac{0.60}{(1 + r)^2} + \frac{1.15}{(1 + r)^3} + \frac{1}{(1 + r)^3}\left[\frac{1.24}{r - 0.08}\right]$$

We have to use trial and error to find the value of $r$ that makes $P_0$ equal \$50. It turns out that the $r$ implicit in these more realistic forecasts is approximately 0.099, quite a difference from our 'constant-growth' estimate of 0.21.

A final warning: Do not use the simple constant-growth formula to test whether the market is correct in its assessment of a share's value. If your estimate of the value is different from that of the market, it is probably because you have used poor dividend forecasts. Remember what we said at the beginning of this chapter about simple ways of making money on the share market: there are none.

## 4.4 The link between share price and earnings per share

Investors often use the terms *growth shares* and *income shares*. They seem to buy growth shares primarily for the expectation of capital gains, and they are interested in the future growth of earnings[13] rather than in next year's dividends. On the other hand, they buy income shares primarily for the cash dividends. Let us see whether these distinctions make sense.

---

[13]  In the analysis that follows we assume that earnings represents the distributable cash flow. That is, the cash that could be distributed to shareholders without reducing the future capacity of the company to sustain this cash flow. This may or may not be true for accounting earnings!

Imagine first the case of a company that does not grow at all. It does not plough back any earnings and simply produces a constant stream of dividends. Its share would be rather like the perpetual bond described in the last chapter. Remember that the return on a perpetuity is equal to the yearly cash flow divided by the present value. The expected return on our share would thus be equal to the yearly dividend divided by the share price (i.e. the dividend yield). Since all the earnings are paid out as dividends, the expected return is also equal to the earnings per share divided by the share price (i.e. the earnings yield, or earnings to price ratio). For example, if the dividend is $1 a share and the equilibrium share price is $10, we have

$$\text{Equilibrium expected return} = \text{dividend yield} = \text{earnings yield} = \text{required return}$$

$$= \frac{DIV_1}{P_0} = \frac{EPS_1}{P_0}$$

$$= \frac{1.00}{10} = 0.10$$

The price equals

$$P_0 = \frac{DIV_1}{r} = \frac{EPS_1}{r} = \frac{1.00}{0.10} = \$10$$

The required return $r$ for firms that do not pay out all their earnings can also equal the earnings yield. The key is whether earnings are reinvested to provide a return greater or less than the required return. For example, suppose our monotonous company suddenly hears of an opportunity to invest $1 a share *next year*. This would mean no dividend at $t = 1$. However, the company expects that in each subsequent year the project would earn $0.10 per share, so that the dividend could be increased to $1.10 a share.

Let us assume that this investment opportunity has about the same risk as the existing business. Then we can discount the investment's cash flow at the 10 per cent rate to find its net present value at year 1:

$$\text{Net present value (of investment) per share at year 1} = -1 + \frac{1.1}{0.10} = 0$$

Thus, the investment opportunity will make no contribution to the company's value. Its prospective return is equal to the opportunity cost of capital.

What effect will the decision to undertake the project have on the company's share price? Clearly none: the NPV of the investment is zero. The reduction in value caused by the nil dividend in year 1 is exactly offset by the increase in value caused by the extra dividends in later years. Therefore, since the current price is unchanged and next year's earnings remain at $1, the market capitalisation rate $r$ is again equal to the earnings yield:

$$r = \frac{EPS_1}{P_0} = \frac{1}{10} = 0.10$$

Table 4.3 repeats our example for different assumptions about the cash flow generated by the new project. Note that the earnings to price ratio, measured in terms of $EPS_1$, next year's expected earnings, equals the market capitalisation rate ($r$) *only* when the new project's NPV = 0. This is an extremely important point—managers frequently make poor financial decisions because they confuse earnings yields with the market capitalisation rate.

In general, we can think of share price as the capitalised value of average earnings (the no-growth value) plus **PVGO**, the **present value of growth opportunities**.

$$P_0 = \frac{EPS_1}{r} + PVGO$$

$$= \text{Value of assets in place} + PVGO$$

**table 4.3**

Effect on share price of investing an additional $1 in year 1 at different rates of return. Notice that the earnings-price ratio (earnings yield) overestimates $r$ when the project has a negative NPV and underestimates it when the NPV is positive.

| Project rate of return | Incremental cash flow C | Project NPV in Year 1[a] | Project's impact on share price in year 0[b] | Share price in year 0, $P_0$ | $\dfrac{EPS_1}{P_0}$ | $r$ |
|---|---|---|---|---|---|---|
| 0.05 | 0.05 | −0.50 | −0.45 | 9.55 | 0.105 | 0.10 |
| 0.10 | 0.10 | 0.00 | 0.00 | 10.00 | 0.10 | 0.10 |
| 0.15 | 0.15 | 0.50 | 0.45 | 10.45 | 0.096 | 0.10 |
| 0.20 | 0.20 | 1.00 | 0.909 | 10.909 | 0.092 | 0.10 |
| 0.25 | 0.25 | 1.50 | 1.36 | 11.36 | 0.088 | 0.10 |

Notes:

[a]  The project costs $1.00 ($EPS_1$). NPV $= -1.00 - C/r$ where r = 0.10.

[b]  NPV is calculated at year 1. To find the impact on $P_0$ discount the NPV for one year at r = 0.10.

The earnings-price ratio therefore equals

$$\frac{EPS_1}{P_0} = r(1 - \frac{PVGO}{P_0})$$

The earnings-price ratio (earnings yield) will underestimate $r$ if PVGO is positive and overestimate $r$ if PVGO is negative. (The latter case is less likely, since firms are rarely *forced* to take projects with negative net present values.)

# *Calculating the present value of growth opportunities for Fledgling Electronics

In our last example both dividends and earnings were expected to grow, but this growth made no net contribution to the share price. The share was in this sense an 'income share'. Be careful not to equate firm performance with the growth in earnings per share. A company that reinvests earnings at below the market capitalisation rate may increase earnings but will certainly reduce the share value.

Now let us turn to that well-known *growth share*, Fledgling Electronics. You may remember that Fledgling's market capitalisation rate, $r$, is 15 per cent. The company is expected to pay a dividend of $0.50 in the first year, and thereafter the dividend is predicted to increase indefinitely by 10 per cent a year. We can therefore use the simplified constant-growth formula to work out Fledgling's price:

$$P_0 = \frac{DIV_1}{r - g} = \frac{0.50}{0.15 - 0.10} = \$10$$

Suppose that Fledgling has earnings per share of $0.833. Its payout ratio is then

$$\text{Payout ratio} = \frac{DIV_1}{EPS_1} = \frac{0.50}{0.833} = 0.6$$

In other words, the company is ploughing back $1 - 0.6$, or 40 per cent, of earnings. Suppose also that Fledgling's ratio of earnings to book equity is ROE = 0.25. This explains the growth rate of 10 per cent:

$$\text{Growth rate} = g = \text{ploughback ratio} \times \text{ROE} = 0.4 \times 0.25 = 0.10$$

The capitalised value of Fledgling's earnings per share if it had no growth would be

$$\frac{EPS_1}{r} = \frac{0.833}{0.15} = \$5.55$$

But we know that the value of Fledgling's shares is $10. The difference of $4.45 must be the amount that investors are paying for growth opportunities. Let us see if we can explain that figure.[14]

Each year Fledgling ploughs back 40 per cent of its earnings into new assets. In the first year Fledgling invests $0.33 ($0.833 \times 0.4 = 0.33$) at a permanent 25 per cent return on equity. Thus, the cash generated by this investment is $0.25 \times 0.33 = \$0.083$ per year, in perpetuity, starting at $t = 2$. The net present value of the investment as of $t = 1$ is

$$NPV_1 = -0.33 + \frac{0.083}{0.15} = \$0.22$$

Everything is the same in year 2 except that Fledgling will invest just over $0.36, 10 per cent more than in year 1 (remember $g = 0.10$). Similarly, the earnings will be 10 per cent higher. Therefore, at $t = 2$ an investment is made with a net present value, at t = 2, of

$$NPV_2 = -0.33 \times 1.10 + \frac{0.083 \times 1.10}{0.15} = \$0.24$$

Thus, the payoff to the owners of Fledgling Electronics shares can be represented as the sum of (1) a level stream of earnings, which could be paid out as cash dividends if the firm did not grow and (2) a set of tickets, one for each future year, representing the opportunity to make investments having positive NPVs. We know that the first component of the value of the share is

$$\text{Present value of level stream of earnings} = \frac{EPS_1}{r} = \frac{0.833}{0.15} = \$5.55$$

How do we value the growth opportunities? The first ticket is worth $0.22 in $t = 1$; the second is worth $0.22 \times 1.10 = \$0.24$ in $t = 2$; and the third is worth $0.24 \times 1.10 = \$0.26$ in $t = 3$. These are the forecasted cash values of the tickets. We know how to value a stream of future cash values that grows at 10 per cent per year: we use our growing perpetuity formula, with the forecast ticket values at year 1—$NPV_1$—as the initial cash flow. To three decimal places the $NPV_1$ of the first ticket is 0.222.

$$\text{Present value of growth opportunities} = PVGO = \frac{NPV_1}{r - g} = \frac{0.222}{0.15 - 0.10}$$

$$= \$4.44$$

Now everything checks:

Share price = present value of level stream of earnings (i.e. PV of assets in place)
    + present value of growth opportunities

$$= \frac{EPS_1}{r} + PVGO$$

$$= \$5.55 + \$4.44$$

$$= \$10 \text{ (after allowing for a one cent rounding error)}$$

Why is Fledgling Electronics a growth share? Not because it is expanding at 10 per cent per year. It is a growth share because the net present value of its future investments accounts for a significant fraction (about 44 per cent) of the *share*'s price. These net present values are positive because the *expected ROE exceeds the required rate of return*. It is this capacity to make *abnormally profitable* investments that is the hallmark of *growth share*s.

---

[14]  To simplify the presentation, figures are rounded to two decimal places or, in some cases for earnings, three decimal places. As a consequence of rounding, the no-growth value and the value of growth are understated by about one cent in total.

Share prices today reflect investors' expectations of future operating *and investment* performance. The expectation of future growth is a significant component of value for most companies. We would usually expect the present value of growth opportunities to be in the range of 20 per cent to 75 per cent of the share price. High-flying growth shares like Microsoft would lie at the top of this range. Such growth shares sell at high price-earnings ratios because investors are willing to pay now for expected *superior* returns on investments that have not yet been made.[15]

# Free cash flow

The Greek god Zeus made a habit of appearing in unusual disguises to unsuspecting maidens. The general DCF formula for valuing shares is rather like that: it keeps cropping up in different forms. Here is another useful version of the formula. We can take the cash revenue, deduct the cash operating costs, then deduct the cash reinvested—the balance left is often known as **free cash flow**:[16]

$$\text{Free cash flow} = \text{revenue} - \text{costs} - \text{investment}$$

So far, we have not allowed for companies raising extra finance externally. Remember we have been assuming that retained earnings finance all investment and that any cash not reinvested in the business is paid out as dividends. In this case the dividend per share is the same as the free cash flow per share, and the general DCF formula can be written in terms of per share revenues, costs and investment:

$$P_0 = \sum_{t=1}^{\infty} \frac{\text{E[free cash flow per share}_t]}{(1 + r)^t}$$

Notice that it is *not* correct to say that a share's value is equal to the discounted stream of its future earnings per share. That would recognise the *rewards* of investment (in the form of increased revenues) but not the *sacrifice* (in the form of investment). The correct formulation states that share value is equal to the discounted stream of free cash flow per share.

To summarise, we can think of a share's value as representing either: (1) the present value of the stream of expected future dividends; (2) the present value of free cash flow; or (3) the present value of average future earnings under a no-growth policy plus the present value of future growth opportunities.

## example

Investors are willing to forgo cash dividends today in exchange for higher earnings and the expectation of high dividends sometime in the future. This is well demonstrated by Woodside's development of Australia's Northwest Shelf for gas and oil. This was a multi-billion dollar project, and for many years during the development Woodside never paid a dividend. Despite this, Woodside was consistently in the top 20 shares by value listed on the ASX. Woodside is not a counter-example to the statement that share price equals the present value of expected future dividends. Companies like Woodside may have zero dividends for many years, but their dividends are expected to be positive sooner or later. Eventually growth must slow down, or developments come on stream, releasing funds that can be paid to the shareholders. This is the prospect that made Woodside shares valuable. Woodside now pays dividends.

---

15   Michael Eisner, the chairman of Walt Disney Productions, made the point this way: 'In school you had to take the test and then be graded. Now we're getting graded, and we haven't taken the test.' This was in late 1985, when Disney stock was selling at nearly 20 times earnings. See Kathleen K. Wiegner, 'The Tinker Bell Principle', *Forbes*, 2 December 1985, p. 102.

16   Confusingly, this is a term with more than one definition. Sometimes, for example, free cash flow is defined as revenue less costs, investment *and* payments to debtholders.

# *Why free cash flow is the fundamental source of value

You may be wondering: What happens when we do allow external financing? We defer detailed discussion of this issue till Chapters 16 to 19. However, there are some important principles that we can establish here. In efficient capital markets the purchasers of securities will pay what they are worth. Therefore, when the company sells securities it can expect to be paid the present value of the cash flows that accrue to those securities. If so, the issue of securities is a zero NPV transaction. In other words, it is not likely to have an effect on the wealth of the existing shareholders.

Remember our observation earlier in the chapter that when a company sells additional shares the old shareholders are no longer entitled to all future dividends, but just a portion of them. Also remember our discussion of the separation theorem in Chapter 2. There we showed how investors could use the capital market to convert the cash flows from a real investment to a pattern that satisfied their consumption plans. The only restriction was that the present value of the consumption cash flows had to be equal to the present value of the cash flows from the real investment. Well, the firm can do the same thing. It can use the capital market to transform the cash flows from its investments to a different pattern of cash flows, but with the same present value. For example, it might make a share issue and use the proceeds to pay a bigger dividend to existing shareholders. The cost to the existing shareholders is, of course, a smaller share of future dividends. The restriction on this process is that the present value of total dividends cannot exceed the present value of the total cash flows from the underlying investment. We can write this as

$$P_0 = \sum_{t=1}^{\infty} \frac{E[DIV_t]}{(1 + r)^t} = \sum_{t=1}^{\infty} \frac{E[FCFS_t]}{(1 + r)^t}$$

The important thing to recognise is that the expected dividend per share $E[DIV_t]$ in any *particular* period is no longer required to be equal to the expected free cash flow per share $E[FCFS_t]$ for that period. Subject to the present value constraint above, the firm can supply existing shareholders with dividends that offer gluttony today and starvation tomorrow, or vice versa, or any combination in between. We can value the shares either by discounting expected future dividends *after* allowing for the future dilution caused by extra share issues, or by discounting expected free cash flow based on the existing number of shares on issue. Recognise, however, that it is the free cash flow from the company's investments that is driving the company's share value.

# What do price-earnings ratios mean?

The **price-earnings ratio** is part of the everyday vocabulary of investors in the share market. People casually refer to growth shares as 'selling at a high P/E'. You can look up P/Es in share quotations given in the newspaper. However, the newspaper gives the ratio of current price to the most recent earnings. Investors are more concerned with price relative to *future* earnings. You should be alert to what price-earnings ratios really signify because you will find them used in odd and misleading ways.

### example

For example, in February 1994 the share statistics in the *Australian Financial Review* showed that Westpac had a P/E of greater than 500, or about 50 times higher than the other banks. Did this mean Westpac had fantastic growth potential? No, it meant that they were having a very bad year and as a consequence had low *current* earnings. Westpac's share price fell, but it did not collapse because investors were forecasting that earnings would recover. Because earnings fell much more than the share price, the P/E ratio based on *current* earnings went through the roof.

Should the financial manager celebrate if the firm's shares sell at a high P/E? The answer is usually yes. The high P/E shows either that investors think that the firm has good growth opportunities (high PVGO), or that its earnings are relatively safe and deserve a low capitalisation rate (low $r$), or sometimes both. However, as we saw above, firms can have high price-earnings ratios not because price is high but because earnings are low. A firm which earns *nothing* (EPS = 0) in a particular period will have an *infinite* P/E relative to those earnings, as long as its shares retain any value at all. Therefore, a high P/E can simply mean that a company is having bad times, but that there is a prospect of improvement sometime in the future.

Are relative P/Es helpful in evaluating shares? Sometimes. Suppose you own shares in a family corporation whose shares are not actively traded. What are those shares worth? A decent estimate is possible if you can find traded firms that have roughly the same risks, growth opportunities and return on equity as your firm. Multiply your firm's earnings per share by the average P/E of the counterpart firms.[17]

Does a high P/E indicate a low market capitalisation rate? No. There is *no* reliable association between a share's price-earnings ratio and the capitalisation rate $r$. The ratio of EPS to $P_0$ measures $r$ only if PVGO = 0 and only if reported EPS is the average future earnings the firm could generate under a no-growth policy.

## What do earnings mean?

Another reason P/Es are hard to interpret is the difficulty of interpreting and comparing earnings per share, the denominator of the price-earnings ratio. What do earnings per share mean? They mean different things for different firms. For some firms they mean more than for others.

The problem is that the earnings that firms report are book, or accounting, figures, not sustainable cash flow. As accounting numbers they reflect a series of more or less arbitrary choices of accounting methods. Almost any firm's reported earnings can be changed substantially by adopting different accounting procedures. A switch in the depreciation method used for reporting purposes directly affects reported EPS, for example. Yet it has *no* effect on cash flow, since depreciation is a non-cash charge. (The depreciation method used for tax purposes *does* affect cash flow.) Other accounting choices that may affect reported earnings are the valuation of assets, the procedures by which the accounts of groups of related firms are combined and the choice between expensing or capitalising research and development. The list could go on and on. In excess of one million alternative measurements of earnings are possible for the consolidated accounts of a moderately complex holding company.

We shall discuss the biases in accounting income and profitability measures in Chapter 12, after we have used present value concepts to develop measures of true, economic income. For the moment, we just want you to remember that accounting earnings are slippery animals. This is one reason why we prefer to work with cash flows.

## 4.5 Valuing a business by discounted cash flow

Investors routinely buy and sell shares. Companies frequently buy and sell entire businesses. For example, when BHP paid $593 million dollars to acquire Tubemakers of Australia, you can be sure that both companies burned a lot of midnight oil to make sure that the deal was fairly priced.

Do the discounted cash flow formulas we presented in this chapter work for entire businesses as well as for shares? Sure: it does not matter whether you forecast dividends per share or the total free cash flow of a business. Value today always equals future cash flow discounted at the opportunity cost of capital.

---

17  When valuing private companies you need to be aware that they have lower P/Es than equivalent listed companies. They suffer a discount for illiquidity.

You may be tempted to estimate the *total* value of a firm's outstanding ordinary shares as the discounted stream of *all* future dividends. But remember our earlier warning: the total value of the company's *issued* shares is equal to the discounted value of that *portion* of the total dividend stream which will be paid to the shares on issue today.

There is another approach to this issue. You could assume that existing shareholders buy any new shares the company issues. In this case, shareholders would bear *all* the costs of future investments and receive *all* the rewards. In other words, existing shareholders would receive every penny of free cash flow. Company value can therefore be calculated as:

$$PV(\text{firm}) = PV(\text{free cash flow}) = PV(\text{revenues} - \text{costs} - \text{investment})$$

## example

Icarus Air has 10 million shares outstanding and expects to earn a constant $10 million per year on its existing assets. All earnings will be paid out as dividends, so:

$$\textbf{Earnings per share = dividends per share}$$

$$EPS = DIV = \frac{\$10 \text{ million}}{10 \text{ million shares}} = \$1$$

If investors' opportunity cost of capital is 10 per cent,

$$P_0 = \frac{DIV_1}{r} = \frac{EPS_1}{r} = \frac{1}{0.10} = \$10$$

Suppose that next year Icarus plans to double in size by issuing a further 10 million shares at $10 a share. Everything is the same as before but twice as big. Thus from year 2 onwards the company earns a constant $20 million, all of which is paid out as dividends on the 20 million shares.

What is the value of Icarus Air? With our first approach we simply discount the total dividends that are expected to be paid on *existing* shares. These are unaffected by next year's expansion, which is entirely paid for by investors in the newly issued shares. These investors get the extra profits and dividends too.[18]

The second approach discounts the net cash flow to existing shareholders if they buy those additional shares that Icarus plans to issue. In this case they will receive the entire profits *less* the cost of the investments to generate those profits:

Cash flows ($million)

| Year | 1 | 2 | 3 | 4 . . . |
|---|---|---|---|---|
| Total profits | 10 | 20 | 20 | 20 |
| *Less* investments | −100 | | | |
| Free cash flow | −90 | 20 | 20 | 20 |

Now discount the free cash flows at 10 per cent:

$$PV = -\frac{90}{1.1} + \frac{20}{(1.1)^2} + \frac{20}{(1.1)^3} + \frac{20}{(1.1)^4} + \cdots$$

[18] That is, the new shareholders earn a fair rate of return on their investment. They get *only* a fair rate of return. If Icarus' expansion had a positive NPV, the company's *current* share price would increase, due to positive PVGO, and new shares could be sold at a higher price. With fewer new shares issued, the 'old' shareholder would receive part of the profits from the expansion.

This series includes a perpetuity of $20 million per year starting in year 2.

$$PV = -\frac{90}{1.1} + \frac{1}{1.1}\left(\frac{20}{0.10}\right) = \$100 \text{ million}$$

The two methods give exactly the same answer.[19]

# Valuing the concatenator business

Of course, things are never as easy in practice as they seem in principle. However, smart application of some basic financial concepts can make discounted cash flow less mechanical and more trustworthy. We illustrate these ideas by walking you through a practical example.

Rumour has it that Establishment Industries is interested in buying your company's concatenator manufacturing operation. Your company is willing to sell if it can get the full value of this rapidly growing business. The problem is to figure out what the present value is.

Table 4.4 gives a forecast of free cash flow. The table is similar to Table 4.2, which forecast earnings and dividends per share for Growth-Tech, based on assumptions about Growth-Tech's assets per share, return on equity and the growth of its business. For the concatenator business, we also have assumptions about assets, growth and profitability (in this case, after-tax operating earnings relative to assets). Growth starts out at a rapid 20 per cent per year, then falls in two steps to a moderate 6 per cent rate for the long run. The growth rate determines the net additional investment required to expand assets, and the profitability rate determines the earnings generated by the business.[20]

**table 4.4**

Forecasts of free cash flow, in millions of dollars, for the Concatenator Manufacturing Division. Rapid expansion in years 1–6 means that free cash flow is negative, because required additional investment outstrips earnings. Free cash flow turns positive when growth slows down after year 6.

| | Year | | | | | | | | | |
|---|---|---|---|---|---|---|---|---|---|---|
| | 1 | 2 | 3 | 4 | 5 | 6 | 7 | 8 | 9 | 10 |
| Asset value | 10.00 | 12.00 | 14.40 | 17.28 | 20.74 | 23.43 | 26.47 | 28.05 | 29.73 | 31.51 |
| Earnings | 1.20 | 1.44 | 1.73 | 2.07 | 2.49 | 2.81 | 3.18 | 3.36 | 3.57 | 3.78 |
| Investment | 2.00 | 2.40 | 2.88 | 3.46 | 2.69 | 3.04 | 1.59 | 1.68 | 1.78 | 1.89 |
| Free cash flow | −0.80 | −0.96 | −1.15 | −1.39 | −0.20 | −0.23 | 1.59 | 1.68 | 1.79 | 1.89 |
| Earnings growth from previous period (%) | 20 | 20 | 20 | 20 | 20 | 13 | 13 | 6 | 6 | 6 |

Notes:
1. Starting asset value is $10 million. Assets required for the business grow at 20 per cent per year to year 4, at 13 per cent in years 5 and 6, and at 6 per cent afterwards.
2. Profitability is constant at 12 per cent.
3. Free cash flow equals earnings minus net investment. Net investment equals total capital expenditures less depreciation. Note that earnings are also calculated net of depreciation.

[19] They have to as long as the company is expected to issue shares at fair value. The new shares cost $100 million. They are expected to provide dividends worth $100 million. Subtracting the cost of the shares and recognising the dividends they generate does not affect value.

[20] Table 4.4 shows *net* investment, which is total investment less depreciation. We are assuming that investment for replacement of existing assets is covered by depreciation and that net investment is devoted to growth. We are also assuming that earnings represent sustainable cash flows from existing investments. We could have reported gross investment in Table 4.4. However, that would have required adding depreciation back to earnings to get operating cash flow. The bottom line, free cash flow, would be the same.

It turns out that free cash flow, the bottom line in Table 4.4, is negative in years 1 to 6. The concatenator business is absorbing more cash than it is generating.

Is that a bad sign? Not really. The business is running a cash deficit not because it is unprofitable, but only because it is growing so fast. Rapid growth is good news, not bad, so long as the business is earning more than the opportunity cost of capital. Your company, or Establishment Industries, will be happy to invest an extra $800 000 in the concatenator business next year, so long as the business offers a superior rate of return.

## Valuation format

The value of a business is usually computed as the discounted value of free cash flows out to a *valuation horizon* (H), plus the forecasted value of the business at the horizon, also discounted back to present value. That is,

$$PV = \underbrace{\frac{FCF_1}{(1 + r)} + \frac{FCF_2}{(1 + r)^2} + \ldots + \frac{FCF_H}{(1 + r)^3}}_{PV(\text{free cash flow})} + \underbrace{\frac{PV_H}{(1 + r)^t}}_{PV(\text{horizon value})}$$

Of course, the concatenator business will continue after the horizon, but it is not practical to forecast free cash flow year by year to infinity. $PV_H$ stands in for free cash flow in periods $H + 1$, $H + 2$, etc.

Valuation horizons are often chosen arbitrarily. Sometimes the boss tells everybody to use 10 years because that is a round number. We will try year 6, because growth of the concatenator business seems to settle down to a long-run trend from year 7 onwards.

## Estimating horizon value

There are several common formulas or rules of thumb for estimating horizon value. First, let us try the constant-growth formula. This requires free cash flow for year 7, which we have from Table 4.4; a long-run growth rate, which appears to be 6 per cent; and a discount rate, which some high-priced consultant has told us is 10 per cent. Therefore,

$$PV(\text{horizon value}) = \frac{1}{(1.1)^6}\left[\frac{1.59}{0.10 - 0.06}\right] = 22.4$$

The present value of the near-term free cash flows is:

$$PV(\text{cash flows}) = \frac{0.80}{1.1} - \frac{0.96}{(1.1)^2} - \frac{1.15}{(1.1)^3} - \frac{1.39}{(1.1)^4} - \frac{0.20}{(1.1)^5} - \frac{0.23}{(1.1)^6}$$

$$= -3.6$$

and therefore, the present value of the business is:

$$PV(\text{business}) = PV(\text{free cash flow}) + PV(\text{horizon value})$$

$$= -3.6 + 22.4$$

$$= \$18.8 \text{ million}$$

Now, are we done? Well, the mechanics of this calculation are perfect. But does it not make you just a little nervous to find that 119 per cent of the value of the business rests on the horizon value? Moreover, a little checking shows that the horizon value can change dramatically in response to apparently minor changes in assumptions. For example, if the long-run growth rate is 8 per cent rather than 6 per cent, the value of the business increases from $18.8 to $26.3 million.[21]

In other words, it is easy for a business valuation by discounted cash flow to be mechanically perfect and practically wrong. Smart financial managers try to check their results by calculating horizon value in several different ways.

Suppose you can observe share prices for mature manufacturing companies whose scale, risk and growth prospects today roughly match those projected for the concatenator business in year 6. Suppose further that these companies tend to sell at price-earnings ratios of about 11. Then you could reasonably guess that the price-earnings ratio of a mature concatenator operation would likewise be 11.[22] This implies:

$$PV(\text{horizon value}) = \frac{1}{(1.1)^6}(11 \times 3.18) = 19.7$$

$$PV(\text{business}) = -3.6 + 19.7 = \$16.1 \text{ million}$$

Notice that to get the value in year 6, we multiply the prospective (year 7) earnings by the P/E ratio.

Suppose also that the market-book ratios of the sample of mature manufacturing companies tend to cluster around 1.4. (The market-book ratio is just the ratio of share price-to-book value per share.[23]) If the concatenator business' market-book ratio is 1.4 in year 6 we just multiply the year 6 asset value by 1.4 to get the horizon value.

$$PV(\text{horizon value}) = \frac{1}{(1.1)^6}(1.4 \times 23.43) = 18.5$$

$$PV(\text{business}) = -3.6 + 18.5 = \$14.9 \text{ million}$$

It is easy to poke holes in these last two calculations. Book value, for example, often is a poor measure of the true value of a company's assets. It can fall far behind actual asset values when there is rapid inflation, and it often entirely misses important intangible assets, such as your patents for concatenator design. Inflation and a long list of arbitrary accounting choices may also bias earnings. Finally, you never know when you have found a sample of truly similar companies.

But remember the purpose of discounted cash flow is to estimate market value—to estimate what investors would pay for a share or business. When you can *observe* what they actually pay for similar companies, that is valuable evidence. Try to work out a way to use it. One way to use it is through valuation rules of thumb, based on price-earnings or market-book ratios.

## A further reality check

Here is another approach to valuing a business. It is based on what you have learned about price-earnings ratios and the present value of growth opportunities.

Suppose the valuation horizon is set not by looking for the first year of stable growth, but by asking when the industry is likely to settle into competitive equilibrium. You might go to the operating manager most familiar with the concatenator business and ask:

---

21  If long-run growth is 8 rather than 6 per cent, an extra 2 per cent of period 7 assets will have to be ploughed back into the concatenator business. This reduces free cash flow by $0.53 to $1.06 million. So

$$PV (\text{horizon value}) = \frac{1}{(1.1)^6}\left(\frac{1.06}{0.10 - 0.08}\right) = \$29.9$$

$$PV (\text{business}) = -3.6 + 29.9 = \$26.3 \text{ million}$$

22  We ignore any effect that the use of debt may have on the P/E because we are assuming all equity financing.

23  Because we are assuming all equity financing, the distinction between net book value and total assets is not necessary—they have the same value. Where the firm is financed with debt the distinction becomes important. We would then use the market to book value per share to value the equity only, not the total assets.

'Sooner or later you and your competitors will be on an equal footing when it comes to major new investments. You may still be earning a superior return on your core business, but you will find that introductions of new products or attempts to expand sales of existing products trigger intense resistance from competitors who are just about as smart and efficient as you are. Give a realistic assessment of when that time will come.'

'That time' is the horizon after which PVGO, the net present value of subsequent growth opportunities, is zero. After all, PVGO is positive only when investments can be expected to earn more than the cost of capital. When your competition catches up, that happy prospect disappears.[24]

We know that present value in any period equals the capitalised value of next period's earnings, plus PVGO:

$$PV_1 = \frac{earnings_{t+1}}{r} + PVGO$$

But what if PVGO = 0? At the horizon period $H$, then:

$$PV_H = \frac{earnings_{H+1}}{r}$$

In other words, when the competition catches up, the price-earnings ratio equals $1/r$, because PVGO disappears.

Suppose competition is expected to catch up by period 8. We can recalculate the value of the concatenator business as follows:

$$PV(\text{horizon value}) = \frac{1}{(1 + r)^8}\left(\frac{\text{earnings in period 9}}{r}\right)$$

$$= \frac{1}{(1 + 0.1)^8}\left(\frac{3.57}{0.10}\right) = \$16.7 \text{ million}$$

$$PV(\text{business}) = -2.0 + 16.7 = \$14.7 \text{ million}$$

The present value of the free cash flow before the horizon improves from −3.6 million to −2 million because the positive cash flows from years 7 and 8 are now included.

We now have four estimates of what Establishment Industries ought to pay for the concatenator business. The estimates reflect four different methods of estimating horizon value. There is no 'best' method, although in many cases we put most weight on the last method, which sets the horizon date at the point when management expects PVGO to disappear. The last method forces managers to remember that sooner or later competition catches up.

Our calculated values for the concatenator business range from $14.7 to $18.8 million, a difference of about $4 million. The width of the range may be disquieting, but it is not unusual. Discounted cash flow formulas only estimate market value, and the estimates change as forecasts and assumptions change. Managers cannot *know* market value until an actual transaction takes place.

---

[24] We cover this point in more detail in Chapter 11.

## 4.6 Summary

In this chapter we have used our new found knowledge of present values to examine the market price ordinary shares. In each case the value of the shares is just like that of any other asset: It is equal to the stream of cash payments discounted at the rate of return that investors expect to receive on comparable securities.

Ordinary shares do not have a fixed maturity; their cash payments consist of an indefinite stream of dividends. Therefore, the present value of an ordinary share is

$$P_0 = \sum_{t=1}^{\infty} \frac{E[DIV_t]}{(1 + r)^t}$$

However, we did not *derive* our DCF formula just by substituting $DIV_t$ for $C_t$. We did not *assume* that the investors purchase ordinary shares solely for dividends. In fact, we began with the assumption that investors have relatively short horizons and invest for both dividends and capital gains. Our fundamental valuation formula is therefore

$$P_0 = \frac{DIV_1 + P_1}{(1 + r)}$$

This is a condition of market equilibrium: If it did not hold, the share would be overpriced or underpriced, and investors would rush to sell or buy it. The flood of sellers or buyers would force the price to adjust so that the fundamental valuation formula holds.

This formula will hold in each future period as well as the present. That allowed us to express next year's forecast price in terms of the subsequent stream of dividends $DIV_1$, $DIV_2$, ...

We also made use of the formula for a growing perpetuity presented in Chapter 3. If dividends are expected to grow forever at a constant rate of $g$, then

$$P_0 = \frac{DIV_1}{r - g}$$

We showed how it can be helpful to twist this formula around and use it to estimate the capitalisation rate $r$, given $P_0$ and estimates of $DIV_1$ and $g$. We also discovered that when the growth rate initially changes, and then settles down to a steady state at some horizon date $H$, we can use the following formula

$$P_0 = \sum_{t=1}^{H} \frac{E[DIV_t]}{(1 + r)^t} + \frac{1}{(1 + r)^H} \times \frac{DIV_{H+1}}{r - g}$$

The general DCF formula can be transformed into a statement about earnings and growth opportunities:

$$P_0 = \frac{EPS_1}{r} + PVGO$$

The ratio $EPS_1/r$ is the capitalised value of the earnings per share that the firm would generate under a no-growth policy. This is sometimes called the value of assets in place. PVGO is the net present value of the investments that the firm will make in order to grow. We used this formula to point out that $EPS_1/P_0$ is only equal to $r$ if PVGO = 0. We also pointed out some of the problems with accounting earnings as a measure of EPS.

A growth share is one for which PVGO is large relative to the capitalised value of EPS. Most growth shares are shares of rapidly expanding firms, but expansion alone does not create a high PVGO. What matters is whether the profitability of the new investments is greater than the required return.

We also showed that it is the free cash flow of the company that fundamentally determines company value. The present value of dividends is fixed to be equal to the present value of the free cash flow. But that fixed present value can be distributed over time in whatever pattern of dividends the company chooses.

The same formulas that are used to value a single share can also be applied to valuing the total package of shares that a company has issued. In other words, we can use them to value an entire business. Applying our present value formulas to a firm or line of business is easy in principle, but messy in application. That is why we concluded the chapter with a practical valuation problem. The methods of valuation that we showed you are not the only possible methods. We will discuss some of the alternatives in the appendix to this chapter.

In earlier chapters you should have acquired—we hope painlessly—a knowledge of the basic principles of valuing assets and a facility with the mechanics of discounting. Now you know something of how ordinary shares are valued and market capitalisation rates estimated. In Chapter 5 we can begin to apply all this knowledge in a more specific analysis of capital budgeting decisions.

# *APPENDIX Some more twists to the valuation story

We simplified things a little when we valued the concatenator manufacturing division. We valued the division as though it were a single investment project. But what if we had to value a firm that consisted of lots of distinct projects? There are two approaches that we could use. The first is to aggregate all the different projects' cash flows to get the global cash flow for the business. Having calculated the total free cash flow for the business we can then proceed in the same way as in our concatenator example. We face one difficult problem: determining the appropriate discount rate for the global cash flow. This is an issue we defer to later chapters.

The second approach is to invoke value additivity—PVs add up. We value each project individually, using a discount rate appropriate to the risk of each project. We then add up the present values for each project to get the total value of the business. Again, selecting the appropriate discount rates will be troublesome. If we get it all right, then the value we get should be *exactly* the same as under the first approach.

$$\text{Value} = \text{PV (free cash flow to business)}$$
$$= \text{sum [PVs net cash flow to individual projects]}$$

We could try another approach—calculate the total value of the company's issued securities. Say the firm has issued debt and shares. We estimate the total expected payments to both debtholders and shareholders that will accrue to the securities currently on issue. We then discount these cash flows at rates appropriate to their risks and add the securities' present values together to get the value of the firm. We should end up with the same total value as in our previous methods. After all, the cash flows to security holders ultimately must come from the free cash flow generated by the company's investments. In other words, the value of the company's portfolio of assets should equal the value of the portfolio of securities issued against those assets.

$$\text{Value} = \text{PV (debt payments)} + \text{PV (payments to shareholders)}$$
$$= \text{PV (free cash flow to business)}$$

Let us look at a simple example of some of these ideas in action. You are a shareholder in the newly established company Hopping Soup Ltd. The company's only project is an investment of $1.5 million in a production plant for kangaroo soup. This project has a five-year life. After five years the company will be closed down for environmental reasons. Given the 'risk class' of the project, the required return on the investment is 12.5 per cent.

The investment is financed by $1 million of debt and $0.5 million of shares. The debt has an interest rate of 10 per cent and is due for repayment at the end of year 5. The required return on equity is 15 per cent.[25]

The expected cash flows for the project are shown as the first five lines of Table 4.5. We assume that there is no tax. Note that an additional investment in plant is required in year 3 and that $1.8 million is salvaged from the sale of assets in year 5. The line labelled free cash flow represents the cash available for distribution to debtholders and shareholders. Payments to debtholders and shareholders are shown in lines 6 and 7 of the table. The shareholders receive whatever cash is left after all other payments have been made.

**table 4.5**

Cash flow forecasts for Hopping Soup Ltd

| | | Cash flow $'000 | | | | | | | | |
|---|---|---|---|---|---|---|---|---|---|---|
| Year | 0 | 1 | 2 | 3 | 4 | 5 | Present value | NPV | Discount rate |
| Cash revenue | | $1000 | $1450 | $1500 | $1400 | $1850 | | | |
| Less cash costs | | ($750) | ($1200) | ($650) | ($1150) | ($1400) | | | |
| Net operating cash flow | | $250 | $250 | $850 | $250 | $450 | | | |
| Less investment/plus salvage | ($1500) | | | ($600) | | $1800 | | | |
| Free cash flow | ($1500) | $250 | $250 | $250 | $250 | $2250 | $2000 | $500 | 12.50% |
| Less payment to debtholders | ($1000) | $100 | $100 | $100 | $100 | $1100 | $1000 | $0 | 10.00% |
| Cash available for shareholders | ($500) | $150 | $150 | $150 | $150 | $1150 | $1000 | $500 | 15.00% |

At the right-hand end of the table the present values of the cash flows from years 1 to 5 have been calculated. Next to the present values are the NPVs. The NPVs are calculated by deducting the initial cash outflow in period 0 from the present value of the cash flow for years 1 to 5. The value of the company is $2 million, as follows:

Value of company = PV (free cash flow) = $2 million
= PV (debt) + PV (equity) = $1 million + $1 million = $2 million

The debtholders make a zero NPV investment. The present value of the payments they receive are exactly equal to the debt finance that they provide. The debt is fairly priced, but as a shareholder you got a bargain. Shareholders are half a million dollars better off as a result of the kangaroo soup venture. They invest half a million dollars and end up holding shares with a market value of a million dollars. Their increase in wealth can be calculated either as the NPV of the free cash flows (the NPV of the project), or as the NPV of the payments to the shareholders. Whichever calculation you make the result will be

---

[25] Some of you may be tempted to try and calculate the cost of capital from this data. You cannot do so because you need the market value of equity for the calculation and you only have the book value of $0.5 million.

the same,[26] as long as the debt is fairly priced.[27] The tricky part is working out the correct discount rate for the shareholders' cash flow.

This example was carefully constructed so that there was one project with constant risk, *and* the *ratio* of the *market* value of debt to the *market* value of equity was *constant* for *every* year of the project. *Given these conditions*, the relationship between the required return on the project and the cost of debt and equity is[28]

$$\text{Weighted average cost debt and equity} = r_D\frac{D}{D+E} + r_E\frac{E}{D+E} = r = \text{required return}$$

Where $r_D$ = the required return on debt
$r_E$ = the required return on equity
$D$ = the market value of debt
$E$ = the market value of equity

You may see this equation written with the required return on investment on the left-hand side. We have it on the right-hand side to emphasise that the required returns for equity and debt are determined by the required return on the underlying investment. People often make the mistake of thinking it is the other way round. In the case of Hopping Soup, suppose we know the required return on investment and our bankers tell us the cost of debt. Then we can work out the return required on equity by substituting in the above equation and solving for $r_E$.

$$0.125 = 0.10\frac{1M}{2M} + r_E\frac{1M}{2M} = 0.10(0.05) + r_E(0.5)$$

Therefore $r_E = 0.15$

The point to be emphasised is that the required return on equity is jointly determined by the required return on the company's investment and the quantity of debt that the company uses. We will have more to say about this in Chapter 17.

# The story so far

We have seen that there are several ways to value a business using discounted cash flow. But ultimately it all comes back to one thing: how much cash the assets of the business are expected to generate. The fundamental determinant of business value is free cash flow. We can value the business as follows:

PV (company free cash flow) = $\sum$ PV (individual projects' cash flow) = PV (debt) + PV (shares) = PV (current earnings) + PVGO

In principle, all the methods we have discussed should give the same estimate of value. In practice they will not. Locating the source of the differences will help you refine your estimates.

---

[26] In many cases it will be more convenient to calculate the NPV of the free cash flows and work out the financing later.
[27] Of course, if the debtholders capture more than a fair share of the free cash flow, the NPV of the project is shared between the debtholders and the shareholders. Therefore, the NPV to shareholders is less than the NPV of the project's free cash flow.
[28] We must warn you that under the title of the weighted average cost of capital this relationship is widely misapplied in circumstances where the required conditions do not hold.

# *A general free cash flow model and PVGO

In this final section we develop a free cash flow model for the value of the firm. In doing so we allow the amount invested and the profitability of that investment to vary from period to period. A by-product of the model is a formula for estimating the present value of growth opportunities.

Consider a company that is generating a total free cash flow of $FCF_1$ and that plans to continue sufficient reinvestment to maintain that cash flow in perpetuity. The first line of cash flows in Figure 4.2 gives the expected free cash flow for such a company. Now suppose new investment opportunities arise, and the company plans to undertake these additional investments. These investments reduce the free cash flow. They are therefore shown with a negative sign as the second line of cash flows in Figure 4.2. As the investments come on stream they start to generate additional cash flows. These cash flows are the product of the size of the investment and the rate of return the investment generates. They are shown as the third line of cash flows in Figure 4.2. How do we value such a company: by discounting the cash flows. The present value of the first line of cash flows is

$$PV = \frac{FCF_I}{r}$$

**figure 4.2**

Time line for free cash flows. $R_t$ is the expected return on investment in period $t$.

| Year | 0 | 1 | 2 | 3 | $n$ → Infinity |
|---|---|---|---|---|---|
| Cash flow | | $FCF_1$ | $FCF_1$ | $FCF_1$ | $FCF_1$ |
| New investment | | $-I_1$ | $-I_2$ | $-I_3$ | $-I_n$ |
| Cash flow from new investment | | | $R_1I_1$ | $R_1I_1 + R_2I_2$ | $\sum_{t=1}^{n} R_t I_t$ |

The present value of the investment outlays is

$$PV = \sum_{t=1}^{\infty} \frac{-I_t}{(1+r)^t}$$

While the present value of the extra cash flows is

$$PV = \frac{\frac{R_1I_1}{r}}{(1+r)} + \frac{\frac{R_2I_2}{r}}{(1+r)^2} + \frac{\frac{R_3I_3}{r}}{(1+r)^3} + \ldots$$

$$= \sum_{t=1}^{\infty} \frac{\frac{R_tI_t}{r}}{(1+r)^t}$$

Putting all this together gives the value of the company

$$PV = \frac{FCF_1}{r} + \sum_{t=1}^{\infty} \frac{\frac{R_tI_t}{r}}{(1+r)^t} - \sum_{t=1}^{\infty} \frac{I_t}{(1+r)^t}$$

This can be rewritten as

$$PV = \frac{FCF_1}{r} + \sum_{t=1}^{\infty} \frac{I_t(R_t - r)}{r(1 + r)^t}$$

$$= \text{Value of} + \text{Present value of}$$
$$\quad\text{assets in} \quad\;\; \text{future growth}$$
$$\quad\;\;\text{place} \qquad\;\; \text{opportunities}$$

This formula makes explicit the components of PVGO: these are the amounts invested each period and the difference between the expected return on the investment and the market's required rate of return. Notice that when $R = r$, no matter how much you invest, today's value for the firm remains the capitalised value of current earnings. The formula we have developed is a useful tool for analysing company value, but it assumes cash flows continue forever into the future. Sometimes it is more convenient to forecast free cash flows for several years and then assume some horizon value for the company. Then, as we demonstrated in our concatenator example, you can discount the free cash flow forecasts and the horizon value to get the present value of the company.

## FURTHER READING

The valuation of ordinary shares is discussed in a number of investment texts. We suggest:

> Z. Bodie, A. Kane and A. J. Marcus, *Investments*, 2nd ed., Richard D. Irwin, Homewood, Ill., 1992.
>
> W. F. Sharpe and G. J. Alexander, *Investments*, 4th ed., Prentice-Hall, Englewood Cliffs, N. J., 1989.

J. B. Williams' original work remains very readable. See particularly Chapter V of:

> J. B. Williams, *The Theory of Investment Value*, Harvard University Press, Cambridge, Mass., 1938.

The following articles provide important developments of Williams' early work. We suggest, however, that you leave the third article until you have read Chapter 16:

> D. Durand, 'Growth Stocks and the Petersburg Paradox', *Journal of Finance*, **12**: 348–63 (September 1957).
>
> M. J. Gordon and E. Shapiro, 'Capital Equipment Analysis: The Required Rate of Profit', *Management Science*, **3**: 102–10 (October 1956).
>
> M. H. Miller and F. Modigliani, 'Dividend Policy, Growth and the Valuation of Shares', *Journal of Business*, **34**: 411–33 (October 1961).

The dangers of using simple growth models in times of inflation are discussed in:

> M. Lally, 'The Gordon-Shapiro Dividend Growth Formula and Inflation', *Accounting and Finance*, **28**: 45–51 (November 1998).

Liebowitz and Kogelman call PVGO the 'franchise factor'. They analyse it in detail in:

> M. L. Liebowitz and S. Kogelman, 'Inside the P/E Ratio: The Franchise Factor', *Financial Analysts Journal*, **46**: 17–35 (November–December 1990).

Myers and Borucki cover the practical problems encountered in estimating DCF costs of equity for regulated companies. Harris and Marston report DCF estimates of rates of return for the stock market as a whole:

> S. C. Myers and L. S. Borucki, 'Discounted Cash Flow Estimates of the Cost of Equity Capital—A Case Study', *Financial Markets, Institutions and Instruments*, **3**: 9–45 (August 1994).
>
> R. S. Harris and F. C. Marston, 'Estimating Shareholder Risk Premia Using Analysts' Growth Forecasts', *Financial Management*, **21**: 63–70 (Summer 1992).

## QUIZ

1. Company X is expected to pay an end-of-year dividend of $10 a share. After the dividend its shares are expected to sell at $110. If the market capitalisation rate is 10 per cent, what is the current share price?

2. Company Y does not plough back any earnings and is expected to produce a level dividend stream of $5 a share. If the current share price is $40, what is the market capitalisation rate?

3. Company Z's dividends per share are expected to grow indefinitely by 5 per cent a year. If next year's dividend is $10 and the market capitalisation rate is 8 per cent, what is the current share price?

4. Company Z-prime is like Z in all respects save one: its growth will stop after year 4. In years 5 and afterwards, it will pay out all earnings as dividends. What is Z-prime's share price? Assume next year's EPS is $15.

5. If company Z (see Question 3) were to distribute all its earnings, it could maintain a level dividend stream of $15 a share. How much therefore is the market actually paying per share for growth opportunities?

6. Which of the following statements are correct?
   a. The value of a share equals the discounted stream of future earnings per share.
   b. The value of a share equals the present value of earnings per share assuming the firm does not grow, plus the net present value of future growth opportunities.
   c. The value of a share equals the discounted stream of future dividends per share.

7. What do financial managers mean by 'free cash flow'? How is free cash flow related to dividends paid out? Briefly explain.

8. Consider three investors.
   a. Mr Single invests for one year.
   b. Ms Double invests for two years.
   c. Mrs Triple invests for three years.
   Assume each invests in company Z (see Question 3). Show that each expects to earn an expected rate of return of 8 per cent per year.

9. Under what conditions does $r$, a share's market capitalisation rate, equal its earnings-price ratio $EPS_1/P_0$?

## QUESTIONS AND PROBLEMS

1. Rework Table 4.1 under the assumption that the dividend on Fledgling Electronics is $1 next year and that it is expected to grow by 5 per cent a year. The capitalisation rate is 15 per cent.

2. Japanese price-earnings ratios are typically much higher than P/Es in Australia, the United Kingdom or the United States, while Japanese dividend yields are typically much lower. Assume you observe the following:[29]

---

29   The Japanese figures were calculated for the NRI 350 index (Japan) by K. R. French and J. M. Poterba, 'Are Japanese Stock Prices Too High?', *Journal of Financial Economics*, 29: 337–63 (1991). Poterba and French adjusted for accounting differences that make commonly reported Japanese price-earning ratios artificially high. The unadjusted Japanese 1988 price-earnings ratio was 54!

|                                    | Japan | Australia |
|------------------------------------|-------|-----------|
| Price-earnings ratio               | 32.1  | 14.4      |
| Dividend yield (per cent)          | 0.6   | 3.5       |
| Nominal interest rate (per cent)   | 4.8   | 10.2      |
| Estimated real interest rate (per cent) | 3.0   | 5.0       |

Reprinted from K. R. French and J. M. Poterba, 'Are Japanese Stock Prices Too High?', *Journal of Financial Economics*, **29**: 337–63, ©1991, with permission from Elsevier Science.

Does this information suggest or imply that expected rates of return demanded by investors were lower in the Japanese market than in the Australian market? Before you answer, be sure to think through the possible explanations of the Japanese market's higher price-earnings ratio and lower dividend yield.

3. Look in a recent issue of the *Australian Financial Review* at the share prices reported in the Markets section near the back of the paper.
   a. What is the latest price of BHP's shares?
   b. What are the annual dividend payment and the dividend yield on BHP shares?
   c. What would the dividend yield be if BHP changed its yearly dividend to $2?
   d. What is the P/E ratio on BHP shares?
   e. Use the P/E ratio to calculate BHP's earnings per share.
   f. Is BHP's P/E higher or lower than that of the National Australia Bank?
   g. What are the possible reasons for the difference in P/E?
   h. Assume that BHP's dividend payment is expected to grow at a constant rate $g$. What expected rate of return is indicated by (i) $g = 0.02$, (ii) $g = 0.05$, (iii) $g = 0.10$?
   i. Make an estimate of $g$ from the company's ploughback rate and return on equity. What expected rate of return is indicated by your estimate?

4. P/E ratios reported in the *Australian Financial Review* use the latest closing prices and the last 12 months reported earnings per share. Explain why the corresponding earnings-price ratios (the reciprocals of reported P/Es) are *not* accurate measures of the expected rates of return demanded by investors.

5. International Growth sold for about $73 last year. Security analysts were forecasting a long-term earnings growth rate of 8.5 per cent. The company was paying dividends of $1.68 per share.
   a. Assume dividends are expected to grow along with earnings at $g = 8.5$ per cent per year in perpetuity. What rate of return $r$ were investors expecting?
   b. International Growth was expected to earn about 12 per cent on book equity and to pay out about 50 per cent of earnings on dividends. What do these forecasts imply for $g$? For $r$? Use the perpetual growth DCF formula.

6. Harrow Ltd ploughs back 40 per cent of its earnings and earns a return of 20 per cent on this investment. The dividend yield on the share is 4 per cent.
   a. Assuming that Harrow can continue to plough back this proportion of earnings and earn a 20 per cent return on the investment, how rapidly will earnings and dividends grow? What is the expected return on Harrow's shares?

b. Suppose that management suddenly announces that future investment opportunities have dried up. Now Harrow intends to pay out all its earnings. How will the share price change?

c. Suppose that management simply announces that the expected return on new investment would in the future be the same as the market capitalisation rate. Now what is Harrow's share price?

**7.** Consider the following three shares:

a. Share A is expected to provide a dividend of $10 a share forever.

b. Share B is expected to pay a dividend of $5 next year. Thereafter dividend growth is expected to be 4 per cent a year forever.

c. Share C is expected to pay a dividend of $5 next year. Thereafter dividend growth is expected to be 20 per cent a year for five years (i.e. until year 6) and zero thereafter.

If the market capitalisation rate for each share is 10 per cent, which share is the most valuable? What if the capitalisation rate is 7 per cent?

**8.** You believe that next year the Dong Lumination Company will pay a dividend of $2 on its ordinary shares. Thereafter you expect dividends to grow at a rate of 4 per cent a year in perpetuity. If you require a return of 12 per cent on your investment, how much should you be prepared to pay for the share?

**\*9.** Rework the analysis of the present value of the growth opportunities for Fledgling Electronics, assuming (i) that the dividend is $1 next year, (ii) that it is expected to grow by 5 per cent a year, (iii) that it ploughs back a constant 20 per cent of earnings, (iv) that the market capitalisation rate is 14 per cent.

a. What is next year's expected earnings per share ($EPS_1$)?

b. What is the return on book equity (ROE)?

c. What is PVGO?

**10.** Explain carefully why different shares may have different P/Es. Show how the price-earnings ratio is related to growth, dividend payout and the required return.

**11.** Look one more time at Table 4.1, which applies the DCF share valuation formula to Fledgling Electronics. The CEO, having just learned that share value is the present value of future dividends, proposes that Fledgling pay a bumper dividend of $1.50 a share in Period 1. The extra cash would have to be raised by an issue of new shares. Recalculate Table 4.1 assuming that profits and payout ratios in all subsequent years are unchanged. You should find that the total present value of dividends *per existing share* is unchanged at $10. Why?

**12.** The constant-growth DCF formula

$$P_0 = \frac{DIV_1}{r - g}$$

is sometimes written as

$$P_0 = \frac{ROE(1 - b)BVPS}{r - bROE}$$

where BVPS is book equity value per share, $b$ the ploughback ratio and ROE the ratio of earnings per share to BVPS. Use this equation to show how the price-to-book ratio varies as ROE changes. What is price-to-book when $ROE = r$?

**13.** Each of the following formulas for determining shareholders' required rate of return can be right or wrong depending on the circumstances:

a. $r = \dfrac{DIV_1}{P_0} + g$

b. $r = \dfrac{EPS_1}{P_0}$

For each formula construct a *simple* numerical example showing that the formula can give wrong answers and explain why the error occurs. Then construct another simple numerical example for which the formula gives the right answer.

**14.** Phoenix Motor Corporation has pulled off a miraculous recovery. Four years ago, it was near liquidation. Now its charismatic leader, a corporate folk hero, may run for Prime Minister.

Phoenix has just announced a $1 per share dividend, the first since the crisis hit. Analysts expect an increase to a 'normal' $3 as the company completes its recovery over the next three years. After that, dividend growth is expected to settle down to a moderate long-term growth rate of 6 per cent.

Phoenix shares are selling at $50 per share. What is the expected long-run rate of return from buying the share at this price? Assume dividends of $1, $2 and $3 for years 1, 2 and 3. A little trial and error will be necessary to find $r$.

**\*15.** Look again at the financial forecasts for Growth-Tech given in Table 4.2. This time assume you *know* that the opportunity cost of capital is $r = 0.12$ (discard the 0.099 figure calculated in the text). Assume you do *not* know Growth-Tech's share value. Otherwise follow the assumptions given in the text.
  a. Calculate the value of Growth-Tech shares.
  b. What part of that value reflects the discounted value of $P_3$, the price forecasted for year 3?
  c. What part of $P_3$ reflects the present value of growth opportunities (PVGO) after year 3?
  d. Suppose that competition will catch up with Growth-Tech by year 4, so that it can only earn its cost of capital on any investments made in year 4 or subsequently. What are Growth-Tech's shares worth now under this assumption? (Make additional assumptions if necessary.)

**16.** Consider a firm with existing assets that generate an EPS of $5. If the firm does not invest except to maintain existing assets, EPS is expected to remain constant at $5 a year. However, starting next year the firm has the chance to invest $3 per share a year in developing a newly discovered geothermal steam source for electricity generation. Each investment is expected to generate a permanent 20 per cent return. However, the source will be fully developed by the fifth year. What will be the share price and earnings-price ratio assuming investors require a 12 per cent rate of return? Show that the earnings-price ratio is 0.20 if the required rate of return is 20 per cent.

**17.** Compost Science and Incineration Ltd (CSI) is in the business of converting Melbourne's waste into fertiliser. The business is not in itself very profitable. However, to induce CSI to remain in business, the Victorian government (VG) has agreed to pay whatever amount is necessary to yield CSI a 10 per cent book return on equity. At the end of the year CSI is expected to pay a $4 dividend. It has been reinvesting 40 per cent of earnings and growing at 4 per cent a year.

a. Suppose CSI continues on this growth trend. What is the expected long-run rate of return from purchasing the shares at $100? What part of the $100 price is attributable to the present value of growth opportunities?

b. Now the VG announces a plan for CSI to treat more sewage. CSI's plant will therefore be expanded gradually over five years. This means that CSI will have to reinvest 80 per cent of its earnings for five years. Starting in year 6, however, it will again be able to pay out 60 per cent of earnings. What will be CSI's share price once this announcement is made and its consequences for CSI are known?

**18.** Look back at our valuation of the concatenator division in Section 4.5. Since the division is owned by a single shareholder, it was natural to think of that shareholder as receiving all the profits and paying for all the investments. This question is designed to show that you get the same answer if you value the dividends on the existing shares. Think of the concatenator division as a separate company financed by 1000 shares. After year 6, all free cash flows are paid out as dividends, but in each of years 1 to 6 the company has no cash to pay dividends and finances the deficits by selling new shares.

a. Suppose that our $18.8 million valuation using the constant-growth formula is correct. (Actually the value is $18.85 million: we rounded.) Given that the market capitalisation rate is 10 per cent, what is the expected value of existing shares in year 1?

b. Concatenator now needs to issue new shares to finance the year 1 deficit of $0.80 million. Suppose that it offers them to investors. How many shares does it need to issue? (Remember, you have just calculated the price per share.)

c. Now calculate the expected share price in year 2. How many new shares need to be issued to finance the year 2 deficit of $0.96 million?

d. Repeat the exercise for each year through to year 6. After financing the deficit in year 6, what is the total number of shares outstanding? What proportion of the company is owned by the initial shareholders?

e. Now calculate the stream of dividends beginning in year 7 that goes to *initial* shareholders and discount at 10 per cent. The answer should be $18.85 million, the same figure as we got by discounting free cash flow.

**19.** Portfolio managers are frequently paid a proportion of the funds under management. Suppose you manage a $100 million equity portfolio offering a dividend yield ($DIV_1/P_0$) of 5 per cent. Dividends and portfolio value are expected to grow at a constant rate. Your annual fee for managing this portfolio is 0.5 per cent of portfolio value and is calculated at the end of each year. Assuming that you will continue to manage the portfolio from now to eternity, what is the present value of the management contract?

# chapter 5

# WHY NPV LEADS TO BETTER INVESTMENT DECISIONS THAN OTHER CRITERIA

In the first four chapters we have introduced, at times surreptitiously, most of the basic principles of the investment decision. In this chapter we consolidate that knowledge. We also take a critical look at other criteria that companies sometimes use to make investment decisions. These rules are the payback rule, the average return on book rule and the internal rate of return rule. The first two are ad hoc rules and may lead to silly decisions. If correctly used the internal rate of return rule should always select those projects that increase shareholder wealth, but we shall see that there are also a number of traps for the unwary.

We conclude the chapter by showing how to cope with situations where the firm has only limited capital or other resources. There are two aspects to this problem. One is computational. In simple cases we just choose those projects that give the highest NPV per dollar of investment. But resource constraints and project interactions often create problems of such complexity that mathematical programming techniques are needed to find the best combination of projects. Linear programming is one such technique. The other part of the problem is to decide whether capital rationing really exists and whether it invalidates net present value as a criterion for capital budgeting.[1]

---

Guess what? NPV, properly interpreted, wins out in the end.

## 5.1 A review of the basics

Vegetron's financial manager is wondering how to analyse a proposed $1 million investment in a new venture called project X. He asks what you think.

Your response should be as follows: 'First, forecast the cash flows generated by project X over its economic life. Second, determine the appropriate opportunity cost of capital. This should reflect both the time value of money and the risk involved in project X. Third, use this opportunity cost of capital to discount the future cash flows of project X. The sum of the discounted cash flows is called present value (PV). Fourth, calculate *net* present value (NPV) by subtracting the $1 million investment from PV. Invest in project X if its NPV is greater than zero.'

However, Vegetron's financial manager is unmoved by your sagacity. He asks why NPV is so important.

You reply: 'Let us look at what is best for Vegetron shareholders. They want you to make their Vegetron shares as valuable as possible.

'Right now Vegetron's total market value (price per share times the number of shares outstanding) is $10 million. That includes $1 million cash we can invest in project X. The value of Vegetron's other assets and opportunities must therefore be $9 million. We have to decide whether it is better to keep the $1 million cash and reject project X or to spend the cash and accept project X. Let us call the value of the new project PV. Then the choice is as follows:

|  | Market value ($million) | |
| --- | --- | --- |
| Asset | Reject project X | Accept project X |
| Cash | 1 | 0 |
| Other assets | 9 | 9 |
| Project X | 0 | PV |
| | 10 | 9 + PV |

'Clearly, project X is worthwhile if its present value, PV, is greater than $1 million—that is, if net present value is positive.'

The financial manager asks: 'How do I know that the PV of project X will actually show up in Vegetron's market value?'

You reply: 'Suppose we set up a new, independent firm X, whose only asset is project X. What would be the market value of firm X?

'Investors would forecast the dividends firm X would pay and discount those dividends by the expected rate of return of securities having risks comparable to firm X. We know that share prices are equal to the present value of forecasted dividends.

'Since project X is firm X's only asset, the dividend payments we would expect firm X to pay are exactly the cash flows we have forecast for project X. Moreover, the rate investors would use to discount firm X's dividends is exactly the rate we should use to discount project X's cash flows.

'I agree that firm X is entirely hypothetical. But if project X is accepted, investors holding Vegetron shares will really hold a portfolio of project X and the firm's other assets. We know the other assets are worth $9 million considered as a separate venture. Since asset values are additive, we can easily figure out the portfolio value once we calculate the value of project X as a separate venture.

'By calculating the present value of project X, we are replicating the process by which the shares of firm X would be valued in capital markets.'

The financial manager asks: 'The one thing I don't understand is where the discount rate comes from.'

You reply: 'I agree that the discount rate is difficult to measure precisely. But it is easy to see what we are *trying* to measure. The discount rate is the opportunity cost of investing in the project rather than in the capital market. In other words, instead of accepting a project, the firm can always give the cash to the shareholders and let them invest it in financial assets.

'Figure 5.1 shows the trade-off. The opportunity cost of taking the project is the return shareholders could have earned had they invested the funds on their own. When we discount the project's cash flows by the expected rate of return on comparable financial assets, we are measuring how much investors would be prepared to pay for your project.'

**figure 5.1**

The firm can either keep and reinvest cash or return it to investors. (Arrows represent possible cash flows or transfers.) If cash is reinvested, the opportunity cost is the expected rate of return that shareholders could have obtained by investing in financial assets.

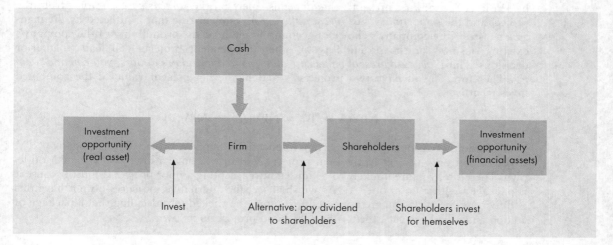

'But which financial assets?' Vegetron's financial manager queries. 'The fact that investors expect only 12 per cent on BHP shares does not mean that we should purchase Wildcat Oil Exploration if it offers 14 per cent.'

You reply: 'The opportunity-cost concept makes sense only if assets of equivalent risk are compared. In general, you should identify financial assets with risks equivalent to the project under consideration, estimate the expected rate of return on these assets and use this rate as the opportunity cost.'

It appears that generations of graduates have put this argument persuasively. The use of NPV has grown strongly since the 1950s, and it is now the most popular investment evaluation technique for large Australian companies.[2]

## 5.2 Net present value's competitors

Let us hope that your financial manager is convinced by now of the correctness of the net present value rule. But it is possible that the manager would like to know why you do not

---

[2]    This does not mean that it is used for all investments. For example, NPV would probably not be used to evaluate the purchase of one personal computer, but it would be used to evaluate investment in a computerised warehouse and distribution system. A useful survey of Australian practice is provided by Mark Freeman and Garry Hobbes, 'Capital Budgeting: Theory Versus Practice', *Australian Accountant*, **61**: 36–41 (September 1991).

recommend any of the alternative investment criteria. Just so that you are prepared, we will now look at the three most popular alternatives to the NPV rule. These are:

1. Payback
2. Average return on book value
3. Internal rate of return

Later in the chapter we will consider a fourth criteria, the profitability index. This has special advantages when capital is rationed.

As we look at these alternative criteria, it is worth keeping in mind the following key features of the net present value rule. First, the NPV rule recognises that *a dollar today is worth more than a dollar tomorrow*, because the dollar today can be invested to start earning interest immediately. Any investment rule that does not recognise the time value of money cannot be sensible. Second, net present value depends solely on the *forecasted cash flows* from the project and the *opportunity cost of capital*. Any investment rule that is affected by the manager's tastes,[3] the company's choice of accounting method, the profitability of the company's existing business or the profitability of other independent projects will lead to inferior decisions. Third, *because present values are all measured in today's dollars, you can add them up*. Therefore, if you have two projects A and B, the net present value of the combined investment is

$$NPV(A + B) = NPV(A) + NPV(B)$$

This additivity property has important implications. Suppose project B has a negative NPV. If you tack it onto project A, the joint project (A + B) will have a lower NPV than A on its own. Therefore, you are unlikely to be misled into accepting a poor project (B) just because it is packaged with a good one (A). As we shall see, the alternative measures do not have this additivity property. If you are not careful, you may be tricked into deciding that a package of a good and a bad project is better than the good project on its own.[4]

## 5.3 Payback

Companies frequently require that the initial outlay on any project should be recoverable within some specified cutoff period. The **payback period** of a project is found by counting the number of years that it takes before cumulative forecasted cash flows equal the initial investment. Consider projects A and B:

| | Cash flows ($) | | | | Payback period (years) | NPV at 10% |
|---|---|---|---|---|---|---|
| Project | $C_0$ | $C_1$ | $C_2$ | $C_3$ | | |
| A | −2000 | +2000 | 0 | 0 | 1 | −182 |
| B | −2000 | +1000 | +1000 | +5000 | 2 | +3492 |

---

[3]   Notice that we said tastes not judgement.

[4]   Sometimes you have to take the good project with the bad because they are dependent on each other. For example, a quarry may be a negative NPV investment, but its subsequent conversion to a tip may have a positive NPV. In this case, to evaluate the tip you have to add the negative NPV of the quarry.

Project A involves an initial investment of $2000 ($C_0 = -2000$) followed by a single cash inflow of $2000 in year 1. Suppose the opportunity cost of capital is 10 per cent. Then project A has an NPV of $-\$182$:

$$\text{NPV(A)} = -2000 + \frac{2000}{1.10} = -\$182$$

Project B also requires an initial investment of $2000 but produces a cash inflow of $1000 in years 1 and 2 and $5000 in year 3. At a 10 per cent opportunity cost of capital project B has an NPV of $+\$3492$:

$$\text{NPV(B)} = -2000 + \frac{1000}{1.10} + \frac{1000}{(1.10)^2} + \frac{5000}{(1.10)^3} = +\$3492$$

Thus, the net present value rule tells us to reject project A and accept project B.

# The payback rule

Now let us look at how rapidly each project pays back its initial investment. With project A you take one year to recover your $2000; with project B you take two years. If the firm used the payback *rule* with a cutoff period of one year, it would accept only project A. If it used the payback rule with a cutoff period of two or more years, it would accept both A and B. Therefore, regardless of the choice of cutoff period, the payback rule gives a different answer from the net present value rule.

The reason for the difference is that payback gives equal weight to all cash flows before the payback date and no weight at all to subsequent flows. For example, the following three projects all have a payback period of two years:

| Project | Cash flows ($) | | | | Payback period (years) | NPV at 10% |
|---------|-------|-------|-------|-------|-------------------------|------------|
|         | $C_0$ | $C_1$ | $C_2$ | $C_3$ |                         |            |
| B | −2 000 | +1 000 | +1 000 | +5 000 | 2 | 3 492 |
| C | −2 000 | 0 | +2 000 | +5 000 | 2 | 3 409 |
| D | −2 000 | +1 000 | +1 000 | +100 000 | 2 | 74 867 |

The payback rule says that these projects are all equally attractive. But project B has a higher NPV than project C for *any* positive interest rate ($1000 in each of years 1 and 2 is more valuable than $2000 in year 2). Project D is obviously the best choice. Not surprisingly, it has a higher NPV than either B or C.

In order to use the payback rule a firm has to decide on an appropriate cutoff date. In general, there is no *reliable* association between NPV and payback. Therefore, whatever payback period is chosen as the cutoff, some positive NPV projects will be rejected and some negative NPV projects will be accepted.

Many firms that use payback choose the cutoff period essentially by guesswork. It is possible to do better than that. If you know the typical pattern of cash flows, then you can find the cutoff period that would come closest to maximising net present value.[5] However, this 'optimal' cutoff point works only for those projects that have 'typical' patterns of cash flows.

---

[5]  If the inflows are, on average, spread evenly over the life of the project, the optimal cutoff for the payback rule is

Optimal cutoff period $= 1/r - 1/r(1 + r)^n$

where $n$ denotes the project life. This expression for the optimal payback was first noted in M. J. Gordon, 'The Pay-Off Period and the Rate of Profit', *Journal of Business*, **28**: 253–60 (October 1955). Did you recognise the expression as the present value annuity factor from Chapter 3?

So it is still better to use the net present value rule. To summarise, the deficiencies of the payback period are:

1. It does not properly account for the time value of money. For example, it fails to account for different timing of cash flows within the payback period.
2. It completely disregards cash flows beyond the payback period. In effect, such cash flows are being treated as though they have infinite risk and therefore zero present value.
3. The choice of the cutoff period is usually arbitrary.

So why is payback used? It is simple, quick and cheap. For decisions involving *small* sums of money, the payback method *may* be a cost-effective and convenient filter. Many firms seem to use it that way for small projects. It is also frequently used as one of a set of multiple criteria used to evaluate project desirability. We can always be sure that if the project *never* pays back its initial investment then it must have a negative NPV.

## Discounted payback

Some companies discount the cash flows before they compute the payback period. The *discounted* payback rule asks, 'How many periods does the project have to last in order to make sense in terms of net present value?' This modification to the payback rule surmounts the objection that equal weight is given to all flows before the cutoff date. However, the discounted payback rule still takes no account of any cash flows after the cutoff date.

Discounted payback is a whisker better than undiscounted payback. It recognises that a dollar at the beginning of the payback period is worth more than a dollar at the end of the payback period. This helps, but it may not help much. The discounted payback rule still depends on the choice of an arbitrary cutoff date and it still ignores all cash flows after that date.

## 5.4 Average return on book value

Some companies judge an investment project by looking at its accounting or **book rate of return**. One way to calculate book rate of return is to divide the average forecasted profits of a project after depreciation and taxes by the average book value of the investment.

$$\text{Book rate of return} = \frac{\text{Average net profit after tax}}{\text{Average book value}}$$

An alternative is to use the initial book value in the denominator, then

$$\text{Book rate of return} = \frac{\text{Average net profit after tax}}{\text{Initial book value}}$$

The book rate of return for the investment is assessed by comparison against the book rate of return for the firm as a whole, or against some external yardstick, such as the average book rate of return for the industry.

Table 5.1a shows projected income statements for project A over its three-year life. Its average net income is $2000 per year (we assume for simplicity that there are no taxes). The required investment is $9000 at $t = 0$. This amount is then depreciated at a constant rate of $3000 per year. So the book value of the new investment will decline from $9000 in year 0 to zero in year 3. This gives an average investment of $4500, that is ($9000 + 0)/2.

Given that the average net income is $2000 and the average net investment is $4500, then the average book rate of return is 2000/4500 = 0.44. Project A would be undertaken if the firm's target book rate of return were less than 44 per cent. If we had used initial book value rather than average book value the ratio would have been 2000/9000 = 0.22, or 22 per cent.[6]

|  | Year 0 ($) | Year 1 ($) | Year 2 ($) | Year 3 ($) |
|---|---|---|---|---|
| Gross book value of investment | 9000 | 9000 | 9000 | 9000 |
| Accumulated depreciation | 0 | 3000 | 6000 | 9000 |
| Net book value of investment | 9000 | 6000 | 3000 | 0 |

This criterion suffers from several serious defects. First, the results depend upon which of several possible formulas you select. Second, there is no allowance for the fact that immediate receipts are more valuable than distant ones. Whereas payback gives no weight to the more distant flows, return on book gives them too much weight. Thus, in Table 5.1b we can introduce two projects, B and C, which have the same average book investment, the same average book income and the same average book profitability as project A. Yet A clearly has a higher NPV than B or C because a greater proportion of the cash flows for project A occur in the early years.

Notice also that the average return on book depends on accounting income and book values of assets. It is not based on the cash flows of a project. Cash flows and accounting income are often very different. For example, the accountant labels some cash outflows *capital investment* and others *operating expenses*. The operating expenses are deducted immediately from each year's income. The capital expenditures are depreciated according to an arbitrary schedule chosen by the accountant. Then the depreciation charge is deducted from each year's income. Thus, the average return on book depends on which items the accountant treats as capital investments and how rapidly they are depreciated. It also depends on a number of other more or less arbitrary accounting decisions that affect both profit and book value. However, the accountant's decisions have nothing to do with the cash flow[7] and therefore should not affect the decision to accept or reject an investment.

A firm that uses average return on book has to decide on a yardstick for judging a project. This decision is also arbitrary. Sometimes the firm uses its current book return as a yardstick. In this case, companies with high rates of return on their existing business may be led to reject good projects, and companies with low rates of return may be led to accept bad ones.

Payback is a bad rule. Average return on book is probably worse. It ignores the opportunity cost of money and is not based on the cash flows of a project. It may also result in the investment decision for new assets being related to the profitability of the firm's existing business.

With such obvious defects why does the accounting rate of return continue to be used? First, people have a natural tendency to use data that is readily available, and the company's financial information system typically produces accounting data. Second, when companies assess a manager's performance it is often based on accounting numbers, such as profit. If you assess and reward people according to accounting profit, then you ensure that the accounting rate of return will be considered in any investment evaluation. Even if investment evaluation using NPV is company policy, there will be hidden use of accounting-based evaluation as long as accounting reports determine management rewards. Third, many managers believe that the share market's reward for performance also depends on accounting numbers. In other words, they believe that accounting results affect market value, independently of the economic reality

---

[6] There are many variants on this rule. For example, some companies measure the *accounting return on cost*, that is, the ratio of average profits before depreciation but after tax to the initial cost of the asset.

[7] Of course, the depreciation method used for tax purposes does have cash consequences that should be taken into account in calculating NPV.

that underlies the accounting numbers. We think they are mostly wrong and explain why in Chapters 12 and 13.

Evidence that senior managers increasingly share our view comes from the growing popularity of economic value added (EVA) as a technique for measuring performance. The use of EVA is designed to focus managers' attention on the cost of using capital and encourage them to select positive NPV projects. EVA is primarily a tool for evaluating the periodic performance of investments once they have been made, so we defer more detailed discussion to Chapter 12.

**table 5.1a**

Computing the average book rate of return on an investment of $9000 in project A

| Project A | Cash flows ($) | | |
|---|---|---|---|
| | Year 1 | Year 2 | Year 3 |
| Revenue | 12 000 | 10 000 | 8 000 |
| Out-of-pocket cost | 6 000 | 5 000 | 4 000 |
| Cash flow | 6 000 | 5 000 | 4 000 |
| Depreciation | 3 000 | 3 000 | 3 000 |
| Net income | 3 000 | 2 000 | 1 000 |

$$\text{Average book rate of return} = \frac{\text{average annual income}}{\text{average annual investment}} = \frac{2\,000}{4\,500} = 0.44$$

**table 5.1b**

Projects A, B and C all cost $9000 and produce an average income of $2000. Therefore, they all have a 44 per cent book rate of return.

| Project | Cash flows ($) | | |
|---|---|---|---|
| | Year 1 | Year 2 | Year 3 |
| A  Cash flow | 6000 | 5000 | 4000 |
|     Net income | 3000 | 2000 | 1000 |
| B  Cash flow | 5000 | 5000 | 5000 |
|     Net income | 2000 | 2000 | 2000 |
| C  Cash flow | 4000 | 5000 | 6000 |
|     Net income | 1000 | 2000 | 3000 |

## 5.5 Internal (or discounted cash flow) rate of return

Whereas payback and average return on book are ad hoc rules, internal rate of return has a much more respectable ancestry and is recommended in many finance texts. If therefore we dwell more on its deficiencies, it is not because they are more numerous but because they are less obvious.

In Chapter 2 we noted that net present value could also be expressed in terms of rate of return, which would lead to the following rule: 'Accept investment opportunities offering rates of return in excess of their opportunity costs of capital.' That statement, properly interpreted, is absolutely correct. However, interpretation is not always easy for long-lived investment projects.

There is no ambiguity in defining the true rate of return of an investment that generates a single payoff after one period:

$$\text{Rate of return} = \frac{\text{payoff}}{\text{investment}} - 1$$

Alternatively, we could write down the NPV of the one period investment and find that discount rate which makes NPV = 0.

Of course, $C_1$ is the payoff and $-C_0$ the required investment,[8] and so our two equations show

$$NPV = C_0 + \frac{C_1}{1 + \text{discount rate}} = 0$$

implies

$$\text{Discount rate} = \frac{C_1}{-C_0} - 1$$

exactly the same thing. *The discount rate that makes NPV = 0 is also the rate of return.*

Thus, if $C_1$ is 110 and $-C_0$ is 100, then the discount rate is [(110/100) − 1] = 0.10, or 10 per cent.

Unfortunately, there is no wholly satisfactory way of defining the true rate of return of a long-lived asset. The best available concept is the so-called **discounted cash flow (DCF) rate of return** or **internal rate of return (IRR)**. The internal rate of return is used frequently in finance. It can be a handy measure, and managers are sometimes seduced by the comfort of working with a percentage. But as we shall see, the IRR gives a percentage that can easily mislead. Therefore, you should know how to calculate it and how to use it properly.

The internal rate of return is defined as the rate of discount which makes NPV = 0. This means that to find the IRR for an investment project lasting $T$ years, we must solve for IRR in the following expression:

$$NPV = C_0 + \frac{C_1}{1 + \text{IRR}} + \frac{C_1}{(1 + \text{IRR})^2} + \dots + \frac{C_1}{(1 + \text{IRR})^T} = 0$$

Actual calculation of IRR usually involves trial and error. For example, consider a project that produces the following cash flows:

| Cash flows ($) | | |
|---|---|---|
| $C_0$ | $C_1$ | $C_2$ |
| −4000 | +2000 | +4000 |

To find the internal rate of return we solve for the IRR in the following equation

$$NPV = -4000 + \frac{2000}{1 + \text{IRR}} + \frac{4000}{(1 + \text{IRR})^2} = 0$$

---

8    $C_0$, the initial investment, is a negative number, so $-C_0$ is a positive number.

Let us arbitrarily try a zero discount rate. In this case NPV is not zero but +$2000:

$$NPV = -4000 + \frac{2000}{1.0} + \frac{4000}{(1.0)^2} = +\$2000$$

The NPV is positive; therefore, the IRR must be greater than zero. The next step might be to try a discount rate of 50 per cent. In this case net present value is −$889:

$$NPV = -4000 + \frac{2000}{1.5} + \frac{4000}{(1.5)^2} = -\$889$$

The NPV is negative; therefore, the IRR must be less than 50 per cent. In Figure 5.2 we have plotted the net present values implied by a range of discount rates. From this we can see that a discount rate of 28 per cent gives the desired net present value of zero. Therefore, IRR is 28 per cent.

The easiest way to calculate IRR, if you have to do it by hand, is to plot three or four combinations of NPV and discount rate on a graph like Figure 5.2. Then connect the points with a smooth line and read off the discount rate at which NPV = 0. Having got an approximate value you can then refine your estimate. You should note that it is possible for your calculated IRR to be a negative number. It is, of course, quicker and more accurate to use the IRR function in a computer spreadsheet or a financial calculator to find the IRR.

**figure 5.2**
This project costs $4000 and then produces cash inflows of $2000 in year 1 and $4000 in year 2. Its internal rate of return (IRR) is 28 per cent, the rate of discount at which NPV is zero.

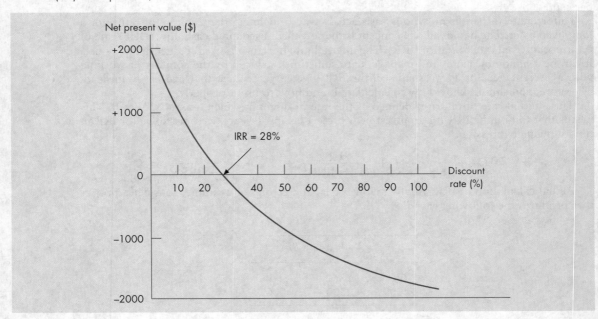

Now, the internal rate of return *rule* is to accept an investment project if the opportunity cost of capital is less than the internal rate of return. You can see the reasoning behind this idea if you look again at Figure 5.2. If the opportunity cost of capital is less than the 28 per cent IRR, then the project has a *positive* NPV when discounted at the opportunity cost of capital. If it is equal to the IRR, the project has a *zero* NPV. And if it is greater than the IRR, the project has a *negative* NPV. Therefore, when we compare the opportunity cost of capital with the IRR on our project, we are effectively asking whether our project has a positive NPV. This is true not only for our example. The rule will give the same answer as the net present value rule *whenever the NPV of a project is a smoothly declining function of the discount rate*, like Figure 5.2.[9]

Many firms use internal rate of return as a criterion in preference to net present value. We think that this is a pity. Although, properly stated, the two criteria are formally equivalent, the internal rate of return rule contains several pitfalls.

# Pitfall 1    Lending or borrowing?

Not all cash flow streams have NPVs that decline as the discount rate increases. Consider the following projects, A and B:

| | Cash flows ($) | | | |
|---|---|---|---|---|
| Project | $C_0$ | $C_1$ | IRR (%) | NPV at 10% |
| A | −1000 | +1500 | +50 | +364 |
| B | +1000 | −1500 | +50 | −364 |

Each project has an IRR of 50 per cent. (In other words, $-1000 + 1500/1.50 = 0$ *and* $+1000 - 1500/1.50 = 0$.)

Does this mean that they are equally attractive? Clearly not, for in the case of project A, where we are initially paying out $1000, we are *lending* money at 50 per cent; in the case of project B, where we are initially receiving $1000, we are *borrowing* money at 50 per cent. When we lend money, we want a *high* rate of return; when we borrow money, we want a *low* rate of return.

If you plot a graph like Figure 5.2 for project B, you will find that NPV increases as the discount rate increases. Obviously, the internal rate of return rule, as we stated it above, will not work in this case; we have to look for an IRR *less* than the opportunity cost of capital.

This is straightforward enough, but now look at project C:

| | Cash flows ($) | | | | | |
|---|---|---|---|---|---|---|
| Project | $C_0$ | $C_1$ | $C_2$ | $C_3$ | IRR (%) | NPV at 10% |
| C | +1000 | −3600 | +4320 | −1728 | +20 | −0.75 |

It turns out that project C has zero NPV at a 20 per cent discount rate. If the opportunity cost of capital is 10 per cent, an IRR of 20 per cent means the project is a good one. Or does it? In part, project C is like borrowing money. This is because we receive money now and pay it out in the first period; it is also partly like lending money because we pay out money in period 1 and recover it in period 2. Should we accept or reject? The only way to find the answer is to look at the net present value. Figure 5.3 shows that the NPV of project C *increases* as the discount rate increases. If the opportunity cost of capital is 10 per cent (i.e. less than the IRR), the project has a very small negative NPV and we should reject the project.

---

[9]  Here is a word of caution. Some people confuse the internal rate of return and the opportunity cost of capital because both appear as discount rates in the NPV formula. The internal rate of return is a *profitability measure* that depends solely on the amount and timing of the project cash flows. The opportunity cost of capital is a *standard of profitability* for the project, which we use to calculate how much the project is worth. The opportunity cost of capital is established in capital markets. It is the expected rate of return offered by other assets equivalent in risk to the project being evaluated.

**figure 5.3**
The net present value of project C increases as the discount rate increases.

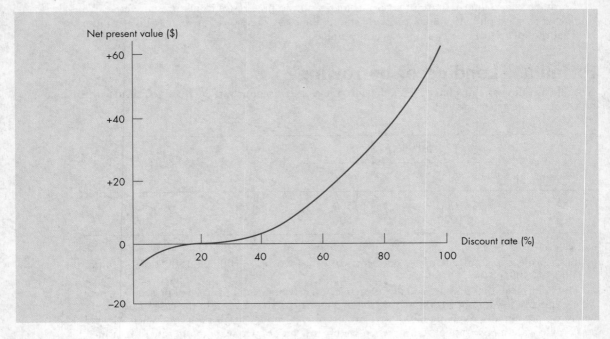

## Pitfall 2    Multiple rates of return

Project C had a unique IRR, but this will not generally be the case when there is more than one change in the sign of the cash flows. Consider, for example, project D. It costs $4000 and brings in $25 000 in the first year. Then in year 2 you have to pay out $25 000:

| Project | Cash flows ($) | | | IRR (%) | NPV at 10% |
|---|---|---|---|---|---|
| | $C_0$ | $C_1$ | $C_2$ | | |
| D | −4000 | +25 000 | −25 000 | 25 and 400 | −1934 |

Note there are *two* discount rates that make NPV = 0. That is, *each* of the following statements holds:

$$NPV = -4000 + \frac{25\,000}{(1 + 0.25)} - \frac{25\,000}{(1 + 0.25)^2} = 0$$

and

$$NPV = -4000 + \frac{25\,000}{(1 + 4)} - \frac{25\,000}{(1 + 4)^2} = 0$$

In other words, the investment has an IRR of both 25 *and* 400 per cent. Figure 5.4 shows how this comes about. As the discount rate increases, NPV initially rises and then declines. The reason for this is the double change in the sign of the cash-flow stream. There can be as

**figure 5.4**

Project D has two internal rates of return. NPV = 0 when IRR = 25 per cent and when IRR = 400 per cent.

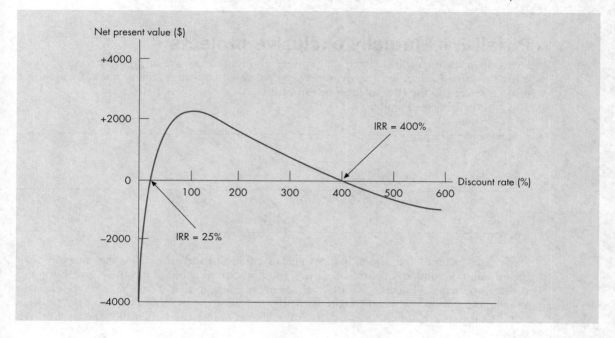

many different internal rates of return for a project as there are changes in the sign of the cash flows.[10]

The change of sign in project D came about because of the negative cash outflow at the end of the project. Does this happen in reality? Yes, many projects have terminal cash outflows. For example, if you mine coal in an open cut, you will probably have to invest substantial amounts to restore the land after the coal is mined. Thus, a new mine creates an initial investment (negative cash flow up-front), a positive series of inflows and an ending cash outflow for restoration. The cash flow stream changes sign twice and mining companies typically see two IRRs.[11]

As if this is not difficult enough, there are also cases in which *no* internal rate of return exists. For example, project E has a positive net present value at all discount rates:

| Project | Cash flows ($) | | | IRR (%) | NPV at 10% |
| | $C_0$ | $C_1$ | $C_2$ | | |
|---|---|---|---|---|---|
| E | +1000 | −3000 | +2500 | none | +339 |

---

[10]  By Descartes' 'rule of signs' there can be as many different solutions to a polynomial as there are changes of sign. For a discussion of the problem of multiple rates of return see J. H. Lorie and L. J. Savage, 'Three Problems in Rationing Capital', *Journal of Business*, **28**: 229–39 (October 1955); and E. Solomon, 'The Arithmetic of Capital Budgeting', *Journal of Business*, **29**: 124–9 (April 1956).

[11]  Another source of changing signs for cash flow is where tax payments are made in arrears and so lag the other project cash flows. When the project finishes there remains a negative outflow for the final tax payment.

A number of adaptations of the IRR rule have been devised for such cases. Not only are they inadequate, they are unnecessary, for the simple solution is to use net present value.

## Pitfall 3   Mutually exclusive projects

Firms often have to choose from among several alternative ways of doing the same job or using the same facility. In other words, they need to choose from among **mutually exclusive projects**. Here too the IRR rule can be misleading.

Consider projects F and G:

| Project | Cash flows ($) | | IRR (%) | NPV at 10% |
|---------|---------|---------|---------|---------|
| | $C_0$ | $C_1$ | | |
| F | −10 000 | +20 000 | 100 | +8 182 |
| G | −20 000 | +35 000 | 75 | +11 818 |

Perhaps project F is a manually-controlled machine tool and project G is the same tool with the addition of computer control. Both are good investments, but G has the higher NPV and is therefore better. However, the IRR rule seems to indicate that if you have to choose, you should go for F since it has the higher IRR. If you follow the IRR rule, you have the satisfaction of earning a 100 per cent rate of return; if you follow the NPV rule, you are $11 818 richer.

You can salvage the IRR rule in these cases by looking at the internal rate of return on the incremental cash flows. Here is how to do it. First, consider the smaller project (F in our example). It has an IRR of 100 per cent, which is well in excess of the 10 per cent opportunity cost of capital. You know therefore that F is acceptable. Now suppose a third project comes along. This project offers cash flows that are exactly equal to the difference in cash flows between G and F. Let us call this the incremental project.[12] The cash flows are as follows:

| Project | Cash flows ($) | | IRR (%) | NPV at 10% |
|---------|---------|---------|---------|---------|
| | $C_0$ | $C_1$ | | |
| G-F | −10 000 | +15 000 | 50 | +3 636 |

The IRR on the incremental project is 50 per cent, which is also well in excess of the 10 per cent opportunity cost of capital. So you should be quite happy to accept project G-F.[13]

The IRR rule tells us to prefer F to G, but it also tells us to accept G-F as well. In fact, we would prefer F + (G-F) to F alone. But F + (G-F) = G, so really we prefer G! Our example shows that IRR is unreliable in *ranking* projects of different scale. It is also unreliable in ranking projects that offer different patterns of cash flow over time. For example,

---

12   What we are really doing here is analysing whether it is worth making the additional $10 000 investment in project G.

13   In analysis of the incremental project you may find that you have jumped out of the frying pan into the fire. The series of incremental cash flows may involve several changes in sign. In this case there are likely to be multiple IRRs and you will be forced to use the NPV rule after all.

suppose the firm can take project H *or* project I, but not both (ignore project J for the moment):

| | Cash flows ($) | | | | | | | IRR | NPV |
| Project | $C_0$ | $C_1$ | $C_2$ | $C_3$ | $C_4$ | $C_5$ | Etc | (%) | at 10% |
|---|---|---|---|---|---|---|---|---|---|
| H | −9000 | +6000 | +5000 | +4800 | 0 | 0 | ... | 33 | 3592 |
| I | −9000 | +1800 | +1800 | +1800 | +1800 | +1800 | ... | 20 | 9000 |
| J | | −6000 | +1200 | +1200 | +1200 | +1200 | ... | 20 | 6000 |

Project H has a higher IRR, but project I has the higher NPV. Figure 5.5 shows why the two rules give different answers. The solid line gives the net present value of project H at different rates of discount. Since a discount rate of 33 per cent produces a net present value of zero, this is the internal rate of return for project H. Similarly, the dashed line shows the net present value of project I at different discount rates. The IRR of project I is 20 per cent. (We assume project I's cash flows continue indefinitely.) Note that project I has a higher NPV so long as the opportunity cost of capital is less than 15.6 per cent.

**figure 5.5**

The IRR of project H exceeds that of project I, but the net present value of project H is higher only if the discount rate is greater than 15.6 per cent.

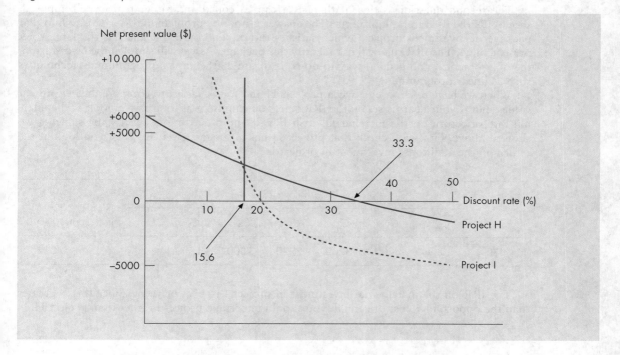

The reason that IRR is misleading is that the total cash inflow of project I is larger but tends to occur later. Therefore, when the discount rate is low, project I has the higher NPV; when the discount rate is high, project H has the higher NPV. (You can see from Figure 5.5 that the two projects have the *same* NPV when the discount rate is 15.6 per cent.) The internal rates of return on the two projects tell us that at a discount rate of 20 per cent project I has a zero NPV (IRR = 20 per cent) and project H has a positive NPV. Thus, if the opportunity cost of capital were 20 per cent, investors would place a higher value on the shorter-lived project H. But in our example the opportunity cost of capital is not 20 per cent but 10 per cent. The loss of value for more distant cash flows is considerably smaller at a discount rate of 10 per cent than at a discount rate of 20 per cent. At a 10 per cent cost of capital, an investment in project I has an NPV of $9000 and an investment in project H has an NPV of only $3592.[14]

This is a favourite example of ours. We have obtained many business people's reaction to it. When asked to choose between projects H and I, many choose H. The reason seems to be the rapid payback generated by project H. In other words, they believe that if they take project H, they will also be able to take a later project like J (note that J can be financed using the cash flows from H), whereas if they take project I, they will not have enough money for project J. In other words, they implicitly assume that it is a *shortage of capital* which forces the choice between projects H and I. When this implicit assumption is brought out, they usually admit that project I is better if there is no capital shortage.

But the introduction of capital constraints raises two further questions. The first stems from the fact that most of the executives preferring project H to I work for firms that would have no difficulty raising more capital. Why would a manager at BHP, say, choose project H on the grounds of limited capital? BHP can raise plenty of capital and can take project J regardless of whether project H or I is chosen; therefore, J should not affect the choice between H and I. The answer seems to be that large firms usually impose capital budgets on divisions and subdivisions as a part of the firm's planning and control system. Since the system is complicated and cumbersome, the budgets are not easily altered and so they are perceived as real constraints by middle management.

The second question is this: If there is a capital constraint, either real or self-imposed, should IRR be used to rank projects? The answer is no. The problem in this case is to find that package of investment projects which satisfies the capital constraint and has the largest net present value. The IRR rule will not identify this package. As we will show in the next section, the only practical and general way to do so is to use mathematical programming techniques such as linear programming.

When we have to choose between projects H and I, it is easiest to compare the net present values. But if your heart is set on the IRR rule, you can use it as long as you look at the internal rate of return on the incremental cash flows. The procedure is exactly the same as we showed above. First, you check that project H has a satisfactory IRR. Then you look at the return on the additional investment in project I:

| | Cash flows ($) | | | | | | | IRR | NPV |
| Project | $C_0$ | $C_1$ | $C_2$ | $C_3$ | $C_4$ | $C_5$ | Etc | (%) | at 10% |
|---|---|---|---|---|---|---|---|---|---|
| I-H | 0 | −4200 | −3200 | −2220 | +1800 | +1800 | ... | 15.6 | +5408 |

The IRR on the incremental investment in project I is 15.6 per cent. Since this is greater than the opportunity cost of capital, you should undertake project I rather than project H.

---

[14] It is often suggested that the choice between the net present value rule and the internal rate of return rule should depend on the probable reinvestment rate. This is wrong. The prospective return on another *independent* investment should *never* be allowed to influence the investment decision. For a discussion of the reinvestment assumption see A. A. Alchian, 'The Rate of Interest, Fisher's Rate of Return over Cost and Keynes' Internal Rate of Return', *American Economic Review*, 45: 938–42 (December 1955).

## Pitfall 4   What happens when we cannot finesse the term structure of interest rates?

We have simplified our discussion of capital budgeting by assuming that the opportunity cost of capital is the same for all the cash flows, $C_1$, $C_2$, $C_3$, etc. This is not the right place to discuss the term structure of interest rates (we do that in Chapter 23). But we must point out certain problems with the IRR rule that crop up when short-term interest rates are different from long-term rates.

Remember our most general formula for calculating net present value:

$$NPV = C_0 + \frac{C_1}{(1 + r_1)} + \frac{C_2}{(1 + r_2)} + \ldots$$

In other words, we discount $C_1$ at the opportunity cost of capital for one year, $C_2$ at the opportunity cost of capital for two years, and so on. The IRR rule tells us to accept a project if the IRR is greater than the opportunity cost of capital. But what do we do when we have several opportunity costs? Do we compare IRR with $r_1$, $r_2$, $r_3$, ... ? Actually, we would have to compute a complex weighted average of these rates to obtain a number comparable to IRR.

What does this mean for capital budgeting? It means trouble for the IRR rule whenever the term structure of interest rates becomes important.[15] In a situation where the term structure is important, we have to compare the project IRR with the expected IRR (yield to maturity) offered by a traded security. That security must (1) be of equivalent risk to the project and (2) offer the same time pattern of cash flows as the project. Such a comparison is easier said than done. It is much better to forget about IRR and just calculate NPV.

Many firms use the IRR, thereby implicitly assuming that there is no difference between short-term and long-term rates of interest. They do this for the same reason that we have so far finessed the term structure: simplicity.[16]

## Pitfall 5   Interpretation and misinterpretation of IRR

Users of the IRR technique may misinterpret what the IRR is telling them. For example, if you invest $1000 for three years at an IRR of 10 per cent you might think that you are earning 10 per cent compound per year on your $1000 investment. If that is your belief you may be sadly disappointed. Consider investments K and L below: both require an investment of $1000 and both have an IRR of 10 per cent. Investment K is a three-year bank deposit in which interest is retained in the account and compounds until the end of the three years. The interest rate is 10 per cent per year, so in the case of K you do earn 10 per cent compound per year on your $1000. Investment L also has an IRR of 10 per cent, but the sum of cash accumulated from L at the end of three years is less than the cash accumulated from K. Therefore, your $1000 invested in L earns less than 10 per cent compounded each year for three years.

| Project | Cash flows ($) | | | | Accumulated cash |
| | $C_0$ | $C_1$ | $C_2$ | $C_3$ | $(C_1 + C_2 + C_3)$ |
| --- | --- | --- | --- | --- | --- |
| K | −1000 | 0 | 0 | 1331 | 1331 |
| L | −1000 | +600 | +50 | +550 | 1200 |

[15] The problem here is not that the IRR is a nuisance to calculate, but that it is not a very useful number to have.
[16] In Chapter 9 we will look at some special cases in which it would be misleading to use the same discount rate for both short-term and long-term cash flows.

There are two morals to be drawn here. First, be careful how you interpret IRR. Second, even where you have equal initial investments and equal terms to maturity, equal IRRs do not necessarily mean equal investment performance.

'But . . .', you may protest, 'in calculating the cash accumulated from investment L you did not allow for the opportunity to reinvest the cash flows paid out in years 1 and 2.' Absolutely correct, we did not account for such opportunities because by definition the extra returns will depend on other investments, not on L. Several problems can arise if we start considering investment packages consisting of L with other projects. For example, we run the risk of accepting a bad project because it is packaged with good projects.

An intuitive interpretation of IRR is difficult. To say that the IRR is the discount rate that makes NPV equal to zero is correct, but may not be very helpful. As an alternative we can say that the IRR represents the maximum required return that the project can support, *assuming* that payments on the project's financing are *exactly* matched to the net cash flows of the project. Thus, for example, investment L can support a required return of 10 per cent because part of the $1000 initial financing is repaid in year 1. You do earn 10 per cent on each dollar you invest, but only while the money remains invested in the project. In year 1 you get a return of $100 on your investment of $1000, and a $500 repayment of your initial investment. In year 2 you get a return of $50 on the $500 which remains invested in the project. In year 3 you get a return of $50 plus repayment of the remaining $500.

This suggests another way to look at IRR: as the compound rate of return on $1 which remains fully invested in the project. The problem is that all the dollars you put in at the beginning of the project do not necessarily stay fully invested for the project's life. If so, the return on $1 fully invested is not a particularly good measure of the performance of the project.

## The verdict on IRR

We have given five examples of things that can go wrong with IRR. We have given only one example of what could go wrong with payback or return on book value. Does this mean that IRR is five times worse than the other two rules? Quite the contrary. There is little point in dwelling on the deficiencies of payback or return on book. They are clearly ad hoc rules that often lead to silly conclusions. The IRR rule has a much more respectable ancestry. It is a less easy rule to use than NPV, but, *used properly*, it gives the same answer.

There is one advantage to IRR—project analysis can commence without *initially* needing to know the required return. Of course, *ultimately* you have to specify the required return in order to judge whether the IRR exceeds that return. So where is the advantage? Well, if you analyse the project using NPV you first need a discount rate. You select the discount rate according to the risk of the project. Here is the catch-22: often you do not know much about the risk of the project until you have analysed it. But, in order to analyse it, you need to know the discount rate. We are back where we started. Use of the IRR can get you out of this endless loop. Thus, in the exploratory phase of project evaluation there may be a role for IRR, but we suggest you switch to NPV once you have an understanding of the project's risk.

## 5.6 Choosing the capital expenditure program when resources are limited

The entire discussion of methods of capital budgeting rests on the proposition that the wealth of a firm's shareholders is highest if the firm accepts *every* project that has a positive net present value. Suppose, however, that there are limitations on the investment program that prevent the company from undertaking all such projects. Economists call this **capital rationing**. When capital is rationed, we need a method of selecting the package of projects that is within the company's resources, yet gives the highest possible net present value.

# An easy problem in capital rationing

Let us start with a very simple example. Suppose that there is a 10 per cent opportunity cost of capital, that our company has total resources of $10 million and that it has the following opportunities:

| Project | Cash flows ($million) | | | NPV at 10% |
|---------|------|------|------|------------|
| | $C_1$ | $C_2$ | $C_3$ | |
| A | −10 | +30 | +5 | 21 |
| B | −5 | +5 | +20 | 16 |
| C | −5 | +5 | +15 | 12 |

All three projects are attractive, but suppose that the firm is limited to spending $10 million. In that case it can invest *either* in project A *or* in projects B and C. Although individually B and C have lower net present values than project A, when taken together they have the higher net present value. Here, we cannot choose between projects solely on the basis of individual net present values. When funds are limited, we need to concentrate on getting the biggest bang for our buck. In other words, we must pick the projects that offer the highest ratio of present value to initial outlay. This ratio is known as the **profitability index**.[17]

$$\text{Profitability index} = \frac{\text{NPV}}{-C_0}$$

For our three projects the profitability index is calculated as follows:[18]

| Project | Investment ($million) | NPV ($million) | Profitability index |
|---------|----------------------|----------------|---------------------|
| A | 10 | 21 | 2.1 |
| B | 5 | 16 | 3.2 |
| C | 5 | 12 | 2.4 |

Of our three projects, B has the highest profitability index and C the next highest. Therefore, if our budget limit is $10 million, we should accept these two projects.[19]

Unfortunately, there are some limitations to this simple ranking method. One of the most serious is that it breaks down whenever more than one resource is rationed. For example,

---

[17]  If the project requires outlays in two or more periods, the denominator should be the present value of the outlays. (Some companies do not discount the benefits or costs before calculating the profitability index. The less said about these companies, the better.)

[18]  Sometimes the profitability index is defined as the ratio of present value to initial outlay—that is as PV/investment. This measure is also known as the benefit-cost ratio. The benefit-cost ratio equals the profitability index plus 1. Project rankings are unchanged.

[19]  If a project has a positive profitability index, it must also have a positive NPV. Therefore, firms sometimes use the profitability index to select projects when capital is not limited. However, like the IRR, the profitability index can be misleading when used to choose between mutually exclusive projects. For example, suppose you were forced to choose between (a) investing $100 in a project whose payoffs have a present value of $200 or (b) investing $1 million in a project whose payoffs have a present value of $1.5 million. The first investment has the higher profitability index; the latter makes you richer.

suppose that a $10 million budget limit applies to cash flows in *each* of years 0 and 1 and that our menu is expanded to include an investment next year in project D:

| Project | Cash flows ($million) | | | NPV at 10% | Profitability index |
|---|---|---|---|---|---|
| | $C_0$ | $C_1$ | $C_2$ | | |
| A | −10 | +30 | +5 | 21 | 3.1 |
| B | −5 | +5 | +20 | 16 | 4.2 |
| C | −5 | +5 | +15 | 12 | 3.4 |
| D | 0 | −40 | +60 | 13 | 0.4 |

One strategy is to accept projects B and C; however, if we do this, we cannot also accept project D, which costs more than our budget limit for period 1. An alternative is to accept project A in period 0. Although this has a lower net present value than the combination of projects B and C, it provides a $30 million positive cash flow in period 1. With that added to the $10 million budget we can also afford to undertake project D. Projects A and D have *lower* profitability indexes than B and C, but they have a *higher* total net present value.

The reason that ranking on the profitability index fails in this example is that resources are constrained in each of two periods. In fact, this ranking method is inadequate whenever there is *any* other constraint on the choice of projects. This means that it cannot cope with cases in which two projects are mutually exclusive or in which one project is dependent on another.

## *Some more elaborate capital rationing models

The simplicity of the profitability-index method may sometimes outweigh its limitations. For example, it may not pay to worry about expenditures in subsequent years if you have only a hazy notion of future capital availability or investment opportunities. But there are also circumstances in which the limitations of the profitability-index method are intolerable. For such occasions, we need a more general method for solving the capital-rationing problem.

We begin by restating the problem just described. Suppose that we were to accept proportion $x_A$ of project A in our example. Then the net present value of our investment in the project would be $21x_A$. Similarly, the net present value of our investment in project B can be expressed as $16x_B$, and so on. Our objective is to select the set of projects with the highest *total* net present value. In other words, we wish to find the values of $x$ that maximise

$$NPV = 21x_A + 16x_B + 12x_C + 13x_D$$

Our choice of projects is subject to several constraints. First, total cash outflow in period 0 must not be greater than $10 million. In other words,

$$10x_A + 5x_B + 5x_C + 0_D \leq 10$$

Similarly, total outflow in period 1 must not be greater than $10 million,

$$-30x_A - 5x_B - 5x_C + 40_D \leq 10$$

Finally, we cannot invest a negative amount in a project and we cannot purchase more than one of each. Therefore, we have

$$0 \leq x_A \leq 1, 0 \leq x_B \leq 1, \ldots$$

Collecting all these conditions, we can summarise the problem as follows:

$$\text{Maximise } 21x_A + 16x_B + 12x_C + 13x_D$$

Subject to

$$10x_A + 5x_B + 5x_C + 0x_D \le 10$$
$$-30x_A - 5x_B - 5x_C + 40x_D \le 10$$
$$0 \le x_A \le 1, 0 \le x_B \le 1, \ldots$$

One way to tackle such a problem is to keep selecting different values for the $x$s, noting which combination both satisfies the constraints and gives the highest net present value. But it is smarter to recognise that the equations above constitute a linear programming (LP) problem. Mathematicians have devised special techniques for solving LP problems. Nowadays, the mechanics of the solution can be left to a computer equipped to solve LP problems.

The answer given by the LP method is somewhat different from the one we obtained earlier. Instead of investing in one unit of project A and one unit of project D, we are told to take half of project A, all of project B and three-quarters of project D. The reason is simple. The computer is a dumb, but obedient, pet, and since we did not tell it that the $x$s had to be whole numbers, it saw no reason to make them so. By accepting 'fractional' projects, it is possible to increase NPV by $2.25 million. For many purposes this is quite appropriate. If project A represents an investment in 1000 square feet of warehouse space or in 1000 tonnes of steel plate, it might be feasible to accept 500 square feet or 500 tonnes and quite reasonable to assume that cash flow would be reduced proportionately. If, however, project A is a single crane or oil well, such fractional investments make little sense.

When fractional projects are not feasible, we can use a form of linear programming known as *integer* (or *zero-one*) *programming*, which limits all the $x$s to integers. Unfortunately, integer programs are computationally more difficult to solve than LP problems. However, this problem is becoming less and less significant with the growth in power of modern computers.

## Uses of capital rationing models

Linear programming models seem tailor-made for solving capital budgeting problems when resources are limited. Why then are they not universally accepted either in theory or in practice? One reason is that these models are often not cheap to use. We know of an oil company that spent over $4 million in one year on an investment planning model using integer programming. While linear programming is considerably cheaper in terms of computer time, it cannot be used when large, indivisible projects are involved.

Second, as with any sophisticated long-range planning tool there is the general problem of getting good data. It is just not worth applying costly, sophisticated methods to poor data. Furthermore, these models are based on the assumption that all future investment opportunities are known. In reality, the discovery of investment ideas is an unfolding process.

Our most serious misgivings centre on the basic assumption that capital is limited. When we come to discuss company financing, we shall see that most firms do not face capital rationing and can raise very large sums of money on fair terms. Why then do many chief executives tell their subordinates that capital is limited? If they are right, the capital market is seriously imperfect. What then are they doing maximising NPV?[20] We might be tempted to suppose that if capital is not rationed, they do not *need* to use the LP model and, if it is rationed, then surely they *ought* not to use it. But that would be too quick a judgement. Let us look at this problem more deliberately.

---

[20]  Do not forget that we had to assume perfect capital markets to derive the NPV rule.

**Soft rationing**   Many firms' capital constraints are 'soft'. They reflect no imperfections in capital markets. Instead, they are provisional limits adopted by management as an aid to financial control.

Some ambitious divisional managers habitually overstate their investment opportunities. Rather than trying to distinguish which projects really are worthwhile, headquarters may find it simpler to impose an upper limit on divisional expenditures and thereby force the divisions to set their own priorities. In such instances budget limits are a rough but effective way of dealing with biased cash flow forecasts. In other cases management may believe that very rapid corporate growth could impose intolerable strains on management and the organisation. Since it is difficult to quantify such constraints explicitly, the budget limit may be used as a proxy.

Because such budget limits have nothing to do with any inefficiency in the capital market, there is no contradiction in using an LP model in the division to maximise net present value subject to the budget constraint. On the other hand, there is not much point in elaborate selection procedures if the cash flow forecasts of the division are seriously biased.

Even if capital is not rationed, other resources may be. The availability of management time, skilled labour or even capital equipment often constitutes an important constraint on a company's growth. In the appendix to this chapter we show you how the programming model that we have described can be extended to incorporate such constraints. And we also show how such models may be used to cope with project interactions.

**Hard rationing**   Soft rationing should never cost the firm anything. If capital constraints become tight enough to hurt—in the sense that projects with significant positive NPVs are passed up—then the firm raises more money and loosens the constraint. But what if it *cannot* raise more money—what if it faces *hard* rationing?

Hard rationing implies market imperfections, but that does not necessarily mean we have to throw away net present value as a criterion for capital budgeting. It depends on the nature of the imperfection.

Australian Aquaculture Industry Ltd (AAI) borrows as much as the banks will lend it, yet it still has good investment opportunities. This is not hard rationing so long as AAI can issue shares. But perhaps it cannot. Perhaps the founder and majority shareholder vetoes the idea from fear of losing control of the firm: Perhaps a share issue would bring costly red tape or legal complications.[21]

This does not invalidate the NPV rule. AAI's *shareholders* can borrow or lend, sell their shares or buy more. They have free access to security markets. The type of portfolio they hold is independent of AAI's financing or investment decisions. The only way AAI can help its shareholders is to make them richer. Thus, AAI should invest its available cash in the package of projects having the largest aggregate net present value.

A barrier between the firm and capital markets does not undermine net present value so long as the barrier is the *only* market imperfection. The important thing is that the firm's *shareholders* have free access to well-functioning capital markets.

The method of net present value *is* undermined when imperfections restrict shareholders' portfolio choice. Suppose that Nullarbor Aquaculture Industries Ltd (NAI) is solely owned by its founder, Alexander Turbot. Mr Turbot has no cash or credit remaining, but he is convinced that expansion of his operation is a high-NPV investment. He has tried to sell shares but has found that prospective investors, sceptical of prospects for fish farming in the desert, offer him much less than he thinks his firm is worth. For Mr Turbot capital markets hardly exist. It makes little sense for him to discount the prospective cash flows at a market opportunity cost of capital.

---

21   A majority owner who is 'locked in' and has much personal wealth tied up in AAI may be effectively cut off from capital markets. The NPV rule may not make sense to such an owner, though it will to the other shareholders.

# Where NPV falls down

We have preached the virtues of NPV. It is only fair that before we conclude the chapter we should also point out where NPV falls down. Imagine that you have to evaluate a choice between building a hotel in Sydney or in a proposed tourist development in the Simpson Desert. You calculate exactly the same NPV for each venture. Which do you choose? Most people would select the Sydney location. One economically sound reason for selecting Sydney is that you are likely to have more options to convert the hotel to other uses, or sell to other investors, if your venture does not turn out as planned. This flexibility to pursue other options has value, but it is not captured in the traditional NPV calculation.

Mining companies buy leases over ore deposits that cannot be profitably mined at current prices. They do this even when prices are not expected to increase. Such leases have a zero or negative PV and are therefore negative NPV investments according to standard NPV calculations. Nevertheless, the leases have value as long as there is a chance that the price *may* rise to a level where mining is profitable. The company can then exercise its option to mine.

The above examples demonstrate that in some cases NPV analysis may neglect an important component of value. That component of value is the value of **real options**[22] associated with a project. We have more to say about valuing real options in Chapter 21.

We should also warn you about the bigger picture. The decision rule for appraising projects is only one part of the capital budgeting process. The process involves, among other things, generating the ideas that lead to projects, corporate strategy, organisational politics, budgetary control, project implementation, forecasting and setting required returns. Selecting the right decision rule may be the least of your problems. Assuming you do choose NPV, then a major and difficult practical problem will be selecting an appropriate discount rate.

## 5.7 Summary

If you are going to persuade your company to use the net present value rule, you must be prepared to explain why other rules do *not* give correct decisions. That is why we have examined three alternative investment criteria in this chapter.

Some companies use the payback method to make investment decisions. In other words, they accept only those projects that recover their initial investment within some specified period. Payback is an ad hoc rule. It ignores the order in which cash flows come within the payback period, and it ignores subsequent cash flows entirely. It therefore takes no account of the opportunity cost of capital.

The simplicity of payback makes it an easy device for *describing* investment projects. Managers talk casually about 'quick payback' projects in the same way that investors talk about 'high P/E' common shares. The fact that managers talk about the payback periods of projects does not mean that the payback rule governs their decisions. Some managers *do* use payback in judging capital investments. Why they rely on such a grossly oversimplified concept is a puzzle.

Some firms use average return on book value. In this case the company must decide which cash payments are capital expenditures and must pick appropriate depreciation schedules. It must then calculate the ratio of average income to the average book value of the investment and compare it with the company's target return. Average return on book is another ad hoc method. Since it ignores whether the income occurs next year or next century, it takes no account of the opportunity cost of money.

---

22   Such options are called real options to distinguish them from financial options as traded on options exchanges. We discuss the valuation of financial options in Chapter 20.

The internal rate of return is defined as the rate of discount at which a project would have zero NPV. It is a handy measure and widely used in finance; you should therefore know how to calculate it. The IRR rule states that companies should accept any investment offering an IRR in excess of the opportunity cost of capital. The IRR rule, like NPV, is a technique based on discounted cash flows. It will therefore give the correct answer if properly used. The problem is that it is easily misapplied. There are four things to look out for:

1. *Lending or borrowing?* If a project offers positive cash flows followed by negative flows, NPV *rises* as the discount rate is increased. You should accept such projects if their IRR is *less* than the opportunity cost of capital.
2. *Multiple rates of return.* If there is more than one change in the sign of the cash flows, the project may have several IRRs or no IRR at all.
3. *Mutually exclusive projects.* The IRR rule may give the wrong ranking of mutually exclusive projects that differ in economic life or in scale of required investment. If you insist on using IRR to rank mutually exclusive projects, you must examine the IRR on each additional unit of investment.
4. *Short-term interest rates may be different from long-term rates.* The IRR rule requires you to compare the project's IRR with the opportunity cost of capital. But sometimes there is an opportunity cost of capital for one-year cash flows, a different cost of capital for two-year cash flows, and so on. In these cases there is no simple yardstick for evaluating the IRR of a project.

If we are going to the expense of collecting forecasts, we might as well use them properly. Ad hoc criteria should therefore have no role in our firm's decisions, and the net present value rule should be employed in preference to other techniques using discounted cash flows. Having said that, we must be careful not to exaggerate the payoff of proper technique. Technique is important, but it is by no means the only determinant of the success of a capital expenditure program. If the forecasts of cash flows are biased, even the most careful application of the net present value rule may fail. In finance, as in love, excessive emphasis on technique may lead to impotence.[23]

In developing the NPV rules we assumed that the company can maximise shareholder wealth by accepting every project that is worth more than it costs. But, if capital is strictly limited, then it may not be possible to take every project with a positive NPV. If capital is rationed in only one period, then the firm should follow a simple rule: Calculate each project's profitability index, which is the firm's NPV per dollar of investment, then pick the projects with the highest profitability index until you run out of capital. Unfortunately, this procedure fails when capital is rationed in more than one period or when there are other constraints on project choice. The only general solution is linear or integer programming.

'Hard' capital rationing always reflects a market imperfection—a barrier between the firm and capital markets. If that barrier also implies that the firm's shareholders lack free access to a well-functioning capital market, the very foundations of net present value crumble. Fortunately, hard rationing is rare for corporations in developed economies. Many firms do use 'soft' capital rationing, however. That is, they set up self-imposed limits as a means of financial planning and control.

---

[23] These words are not ours, but they have stuck in our mind. Unfortunately, we have forgotten the name of their author so we cannot give him due credit.

# APPENDIX Some embellishments to the capital rationing model

In Section 5.6 we showed that when capital is rationed you can set up the investment decision as a linear programming problem. In this appendix we describe some embellishments to these models, and we show how you can use them to cope with other resource constraints and project interactions.

## Cash carry-forward

A plant manager who is forced to return the unspent part of an annual capital allocation may be goaded into a substantial year-end investment in pink carpeting for the foundry floor or other equally silly assets. (How can you argue for a high budget next year if there is money left over this year?) Headquarters can alleviate this problem by permitting the manager to carry forward any unspent balance. (Then the manager could at least wait until June and get a better selection of carpet colours.) Let us take the sample problem that we described in Section 5.6. To incorporate the possibility of cash carry-forward, we simply need to add another term to our spending constraint. Let $s$ denote funds transferred from year 0 to year 1 and let them earn interest at the rate $r$. Then we can rewrite our constraint for year 0 as

$$10x_A + 5x_B + 5x_C + 0_D + s = 10$$

Similarly, the constraint for year 1 becomes

$$-30x_A - 5x_B - 5x_C + 40_D \le 10 + (1 + r)s$$

Since carrying forward a negative amount is equivalent to borrowing, we will probably wish to add the constraint $s \ge 0$.

## Mutually exclusive projects and contingent projects

Suppose now that projects B and C are mutually exclusive. We can take care of this in an *integer* program by specifying that our *total* investment in the two projects cannot be greater than 1.

$$x_B + x_C \le 1 \quad x_B, x_C = 0 \text{ or } 1$$

In other words, if $x_B$ is 1, $x_C$ must be 0; if $x_C$ is 1, $x_B$ must be 0.

Suppose next that project D is an attachment to project A, and we cannot accept D *unless* we also accept A. In this case we need to add

$$x_D - x_A \le 0 \quad x_D, x_A = 0 \text{ or } 1$$

In other words, if $x_A$ is 1, $x_D$ can be 0 *or* 1; but if $x_A$ is 0, $x_D$ must likewise be 0.

## Constraints on non-financial resources

Money may not be the only scarce resource. Each of our projects may require services from a 12-person technical design department. If project A would employ three designers, project B two and so on, we would need to add a constraint like

$$3x_A + 2x_B + 8x_C + 3x_D \le 12$$

Sometimes it is appropriate to place constraints on the total increase in physical capacity. Suppose that projects A and C produce four and three units, respectively, of the same product. If the company is unable to sell more than five units, it is necessary to add

$$4x_A + 3x_C \leq 5$$

We could go on—but you get the idea.

## FURTHER READING

Most capital budgeting texts contain a discussion of alternative budgeting criteria. See, for example:

> H. Bierman, Jr and S. Smidt, *The Capital Budgeting Decision*, 8th ed., The Macmillan Company, New York, 1992.

A useful survey of Australian practice is provided by:

> M. Freeman and G. Hobbes, 'Capital Budgeting: Theory Versus Practice', *Australian Accountant*, **61**: 36–41, September 1991.

Classic articles on the internal rate of return rule include:

> J. H. Lorie and L. J. Savage, 'Three Problems in Rationing Capital', *Journal of Business*, **28**: 229–39 (October 1955).

> E. Solomon, 'The Arithmetic of Capital Budgeting Decisions', *Journal of Business*, **29**: 124–9 (April 1956).

> A. A. Alchian, 'The Rate of Interest, Fisher's Rate of Return over Cost and Keynes' Internal Rate of Return', *American Economic Review*, **45**: 938–42 (December 1955).

For a discussion of the profitability index, see:

> B. Schwab and P. Lusztig, 'A Comparative Analysis of the Net Present Value and the Benefit-Cost Ratios as Measures of the Economic Desirability of Investment', *Journal of Finance*, **24**: 507–16 ((June 1969).

The classic treatment of linear programming applied to capital budgeting is:

> H. M. Weingartner, *Mathematical Programming and the Analysis of Capital Budgeting Problems*, Prentice-Hall, Inc., Englewood Cliffs, N.J., 1963.

There is a long scholarly controversy on whether capital constraints invalidate the NPV rule. Weingartner has reviewed this literature.

> H. M. Weingartner, 'Capital Rationing: *n* Authors in Search of a Plot', *Journal of Finance*, **32**: 1403–32 (December 1977).

## QUIZ

**1.** What is the opportunity cost of capital supposed to represent? Give a concise definition.

**2.** a. What is the payback period on each of the following projects?

| Project | Cash flows ($) | | | | |
|---|---|---|---|---|---|
| | $C_0$ | $C_1$ | $C_2$ | $C_3$ | $C_4$ |
| A | −5000 | +1000 | +1000 | +3000 | 0 |
| B | −1000 | 0 | +1000 | +2000 | +3000 |
| C | −5000 | +1000 | +1000 | +3000 | +5000 |

b. Given that you wish to use the payback rule with a cutoff period of two years, which projects would you accept?

c. If you use a cutoff period of three years, which projects would you accept?

d. If the opportunity cost of capital is 10 per cent, which projects have positive NPVs?

e. 'Payback gives too much weight to cash flows that occur after the cutoff date.' True or false?

f. 'If a firm uses a single cutoff period for all projects, it is likely to accept too many short-lived projects.' True or false?

g. If the firm uses the discounted payback rule, will it accept any negative NPV projects? Will it turn down any positive NPV projects? Explain.

**3.** A machine costs $8000 and is expected to produce profit before depreciation of $2500 in each of years 1 and 2 and $3500 in each of years 3 and 4. Assuming that the machine is depreciated at a constant rate of $2000 a year and that there are no taxes, what is the average return on book?

**4.** Are the following statements true or false? Why?

a. 'The average return on book rule gives too much weight to the later cash flows.'

b. 'If companies use their existing return on book as a yardstick for new investments, successful companies will tend to undertake too much investment.'

**5.** a. Calculate the net present value of the following project for discount rates of 0, 50 and 100 per cent.

| Cash flows ($) | | |
| --- | --- | --- |
| $C_0$ | $C_1$ | $C_2$ |
| −6 750 | +4 500 | +18 000 |

b. What is the IRR of the project?

**6.** Consider projects A and B:

| | Cash flows ($) | | | |
| --- | --- | --- | --- | --- |
| Project | $C_0$ | $C_1$ | $C_2$ | IRR (%) |
| A | −4000 | +2410 | +2930 | 21 |
| B | −2000 | +1310 | +1720 | 31 |

a. The opportunity cost of capital is less than 10 per cent. Use the IRR rule to determine which project or projects you should accept (i) if you can undertake both and (ii) if you can undertake only one.

b. Suppose that project A has an NPV of $690 and project B has an NPV of $657. What is the NPV of the $2000 incremental investment in project A?

**7.** Projects C and D both involve the same outlay and offer the same IRR which exceeds the opportunity cost of capital. The cash flows generated by project C are larger than those of project D but tend to occur later. Which project has the higher NPV?

**8.** You have the chance to participate in a project that produces the following cash flows:

| | Cash flows ($) | |
|---|---|---|
| $C_0$ | $C_1$ | $C_2$ |
| +5 000 | +4 000 | −11 000 |

The internal rate of return is 13 per cent. If the opportunity cost of capital is 10 per cent, would you accept the offer?

**9.** Suppose you have the following investment opportunities, but only $100 000 available for investment. Which projects should you take?

| Project | NPV | Investment |
|---|---|---|
| 1 | 5 000 | 10 000 |
| 2 | 5 000 | 5 000 |
| 3 | 10 000 | 90 000 |
| 4 | 15 000 | 60 000 |
| 5 | 15 000 | 75 000 |
| 6 | 3 000 | 15 000 |

**10.** What is the difference between 'hard' and 'soft' capital rationing? Does soft rationing mean the manager should stop trying to maximise NPV? How about hard rationing?

## QUESTIONS AND PROBLEMS

**1.** Consider the following projects:

| Project | $C_0$ | $C_1$ | $C_2$ | $C_3$ | $C_4$ | $C_5$ |
|---|---|---|---|---|---|---|
| | | Cash flows ($) | | | | |
| A | −1000 | +1000 | 0 | 0 | 0 | 0 |
| B | −2000 | +1000 | +1000 | +4000 | +1000 | +1000 |
| C | −3000 | +1000 | +1000 | 0 | +1000 | +1000 |

a. If the opportunity cost of capital is 10 per cent, which projects have a positive NPV?
b. Calculate the payback period for each project.
c. Which project(s) would a firm using the payback rule accept if the cutoff period were three years?

**2.** Project A (shown in Table 5.1a) has undergone some revisions. The initial investment has been reduced to $6000, and the firm proposes to depreciate this investment by $2000 a year. Operating costs, unfortunately, have increased by $1000 a year. If the opportunity cost of capital is 7 per cent, how do these changes alter the NPV of the project? How do they affect the average return on book?

**3.** Consider a project with the following cash flows:

| $C_0$ | $C_1$ | $C_2$ |
|-------|-------|-------|
| $-100$ | $+200$ | $-75$ |

a. How many internal rates of return does this project have?
b. The opportunity cost of capital is 20 per cent. Is this an attractive project? Briefly explain.

**4.** Respond to the following comments:
a. 'We like to use payback principally as a way of coping with risk.'
b. 'The great merit of the IRR rule is that one does not have to think about what is an appropriate discount rate.'

**5.** The payback rule is still used by many firms despite its acknowledged theoretical shortcomings. Why do you think this is so?

**6.** Unfortunately, your chief executive officer refuses to accept any investments in plant expansion that do not return their original investment in four years or less. That is, he insists on a *payback rule* with a *cutoff period* of four years. As a result, attractive long-lived projects are being turned down.

The CEO is willing to switch to a *discounted payback rule* with the same four-year cutoff period. Would this be an improvement? Explain.

**7.** Consider the following two mutually exclusive projects

| | Cash flows ($) | | | |
|---------|-------|-------|-------|-------|
| Project | $C_0$ | $C_1$ | $C_2$ | $C_3$ |
| A | $-100$ | $+60$ | $+60$ | 0 |
| B | $-100$ | 0 | 0 | $+140$ |

a. Calculate the NPV of each project for discount rates of 0, 10 and 20 per cent. Plot these on a graph with NPV on the vertical axis and discount rate on the horizontal.
b. What is the approximate IRR for each project?
c. In what circumstances should the company accept project A?
d. Calculate the NPV of the incremental investment (B-A) for discount rates of 0, 10 and 20 per cent. Plot these on your graph. Show that the circumstances in which you would accept A are also those in which the IRR on the incremental investment is less than the opportunity cost of capital.

**8.** Mr Cyrus Clops, the president of Giant Enterprises, has to make a choice between two possible investments:

| | Cash flows ($'000) | | | |
|---|---|---|---|---|
| Project | $C_0$ | $C_1$ | $C_2$ | IRR (%) |
| A | −400 | +241 | +293 | 21 |
| B | −200 | +131 | +172 | 31 |

The opportunity cost of capital is 9 per cent. Mr Clops is tempted to take project B, which has the higher IRR.
a. Explain to Mr Clops why this is not the correct procedure.
b. Show him how to adapt the IRR rule to choose the best project.
c. Show him that this project also has the higher NPV.

**9.** The Titanic Shipbuilding Company has a non-cancellable contract to build a small cargo vessel. Construction involves a cash outlay of $250 000 at the end of each of the next two years. At the end of the third year the company will receive payment of $650 000. The company can speed up construction by working an extra shift. In this case there will be a cash outlay of $550 000 at the end of the first year followed by a cash payment of $650 000 at the end of the second year. Use the IRR rule to show the (approximate) range of opportunity costs of capital at which the company should work the extra shift.

**10.** Look again at projects F and G in Section 5.3. Assume that the projects are mutually exclusive and that the opportunity cost of capital is 10 per cent.
a. Calculate the profitability index for each project.
b. Show how the profitability-index rule can be used to select the superior project.

**11.** Some wealthy investors have been offered a scheme that would allow them to postpone taxes. The scheme involves a debt-financed purchase of a fleet of beer delivery trucks, which will then be leased to a local distributor. The cash flows are as follows:

| Year | Cash flow | |
|---|---|---|
| 0 | −21 750 | |
| 1 | +7 861 | |
| 2 | +8 317 | |
| 3 | +7 188 | Tax savings |
| 4 | +6 736 | |
| 5 | +6 231 | |
| 6 | −5 340 | |
| 7 | −5 972 | Tax paid later |
| 8 | −6 678 | |
| 9 | −7 468 | |
| 10 | +12 578 | Salvage value |

Calculate the approximate IRRs. Is the project attractive at a 14 per cent opportunity cost of capital?

**12.** Borghia Pharmaceuticals has $1 million allocated for capital expenditures. Which of the following projects should the company accept to stay within the $1 million budget? How much does the budget limit cost the company in terms of its market value? The opportunity cost of capital for each project is 11 per cent.

| Project | Investment ($'000) | NPV ($'000) | IRR (%) |
|---|---|---|---|
| 1 | 300 | 66 | 17.2 |
| 2 | 200 | −4 | 10.7 |
| 3 | 250 | 43 | 16.6 |
| 4 | 100 | 14 | 12.1 |
| 5 | 100 | 7 | 11.8 |
| 6 | 350 | 63 | 18.0 |
| 7 | 400 | 48 | 13.5 |

# chapter 6

# MAKING INVESTMENT DECISIONS WITH THE NET PRESENT VALUE RULE

We hope that by now you are convinced that wise investment decisions are based on the net present value rule. In this chapter we can think about how to apply the rule to practical investment problems. Our task is twofold. The first issue is to decide what should be discounted. We know the answer in principle: discount cash flows. But useful forecasts of cash flows do not arrive on a silver platter. Often the financial manager has to make do with raw data supplied by specialists in product design, production, marketing, and so on, and must check such information for relevance, completeness, consistency, and accuracy and then pull everything together into a usable forecast.

Our second task is to explain how the net present value rule should be used when there are project interactions. These occur when a decision about one project cannot be separated from a decision about another. Project interactions can be extremely complex. We will make no attempt to analyse every possible case. But we will work through most of the simple cases, as well as a few examples of medium complexity.

Another source of complexity is the imputation tax system. Unfortunately, this complexity requires us to consider both investment and financing decisions. We must learn to walk before we can run, so in this chapter we do not burden you with the detail of these additional complexities. We content ourselves with briefly alerting you to the need to consider the effects of imputation. A full analysis of this issue is presented in Chapter 19.

## 6.1 What to discount

Up to this point we have been concerned mainly with the mechanics of discounting and with the various methods of project appraisal. We have had almost nothing to say about the problem of what one should discount. When you are faced with this problem, you should always stick to three general rules:

**1.** Be consistent.
**2.** Only cash flow is relevant.
**3.** Always estimate cash flows on an incremental basis.

We will discuss each of these rules in turn.

## Be consistent

We cannot stress strongly enough the importance of being consistent when calculating NPV. The failure to properly understand and apply the principle of consistency in project valuations is a major source of error in practice.[1] We can think of consistency in NPV calculations as being on two levels.

**Level 1** requires consistency between the definition of:

▌ Capital invested
▌ Cash flow
▌ Cost of funds (discount rate)

The purpose of the NPV analysis is to determine whether the net cash flows are sufficient to service the capital invested. Obviously, there is little chance of the right result in this analysis unless the capital invested, the measurement of cash flows and the discount rate are defined on a consistent basis. For example, suppose a project requires $10 million to get it started. Shareholders provide half this sum and the rest is raised as debt. In doing the NPV analysis let us suppose the capital invested is defined to be the cash contributed by shareholders, that is $5 million. Then the cash flows in the NPV calculation should be the cash flows available to shareholders after we have deducted payments to debtholders, and the discount rate should be the rate of return that the shareholders require on the cash they have invested.

The example we give above is unusual. In practice the capital invested is usually defined to be the total funds required for the project.[2] So the cash flows are measured as the cash flows to service all capital supplied, both debt and equity. In this first part of the book, however, we mostly use yet another alternative. We assume that *all* the funds required are contributed by the shareholders. This would mean in our example above that the shareholders would provide the full $10 million. As a consequence, all the net cash flows from the project go to the shareholders and the discount rate is the rate that shareholders require for a firm with no debt.[3] We follow this approach for three reasons. First, to keep things simple. Second, because we want to avoid introducing the effects of debt until we have considered the firm's debt policy in Chapters 17 and 18. Third, because it means that the required return only depends on the risk of the project.

---

1   Errors from this source can easily run into millions of dollars. There are stories of several $100 million plus valuation errors in Australia and even one valuation error of $1 billion. There have been some large companies who failed to heed our advice on this issue, and who subsequently experienced financial distress. Of course, this might have been coincidence.

2   Strictly speaking, this is shareholders' funds plus debt with an explicit cost, excluding spontaneously-generated debt like trade credit.

3   This rate reflects the inherent risk of the business.

**Level 2** requires consistency between the adjustments made to the cash flow and the discount rate. These adjustments are:

- Adjustment for risk
- Adjustment for inflation
- Adjustment for taxes
- Adjustment for the company's financing mix

We recommend the measurement of cash flows on an after-corporate-tax basis and therefore the discount rate should be the required return after corporate tax. If the cash flows are **nominal** cash flows (they include the effect of inflation) then the discount rate should be a nominal discount rate, and so on. As it turns out, the discount rate we observe in the market is an after-corporate-tax discount rate. It is also a discount rate appropriate for discounting nominal cash flows. Market discount rates incorporate an extra component of return to compensate investors for *expected* inflation.

We also need to be careful to ensure that the discount rate we use and the definition of the cash flows are consistent with regard to the effects of the imputation tax system. We will return to these consistency issues in Chapter 19. In this chapter we will concentrate on the inflation adjustment.

# Only cash flow is relevant

A most important point is that the net present value rule is stated in terms of expected cash flows. Cash flow is the simplest possible concept; it is just the difference between dollars received and dollars paid out. Many people nevertheless confuse cash flow with accounting profits.

**Do not rely on accounting numbers**    Accountants start with 'dollars in' and 'dollars out', but in order to obtain accounting income they adjust these data in two important ways. First, they try to show profit as it is earned rather than when the company and the customer get around to paying their bills. Second, they sort cash outflows into two categories: current expenses and capital expenses. They deduct current expenses when calculating profit, but do not deduct capital expenses. Instead they 'depreciate' capital expenses over a number of years and deduct the annual depreciation charge from profits. As a result of these procedures, profits include some cash flows and exclude others and are reduced by depreciation charges, which are not cash flows at all.

It is not always easy to translate the customary accounting data back into actual dollars—dollars you can buy beer with. If you are in doubt about what a cash flow is, simply count the dollars coming in and take away the dollars going out. Do not assume without checking that you can find cash flow by simple manipulation of accounting data.

**Think carefully about the timing of cash flows**    You should also make sure that cash flows are recorded only when they occur and not when the work is undertaken or the liability incurred. For example, taxes should be discounted from their actual payment date, not from the time when the tax liability is recorded in the firm's books.

**Calculate cash flows after corporate tax**    We recommend that you always estimate cash flows on an after-company-tax basis. Some firms do not deduct tax payments in calculating investment cash flows. They try to offset this mistake by discounting the cash flows before taxes at a rate higher than the opportunity cost of capital observed in the market. Unfortunately, there is no reliable *general* formula that can be used for making such adjustments to the discount rate.[4]

---

[4]    It is possible to derive formulas to make such adjustments, but they only work for special cases such as perpetuities or cases where we assume that tax is a fixed proportion of cash flow.

**The effect of the imputation tax system**    Two projects with the same *after-corporate-tax cash flows* and the same risk do not necessarily have the same value under an imputation tax system. Suppose project Notax will be structured in such a way as to pay little or no corporate tax, while the other project, Fulltax, will be fully taxed. Remember the net *after-corporate-tax flows* are identical, so if we discount these cash flows at the same discount rate we will get the same project values. However, project Fulltax will be valued more highly by equity investors because in addition to the project cash flows it creates valuable franking credits[5] as a consequence of paying corporate tax.[6]

One way to handle this is to make a separate estimate of the present value of expected franking credits and add this to the value of the project. However, the franking credits only become usable by investors when dividends are paid. So we have to consider how large a dividend will be paid and when. This creates an interaction between the investment decision and dividend policy. It also turns out that there is an interaction between dividend policy and debt policy under imputation. We must therefore wait until we have discussed dividend policy and debt policy before we can pursue this issue further. Our discussion of imputation and investment decisions must therefore be deferred until Chapter 19.

# Estimate cash flows on an incremental basis

The value of a project depends on all the additional cash flows that follow from project acceptance. Here are some things to watch for when you are deciding which cash flows should be included:

**Do not confuse average with incremental payoffs**    Most managers naturally hesitate to throw good money after bad. For example, they are reluctant to invest more money in a losing division. But occasionally you will encounter 'turnaround' opportunities in which the incremental NPV on new investment in a loser is strongly positive.

Conversely, it does not always make sense to throw good money after good. A division with an outstanding past profitability record may have run out of good opportunities. Sentiment aside, you would not pay a large sum for a 20-year-old stallion, regardless of how many races that horse had won or how many champions it had sired.

Here is another example illustrating the difference between average and incremental returns. Suppose that a railway bridge is in urgent need of repair. With the bridge the railway can continue to operate; without the bridge it cannot. In this case the payoff from the repair work consists of all the benefits of operating the railway. The incremental NPV of the investment may be enormous. Of course, these benefits should be net of all other costs and all subsequent repairs; otherwise, the company may be misled into rebuilding an unprofitable railway piece by piece.

**Include all incidental effects**    It is important to include all incidental effects on the remainder of the business. For example, a branch line for a railway may have a negative NPV when considered in isolation, but still be a worthwhile investment when one allows for the additional traffic that it brings to the main line.

New investments are not always good news for existing investments. It is common for a new product to cannibalise part of the market for the company's existing products. Therefore, you need to consider whether the new product still has a positive NPV after you have accounted for lost sales on existing products.

---

5    When an Australian company pays dividends from profits which have been subject to Australian corporate tax, the Australian shareholders can claim the corporate tax paid as a deduction from their personal tax liability. This tax deduction is known as an imputation tax credit. More detailed discussion can be found in Chapters 16 and 19.

6    Note that this does not imply that the payment of corporate tax increases value. Project Fulltax *might* be even more valuable if it too could be structured to avoid corporate tax and thus increase its total after-tax cash flow. Then again, its value might be unchanged.

## Do not forget working capital requirements[7]

Net working capital (often referred to simply as working capital) is the difference between a company's short-term assets and liabilities. The principal short-term assets are cash, accounts receivable (customers' unpaid bills) and inventories of raw materials and finished goods. The principal short-term liabilities are accounts payable (bills that you have not paid). Most projects entail an additional investment in working capital.[8] This investment should therefore be recognised in your cash flow forecasts. By the same token, when the project comes to an end, you can usually recover some of the investment. This is treated as a cash inflow.

## Forget sunk costs

Sunk costs are like spilled milk: they are past and irreversible outflows. Because sunk costs are bygones, they cannot be affected by the decision to accept or reject the project and so they should be ignored.

This fact is often forgotten. For example, in 1971 Lockheed sought a federal guarantee from the United States government for a bank loan to continue development of the TriStar aeroplane. Lockheed and its supporters argued it would be foolish to abandon a project on which nearly $1 billion had already been spent. Some of Lockheed's critics countered that it would be equally foolish to continue with a project that offered no prospect of a satisfactory return on that $1 billion. Both groups were guilty of the sunk-cost fallacy: the $1 billion was irrecoverable and therefore irrelevant.[9]

## Include opportunity costs

The cost of a resource may be relevant to the investment decision even when no cash changes hands. For example, suppose a new manufacturing operation uses land that could otherwise be sold for $100 000. This resource is not free. It has an opportunity cost, which is the cash it could generate for the company if the project were rejected and the resource sold or put to some other productive use. In using opportunity costs we may appear to have swiftly abandoned our earlier dictum that you should only consider cash flows. However, this is not so. As we discuss below, the proper basis for judging a project is the difference in cash flows with the project and without it. The opportunity cost of the land measures an extra cash flow that would be generated without the project.

The above example prompts us to warn you against judging projects on the basis of 'before versus after'. The proper comparison is 'with or without'. A manager comparing before versus after might not assign any value to the land because the firm owns it both before and after:

| Before | Take project | After | Cash flow, before versus after |
|---|---|---|---|
| Firm owns land | | Firm still owns land | 0 |

The proper comparison, which is with or without, is as follows:

| Before | Decision | After | Cash flow |
|---|---|---|---|
| Firm owns land | Take project | Firm still owns land | $0 with project |
| Firm owns land | Do not take project | Firm sells land for $100 000 | $100 000 without project |

---

[7] Later in the book we devote a whole chapter to working capital—Chapter 29.

[8] If you do your cash flow forecasting with sufficient care, the change in working capital will be captured by items such as increased payments for inventories. Often, however, it is not convenient to make detailed forecasts of these cash flows and instead an estimate is made of the working capital change.

[9] U. E. Reinhardt provides an analysis of the value of the TriStar in 1971 in 'Break-Even Analysis for Lockheed's TriStar: An Application of Financial Theory,' *Journal of Finance*, **28**: 821–38 (September 1973). Reinhardt does not fall into the sunk-cost fallacy.

Comparing the two possible 'afters', we see that the firm gives up a $100 000 cash flow by undertaking the project. This reasoning still holds if the land will not be sold but is worth $100 000 to the firm in some other use.

Sometimes opportunity costs may be very difficult to estimate; however, where the resource can be freely traded, its opportunity cost is simply equal to the market price. Why? It cannot be otherwise. If the value of a parcel of land to the firm is less than its market price, the firm should sell it. On the other hand, the opportunity cost of using land in a particular project cannot exceed the cost of buying an equivalent parcel of land to replace it.

**Beware of allocated overhead costs**    We have already mentioned that the accountant's objective in gathering data is not always the same as the investment analyst's. A case in point is the allocation of overhead costs. Overheads include such items as supervisory salaries, rent, heat and light. These overheads may not be related to any particular project, but they have to be paid for somehow. Therefore, when the accountant assigns costs to the firm's projects, a charge for overheads is usually made. Now our principle of incremental cash flows says that in investment appraisal we should include only the extra cash outlays that would result from the project. A project may generate extra overhead expenditures—and then again it may not. We should be cautious about assuming that the accountant's allocation of overheads represents the true extra expenditure that would be incurred.

# Consistent treatment of inflation

Interest rates are usually quoted in nominal rather than real terms. Suppose you hold a government 8 per cent bond that promises to pay you $1080 at the end of the year. The government guarantees to make the payment, but it makes no promise about what the $1080 will buy. Investors take that into account and factor in inflation when they decide what is a fair rate of interest.

For example, suppose that the rate of interest on a one-year Commonwealth bond is 8 per cent and that next year's inflation is expected to be 6 per cent. If you buy the bond, you get back $1080 in year 1 dollars, which you expect to be worth 6 per cent less than current dollars. The nominal payoff is $1080, but the expected real value of your payoff is $1080/1.06 = $1019. The real rate of return is 19/1000 = 0.019, or 1.9 per cent. Thus, we could say: 'The nominal interest rate on the bond is 8 per cent.' Or: 'It offers a 1.9 per cent expected real rate of return.' Remember from Chapter 3 that the relationship linking the two is:[10]

$$1.08 = 1.019 \times 1.06$$

or

$$1 + E[r_{nominal}] = (1 + E[r_{real}])(1 + E[\text{inflation rate}])$$

If the discount rate is stated in nominal terms, then consistency requires that cash flows be estimated in nominal terms, taking account of trends in selling price, labour and materials cost, etc. This calls for more than simply applying a single assumed inflation rate to all components of cash flow. Labour cost per hour of work, for example, normally increases at a faster rate than the consumer price index because of improvements in productivity and increasing real wages throughout the economy. The tax deduction for depreciation does not increase with inflation; it stays constant in nominal terms because tax law allows only the original cost of assets to be depreciated.

Of course, it is possible to discount real cash flows at a real discount rate, although this is not commonly done.[11] Here is a simple example showing the equivalence of the two methods.

---

10    For government bonds the nominal rate is certain, but because inflation is uncertain so is the real return.
11    It is sometimes done for investments with a very long life, such as forests.

Suppose your firm usually forecasts cash flows in nominal terms and discounts at a 15 per cent nominal rate. In this particular case, however, you are given project cash flows estimated in real terms, that is, current dollars:

| Real cash flows ($'000) | | | |
|---|---|---|---|
| $C_0$ | $C_1$ | $C_2$ | $C_3$ |
| −100 | +35 | +50 | +30 |

It would be inconsistent to discount these real cash flows at 15 per cent. You have two alternatives: Either restate the cash flows in nominal terms and discount at 15 per cent, or restate the discount rate in real terms and use this to discount the real cash flows. We will now show you that both methods produce the same answer.

Assume that inflation is projected at 10 per cent a year. Then the first cash flow for year 1, which is \$35 000 in current dollars, will be $35\,000 \times 1.10 = \$38\,500$ in year 1 dollars. Similarly, the cash flow for year 2 will be $50\,000 \times (1.10)^2 = \$60\,500$ in year 2 dollars, and so on. If we discount these nominal cash flows at the 15 per cent nominal discount rate we have

$$\text{NPV} = -100 + \frac{38.5}{1.15} + \frac{60.5}{(1.15)^2} + \frac{39.9}{(1.15)^3} = 5.5, \text{ or } \$5500$$

Instead of converting the cash flow forecasts into nominal terms, we could convert the discount rate into real terms. To get the nominal rate of interest we compound the real rate of interest by the inflation rate.

$$1 + \text{nominal discount rate} = (1 + \text{real discount rate}) \times (1 + \text{inflation rate})$$

Rearranging this equation gives the real discount rate as:

$$\text{Real discount rate} = \frac{1 + \text{nominal discount rate}}{1 + \text{inflation rate}} - 1$$

In our example this gives

$$\text{Real discount rate} = (1.15/1.10) - 1 = 0.045, \text{ or } 4.5\%$$

If we now discount the real cash flows by the real discount rate, we have an NPV of \$5500, just as before:

$$\text{NPV} = -100 + \frac{35}{1.045} + \frac{50}{(1.045)^2} + \frac{30}{(1.045)^3} = 5.5, \text{ or } \$5500$$

This was a simple example and it was therefore relatively easy to work with either real or nominal values. In practice we usually recommend the use of nominal cash flows and nominal discount rates. There are two reasons for this. First, if you work with nominal cash flows it is usually easier to handle cash flows that inflate at different rates. Second, the discount rates observed in the market are typically nominal rates. Before you can adjust them to real rates you have to estimate the expected rate of inflation that is built into the nominal rates. Having to make this estimate, which you may get wrong, introduces another potential source of error into the analysis.[12]

---

[12] The equation we used for the effect of inflation on nominal interest rates is known as the Fisher equation, having been developed by the great economist Irving Fisher in about 1930. However, not everybody agrees that Fisher's theory is right. So not only do we run the risk of mis-estimating inflation, but we might also be getting the adjustment process wrong.

Note that you can *roughly* estimate the real discount rate as the *difference* between the nominal discount rate of 15 per cent and the inflation rate of 10 per cent. Discounting at 5 per cent would give NPV = $4600—not exactly right, but in the ballpark. This method of estimating the real discount rate gives a much better approximation as the inflation rate gets smaller.

The message of all this is quite simple: be consistent. Discount nominal cash flows at a nominal discount rate. Discount real cash flows at a real rate. Obvious as this rule is, it is sometimes violated. For example, in 1974 there was a political storm in Ireland over the government's acquisition of a stake in Bula Mines. The price paid by the government reflected an assessment of £40 million as the value of Bula Mines; however, one group of consultants thought that the company's value was only £8 million and others thought that it was as high as £104 million. Although these valuations used different cash flow projections, a significant part of the difference in views seemed to reflect confusion about real and nominal discount rates.[13]

## 6.2 Example—IM&C project

As the newly appointed financial manager of International Mulch and Compost Company (IM&C) you have moved to the head office in Queensland. There you are asked to analyse a proposal for marketing guano as a garden fertiliser. (IM&C's planned advertising campaign features a rustic gentleman who steps out of a vegetable patch singing, 'All my troubles have guano way.')[14]

You are given the forecasts shown in Table 6.1. The project requires an investment of $10 million in plant and machinery (line 1). This machinery can be dismantled and sold for net proceeds estimated at $1 million in year 7 (line 1, column 7). This amount is the plant's *salvage value*.

In Table 6.1 and subsequent tables we have made a simplifying assumption about the effects of tax.[15] We assume there is no time lag in the payment of tax or in the receipt of tax benefits. We could allow for tax effects to be lagged one period by shifting all the tax entries one column to the right. However, we think you have enough to do mastering the principles of investment evaluation, without at this stage worrying about tax lags. That said, it is important to understand that such lags can be important in practice.[16] Indeed, firms devote significant effort to deferring tax payments for as long as possible.

Whoever prepared Table 6.1 depreciated the capital investment over six years to an arbitrary salvage value of $500 000, which is less than your forecast of salvage value. *Straight-line depreciation* was assumed. Under this method annual depreciation equals a constant proportion of the initial investment less salvage value ($9.5 million). If we call the depreciable life $T$, then the straight-line depreciation in year $t$ is:

Depreciation in year $t = 1/T \times$ depreciable value $= 1/6 \times 9.5 = $1.583 million

Lines 6 to 12 in Table 6.1 show a simplified income statement for the guano project. This might be taken as a starting point for estimating cash flow. However, you discover that all figures submitted to you are based on costs and selling prices prevailing in year 0. IM&C's production managers realise there will be inflation, but they have assumed that prices can be raised to cover increasing costs. Thus, they claim that inflation will not affect the real value of the project.

---

[13] In some cases it is unclear what procedure was used. At least one expert seems to have discounted nominal cash flows at a real rate. For a review of the Bula Mines controversy see E. Dimson and P. R. Marsh, *Cases in Corporate Finance*, Wiley International, London, 1987.

[14] Sorry.

[15] At the time of writing the Australian corporate tax rate was 36 per cent; not so long ago it was 33 per cent, and not long before that it was 39 per cent. It looks as though it may change again in the not too distant future. So we use a variety of tax rates throughout the book.

[16] The government tries to minimise the effect of such lags by requiring large companies to pay quarterly tax instalments based on estimated taxable profit for the current year.

**table 6.1**

IM&C's guano project—initial projections ($'000)

| Period | 0 | 1 | 2 | 3 | 4 | 5 | 6 | 7 |
|---|---|---|---|---|---|---|---|---|
| 1. Capital investment | 10 000 | | | | | | | −1 000[a] |
| 2. Accumulated depreciation | | 1 583 | 3 167 | 4 750 | 6 333 | 7 917 | 9 500 | 0 |
| 3. Year-end book value | 10 000 | 8 417 | 6 833 | 5 250 | 3 667 | 2 083 | 500 | 0 |
| 4. Working capital | | 500 | 1 065 | 2 450 | 3 340 | 2 225 | 1 130 | 0 |
| 5. Total book value (3 + 4) | 10 000 | 8 917 | 7 898 | 7 700 | 7 007 | 4 308 | 1 630 | 0 |
| 6. Sales | | 475 | 10 650 | 24 500 | 33 400 | 22 250 | 11 130 | |
| 7. Cost of goods sold | | 761 | 6 388 | 14 690 | 20 043 | 13 345 | 6 678 | |
| 8. Other costs[b] | 4 000 | 2 000 | 1 000 | 1 000 | 1 000 | 1 000 | 1 000 | |
| 9. Depreciation | | 1 583 | 1 583 | 1 583 | 1 583 | 1 583 | 1 583 | |
| 10. Pre-tax profit (6 − 7 − 8 − 9) | −4 000 | −3 869 | 1 679 | 7 227 | 10 774 | 6 322 | 1 869 | 500[c] |
| 11. Tax at 33% | −1 320 | −1 277 | 554 | 2 385 | 3 555 | 2 086 | 617 | 165 |
| 12. Profit after tax | −2 680 | −2 592 | 1 125 | 4 842 | 7 219 | 4 236 | 1 252 | 335 |

Notes:

[a]   *Salvage value.*

[b]   *Start-up costs in years 0 and 1, and general and administrative costs in years 1 to 6.*

[c]   *The difference between the salvage value $1 million and the ending book value of $500 000 is a taxable profit.*

Though this line of argument sounds plausible, it will get you into trouble. First, opportunity costs of capital are usually expressed as *nominal* rates. You cannot use a nominal rate to discount real cash flows. Second, not all prices and costs increase at the same rate. For example, wages generally increase faster than the inflation rate. Labour cost per tonne of guano will rise in real terms unless technological advances allow more efficient use of labour. On the other hand, the tax savings provided by depreciation are unaffected by inflation, since the tax department allows you to depreciate only the original cost of the equipment regardless of what happens to prices after the investment is made. However, the tax department also allows you to assume that depreciable assets have zero salvage value. For investment purposes, it is the tax allowable depreciation charge that is relevant. In this case it is ($10 million)/6 or $1.667 million.

Assume that future inflation is forecast at 10 per cent a year. Table 6.2 restates Table 6.1 in nominal terms assuming just for simplicity that sales, investment salvaged, operating costs and required working capital appreciate at this general rate. You can see, however, that depreciation is not affected by inflation. The change from $1.583 million to $1.667 million is due to assuming zero salvage value when calculating depreciation for tax purposes.

Table 6.3 derives cash flow forecasts from the investment and income data given in Table 6.2. Cash flow from operations is defined as sales less cost of goods sold, other costs and taxes.[17] The remaining cash flows include the *changes* in working capital, the initial capital investment and the final recovery of salvage value. If, as you expect, the salvage value turns out higher than zero (the depreciated value of the machinery), you will have to pay tax on the difference. So you must also include this figure in your cash flow forecast.[18]

---

[17]   Sales revenue may not represent actual cash inflow. Costs may not represent cash outflows. This is why change in working capital must be taken into account, as it is in Table 6.3. The 'A further note on estimating cash flow' in Section 6.2 discusses the relationship between operating cash flow and change in working capital in more detail.

[18]   The options, under Australian tax law, for treating gains on disposal are more complex than this simple example suggests. These options are considered more fully in 'A further note on depreciation' later in Section 6.2.

table 6.2
IM&C's guano project—revised projections reflecting inflation ($'000)

| Period | 0 | 1 | 2 | 3 | 4 | 5 | 6 | 7 |
|---|---|---|---|---|---|---|---|---|
| 1. Capital investment | 10 000 | | | | | | | −1949[a] |
| 2. Accumulated depreciation | | 1 583 | 3 167 | 4 750 | 6 333 | 7 917 | 9 500 | 0 |
| 3. Year-end book value | 10 000 | 8 417 | 6 833 | 5 250 | 3 667 | 2 083 | 500 | 0 |
| 4. Working capital | | 550 | 1 289 | 3 261 | 4 890 | 3 583 | 2 002 | 0 |
| 5. Total book value (3 + 4) | 10 000 | 8 967 | 8 122 | 8 511 | 8 557 | 5 666 | 2 502 | 0 |
| 6. Sales | | 523 | 12 887 | 32 610 | 48 901 | 35 834 | 19 717 | |
| 7. Cost of goods sold | | 837 | 7 729 | 19 552 | 29 345 | 21 492 | 11 830 | |
| 8. Other costs | 4 000 | 2 200 | 1 210 | 1 331 | 1 464 | 1 611 | 1 772 | |
| 9. Depreciation | | 1 667 | 1 667 | 1 667 | 1 667 | 1 667 | 1 667 | |
| 10. Pre-tax profit (6 − 7 − 8 − 9) | −4 000 | −4 181 | 2 281 | 10 060 | 16 425 | 11 064 | 4 448 | 1 949[b] |
| 11. Tax at 33% | −1 320 | −1 380 | 753 | 3 320 | 5 420 | 3 651 | 1 468 | 643 |
| 12. Profit after tax (10 − 11) | −2 680 | −2 801 | 1 528 | 6 740 | 11 005 | 7 413 | 2 980 | 1 306 |

Notes:

[a]  Salvage value.

[b]  The difference between the salvage value $1 million and the ending book value for tax purposes of $0 is a taxable profit.

IM&C estimates the nominal opportunity cost of capital for projects of this type as 20 per cent. When all cash flows are added up and discounted, the guano project is seen to offer a net present value of about $3.8 million:

$$\text{NPV} = -12\ 680 + \frac{-1684}{1.20} + \frac{2456}{(1.20)^2} + \frac{6435}{(1.20)^3} + \frac{11\ 043}{(1.20)^4} + \frac{10\ 387}{(1.20)^5} + \frac{6228}{(1.20)^6} + \frac{3307}{(1.20)^7}$$

$$= +3\ 855, \text{ or } \$3\ 855\ 000$$

## Separating investment and financing decisions

Our analysis of the guano project takes no notice of how that project is financed. It may be that IM&C would decide to finance partly by debt, but, if it did, we would not subtract the debt proceeds from the required investment, nor would we recognise interest and principal payments as cash outflows. We treat the project *as if* it is all equity-financed. Shareholders are assumed to supply all the cash for the investment and get all the net cash flow. We also use a discount rate that would be appropriate if the project were all equity financed. This discount rate depends *solely* on the risk of the project. The resulting NPV is often called the base case NPV. It is the value the project *would* have if it were *all equity* financed. We can think of this approach as valuing the project as though it were a separate mini-firm financed entirely by equity.

We approach the problem in this way so that we can separate the analysis of the investment decision from the financing decision. Then, when we have calculated the base case NPV, we can undertake a separate analysis of financing. Financing decisions and their possible interaction with investment decisions are covered in Chapter 19.

**table 6.3**

IM&C's guano project—cash flow analysis ($'000)

| Period | 0 | 1 | 2 | 3 | 4 | 5 | 6 | 7 |
|---|---|---|---|---|---|---|---|---|
| 1. Sales | | 523 | 12 887 | 32 610 | 48 901 | 35 834 | 19 717 | |
| 2. Cost of goods sold | | 837 | 7 729 | 19 552 | 29 345 | 21 492 | 11 830 | |
| 3. Other costs | 4 000 | 2 200 | 1 210 | 1 331 | 1 464 | 1 611 | 1 772 | |
| 4. Tax on operations | −1 320 | −1 380 | 753 | 3 320 | 5 420 | 3 651 | 1 468 | |
| 5. Cash flow from operations (1 − 2 − 3 − 4) | −2 680 | −1 134 | 3 195 | 8 407 | 12 672 | 9 080 | 4 647 | |
| 6. Change in working capital | | −550 | −739 | −1 972 | −1 629 | 1 307 | 1 581 | 2 002 |
| 7. Capital investment and disposal | −10 000 | | | | | | | 1 306[a] |
| 8. Net cash flow (5 + 6 + 7) | −12 680 | −1 684 | 2 456 | 6 435 | 11 043 | 10 387 | 6 228 | 3 307 |
| 9. Present value at 20% | −12 680 | −1 404 | 1 706 | 3 724 | 5 325 | 4 174 | 2 086 | 923 |
| 10. Net present value | 3 855 | | | | | | | |

Note:

[a]  Salvage value of $1949 less tax of $643 on the difference between salvage value and ending book value for tax.

# Mixing investment and financing decisions

Many firms use a different procedure. They define the magnitude of the investment as above, but they recognise that the cash required will be supplied by shareholders and debtholders. They then calculate the net cash flow of the project as in line 8 of Table 6.3. This cash flow is often called the unlevered cash flow, because it is the source of payments to both debtholders and shareholders. So far the numbers are exactly the same as in the base case NPV analysis. The difference comes in the discount rate. Firms attempt to incorporate the financing decision into the analysis by using a discount rate that is a weighted average of the required returns on debt and equity—the weights being the proportions of debt and equity used by the firm. This discount rate is commonly known as the **weighted average cost of capital** (**WACC**). While many firms use this approach it can get you into trouble. Once you get to Chapter 19 we hope that you will understand where trouble lurks and how to use WACC without getting into trouble.

# *A further note on estimating cash flow

Now here is an important point. You can see from line 6 of Table 6.3 that working capital increases in the early and middle years of the project. 'What is working capital?', you may ask, 'and why does it increase?' Working capital summarises the *net* investment in short-term assets associated with a firm, business or project. Its most important components are *inventory*, *accounts receivable* and *accounts payable*. The guano project's total requirements for working capital in year 2 might be as follows:

Working capital = inventory + accounts receivable − accounts payable
1289         =       635     +        1030        −            376

This is an increase of 739 over the previous year's requirements. Why has the increase been necessary? There are several possibilities:

1. Sales recorded on the income statement overstate actual cash receipts from guano shipments because sales are increasing and customers are slow to pay their bills. Therefore, accounts receivable increase.
2. It takes several months for processed guano to age properly. Thus, as projected sales increase, larger inventories have to be held in the ageing sheds.
3. An offsetting effect occurs if payments for materials and services used in guano production are delayed. In this case accounts payable will increase.

The changes in working capital from year 2 to 3 might be

| Change in working capital 1972 | = increase in inventory = 972 | + increase in accounts receivable + 1500 | − increase in accounts payable − 500 |
|---|---|---|---|

A detailed cash flow forecast for year 3 would look like Table 6.4.

Instead of worrying about changes in working capital, you could estimate cash flow directly by counting the dollars coming in and taking away the dollars going out. In other words:

1. If you replace each year's sales with cash received from customers, you do not have to worry about accounts receivable.
2. If you replace cost of goods sold with cash payments for labour, materials and other costs of production, you do not have to keep track of inventory or accounts payable.

However, you would still have to construct a projected income statement to estimate taxes.

We discuss the links between cash flow and working capital in much greater detail in Chapter 29.

**table 6.4**

Details of cash flow forecast for IM&C's guano project in year 3 ($'000)

| Cash flows | Data from forecast income statement | Working capital changes |
|---|---|---|
| Cash inflow | = sales | − increase in accounts receivable |
| $31 110 | = 32 610 | − 1 500 |
| Cash outflow | = cost of goods sold, other costs and taxes | + increase in inventory net of increase in accounts payable |
| $24 675 | = (19 552 + 1 331 + 3 320) | + (972 − 500) |

Net cash flow = cash inflow − cash outflow
$6 435 = 31 110 − 24 675

## A further note on depreciation

Depreciation is a non-cash expense; it is important only because it reduces taxable income. It provides an annual *tax shield* equal to the product of depreciation and the marginal tax rate:

$$\text{Tax shield} = \text{depreciation} \times \text{tax rate} = 1667 \times 0.33 = 550, \text{ or } \$550\,000$$

The present value of the tax shields ($550 000 for six years) is $1 829 000 at a 20 per cent discount rate.[19]

Now if IM&C could just get those tax shields sooner, they would be worth more, right? Fortunately, the *Income Tax Assessment Act* allows corporations to do just that. For tax purposes companies may elect to claim depreciation on a **diminishing value** basis, rather than a straight-line basis. Under the diminishing value method, depreciation is calculated by applying a fixed percentage to the *depreciated* book value of the asset.

For many years the diminishing value rates in Australia were 150 per cent of the straight-line rates. This made diminishing value the tax-preferred depreciation method for most firms. However, there has been much tinkering with the tax system in recent years and both depreciation rates and tax rates have been changed. Table 6.5 gives diminishing value rates which apply after recent changes to allowable deductions.[20] Notice that there is a 100 per cent tax write-off in the first year of operation for assets with a life of less than three years.

**table 6.5**

Tax deduction allowed under diminishing value depreciation (figures in per cent of depreciable investment)

| Asset life (in years) | Less than 3 | 3 to 5 | 5 to 6.66 | 6.66 to 10 | 10 to 13 | 13 to 30 | 30 |
|---|---|---|---|---|---|---|---|
| Rate | 100% | 60% | 40% | 30% | 25% | 20% | 10% |

*Note: Income producing buildings are depreciated at 2.5 per cent per year over 40 years, subject to construction having commenced after July 1985 for residential buildings, and after September 1987 for non-residential buildings.*

In establishing depreciation rates for tax purposes, the first step is to determine the asset's life. Since 1991, taxpayers have been allowed to make their own estimate of the effective life of the asset, or they may use asset lives as published by the commissioner of taxation. Let us assume that for tax purposes we can treat the investment as having a five-year life. We will assume that the 60 per cent depreciation rate can then be applied for each of the six years of the project, rather than writing the undepreciated balance off in year 5. Thus, IM&C can write off 60 per cent of its depreciable investment in year 1, as soon as the assets are placed in service, then 60 per cent of the depreciated book value in year 2, and so on. Here are the tax shields for the guano project:

| Year | 1 | 2 | 3 | 4 | 5 | 6 |
|---|---|---|---|---|---|---|
| Book value less accumulated depreciation | 10 000 | 4 000 | 1 600 | 640 | 256 | 102 |
| Depreciation (60% of depreciated book value) | 6 000 | 2 400 | 960 | 384 | 154 | 61 |
| Tax shield (tax depreciation × tax rate, $T = 0.33$) | 1 980 | 792 | 317 | 127 | 51 | 20 |
| PV | 1 650 | 550 | 183 | 61 | 20 | 7 |
| Total PV of tax shield | 2 472 | | | | | |

---

[19] By discounting the depreciation tax shields at 20 per cent, we assume that they are as risky as the other cash flows. Since they depend only on tax rates, depreciation method, and IM&C's ability to generate taxable income, they may well be less risky. In some contexts—the analysis of financial leases, for example—depreciation tax shields are treated as safe, nominal cash flows and discounted at an after-tax borrowing or lending rate. See Chapter 26.

[20] These changes were made in the early 1990s. As we enter the new millennium, further revisions in depreciation allowances are being proposed. There remain a number of special cases. Examples include assets purchased prior to March 1991, motor vehicles, ships, buildings, investment in research and development, and primary production facilities. From time to time the government also offers special tax concessions to stimulate investment. Sometimes these concessions are quite general, but sometimes they are targeted at specific areas such as mineral exploration or research and development.

The present value of these tax shields is $2 472 000, about $643 000 higher than under the straight-line method. Understand that the total of deductions under both depreciation methods is the same after adjusting for tax effects on asset disposal. It is the later payment of taxes under the diminishing value method that gives rise to the increased value.

Table 6.6 recalculates the guano project's impact on IM&C's future tax bills and Table 6.7 shows revised after-tax cash flows and present value. This time we have incorporated realistic assumptions about taxes as well as inflation. Of course, we arrive at a higher NPV than in Table 6.3 because that table ignored the additional present value of accelerated depreciation.

**table 6.6**

Tax payments on IM&C's guano project ($'000)

| Period | 0 | 1 | 2 | 3 | 4 | 5 | 6 | 7 |
|---|---|---|---|---|---|---|---|---|
| 1. Sales[a] | | 523 | 12 887 | 32 610 | 48 901 | 35 834 | 19 717 | |
| 2. Cost of goods sold[a] | | 837 | 7 729 | 19 552 | 29 345 | 21 492 | 11 830 | |
| 3. Other costs[a] | 4 000 | 2 200 | 1 210 | 1 331 | 1 464 | 1 611 | 1 772 | |
| 4. Depreciation | | 6 000 | 2 400 | 960 | 384 | 154 | 61 | |
| 5. Pre-tax profit (1 − 2 − 3 − 4) | −4 000 | −8 514 | 1 548 | 10 767 | 17 708 | 12 577 | 6 054 | 1 949[b] |
| 6. Tax at 33%[c] | −1 320 | −2 810 | 511 | 3 553 | 5 844 | 4 151 | 1 998 | 643 |

*Notes:*
[a] From Table 6.2.
[b] Book value is zero, for tax purposes, after all tax depreciation has been taken. Thus, tax is payable on the full salvage value of $1949.
[c] A negative tax payment means a cash inflow, assuming IM&C can use the tax loss on its guano project to shield income from other projects.

**table 6.7**

IM&C's guano project—revised cash flow analysis ($'000)

| Period | 0 | 1 | 2 | 3 | 4 | 5 | 6 | 7 |
|---|---|---|---|---|---|---|---|---|
| 1. Sales[a] | | 523 | 12 887 | 32 610 | 48 901 | 35 834 | 19 717 | |
| 2. Cost of goods sold[a] | | 837 | 7 729 | 19 552 | 29 345 | 21 492 | 11 830 | |
| 3. Other costs[a] | 4 000 | 2 200 | 1 210 | 1 331 | 1 464 | 1 611 | 1 772 | |
| 4. Tax on operations[b] | −1 320 | −2 810 | 511 | 3 553 | 5 844 | 4 151 | 1 998 | 643 |
| 5. Cash flow from operations (1 − 2 − 3 − 4) | −2 680 | 296 | 3 437 | 8 174 | 12 248 | 8 580 | 4 117 | |
| 6. Change in working capital | | −550 | −739 | −1 972 | −1 629 | 1 307 | 1 581 | 2 002 |
| 7. Capital investment and disposal | −10 000 | | | | | | | 1 306 |
| 8. Net cash flow (5 + 6 + 7) | −12 680 | −254 | 2 698 | 6 202 | 10 619 | 9 887 | 5 698 | 3 308 |
| 9. Present value at 20% | −12 680 | −212 | 1 874 | 3 589 | 5 121 | 3 974 | 1 908 | 923 |
| 10. Net present value = +4 497 | | | | | | | | |

*Notes:*
[a] From Table 6.2.
[b] From Table 6.6.

In the IM&C case we have assumed that the gain on salvage is taxed as income. In effect the tax recaptures excess depreciation allowances. However, rather than paying tax, companies have the alternative of reducing the depreciable value of the replacement asset (or other depreciable assets if the asset is not replaced). In practice most companies will elect to write-down the value of depreciable assets because this defers the payment of tax.

Had the asset been sold for more than its purchase price a capital gains tax would also have been payable on the *real* gain. The real gain is calculated as the selling price less the original cost indexed for inflation.

## A final comment on taxes

Almost every large corporation keeps two separate sets of books, one for its shareholders and one for the tax department. For example, companies may use straight-line depreciation in the shareholder books and diminishing value depreciation in the tax books. The tax commissioner does not object to this, and it usually makes the firm's reported earnings higher than if diminishing value depreciation were used everywhere. There are many other possible differences between tax books and shareholder books, for example in the valuation of inventory.

The financial analyst must be careful to remember which set of books he or she is looking at. In capital budgeting only the tax books are relevant, but to an outside analyst only the shareholder books are available. Some of the differences between the tax books and the shareholder books are captured by tax effect accounting. For example, where a company reports higher accounting earnings than taxable earnings, due to deferral of taxes, the shareholder books will report a provision for deferred income tax.

## A final comment on project analysis

Let us review. Several pages ago, you embarked on an analysis of IM&C's guano project. It appeared at first that you had all the facts you needed in Table 6.1, but many of those numbers had to be thrown away because they did not reflect expected inflation. So you worked out revised projections and calculated project net present value. However, then you remembered accelerated depreciation; you turned wearily back to your worksheets and finally obtained decent estimates of cash flow and NPV.

You were lucky to get away with just two NPV calculations. In real situations, it often takes several tries to purge all inconsistencies and mistakes. Then there are 'what if' questions. For example: What if inflation rages at 15 per cent per year, rather than 10 per cent? What if technical problems delay start-up to year 2? What if gardeners prefer chemical fertilisers to your natural product?

You will not truly understand the guano project until these questions are answered. *Project analysis* is more than one or two NPV calculations, as we will see in Chapter 10.

However, before you become too deeply immersed in guano, we should now turn to the subject of project interactions.

## 6.3 Project interactions

Almost all decisions about capital expenditure involve 'either-or' choices. The firm can build either a 3000-square metre warehouse or a 4000-square metre warehouse, but it cannot have both on the same site. Head office can be located in one of several locations, most likely Sydney, Melbourne, Brisbane, Adelaide or Perth, but which? A factory can be heated either by oil or by natural gas, and so on. These mutually exclusive options are simple examples of *project interactions*.

Project interactions can arise in countless ways. The literature of operations research and industrial engineering sometimes addresses cases of extreme complexity and difficulty. We will concentrate on five simple but important cases.

# Case 1   Optimal timing of investment

The fact that a project has a positive NPV does not mean that it is best undertaken now. It might be even more valuable if undertaken in the future. Similarly, a project with a currently negative NPV might become a valuable opportunity if we wait a bit. Thus, *any* project has two mutually exclusive alternatives: do it now, or wait and invest later.

The question of optimal timing of investment is not difficult under conditions of certainty. We first examine alternative dates ($t$) for making the investment and calculate its net *future* value as of each date. Then, in order to find which of the alternatives would add most to the firm's *current* value, we must work out the present value for each alternative as:

$$\frac{\text{Net future value as of date } t}{(1 + r)^t}$$

For example, suppose you have invested in a stand of timber. The longer you wait before harvesting, the more interest charges accumulate on your investment. Effectively, the cost of your investment grows each year. On the other hand, the trees are growing too, so the value of the timber is increasing as you wait.

Let us suppose that the net value of the harvest at different future dates is as follows:

| Year of harvest | 0 | 1 | 2 | 3 | 4 | 5 |
|---|---|---|---|---|---|---|
| Net *future* value ($'000) | 50 | 64.4 | 77.5 | 89.4 | 100 | 109.4 |
| Change in value from previous year (%) | | +28.8 | +20.3 | +15.4 | +11.9 | +9.4 |

As you can see, the longer you defer cutting the timber, the more money you will make. However, your concern is with the date that maximises the net *present* value of your investment. You therefore need to discount the net future value of the harvest back to the present. Suppose the appropriate discount rate is 10 per cent. Then, if you harvest the timber in year 1, it has a net *present* value of $58 500:

$$\text{NPV if harvested in year 1} = \frac{64.4}{1.10} = 58.5, \text{ or } \$58\,500$$

The net present value (at $t = 0$) for other harvest dates is as follows:

| Year of harvest | 0 | 1 | 2 | 3 | 4 | 5 |
|---|---|---|---|---|---|---|
| Net present value ($'000) | 50 | 58.5 | 64.0 | 67.2 | 68.3 | 67.9 |

The optimal point to harvest the timber is year 4 because this is the point that maximises NPV.

Notice that before year 4 the net future value of the timber increases by more than 10 per cent a year: The gain in value is greater than the cost of the capital that is tied up in the project. After year 4 the gain in value is still positive but less than the cost of capital. You maximise the net present value of your investment if you harvest your timber as soon as the rate of increase in value drops below the cost of capital.[21]

---

[21]   Our timber-cutting example conveys the right idea about investment timing, but it misses an important practical point: the sooner you cut the first crop of trees, the sooner the second crop can start growing. Thus, the value of the second crop depends on when you cut the first. This more complex and realistic problem might be solved in one of two ways:

1. Find the cutting dates that maximise the net present value of a series of harvests, taking account of the different growth rates of young and old trees.
2. Repeat our calculations, counting the future market value of cut-over land as part of the payoff to the first harvest. The value of cut-over land includes the present value of all subsequent harvests.

The second solution is far simpler if you can figure out what cut-over land will be worth. H. Bierman and S. Smidt discuss the tree-cutting problem in *The Capital Budgeting Decision*, 8th ed., The Macmillan Company, New York, 1992.

The problem of optimal timing of investment under uncertainty is, of course, much more complicated. An opportunity not taken at $t = 0$ might be either more or less attractive at $t = 1$; there is rarely any way of knowing for sure. In terms of our timber harvesting problem, we cannot be sure whether future prices for timber will be higher or lower when we come to harvest. Perhaps it is better to strike while the iron is hot even if there is a chance it will become hotter. On the other hand, if you wait a bit you might obtain more information and avoid a bad mistake. To analyse this problem properly you need to understand how to value options. So we return to this problem in Chapter 21.

# Case 2    Choosing between long- and short-lived equipment

Suppose the firm is forced to choose between two machines, A and B. The two machines are designed differently but have identical capacity and do exactly the same job. Machine A costs $15 000 and will last three years. It costs $5 000 per year to run. Machine B is an 'economy' model costing only $10 000, but it will last only two years and costs $6000 per year to run. These are real cash flows: the costs are forecasted in dollars of constant purchasing power (i.e. real dollars).[22] The project does not terminate at the end of the machine's life and therefore replacement machines will be required.

Because the two machines produce exactly the same product, we can choose between them on the basis of cost. Suppose we compute the present value of cost:

| Machine | Costs ($'000) | | | | Present value at 6% ($'000) |
|---|---|---|---|---|---|
| | $C_0$ | $C_1$ | $C_2$ | $C_3$ | |
| A | +15 | +5 | +5 | +5 | 28.37 |
| B | +10 | +6 | +6 | | 21.00 |

Should we take machine B, the one with the lower present value of costs? Not necessarily, because machine B gives less service and will have to be replaced a year earlier than machine A. In other words, the timing of a future investment decision is contingent on today's choice of machine A or B. So, a machine with total PV (costs) of $21 000 spread over two years is not necessarily better than a competing machine with PV (costs) of $25 690 spread over three years. We have three ways of making a choice. One way is to calculate the PV of costs over some equivalent service horizon.

**The equivalent horizon method**    We could compare machines A and B over a common horizon of six years—two cycles of machine A and three cycles of machine B. Over the six-year horizon we are comparing like service with like service and we can therefore rank them on the PV of total costs over this period.

| Machine | Costs ($'000) | | | | | | | Present value at 6% ($'000) |
|---|---|---|---|---|---|---|---|---|
| | $C_0$ | $C_1$ | $C_2$ | $C_3$ | $C_4$ | $C_5$ | $C_6$ | |
| A | +15 | +5 | +5 | +20 | +5 | +5 | +5 | 52.18 |
| B | +10 | +6 | +16 | +6 | +16 | +6 | +6 | 56.32 |

[22] The following calculations are best done in real terms. Of course, we must be consistent and use a real discount rate. We will assume it is 6 per cent. You can start with inflation adjusted cash flows and discount them with a nominal discount rate. The result of this calculation, the PV, is a real value because it is expressed in current dollars. You then apply a real discount rate to the PV and calculate an equivalent annuity cash flow in real dollars.

As we can see machine A turns out to have a lower PV of costs at 52.18 or $52 180 over six years, compared to machine B at 56.32 or $56 320. Suppose, however, that machines A and B had seven- and nine-year lives respectively. The common horizon now becomes 63 years. Add a third alternative machine with an 11-year life. The common horizon is now 693 years. The calculation is starting to get tedious.

Fortunately, we have another alternative. We can convert total PV (costs) to a cost *per year*.

## The equivalent annual cost method

Suppose the financial manager is asked to *rent* machine A to the plant manager actually in charge of production. There will be three equal rental payments starting in year 1. The three rental payments must recover both the original cost of the machine at time 0 and the cost of running it in years 1 to 3. Obviously, the financial manager has to make sure that the rental payments are worth $28 370, the total PV (costs) of machine A. This fair rental payment, which is usually called the equivalent annual cost, turns out to be 10.61, or $10 610 per year:

| | Costs ($'000) | | | | Present value |
|---|---|---|---|---|---|
| Machine | $C_0$ | $C_1$ | $C_2$ | $C_3$ | at 6% ($'000) |
| A | +15 | +5 | +5 | +5 | 28.37 |
| Equivalent annual cost | | +10.61 | +10.61 | +10.61 | 28.37 |

The fair rental payment, or equivalent annual cost, is an annuity that has exactly the same life and present value as machine A. How did we know that the right cash flow from the annuity was 10.61? It was easy! We set the NPV of the annuity equal to the present value of costs for machine A and solved for the payment of the annuity. Remember our discussion of EACs in Chapter 3?

$$\text{PV of annuity} = \text{PV of cash outflows of machine A} = 28.37$$
$$= \text{annuity payment} \times \text{3-year annuity factor}$$

Therefore, the annuity payment equals the present value divided by the annuity factor, which is 2.673 for three years and a 6 per cent real cost of capital.[23]

$$\text{Annuity payment} = \frac{28.37}{2.673} = 10.61$$

If we make a similar calculation for machine B, we get:

| | Costs ($'000) | | | Present value |
|---|---|---|---|---|
| Machine | $C_0$ | $C_1$ | $C_2$ | at 6% ($'000) |
| B | +10 | +6 | +6 | 21.00 |
| Equivalent 2-year annuity | | +11.45 | +11.45 | 21.00 |

---

[23] This factor can be obtained from an annuity table or from the annuity formula given in Chapter 3.

We see that machine A is better, because its equivalent annual cost is less ($10 610 versus $11 450 for machine B). In other words, machine A could be rented to the production manager for less than machine B.

Our rule for comparing assets of different lives is therefore as follows. Select the machine that has the lowest equivalent annual cost.[24] The equivalent annual cost is simply the net present value of the cost divided by the annuity factor. Note, however, that you need to do these calculations of the equivalent annual cost in real terms.

**Equivalent annual cost and inflation**  The equivalent annual costs we just calculated are *real* annuities based on forecasted *real* costs and a 6 per cent *real* discount rate. We could, of course, restate the annuities in nominal terms. Suppose the expected inflation rate is 5 per cent: we multiply the first cash flow of the annuity by 1.05, the second by $(1.05)^2 = 1.105$, and so on.

|  | $C_0$ | $C_1$ | $C_2$ | $C_3$ |
|---|---|---|---|---|
| A: real annuity |  | 10.61 | 10.61 | 10.61 |
| A: nominal annuity |  | 11.14 | 11.70 | 12.28 |
| B: real annuity |  | 11.45 | 11.45 |  |
| B: nominal annuity |  | 12.02 | 12.62 |  |

Note that machine B is still inferior to machine A. Of course, the present values of the nominal and real annuities are identical. Just remember to discount the real annuity at the real rate and the nominal annuity at the consistent nominal rate.[25]

When you use equivalent annual costs simply for comparison of costs per period, as we did for machines A and B, then we strongly recommend doing the calculations in real terms.[26] You should do this in three steps. First, work out the nominal cash flows for buying and operating the machine. Second, discount them at the nominal discount rate to give you the present value of costs. This present value is a real value, because it is expressed in today's dollars. Third, convert the present value to a real equivalent annual cost by using the annuity factor for the real discount rate.

If you actually rent out the machine to the plant manager, or anyone else, be careful to specify that the rental payments be 'indexed' to inflation. In other words, they should be increasing nominal payments as in our table above. If inflation runs on at 5 per cent per year, and rental payments do not increase proportionally, then the real value of the rental payments must decline and will not cover the full cost of buying and operating the machine.

**Equivalent annual cost and technological change**  So far we have the following simple rule: Two or more streams of cash outflows with different lengths or time patterns can be compared by converting their present values to equivalent annual costs. Just remember to do the equivalent annual cost part of the calculation in real terms.

Now any rule this simple cannot be completely general. For example, it would not make sense to compare the current annual costs for renting machines A and B if the rent on machine A is likely

---

[24]  If the revenues differed between alternatives we would need to calculate the machines' NPVs rather than the PVs of their costs. The decision rule would then be to select the alternative that had the highest equivalent annual cash inflow.

[25]  The nominal discount rate is

$$r_{nominal} = (1 + r_{real})(1 + \text{inflation rate}) - 1$$
$$= (1.06)(1.05) - 1 = 0.113, \text{ or } 11.3\%$$

Discounting the nominal annuities at this rate gives the same present values as discounting the real annuities at 6 per cent.

[26]  Do *not* calculate equivalent annual costs as level *nominal* annuities. You should not, for example, take the present value of machine B ($21 000) and convert this to an equivalent annual cost using the nominal discount rate of 11.3 per cent. If you do this you will be implicitly assuming that the nominal costs of the replacement machines will be the same cost as the machine first acquired. The result can be incorrect rankings of true equivalent annual costs at high inflation rates. See problem Question 10 at the end of this chapter for an example.

to leap in year 3 after machine B has worn out in year 2. When we compare the equivalent annual real costs, we are implicitly assuming that the real rental for machine A will *continue* to be $10 610. This will be so only if the *real* costs of buying and operating the machine stay the same.

Suppose that this is not the case. Specifically, suppose that thanks to technological improvements new machines each year cost 20 per cent less in real terms to buy and operate. In this case future owners of brand new, lower-cost machines will be able to cut the rental cost by 20 per cent and owners of old machines will be forced to match this reduction. Thus, we now need to ask: If the real level of rents declines by 20 per cent a year, how much will it cost to rent each machine?

If the rent for year 1 is $rent_1$, the rent for year 2 is $rent_2 = 0.8 \times rent_1$. $rent_3$ is $0.8 \times rent_2$ or $0.64 \ rent_1$. The owner of each machine must set the rent sufficiently high to recover the present value of the costs. In the case of machine A,

$$\text{PV of renting machine A} = \frac{rent_1}{(1.06)} + \frac{rent_2}{(1.06)^2} + \frac{rent_3}{(1.06)^3} = 28.37$$

$$= \frac{rent_1}{(1.06)} + \frac{0.8(rent_1)}{(1.06)^2} + \frac{0.64(rent_1)}{(1.06)^3} = 28.37$$

Solving for $rent_1$ gives 12.94, or $12 940.
And for machine B,

$$\frac{rent_1}{(1.06)} + \frac{0.8(rent_1)}{(1.06)^2} = 21.00$$

Solving for $rent_1$ for machine B gives 12.69, or $12 690.

The merits of the two machines are now reversed; machine B will have the lower rental each year over its two-year life. Once we recognise that technology is expected to reduce the real costs of new machines, then it pays to buy the shorter-lived machine B rather than becoming locked in to an ageing technology for year 3.

You can imagine other complications. Perhaps machine C will arrive in year 1 with an even lower equivalent annual cost. You would then need to consider scrapping or selling machine B at year 1 (more on this decision below). The financial manager could not choose between machines A and B in year 0 without taking a detailed look at what each machine could be replaced with.

Our point is a general one. Comparing equivalent annual costs should never be a mechanical exercise; always think about the assumptions that are implicit in the comparison.

It might be the case that the alternatives being compared involve different risks and therefore should be evaluated at different discount rates. If so, using the EACs alone can give the wrong results. We need to add one step to the calculation and find the PV assuming machine replacement to infinity.[27] For example, assume that the real cash flows from machine A should be evaluated at a 6 per cent discount rate, while the real cash flows for machine B should be discounted at a 10 per cent rate. The EAC for machine A is unchanged at $10 610, while the EAC of machine B rises to $11 760. Thus, judging on the EAC alone we would still conclude that machine A is the better choice. To compute the PV assuming infinite replacement is easy, we treat the EACs as perpetuities and divide them by the discount rate, as below.

| PV with infinite replacement ($'000) | |
|---|---|
| Machine A | Machine B |
| $PV = \dfrac{10.61}{0.06} = 160.16$ | $PV = \dfrac{11.76}{0.10} = 117.60$ |

---

[27] We could instead compute the PV for the lowest common life of the replacement chain—six years in this example. However, it is often more convenient to compute the PV to infinity, and we get exactly the same decision.

We can now see that the difference in the discount rates has changed our choice. Machine B is now the better alternative.

There is one other problem with risk. We have assumed that the replacement decision will be as risky as the decision to purchase the initial machine. This may not be so. Once we have experience in operating a new machine we are likely to be much more certain of the operating cost of an identical replacement. Using a constant discount rate may no longer be appropriate in these circumstances. But we must defer discussion of this issue till Chapters 9 and 10.

Finally, remember why equivalent annual costs are necessary in the first place. The reason is that A and B *will be replaced* at *different* future dates. The choice between them therefore affects future investment decisions. If subsequent decisions are not affected by the initial choice—for example, because neither machine will be replaced—then we do *not need to take future decisions into account*.[28]

## The planned replication with abandonment method

One reason for considering the equivalent annual cost approach was to make our analysis easier. However, you probably noticed that once we moved from a very simple example the equivalent annual cost approach started to get quite complicated.[29] It has another disadvantage. It only acts as a ranking procedure, it does not tell us the impact the decision will have on shareholder wealth.

The computational advantages of using the equivalent annual cost approach are less compelling in these times of computer spreadsheets. With spreadsheets it is much less of a chore to consider competing alternatives over a long time horizon. Perhaps we should re-think our approach to the replacement problem. The first step would be to decide how long we expect the total sequence of replacement cycles to run. Having made that decision we can then compare the costs over that horizon. Taking our example of machines A and B, suppose that we anticipated that replacements would continue over 12 years. The result is given below.

| Machine | Costs ($'000) | | | | | | | | | | | | | Present value at 6% ($'000) |
|---|---|---|---|---|---|---|---|---|---|---|---|---|---|---|
| | $C_0$ | $C_1$ | $C_2$ | $C_3$ | $C_4$ | $C_5$ | $C_6$ | $C_7$ | $C_8$ | $C_9$ | $C_{10}$ | $C_{11}$ | $C_{12}$ | |
| A | 15 | 5 | 5 | 20 | 5 | 5 | 20 | 5 | 5 | 20 | 5 | 5 | 5 | $88.97 |
| B | 10 | 6 | 16 | 6 | 16 | 6 | 16 | 6 | 16 | 6 | 16 | 6 | 6 | $96.03 |

We therefore estimate that shareholders will be better off by 96.03 − 88.97 = 7.07, or $7070, if we choose machine A rather than machine B.

In this example the full replacement cycle happily coincided with a common horizon for the lives of the individual machines, but suppose we only anticipate a need for the machines for eight years. For machine type B we will have just come to the end of the life of the fourth machine. But we will still have one year's useful life remaining from the third replacement of machine type A. We can account for this by taking a scrap, or abandonment, value for machine A, say $3000. Thus, the cash flow in year 8 for machine A will be a negative $5000

---

[28]　However, if neither machine will be replaced, we have to consider the extra revenue generated by machine A in its third year, when it will be operating but B will not.

[29]　We did not investigate all the complexities. For example, there are those who argue that we should compute the equivalent annual cost using the risk-free rate, and some who argue that we should discount risky cash outflows (costs) at a lower rate than more certain outflows. We are not convinced by either of these arguments.

of operating expenses offset by a positive $3000 salvage, to give a net outflow of $2000. The resulting PV is given by:

| Machine | Costs ($'000) | | | | | | | | | Present value at 6% ($'000) |
|---|---|---|---|---|---|---|---|---|---|---|
| | $C_0$ | $C_1$ | $C_2$ | $C_3$ | $C_4$ | $C_5$ | $C_6$ | $C_7$ | $C_8$ | |
| A | 15 | 5 | 5 | 20 | 5 | 5 | 20 | 5 | 2 | $67.34 |
| B | 10 | 6 | 16 | 6 | 16 | 6 | 16 | 6 | 6 | $71.30 |

In this case machine A still comes out ahead but its advantage is smaller than over the 12-year horizon.

This approach to the problem is quite flexible. For example, if we expect new technology to provide machines with a different cost structure we can incorporate this into the expected cash flows over the planned period of replication. Of course, if there is technological change we may want to consider retiring some machines early. This brings us to our next case.

## Case 3    Deciding when to replace an existing machine

The previous example took the life of each machine as fixed. In practice the point at which equipment is replaced reflects economic considerations rather than total physical collapse. We must decide when to replace. The machine will rarely decide for us.

Here is a common problem. You are operating an elderly machine that is expected to produce a net cash *inflow* of $4000 in the coming year and $4000 in the next year. After that it will give up the ghost. You can replace it now with a new machine, which costs $15 000 but is much more efficient and will provide a cash inflow of $8000 a year for three years. You want to know whether you should replace your equipment now or wait a year.

We can calculate the NPV of the new machine and also its equivalent annual cash flow, that is, the three-year annuity that has the same net present value.

| | Cash flows ($'000) | | | | NPV at 6% ($'000) |
|---|---|---|---|---|---|
| | $C_0$ | $C_1$ | $C_2$ | $C_3$ | |
| New machine | −15 | +8 | +8 | +8 | 6.38 |
| Equivalent 3-year annuity | | +2.387 | +2.387 | +2.387 | 6.38 |

In other words, the cash flows of the new machine are equivalent to an annuity of $2387 per year. So we can equally well ask at what point we would want to replace our old machine with a new one producing $2387 a year. When the question is put this way, the answer is obvious. As long as your old machine can generate a cash flow of $4000 a year, who wants to put in its place a new one that generates the equivalent of only $2387 a year?

It is a simple matter to incorporate salvage values into this calculation. Suppose that the current salvage value is $8000 and next year's value is $7000. Let us see where you come out next year if you wait and then sell. On one hand, you gain $7000, but you lose today's salvage value *plus* a year's return on that money. That is, $8000 × 1.06 = $8480. Your net loss is $8480 − $7000 = $1480, which only partly offsets the operating gain. You should not replace yet. Alternatively, you can work out the EAC of operating the old machine treating the salvage value as the cost of your investment in keeping the old machine going.

Remember that the logic of such comparisons requires that the new machine be the best of the available alternatives and that it in turn be replaced at the optimal point. How do you find that optimal life? Easy, you just calculate the EAC of the new machine for different replacement horizons and select the one with the lowest EAC if you are doing a cost analysis, or the one with the highest positive EAC in a cost and revenue analysis.

## Case 4    Cost of excess capacity

Any firm with a computer encounters many proposals for using it. Recently installed computers tend to have excess capacity and, since the immediate marginal cost of using such computers seems to be negligible, management often encourages new uses. Sooner or later, however, the load on the machine will increase to a point at which management must either terminate the uses it originally encouraged or invest in another computer several years earlier than it had planned. Such problems can be avoided if a proper charge is made for the use of spare capacity.

Suppose we have a new investment project that requires heavy use of the computer. The effect of adopting the project is to bring the purchase date of a new computer forward from year 4 to year 3. This new computer has a life of five years, and at a discount rate of 6 per cent the present value of the cost of buying and operating it is $500 000.

We begin by converting the $500 000 present value of the cost of the computer to an equivalent annual cost of $118 700 for each of five years. Of course, when the new computer in turn wears out, we will replace it with another. So we face the prospect of computing expenses of $118 700 a year. If we undertake the new project, the series of expenses begins in year 4; if we do not undertake it, the series begins in year 5. The new project therefore results in an *additional* computing cost of $118 700 in year 4. This has a present value of $118\ 700/(1.06)^4$, or about $94 000. This cost is properly charged against the new project. When we recognise it, the NPV of the project may prove to be negative. If so, we still need to check whether it is worthwhile undertaking the project now and abandoning it later, when the excess capacity of the present computer disappears.

## Case 5    Fluctuating load factors

Although a $10 million warehouse may have a positive net present value, it should be built only if it has a higher NPV than a $9 million alternative. In other words, the NPV of the $1 million *marginal* investment required to buy the more expensive warehouse must be positive.

One case in which this is easily forgotten is when equipment is needed to meet fluctuating demand. Consider the following problem. A widget manufacturer operates two machines, each of which has a capacity of 1000 units a year. They have an indefinite life and no salvage value and so the only costs are the operating expenses of $2 per widget. Widget manufacture, as everyone knows, is a seasonal business, and widgets are perishable. During the autumn and winter, when demand is high, each machine produces at capacity. During the spring and summer, each machine works at 50 per cent of capacity. Production is therefore 750 widgets per machine. With a discount rate of 10 per cent and if the machines are kept indefinitely, the present value of the costs is $30 000:

|  | Two old machines |
|---|---|
| Annual output per machine | 750 units |
| Operating cost per machine | 2 × 750 = $1 500 |
| PV operating cost per machine | 1 500/0.10 = $15 000 |
| PV operating cost of two machines | 2 × 15 000 = $30 000 |

The company is considering whether to replace these machines with newer equipment. The new machines have a similar capacity and so two would still be needed to meet peak demand. Each new machine costs $6000 and lasts indefinitely. Operating expenses are only $1 per unit. On this basis the company calculates that the present value of the costs of two new machines would be $27 000:

|  | Two new machines |
| --- | --- |
| Annual output per machine | 750 |
| Capital cost per machine | $6 000 |
| Operating cost per machine | $1 \times 750 = \$750$ |
| PV operating cost per machine | $6\,000 + 750/0.10 = \$13\,500$ |
| PV operating cost of two machines | $2 \times 13\,500 = \$27\,000$ |

Therefore, it scraps both old machines and buys two new ones.

The company was quite right in thinking that two new machines are better than two old ones, but unfortunately it forgot to investigate a third alternative; to replace just one of the old machines. Since the new machine has low operating costs, it would pay to operate it at capacity all year. The remaining old machine could then be kept simply to meet peak demand. The present value of the costs under this strategy is $26 000:

|  | One old machine | One new machine |
| --- | --- | --- |
| Annual output per machine | 500 units | 1 000 units |
| Capital cost per machine | 0 | $6 000 |
| Operating cost per machine | $2 \times 500 = \$1\,000$ | $1 \times 1\,000 = \$1\,000$ |
| PV total cost per machine | $1\,000/0.10 = \$10\,000$ | $6\,000 + 1\,000/0.10 = \$16\,000$ |
| PV total cost of both machines | $26 000 | |

Replacing one machine saves $4000; replacing two machines saves only $3000. The net present value of the *marginal* investment in the second machine is −$1000.

## 6.4 Summary

By now present value calculations should be a matter of routine. However, forecasting cash flows will never be routine. It will always be a skilled, hazardous occupation. Mistakes can be minimised by following three rules.

1. Make sure you are consistent in your definition of investment, cash flow and discount rate. And make sure that you discount nominal cash flow forecasts at nominal discount rates and real cash flow forecasts at real rates.
2. Concentrate on cash flows after taxes. Be wary of accounting data masquerading as cash flow data.
3. Always judge investments on an incremental basis. Tirelessly track down all cash flow consequences of your decision.

It is possible to analyse projects with the investment and financing decisions mixed in, or the two decisions can be analysed separately. Where possible, we recommend separating the decisions in a two-step procedure. First, calculate the value of the project as though it was all equity financed. Remember that the discount rate you use for this process depends only on the risk of the project. Second, adjust the value of the project to allow for any financing side effects. We show you how to do this in Chapter 19.

We might add a further rule, which relates to another kind of mixing: recognise project interactions. Decisions involving only a choice of accepting or rejecting a project rarely exist, since capital projects can rarely be isolated from other projects or alternatives. The simplest decision normally encountered is accept or reject or delay. A project having a positive NPV if undertaken today may have a still higher NPV if undertaken tomorrow.

Projects also interact because they are mutually exclusive. You can install machine A or B, but not both. When mutually exclusive choices involve different lengths or time patterns of cash outflows comparison can be quite difficult. The traditional solution to this problem is to convert present values to equivalent annual costs. Think of the equivalent annual cost as the period by period rental payment necessary to cover all the cash outflows. Choose A over B, other things being equal, if it has the lower equivalent annual cost. Remember though, you *must* calculate equivalent annual costs in real terms. With the availability of spreadsheet technology a more direct alternative than the EAC method can be used. You can compare the total of the present value of costs over the *full* sequence of anticipated replacements. We think this has some advantages over the EAC method, but only time will tell whether it will displace the use of the EAC.

This chapter is concerned with the mechanics of applying the net present value rule in practical situations. All our analysis boils down to two simple themes. First, be careful about the definition of alternative projects. Make sure you are comparing like with like. Second, make sure that your calculations include all incremental cash flows.

## FURTHER READING

There are several good general texts on capital budgeting that cover project interactions. Two examples are:

E. L. Grant, W. G. Ireson and R. S. Leavenworth, *Principles of Engineering Economy*, 8th ed., Ronald Press, New York, 1990.

H. Bierman and S. Smidt, *The Capital Budgeting Decision*, 8th ed., The Macmillan Company, New York, 1992.

Reinhardt provides an interesting case study of a capital investment decision in:

U. E. Reinhardt: 'Break-Even Analysis for Lockheed's TriStar: An Application of Financial Theory', *Journal of Finance*, **32**: 821–38 (September 1973).

## QUIZ

1. Which of the following should be treated as incremental cash flows when deciding whether to invest in a new manufacturing plant? The site is already owned by the company, but existing buildings would need to be demolished.
   a. The market value of the site and existing buildings.
   b. Demolition costs and site clearance.
   c. The cost of a new access road put in last year.
   d. Lost earnings on other products due to executive time spent on the new facility.
   e. A proportion of the cost of leasing the chief executive's jet aeroplane.
   f. Future depreciation of the new plant.
   g. The reduction in the corporation's tax bill resulting from tax depreciation of the new plant.

h. The initial investment in inventories of raw materials.
i. Money already spent on engineering design of the new plant.

2. Monsieur Loup Garou will be paid 100 000 French francs one year hence. This is a nominal flow, which he discounts at a 15 per cent nominal discount rate:

$$PV = \frac{100\ 000}{1.15} = 86\ 957 \text{ francs}$$

The inflation rate is 10 per cent.
Calculate the present value of Monsieur Garou's payment using the real cash flow and real discount rate. (You should get exactly the same answer as he did.)

3. 'Those egghead finance MBAs make everything too complicated. Take inflation, for example. We don't worry about it. We just take today's selling prices, less labour, raw material and other unit manufacturing costs, and multiply by forecasted unit sales. Who cares what inflation turns out to be? It doesn't matter because costs and revenues will rise or fall together.'
    Could this be true? Does the net present value of a typical capital investment project not depend on whether forecasted future inflation is high or low? Explain briefly. (*Hint*: Compare Tables 6.1 and 6.2. Does inflation affect all of each year's entries proportionally?)

4. How does the present value of depreciation tax shields vary across the recovery period classes shown in Table 6.5? Give a general answer and then check it by calculating the present values of depreciation tax shields with 5-year and 7-year asset lives. The tax rate is 35 per cent. Use any reasonable discount rate.

5. Each of the following statements is true. Explain why they are consistent.
    a. When a company introduces a new product, or expands production of an existing product, investment in net working capital is usually an important cash outflow.
    b. Forecasting changes in net working capital is not necessary if the timing of all cash inflows and outflows is carefully specified.

6. When appraising mutually exclusive projects, many companies calculate the projects' equivalent annual costs and rank the projects on this basis. Why is this necessary? Why not just compare the projects' NPVs? Explain briefly. What alternative could you use?

7. Machines A and B are mutually exclusive and are expected to produce the following cash flows:

| Machine | Cash flows ($'000) | | | |
|---|---|---|---|---|
| | $C_0$ | $C_1$ | $C_2$ | $C_3$ |
| A | −100 | +110 | +121 | |
| B | −120 | +110 | +121 | +133 |

The opportunity cost of capital is 10 per cent.
a. Calculate the NPV of each machine.
b. Use present value tables to calculate the equivalent annual cash flow from each machine.

c. Calculate the total PV of costs if the full sequence of replacements is expected to run for 12 years.

d. Which machine should you buy?

**8.** Machine C was purchased five years ago for $200 000 and produces an annual cash flow of $80 000. It has no salvage value but is expected to last another five years. The company can replace machine C with machine B (see Question 7 above) *either* now *or* at the end of five years. Which should it do?

## QUESTIONS AND PROBLEMS

**1.** Restate the cash flows for the Guano project in real terms (see Table 6.7). Discount the restated cash flows at a real discount rate. Assume a 20 per cent nominal rate and 10 per cent expected inflation. Net present value should be unchanged at $4 497 000.

**2.** Calculate the NPV of some personal investment decision, such as buying a solar hot water system, insulating the roof or replacing the car. Ignore the extra convenience of the new asset. Just focus on the cash costs and benefits.

**3.** Discuss the following statement: 'We don't want individual plant managers to get involved in the firm's tax position. So instead of telling them to discount after-tax cash flows at 10 per cent, we just tell them to take the pre-tax cash flows and discount at 15 per cent. With a 36 per cent tax rate, 15 per cent pre-tax generates approximately 10 per cent after tax.'

**4.** What do you think of the following statement: 'We like to do all our capital budgeting calculations in real terms. It saves making any forecasts of the inflation rate.'

**5.** A project requires use of spare computer capacity. If the project is not terminated, the company will need to buy an additional graphics-server at the end of year 2. If it is terminated, the graphics-server will not be required until the end of year 4. If graphics-servers cost $10 000 and last five years, and if the opportunity cost of capital is 10 per cent, what is the present value of the cost of this extra usage if the project is terminated at the end of year 2? What if the project continues indefinitely?

**6.** Mrs T. Potts, the treasurer of Ideal China, has a problem. The company has just ordered a new kiln for $400 000. Of this sum, $50 000 is described by the supplier as 'installation cost'. Mrs Potts does not know whether the commissioner for taxation will permit the company to treat this cost as a current tax-deductible expense or as a capital investment. In the latter case, the company could depreciate the $50 000 using a five-year life for depreciation. If the tax rate is 36 per cent and the opportunity cost of capital is 5 per cent, what is the present value of the tax shield in either case?

**7.** You own 125 hectares of timberland in South Australia. The young timber is worth $40 000 if logged now. This represents 1000 cubic metres of wood worth $40 per cubic metre net of costs of cutting and transport. A paper company has offered to purchase your tract for $140 000. Should you accept the offer?

■ You have the following information:

| Years from the present | Yearly growth rate (cubic metres/hectare) |
|---|---|
| 1–4 | 16% |
| 5–8 | 11% |
| 9–13 | 4% |
| 14 and subsequent years | 1% |

■ You expect price per cubic metre to increase at 4 per cent per year indefinitely.
■ The cost of capital is 9 per cent. Ignore taxes.
■ The market value of your land would be $400 per hectare if you cut and removed the timber this year. The value of cut-over land is also expected to grow at 4 per cent per year indefinitely.

**8.** The Borstal Company has to choose between two machines that do the same job but have different lives. The two machines have the following costs:

| Year | Machine A | Machine B |
|---|---|---|
| 0 | $40 000 | $50 000 |
| 1 | 10 000 | 8 000 |
| 2 | 10 000 | 8 000 |
| 3 | 10 000 + replace | 8 000 |
| 4 | | 8 000 + replace |

These costs are expressed in real terms.

a. Suppose you are Borstal's financial manager. If you had to buy one or other machine, and rent it to the production manager for that machine's economic life, what annual rental payment would you have to charge? Assume a 6 per cent real discount rate and ignore taxes.
b. Which machine should Borstal buy?
c. Usually the rental payments you derived in Part (a) are just hypothetical—a way of calculating and interpreting equivalent annual cost. Suppose you actually do buy one of the machines and rent it to the production manager. How much would you actually have to charge in each future year if there is steady 8 per cent per year inflation? (*Note:* The rental payments calculated in Part (a) are real cash flows. You would have to mark those payments up to cover inflation.)
d. Calculate the total PV of costs if the sequence of replacements is expected to last 12 years.
e. Recalculate the total PV of costs if the machine will only be needed for 10 years. Assume that on disposal before the end of their operating lives, A's scrap value is $10 000 and B's scrap value is $15 000.

**9.** Look again at your calculations for Question 8. Suppose that technological change is expected to reduce costs by 3 per cent per year. There will be new machines in year 1 that cost 3 per cent less to buy and operate than machines A and B. In year 2 there will be a second crop of new machines incorporating a further 3 per cent reduction, and so on. How does this change the equivalent annual costs of machines A and B?

10. We warned that equivalent annual costs should be calculated in real terms. We did not fully explain why. This problem will show you.

    Look back to the cash flows for machines A and B in 'Case 2 Choosing between short- and long-lived equipment'. The present values of purchase and operating costs in thousands of dollars are 28.37 (over three years for machine A) and 21.00 (over two years for machine B). The real discount rate is 6 per cent and the inflation rate is 5 per cent.

    a. Calculate the three- and two-year level nominal annuities that have present values of 28.37 and 21.00. Explain why these annuities are not realistic estimates of equivalent annual costs. (*Hint*: In real life machinery rentals increase with inflation.)

    b. Suppose the inflation rate increases to 25 per cent. The real interest rate stays at 6 per cent. Recalculate the level nominal annuities. Note that the *ranking* of machines A and B appears to change. Why? (*Hint*: Think of renting out machines A and B. Suppose you are locked into level nominal rental payments, with no increase to cover inflation at 25 per cent. You then suffer more from inflation over the three-year life of machine A than over the two-year life of machine B. Therefore, the required immediate payment for machine A goes up more than for machine B, and A *appears* more expensive.)

11. As a result of improvements in product engineering, United Automation is able to sell one of its two milling machines. Both machines perform the same function but differ in age. The newer machine could be sold today for $50 000. Its operating costs are $20 000 a year, but in five years the machine will require a $20 000 overhaul. Thereafter operating costs will be $30 000 until the machine is finally sold in year 10 for $5000.

    The older machine could be sold today for $25 000. If it is kept, it will need an immediate $20 000 overhaul. Thereafter operating costs will be $30 000 a year until the machine is finally sold in year 5 for $5000.

    Both machines are fully depreciated for tax purposes. The company pays tax at 36 per cent due immediately. Cash flows have been forecast in real terms. The real cost of capital is 12 per cent.

    Which machine should United Automation sell? Explain the assumptions underlying your answer.

12. Hayden Ltd has a number of copiers that were bought four years ago for $20 000. Currently maintenance costs $2000 a year, but the maintenance agreement expires at the end of two years and thereafter the annual maintenance charge will rise to $8000. The machines have a current resale value of $8000, but at the end of year 2 their value will have fallen to $3500. By the end of year 6 the machines would be valueless and would be scrapped.

    Hayden is considering replacing the copiers with new machines that would do essentially the same job. These machines cost $25 000, and the company can take out an eight-year maintenance contract for $1000 a year. The machines have no value by the end of the eight years and would be scrapped.

    Both machines are depreciated by straight-line to a zero salvage value, using a seven-year life for tax purposes, and the tax rate is 36 per cent. Assume for simplicity that the inflation rate is zero. The real cost of capital is 7 per cent. When should Hayden replace its copiers?

13. The *Financial Analysts Journal* has offered the following subscription options: one year, $150; two years, $260; three years, $345. These rates are expected to increase at the general rate of inflation. What is your optimal strategy assuming you intend to be a permanent subscriber? Make other assumptions as appropriate.

**14.** The chief executive's jet is not fully utilised. You judge that its use by more executives would increase direct operating costs by only $20 000 a year and would save $100 000 a year in airline bills. On the other hand, you believe that with the increased use the company will need to replace the jet at the end of three years rather than four. A new jet costs $1.1 million and (at its current low rate of use) has a life of six years. Assume that the company does not pay taxes. All cash flows are in real terms and the real opportunity cost of capital is 8 per cent. Should you try to persuade the chief executive to allow other managers to use the aeroplane?

**15.** A project requires an initial investment of $100 000 and is expected to produce a cash inflow before tax of $26 000 per year for five years. Company A has substantial accumulated tax losses and is unlikely to pay taxes in the foreseeable future. Company B pays corporate taxes at a rate of 33 per cent and can depreciate the investment for tax purposes using a five-year life. Suppose the opportunity cost of capital is 8 per cent. Ignore inflation.
  a. Calculate project NPV for each company.
  b. What is the IRR of the after-tax cash flows for each company? What does comparison of the IRRs suggest is the effective corporate tax rate?

**16.** A widget manufacturer currently produces 200 000 units a year. It buys widget lids from an outside supplier at a price of $2 a lid. The plant manager believes that it would be cheaper to make these lids rather than buy them. Direct production costs are estimated to be only $1.50 a lid. The necessary machinery would cost $150 000. This investment could be written off for tax purposes using a seven-year life. The plant manager estimates that the operation would require additional working capital of $30 000 but argues that this sum can be ignored since it is recoverable at the end of the 10 years. If the company pays tax at a rate of 36 per cent and the opportunity cost of capital is 15 per cent, would you support the plant manager's proposal? State clearly any additional assumptions that you need to make.

**17.** Reliable Electric is considering a proposal to manufacture a new type of industrial electric motor that would replace most of its existing product line. A research breakthrough has given Reliable a two-year lead on its competitors. The project proposal is summarised in Table 6.8 opposite.
  a. Read the notes to the table carefully. Which entries make sense? Which do not? Why or why not?
  b. What additional information would you need to construct a version of Table 6.8 that makes sense?
  c. Construct such a table and recalculate NPV. Make additional assumptions as necessary.

**18.** United Pigpen is considering a proposal to manufacture high-protein pig feed. The project would make use of an existing warehouse, which is currently rented out to a neighbouring firm. The next year's rental charge on the warehouse is $100 000, and thereafter the rent is expected to grow in line with inflation at 4 per cent a year. In addition to using the warehouse, the proposal envisages an investment in plant and equipment of $1.2 million. This could be depreciated for tax purposes straight-line over 10 years. However, Pigpen expects to terminate the project at the end of eight years and to resell the plant and equipment in year 8 for $400 000. Finally, the project requires an initial investment in working capital of $350 000. Thereafter, working capital is forecast to be 10 per cent of sales in each of years 1 to 7.

**table 6.8** _____

Cash flows and present value of Reliable Electric's proposed investment (annual cash flows in $'000)

|  | 1995 | 1996 | 1997 | 1998–2005 |
|---|---|---|---|---|
| 1. Capital expenditure | −10 400 | | | |
| 2. Research and development | −2 000 | | | |
| 3. Working capital | −4 000 | | | |
| 4. Revenue | | +8 000 | +16 000 | +40 000 |
| 5. Operating costs | | −4 000 | −8 000 | −20 000 |
| 6. Overhead | | −800 | −1 600 | −4 000 |
| 7. Depreciation | | −1 040 | −1 040 | −1 040 |
| 8. Interest | | −2 160 | −2 160 | −2 160 |
| 9. Income | −2 000 | 0 | +3 200 | +12 800 |
| 10. Tax | 0 | 0 | −420 | −4 480 |
| 11. Net cash flow | −16 400 | 0 | +2 780 | +8 320 |
| Net present value | 13 932 | | | |

_Notes:_

1. Capital expenditure: _$8 million for new machinery and $2.4 million for a warehouse extension. The full cost of the extension has been charged to this project, although only about half of the space is currently needed. Since the new machinery will be housed in an existing factory building, no charge has been made for land and building._
2. Research and development: _$1.82 million spent in 1989. This figure was corrected for 10 per cent inflation from the time of expenditure to date. Thus 1.82 × 1.1 = $2 million._
3. Working capital: _Initial investment in inventories._
4. Revenue: _These figures assume sales of 2000 motors in 1991, 4000 in 1992 and 10 000 per year from 1993 to 2000. The initial unit price of $4000 is forecast to remain constant in real terms._
5. Operating costs: _These include all direct and indirect costs. Indirect costs (heat, light, power, fringe benefits, etc.) are assumed to be 200 per cent of direct labour costs. Operating costs per unit are forecast to remain constant in real terms at $2000._
6. Overhead: _Marketing and administrative costs, assumed equal to 10 per cent of revenue._
7. Depreciation: _Straight-line for 10 years._
8. Interest: _Charged on capital expenditure and working capital at Reliable's current borrowing rate of 15 per cent._
9. Income: _Revenue less the sum of research and development, operating costs, overhead, depreciation and interest._
10. Tax: _35 per cent of income. However, income is negative in 1990. This loss is carried forward and deducted from taxable income in 1992._
11. Net cash flow: _Assumed equal to income less tax._
12. Net present value: _NPV of net cash flow at a 15 per cent discount rate._

Year 1 sales of pig feed are expected to be $4.2 million, and thereafter sales are forecast to grow by 5 per cent a year, slightly faster than the inflation rate. Manufacturing costs are expected to be 90 per cent of sales and profits are subject to tax at 35 per cent payable immediately. The cost of capital is 12 per cent. What is the net present value of Pigpen's project?

**19.** In the International Mulch and Compost example (Section 6.2), we assumed that losses on the project could be used to offset taxable profits elsewhere in the corporation. Suppose that the losses had to be carried forward and offset against future taxable profits from the project. How would the project NPV change? What is the value of the company's ability to use the tax deductions immediately?

**20.** In 2009 Peter Handy, the finance director of New Economy Transport Company (NETCO), was evaluating a proposed $610 000 outlay for an overhaul of its dry cargo boat, the *Vital Spark*. Estimated costs were as follows:

|                      |           |
|----------------------|-----------|
| Install new engine   | $250 000  |
| New navigation system|   200 000 |
| Repair hull          |   160 000 |
|                      | $610 000  |

The hull repair was chargeable against taxable profits in year 0. Items 1 and 2 were regarded as capital expenditure and could be depreciated for tax purposes straight-line over years 1 to 5.

NETCO's chief engineer, Scott McPhail, estimated post-overhaul operating costs as $985 000 per annum. However, the company could decide not to go ahead with the navigation system, in which case operating costs would rise to $1 181 000.

The *Vital Spark* is fully depreciated and, even if rehabilitated, could not last more than 10 years. Instead of overhauling the *Vital Spark*, NETCO could sell it as is for $140 000 and invest in a new boat. The new boat would cost $2 000 000, and this expenditure could be depreciated straight-line over 10 years. The new boat would have an economic life of 15 years and would cost only $900 000 a year to operate.

The cost of capital is 10 per cent and the company tax rate is 40 per cent. Inflation was eliminated when Australia adopted the gold standard in the year 2006. What should NETCO do?

# part 2

## RISK

# chapter 7

# RISK, RETURN, DIVERSIFICATION AND THE OPPORTUNITY COST OF CAPITAL

**W**e have managed to go through six chapters without directly addressing the problem of risk, but now the jig is up. We can no longer be satisfied with vague statements like 'The opportunity cost of capital depends on the risk of the project'. We need to know how risk is defined and measured, what the links are between risk and the opportunity cost of capital, and how the financial manager can cope with risk in practical situations.

In this chapter we concentrate on the first of these issues—how risk is defined and measured—and leave the other two to Chapters 8 and 9. We start by summarising the twentieth century's evidence on rates of return in capital markets. Then we take a first look at investment risks and show how they can be reduced by portfolio diversification. We introduce you to variance—a risk measure used for portfolios—then we introduce you to **beta**—a risk measure used for individual securities.

The themes of this chapter, then, are portfolio risk, security risk and diversification. For the most part, we take the view of the individual investor. But at the end of the chapter we turn the problem around and ask whether diversification makes sense as a *corporate* objective.

## 7.1 The twentieth century's capital market history in one easy lesson

### American evidence

Financial analysts are blessed with an enormous quantity of data on security prices and returns. The best known and most researched data files were developed by the University of Chicago's Center for Research in Security Prices (CRSP). CRSP has developed a file of prices and dividends for each month since 1926 for every share that has been listed on the New York Share Exchange (NYSE). Other files give daily prices and data for shares that are traded on the American Share Exchange and the over-the-counter market, data for bonds, for options, and so on.

Similar data is available in Australia,[1] but detailed data typically covers less than 25 years of prices, and for some securities such as corporate bonds very few trades are reported. We therefore concentrate on the classic study undertaken in the United States by Ibbotson Associates. The Australian research, which we discuss below, yields similar results to American studies.

Ibbotson Associates consider the historical performance of five portfolios of securities:[2]

1. A portfolio of Treasury bills, that is, United States government debt securities maturing in less than one year.
2. A portfolio of long-term United States government bonds.
3. A portfolio of long-term corporate bonds.[3]
4. Standard and Poor's Composite Index, which represents a portfolio of common stocks of 500 large firms.
5. A portfolio of the common stocks of small firms.

These portfolios offer different degrees of risk. Treasury bills are about as safe an investment as you can make. There is negligible risk of default and their short maturity means that the prices of Treasury bills are relatively stable. In fact, an investor who wishes to lend money for, say, three months can achieve a perfectly certain payoff by purchasing a Treasury bill maturing in three months. However, the investor cannot lock in a *real* rate of return: There is still some uncertainty about inflation.

By switching to long-term government bonds, the investor acquires an asset whose prices fluctuate as interest rates vary. (Bond prices fall when interest rates rise and rise when interest rates fall.) An investor who switches from government to corporate bonds accepts an additional *default* risk. An investor who shifts from corporate bonds to common stocks has a direct share in all the risks of the enterprise.

Figure 7.1 shows how your money would have grown if you had invested one dollar at the start of 1926 and reinvested all dividend or interest income in each of the five portfolios.[4] Figure 7.2 is identical except that it depicts the growth in the real value of the portfolio. We focus here on nominal values.

Portfolio performance coincides with our intuitive risk ranking. A dollar invested in the safest investment, Treasury bills, would have grown to just over $12 by 1994, barely enough to keep up with inflation. An investment in long-term Treasury bonds would have produced $26 and corporate bonds a pinch more. Common stocks were in a class by themselves. An investor who placed a dollar in the stocks of large American firms would have received $811.

---

1   Sources of such data include the Australian Stock Exchange, the Sydney Futures Exchange, Reuters, Datastream, Standard and Poor's Global Vantage product, the Australian Graduate School of Management and SIRCA.

2   In reference to the Ibbotson and Associates study we will use the American terminology—Treasury bills are equivalent to Australian Treasury notes, and common stocks are equivalent to Australian ordinary shares.

3   The two bond portfolios were revised each year in order to maintain a constant maturity.

4   Portfolio values are plotted on a log scale. If they were not, the ending values for the two ordinary share portfolios would run off the top of the page.

**figure 7.1**

How an investment of $1 at the start of 1926 would have grown, assuming reinvestment of all dividend and interest payments.

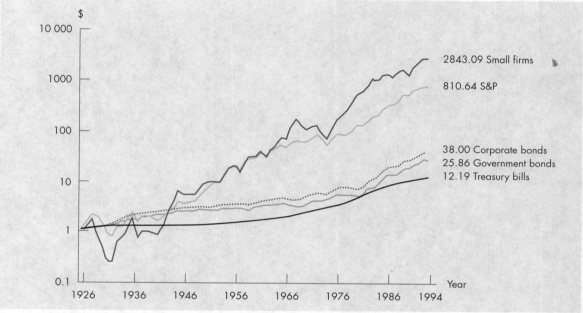

*Source: Stocks, Bonds, Bills, and Inflation, 1995 Yearbook*, Chicago, © 1995 Ibbotson Associates, Inc. Based on copyright works by Ibbotson and Sinquefield. All rights reserved. Used with permission.

The jackpot, however, went to investors in stocks of small firms—$2843 for each dollar invested.

Ibbotson Associates also calculated a rate of return for each of these portfolios for each year from 1926 to 1994. This rate of return reflects both cash receipts—dividends or interest—and the capital gain realised during the year. Averages of the annual rates of return for each portfolio are shown in Table 7.1.

The safest investment, Treasury bills, also gave the lowest rate of return—3.7 per cent a year in *nominal* terms and 0.6 per cent in *real* terms. In other words, the average rate of inflation for the United States over this period was just over 3 per cent a year. Investors who accepted the extra risk of common stocks received on average a premium of 8.4 per cent a year over the return on Treasury bills and a premium of 7.0 per cent over government bonds. Stocks in small firms offered an even higher premium.

You may ask why we look back over such a long period to measure average rates of return. The reason is that annual rates of return for common stocks fluctuate so much that averages taken over short periods are meaningless. Our only hope of gaining insights from historical rates of return is to look at a very long period.[5] These are arithmetic averages. Ibbotson

---

[5]  Even with 69 years of data we cannot be sure that this period is truly representative and that the average is not distorted by a few unusually high or low returns. The reliability of an estimate of the average is usually measured by its *standard error*. For example, for the American data the standard error of our estimate of the average risk premium on ordinary shares is about 2.5 per cent. There is a 95 per cent chance that the *true* average is within plus or minus 2 standard errors of the 8.4 per cent estimate. In other words, if you said that the true average was between 3.4 and 13.4 per cent, you would have a 95 per cent chance of being right. (*Technical note:* The standard error of the mean is equal to the standard deviation divided by the square root of the number of observations. In the current case this is $20.6/\sqrt{69} = 2.5$.)

**figure 7.2**

How an investment of $1 at the start of 1926 would have grown in real terms, assuming reinvestment of all dividend and interest payments. Compare this plot to Figure 7.1 and note how inflation has eroded the purchasing power of returns to investors.

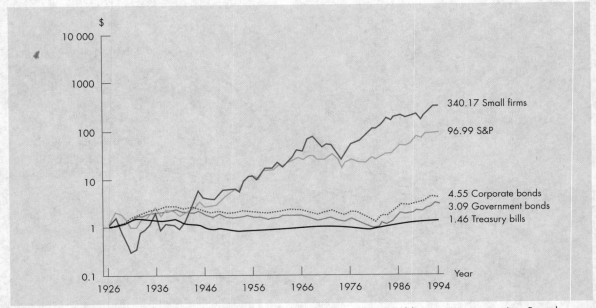

*Source: Stocks, Bonds, Bills, and Inflation, 1995 Yearbook*, Chicago, © 1995 Ibbotson Associates, Inc. Based on copyright works by Ibbotson and Sinquefield. All rights reserved. Used with permission.

Associates simply added the 69 annual returns and divided by 69.[6] The arithmetic average return is higher than the compound annual return over the period, which was 10.2 per cent.[7]

## Australian evidence

Table 7.1a presents estimates of the historic returns for shares and government bonds in Australia. This table is based on the work of Bob Officer who used more than 100 years of data on shares and bonds.[8] The results closely parallel the data for the United States. Note the absence of Australian Treasury note data—thus the average risk premium of almost 8.0 per cent is the excess of returns to shares over government bonds. The comparable figure from the American study is 7 per cent. Assuming Australian Treasury bonds have about a one per cent yield premium over Treasury notes, then the Australian premium for ordinary shares over Treasury notes would be about 9 per cent. This is not far from the American figure of 8.4 per

---

6    The choice between arithmetic averages and geometric averages (compound returns) is open to debate, and it can have a substantial effect. For example, suppose a share doubles in value one year and halves the next. Since you are back where you started, the compound annual return is zero. But the arithmetic average return is $(+100 − 50)/2 = +25$ per cent. For estimating annual *expected returns* the use of arithmetic averages is usually preferred when returns are uncorrelated over time and the distribution of returns remains unchanged over time.

7    This was calculated from $(1+r)^{69} = 811$, which implies $r = 0.102$. (*Technical note:* For lognormally distributed returns the annual compound return is equal to the arithmetic average return minus half the variance. For example, equity returns in the American market have a standard deviation of about 0.2, or 20 per cent per year. Squaring this to get the variance gives 0.04. If the returns are lognormal the compound return is $0.04/2 = 0.02$, or 2 per cent less than the arithmetic average.

8    See R. Officer, 'Rates of Return to Shares, Bond Yields and Inflation Rates: An Historical Perspective', in R. Ball et al. (eds.), *Share Markets and Portfolio Theory*, 2nd ed., Queensland University Press, 1989, pp. 207–11. Evidence on the performance of the mining industry, an important sector in Australia, can be found in R. Ball and P. Brown, 'Risk and Return from Equity Investments in the Australian Mining Industry', *Australian Journal of Management*, 5: 45–66 (October 1980).

**table 7.1**

Average rates of return on Treasury bills, government bonds, corporate bonds and common stocks, 1926–94 (figures in % per year)

| Portfolio | Average annual rate of return | | Average risk premium (extra return versus Treasury bills) |
|---|---|---|---|
| | Nominal | Real | |
| Treasury bills | 3.7 | 0.6 | 0 |
| Government bonds | 5.2 | 2.1 | 1.4 |
| Corporate bonds | 5.7 | 2.7 | 2.0 |
| Common stocks (S&P 500) | 12.2 | 8.9 | 8.4 |
| Small-firm common stocks | 17.4 | 13.9 | 13.7 |

*Source: Stocks, Bonds, Bills, and Inflation, 1995 Yearbook*, Chicago, © 1995 Ibbotson Associates, Inc. Based on copyright works by Ibbotson and Sinquefield. All rights reserved. Used with permission.

**table 7.1a**

Average rates of return for government bonds and ordinary shares for Australia, 1882–1987

| Portfolio | Average annual rate of return (nominal) (%/yr) | Average annual rate of return (real) (%/yr) | Average risk premium (*over bonds*) (%/yr) |
|---|---|---|---|
| 10-year government bonds | 5.21 | | |
| Ordinary shares | 13.06 | 9.56 | 7.85 |

*Source*: Compiled from R. Officer, op. cit., Footnote 8.

cent. Interestingly, the average risk premium for shares over Treasury bills in the United Kingdom is also about 8.5 per cent. In Canada it is slightly lower at 7.5 per cent.

# *Imputation and rates of return

In 1987 the imputation tax system was introduced to Australia. As a consequence, the tax burden on dividend receipts was reduced for *some* investors. This was achieved by allowing *some* investors a tax credit for corporate tax paid on dividends received. Such credits attach to the dividend and are known as franking credits.

This change in the tax system had two implications for rates of return. First, if it succeeded in reducing investors' taxes then it is likely that investors would accept a lower before tax rate of return on shares.[9] Since the imputation system does not affect taxes on debt returns, interest rates would not be directly affected. With required pre-tax returns on shares lower and required pre-tax returns on debt relatively unchanged, the pre-tax risk premium would appear to fall.[10] This is important in the context of the current chapter, because the returns observed

---

[9]  Investor's after-tax required rate of return is likely to remain unchanged since it depends only on time preference and risk aversion. If the after-tax required return is constant and the extra return pre-tax, required to compensate for taxes, goes down, then the required pre-tax return also goes down.

[10]  This is slightly misleading—the return investors demand in dividends and capital gains goes down, but only to the extent that there is an offsetting increase in the component of return coming from the imputation tax credits.

in the market, like those in the Tables 7.1 and 7.1a above, are pre-investor tax returns.[11] Assume for a moment that the imputation system did result in a lower equilibrium for pre-tax required returns on shares. If this assumption is correct, our historic estimates of the long-run share market return, and the market risk premium, may be too high for firms that supply investors with franking credits. If the estimate of the market return is too high, then the estimate of the risk premium will also be too high.

The second issue is that share returns now have an 'invisible' component of value: the franking credit. This substantially complicates the measurement of returns. Consider two shares both paying a one-dollar dividend and both having a share price of $25. The first company—Franked Ltd—pays a fully franked dividend; the second company—Unfranked Ltd—pays a dividend with no franking credit. If you ignore the franking credits, both firms have the same dividend yield at 4 per cent, but this hardly seems a satisfactory comparison. Simple, you may say, just add the value of the franking credit to the dividend when calculating the dividend yield. The problem with this suggestion is that we do not know how much to add. This is because the market value of the franking credit is likely to differ from its face value. We do not know exactly what the market value is, but the evidence suggests that franking credits are valued at a significant discount to their face value.

The common solution to this problem is to report both the dividend yield and the extent to which it is franked. Thus, Franked Ltd would be reported as having a 4 per cent dividend yield which is 100 per cent franked, while Unfranked Ltd would be reported as having a 4 per cent dividend yield which is 0 per cent franked. Depending on the amount of corporate tax paid, it is possible to pay partially-franked dividends, in which case the percentage franked lies between 0 and 100 per cent. Using this approach we sidestep the problem of how much the franking credit is worth. Another approach is to tackle this issue head on and define the dividend yield as[12]

$$\text{Dividend yield} = \frac{\gamma F + D_t}{P_{t-1}}$$

where $\gamma$ = the market value of franking credits as a percentage of face value
$F$ = the face value of the franking credit

This approach, however, still leaves us with the problem of determining $\gamma$.

## A small effect from imputation?

The problems above need to be resolved. But perhaps we should not worry about them too much. The impact of imputation may not have been that big. There are several reasons for this. As suggested by Bob Officer,[13] in a small open economy like Australia, equilibrium rates of return are likely to be determined by capital flows from *international* investors. If so, *domestic* tax changes are likely to have a reduced effect, or no effect at all, on equilibrium rates of return. This argument, of course, assumes that the offshore investors, who cannot use the credits, cannot sell them either. Only if the credits have no value to such investors will they have no effect on returns.

We should also remember that the long average returns we reported in Table 7.1a were calculated over several different tax regimes. Indeed, from 1900 until the start of World War II, the Australian tax system largely followed the principles of an imputation system. The tax rebate, for dividends paid out of profits on which company tax had been paid, was abolished in order to help finance the war.

The long-run average risk premium is therefore an average taken over both time and different tax systems. Its value is remarkably similar to the risk premium estimated for the United

---

11   To be precise, they are after-corporate-tax but before investor-tax returns.

12   This approach was suggested in R. Officer, 'The Cost of Capital of a Company Under an Imputation Tax System', *Accounting and Finance*, 34: 1–17 (May 1994).

13   See R. Officer, 'The Required Rate of Return on Tax Imputation, Estimating the Effect of the Imputation Tax on Investment Appraisal', *Australian Tax Forum*, 4(3): 405–17.

Kingdom and the United States and is of a comparable order of magnitude to Canada. This is a source of some comfort.

We should also consider whether tax savings derived from the 1987 switch to the imputation system were really that significant. Prior to imputation, of the order of 70 per cent of dividends were received tax-free. These dividends went to tax-exempt investors such as charities, to insurance company life offices who paid no tax on dividends and to companies. The intercompany dividend payments were subject to a tax rebate that effectively made them tax-free. This left a balance of about 30 per cent of dividends taxable. Finding a means to avoid tax on these dividends was not a particularly difficult task. And in the 1970s and early 1980s tax avoidance was a major Australian sport. Most likely, this left taxes on dividends being paid only by public-spirited investors and small investors without the resources to engage in tax avoidance. Even for these investors there was a tax break. For a short period, which ended about two years before the introduction of imputation, there was a tax rebate on the first $1000 of dividend income. The effective tax savings from imputation may therefore have been quite small. Particularly when we remember that not all investors receive the benefits of imputation.

### Some empirical evidence

A study by Brown and Clarke found that in the year following the switch to the imputation system there was no significant effect of imputation on ex-dividend day returns.[14] This was a surprising result. It suggested that, immediately after the introduction of imputation, franking credits had little value. Other researchers have attempted to estimate the market value of imputation credits as a percentage of their face value.[15] The results have been mixed, but they suggest the market value of franking credits is positive, but significantly less than the credit's face value.

Our own research indicates that in 1996 a dollar of fully-franked dividends was valued in the market at about $1.20.[16] Using this value to compute a dividend plus franking credit yield for Franked Ltd gives 1.2/25 = 0.048, or 4.8 per cent. Not a big increase over the previously calculated dividend only yield of 4 per cent. In Section 7.2 we also point out that the dividend component of annual returns is small in relation to the component from price changes. If the imputation credit does not have a big effect on the measurement of dividend yield, and the dividend yield is a small component in the estimation of annual returns, then we may have a problem in accurately estimating *annual* market returns, but not a big one.[17]

Our bottom line is simple. It is premature to jettison the evidence of our financial history. The generally accepted view is that the risk premium lies in the range of 6 per cent to 8 per cent, and we tend to favour the 8 per cent end of the range.

Currently, some practitioners are favouring the 6 per cent end. They may have a case to do so. Investors' risk aversion and the level of risk of the market drive the risk premium. It can be argued that equity returns are less volatile now than earlier in the twentieth century. If so, the risk premium should be lower. Investors are certainly wealthier. Other things being equal, this should make them less risk averse. Again, this will tend to reduce the risk premium. But we should be careful not to fall into a trap. That trap is forgetting about imputation credits. The risk premium may appear to be lower because we do not allow for the value of the imputation

---

14  The ex-dividend day is the day on which the share switches from being cum-dividend to being ex-dividend. If you buy the share cum-dividend you get the share plus the current dividend and with imputation you get the imputation credit as well. If you buy the share ex-dividend you just get the share. So the ex-dividend share is worth less than the cum-dividend share. Brown and Clarke expected the cum-dividend to ex-dividend price drop to be more following imputation, reflecting the greater value loss of dividend plus imputation credit. Their expectations, however, were not realised. There was some evidence of an imputation effect in later years, but that was after changes to the taxation of superannuation funds—a story that we leave to later in the book. See P. Brown and A. Clarke, 'The Ex-Dividend Day Behaviour of Australian Share Prices Before and After Dividend Imputation', *Australian Journal of Management*, **18**: 1–40 (1993).

15  See, for example, N. Hathaway and R. Officer, *The Value of Imputation Tax Credits*, Working Paper, Graduate School of Management, University of Melbourne, 1992.

16  S. Walker and G. H. Partington, *The Ex-Dividend Drop Off: Estimating the Value of Dividends from Cum-Dividend Trading in the Ex-Dividend Period*, Accounting Association of Australia and New Zealand Conference, Hobart, 1997.

17  We do, however, have a problem if we want to estimate accumulated returns. As we explain in Section 7.2, dividend yields make a big difference if we allow for compounding through dividend re-investment.

credits when we compute the risk premium on the market. So when we look at the risk premium we need to ask ourselves is this with, or without, the imputation tax credit.

# Using historical evidence to evaluate today's cost of capital

Suppose there is an investment project which you *know*—do not ask how—has the same risk as the ASX All Ordinaries Index. In other words, it has the same degree of risk as a broadly-based *share market portfolio*.[18] What rate should you use to discount this project's forecasted cash flows?

Clearly, you should use the currently expected rate of return on the market portfolio; that is, the return investors would forgo by investing in the proposed project. Let us call this market return $r_m$. One way to estimate $r_m$ is to assume that the future will be like the past and that today's investors expect to receive the same 'normal' rates of return revealed by the averages shown in Table 7.1 or Table 7.1a. In this case, you would set $r_m$ at 13 per cent, the average of past market returns.

Unfortunately, this is *not* the way to do it. The value of $r_m$ is not likely to be stable over time. Remember that it is the sum of the risk-free interest rate $r_f$ and a premium for risk. We know that $r_f$ varies over time. For example, during the 1990s there were times when Australian government bonds were yielding over 13 per cent, more than twice the historic average for government bonds. During the 1980s they got even higher, reaching almost 16 per cent, while Treasury note yields reached almost 20 per cent.

What if you were called upon to estimate $r_m$ when government bond rates were 13 per cent? Would you have said 13 per cent? That would have squeezed the historic risk premium to zero. Would you still have said $r_m$ was 13 per cent when government bonds offered 16 per cent? We hope not! A more sensible procedure is to take the current interest rate on government bonds plus 8 per cent, roughly the average *risk premium* from Table 7.1a.[19] With a rate of 13 per cent for Treasury bonds, that gives

$$r_m = r_f + \text{normal risk premium} = 0.13 + 0.08 = 0.21, \text{ or } 21\%$$

Whereas if you had been doing your analysis in early 1996, your calculation would have been

$$r_m = r_f + \text{normal risk premium} = 0.06 + 0.08 = 0.14, \text{ or } 14\%$$

The crucial assumption here is that there is a normal, stable risk premium on the market portfolio, so that the expected *future* risk premium can be measured by the average past risk premium. One could quarrel with this assumption, but at least it does yield estimates of $r_m$ that seem sensible. It is only fair to point out that some would indeed quarrel with us and argue for a lower risk premium, but not much lower than 6 per cent.

Even though we have data for the best part of the twentieth century, we cannot estimate the market risk premium exactly, nor can we be sure that today's investors are demanding the same reward for risk that their parents and grandparents were 70 years ago. So it would be

---

18  In the finance literature a tradition has arisen of referring to the share market portfolio as the market portfolio. Strictly speaking, the market portfolio contains all capital assets, for example debt securities, property and even human capital. As we will see when we discuss the capital asset pricing model, the distinction between the share market portfolio and the market portfolio is more than a question of semantics.

19  There is a debate in academic circles about whether to use the note rate, or the bond rate, as the risk-free base $r_f$ to which you add the risk premium. Treasury notes are certainly the closest thing we have to a risk-free security; however, their yields are not set in a free market. Note yields are strongly influenced by Reserve Bank announcements and open market operations as the Bank implements monetary policy. We have chosen to use bond yields because they are market determined; also because we have better Australian data on the risk premium to add to bonds and because bond yields provide a natural benchmark for longer-term investments. Bond yields also tend to be less volatile than note yields.

good to have a check to see if our figures are in the ballpark. Robert Harris and Felicia Marston have used the constant growth DCF formula to estimate the average rates of return that security analysts expected on a large sample of ordinary shares.[20] Their findings are summarised in Figure 7.3. Over the period 1982 to 1991 analysts in the United States appeared to be forecasting a market return that was 8.5 per cent above the Treasury bill rate.

**figure 7.3** _____

Expected market returns estimated using the constant-growth DCF formula. The spread between these estimates and Treasury bill yields varies, but it is consistent with the long-run average risk premium of 8.4 per cent shown in Table 7.1.

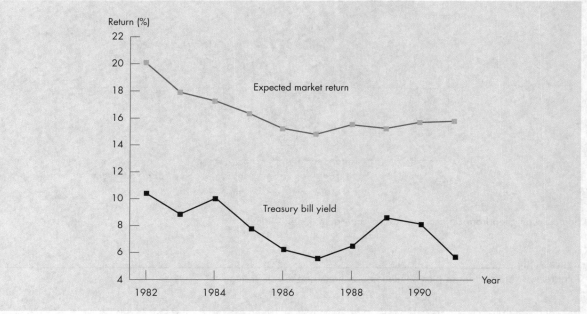

*Source*: R. S. Harris and F. C. Marston, 'Estimating Shareholder Risk Premia Using Analysts' Growth Forecasts', *Financial Management*, **21**: 63–70 (Summer 1992).

## 7.2 Measuring portfolio risk

You now have a couple of benchmarks. You know the discount rate for safe projects and you know the rate for 'average risk' projects. But you *do not* know yet how to estimate discount rates for assets that do not fit these simple cases. To do that, you have to learn (1) how to measure risk and (2) the relationship between risks borne and risk premiums demanded.

Figure 7.4(a) shows the annual rates of return from 1973 to 1996 arising from price changes in the Australian share market. The fluctuations in year-to-year returns due to price changes are remarkably wide. The highest return was in 1983 at nearly 59 per cent, while the worst year, 1974, returned a loss of about 27.5 per cent. The returns from dividends are much more stable. In Figure 7.4(b) we plot total returns (price changes plus dividends)—notice the similarity in the pattern of returns in Figures 7.4(a) and 7.4(b). Depending on the year, dividends add between plus 2 and plus 6 per cent to the return from price changes.

---

[20]   See R. S. Harris and F. C. Marston, 'Estimating Shareholder Risk Premia Using Analysts' Growth Forecasts', *Financial Management*, **21**: 63–70 (Summer 1992). Harris and Marston used five-year earnings forecasts regularly published by I/B/E/S. See Section 4.3.

**figure 7.4(a)**
Returns from price changes on the Australian share market have been profitable but extremely variable.

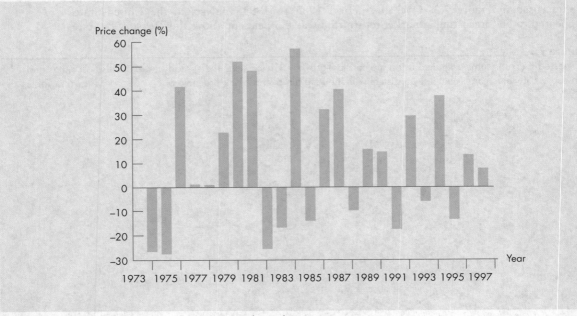

*Source*: Compiled from Datastream Australian Market Index—Prices.

**figure 7.4(b)**
Total returns, price changes plus dividends, for the Australian share market.

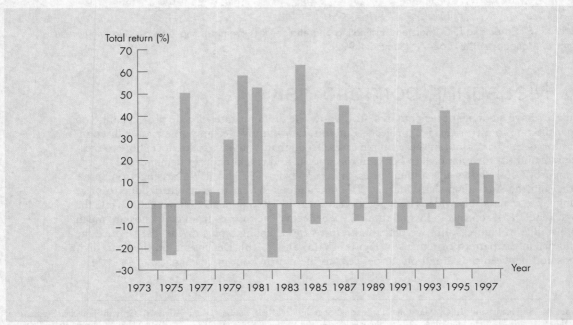

*Source*: Compiled from Datastream Australian Market Index—Total Returns.

The difference in annual returns due to dividends may not seem like much. But reinvesting the dividends and compounding this extra return over time has a big effect. Suppose you invested $100 in the Australian share market at the beginning of 1973. If you only earned the return from price changes the investment would have grown to $647 by the beginning of 1997. With reinvestment of dividends your $100 would have grown to $1834.[21]

Another way of presenting the returns data is by a histogram or frequency distribution. This is done in Figure 7.5, where the variability of year-to-year returns shows up in the wide 'spread' of outcomes.

**figure 7.5** _____

Histogram of the total return on the Australian share market, 1973–96.

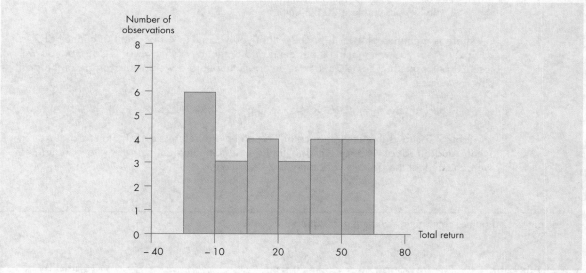

*Source*: Compiled from Datastream Australian Market Index—Total Returns.

# Variance and standard deviation

The standard statistical measures of spread are **variance** and **standard deviation**.[22] The variance of the market return is the expected squared deviation from the expected return. In other words,

$$\text{Variance } (\tilde{r}_m) = \text{the expected value of } (\tilde{r}_m - r_m)^2$$

where $\tilde{r}$ is the actual return and $r_m$ is the expected return.[23] The standard deviation is simply the square root of the variance:

$$\text{Standard deviation of } \tilde{r}_m = \sqrt{\text{variance } (\tilde{r}_m)}$$

---

[21] Special indices are constructed to capture the return from price changes, dividends and the reinvestment of those dividends. Such indices are known as accumulation indices.

[22] Standard deviation is often denoted by $\sigma$ and variance by $\sigma^2$.

[23] Here is a technical point. When variance is estimated from a sample of observed returns, we add the squared deviations and divide by $N - 1$, where $N$ is the number of observations. We divide by $N - 1$ rather than $N$ to correct for what is called the loss of a degree of freedom. The formula is:

$$\text{Variance} = \frac{1}{N-1} \sum_{t=1}^{N} (\tilde{r}_{mt} - r_m)^2$$

where $\tilde{r}_m$ = market return observed in period $t$
$r_m$ = mean of the values of $\tilde{r}_{mt}$.

## example

Here is a very simple example showing how variance and standard deviation are calculated. Suppose that you are offered the chance to play the following game. You start by investing $100. Then two coins are flipped. For each head that comes up you get back your starting balance *plus* 20 per cent, and for each tail that comes up you get back your starting balance *less* 10 per cent. Clearly there are four equally likely outcomes:

▐ Head + head: you gain 40 per cent.
▐ Head + tail: you gain 10 per cent.
▐ Tail + head: you gain 10 per cent.
▐ Tail + tail: you lose 20 per cent.

There is a chance of 1 in 4, or 0.25, that you will make 40 per cent; a chance of 2 in 4, or 0.5, that you will make 10 per cent; and a chance of 1 in 4, or 0.25, that you will lose 20 per cent. The game's expected return is therefore a weighted average of the possible outcomes:

**Expected return** = (0.25 × 40) + (0.5 × 10) + (0.25 × −20) = +10%

Table 7.2 shows that the variance of the percentage returns is 450. Standard deviation is the square root of 450, or 21. This figure is in the same units as the rate of return, so we can say that the game's variability is 21 per cent.

**table 7.2**

The coin-tossing game: calculating variance and standard deviation

| (1)<br>Per cent<br>rate of<br>return ($\tilde{r}$) | (2)<br>Deviation<br>from expected<br>return ($\tilde{r} - r$) | (3)<br>Squared<br>deviation<br>$[(\tilde{r} - r)^2]$ | (4)<br>Probability | (5)<br>Probability ×<br>squared<br>deviation |
|---|---|---|---|---|
| +40 | +30 | 900 | 0.25 | 225 |
| +10 | 0 | 0 | 0.5 | 0 |
| −20 | −30 | 900 | 0.25 | 225 |

Variance = expected value of $(\tilde{r} - r)^2$ = 450

Standard deviation = $\sqrt{\text{variance}} = \sqrt{450} = 21$

One way of defining uncertainty is to say that more things can happen than will happen. The risk of an asset can be completely expressed, as we did for the coin-tossing game, by writing all possible outcomes and the probability of each. For real assets this is cumbersome and often impossible. Therefore, we use variance or standard deviation to summarise the spread of possible outcomes.[24]

---

[24] Which of the two we use is solely a matter of convenience. Since standard deviation is in the same units as the rate of return, it is generally more convenient to use standard deviation. However, when we are talking about the *proportion* of risk that is due to some factor, it is usually less confusing to work in terms of the variance.

These measures are natural indices of risk.[25] If the outcome of the coin-tossing game had been certain, the standard deviation would have been zero. The actual standard deviation is positive because we *do not* know what will happen.

Consider a second game, the same as the first except that each head means a 35 per cent gain and each tail means a 25 per cent loss. Again, there are four equally likely outcomes:

- Head + head: you gain 70 per cent.
- Head + tail: you gain 10 per cent.
- Tail + head: you gain 10 per cent.
- Tail + tail: you lose 50 per cent.

For this game the expected return is 10 per cent, the same as that of the first game. But its standard deviation is double that of the first game, 42 versus 21 per cent. By this measure the second game is twice as risky as the first.

## Measuring variability

In principle you could estimate the variability of any portfolio of shares or bonds by the procedure just described. You would identify the possible outcomes, assign a probability to each outcome and grind through the calculations. But where do the probabilities come from? You cannot look them up in the newspaper; newspapers seem to go out of their way to avoid definite statements about prospects for securities. We once saw an article headlined 'Bond Prices Possibly Set To Move Sharply Either Way'. Stockbrokers are much the same. Yours may respond to your query about possible market outcomes with a statement like this:

'The market currently appears to be undergoing a period of consolidation. For the intermediate term, we would take a constructive view, provided economic recovery continues. The market could be up 20 per cent a year from now, perhaps more if inflation moderates. On the other hand, . . .'

The Delphic oracle gave advice, but no probabilities.

Most financial analysts start by observing past variability. Of course, there is no risk in hindsight, but it is reasonable to assume that portfolios with histories of high variability also have the least predictable future performance.

The annual standard deviations and variances observed for our five Ibbotson Associates portfolios over the period 1926–1994 and for Australian shares from 1882–1987 are given in Table 7.3.[26] As expected, Treasury bills were the least variable security and ordinary shares were the most variable. Government and corporate bonds hold the middle ground.[27]

You may find it interesting to compare the coin-tossing game and the share market as alternative investments. The American data shows an average annual return from the share market of 12.1 per cent with a standard deviation of 20.2 per cent, while the Australian data shows a return of 13.1 per cent and a standard deviation of 17 per cent. The game offers 10 and 21 per cent, respectively. Your gambling friends may have come up with a crude representation of the share market.

---

[25]  As we explain in Chapter 8, standard deviation and variance are the correct measures of risk if the returns are normally distributed.

[26]  Notice that in discussing the riskiness of *bonds* we must be careful to specify the time period and whether we are speaking in real or nominal terms. The *nominal* return on a long-term government bond is absolutely certain to an investor who holds on until *maturity*; in other words, it is risk-free if you forget about inflation. After all, the government can always print money to pay off its debts. However, the real return on government securities is uncertain because no one knows how much each future dollar will buy. The bond returns reported by Ibbotson Associates were measured annually. The returns reflect year-to-year changes in bond prices as well as interest received. The *one-year* returns on long-term bonds are risky in *both* real and nominal terms.

[27]  You may have noticed that corporate bonds come in just ahead of government bonds in terms of low variability. You should not get excited about this. The problem is that it is difficult to get two sets of bonds that are alike in all other respects. For example, particularly in the United States, corporate bonds may be *callable* (i.e. the company has an option to repurchase them for their face value). Government bonds are not callable. Also, interest payments are higher on corporate bonds. So investors in corporate bonds get their initial investment back sooner. As we will see in Chapter 25, this also reduces the bond's variability.

**table 7.3**

Standard deviation and variance of portfolio returns

| Portfolio | Standard deviation ($\sigma$) | Variance ($\sigma^2$) |
|---|---|---|
| **UNITED STATES** | | |
| Treasury bills | 3.3 | 10.7 |
| Long-term government bonds | 8.7 | 75.5 |
| Corporate bonds | 8.3 | 69.7 |
| Common stock (Standard & Poor's 500) | 20.2 | 408.0 |
| Small firm common stock | 34.3 | 1177.4 |
| **AUSTRALIA** | | |
| Ordinary shares | 17.01 | 289.34 |

Of course, there is no reason to believe that the market's variability should stay the same over more than 60 years. For example, it is likely to be less now than in the Great Depression of the 1930s. The volatility of Australian government bonds has also changed. Bond volatility has increased greatly since the start of the 1970s. For most of the century prior to 1970 government bonds typically had yields ranging between 2 and 5 per cent. Since the start of the 1970s fluctuations have been in the range of 5 to 16 per cent. In contrast, equity markets do not appear to be markedly more volatile. If anything, the equity market's variance has fallen in the last quarter of the twentieth century. In that period, however, there have been brief episodes of extremely high volatility.

On Monday 19 October 1987 sentiment in the Australian market was somewhat negative, following a Black Friday on Wall Street. The Australian market index fell by about 4 per cent, but there was little indication of what was to come. The Earth moved round the Sun and the day of 19 October dawned in the United States. On that day the share prices in the United States dropped by 23 per cent. Night fell on Wall Street's financial slaughter and the Sun moved on. The dawn of 20 October began in Australia, and the market fell by almost exactly 25 per cent.[28] The standard deviation of the return on All Ordinaries for the week of the crash was equivalent to 73 per cent per year. Fortunately, volatility dropped back to normal levels within a few weeks after the crash.

## Diversification reduces risk

We can calculate our measures of variability equally well for individual securities and portfolios of securities. Of course, the level of variability over many years is less interesting for specific companies than for the market portfolio—it is a rare company that faces the same business risks today as it did in 1882. Company risk can shift substantially over a five-year period.

Table 7.4 presents estimated standard deviations for eight well-known ordinary shares over a recent five-year period.[29] Do these standard deviations look high to you? Most of them should. Remember that the Australian market's standard deviation was 17 per cent averaged

---

[28]   The timing of the crash could not have been worse for the ASX. That week the exchange had just begun to switch from floor trading to computerised trading using their system, SEATS.

[29]   These estimates are derived from monthly rates of return. Five annual observations are insufficient for estimating variability. We converted the monthly variance to an annual variance by multiplying by 12. That is, the variance of the monthly return is one-twelfth of the annual variance. The longer you hold a security or portfolio, the more risk you have to bear.

   This conversion assumes that successive monthly returns are statistically independent. This is, in fact, a good assumption, as we will show in Chapter 13.

   Because variance is approximately proportional to the length of time interval over which a security or portfolio return is measured, standard deviation is proportional to the square root of the interval.

**table 7.4**

Standard deviations for selected ordinary shares, 1992–96

| Company | Standard deviation (%/yr) | Company | Standard deviation (%/yr) |
|---|---|---|---|
| BHP | 20.2 | Capral Aluminium | 30.8 |
| Coles Myer | 17.5 | George Weston | 16.1 |
| Comalco | 28.5 | Arnotts | 16.5 |
| Newcrest Mining | 39.9 | News Corporation | 25.1 |

over the twentieth century, while for 1992 to 1996 the market's standard deviation was even lower at only 13.5 per cent. The average standard deviation for our sample of shares for the same period was 24.3 per cent. Of our individual shares only two managed to just creep below the market's long run average of 17 per cent. The results of Table 7.4 are typical. Most shares are substantially more variable than the market portfolio; only a handful are less variable.

This raises an important question: The market portfolio is made up of individual shares, so why does its variability not reflect the average variability of its components? The answer is that *diversification reduces variability*. This is an important point so we will repeat it. The standard deviation of a diversified portfolio is *less* than the average standard deviation of its constituent securities.

Even a little diversification can provide a substantial reduction in variability. Suppose you calculate the standard deviations of randomly chosen portfolios comprising shares in one company, two companies, five companies, etc. You then randomly select another one-share portfolio, another two-share portfolio, another five-share portfolio and so on, and calculate the standard deviation for each of these new portfolios. You repeat this process several times and calculate the *average* of portfolio standard deviations for the one-share portfolio, the two-share portfolio, etc. If you plot the results they will look like Figure 7.6. One of the interesting

**figure 7.6**

Diversification reduces risk (standard deviation) rapidly at first, then more slowly.

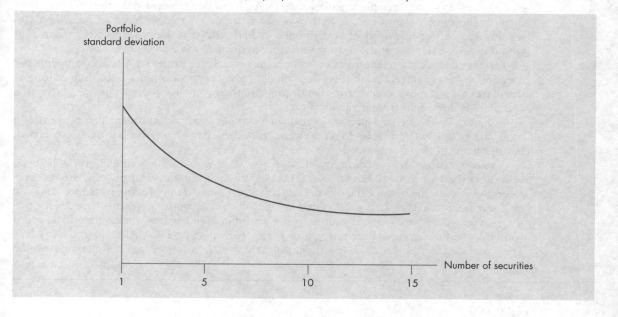

attributes of Figure 7.6 is that you are almost certain to get a similar result for most active share markets in the world.

You can see that diversification can cut the variability of returns roughly in half. But you can get most of this benefit with relatively few shares. Shares in between six to 14 companies will capture much of the benefit of diversification. The diversification improvement is very slight when the number of securities is increased beyond say 20 or 30.

Remember that Figure 7.6 represents the *average* outcome from random portfolio selection. If you select your own portfolio of say 15 shares at random you would expect to be quite well diversified. But not all randomly selected 15-share portfolios will be well diversified; you might be unlucky and get one of badly diversified ones. Spreading your eggs over several baskets helps, but if those baskets are all on the same truck and it goes over a cliff it does not help much (unless you like omelettes!). Fortunately, we do not have to rely on random portfolio selection. We show you in Chapter 8 how to pick portfolios that minimise risk for a given level of return.

## How diversification works

Diversification works because prices of different shares do not move exactly together. Statisticians make the same point when they say that share price changes are less than perfectly correlated. Look, for example, at Figure 7.7(a). In the upper panel we have a histogram which shows the returns for BHP for each month from January 1992 to December 1996. As you can see the returns were quite variable, fluctuating between positive and negative values. But on average over this period the monthly return was positive and equivalent to 0.98 per cent per month, or just under 1 per cent.

Now suppose you can find a stock like Nega Corella (the second panel of Figure 7.7(a)). Nega Corella also has an average return of 0.98 per cent per month, but its return moves in exactly the opposite direction to BHP's. It goes down when BHP's return goes up, and up when BHP's return goes down. In fact, the two stocks are *perfectly negatively* correlated. If you put half your money into BHP and half into Nega Corella, the resulting return for the portfolio is shown in the third panel of Figure 7.7(a). You get a constant 0.98 per cent per month. There is no variability; you have eliminated all the risk.

This is a general result. If you can find two securities that are perfectly negatively correlated you can eliminate all the risk, provided you hold them in the right proportions. In this case the securities are equally volatile; they have the same standard deviation, so you hold them in the same proportions. If BHP was say twice as volatile as Nega Corella then you would need to put one-third of your money in BHP and two-thirds in Nega Corella. That would exactly balance out the movements in the returns of the two shares.

Perfect negative correlation between shares is rare. Share prices tend to move together—they are positively correlated. But we can still get some benefits from diversification as long as the shares do not move *exactly* together. If they do, then you have *perfect positive* correlation and there is no benefit from diversification.

In Figure 7.7(b) we present a more realistic example. In this case we construct a portfolio using shares in BHP and Coles Myer. Returns from these two shares are positively correlated, but the correlation is not perfect.[30]

You can see that an investment in BHP or Coles Myer would have been quite variable if you held either share on its own. But on several occasions a decline in the value of one share was cancelled by a rise in the price of the other. Therefore, there was an opportunity to reduce your risk by diversification. Figure 7.7(b) shows that if you had divided your funds evenly between the two shares, you would have reduced your risk. The portfolio is clearly less volatile than BHP, and if you look carefully (compare the histograms bar by bar) it is also less volatile than Coles Myer. The variability of your portfolio (portfolio standard deviation = 15.3 per cent per year) would

---

30   Over the period in question the correlation was 0.31.

**figure 7.7(a)** _____

There is no variability for a portfolio with equal holdings in BHP and Nega Corella. Each bar in the histogram represents one month running from January 1992 to December 1996.

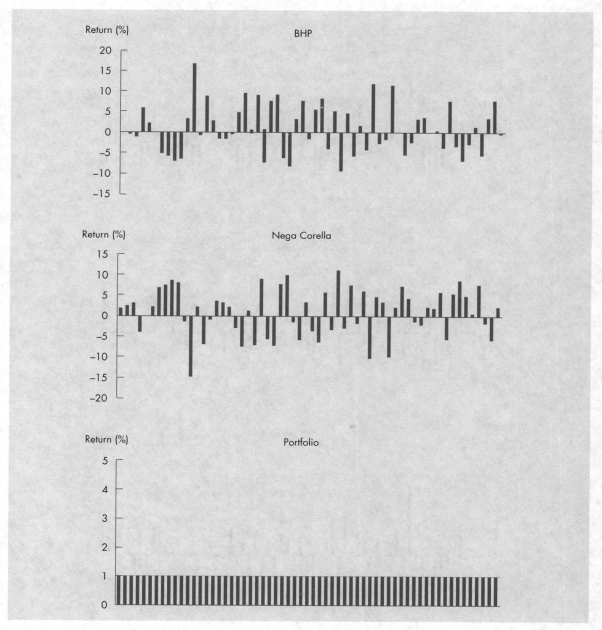

have been significantly less than the average variability of the two shares (average standard deviation = 18.9 per cent). So you get the *average* of the two shares' *returns* for *less than the average* of their *risks*. In this *particular* case the portfolio actually has *less risk* than *either* of the securities in it. This will not always be the case. But the risk of a portfolio will always be less than the average risk of its constituent securities, except for the special case of perfectly correlated returns. This is the magic of diversification; it does not just average risk, it makes some of the risk disappear.

**figure 7.7(b)**
The variability of a portfolio with equal holdings in BHP and Coles Myer would have been less than the average variability of the individual stocks. Each bar in the histogram represents one month running from January 1992 to December 1996.

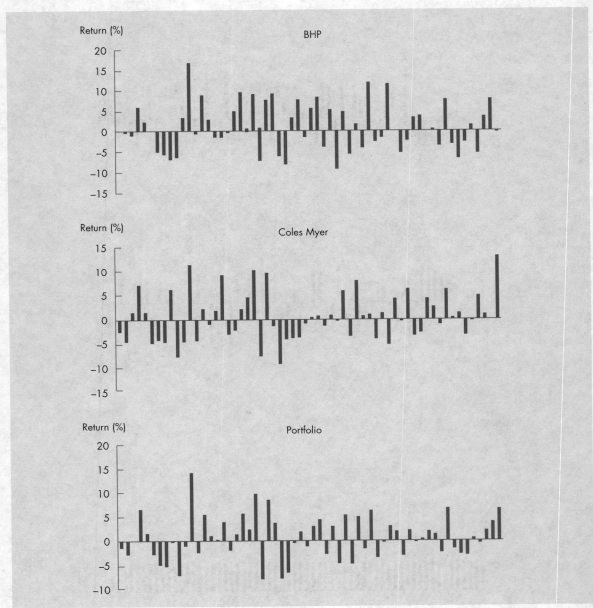

The risk that potentially can be eliminated by diversification is called **unique risk.**[31] Unique risk stems from the fact that many of the perils that surround an individual company are peculiar to that company and perhaps its immediate competitors. You might have a strike at one of your factories,

31   Unique risk may be called *unsystematic risk*, *residual risk*, *specific risk* or *diversifiable risk*.

you may have a cost overrun or delays in bringing new equipment into production, retailers may decide not to stock your product, and so on. BHP, for example, experienced a cost overrun of several hundred million dollars in its construction of a hot briquetted iron plant to process iron ore in Western Australia, and Coles Myer had a very public brawl over its corporate governance. Such events have an adverse effect on the returns of an individual stock, but wash out in a diversified portfolio. For example, BHP's cost overrun is a revenue gain to the contractor for the project. So if you hold shares in BHP and the contractor, you have diversified the risk of cost overruns.[32]

But there is also some risk that you cannot avoid, regardless of how much you diversify. This risk is generally known as **market risk**.[33] Market risk stems from the fact that there are other economy-wide perils that threaten all businesses. For example, rising interest rates, recessions, major droughts, inflation, falling consumer spending, and so on. That is why shares have a tendency to move together. And that is why investors are exposed to 'market uncertainties', no matter how many shares they hold.

In Figure 7.8 we have divided the risk into its two parts—unique risk and market risk. If you have only a single share, unique risk is very important; but once you have a portfolio of 20 or more shares, diversification has done the bulk of its work. For a reasonably well-diversified portfolio, only market risk matters. Therefore, the predominant source of uncertainty for a diversified investor is that the market will rise or plummet, carrying the investor's portfolio with it.

**figure 7.8**

Diversification reduces risk (standard deviation) rapidly at first, then more slowly.

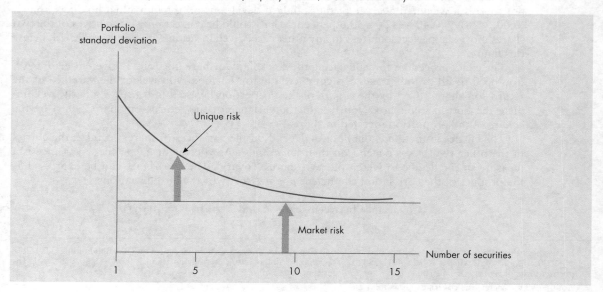

## 7.3 Calculating portfolio risk

We have given you an intuitive idea of how diversification reduces risk, but to understand fully the effect of diversification, you need to know how the risk of a portfolio depends on the risk of the individual shares.

---

32  But what if the contractor's reputation and hence share value is affected by the bad publicity about the cost overrun? To diversify that risk you can hold the shares of all construction firms. Can you see where this is leading?

33  Market risk may be called *systematic risk* or *undiversifiable risk*.

Suppose that 60 per cent of your portfolio is invested in the shares of Budget Horse Power—Bhp for short—and the remainder in Coals Mire. You expect that over the coming year Bhp will give a return of 15 per cent and Coals Mire 21 per cent. The expected return on your portfolio is simply a weighted average of the expected returns on the individual shares:[34]

$$\text{Expected portfolio return} = (0.60 \times 15) + (0.40 \times 21) = 17.4\%$$

The general formula is:

$$E[r_p] = \sum_{i=1}^{n} x_i E[r_i]$$

where $E[r_p]$ is the expected return on the portfolio
  $x_i$ is the proportion of your portfolio invested in security $i$
  $E[r_i]$ is the expected return on security $i$
  $n$ is the number of securities in the portfolio

Calculating the expected portfolio return is easy. The hard part is to work out the risk of your portfolio. You estimate that the standard deviation of returns will be about 28 per cent for Bhp and 42 per cent for Coals Mire. You can form such estimates using historical values for standard deviation, provided you believe that the past figures are a fair measure of the spread of possible *future* outcomes.

Your first inclination may be to assume that the standard deviation of the returns on your portfolio is a weighted average of the standard deviations on the individual holdings, that is $(0.60 \times 28) + (0.40 \times 42) = 33.6$ per cent. That would be correct *only* if the prices of the two shares moved in perfect lockstep. In any other case, diversification would reduce the risk below this figure.

The exact procedure for calculating the risk of a two-share portfolio is given in Figure 7.9. You need to fill in four boxes. To complete the top left box, you weight the variance of the returns on share 1 $(\sigma_1^2)$ by the *square* of the proportion invested in it $(x_1^2)$. Similarly, to complete the bottom right box, you weight the variance of the returns on share 2 $(\sigma_2^2)$ by the *square* of the proportion invested in share 2 $(x_2^2)$.

The entries in these diagonal boxes depend on the variances of shares 1 and 2; the entries in the other two boxes depend on their *covariance*. As you might guess, the covariance is a measure of the degree to which the two shares 'covary'. The covariance can be expressed as the product of the correlation coefficient $\rho_{12}$ and the two standard deviations:[35]

$$\text{Covariance between shares 1 and 2} = \sigma_{12} = \rho_{12}\sigma_1\sigma_2$$

---

[34]  Let us check this. Suppose you invest $60 in Bhp and $40 in Coals Mire. The expected dollar return on your Bhp holding is $0.15(60) = \$9.00$, and on Coals Mire it is $0.21(40) = \$8.40$. The expected dollar return on your portfolio is $9.00 + 8.40 = \$17.40$. The portfolio *rate* of return is $17.40/100 = 0.174$, or 17.4 per cent.

[35]  Another way to define the covariance is as follows:
Covariance between shares 1 and 2 $= \sigma_{12} =$ expected value of $(\tilde{r}_1 - r_1) \times (\tilde{r}_2 - r_2)$

Note that the covariance formula is very like the variance formula. In fact, a security's covariance with itself is just its variance:

$$\sigma_{11} = \text{expected value of } (\tilde{r}_1 - r_1) \times (\tilde{r}_1 - r_1)$$
$$= \text{expected value of } (\tilde{r}_i - r_i)^2 = \text{variance of share 1}$$

Remember we suggested the following formula to estimate the variance from data (Footnote 23):

$$\text{Variance} = \frac{1}{N-1}\sum_{t=1}^{N}(\tilde{r}_t - r)^2$$

You can use a similar formula for estimating covariance:

$$\text{Co-variance} = \frac{1}{N-1}\sum_{t=1}^{N}(\tilde{r}_{1t} - r_1) \times (\tilde{r}_{2t} - r_2)$$

where $(\tilde{r}_{1t} - r_1)$ and $(\tilde{r}_{2t} - r_2)$ are the paired observations of returns on securities 1 and 2, jointly observed at time $t$.

**figure 7.9**

The variance of a two-share portfolio is the sum of these four boxes, $x_i$ = proportion invested in share $i$; $\sigma_i^2$ = variance of return on share $i$; $\sigma_{ij}$ = covariance of returns on shares $i$ and $j$ ($\rho_{ij}\sigma_i\sigma_j$); $\rho_{ij}$ = correlation between returns on shares $i$ and $j$.

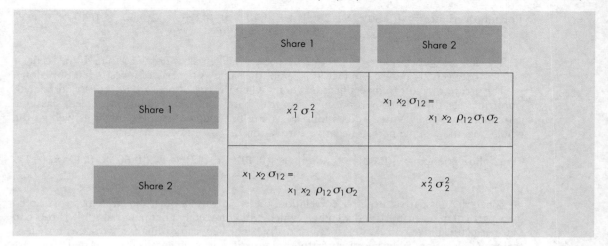

For the most part, shares tend to move together. In this case the correlation coefficient $\rho_{12}$ is positive and therefore the covariance $\sigma_{12}$ is also positive. If the prospects of the shares were wholly unrelated, both the correlation coefficient and the covariance would be zero; and if the shares tended to move in opposite directions, the correlation coefficient and the covariance would be negative. Just as you weighted the variances by the square of the proportion invested, so you must weight the covariance by the *product* of the two proportionate holdings $x_1$ and $x_2$.

Once you have completed these four boxes, you simply add the entries to obtain the portfolio variance:

$$\text{Portfolio variance} = x_1^2\sigma_1^2 + x_2^2\sigma_2^2 + 2(x_1 x_2\,\rho_{12}\sigma_1\sigma_2)$$

The portfolio standard deviation is, of course, the square root of the variance.

Now you can try putting in some figures for Bhp and Coals Mire. We said earlier that if the two shares were perfectly correlated, the standard deviation of the portfolio would be a weighted average of the standard deviations of the two shares. Let us check this out by filling in the boxes with $\rho_{12} = +1$, perfect positive correlation:

|  | Bhp | Coals Mire |
|---|---|---|
| Bhp | $x_1^2\sigma_1^2 = (0.60)^2 \times (28)^2$ | $x_1 x_2\rho_{12}\sigma_1\sigma_2 = 0.60 \times 0.40 \times 1 \times 28 \times 42$ |
| Coals Mire | $x_1^2 x_2^2\rho_{12}\sigma_1\sigma_2 = 0.60 \times 0.40 \times 1 \times 28 \times 42$ | $x_2^2\sigma_2^2 = (0.40)^2 \times (42)^2$ |

The variance of your portfolio is the sum of these entries:

$$\text{Portfolio variance} = [(0.60)^2 \times (28)^2] + [(0.40)^2 \times (42)^2] + 2(0.60 \times 0.40 \times 1 \times 28 \times 42) = 1129$$

The standard deviation is $\sqrt{1129} = 33.6$ per cent, or 40 per cent of the way between 28 and 42. In this case there is no gain from diversification because the returns have *perfect positive correlation*.

However, Bhp and Coals Mire do not move in perfect lockstep. Using past experience and your judgement, you estimate that the correlation between the two shares is about 0.4. If we go through the same exercise again with $\rho_{12} = +0.4$ we find:

$$\text{Portfolio variance} = [(0.60)^2 \times (28)^2] + [(0.40)^2 \times (42)^2] + 2(0.60 \times 0.40 \times 0.4 \times 28 \times 42) = 790$$

The standard deviation is $\sqrt{790} = 28.1$ per cent. The risk is now *less* than 40 per cent of the way between 28 and 42—in fact, it is about the same as the risk of investing in Bhp alone.

The greatest payoff to diversification comes when the two shares are *negatively* correlated. Unfortunately, this almost never occurs with real shares, but just for illustration, let us assume it for Bhp and Coals Mire. And as long as we are being unrealistic, we might as well go the whole hog and assume perfect negative correlation ($\rho_{12} = -1$). In this case

$$\text{Portfolio variance} = [(0.60)^2 \times (28)^2] + [(0.40)^2 \times (42)^2] + 2[0.60 \times 0.40 \times (-1) \times 28 \times 42] = 0$$

When there is perfect negative correlation, there is always a portfolio strategy (represented by a particular set of portfolio weights) which will completely eliminate risk.[36] It is too bad that perfect negative correlation does not really occur between ordinary shares. Nevertheless, the principle is important because portfolios consisting of two negatively correlated assets are frequently used to hedge against various forms of financial risk (see Chapter 25).

Let us pause for a review. Look back at the formula for portfolio variance. What it tells us is that the variance of a portfolio depends upon:

1. The share's own risk, measured by variance $\sigma_i^2$.
2. The share's risk in combination with other shares, measured by covariance $\sigma_{ij}$. The covariance in turn depends upon the correlation coefficient $\rho_{ij}$.
3. The quantity of the share in the portfolio, measured by its proportion $x_{i.}$.

## *General formula for computing portfolio risk

The method for calculating portfolio risk can easily be extended to portfolios of three or more securities. We just have to fill in a larger number of boxes. Each of those down the diagonal—the shaded boxes in Figure 7.10—contains the variance weighted by the square of the proportion invested. Each of the other boxes contains the covariance between that pair of securities, weighted by the product of the proportions invested. The formal equivalent to 'add all the boxes' is

$$\text{Portfolio variance} = \sum_{i=1}^{N} \sum_{j=1}^{N} x_i x_j \sigma_{ij}$$

Notice that when $j = i$, $\sigma_{ij}$ is just the variance of share $i$.
What you are adding up is a weighted variance-covariance matrix.

## *Limits to diversification

Did you notice in Figure 7.10 how much more important the covariances became as we added more securities to the portfolio? When there are just two securities, there are equal numbers of variance boxes and covariance boxes. When there are many securities, the number of covariances is much larger than the number of variances. Thus, the variability of a well-diversified portfolio reflects mainly the covariances.

---

36  Since the standard deviation of Coals Mire is 1.5 times that of Bhp, you need to invest 1.5 times as much in Bhp to eliminate risk in this two-share portfolio.

**figure 7.10**

To find the variance of an N-share portfolio, we must add the entries in the matrix like this. The diagonal boxes contain variance terms $(x_i^2 \sigma_i^2)$ and the off-diagonal boxes contain covariance terms $(x_i x_j \sigma_{ij})$.

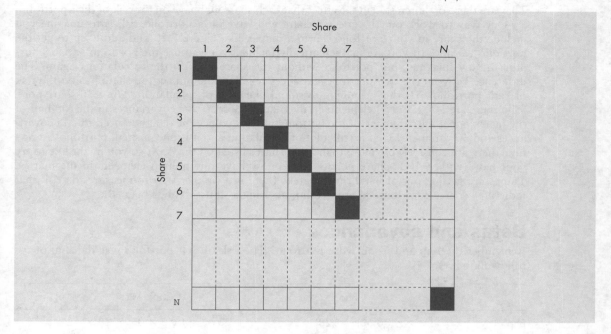

Suppose we are dealing with portfolios in which equal investments are made in each of $N$ shares. The proportion invested in each share is therefore $1/N$. So in each variance box we have $(1/N)^2$ times the variance, and in each covariance box we also have $(1/N)^2$ times the covariance. There are $N$ variance boxes and that leaves $N^2 - N$ covariance boxes. Therefore,

$$\text{Portfolio variance} = N\left(\frac{1}{N}\right)^2 \times \text{average variance} + (N^2 - N)\left(\frac{1}{N}\right)^2 \times \text{average covariance}$$

$$= \frac{1}{N} \times \text{average variance} + \left(1 - \frac{1}{N}\right) \times \text{average covariance}$$

Notice that as $N$ increases $1/N$ tends towards zero, and therefore the first term on the right-hand side of the equation approaches zero. Consequently, the portfolio variance steadily approaches the average covariance. If the average covariance were zero, it would be possible to eliminate *all* risk by holding a sufficient number of securities. Unfortunately, ordinary shares move together, not independently. Thus, most of the shares that the investor can actually buy are tied together in a web of positive covariances which set the limit to the benefits of diversification. Now we can understand the precise meaning of the market risk portrayed in Figure 7.8. It is the average covariance that constitutes the bedrock of risk remaining after diversification has done its work.

# 7.4 How individual securities affect portfolio risk

We presented earlier some data on the variability of selected individual securities. Newcrest Mining had the highest standard deviation and George Weston had the lowest. If you had held

Newcrest on its own, the spread of possible returns would have been almost 2.5 times greater than if you had held George Weston on its own. But that is not a very interesting fact. Wise investors do not put all their eggs into just one basket: they reduce their risk by diversification. They are therefore interested in the effect that each share will have on the risk of their portfolio.

One way to work out the effect a share will have on a portfolio risk is to imagine you include the share in your portfolio. Form a matrix like Figure 7.10 and add it up to get the portfolio variance (if you are mathematically inclined you can use the portfolio variance formula). Now imagine your portfolio without the share and do the calculations again. The difference between the two portfolio variances tells you the impact the share has on the risk of your portfolio.[37] Is this beginning to sound like a lot of calculation? For a 30-share portfolio there are 900 (i.e. $N^2$) elements in the matrix. Because the covariances in the top half of the matrix are a mirror image of the bottom half you reduce the data you need to 435 covariances and 30 variances. That is still a lot of calculation and it is only a small portfolio! At any time there are considerably more than 1000 shares listed on the ASX, so you might like to try your hand with a 1000-share portfolio. We now have one million elements in the matrix. Things are getting out of hand. Fortunately, there is a simpler way to measure the risk that individual shares contribute to a portfolio, by using a statistic called **beta ($\beta$)**.

## Betas and covariances

Remember the Bhp and Coals Mire portfolio? The risk of that portfolio was the sum of the following boxes:

|  | Bhp | Coals Mire |
|---|---|---|
| Bhp | $(0.60)^2 \times (28)^2$ | $0.60 \times 0.40 \times 0.4 \times 28 \times 42$ |
| Coals Mire | $0.60 \times 0.40 \times 0.4 \times 28 \times 42$ | $(0.40)^2 \times (42)^2$ |

If we add each *row* of boxes, we can see how much of the portfolio's risk comes from Bhp and how much from Coals Mire:

| Share | Contribution to risk | |
|---|---|---|
| Bhp | $(0.60)2 \times (28)2 + (0.60 \times 0.40 \times 0.4 \times 28 \times 42)$ | = 395 |
| Coals Mire | $(0.40 \times 0.60 \times 0.4 \times 28 \times 42) + (0.40)2 \times (42)2$ | = 395 |
| | Total portfolio | = 790 |

In this case both securities contribute equally to the risk of the portfolio. But, of course, that is only for the current 60 per cent to 40 per cent weighting of the securities. We could think of each security's contribution to the risk of the portfolio as being determined by their inherent risk and their weight in the portfolio. We could write this as:

Risk contribution = proportion of the security in the portfolio × risk measure for the security

For Bhp this means that:

$$395 = 0.6 \times \text{risk measure for Bhp}$$

Therefore, risk measure for Bhp = 395/0.6 = 658

---

[37] The change so calculated has two components: first, the contribution of the new share to changing the risk of the portfolio; and second, the contribution due to changes in the proportions of shares already in the portfolio.

As it turns out, 658 is a significant number. It is equal to the covariance of Bhp returns with the returns from the *portfolio* $\sigma_{ip}$. This is a general result.[38] The effect of a security on the risk of a portfolio can be summarised by two numbers: the proportion of the security in the portfolio and the covariance of the security *with the portfolio*.

It is convenient to express the covariance as a proportion of the risk of the portfolio. We do this by dividing the covariance of the share with the portfolio by the standard deviation of the portfolio. For Bhp this is $658/790 = 0.83$. If we multiply 0.83 by Bhp's weight in the portfolio of 0.6 we get 0.5—the proportion of risk that Bhp contributes to the risk of the portfolio. If we did the same calculations for Coals Mire we would get $1.25 \times 0.4$ equals 0.5.

In each case the proportion of risk contributed to the portfolio depends on two numbers—the relative size of the holding (0.60 or 0.40) and a measure of the effect of that holding on portfolio risk (0.83 or 1.25). The latter values are the betas of Bhp and Coals Mire *relative to the portfolio*. A useful property of these betas is that they measure how sensitive the returns on the securities are to changes in the return on the portfolio. *On average*, an extra 1 per cent in the rate of return of the portfolio would be associated with an extra 0.83 per cent in the rate of return of Bhp and an extra 1.25 per cent return from Coals Mire.

A statistician would define the beta of share $i$ relative to portfolio $p$ as

$$\beta_{ip} = \sigma_{ip}/\sigma_p^2$$

where $\sigma_{ip}$ is the covariance between share $i$'s return and the portfolio return and $\sigma_p^2$ is the variance of the portfolio return.

To calculate Bhp's beta relative to the portfolio, we simply took the covariance of Bhp with the portfolio and divided by the portfolio variance. The idea is exactly the same if we wish to calculate the beta of Bhp *relative to some other portfolio, such as the share market portfolio*. We just calculate its covariance with the market portfolio and divide by the variance of the market:[39] It is traditional to refer to beta relative to the share market portfolio simply as beta.

$$\text{Beta relative to market portfolio} = \frac{\text{covariance with market}}{\text{variance of market}} = \frac{\sigma_{im}}{\sigma_m^2}$$

Say we estimate the variance on the market to be about 300, and we estimate Bhp's covariance with the market to be 496, then Bhp's beta relative to the share market is given by

$$\text{Beta} = \frac{496}{300} = 1.65$$

This brings us to one of the principal themes of this chapter: *The variance of a well-diversified portfolio depends on the market (beta) risk of the securities included in the portfolio.* Tattoo that statement on your forehead if you cannot remember it any other way. It is one of the most important ideas in this book.

## Market risk and beta

If you want to know the contribution of an individual security to the risk of a well-diversified portfolio, it is no good thinking about how risky that security is if held in isolation. You need to measure its *market* risk and that boils down to measuring how sensitive it is to market movements. This sensitivity is conveniently measured by beta.

Shares with betas greater than 1.0 tend to amplify the overall movements of the market. Shares with betas between 0 and 1.0 tend to move in the same direction as the market, but not as far. Of course, the market is the portfolio of all shares, so the 'average' share has a beta of 1.0.

---

[38]  In the limit, as the number of securities increases, the covariance of the security with the portfolio converges to the average of its covariances with the other securities in the portfolio.

[39]  We show you in the next chapter that you can also estimate market beta from a regression of the returns from the share against the returns from the market portfolio.

Table 7.5 reports some estimates of betas for 10 ordinary shares. The shares are ranked from highest to lowest beta. Most of the shares are well known and we have encountered many of them earlier in this chapter. Beta was estimated for the four-year period preceding June 1996.

**table 7.5**

Betas for selected ordinary shares

| Company name | Beta |
|---|---|
| Newcrest Mining | 1.89 |
| John Fairfax | 1.53 |
| BHP | 1.45 |
| Comalco | 1.34 |
| Capral Aluminium | 1.30 |
| News Corporation | 0.97 |
| Coles Myer | 0.58 |
| George Weston | 0.57 |
| Arnotts | 0.33 |
| Nullarbor Holdings | −0.61 |

*Source*: Compiled from AGSM Risk Measurement Service, June 1996. (Ordinary least squares estimates of beta.)

Newcrest Mining, a company with substantial interests in gold mining, had the largest beta, 1.89. *If* the future resembles the past, then *on average* when the market rises an extra 1.0 per cent, Newcrest's shares will rise an extra 1.89 per cent. When the market falls an extra 2 per cent, Newcrest will *on average* fall an extra 3.78 per cent, and so on. Thus, a line fitted to a plot of Newcrest's returns versus market returns has a slope of 1.89. See Figure 7.11.

Of course, Newcrest's share returns are not perfectly correlated with market returns. The company is also subject to unique risk, so the actual returns will be scattered about the fitted line in Figure 7.11. Sometimes Newcrest will head south while the market goes north, or vice versa.

Notice also in Table 7.5 how firms in similar lines of business have similar betas, for example Comalco and Capral. This is usual, but it is not always the case. Consider the difference in betas between Newcrest and Nullarbor. Both are involved in gold mining, but they are at opposite ends of the ranking by beta. Nullarbor's beta is particularly unusual: it is negative. Negative betas for shares are as rare as the proverbial hen's teeth. So we should take another look at the estimate. Nullarbor is much smaller than the other companies in the table, so it probably does not trade very often. Thin trading makes beta estimates much less reliable. The statistics from the AGSM risk measurement service also show that the absolute value of the correlation between the return on Nullarbor's shares and the return on the market is very low (correlation = −0.14). For most of the other shares in the table the correlation with the market exceeds 0.5. It seems that most of Nullarbor's risk is firm-specific.[40]

---

[40] The $R^2$ statistic for the regression was about 2 per cent, which means that only 2 per cent of the variability of Nullarbor's returns could be explained by movements in the market.

**figure 7.11** _____

The return on Newcrest shares changes on average by 1.89 per cent for each 1 per cent change in the market return. Beta is therefore 1.89.

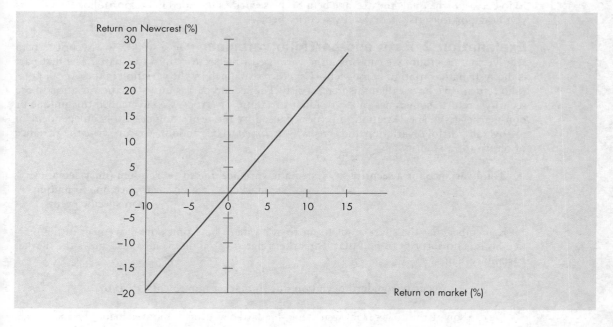

# Why security betas determine portfolio risk

Let us review the two crucial points about security risk and portfolio risk:

- Market risk accounts for most of the risk of a well-diversified portfolio.
- The beta of an individual security measures its sensitivity to market movements.

It is easy to see where we are heading. In a portfolio context, a security's risk is measured by beta. We hope that you are beginning to understand why. In any event, we offer one last intuitive explanation and one more rigorous one. If you look carefully you will see that they both say the same thing.

**Explanation 1  Where is bedrock?**  Look back to Figure 7.8, which shows how the standard deviation of portfolio return depends on the number of securities in the portfolio. With more securities, and therefore better diversification, portfolio risk declines until all unique risk is eliminated and only the bedrock of market risk remains. Where is bedrock? It depends on the average beta of the securities selected.

Suppose we constructed a portfolio containing a large number of shares—500 say—drawn randomly from the whole market. What would we get? The market itself—or a portfolio *very* close to it. The portfolio beta would be 1.0 and the correlation with the market would be 1.0. If the standard deviation of the market were 20 per cent, then the portfolio standard deviation would also be 20 per cent.

But suppose we constructed the portfolio from a large group of shares with an average beta of 1.5. Again, we would end up with a 500-share portfolio with virtually no unique risk—a portfolio that moves almost in lockstep with the market. However, *this* portfolio's standard deviation would be 30 per cent, 1.5 times that of the market.[41] A well-diversified portfolio with a beta of 1.5 will amplify every market move by 50 per cent and end up with 150 per cent of the market's risk.

Of course, we could repeat the same experiment with shares with a beta of 0.5 and end up with a well-diversified portfolio half as risky as the market. Figure 7.12 shows these three cases.

The general point is this: The risk of a well-diversified portfolio is proportional to the portfolio beta, which equals the average beta of the securities included in the portfolio. This shows you how portfolio risk is driven by security betas.

## Explanation 2 Beta and portfolio variance

Once we know a security's beta relative to a portfolio, we can break the variance of the security into two parts. The first part is the systematic variation in the security's return explained by the variation in the overall portfolio return—we have called this market risk. The second part is unsystematic variation in the security's return, sometimes called residual variation, or error—we have called this unique or non-market risk. The variation in returns caused by the firm's unique risk is independent of the overall portfolio variation and is *usually assumed* to be random. We can write the variance of return for a security as:

Total variance for a security = systematic variance due to + residual (unsystematic)
the market                          variance due to unique
                                        firm specific events

Remember that the share tends to move at a rate of beta times the movement of the market. So it is no surprise to find that its market related variability is also beta times the market variability. Thus:

$$\text{Security standard deviation due to market movements} = \beta_i \sigma_m$$

We can square this to get from systematic standard deviation to the systematic variance $\beta_i^2 \sigma_m^2$. The variance that is left over reflects the firm-specific risk. We usually write the firm-specific component of variance (the residual or error variance) as $\sigma_{\varepsilon i}^2$. So we can write the total variance as:

$$\sigma_i^2 = \beta_i^2 \sigma_m^2 + \sigma_{\varepsilon i}^2$$

The risk of any portfolio can similarly be written as

$$\sigma_p^2 = \beta_p^2 \sigma_m^2 + \sigma_{\varepsilon p}^2$$

where $\beta_p = \sum_{i=1}^{N} x_i \beta_i$

As we increase the level of diversification, the unsystematic variance of the portfolio gets smaller and smaller, until eventually it reaches zero. So in the formula for portfolio variance that follows we drop the unsystematic risk term $\sigma_{\varepsilon i}$. The resulting formula provides an approximation for portfolio variance which is increasingly accurate as diversification is increased.[42]

$$\sigma_p^2 \approx \beta_p^2 \sigma_m^2$$
$$\approx \sum_{i=1}^{N} \beta_i^2 \sigma_m^2$$

The market portfolio contains no unsystematic risk, and therefore a security's contribution to the risk of the market portfolio is exactly $\beta_i^2 \sigma_m^2$.

---

[41]  A 500-share portfolio with $\beta = 1.5$ would still have some unique risk because it would be unduly concentrated in high-beta industries. Its actual standard deviation would be a bit higher than 30 per cent. If that worries you, relax; we will show you in Chapter 8 how you can construct a fully-diversified portfolio with a beta of 1.5 by borrowing and investing in the market portfolio.

[42]  The residual returns are usually assumed to be uncorrelated between securities. If they are not, then there are factors *in addition* to general market movements which cause systematic variation in returns. In this case this shortcut method for calculating portfolio variance may be quite inaccurate. For accurate portfolio variances we would have to add up the full variance-covariance matrix.

**figure 7.12**

(a) A randomly selected 500-share portfolio ends up with $\beta = 1$ and a standard deviation equal to the market's—in this case 20 per cent; (b) A 500-share portfolio constructed with shares with average $\beta = 1.5$ has a standard deviation of about 30 per cent—150 per cent of the market's; (c) A 500-share portfolio constructed with shares with average $\beta = 5$ has a standard deviation of about 10 per cent—half the market's.

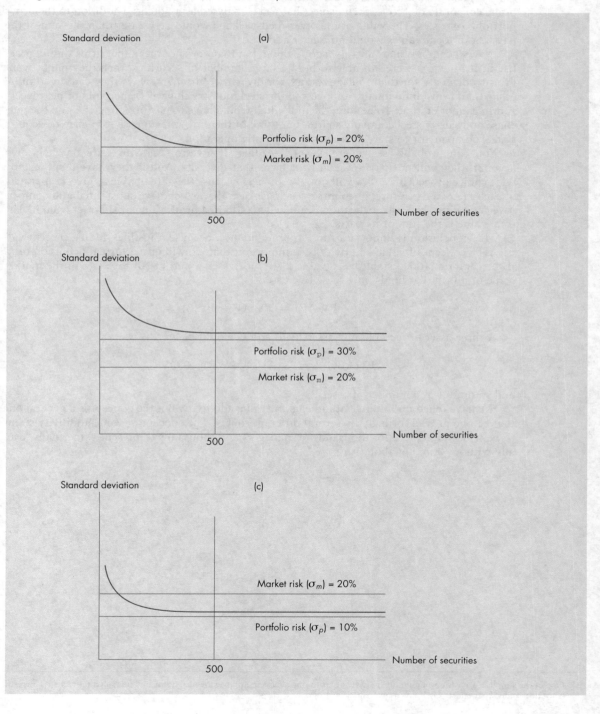

## 7.5 Diversification and value additivity

We have seen that diversification reduces risk and therefore makes sense for investors. But does it also make sense for the firm? Is a diversified firm more attractive to investors than an undiversified one? If it is, we have an *extremely* disturbing result. If diversification is an appropriate corporate objective, each project has to be analysed as a potential addition to the firm's portfolio of assets. The value of the diversified package would be greater than the sum of the parts. So present values would no longer add.

Diversification is undoubtedly a good thing, but that does not mean that firms should practise it. If investors were *not* able to hold a large number of securities, then they might want firms to diversify for them. But investors *can* diversify.[43] In many ways they can do so more easily than firms. Individuals can invest in the steel industry this week and pull out next week. A firm cannot do that. To be sure, the individual would have to pay brokerage fees on the purchase and sale of steel company shares, but think of the time and expense for a firm to acquire a steel company or to start up a new steel-making operation.

You can probably see where we are heading. If investors can diversify on their own account, they will not pay any *extra* for firms that diversify. And if they have a sufficiently wide choice of securities, they will not pay any *less* because they are unable to invest separately in each factory. Therefore, in countries such as Australia, which have substantial and competitive capital markets, diversification is unlikely to add to a firm's value or subtract from it. The total value is the sum of its parts.

This conclusion is important for corporate finance, because it justifies adding present values. The concept of value additivity is so important that we will give a formal definition of it. If the capital market establishes a value PV(A) for asset A and PV(B) for asset B, the market value of a firm that holds only these two assets is:

$$PV(AB) = PV(A) + PV(B)$$

A three-asset firm combining assets A, B and C would be worth

$$PV(ABC) = PV(A) + PV(B) + PV(C)$$

and so on, for any number of assets.

We have relied on intuitive arguments for value additivity. But the concept is a general one that can be proved formally by several different routes. The concept of value additivity seems to be widely accepted, for thousands of managers add thousands of present values daily, usually without thinking about it.

---

43   One of the simplest ways for an individual to diversify is to buy shares in an investment fund or buy units in a unit trust. The result is that the individual effectively holds a diversified portfolio.

# 7.6 Summary

Our review of capital market history showed that the returns to investors have varied according to the risks they have borne. At one extreme, very safe securities like Australian government bonds have provided an average return over more than 100 years of a little in excess of 5 per cent a year. The riskiest securities that we looked at were ordinary shares. Australian shares have provided an average return of 13 per cent, a premium of 8 per cent over the bond rate.

This gives us two benchmarks for the opportunity cost of capital. If we are evaluating a safe project, we discount at the current risk-free rate of interest appropriate to the maturity of the investment. We would use the Australian government bond rate for longer-term investments and the Treasury note rate for very short-term investments. If we are evaluating a project of average risk, we discount at the expected return on the average ordinary share. Historical evidence suggests that this is about 8 per cent above the bond rate. That still leaves us with a lot of assets that do not fit these simple cases. Before we can deal with them, we need to learn how to measure risk.

Risk is best judged in a portfolio context. Most investors do not put all their eggs into one basket: they diversify. Thus, the effective risk of any security cannot be judged by an examination of that security alone. Part of the uncertainty about the security's return is 'diversified away' when the security is grouped with others in a portfolio.

Risk in investment means that future returns are unpredictable. This spread of possible outcomes is usually measured by standard deviation. The standard deviation of the *market portfolio*—generally represented by a stock market index such as the All Ordinaries Accumulation Index—is of the order of 15 to 20 per cent a year.

Most individual shares have higher standard deviations than this, but much of their variability represents *unique* risk that can be eliminated by diversification. Diversification cannot eliminate *market* risk. Diversified portfolios are exposed to variations in the general level of the market.

A security's contribution to the risk of a well-diversified portfolio depends on how the security is liable to be affected by a general market decline. This sensitivity to market movements is known as *beta* ($\beta$). Beta measures the amount that investors *expect* the share price to change for each additional 1 per cent change in the market. Of course, these expectations are not always realised. Because of unsystematic risk there are times when the share and the market will be travelling in different directions.

The average beta of all shares is 1.0. A share with a beta greater than 1 is unusually sensitive to market movements; a share with a beta below 1 is unusually insensitive to market movements. The standard deviation of a well-diversified portfolio is proportional to its beta. Thus, a diversified portfolio invested in shares with a beta of 2.0 will have twice the risk of a diversified portfolio with a beta of 1.0.

One theme of this chapter is that diversification is a good thing *for the investor*. This does not imply that *firms* should diversify. Corporate diversification is redundant if investors can diversify on their own account. Since diversification does not affect the firm value, present values add up even when risk is explicitly considered. Thanks to this *value additivity*, the net present value rule for capital budgeting works even under uncertainty.

Before we leave this chapter it is important to distinguish the statistical analysis of portfolio risk that we have discussed here from the theory of asset pricing models which we discuss in the next chapter. Unlike the formulas describing asset pricing models, the formulas for portfolio statistics are statements of fact. They do not rely on assumptions about economic behaviour and they are not controversial subjects of debate. In particular you should understand that beta as we have discussed it in this chapter has no economic content; it only involves statistical concepts. In the next chapter we discuss the statistical estimation of beta and also show that *given certain assumptions* beta has a critical role to play in the pricing of securities.

Given that the portfolio formulas are correct we only have to worry about supplying the data. This is the difficult bit. We can estimate a share's mean return, variance and covariances or beta from past observations of return data. But, maybe history will not repeat itself—in which case our historical data is a poor predictor of future values. Remember that for the portfolio formulas to be useful we have to start with useful estimates as our data input.

## FURTHER READING

The study by Officer (1989) that we used in the chapter covers more than 100 years of Australian share returns. For an Australian study that covers a shorter time frame but more asset classes see:

R. Ball and J. Bowers, 'Shares, Bonds, Treasury Notes, Property Trusts and Inflation: Historical Returns and Risks, 1974–1985', *Australian Journal Of Management*, **11**: 117–37 (December 1986).

The problems encountered in measuring average returns from historical data are covered in the following:

R. C. Merton, 'On Estimating the Expected Return on the Market: An Exploratory Investigation', *Journal of Financial Economics*, **8**: 323–61 (December 1980).

R. Ball and J. Bowers, 'A Corrected Statex-Actuaries Daily Accumulation Index', *Australian Journal of Management*, **12**: 1–18 (June 1987).

Much work in finance assumes that asset returns are normally distributed. For Australian evidence that this is not always the case. See:

W. L. Beedles, 'Asymmetry in Australian Equity Returns', *Australian Journal of Management*, **11**: 1–12 (June 1986).

For a consultant's view on the value of the imputation credit as a component of returns see:

K. Bruckner, N. Dews and D. White, *Capturing Value from Dividend Imputation*, McKinsey and Company, 1994.

Most investment texts devote a chapter or two to the distinction between market and unique risk and to the effect of diversification on risk. See, for example:

Z. Bodie, A. Kane and A. J. Marcus, *Investments*, 2nd ed., Richard D. Irwin, Inc, Homewood, Ill., 1992.

W. F. Sharpe and G. J. Alexander, *Investments*, 4th ed., Prentice-Hall, Englewood Cliffs, N.J., 1989.

The classic analysis of the degree to which shares move together is:

B. F. King, 'Market and Industry Factors in Share Price Behavior', *Journal of Business*, Security Prices: A Supplement, **39**: 179–90 (January 1966).

There have been several studies of the way that standard deviation is reduced by diversification, including:

M. Statman, 'How Many Shares Make a Diversified Portfolio?', *Journal of Financial and Quantitative Analysis*, **22**: 353–64 (September 1987).

Formal proofs of the value additivity principle can be found in:

S. C. Myers, 'Procedures for Capital Budgeting under Uncertainty', *Industrial Management Review*, **9**: 1–20 (Spring 1968).

L. D. Schall, 'Asset Valuation, Firm Investment and Firm Diversification', *Journal of Business*, **45**: 11–28 (January 1972).

### QUIZ

**1.** a. What has been the average long-run annual return on Australian ordinary shares (approximately)?
  b. What was the average difference between this return and the return on Australian Treasury bonds?
  c. What was the average return on American Treasury bills in real terms?
  d. What was the standard deviation of returns on the market index (approximately)?
  e. Was this standard deviation more or less than on most individual shares?

**2.** Fill in the missing words:
  Risk is usually measured by the variance of returns or the _____, which is simply the square root of the variance. As long as the share price changes are not perfectly _____, the risk of a diversified portfolio is _____ than the average risk of the individual shares.
  The risk that can be eliminated by diversification is known as _____ risk. But diversification cannot remove all risk; the risk that it cannot eliminate is known as _____ risk.

**3.** A game of chance offers the following odds and payoffs. Each play of the game costs $100, so the net profit is the payoff less $100.

| Probability | Payoff | Net profit |
|---|---|---|
| 0.10 | $500 | $400 |
| 0.50 | $100 | $0 |
| 0.40 | $0 | −$100 |

  What is the expected cash payoff and what is the expected rate of return? Calculate the variance and standard deviation of the rate of return.

**4.** Av Ago, ace fund manager, produced the following percentage rates of return over a five-year period. Rates of return on the Market Index are given for comparison.

| | 1991 | 1992 | 1993 | 1994 | 1995 |
|---|---|---|---|---|---|
| Mr Ago | 2.0 | 25.1 | 10.0 | −2.3 | −5.0 |
| Market Index | 7.06 | −1.91 | 43.71 | −10.51 | 19.60 |

  Calculate the average return and standard deviation of Mr Ago's investment fund. Did he do better or worse than the Australian share index by these measures?

**5.** True or false?
  a. Investors prefer diversified companies because they are less risky.
  b. If shares were perfectly positively correlated, diversification would not reduce risk.
  c. The contribution of a share to the risk of a well-diversified portfolio depends on its market risk.
  d. A well-diversified portfolio with a beta of 2.0 is twice as risky as the market portfolio.
  e. An undiversified portfolio with a beta of 2.0 is less than twice as risky as the market portfolio.

**6.** What is the beta of each of the shares shown in the table below?

| Share | Expected share return if market return is −10% | Expected share return if market return is +10% |
|-------|-----------------------------------------------|-----------------------------------------------|
| A | 0 | +20 |
| B | −20 | +20 |
| C | −30 | 0 |
| D | +15 | +15 |
| E | +10 | −10 |

**7.** Suppose the standard deviation of the market return is 20 per cent.
   a. What is the standard deviation of returns on a well-diversified portfolio with a beta of 1.3?
   b. What is the standard deviation of returns on a well-diversified portfolio with a beta of 0?
   c. A well-diversified portfolio has a standard deviation of 15 per cent. What is its beta?
   d. A poorly-diversified portfolio has a standard deviation of 20 per cent. What can you say about its beta?

**8.** A portfolio contains equal investments in 10 shares. Five have a beta of 1.2; the remainder have a beta of 1.4. What is the portfolio beta?
   a. 1.3.
   b. Greater than 1.3 because the portfolio is not completely diversified.
   c. Less than 1.3 because diversification reduces beta.

**9.** In which of the following situations would you get the largest reduction in risk by spreading your investment across two shares?
   a. The two shares are perfectly correlated.
   b. There is no correlation.
   c. There is modest negative correlation.
   d. There is perfect negative correlation.

**10.** To calculate the variance of a three-share portfolio, you need to add nine boxes:

|  |  |  |
|---|---|---|
|  |  |  |
|  |  |  |
|  |  |  |

   Use the same symbols that we used in this chapter; for example, $x_1$ = proportion invested in share one and $\sigma_{12}$ = covariance between shares one and two. Now complete the nine boxes.

**11.** 'Diversification reduces risk. Therefore, corporations ought to favour capital investments with low correlations with their existing lines of business.' True or false? Why?

# QUESTIONS AND PROBLEMS

**1.** Here are some estimated inflation rates, returns on the stock market and representative government bond rates between 1992 and 1996:

| Year | Inflation | Return on market | Government bond yields |
|------|-----------|------------------|------------------------|
| 1992 | 0.9% | −1.9% | 9.39% |
| 1993 | 1.8% | 43.7% | 8.0% |
| 1994 | 1.9% | −10.5% | 6.7% |
| 1995 | 4.5% | 19.6% | 10.0% |
| 1996 | 2.6% | 13.4% | 8.1% |

   a. What was the real return on the market index in each year?
   b. What was the average real return?
   c. What was the risk premium of shares over government bonds in each year?
   d. What was the standard deviation of this risk premium?

**2.** You roll a die. If the number you roll is less than three you receive $10. If it is greater than four you pay $10. Otherwise you call it quits. What is the expected payoff? What is the standard deviation?

**3.** Each of the following statements is dangerous or misleading. Explain why.
   a. A long-term Australian government bond is absolutely safe.
   b. All investors should prefer shares to bonds because shares offer higher long-run returns.
   c. The best practical forecast of future rates of return on the share market is a five- or 10-year average of historical returns.

**4.** There are few, if any, real companies with negative betas. But suppose you found one with $\beta = -0.25$.
   a. How would you expect this share's price to change if the overall market rose by an extra 5 per cent? What if the market fell by an extra 5 per cent?
   b. You have $1 million invested in a well-diversified portfolio of shares. Now you receive an additional $20 000 bequest. Which of the following actions will yield the safest overall portfolio return?
      i.   Invest $20 000 in Treasury notes (which have $\beta = 0$).
      ii.  Invest $20 000 in shares with $\beta = 1$.
      iii. Invest $20 000 in the shares with $\beta = -0.25$.
   Explain your answer.

**5.** Simpson Mines has a standard deviation of 42 per cent per year and a beta of +0.10. Amalgamated Copper has a standard deviation of 31 per cent a year and a beta of +0.66. Explain why Simpson Mines is the safer investment for a diversified investor.

**\*6.** The data below gives the standard deviations and correlation coefficients for three shares. Calculate the variance of a portfolio invested 40 per cent in BHP, 40 per cent in Coles Myer and 20 per cent in Comalco.

|  | BHP | Coles Myer | Comalco | Standard deviation |
|--|-----|------------|---------|--------------------|
| BHP | 1.000000 | 0.31 | 0.60 | 20.18% |
| Coles Myer |  | 1.000000 | 0.14 | 17.54% |
| Comalco |  |  | 1.000000 | 28.47% |

**\*7.** Look back at your calculations for Question 6. Calculate each share's contribution to the overall portfolio variance. What is each share's beta relative to the three-share portfolio?

**\*8.** Your eccentric Aunt Claudia has left you $50 000 in BHP shares plus $50 000 cash. Unfortunately, her will requires that the BHP shares not be sold for one year and the $50 000 cash must be entirely invested in one of the shares from Question 6. What is the safest attainable portfolio under these restrictions?

**9.** Suppose that Treasury notes offer a return of about 6 per cent and the expected risk premium of shares over notes is 8.5 per cent. The standard deviation of Treasury notes is zero and the standard deviation of the market is 20 per cent. Use the formula for portfolio risk to calculate the standard deviation of portfolios with different proportions in Treasury notes and the market. Graph the expected portfolio returns and standard deviations.

**10.** Lucky Strike, a gold exploration and production company, has just secured exploration rights to a mining lease in central Australia. Geologists are divided over the merits of this lease. Some suggest that the geological evidence in favour of significant gold deposits is strong. Other geologists are doubtful about the prospect of finding any gold at all. Is this a risky investment for Lucky Strike's shareholders? Explain.

**11.** 'The variance of a stock has *no* effect whatsoever on portfolio risk, providing the portfolio is diversified.' Is that correct? Explain.

**12.** 'There's upside risk and downside risk. Standard deviation doesn't distinguish between them.' Do you think the speaker has a fair point?

**13.** Respond to the following comments:
   a. 'Risk is not variability. If I know a share is going to fluctuate between $10 and $20, I can make myself a bundle.'
   b. 'There are all sorts of risk in addition to beta risk. There's the risk that we'll have a downturn in demand, there's the risk that my best plant manager will drop dead, and there's the risk of a jump in steel prices. You've got to take all these things into consideration.'
   c. 'Risk to me is the probability of loss.'
   d. 'Those who suggest that beta is a measure of risk make the big assumption that betas don't change.'

**\*14.** Here are some historical data on the risk characteristics of News Corporation and Newcrest Mining:

|  | News Corporation | Newcrest Mining |
| --- | --- | --- |
| $\beta$ (beta) | 0.97 | 1.89 |
| Yearly standard deviation of return | 25% | 38% |

Assume that the standard deviation of the return on the market was 17 per cent.
   a. The correlation coefficient of News Corporation's return versus Newcrest Mining's is negative at −0.10. What is the standard deviation of a portfolio half invested in News Corporation and half in Newcrest Mining?

b.  What is the standard deviation of a portfolio one-third invested in News Corporation, one-third in Newcrest Mining and one-third in Treasury notes?

**\*15.** You believe that there is a 40 per cent chance that share A will decline by 10 per cent and a 60 per cent chance that it will rise by 20 per cent. Correspondingly, there is a 30 per cent chance that share B will decline by 10 per cent and a 70 per cent chance that it will rise by 20 per cent. The correlation coefficient between the two shares is 0.7. Calculate the expected return, the variance and the standard deviation for each share. Then calculate the covariance between their returns.

**\*16.** An individual invests 60 per cent of her funds in share I and the balance in share J. The standard deviation of returns on I is 10 per cent and on J it is 20 per cent. Calculate the variance of portfolio returns, assuming:
a.  The correlation between the returns is 1.0.
b.  The correlation is 0.5.
c.  The correlation is 0.

**\*17.** a.  How many variance terms and how many covariance terms do you need to calculate the risk of a 100-share portfolio?
b.  Suppose all shares had a standard deviation of 30 per cent and a correlation with each other of 0.4. What is the standard deviation of the returns on a portfolio that has equal holdings in 50 shares?
c.  What is the standard deviation of a fully-diversified portfolio of such shares?

**\*18.** Suppose that the standard deviation of returns from a typical share is about 0.40 (or 40 per cent) a year. The correlation between the returns of each pair of shares is about 0.3. Calculate the variance and standard deviation of the returns on a portfolio that has equal investments in two shares, three shares, and so on up to 10 shares.
a.  Use your estimates to draw two graphs like Figure 7.8 (one for variance, the other for standard deviation). How large is the underlying market risk that cannot be diversified away?
b.  Now repeat the problem, assuming that the correlation between each pair of shares is zero.

**\*19.** The market portfolio has a standard deviation of 20 per cent, and the covariance between the returns on the market and those on share Z is 800.
a.  What is the beta of share Z?
b.  What is the standard deviation of a fully-diversified portfolio of shares like Z?
c.  What is the average beta of all shares?
d.  If the market portfolio gave an extra return of 5 per cent, how much extra return can you expect from share Z?
e.  Are you certain to get the extra return calculated in Part (d)?

**\*20.** It is often useful to know how well your portfolio is diversified. Two measures have been suggested:
a.  The variance of the returns on a fully-diversified portfolio as a proportion of the variance of returns on your portfolio.
b.  The number of shares in a portfolio that (i) has the same risk as yours, (ii) is invested in 'typical' shares and (iii) has equal amounts invested in each share.
Suppose that you hold eight shares. All are fairly typical—they have a standard deviation of 0.40 a year and the correlation between each pair is 0.3. Of your fund,

20 per cent is invested in one share, 20 per cent in a second share and the remaining 60 per cent is spread evenly over a further six shares.
    Calculate each of the above two measures of portfolio diversification.

**21.** Diversification has enormous value to investors, yet opportunities for diversification should not sway capital investment decisions by corporations. How would you explain this apparent paradox?

# chapter 8

# RISK AND RETURN

In order to value a risky investment, the financial manager needs to know how much investors expect to be paid for taking risk. That is why in Chapter 7 we began to come to grips with the problem of measuring risk. Here is the story so far.

The share market is risky because there is a spread of possible outcomes. The usual measure of this spread is the standard deviation or variance. The risk of any share can be broken down into two parts. There is the *unique risk* that is peculiar to that share, and there is the *market risk* that is associated with market-wide variations. Investors can eliminate unique risk by holding a well-diversified portfolio, but they cannot eliminate market risk. *All* the risk of a fully diversified portfolio is market risk.

A share's contribution to the risk of a fully-diversified portfolio depends on its sensitivity to market changes. This sensitivity is generally known as *beta*. A security with a beta of 1.0 has average market risk—*a well-diversified portfolio* of such securities has the same standard deviation as the market index and will closely track the movement of the market.[1] A security with a beta of 0.5 has below average market risk—*a well-diversified portfolio* of these securities tends to move half as far as the market moves and has half the market's standard deviation.

In this chapter we use this new-found knowledge to develop some theories linking risk and return in a competitive economy, and we show you how to use these theories to estimate the return that investors require in different share market investments. Then in Chapter 9 we look at how these ideas can help the financial manager cope with risk in practical capital budgeting situations.

---

[1] An individual security with a beta of 1.0 will not follow the market so closely. It will *tend* to move as the market does, but because of risk unique to the security, it is quite likely that there will be times when the security and the market are moving in opposite directions.

## 8.1 Harry Markowitz and the birth of portfolio theory

Most of the ideas in Chapter 7 date back to an article written in 1952 by Nobel prize winner Harry Markowitz.[2] Markowitz drew attention to the common practice of portfolio diversification and showed exactly how an investor can reduce the standard deviation of portfolio returns by choosing shares that do not move exactly together. But Markowitz did not stop there—he went on to work out the basic principles of choosing the best portfolio. These principles are the foundation for much of what has been written about the relationship between risk and return.

We begin with Figure 8.1, which shows a histogram of the daily returns on BHP. These returns are the result of daily price changes for the five years from 1992 to 1996.[3] On this histogram we have superimposed a bell-shaped normal distribution. The result is typical: When returns are measured over some fairly short intervals (daily returns in this case), the past rates of return on shares *approximate* a normal distribution.[4]

One important feature of a normal distribution is that it can be completely defined by two numbers. One is the average or 'expected' return; the other is the variance or standard deviation. Now you can see why in Chapter 7 we discussed the calculation of expected return and standard deviation. They are not just arbitrary measures. *If* returns are normally distributed, they are the *only* two measures that an investor need consider.

**figure 8.1** _____

Daily price changes for BHP (1992 to 1996) are approximately normally distributed.

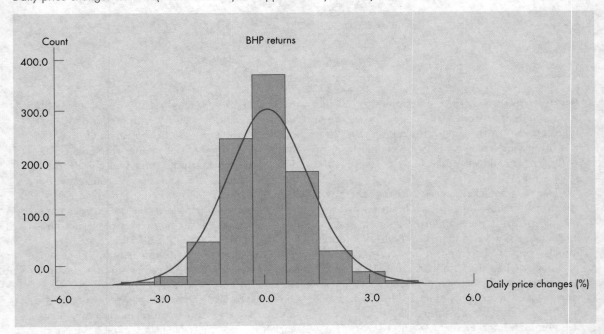

---

2   H. M. Markowitz, 'Portfolio Selection', *Journal of Finance*, 7: 77–91 (March 1952).

3   The returns plotted in Figure 8.1 are continuously compounded returns. They are computed as the natural logarithm of the price relative, that is, $\log_e (P_t / P_{t-1})$, where $P_t$ is the current price and $P_{t-1}$ is last period's price.

4   How closely the distribution of share returns approximates a normal distribution is still subject to debate. However, there is general agreement that if you were to measure returns over a long interval, the distribution would be skewed. For example, you would encounter returns greater than 100 per cent but none less than −100 per cent. The effect of this skew is that the distribution of yearly, and perhaps even monthly, returns would be better approximated by a lognormal distribution. The lognormal distribution, like the normal, is completely specified by its mean and standard deviation.

Figure 8.2 shows the distribution of possible returns from two investments. Both offer an expected return of 10 per cent, but investment A has much the wider spread of possible outcomes. Its standard deviation is 30 per cent; the standard deviation of investment B is 15 per cent. Most investors dislike uncertainty and would therefore prefer B to A.

**figure 8.2**

These two investments both have an *expected* return of 10 per cent; but because investment A has the greater spread of *possible* returns, it is more risky than B. We can measure this spread by the standard deviation. Investment A has a standard deviation of 30 per cent and investment B 15 per cent. Most investors would prefer B to A.

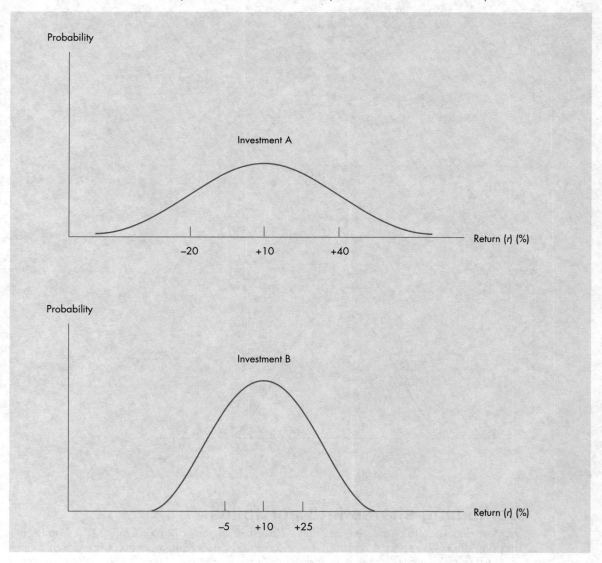

Figure 8.3 shows the distribution of returns from two other investments. This time both have the *same* standard deviation, but the expected return is 20 per cent from share C and only 10 per cent from share D. Most investors like high expected return and would therefore prefer C to D.

**figure 8.3**

The standard deviation of possible returns is 15 per cent for both these investments, but the expected return from investment C is 20 per cent compared with an expected return from D of only 10 per cent. Most investors would prefer C to D.

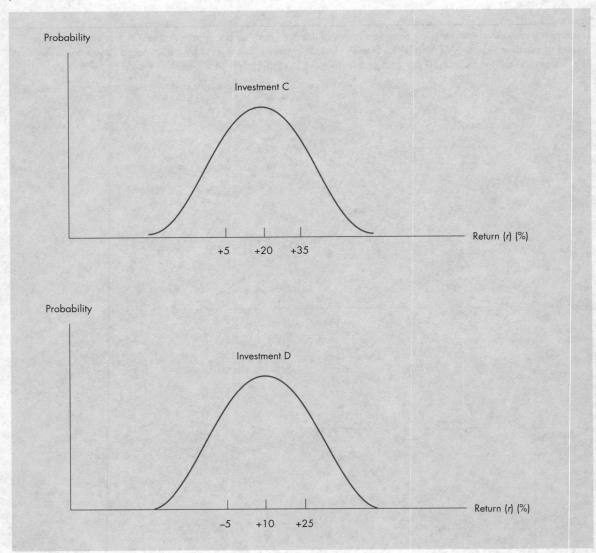

## Combining shares into portfolios

Suppose that you are wondering whether to invest in shares of Bhp or Coals Mire. You decide that Bhp offers an expected return of 15 per cent and Coals Mire an expected return of 21 per cent. After looking back at the past variability of the two shares, you also decide that the standard deviation of returns is 28 per cent for Bhp and 42 per cent for Coals Mire. Coals Mire offers the higher expected return, but it is considerably more risky.

Now there is no reason to restrict yourself to holding only one share. For example, in Section 7.3 we analysed what would happen if you invested 60 per cent of your money in Bhp and 40 per cent in Coals Mire. The expected return on this portfolio is 17.4 per cent, which is simply a weighted average of the expected returns on the two holdings. What about the risk of such a portfolio? We know that thanks to diversification the portfolio risk is less than the average of the risks of the separate shares. In fact, on the basis of past experience we can calculate that the standard deviation of this portfolio is 28.1 per cent.[5]

**figure 8.4**

The curved line illustrates how expected return and standard deviation change as you hold different combinations of two shares. For example, if you invest 40 per cent in Coals Mire and the remainder in Bhp your expected return is 17.4 per cent, which is 40 per cent of the way between the expected returns on the two shares. The standard deviation is 17.3 per cent, which is *much less* than 40 per cent of the way between the standard deviations on the two shares. This is because diversification reduces risk.

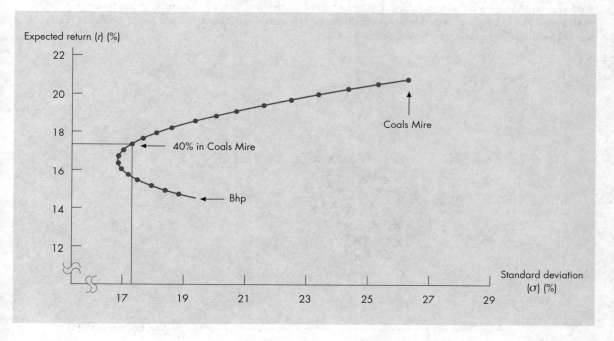

In Figure 8.4 we have plotted the expected return and risk that you could achieve by different combinations of the two shares. Which of these combinations is best? That depends on your stomach. If you want to stake all on getting rich quickly, you will do best to put all your money in Coals Mire. If you want a more peaceful life, you should invest most of your money in Bhp—to minimise risk you should keep a small investment in Coals Mire. The portfolio with the minimum risk has 19.5 per cent in Coals Mire.

In practice you are unlikely to be limited to investing in only two shares. Figure 8.5 shows what happens when you have a larger choice of securities. Each cross represents the combination of risk and return offered by a different individual security. By mixing these securities in different proportions you can obtain an even wider selection of risk and expected return.

---

[5]  Given a correlation between the two firms of about 0.4, the variance of a portfolio which is invested 60 per cent in Bhp and 40 per cent in Coals Mire is:

$$Variance = x_1\sigma_1 + x_2\sigma_2 + 2x_1x_2\rho_{12}\sigma_1\sigma_2$$
$$= [(0.60)^2 \times (28)^2] + [(0.40)^2 \times (42)^2] + 2(0.60 \times 0.40 \times 0.4 \times 28 \times 42)$$
$$= 790$$

The portfolio standard deviation is $\sqrt{790} = 28.1\%$

For example, the range of attainable combinations might look something like the broken-egg-shaped area in Figure 8.5. Since you wish to increase expected return and to reduce standard deviation, you will be interested in only those portfolios that lie along the heavy solid line. Markowitz called them **efficient portfolios** and the heavy line is known as the efficient set or efficient frontier. At any point along the heavy line you get the maximum return for a given level standard deviation. Once again, whether you want to choose the minimum risk portfolio (portfolio A) or the maximum-expected-return portfolio (portfolio B) or some other efficient portfolio depends on how much you dislike taking risk.

**figure 8.5**

Each cross shows the expected return and standard deviation from investing in a single share. The broken-egg shaped area shows the possible combinations of expected returns and standard deviation if you invest in a *mixture* of shares. If you like high expected returns and dislike high standard deviations you will prefer portfolios along the heavy line. These are *efficient* portfolios.

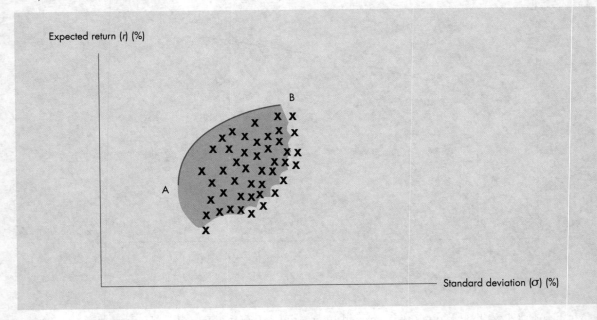

The problem of finding these efficient portfolios is rather similar to the capital rationing problem that we encountered in Chapter 5. There we wanted to deploy a limited amount of capital in a mixture of projects to give the highest total NPV. Here we want to deploy a limited amount of capital to give the highest expected return for a given standard deviation. In principle both problems can be solved by a hunt-and-peck procedure—but only in principle. To solve the capital rationing problem in practice we can employ linear programming techniques; to solve the portfolio problem we can employ a variant of linear programming known as *quadratic programming*. If we estimate the expected return and standard deviation for each share in Figure 8.5, as well as the correlation between each pair of shares, then we can use a standard computer quadratic program to calculate the set of efficient portfolios.[6]

We should point out that the proportions invested in each security are not necessarily constrained to be positive. Where short selling is possible you can hold negative proportions of some shares and this will expand the efficient set.

---

6   You will also find that you can use the Solver add-in program in EXCEL to select efficient portfolios.

# We introduce borrowing and lending

Now we introduce yet another possibility. Suppose that you can also lend and borrow money at some risk-free rate of interest $r_f$. By definition the risk-free asset has zero variance. Traditionally, we view Australian government securities as satisfactory approximations to a risk-free asset. If you invest some of your money in Treasury notes (i.e. lend money) and place the remainder in ordinary share portfolio S, you can obtain any combination of expected return and risk along the straight line joining $r_f$ and S in Figure 8.6. Since borrowing is merely negative lending, you can extend the range of possibilities to the right of S by borrowing funds at an interest rate of $r_f$ and investing them as well as your own money in portfolio S.

**figure 8.6** _____

Lending and borrowing extend the range of investment possibilities. If you invest in portfolio S and lend or borrow at the risk-free interest rate $r_f$ you can achieve any point along the straight line from $r_f$ to S. This gives you a higher expected return for any level of risk than if you just invest in ordinary shares.

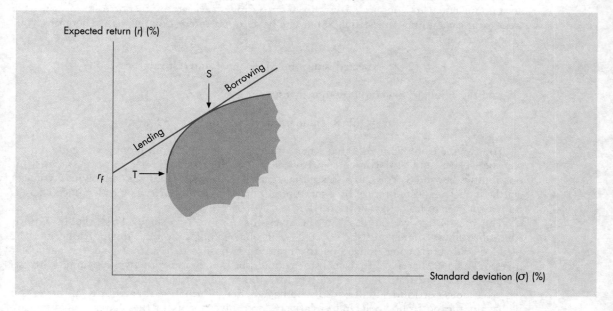

You may be wondering why we now get a straight line for the relation between risk and return instead of a curve like the original efficient set. Remember the formula for the standard deviation of a two-security portfolio:

$$\text{Variance} = x_1\sigma_1 + x_2\sigma_2 + 2x_1x_2\rho_{12}\sigma_1\sigma_2$$

When security two is riskless (i.e. when $\sigma_2$ is zero) then all the terms containing $\sigma_2$ are also equal to zero. So the equation for the risk of the portfolio reduces to:

$$\text{Variance} = x_1\sigma_1$$

In other words, the risk of the portfolio is an increasing linear function of how much you invest in the risky asset. The expected return is also an increasing linear function of how much you invest in the risky asset. We can see this by recognising that the expected return for the combination of risky asset and risk-free asset is:

$$r_p = x_t r_1 + x_2 r_f = x_1 r_1 + (1 - x_1) r_f$$

Let us put some numbers on this. Suppose that portfolio S has an expected return of 15 per cent and a standard deviation of 16 per cent. Treasury notes offer an interest rate ($r_f$) of 5 per cent and are risk-free (i.e. their standard deviation is zero). If you invest half your money in portfolio S and lend the remainder at 5 per cent, the expected return on your investment is halfway between the expected return on S and the interest rate on Treasury notes:

$$r = (\frac{1}{2} \times \text{expected return on S}) + (\frac{1}{2} \times \text{interest rate}) = 10\%$$

And the standard deviation is halfway between the standard deviation of S and the standard deviation of Treasury notes. Since the standard deviation of Treasury notes is zero, the standard deviation of the portfolio is simply half the standard deviation of S

$$\sigma = (\frac{1}{2} \times \text{standard deviation of S}) = 8\%$$

Or suppose that you decide to go for the big time: You borrow at the Treasury note rate an amount equal to your initial wealth and you invest everything in portfolio S. You have twice your own money invested in S, but you have to *pay* interest on the loan. Therefore, your expected return is

$$r = (2 \times \text{expected return on S}) - (1 \times \text{interest rate}) = 25\%$$

And the standard deviation of your investment is

$$\sigma = (2 \times \text{standard deviation of S}) = 32\%$$

You can see from Figure 8.6 that when you lend a portion of your money, you end up part-way between $r_f$ and S; if you can borrow money at the risk-free rate, you can extend your possibilities beyond S. You can also see that regardless of the level of risk you choose, you can get the highest expected return by a mixture of portfolio S and borrowing or lending. There is no reason ever to hold, say, portfolio T.

This means that we can separate the investor's job into two stages. First, the 'best' portfolio of ordinary shares must be selected—S in our example.[7] Second, this portfolio must be blended with borrowing or lending to obtain an exposure to risk that suits the particular investor's taste. Therefore, each investor should put money into just two benchmark investments—a risky portfolio S and a risk-free loan (borrowing or lending).[8]

What does portfolio S look like? If you have better information than your rivals have, you will want the portfolio to include relatively large investments in the shares you think are undervalued. But in a competitive market you are unlikely to have a monopoly of good ideas. In that case there is no reason to hold a different portfolio of ordinary shares from anybody else. In other words, you might just as well hold the market portfolio. That is why many professional investors invest in a market-index portfolio and why many others hold well-diversified portfolios.[9]

---

[7]   Portfolio S is the point of tangency to the set of efficient portfolios. It offers the highest expected risk premium ($r - r_f$) per unit of standard deviation $\sigma$.

[8]   This *separation theorem* was first pointed out by J. Tobin in 'Liquidity Preference as Behaviour toward Risk, '*Review of Economic Studies*, **25**: 65–86 (February 1958).

[9]   While institutional shareholders, who are a dominant force in the Australian share market, generally hold well-diversified equity portfolios, the same is not true for individual investors. Surveys by the ASX suggest that about 80 per cent of individual share-holders have shares in less than six different companies. Transaction costs might be one factor inhibiting diversification, or it might be that many such investors already have diversified shareholdings through institutional investments such as their superannuation funds. Some investors may also be diversified across other classes of assets such as real estate and bank deposits.

# 8.2 The capital market line

If we make the assumptions listed below, then *all* investors will select the market portfolio as the portfolio of risky assets, and we can then determine how portfolios consisting of the market portfolio and the risk-free asset will be priced.

1.  Investors make investment decisions for one period only. The objective of these decisions is to maximise the utility of *expected* end-of-period wealth created by the investments. Investors' utility is increased by more expected wealth and reduced by more risk.
2.  The mean and variance of portfolio return are sufficient statistics for choosing a portfolio.
3.  Investors have homogeneous expectations. In other words, they all agree on the expected returns, variances and covariances for available assets, and therefore they all compute the same efficient set.
4.  There are no frictions preventing investors from investing in their desired portfolios. All assets are assumed infinitely divisible; there are no taxes and no transactions costs.
5.  Investors can borrow and lend at the risk-free rate.

Given these assumptions all investors agree what the best portfolio of risky assets is, and they all hold it since there are no frictions preventing them from doing so. Highly risk-averse investors only invest a small proportion of their wealth in the optimal portfolio of risky assets and they invest the rest in the risk-free asset. Other investors spread their wealth between the portfolio of risky assets and the risk-free asset according to their risk preferences. The result is that all investors hold portfolios that lie along the line extending through $r_f$ and S in Figure 8.6.

## Share portfolios and the market portfolio

For ease of explanation we talk about risk and diversification in terms of share portfolios. As a consequence we have viewed the share market as the source of the market portfolio. But the theory we are developing is broader than that. The market portfolio consists of all risky assets—not only shares in listed companies, but also shares in private companies, risky debt securities, real estate, commodities and other physical assets, and even human capital.[10] Thus, we should not restrict our analysis to the share portfolio S, but instead think about a broader portfolio M, where M is known as the market portfolio and is the optimal portfolio of risky assets held by all investors.

Suppose an asset, say BHP debentures, were not in portfolio M. If BHP debentures were not in the optimal portfolio there would be no demand for BHP debentures. The BHP debenture price would drop like a stone. As price falls, BHP debentures start to look more and more attractive and eventually they will be included in the optimal portfolio. This sort of process ensures that all assets are included in portfolio M.

According to the theory, each investor should diversify by holding a portfolio of risky assets that mimics the market portfolio. This means a risky portfolio containing all assets with weights in the portfolio that match the proportion of each asset in the total market portfolio. Thus, if houses represent 50 per cent of the wealth in the economy then houses should have a 50 per cent weight in each investor's risky portfolio.

In practice it is extremely difficult to obtain good data on the returns to assets other than shares in listed companies. Therefore, in the finance literature most examples, discussion and empirical work are based on share markets, and a share market index is usually taken to represent the market portfolio. The fact that this is common practice does not necessarily mean it is right. However, this is one of those cases where there is little choice but to go with the flow.

---

[10]   You will be pleased to learn, we hope, that reading this book is an investment in your own human capital.

# The price of risk

Having pointed out an important practical problem let us return to the theory. Imagine that we replace the label S in Figure 8.6 with the label M, for the market portfolio. The line extending through $r_f$ and M is known as the **capital market line**. This line provides us with an equation for pricing *efficient* portfolios.

Because they want the highest expected return for a given risk (standard deviation) no investor will hold other than the **mean variance efficient portfolios** which lie along the capital market line. The capital market line therefore delineates the efficient portfolio set for all investors and shows us how investors trade off risk for expected return. For example, they require a return $r_f$ when there is no risk, and when there is risk equal to the market risk $\sigma_m$ they require an additional risk premium of $r_m - r_f$. We can see that the intercept of the capital market line must be $r_f$, and we can work out the slope as

$$\text{Slope} = \frac{\text{rise}}{\text{run}} = \frac{r_m - r_f}{\sigma_m}$$

Therefore, the equation of the capital market line is

$$r_p = r_f + \frac{r_m - r_f}{\sigma_m}(\sigma_p)$$

where $\sigma_p$ is the standard deviation of an *efficient* portfolio and $r_p$ is its return.

We now have an equation that gives us the required return for *efficient portfolios* only exposed to market risk. Suppose we have such a portfolio with an expected value in one year's time of $100 000 and a standard deviation of returns of 15 per cent. In Chapter 7 we suggested that the share market risk premium $(r_m - r_f)$ was of the order of 8 per cent, and that the standard deviation of share market returns $(\sigma_m)$ was of the order of 20 per cent. This provides an estimate of the slope of the capital market line, sometimes called the **price of risk**, of 0.08/0.20, or 0.4 per cent. For each one per cent of extra market risk in a well-diversified portfolio investors demand 0.4 per cent of extra return. If we estimate the variance of the market to be 16 per cent rather than 20 per cent, then the price of risk goes up to 0.5 per cent. If the risk-free rate of return is 6 per cent and the price of risk is 0.4 per cent, then the required return on our portfolio is

$$r_p = 0.06 + 0.04 \times 0.15 = 0.12, \text{ or } 12\%$$

The value of the portfolio today is therefore $100 000/1.12 = $89 286

We can now price efficiently diversified portfolios only exposed to market risk. Our next task is to extend our analysis to pricing individual assets and any portfolio, efficient or not.

## 8.3 The security market line

We have established that the required return for an efficiently diversified portfolio depends on the standard deviation for the portfolio. As we saw in Chapter 7, the contribution of individual securities to the standard deviation of a diversified portfolio is measured by beta. We might suspect then that beta has a role to play in determining the required returns for individual securities. Proving the relationship is quite difficult,[11] so we start with an intuitive explanation.

In Figure 8.7 we have plotted the risk and expected return from the risk-free asset and the market portfolio. You can see that the risk-free asset has a beta of 0 and a risk premium of 0. The market portfolio has a beta of 1.0 and a risk premium of $r_m - r_f$. This gives us two benchmarks for the expected risk premium. But what is the expected risk premium when beta is not 0 or 1?

---

11   Building on the foundation of Markowitz's work on diversification it took about 12 years to develop the concept of beta and an equation for pricing individual securities. The significance of this breakthrough was recognised with the award of Nobel prizes nearly two decades later.

**figure 8.7**

The capital asset pricing model stated that the expected risk premium on each investment is proportional to its beta. This means that each investment should lie on the sloping security market line connecting Treasury notes and the market portfolio.

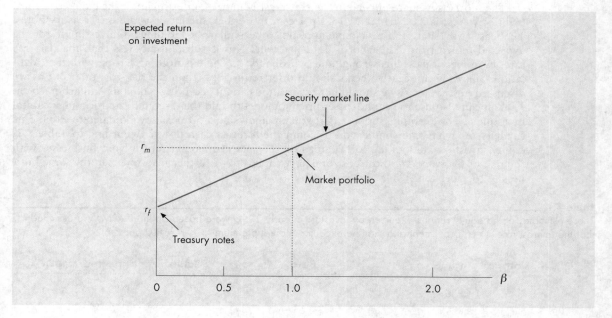

In the mid-1960s three economists—William Sharpe, John Lintner and Jack Treynor—produced an answer to this question.[12] Their answer is known as the **capital asset pricing model (CAPM)**. The model's message is surprisingly simple. In a competitive market the expected risk premium varies in direct proportion to beta. This means that in Figure 8.7 all investments must plot along the sloping line, known as the **security market line**. The expected risk premium on an investment with a beta of 0.5 is therefore *half* the expected risk premium on the market; and the expected risk premium on an investment with a beta of 2.0 is *twice* the expected risk premium on the market. We can write this relationship as:

Expected risk premium on share = beta × expected risk premium on market

$$r - r_f = \beta(r_m - r_f)$$

## Some estimates of expected returns

Before we tell you where this formula comes from, let us use it to figure out what returns investors are looking for from particular shares. To do this, we need three numbers: $r_f$, $r_m - r_f$ and $\beta$. In early 1996 the interest rate on Treasury notes was about 6 per cent.[13] From

---

12   See W. F. Sharpe, 'Capital Asset Prices: A Theory of Market Equilibrium under Conditions of Risk', *Journal of Finance*, **19**: 425–42 (September 1964); J. Lintner, 'The Valuation of Risk Assets and the Selection of Risky Investments in Share Portfolios and Capital Budgets', *Review of Economics and Statistics*, **47**: 13–37 (February 1965). Treynor's 1961 article has not been published.

13   We could equally well have used the government bond rate. The difficulty we face here is attempting to use a single-period model in a multi-period setting. Treasury notes are the closest thing that we have to a risk-free security, but they have a short life. A long-dated government bond may therefore be a better benchmark for shares which have a perpetual life. Given that we used the Treasury note rate in this case, history suggests that perhaps a higher risk premium should be used. On the other hand, some would argue that 8 per cent is too high. This may be confusing for the novice. However, it is important not to gloss over these issues—they make finance challenging and rewarding.

past evidence we would judge that $r_m - r_f$ is about 8 per cent. Finally, in Table 7.4 we gave you estimates of the ordinary least squares (OLS) betas of several shares as estimated by the AGSM risk measurement service. In Table 8.1 we have selected some of these shares and put the numbers together to give an estimate of the expected return on each share.

The *most* risky share appears to be Newcrest Mining. Our estimate of the expected return from Newcrest is 21.2 per cent, 15.2 per cent more than the interest rate on Treasury notes. The least risky share in our sample appears to be Nullarbor Holdings. Our estimate for the expected return from Nullarbor is 1.12 per cent. This is substantially less than the risk-free rate. Intuitively this seems wrong, and it probably is. There is nothing wrong with the calculation. Shares with negative betas should offer returns less than the risk-free rate. But as we discussed in Chapter 7, we should be very cautious about accepting −0.61 as Nullarbor's beta.

You can also use the capital asset pricing model to find the discount rate for a new capital investment. For example, suppose that you are analysing a proposal by Comalco to expand its capacity. At what rate should you discount the forecast cash flows? According to Table 8.1, equity investors are looking for a return of 16.7 per cent equity return from businesses with the risk of Comalco.[14] So the cost of equity capital for a further investment in the same business is 16.7 per cent.[15]

**table 8.1** _____

These estimates of the equity returns *expected* by investors in early 1996 were based on the CAPM. We assumed that the interest rate $r_f = 6.0$ per cent and that the expected market premium $r_m - r_f = 8.0$ per cent.

| Company name | Beta | Equilibrium expected return |
|---|---|---|
| Newcrest Mining | 1.89 | 21.12 |
| Nullarbor Holdings | −0.61 | 1.12 |
| Capral Aluminium | 1.30 | 16.40 |
| Comalco Ltd | 1.34 | 16.72 |
| George Weston | 0.57 | 10.56 |
| Arnotts Limited | 0.33 | 8.64 |
| News Corporation | 0.97 | 13.76 |
| John Fairfax | 1.53 | 18.24 |

In practice choosing a discount rate is seldom so easy. (After all, you cannot expect to be paid a fat salary just for plugging numbers into a formula.) For example, you must learn how to adjust for the extra risk caused by company borrowing and how to estimate the discount rate for projects that do not have the same risk as the company's existing business. There are also tax issues. But these refinements can wait until later.[16]

_____

[14] Strictly speaking, this rate reflects both the business risk and the risk created by the company's use of debt. To get the rate for business risk alone we have to 'unlever' the equity beta and then use the unlevered beta to calculate the required return from the CAPM.

[15] Remember that instead of investing in plant and machinery, the firm could return the money to the shareholders. The opportunity cost of investing is the return that shareholders could expect to earn by buying financial assets. This expected return depends on the market risk of the assets.

[16] Tax issues arise because a corporation must pay tax on income from an investment in Treasury notes or other interest-paying securities. It turns out that the correct discount rate for risk-free investments is the after-tax Treasury note rate. We come back to this point in Chapters 19 and 26. Various other points on the practical use of betas and the capital asset pricing model are covered in Chapter 9.

# A summary of the capital asset pricing model

Let us review four basic principles of portfolio selection:

**1.** Investors like high expected return and low standard deviation. Ordinary share portfolios that offer the highest expected return for a given standard deviation are known as *efficient portfolios*.

**2.** If you want to know the marginal impact of a share on the risk of a portfolio, you must look not at the risk of that share in isolation, but at its contribution to the portfolio risk. That contribution depends on the share's sensitivity to changes in the value of the portfolio.

**3.** A share's sensitivity to changes in the value of the *market* portfolio is known as *beta*. Beta therefore measures the marginal contribution of a share to the risk of the market portfolio.

**4.** If investors can borrow and lend at the risk-free rate of interest then they should always hold a mixture of the risk-free investment and one particular ordinary share portfolio. The composition of this share portfolio depends only on investors' assessment of the prospects for each share and not on their attitude to risk. If they have no superior information, investors should hold the same share portfolio as everybody else—in other words, they should hold the market portfolio.

Now if everyone holds the market portfolio, and if beta measures each security's contribution to the market portfolio risk, then it is no surprise that the risk premium demanded by investors is proportional to beta.

Risk premiums always reflect the contribution to portfolio risk. Suppose you are constructing a portfolio. Some shares will add to the risk of the portfolio and so you will buy them only if they also increase the expected return. Other shares will reduce portfolio risk and you may therefore be prepared to buy them even if they also reduce the portfolio's expected return. If the portfolio you have chosen is efficient, each of your investments must be working equally hard for you. So if one share has a greater marginal effect on portfolio risk than another share, it must also have proportionately greater expected return. This means that if you plot each share's expected return against its marginal contribution to the risk of your efficient portfolio, you will find that the shares lie along a straight line, as in Figure 8.8. This is

**figure 8.8** _____

If a portfolio is efficient, each share should lie along a straight line linking the share's expected return with its marginal contribution to the portfolio's risk.

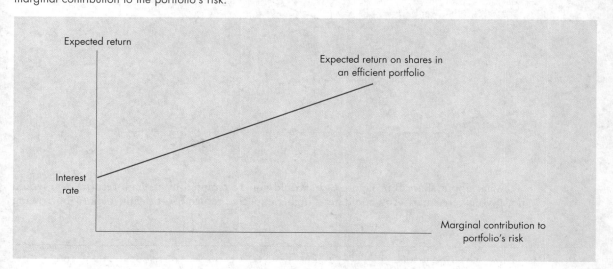

*always* the case: If a portfolio is efficient, there *must* be a straight-line relationship between each share's expected return and its marginal contribution to portfolio risk. The converse is also true: if there is not a straight-line relationship, the portfolio is not efficient.

Now you can see that Figures 8.7 and 8.8 are identical *if* the efficient portfolio in Figure 8.8 is the market portfolio. (Remember that the beta of a share measures its marginal contribution to the risk of the market portfolio.) So the capital asset pricing model boils down to the statement that the market portfolio is efficient. As we have already seen, this will be so if each investor has the same information and faces the same opportunities as everyone else. In these circumstances, each investor should hold the same portfolio as everyone else—in other words, each should hold the market portfolio.

## What would happen if a share did *not* lie on the security market line?

Imagine that you encounter share A in Figure 8.9. Would you buy it? We hope not[17]—if you want an investment with a beta of 0.5, you could get a higher expected return by investing half your money in Treasury notes and half in the market portfolio. If everybody shares your view of the share's prospects, the price of A will have to fall until the expected return matches what you could get elsewhere.

**figure 8.9**

In equilibrium no share can lie below the security market line. For example, instead of buying share A, investors would prefer to lend part of their money and put the balance in the market portfolio. And instead of buying share B, they would prefer to borrow and invest in the market portfolio.

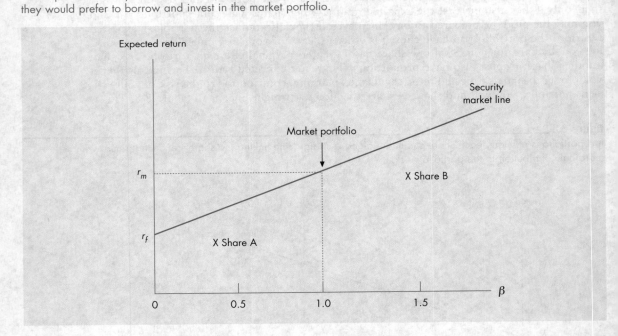

What about share B in Figure 8.9? Would you be tempted by its high return? You would not if you were smart. You could get a higher expected return for the same beta by borrowing

---

[17]   Unless, of course, we were trying to sell it.

50 cents for every dollar of your own money and investing in the market portfolio. Again, if everybody agrees with your assessment, the price of share B cannot hold. It will have to fall until the expected return on B is equal to the expected return on the combination of borrowing and investment in the market portfolio.

We have made our point. An investor can always obtain an expected risk premium of $\beta(r_m - r_f)$ by holding a mixture of the market portfolio and a risk-free loan. So in well-functioning markets nobody will hold a share that offers an expected risk premium of *less* than $\beta(r_m - r_f)$. But what about the other possibility? Are there shares that offer a higher expected risk premium? In other words, are there any that lie above the security market line in Figure 8.9? If we take all shares together, we have the market portfolio. Therefore, we know that shares *on average* lie on the line. Since none lies *below* the line, then there also cannot be any that lie *above* the line.[18] Thus, each and every share must lie on the security market line and offer an expected risk premium of:

$$r - r_f = \beta(r_m - r_f)$$

# A proof of the capital asset pricing model

Suppose you currently hold an efficient portfolio. From the capital market line we know that the efficient portfolio you should hold consists of the market portfolio plus borrowing, or lending, at the risk-free rate. Suppose you hold such a portfolio and you are prepared to make a tiny proportional increase $\delta$ in your investment, which you will finance by borrowing at the risk-free rate. You are deciding whether it would be better to increase your investment by buying more of the market portfolio or more shares of BHP.

If you buy more of the market portfolio your return will increase by $\delta r_m - \delta r_f$. If you buy more of BHP your return will increase by $\delta r_{BHP} - \delta r_f$. You do not get your increase in return for nothing—risk will also increase. We showed you in Chapter 7 that the contribution of an investment to the risk of a portfolio was given by the beta of the investment multiplied by the standard deviation of the market multiplied by the proportion of your portfolio invested in the asset. By definition the beta of the risk-free asset is zero so it drops out of our calculations. We only have to worry about the betas of BHP and the market. For the investment in the market the standard deviation of your portfolio will increase by $\delta(\beta_m \sigma_m) = \delta \sigma_m$, (remember $\beta_m = 1$). If instead you invest in BHP, the increase in your portfolio standard deviation will be $\delta(\beta_{BHP} \sigma_m)$.[19]

Which is the better deal depends on the trade-off between extra return and extra risk. Now suppose BHP offers the better deal. This means that BHP offers a higher return per unit of risk. Then you and other astute investors like you will start buying BHP and push the price up. As a consequence the extra return from BHP comes down. The now familiar result is that in equilibrium the marginal risk-return trade-off for an investment in BHP must be the same as for an investment in the market portfolio. Both must offer the same return per unit of risk, thus:

$$\frac{\delta r_m - \delta r_f}{\delta \sigma_m} = \delta r_{BHP} - \frac{\delta r_f}{\delta(\beta_{BHP}\sigma_m)}$$

re-arranging and simplifying gives

$$r_{BHP} - r_f = \beta_{BHP}(r_m - r_f)$$

---

[18] Suppose you did find such a share: it offers more return than is necessary to compensate for its risk. So you and other astute investors would rush to buy it. The sudden growth in demand would push its price up and return would fall.

[19] Strictly speaking, your investment in BHP will also add some unsystematic risk to your portfolio. However, we started from the assumption that you were already well-diversified, and for the purpose of our argument we can make $\delta$ so small that the effect of the unsystematic risk on your portfolio is negligible. Given these conditions the unsystematic risk can safely be ignored.

or

$$r_{BHP} = r_f + \beta_{BHP}(r_m - r_f)$$

The logic we applied to BHP could be applied to other assets and therefore the formula we have derived is a general model for determining the required return on any asset. Note that the equation for the security market line can be used to price *both* individual assets and portfolios. In contrast, the capital market line can only be used to price efficient portfolios.

## 8.4 Validity and role of the capital asset pricing model

Any economic model is a simplified statement of reality. We need to simplify in order to interpret what is going on around us. But we also need to know how much faith we can place in our model.

Let us begin with some matters about which there is broad agreement. First, few people quarrel with the idea that investors require some extra return for taking on risk. That is why ordinary shares have given on average a higher return than Australian government securities. Who would want to invest in risky shares if they offered only the *same* expected return as Treasury notes or government bonds? We would not, and we suspect you would not either.

Second, investors appear to be concerned principally with those risks that they cannot eliminate by diversification. If this were not so, we should find that share prices increase whenever two companies merge to spread their risks. And we should find that investment companies that invest in the shares of other firms are more highly valued than the shares they hold. But we do not observe either phenomenon. Mergers undertaken just to spread risk do not increase share prices, and investment funds are no more highly valued than the shares they hold.[20]

The capital asset pricing model captures these ideas in a simple way and in so doing provides a quantitative measure of risk. That is why many financial managers find it the most convenient tool for coming to grips with the slippery notion of risk. In the investment fund industry there has been extensive use of beta as a tool in portfolio management and this affects the investment of hundreds of billions of dollars worldwide. Application of the capital asset pricing model to investment in real assets is less common, particularly in Australia. This is because beta estimation for real assets is much more difficult than it is for securities.

The simplicity and elegance of the capital asset pricing model is why economists often use the capital asset pricing model to demonstrate important ideas in finance, even when there are other ways to prove these ideas. But that does not mean that the capital asset pricing model is ultimate truth. We will see later that it has several unsatisfactory features, and we will look at some alternative theories. Nobody knows whether one of these alternative theories is eventually going to come out on top or whether there are other, better models of risk and return that have not yet seen the light of day.

### Tests of the capital asset pricing model

The ultimate test of any model is whether it fits the facts. The prediction of the capital asset pricing model is that in equilibrium securities will be priced such that their *expected* returns plot along the security market line. This is so because the security market line gives the

---

20    In fact, closed-end investment funds have often appeared to have sold at a discount to the value of the shares they hold. This is something that has puzzled financial economists, but perhaps it is because these funds have hidden liabilities, such as unrealised capital gains taxes. In contrast, open-ended investment funds such as unit trusts sell at the value of the shares in the fund, with minor adjustments for management fees.

required returns and in equilibrium expected and required returns are equal. Unfortunately, there are two problems in testing whether expected returns do plot along the security market line. First, we cannot observe the return that investors *expected*; we can only observe the returns they actually got—the *realised* return. The nature of risk is that we do not necessarily get what we expect. Share returns reflect expectations, but they also embody lots of 'noise'— the steady flow of surprises that gives many shares standard deviations of 30 or 40 per cent or more per year. Second, the market portfolio should comprise all risky investments, including shares, bonds, commodities, real estate—even human capital. Most market indexes contain only a sample of ordinary shares.

What most studies have actually done is examine the realised returns on shares and measure the betas of those shares relative to some share market index. The research usually boils down to answering the following questions:

1. Do the *realised* returns on individual shares vary systematically with the market? In particular, can the variation in a share's returns over time be explained in terms of a systematic linear relationship with the return on the market?
2. Do the *realised* returns on individual shares vary such that on average[21] higher beta shares have higher returns? In other words, is the cross-sectional variation in returns explained by cross-sectional variation in beta?
3. Do variables other than beta help explain realised returns?

Definitive answers to these questions have proved elusive, but the answer to the first question appears to be yes. However, this is not compelling evidence in favour of the CAPM. It reflects the fact that most shares tend to move with the market over time. We should also note that for many shares the relationship is quite weak, and it also appears that company betas change over time.

Attempts to answer the second question have provided a mixed bag. It appears that beta does a reasonable job of explaining cross-sectional differences in return in some periods, but a poor job in other periods. However, such tests tend to suggest that the intercept of the security market line is typically higher than the risk-free rate and that the slope is flatter than the theory predicts.

The answer to the third question is yes. Later in the chapter we discuss results which show that the average return on small-firm shares has been substantially larger than predicted by the capital asset pricing model.[22] This is a problem because the capital asset pricing model predicts that beta is the *only* reason that expected returns differ. We defer discussion of this problem until later in the chapter.

## What is being tested?

The early tests were generally supportive of the capital asset pricing model. In Australia, for example, a study in 1976 by Ray Ball, Philip Brown and Bob Officer found evidence that returns on industrial shares were related to beta in a way that was consistent with the CAPM.[23] However, about that date testing halted and then changed direction in response to Richard Roll's critique that the capital asset pricing model had not really been tested and was never likely to be.[24] Roll argued that a proper test requires the use of the proper market

---

21   We consider returns on average because when the market is falling *realised returns* on high beta shares will be less than on low beta shares.

22   In the United States small-firm shares have higher betas, but the difference in betas does not appear to be nearly sufficient to explain the difference in returns. In Australia thin trading makes it virtually impossible to estimate reliable betas for shares in small public companies.

23   See R. Ball, P. Brown and R. Officer, 'Asset Pricing in the Australian Industrial Equity Market,' *Australian Journal of Management*, 1: 1–32 (April 1976).

24   See R. Roll, 'A Critique of the Asset Pricing Theory's Tests; Part 1: On Past and Potential Testability of the Theory', *Journal of Financial Economics*, 4: 129–76 (March 1977).

portfolio, not just some proxy like a share market index. This is unfortunate, because it is not practical to observe the market portfolio for all assets.

Roll's critique, however, is deeper than this. He points out that deriving the capital market line and security market line (CAPM) depends on the efficiency of the market portfolio. Once you have an efficient market portfolio the security market line automatically follows as a direct consequence of the portfolio mathematics. Thus, the theory only depends upon whether the market portfolio is efficient. If it is, and the betas are measured relative to it, then there will automatically be a perfect linear relationship between the return on assets in the market portfolio and the betas of those assets. In fact, for *any portfolio on the efficient set* there will be a perfect linear relationship between return and beta, if beta is measured relative to that efficient portfolio. So, if you select some index as a proxy for the market portfolio and find that there is a perfect linear relationship between returns and your measurement of beta, all you have demonstrated is that the index lies on the efficient set.[25] To test the capital asset pricing model you need to test whether the market portfolio for all assets is on the efficient set.

There have been tests of the efficiency of share market indices. Efficient portfolios offer the highest *expected* return for their risk. That does not mean that they will always *with hindsight* provide the highest *realised* return, but at least we can see whether any shortfall could have been due simply to bad luck. It turns out that the standard share market indices were *not* efficient portfolios, but we do not know whether a more comprehensive market index would have performed better.[26]

## Recent evidence

Despite the assault by Roll, tests of the CAPM eventually revived. But some of the authors whose original works supported the CAPM now changed sides. Notable among these was Eugene Fama who, in an influential paper with Ken French, claimed to show that equity beta had almost no real power to explain equity returns.[27] Fama and French do not dispute that share returns vary systematically with the market movements over time, but they argue that the share betas which describe this relationship do not explain the differences in returns *between* shares. According to their results a strategy of investing in high beta shares has little prospect of earning higher returns than a strategy of investing in low beta shares.

Thus, beta as a risk measure and the capital asset pricing model are under attack. It will be interesting to see if they survive.[28] However, as we discuss shortly, the basic elements of the theory have proved remarkably robust when researchers have investigated the consequences of relaxing the standard CAPM assumptions. The CAPM also seems to do better in empirical studies when we consider longer histories of share returns.

## 8.5 The evidence of history

All this is probably leaving you feeling tired and thirsty, so let us adjourn to a Wall Street bar and let us also go back in time over 60 years.[29]

---

25  Since you have to use realised returns for your test, what you demonstrate is that the portfolio is *ex-post* efficient.

26  See, for example,. S. Kandel and R. F. Stambaugh, 'On Correlations and Inferences about Mean-Variance Efficiency', *Journal of Financial Economics*, **18**: 61–90 (March 1987).

27  See E. Fama and K. French, 'The Cross-Section of Expected Share Returns', *Journal of Finance*, **47**: 427–65 (1992).

28  Of course, not everyone agrees with Fama and French. S. Kothari, J. Shanken and R. Sloan in 'Another Look at the Cross-Section of Expected Share Returns', *Journal of Finance*, **50**: 185–224 (1995) are highly critical of the Fama and French study; criticism which Fama and French attempt to rebut in 'The CAPM is Wanted, Dead or Alive', *Journal of Finance*, **51**: 1947–58 (1996). We should note that Fama and French now agree that the market factor makes some contribution to explaining returns. But they argue that three factors—a market factor, a market to book factor and a size factor—explain returns. It is the significance of these later two factors that is inconsistent with the CAPM. See, for example, E. F. Fama and K. R. French, 'Common Risk Factors in the Returns on Stocks and Bonds', *Journal of Financial Economics*, **33**: 3–56 (February 1993).

29  We would like to have made this the famous Marble Bar at the Sydney Hilton. Unfortunately, we do not have the Australian data to go back 60 years.

Imagine that, in 1931, 10 investors gathered together in a Wall Street bar to discuss their portfolios. Each agreed to follow a different investment strategy. Investor 1 opted to buy the 10 per cent of New York Stock Exchange shares with the lowest estimated betas. Investor 2 chose the 10 per cent with the next lowest betas, and so on, up to Investor 10, who agreed to buy the shares with the highest betas. They also undertook that at the end of every year they would re-estimate the betas of all NYSE shares and reconstitute their portfolios.[30] Finally, they promised that they would return 60 years later to compare results, and so parted with much cordiality and good wishes.

In 1991 the same 10 investors, now much older and wealthier, met again in the same bar. Figure 8.10 shows how they had fared. Investor 1's portfolio turned out to be much less risky than the market: its beta was only 0.49. However, Investor 1 also realised the lowest return, 9 per cent above the risk-free rate of interest. At the other extreme, the beta of Investor 10's portfolio was 1.52, about three times that of Investor 1. But investor 10 was rewarded with the highest return, averaging 17 per cent a year above the interest rate. So over this 60-year period returns did indeed increase with beta.

As you can see from Figure 8.10, the market portfolio over the same 60-year period provided an average return of 14 per cent above the interest rate[31] and (of course) had a beta of

## figure 8.10

The capital asset pricing model states that the expected risk premium from any investment should lie on the market line. The dots show the actual average risk premiums from portfolios with different betas. The high-beta portfolios generated higher average returns, just as predicted by the CAPM. But the high-beta portfolios plotted below the market line and four of the five low-beta portfolios plotted above. A line fitted to the 10 portfolio returns would be 'flatter' than the market line.

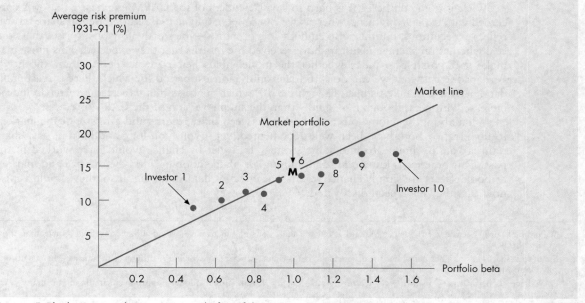

*Source*: F. Black, 'Beta and Return', *Journal of Portfolio Management*, **20**: 8–18 (Fall 1993). Reprinted with permission of Institutional Investor, Inc.

---

[30]  Betas were estimated using returns over the previous 60 months.

[31]  In Figure 8.10 the shares in the 'market portfolio' are weighted equally. Since the shares of small firms have provided higher average returns than those of large firms, the risk premium on an equally-weighted index is higher than on a value-weighted index. This accounts for the difference between the 14 per cent market risk premium in Figure 8.10 and the 8.4 per cent premium reported in Table 7.1.

1.0. The CAPM predicts that the risk premium should increase in proportion to beta, so that the returns of each portfolio should lie on the upward-sloping security market line in Figure 8.10. Since the market provided a risk premium of 14 per cent, Investor 1's portfolio, with a beta of 0.49, should have provided a risk premium of a shade under 7 per cent and Investor 10's portfolio, with a beta of 1.52, should have given a premium of a shade over 21 per cent. You can see that, while high-beta shares performed better than low-beta shares, the difference was not as great as the CAPM predicts.

Figure 8.10 provides broad support for the CAPM, though it suggests that the line relating return to beta has been 'too flat'. But the model has come under fire on two fronts. First, the slope of the line has been particularly flat in recent years. For example, Figure 8.11 shows how our 10 investors fared between 1966 and 1991. Now it is less clear who is buying the drinks: the portfolios of Investors 1 and 10 had very different betas but both earned the same average return over these 25 years. Of course, the line was correspondingly steeper before 1966. This is also shown in Figure 8.11.

Critics of the CAPM also point out that, while return has not risen with beta in recent years, it has been related to other measures. For example, Figure 8.12 shows that from 1963 to 1990 small-company shares performed substantially better than large-company shares,[32] and shares with low ratios of market-to-book value performed much better than shares with a high ratio of market-to-book.[33] Possibly, small companies and companies with low market-to-book ratios were exposed to risks not captured in the CAPM; this could account for their higher returns.

But the CAPM predicts that beta is the *only* reason that expected returns differ. If investors *expected* the returns to depend on firm size or market-to-book ratio, then the simple version of the CAPM cannot be the whole truth. Such findings have prompted headlines like 'Is Beta Dead?' in the business press.[34]

What is going on here? It is hard to say. Defenders of the CAPM emphasise that it is concerned with *expected* returns, whereas we can observe only *actual* returns. Actual share returns reflect expectations, but they also embody lots of 'noise'—the steady flow of surprises that conceal whether on average investors have received the returns that they expected. This noise may make it impossible to judge whether the model holds better in one period than another.[35] Perhaps the best that we can do is to focus on the longest period for which there is reasonable data. This would take us back to Figure 8.10, which suggests that expected returns do indeed increase with beta, though less rapidly than the simple version of the CAPM predicts.[36]

What about the anomalous relationship between share returns and firm size or the market-to-book ratio? Both have been well-documented, yet if you look long and hard at past share returns you are bound to find some strategy that just by chance would have worked in the past. This practice is known as 'data mining' or 'data snooping'. Maybe the size and market-to-book effects are simply chance results, the effect of data snooping. If so, they should vanish now that they have been discovered.[37]

---

[32]  We pointed out in Section 7.1 that since the mid-1960s the shares of small firms have provided higher average returns than those of large firms.

[33]  Small-firm shares have higher betas, but the difference in betas is not sufficient to explain the difference in returns. There is no simple relationship between market-to-book ratios and beta.

[34]  A. Wallace, 'Is Beta Dead?', *Institutional Investor*, 14: 22–30 (July 1980). Similar obituaries have been circulating for many years. Perhaps this is to the CAPM's credit: only a strong theory can survive several funerals.

[35]  A second problem with testing the model that we have mentioned earlier is that the market portfolio should contain all risky investments, including shares, bonds, commodities, real estate—even human capital. Most market indexes contain only a sample of ordinary shares. See R. Roll, 'A Critique of the Asset Pricing Theory's Tests; Part 1: On Past and Potential Testability of the Theory', *Journal of Financial Economics*, 4: 129–76 (March 1977).

[36]  We say 'simple version' because Fischer Black has shown that, if there are borrowing restrictions, there should still exist a positive relationship between expected return and beta, but the security market line would be less steep as a result. See F. Black, 'Capital Market Equilibrium with Restricted Borrowing', *Journal of Business*, 45: 444–55 (July 1972).

[37]  For example, there is some evidence that the size effect has become less important since Rolf Banz first discovered it in 1981. See R. Banz, 'The Relationship Between Return and Market Values of Common Stock,' *Journal of Financial Economics*, 9: 3–18 (1981).

**figure 8.11**

The relationship between beta and actual average return has been much weaker since the mid-1960s.

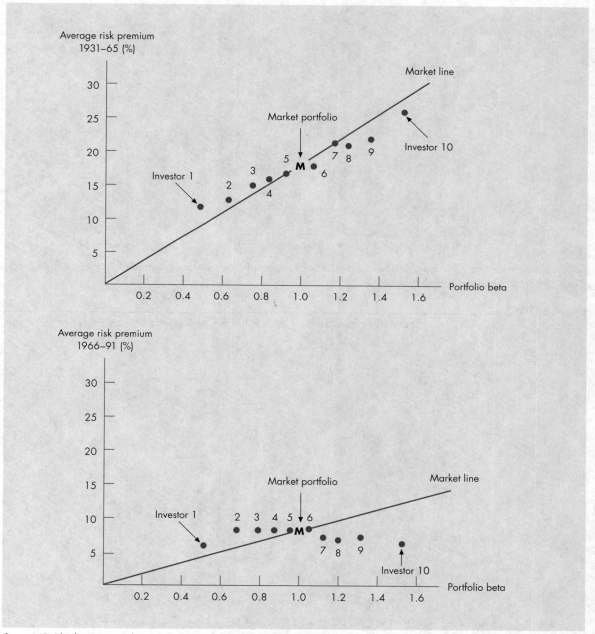

*Source*: F. Black, 'Beta and Return', *Journal of Portfolio Management*, **20**: 8–18 (Fall 1993). Reprinted with permission of Institutional Investor, Inc.

One thing is sure: it will be very hard to reject the CAPM beyond all reasonable doubt. Data and statistics will probably not give final answers soon, so the plausibility of the CAPM *theory* will have to be weighed along with the 'facts'.

**figure 8.12(a)**

Since the mid-1960s shares of small companies have done systematically better than shares of large companies.

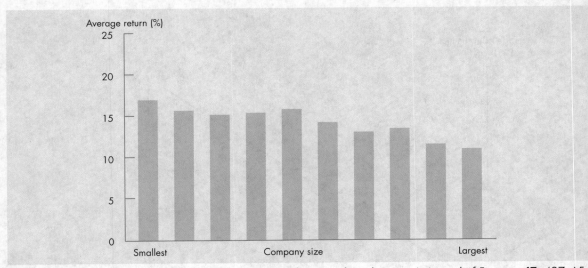

*Source*: E. F. Fama and K. R. French, 'The Cross-Section of Expected Stock Returns', *Journal of Finance*, **47**: 427–65 (June 1992). © Blackwell Publishers.

**figure 8.12(b)**

Shares with low ratios of price to book value per share have done better than shares with high price to book ratios.

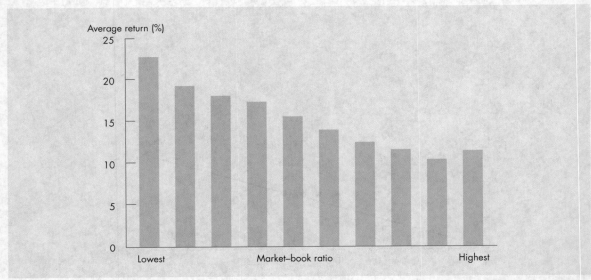

*Source*: E. F. Fama and K. R. French, 'The Cross-Section of Expected Stock Returns', *Journal of Finance*, **47**: 427–65 (June 1992). © Blackwell Publishers.

## 8.6  Relaxing the assumptions

Earlier in the chapter we listed the assumptions that are required to derive the capital market line, which in turn underpins the capital asset pricing model. For example, we assumed there was a risk-free investment. Usually we take this to be Treasury notes or government bonds. However, the return is not certain if we sell these securities before they mature. Even if we hold government securities to maturity, uncertainty about inflation means that the real rate of return is uncertain.[38] We also assumed that you could borrow and lend at the risk-free rate. Usually, your borrowing rate is higher than your lending rate.[39]

It turns out that many of the assumptions are not crucial, and with a little pushing and pulling it is possible to modify the CAPM to handle variation in the assumptions. The really important idea is that investors are content to invest their money in a limited number of benchmark port-folios. (In the basic CAPM these benchmarks are Treasury notes and the market portfolio.)

In these modified CAPMs expected return still depends on market risk, but the definition of market risk depends on the nature of the benchmark portfolios.[40] In practice none of these alternative CAPMs is as widely used as the standard version.

Remember, however, when you use the standard version that there can be problems. The model is a single-period model, but you are likely to be using it in a multi-period setting. Furthermore, the mean and variance of returns may not be sufficient statistics for portfolio choice. Taxes and transactions costs assumed away in the model do affect investment decisions in reality. Investors may also have divergent expectations about returns. It would be bad news for stockbrokers if investors were all in agreement about expected returns. If this were the case the volume of trading would be much lower. In the next section we examine alternatives to the standard CAPM which incorporate the impact of some of these factors.

# *8.7 Some alternative theories

## Consumption betas versus market betas

The CAPM pictures investors as solely concerned with the level and uncertainty of their future wealth. But for most people wealth is not an end in itself. What good is wealth if you cannot spend it? People invest now to provide future consumption for themselves or for their families and heirs. The most important risks are those which might force a cutback of future consumption.

Douglas Breeden has developed a model in which a security's risk is measured by its sensitivity to changes in investors' consumption.[41] If he is right, a share's expected return should move in line with its *consumption beta* rather than its market beta. Figure 8.13 summarises the chief differences between the standard and consumption CAPMs. In the standard model investors are concerned exclusively with the amount and uncertainty of their future wealth. Each investor's wealth ends up perfectly correlated with the return on the market portfolio; the demand for shares and other risky assets is thus determined by their market risk. The deeper motive for investing—to provide for consumption—is outside the model.

In the consumption CAPM uncertainty about share returns is connected directly to uncertainty about consumption. Of course, consumption depends on wealth (portfolio value), but wealth does not appear explicitly in the model. The consumption CAPM has several appealing features. For example, you do not have to identify the market or any other benchmark portfolio. You do not have to worry that the All Ordinaries Index does not track returns on bonds, commodities and real estate. Another appealing feature of the consumption CAPM is that it is a multi-period model.

---

38  Unless, of course, you hold an index-linked bond.

39  Unless you are in the fortunate position of being a bank.

40  For example, see M. C. Jensen (ed.), *Studies in the Theory of Capital Markets*, Frederick A. Praeger, Inc., New York, 1972. In the introduction Jensen provides a very useful summary of some of these variations on the CAPM. N. Sinclair also provides a good summary in 'Multifactor Asset Pricing Models', *Accounting and Finance*, 27: 17–36 (1987).

41  D. T. Breeden, 'An Intertemporal Asset Pricing Model with Stochastic Consumption and Investment Opportunities', *Journal of Financial Economics*, 7: 265–96 (September 1979).

**figure 8.13**

(a) The standard CAPM concentrates on how shares contribute to the level and uncertainty of investors' wealth. Consumption is outside the model (b) The consumption CAPM defines risk as a share's contribution to uncertainty about consumption. Wealth (the intermediate step between share returns and consumption) drops out of the model.

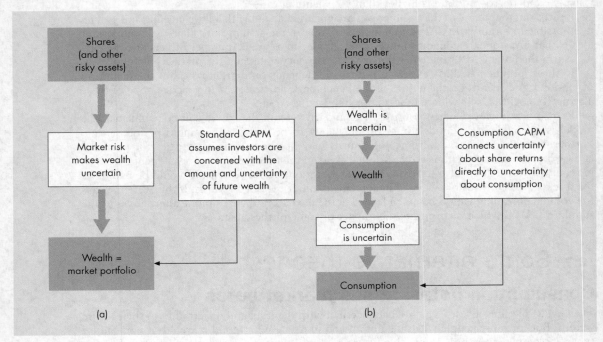

However, you do have to be able to measure consumption. *Quick:* How much did you consume last month? Perhaps it was easy to count the hamburgers and movie tickets, but what about the depreciation on your car or washing machine, or the daily cost of your home insurance policy? We suspect that your estimate of total consumption will rest on rough or arbitrary allocations and assumptions. And if it is hard for you to put a dollar value on your total consumption, think of the task facing a government statistician asked to estimate month-by-month consumption for all of us.

Compared to share prices, estimated aggregate consumption changes smoothly and gradually over time. Changes in consumption often seem to be out of phase with the share market. Individual shares seem to have low or erratic consumption betas. Moreover, the volatility of consumption appears too low to explain the past average rates of return on ordinary shares unless one assumes unreasonably high investor risk aversion.[42] These problems may reflect our poor measures of consumption or perhaps poor models of how individuals distribute consumption over time. In empirical testing, consumption-based asset pricing models seem to perform worse than the standard CAPM. It therefore seems too early for the consumption CAPM to see practical use.

## Arbitrage pricing theory

The capital asset pricing theory begins with an analysis of how investors construct efficient portfolios. Steven Ross's **arbitrage pricing theory (APT)** comes from a different family entirely.

42    See R. Mehra and E. C. Prescott, 'The Equity Risk Premium: A Puzzle', *Journal of Monetary Economics*, **15**: 145–61 (1985).

It does not ask which portfolios are efficient. Instead, it starts by *assuming* that each share's return depends partly on pervasive macroeconomic influences or 'factors' and partly on 'noise'—events that are unique to that company. Moreover, the return is assumed to obey the following simple relationship:

$$\text{Return} = a + b_1(r_{\text{factor 1}}) + b_2(r_{\text{factor 2}}) + b_3(r_{\text{factor 3}}) + \ldots + \text{noise}$$

The theory does not say what the factors are: there could be an oil price factor, an interest rate factor, and so on. The return on the market portfolio *might* serve as one factor, but then again it might not.

Some shares will be more sensitive to a particular factor than other shares. Westpac would be more sensitive to an interest rate factor than say Woolworths. If factor 1 picks up unexpected changes in interest rates, $b_1$ will be higher for Westpac.

For any individual share there are two sources of risk. First, there is the risk that stems from the pervasive macroeconomic factors that cannot be eliminated by diversification. Second, there is the risk arising from possible events that are unique to the company. Diversification *does* eliminate unique risk, and diversified investors can therefore ignore it when deciding whether to buy or sell a share. The expected risk premium on a share is affected by 'factor' or 'macroeconomic' risk; it is *not* affected by unique risk.

Arbitrage pricing theory states that the expected risk premium on a share should depend on the expected risk premium associated with each factor and the share's sensitivity to each of the factors ($b_1$, $b_2$, $b_3$, etc). Thus the formula is[43]

$$\text{Expected risk premium on investment} = r - r_f = b_1(r_{\text{factor 1}} - r_f) + b_2(r_{\text{factor 2}} - r_f) + \ldots$$

Notice that this formula makes two statements:

**1.** If you plug in a value of zero for each of the $b$s in the formula, the expected risk premium is zero. A diversified portfolio that is constructed to have zero sensitivity to each macroeconomic factor is essentially risk-free and therefore must be priced to offer the risk-free rate of interest. If the portfolio offered a higher return, you could make a risk-free (or 'arbitrage') profit by borrowing to buy the portfolio. If it offered a lower return, you could make an arbitrage profit by running the strategy in reverse—in other words, you would *sell* the diversified 'zero-sensitivity' portfolio and invest the proceeds in Australian government securities.

**2.** A diversified portfolio that is constructed to have exposure to, say, factor 1, will offer a risk premium, which will vary in direct proportion to the portfolio's sensitivity to that factor. For example, imagine that you construct two portfolios, A and B, which are affected only by factor 1. If portfolio A is twice as sensitive to factor 1 as portfolio B, portfolio A must offer twice the risk premium. Therefore, if you divided your money equally between government securities and portfolio A, your combined portfolio would have exactly the same sensitivity to factor 1 as portfolio B and would offer the same risk premium.

Suppose that the arbitrage pricing formula did *not* hold. For example, suppose that the combination of Treasury notes and portfolio A offered a higher return. In that case you could make an arbitrage profit by selling portfolio B and investing the proceeds in the mixture of notes and portfolio A.

---

[43]  There may be some macroeconomic factors that investors are simply not worried about. (For example, some macroeconomists believe that money supply does not matter and therefore investors are not worried about inflation.) Such factors would not command a risk premium. They would drop out of the APT formula for expected return.

The arbitrage that we have described applies to well-diversified portfolios, where the unique risk has been diversified away. But if the arbitrage pricing relationship holds for all diversified portfolios, it must generally hold for the individual shares. Each share must offer an expected return commensurate with its contribution to portfolio risk. In the APT, this contribution depends on the sensitivity of the share's return to unexpected changes in the macroeconomic factors.

## A comparison of the CAPM and APT

Like the CAPM, APT stresses that expected return depends on the risk stemming from economy-wide influences and is not affected by unique risk. You can think of the factors in arbitrage pricing as representing special portfolios of shares that tend to be subject to a common influence. If the expected risk premium on each of these portfolios is proportional to the portfolio's market beta, then the APT and the CAPM will give the same answer. In any other case they will not.

How do the two theories stack up? Arbitrage pricing has some attractive features. For example, the market portfolio that plays such a central role in the CAPM does not feature in APT.[44] So we do not have to worry about the problem of measuring the market portfolio, and in principle we can test the APT even if we have data on only a sample of risky assets.

Unfortunately, you win some and lose some. APT does not tell us what the underlying factors are—unlike the CAPM, which collapses *all* macroeconomic risks into a well-defined *single* factor, the return on the market portfolio.

Although it is tricky to estimate factor sensitivities and risk premiums, there are already several billion dollars of investment funds under management using the APT. Some companies in the United States are also beginning to use APT to estimate the cost of capital for investment in real assets.

## APT example

APT will provide a good handle on expected returns only if we can (1) identify a reasonably short list of macroeconomic factors,[45] (2) measure the expected risk premium on each of these factors and (3) measure the sensitivity of each share to these factors. Let us look briefly at how Elton, Gruber and Mei tackled each of these issues and estimated the cost of equity for a group of nine New York utilities.[46]

**Step 1  Identify the macroeconomic factors**    Although APT does not tell us what the underlying economic factors are, Elton, Gruber and Mei identified five principal factors that could affect either the cash flows themselves or the rate at which they are discounted. These factors are:

| Factor | Measured by |
| --- | --- |
| Yield spread | Return on long government bond *less* return on 30-day Treasury bills |
| Interest rate | Change in Treasury bill return |

---

[44]  Of course, the market portfolio *may* turn out to be one of the factors, but that is not a necessary implication of APT.

[45]  Some researchers have argued that there are four or five principal pervasive influences on share prices, but others are not so sure. They point out that the more shares you look at, the more factors you need to take into account. See, for example, P. J. Dhrymes, I. Friend and N. B. Gultekin, 'A Critical Re-examination of the Empirical Evidence on the Arbitrage Pricing Theory', *Journal of Finance*, **39**: 323–46 (June 1984).

[46]  See E. J. Elton, M. J. Gruber and J. Mei, 'Cost of Capital Using Arbitrage Pricing Theory: A Case Study of Nine New York Utilities', *Financial Markets, Institutions and Instruments*, **3**: 46–73 (August 1994). The study was prepared for the New York State Public Utility Commission.

| Factor | Measured by |
|---|---|
| Exchange rate | Change in value of dollar relative to basket of currencies |
| Real GNP | Change in forecasts of real GNP |
| Inflation | Change in forecasts of inflation |

To capture any remaining pervasive influences, Elton, Gruber and Mei also included a sixth factor: the portion of the market return that could not be explained by the first five.

## Step 2  Estimate the risk premium for each factor

Some shares are more exposed than others to a particular factor, so we can estimate the sensitivity of a sample of shares to each factor and then measure how much extra return investors would have received in the past for taking on factor risk. The results are shown in Table 8.2.

For example, shares with positive sensitivity to real GNP tended to have higher returns when real GNP increased. A share with an average sensitivity gave investors an additional return of 0.49 per cent a year compared with a share that was completely unaffected by changes in real GNP. In other words, investors appeared to dislike 'cyclical' shares whose returns were sensitive to economic activity and demanded a higher return from these shares.

By contrast, Table 8.2 shows that a share with average exposure to *inflation* gave investors 0.83 per cent a year *less* return than a share with no exposure to inflation. Thus investors seemed to prefer shares that protected them against inflation (shares that did well when inflation accelerated) and were willing to accept a lower expected return from such shares.

## Step 3  Estimate the factor sensitivities

These estimates of the premiums for taking on factor risk can now be used to estimate the cost of equity for the group of New York State utilities. Remember, APT states that the risk premium for any asset depends on its sensitivities to factor risks ($b$) and the expected risk premium for each factor ($r_{factor} - r_f$). In this case there are six factors, so:

$$r - r_f = b_1(r_{factor\ 1} - r_f) + b_2(r_{factor\ 2} - r_f) + \ldots + b_6(r_{factor\ 6} - r_f)$$

The first column of Table 8.3 shows the factor risks for the portfolio of utilities and the second column shows the required risk premium for each factor (taken from Table 8.2). The third column is simply the product of these two numbers. It shows how much return investors demanded for taking on each factor risk. To find the expected risk premium, just add the figures in the final column:

$$\text{Expected risk premium} = r - r_f = 8.53\%$$

The one-year Treasury rate in December 1990, the end of the Elton, Gruber and Mei sample period, was about 7 per cent, so the APT estimate of the expected return on New York State utility shares was:[47]

$$
\begin{aligned}
\text{Expected return} &= \text{risk-free interest rate} + \text{expected risk premium} \\
&= 7 + 8.53 \\
&= 15.53, \text{ or about } 15.5\%
\end{aligned}
$$

---

[47]  This estimate rests on risk premiums actually earned from 1978 to 1990, an unusually rewarding period for ordinary share investors. Estimates based on long-run market risk premiums would be lower. See Elton, et al., op. cit., Footnote 46, p. 61.

**table 8.2**

Estimated risk premium for taking on factor risks, 1978–90

| Factor | Estimated risk premium ($r_{factor} - r_f$) |
|---|---|
| Yield spread | 5.10% |
| Interest rate | −0.61 |
| Exchange rate | −0.59 |
| Real GNP | 0.49 |
| Inflation | −0.83 |
| Market | 6.36 |

*Note*: The risk premiums have been scaled to represent the annual premiums for the average industrial share in the Elton, Gruber and Mei sample.
*Source*: E. Elton, M. Gruber and J. Mei, op cit., Footnote 46.

**table 8.3**

Using APT to estimate the expected risk premium for a portfolio of nine New York State utility shares

| Factor | Factor risk ($b$) | Expected risk premium ($r_{factor} - r_f$) | Factor risk × risk premium [$b(r_{factor} - r_f)$] |
|---|---|---|---|
| Yield spread | 1.04 | 5.10 | 5.30% |
| Interest rate | −2.25 | −0.61 | 1.37 |
| Exchange rate | 0.70 | −0.59 | −0.41 |
| GNP | 0.17 | 0.49 | 0.08 |
| Inflation | −0.18 | −0.83 | 0.15 |
| Market | 0.32 | 6.36 | 2.04 |
| Total | | | 8.53% |

*Source*: E. Elton, M. Gruber and J. Mei, op cit., Footnote 46. Risk premiums have been restated as approximate annual rates.

## 8.8 Summary

The basic principles of portfolio selection boil down to a commonsense statement that investors try to increase the expected return on their portfolios and to reduce the standard deviation of that return. A portfolio that gives the highest expected return for a given standard deviation, or the lowest standard deviation for a given expected return, is known as an *efficient portfolio*. To work out which portfolios are efficient, an investor must be able to state the expected return and standard deviation of each share and the degree of correlation between each pair of shares.

Investors who are restricted to holding ordinary shares should choose an efficient portfolio that suits their attitudes to risk. But investors who can also borrow and lend at the risk-free rate of interest should choose the 'best' ordinary share portfolio *regardless* of their attitudes to risk. Having done that, they can then set the risk of their overall portfolio by deciding what proportion of their money they are willing to invest in shares. For an investor who has only the same opportunities and information as everybody else, the best share portfolio is the same as the best share portfolio for other investors. In other words, she or he should invest in a mixture of the market portfolio and a risk-free loan (i.e. borrowing or lending).

A share's marginal contribution to portfolio risk is measured by its sensitivity to changes in the value of the portfolio. If a portfolio is efficient, there will be a straight-line relationship between each share's expected return and its marginal contribution to the risk of the portfolio. The marginal contribution of a share to the risk of the *market portfolio* is measured by *beta*. So if the market portfolio is efficient, there will be a straight-line relationship between the expected return and beta of each share. That is the fundamental idea behind the CAPM which concludes that each security's expected risk premium should increase in proportion to its beta:

$$\text{Expected risk premium} = \text{beta} \times \text{market risk premium}$$
$$r - r_f = \beta(r_m - r_f)$$

The capital asset pricing theory is the best-known model of risk and return. It is plausible and widely used but far from perfect. Actual returns are related to beta over the long run, but the relationship is not as strong as the CAPM predicts, and other factors may explain return better since the mid-1960s. Shares of small companies, and shares with low market prices relative to book value per share, appear to have risks not captured by the CAPM. The CAPM has also been criticised for its strong simplifying assumptions.

A new theory called the *consumption* capital asset pricing model suggests that security risk reflects the sensitivity of returns to changes in investors' *consumption*. This theory calls for a consumption beta rather than a beta relative to the market portfolio.

The APT offers an alternative theory of risk and return. It states that the expected risk premium on a share should depend on the share's exposure to several pervasive macro-economic factors that affect share returns:

$$\text{Expected risk premium} = b_1(r_{\text{factor 1}} - r_f) + b_2(r_{\text{factor 2}} - r_f) + \ldots$$

Here the $b$s represent the individual security's sensitivities to the factors, and $r_{\text{factor}} - r_f$ is the risk premium demanded by investors who are exposed to this factor.

APT does not say what these factors are. It asks economists to hunt for unknown game with their statistical tool kits. The hunters have returned with several candidates, including unanticipated changes in:

- The level of industrial activity
- The rate of inflation
- The spread between short- and long-term interest rates
- The spread between the yields of low- and high-risk corporate bonds

Each of these different models of risk and return has its fan club. However, all financial economists agree on two basic ideas: (1) investors require extra expected return for taking on risk and (2) they appear to be concerned predominantly with the risk that they cannot eliminate by diversification.

## FURTHER READING

The pioneering article on portfolio selection is:

H. M. Markowitz, 'Portfolio Selection', *Journal of Finance*, 7: 77–91 (March 1952).

There are a number of textbooks on portfolio selection which explain both Markowitz's original theory and some ingenious simplified versions. See, for example:

E. J. Elton and M. J. Gruber, *Modern Portfolio Theory and Investment Analysis*, 4th ed., John Wiley & Sons, New York, 1991.

Of the three pioneering articles on the capital asset pricing model, Jack Treynor's has never been published. The other two articles are:

W. F. Sharpe, 'Capital Asset Prices: A Theory of Market Equilibrium under Conditions of Risk', *Journal of Finance*, **19**: 425–42 (September 1964).

J. Lintner, 'The Valuation of Risk Assets and the Selection of Risky Investments in Share Portfolios and Capital Budgets', *Review of Economics and Statistics*, **47**: 13–37 (February 1965).

The subsequent literature on the CAPM is enormous. The following book provides a collection of some of the more important early articles plus a very useful survey by Jensen:

M. C. Jensen (ed.), *Studies in the Theory of Capital Markets*, Frederick A. Praeger, Inc., New York, 1972.

A useful article which provides a compact summary of developments in asset pricing models including extensions to the CAPM is:

N. Sinclair, 'Multifactor Asset Pricing Models', *Accounting and Finance*, **27**: 17–37 (May 1987).

There have been a number of tests of the CAPM. Some of the more important tests are:

E. F. Fama and J. D. MacBeth, 'Risk, Return and Equilibrium: Empirical Tests', *Journal of Political Economy*, **81**: 607–36 (May 1973).

F. Black, M. C. Jensen and M. Scholes, 'The Capital Asset Pricing Model: Some Empirical Tests', in M. C. Jensen (ed.), *Studies in the Theory of Capital Markets*, Frederick A. Praeger, Inc., New York, 1972.

M. R. Gibbons, 'Multivariate Tests of Financial Models', *Journal of Financial Economics*, **10**: 3–27 (March 1982).

For a critique of empirical tests of the model see:

R. Roll, 'A Critique of the Asset Pricing Theory's Tests; Part I: On Past and Potential Testability of the Theory', *Journal of Financial Economics*, **4**: 129–76 (March 1977).

Fama and French's 1992 paper prompted much of the recent controversy about the performance of the CAPM. The paper by Black takes issue with Fama and French and updates the Black, Jensen and Scholes test of the CAPM. In further work Fama and French suggest that returns can be explained by three factors: a market factor, a market to book factor and a size factor:

E. F. Fama and K. R. French, 'The Cross-Section of Expected Share Returns', *Journal of Finance*, **47**: 427–65 (June 1992).

F. Black, 'Beta and Return', *Journal of Portfolio Management*, **20**: 8–18 (Fall 1993).

E. F. Fama and K. R. French, 'Common Risk Factors in the Returns on Stocks and Bonds', *Journal of Financial Economics*, **33**: 3–56 (February 1993).

E. F. Fama and K. R. French, 'Multifactor Explanations of Asset Pricing Anomalies', *Journal of Finance*, **51**: 55–84 (March 1996).

Breeden's 1979 article describes the CAPM, and the Breeden, Gibbons and Litzenberger paper tests the model and compares it with the standard CAPM:

D. T. Breeden, 'An Intertemporal Asset Pricing Model with Stochastic Consumption and Investment Opportunities', *Journal of Financial Economics*, 7: 265–96 (September 1979).

D. T. Breeden, M. R. Gibbons and R. H. Litzenberger, 'Empirical Tests of the Consumption-Oriented CAPM', *Journal of Finance*, **44**: 231–62 (June 1989).

APT is described in Ross's 1976 paper. These three papers test the model and attempt to identify the principal factors:

S. A. Ross, 'The Arbitrage Theory of Capital Asset Pricing', *Journal of Economic Theory*, 13: 341–60 (December 1976).

R. Roll and S. A. Ross, 'An Empirical Investigation of the Arbitrage Pricing Theory', *Journal of Finance*, 35: 1073–103 (December 1980).

N. F. Chen, R. Roll and S. A. Ross, 'Economic Forces and the Share Market', *Journal of Business*, 59: 383–403 (July 1986).

Australian studies of asset pricing models include:

R. Ball, P. Brown and R. Officer, 'Asset Pricing in the Australian Industrial Equity Market', *Australian Journal of Management*, 1: 1–32 (April 1976)

R. Ball and P. Brown, 'Risk and Return in the Australian Mining Industry: January 1958–February 1979', *Australian Journal of Management*, 5: 45–66 (October 1980).

R. Faff, 'An Empirical Test of the Arbitrage Pricing Theory on Australian Share Returns', *Accounting and Finance*, 28: 23–44 (November 1988).

For an example of an efficient markets anomaly in an Australian context see:

P. Brown, A. Kleidon and T. Marsh, 'Stock Return Seasonalities and the Tax-Loss Selling Hypothesis: Analysis of the Arguments and Australian Evidence', *Journal of Financial Economics*, 12: 105–27 (1983)

The most accessible recent implementation of APT is:

E. Elton, M. Gruber and J. Mei, 'Cost of Capital Using Arbitrage Pricing Theory: A Case Study of Nine New York Utilities', *Financial Markets, Institutions and Instruments*, 3: 46–73 (August 1994).

## QUIZ

**1.** Figures 8.14 and 8.15 purport to show the range of attainable combinations of expected return and standard deviation.

**figures 8.14 and 8.15**

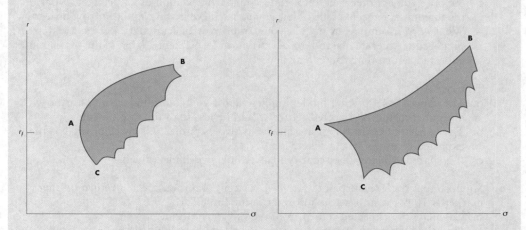

a. Which diagram is incorrectly drawn and why?
b. Which is the efficient set of portfolios?
c. If $r_f$ is the rate of interest, mark with an X the optimal share portfolio.

**2.** For each of the following pairs of investments, state which would always be preferred by a rational investor (assuming that these are the *only* investments available to the investor):

 a. Portfolio A $r$ = 18 per cent $\sigma$ = 20 per cent.
    Portfolio B $r$ = 14 per cent $\sigma$ = 20 per cent.
 b. Portfolio C $r$ = 15 per cent $\sigma$ = 18 per cent.
    Portfolio D $r$ = 13 per cent $\sigma$ = 8 per cent.
 c. Portfolio E $r$ = 14 per cent $\sigma$ = 16 per cent.
    Portfolio F $r$ = 14 per cent $\sigma$ = 10 per cent.

**3.** Consider the following four portfolios:

 a. 50 per cent in Treasury notes, 50 per cent in share W.
 b. 50 per cent in share W, 50 per cent in share X, where the returns are perfectly positively correlated.
 c. 50 per cent in share X, 50 per cent in share Y, where the returns are uncorrelated.
 d. 50 per cent in share Y, 50 per cent in share Z, where the returns are perfectly negatively correlated.

In which of these cases would the standard deviation of the portfolio lie exactly midway between that of the two securities?

**4.** a. Plot the following risky portfolios on a graph:

| Portfolio | A | B | C | D | E | F | G | H |
|---|---|---|---|---|---|---|---|---|
| Expected return ($r$) (%) | 10 | 12.5 | 15 | 16 | 17 | 18 | 18 | 20 |
| Standard deviation ($\sigma$) (%) | 23 | 21 | 25 | 29 | 29 | 32 | 35 | 45 |

 b. Five of these portfolios are efficient and three are not. Which are the *in*efficient ones?
 c. Suppose you can also borrow and lend at an interest rate of 12 per cent. Which of the above portfolios is best?
 d. Suppose you are prepared to tolerate a standard deviation of 25 per cent. What is the maximum expected return that you can achieve if you cannot borrow or lend?
 e. What is your optimal strategy if you can borrow or lend at 12 per cent and are prepared to tolerate a standard deviation of 25 per cent? What is the maximum expected return that you can achieve?

**5.** True or false?

 a. The capital asset pricing model implies that if you could find an investment with a negative beta, its expected return would be less than the interest rate.
 b. The expected return on an investment with a beta of 2.0 is twice as high as the expected return on the market.
 c. If a share lies below the security market line, it is undervalued.

**6.** Suppose that the Treasury note rate is 4 per cent and the expected return on the market is 10 per cent. Use the information in Table 8.1.

 a. Calculate the expected return from News Corporation.
 b. Find the highest expected return that is offered by one of these shares.
 c. Find the lowest expected return that is offered by one of these shares.
 d. Would Arnotts offer a higher or lower expected return if the interest rate were 8 per cent rather than 4 per cent? Assume that the expected return on the market stays at 10 per cent.

e. Would Comalco offer a higher or lower expected return if the interest rate were 8 per cent?

**7.** The capital asset pricing model states that a share has the same market risk and expected return as:
 a. A portfolio with proportion $\beta$ invested in Treasury notes and $1 - \beta$ in the market.
 b. A portfolio with $\beta$ invested in the market and $1 - \beta$ in Treasury notes.
 c. A portfolio evenly divided between the market and Treasury notes.
 Which is the correct answer?

**8.** By 2020, after several years of frenzied merger activity, only two giant conglomerates remain on the ASX. For convenience, we will label these firms A and B. Each accounts for half the value of the market portfolio. You are given the following data:

|  | A | B |
| --- | --- | --- |
| Expected rate of return ($r$) | 23 | 13 |
| Standard deviation of return ($\sigma$) (%/year) | 40 | 24 |

The correlation coefficient of A and B is $\rho_{AB} = 0.8$.
 a. What is the expected rate of return on the market portfolio ($r_m$)?
 b. What is the standard deviation of the market portfolio ($\sigma_m$)?
 c. What are the betas of shares A and B with respect to the market portfolio?
 d. Assume the risk-free rate is 10 per cent. Are the expected rates of return on A and B consistent with the CAPM?

**9.** Write out the APT equation for the expected rate of return on a risky share. Identify and interpret each of the variables entering the equation.

**10.** Consider a three-factor APT model. The factors and associated risk premia are:

| Factor | Risk premia |
| --- | --- |
| Change in GNP | 5% |
| Change in energy prices | −1% |
| Change in long-term interest rates | 2% |

Calculate expected rates of return on the following shares. The risk-free interest rate is 7 per cent.
 a. A share whose return is uncorrelated with all three factors.
 b. A share with average exposure to each factor (i.e. with $b = 1$ for each).
 c. A pure-play energy share with high exposure to the energy factor ($b = 2$) but zero exposure to the other two factors.
 d. An aluminium company share with average sensitivity to changes in interest rates and GNP, but negative exposure to $b = -1.5$ to the energy factor. (The aluminium company is energy-intensive and suffers when energy prices rise.)

# QUESTIONS AND PROBLEMS

**1.** True or false? Explain or qualify as necessary.
   a. Investors demand higher expected rates of return on shares with more variable rates of return.
   b. The capital asset pricing model predicts that a security with a beta of zero will offer a zero expected return.
   c. An investor who puts $10 000 in Treasury notes and $20 000 in the market portfolio will have a beta of 2.0.
   d. Investors demand higher expected rates of return from shares with returns that are highly exposed to macroeconomic changes.
   e. Investors demand higher expected rates of return from shares with returns that are very sensitive to fluctuations in the share market.

**2.** 'There may be some truth in these CAPM and APT theories, but last year some shares did much better than these theories predicted and other shares did much worse.' Is this a valid criticism?

**3.** Here are betas estimated in 1996 for several well-known shares:

| Share | Beta |
|-------|------|
| Ampolex | 1.4 |
| Lend Lease | 1.0 |
| Coca Cola Amatil | 0.7 |
| Seven Network | 1.9 |

   a. Estimate the expected rate of return using the CAPM formula. The risk-free rate (government bonds) was about 7.5 per cent and the market risk premium was 8.0 per cent.
   b. The standard deviation of Ampolex shares was about 33 per cent per year. Seven Network's standard deviation was about 29 per cent. Yet the CAPM says Ampolex was the safer investment. Explain why this makes sense.

**4.** Sketch the efficient set of ordinary share portfolios. Show the combinations of expected return and risk that you could achieve if you could borrow and lend at the same risk-free rate of interest. Now show the combinations of expected return and risk that you could achieve if the rate of interest is higher for borrowing than for lending.

**5.** Look back at the calculation for Bhp and Coals Mire in Section 8.1. Recalculate the expected portfolio return and standard deviation for different values of $x_1$ and $x_2$, assuming $\rho_{12} = 0$. Plot the range of possible combinations of expected return and standard deviation as in Figure 8.4. Repeat the problem for $\rho_{12} = +1$ and for $\rho_{12} = -1$.

**6.** Mark Harrywitz proposes to invest in two shares, X and Y. He expects a return of 12 per cent from X and 8 per cent from Y. The standard deviation of returns is 8 per cent for X and 5 per cent for Y. The correlation coefficient between the returns is 0.2.
   a. Compute the expected return and standard deviation of the following portfolios:

| Portfolio | Percentage in X | Percentage in Y |
|-----------|-----------------|-----------------|
| 1 | 50 | 50 |
| 2 | 25 | 75 |
| 3 | 75 | 25 |

b. Sketch the set of portfolios composed of X and Y.
c. Suppose that Mr Harrywitz can also borrow or lend at an interest rate of 5 per cent. Show on your sketch how this alters his opportunities. Given that he can borrow or lend, what proportions of the ordinary share portfolio should be invested in X and Y?

**7.** Hilda Hornbill has invested 60 per cent of her money in share A and the remainder in share B. She assesses their prospects as follows:

|  | A | B |
|--|---|---|
| Expected return (%) | 15 | 20 |
| Standard deviation (%) | 20 | 22 |
| Correlation between returns | 0.5 | |

a. What are the expected return and the standard deviation of returns on her portfolio?
b. How would your answer change if the correlation coefficient were 0 or $-0.5$?
c. Is Ms Hornbill's portfolio better or worse than one invested entirely in share A, or is it not possible to say?

**8.** The Treasury note rate is 4 per cent and the expected return on the market portfolio is 12 per cent. On the basis of the capital asset pricing model:
a. Draw a graph similar to Figure 8.7 showing how the expected return varies with beta.
b. What is the risk premium on the market?
c. What is the required return on an investment with a beta of 1.5?
d. If an investment with a beta of 0.8 offers an expected return of 9.8 per cent, does it have a positive NPV?
e. If the market expects a return of 11.2 per cent from share X, what is the beta?

**9.** Estimate the returns expected by investors today for the 8 shares in Table 8.1. Plot the expected returns against beta as in Figure 8.7.

**10.** A company is deciding whether to issue shares to raise money for an investment project which has the same risk as the market and an expected return of 20 per cent. If the risk-free rate is 10 per cent and the expected return on the market is 15 per cent, the company should go ahead:
a. Unless the project's beta is greater than 2.0.
b. Unless the project's beta is less than 2.0.
c. Whatever the project's beta.
Which answer is correct? Say briefly why.

**11.** The shares of United Merchants have a beta of 1.0 and very high unique risk. If the expected return on the market is 20 per cent, the expected return on United Merchants will be:

   a.  10 per cent if the interest rate is 10 per cent.

   b.  20 per cent.

   c.  More than 20 per cent because of the high unique risk.

   d.  Indeterminate unless you also know the interest rate.

Which is the right answer? Explain *briefly* why.

**12.** The expected return on a share is frequently written as $r = \alpha + \beta r_m$, where $r_m$ is the expected return on the market. The capital asset pricing model says that in equilibrium:

   a.  $\alpha = 0$.

   b.  $\alpha = r_f$ (the risk-free rate of interest).

   c.  $\alpha = (1 - \beta)\, r_f$.

   d.  $\alpha = (1 - r_f)$.

Which is correct?

**13.** Suppose that there is *no* relationship between beta and expected returns. Does that mean that beta is an uninteresting statistic? What would you do as an investor? What strategies should a corporation adopt?

**14.** In the table below we give you some data on the standard deviation of returns for a sample of shares and on the correlation between the returns. Suppose that after intensive analysis you have made the forecast of returns that also appears in the table.

|  | BHP | Coles Myer | Comalco | Standard deviation | Expected return |
|---|---|---|---|---|---|
| BHP | 1.00 | 0.31 | 0.60 | 20.18% | 18% |
| Coles Myer |  | 1.00 | 0.14 | 17.54% | 12% |
| Comalco |  |  | 1.00 | 28.47% | 16% |

   a.  Calculate the set of efficient portfolios.

   b.  What is the portfolio with the highest expected return?

   c.  What is the minimum-risk portfolio?

**\*15.** Look again at Question 14. Take one of the efficient portfolios (other than the minimum-variance portfolio) and calculate the beta of each holding relative to that portfolio. Show that there is a straight-line relationship between the expected returns on the shares held and their betas *relative to the efficient portfolio.*

**16.** In Section 8.1 we noted that the minimum risk portfolio contained an investment of 19.5 per cent in Coals Mire and 80.5 per cent in Bhp. Prove this. (*Hint*: You need a little calculus to do so.)

**\*17.** The following question illustrates the arbitrage pricing theory. Imagine that there are only two pervasive macroeconomic factors. Investments X, Y and Z have the following sensitivities to these two factors:

| Investment | $b_1$ | $b_2$ |
|------------|-------|-------|
| X | 1.75 | 0.25 |
| Y | −1.00 | 2.00 |
| Z | 2.00 | 1.00 |

We assume that the expected risk premium is 4 per cent on factor 1 and 8 per cent on factor 2. Treasury notes obviously offer a zero risk premium.

a. According to arbitrage pricing theory, what is the risk premium on each of the three shares?

b. Suppose you buy $200 of X and $50 of Y and sell $150 of Z. What is the sensitivity of your portfolio to each of the two factors? What is the expected risk premium?

c. Suppose you buy $80 of X and $60 of Y and sell $40 of Z. What is the sensitivity of your portfolio to each of the two factors? What is the expected risk premium?

d. Finally, suppose you buy $160 of X and $20 of Y and sell $80 of Z. What is your portfolio's sensitivity now to each of the two factors? And what is the expected risk premium?

e. Suggest two possible ways that you could construct a fund that had a sensitivity of 0.5 to factor 1 only. Now compare the expected risk premiums on each of these investments.

f. Suppose that the arbitrage pricing relationship did *not* hold and that X offered a risk premium of 8 per cent, Y offered a premium of 14 per cent and Z a premium of 16 per cent. Devise an investment that had zero sensitivity to each factor and that offered a positive risk premium.

**18.** Some true or false questions about the APT:
a. The APT factors cannot reflect diversifiable risks.
b. The market rate of return cannot be an APT factor.
c. Each APT factor must have a positive risk premium associated with it—otherwise the model is inconsistent.
d. There is no theory that specifically identifies the APT factors.
e. The APT model could be true but not very useful—for example, if the relevant factors change unpredictably.

**19.** 'Suppose you could forecast the behaviour of APT factors, such as industrial production, interest rates, etc. You could then identify shares' sensitivities to these factors, pick the right shares and make lots of money.' Is this a good argument favouring the APT? Explain why or why not.

**20.** Percival Hygiene has $10 million invested in long-term corporate bonds. This bond portfolio's expected annual rate of return is 9 per cent and the annual standard deviation is 10 per cent.

Amanda Reckonwith, Percival's financial adviser, recommends that Percival consider investing in an index fund which closely tracks the All-Ordinaries Index. The Index has an expected return of 14 per cent and its standard deviation is 16 per cent.

a. Suppose Percival puts all his money in a combination of the Index fund and Treasury notes. Can he improve his annual rate of return without changing the risk of his portfolio? The Treasury note yield is 6 per cent.

b.  Could Percival do even better by investing equal amounts in the corporate bond portfolio and the Index fund? The correlation between the bond portfolio and the Index fund is +0.1.

**21.** Explain the difference between the capital market line and the security market line.

**22.** In many of the questions above we have been doing calculations with the betas of individual shares. Why should we be careful in using the results of such calculations?

# chapter 9

# CAPITAL BUDGETING AND RISK

Long before the development of modern theories linking risk and expected return, smart financial managers adjusted for risk in capital budgeting. They realised intuitively that, other things being equal, risky projects are less desirable than safe ones. Therefore, financial managers demanded a higher rate of return from risky projects, or they based their decisions on conservative estimates of the cash flows.

Various rules of thumb are often used to make these risk adjustments. For example, many companies estimate the rate of return required by investors in their securities and use this *company cost of capital* to discount the cash flows on all new projects. Since investors require a higher

rate of return from a more risky company, such a firm will have a higher company cost of capital and will set a higher discount rate for its new investment opportunities. For example, in Table 8.1 we estimated that investors expected a rate of return of 21.2 per cent from the shares of Newcrest Mining. If we assume that Newcrest is 100 per cent financed by equity, then according to the company cost of capital rule, a 21.2 per cent discount rate should be used to compute project net present values.[1]

This is a step in the right direction. Even though we cannot measure risk or the expected return on risky securities with absolute precision, it is still reasonable to assert that Newcrest faced

---

[1] Since Newcrest is not 100 per cent equity financed its cost of capital will not really be 21.2 per cent. If Newcrest really were 100 per cent equity financed its cost of equity would be lower. The 21.2 per cent required return on Newcrest shares that we calculated in Table 8.1 compensates shareholders for both the company's business risk and the risk to shareholders created by the use of debt in the company.

more risk than the average firm and therefore should have demanded a higher rate of return from its capital investments. But this company cost of capital rule can also get the firm into trouble if the new projects are more or less risky than its existing business.

**Cost of capital: project v company.** *Each project should be evaluated at its **own** opportunity cost of capital.* This is a clear implication of the value additivity principle introduced in Chapter 7. For a firm composed of assets A and B, the firm value is

Firm value = PV(AB) = PV(A) + PV(B) = sum of separate asset values

Here PV(A) and PV(B) are valued just as if they were mini-firms in which shareholders could invest directly. Investors would value A by discounting its forecast cash flows at a rate reflecting the risk of A. They would value B by discounting at a rate reflecting the risk of B. The two discount rates will, in general, be different.

If the firm considers investing in a third project, C, it should also value C as if C were a mini-firm. That is, the firm should discount the cash flows of C at the expected rate of return that investors would demand to make a separate investment in C. *The true cost of capital depends on the use to which the capital is put.*

This means that Newcrest should accept any project that more than compensates for the *project's beta.* In other words, Newcrest should accept any project lying above the upward-sloping line that links expected return to risk in Figure 9.1. If the project has a high risk, Newcrest needs a higher prospective return than if the project has a low risk. Now contrast this with the company cost of capital rule, which is to accept any project *regardless of its risk* as long as it offers a higher return than the *company's* cost of capital. In terms of Figure 9.1, the rule tells Newcrest to accept any project above the horizontal cost of capital line, that is, any project offering a return of more than 21.2 per cent.

---

**figure 9.1**

A comparison between the company cost of capital rule and the required return under the capital asset pricing model. Newcrest's company cost of capital is about 21.1 per cent. This is the correct discount rate only if the project beta is 1.89. In general the correct discount rate increases as project beta increases. Newcrest should accept projects with rates of return above the security market line relating required return to beta.

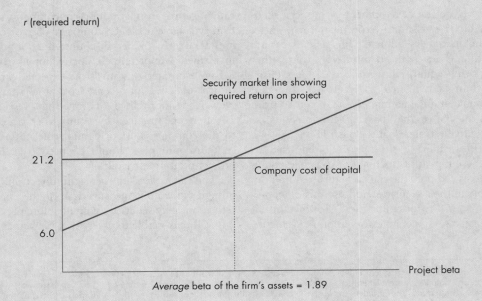

*Average* beta of the firm's assets = 1.89

It is clearly silly to suggest that Newcrest should demand the same rate of return from a very safe project as from a very risky one. If Newcrest used the company cost of capital rule, it would reject many good low-risk projects and accept many poor high-risk projects. It is also silly to suggest that just because another firm has a low company cost of capital, it is justified in accepting projects that Newcrest would reject. Consider an investment in Treasury notes: it does not matter whether that investment is made by a company with a low cost of capital or a high cost of capital, the value of the investment is the same in both cases.[2]

The dangerous notion that each company has some individual discount rate or cost of capital is widespread, but fortunately it is far from universal. Many firms require different returns from different categories of investment. Discount rates might be set as follows:

| Category | Discount rate (%) |
| --- | --- |
| Speculative ventures | 30 |
| New products | 20 |
| Expansion of existing business | 15 (company cost of capital) |
| Cost improvement, known technology | 10 |

While this is better than a single discount rate for all investments it is still somewhat arbitrary. If we want to be more scientific we can use a model like the capital asset pricing model. But using the CAPM will not be easy, nor can we honestly claim that it will always be accurate.

**Project betas and the CAPM.** Some large companies use the CAPM to estimate the required return on equity, and this can provide a starting point for estimating company discount rates. Some companies go a step further and estimate *project* betas. They then use the project beta and the CAPM to estimate the required

return on the project. However, this is not common in Australia. A major stumbling block is the difficulty in estimating project betas.[3] Assuming that you can solve the difficult task of estimating the project beta then you can also estimate the discount rate required for the project as follows:

$$\text{Required project return} = r = r_f + (\text{project beta})(r_m - r_f)$$

Before thinking about the betas of individual projects, we will look at some problems you would encounter in using beta to estimate a company's cost of capital. It turns out that beta is easier to measure for shares than it is for projects, although even this is far from easy. It is difficult to accurately estimate the beta for the shares of an individual firm: much greater accuracy can be achieved by looking at an average of similar companies. But then we have to define *similar*. Among other things, we will find that a firm's borrowing policy affects its share beta. It would be misleading, for example, to average the betas of Chrysler, which has been a heavy borrower, and General Motors, which has borrowed less.

The company cost of capital is the correct discount rate for projects that have the same risk as the company's existing business but *not* for those projects that are safer or riskier than the company's average. The problem is to judge the relative risks of the projects available to the firm. To handle that problem, we will need to dig a little deeper and look at what features make some investments riskier than others. After you know *why* Coles Myer shares have less market risk than, say, Comalco, you will be in a better position to judge the relative risks of capital investment opportunities.

There is still another complication: project betas can shift over time. Some projects are safer in youth than in old age; others are riskier. In this case, what do we mean by *the* project beta? There may be a separate beta for each year of the project's life. To put it another way, can we jump from the capital asset pricing model, which looks

---

2   Consider an asset like a Treasury note, where the cash flows are independent of who owns the asset. If the present value of the asset depended on the identity of the company buying the asset, then present values would not add up. Remember, a good project is a good project is a good project.

3   We do not know for sure that beta is the correct index for risk. At the moment, however, we do not have anything better, and in an imperfect world you have to use the best you have got. In any event, beta usefully illustrates the fundamental principle that the project's required return is determined by the characteristics of the project.

out one period into the future, to the discounted cash flow formula that we developed in Chapters 2 to 6 for valuing long-lived assets? Current practice assumes it is safe to do so, but you should be able to recognise and deal with the exceptions.

We will use the CAPM throughout this chapter. But you should not infer that the CAPM is the last word on risk and return. The principles and procedures covered in this chapter work just as well with other models, such as arbitrage pricing theory (APT). For example, we could have started with an APT estimate of the required return on Newcrest shares; the discussion of company and project cost of capital would have followed exactly as it is presented here.

## 9.1 Measuring betas

Suppose that you were considering an across-the-board expansion by your firm. Such an investment would have about the same degree of risk as the existing business. Therefore, you should discount the projected flows at the company cost of capital. To estimate the company cost of capital, you could begin by estimating the beta of the company's shares.

An obvious way to measure the beta of the share is to look at how its price has responded in the past to market movements. For example, in Figure 9.2 we have plotted monthly rates of return for BHP and News Corporation against market returns for the same months. In each case we have fitted a line through the points. Beta is the slope of the line. It varied slightly from one period to the other, but there is little doubt that BHP's beta was greater than News Corporation's. If you had used the past beta of either share to predict its future beta, you would not have been too far off in most cases.

Notice also that there is much less scatter of the points about the fitted line in the case of BHP. This means that BHP's return follows the market more closely than News Corporation's. To put it another way, BHP is less affected by the unsystematic component of returns.

### Stability of betas over time

We would not want you to go away with the idea that all betas are as stable as they appear from Figure 9.2. Nevertheless, betas for some firms do appear to be reasonably stable. An extensive study of stability was provided by Sharpe and Cooper.[4] They divided shares into 10 classes according to the estimated beta in each five-year period from 1931–67. Each class contained one-tenth of the shares in the sample. The shares with the lowest betas went into class 1; class 2 contained shares with slightly higher betas, and so on. Sharpe and Cooper then looked at where these shares were five years later. The more they had moved from their initial risk class, the less stable they were. If you are willing to stretch the definition of stable to include a jump to an adjacent risk class, then from 40 to 70 per cent of betas were stable over the subsequent five years. We also know that if we put the shares into portfolios, then the portfolio betas would vary much less over time than the betas for individual shares.

### Moving betas and mean reversion

One reason that estimates of beta are only imperfect guides to the future is that the shares can genuinely change their market risk. However, an important reason is that the betas in any one period are just estimates based on a limited number of observations. If good company news coincides by chance with high market returns, the share's beta will appear higher than if the news coincides with low market returns. We can twist this the other way around. If a share

---

4    W. F. Sharpe and G. M. Cooper, 'Risk-Return Classes of New York Stock Exchange Common Stocks, 1931–1967', *Financial Analysts Journal*, **28**: 46–54, 81 (March–April 1972).

**figure 9.2**

We can use data on past returns to obtain an estimate of beta for BHP and News Corporation. Notice how BHP's beta was above 1 in both periods while News Corporation's beta was below 1.

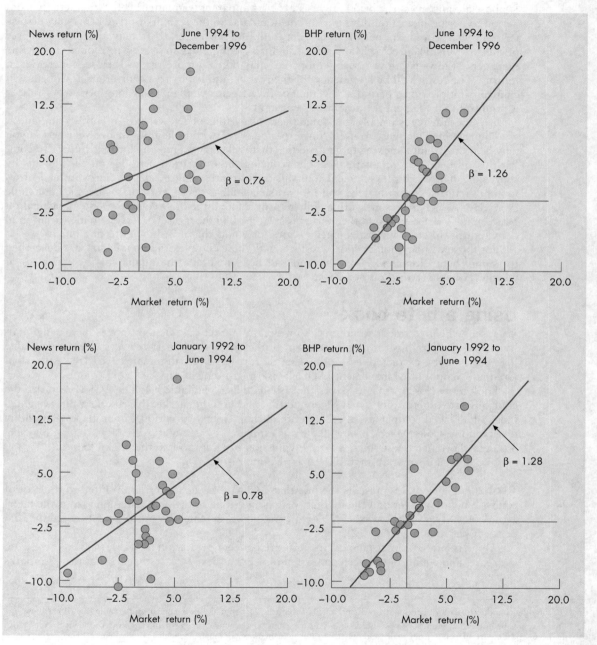

appears to have a high beta, it may be because it genuinely does have a high beta, or it may be because we have overestimated it. The largest overestimates tend to be associated with the largest values of beta and the largest underestimates tend to be associated with the smallest values for beta. Over time the errors in estimation will average out and thus high betas tend to drift down and low betas tend to drift up, both converging towards 1. This is known as **mean reversion in beta.**

Some of the observed fluctuation in beta is therefore an artefact of the estimation process. Suppose a company's true beta really is stable. Its apparent (estimated) beta will fluctuate from period to period due to random measurement errors. So the stability of true betas may be better than Sharpe and Cooper's results seem to imply.[5] However, there may also be real causes of mean reversion in beta. Managers of high-risk companies may seek to reduce risk, while managers of low-risk (low-return) companies may take on more risk as they seek increases in return.[6] The result will be a tendency for the real beta to revert to 1. For other firms beta will change from period to period as leverage or investments change. Over long periods of time it is doubtful that the beta for any firm is constant.

Current practice is usually to estimate beta using four or five years of monthly data, and it would probably be unwise to use a longer period. Even within the four- or five-year period you may be trying to hit a moving target, and one that will carry on moving into the future. To combat this problem you might think about reducing the estimation period. You can do this by shortening the return measurement interval; for instance using 60 daily returns instead of 60 monthly returns. Unfortunately, you hit two snags. First, many Australian shares do not trade every day—which makes measuring daily returns rather difficult. Second, the systematic relation between the share return and the market is swamped by the 'noise' of unsystematic variation in daily returns. In other words, you get a scatter of points that it is difficult to fit a line to.

For those who are not keen on wrestling with these complexities an industry has developed to supply beta estimates. However, you still need to judge the quality of the estimates of whichever beta service you purchase.[7]

## Using a beta book

Because of the investment community's interest in market risk, beta estimates of varying quality are regularly published by a number of brokerage and advisory services worldwide. Table 9.1 shows data extracted from the Centre for Research in Finance (CRIF), Australian Graduate School of Management (AGSM) risk measurement service.[8]

Look more closely at Coles Myer, the last share listed in Table 9.1. The AGSM recorded the company rate of return for Coles Myer and the return on the market (based on a value-weighted index of all listed companies) in each month during a four-year period.[9] That made 48 monthly observations. Coles Myer's beta of 0.58 was estimated by 'straight' regression, that is, by using a standard ordinary least squares (OLS) regression program to find the line of 'best fit'.

The other information in Table 9.1 is also interesting.

**Alpha**    Figure 9.3 represents the line that AGSM's regression program fitted to the plot of returns on Coles Myer and the market. Beta is the slope of the line, and alpha ($\alpha$) is the intercept. Coles Myer's alpha was $-7.29$ on an annual basis, which is approximately equal to $-0.6$ per cent per month ($-7.29/12$).

Alpha is a rate of price change. Its units are per cent per period (in Table 9.1 the value from the regression equation has been converted to per cent per year). It appears that the 48 months

---

5    On the other hand, estimates of beta made in the presence of thin trading can make beta appear more stable than it really is.

6    This may not be in the best interest of shareholders, but a safety first strategy for managers is not to stray too far from the rest of the herd—particularly if you are not really sure whether returns earned are commensurate with risks taken.

7    Although it is easy in principle to find a line of best fit, there are some tricks to finding the best time period over which to measure returns, for dealing with shares that trade only infrequently, and so on. Some 'beta services' are much more careful than others.

8    Datastream also supplies an extensive array of beta forecasts.

9    The company rate of return includes both price changes and dividends adjusted for capitalisation changes, as does the market index used. The AGSM converts the monthly returns to continuously compounded returns. Because the market index includes dividends it is known as an accumulation index. The dividends are assumed to be reinvested monthly. Some beta estimation services ignore dividends and just use the returns due to price changes.

**table 9.1**

Regression estimates of beta

| ASX code | Company name | OLS beta | OLS alpha | RSQ | Std dev ret | Std beta | Err alpha | S-W beta | Std err S-W beta | OBS |
|---|---|---|---|---|---|---|---|---|---|---|
| ncm | Newcrest Mining | 1.89 | −5.57 | 0.33 | 11.70 | 0.39 | 16.11 | 1.91 | 0.77 | 48 |
| nlb | Nullarbor Holdings | −0.61 | 8.48 | 0.02 | 16.90 | 0.70 | 33.21 | −0.99 | 1.30 | 46 |
| caa | Capral Aluminium | 1.30 | 8.74 | 0.24 | 9.50 | 0.34 | 16.01 | 1.03 | 0.68 | 48 |
| cmc | Comalco Ltd | 1.34 | 4.42 | 0.31 | 8.70 | 0.30 | 13.35 | 0.93 | 0.60 | 48 |
| weg | George Weston | 0.57 | −6.99 | 0.21 | 4.40 | 0.17 | 6.49 | 0.73 | 0.32 | 48 |
| arn | Arnotts Limited | 0.33 | 0.12 | 0.05 | 5.00 | 0.20 | 8.66 | 0.36 | 0.39 | 48 |
| fxj | John Fairfax | 1.53 | 3.04 | 0.58 | 7.20 | 0.19 | 8.44 | 1.23 | 0.39 | 48 |
| cml | Coles Myer | 0.58 | −7.29 | 0.18 | 4.90 | 0.18 | 7.23 | 0.21 | 0.37 | 48 |

*Source*: Compiled from CRIF, AGSM Risk Measurement Service, June 1996. Note that alpha has been expressed in per cent per year.

preceding June 1996 were not such good ones for Coles Myer. This is reflected in the negative value for alpha. From Figure 9.3 we see that alpha was the average rate of price depreciation borne by Coles Myer shareholders when investors in the market as a whole earned nothing. Investors in some other shares in Table 9.1 were more fortunate. What about the future? Will Coles Myer continue to underperform? Possibly, but you should not bet on it. The most likely outcome is that the return (price change plus dividend yield) will simply compensate for the market risk.

**figure 9.3**

Results of regressing Coles Myer monthly returns against monthly returns on the market. The slope of the fitted line is beta. The intercept is alpha.

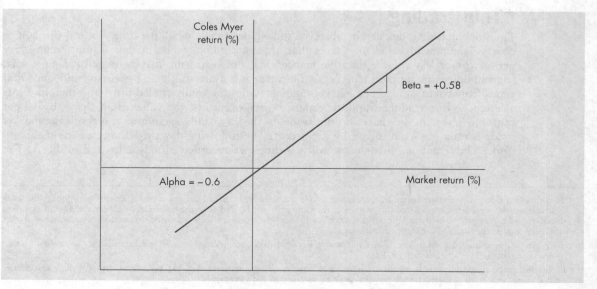

**R-squared and standard deviation of return**    The column headed 'RSQ' shows the proportion of the total *variance* of Coles Myer share returns that can be explained by market movements. That is, 18 per cent of its risk is market risk and 82 per cent is unique risk. The next column 'Std dev ret' is the total risk, measured as a standard deviation of return: 4.9 per cent per month for Coles Myer, equivalent to 16.97 per cent per year.[10] Eighty-two per cent of the variance is unique risk. So the unique component of variance per year is given by $(16.97)^2 \times 0.82$. Taking the square root to get the standard deviation gives 15.4 per cent per year. This is the annual standard deviation of the unique price change, that part of the actual change that was not explained by the change in the market index.

**Standard errors of beta and alpha**    The AGSM's betas are simply *estimates* based on 48 particular months. Therefore, we would like to have an idea of the extent of the possible error in these estimates. The column labelled 'Std err beta' provides this information. Statisticians set up a *confidence interval* of the estimated value plus or minus two standard errors. Thus, the confidence interval for Coles Myer's beta is between 0.58 plus or minus 2 × 0.18. If you state that the *true* beta for Coles Myer was between 0.22 and 0.94, you have a 95 per cent chance of being right. You have to do the best you can when estimating risk, but never forget the huge margin for error when estimating beta for individual shares.

Similarly, the standard error of alpha tells us to be cautious about inferring anything as to Coles Myer's 'true' or 'normal' alpha. It could easily be zero.

## Adjusted beta

We can adjust betas for both mean reversion and thin trading. In order to allow for mean reversion, equations to modify the raw beta estimate have been proposed. Tony Castagna and Zoltan Matolcsy suggest the following adjustment for Australia:[11]

$$\text{Adjusted beta} = 0.54 + 0.46 \, (\text{raw } \beta)$$

The result of this adjustment is to push high betas down and low betas up, so both move towards 1. For Coles Myer the adjusted beta would be 0.84. Adjusted betas are tricky to work with, and the Bayesian statistics needed to understand them properly are beyond the scope of this book. Thus, we will stick to 'raw' betas.

## *Thin trading

The stock market index can be observed to be changing value all the time. But it is difficult to observe changes in value for shares that are not trading.[12] Shares that do not trade every period *appear* less volatile than the market. It is not surprising that estimated betas for such shares underestimate their true betas. But there is a more subtle and pervasive influence that arises from thin trading. The market index includes the thinly traded firms and therefore it is affected by thin trading. Suppose a market-wide event lifts the value of all shares by 10 per cent. However, all the shares do not trade on the day of the event and as a result the market index is only observed to rise by 7 per cent. The following day the balance of the shares do trade. The remaining 3 per cent return is therefore recorded on day 2 instead of day 1. The

---

10    To compute the annual standard deviation you cannot simply multiply the standard deviation by 12. You have to square the standard deviation to get back to the monthly variance, then multiply by 12 and take the square root to get the annual standard deviation. This assumes that we can ignore the covariance in monthly returns, which is mostly a reasonable assumption—market efficiency implies that returns are independent over time.

11    See A. D. Castagna and Z. P. Matolcsy, 'The Relationship Between Accounting Variables and Systematic Risk', *Australian Journal of Management*, 3: 113–19 (October 1978).

12    Even when there are no trades it is sometimes possible to observe changes in value. The bid and ask prices for a share can change even if there is no trade. However, such changes must be interpreted with caution.

return recorded for day 2 is a mixture of returns for day 2 and day 1.[13] A consequence of the spreading of returns over more than one period is that the observed market returns appear to be smoother than the true market returns and so the variance estimate for the market $\sigma_m^2$ is understated. The covariance of any share $i$ with the market $\sigma_{im}$ is also understated. So both the numerator and denominator of the beta calculation ($\sigma_{im}/\sigma_m^2$) are in error. The effect is such that for shares which trade more frequently than average beta is overestimated, and for shares that trade less frequently than average beta is underestimated.

Many firms in the Australian market do not trade daily and some do not even trade monthly. Therefore, thin trading is a significant problem in the Australian market. There are several techniques to adjust betas for thin trading. The most popular is the Scholes Williams beta and this is used by the AGSM risk measurement service.[14] The formula for the Scholes Williams beta is

$$\text{Scholes Williams } \beta = \frac{(\beta_{i-1} + \beta_i + \beta_{i+1})}{(1 + 2\rho_m)}$$

where $\beta_{i-1}, \beta_i, \beta_{i+1}$ are the slopes of simple regressions of the return for share $i$ at time $t$ ($r_{i,t}$) against the return on the market: lagged one period ($r_{m,t-1}$), for the same period ($r_{m,t}$) and for the next period ($r_{m,t+1}$), $\rho_m$ is the first order serial correlation coefficient for the market return—this means that it is the correlation coefficient between today's return and yesterday's return.

## Fundamental betas

Rather than worrying about the problem of estimating a company's past market beta from rates of return, and then hoping that the company will have the same beta in the future, we can follow a different tack. We can attempt to use some fundamental characteristics of the firm to forecast beta. BARRA is one well-known commercial service that supplies such fundamental betas. The first step is to identify variables that are significantly related to beta, such as size, leverage, growth rate and industry. The variables are selected by estimating market betas for one period and then using multiple regression to find out which firm characteristics from the prior period are the best forecasters of beta. We can then use an equation of the following form to predict beta for subsequent periods:[15]

$$\text{Predicted } \beta = b_0 + b_1 x_1 + b_2 x_2 + b_2 x_3 \ldots + b_n x_n$$

where $x_1$ to $x_n$ are the variables used to predict beta for a given firm, and $b_0$ to $b_n$ are the estimated coefficients for those variables.

The BARRA service uses of the order of 100 variables in its beta prediction model for American shares. BARRA has also offered a similar service in Australia, but only using about 10 variables.

## Industry betas and the divisional cost of capital

That concludes our lesson on how to estimate and predict betas for individual shares. You should now understand the basic idea of how to estimate a share's beta by fitting a line to past data, and you should be able to read and understand publications such as the AGSM's beta estimates. Bear in mind that such estimates should enable you to pick up major differences in market risk, but they do not allow you to draw fine distinctions. This is because you are exposed to potentially large estimation errors when you estimate betas of individual shares

---

[13]  Because of this the market index may *appear* to be positively correlated from period to period. Positive correlation over time is known as positive serial correlation.

[14]  Myron Scholes and Joseph T. Williams, 'Estimating Betas From Nonsynchronous Data', *Journal of Financial Economics*, 5(3): 309–27 (1977).

[15]  Of course, in doing this we are relying on the regression relationship being stable over time.

from a limited sample of data. Fortunately these errors tend to cancel when you estimate betas of *portfolios*. Suppose that you were to compute the average of the betas of 100 shares. The standard error of the average would be about one-tenth of the average standard error of the 100 individual betas.[16] That is why it is often easier to estimate *industry betas* than betas for individual firms. Another advantage of working with portfolio betas is that they are much more stable over time than the betas of individual shares.

If Coles Myer is contemplating an across-the-board expansion, it is reasonable to discount the cash flows at the company cost of capital. To estimate this company cost of capital, Coles Myer could use its share beta or, better still, the average beta of several similar retailers.[17] Suppose, however, that Coles Myer proposed instead to invest in the production and sale of building materials. The company cost of capital is not likely to be the right discount rate for its new building materials division. For such a venture the company needs an estimate of the division's cost of capital. This is where the notion of an industry beta comes into its own. Probably the best way to estimate the discount rate for such an expansion is to use the beta of a portfolio of firms in the building materials industry.

Thus, we can think of *divisional* costs of capital as a way station between company and project costs of capital. Company costs of capital are nearly useless for diversified firms. If Coles Myer's building materials venture becomes at all significant, Coles Myer's beta will not measure the risk of *either* the building materials business *or* the retail store business. It will measure just the average risk of the two divisions. A company cost of capital based on Coles Myer's beta will almost inevitably be too high for one division and too low for the other.

## Perfect pitch and the cost of capital

Why is so much time spent estimating company and industry costs of capital? The true cost of capital depends on project risk, not on the company undertaking the project.

There are two reasons. First, many, maybe most, projects can be treated as average risk—that is, neither more nor less risky than the average of the company's other assets. For these projects the company cost of capital is the right discount rate. Second, the company cost of capital is a useful starting point for setting discount rates for unusually risky or safe projects. It is easier to add to or subtract from the company cost of capital than to estimate each project's cost of capital from scratch.

There is a good musical analogy here.[18] Most of us, lacking perfect pitch, need a well-defined reference point like middle C before we can sing on key. But anyone who can carry a tune gets relative pitch right. Business people have good intuition about *relative* risks, at least in industries they are used to, but not absolute risks or required rates of return. Therefore, they set a company- or industry-wide cost of capital as a benchmark. This is not the right hurdle rate for everything the company does, but adjustments can be made for more or less risky ventures.

## 9.2 Capital structure and the company cost of capital

The cost of capital is a hurdle rate for capital budgeting decisions. It depends on the *business risk* of the firm's investment opportunities. The risk of ordinary shares reflects the business risk of the real assets held by the firm. But shareholders also bear *financial risk* to the extent that

---

16   If the observations are independent, the standard error of the estimated mean declines in proportion to the square root of the number of observations.

17   But we would have to adjust the observed betas for differences in the debt policies of the firms. This is explained in the next section.

18   The analogy is borrowed from S. C. Myers and L .S. Borucki, 'Discounted Cash Flow Estimates of the Cost of Equity Capital – A Case Study', *Financial Markets, Institutions and Investments*, 3: 18 (August 1994).

the firm issues debt to finance its real investments. The more a firm relies on debt financing, the riskier its ordinary shares are. The financial risk can be substantial. For many companies, outstanding debt is worth more than their outstanding equity.

Borrowing is said to create **financial leverage** or **gearing**. Financial leverage does not affect the risk or the expected return on the firm's assets, but it does push up the risk of the ordinary shares and leads the shareholders to demand a correspondingly higher return. For this reason the required return on equity for Newcrest (21.2 per cent) is too high as a measure of the required return on the company's assets.

There are two risks that the use of debt creates. First, the firm may be unable to meet its debt obligations and may be forced into liquidation. This is a remote prospect for most firms and typically has a small effect on required equity returns. Second, and far more important, leverage magnifies the effect on equity returns of good times and bad. Thus, leverage makes equity returns more volatile increasing both systematic (measured by the equity beta) and unsystematic risk. Since leverage increases the equity beta it also increases the required return on equity.

## How changing capital structure affects equilibrium expected returns

Think again of what the *company* cost of capital is and what it is used for. We *define* it as the opportunity cost of capital for the firm's existing assets; we *use* it to value new assets that have the same risk as the old ones.

If you owned a portfolio of all the firm's securities—100 per cent of the debt and 100 per cent of the equity—you would own the firm's assets lock, stock and barrel. You would not share the cash flows with anyone; every dollar of cash the firm paid out would be paid to you.

You can think of the company cost of capital as the equilibrium expected return (required return) on this hypothetical portfolio. To calculate it, you just take a weighted average of the expected returns on the debt and the equity:

$$\text{Company cost of capital} = r_{\text{assets}} = r_{\text{portfolio}}$$

$$= \frac{\text{debt}}{\text{debt} + \text{equity}} r_{\text{debt}} + \frac{\text{equity}}{\text{debt} + \text{equity}} r_{\text{equity}}$$

For example, suppose that the firm's market value balance sheet is as follows:

| Asset value | 100 | Debt value (D) | 40 |
|---|---|---|---|
|  |  | Equity value (E) | 60 |
| Asset value | 100 | Firm value (V) | 100 |

Note that the values of debt and equity add up to the firm value ($D + E = V$) and that the firm value equals the asset value. (These figures are *market* values, not *book* values: The market value of the firm's equity is often substantially different from its book value.)

If investors expect a return of 8 per cent on the debt and 15 per cent on the equity, then the expected return on the assets is

$$r_{\text{assets}} = \frac{D}{V} r_{\text{debt}} + \frac{E}{V} r_{\text{equity}}$$

$$= \frac{40}{100} \times 8 + \frac{60}{100} \times 15 = 12.2\%$$

If the firm is contemplating investment in a project that has the same risk as the firm's existing business, the opportunity cost of capital for this project is the same as the firm's cost of capital; in other words, it is 12.2 per cent.

What would happen if the firm issued an additional 10 of equity and used the cash to repay 10 of its debt? The revised market value balance sheet is:

| Asset value | 100 | Debt value (D) | 30 |
| | | Equity value (E) | 70 |
| Asset value | 100 | Firm value (V) | 100 |

The change in financial structure does not affect the amount or risk of the cash flows on the total package of the debt and the equity. Therefore, if investors require a return of 12.2 per cent on the total package before the refinancing, they must require a 12.2 per cent return on the firm's assets afterwards.

Although the required return on the *package* of the debt and equity is unaffected, the change in financial structure does affect the required return on the individual securities. Since the company has less debt than before, the debtholders are likely to be satisfied with a lower return. We will suppose that the expected return on the debt falls to 7.3 per cent. Now you can write down the basic equation for the return on assets:

$$r_{assets} = \frac{D}{V} r_{debt} + \frac{E}{V} r_{equity}$$

$$= \frac{30}{100} \times 7.3 + \frac{70}{100} \times r_{equity} = 12.2\%$$

and solve for the return on equity

$$r_{equity} = 14.3\%$$

Reducing the amount of debt reduced debtholders' risk and led to a fall in the return that debtholders required ($r_{debt}$ fell from 8 to 7.3 per cent). The lower leverage also made the equity safer and reduced the return that shareholders required ($r_{equity}$ fell from 15 to 14.3 per cent). The weighted average return on debt and equity remained at 12.2 per cent:

$$r_{assets} = (0.3 \times r_{debt}) + (0.7 \times r_{equity})$$

$$= (0.3 \times 7.3) + (0.7 \times 14.3) = 12.2\%$$

You may be wondering: If the cost of debt has gone down and the cost of equity has gone down, how is it that the required return has not gone down? Simple, you are replacing 'cheap' debt with more 'expensive' equity. We remind you that it is the required return on the assets that matters, not how those assets are financed.

Suppose that the company issues enough equity to repay all the debt. In that case all the cash flows will go to the equity holders. The firm cost of capital, $r_{assets}$, stays at 12.2 per cent, and $r_{equity}$ is also 12.2 per cent.

## How changing capital structure affects beta

We have looked at how changes in financial structure affect expected return. Let us now look at the effect on beta.

The shareholders and debtholders both receive a share of the firm's cash flows, and both bear part of the risk. For example, if the firm's assets turn out to be worthless, there will be no cash to pay shareholders *or* debtholders. But debtholders bear much less risk than shareholders. Debt betas of large blue-chip firms are typically close to zero—close enough that for such companies many financial analysts just assume that $\beta_{debt} = 0$.[19]

If you owned a portfolio of all the firm's securities, you would not share the cash flows with anyone. You would not share the risks with anyone either; you would bear them all. Thus, the firm's asset beta is equal to the beta of a portfolio of all the firm's debt and its equity.

The beta of this hypothetical portfolio is just a weighted average of the debt and equity betas:

$$\beta_{assets} = \beta_{portfolio} = \frac{D}{V}\beta_{debt} + \frac{E}{V}\beta_{equity}$$

Think back to our example. If the debt before the refinancing has a beta of 0.2 and the equity a beta of 1.2, then

$$\beta_{assets} = (0.4 \times 0.2) + (0.6 \times 1.2) = 0.8$$

What happens after the refinancing? The risk of the total package is unaffected, but both the debt and the equity are now less risky. Suppose that debt beta falls to 0.1. We can work out the new equity beta:

$$\beta_{assets} = \frac{D}{V}\beta_{debt} + \frac{E}{V}\beta_{equity}$$
$$0.8 = (0.3 \times 0.1) + (0.7 \times \beta_{equity})$$
$$\beta_{equity} = 1.1$$

Figure 9.4 shows the expected return and beta of the firm's assets. It also shows how expected return and risk are shared between the debtholders and equity holders before the refinancing. Figure 9.5 shows what happens after the refinancing. Both debt and equity are less risky, and therefore investors are satisfied with a lower expected return. But equity (which is more expensive than debt) now accounts for a larger proportion of firm value than before. As a result, the weighted average of the expected returns is constant and the weighted average of the betas is also constant.

Now you can see how to unlever betas—that is, how to go from an observed $\beta_{equity}$ to $\beta_{assets}$. You have the equity beta, say 1.1. You also need the debt beta, say 0.1, and the relative market values for debt D/V and equity E/V. If debt accounts for 30 per cent of the overall value V,

$$\beta_{assets} = (0.3 \times 0.1) + (0.7 \times 1.1) = 0.8$$

This runs the previous example in reverse. Just remember the basic relationship,

$$\beta_{assets} = \frac{D}{V}\beta_{debt} + \frac{E}{V}\beta_{equity}$$

# A word of caution and a few observations

In many ways we have given an oversimplified version of how financial leverage affects equity risks and returns. For example, later we will need to amend our formulas to recognise the fact that interest can be deducted from taxable income. These finer points can wait.[20] For now, there are just a few points to remember:

▌ It is the company cost of capital that is relevant in capital budgeting decisions, not the expected return on the shares. But we only use the company cost of capital for analysing projects that have the same business risk as the company's existing investments.

---

[19] This assumption should be challenged in periods of volatile interest rates, when prices of long-term corporate and government bonds can fluctuate dramatically. There were such periods in the 1980s when bond betas were as high as 0.3 to 0.4. We would expect them to be much lower now, say about 0.2.

[20] In fact, they will have to wait till Chapters 18 and 19.

- The company cost of capital is a weighted average of the returns that investors expect from the various debt and equity securities issued by the firm.
- The company cost of capital is related to the firm's asset beta, not to the beta of the shares.
- The asset beta can be calculated as a weighted average of the betas of the various securities.
- When the firm changes its financial leverage, the risk and expected returns of the individual securities change. The asset beta and the company cost of capital do *not* change.

**figure 9.4** _____

Expected returns and betas before refinancing. The expected return and beta of the firm's assets are weighted averages of the expected return and betas of the debt and equity.

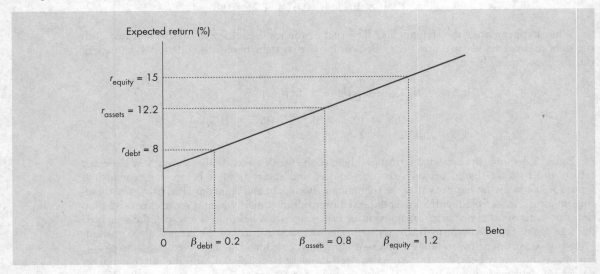

**figure 9.5** _____

Expected returns and betas after refinancing.

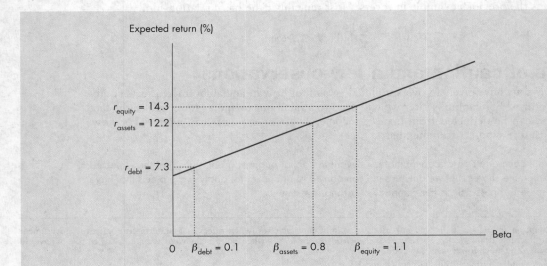

# 9.3 How to estimate the cost of capital— an example

## The expected return on Australasian P&L's ordinary shares

Suppose that after the year 2005 several power companies have been created in the wake of the privatisation of the electricity industry. You are asked to estimate the company cost of capital of one of them, Australasian Power and Light (P&L). Remember that the company cost of capital is the expected return on a portfolio of all the firm's securities. Thus, it can be calculated as a weighted average of the returns on the separate parts.

The tough part in calculating the weighted average is to estimate the equilibrium expected return on Australasian P&L's ordinary shares. It is the same problem that we encountered in Chapter 4 where we showed you how to use the constant-growth DCF formula to estimate equilibrium expected returns. The constant-growth formula and the capital asset pricing model are two different ways of getting a handle on the same problem.[21]

Table 9.2 shows estimates of beta and the standard errors of these estimates for the ordinary shares of five power companies. Most of the standard errors are less than 0.15 but they are still large enough to preclude a precise estimate of any particular power companies' beta. But our confidence about the average beta of the five power companies is rather better.

Are these power company shares really equivalent-risk securities? Judging from Table 9.2 that appears to be a reasonable assumption. Much of the spread of estimated betas could be attributed to random measurement errors. It would be hard to reject the hypothesis that the 'true' beta was the same for each of the firms.

**table 9.2**

Betas for five power companies. The average beta was calculated from the monthly returns on a portfolio of the five companies

| | Beta | Standard error |
| --- | --- | --- |
| Specific Power | 0.38 | 0.15 |
| Apple Hydro | 0.46 | 0.18 |
| Western Watts | 0.53 | 0.17 |
| Australasian P&L | 0.42 | 0.15 |
| Reef Generators | 0.35 | 0.19 |
| Portfolio | 0.43 | 0.11 |

You now have two clues about the true beta of Australasian P&L: the direct estimate of 0.42 and the average estimate for the industry of 0.43.[22] Fortunately, these two pieces of evidence are in broad agreement, so let us suppose that you take the easy way out and elect to use the figure of 0.42. Inflation took off in the year 2005, pushing up short-term interest rates, so the risk-free rate of interest $r_f$ is about 8 per cent. Therefore, if you accept an estimate of

---

21 In Chapter 4 we pointed out that the constant-growth formula will not give you good estimates of the required return for shares with rapid or unstable growth. But in other cases the constant-growth formula could give you a useful check on the estimate of $r$ that you get from the capital asset pricing model.

22 Using the average beta of power shares as a guide to the beta of Australasian P&L could be misleading if Australasian P&L had abnormally high or low leverage. A more complete analysis would adjust the betas of the sample to the debt to value ratio for Australasian P&L. We discussed leverage adjustments for beta in the last section.

8.4 per cent for the risk premium on the market, you will conclude that the expected return on Australasian P&L's share was about 11.5 per cent:[23]

$$r_{\text{equity}} = r_f + \beta_{\text{equity}}(r_m - r_f)$$

$$= 0.080 + 0.42(0.084)$$

$$= 0.115, \text{ or } 11.5\%$$

We have focused on using the capital asset pricing model to estimate the expected return on Australasian P&L's ordinary shares. But it would be useful to get a check on this figure. We have already mentioned one possibility—the constant-growth DCF formula.[24] You could also use DCF models with varying growth rates. Perhaps you might use the APT, as we showed you in Section 8.4.

## Estimating Australasian P&L's company cost of capital

If Australasian P&L were financed with shares only, the company cost of capital would be the same as the expected return on its shares. We will assume that after the year 2005 ordinary shares account for about 55 per cent of the market value of the company's securities. Debt accounts for the remaining 45 per cent.

We estimated the expected return from Australasian P&L's ordinary shares as 11.5 per cent. The yield on the company's debt is about 9.7 per cent.[25] To find the company cost of capital, we simply calculate a weighted average of the expected returns on the different securities:

$$\text{Company cost of capital} = r_{\text{assets}} = \frac{D}{V}r_{\text{debt}} + \frac{E}{V}r_{\text{equity}}$$

$$= 0.45(9.7) + 0.55(11.5)$$

$$= 0.107, \text{ or } 10.7\%\text{[26]}$$

---

[23]  This is really a discount rate for near-term cash flows, since it rests on a risk-free rate measured by the yield on Treasury notes with maturities less than one year. Is this, you may ask, the right discount rate for cash flows from an asset with, say, a 10- or 20-year expected life?

Well, now that you mention it, possibly not. The risk-free rate could be defined as a long-term Treasury bond yield. If you do this, however, you should subtract the risk premium of Treasury bonds over notes, say about 1 per cent. This gives a rough-and-ready estimate of the expected yield on short-term Treasury *notes* over the life of the bond:

Expected average T-note rate = T-bond yield − premium of bonds over notes.

[24]  We can also use the constant-growth model to estimate the expected return for individual shares, although such estimates are likely to be less reliable. Suppose that in the spring of 2005 Australasian P&L shares had a 6.6 per cent dividend yield. The company has traditionally ploughed back one-third of its earnings, and the current return on book equity (ROE) is about 13.5 per cent. If these relationships continue to hold, Australasian P&L's earnings and dividends will grow at $0.33 \times 13.5 = 4.5$ per cent (This is explained in Section 4.3.) Putting this information together gives

Expected return on share = dividend yield + expected dividend growth = 6.6 + 4.5 = 11.1%

In this case it checks fairly well with our estimates made by using the capital asset pricing model.

[25]  This is a *promised* yield; i.e. it is the yield if Australasian P&L makes all the promised payments. Since there is some risk of default, the *expected* return is less than the promised yield. For a blue-chip company like Australasian P&L, the difference is small. But for a company that is hovering on the brink of bankruptcy, it can be important.

[26]  Note you should get exactly the same result if you estimated the asset beta and then plugged this into the capital asset pricing model. Let us check.

$$r_{\text{debt}} = r_f + \beta_{\text{debt}}(r_m - r_f)$$
$$9.7 = 8.0 + \beta_{\text{debt}}(8.4)$$
$$\beta_{\text{debt}} = 0.20$$

Now calculate the beta of the firm's assets:
$$\beta_{\text{assets}} = \frac{D}{V}\beta_{\text{debt}} + \frac{E}{V}\beta_{\text{equity}}$$
$$= 0.45(0.20) + 0.55(0.42) = 0.32$$

Finally, use the capital asset pricing model to calculate $r_{\text{assets}}$:
$$r_{\text{assets}} = r_f + \beta_{\text{assets}}(r_m - r_f)$$
$$= 8.0 + 0.32(8.4) = 10.7\%$$

## 9.4 Setting discount rates when you cannot use a beta book

Share betas, industry betas or asset betas provide a rough guide to the risk encountered in various lines of business. But an asset beta for, say, the steel industry can take us only so far. Not all investments made in the steel industry are 'typical'. What other kinds of evidence about business risk might a financial manager examine?

In some cases the asset is publicly traded. If so, we can simply estimate its beta from past price data. For example, suppose a firm wants to analyse the risks of holding a large inventory of copper. Because copper is a standardised, widely-traded commodity, it is possible to calculate rates of return from holding copper and to calculate a beta for copper.

What should a manager do if the asset has no such convenient price record? What if the proposed investment is not close enough to business as usual to justify using a company or divisional cost of capital?

These cases clearly call for judgement. For managers making that kind of judgement, we offer two pieces of advice.

1. *Avoid fudge factors* Do not give in to the temptation to add fudge factors to the discount rate to offset things that could go wrong with the proposed investment. Adjust cash flow forecasts first.

2. *Think about the determinants of asset betas* Often the characteristics of high- and low-beta assets can be observed when the beta itself cannot be.

Let us expand on these two points.

## Avoiding fudge factors in discount rates

We have defined risk, from the investor's viewpoint, as the standard deviation of portfolio return or the beta of an ordinary share or other security. But in everyday usage *risk* simply equals 'bad outcome'. People think of the risks of a project as a list of things that can go wrong. For example,

▮ A geologist looking for oil worries about the risk of a dry hole.

▮ A pharmaceutical manufacturer worries about the risk that a new drug which cures baldness may not be approved for release by health authorities.

▮ The owner of a hotel in a politically unstable part of the world worries about the 'political risk' of expropriation.

Managers often add fudge factors to discount rates to offset worries such as these.

This sort of adjustment makes us nervous. First, the bad outcomes we cited appear to reflect unique (ie. diversifiable) risks that would not affect the expected rate of return demanded by investors. Second, the need for a discount rate adjustment usually arises because managers fail to give bad outcomes their due weight in cash flow forecasts. The managers then try to offset that mistake by adding a fudge factor to the discount rate.

### example

Project Z will produce just one cash flow, forecasted at $1 million at year 1. It is regarded as average risk, suitable for discounting at a 10 per cent company cost of capital:

$$\text{PV} = \frac{C_1}{(1 + r)} = \frac{1\,000\,000}{1.1} = \$909\,100$$

But now you discover that the company's engineers are behind schedule in developing the technology required for the project. They are 'confident' it will work, but they admit to a small chance that it will not. You still see the *most likely* outcome as $1 million, but you also see some chance that project Z will generate *zero* cash flow next year.

Now the project's prospects are clouded by your new worry about technology. It must be worth less than the $909 100 you calculated before that worry arose. But how much less? There is *some* discount rate (10 per cent plus a fudge factor) which will give the right value, but we do not know what that adjusted discount rate is.

We suggest you reconsider your original $1 million forecast for project Z's cash flow. Project cash flows are supposed to be *unbiased* forecasts, which give due weight to all possible outcomes, favourable and unfavourable. Managers making unbiased forecasts are correct on average. Sometimes their forecasts will turn out high, other times low, but their errors will average out over many projects.

If you forecast cash flow of $1 million for projects like Z, you will overestimate the average cash flow, because every now and then you will hit a zero. Those zeros should be 'averaged in' to your forecasts.

For many projects, the most likely cash flow is also the unbiased forecast. If there are three possible outcomes, then with the probabilities shown below, the unbiased forecast is $1 million. (The unbiased forecast is the sum of the probability-weighted cash flows.)

| Possible cash flow | Probability | Probability-weighted cash flow | Unbiased cash flow |
|---|---|---|---|
| 1.2 | 0.25 | 0.3 | |
| 1.0 | 0.5 | 0.5 | 1.0 or $1 million |
| 0.8 | 0.25 | 0.2 | |

This might describe the initial prospects of project Z. But if technological uncertainty introduces the chance of a zero cash flow, the unbiased forecast could drop to $833 300:

| Possible cash flow | Probability | Probability-weighted cash flow | Unbiased cash flow |
|---|---|---|---|
| 1.2 | 0.25 | 0.3 | |
| 1.0 | 0.333 | 0.333 | 0.833, or $833 000 |
| 0.8 | 0.25 | 0.2 | |
| 0 | 0.167 | 0 | |

The present value is

$$PV = \frac{0.833}{1.1} = 0.757, \text{ or } \$757\,000$$

Now, of course, you can figure out the right fudge factor to add to the discount rate to apply to the original $1 million forecast to get the correct answer. But you have to think through possible cash flows in order to get that fudge factor; and once you have thought through the cash flows, you do not *need* the fudge factor.

Managers often work out a range of possible outcomes for major projects, sometimes with explicit probabilities attached. We give more elaborate examples and further discussion in Chapter 10. But even when a range of outcomes and probabilities is not explicitly written down, the manager can still consider the good and bad outcomes as well as the most likely one. When the bad outcomes outweigh the good, the cash flow forecast should be reduced until balance is regained.

Step 1, then, is to do your best to make unbiased forecasts of a project's cash flows. Step 2 is to consider whether *investors* would regard the project as more or less risky than typical for a company or division. Here our advice is to search for characteristics of the asset that are associated with high or low betas. We wish we had a more fundamental scientific understanding of what these characteristics are. We see business risks surfacing in capital markets, but as yet there is no satisfactory theory describing how these risks are generated. Nevertheless, some things are known.

# What determines asset betas?

**Cyclicality**     Many people intuitively associate risk with the variability of book, or accounting, earnings. But much of this variability reflects unique or diversifiable risk. Lone prospectors searching for gold in the Western Australian bush look forward to extremely uncertain future earnings. But whether they strike it rich is not likely to depend on the performance of the market portfolio. Therefore, an investment in gold exploration has a high standard deviation but a relatively low beta. Of course, once you strike gold your beta is likely to increase because your earnings are now closely tied to fluctuations in the gold price. How much beta increases depends on how closely the gold price is linked to returns on the market portfolio.

What really counts is the strength of the relationship between the firm's earnings and the aggregate earnings on all real assets. We can measure this either by the *accounting beta* or by the *cash flow beta*. These are just like a real beta except that changes in book earnings or cash flow are used in place of rates of return on securities. We would predict that firms with high accounting or cash flow betas should also have high share betas—and the prediction is correct.[27]

This means that cyclical firms—firms whose revenues and earnings are strongly dependent on the state of the business cycle—tend to be high-beta firms. Thus, you should demand a higher rate of return from investments whose performance is strongly tied to the performance of the economy.

# *Operating leverage

We have already seen that financial leverage—in other words, the commitment to fixed debt charges—increases the beta of an investor's portfolio. In just the same way, operating leverage—in other words, the commitment to fixed *production* charges—must add to the beta of a capital project. Let us see how this works.

The cash flows generated by any productive asset can be broken down into revenue, fixed costs and variable costs:

$$\text{Cash flow} = \text{revenue} - \text{fixed cost} - \text{variable cost}$$

Costs are variable if they depend on the rate of output. Examples are raw materials, sales commissions and some labour and maintenance costs. Fixed costs are cash outflows that occur regardless of whether the asset is active or idle—for example, rates on property or the wages of workers under contract.

---

[27]  For example, see W. H. Beaver and J. Manegold, 'The Association between Market-Determined and Accounting-Determined Measures of Systematic Risk: Some Further Evidence', *Journal of Financial and Quantitative Analysis*, **10**: 231–84 (June 1975); or A. D. Castagna and Z. P. Matolcsy, op. cit, Footnote 11.

We can break down the asset's present value in the same way:

$$PV(\text{asset}) = PV(\text{revenue}) - PV(\text{fixed cost}) - PV(\text{variable cost})$$

Or equivalently:

$$PV(\text{revenue}) = PV(\text{fixed cost}) + PV(\text{variable cost}) + PV(\text{asset})$$

Those who *receive* the fixed costs are like debtholders in the project—they simply get a fixed payment. Those who receive the net cash flows from the asset are like holders of ordinary shares—they get whatever is left after payment of the fixed costs.

We can now figure out how the asset's beta is related to the betas of the values of revenue and costs. We just use our previous formula with the betas relabelled:

$$\beta_{\text{revenue}} = \beta_{\text{fixed cost}} \frac{PV(\text{fixed cost})}{PV(\text{revenue})} + \beta_{\text{variable cost}} \frac{PV(\text{variable cost})}{PV(\text{revenue})} + \beta_{\text{asset}} \frac{PV(\text{asset})}{PV(\text{revenue})}$$

In other words, the beta of the value of the revenues is simply a weighted average of the beta of its component parts. Now the fixed-cost beta is zero by definition. Whoever receives the fixed costs holds a safe asset. The betas of the revenues and variable costs should be approximately the same, because they respond to the same underlying variable, the rate of output. Therefore, we can substitute $\beta_{\text{revenue}}$ for $\beta_{\text{variable cost}}$ and solve for the asset beta. Remember that $\beta_{\text{fixed cost}} = 0$.

$$\beta_{\text{asset}} = \beta_{\text{revenue}} \frac{PV(\text{revenue}) - PV(\text{variable cost})}{PV(\text{asset})}$$

$$= \beta_{\text{revenue}} \left[ 1 + \frac{PV(\text{fixed cost})}{PV(\text{asset})} \right]$$

Thus, given the cyclicality of revenues (reflected in $\beta_{\text{revenue}}$), the asset beta is proportional to the ratio of the present value of fixed costs to the present value of the project.

Now you have a rule of thumb for judging the relative risks of alternative designs or technologies for producing the same project. Other things being equal, the alternative with the higher ratio of fixed costs to project value will have the higher project beta. Empirical tests confirm that companies with high operating leverage actually do have high betas.[28]

## Searching for clues

Recent research suggests a variety of other factors that affect an asset's beta.[29] But going through a long list of these possible determinants would take us too far afield.

You cannot hope to estimate the relative risk of assets with any precision, but good managers examine any project from a variety of angles and look for clues as to its riskiness. They know that high market risk is a characteristic of cyclical ventures and of projects with high fixed costs. They think about the major uncertainties affecting the economy and consider how projects are affected by these uncertainties.[30]

---

28  See B. Lev, 'On the Association between Operating Leverage and Risk', *Journal of Financial and Quantitative Analysis*, 9: 627–42 (September 1974), and G. N. Mandelker and S. G. Rhee, 'The Impact of the Degrees of Operating and Financial Leverage on Systematic Risk of Ordinary Shares', *Journal of Financial and Quantitative Analysis*, 19: 45–57 (March 1984).

29  Some of this work is reviewed in G. Foster, *Financial Statement Analysis*, 2nd ed., Prentice-Hall, Englewood Cliffs, N.J., 1986, Chapter 10.

30  Sharpe's article on a 'multi-beta' interpretation of market risk offers a useful way of thinking about these uncertainties and tracing their impact on a firm or project's risk. See W. F. Sharpe, 'The Capital Asset Pricing Model: A "Multi-Beta" Interpretation', in H. Levy and M. Sarnat (eds.), *Financial Decision Making under Uncertainty*, Academic Press, New York, 1977.

# *9.5 Another look at risk and discounted cash flow

In practical capital budgeting, a single discount rate is usually applied to all future cash flows. For example, an expected return may be calculated from the capital asset pricing model:

$$r = r_f + \beta(r_m - r_f)$$

The resulting $r$ would be plugged directly into the standard discounted cash flow formula:

$$PV = \sum_{t=1}^{T} \frac{C_t}{(1 + r)^t}$$

Among other things, this procedure assumes that beta is constant over the project's entire life.[31] Here is an example which shows what that assumption really means.

---

## example

Project A is expected to produce a cash inflow of $100 million for each of three years. The risk-free interest rate is 6 per cent, the market risk premium is 8 per cent and project A's beta is 0.75. You therefore calculate A's opportunity cost of capital as follows:

$$r = r_f + \beta(r_m - r_f)$$

$$= 6 + 0.75(8) = 12\%$$

Discounting at 12 per cent gives the following present value for each cash flow:

Project A

| Year | Cash flow | PV at 12% |
|------|-----------|-----------|
| 1 | 100 | 89.3 |
| 2 | 100 | 79.7 |
| 3 | 100 | 71.2 |
| | Total PV | 240.2 |

Now compare these figures with the cash flows of project B. Notice that B's cash flows are lower than A's; but B's flows are safe, and therefore they are discounted at the risk-free interest rate. The *present value* of each year's cash flow is identical for the two projects.

---

[31]   See E. F. Fama, 'Risk-Adjusted Discount Rates and Capital Budgeting under Uncertainty', *Journal of Financial Economics*, **5**: 3–24 (August 1977); or S. C. Myers and S. M. Turnbull, 'Capital Budgeting and the Capital Asset Pricing Model: Good News and Bad News', *Journal of Finance*, **32**: 321–32 (May 1977).

| Project B | | |
|---|---|---|
| Year | Cash flow | PV at 6% |
| 1 | 94.6 | 89.3 |
| 2 | 89.6 | 79.7 |
| 3 | 84.8 | 71.2 |
| | Total PV | 240.2 |

In year 1 project A has a risky cash flow of 100. This has the same present value as the safe cash flow of 94.6 from project B. Economists would describe the 94.6 as the **certainty equivalent** of 100. Since the two cash flows have the same present value, investors are willing to give up $100 - 94.6 = 5.4$ in expected year 1 income in order to get rid of the uncertainty.

In year 2 project A has a risky cash flow of 100 and B has a safe cash flow of 89.6. Again both flows have the same present value. Thus, to eliminate the uncertainty in year 2, investors are prepared to give up $100 - 89.6 = 10.4$ of future income. And to eliminate uncertainty in year 3, they are willing to give up $100 - 84.8 = 15.2$ of future income.

To value project A, you discounted each cash flow at the same risk-adjusted discount rate of 12 per cent. Now you can see what is implied when you did that. By using a constant rate you effectively made a larger deduction for risk from the later cash flows:

| Year | Forecasted flow for project A | Certainty-equivalent cash flow | Deduction for risk |
|---|---|---|---|
| 1 | 100 | 94.6 | 5.4 |
| 2 | 100 | 89.6 | 10.4 |
| 3 | 100 | 84.8 | 15.2 |

The second cash flow is riskier than the first because it is exposed to two years of market risk. The third cash flow is riskier still because it is exposed to three years of market risk. You can see this increased risk reflected in the steadily declining certainty equivalents.

In the first year, investors would be willing to accept a 5.4 per cent lower cash flow if it were risk-free:

$$\frac{\text{Risk cash flow}}{1.054} = \text{certainty-equivalent cash flow}$$

$$\frac{100}{1.054} = 94.6$$

Later years certainty equivalents decrease by 5.4 per cent per year:

$$\text{Second year: } \frac{100}{(1.054)^2} = 89.6$$

$$\text{Third year: } \frac{100}{(1.054)^3} = 84.8$$

There is no law of nature stating that certainty equivalents have to decrease in this smooth and regular way. In just a moment we will sketch a real example in which they did not. But first let us formalise and review the concept of certainty equivalents.

## Valuing certainty-equivalent flows

Let us start again with a single future cash flow $C_1$. If $C_1$ is certain, its present value is found by discounting at the risk-free rate $r_f$:

$$PV = \frac{C_1}{1 + r_f}$$

If the cash flow is risky, the normal procedure is to discount its forecasted (expected) value at a *risk-adjusted discount rate r*, which is greater than $r_f$.[32] The risk-adjusted discount rate adjusts for both time and risk. This is illustrated by the clockwise route in Figure 9.6.

**figure 9.6** _____
Two ways to calculate present value.

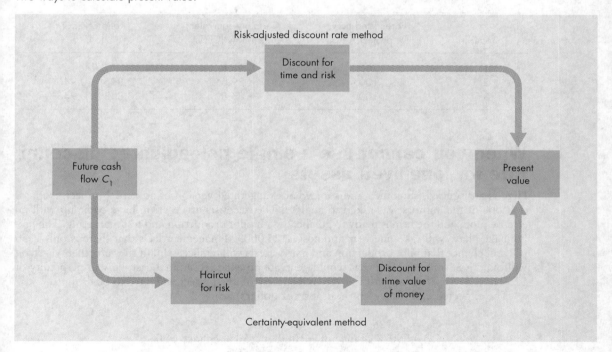

The alternative certainty-equivalent method makes separate adjustments for risk and time. This is illustrated by the counterclockwise route in Figure 9.6. When we use this method, we ask: 'What is the smallest *certain* payoff for which I would exchange the risky cash flow $C_1$?' This is called the *certainty equivalent* of $C_1$, denoted by $CEQ_1$.[33]

---

[32] The quantity $r$ can be less than $r_f$ for assets with negative betas. But the betas of the assets which corporations hold are almost always positive.

[33] $CEQ_1$ can be calculated directly from the capital asset pricing model. The formula is given in the appendix to this chapter.

Since $CEQ_1$ is the value equivalent of a safe cash flow, it is discounted at the risk-free rate $r_f$. Thus, we have two identical expressions for PV:

$$PV = \frac{C_1}{(1 + r)} = \frac{CEQ_1}{(1 + r_f)}$$

For cash flows two, three or $t$ years away,

$$PV = \frac{C_t}{(1 + r)^t} = \frac{CEQ_t}{(1 + r_f)^t}$$

So if we want to covert $C_t$ to a certainty equivalent we have to multiply it by a factor equal to

$$\frac{(1 + r_f)^t}{(1 + r)^t} = \left[\frac{(1 + r_f)}{(1 + r)}\right]^t$$

If we are to use the same discount rate for every future cash flow, then the certainty equivalents must decline steadily as a fraction of the cash flow. We saw this with project A, where the ratio of the certainty-equivalent cash flow to the forecasted flow declined by 5.4 per cent a year:

| Year | Forecasted flow for project A ($C_t$) | Certainty-equivalent cash flow ($CEQ_t$) | Ratio of $CEQ_t$ to $C_t$ |
|---|---|---|---|
| 1 | 100 | 94.6 | 0.946 |
| 2 | 100 | 89.6 | $0.896 = 0.946^2$ |
| 3 | 100 | 84.8 | $0.848 = 0.946^3$ |

## When you *cannot* use a single risk-adjusted discount rate for long-lived assets

Here is a disguised, simplified and somewhat exaggerated version of an actual project proposal that one of the authors was asked to analyse. The scientists at Vegetron have come up with an electric mop, and the firm is ready to go ahead with pilot production and test marketing. The preliminary phase will take one year and cost $125 000. Management feels that there is only a 50 per cent chance that pilot production and market tests will be successful. If they are, then Vegetron will build a $1 million plant that would generate an expected annual cash flow in perpetuity of $250 000 a year after taxes. If they are not successful, the project will have to be dropped.

The expected cash flows (in thousands of dollars) are

$$C_0 = -125$$
$$C_1 = 50\% \text{ chance of } -1000 \text{ and } 50\% \text{ chance of } 0$$
$$= 0.5(-1000) + 0.5(0) = -500$$
$$C_t \text{ for } t \text{ of } 2, 3, \ldots = 50\% \text{ chance of } 250 \text{ and } 50\% \text{ chance of } 0 = 0.5(250) + 0.5(0) = 125$$

Management has little experience with consumer products and considers this a project of extremely high risk.[34] Therefore, they discount the cash flows at 25 per cent, rather than at Vegetron's normal 10 per cent standard:

$$NPV = -125 - \frac{500}{1.25} - \sum_{t=2}^{\infty} \frac{125}{(1.25)^t} = -125, \text{ or } -\$125 \ 000$$

---

[34] We will assume that they mean high *market* risk and that the difference between 25 and 10 per cent is *not* a fudge factor introduced to offset optimistic cash flow forecasts.

This seems to show that the project is not worthwhile.

Management's analysis is open to criticism if the first year's experiment resolves a high proportion of the risk. If the test phase is a failure, then there's no risk at all—the project is *certain* to be worthless. If it is a success, there could well be only normal risk from there on. Let us assume that there is only normal risk if the first year is a success. Then it is no longer appropriate to discount at a rate that assumes year 1 risks continue into the future.

We should make sure that the expected cash flows from year 1 onwards are correctly adjusted for the risk in year 1, and then discount them at the normal discount rate. There is a 50 per cent chance that at the end of year 1 Vegetron will have the opportunity to invest in a project of *normal* risk, for which the *normal* discount rate of 10 per cent would be appropriate. Thus, they have a 50 per cent chance to invest $1 million in a project with a net present value of $1.5 million:

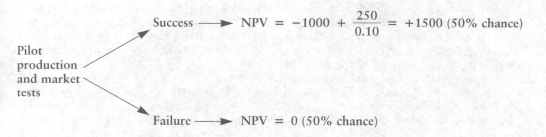

$$\text{Success} \longrightarrow \text{NPV} = -1000 + \frac{250}{0.10} = +1500 \text{ (50\% chance)}$$

Pilot production and market tests

$$\text{Failure} \longrightarrow \text{NPV} = 0 \text{ (50\% chance)}$$

Thus, we could view the project as offering an expected payoff of $0.5(1500) + 0.5(0) = 750$ or $750\,000 at $t = 1$ on a $125\,000 investment at $t = 0$. We still have the problem of determining a discount rate for the $750\,000. Does the 25 per cent rate properly reflect year 1 risks? If it does, the project clearly has a positive NPV.

Alternatively, we could use the certainty-equivalent approach. The certainty equivalent of the payoff is less than $750\,000, but the difference would have to be very large to justify rejecting the project. For example, if the certainty equivalent is half the forecasted cash flow and the risk-free rate is 7 per cent, the project is worth $225\,500:

$$\text{NPV} = C_0 + \frac{\text{CEQ}_1}{(1 + r_f)}$$

$$= -125 + \frac{0.5(750)}{1.07} = 225.5, \text{ or } \$225\,500$$

This is not bad for a $125\,000 investment—and quite a change from the negative NPV that management got by discounting all future cash flows at 25 per cent.

## A common mistake

You sometimes hear people say that because distant cash flows are 'riskier' they should be discounted at a *higher rate* than earlier cash flows. That is quite wrong. Using the same risk-adjusted discount rate for each year's cash flow *implies* a larger deduction for risk from the later cash flows. The reason is that the discount rate compensates for the risk borne *per period*. The more distant the cash flows, the greater the number of periods and the larger the *total* risk adjustment.

It makes sense to use a single risk-adjusted discount rate as long as the project has the same market risk at each point in its life. But look out for exceptions like the electric mop project, where market risk changes as time passes.

## 9.6 Summary

In Chapter 8 we set out some basic principles for valuing risky assets. In this chapter we have shown you how to apply these principles to practical situations, such as estimating equity betas.

The problem of selecting a discount rate is easiest when you believe that the project has the same market risk as the company's existing assets. In this case, the required return equals the required return on a portfolio of the company's securities. This is often called the *company cost of capital.*

Capital asset pricing theory states that the required return on any asset depends on its risk. In this chapter we have defined risk as beta and used the capital asset pricing model to calculate expected returns.

The most common way to estimate the beta of a share is to figure out how the share price has responded to market changes in the past. Of course, this will give you only an estimate of the share's true beta. You may get a more reliable figure if you calculate an industry beta for a group of similar companies. Alternatively, you may prefer to use a fundamental estimate of the equity beta.

Suppose that you now have an estimate of the equity beta. Can you plug that into the capital asset pricing model to find the company's cost of capital? No, the equity beta for levered firms reflects both business and financial risk. Whenever a company borrows money, it increases the beta (and the expected return) of its share. Remember that the company cost of capital is the required return on a portfolio of all the firm's securities, not just the ordinary shares. You can calculate it by estimating the required return on each of the securities and then taking a weighted average of these separate returns. Or you can calculate the beta of the portfolio of securities and then plug this *asset beta* into the capital asset pricing model.

The company cost of capital is the correct discount rate for projects that have the same risk as the company's existing business. Many firms, however, use the company cost of capital to discount the forecasted cash flows on all new projects. This is a dangerous procedure. Each project should be evaluated at its own opportunity cost of capital; the true cost of capital depends on the use to which the capital is put. If we wish to estimate the cost of capital for a particular project, it is *project risk* that counts. Of course, the company cost of capital is fine as a discount rate for average risk projects. It is also a useful starting point for estimating discount rates for safer or riskier projects.

We cannot give you a neat formula that will allow you to estimate project betas. This has greatly restricted the use of beta in evaluating real investments. Many firms start with the company cost of capital and adjust it up or down according to their assessment of project risk. While we cannot give you beta estimates on a plate, we can give you some clues about what you should consider when setting the discount rate. First, avoid adding fudge factors to discount rates to offset your worries about bad project outcomes. Adjust cash flow forecasts to give due weight to bad outcomes as well as good; *then* ask whether the chance of bad outcomes adds to the project's market risk. Second, you can often identify the characteristics of a high- or low-beta project even when the project beta cannot be calculated directly. For example, you can try to figure out how much the cash flows are affected by the overall performance of the economy: Cyclical investments are generally high-beta investments. You can also look at the project's operating leverage: fixed production charges work like fixed debt charges—that is, they increase beta.

There is one more fence to jump. Most projects produce cash flows for several years. Firms generally use the same risk-adjusted rate $r$ to discount each of these cash flows. When they do this, they are implicitly assuming that cumulative risk increases at a constant rate, as you look further into the future. That assumption is usually reasonable. It is precisely true when the project's future beta will be constant—that is, when risk *per period* is constant.

It is the exceptions that prove the rule, or so the saying goes.[35] So be on the alert for projects where risk clearly does *not* increase steadily. In these cases, you should break the project into segments within which the same discount rate can be reasonably used. Or you should use the certainty-equivalent version of the DCF model, which allows separate risk adjustments to each period's cash flow.

Finally, we must point out that the capital asset pricing model may not give us the whole story on required returns. It is a relatively simple model derived under some fairly restrictive assumptions. However, it has proved to be quite robust, and so far we have failed to come up with any measure of risk that is convincingly better than beta.

## APPENDIX Using the capital asset pricing model to calculate certainty equivalents

When calculating present value, you can take account of risk in either of two ways. You can discount the expected cash flow $C_1$ by the risk-adjusted discount rate $r$:

$$PV = \frac{C_1}{(1 + r)}$$

Alternatively, you can discount the certainty-equivalent cash flow $CEQ_1$ by the risk-free rate of interest $r_f$:

$$PV = \frac{CEQ_1}{(1 + r_f)}$$

In this appendix we show how you can derive $CEQ_1$ from the capital asset pricing model.

We know from our present value formula that $1 + r$ equals the expected dollar payoff on the asset divided by its present value:

$$1 + r = \frac{C_1}{PV}$$

The capital asset pricing model also tells us that

$$1 + r = 1 + r_f + \beta(r_m - r_f)$$

Therefore,

$$\frac{C_1}{PV} = 1 + r_f + \beta(r_m - r_f)$$

In order to find beta, we calculate the covariance between the asset return and the market return and divide by the market variance:

$$\beta = \frac{\text{cov}(\tilde{r}, \tilde{r}_m)}{\sigma_m^2} = \frac{\text{cov}(\tilde{C}_1/PV - 1, \tilde{r}_m)}{\sigma_m^2}$$

---

[35]  This is one of those sayings that have become misused with the passage of time. 'Prove' in this context has the old English meaning of test. So the saying is really—the exception tests the rule.

The quantity $\widetilde{C}_1$ is the future cash flow and is therefore uncertain. But PV is the asset's present value: it is *not* unknown and therefore does not 'covary' with $r_m$—it is a constant. The $-1$ is also a constant and drops out. Therefore, we can rewrite the expression for beta as

$$\beta = \frac{\text{cov}(\widetilde{C}_1, \widetilde{r}_m)}{\text{PV}\,\sigma_m^2}$$

Substituting this expression back into our equation for $C_1/\text{PV}$ gives

$$\frac{C_1}{\text{PV}} = 1 + r_f + \frac{\text{cov}(\widetilde{C}_1, \widetilde{r}_m)}{\text{PV}} \times \frac{r_m - r_f}{\sigma_m^2}$$

The expression $(r_m - r_f)/\sigma^2$ is the expected risk premium on the market per unit of variance. It is often known as the *market price of risk* and is written as $\lambda$. Thus,

$$\frac{C_1}{\text{PV}} = 1 + r_f + \frac{\lambda\,\text{cov}(\widetilde{C}_1, \widetilde{r}_m)}{\text{PV}}$$

Multiplying through by PV and rearranging gives

$$\text{PV} = \frac{C_1 - \lambda\,\text{cov}(\widetilde{C}_1, \widetilde{r}_m)}{1 + r_f}$$

This is the certainty-equivalent form of the capital asset pricing model. It tells us that, if the asset is risk-free, cov $(\widetilde{C}_1, \widetilde{r}_m)$ is zero and we simply discount $C_1$ by the risk-free rate. But, if the asset is risky, we must discount the certainty equivalent of $C_1$. The deduction that we make from $C_1$ depends on the market price of risk and on the covariance between the cash flows on the project and the return on the market.

## FURTHER READING

There is a good review article by Rubinstein on the application of the capital asset pricing model to capital investment decisions:

M. E. Rubinstein, 'A Mean-Variance Synthesis of Corporate Financial Theory', *Journal of Finance*, **28**: 167–82 (March 1973).

For evidence on the stability of betas estimated from past share price data, see:

M. E. Blume, 'On the Assessment of Risk', *Journal of Finance*, **26**: 1–10 (March 1971).

W. F. Sharpe and G. M. Cooper, 'Risk-Return Classes of New York Share Exchange Ordinary Shares, 1931–1967,' *Financial Analysts Journal*, **28**: 46–54, 81 (March–April 1972).

There have been a number of studies of the relationship between accounting data and beta. Foster provides a review of many of the studies and Castagna and Matolcsy provide some Australian evidence:

G. Foster, *Financial Statement Analysis*, 2nd ed., Prentice-Hall, Inc., Englewood Cliffs, N.J., 1986.

A. D. Castagna and Z. P. Matolcsy, 'The Relationship Between Accounting Variables and Systematic Risk', *Australian Journal of Management*, 113–19 (October 1978).

For some ideas on how one might break down the problem of estimating beta, see:

W. F. Sharpe, 'The Capital Asset Pricing Model: A "Multi-Beta" Interpretation', in H. Levy and M. Sarnat (eds.), *Financial Decision Making Under Uncertainty*, Academic Press, New York, 1977.

The assumptions required for use of risk-adjusted discount rates are discussed in:

E. F. Fama, 'Risk-Adjusted Discount Rates and Capital Budgeting under Uncertainty', *Journal of Financial Economics*, **5**: 3–24 (August 1977).

S. C. Myers and S. M. Turnbull, 'Capital Budgeting and the Capital Asset Pricing Model: Good News and Bad News', *Journal of Finance*, **32**: 321–32 (May 1977).

The relationship between the certainty-equivalent and risk-adjusted discount rate valuation formulas was first discussed by:

A. A. Robichek and S. C. Myers, 'Conceptual Problems in the Use of Risk-Adjusted Discount Rates', *Journal of Finance*, **21**: 727–30 (December 1966).

## QUIZ

**1.** Suppose a firm uses its company cost of capital to evaluate all capital projects. What kinds of mistakes will it make?

**2.** A project costs $100 000 and offers a single $150 000 cash flow one year hence. The project beta is 2.0, and the market risk premium $(r_m - r_f)$ is 8.5 per cent. Look up current risk-free interest rates in the *Australian Financial Review* or another newspaper. Use the capital asset pricing model to find the opportunity cost of capital and the present value of the project.

**3.** Look again at Table 9.1 and the row of statistics shown for Comalco. Define and interpret each of these statistics.

**4.** A company is financed 40 per cent by risk-free debt. The interest rate is 10 per cent, the expected market return is 18 per cent, and the share's beta is 0.5. What is the company cost of capital?

**5.** The total market value of the ordinary shares of the Booker Real Estate Company is $6 million, and the total value of its debt is $4 million. The treasurer estimates that the beta of the shares is currently 1.5 and that the expected risk premium on the market is 9 per cent. The Treasury note rate is 8 per cent.
  a. What is the required return on Booker shares?
  b. What is the beta of the company's existing portfolio of assets?
  c. Estimate the company's cost of capital.
  d. Estimate the discount rate for an expansion of the company's present business.
  e. Suppose the company wants to diversify into the manufacture of rose-coloured spectacles. The beta of unleveraged optical manufacturers is 1.2. Estimate the required return on Booker's new venture.

**6.** An oil company is drilling a series of new wells on the perimeter of a producing oil field. About 20 per cent of the new wells will be dry holes. Even if a new well strikes oil, there will still be uncertainty about the amount of oil produced. Forty per cent of new wells that strike oil only produce 1000 barrels a day. Sixty per cent produce 5000 barrels per day.
  a. Forecast the annual cash revenues from a new perimeter well. Use a future oil price of $18 per barrel.
  b. A geologist proposes to discount the cash flows of the new wells at 30 per cent to offset the risk of dry holes. The oil company's normal cost of capital is 10 per cent. Does the geologist's proposal make sense? Briefly explain why or why not.

**\*7.** Which of these companies is likely to have the higher cost of capital?
  a. A's sales force is paid a fixed annual rate; B's is paid on a commission basis.
  b. C produces machine tools; D produces breakfast cereal.

**\*8.** Select the appropriate phrase from within each pair of brackets:
'In calculating PV there are two ways to adjust for risk. One is to make a deduction from the expected cash flows. This is known as the *certainty-equivalent method*. It is usually written as PV = $[CEQ_t/(1 + r_f)^t$; $CEQ_t/(1 + r_m)^t]$. The certainty-equivalent cash flow, $CEQ_t$, is always [more than; less than] the forecasted risky cash flow. Another way to allow for risk is to discount the expected cash flows at a rate of $r$. If we use the capital asset pricing model to calculate $r$, then $r$ is $[r_f + \beta r_m$; $r_f + \beta(r_m - r_f)$; $r_m + \beta(r_m - r_f)]$. This method is exact only if the ratio of the certainty-equivalent cash flow to the forecasted risky cash flow [is constant; declines at a constant rate; increases at a constant rate]. For the majority of projects, the use of a single discount rate, $r$, is probably a perfectly acceptable approximation.'

**\*9.** A project has a forecasted cash flow of $110 in year 1 and $121 in year 2. The interest rate is 5 per cent, the estimated risk premium on the market is 10 per cent and the project has a beta of 0.5. If you use a constant risk-adjusted discount rate, what is:
  a. The present value of the project?
  b. The certainty-equivalent cash flow in year 1 and year 2?
  c. The ratio of the certainty-equivalent cash flows to the expected cash flows in years 1 and 2?

## QUESTIONS AND PROBLEMS

**1.** Look at Table 9.1.
  a. How much did Capral Aluminium's share price tend to change in an unchanged market?
  b. Which share had price changes that were most closely related to the market? What proportion of the share's risk was market risk and what proportion was unique risk?
  c. What was the confidence interval on George Weston's beta?
  d. Calculate the adjusted beta for Newcrest mining.
  e. What was the total risk of John Fairfax shares *per year*?

**2.** Explain the estimate of alpha for Comalco shares in Table 9.1. Why is this not a good guide to the share's future alpha? What is your best forecast of alpha?

**3.** Nullarbor's beta in Table 9.1 is unusual. Why? Would you feel comfortable relying on Nullarbor's beta when calculating the cost of capital?

**4.** Look again at the estimates for Comalco shares in Table 9.1.
  a. Calculate the required return of Comalco assuming the capital asset pricing model is correct. Use current one-year Treasury rates and a reasonable forecast of the market risk premium. How much confidence would you have in this estimate?
  b. What are the pros and cons of using an aluminium industry cost of capital as a benchmark discount rate for Comalco?

**5.** 'The cost of capital depends on the risk of the project being evaluated. Therefore, company costs of capital are useless.' Is this correct? Evaluate this statement.

**6.** a. Nero Violins has the following capital structure:

| Security | Beta | Total market value ($million) |
|----------|------|-------------------------------|
| Debt | 0 | 100 |
| Preferred shares | 0.20 | 40 |
| Ordinary shares | 1.20 | 200 |

What is the firm's asset beta (i.e. the beta of a portfolio of all the firm's securities)?

b. How would the asset beta change if Nero issued an additional $140 million of ordinary shares and used the cash to repurchase all the debt and preferred shares?

c. Assume that the capital asset pricing model is correct. What discount rate should Nero set for investments that expand the scale of its operations without changing its asset beta? Assume any new investment is all equity-financed. Plug in numbers that are reasonable today.

**7.** You are given the following information for Rouge Centre Tours:

- Long-term debt outstanding     $300 000
- Current yield to maturity, $r_D$     8 per cent
- Number of ordinary shares     10 000
- Price per share     $50
- Book value per share     $25
- Expected rate of return on the stock, $r_E$     15 per cent

a. Calculate Rouge's weighted average cost of capital.

b. How would $r_E$ and the weighted average cost of capital change if Rouge's share price fell to $25 due to declining profits? Business risk is unchanged.

**8.** Amalgamated Products has three operating divisions:

| Division | Percentage of firm value |
|----------|--------------------------|
| Food | 50 |
| Electronics | 30 |
| Chemicals | 20 |

To estimate the cost of capital for each division, Amalgamated has identified the following three principal competitors:

| | Estimated equity beta | Debt/(debt + equity) |
|---|-----------------------|----------------------|
| United Foods | 0.8 | 0.3 |
| General Electronics | 1.6 | 0.2 |
| Associated Chemicals | 1.2 | 0.4 |

Assume these betas are accurate estimates and that the capital asset pricing
model is correct.

a. Assuming that the debt of these firms is risk-free, estimate the asset beta for
   each of Amalgamated's divisions.
b. Amalgamated's ratio of debt to debt plus equity is 0.4. If your estimates of
   divisional betas are right, what is Amalgamated's equity beta?
c. Assume that the risk-free interest rate is 7 per cent and that the expected return
   on the market index is 15 per cent. Estimate the cost of capital for each of
   Amalgamated's divisions.
d. How much would your estimates of each division's cost of capital change if you
   assumed that each division's debt had a beta of 0.2?

9. 'The errors in estimating beta are so great that you might just as well assume that
   all betas are 1.0.' Do you agree?

10. Assume you have identified a group of six food companies with similar products
    and operating strategies. Explain how you would calculate an industry beta and
    cost of capital for this sample of companies. Assume for simplicity that the
    companies have no debt outstanding, How would you check the range of potential
    error in the industry beta?

11. Mum and Dad Groceries has just dispatched a year's supply of groceries to the
    government of the Central Antarctic Republic. Payment of $250 000 will be made
    one year hence after the shipment arrives by snow train. Unfortunately, there is a
    good chance of a coup d'état, in which case the new government will not pay. Mum
    and Dad's controller therefore decides to discount the payment at 40 per cent,
    rather than at the company's 12 per cent cost of capital.

a. What is wrong with using a 40 per cent rate to offset 'political risk'?
b. How much is the $250 000 payment really worth if the odds of a coup d'état
   are 25 per cent?

12. Here is a more challenging problem involving cash flow forecasts, discount rates
    and fudge factors. An oil company executive is considering investing $10 million in
    one or both of two wells. Well 1 is expected to produce oil worth $3 million a year
    for 10 years; well 2 is expected to produce oil worth $2 million a year for 15 years.
    These are *real* (inflation-adjusted) cash flows.

    The beta for *producing wells* is 0.9. The market risk premium is 8 per cent, the
    nominal risk-free interest rate is 6 per cent and expected inflation is 4 per cent.

    The two wells *are* intended to develop a previously discovered oil field.
    Unfortunately, there is still a 20 per cent chance of a dry hole in each case. A dry
    hole means zero cash flow and a complete loss of the $10 million investment.

    Ignore taxes and make further *assumptions* as necessary.

a. What is the correct real *discount* rate for cash flows from developed wells?
b. The oil company executive proposes to add 20 *percentage* points to the real
   discount rate to offset the risk of a dry hole. Calculate the NPV of each well
   with this adjusted discount rate.
c. What do *you* say the NPVs of the two wells are?
d. Is there any *single* fudge factor that could be added to the discount rate for
   developed wells that would yield the correct NPV for both wells? Explain.

13. 'For a high-beta project, you should use a high discount rate to value positive cash
    flows and a low discount rate to value negative cash flows.' Is this statement
    correct? Should the sign of the cash flow affect the appropriate discount rate?

**\*14.** A project has the following forecasted cash flows:

| Cash flows ($'000) | | | |
|---|---|---|---|
| $C_0$ | $C_1$ | $C_2$ | $C_3$ |
| +100 | +40 | +60 | +50 |

The estimated project beta is 1.5. The market return $r_m$ is 16 per cent, and the risk-free rate $r_f$ is 7 per cent.
a. Estimate the opportunity cost of capital and the project's present value (using the same rate to discount each cash flow).
b. What are the certainty-equivalent cash flows in each year?
c. What is the ratio of the certainty-equivalent cash flow to the expected cash flow in each year?
d. Explain why this ratio declines.

**\*15.** Look back at project A in Section 9.5. Now assume that:
a. Expected cash flow is $150 per year for five years.
b. The risk-free rate of interest is 5 per cent.
c. The market risk premium is 9 per cent.
d. The estimated beta is 1.2.
Recalculate the certainty-equivalent cash flows and show that the ratio of these certainty-equivalent cash flows to the risky cash flows declines by a constant proportion each year.

**\*16.** The McGregor Whisky Company is proposing to market diet scotch. The product will first be test-marketed for two years in South Australia at an initial cost of $500 000. This test launch is not expected to produce any profits but should reveal consumer preferences. There is a 60 per cent chance that demand will be satisfactory. In this case, McGregor will spend $5 million to launch the scotch nationwide and will receive an expected annual profit of $700 000 in perpetuity. If demand is not satisfactory, diet scotch will be withdrawn.
Once consumer preferences are known, the product will be subject to an average degree of risk and therefore McGregor requires a return of 12 per cent on its investment. However, the initial test-market phase is viewed as much riskier, and McGregor demands a return of 40 per cent on this initial expenditure.
What is the NPV of the diet scotch project?

**\*17.** Use past share price data to estimate the betas of a sample of ordinary shares. Plug these betas into the capital asset pricing model to estimate the return that investors require on these shares today. Now use a different sample period to re-estimate the betas of each share. How much difference would it have made to your estimates of the required return if you had used these betas?

# part 3

# PRACTICAL PROBLEMS IN CAPITAL BUDGETING

# chapter 10

# A PROJECT IS NOT A BLACK BOX

**A** *black box* is something that we accept and use but do not understand. For most of us a computer is a black box. We may know what it is supposed to do, but we do not understand how it works and, if something breaks, we cannot fix it.

We have been treating capital projects as black boxes. In other words, we have talked as if managers are handed unbiased cash flow forecasts and their only task is to assess risk, choose the right discount rate and crank out net present value. Actual financial managers will not rest until they understand what makes the project tick and what could go wrong with it. Remember Murphy's law, 'If anything can go wrong, it will' and O'Reilly's corollary, 'at the worst possible time'.

*Even if the project's risk is wholly diversifiable,* you still need to understand why the venture could fail. Once you know that, you can decide whether it is worth trying to resolve the uncertainty. Maybe further expenditure on market research would clear up these doubts about acceptance by consumers; maybe another drill hole would give you a better idea of the size of the ore body; and maybe some further work on the test bed would confirm the durability of those welds. If the project really has a negative NPV, the sooner you can identify it, the better. And even if you decide that it is worth going ahead on the basis of present information, you do not want to be caught by surprise if things subsequently go wrong. You want to know the danger signals and the actions you might take.

In short, managers avoid black boxes whenever they can, and they reward whoever can help them look inside. Consequently, consultants and academics have developed procedures for what we will call *project analysis*. We will discuss several of the procedures in this chapter, mainly sensitivity analysis, break-even analysis, Monte Carlo simulation and decision trees. These techniques not only help you understand the project, they may also help you identify and value the options associated with projects.[1] There is no magic in these techniques, just computer-assisted common sense. You do not need a licence to use them.

Some analysts have proposed these techniques not only for project analysis but also as a supplement or replacement for net present value. You can imagine our reaction to that. Their proposals seem to reflect a belief that net present value cannot cope with risk. But we have seen that it can cope. At the end of the day, after project analysis is complete, the final decisions should flow from NPV, adjusted if necessary for any option values embedded in the project.

## 10.1 Sensitivity analysis

Uncertainty means that more things can happen than will happen. Therefore, whenever you are confronted with a cash flow forecast, you should try to discover what else could happen.

Put yourself in the well-heeled shoes of the treasurer of the Jalopy Motor Company. You are considering the introduction of an electrically-powered motor scooter for city use. Your staff members have prepared the cash flow forecasts shown in Table 10.1. Since NPV is positive at the 10 per cent opportunity cost of capital, it appears to be worth going ahead.

$$NPV = -150 + \sum_{t=1}^{10} \frac{30}{(1.10)^t} = \$34.3 \text{ million}$$

Before you decide, you want to delve into these forecasts[2] and identify the key variables that determine whether the project will succeed or fail. It turns out that the marketing department has estimated revenue as follows:

Unit sales = new product's share of market × size of motor scooter market
    = 0.1 × 1 million = 100 000 motor scooters
Revenue = unit sales × price per unit
    = 100 000 × 3750 = $375 million

The production department has estimated variable costs per unit as $3000. Since projected volume is 100 000 motor scooters per year, *total* variable cost is $300 million. Fixed costs are $30 million per year. The initial investment can be depreciated on a straight-line basis over the 10-year period, and profits are taxed at a rate of 50 per cent.

These seem to be the important things you need to know, but look out for unidentified variables. Perhaps there are patent problems, or perhaps you will need to invest in service stations that will recharge the motor scooter batteries. The greatest dangers often lie in these *unknown* unknowns, or 'unk-unks' as scientists call them.

Having found no unk-unks (no doubt you will find them later), you conduct a **sensitivity analysis** with respect to market size, market share, and so on.[3] In order to do this, the marketing and production staff are asked to give optimistic and pessimistic estimates for the underlying variables. These are set out in the left-hand columns of Table 10.2. The right-hand

---

[1]   Remember, we introduced the idea of such options in Chapter 5.

[2]   Bear in mind when you are working with cash flow forecasts the distinction between the expected value and the most likely (or modal) value. Present values are concerned with *expected* cash flows—i.e. the probability weighted average of the possible future cash flows. If the distribution of possible outcomes is skewed, the expected cash flow will not be the same as the most likely cash flow.

[3]   You might also test the sensitivity of the project to changes in the corporate tax rate. We have chosen a 50 per cent tax rate for convenience in calculation. The real Australian corporate tax rate is currently 36 per cent, but it has varied between 33 per cent and 39 per cent over the last decade, and before that it was not far from 50 per cent.

side shows what happens to the project's NPV if the variables are set *one at a time* to their optimistic and pessimistic values. Your project appears to be by no means a sure thing. The most dangerous variables appear to be market share and unit variable cost. If market share is only 0.04 (and all other variables are as expected), then the project has an NPV of −$104 million. If unit variable cost is $3600 (and all other variables are as expected), then the project has an NPV of −$150 million.

**table 10.1**

Preliminary cash flow forecasts for Jalopy Motor's electric scooter project ($million)

|  | Year 0 | Years 1–10 |
|---|---|---|
| Investment | 150 | |
| 1. Revenue | | 375 |
| 2. Variable cost | | 300 |
| 3. Fixed cost | | 30 |
| 4. Depreciation | | 15 |
| 5. Pre-tax profit (1 − 2 − 3 − 4) | | 30 |
| 6. Tax | | 15 |
| 7. Net profit (5 − 6) | | 15 |
| 8. Operating cash flow (4 + 7) | | 30 |
| Net cash flow | −$150 | +$30 |

*Assumptions:*
1. Investment is depreciated over 10 years straight-line.
2. Income is taxed at a rate of 50 per cent.

**table 10.2**

To undertake a sensitivity analysis of the electric motor scooter project, we set each variable *in turn* at its most pessimistic or optimistic value and recalculate the net present value of the project.

| Variable | Range | | | NPV ($million) | | |
|---|---|---|---|---|---|---|
|  | Pessimistic | Expected | Optimistic | Pessimistic | Expected | Optimistic |
| Market size | 0.9 million | 1 million | 1.1 million | +11 | +34 | +57 |
| Market share | 0.04 | 0.1 | 0.16 | −104 | +34 | +173 |
| Unit price | $3500 | $3750 | $3800 | −42 | +34 | +50 |
| Unit variable cost | $3600 | $3000 | $2750 | −150 | +34 | +111 |
| Fixed cost | $40 million | $30 million | $20 million | +4 | +34 | +65 |

# Value of information

Now you can check whether an investment of time or money could resolve some of the uncertainty *before* your company parts with the $150 million investment. Suppose that the pessimistic value for unit variable cost partly reflects the production department's worry that a particular machine will not work as designed and that the operation will have to be performed by other methods at an extra cost of $200 per unit. The chance that this will occur is only 1 in 10. But, if it did occur, the extra $200 unit cost would reduce after-tax cash flow by

$$\text{Unit sales} \times \text{additional unit cost} \times (1 - \text{tax rate}) = 100\ 000 \times 200 \times 0.50$$
$$= \$10 \text{ million}$$

It would reduce the net present value of your project by

$$\text{Extra PV of costs} = \sum_{t=1}^{10} \frac{10}{(1.10)^2} = \$61.4 \text{ million}$$

This would be sufficient to sink the project, because the NPV would be $+34 - 61.4 = -\$27.4$ million.

Suppose further that a $100 000 pre-test of the machine will reveal whether it will work or not and allow you to clear up the problem. It clearly pays to invest $100 000 to avoid a 10 per cent probability of $61.4 million fall in NPV. You are ahead by $-100\ 000 + 0.10 \times 61\ 400\ 000 = +\$6\ 040\ 000$.

On the other hand, the value of additional information about market size is small. Because the project is acceptable even under pessimistic assumptions about market size, you are unlikely to be in trouble if you have misestimated that variable.[4]

## Limits to sensitivity analysis

Sensitivity analysis boils down to expressing cash flows in terms of key project variables and then calculating the consequences of misestimating the variables. It forces the manager to identify the underlying variables, indicates where additional information would be most useful and helps to expose confused or inappropriate forecasts.

One drawback to sensitivity analysis is that it always gives somewhat ambiguous results. For example, what exactly does *optimistic* or *pessimistic* mean? The marketing department may be interpreting the terms in a different way from the production department. Ten years from now, after hundreds of projects, hindsight may show that the marketing department's pessimistic limit was exceeded twice as often as the production department's; but what you may discover 10 years hence is no help now. One solution is to ask the two departments for a *complete* description of the various odds. However, it is far from easy to extract a forecaster's subjective notion of the complete probability distribution of possible outcomes.[5]

Another problem with sensitivity analysis is that the underlying variables are likely to be interrelated. What sense does it make to look at the effect in isolation of an increase in market size? If market size exceeds expectations, it is likely that demand will be stronger than you anticipated and unit prices will be higher. And why look in isolation at the effect of an increase in price? If inflation pushes prices to the upper end of our range, it is quite probable that costs will also be inflated.

Sometimes the analyst can get around these problems by defining underlying variables so that they are roughly independent. But you cannot push *one-at-a-time* sensitivity analysis too far. It is impossible to obtain expected, optimistic and pessimistic values for total *project* cash flows from the information in Table 10.2.

---

4    Of course, these are very simple examples. The derivation of optimal rules for investing in information is a well-developed part of Bayesian statistics. See H. Raiffa, *Decision Analysis: Introductory Lectures on Choices under Uncertainty*, Addison-Wesley Publishing Company, Inc., Reading, Mass., 1968.

5    If you doubt this, try some simple experiments. Ask the person who repairs your television to state a numerical probability that your set will work for at least one more year. Or construct your own subjective probability distribution of the number of telephone calls you will receive next week. That ought to be easy. Try it.

# Examining the project under different scenarios

If the variables are interrelated, it may help to consider some alternative plausible combinations. For example, perhaps the company economist is worried about the possibility of another sharp rise in world oil prices. The direct effect of this would be to encourage the use of electrically-powered motor scooters. The popularity of smaller cars after the oil price increases in the 1970s leads you to estimate that an immediate 20 per cent price rise in oil would enable you to capture an extra 0.3 per cent of the car market. On the other hand, the economist also believes that higher oil prices would prompt a world recession and at the same time stimulate inflation. In that case, market size might be in the region of 8 million motor scooters and both prices and cost might be 15 per cent higher than your initial estimates. Table 10.3 shows that this scenario of higher oil prices and recession would on balance help your new venture. Its net present value would increase to $65 million.

**table 10.3** _____

How the net present value of the electric scooter project would be affected by higher oil prices and a world recession

| | Cash flows, years 1–10 ($million) | |
|---|---|---|
| | **Base case** | **High oil prices and recession case** |
| 1. Revenue | 375 | 449 |
| 2. Variable cost | 300 | 359 |
| 3. Fixed cost | 30 | 35 |
| 4. Depreciation | 15 | 15 |
| 5. Pre-tax profit (1 − 2 − 3 − 4) | 30 | 40 |
| 6. Tax | 15 | 20 |
| 7. Net profit (5 − 6) | 15 | 20 |
| 8. Net cash flow (4 + 7) | 30 | 35 |
| Present value of cash flows | +184 | +215 |
| Net present value | +34 | +65 |

| | Assumptions | |
|---|---|---|
| | **Base case** | **High oil prices and recession case** |
| Market size | 1 million | 0.8 million |
| Market share | 0.1 | 0.13 |
| Unit price | $3750 | $4313 |
| Unit variable cost | $3400 | $3450 |
| Fixed cost | $30 million | $35 million |

Managers often find it helpful to look at how their project would fare under different scenarios. It allows them to look at different but *consistent* combinations of variables. Forecasters generally prefer to give an estimate of revenues or costs under a particular scenario than to give some absolute optimistic or pessimistic value.

# Break-even analysis

When we undertake a sensitivity analysis of a project or when we look at alternative scenarios, we are asking how serious it would be if sales or costs turned out to be worse than we forecasted. Managers sometimes prefer to rephrase this question and ask how bad sales can get before the project begins to lose money. This exercise is known as **break-even analysis**.

In the left-hand portion of Table 10.4 we set out the revenues and costs of the electric motor scooter project under different assumptions about annual sales.[6] In the right-hand portion of the table we discount these revenues and costs to give us the *present value* of the inflows and the *present value* of the outflows. *Net* present value is, of course, the difference between these numbers.

You can see that NPV is strongly negative if the company does not produce a single motor scooter. It is just positive if (as expected) the company sells 100 000 motor scooters and is strongly positive if it sells 200 000 motor scooters. Clearly the *zero NPV* point occurs at a little under 100 000 motor scooters.

In Figure 10.1 we have plotted the present value of the inflows and outflows under different assumptions about annual sales. The two lines cross when sales reach 85 000 motor scooters. This is the point at which the project has zero NPV. As long as sales are greater than 85 000, the project has a positive NPV.[7]

table 10.4 _____

NPV of electric scooter project under different assumptions about unit sales ($million)

| | Inflow | Outflow | | | | | | |
|---|---|---|---|---|---|---|---|---|
| | | Year 0 | Years 1–10 | | | | | |
| Unit sales (thousands) | Revenue Years 1–10 | Investment | Variable cost | Fixed cost | Taxes | PV inflows | PV outflow | NPV |
| 0 | 0 | 150 | 0 | 30 | −22.5 | 0 | 196 | −196 |
| 100 | 375 | 150 | 300 | 30 | 15 | 2304 | 2270 | 34 |
| 200 | 750 | 150 | 600 | 30 | 52.5 | 4608 | 4344 | 264 |

Managers frequently calculate the break-even point in terms of accounting profits rather than present values. Table 10.5 shows the effect on Jalopy's after-tax profit of differences in electric motor scooter sales. Once again, in Figure 10.2 we have plotted revenues and costs against unit sales. But the story this time is different. Figure 10.2, which is based on accounting profits, shows a break-even point of 60 000 motor scooters. Figure 10.1, which is based on present values, shows a break-even point of 85 000 motor scooters. Why the difference?

When we work in terms of accounting profit, we deduct depreciation of $15 million each year to cover the cost of the initial investment. If Jalopy sells 60 000 motor scooters a year, revenues will be sufficient both to pay operating costs and to recover the initial outlay of $150 million. But they will *not* be sufficient to repay the *opportunity cost* of that $150 million. If

---

[6]  Notice that if the project makes a loss, this loss can be used to reduce the tax bill on the rest of the company's business. In this case the project produces a tax saving—the tax outflow is negative.

[7]  Instead of working with the present values of the inflows and outflows, we could work equally well with the equivalent annual revenues and costs. The annual cost of the project includes the recurring costs (variable costs, fixed costs and taxes) *plus* the equivalent annual cost of the $150 million initial investment. To calculate the equivalent annual cost of the initial investment we divide the investment by the 10-year annuity factor. Of course, when we plot the equivalent annual costs and revenues the break-even point would be identical at 85 000 motor scooters.

**figure 10.1**

A break-even chart showing the present value of Jalopy's cash inflows and outflows under different assumptions about unit sales. NPV is zero when sales are 85 000.

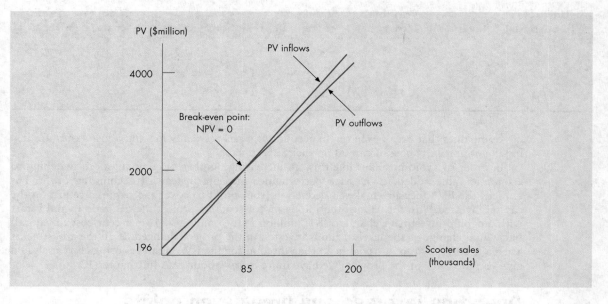

**figure 10.2**

Sometimes break-even charts are constructed in terms of accounting numbers. After-tax profit is zero when sales are 60 000.

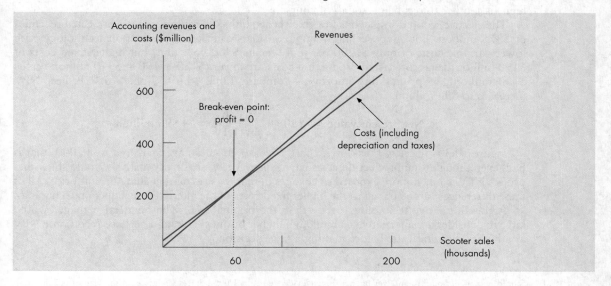

we allow for the fact that the $150 million could have been invested elsewhere to earn 10 per cent, the equivalent annual cost of the investment is not $15 million but $24.4 million.[8]

---

[8]　Equivalent annual cost of investment = (investment)/(10-year annuity factor at 10%) = 150/6.145 = $24.4 million.

　　The annual revenues at 85 000 motor scooters per year are about $319 million. You can check that this is sufficient to cover fixed costs, variable costs and taxes, and still leave $24.4 million per year to recover the $150 million initial investment and a 10 per cent return on that investment.

**table 10.5**

The effect of the electric motor scooter project on accounting profit under different assumptions about unit sales ($million)

| Unit sales (thousands) | Revenue | Variable costs | Fixed costs | Depreciation | Taxes | Total costs | Profit after tax |
|---|---|---|---|---|---|---|---|
| 0 | 0 | 0 | 30 | 15 | −22.5 | 22.5 | −22.5 |
| 100 | 375 | 300 | 30 | 15 | 15 | 360 | 15 |
| 200 | 750 | 600 | 30 | 15 | 52.5 | 697.5 | 52.5 |

Companies that break even on an accounting basis are really making a loss—they are losing the opportunity cost of capital on their investment.[9]

In order to avoid mistakes like this, an increasing number of companies are switching to economic value added (EVA) as a performance measure instead of accounting profit. Put crudely, the EVA measure makes a deduction from profit to cover the required return on the capital invested.[10] In the case of the Jalopy motor scooters project the deduction would start with a capital investment charge of $15 million ($150 million × 10 per cent cost of capital) but would change as the level of funds invested in the project changed. If all the adjustments are made correctly (not a trivial task) then discounting the EVA numbers for each year should give you the NPV of the project. We have more to say about EVA in Chapter 12.

## Operating leverage and break-even points

Break-even charts like Figure 10.1 help managers appreciate *operating leverage*—that is, project exposure to fixed costs. Remember from Section 9.4 that high operating leverage means high risk, other things being equal, of course.

The electric scooter project has low fixed costs; only $30 million against projected revenues of $375 million. But suppose Jalopy now considers a different production technology with lower variable costs of only $1200 per unit (versus $3000 per unit) but higher fixed costs of $190 million. Total forecasted production costs are lower ($120 + 190 = $310 million versus $330 million), so profitability improves—compare Table 10.6 to Table 10.1. Project NPV increases to $96 million.

$$\text{Net present value} = 150 + \sum_{t=1}^{10} \frac{40}{(1.1)^t} = +\$96 \text{ million}$$

Figure 10.3 is the new break-even chart. Break-even sales have *increased* to 88 000 (that is bad) even though total production costs have *fallen*. A new sensitivity analysis would show that project NPV is much more exposed to changes in market size, market share or unit price. All of these differences can be traced to the higher fixed costs of the alternative production technology.

Is the alternative technology better than the original one? The financial manager would have to consider the alternative technology's higher business risk, and perhaps recompute NPV at a higher discount rate, before making a final decision.[11]

---

9   In 1971 Lockheed managers found themselves having to give evidence to the United States Congress on the viability of the company's L-1011 TriStar program. They argued that the program appeared to be 'commercially attractive' and that TriStar sales would eventually exceed the break-even point of about 200 aircraft. But in calculating this break-even point, Lockheed appears to have ignored the opportunity cost of the huge $1 billion capital investment on this project. Had it allowed for this cost, the break-even point would probably have been nearer to 500 aircraft. See U. E. Reinhardt, 'Break-Even Analysis for Lockheed's TriStar: An Application of Financial Theory', *Journal of Finance*, 28: 821–38 (September 1973).

10  This is not a new idea. It has been around for a long time under the label 'residual income'. It has been re-badged and re-packaged with computer software and made more palatable by consultants.

11  He or she could use the procedures outlined in Section 9.4 to recalculate beta and come up with a new discount rate.

**table 10.6**
Cash flow forecasts and present value for the electric scooter project, here assuming a production technology with high fixed costs but low total costs (compare with Table 10.1).

|  | Year 0 | Years 1–10 |
|---|---|---|
| Investment | 150 | |
| 1. Revenue | | 375 |
| 2. Variable costs | | 120 |
| 3. Fixed cost | | 190 |
| 4. Depreciation | | 15 |
| 5. Pre-tax profit (1 − 2 − 3 − 4) | | 50 |
| 6. Tax | | 25 |
| 7. Net profit (5 − 6) | | 25 |
| 8. Operating cash flow (4 + 7) | | 40 |
| Net cash flow | −$150 | +$40 |

**figure 10.3**
Break-even chart for an alternative production technology with higher fixed costs. Notice that break-even sales increase to 88 000. Compare with Figure 10.1.

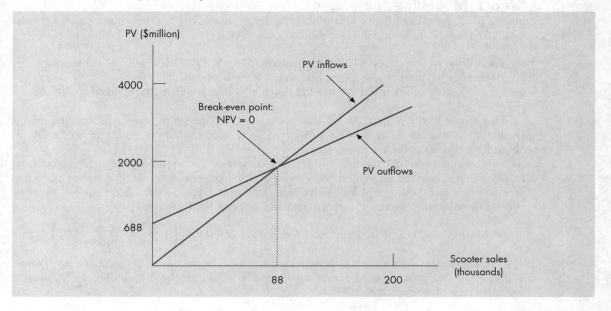

## 10.2 Monte Carlo simulation

Sensitivity analysis allows you to consider the effect of changing one variable at a time. By looking at the project under alternative scenarios, you can consider the effect of a *limited number* of plausible combinations of variables. **Monte Carlo simulation** is a tool for considering *all* possible combinations. It therefore enables you to inspect the entire distribution of project outcomes. Its use in capital budgeting was first advocated by David Hertz and McKinsey and Company, the management consultants.[12]

Imagine that you are a gambler at Monte Carlo. You know nothing about the laws of probability (few casual gamblers do), but a friend has suggested to you a complicated strategy for playing roulette. Your friend has not actually tested the strategy but is confident that it will *on the average* give you a 2.5 per cent return for every 50 spins of the wheel. Your friend's optimistic estimate for any series of 50 spins is a profit of 55 per cent; your friend's pessimistic estimate is a loss of 50 per cent. How can you find out whether these really are the odds? An easy but possibly expensive way is to start playing and record the outcome at the end of each series of 50 spins. Then after, say, 100 series of 50 spins each, plot a frequency distribution of the outcomes and calculate the average and upper and lower limits. If things look good, you can then get down to some serious gambling.

An alternative is to tell a computer to simulate the roulette wheel and the strategy. In other words, you could instruct the computer to draw numbers out of its hat to determine the outcome of each spin of the wheel and then to calculate how much you would make or lose from the particular gambling strategy.

That would be an example of Monte Carlo simulation. In capital budgeting we replace the gambling strategy with a model of the project, and the roulette wheel with a model of the world in which the project operates. Let us see how this might work with our project for an electrically-powered scooter.

## Simulating the electric scooter project

### Step 1 Modelling the project

The first step in any simulation is to give the computer a precise model of the project. For example, the sensitivity analysis of the scooter project was based on the following implicit model of cash flow:

Cash flow = (revenues − costs − depreciation) × (1 − tax rate) + depreciation
Revenues = market size × market share × unit price
Costs = (market size × market share × variable unit cost) + fixed cost

This model of the project was all that you needed for the simple-minded sensitivity analysis that we described above. But if you wish to simulate the whole project, you need to think about how the variables are interrelated.

For example, consider the first variable—market size. The marketing department has estimated a market size of 10 million scooters in the first year of the project's life, but of course you do not *know* how things will work out. Actual market size will exceed or fall short of expectations by the amount of the department's error in the forecast:

$$\text{Market size, year 1} = \text{expected market size, year 1} \times \left(1 + \frac{\text{forecast error,}}{\text{year 1}}\right)$$

You *expect* the forecast error to be zero but it could turn out to be positive or negative. Suppose, for example, that the actual market size turns out to be 1.1 million. That means a forecast error of 10 per cent or +0.1:

$$\text{Market size, year 1} = 1 \times (1 + 0.1) = 1.1 \text{ million}$$

12   See D. B. Hertz, 'Investment Policies that Pay Off', *Harvard Business Review*, **46**: 96–108 (January–February 1968).

You can write the market size in the second year in exactly the same way:

$$\text{Market size, year 2} = \text{expected market size, year 2} \times \left(1 + \frac{\text{forecast error, year 2}}{}\right)$$

But at this point you must consider how the expected market size in year 2 is affected by what happens in year 1. If scooter sales are below expectations in year 1, it is likely that they will continue to be below in subsequent years. Suppose that a shortfall in sales in year 1 would lead you to revise down your forecast of sales in year 2 by a like amount. Then

$$\text{Expected market size, year 2} = \text{actual market size, year 1}$$

Now you can rewrite the market size in year 2 in terms of the actual market size in the previous year plus a forecast error:

$$\text{Market size, year 2} = \text{market size, year 1} \times \left(1 + \frac{\text{forecast error, year 2}}{}\right)$$

In the same way you can describe the expected market size in year 3 in terms of market size in year 2, and so on.

This set of equations illustrates how you can describe interdependence between different *periods*. But you also need to allow for interdependence between different *variables*. For example, the price of electrically-powered scooters is likely to increase with general inflation and with market size. Suppose that this is the only uncertainty and that each 10 per cent shortfall in market size would lead you to predict a 3 per cent reduction in price, and for each 10 per cent demand greater than expected you predict a 3 per cent price increase. Then you could model the first year's price as follows:

$$\text{Price, year 1} = \text{expected price, year 1} \times \left(1 + 0.03 \times \frac{\text{error in market size forecast, year 1}}{}\right)$$

Then, if variations in market size exert a permanent effect on price, you can define the second year's price as

$$\text{Price, year 2} = \text{expected price, year 2} \times \left(1 + 0.03 \times \frac{\text{error in market size forecast, year 2}}{}\right)$$

$$= \text{actual price, year 1} \times \left(1 + 0.03 \times \frac{\text{error in market size forecast, year 2}}{}\right)$$

The complete model of your project would include a set of equations for each of the variables—market size, price, market share, unit variable cost and fixed cost. Even if you allowed for only a few interdependencies between variables and across time, the result would be quite a complex list of equations.[13] Perhaps that is not a bad thing if it forces you to understand what the project is all about. Model building is like spinach: you may not like the taste, but it is good for you.

## Step 2 Specifying probabilities

Remember the procedure for simulating the gambling strategy? The first step was to specify the strategy, the second was to specify the numbers on the roulette wheel, and the third was to tell the computer to select these numbers at random and calculate the results of the strategy:

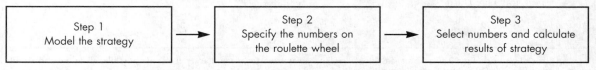

| Step 1<br>Model the strategy | → | Step 2<br>Specify the numbers on<br>the roulette wheel | → | Step 3<br>Select numbers and calculate<br>results of strategy |

---

[13]  Specifying the interdependencies is the hardest and most important part of a simulation. If all components of project cash flows were unrelated, simulation would rarely be necessary.

The steps are just the same for your scooter project:

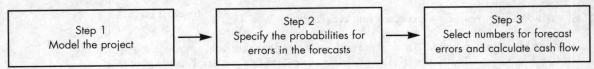

Figure 10.4 illustrates how you might go about specifying your possible errors in forecasting market size. You *expect* market size to be 10 million scooters. You obviously do not think that you are underestimating or overestimating market size; therefore, your expected forecast error is zero. On the other hand, the marketing department has given you a range of possible estimates. Market size could be as low as 0.85 million scooters or as high as 1.15 million scooters. Thus, the forecast error has an expected value of 0 and a range of plus or minus 15 per cent.[14] You need to draw up similar patterns of the possible forecast errors for each of the other variables that are in your model.

**figure 10.4**
Distribution of forecast errors for market size. The expected error is 0, but extreme errors could be as large as plus or minus 0.15. We have assumed a normal, bell-shaped distribution with a standard deviation of 0.05.

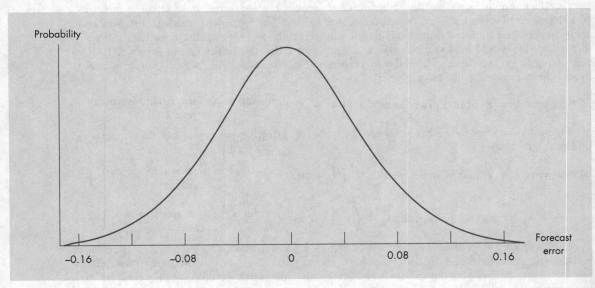

**Step 3   Simulate the cash flows**   The computer now *samples* from the distribution of the forecast errors, calculates the resulting cash flows for each period and records them. After many iterations you begin to get accurate estimates of the probability distributions of the project cash flows—accurate, that is, only to the extent that your model and the probability distributions of the forecast errors are accurate. Remember the GIGO principle: 'Garbage in, garbage out'.

---

14   An error of plus or minus 0.15 is three standard deviations away from the mean. Larger errors are possible, given the normal distribution in Figure 10.4, but extremely improbable.

   Other distributions could, of course, be used. For example, the marketing department may view any market size between 0.9 and 1.1 million scooters as equally likely. In that case the simulation would require a uniform (rectangular) distribution of forecast errors, with a range of −0.10 to +0.10.

Figure 10.5 shows some of the outputs from an actual simulation of the electric scooter project. The mean cash flow is about $31 million for both years shown, but the range of possible outcomes is considerably higher in year 10 than in year 5.[15] Note also the positive skewness of the outcomes—very large outcomes are somewhat more likely than very small ones. This is common—and realistic—when forecast errors accumulate over time. Because of the skewness the average cash flow is somewhat higher than the most likely outcome—in other words, a bit to the right of the peak of the distribution.

Let us look at this a bit more closely. Our simulations tell us that the expected cash flow in each year is about $31 million, but the new products group told you that the expected cash flow is $30 million. They evidently arrived at this figure by taking the expected sales, multiplying by the expected profit per unit and deducting the expected fixed cost and tax:

$$\text{Expected} = \text{expected sales (units)} \times (\text{expected unit price} - \text{variable unit cost})$$
$$- \text{ expected fixed costs} - \text{ expected tax}$$

$$100\ 000(\$3750 - \$3000) - \$30 \text{ million} - \$15 \text{ million} = \$30 \text{ million}$$

Unfortunately, there was an error in the logic of the new products group. The expected revenues are *not* equal to the expected unit sales multiplied by the expected unit price unless sales and price are unrelated. If that sounds odd to you, consider the following example. Suppose a firm is equally likely to sell 100 items at a price of $1 each or 300 items at a price of $3 each. Its expected unit sales are $(100 + 300) \times 0.5 = 200$, and the expected price is $(1 + 3) \times 0.5 = \$2$. The expected unit sales multiplied by the expected price is therefore $200 \times 2 = \$400$. But the expected *revenue* is $[(100 \times 1) + (300 \times 3)] \times 0.5 = \$500$. The expected revenue is higher because in this example price and sales levels are positively correlated.

Similarly in the case of Jalopy, price tends to go up and down with sales volume. Therefore, the calculations of the new products group have *underestimated* the expected cash flow.

## Simulation of pharmaceutical research and development

Simulation, though sometimes costly and complicated, has the obvious merit of compelling the forecaster and the decision maker to face up to uncertainty and to interdependencies. By constructing a detailed Monte Carlo simulation model you will gain a better understanding of how the project works and what could go wrong with it. You will have confirmed, or improved, your forecasts of future cash flows, and you can be more confident about your calculations of the project's NPV.

Australian industrial companies such as CSR have used simulation to evaluate new projects, while some Australian mining companies use simulation when deciding whether to open a new mine. Internationally, several large pharmaceutical companies have used Monte Carlo simulation to analyse investments in research and development (R&D) of new drugs. These companies spend billions of dollars annually on R&D, in the face of massive uncertainty.

Figure 10.6 sketches the life cycle of a new drug from its infancy, when it is identified as a promising chemical compound, to old age, when the drug's patents expire and 'generic' competitors enter and drive down selling prices. The R&D phase may last 10 to 12 years before health authorities approve the new drug and the company begins to market it. The total life cycle may span 25 to 30 years.

---

[15]   These are actual outputs from Crystal Ball™ software used with an EXCEL spreadsheet program. The simulation ran through 10 000 trials. We thank Christopher Howe for running the simulation.

**figure 10.5**

Simulations of cash flows in years 5 and 10 for the electric scooter project.

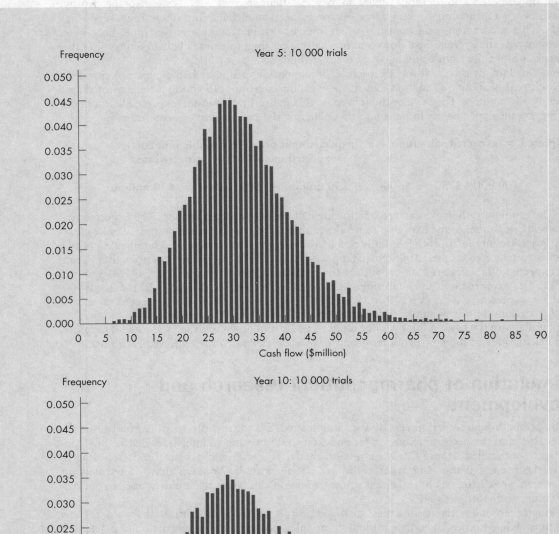

**figure 10.6**
Research and testing of a potential new drug from discovery to initial sales. This figure concentrates on the odds that the drug will pass all required clinical tests and be approved by the health authorities. Some of the hazards or uncertainties facing an approved drug are listed at bottom right. Only a small fraction of drug candidates identified in basic research prove to be safe and effective and achieve profitable production. The 'Stop' signs indicate failure and abandonment of the candidate.

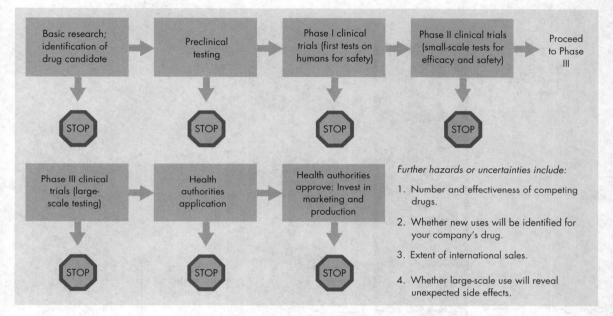

The pharmaceutical companies' scientists and marketing and financial managers face three kinds of uncertainty.

1. *Scientific and clinical* Will the compound work? Will it have harmful side effects? Will it ultimately gain public health approval? (Most drugs do not: of 10 000 promising compounds, only one or two may ever get to market. These one or two have to generate enough cash flow to make up for the 9999 or 9998 that fail.)
2. *Production and distribution* Heavy investments in R&D have to be made with only a vague idea of costs of production and distribution.
3. *Market success* Health authority approval does not guarantee that a drug will sell. A competitor may be there first with a similar (or better) drug. The company may or may not be able to sell the drug worldwide. Selling prices and marketing costs are unknown.

Imagine you are standing at the top left of Figure 10.6. A proposed research program will investigate a promising class of compounds. Could you write down expected cash inflows and outflows of the program out to 25 or 30 years in the future? We suggest that no mortal could do so without a model to help.

Figure 10.7 reproduces a flow chart for a Monte Carlo simulation model used by Merck & Co. This 'Research Planning Model' has been used for more than 10 years and is 'integral to [Merck's] strategic decision making process'.[16]

---

[16] N. A. Nichols, 'Scientific Management at Merck: An Interview with CFO Judy Lewent', *Harvard Business Review*, **72**: 91 (January–February 1994).

**figure 10.7**

Flowchart of a simulation model used by Merck & Company to analyse investments in pharmaceutical R&D.

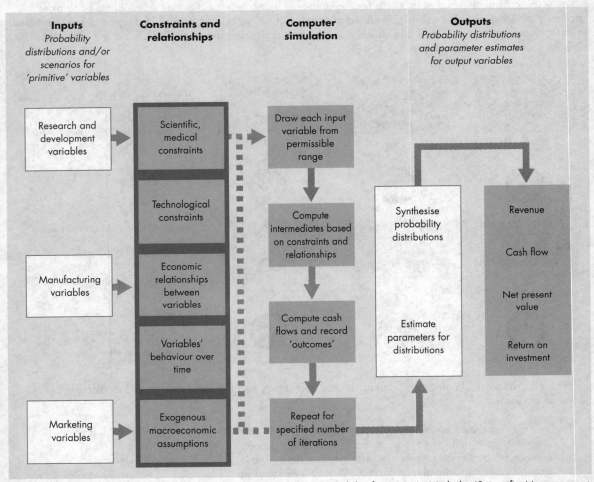

*Source*: Reprinted by permission of *Harvard Business Review*. An exhibit from N. A. Nichols, 'Scientific Management at Merck: An Interview with CFO Judy Lewent', *Harvard Business Review*, **72**: 96 (January–February 1994). Copyright © 1994 by the President and Fellows of Harvard College; all rights reserved.

## Assessing simulation: you pay for what you get

With the advent of computer spreadsheet packages, simulation has become much easier and cheaper. To make the task even easier there are simulation packages that you can purchase as spreadsheet add-ins. Once you have constructed your model, it is simple to analyse changes in the variables: What would happen, for example, if through more market research you were able to narrow down the range of uncertainty about any of the variables? You can also use the simulation to explore the effect of modifications to the project.

Simulation may sound like a panacea for the world's ills. But, as usual, you pay for what you get. Sometimes you pay for more than you get. It is not just a matter of the time and money spent in building the model. It is extremely difficult to estimate interrelationships between variables and the underlying probability distributions, even when you are trying to be honest.[17] But in capital budgeting, forecasters are seldom impartial and the probability distributions on which simulations are based can be highly biased.

In practice a simulation that attempts to be realistic will also be complex. Therefore, the decision maker may delegate the task of constructing the model to management scientists or consultants. The danger here is that, even if the builders understand their creation, the decision maker cannot and therefore does not rely on it. This is a common but ironic experience: the model that was intended to open up black boxes ends up creating another one.

## Misusing simulation

The financial manager, like a detective, must use every clue. Simulation should be regarded as one of several ways to obtain information about expected cash flows and risk. But the final investment decision involves only one number: NPV.

Some of the early champions of simulation made much greater claims for the method. They started with the premise that NPV cannot in itself reflect risk properly and therefore they bypassed that last crucial step. In this alternative approach the financial manager is given distributions not of cash flows but of NPVs or internal rates of return. Now that may sound attractive—surely a whole distribution of NPVs is better than a single number? But we shall see that this 'more is better' reasoning leads the financial manager into a trap.

First, we should explain what is meant by a distribution of NPVs. To get the distribution, the NPV calculation is incorporated into the simulation. The cash flows for each iteration of the simulation model are translated into a net present value by *discounting at the risk-free rate*. Notice that it is the cash flows from each iteration of the simulation that are being discounted and *not* the *expected cash flows*. Why are they not discounted at the opportunity cost of capital? Because, if you know what that is, you do not need a simulation model, except perhaps to help forecast expected cash flows. The risk-free rate is used to avoid prejudging risk.[18]

A project's 'risk' is then reflected in the dispersion of its NPV distribution. Thus, the term *net present value* takes on a very different meaning from the usual one. If an asset has a number of possible 'present values', it makes little sense to associate PV with *the* price the asset would sell at in a competitive capital market.[19]

The 'risk' of this distribution ignores the investors' opportunity to diversify. Moreover, it is sensitive to the definition of the project. If two unrelated projects are combined, the 'risk' of the NPV of the combined projects will be less than the average 'risk' of the NPVs of the two separate projects. That not only offends the value additivity principle, but it also encourages sponsors of marginal projects to beat the system by submitting joint proposals.

Finally, it is very difficult to interpret a distribution of NPVs. Since the risk-free rate is not the opportunity cost of capital, there is no economic rationale for the discounting process. Because the whole edifice is arbitrary, managers can only be told to stare at the distribution until inspiration dawns. No one can tell them how to decide or what to do if inspiration never dawns.

Do not use simulation just to generate distributions of NPVs. Use it to understand the project, forecast its expected cash flows and assess its risk. Then calculate NPV the old-fashioned way, by discounting expected cash flows at a discount rate appropriate for the project's risk.

---

[17] These difficulties are less severe for pharmaceutical companies then for most other industries. Pharmaceutical companies have accumulated a great deal of information on the probabilities of scientific and clinical success and on the time and money required for clinical testing and public health approval.

[18] Some analysts used risk-adjusted discount rates, which they varied during the simulation. They included the NPV calculation as part of the simulation model, and as one of the inputs to the model they provided a distribution of possible discount rates. The problem with this approach was and is that the cash flows being discounted are not the expected cash flows.

[19] The only interpretation we can put on these bastard NPVs is the following: Suppose all uncertainty about the project's ultimate cash flows were resolved the day after the project was undertaken. On that day the project's opportunity cost of capital would fall to the risk-free rate. The distribution of NPVs represents the distribution of possible project values on that second day of the project's life.

There is one exercise which managers may find worthwhile if they are uncertain about the correct discount rate for a project. The first step is to derive the *expected cash flow* for the project using the Monte Carlo technique; then calculate NPV using the best estimate of the discount rate; and finally compute NPV using other possible discount rates. The resulting NPVs indicate the sensitivity of the project to errors in the discount rate. Remember the order of the steps; work out the expected cash flow before you do any discounting.

## 10.3 Decision trees and subsequent decisions

If financial managers treat projects as black boxes, they may be tempted to think only of the first accept-reject decision and to ignore the subsequent investment decisions that may be tied to it. But if subsequent investment decisions depend on those made today, then today's decision may depend on what you plan to do tomorrow.

### An example: Vegetron

We have already solved in the last chapter a simple sequential decision problem, Vegetron's electric mop project. The problem was as follows:

The scientists at Vegetron have come up with an electric mop and the firm is ready to go ahead with pilot production and test marketing. The preliminary phase will take a year and cost $125 000. Management feels that there is only a 50–50 chance that the pilot production and market tests will be successful. If they are, then Vegetron will build a $1 million plant, which will generate an expected annual cash flow in perpetuity of $250 000 a year after taxes. If they are not successful, Vegetron will not continue with the project.

Of course, Vegetron *could* go ahead even if the tests fail. Let us suppose that in that case the $1 million investment would generate only $75 000 per year.

Financial managers often use **decision trees** for analysing projects involving sequential decisions. Figure 10.8 displays the electric mop problem as a decision tree. You can think of it as a game between Vegetron and fate. Each square represents a separate decision point for Vegetron; each circle represents a decision point for fate. Vegetron starts the play at the left-hand box. If Vegetron decides to test, then fate casts the enchanted dice and decides the result of the tests. If the tests are successful—there is a probability of 0.5 that they will be—then the firm faces a second decision: invest $1 million in a project offering a $1.5 million net present value or stop. If the tests fail, Vegetron has a similar choice but the investment yields a net present value of −$250 000.

It is obvious what the second stage decisions will be: invest if the tests are successful and if they fail. The net present value of stopping is zero, so the decision tree boils down to a simple problem: Should Vegetron invest $125 000 now to obtain a 50 per cent chance of $1.5 million a year later? What decision would you make?

### *A tougher example: Magna Charter

Magna Charter is a new corporation formed by Agnes Magna to provide an executive flying service for the eastern states of Australia. The founder thinks there will be a ready demand from businesses that cannot justify a full-time company aeroplane but nevertheless need one from time to time. However, the venture is not a sure thing. There is a 40 per cent chance that demand in the first year will be low. If it is low, there is a 60 per cent chance that it will remain low in subsequent years. On the other hand, if the initial demand is high, there is an 80 per cent chance that it will stay high.

The immediate problem is to decide what kind of aeroplane to buy. A turboprop costs $550 000. A piston-engine plane costs only $250 000 but has less capacity and customer

**figure 10.8**_____

The electric mop example from Chapter 9 expressed as a decision tree. This is a project involving sequential decisions. The investment in testing generates the opportunity to invest in full-scale production. (All figures are in thousands; probabilities are in parentheses.)

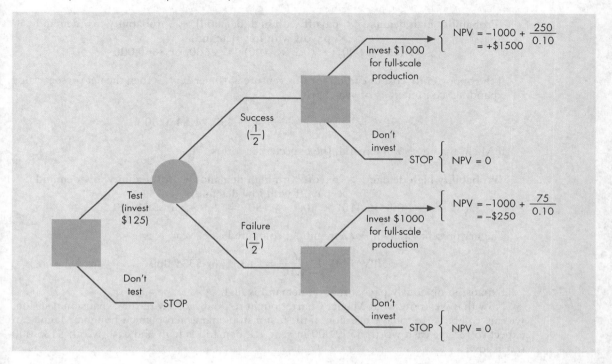

appeal. Moreover, the piston-engine plane is an old design and likely to depreciate rapidly. Ms Magna thinks that next year second-hand piston aircraft will be available for only $150 000.

That gives Ms Magna an idea: Why not start out with one piston aeroplane and buy another if demand is still high? It will cost only $150 000 to expand. If demand is low, Magna Charter can sit tight with one small, relatively inexpensive aircraft.

Figure 10.9 displays these choices. The square on the left marks the company's initial decision to purchase a turboprop for $550 000 or a piston aircraft for $250 000. After the company has made its decision, fate decides on the first year's demand. You can see in parentheses the probability that demand will be high or low, and you can see the expected cash flow for each combination of aircraft and demand level. At the end of the year the company has a second decision to make if it has a piston-engine aircraft: It can either expand or sit tight. This decision point is marked by the second square. Finally, fate takes over again and selects the level of demand for year 2. Again you can see in parentheses the probability of high or low demand. Notice that the probabilities for the second year depend on the first-period outcomes. For example, if demand is high in the first period, then there is an 80 per cent chance that it will also be high in the second. The chance of high demand in *both* the first and second periods is $0.6 \times 0.8 = 0.48$. After the parentheses we again show the profitability of the project for each combination of aircraft and demand level. You can interpret each of these figures as the present value at the end of year 2 of the cash flows for that and all subsequent years.

The problem for Ms Magna is to decide what to do today. We solve that problem by thinking first what she would do next year. This means that we start at the right side of the tree and work backwards to the beginning on the left. This is called a recursive solution. We will encounter it again when we look at option pricing.

The only decision that Ms Magna needs to make next year is whether to expand if purchase of a piston-engine aeroplane is succeeded by high demand. If she expands, she invests $150 000 and receives a payoff of $800 000 if demand continues to be high and $100 000 if demand falls. So her *expected* payoff is

$$(\text{Probability high demand} \times \text{payoff with high demand}) + (\text{probability low demand} \times \text{payoff with low demand})$$
$$= (0.8 \times 800) + (0.2 \times 100) = +660, \text{ or } \$660\,000$$

If the opportunity cost of capital for this venture is 10 per cent,[20] then the net present value of expanding, computed as of year 1, is

$$\text{NPV} = -150 + \frac{660}{1.10} = +450, \text{ or } \$450\,000$$

If Ms Magna does *not* expand, the expected payoff is

$$(\text{Probability high demand} \times \text{payoff with high demand}) + (\text{probability low demand} \times \text{payoff with low demand})$$
$$= (0.8 \times 410) + (0.2 \times 180) = +364, \text{ or } \$364\,000$$

The net present value of *not* expanding, computed as of year 1, is

$$\text{NPV} = 0 + \frac{364}{1.10} = +331, \text{ or } \$331\,000$$

Expansion obviously pays if market demand is high.

Now that we know what Magna Charter ought to do if faced with the expansion decision, we can 'roll back' to today's decision. If the first piston-engine aeroplane is bought, Magna can expect to receive cash worth $550 000 in year 1 if demand is high and cash worth $185 000 if it is low:

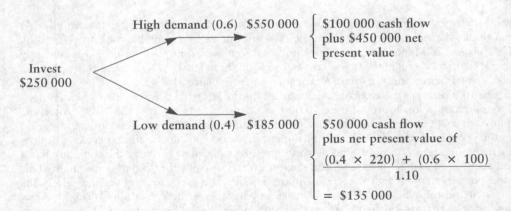

The net present value of the investment in the piston-engine aeroplane is therefore $117 000:

$$\text{NPV} = -250 + \frac{0.6(550) + 0.4(185)}{1.10} = +117, \text{ or } \$117\,000$$

---

20  We are guilty here of assuming away one of the most difficult questions. Just as in the Vegetron mop case, the most risky part of Ms Magna's venture is likely to be the initial prototype project. Perhaps we should use a lower discount rate for the second piston-engine aeroplane than for the first.

**figure 10.9**
Decision tree for Magna Charter. Should it buy a turboprop or a smaller piston-engine aeroplane? A second piston aeroplane can be purchased in year 1 if demand turns out to be high. (All figures are in thousands.)

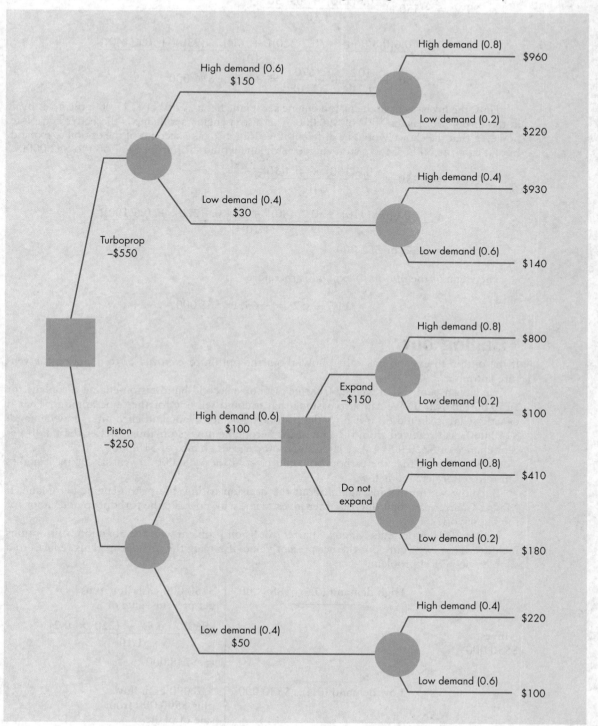

If Magna buys the turboprop, there are no future decisions to analyse and so there is no need to roll back. We just calculate expected cash flows and discount:

$$\text{NPV} = -550 + \frac{0.6(150) + 0.4(30)}{1.10}$$

$$+ \frac{0.6[0.8(960) + 0.2(220)] + 0.4[0.4(930) + 0.6(140)]}{(1.10)^2}$$

$$= -550 + \frac{102}{1.10} + \frac{670}{(110)^2} = +96, \text{ or } \$96\,000$$

Thus, the investment in the piston-engine aeroplane has an NPV of $117\,000; the investment in the turboprop has an NPV of $96\,000. The piston-engine aeroplane is the better bet. Note, however, that the choice would be different if we forgot to take account of the option to expand. In that case the NPV of the piston-engine aeroplane would drop from $117\,000 to $52\,000:

$$\text{NPV} = -250 + \frac{0.6(100) + 0.4(50)}{1.10}$$

$$+ \frac{0.6[0.8(410) + 0.2(180)] + 0.4[0.4(220) + 0.6(100)]}{(1.10)^2}$$

$$= +52, \text{ or } \$52\,000$$

The value of the *option to expand* is therefore

$$117 - 52 = +65, \text{ or } \$65\,000$$

## *Bailing out

If the option to expand has value, how about the option to *contract* or to abandon the venture entirely?

We have assumed that Magna Charter can buy a second-hand piston-engine aeroplane for $150\,000 in year 1. We can also assume that it could sell one for the same amount. That is exactly what it should do if it buys the piston-engine aeroplane and encounters low demand: $150\,000 cash received from the sale of the aeroplane now is obviously better than a 40 per cent chance of $220\,000 a year later and a 60 per cent chance of $100\,000.

Let us suppose that the turboprop could be sold for $500\,000 in year 1. Again, it makes sense to sell if demand is low.

But now we must think again about the decision to buy the piston-engine aeroplane. If Magna Charter can 'bail out' of either investment, why not take the turboprop and shoot for the big payoff?

Figure 10.10 represents Magna Charter's decision problem with the abandonment options included. First, we figure out the net present value of buying the turboprop. This reduces to a simple one-period problem:

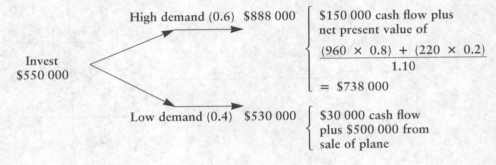

**figure 10.10**

Revised decision tree for Magna Charter, taking account of the possibility of abandoning the business if demand turns out to be low. (All figures are in thousands.)

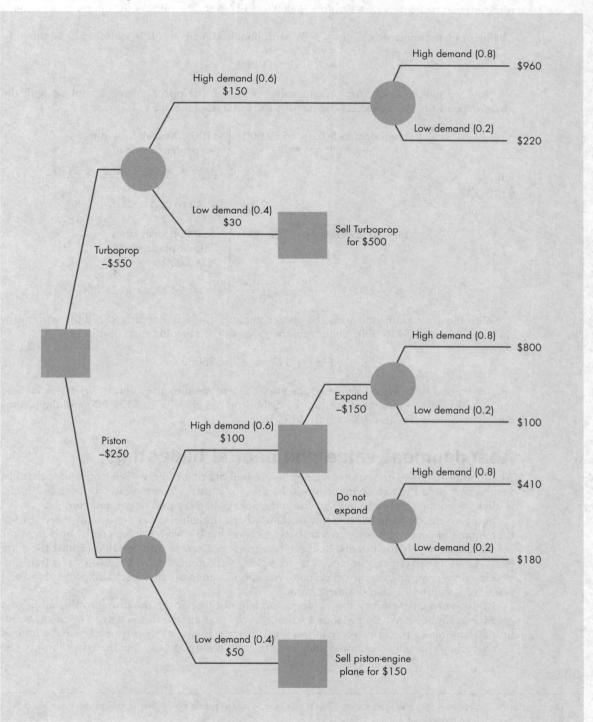

$$NPV = -550 + \frac{0.6(888) + 0.4(530)}{1.10} = +127, \text{ or } \$127\ 000$$

Thus, when we allow for the possibility of abandonment, the net present value of the turboprop investment increases from $96 000 to $127 000. The value of the *option to abandon* is

$$
\begin{aligned}
\text{Value of abandonment option} &= \text{NPV with abandonment} - \text{NPV without abandonment} \\
&= 127 - 96 \\
&= 31, \text{ or } \$31\ 000
\end{aligned}
$$

Now we figure out the net present value of buying the piston-engine aeroplane with the abandonment option included. The payoffs for this aeroplane are as follows:

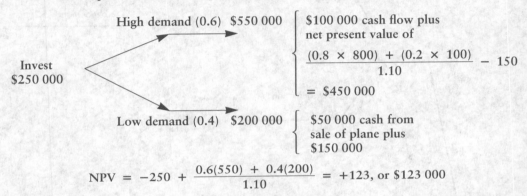

$$NPV = -250 + \frac{0.6(550) + 0.4(200)}{1.10} = +123, \text{ or } \$123\ 000$$

With the abandonment option the piston-engine aeroplane is worth $123 000; without it, the plane is worth $117 000. Therefore, the value of the abandonment option is

$$123 - 117 = 6, \text{ or } \$6000$$

It is a good thing we remembered the possibility of reselling the aircraft. When we include the value of the abandonment option, the turboprop has an NPV of $127 000 and the piston-engine aeroplane has an NPV of only $123 000.

## Abandonment value and capital budgeting

Abandonment value—the value of the option to bail out of a project—is a simple idea that has surprisingly broad practical implications. In a way it is just common sense; disaster, like a cat, is always waiting to pounce, and so you must always be prepared to cut and run.

Some assets are easier to bail out of than others. Tangible assets are usually easier to sell than intangible ones.[21] It helps to have active second-hand markets, which really only exist for standardised, widely used items. Real estate, aeroplanes, trucks and certain machine tools are likely to be relatively easy to sell. The knowledge accumulated by Vegetron's research and development program, on the other hand, is a specialised intangible asset and probably would not have a significant abandonment value.

In the worst case a firm's shareholders can bail out by putting the firm into the hands of a receiver or liquidator.[22] It may sound strange to say that an investor is helped by the possibility of abandoning the firm to creditors, but it is true. Investors in corporations have *limited liability*: they risk only the money they invest. From their point of view there is a limit to the

---

21  This is, of course, not always the case. Some tangible assets you have to *pay* to get rid of—worn-out refrigerators, for instance.
22  We will discuss financial distress in Chapters 18 and 30.

money the firm can lose. They always have the option of walking away from the firm and leaving its problems in the hands of the creditors and the courts.

Expansion value can be just as important as abandonment value. When things turn out well, the quicker and easier the business can be expanded the better. The best of all possible worlds occurs when good luck strikes and you find that you can expand quickly *but your competitors cannot*.

# Pro and con decision trees

Our examples of abandonment and expansion are extreme simplifications of the sequential decision problems that financial managers face. But they make an important general point. If today's decisions affect what you can do tomorrow, then tomorrow's decisions have to be analysed before you can act rationally today.

Any cash flow forecast rests on some assumption about the firm's future investment and operating strategy. Often that assumption is implicit. Decision trees force the underlying strategy into the open. By displaying the links between today and tomorrow's decisions, they help the financial manager to find the strategy with the highest net present value.[23]

The trouble with decision trees is that they get so _____ complex so _____ quickly (insert your own expletives). What will Magna Charter do if demand is neither high nor low but just middling? In that event Ms Magna might sell the turboprop and buy a piston-engine aeroplane, or she might defer expansion and abandonment decisions until year 2. Perhaps middling demand requires a decision about a price cut or an intensified sales campaign.

There are other possibilities. Perhaps there is uncertainty about future prices of second-hand aircraft. If so, abandonment will depend not just on the level of demand but also on the level of second-hand prices. What is more, second-hand prices are likely to be depressed if demand is low and buoyant if demand is high.

We could draw a new decision tree covering this expanded set of events and decisions. Try it if you like. You will see how fast the circles, squares and branches accumulate.

Life is complex, and there is very little we can do about it. It is therefore unfair to criticise decision trees because they can become complex. Our criticism is reserved for analysts who let the complexity become overwhelming. The point of decision trees is to allow explicit analysis of possible future events and decisions. They should be judged not on their comprehensiveness but on whether they show the most important links between today and tomorrow's decisions. Decision trees used in real life will be more complex than Figures 10.9 and 10.10, but they will nevertheless display only a small fraction of possible future events and decisions. Decision trees are like grapevines: they are productive only if they are vigorously pruned.

Our analysis of the Magna Charter project begged an important question. The option to expand enlarged the spread of possible outcomes and therefore increased the risk of investing in a piston aircraft. Conversely, the option to bail out narrowed the spread of possible outcomes. So it reduced the risk of investment. We should have used different discount rates to recognise these changes in risk, but decision trees do not tell us how to do this. In fact, decision trees do not tell us how to value options at all; they are just a convenient way to summarise cash flow consequences. But the situation is not hopeless. Modern techniques of option valuation are beginning to help value these investment options. We will describe these techniques in Chapters 20 and 21.

# Decision trees and Monte Carlo simulation

We have said that any cash flow forecast rests on assumptions about future investment and operating strategy. Think back to the Monte Carlo simulation model that we constructed for

---

23  Some analysts go further than that. Like the early advocates of simulation models, they start with the premise that NPV cannot take account of risk. They therefore propose that the decision tree be used to calculate a *distribution* of 'NPVs' or internal rates of return for each possible sequence of company decisions. That may sound like a gingerbread house, but you should know by now that there is a witch inside.

the Jalopy Motor Company. What strategy was that based on? We do not know. Inevitably Jalopy will face decisions about pricing, production, expansion and abandonment, but the model builder's assumptions about these decisions are buried in the model's equations. At some point the model builder may have implicitly identified a future strategy for Jalopy, but it is clearly not the optimal one. There will be some runs of the model when nearly everything goes wrong and when in real life Jalopy would abandon to cut its losses. Yet the model goes on period after period, heedless of the drain on Jalopy's cash resources. The most unfavourable outcomes reported by the simulation model would never be encountered in real life.

On the other hand, the simulation model probably understates the project's potential value if nearly everything goes right: there is no provision for expanding to take advantage of good luck.

Most simulation models incorporate a 'business as usual' strategy, which is fine as long as there are no major surprises. The greater the divergence from expected levels of market growth, market share, cost, and so on, the less realistic is the simulation. Therefore, the extreme high and low simulated values—the 'tails' of the simulated distributions—should be treated with extreme caution. Do not take the area under the tails as realistic probabilities of disaster or bonanza.

## 10.4 Summary

There is more to capital budgeting than grinding out calculations of net present value. If you can identify the major uncertainties, you may find that it is worth undertaking some additional preliminary research that will *confirm* whether the project is worthwhile. And even if you decide that you have done all you can to resolve the uncertainties, you still want to be aware of the potential problems. You do not want to be caught by surprise if things go wrong: You want to be ready to take corrective action.

There are three ways in which companies try to identify the principal threats to a project's success. The simplest is to undertake a sensitivity analysis. In this case the manager considers in turn each of the determinants of the project's success and estimates how far the present value of the project would be altered by taking a very optimistic view or a very pessimistic view of that variable.

Sensitivity analysis of this kind is easy, but it is not always helpful. Variables do not usually change one at a time. If costs are higher than you expect, it is a good bet that prices will have to be higher also. And if prices are higher, it is a good bet that sales volume will be lower. If you do not allow for the dependencies between the swings and the merry-go-rounds, you may get a false idea of the hazards of the fairground business. Many companies try to cope with this problem by examining the effect on the project of alternative plausible combinations of variables. In other words, they estimate the net present value of the project under different scenarios and compare this estimate with the base case.

In a sensitivity analysis you change variables one at a time: When you analyse scenarios, you look at a limited number of alternative combinations of variables. If you want to go the whole hog and look at *all* possible combinations of variables, then you will probably need to use Monte Carlo simulation to cope with the complexity. In that case you must construct a complete model of the project and specify the probability distribution of each of the determinants of cash flow. You can then ask the computer to select a value at random from the distribution for each of these determinants. If you gave the computer the correct specification for the distribution, the chance of any value being picked is the same as the chance that it will really occur. Having picked the values for all the relevant variables the computer can then work out the cash flows that would result. After the computer has repeated this process a thousand or so times, you should have a fair idea of the expected cash flow in each year and the spread of possible cash flows.

Simulation can be a very useful tool. The discipline of building a model of the project can in itself lead you to a deeper understanding of the project. And once you have constructed your model, it is a simple matter to see how the outcomes would be affected by altering the scope of the project or the distribution of any of the variables. There are, of course, limits to what you can learn from simulations. A marine engineer uses a water tank to simulate the performance of alternative hull designs but knows that it is impossible to fully replicate the conditions that the ship will encounter. In the same way, the financial manager can learn a lot from 'laboratory' tests but cannot hope to build a model that accurately captures all the uncertainties and interdependencies that really surround a project.

Books about capital budgeting sometimes create the impression that, once the manager has made an investment decision, there is nothing to do but sit back and watch the cash flows unfold. In practice companies are constantly modifying their operations. If cash flows are better than anticipated, the project may be expanded; if they are worse, it may be contracted or abandoned altogether. Good managers take account of these options when they value a project. In fact, they are nearly always looking for projects that contain options. Such projects not only have more value than projects that do not have options, they also give the managers something to manage.

Valuing projects that have options is tricky. Simple NPV analysis will usually understate the project's value. One convenient way to analyse project options is by means of a decision tree. You identify the principal things that could happen to the project and the main counteractions that you might take. Then, working back from the future to the present, you calculate which action you *should* take in each case. Once you know that, you can work out how much the value of the project is increased by these opportunities to react to changing circumstances. One thing to look out for is that the availability of these options change the risk of the project over its life. However, we shall have to wait until we reach the chapters on option valuation before we can satisfactorily address this problem.

Many of the early articles on simulation and decision trees were written before we knew how to introduce risk into calculations of net present value. Their authors believed that these techniques might allow the manager to make investment decisions without estimating the opportunity cost of capital and calculating net present value. Today we know that simulation and decision analysis cannot save you from having to calculate net present value. The value of these techniques is to help the manager get behind the cash flow forecast; they help the manager to understand what could go wrong and what opportunities are available to modify the project. That is why we described them as tools to open up black boxes.

## FURTHER READING

For an excellent case study of break-even analysis see:

  U. E. Reinhardt, 'Break-Even Analysis for Lockheed's TriStar: An Application of Financial Theory', *Journal of Finance*, **28**: 821–38 (September 1973).

The first advocate of simulation was David Hertz. See:

  D. B. Hertz, 'Risk Analysis in Capital Investment', *Harvard Business Review*, **42**: 95–106 (January–February 1964).

  D. B. Hertz, 'Investment Policies that Pay Off', *Harvard Business Review*, **46**: 96–108 (January–February 1968).

Merck's use of Monte Carlo simulation is discussed in:

  N. A. Nichols, 'Scientific Management at Merck: An Interview with Judy Lewent', *Harvard Business Review*, **72**: 89–99 (January–February 1994).

Myers discusses the interpretation and use of simulations in:

  S. C. Myers, 'Postscript: Using Simulation for Risk Analysis', in S. C. Myers (ed.), *Modern Developments in Financial Management*, Praeger Publishers, Inc., New York, 1976.

The use of decision trees in investment appraisal was first discussed in:

J. Magee, 'How to Use Decision Trees in Capital Investment', *Harvard Business Review*, **42**: 79–96 (September–October 1964).

Hax and Wiig discuss how Monte Carlo simulation and decision trees were used in an actual capital budgeting decision:

A. C. Hax and K. M. Wiig, 'The Use of Decision Analysis in Capital Investment Problems', *Sloan Management Review*, **17**: 19–48 (Winter 1976).

The abandonment option in capital budgeting was first analysed by:

A. A. Robichek and J. C. Van Horne, 'Abandonment Value in Capital Budgeting', *Journal of Finance*, **22**: 577–90 (December 1967).

## QUIZ

**1.** Define and briefly explain each of the following terms or procedures:
   a. Project analysis.
   b. Sensitivity analysis.
   c. Break-even analysis.
   d. Monte Carlo simulation.
   e. Decision tree.
   f. Abandonment value.
   g. Expansion value.

**2.** What is the NPV of the electric scooter project under the following scenario?

| | |
|---|---|
| ▌ Market size | 1.1 million |
| ▌ Market share | 0.1 |
| ▌ Unit price | $4000 |
| ▌ Unit variable cost | $3600 |
| ▌ Fixed cost | $20 million |

**3.** Jalopy Motor Company is considering still another production method for its electric scooter. It would require an additional investment of $150 million but would reduce variable costs by $40 million a year. Other assumptions follow Table 10.1.
   a. What is the NPV of this alternative scheme?
   b. Draw break-even charts for this alternative scheme along the lines of Figure 10.1.
   c. Explain how you would interpret the break-even figure.

**4.** Summarise the problems that a manager would encounter in interpreting a standard sensitivity analysis such as the one shown in Table 10.2. Which of these problems are alleviated by examining the project under alternative scenarios?

**5.** True or false?
   a. Project analysis is unnecessary for projects with asset betas that are equal to zero.
   b. Sensitivity analysis can be used to identify the variables most crucial to a project's success.
   c. Sensitivity analysis gives 'optimistic' and 'pessimistic' values for project cash flow and NPV.
   d. The break-even sales level of a project is higher when *break-even* is defined in terms of NPV rather than accounting income.
   e. Monte Carlo simulation can be used to help forecast cash flows.

   f.  Monte Carlo simulation eliminates the need to estimate a project's opportunity cost of capital.
   g.  Decision trees are useful when future investment decisions may depend on today's decision.
   h.  High abandonment value increases NPV, other things being equal.

6.  Suppose a manager has already estimated a project's cash flows, calculated its NPV and done a sensitivity analysis like the one shown in Table 10.2. List the additional steps required to carry out a Monte Carlo simulation of project cash flows.

7.  Use a decision tree to show that it pays Jalopy Motor Company to conduct a pre-test of the suspect machine (see Section 10.1).

8.  Big Oil is wondering whether to drill for oil near Broken Hill. The prospects are as follows:

| Depth of well (feet) | Total cost ($million) | Cumulative probability of finding oil | PV of oil (if found) ($million) |
|---|---|---|---|
| 1000 | 2 | 0.5 | 5 |
| 2000 | 2.5 | 0.6 | 4.5 |
| 3000 | 3 | 0.7 | 4 |

   Draw a decision tree showing the successive drilling decisions to be made by Big Oil. How deep should it be prepared to drill?

## QUESTIONS AND PROBLEMS

*1. Your staff have come up with the following revised estimates for the electric scooter project:

|  | Pessimistic | Expected | Optimistic |
|---|---|---|---|
| Market size | 0.8 million | 1.0 million | 1.2 million |
| Market share | 0.04 | 0.1 | 0.16 |
| Unit price | $3000 | $3750 | $4000 |
| Unit variable cost | $3500 | $3000 | $2750 |
| Fixed cost | $50 million | $30 million | $10 million |

   Conduct a sensitivity analysis. What are the principal uncertainties in the project?

*2. The Goodyear Welt Company is proposing to replace its old welt-making machinery with more modern equipment. The new equipment costs $10 million and the company expects to sell its old equipment for $1 million. The attraction of the new machinery is that it is expected to cut manufacturing costs from their current level of $8 a welt to $4. However, as the following table shows, there is some uncertainty both about future sales and about the performance of the new machinery:

|  | Pessimistic | Expected | Optimistic |
|---|---|---|---|
| Sales (millions of welts) | 0.4 | 0.5 | 0.7 |
| Manufacturing cost with new machinery (dollars per welt) | 6 | 4 | 3 |
| Economic life of new machinery (years) | 7 | 10 | 13 |

Conduct a sensitivity analysis of the replacement decision, assuming a discount rate of 12 per cent. Goodyear Welt does not pay taxes.

**\*3.** Goodyear Welt could commission engineering tests to determine the actual improvement in manufacturing costs generated by the proposed new welt machines (see Question 2 above). The study would cost $450 000. Would you advise the company to go ahead with the study?

**4.** Waldo County, the well-known real estate developer, plans to build still another shopping centre designed to intercept tourists heading towards the Homebush Olympic site. Table 10.10 shows Mr County's projections. Note that the centre's revenues come from two sources. Mr County will (1) charge retail stores for the space they occupy and (2) receive 5 per cent of each store's gross sales. Projected cash flows (in millions of dollars) are as follows:

|  | Year | | | | | |
|---|---|---|---|---|---|---|
|  | 0 | 1 | 2 | 3 | 4 | 5–17 |
| **Investment:** | | | | | | |
| Land | 15 | | | | | |
| Construction | 10 | 15 | 5 | | | |
| **Operations:** | | | | | | |
| Rentals | | | | 6 | 6 | 6 |
| Share of 5% of retail sales | | | | 12 | 12 | 12 |
| Operating and maintenance cost | 1 | 2 | 2 | 5 | 5 | 5 |
| Rates | 1 | 1 | 1.5 | 2 | 2 | 2 |

Construction costs can be depreciated over 15 years starting in year 3. For simplicity you can assume straight-line depreciation. Land cannot be depreciated. The tax rate is 35 per cent and the real cost of capital is 9 per cent.

Mr County believes that the shopping centre will have to be rebuilt in year 17. The $30 million construction cost outlay will have no value at that time. The land should retain its value, however.

a. What is the net present value of Mr County's project?

b. The centre's sales are highly uncertain. They could be as much as 40 per cent higher or lower than forecast. Do a sensitivity analysis for this variable.

c. Calculate the break-even level of sales for the project.

d. Calculate the sales level for which the project breaks even in terms of accounting profits. Explain why this sales level is lower than your answer to Part (c).

e. Mr County worries that rapid growth in the centre's sales would also mean higher costs and higher council rates. Calculate the project's net present value for a *scenario* with 20 per cent higher sales, 15 per cent higher operating and maintenance costs and 20 per cent higher rates.

f. Mr County also worries about construction cost overruns and delays due to required zoning changes and environmental approvals. He has seen cases of 25 per cent cost overruns and delays up to 12 months. What effect would this have on project net present value? And on its break-even revenue level?

**5.** Waldo County has received a brochure from Hotshot Consultants advocating Monte Carlo simulation. Mr County is intrigued and wants to try the method out on the Olympic tourist centre described in Question 4.

a. Outline the steps required to set up and run the Monte Carlo simulation for this project. Which key uncertainties would you advise Mr County to concentrate on?

b. What would the output of the simulation be? What could Mr County learn from it?

c. The brochure from Hotshot Consultants says that the most important simulation output is the probability distribution of project NPVs. Hotshot implies that projects should not be accepted unless the probability of negative NPVs (as calculated by the simulation) is small. What do you think of this? Explain.

**\*6.** Agnes Magna has found some errors in her data (see Section 10.3). The corrected figures are as follows:

- Price of turboprop, year 0 = $350 000.
- Price of piston-engine, year 0 = $180 000.
- Price of turboprop, year 1 = $300 000.
- Price of piston-engine, year 1 = $150 000.
- Discount rate = 8 per cent.

Redraw the decision tree with the changed data. Calculate the value of the option to expand. Recalculate the value of the abandonment option. Which aeroplane should Ms Magna buy?

**\*7.** Ms Magna has thought of another idea. Perhaps she should buy a piston-engine aeroplane now. Then, if demand is high in the first year, she can sell it and buy a turboprop. Redraw Figure 10.8 to incorporate this possibility. What should Ms Magna do?

**\*8.** For what kinds of capital investment projects do you think Monte Carlo simulation would be most useful? For example, can you think of some industries in which this technique would be particularly attractive? Would it be more useful for large-scale investments than small ones? Discuss.

**\*9.** You own an unused gold mine near Broome that will cost $100 000 to reopen. If you open the mine, you expect to be able to extract 1000 ounces of gold a year for each of three years. After that, the deposit will be exhausted. The gold price is currently $500 an ounce, and each year the price is equally likely to rise or fall by $50 from its level at the start of the year. The extraction cost is $460 an ounce and the discount rate is 10 per cent.

a. Should you open the mine now or delay one year in the hope of a rise in the gold price?

b. What difference would it make to your decision if you could costlessly (but irreversibly) shut down the mine at any stage?

**\*10.** Read and criticise the Hax–Wiig article listed in the 'Further Reading' for this chapter. Are all their recommendations consistent with finance theory?

**\*11.** You are considering offering a new computer-based consulting service. There is a 60 per cent chance the demand will be high in the first year. If it is high, there is an 80 per cent chance that it will continue high indefinitely. If demand is low in the first year, there is a 60 per cent chance that it will continue low indefinitely.

If demand is high, forecasted revenue is $90 000 a year; if demand is low, forecasted revenue is $70 000 a year. You can cease to offer the service at any point, in which case, of course, revenues are zero. Costs other than computing are forecasted at $50 000 a year regardless of demand. These costs also can be terminated at any point. You have a choice on computing costs. One possibility is to buy your own minicomputer. This involves an initial outlay of $200 000 and no subsequent expenditure. It has an economic life of 10 years and no salvage value. The alternative is to rent computer time as you need it. In this case computer costs are 40 per cent of revenues.

Assume that the computing decision cannot be reversed (i.e. if you buy a computer, you cannot resell it; if you do *not* buy it today, you cannot do so later).

There are no taxes and the opportunity cost of capital is 10 per cent.

Draw a decision tree showing the alternatives. Is it better to buy a computer or rent?

State clearly any additional assumptions that you need to make.

# chapter 11

# WHERE POSITIVE NET PRESENT VALUES COME FROM

**W**hy is an MBA student who has learned about DCF like a baby with a hammer? Answer: Because to a baby with a hammer, everything looks like a nail.

Our point is that you should not focus on the arithmetic of DCF and thereby ignore the forecasts that are the basis of every investment decision. Senior managers are continuously bombarded with requests for funds for capital expenditures. All these requests are supported with detailed DCF analyses showing that the projects have positive NPVs.[1] How, then, can managers distinguish the NPVs that are truly positive from those that are merely the result of forecasting errors? We suggest that they should ask some probing questions about the possible sources of economic gain.

We all know what sort of ideal project we are looking for. One that has high returns, little or no risk and that requires little or no investment. Unfortunately, this is what everybody is looking for, and therefore there is little chance of finding such a project in competitive markets. This gives us a clue about where we should look and what we should look for. We should seek out some source of comparative advantage that will give us an edge over our competitors. In practice it turns out that it is often the identification of such opportunities that leads to proposals for major new projects. The NPV calculation provides a

---

[1] Here is another riddle: Are projects proposed because they have positive NPVs, or do they have positive NPVs because they are proposed? No prizes for the correct answer.

formal estimate of the value of the competitive advantage. In order to believe the numbers you should understand the source of the advantage and how long it is likely to last.

The first section in this chapter reviews certain common pitfalls in capital budgeting, notably the tendency to apply DCF when market values are already available and no DCF calculations are needed. The second section covers the *economic rents* that underlie all positive NPV investments. The third section presents a case study describing how Marvin Enterprises, the gargle blaster company, analysed the introduction of a radically new product.

## 11.1 Look first to market values

Let us suppose that you have persuaded all your project sponsors to give honest forecasts. Although those forecasts are unbiased, they are still likely to contain errors, some positive and others negative. The average error will be zero, but that is little consolation because you want to accept only projects with *truly* superior profitability.

Think, for example, of what would happen if you were to jot down your estimates of the cash flows from operating various items of equipment. You would probably find that about half *appeared* to have positive NPVs. This may not be because you personally possess any superior skill in operating jumbo jets or running a chain of laundromats but because you have inadvertently introduced large errors into your estimates of the cash flows. The more projects you contemplate, the more likely you are to uncover projects that *appear* to be extremely worthwhile. Indeed, if you were to extend your activities to making cash flow estimates for various companies, you would also find a number of *apparently* attractive takeover candidates. In some of these cases you might have genuine information and the proposed investment really might have a positive NPV. But in many other cases the investment would only look good because you made a forecasting error.

What can you do to prevent forecast errors from swamping genuine information? We suggest that you begin by looking at market values.

### The Holden and the film star

The following parable should help to illustrate what we mean. Your local car dealer is announcing a special offer. For $35 001 you get not only a brand new Holden but also the chance to shake hands with your favourite film star. You wonder how much you are paying for that handshake.

There are two possible approaches to the problem. You could evaluate the worth of the Holden's power steering, disappearing windshield wipers and other features and conclude that the Holden is worth $36 000. This would seem to suggest that the dealership is willing to pay $999 to have a movie star shake hands with you. Alternatively, you might note that the market price for Holdens is $35 000, so that you are paying $1 for the handshake. As long as there is a competitive market for Holdens, the latter approach is more appropriate.

Security analysts face a similar problem whenever they value a company's shares. They must consider the information that is already known to the market about a company, *and* they must evaluate the information that is known only to them. The information that is known to the market is the Holden; the private information is the handshake with the movie star. Investors have already evaluated the information that is generally known. Security analysts do not need to evaluate this information again. They can *start* with the market price of the share and concentrate on valuing their private information.

While lesser mortals would instinctively accept the Holden's market value of $35 000, the financial manager is trained to enumerate and value all the costs and benefits from an investment and is therefore tempted to substitute his or her own opinion for the market's. Unfortunately, this approach increases the chance of error. Many capital assets are traded in a competitive market, and so it makes sense to *start* with the market price and then ask why these assets should earn more in your hands than your rivals'.

## example: investing in a new department store

We encountered a department store chain that estimated the present value of the expected cash flows from each proposed store, including the price at which it could eventually sell the store. Although the firm took considerable care with these estimates, it was disturbed to find that its conclusions were heavily influenced by the forecasted selling price of each store. Although management disclaimed any particular real estate expertise, it discovered that its investment decisions were unintentionally dominated by its assumptions about future real estate prices.

Once the financial managers realised this, they always checked the decision to open a new store by asking the following question: 'Let us assume that the property is fairly priced. What is the evidence that it is best suited to one of our department stores rather than to some other use?' In other words, *if an asset is worth more to others than it is to you, then beware of bidding for the asset against them.*

Let us take the department store problem a little further. Suppose that the new store costs $100 million.[2] You forecast that it will generate after-tax cash flow of $8 million a year for 10 years. Real estate prices are estimated to grow by 3 per cent a year, so the expected value of the real estate at the end of 10 years is $100 \times (1.03)^{10} = \$134$ million. At a discount rate of 10 per cent, your proposed department store has an NPV of $1 million:

$$\text{NPV} = -100 + \frac{8}{1.10} + \frac{8}{(1.10)^2} + \ldots + \frac{8 + 134}{(1.10)^{10}} = \$1 \text{ million}$$

Notice how sensitive this NPV is to the ending value of the real estate. For example, an ending value of $120 million implies an NPV of $-$5 million.

It is helpful to imagine such a business as divided into two parts—a real estate subsidiary which buys the building and a retailing subsidiary which rents and operates it. Then figure out how much rent the real estate subsidiary would have to charge, and ask whether the retailing subsidiary could afford to pay the rent.

In some cases a fair market rental can be estimated from real estate transactions. For example, we might observe that similar retail space recently rented for $10 million a year. In that case we would conclude that our department store was an unattractive use for the site. Once the site had been acquired, it would be better to rent it out at $10 million than to use it for a store generating only $8 million.

Suppose, on the other hand, that the property could be rented for only $7 million per year. The department store could pay this amount to the real estate subsidiary and still earn a net operating cash flow of $8 - 7 = \$1$ million. It is therefore the best *current* use for the real estate.[3]

Will it also be the best *future* use? Maybe not, depending on whether retail profits keep pace with any rent increases. Suppose that real estate prices and rents are expected to increase by 3 per cent per year. The real estate subsidiary must charge $7 \times 1.03 = \$7.21$ million in year

---

[2]  For simplicity we assume all the $100 million goes to real estate. In real life there would also be substantial investments in fixtures, information systems, training and start-up costs.

[3]  The fair market rent equals the profit generated by the real estate's *second*-best use.

2, 7.21 × 1.03 = $7.43 million in year 3, and so on.[4] Figure 11.1 shows that the store's income fails to cover the rental after year 5.

If these forecasts are right, the store has only a five-year economic life; from that point on the real estate is more valuable in some other use. If you stubbornly believe that the department store is the best long-term use for the site, you must be ignoring potential growth in income from the store.[5]

**figure 11.1** _____

Beginning in year 6, the department store's income fails to cover the rental charge.

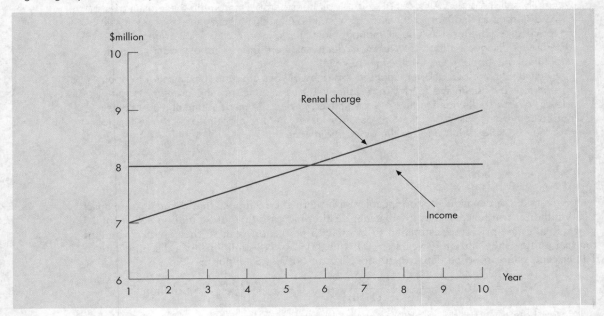

There is a general point here. Whenever you make a capital investment decision, think what bets you are placing. Our department store example involved at least two bets—one on real estate prices and another on the firm's ability to run a successful department store. But that suggests some alternative strategies. For instance, it would be foolish to make a lousy department store investment just because you are optimistic about real estate prices. You would do better to buy real estate and rent it out to the highest bidders. The converse is also true. You should not be deterred from going ahead with a profitable department store because you are pessimistic about real estate prices. You would do better to sell the real estate and *rent* it back for the department store. We suggest that you separate the two bets by first asking, 'Should we open a department store on this site, assuming that the real estate is fairly priced?' and then deciding whether you also want to go into the real estate business.

---

[4]  This rental stream yields a 10 per cent rate of return to the real estate subsidiary. Each year it gets a 7 per cent 'dividend' and 3 per cent capital gain. Growth at 3 per cent would bring the value of the property to $134 million by year 10.

The present value (at $r = 0.10$) of the growing stream of rents is

$$PV = \frac{7}{r - g} = \frac{7}{0.10 - 0.03} = \$100 \text{ million}$$

This PV is the initial market value of the property.

[5]  Another possibility is that real estate rents and values are expected to grow at less than 3 per cent a year. But in that case the real estate subsidiary would have to charge more than $7 million rent in year 1 to justify its $100 million real estate investment (see Footnote 4). That would make the department store even less attractive.

## another example: opening a gold mine

Here is another example of how market prices can help you make better decisions. Kingsley Solomon is considering a proposal to open a new gold mine near Ballarat. He estimates that the mine will cost $200 million to develop and that in each of the next 10 years it will produce 0.1 million ounces of gold at a cost, after mining and refining, of $200 an ounce. The extraction costs can be predicted with reasonable accuracy and are expected to remain unchanged. However, Mr Solomon is much less confident about future gold prices. His best guess is that the price will rise by 5 per cent per year from its current level of $400 an ounce. At a discount rate of 10 per cent, this gives the mine an NPV of −$10 million.

$$NPV = -200 + \frac{0.1(420 - 200)}{1.10} + \frac{0.1(441 - 200)}{(1.10)^2} + \cdots$$

$$+ \frac{0.1(652 - 200)}{(1.10)^{10}}$$

$$= -\$10 \text{ million}$$

Therefore, the gold mine project is rejected.

Unfortunately, Mr Solomon did not look at what the market was telling him. What is the present value of an ounce of gold? Clearly, if the gold market is functioning properly, it is the current price—$400 an ounce. Gold does not produce any income, so $400 is the discounted value of the expected future gold price.[6] Since the mine is expected to produce a total of 1 million ounces (0.1 million ounces per year for 10 years), the present

---

6    Investing in an ounce of gold is like investing in a share that pays no dividends: the investor's return comes entirely as capital gains. Look back at Section 4.2, where we showed that $P_0$, the price of the share today, depends on $DIV_1$ and $P_1$, the expected dividend and price for next year, and the opportunity cost of capital $r$:

$$P_0 = \frac{DIV_1 + P_1}{1 + r}$$

But for gold $DIV_1 = 0$, so

$$P_0 = \frac{P_1}{1 + r}$$

Expressed in words, *today's price is the present value of next year's price.* Therefore, we do not have to know either $P_1$ or $r$ to find the present value. Also since $DIV_2 = 0$,

$$P_1 = \frac{P_2}{1 + r}$$

and we can express $P_0$ as

$$P_0 = \frac{P_1}{1 + r} = \frac{1}{(1 + r)}\left(\frac{P_2}{1 + r}\right) = \frac{P_2}{(1 + r)^2}$$

In general,

$$P_0 = \frac{P_t}{(1 + r)^t}$$

This holds for any asset which pays no dividends, is traded in a competitive market and costs nothing to store. Storage costs for gold or shares are very small compared to asset value. We also assume that guaranteed future delivery of gold is just as good as having gold in hand today. This is not quite right. As we will see in Chapter 24, gold in hand can generate a small 'convenience yield'.

value of the revenue stream is $1 \times 400 = \$400$ million.[7] We assume that 10 per cent is an appropriate discount rate for the relatively certain extraction costs. Thus

$$NPV = -\text{initial investment} + PV(\text{revenues}) - PV(\text{costs})$$

$$= -200 + 400 - \sum_{t=1}^{10} \frac{0.1 \times 200}{(1.10)^t} = \$77 \text{ million}$$

It looks as if Kingsley Solomon's mine is not such a bad bet after all.[8]

Mr Solomon's gold was just like anyone else's gold. So there was no point in trying to value it separately. By taking the present value of the gold sales as given, Mr Solomon was able to focus on the crucial issue: Were the extraction costs sufficiently low to make the venture worthwhile? That brings us to another of those fundamental truths: If others are producing an article profitably and (like Mr Solomon) you can make it more cheaply, then you do not need any NPV calculations to know that you are probably onto a good thing.

We confess that our example of Kingsley Solomon's mine is somewhat special. Unlike gold, most commodities are not kept primarily for investment purposes, and therefore you cannot automatically assume that today's price is equal to the present value of the future price.[9] But when you do have the market value of an asset, *use it*, at least as a starting point for your analysis.

One more example. Suppose that BHP is contemplating an investment in tankers to ship Bass Strait oil. Tankers are freely traded in a competitive market. Therefore, the present value of a tanker to BHP is equal to the tanker's price *plus* any extra gains that are likely to come from having BHP, rather than another owner, operate the vessel.

## 11.2 Forecasting economic rents

We recommend that financial managers ask themselves whether an asset is more valuable in their hands than in another's. A bit of classical microeconomics can help to answer that question. When an industry settles into long-run competitive equilibrium, all its assets are expected to earn their opportunity costs of capital—no more and no less. If the assets earned more, firms in the industry would expand or firms outside the industry would try to enter it.

Profits that *more* than cover the opportunity cost of capital are known as economic rents. These rents may be either temporary (in the case of an industry that is not in long-run equilibrium) or persistent (in the case of a firm with some degree of monopoly or market power). The NPV of an investment is simply the discounted value of the economic rents that it will produce. Therefore, when you are presented with a project that appears to have a positive

---

7   We assume that the extraction rate does not vary. If it can vary, Mr Solomon has a valuable operating option to increase output when gold prices are high or to cut back when prices fall. Option pricing techniques are needed to value the mine when operating options are important. See Chapters 20 and 21.

8   As in the case of our department store example, Mr Solomon is placing two bets—one on his ability to mine gold at a low cost and the other on the price of gold. Suppose that he really does believe that gold is overvalued. That should not deter him from running a low-cost gold mine as long as he can place separate bets on gold prices. For example, he might be able to enter into a long-term contract to sell the mine's output or he could sell gold futures. (We explain *futures* in Chapter 25.)

9   However, Hotelling has pointed out that if there are constant returns to scale in mining any mineral, the expected rise in the price of the mineral *less* extraction costs should equal the cost of capital. If the expected growth were faster, everyone would want to postpone extraction; if it were slower, everyone would want to exploit the resource today. In this case the value of a mine would be independent of when it was exploited, and you could value it by calculating the value of the mineral at today's price less the current cost of extraction. If (as is usually the case) there are declining returns to scale, then the expected price rise net of costs must be less than the cost of capital. For a review of Hotelling's Principle see S. Devarajan and A. C. Fisher, 'Hotelling's "Economics of Exhaustible Resources": Fifty Years Later', *Journal of Economic Literature*, **19**: 65–73 (March 1981). And for an application to the problem of valuing mineral deposits see M. H. Miller and C. W. Upton, 'A Test of the Hotelling Valuation Principle', *Journal of Political Economy*, **93**: 1–25 (1985).

NPV, do not just accept the calculations at face value. They may reflect simple estimation errors in forecasting cash flows. Probe behind the cash flow estimates and *try to identify the source of economic rents*. A positive NPV for a new project is believable only if *you* believe that your company has some special advantage.

Such advantages can arise in several ways. You may be smart or lucky enough to be first to the market with a new, improved product for which customers are prepared to pay premium prices (until your competitors enter and squeeze out excess profits). You may have a patent, proprietary technology or production cost advantage that competitors cannot match, at least for several years. You may have some valuable contractual advantage. For example, Telstra once had the advantage of a monopoly on telecommunications.[10] The hefty price that Optus paid for the right to be the first competitor to Telstra is an indicator of how valuable such competitive advantages are.

Thinking about competitive advantage can also help ferret out negative-NPV calculations that are negative by mistake. If you are the lowest-cost producer of a profitable product in a growing market, then you should invest to expand along with the market. If your calculations show a negative NPV for such an expansion, then you have probably made a mistake.

Do not forget what your competition is doing. There are two important questions that apply to nearly all projects: How long before the competition catches up? Meanwhile, are there sufficient excess returns to make the project worthwhile?

## How one company avoided a $100 million mistake

An Australian chemical producer was about to modify an existing plant to produce a specialty product, Polyzone, which was in short supply on world markets.[11] At prevailing raw material and finished product prices the expansion would have been strongly profitable.

Table 11.1 shows a simplified version of their analysis. Note the NPV of about $64 million at the company's 8 per cent real cost of capital—not bad for a $100 million outlay.

Then doubt began to creep in. Notice the outlay for transportation costs. A substantial proportion of the project's raw materials were special chemicals, largely imported from Europe, and much of the Polyzone production was to be exported back to Europe. Moreover, the Australian company had no long-run technological edge over potential European competitors; it simply had productive capacity and modern equipment not yet installed in Europe. It had a head start, but was that really enough to generate a positive NPV?

Notice the importance of the price spread between raw materials and finished product. Table 11.1 forecasts the spread at a constant $1.20 per kilogram of Polyzone for 10 years. That had to be wrong: European producers, who did not face the Australian company's transportation costs, would see an even larger NPV and expand capacity. Increased competition would almost surely squeeze the spread.

The Australian company decided to calculate the competitive spread—the spread at which a European competitor would see Polyzone capacity as zero NPV. Table 11.2 shows their analysis. The resulting spread of $0.95 per kilogram is the best *long-run* forecast for the Polyzone market, other things being constant, of course.

How much of a head start did the Australian producer have? How long before competitors forced the spread down to $0.95? Management's best guess was five years. They prepared Table 11.3, which is identical to Table 11.1 except for the forecast spread, which now shrinks to $0.95 by the start of year 5. Now the NPV was negative.

The project might have been saved if production could have been started in year 1 rather than year 2, or if local markets could have been expanded, thus reducing transportation costs. But these changes were not feasible, so management cancelled the project, albeit with a sigh of relief that they had not stopped at Table 11.1.

---

[10]   At the time of the monopoly Telstra was fully government-owned and was known as Telecom.

[11]   This is a true story, but names, places and details have been changed to protect the guilty.

This was a perfect example of the importance of thinking through sources of economic rents. Positive NPVs are suspect without some long-run competitive advantage.

table 11.1 _____

NPV calculation for proposed investment in Polyzone production by an Australian chemical company (figures in $million, except for production and spread).

| Year | 0 | 1 | 2 | 3–10 |
|---|---|---|---|---|
| Investment | 100 | | | |
| Production (millions of kilograms/year) | 0 | 0 | 40 | 80 |
| Spread ($/kilogram) | 1.20 | 1.20 | 1.20 | 1.20 |
| Net revenues (spread × production) | 0 | 0 | 48 | 96 |
| *Less* | | | | |
| Production costs | 0 | 0 | 30 | 30 |
| Transport costs | 0 | 0 | 4 | 8 |
| Other costs | 0 | 20 | 20 | 20 |
| Cash flow | −100 | −20 | −6 | +38 |

NPV (at $r = 8\%$) = $63.6 million

*Notes:*
1. For simplicity, we assume no inflation and no taxes.
2. Production capacity is 80 million kilograms per year.
3. Forecasted spread between output and raw material costs is $1.20 per kilogram.
4. Production costs are $0.375 per kilogram after startup ($0.75 per kilogram in year 2, when production is only 40 million kilograms).
5. Transportation costs are $0.10 per kilogram to European ports.
6. Plant and equipment have no salvage value after 10 years.

table 11.2 _____

What is the competitive spread to a European producer? About $0.95 per kilogram of Polyzone. Note that European producers face no transportation costs. Compare with Table 11.1 (figures in $million, except for production and spread).

| Year | 0 | 1 | 2 | 3–10 |
|---|---|---|---|---|
| Investment | 100 | | | |
| Production (millions of kilograms/year) | 0 | 0 | 40 | 80 |
| Spread ($/kilogram) | 0.95 | 0.95 | 0.95 | 0.95 |
| Net revenues | 0 | 0 | 38 | 76 |
| *Less* | | | | |
| Production costs | 0 | 0 | 30 | 30 |
| Transport costs | 0 | 0 | 0 | 0 |
| Other costs | 0 | 20 | 20 | 20 |
| Cash flow | −100 | −20 | −12 | +26 |

NPV (at $r = 8\%$) = 0

**table 11.3**

If expansion by European producers forces competitive spreads by year 5, the Australian producer's NPV falls to −$10.3 million. Compare with Table 11.1 (figures in $million, except for production and spread).

| Year | 0 | 1 | 2 | 3 | 4 | 5–10 |
|---|---|---|---|---|---|---|
| Investment | 100 | | | | | |
| Production (millions of kilograms/year) | 0 | 0 | 40 | 80 | 80 | 80 |
| Spread ($/kilogram) | 1.2 | 1.2 | 1.2 | 1.2 | 1.1 | 0.95 |
| Net revenues | 0 | 0 | 48 | 96 | 88 | 76 |
| *Less* | | | | | | |
| Production costs | 0 | 0 | 30 | 30 | 30 | 30 |
| Transport | 0 | 0 | 4 | 8 | 8 | 8 |
| Other costs | 0 | 20 | 20 | 20 | 20 | 20 |
| Cash flow | −100 | −20 | −6 | +38 | +30 | +18 |

NPV (at $r = 8\%$) = −$10.3 million

When a company contemplates investing in a new product, or expanding production of an existing product, it should specifically identify its advantages or disadvantages over its most dangerous competitors. It should calculate NPV from those competitors' points of view. If competitors' NPVs come out strongly positive, the company had better expect decreasing prices (or spreads) and evaluate the proposed investment accordingly.

# 11.3 Example—Marvin Enterprises decides to exploit a new technology

To illustrate some of the problems involved in predicting economic rents, let us leap forward to the twenty-first century and look at the decision by Marvin Enterprises to exploit a new technology.[12]

One of the most unexpected developments of these years was the remarkable growth of a completely new industry. By 2013 annual sales of gargle blasters totalled $1.68 billion, or 240 million units. Although it controlled only 10 per cent of the market, Marvin Enterprises was among the most exciting growth companies of the decade. Marvin had come late into the business, but it had pioneered the use of integrated microcircuits to control the genetic engineering processes used to manufacture gargle blasters. This development had enabled producers to cut the price of gargle blasters from $9 to $7 and had thereby contributed to the dramatic growth in the size of the market. The estimated demand curve in Figure 11.2 shows just how responsive demand is to such price reductions.

Table 11.4 summarises the cost structure of the old and new technologies. While companies with the new technology were earning 20 per cent on their initial investment, those with first-generation equipment had been hit by the successive price cuts. Since all Marvin's investment was in the 2009 technology, it had been particularly well placed during this period.

---

[12] We thank Stewart Hodges for permission to adapt this example from a case prepared by him and we thank the BBC for permission to use the term *gargle blasters*.

**figure 11.2**

The demand 'curve' for gargle blasters shows that for each $1 cut in price there is an increase in demand of 80 million units.

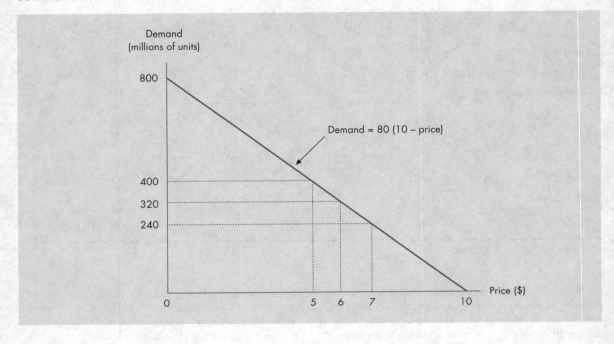

**table 11.4**

Size and cost structure of the gargle blaster industry before Marvin announced its expansion plans.

| | **Capacity (millions of units)** | | | | |
|---|---|---|---|---|---|
| **Technology** | **Industry** | **Marvin** | **Capital cost per unit ($)** | **Manufacturing cost per unit ($)** | **Salvage value per unit ($)** |
| First generation (2001) | 120 | — | 17.50 | 5.50 | 2.50 |
| Second generation (2009) | 120 | 24 | 17.50 | 3.50 | 2.50 |

*Notes:*

1. *Selling price is $7 per unit. One 'unit' means one gargle blaster.*
2. *Capital cost per unit is the average investment required per unit of production capacity.*

Rumours of new developments at Marvin had been circulating for some time, and the total market value of Marvin's shares had risen to $460 million by January 2014. At that point Marvin called a press conference to announce another technological breakthrough. Management claimed that their new third-generation process involving mutant neurons enabled the firm to reduce capital costs to an investment of $10 per unit and manufacturing costs to $3 per unit. Marvin proposed to capitalise on this invention by embarking on a huge $1 billion expansion program that would add 100 million units to capacity. The company expected to be in full operation within 12 months.

Before deciding to go ahead with this development, Marvin had undertaken extensive calculations on the effect of the new investment. The basic assumptions were as follows:

1. The cost of capital was 20 per cent.
2. The production facilities had an indefinite physical life.
3. The demand curve and the costs of each technology would not change.
4. There was no chance of a fourth-generation technology in the foreseeable future.
5. The corporate income tax, which had been abolished in 2010, was not likely to be reintroduced.

Marvin's competitors greeted the news with varying degrees of concern. There was general agreement that it would be five years before any of them would have access to the new technology. On the other hand, many consoled themselves with the reflection that Marvin's new plant could not compete with fully depreciated existing plant.

Suppose that you were Marvin's financial manager. Would you have agreed with the decision to expand? Do you think it would have been better to go for a larger or smaller expansion? How do you think Marvin's announcement is likely to affect the price of its shares?

You have a choice. You can go on *immediately* to read *our* solution to these questions. But you will learn much more if you stop and work out your own answer first. Try it.

## *Forecasting prices of gargle blasters

Up to this point in any capital budgeting problem we have always given you the set of cash flow forecasts. In the present case you have to *derive* those forecasts.

The first problem is to decide what is going to happen to the price of gargle blasters. Marvin's new venture will increase industry capacity to 340 million units. From the demand curve in Figure 11.2, you can see that the industry can sell this number of gargle blasters only if the price declines to $5.75:

$$\text{Demand (millions of units)} = 80 \,(10 - \text{price})$$
$$= 80 \,(10 - 5.75) = 340 \text{ million units}$$

If the price falls to $5.75, what will happen to companies with the 2001 technology? They also have to make an investment decision: Should they stay in business, or should they sell their equipment for its salvage value of $2.50 per unit? With a 20 per cent opportunity cost of capital, the NPV of staying in business is

$$\text{NPV} = -\text{investment} + \text{PV}(\text{price} - \text{manufacturing cost})$$
$$= -2.50 + \frac{5.75 - 5.50}{0.20} = -\$1.25 \text{ per unit}$$

Smart companies with 2001 equipment will therefore see that it is better to sell off capacity. No matter what their equipment originally cost or how far it is depreciated, it is more profitable to sell the equipment for $2.50 per unit than to operate it and lose $1.25 per unit.

As capacity is sold off, the supply of gargle blasters will decline and the price will rise. An equilibrium is reached when the price gets to $6. At this point 2001 equipment has a zero NPV:

$$\text{NPV} = -2.50 + \frac{6.00 - 5.50}{0.20} = \$0 \text{ per unit}$$

How much capacity will have to be sold off before the price reaches $6? You can check that by going back to the demand curve:

$$\text{Demand (millions of units)} = 80(10 - \text{price})$$
$$= 80(10 - 6) = 320 \text{ million units}$$

Therefore, Marvin's expansion will cause the price to settle down at $6 a unit and will induce first-generation producers to withdraw 20 million units of capacity.

But after five years Marvin's competitors will also be in a position to build third-generation plants. As long as these plants have positive NPVs, companies will increase their capacity and force prices down once again. A new equilibrium will be reached when the price reaches $5. At this point, the NPV of new third-generation plants is zero and there is no incentive for companies to expand further:

$$NPV = -10 + \frac{5.00 - 3.00}{0.20} = \$0 \text{ per unit}$$

Looking back once more at our demand curve, you can see that with a price of $5 the industry can sell a total of 400 million gargle blasters:

Demand (millions of units) $= 80(10 - \text{price}) = 80(10 - 5) = 400$ million units

The effect of the third-generation technology is therefore to cause industry sales to expand from 240 million units in 2013 to 400 million five years later. But that rapid growth is no protection against failure. By the end of five years any company that has only first-generation equipment will no longer be able to cover its manufacturing costs and will be *forced* out of business.

## *The value of Marvin's new expansion

We have shown that the introduction of third-generation technology is likely to cause gargle blaster prices to decline to $6 for the next five years and to $5 thereafter. We can now set down the expected cash flows from Marvin's new plant:

|  | Year 0 (investment) | Years 1–5 (revenue – manufacturing cost) | Years 6, 7, 8, . . . (revenue – manufacturing cost) |
|---|---|---|---|
| Cash flow, per unit ($) | −10 | 6 − 3 = 3 | 5 − 3 = 2 |
| Cash flow, 100 million units ($million) | −1000 | 600 − 300 = 300 | 500 − 300 = 200 |

Discounting these cash flows at 20 per cent gives us

$$NPV = -1000 + \sum_{t=1}^{5}\frac{300}{(1.20)^t} + \frac{1}{(1.20)^5}\left(\frac{200}{0.20}\right) = \$299 \text{ million}$$

It looks as if Marvin's decision to go ahead was correct. But there is something we have forgotten. When we evaluate an investment, we must consider *all* incremental cash flows. One effect of Marvin's decision to expand is to reduce the value of its existing 2009 plant. If Marvin decided not to go ahead with the new technology, the $7 price of gargle blasters would hold until Marvin's competitors started to cut prices in five years time. Marvin's decision therefore leads to an immediate $1 cut in price. This reduces the present value of its 2009 equipment by

$$24 \text{ million} \times \left[\sum_{t=1}^{5}\frac{1.00}{(1.20)^t}\right] = \$72 \text{ million}$$

Considered in isolation, Marvin's decision has an NPV of $299 million. But it also reduces the value of existing plant by $72 million. The net present value of Marvin's venture is therefore $299 − 72 = \$227$ million. The cannibalisation of existing business by a new product or technology is an important but sometimes overlooked aspect of the capital budgeting decision.

# *Alternative expansion plans

Marvin's expansion has a positive NPV, but perhaps Marvin could do better to build a larger or smaller plant. You can check that by going through the same calculations as above. First, you need to estimate how the additional capacity will affect gargle blaster prices. Then you can calculate the net present value of the new plant and the change in the present value of the existing plant. The total NPV of Marvin's expansion plan is

$$\text{Total NPV} = \text{NPV of new plant} + \text{change in PV of existing plant}$$

We have undertaken these calculations and plotted the results in Figure 11.3. You can see how total NPV would be affected by a smaller or larger expansion.

**figure 11.3** _____

Effect on NPV of alternative expansion plans. Marvin's 100 million unit expansion has a total NPV of $227 million (total NPV = NPV new plant + change in PV existing plant = 299 − 72 = 227). Total NPV is maximised if Marvin builds 200 million units of new capacity. If Marvin builds 280 million units of new capacity, total NPV is −$144 million.

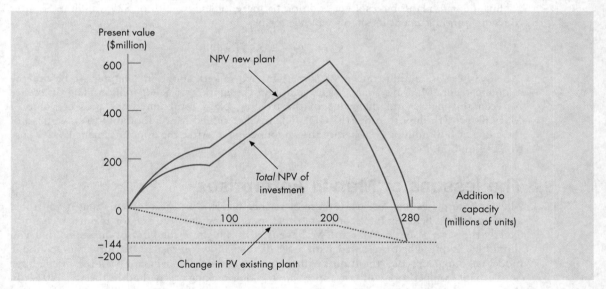

When the new technology becomes generally available in 2019 firms will construct a total of 280 million units of new capacity.[13] But Figure 11.3 shows that it would be foolish for Marvin to go that far. If Marvin added 280 million units of new capacity in 2014, the discounted value of the cash flows from the new plant would be zero *and* the company would have reduced the value of its old plant by $144 million. To maximise NPV, Marvin should construct 200 million units of new capacity and set the price just below $6 to drive out the 2001 manufacturers. Output is therefore less and price is higher than either would be under free competition.[14]

---

[13] Total industry capacity in 2019 will be 400 million units. Of this, 120 million units are second-generation capacity, and the remaining 280 million units are third-generation capacity.

[14] Notice that we are assuming that all customers have to pay the same price for their gargle blasters. If Marvin could charge each customer the maximum price that that customer would be willing to pay, output would be the same as under free competition. Such direct price discrimination is illegal and in any case difficult to enforce. But firms do search for indirect ways to differentiate between customers. For example, stores often offer free delivery, which is equivalent to a price discount for customers who live at an inconvenient distance. Publishers differentiate their products by selling hardback copies to libraries and paperbacks to impecunious students. In the early years of electronic calculators, manufacturers put a high price on their product. Although buyers knew that the price would be reduced in a year or two, the additional outlay was more than compensated for by the convenience of having the machines for the extra time.

## *The value of Marvin shares

Let us think about the effect of Marvin's announcement on the value of its shares. Marvin has 24 million units of second-generation capacity. In the absence of any third-generation technology, gargle blaster prices would hold at $7 and Marvin's existing plant would be worth

$$PV = 24 \text{ million} \times \frac{7.00 - 3.50}{0.20}$$

$$= \$420 \text{ million}$$

Marvin's new technology reduces the price of gargle blasters initially to $6 and after five years to $5. Therefore, the value of existing plant declines to

$$PV = 24 \text{ million} \left[ \sum_{t=1}^{5} \frac{6.00 - 3.50}{(1.20)^t} + \frac{5.00 - 3.50}{0.20 \times (1.20)^5} \right]$$

$$= \$252 \text{ million}$$

But the *new* plant makes a net addition to shareholders' wealth of $299 million. So after Marvin's announcement its shares will be worth

$$252 + 299 = \$551 \text{ million}[15]$$

Now here is an illustration of something we talked about in Chapter 4. Before the announcement, Marvin's shares were valued in the market at $460 million. The difference between this figure and the value of the existing plant represented the present value of Marvin's growth opportunities (PVGO). The market valued Marvin's ability to stay ahead of the game at $40 million even before the announcement. After the announcement PVGO rose to $299 million.[16]

## The lessons of Marvin Enterprises

Marvin Enterprises may be just a piece of science fiction, but the problems that it confronts are very real. Whenever Intel considers developing a new microprocessor it must face up to exactly the same issues as Marvin. We have tried to illustrate the *kind* of questions that you should be asking when presented with a set of cash flow forecasts. Of course, no economic model is going to predict the future with accuracy. Perhaps Marvin can hold the price above $6. Perhaps competitors will not appreciate the rich pickings to be had in the year 2014. In that case, Marvin's expansion would be even more profitable. But would you want to bet $1 billion on such possibilities?

Investments often turn out to earn far more than the cost of capital because of a favourable surprise. This surprise may in turn create a temporary opportunity for further investments earning more than the cost of capital. But anticipated and more prolonged rents will naturally lead to the entry of rival producers. That is why you should be suspicious of any investment proposal that predicts a stream of economic rents into the indefinite future. Try to estimate *when* competition will drive the NPV down to zero, and think what that implies for the price of your product.

---

[15]  In order to finance the expansion, Marvin is going to have to sell $1000 million of new shares. Therefore, the *total* value of Marvin's shares will rise to $1551 million. But investors who put up the new money will receive shares worth $1000 million. The value of Marvin's old shares after the announcement is therefore $551 million.

[16]  Notice that the market value of Marvin shares will be greater than $551 million if investors expect the company to expand again within the five-year period. In other words, PVGO after the expansion may still be positive. Investors may expect Marvin to stay one step ahead of its competitors or to successfully apply its special technology in other areas.

Many companies try to identify the major growth areas in the economy and then concentrate their investment in these areas. But the sad fate of first-generation gargle blaster manufacturers illustrates how rapidly existing plants can be made obsolete by changes in technology. It is fun being in a growth industry when you are at the forefront of the new technology, but a growth industry has no mercy on technological laggards.

You can expect to earn economic rents only if you have some superior resource such as management, sales force, design team, production facilities, distribution network or special reputation. Therefore, rather than trying to move into growth areas, you would do better to identify your firm's comparative advantages and try to capitalise on them. Unfortunately, superior profits will not accrue to the firm unless it can also avoid paying the full value of the superior resources. For example, the Boeing 777 is a much more efficient aeroplane to operate than older aircraft. But that does not mean that the airlines which operate the 777 can expect to earn supernormal profits. The greater efficiency is likely to be reflected in the price that Boeing charges for the 777. An airline will earn superior profits (i.e. economic rents) only if the 777 is more valuable to it than to other operators.[17]

We do not wish to imply that good investment opportunities do not exist. For example, such opportunities frequently arise because the firm has invested money in the past, which gives it the option to expand cheaply in the future. Perhaps the firm can increase its output just by adding an extra production line, whereas its rivals would need to construct an entire new factory. In such cases, you must take into account not only *whether* it is profitable to exercise your option, but also *when* it is best to do so.

Marvin also reminded us of project interactions, which we first discussed in Chapter 6. When you estimate the incremental cash flows from a project, you must remember to include the project's impact on the rest of the business. By introducing the new technology immediately, Marvin reduced the value of its existing plant by $72 million. Sometimes the losses on existing plant may completely offset the gains from a new technology. That is why we sometimes see established, technologically-advanced companies deliberately slowing down the rate at which they introduce new products.

Notice that Marvin's economic rents were equal to the difference between its costs and those of the marginal producer. The costs of the marginal 2001-generation plant consisted of the manufacturing costs plus the opportunity cost of not selling the equipment. Therefore, if the salvage value of the 2001 equipment were higher, Marvin's competitors would incur higher costs and Marvin could earn higher rents. We took the salvage value as given, but it in turn depends on the cost savings from substituting outdated gargle blaster equipment for some other asset. In a well-functioning economy, assets will be used so as to minimise the *total* cost of producing the chosen set of outputs. The economic rents earned by any asset are equal to the total extra costs that would be incurred if that asset were withdrawn.

Here is another point about salvage value that takes us back to our discussion of Magna Charter in the last chapter. A high salvage value gives the firm an option to abandon a project if things start to go wrong. However, if competitors *know* that you can bail out easily, they are more likely to enter your market. If it is clear that you have no alternative but to stay and fight, they will be more cautious about competing.

When Marvin announced its expansion plans, many owners of first-generation equipment took comfort in the belief that Marvin could not compete with their fully depreciated plant. Their comfort was misplaced. Regardless of past depreciation policy, it paid to scrap first-generation equipment rather than keep it in production. Do not expect that numbers in your balance sheet can protect you from harsh economic reality.

---

[17]  The rent that you earn because equipment is worth more to you than to your rivals is known as *consumer surplus*. If Boeing were able to charge each customer the maximum price that it was prepared to pay, no airline could expect to earn a consumer surplus from operating the 777, and Boeing would capture all the benefits.

# 11.4 Summary

It helps to use present value when you are making investment decisions, but that is not the whole story. Good investment decisions depend on both a sensible criterion and sensible forecasts. In this chapter we have looked at the problem of forecasting.

Projects may look attractive for two reasons: (1) there may be some errors in the sponsor's forecasts and (2) the company can genuinely expect to earn excess profit from the project. Good managers therefore try to ensure that the odds are stacked in their favour by expanding in areas in which the company has a comparative advantage. We like to put this another way by saying that good managers try to identify projects that will generate 'economic rents'. Good managers carefully avoid expansion when competitive advantages are absent and economic rents unlikely. They do not project favourable current product prices into the future without checking whether entry or expansion by competitors will drive future prices down.

Our story of Marvin Enterprises illustrates the origin of rents and how they determine a project's cash flows and net present value.

Any present value calculation, including our calculation for Marvin Enterprises, is subject to error. That is life: there is no other sensible way to value most capital investment projects. But some assets, such as gold, real estate, crude oil, ships and aeroplanes, and financial assets, such as shares and bonds, are traded in reasonably competitive markets. When you have the market value of such an asset, *use it*, at least as a starting point for your analysis.

## FURTHER READING

Most microeconomics texts contain a discussion of the determinants of economic rents. See, for example:

> S. Fischer et al., *Introduction to Microeconomics*, 2nd ed., McGraw-Hill Book Company, New York, 1988.
>
> D. McTaggart et al., *Economics*, 2nd ed., Addison-Wesley, Sydney, 1996.

For an interesting analysis of the likely effect of a new technology on the present value of existing assets see

> S. P. Sobotka and C. Schnabel, 'Linear Programming as a Device for Predicting Market Value: Prices of Used Commercial Aircraft, 1959–65', *Journal of Business*, 34: 10–30 (January 1961).

## QUIZ

**1.** Why is an MBA student who has learned about DCF like a baby with a hammer? What was the point of our answer?

**2.** You have inherited 250 acres of prime farmland in Victoria. There is an active market in land of this type, and similar properties are selling for $1000 per acre. Net cash returns per acre are $75 per year. These cash returns are expected to remain constant in real terms. How much is the land worth? A local banker has advised you to use a 12 per cent discount rate.

**3.** True or false?
   a. A firm that earns the opportunity cost of capital is earning economic rents.
   b. A firm that invests in positive NPV ventures expects to earn economic rents.

c. Financial managers should try to identify areas where their firms can earn economic rents, because it is there that positive NPV projects are likely to be found.

d. Economic rent is the equivalent annual cost of operating capital equipment.

**4.** Demand for concave utility meters is expanding rapidly, but the industry is highly competitive. A utility meter plant costs $50 million to set up, and it has an annual capacity of 500 000 meters. The production cost is $5 per meter, and this cost is not expected to change. If the machines have an indefinite physical life and the cost of capital is 10 per cent, what is the price of a utility meter?

a. $5.

b. $10.

c. $15.

**5.** The following comment appeared in *Aviation Week and Space Technology*, 25 July 1966: 'Alitalia has decided against ordering an advanced-technology jet transport. The carrier's analysis, in common with some other airlines, indicates that it can operate fully depreciated Douglas DC-8s at fare levels competitive with a Boeing 747. This is because seat or ton-mile costs of a fully depreciated current generation subsonic jet may not differ greatly from the advanced-technology jet.' Here 'fully depreciated' means fully written-off for accounting purposes. Discuss whether the low depreciation charge on a DC-8 justifies the continued use of that aeroplane. Under what circumstances would it pay to operate 747s?

**6.** If a capital equipment producer brings out a new, more efficient product, who is likely to get the benefits? In what circumstances would purchase of the new equipment be a positive NPV investment?

**7.** Look back to the Polyzone example at the end of Section 11.2. Explain why it was necessary to calculate the NPV of investment in Polyzone capacity from the point of view of a potential European competitor.

**8.** Your brother-in-law wants you to join him in purchasing a building on the outskirts of town. You and he would then develop and run a Taco Palace restaurant. Both of you are extremely optimistic about future real estate prices in this area, and your brother-in-law has prepared a cash flow forecast, which implies a large positive NPV. This calculation assumes sale of the property after 10 years. What further calculations should you do before going ahead?

**9.** A new leaching process allows your company to recover some gold as a by-product of its aluminium mining operations. How would you calculate the present value of the future cash flows from gold sales?

## QUESTIONS AND PROBLEMS

**1.** Suppose that you are considering investing in an asset for which there is a reasonably good secondary market. Specifically, you are Ansett Airlines and the asset is a Boeing 777—a very widely used aeroplane. How does the presence of a secondary market simplify your problem in principle? Do you think these simplifications could be realised in practice? Explain.

**2.** There is an active, competitive leasing (i.e. rental) market for most standard types of commercial jets. Many of the aeroplanes flown by the major domestic and international airlines are not owned by them, but leased for periods ranging from a few months to several years.

Gamma Airlines, however, owns two long-range DC-11s just withdrawn from service in Papua New Guinea. Gamma is considering using these aeroplanes to develop the potentially lucrative new route from the Northern Territory to Indonesia. A considerable investment in terminal facilities, training and advertising will be required. Once committed, Gamma will have to operate the route for at least three years.

One further complication: the manager of Gamma's international division is opposing commitment of the aeroplanes to the Northern Territory–Indonesia route because of anticipated future growth in traffic through Gamma's new hub in Ulan Bator.

How would you evaluate the proposed Northern Territory–Indonesia project? Give a detailed list of the necessary steps in your analysis. Explain how the aeroplane leasing market would be taken into account. If the project is attractive, how would you respond to the manager of the international division?

**3.** New-model commercial aeroplanes are much more fuel-efficient than older models. How is it possible for an airline flying older models to make money when its direct competitors are flying newer aeroplanes? Explain.

**4.** Thanks to acquisition of a key patent, your company now has exclusive production rights for barkelgassers (BGs) in Australia.

Production facilities for 200 000 BGs per year will require a $25 million immediate capital expenditure. Production costs are estimated at $65 per BG. The BG marketing manager is confident that all 200 000 units can be sold for $100 per unit (in real terms) until the patent runs out five years hence. After that the marketing manager does not have a clue about what the selling price will be.

What is the NPV of the BG project? Assume the real cost of capital is 9 per cent. To keep things simple, also make the following assumptions:

■ The technology for making BGs will not change. Capital and production costs will stay the same in real terms.
■ Competitors know the technology and can enter as soon as the patent expires, that is, in year 6.
■ If your company invests immediately, full production begins after 12 months, that is, in year 1.
■ There are no taxes.
■ BG production facilities last 12 years. They have no salvage value at the end of their useful life.

**5.** How would your answer to Question 4 change if technological improvements reduce the cost of new BG production facilities by 3 per cent per year? Thus, a new plant built in year 1 would only cost $25 (1 − 0.03) = $24.25$ million; a plant built in year 2 would cost $23.52 million, and so on. Assume that production costs per unit remain at $65.

**6.** Re-evaluate the NPV of the proposed Polyzone project under each of the following assumptions. Follow the format of Table 11.3. What is the right management decision in each case?
a. Competitive entry does not begin until year 5, when the spread falls to $1.10 per kilogram, and is complete in year 6, when the spread is $0.95 per kilogram.
b. The Australian chemical company can start up Polyzone production at 40 million kilograms in year 1 rather than year 2.
c. The Australian company makes a technological advance, which reduces its annual production costs to $25 million. Competitors' production costs do not change.

**7.** Photographic laboratories recover and recycle the silver used in photographic film. Murray River Photo is considering purchase of improved equipment for their laboratory at Telegraph Creek. Here is the information they have:

- The equipment costs $100 000.
- It will cost $80 000 per year to run.
- It has an economic life of 10 years but for tax purposes it will be depreciated over five years by the straight-line method.
- It will recover an additional 5000 ounces of silver per year.
- Silver is selling for $20 per ounce. Over the past 10 years the price of silver has appreciated by 4.5 per cent per year in real terms. Silver is traded in an active, competitive market.
- Murray's marginal tax rate is 33 per cent.
- Murray's company cost of capital is 8 per cent in real terms.

What is the NPV of the new equipment? Make additional assumptions as necessary.

**8.** The manufacture of polysyllabic acid is a competitive industry. Most plants have an annual output of 100 000 tonnes. Operating costs are 90 cents a tonne, and the sales price is $1 a tonne. A 100 000-tonne plant costs $100 000 and has an indefinite life. Its current scrap value of $60 000 is expected to decline to $57 900 over the next two years.

Phlogiston Ltd proposes to invest $100 000 in a plant that employs a new low-cost process to manufacture polysyllabic acid. The plant has the same capacity as existing units, but operating costs are 85 cents a tonne. Phlogiston estimates that it has two years lead over each of its rivals in use of the process but is unable to build any more plants itself before year 2. Also, it believes that demand over the next two years is likely to be sluggish and that its new plant will therefore cause temporary overcapacity.

You can assume that there are no taxes and that the cost of capital is 10 per cent.

a. By the end of year 2, the prospective increase in acid demand will require the construction of several new plants using the Phlogiston process. What is the likely NPV of such plants?
b. What would be the present value of each of these new plants?
c. What does that imply for the price of polysyllabic acid in year 3 and beyond?
d. Would you expect existing plant to be scrapped in year 2? How would your answer differ if scrap value were $40 000 or $80 000?
e. The acid plants of United Alchemists Ltd have been fully depreciated. Can it operate them profitably after year 2?
f. Acidosis, Inc purchased a new plant last year for $100 000 and is writing it down by $10 000 a year. Should it scrap this plant in year 2?
g. What would be the present value of Phlogiston's venture?

**9.** The Opera Association has come up with a unique door prize for its December 1998 fund-raising ball: 20 door prizes will be distributed, each one a ticket entitling the bearer to receive a cash award from the Association on 30 December 1999. The cash award is to be determined by calculating the ratio of the level of the ASX industrial share price index on 30 December 1999 to its level on 30 June 1999, and multiplying by $100. Thus, if the index turns out to be 2500 on 30 June 1999 and 3000 on 30 December 1999, the payoff will be $100 \times (3000/2500) = \$120$.

After the ball, a black market springs up in which the tickets are traded. What will the tickets sell for on 1 January 1999? On 30 June 1999? Assume the risk-free interest rate is 10 per cent per year. Also assume the Opera Association will be solvent at year-end 1999 and will, in fact, pay off on the tickets. Make other assumptions as necessary.

Would ticket values be different if the tickets' payoffs depended on the All-Ordinaries Index rather than the All-Industrials Index?

**10.** You are asked to value a large building in northern New South Wales. The valuation is needed for a bankruptcy settlement. Here are the facts:

■ The settlement *requires* that the building's value equal the present value of the *net cash proceeds* the owner would receive if the building is emptied and sold for its highest and best use, which is as a warehouse.

■ The building has been appraised at $1 million. This figure is based on recent selling prices of a sample of similar buildings in the area used as, or available for use as, warehouses.

■ If rented today as a warehouse, the building could generate $80 000 per year. This cash flow is calculated *after* out-of-pocket operating expenses and *after* rates of $50 000 per year:

| | |
|---|---|
| Gross rents | $180 000 |
| Operating expenses | 50 000 |
| Rates | 50 000 |
| Net | $ 80 000 |

Gross rents, operating expenses and rates are uncertain but are expected to grow with inflation.

■ However, it would take one year and $200 000 to clear out the existing equipment and prepare the building for use as a warehouse. This expenditure would be spread evenly over the next year.

■ The property will be put on the market when ready for use as a warehouse. Your real estate adviser says that properties of this type take, on average, one year to sell after they are put on the market. However, the owner could rent the building as a warehouse while waiting for it to sell.

■ The opportunity cost of capital for investment in real estate is 8 per cent in *real* terms.

■ Your real estate adviser notes that selling prices of comparable buildings in northern New South Wales have declined, in real terms, at an average rate of 2 per cent per year over the last 10 years.

■ The owner would pay a 5 per cent sales commission at the time of the sale.

■ The owner pays no income taxes, but does pay rates.

**\*11.** The world airline system is composed of the routes X and Y, each of which requires 10 aircraft. These routes can be serviced by three types of aircraft—A, B and C. There are five type A aircraft available, 10 type B and 10 type C. These aircraft are identical except for their operating costs, which are as follows:

| | Annual operating cost ($'000) | |
|---|---|---|
| Aircraft type | Route X | Route Y |
| A | 15 | 15 |
| B | 25 | 20 |
| C | 45 | 35 |

The aircraft have a useful life of five years and a salvage value of $10 000.

The aircraft owners do not operate the aircraft themselves but rent them to the operators. Owners act competitively to maximise their rental income, and operators attempt to minimise their operating costs. Airfares are also competitively determined.

Assume the cost of capital is 10 per cent.

a.  Which aircraft would be used on which route, and how much would each aircraft be worth?

b.  What would happen to usage and prices of each aircraft if the number of type A aircraft increased to 10?

c.  What would happen if the number of type A aircraft increased to 15?

d.  What would happen if the number of type A aircraft increased to 20? State any additional assumptions you need to make.

**\*12.** Taxes are a cost and therefore changes in tax rates can affect consumer prices, project lives and the value of existing firms. The following (quite hard) problem illustrates this. It also illustrates that tax changes that appear to be 'good for business' do not always increase the value of existing firms. Indeed, unless new investment incentives increase consumer demand, they can work only by rendering existing equipment obsolete.

The manufacture of bucolic acid is a competitive business. Demand is steadily expanding, and new plants are constantly being opened. Expected cash flows from an investment in plant are as follows:

|  | 0 | 1 | 2 | 3 |
|---|---|---|---|---|
| 1. Initial investment | 100 | | | |
| 2. Revenues | | 100 | 100 | 100 |
| 3. Cash operating costs | | 50 | 50 | 50 |
| 4. Tax depreciation | | 33.33 | 33.33 | 33.33 |
| 5. Income pre-tax | | 16.67 | 16.67 | 16.67 |
| 6. Tax at 40% | | 6.67 | 6.67 | 6.67 |
| 7. Net income | | 10 | 10 | 10 |
| 8. After-tax salvage | | | | 15 |
| 9. Cash flow (7 + 8 + 4 − 1) | −100 | +43.33 | +43.33 | +58.33 |
| NPV at 20% = 0 | | | | |

*Assumptions:*

1. Tax depreciation is straight-line over three years.
2. Pre-tax salvage value is 25 in year 3 and 50 if the asset is scrapped in year 2.
3. Tax on salvage value is 40 per cent of the difference between salvage value and depreciated investment.
4. The cost of capital is 20 per cent.

a.  What is the value of a one-year-old plant? Of a two-year-old plant?

b.  Suppose that the government now changes tax depreciation to allow a 100 per cent write-off in year 1. How does this affect the value of existing one-year and two-year-old plants? Existing plants must continue using the original tax depreciation schedule.

c.  Would it now make sense to scrap existing plants when they are two rather than three years old?

d.  How would your answers change if the corporate income tax were abolished entirely?

# chapter 12

# ORGANISING CAPITAL EXPENDITURE AND EX-POST EVALUATION

Up to this point we have considered how a firm *should* set its capital budget. In this chapter we discuss how it is done in practice. We pay particular attention to the organisation of capital budgeting and to the administrative problems that inevitably crop up.

A good capital budgeting system does more than just make accept–reject decisions on individual projects. It must tie into the firm's long-range planning process—the process that chooses the direction of the firm's business and sets out plans for financing, production, marketing, research, and so on. It must also tie into a procedure for measurement of performance. Otherwise the firm has no way of knowing how its expenditure decisions finally turn out. Measurement of performance occupies a substantial part of this chapter. The pitfalls in measuring profitability are serious but not as widely recognised as they should be.

## 12.1 Capital budgets and project authorisations

For most sizeable firms, the investment process is formalised in the preparation of an annual **capital budget**, which is a list of planned investments by plant and division. (In this chapter we will think of plants as building blocks for divisions and divisions as building blocks for firms. That is arbitrary: there may be more than two layers. Also, divisions are often organised by product line, region, or some other business unit.) In principle, the capital budget should be a list of all positive NPV opportunities open to the firm.

Most firms let project proposals bubble up from plants for review by division management and from divisions for review by senior management. The administrative process typically works as follows.

Plant managers identify 'interesting' opportunities, analyse them and decide which ones are really worthwhile. Proposed expenditures for these projects are then submitted to division managers for further review. Some of the proposals by the plants do not 'make the cut' at the divisional level. Divisional management may add its own ideas, usually new, larger ventures, such as manufacturing a new product, that plant managers could not be expected to initiate. Projects coming from divisional management may also reflect a vision for new strategic initiatives for the division. This may be the divisional manager's own vision, or it may be a response to instructions from head office to seek out new strategic opportunities in specified areas. The lists of the divisions are forwarded to the corporate controller or treasurer, who prunes and consolidates them into a proposed company budget. For very large, diversified firms there may be several intermediate review stages.

The resulting budget is a list of proposed new projects for the coming year and any projects from former years that are incomplete. Supporting information is usually provided on standard forms, supplemented by descriptive memoranda for larger projects. Since approval of the budget does not give the final go-ahead to spend money, backup information is not as detailed at this stage as it is later. Projects below a specific size are typically not even listed separately, but are simply included under a blanket approval for a given division or plant. In many companies the budget also contains rough estimates of likely expenditures over a five-year period, and in some cases even longer. At one time, for example, General Motor's operation in Australia—Holden—had indicative planning budgets going out as far as 20 years.

Senior management and staff specialising in planning and financial analysis then review the suggested budget. Usually there are negotiations between the firm's senior management and its divisional management, and perhaps there will also be special analyses of major outlays or ventures into new areas before the budget is submitted to the board for approval. Once approved, the budget generally remains the basis for planning over the ensuing year. In a few firms, however, it is updated each quarter.

Because each proposal in the budget needs to be authorised subsequently, the use of a budget involves some duplication of effort. But it allows information exchange up and down the management hierarchy before attitudes have hardened and personal commitments have been made. The danger with the whole procedure is loss of flexibility. There is a tendency for most projects to appear for the first time in the annual budget, and in some companies it is difficult to initiate project ideas at any other time of the year.

# Processes in project development[1]

There are several recognisable processes in project development. Although we present them in a sequential list they do not necessarily form a sequence of steps one following the other. Sometimes there will be doubling back from later processes to earlier processes, and sometimes processes will overlap with two or more going on simultaneously. The effort that goes into the processes will vary enormously from project to project. Obviously, less effort will be devoted to a routine machine replacement proposal than will be devoted to a major strategic initiative such as the development of a new product or the building of a new factory. The processes are as follows:

---

[1]   We acknowledge that this section is based largely on the work of Simon Draper (Valuation, Creation and Discretion: Value Analysis and Investment Decision Making for Real Assets, M.Bus. thesis, UTS, 1997), who in turn builds on the work of P. King, 'Is the Emphasis on Capital Budgeting Theory Misplaced?', *Journal of Business Finance and Accounting*, (Spring 1975).

**Triggering**    This is the starting process for a project, where there is either recognition that the opportunity exists for a new project (for example, a cost reducing method of production), or that a need exists to develop a new project (for example, recognition that the company needs to change its product line, as was the case with James Hardie's asbestos products). Often, and particularly for large projects, the trigger is a belief that there is an opportunity to develop, or exploit, a competitive advantage. At this stage in the process the project exists as little more than an idea.

**Screening**    The initial idea is subject to further, and often informal analysis, to determine whether more detailed investigation is justified. The purpose here is to determine whether the idea really has the potential to create value. As we discuss later in the chapter, methods of measuring managers' performance may have a substantial impact on which projects get past this point.

**Definition**    This is the process where the project starts to take shape. The technical and economic form of the project are developed. The project may be quite fluid at this stage and may be subject to considerable tailoring to get it into a form that will be acceptable both economically and politically within the company. This process may be revisited several times during the life of the project proposal. Initially, the definition may be quite crude, but before the project is finally approved considerable time, effort and money may have been consumed in this process. If the project reaches this stage the task of building commitment to the project has begun and managers' reputations and egos may now be at stake.

**Evaluation**    This provides the formal case and the formal test for the particular project. Evaluation may have been taking place throughout the project's development, but it eventually reaches a stage of formalisation. Such formal evaluations may be used in two ways: as a test to confirm that the proposed project is likely to add value; and/or as a justification and validation of earlier decision making. The formal evaluation may reveal that the project is unacceptable in its current form, but worthy of more work in the definition process.

**Transmission**    Information about the proposal is passed up and down the organisation. This will involve both formal and informal processes. The sponsors of the project will try and build commitment to the project at different levels within the company. To do this they will attempt to anticipate the concerns and information requirements of other parties in the decision process. They may also tailor the project and the formal proposal in such a way as to minimise resistance to acceptance of the project.

**Decision**    This is the formal part of the decision process. It allows senior management to assess whether the proposal is solid. The decision process also allows them to review the strategic fit of the proposal and formalises their commitment to it. This assessment by senior management also motivates the project sponsors to develop a thorough and rigorous case. It will likely reflect badly on the project sponsors if the proposal gets to this stage and is rejected.

**Post-audit**    This is the process where the implementation of the project is reviewed to determine whether the capital expenditures, the project and its outcomes were as planned. Formal post-audits, it turns out, are surprisingly infrequent events. However, there does appear to be an increasing trend towards their use. In many companies, however, the last act of formal control has been the authorisation to spend the money.

# Project authorisations

The approval of the total capital budget rarely provides the go-ahead to make the expenditures for each project listed in the budget. Most companies demand that formal **appropriation requests** be prepared for each proposal. These requests are accompanied by more or less elaborate backup, depending on the project's size, novelty and strategic importance. Also, the type of backup information required depends on the project category. Some firms use a four-fold breakdown:

1. Safety or environmental outlays required by law or company policy, e.g. for pollution control equipment.
2. Maintenance or cost reduction, e.g. machine replacement.
3. Capacity expansion in existing businesses.
4. Investment for new products or ventures.

The information requirements for projects differ across these categories:

1. Pollution control does not have to pay its own way. The main issue is whether standards are met at minimum present value of cost. The decision is likely to hinge on engineering analyses of alternative technologies.
2. Engineering analysis is also important in machine replacement, but new machines have to pay their own way. In category 2, the firm faces the classical capital budgeting problems described in Chapter 6.
3. Projects in category 3 are less straightforward; these decisions may hinge on forecasts of demand, possible shifts in technology and competitors' strategies. We looked at these issues in Chapter 11.
4. Projects in category 4 are most likely to depend on intangibles. The first projects in a new area may not have positive NPVs if they are considered in isolation, yet the firm may go ahead in order to establish a position in a market and to pave the way for profitable future projects. The first projects are not undertaken for their own sake, but because they generate valuable *options* to undertake follow-up projects.[2] Thus, for projects in category 4, cash flow forecasts may be less important than the issue of whether the firm enjoys some technological or other advantage, which promises to generate economic rents for the firm. That issue becomes the main focus of project analysis.

Most large firms have manuals providing checklists to make sure that all relevant costs and alternatives are considered. The manuals may contain instructions showing how to forecast cash flows and how to compute NPV, internal rate of return or other measures of project value. Usually the manuals also specify the opportunity cost of capital.[3]

Although the project originator may prepare appropriation requests, the plant manager is usually responsible for submitting them. These requests come up through the ranks of operating management for approval at each succeeding level. If the project is large, staff accountants, engineers and economists may check the request at some stage. The number of hurdles the proposal must pass depends on the expenditure involved.

Because the investment decision is central to the development of the firm, authorisation tends to be reserved for senior management. Almost all companies set ceilings on the size of capital projects that divisional managers can authorise without specific approval from their superiors. Moreover, the ceilings are surprisingly low. Scapens and Sale surveyed 203 larger firms, with average capital budgets of $130 million per year, and found that the average ceiling

---

[2]  We discuss how to value these capital investment options in Chapter 21.

[3]  As the following conversation with one finance director suggests, having a manual is not the same as using it:

*Finance director*: 'I can give you a copy of our capital expenditure control manual.'
*Interviewer*: 'Did you have any hand in putting it together?'
*Finance director*: 'Absolutely not. I think they're extremely boring. I have no idea of my way around it.'

Cited in P. R. Marsh, T. P. Barwise, K. Thomas and J. R. C. Wensley, 'Managing Strategic Investment Decisions in Large Diversified Companies', in A. M. Pettigrew (ed.), *Competitiveness and the Management Process*, Basil Blackwell, Oxford, 1988, p. 101.

for individual projects was only \$136 000.[4] Ceilings have risen since this survey, but are still small fractions of total capital expenditures. When you consider that a large company may generate thousands of appropriation requests each year, the limited extent of delegation is striking.

## The decision criteria managers actually use

These days almost all large companies use discounted cash flow in some form, but many companies also compute flawed measures such as payback. Why does payback survive even in successful and sophisticated companies?

When pressed, managers usually concede that, if followed literally, the payback rule does not make sense. But they may point out that payback is the simplest way to *communicate* an idea of project profitability. Capital budgeting is a process of discussion and negotiation involving people from all parts of the firm, and therefore it is important to have a measure that everyone can understand. Insisting that everyone commenting on a project do so in terms of NPV may cut out those who do not understand NPV but who can still contribute useful information.

Other managers will check on the project's payback because they know that in a competitive world high profits do not last forever, and therefore they may distrust the more distant cash flow forecasts. Looking at payback, which ignores the later cash flows completely, provides a rough-and-ready check on project profitability. Of course, it would be better to do a careful analysis of when competition will intensify and what effect that will have on cash flows.

The use of intelligent techniques does not guarantee intelligent decisions. You can have good technique and poor judgement, or vice versa. You can be conceptually perfect, by relying on NPV, and still fall down in the execution of your NPV calculation. Some firms fail to understand the importance of Level 1 and Level 2 consistency (discussed in Chapter 6) and as a consequence we have seen errors that have cost firms millions and millions of dollars. For example, some companies use nominal discount rates without properly adjusting for future inflation in their cash flow forecasts. Other companies think they can ignore inflation in cash flow forecasts because 'on the average revenues increase to cover inflated costs'. Others simply do not understand the opportunity cost of capital. Several years ago a leading Australian property development company got into financial distress; perhaps this was no surprise. One of the most senior finance executives insisted to one of the authors that the cost of equity capital was the dividend yield. Managers who hold such views may make much better decisions if they use payback rather than NPV. We discussed these sorts of elementary mistakes in Chapter 6.

Before we get too smug, remember that business people often act smarter than they talk. (For students and scholars it is often the other way around.) They may make correct decisions, but they may not be able to explain them in the language of finance and economics. Many decisions are fundamentally intuitive. If *intuitive* sounds capricious, replace the word with *informed judgement*. As we argued in Chapter 11, if a firm enjoys an advantage that promises to generate economic rents, it should probably press on regardless of calculated payback or present value. Experience helps in identifying such opportunities.

## Controlling capital investment decisions

Most large companies have corporate capital budgeting staff who help to enforce consistency, uncover unspecified assumptions and undertake sophisticated analyses of major projects.

---

4   R. W. Scapens and J. T. Sale, 'Performance Measurement and Formal Capital Expenditure Controls in Divisionalized Companies', *Journal of Business Finance and Accounting*, 8: 389–420 (Autumn 1981).

Their analyses may also have to ferret out local managers who are evading the controls in the capital investment process. For example, managers may be permitted to approve projects only up to a certain value. But this authority may become infinite if each project can be broken down into a large number of small parts. The following story illustrates this problem:

'Our [top managers] like to make all the major capital decisions. They think they do, but I've just seen one case where a division beat them.

'I received for editing a capital request from the division for a large chimney. I couldn't see what anyone could do with just a chimney so I flew out for a visit. They've built and equipped a whole plant on plant expense orders. The chimney is the only indivisible item that exceeded the $50 000 limit we put on the expense orders. Apparently they learned informally that a new plant wouldn't be favourably received, and since they thought the business needed it, and the return would justify it, they built the damn thing.'[5]

This embarrassment might have been avoided if the firm had imposed a limit on individual discretionary expenditures *and* on the total amount of such expenditures by each manager in any one year.

The boundaries of 'capital expenditure' are often imprecise. Consider the investments in information technology or 'IT' (computers, software and systems, training and telecommunications) made by large banks and securities firms. These investments soak up *hundreds* of millions of dollars annually, and some multi-year IT projects have cost well over $1 billion. Yet much of this expenditure goes to intangibles such as system design, testing or training. Such outlays often bypass capital expenditure controls, particularly if they are made piecemeal rather than as large, discrete commitments. The problems here are obvious. Authorisation procedures should be broadly construed and not encourage the inefficient substitution of one kind of an investment for another. Neither should they encourage the substitution of different forms of financing to bypass expenditure controls. Leasing, for example, involves rental payments rather than capital expenditures. So leasing an asset may allow a manager to acquire the use of the asset without any formal capital expenditure approval.

Authorisation requests should draw attention to all likely contingent expenditures. Too often, seemingly small and innocuous investments are the first step in a chain of economically dependent investments. Management should be aware of the full consequences of letting a plant or division get its foot in the door.

A final problem is to check that the money is spent on the projects approved and that the projects are implemented successfully. Often in the past there was little control other than in the approval process. It was often left to divisional managers to spend the money with relatively little restriction or follow-up of project outcomes. Now more large firms are conducting post-audits on major projects.

## 12.2 Problems and some solutions

Good investment decisions require good data. How can you organise the capital budgeting operation to get the kind of information that you need? We suggest five problems that you need to think about.

### Ensuring that forecasts are consistent

Inconsistent assumptions often creep into investment proposals. Suppose that the manager of your furniture division is bullish on housing starts but the manager of your appliance division is bearish. This inconsistency makes the furniture division's project look better than the

---

5   Cited in J. L. Bower, *Managing the Resource Allocation Process: A Study of Corporate Planning and Investment*, Division of Research, Graduate School of Business Administration, Harvard University, Boston, 1970, p. 15.

appliance division's. Senior management ought to negotiate a consensus estimate and make sure that all NPVs are recomputed using that joint estimate. Then a rational decision can be made.

This is why many firms begin the capital budgeting process by establishing forecasts of economic indicators, such as inflation and growth in gross national product, as well as forecasts of particular items that are important to the firm's business, such as housing starts or the price of raw materials. These forecasts can then be used as the basis for all project analyses.

# Eliminating conflicts of interest

Plant and divisional managers are concerned about their own futures. Sometimes their interests conflict with shareholders', and that may lead to investment decisions that do not maximise shareholder wealth. For example, new plant managers naturally want to demonstrate good performance right away, in order to move up the corporate ladder. Perhaps they will propose quick-payback projects even if NPV is sacrificed. And if their performance is judged on book earnings, they will also be attracted by projects whose accounting results look good.

The problem lies in the way many firms measure performance and reward managers. Do not expect managers to concentrate only on NPV if you always demand quick results, or if you will reward them later on the basis of book return. More on this later in the chapter.

Another potential conflict of interest arises because some managers are less willing to take risks than others are. They may let their personal attitude towards risk interfere with their business judgement. Managers of divisions that have assured good performance are more likely to propose high-risk projects than managers of faltering divisions with an uncertain future. Also, a large division is more likely to risk a $1 million loss than a small division. Such a loss might merely make a dent in the profits of the larger division, but it could put the manager of the small division out of work.

This problem ties back to how managers' performance is measured and rewarded. A good measurement and reward system should have some tolerance for mistakes and should be able to discriminate between good decisions and lucky ones. Ideally, managers should be rewarded for good decisions thwarted by bad luck and penalised for bad decisions rescued by good luck.[6]

# Reducing forecast bias

Anyone who is keen to get a project proposal accepted is likely to look on the bright side when forecasting the project's cash flows. Such overoptimism seems to be a common feature in financial forecasts. How often have you heard of a new tunnel, opera house or motorway, which actually cost *less* than was originally forecast?

You will probably never be able to eliminate bias completely, but if you are aware of why bias occurs, you are at least part of the way there. Project sponsors are likely to overstate their case deliberately only if you, the manager, encourage them to do so. For example, if they believe that success depends on having the largest division rather than the most profitable one, they will propose large expansion projects that they do not truly believe have positive NPVs. Or if they believe that you will not listen to them unless they paint a rosy picture, you will be presented with many rosy pictures. Or if you invite each division to compete for limited resources, you will find that each attempts to outbid the other for those resources. The fault in such cases is your own—if you hold up the hoop, others will try to jump through it.

---

[6]   If you can devise a reliable way to do this we would like to hear from you!

# Getting senior management the information that it needs

Valuing capital investment opportunities is hard enough when you can do the entire job yourself. In real life it is a cooperative effort. Although cooperation brings more knowledge to bear, it has its own problems. Some are unavoidable—just another cost of doing business. Others can be alleviated by adding checks and balances to the investment process.

Many of the problems stem from sponsors' eagerness to obtain approval for their favourite projects. As the proposal travels up the organisation, alliances are formed. Preparation of the request inevitably involves discussions and compromises that limit subsequent freedom of action. Thus, once a division has screened its plants' proposals, the plants unite in competing against 'outsiders'.

This competition among divisions can be put to good use if it forces division managers to develop a well thought-out case for what they want to do. But the competition has its costs as well. Several thousand appropriation requests may reach the senior management level each year; all essentially sales documents presented by united fronts and designed to persuade. Alternative schemes have been filtered out at an earlier stage. The danger is that senior management cannot obtain (let alone absorb) the information to evaluate each project rationally.

The dangers are illustrated by the following practical question: Should we establish a definite opportunity cost of capital for computing the NPV of projects in our furniture division? The answer in theory is a clear yes, providing that the projects of the division are all in the same risk class. Remember that most project analysis is done at the plant or divisional level.[7] Only a small proportion of project ideas analysed survive for submission to top management. Plant and division managers cannot judge projects correctly unless they know the true opportunity cost of capital.

Suppose that senior management settles on 12 per cent. That helps plant managers make rational decisions. But it also tells them exactly how optimistic they have to be to get their pet project accepted. We propose the following law: *the proportion of proposed projects having a positive NPV is independent of top management's estimate of the opportunity cost of capital.*

This is not a facetious conjecture. The law was tested in a large oil company, whose capital budgeting staff kept careful statistics on forecasted profitability of proposed projects. One year top management announced a big push to conserve cash. They imposed discipline on capital expenditures by increasing the corporate hurdle rate by several percentage points. But staff statistics showed the fraction of proposals with positive NPVs stayed rock-steady at about 85 per cent of all proposals. Top management's tighter discipline was repaid with expanded optimism.

A firm that accepts poor information at the top faces two consequences. First, senior management cannot evaluate individual projects. In a study by Bower of a large multi-divisional company, projects that had the approval of a division general manager were seldom turned down by his or her group of divisions, and those reaching the top management were almost never rejected.[8] Second, since senior managers have limited control over project-by-project decisions, capital investment decisions are effectively decentralised regardless of what formal procedures specify. Some senior managers try to impose discipline and offset optimism by setting rigid capital expenditure limits. This artificial capital rationing forces plant or division managers to set priorities. The firm ends up using capital rationing not because capital is truly unobtainable but as a way of decentralising decisions.

There is a general point here. When we say that firms should accept all projects with positive NPVs, we implicitly assume that the forecasts on which those NPVs are based are unbiased. But if managers are fed optimistic forecasts, you may find that ad hoc procedures may actually lead to better decisions than the NPV rule. We should stress that we are not *recommending* the use of ad hoc criteria. The essential point is that improvements in one aspect of the decision-making process must take account of deficiencies in other areas.

---

7   It is quite common for different hurdle rates to be applied to different divisions.
8   See J. L. Bower, op. cit., Footnote 5.

# Recognising strategic 'fit'

We have pictured the capital investment process as if all proposals bubbled up from the bottom of the organisation. That is never the whole story. The managers of plants A and B cannot be expected to see the potential economies of scale of closing their plants and consolidating production at a new plant C. We expect divisional management to propose plant C. Similarly, divisions 1 and 2 may not be eager to give up their own data processing operations to a large, central computer. That proposal would come from senior management.

The final capital budget must also reflect strategic choices made by senior management. Strategic planning attempts to identify businesses in which the firm has a real competitive advantage. It also attempts to identify businesses to sell or liquidate as well as declining businesses that should be allowed to run down. Strategic planning is really capital budgeting on a grand scale.

The problem is that a firm's capital investment choices should reflect both 'bottom-up' and 'top-down' processes—capital budgeting and strategic planning, respectively. The two processes should complement each other. Plant and division managers, who do most of the work in bottom-up capital budgeting, may not see the forest for the trees. Strategic planners may have a mistaken view of the forest because they do not look at the trees one by one.

# 12.3 Evaluating performance

Managers are likely to act in shareholders' interests only if they have the right incentives. Therefore, the way that managerial performance is measured and rewarded must tie in with the capital investment process.

Most firms have formal procedures for evaluating the performance of their capital investments. There are three aspects to performance measurement. First, companies need to monitor projects under construction to ensure that there are no serious delays or cost overruns. Second, companies may conduct a post-audit on major projects shortly after they have begun to operate. These help to identify problems that need fixing, to check the accuracy of forecasts and to suggest questions that should have been asked before the project was undertaken. Post-audits pay off mainly by helping managers do a better job when they come to analyse the next round of investment proposals. Finally, there is ongoing performance measurement, which is done through the firm's accounting and control system. We will explain how that system should work to support the capital investment process and why it sometimes fails.

## Controlling projects in progress

A decision to authorise expenditure usually specifies how much money may be spent and when. Control is established by accounting procedures for recording expenditures as they occur. Typically, companies will permit up to 10 per cent expenditure overruns, but beyond that the sponsor is required to submit a supplemental request for funds. To ensure that the money is not diverted to other uses, the sponsor may be required to submit a revised request if there is any significant change in the nature of the project.

To avoid delays, a few companies attempt to set limits on the length of time before construction begins. Almost all firms require the project sponsor to submit a formal notice of completion, so that the accumulated costs can be transferred to the permanent accounts and any unspent cash can be recovered rather than kept in a hidden kitty for miscellaneous uses.

These procedures are necessary aspects of control. More general information on progress is usually contained in monthly or quarterly status reports.

## Post-audits

Post-audits of capital expenditures are now increasingly undertaken in large firms. Not all projects are audited, and those that are are usually audited only once. A few firms require further audits for 'problem' projects. The most common time for audits is one year after construction has been completed.

It makes sense to check on the progress of recent investments. Otherwise problems may go undetected and uncorrected. Post-audits can also provide useful insights to the next round of decision making on capital investments. After a post-audit the controller may say, 'We should have anticipated the extra working capital needed to support the project.' So the next time working capital will get the attention it deserves.

The post-audit is sometimes used to monitor the quality of forecasts made by project proposers. However, it is worth sounding a note of caution here. The audit is usually taken far too soon after installation to provide any clear assessment of the project's success. And since the forecasters rarely specify the economic assumptions underlying their forecasts, it is hard to tell whether they really got it right or whether they were bailed out by a buoyant economy. Finally, the number of audited projects is so small and their authorship so imprecise that it is difficult to associate forecasting ability with a particular type of project or proposer.

Of course, the mere threat of post-audit may spur the proposer to greater accuracy. But it can work the other way around. Many managers make conservative forecasts in the belief that what matters is to beat one's forecasts. This is illustrated in the following conversation:

First project team member: 'The other question we need to decide in a wider context is how much we want to declare we want to save.'

Second project team member: 'Yes, we'll decide on the politics. . . . Don't want to be putting in too much savings. . . . We can come back with another little bit later on.'[9]

## Problems in measuring incremental cash flows after the fact

Often, post-audits cannot measure all cash flows generated by a project. It may be impossible to split the project away from the rest of the business.

Suppose that you have just taken over a transport firm in Auckland that operates a package delivery service for local stores. You decide to try to revitalise the business by cutting costs and improving service. This requires three investment projects:

1.  Buy five new trucks.
2.  Construct two additional dispatching centres.
3.  Buy a small computer to keep track of packages and schedule trucks.

A year later you try a post-audit of the computer. You verify that it is working properly and check actual costs of purchase, installation and training against projections. But how do you identify the incremental *inflows* generated by the computer? No one has kept records of the extra petrol that *would have been used* or the extra packages that *would have been lost*, had the computer not been installed. You may be able to verify that service is better, but how much of the improvement comes from the new trucks, how much from the dispatching centres and how much from the new computer? It is impossible to say. The only meaningful way to judge success or failure of your re-vitalisation program is to examine the delivery business as a whole.[10]

## Evaluating operating performance

Think again of your package delivery business. We could measure its performance in two ways:

1.  *Actual versus projected*   We could compare actual operating earnings or cash flow with what you predicted.

---

9   Cited in P. R. Marsh et al. , op. cit., Footnote 3.
10  Even here you do not know the incremental cash flows that have resulted from your efforts unless you can establish what the business would have earned if you had not made the changes. It is often far from clear what the appropriate base case is from which to measure these incremental cash flows.

**2.** *Actual profitability versus an absolute standard of profitability*  We could also compare actual profitability with the cost of capital. In other words, we could look at whether with hindsight the project has provided the return that investors required.

The first measure is relatively easy to understand and implement, although it may be difficult to tell whether the deviations from forecast reflect poor analysis or bad luck. The second measure is full of pitfalls, as we will now see.

# Biases in accounting rates of return

Many firms compute accounting rates of return on investment (ROI).[11] ROI is just the ratio of after-tax operating income to the net (depreciated) book value of assets. We rejected book ROI as a capital investment criterion in Chapter 5, and in fact few companies now use it for that purpose. But they do use it to evaluate profitability of existing businesses, because there is usually no alternative.

Consider the pharmaceutical and chemical industries. If you compare the ROI in these industries you will find that pharmaceutical companies around the world generally have much higher ROIs than chemical companies. It is not difficult to find pharmaceutical ROIs that are more than five times the ROIs of chemical companies. Are the pharmaceutical companies *really* that profitable? If so, lots of companies should be rushing into the pharmaceutical business. Or is there something wrong with the ROI measure?

Pharmaceutical companies have done well, but they look more profitable than they really are. Book ROIs are biased upwards for companies with intangible investments such as research and development (R&D). There are two reasons for this. First, many of the costs incurred in R&D may be expensed rather than capitalised and so never appear in the balance sheet. Second, the payoff from successful R&D greatly exceeds the cost; thus, such costs as are capitalised grossly underestimate the market value of the R&D asset.

Table 12.1 shows cash inflows and outflows for two mature companies. Neither is growing. Each must plough back $400 million to maintain its existing business. The *only* difference

**table 12.1**

Comparison of a pharmaceutical company and a chemical company, each in a no-growth steady state. Revenues, costs, total investment and annual cash flow are identical, but the pharmaceutical company invests more in R&D (figures in $million).

|  | **Pharmaceutical company** | **Chemical company** |
|---|---|---|
| Revenues | 1000 | 1000 |
| Cash operating costs | 500 | 500 |
| Net operating cash flow | 500 | 500 |
| *Investment* |  |  |
| Plant and equipment | 100 | 300 |
| R&D | 300 | 100 |
| Total investment | 400 | 400 |
| Annual cash flow |  |  |
| (revenue − cash operating costs − total investment) | +100 | +100 |

---

[11]  This is also known as the return on book value—see Chapter 5.

is that the chemical company's ploughback goes mostly to plant and equipment; the pharmaceutical company invests mostly in R&D. We assume that all the R&D costs are expensed against profits at the time the costs are incurred. The chemical company invests only one-third as much in R&D ($100 versus $300 million) but triples the pharmaceutical company's investment in fixed assets.

Table 12.2 calculates the annual depreciation charges. Notice that the sum of R&D and total annual depreciation is identical for the two companies.

The companies' cash flows, true profitability and true present values are also identical, but as Table 12.3 shows, the pharmaceutical company's book ROI is 18 per cent, *triple* the chemical company's. The accountants would get annual income right (in this case it is identical to cash flow), but understate the value of the pharmaceutical company's assets relative to the chemical company's. Lower asset value creates the upward-biased pharmaceutical company's ROI.

The moral is this: do not assume that businesses with high book ROIs are necessarily performing better. They may just have more 'hidden' assets, that is, assets which accountants do not put on balance sheets.

This 'hidden assets' problem is only one of several reasons why accounting rates of return are biased. We take a closer look at this bias in the next section.

**table 12.2**

Book asset values and annual depreciation for the companies described in Table 12.1 (figures in $million).

| Age in years | Pharmaceutical company | | Chemical company | |
|---|---|---|---|---|
| | Original cost of investment | Net book value | Original cost of investment | Net book value |
| 0 (new) | 100 | 100 | 300 | 300 |
| 1 | 100 | 90 | 300 | 270 |
| 2 | 100 | 80 | 300 | 240 |
| 3 | 100 | 70 | 300 | 210 |
| 4 | 100 | 60 | 300 | 180 |
| 5 | 100 | 50 | 300 | 150 |
| 6 | 100 | 40 | 300 | 120 |
| 7 | 100 | 30 | 300 | 90 |
| 8 | 100 | 20 | 300 | 60 |
| 9 | 100 | 10 | 300 | 30 |
| Total net book value | | 550 | | 1650 |

| | Pharmaceutical company | Chemical company |
|---|---|---|
| Annual depreciation[a] | 100 | 300 |
| R&D expense | 300 | 100 |
| Total depreciation and R&D | 400 | 400 |

Note:

[a] The pharmaceutical company has 10 vintages of assets, each depreciated by $10 per year. Total depreciation per year is $10 \times 10 = \$100$ million. The chemical company's depreciation is $10 \times 30 = \$300$ million.

**table 12.3**

Book ROIs for the companies described in Table 12.1 (figures in $million). The companies' cash flows and values are identical. But the pharmaceutical company's accounting rate of return is triple the chemical company's. This bias occurs because the accounts do not show the value of the investment in R&D in the balance sheet.

|  | Pharmaceutical company | Chemical company |
|---|---|---|
| Revenues | 1000 | 1000 |
| Cash operating costs | 500 | 500 |
| R&D expense | 300 | 100 |
| Depreciation[a] | 100 | 300 |
| Net income | 100 | 100 |
| Net book value[a] | 550 | 1650 |
| Book ROI | 18% | 6% |

*Note:*
[a]  *Calculated in Table 12.2.*

## 12.4 Example—measuring the profitability of the Nodhead supermarket

Supermarket chains invest heavily in building and equipping new stores. The regional manager of a chain is about to propose investing $1 million in a new store in Nodhead. Projected cash flows are:

| Year | 1 | 2 | 3 | 4 | 5 | 6 | After year 6 |
|---|---|---|---|---|---|---|---|
| Cash flow ($'000) | 100 | 200 | 250 | 298 | 298 | 298 | 0 |

Of course, real supermarkets last more than six years. But these numbers are realistic in one important sense: it may take two or three years for a new store to catch on—that is, to build up a substantial, habitual clientele. Thus, cash flow is low for the first few years even in the best locations.

We will assume the opportunity cost of capital is 10 per cent. The Nodhead store's NPV at 10 per cent is zero. It is an acceptable project, but not an unusually good one:

$$NPV = -1000 + \frac{100}{1.10} + \frac{200}{(1.10)^2} + \frac{250}{(1.10)^3} + \frac{298}{(1.10)^4} + \frac{298}{(1.10)^5} + \frac{298}{(1.10)^6} = 0$$

With NPV = 0, the true (internal) rate of return of this cash flow stream is also 10 per cent.

Table 12.4 shows the store's forecasted *book* profitability, assuming straight-line depreciation over its six-year life. The book ROI is lower than the true return for the first two years and higher afterwards.[12]

---

12  The errors in book ROI always catch up with you in the end. If the firm chooses a depreciation schedule that overstates a project's return in some years, it must also understate the return in other years. In fact, you can think of a project's IRR as a kind of average of the book returns. It is not a simple average, however. The weights are the project's book values discounted at the IRR. See J. A. Kay, 'Accountants, Too, Could Be Happy in a Golden Age: The Accountant's Rate of Profit and the Internal Rate of Return', *Oxford Economic Papers*, 28: 447–60 (1976).

**table 12.4**

Forecasted book income and ROI for the proposed Nodhead store. Book ROI is lower than the true rate of return for the first two years and higher thereafter.

|  | Year | | | | | |
|---|---|---|---|---|---|---|
|  | **1** | **2** | **3** | **4** | **5** | **6** |
| Book value at start of year, straight-line depreciation | 1000 | 833 | 667 | 500 | 333 | 167 |
| Book value at end of year, straight-line depreciation | 833 | 667 | 500 | 333 | 167 | 0 |
| Change in book value during year | −167 | −167 | −167 | −167 | −167 | −167 |
| Cash flow | 100 | 200 | 250 | 298 | 298 | 298 |
| Book income | −67 | +33 | +83 | +131 | +131 | +131 |
| Book ROI | −0.067 | +0.04 | +0.124 | +0.262 | +0.393 | +0.784 |
| Book depreciation | 167 | 167 | 167 | 167 | 167 | 167 |

# Book earnings versus true earnings

At this point the regional manager steps up on stage for the following soliloquy:

'The Nodhead store's a decent investment. I really should propose it. But if we go ahead, I won't look very good at next year's performance review. And what if I also go ahead with the new stores in Russet, Gravenstein and Sheepnose? Their cash flow patterns are pretty much the same. I could actually appear to lose money next year. The stores I've got won't earn enough to cover the initial losses on four new ones.

'Of course, everyone knows new supermarkets lose money at first. The loss would be in the budget. My boss will understand—I think. But what about her boss? What if the board of directors starts asking pointed questions about profitability in my region? I'm under a lot of pressure to generate better earnings. Pamela Quince, the north region manager, got a bonus for generating a 40 per cent increase in book ROI. She didn't spend much on expansion. . . .'

The regional manager is getting conflicting signals. On one hand, he is told to find and propose good investment projects. *Good* is defined by discounted cash flow. On the other hand, he is also urged to increase book earnings. But the two goals conflict because book earnings do not measure true earnings. The greater the pressure for immediate book profits, the more the regional manager is tempted to forgo good investments or to favour quick-payback projects over longer-lived projects, even if the latter have higher NPVs.

# Measuring economic rates of return

Let us think for a moment about how profitability should be measured in principle. It is easy enough to compute the true, or 'economic', rate of return for a share that is continuously traded. We just record cash receipts (dividends) for the year, add the change in price over the year and divide by the beginning price:

$$\text{Rate of return} = \frac{\text{cash receipts} + \text{change in price}}{\text{beginning price}}$$
$$= \frac{C_1 + (P_1 - P_0)}{P_0}$$

The numerator of the expression for rate of return (cash flow plus change in value) is called **economic income:**

$$\text{Economic income} = \text{cash flow} + \text{change in present value}$$

Any reduction in present value represents **economic depreciation**; any increase in present value represents *negative* economic depreciation. Therefore,

$$\text{Economic depreciation} = \text{reduction in present value}$$

and

$$\text{Economic income} = \text{cash flow} - \text{economic depreciation}$$

The concept works for any asset. Rate of return equals cash flow plus change in value divided by starting value:

$$\text{Rate of return} = \frac{C_1 + (PV_1 - PV_0)}{PV_0}$$

where $PV_0$ and $PV_1$ indicate the present values of the business at the ends of years 0 and 1.

The only hard part in measuring economic income and return is calculating present value. You can observe market value if shares in the asset are actively traded, but few plants, divisions or capital projects have *their own* shares traded in the share market. You can observe the present market value of *all* the firm's assets but not of any one of them taken separately.

Accountants rarely ever attempt to measure present value. Instead they give us net book value (BV), which is original cost less depreciation computed according to some arbitrary schedule. Many companies use the book value to calculate the book return on investment (ROI). Therefore, book income is given by:[13]

$$\begin{aligned}\text{Book income} &= \text{cash flow} - \text{depreciation} \\ &= C_1 + (BV_1 - BV_0)\end{aligned}$$

Therefore,

$$\text{Book ROI} = \frac{C_1 + (BV_1 - BV_0)}{BV_0}$$

If book depreciation and economic depreciation are different (they are rarely the same), then the book profitability measures will be wrong; that is, they will not measure true profitability. (In fact, it is not clear that accountants should even *try* to measure true profitability. They could not do so without heavy reliance on subjective estimates of value. Perhaps they should stick to supplying objective information and leave the estimation of value to managers and investors.)

It is not too hard to forecast economic income and rate of return. Table 12.5 shows the calculations. From the cash flow forecasts we can forecast present value at the start of periods 1 to 6. For example, the present value of $901 at the *start* of year 3 is the PV of the four remaining cash flows, $250, $298, $298 and $298. The present value at the *end* of year 3 is the same as the present value at the *start* of year 4, being the PV of the three remaining cash flows of $298 each. The cash flow in each period plus the *change* in present value between the start and end of the period equals economic income. Rate of return equals economic income divided by start-of-period value.

Of course, these are forecasts. Actual future cash flows and values will be higher or lower. Table 12.5 shows that investors *expect* to earn 10 per cent in each year of the store's six-year life. In other words, investors expect to earn the opportunity cost of capital each year from holding this asset.[14]

---

[13]  To keep things simple we ignore other non-cash adjustments that accountants make in calculating income under an accrual accounting system. We remind you, however, that over the life of an enterprise accounting profit equals net cash flow.

[14]  This is a general result. If we use the present value of the investment (as distinct from the cash invested) as the basis for our depreciation charge, forecasted profitability always equals the discount rate used to calculate the estimated present values of the asset in future years.

table 12.5 _____

Forecasted economic income and ROI for the proposed Nodhead store. Economic income equals cash flow plus change in present value. Rate of return equals economic income divided by present value at the start of the year.

| | Year | | | | | |
|---|---|---|---|---|---|---|
| | 1 | 2 | 3 | 4 | 5 | 6 |
| Present value at *start* of year, 10% discount rate | 1000 | 1000 | 901 | 741 | 517 | 271 |
| Present value at *end* of year, 10% discount rate | 1000 | 901 | 741 | 517 | 271 | 0 |
| Change in value during year | 0 | −99 | −160 | −224 | −246 | −271 |
| Cash flow | 100 | 200 | 250 | 298 | 298 | 298 |
| Economic income | 100 | 101 | 90 | 74 | 52 | 27 |
| Rate of return | 0.10 | 0.10 | 0.10 | 0.10 | 0.10 | 0.10 |
| Economic depreciation | 0 | 99 | 160 | 224 | 246 | 271 |

*Note: There are minor rounding errors in some annual figures.*

## Does ROI give the right answer in the long run?

Some people downplay the problem we have just described. Is a temporary dip in book profits a major problem? Do not the errors wash out in the long run, when the region settles down to a steady state with an even mix of old and new stores?

It turns out that the errors diminish but do *not* exactly offset. The simplest steady-state condition occurs when the firm does not grow but reinvests just enough each year to maintain earnings and asset values. Table 12.6 shows steady-state book ROIs for a regional division that opens one store a year. For simplicity we assume that the division starts from scratch and that each store's cash flows are carbon copies of the Nodhead store. The true rate of return on each store is therefore 10 per cent. But as Table 12.6 demonstrates, steady-state book ROI, at 12.6 per cent, overstates the true rate of return. Therefore, you cannot assume that the errors in book ROI will wash out in the long run.

Thus, we still have a problem even in the long run. The extent of error depends on how fast the business grows. We have just considered one steady state with a zero growth rate. Think of another firm with a 5 per cent steady-state growth rate. Such a firm would invest $1000 the first year, $1050 the second, $1102.50 the third, and so on. Clearly the faster growth means more new projects relative to old ones. The greater the weight given to young projects, which have low book ROIs, the lower the business' apparent profitability. Figure 12.1 shows how this works out for a business composed of projects like the Nodhead store. Book ROI will either overestimate or underestimate the true rate of return unless the amount that the firm invests each year grows at the same rate as the true rate of return.[15]

15  This also is a general result. Biases in steady-state book ROIs disappear when the growth rate equals the true rate of return. This was discovered by E. Solomon and J. Laya, 'Measurement of Company Profitability: Some Systematic Errors in Accounting Rate of Return', in A. A. Robichek (ed.), *Financial Research and Management Decisions*, John Wiley & Sons, Inc., New York, 1967, pp. 152–83.

**table 12.6**

Book ROI for a group of stores like the Nodhead store. The steady-state book ROI overstates the 10 per cent economic rate of return.

| | Year | | | | | |
|---|---|---|---|---|---|---|
| | **1** | **2** | **3** | **4** | **5** | **6** |
| Book income for store[a] | | | | | | |
| 1 | −67 | +33 | +83 | +131 | +131 | +131 |
| 2 | | −67 | +33 | +83 | +131 | +131 |
| 3 | | | −67 | +33 | +83 | +131 |
| 4 | | | | −67 | +33 | +83 |
| 5 | | | | | −67 | +33 |
| 6 | | | | | | −67 |
| Total book income | −67 | −34 | +49 | +180 | +311 | +442 |
| Book value for store | | | | | | |
| 1 | 1000 | 833 | 667 | 500 | 333 | 167 |
| 2 | | 1000 | 833 | 667 | 500 | 333 |
| 3 | | | 1000 | 833 | 667 | 500 |
| 4 | | | | 1000 | 833 | 667 |
| 5 | | | | | 1000 | 833 |
| 6 | | | | | | 1000 |
| Total book value | 1000 | 1833 | 2500 | 3000 | 3333 | 3500 |
| Book ROI for all stores = $\frac{\text{total book income}}{\text{total book value}}$ | −0.067 | −0.019 | +0.02 | +0.06 | +0.093 | **+0.126**[b] |

*Notes:*
[a] *Book income = cash flow + change in book value during year.*
[b] *Steady-state book ROI.*

## 12.5 What can we do about biases in accounting profitability measures?

The dangers in judging profitability by accounting measures are clear from this chapter's discussion and examples. To be forewarned is to be forearmed. But we can say something beyond just 'be careful'.

It is natural for firms to set an absolute standard of profitability for plants or divisions. Ideally that standard should be the opportunity cost of capital for investment in the plant or division. But if performance is measured by book ROI, then the standard should be adjusted to reflect accounting biases.

This is easier said than done, because accounting biases are notoriously hard to measure in complex practical situations. Thus, many firms end up asking not 'Did the widget division earn more than its cost of capital last year?', but 'Was the widget division's book ROI typical of a

**figure 12.1**
The faster a firm grows, the lower its book rate of return, providing true profitability is constant and cash flows are constant or increasing over the project life. This graph is drawn for a firm composed of identical projects, all like the Nodhead store (see Table 12.4), but growing at a constant compound rate.

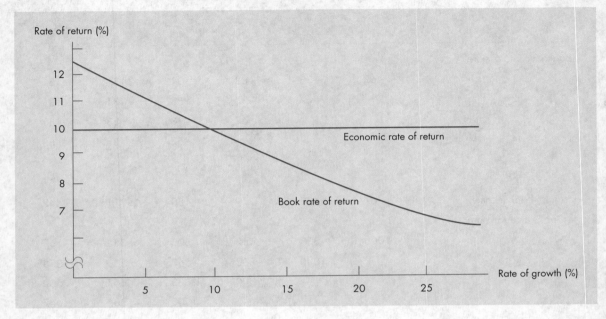

successful firm in the widget industry?' The underlying assumptions are that (1) similar accounting procedures are used by other widget manufacturers and (2) successful widget companies earn their cost of capital.

There are some simple accounting changes that could reduce biases in book ROI. Remember that the biases primarily stem from *not* using economic depreciation. Therefore, why not switch to economic depreciation? The main reason is that each asset's present value would have to be re-estimated every year. Imagine the confusion if this were attempted. You can understand why accountants set up a depreciation schedule when an investment is made and then stick to it apart from in exceptional circumstances. But why restrict the choice of depreciation schedules to the old stand-bys such as straight-line depreciation? Why not specify a depreciation pattern that at least matches *expected* economic depreciation? For example, the Nodhead store could be depreciated according to the expected economic depreciation schedule shown in Table 12.6. This would avoid any systematic biases.[16] This step seems so simple and effective that we are at a loss to explain why firms did not adopt it long ago.[17]

One final comment. Suppose that you *do* conclude that a project has earned less than its cost of capital. This indicates that you made a mistake in taking on the project and, if you could have your time over again, you would not accept it. But does that mean you should bail out now? Not necessarily. That depends on how much the assets would be worth if you sold them or put them to an alternative use. A plant that produces low profits may still be worth operating if it has few alternative uses. Conversely, on some occasions it may pay to sell or redeploy a highly profitable plant.

---

[16] Using expected economic depreciation will not generate book ROIs that are exactly right unless realised cash flows exactly match forecasted flows. But we expect forecasts to be right, on average.

[17] This procedure has been suggested by several authors. See, for example, Zvi Bodie, 'Compound Interest Depreciation in Capital Investment', *Harvard Business Review*, **60**: 58–60 (May–June 1982).

# Do managers worry too much about book profitability?

Book measures of profitability can be wrong or misleading because:

1. Errors occur at different stages of a project's life. When true depreciation is low early in the project's life, book measures are likely to understate true profitability for new projects and overstate it for old ones.
2. Errors also occur when firms or divisions have a balanced mix of old and new projects. Our 'steady-state' analysis of Nodhead shows this.
3. Errors occur because of inflation, basically because inflation shows up in revenue faster than it shows up in costs. For example, a firm owning a plant built in 1970 will, under standard accounting procedures, calculate depreciation in terms of the plant's original cost in 1970 dollars. The plant's output is sold for current dollars. This is why some firms report corporate profits calculated under replacement cost accounting. This procedure bases depreciation not on the original cost of firms' assets, but on what it would cost to replace the assets at current prices.
4. Book measures are often confused by 'creative accounting'. Some firms pick and choose among available accounting procedures, or even invent new ones, in order to make their income statements and balance sheets look good. This was done with particular imagination in the 'go-go years' of the mid-1960s and again in the mid-1980s.

Investors and financial managers, having been burned by inflation and creative accounting, have learned not to take accounting profitability at face value. Yet many people do not realise the depth of the problem. They think that if firms adopted inflation accounting and eschewed creative accounting, everything would be all right except perhaps for temporary problems with very old or very young projects. In other words, they worry about reasons 3 and 4 above, and a little about reason 1, but not at all about reason 2. We think reason 2 deserves more attention.

Much of the pressure for good book earnings comes from top management. Chief executives have good reasons to shoot for good short-run earnings. Probably their bonuses depend on it. The market watches current earnings per share (partly because it is not allowed to look over top management's shoulder at the five-year plan). Is it surprising that top management does not always jump happily into high NPV projects that will depress next year's earnings per share?

We do not mean to imply that chief executives typically sacrifice long-run value for immediate earnings. But they at least *worry* about earnings, and their worries affect attitudes and decisions down the line.

We think managers worry too much. They are uptight about book earnings. They often picture investors as mindless creatures who respond only to the latest earnings announcement. Investors are more sophisticated than that.

Financial managers can help investors do better by *not* playing the earnings game. That is, they should not hire creative accountants or emphasise book earnings while downplaying more fundamental information about their firm's performance.

# Other performance measures

Managers are not oblivious to the problems of:

▮ Encouraging decision making consistent with value maximisation.
▮ Measuring performance and tying performance bonuses to measures that encourage managers to select value-increasing investments.
▮ DCF decision criteria that not all decision makers understand.

There was a market for solving these problems and given this profit opportunity consultants took existing finance concepts and packaged them as answers to the problem. One of the most popular of these packages is economic value added (EVA) and the related measure of market value added (MVA).[18]

## Market value added (MVA)

This is a measure of management performance most easily applied at the level of the company. The idea is a simple one; we are trying to measure how much value has been created over and above the total equity capital supplied by owners. This capital consists of the owners' initial investment together with the cash that has subsequently been retained and reinvested in the business.

$$\text{MVA} = \text{market value of equity} - \text{equity capital provided to managers}$$

In principle this measure can easily be obtained by comparing the market value of equity with the book value of equity. One of the attractive features of this measure is that it distinguishes between maximising the value of the firm and shareholder wealth maximisation. Suppose an existing company with a market value of \$10 million raises an extra million dollars from its shareholders. Further, suppose that the million dollars is badly invested and that the resulting market value of the investment is only \$600 000. The value of the firm will be \$10.6 million, or \$600 000 greater than its value before the finance was raised. However, shareholders are \$400 000 worse off, and this is exactly what the MVA measure will show.

The MVA measure is a natural choice if you select investments on the basis of NPV. MVA is simply the sum of positive NPV investments that the firm has undertaken. So the use of MVA should encourage managers to select positive NPV investments. However, some people object to MVA as a measure of managers' performance because it is based on both what managers have done and unverifiable expectations about what they will do. Expectations naturally enter into MVA because the market value of an asset depends on its expected future cash flows.

In any event the MVA measure should be interpreted with some care. Suppose you observe that a company has a negative MVA. There are three possible explanations:

1. Bad management—management are destroying value rather than creating it.
2. Bad luck—good management has been overtaken by circumstances beyond management's control, and these circumstances could not have reasonably been anticipated.
3. Bad accounting—the method of accounting adopted is such that book value of equity overstates the value of the equity capital provided to managers.

Conversely, if the MVA is positive this may be due to good management, good luck or an understatement of owners' equity.

## Economic value added (EVA)

The MVA measure is difficult to apply other than at the level of the whole company. However, we can use economic value added (EVA) to measure the performance of sub-units of the organisation such as divisions, or even individual projects. EVA can be used as both a tool for selecting projects and for evaluating subsequent performance. This makes it an attractive procedure, the more so since it is entirely consistent with NPV. The idea behind EVA is simple: deduct a charge from operating profits for capital employed. This is quite an old idea originally known as residual income; the new twist is to link EVA to NPV. MVA, EVA and NPV are linked in the following way:

$$\text{Shareholder wealth created} = \text{total market value (i.e. total PV)} - \text{total capital (i.e. total investment)}$$

$$= \text{MVA}$$

---

[18]  We only provide a summary treatment of these measures. For a more complete discussion see G. Bennett Stewart III, *The Quest for Value*, Harper Business, New York, 1991.

MVA for the firm is simply the sum of project NPVs since:

Project NPV = PV of cash flows (i.e. project market value) − project investment (i.e. capital)

The relationship between EVA and NPV is:

$$\text{NPV} = \text{present value of future EVAs for the project}$$

Thus, EVA attempts to measure the surplus cash flows that give rise to NPV. It does this by deducting the following charges from operating cash flows for each period:

1. Operating expenses including taxes.
2. A charge to recover the capital invested.
3. A charge to cover the required return on the capital invested.

Any surplus cash flow left over is the project's EVA. Of course, if there is no surplus but rather a continuing deficit then the project has a negative NPV.

In applying EVA there is a difficult balancing trick to be mastered. The attraction of EVA is that it supplies a simple income-like number that can be integrated with each period's accounting data. However, to make that number consistent with NPV complex adjustments to the accounting data may be required. As many as 164 adjustments have been suggested, although in practice as few as five to 10 adjustments may actually be made.[19] The required adjustments will also vary between companies. Note also that the principles of Level 1 and Level 2 consistency still need to be applied. The balancing trick is to provide a convenient measure that can easily be understood and calculated by managers, while at the same time not doing too much violence to the valuation concepts on which the measure is based.

A common basis for implementation of EVA is as follows:

$$\text{EVA}_t = \text{EBIT}_t(1 - \text{tax rate}) - (\text{WACC after tax})(\text{capital invested})$$

This is not as simple as it seems. First, the weighted average cost of capital (WACC) should reflect the risk of the project or division, not the risk of the company. Second, the capital invested changes from period to period. Another important point to understand is that the earnings before interest and taxes (EBIT) in the above formula is an accounting EBIT that includes depreciation as an expense.[20] This is a necessary requirement for EVA. Without a depreciation charge there would be no allowance for recovery of the initial capital investment. This takes us back to our discussion earlier in the chapter on the distortions caused by using accounting depreciation.

In our example of the Nodhead supermarket we solved the depreciation problem by applying economic depreciation to the market value of the investment. We suggest a similar approach in calculating EVA. In this case we calculate a sinking fund depreciation charge based on the initial capital invested in the project. The result is rather like the amortisation payments on a home mortgage. Over the life of the project the amortisation returns the initial capital investment and covers the required return on the capital remaining in the project. In the early years most of the charge is the required return, with a little repayment of principal, while in the latter years it is exactly the reverse. The capital repayment component is used as the depreciation charge.

---

[19] G. Bennett Stewart III, 'EVA: Fact and Fantasy', *Journal of Applied Corporate Finance*, 7(2): 71–84 (Summer 1994).

[20] In contrast, the finance literature often uses EBIT to mean cash operating revenues minus cash operating expenses.

## 12.6 Summary

We began this chapter by describing how capital budgeting is organised and ended by exposing serious biases in accounting measures of financial performance. Inevitably such discussions stress the mechanics of organisation, control and accounting. It is harder to talk about the informal procedures that reinforce the formal ones. But remember that it takes informal communication and personal initiative to make capital budgeting work. Also, the accounting biases are partly or wholly alleviated because managers and shareholders are smart enough to look behind reported book earnings.

Formal capital budgeting systems usually have four stages:

1. Preparation of a *capital budget* for the firm. This is a plan for capital expenditure by plant, division, or other business unit.
2. *Project authorisations*, which give authority to go ahead with specific projects.
3. Procedures for *control of projects under construction*, which warn if projects are behind schedule or costing more than planned.
4. *Post-audits*, which check on the progress of recent investments.

Of course, to get into the capital budgeting process the project proposal first has to be generated. There are several identifiable processes in the development of a project: the triggering of an idea, the preliminary screening of that idea, the fleshing out of the idea into a definable project, the formal evaluation of the project, the transmission of information about the project up and down the organisation, the decision whether or not to proceed and, for projects that proceed, perhaps a post-audit.

The formal criteria used in project evaluation are a mixture of modern rules such as net present value and internal rate of return and old-fashioned rules such as payback. Consideration may also be given to whether the proposal is consistent with company strategy.

The old rules survive partly because everyone understands them; they provide a common language for discussing the project. They also survive because of the way performance is evaluated and rewarded. If managers are expected to generate quick results, then management is naturally interested in payback and book return. These problems, however, are increasingly being recognised and more companies are turning to performance measurement systems such as economic value added (EVA).

Most specific project proposals originate at the plant or division level. If the project does not cost much, it may be approved by middle management. But the final say on major capital outlays belongs to top management. The desire of top management to retain control of capital budgeting is understandable. But the chief executive cannot undertake a detailed analysis of every project he or she approves. Information at the top is often limited; project proposals may be designed more to persuade than inform.

Top management copes by relying on staff financial analysts, by making capital budgeting part of a broader budgeting and planning process and by keeping the capital budgeting process flexible and open to informal communication.

Capital budgeting is not entirely a bottom-up process. Strategic planners practise 'capital budgeting on a grand scale' by attempting to identify those businesses in which the firm has a special advantage. Project proposals that support the firm's accepted overall strategy are much more likely to have clear sailing as they come up through the organisation.

Usually the plant or division proposing a capital investment will be responsible for making the project work. A project's sponsors naturally want the project to perform well and to *appear* to perform well. Thus, the way the firm evaluates operating performance can affect the kinds of projects that middle management is willing to propose.

There are two approaches to performance measurement. The first and easiest is to compare actual cash flow with forecasted cash flow. The second is to compare actual profitability with the opportunity cost of capital. Both approaches are needed.

The second approach is the difficult and dangerous one. Many firms measure performance in terms of accounting or book profitability. Unfortunately, book income and ROI are often seriously biased measures of true profitability and thus should not be compared directly to the opportunity cost of capital.

In principle true or economic income is easy to calculate: you just subtract economic depreciation from the asset's cash flow for the period you are interested in. Economic depreciation is simply the decrease in the asset's present value during the period. (If the asset's value increases, then economic depreciation is negative.)

Unfortunately, we cannot ask accountants to recalculate each asset's present value every time income is calculated. But it does seem fair to ask why they do not try at least to match book depreciation schedules to typical patterns of economic depreciation.

An alternative approach to calculating economic income is to calculate the 'surplus cash flow' generated by the asset. It is this 'surplus cash flow' that gives rise to NPV or value added. EVA provides a measurement of this 'surplus cash flow'. Getting this measurement right is more complex than it seems. We suspect that for the measurements used in practice the present value of EVA is not exactly equal to the asset's NPV. It is not clear how often this difference is a significant practical problem. It is clear that EVA is becoming increasingly popular and is used by many large and successful companies as a value adding management tool.

## FURTHER READING

For an extensive study of the capital budgeting process see:

J. L. Bower, *Managing the Resource Allocation Process*, Division of Research, Graduate School of Business Administration, Harvard University, Boston, 1970.

The articles by Scapens and Sale, and Pohlman, Santiago and Markel are more up-to-date surveys of current practice. Freeman and Hobbes provide some evidence on Australian practice:

M. Freeman and G. Hobbes, 'Capital Budgeting: Theory versus Practice', *Australian Accountant*, **61**: 36–41 (September 1991).

R. A. Pohlman, E. S. Santiago and F. L. Markel, 'Cash Flow Estimation Practices of Large Firms', *Financial Management*, **17**: 71–9 (Summer 1988).

R. W. Scapens and J. T. Sale, 'Performance Measurement and Formal Capital Expenditure Controls in Divisionalised Companies', *Journal of Business Finance and Accounting*, **8**: 389–420 (Autumn 1981).

Swalm and Weingartner discuss some of the incentive problems arising in corporations:

R. O. Swalm, 'Utility Theory: Insights into Risk-Taking', *Harvard Business Review*, **44**: 123–36 (November–December 1966).

H. M. Weingartner, 'Some New Views on the Payback Period and Capital Budgeting', *Management Science*, **15**: B594–607 (August 1969).

Biases in book ROI and procedures for reducing the biases are discussed by:

Z. Bodie, 'Compound Interest Depreciation in Capital Investment', *Harvard Business Review*, **60**: 58–60 (May–June 1982).

F. M. Fisher and J. I. McGowan, 'On the Misuse of Accounting Rates of Return to Infer Monopoly Profits', *American Economic Review*, **73**: 82–97 (March 1983).

J. A. Kay, 'Accountants, Too, Could Be Happy in a Golden Age: The Accountant's Rate of Profit and the Internal Rate of Return', *Oxford Economic Papers*, **28**: 447–60 (1976).

E. Solomon and J. Laya:, 'Measurement of Company Profitability: Some Systematic Errors in the Accounting Rate of Return', in A. A. Robichek (ed.), *Financial Research and Management Decisions*, John Wiley & Sons, Inc., New York, 1967, pp. 152–83.

# QUIZ

1. True or false?
   a. The approval of a capital budget allows managers to go ahead with any projects included in the budget.
   b. In most companies the controller authorises all appropriation requests for capital expenditures.
   c. Typically, companies will permit up to 10 per cent expenditure overruns, but beyond that the sponsor is required to submit a supplemental appropriation request.
   d. Most firms use only NPV for project selection.
   e. Post-audits are usually undertaken about five years after project completion.
   f. Setting capital budgets and project authorisations is a bottom-up process. Strategic planning, in so far as it affects capital investment decisions, is a top-down process.

2. Explain how each of the following actions or problems can distort or disrupt the capital budgeting process.
   a. Overoptimism by project sponsors.
   b. Inconsistent forecasts of industry and macroeconomic variables.
   c. Capital budgeting organised solely as a bottom-up process.
   d. Demanding quick results from an operating manager, for example by requiring new capital expenditures to meet a payback constraint.
   e. Top management, anticipating a fall in operating cash flow, raising the hurdle rate for capital investment from 12 to 20 per cent.

3. Fill in the blanks:

   A project's economic income for a given year equals the project's _____ less its _____ depreciation. Book income is typically _____ than economic income early in the project's life and _____ than economic income later in its life.

4. Consider the following project:

   | Period | 0 | 1 | 2 | 3 |
   | --- | --- | --- | --- | --- |
   | Net cash flow | −100 | 0 | 78.55 | 78.55 |

   The internal rate of return is 20 per cent. The NPV, assuming a 20 per cent opportunity cost of capital, is exactly zero. Calculate the expected *economic* income and economic depreciation in each year.

5. True or false? Explain briefly.
   a. Book profitability measures are biased measures of true profitability for individual assets. However, these biases 'wash out' when firms hold a balanced mix of old and new assets.
   b. Systematic biases in book profitability would be avoided if companies used depreciation schedules that matched expected economic depreciation. However, few, if any, firms have done this.

# QUESTIONS AND PROBLEMS

**1.** Discuss the value of post-audits. Who should conduct them? When? Should they consider solely financial performance? Should they be confined to the larger projects?

**2.** Draw up an outline or flow chart tracing the capital budgeting process from the initial idea for a new investment project through the commissioning of the project and its initial operations. Assume the idea for a new obfuscator machine comes from a plant manager in the Deconstruction Division of the Modern Language Corporation.

Here are some questions your outline or flow chart should consider: Who will prepare the original proposal? What information will the proposal contain? Who will evaluate it? What approvals will be needed and who will give them? What would happen if the machine costs 40 per cent more to purchase and install than originally forecasted? What will happen when the machine is finally up and running?

**3.** Suppose that the cash flows from Nodhead's new supermarket are as follows:

| Year | 0 | 1 | 2 | 3 | 4 | 5 | 6 |
|---|---|---|---|---|---|---|---|
| Cash flows ($'000) | −$1000 | +298 | +298 | +298 | +138 | +138 | +138 |

a. Recalculate economic depreciation. Is it accelerated or decelerated?
b. Rework Tables 12.4 and 12.5 to show the relationship between the 'true' rate of return and book ROI in each year of the project's life.

**4.** Reconstruct Figure 12.1 assuming a steady-state growth rate of 10 per cent per year. Your answer will illustrate a fascinating theorem, namely that book rate of return equals the economic rate of return when the economic rate of return and the steady-state growth rate are the same.

**5.** Consider an asset with the following cash flows:

| Year | 0 | 1 | 2 | 3 |
|---|---|---|---|---|
| Cash flows ($million) | −12 | +5.20 | +4.80 | +4.40 |

The firm uses straight-line book depreciation. Thus, for this project, it writes off $4 million per year in years 1, 2 and 3. The discount rate is 10 per cent.
a. Show that economic depreciation equals book depreciation.
b. Show that the book rate of return is the same in each year.
c. Show that the project's book profitability is its true profitability.

Notice that you have just illustrated another interesting theorem: If the book rate of return is the same in each year of a project's life, the book rate of return equals the IRR.

**6.** Suppose operating managers' bonuses in the Modern Language Corporation are based on the book ROI of their plants or divisions. What kinds of capital investments will the managers tend to favour?

**7.** Some large companies' strategic (i.e. 'top-down') analyses emphasise accounting performance and tend to direct new investment towards businesses with high book ROIs. What kinds of problems would this create in a large, diversified company?

**8.** A project is expected to produce the following cash flows:

| $C_0$ | $C_1$ | $C_2$ | $C_3$ |
|-------|-------|-------|-------|
| −900 | +300 | +400 | +500 |

a. Find the IRR of the project.
b. Calculate the accounting return in each year, assuming straight-line depreciation.
c. In Footnote 12, we stated that the IRR is a weighted average of the accounting returns where the weights are equal to the book values (at start of year) discounted by the IRR. Show that this is true for the above project.

**9.** Here is a harder question. It is often said that book income is overstated when there is rapid inflation because book depreciation understates true depreciation. What definition of *true depreciation* is implicit in this statement? Does *true depreciation* equal *economic depreciation*, as we have defined the latter term?

**10.** Instead of looking at past market returns for a guide to the cost of capital, some financial managers look at past accounting returns. What do you think are the advantages and disadvantages of doing this?

**11.** Calculate the year-by-year book and economic profitability for investment in Polyzone production, as described in Chapter 11. Use the cash flows and competitive spreads shown in Table 11.2.

What is the steady-state book rate of return (ROI) for a mature company producing Polyzone? Assume no growth and competitive spreads.

**12.** The following are extracts from two newsletters sent to a stockbroker's clients:

*Investment letter—March 1995*
Kipper Parlours was founded earlier this year by its president, Albert Herring. It plans to open a chain of kipper parlours where young people can get together over a kipper and a glass of wine in a pleasant, intimate atmosphere. In addition to the traditional grilled kipper, the parlours serve such delicacies as Kipper Schnitzel, Kipper Grandemere and (for dessert) Kipper Sorbet.

The economics of the business are simple. Each new parlour requires an initial investment in fixtures and fittings of $200 000 (the property itself is rented). These fixtures and fittings have an estimated life of five years and are depreciated straight-line over that period. Each new parlour involves significant start-up costs and is not expected to reach full profitability until its fifth year. Profits per parlour are estimated as follows:

| Year after opening | 1 | 2 | 3 | 4 | 5 |
|---|---|---|---|---|---|
| Profit | 0 | 40 | 80 | 120 | 170 |
| Depreciation | 40 | 40 | 40 | 40 | 40 |
| Profit after depreciation | −40 | 0 | 40 | 80 | 130 |
| Book value at start of year | 200 | 160 | 120 | 80 | 40 |
| Return on investment (%) | −20 | 0 | 33 | 100 | 325 |

Kipper has just opened its first parlour and plans to open one new parlour each year. Despite the likely initial losses (which simply reflect start-up costs), our calculations show a dramatic profit growth and a long-term return on investment that is substantially higher than Kipper's 20 per cent cost of capital.

The total market value of Kipper shares is currently only $250 000. In our opinion, this does not fully reflect the exciting growth prospects, and we strongly recommend clients to buy.

*Investment letter—April 1995*
Albert Herring, president of Kipper Parlours, yesterday announced an ambitious new building plan. Kipper plans to open two new parlours next year, three the year after, and so on.

We have calculated the implications of this for Kipper's earnings per share and return on investment. The results are extremely disturbing and, under the new plan, there seems to be no prospect of Kipper's *ever* earning a satisfactory return on capital.

Since March, the value of Kipper's shares has fallen by 40 per cent. Any investor who did not heed our earlier warnings should take the opportunity to sell the shares now.

Compare Kipper's accounting and economic income under the two expansion plans. How does the change in plan affect the company's return on investment? What is the present value of Kipper's shares? Ignore taxes in your calculations.

13. In our Nodhead example, true depreciation was lower in the early years of the asset's life and higher later. That is not always the case. For instance, the value of a Boeing 737 falls more swiftly in the early years of the aeroplane's life compared to later in its life. Table 12.7 shows the market value at different points in the aeroplane's life[21] and the net cash flow needed in each year to provide a 10 per cent return. (For example, given these cash flows, if you bought a 737 for $19.69 million at the start of year 1 and sold it a year later, your total profit would be 17.99 + 3.67 − 19.69 = $1.97 million: 10 per cent of the purchase cost.)

Many airlines write off their aircraft straight-line over 15 years to a salvage value equal to 20 per cent of the original cost.
a. Calculate economic and book depreciation for each year of the aeroplane's life.
b. Compare the true and book rate of return in each year.
c. Suppose an airline invested in a fixed number of Boeing 737s each year. Would steady-state book return overstate or understate true return?

---

21   We are grateful to Mike Staunton for providing us with these estimates.

**table 12.7** _____

Estimated market values of a Boeing 737 in January 1987 as a function of age, plus the cash flows needed to provide a 10 per cent true rate of return (figures in $million)

| Age | Market value | Cash flow |
|:---:|:---:|:---:|
| 1 | $19.69 | — |
| 2 | 17.99 | $3.67 |
| 3 | 16.79 | 3.00 |
| 4 | 15.78 | 2.69 |
| 5 | 14.89 | 2.47 |
| 6 | 14.09 | 2.29 |
| 7 | 13.36 | 2.14 |
| 8 | 12.68 | 2.02 |
| 9 | 12.05 | 1.90 |
| 10 | 11.46 | 1.80 |
| 11 | 10.91 | 1.70 |
| 12 | 10.39 | 1.61 |
| 13 | 9.91 | 1.52 |
| 14 | 9.44 | 1.46 |
| 15 | 9.01 | 1.37 |
| | 8.59 | 1.32 |

# part 4

# FINANCING DECISIONS AND MARKET EFFICIENCY

# chapter 13

# CORPORATE FINANCING AND THE SIX LESSONS OF MARKET EFFICIENCY

**U**p to this point we have concentrated almost exclusively on the assets side of the balance sheet—the firm's capital expenditure decision. Now we move to the liabilities side and to the problems involved in providing finance for the capital expenditures. To put it crudely, you have learned how to spend money—now learn how to raise it.

Of course, we have not totally ignored financing in our discussion of capital budgeting. But we recommended the simplest possible assumption: all equity financing. That means we assumed the firm raises its money by selling shares and then invests the proceeds in real assets. Later, when those assets generate cash flows, the cash is either returned to shareholders or invested in a second generation of real assets. Shareholders supply all the firm's capital, bear all the business risks and receive all the rewards.

Now we are turning the problem around. We take the firm's present portfolio of real assets and its future investment strategy as given, and then we determine what the best financing strategy is. We will analyse trade-offs between different financing alternatives. For example:

- Should the firm reinvest most of its earnings in the business or should it pay them out as dividends?
- If the firm needs more money, should it issue more shares or should it borrow?
- Should it borrow short-term or long-term?
- Should it borrow by issuing normal long-term debt or convertible debt (i.e. debt which can be exchanged by the debtholders for ordinary shares of the firm)?

There are countless other financing trade-offs, as you will see.

The purpose of holding the firm's capital budgeting decision constant is to separate those decisions from the financing decision. Strictly speaking, this assumes that capital budgeting and financing decisions are *independent*. In many circumstances this is a quite reasonable assumption. The firm is generally free to change its capital structure by repurchasing one security and issuing another. In that case there is no need to associate a particular investment project with a particular source of cash. The firm can think first about what projects to accept and second about how they should be financed.

Sometimes decisions about capital structure depend on project choice or vice versa, and in those cases the investment and financing decisions have to be considered jointly. However, we defer discussion of such interactions of financing and investment decisions until later in the book.

## 13.1 We always come back to NPV

Although it is helpful to separate investment and financing decisions, there are basic similarities in the criteria for making them. The decisions to purchase a machine tool or to issue some debt each involve valuation of a risky asset. The fact that one asset is real and the other financial does not matter. In both cases we end up computing net present value.

The phrase *net present value of borrowing* may seem odd to you. But the following example should help to explain what we mean. As part of its policy of encouraging small business, the government offers to lend your firm $100 000 for 10 years at an interest rate of 3 per cent. This means that the firm is liable for interest payments of $3000 in each of the years 1 to 10 and that it is responsible for repaying the $100 000 in the final year. Should you accept the offer?

We can compute the NPV of the loan agreement in the usual way. The one difference is that the first cash flow is *positive* and the subsequent flows are *negative*:

$$\text{NPV} = \text{amount borrowed} - \text{present value of interest payments}$$
$$- \text{present value of loan repayment}$$

$$= +100\,000 - \sum_{t=1}^{10} \frac{3000}{(1+r)^t} - \frac{100\,000}{(1+r)^{10}}$$

The only missing variable is $r$, the opportunity cost of capital. You need that to value the liability created by the loan. We reason this way. The government's loan to you is a financial asset: a piece of paper representing your promise to pay $3000 per year plus the final repayment of $100 000. How much would that paper sell for if freely traded in capital markets? It would sell for the present value of those cash flows, discounted at $r$, the rate of return offered by other securities of equivalent risk. Now, the class of equivalent-risk securities includes other debt issued by your firm, so that all you have to do to determine $r$ is to answer this question: 'What interest rate would my firm have to pay to borrow money directly from the capital markets rather than from the government?'

Suppose that this rate is 10 per cent. Then

$$\text{NPV} = +100\,000 - \sum_{t=1}^{10} \frac{3000}{(1.10)^t} - \frac{100\,000}{(1.10)^{10}} = +100\,000 - 56\,988 = +\$43\,012$$

Of course, you do not need any arithmetic to tell you that borrowing at 3 per cent is a good deal when the fair rate is 10 per cent. But the NPV calculation tells you just how much that opportunity is worth ($43 012).[1] It also brings out the essential similarity of investment and financing decisions.

---

[1]     We ignore here any tax consequences of borrowing. These are discussed in Chapter 19.

# Differences between investment and financing decisions

In some ways investment decisions are simpler than financing decisions. The number of different financing instruments (i.e. securities) is continually expanding. You will have to learn the major families, genera and species. You should also be aware of the major financial institutions which provide financing for business firms. Finally, the vocabulary of financing has to be acquired. You will learn about tombstones, red herrings, balloons, sinking funds and many other exotic beasts—behind each of these terms lies an interesting story.

There are also ways in which financing decisions are much easier than investment decisions. First, financing decisions do not have the same degree of finality as investment decisions. They are easier to reverse. In other words, their abandonment value is higher.

Second, it is harder to make or lose money by smart or stupid financing strategies. In other words, it is difficult to find financing schemes with NPVs significantly different from zero. That reflects the nature of the competition.

When the firm looks at capital investment decisions, it does not assume that it is facing perfect, competitive markets. It may have only a few competitors that specialise in the same line of business in the same geographical area. And it may own some unique assets that give it an edge over its competitors. Often these assets are intangible items, such as patents, expertise, reputation or market position. All this opens up the opportunity of making superior profits and of finding projects with positive NPVs. It also makes it difficult to tell whether any specific project has a positive NPV.

In financial markets your competition is all other companies seeking funds, to say nothing of the state and federal governments, financial institutions, individuals, and foreign firms and governments that also come to capital markets such as London, Wall Street, Tokyo or even Sydney for financing. The investors who supply financing are also numerous, and they are smart: money attracts brains. The financial amateur often views capital markets as segmented, that is, broken down into distinct sectors. But money moves between those sectors and it moves fast. The 1998 financial turmoil in Asia provided plenty of evidence of how fast money can move!

Remember that a good financing decision generates a positive NPV. It is one in which the amount of cash raised exceeds the value of the liability created. But turn that statement around. If selling a security generates a positive NPV for you, it must generate a negative NPV for the buyer. Thus, the loan we discussed was a good deal for your firm, but a negative NPV investment from the government's point of view. By lending at 3 per cent it offered a $43 012 subsidy.

What are the chances that your firm could consistently trick or persuade investors into purchasing securities with negative NPVs to them? Pretty low. *In general, firms should assume that the securities they issue are fairly priced—there are no free lunches!* This is a very important idea. It should be the starting point for any analysis of a financing decision. Do not forget it.

# Efficient capital markets

We are leading up to the fundamental financial concept of **efficient capital markets**. If capital markets are efficient, then purchase or sale of any security at the prevailing market price is never a positive NPV transaction.

Does that sound like a sweeping statement? It is. That is why we have devoted all the rest of this chapter to the history, logic and tests of the efficient-market hypothesis.

You may ask why we start our discussion of financing issues with this conceptual point, before you have even the most basic knowledge about securities, issue procedures and financial institutions. We do it this way because financing decisions seem overwhelmingly complex if you do not learn to ask the right questions. We are afraid you might flee from confusion to the myths that often dominate popular discussion of corporate financing.

You need to understand the efficient-market hypothesis, not because it is *universally* true, but because it leads you to ask the right questions.

## 13.2 What is an efficient market?

When economists say that the security market is efficient, they are not talking about whether the filing is up-to-date or whether desk tops are tidy. They mean that information is widely and cheaply available to investors and that all relevant and ascertainable information is *already reflected* in security prices. That is why purchases or sales in an efficient market cannot be positive NPV transactions.

### A startling discovery: price changes are random

As is so often the case with important ideas, this concept of efficient markets was a by-product of a chance discovery. In 1953 the Royal Statistical Society met in London to discuss a rather unusual paper.[2] Its author, Maurice Kendall, was a distinguished statistician, and the subject was the behaviour of share and commodity prices. Kendall had been looking for regular price cycles, but to his surprise he could not find them. Each series appeared to be 'a "wandering" one, almost as if once a week the Demon of Chance drew a random number and added it to the current price to determine the next week's price'. In other words, prices seemed to follow a *random walk*.

You can write the random walk as:

$$P_t = P_{t-1} + \varepsilon_t$$

where $P_t$ = price today, $P_{t-1}$ is yesterday's price and $\varepsilon_t$ is the random change in price.

Shares tend to increase in value in the long run. So it often makes sense to add a small constant to the random walk to allow for this increase. We call this a random walk with drift, because the value of $P_t$ then drifts up over time. This is written as:[3]

$$P_t = \alpha + P_{t-1} + \varepsilon_t$$

where $\alpha$ is the drift per period.

Saying that share prices follow a random walk is not the same as saying that we cannot predict prices. We can. The random walk tells us that the best prediction of tomorrow's price is today's price. Try it. You will find it does a pretty good job most of the time. What we cannot predict are *changes* in price, which, of course, is where most of our return comes from. However, we can estimate some statistics for the distribution of the changes. For example, we can estimate the mean or expected value of the change. It will be zero if the random walk without drift applies, or $\alpha$ if there is drift. We can also compute the variance of the change. What we cannot do is say whereabouts in the distribution the change will land up on any particular day.

### An example of a random walk

If you are not sure what we mean by random walk, you might like to think of the following example. You are given $100 to play a game. At the end of each month a coin is tossed. If it comes up heads, you win 6 per cent of your investment; if it is tails you lose 4 per cent. Therefore, your capital at the end of the first month is either $106 or $96. At the end of the second month the coin is tossed again. The possible outcomes are given in Figure 13.1.

---

2    See M. G. Kendall, 'The Analysis of Economic Time-Series, Part I. Prices', *Journal of the Royal Statistical Society*, 96: 11–25 (1953).

3    As an alternative we could think of prices being generated by a compound growth process but also having a random component. In which case prices are given by: $P_t = P_{t-1}(1 + \text{expected return}) + \varepsilon_t$.

# Textbook Evaluation Card

Date Received _____

Author _____

ISBN _____

Title _____

Purpose for this text:
☐ Prescribed text
☐ Recommended text
☐ Reference

Course Name _____

Course No. _____

Present Text _____

Bookshop advised of text? ☐ Yes ☐ No

Est Student Enrolment _____

Est Book Quantity _____

Academic Year _____

Semester _____

## General Comments

Name _____

Department _____

Institution _____

Address _____

Email Address _____

Phone No. _____

Fax No. _____

. . . . . . . . . . . . . . . . . . . . . . . . .
. . . . . . . . . . . . . . . . . . . . . . . . .
. . . . . . . . . . . . . . . . . . . . . . . . .
. . . . . . . . . . . . . . . . . . . . . . . . .
. . . . . . . . . . . . . . . . . . . . . . . . .
. . . . . . . . . . . . . . . . . . . . . . . . .
. . . . . . . . . . . . . . . . . . . . . . . . .
. . . . . . . . . . . . . . . . . . . . . . . . .
. . . . . . . . . . . . . . . . . . . . . . . . .
. . . . . . . . . . . . . . . . . . . . . . . . .
. . . . . . . . . . . . . . . . . . . . . . . . .

We look forward to hearing from you.

Thank you for taking the time to examine the text and letting us have your reactions to it. Your comments will help us in the following ways:

1. Learning whether or not you plan to use the text will help us to plan our inventory to satisfy your requirements.
2. Receipt of the card will assist us in evaluating our delivery systems.
3. Your comments may be passed to the Author and used for review purposes.

*McGraw-Hill Book Company*
*Australia Pty Ltd*
*Higher Education Division*
*4 Barcoo Street (P.O. Box 239)*
*East Roseville   NSW   2069*
*Phone (02) 9415 9887*
*Fax (02) 9417 3428*

**Delivery Address:**
PO Box 239
ROSEVILLE NSW 2069

ıl,ıl,ıll,lllıll,ıll,ıl,llllllll,.........,ıl,ıl,ıll,ıll.

McGraw Hill Book Company Australia
Account - Higher Education Division
Reply Paid 239
ROSEVILLE   NSW   2069

*McGraw-Hill Australia*
**Book Evaluation Card**

**figure 13.1**

Possible results for two rounds of the coin-tossing game.

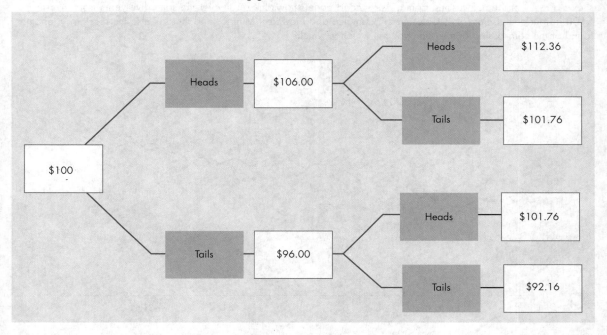

This process is a random walk with a positive drift of 1 per cent per month.[4] It is a random walk because successive changes in value are independent. That is, the odds of a positive change each week are 50 per cent, regardless of the value of your investment at the start of the week or of the pattern of heads and tails in the previous weeks.

If you find it difficult to believe that there are no patterns in share price changes, look at the two charts in Figure 13.2. One of these charts shows the outcome from playing our game for five years; the other shows the actual performance of the Australian share market as measured by Datastream's total return index for a five-year period. Can you tell which one is which? Maybe you can do better with individual shares. Look at the lower panel of Figure 13.2. Can you tell which series represents real Australian companies and which represents a sequence of random numbers with positive drift?

When Maurice Kendall suggested that share prices follow a random walk, he was implying that the price changes are as independent of one another as the gains and losses in our game. To most economists this was a startling and bizarre idea. In fact, the idea was *not* completely novel. It had been proposed in an almost forgotten doctoral thesis written 53 years earlier by a Frenchman, Louis Bachelier.[5] Bachelier's suggestion was original enough, but his accompanying development of the mathematical theory of random processes anticipated by five years Einstein's famous work on the random motion of colliding gas molecules.

Kendall's work did not suffer the neglect that Bachelier's did. As computers and data became more readily available, economists and statisticians rapidly amassed a large volume of supporting evidence. Let us look very briefly at the kinds of tests that they have used.

---

[4]   The drift is equal to the expected outcome: $0.5(6\%) + 0.5(-4\%) = 1\%$.

[5]   See L. Bachelier, *Theorie de la Speculation,* Gauthier-Villars, Paris, 1900. Reprinted in English (A. J. Boness, trans.) in P. H. Cootner (ed.), *The Random Character of Share Market Prices*, M.I.T. Press, Cambridge, Mass., 1964, pp. 17–78. During the 1930s the food economist Holbrook Working had also noticed the random behaviour of commodity prices. See H. Working, 'A Random Difference Series for Use in the Analysis of Time Series', *Journal of the American Statistical Association*, **29**: 11–24 (March 1934).

**figure 13.2** _____

In the top panel, one of the lines shows the returns on the ASX for the five years from 1991 to 1996; the other line shows a result of the coin-tossing game. The second panel shows the result over the same five years from investing $100 in four companies, BHP, Coles Myer, Comalco and Newcrest Mining, and there is also the result from another round of the coin-tossing game. Can you tell which is which? [6]

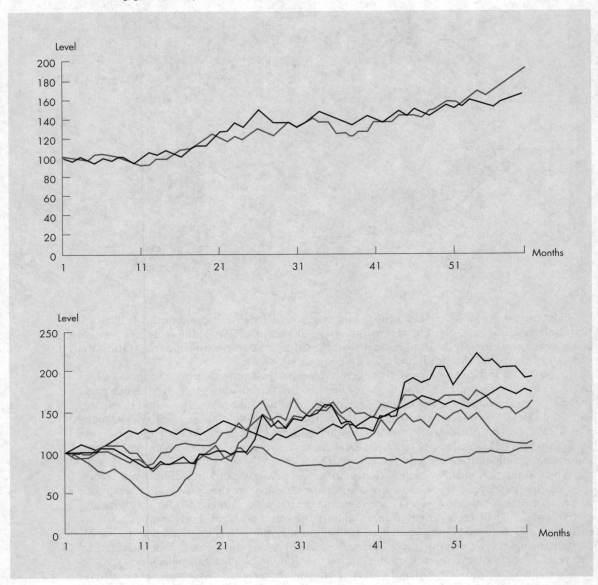

6    In Figure 13.2 the lower line cutting the right-hand axis shows the share index for the years 1991 to 1996; the other line is a series of numbers cumulated at random from the payoffs to the game. Of course, 50 per cent of you will have guessed right, but we bet it was just a guess. In the lower panel the random numbers finish second from the top on the right-hand vertical axis. Comalco finishes above the random series, while BHP is just below, followed by Newcrest and then Coles. A similar comparison between cumulated random numbers and actual price series was first suggested by H. V. Roberts, 'Share Market "Patterns" and Financial Analysis: Methodological Suggestions', *Journal of Finance*, **14**: 1–10 (March 1959).

   Suppose that you wished to assess whether there is any tendency for price changes to per-sist from one day to the next. You might begin by drawing a scatter diagram of changes on successive days. Figure 13.3 is an example of such a diagram. Each dot shows the change in the price of the American shares of Weyerhaeuser on successive days. If there had been a sys-tematic tendency for increases to be followed by decreases, there would be many dots in the southeast quadrant and few in the northeast quadrant (increases followed by increases). It is obvious from a glance that there is very little pattern in these price movements. The points are equally scattered between the four quadrants. However, the points on the chart do resemble a starburst with clustering along a series of rays emanating from the centre.[7] The reason? The minimum amount by which prices can change on the New York Stock Exchange—the **tick** size—was one-eighth of a dollar ($0.125). For example, suppose the share price is $50. Suppose also that we observe a number of cases where there is a rise of 0.25 per cent, which is $0.125. This is followed on the second day by another rise of $0.125, or 0.249 per cent (0.125/50.125 = 0.00249). However, we can never observe a second day rise less than 0.249 per cent, nor can we observe a rise of greater than 0.249 per cent but less than 0.499 per cent (i.e. between $0.125 and $0.25). The rules of the market create the pattern.[8] This is an exam-ple of **market microstructure**, an area increasingly attracting researchers' attention.[9]

**figure 13.3**

Each dot shows a pair of returns for Weyerhaeuser shares on two successive days between 1963 and 1993. (Some dots, such as those reflecting the stock market crash of 19 October 1987, are off-scale and thus not shown.) The scatter diagram shows no significant relationship between returns on successive days.

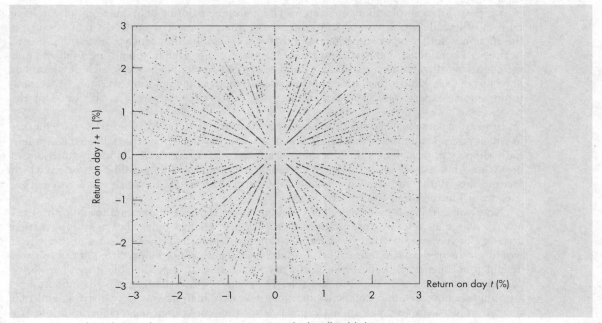

*Source*: T. Crack and O. Ledoit, op. cit., Footnote 7. © Blackwell Publishers.

7   This pattern was discovered by Timothy Crack and Oliver Ledoit. See their paper, 'Robust Structure Without Predictability: The "Compass Rose" Pattern of the Stock Market', *Journal of Finance*, 51: 751–62 (June 1996).

8   For a similar reason, if you look very carefully at our plots in Figure 13.2 you may see that the line for the coin-tossing game seems a bit smoother than the other plots.

9   The microstructure of tick movements on the ASX differs from the NYSE. On the ASX the minimum tick size varies with the price of the share. It starts at half a cent for the penny dreadfuls, increasing to one cent and then two, and so on, as prices increase.

Eyeballing the plot lacks precision. A more precise test of predictability in returns is to calculate the coefficient of correlation between each day's price change and the next. If price movements persisted the correlation would be significantly positive; if there were no relationship it would be 0. In our example above, the correlation was +0.07. This is not enough to make our fortunes; for practical purposes there was a negligible tendency for price rises to be followed by further rises.

Figure 13.3 shows the behaviour of only one share, but the result is typical. Researchers have looked at daily changes, weekly changes and monthly changes; they have looked at many different shares in many different countries and for many different periods; they have calculated the coefficient of correlation between these price changes; they have looked for runs of positive (positive following positive following positive . . .) price changes, and for runs of negative (negative following negative . . .) price changes; they have examined some of the *technical rules* that have been used by some investors to exploit the 'patterns' they claim to see in past share prices. With remarkable unanimity researchers have concluded that there is no useful information in the sequence of past changes in share price. As a result, many of the researchers have become famous. None has become rich.[10]

## A theory to fit the facts

We have mentioned that the initial reaction to the random walk finding was surprise. It was several years before economists appreciated that this price behaviour is exactly what one should expect in any competitive market.

Suppose, for example, that you wish to sell an antique painting at an auction but you have no idea of its value. Can you be sure of receiving a fair price? The answer is that you can if the auction is sufficiently competitive. In other words, you need to satisfy yourself that it is to be properly conducted,[11] that there is no substantial cost involved in submitting a bid and that the auction is attended by a reasonable number of skilled potential bidders, each of whom has access to the available information. In this case, no matter how ignorant *you* may be, competition among experts will ensure that the price you realise fully reflects the value of the painting.

In just the same way, competition among investment analysts will lead to a share market in which prices at all times reflect true value. But what do we mean by *true value*? It is a potentially slippery phrase. True value does not mean what the *future* value ultimately turns out to be—we do not expect investors to be fortune-tellers. It means an equilibrium price, which incorporates *all* the information available to investors at the time the price was formed. That was our definition of an efficient market.

Now you can begin to see why price changes in an efficient market are random. If prices always reflect all relevant information, then they will change only when new information arrives. But new information *by definition* cannot be predicted ahead of time (otherwise it would not be new information). Therefore, price changes cannot be predicted ahead of time. To put it another way, if share prices already reflect all that is predictable, then share price *changes* must reflect only the unpredictable. The series of price changes must be random.[12]

Suppose, however, that competition among research analysts was not so strong and that there were predictable cycles in share prices. Investors could then make superior profits by trading on the basis of these cycles. Figure 13.4, for example, shows a two-month upswing for Establishment Industries (EI). The upswing started last month, when EI's share price was $5,

---

10  Of course, if you did find a way of forecasting share prices from past prices and you wanted to become rich then you would be foolish to reveal your discovery.

11  This includes no collusion among bidders.

12  When economists speak of share prices following a random walk, they are being a little imprecise. A statistician reserves the term random walk to describe a series that has a constant expected change each period and a constant degree of variability. But market efficiency does not imply that expected risks and expected returns cannot shift over time.

**figure 13.4**

Cycles self-destruct as soon as they are recognised by investors. The share price instantaneously jumps to the present value of the expected future price.

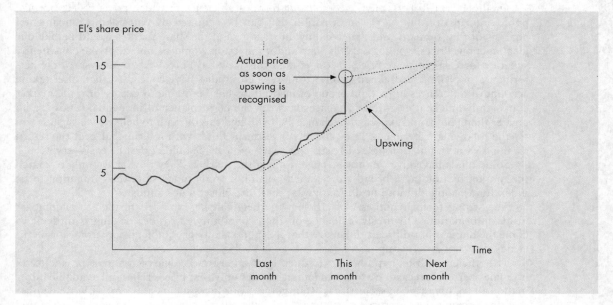

and it is expected to carry the share price to $15 next month. What will happen when investors perceive this bonanza? It will self-destruct. Since EI shares are still a bargain at $10, investors will rush to buy. They will stop buying only when the share offers a normal rate of return. Therefore, as soon as a cycle becomes apparent to investors, they immediately eliminate it by their trading.

Two types of investment analyst help to make price changes random. Many analysts study the company's business and try to uncover information about its profitability that will shed new light on the value of the share. These analysts are often called *fundamental analysts*. Competition in fundamental research will tend to ensure that prices reflect *all* relevant information and that price changes are unpredictable. The other analysts study the past price and volume records and look for cycles. These analysts are called *technical analysts*. Since they often look for patterns by studying charts of price and volume, technical analysts are often called *chartists*. Competition in technical research will tend to ensure that current prices reflect all information in the past sequence of prices and that future price changes cannot be predicted from past prices.

# Three forms of the efficient-market theory

Harry Roberts has defined three levels of market efficiency.[13] The first is the case in which prices reflect all information contained in the record of past prices. Roberts called this a *weak* form of efficiency. The random walk research shows that the market is *at least* efficient in this weak sense.

The second level of efficiency is the case in which prices reflect not only past prices but all other published information. Roberts called this a *semistrong* form of efficiency. Researchers

---

13   See H. V. Roberts, Statistical versus Clinical Prediction of the Share Market, unpublished paper presented to the Seminar on the Analysis of Security Prices, University of Chicago, May 1967.

have tested this by looking at specific items of news such as announcements of earnings and dividends, forecasts of company earnings, changes in accounting practices and mergers.[14] Most of this information was rapidly and accurately impounded in the price of the share.[15]

Finally, Harry Roberts envisaged a *strong* form of efficiency in which prices reflect not just public information but *all* the information that can be acquired by painstaking fundamental analysis of the company and the economy. In such a case, the share market would be like our ideal auction: Prices would *always* be fair and *no* investor would be able to make consistently superior forecasts of share prices. Most tests of this view have involved an analysis of the performance of professionally managed portfolios. These studies have concluded that, after taking account of differences in risk, no group of institutions has been able to outperform the market consistently and that even the differences between the performance of individual funds are no greater than you would expect from chance.[16] If you find this difficult to believe, we suggest you try the following experiment. Look for any investment funds with returns that beat the return on the ASX accumulation index five straight years in a row. Shouldn't that be easy—try it.[17]

Some funds have given up the struggle to beat the market. They now strive only to match the market by holding a broadly diversified portfolio. Some funds state their intention to be index funds, some do not but do it anyway; these are closet index funds.

The strong form hypothesis of efficient markets can be extended further to encompass inside information. Obviously, evidence on the profitability of insider trading is difficult to come by. But it is not difficult to believe that it is abnormally profitable; if so, strong form efficiency does not strictly apply.

The efficient-market hypothesis is frequently misinterpreted. One common error is to think it implies perfect forecasting ability. In fact, it implies only that prices reflect all available information. If so, investing in securities is a fair game. Your investments are zero NPV. Remember this does not mean no return, it means that *on average* you can expect to earn the required return commensurate with the risk of your investment.

Some have suggested that prices cannot represent fair value because they go up and down. The answer, however, is that they would not represent fair value *unless* they went up and down. It is because the future is so uncertain and people are so often surprised that prices fluctuate. (Of course, when we look *back,* nothing seems quite so surprising. It is easy to convince ourselves that we really knew all along how prices were going to change.) A rather different temptation is to believe that the inability of institutions to achieve superior portfolio performance is an indication that their portfolio managers are incompetent. This is incorrect. Market efficiency exists only because competition is keen and managers are doing their job.

Another error is to think that the random behaviour of share prices implies that the share market is irrational. *Randomness* and *irrationality* are not synonymous. Share price changes are random because investors are rational and competitive.

---

[14] See, for example, R. Ball and P. Brown, 'An Empirical Evaluation of Accounting Income Numbers', *Journal of Accounting Research*, 6: 159–78 (Autumn 1968); R. R. Pettit, 'Dividend Announcements, Security Performance and Capital Market Efficiency', *Journal of Finance*, 27: 993–1007 (December 1972); G. Foster, 'Share Market Reaction to Estimates of Earnings per Share by Company Officials', *Journal of Accounting Research*, 11: 25–37 (Spring 1973); R. S. Kaplan and R. Roll, 'Investor Evaluation of Accounting Information: Some Empirical Evidence', *Journal of Business*, 45: 225–57 (April 1972); G. Mandelker, 'Risk and Return: The Case of Merging Firms', *Journal of Financial Economics*, 1: 303–35 (December 1974).

[15] The price reaction to news appears to be almost immediate. For example, within five to 10 minutes of earnings or dividend announcements, most of the price adjustment has occurred and any remaining gain from acting on the news is less than the transaction costs. See J. M. Patell and M. A. Wolfson, 'The Intraday Speed of Adjustment of Share Prices to Earnings and Dividend Announcements', *Journal of Financial Economics*, 13: 223–52 (June 1984). The price reaction to the sale of a large block of shares seems to be equally rapid. See L. Dann, D. Mayers and R. Raab, 'Trading Rules, Large Blocks and the Speed of Adjustment', *Journal of Financial Economics*, 4: 3–22 (January 1977).

[16] The classic study was M. C. Jensen, 'The Performance of Mutual Funds in the Period 1945–64', *Journal of Finance*, 23: 389–416 (May 1968). More recent studies include J. C. Bogle and J. M. Twardowski, 'Institutional Investment Performance Compared: Banks, Investment Counselors, Insurance Companies and Mutual Funds', *Financial Analysts Journal*, 36: 33–41 (January–February 1980); M. Grinblatt and S. Titman, 'Mutual Fund Performance: An Analysis of Quarterly Portfolio Holdings', *Journal of Business*, 62: 393–416 (July 1989); and R. A. Ippolito, 'Efficiency with Costly Information: A Study of Mutual Fund Performance, 1965–84', *Quarterly Journal of Economics*, 104: 1–23 (February 1989).

[17] To do this properly, of course, you should adjust for differences in risk. But for the purpose of the experiment you can neglect this nicety.

## Some alternative views

Although there is much to be said in favour of the efficient-market hypothesis there are some other ideas which have merit. For example, the market may be better at preventing under-pricing than overpricing. If you find a security that you believe is underpriced the remedy is simple: you buy it. Your efforts and those of like-minded investors will tend to push the price up and thus eliminate any underpricing. Now suppose you find a security you believe is over-priced. The remedy is to sell the security short. This is not so simple as buying a security and is more costly, particularly if you have to hold the short position for a long period.[18] In some cases short selling may not be feasible. For example, in the not so recent past short selling was illegal in Australia. Now, if you want to short sell a security on the ASX it has to be one which is on the list of securities approved for short selling. On the New York Stock Exchange short sales are only permitted on upticks (after an upward price movement). The difficulty in short selling means that overpricing may be more common and persistent than underpricing. The effect, however, is not likely to be very large. Financial institutions can and do take short positions with greater ease and at lower cost than individual investors. Action by such institutions therefore helps prevent gross overpricing.

Another line of argument suggests that the dominance of institutional investors may inhibit market efficiency. A fund manager is not subject to the full cost of bad investment decisions nor does she get the full benefit of good ones. Thus, the interests of the fund manager and the investors she represents are not the same. The fund manager is likely to be at least as con-cerned about keeping her job as she is about fund performance. The safety first strategy for such a manager is to perform well when other managers perform well and badly when other managers perform badly. In other words, she should stay with the herd. It takes a brave man-ager to sell when the majority are buying and to buy when the majority are selling. Thus, institutional investment may encourage speculative bubbles.

However, there are limits to this process. First, fund managers' rewards and job security are at least partially linked to fund performance. Second, institutions have considerable exper-tise in security pricing and this should help reduce any mispricing. Third, if, despite their expertise, institutions consistently mispriced securities then profit opportunities would induce corrective trades by individuals, brokers and fund managers trading on their own account.

Our view is that securities markets are efficient most of the time. But they are not 100 per cent efficient 100 per cent of the time. Inefficiency is likely to be greatest where trades are thinnest.

## 13.3 The crash of 1987

On Monday 19 October 1987, while Australian markets were closed overnight, the Dow Jones Industrial Average fell 23 per cent in one day. From its opening on Tuesday morning the Australian market fell and fell, dropping about 25 per cent on the day. Immediately after the crash, everybody started to ask two questions: 'Who were the guilty parties?' and 'Do prices really reflect fundamental values?'

It is nearly always easy and convenient to blame computers, in this case computer-originated trades generated by index arbitrage and portfolio insurance programs. This expla-nation was gleefully seized on by journalists. But, like much journalistic reporting of financial matters, it needs to be taken with a very large grain of salt.

As in most murder mysteries, the immediate suspects are not the ones 'who done it'. The first group of suspects were the 'index arbitrageurs' who trade back and forth between index futures[19] and the shares comprising the market index, taking advantage of any price discrep-ancies. On Black Monday in the United States futures fell first and fastest because investors

---

18   When you sell a share short you usually borrow the share through your broker. In return you lodge a security deposit and pay a fee. In some cases you can create a short position using derivative securities such as options or futures.

19   An index future provides a way of trading in the share market as a whole. It is a contract that pays investors the value of the shares in the index at a specified future date. We discuss futures in Chapter 25.

found it easier to bail out of the share market by way of futures than by selling individual shares. This appeared to push the futures price below the share market index.[20] Then the arbitrageurs tried to make money by selling shares and buying futures, but they found it difficult to get up-to-date quotes on the shares they wished to trade. Thus, the futures and share markets were for a time disconnected. Arbitrageurs contributed to the trading volume that swamped the New York Stock Exchange, but they did not cause the crash—they were the messengers that tried to transmit the selling pressure in futures markets back to the exchange.

The second suspects were the large institutional investors who were trying to implement portfolio insurance schemes. Portfolio insurance aims to put a floor on the value of an equity portfolio by progressively selling shares and buying safe, short-term debt securities as share prices fall. Thus, the selling pressure that drove prices down on Black Monday led portfolio insurers to sell still more. One institutional investor on 19 October sold shares and futures totalling $1.7 billion. On this view, the immediate cause of the price fall on Black Monday may have been a herd of elephants all trying to leave by the same exit.

Perhaps some large portfolio insurers can be convicted of disorderly conduct, but portfolio insurance trades did not constitute the bulk of trading, and why did share prices fall *worldwide*—see Table 13.1—when portfolio insurance is significant only in the United States? Moreover, if sales were triggered mainly by portfolio insurance or trading tactics, they should have conveyed little fundamental information, and prices should have bounced back after Black Monday's confusion had dissipated.

So why did prices fall so sharply? There are two questions to answer: Why did the American market fall? Why did most other markets follow suit? We start by answering the second question first.

## The American economy and the rest of the world

America's role as the engine of growth for the world economy has diminished in importance. But in 1987 there was still some truth in the adage 'When America sneezes the rest of the world catches a cold'. If the crash in American market was predicting bad news for the American economy, then it was also predicting bad news for most other economies. The more so since growing protectionist sentiment in the American Senate was an increasing threat to world trade.

As a sensitive barometer of the value of future economic activity share markets fall rapidly in response to bad news about the economy. Therefore, it was appropriate that the American crash was immediately felt in most other financial markets. However, in the other economic superpower of the time—Japan—the Tokyo market was actually rising as other markets fell. By the end of October the Japanese market was only down 7.7 per cent in US$ terms. In contrast, Australia, which depends heavily on world trade and a strong world economy, suffered almost a 45 per cent decline over the month (measured in US$).

Before discussing possible causes of the crash in American markets we must make the point that there is *nothing* in the theory of efficient markets which is inconsistent with dramatic price movements, such as the 1987 crash. However, some financial economists were puzzled because there was no obvious, new fundamental information to justify such a sharp decline in share values. For this reason, the idea that market price is the best estimate of intrinsic value seemed less compelling than before. Perhaps prices were either irrationally high before Black Monday or irrationally low afterwards. Could the theory of efficient markets be another casualty of the crash? Perhaps, but perhaps a small revision in expectations was sufficient to trigger the crash and perhaps the triggering event was no event at all. Let us explain.

---

20   That is, sellers appeared to push the futures prices below its *proper relation* to the index—again, see Chapter 25. The proper relation is not exact equality. Part of the problem was that at times during the day the reported index was out-of-date. The start of trading on the New York Stock Exchange was substantially delayed because the procedure for setting opening prices could not cope with the volume of sell orders. Later in the day the volume of trades swamped the exchange computer. Because of these events it was not possible to continuously provide an up-to-date index that reflected the true state of the market.

**table 13.1**

Percentage changes in share price indexes in October 1987. The column headed 'US$' provides a consistent benchmark across the countries. This table shows that the crash of 1987 was worldwide. Therefore, it is hard to attribute the crash to index arbitrage, portfolio insurance or other special customs of the New York market.

| Country | Local currency | US$ |
|---|---|---|
| Australia | −41.8 | −44.9 |
| Austria | −11.4 | −5.8 |
| Belgium | −23.2 | −18.9 |
| Canada | −22.5 | −22.9 |
| Denmark | −12.5 | −7.3 |
| France | −22.9 | −19.5 |
| Germany | −22.3 | −17.1 |
| Hong Kong | −45.8 | −45.8 |
| Ireland | −29.1 | −25.4 |
| Italy | −16.3 | −12.9 |
| Japan | −12.8 | −7.7 |
| Malaysia | −39.8 | −39.3 |
| Mexico | −35.0 | −37.6 |
| Netherlands | −23.3 | −18.1 |
| New Zealand | −29.3 | −36.0 |
| Norway | −30.5 | −28.8 |
| Singapore | −42.2 | −41.6 |
| South Africa | −23.9 | −29.0 |
| Spain | −27.7 | −23.1 |
| Sweden | −21.8 | −18.6 |
| Switzerland | −26.1 | −20.8 |
| United Kingdom | −26.4 | −22.1 |
| United States | −21.6 | −21.6 |

*Source:* R. Roll, 'The International Crash of October 1987', in R. Kamphis (ed.), *Black Monday and the Future of Financial Markets,* Richard D. Irwin, Inc., Homewood, Ill., 1989. See Table 1, p. 37.

We show below, for the Australian market, that a comparatively small revision in expected growth rates could at the time of the crash have caused a 25 per cent change in share prices. A similar result can be demonstrated for the American market. The key question therefore is what might have caused this revision of expected growth rates.

# No news is bad news

In the weeks prior to the crash there were a number of events that did not augur well for the American economy. There was an exchange of views between the American, German and Japanese governments which verged on a diplomatic punch up. America had a very large and growing trade problem, and the message of the diplomatic exchange was that Germany and Japan were increasingly reluctant to keep accommodating the American current account deficit. America had to take its medicine and get its own house in order. The American response was not positive, and these events were taking place against a background of growing support for protectionism in the Senate. American interest rates were high by historic standards and still rising, and on Thursday 15 October the largest ever American trade deficit was announced. Uncertainty was in the air, and there was speculation about further interest rate increases. In such circumstances, governments often make an announcement about their plan of action, with the objective of reassuring the financial markets. But no announcement was forthcoming. On Friday 16 October prices on the New York Stock Exchange fell sharply as investors sold their shares. At least one weekend newspaper labelled the Friday price fall in response to the sell-off as a Black Friday. Perhaps there would be a policy announcement over the weekend. Investors waited. The American administration remained silent. Monday 19 October dawned and the sell orders flooded in.

It is doubtful that we will ever know whether it really was the lack of a government announcement that triggered the crash. However, it does seem likely, under the circumstances, that investors were revising their estimates of expected growth downwards. Let us see how a one percentage point reduction of equity growth rates could have affected the Australian share market.

## The magnitude of the price change

Suppose that in October 1987 you wanted to check whether Australian ordinary shares were fairly valued. At least as a first stab you might use the constant-growth formula that we introduced in Chapter 4. The average annual dividend on the ASX was about 3 per cent per annum in 1987. The required return on the share market at that time was about 23 per cent per annum.[21] This implied an expectation of capital gains of 20 per cent a year, which in turn implied dividend and profit growth of 20 per cent a year. If we take a share with an expected $1.20 dividend the constant-growth formula gives a value for the share as:

$$\text{Price} = \text{PV} = \frac{\text{DIV}_1}{r - g} = \frac{1.20}{0.23 - 0.20} = \$40$$

Now let us revise the expected growth rate to 19 per cent and the expected dividend to $1.19. Then the price becomes

$$\text{Price} = \frac{1.19}{0.23 - 0.19} = \$29.75$$

The price falls by 25.63 per cent. In other words, most of the price drop that occurred in Australia on 20 October 1987 could be explained by investors suddenly becoming 1 percentage point less optimistic about future dividend growth.

Of course, this sort of calculation is much easier with the benefit of hindsight. Table 13.2 shows the diversity of views about market prospects published on the Sunday immediately before Black Monday. Notice that the brokers' estimates of price growth are consistently positive. Was this overoptimism, or was it consistent with a view that the market was correctly priced at the time of the survey, which was one week before the crash?[22]

The crash reminds us how exceptionally difficult it is to value ordinary shares from scratch and this has two important consequences. First, investors almost always price an ordinary share relative to yesterday's price or relative to today's price of comparable securities. In other words, they generally take yesterday's price as correct; adjusting upwards or downwards based on today's information. If information arrives smoothly then, as time passes, investors become more and more confident that today's market level is correct. However, when investors lose confidence in the benchmark of yesterday's price, there may be a period of confused trading and volatile prices before a new benchmark is established.

---

[21]  This seems high by today's standards, but inflation rates were much higher then.

[22]  We leave you to supply your own answer.

**table 13.2** _____

Economists and share market analysts were asked to predict where the Australian share market would be by 30 June 1988. Their answers are accompanied by abridged comments on changes in the fundamentals driving the market.

| **Brokers** | | |
|---|---|---|
| Don Stammer, Bain & Co | Up 20% | Recent strong share price rises have meant more of the good news on fundamentals (low world interest rates, worldwide P/E rerating and high corporate profits) is now incorporated in share prices. |
| Frank Shostak, Ord Minnett | Up 20% | Excess monetary growth will continue to support the market in the short term. Inflation is beginning to show there is a 90% chance of a collapse as bad, or worse, than in 1929 in the next couple of years. |
| Ian Story, BZW Meares | Around current levels | $US will fall reducing the US trade deficit which has given European and Japanese investors record funds. New production will depress commodity prices with a 6–12 months lead time. |
| Mark Fulton, County NatWest | Up 20% | High liquidity, growth in commodity prices and gold production will continue to support the market. Late 1988 US interest rates may rise, and could tip the next, very detrimental, world recession. |
| Patrick O'Leary, McCaughan D | Up 15–20% | Financial deregulation is still with us and high world liquidity levels are rising even higher. A decline will eventually come from reregulation of markets and attempts to refix exchange rages. |
| Tim Knapton, Rivkin J Capel | Up 20–30% | OECD growth and stronger base metal prices have eased. Corporate profit growth in 87/88 will be high but lower than last year and similarly global money supply is high but decelerating. |
| Peter Quinton, Roach Tilley | Up 20% | Corporate profit growth and a high gold price continue to support shares. Takeovers, investor liquidity will be less significant. US interest rates will rise moderately; share markets will recover and grow. |
| David Jarman, J B Were | Up 20% | Domestic fundamentals for a continued bull run are still in place: earnings of listed companies should grow 17–20% in 87/88 and there is scope for further industry rationalisation. |
| **Financial institutions** | | |
| Bill Shields, Macquarie Bank | Down 15–20% | Different sectors have successively buoyed the market. Latest is a pick-up in industrial stocks following entrepreneurial, media and gold stocks. Serious chance of downturn in overseas markets. |
| Sam Kavourakis, National Mutual | No comment | Changes in bullish influence—earnings growth, liquidity and overseas markets will have a mixed impact on the market. Recent falls in the local market is probably a correction. |
| Merv Peacock, AMP | Up trend | The bull market rose from a low base. Many fundamentals continue to support the local market but an apparent trend to tighten monetary policy means a consequent tightening of liquidity. *(continues)* |

**table 13.2 (continued)**

Economists and share market analysts were asked to predict where the Australian share market would be by 30 June 1988. Their answers are accompanied by abridged comments on changes in the fundamentals driving the market.

### Financial institutions

| | | |
|---|---|---|
| Ross Finley, BT Asset Mgmt | Down 20% | International rerating of stocks is complete. Rising US interest rates will thwart growth in the US and Australian share markets in the short-term. |
| Andrew Mohl, ANZ Bank | Down 5% | Depreciation of the $A and takeovers fuelled the bull run, but $A is now more robust and high P/E ratios will inhibit takeovers. Healthy corporate profits and world liquidity will continue as supports. |
| Phil O'Sullivan, Commonwealth | Up 10–15% | Local fundamentals will sustain the local sharemarket. The major question overhangs world economic growth. Slower growth would depress commodity prices, a major prop for local markets. |
| Ian Bright, NM Royal Bank | Up 15% | The slowdown in world economic growth will limit the potential for continued share market growth. Gold price may come under pressure in the next year, reducing the attractiveness of local shares. |
| Colin Moore, MLC | Up 15% | The global weight of money will continue to support the market. Expanding resource sector and healthy economy will shield the local market from downward effects of rising US interest rates. |
| Bob Vagg, Equitilink | Up 25% | Bullish influences including a consistent government attitude, takeover pressure on the old guard (epitomised by 'no company is safe unless it performs') and upturn in metals stocks are still in place. |

### Industry and academics

| | | |
|---|---|---|
| Carol Austin, AIDC | Down 25% | Danger of a global collapse because of unwinding of the bullish fundamentals—disinflation and the $A depreciation. Also world growth and low bond yields have reversed or turned neutral. |
| Des Moore, IPA | Down 25% | Loose monetary policies worldwide pushed interest rates and yields down to artificially low levels. Increasing signs of tightening in monetary policies overseas, if continued, will depress markets. |
| Graham Partington, Macquarie Uni | Lower | Critically, the growth in expected returns will not keep pace with required rates of return. Difficulty in sustaining current corporate profit growth levels of around 20%. |
| Ian Sharpe, NSW Uni | Current levels | External demand for Australian stocks will continue. If US inflation rises US interest rates will also rise and soften the US and Australian share markets. |
| Peter Swan, AGSM | No comment | The prospect of a highly protectionist US Congress/Senate could have serious adverse consequences for world trade and thus weaken world share markets. |
| Tom Valentive, Macquarie Uni | Down 30% | Overseas share markets are weakening which will flow on to Australian markets. In the next couple of years there is a chance of a severe depression (big unemployment, falling property values). |

*Source*: Caroline Falls, *The Times on Sunday*, 18 October 1987, p. 15.

Second, the hypothesis that share price *always* equals intrinsic value is nearly impossible to test, precisely because it is so difficult to calculate intrinsic value without referring to prices. Thus, the crash did not disprove the hypothesis. But many people now find it less *plausible*.[23]

However, the crash does not undermine the evidence for market efficiency with respect to *relative* prices. Take, for example, Advance Bank, which sold for about $10.80 per share in mid-February 1994. The dividend was $0.60 per share and reported earnings were $0.66 per share. Could we *prove* that true intrinsic value was $10.80? No, but we could be more confident that Advance Bank's price should be close to that of National Australia Bank which had a slightly lower dividend at $0.50 but somewhat higher earnings per share at $0.87. Given similar dividend and earnings prospects you would expect the banks' prices to be similar. In the event, National Australia Bank sold at the slightly higher price of $12.30. Given the better earnings of the National Australia Bank this relation between the prices of the two banks seems quite reasonable. Moreover, if Advance Bank announced unexpectedly higher earnings, we could be quite confident that its share price would respond instantly and without bias. In other words, the subsequent price would be set correctly relative to the prior price.

Most of the corporate finance lessons of the efficient-market hypothesis depend on these kinds of relative efficiency. Let us turn now to consider some of these lessons and at the same time introduce briefly some of the issues discussed in subsequent chapters.

# No theory is perfect

Although few simple economic ideas are as well-supported by the evidence as the efficient-market theory, it would be wrong to pretend that there are no puzzles or apparent exceptions. After the 1960s and 1970s, when finance journals were brim full of articles demonstrating market efficiency, researchers got more notice by finding puzzles and anomalies inconsistent with market efficiency. With many researchers worldwide aided by powerful computers all looking for pricing anomalies it is not surprising that some were found. Of course, if you torture the data long enough it will give up the story you want. The question is whether the anomalies are real, or whether the extensive searching has just uncovered some unusual coincidences.

It is difficult, however, to dismiss all the evidence against market efficiency as coincidence. There are phenomena that take rather more explaining. For instance, company managers appear to have made consistently superior profits when they have dealt in their own company's shares.[24] This does not seem to square well with the strong form of the efficient market theory.

It may not be so surprising that insiders make superior profits, but it is more difficult to explain the well-known small firm effect. As we discussed in Chapter 7, history shows that an investment in small firms has generated substantially greater returns than an investment in large firms. One study suggests that from 1958 to 1981 the difference in return between the smallest and largest Australian listed companies exceeded 5 per cent per month. This is an

---

[23]  Some economists believe the market is prone to bubbles—situations in which price grows faster than fundamental value, but investors do not sell because they expect price to *keep* rising. Of course, all such bubbles pop eventually, but they can, in theory, be self-sustaining for a while. The *Journal of Economic Perspectives*, 4 (Spring 1990) contains several non-technical articles on bubbles. Such bubbles can be rational. If the price is given by

$P_0 = \sum_{t=1}^{\infty} \dfrac{D_t}{(1 + r)^t}$, this represents a rational price and implies no speculative bubbles. If the price is given by

$P_0 = \sum_{t=1}^{n} \dfrac{D_t}{(1 + r)^t} + \dfrac{P_t}{(1 + r)^t}$, this is also a rational price but implies a speculative bubble if $P_0 = \sum_{t=1}^{n} \dfrac{D_t}{(1 + r)^t} + \dfrac{P_n}{(1 + r)^n}$

$\neq \sum_{t=1}^{\infty} \dfrac{D_t}{(1 + r)^t}$. Such a bubble is rational provided that in forming the expected price $P_n$ investors form an unbiased estimate

of the probability that the bubble will burst.

[24]  See J. Jaffe, 'The Effect of Regulation Changes on Insider Trading', *Bell Journal of Economics and Management Science*, 5: 93–121 (Spring 1974); and H. N. Seyhun, 'Insiders' Profits, Costs of Trading and Market Efficiency', *Journal of Financial Economics*, 16: 189–212 (June 1986).

extraordinarily large difference and perhaps the estimate is biased by thin trading. If we consider the largest and next-to-smallest firms, the return difference shrinks to about 1 per cent per month.[25] On an annual basis this is consistent with the data in Figure 13.5 which shows that the size effect is a common experience across many other countries. This seems too much to be just coincidence.

**figure 13.5** _____

The difference between the average return on small firms and that on large firms has been positive in most countries.

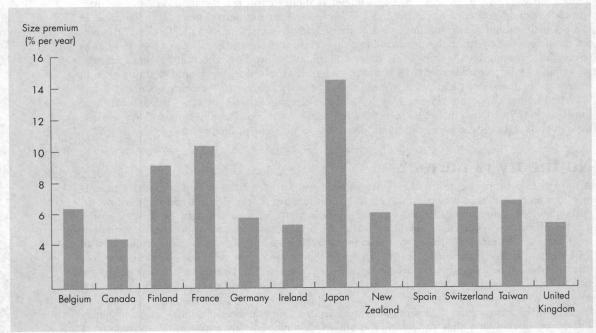

_Source_: Data is drawn from a variety of studies and relates to a variety of periods since 1954. They are summarised in G. Hawawini and D. B. Keim, 'On the Predictability of Common Stock Returns: World-Wide Evidence', in R. A. Jarrow, V. Maksimovic and W. T. Ziemba (eds.), _Finance_, North Holland, Amsterdam, 1994.

In part the higher return to small firms is explained by differences in risk. Small firms typically have higher betas than large firms. But the differences in beta are not large enough to explain all the differences in returns. One explanation may be that investors demand an additional return from shares in small firms to compensate for some extra risk factor that is not captured in the simple form of the CAPM.[26] That is why we asked in Chapter 8 whether the small-firm effect was evidence against the CAPM. For example, it is well known that the spread between prices offered for buying and selling is wider for small-firm shares than for large-firm shares. This indicates thin trading, in other words less liquidity in the market for small-firm shares. Perhaps investors require extra return to compensate for a lack of easy marketability. This kind of effect is not allowed for in our theories or tests. It is always possible, however, that the size effect may simply represent an important exception to the efficient-market theory.

---

25    See P. Brown, D. Keim, A. Kleidon and T. Marsh, 'Stock Return Seasonalities and the Tax Loss Selling Hypothesis: Analysis of the Arguments and Australian Evidence', _Journal of Financial Economics_, **12**: 105–27 (1983).

26    Ray Ball argues persuasively that such missing risk factors are likely to explain many of the anomalies that researchers have uncovered. See 'Anomalies in Relationships Between Securities' Yields and Yield Surrogates', _Journal of Financial Economics_, **6**: 103–26 (1978).

But this is not the end of the story. Now look at Figure 13.6, which shows the difference between small- and large-firm shares in January and the remaining months. Notice that nearly all the gains from investing in small firms came in January. Indeed, nearly all of the gain came in the *first week* of January. This is a particular example of what is known as a seasonal in returns.[27] In Australia there is evidence of a January seasonal and another smaller seasonal in July. There is also a day of the week effect with returns over the weekend and through Monday being abnormally low. What is the explanation? More coincidences, an inefficient and irrational market, or is there an explanation still to be uncovered?

**figure 13.6** _____

The size premium—difference between the average return on small firms and that on large firms—between April 1962 and December 1989, by month. Notice that the small-firm effect occurs entirely in January.

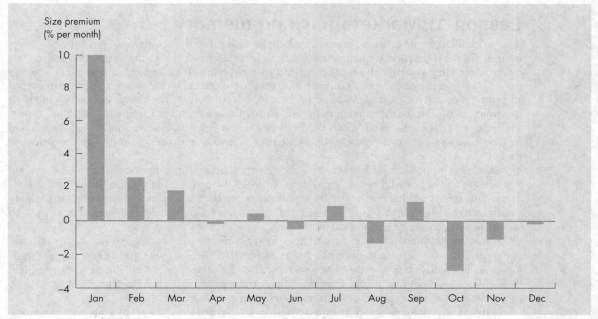

*Source*: Reprinted from G. Hawawini and D. B. Keim, 'On the Predictability of Common Stock Returns: World-Wide Evidence', in R. A. Jarrow, V. Maksimovic and W. T. Ziemba (eds.), *Finance*, North Holland, Amsterdam, © 1994, with permission from Elsevier Science.

Some researchers suggest that part of the explanation for the anomalies may lie in market microstructure. For example, they point to the fact that at certain times there is a higher probability of trades occurring at the bid price offered by buyers, while at other times there is a higher probability of trades occurring at the ask, the price demanded by sellers.[28] Since the bid is the lower boundary for the price spread and the ask is the upper boundary, part of an apparently abnormal return may simply be the spread as prices bounce from the bid to the ask.

---

27  A readable summary of these size and seasonal effects is given by D. B. Keim, 'The CAPM and Equity Return Regularities', *Financial Analysts Journal*, **42**: 19–34 (May–June 1986).

28  For a review of some of this literature and an empirical analysis of Australian data see M. Aitken, P. Brown, H.Y. Izan, A. Kua and T. Walter, 'An Intraday Analysis of the Probability of Trading on the ASX at the Asking Price', *Australian Journal of Management* (1995).

While there is no lack of puzzles, we believe that there is now widespread agreement that capital markets function well and that opportunities for easy profits are rare.[29] So nowadays when economists come across instances where this apparently is not true, they do not throw the efficient-market hypothesis onto the economic garbage heap. Instead, they think carefully about whether there is some missing ingredient that their theories ignore, or some subtle error in their research method with the result that the anomaly is an artefact of their method rather than a real effect.

We suggest that financial managers should assume as a starting point that security prices are fair and that it is very difficult to outguess or fool the market. This has several implications for the financial manager.

## 13.4 The six lessons of market efficiency

### Lesson 1: Markets have no memory

The weak form of the efficient-market hypothesis states that the sequence of past price changes contains no information about future changes. Economists express the same idea more concisely when they say that the market has no memory. Sometimes financial managers *seem* to act as if this were not the case. For example, they are often reluctant to issue shares after a fall in price. They are inclined to wait for a rebound, but, of course, the shares are just as likely to go down as up. Similarly, managers favour equity rather than debt financing after an abnormal price rise. The idea is to 'catch the market while it is high'. But we know that the market has no memory and the predictable cycles that financial managers seem to rely on do not exist.[30]

Managers appear to be behaving as though they believe that their companies' shares are not always fairly priced. If issuing shares is a zero-NPV transaction then it should not matter when you sell your shares—at the time you get what they are worth. After the event it may prove to have been a good deal or a bad deal, but in an efficient market you cannot tell which it will be in advance of making the issue.

Sometimes a financial manager will have inside information indicating that the firm's share is overpriced or underpriced. Suppose, for example, that there is some good news that the market does not know but you do. The share price will rise sharply when the news is revealed. Therefore, if the company sold shares at the current price, it would be offering a bargain to new investors at the expense of present shareholders.

Naturally managers are reluctant to sell new shares when they have favourable inside information. But such inside information has nothing to do with the history of the share price. Your firm's share could be selling now at half its price of a year ago and yet you could have special information suggesting that it is *still* grossly overvalued. Or it may be undervalued at twice last year's price. The puzzle is that managers seem to behave as though selling shares when the share price is historically low is a negative NPV transaction, but is a positive NPV transaction when prices are high.

---

[29]  Everyone thinks they know a duck when they see one, but it is hard to come up with a satisfactory definition. It is rather like that with efficient markets. We have talked about 'well-functioning' markets and 'fair' markets without ever saying what this means. Fama defined efficient markets in terms of the difference between the actual price and the price that investors expected given a particular set of information. An efficient market, Fama argues, is one in which the expected value of this difference is zero. See E. F. Fama, 'Efficient Capital Markets: A Review of Theory and Empirical Work', *Journal of Finance*, **25**: 383–417 (May 1970). Rubinstein defines an efficient market as one in which prices would not be altered if everyone revealed all that they knew. See M. Rubinstein, 'Securities Market Efficiency in an Arrow-Debreu Economy', *American Economic Review*, **65**: 812–24 (December 1975).

[30]  If high prices signal good investment opportunities then we would expect to see the firm raise more funds in total when prices are historically high, but this does not explain why firms prefer to raise the extra finance as equity issues rather than debt.

# Lesson 2: Trust market prices

In an efficient market you can trust prices. They impound all available information about the value of each security. This does not just apply to shares but also to trading in interest rates and exchange rates.

This means that in an efficient market there is no way for most investors to achieve consistently superior rates of return. To do so, you not only need to know more than *anyone* else does, you also need to know more than *everyone* else. This message is important for the financial manager who is responsible for the firm's exchange rate policy or for its purchases and sales of debt. If you operate on the basis that you are smarter than others at predicting currency changes or interest-rate moves, you will trade a consistent financial policy for an elusive will-o'-the-wisp. There is no shortage of examples of managers who have been overconfident about their ability to beat the market and led their companies into financial distress.

The company's assets may also be directly affected by management's faith in its investment skills. For example, one company will often purchase another simply because its management thinks that the share is undervalued. On approximately half the occasions the share of the acquired firm really will turn out to be undervalued. But on the other half it will turn out to be overvalued.[31] On average, the value will be correct, so that the acquiring company is playing a fair game except for the costs of acquisition.

---

### example: AWA's foreign exchange experience

A few years ago the Australian company AWA had a young financial executive who was responsible for managing the company's foreign exchange exposure. He appeared to be something of a hotshot and initially he had some success in taking forward foreign exchange positions. This created significant profits for the company. Unfortunately, it appears his early success was more good luck than superior skill and things began to turn sour. Eventually, the company lost in excess of $20 million and as a consequence was led into serious financial difficulties.

---

Unpleasant as this was for AWA it pales into insignificance beside the experience of Orange County in the United States and the British bank Barings. Both of these organisations lost over a billion dollars because executives backed themselves against the market.

Financial managers take such risks because they believe that they can spot the direction of interest rates, exchange rates or share prices, and sometimes their employers encourage them to speculate. We are not suggesting that such speculation always results in losses, for in efficient markets speculators win as often as they lose. This is a danger because those who have the luck to be early winners can overestimate their true ability. Falling into this trap, they risk shattering their hopes and company fortunes on an unforgiving and efficient market. Corporate treasurers would do better to trust market prices rather than incur large risks in the quest for trading profits.

# Lesson 3: Reading the message in prices

If the market is efficient, prices impound all available information relevant to predicting the future value of securities. Therefore, if only we can learn to read the message embedded in the price, we can tell a lot about the future. For example, in Chapter 27 we will show how

---

[31] We are not suggesting here that the share is initially mispriced. We are suggesting that the market is not all knowing. With the benefit of *hindsight* roughly half your purchases can be seen to have done better than expected and the other half worse.

information in the company's accounts can help the financial manager to estimate the probability of bankruptcy. But, of course, these accounts are only one of many sources of information available to investors. The return offered by the company's debt and equity securities provides another indicator.[32] The debt of Rothwell's, an Australian merchant bank, offered higher rates of return than its competitors. As holders of these securities discovered this was not all good news. The extra return was compensation for extra risk. In Rothwell's case the extra risk proved fatal and the bank failed. The moral is simple: if a company's debt offers a much higher yield than average you can deduce that the company is probably in trouble.

Here is another example. Suppose that investors are confident that interest rates are going to rise over the next year. In that case, they will prefer to wait before they enter into long-term loans. Any firm that wants to borrow long-term money today will have to offer the inducement of a higher rate of interest. In other words, the long-term rate of interest will have to be higher than the one-year rate. Differences between the long-term interest rate and the short-term rate tell you something about what investors expect to happen to short-term rates in the future.[33]

Here is one final example. When St George Bank bid for Advance Bank, who was it good for? The market clearly thought it was good for shareholders in Advance Bank; their share price rose on the announcement of the bid. On the market's view it was bad for shareholders in St George; their share price fell on the announcement. Of course, to do this analysis properly we should not just look at the raw price movements. For example, suppose share prices for both banks had gone up, but that there had also been a general increase in the market at the same time. Could we tell whether the bid was really good news, or whether it was just the banks' prices drifting up with the market? Yes we could, but to do so we need to be able to calculate a share's abnormal return.

$$\text{Abnormal return} \; = \; \text{actual return} \; - \; \text{expected return}$$

We discuss how to do this in the next lesson.

## Lesson 4: There are no financial illusions

In an efficient market there are no financial illusions. Investors are unromantically concerned with the firm's cash flows and the portion of those cash flows to which they are entitled.

### example: bonus dividends and share splits

We can illustrate our fourth lesson by looking at the effect of share splits and bonus dividends. Companies can increase the number of shares on issue in two ways. They can subdivide the shares that are already outstanding, in which case the par value of the shares changes. For example, a share with a $1 par value might be split into two shares each with a $0.50 par value. The other alternative is to distribute extra shares as a bonus dividend.[34] The bonus dividend *was* the alternative chosen by most Australian companies before the introduction of the imputation tax system.[35]

---

32  See W. H. Beaver, 'Market Prices, Financial Ratios and the Prediction of Failure', *Journal of Accounting Research*, 6: 179–92 (Autumn 1968).

33  We will discuss the relationship between short-term and long-term interest rates in Chapter 23. Notice, however, that in an efficient market the difference between the prices of *any* short-term and long-term contracts always says something about how participants expect prices to move.

34  There are some confusing transpacific differences in terminology. In the United States the term share split is more common than the term bonus issue. For example, in the United States an issue of two additional shares for each share currently held would be called a 3-for-1 split, rather than a 2-for-1 bonus. Whatever the name, the outcome is the same; in this case you end up with three shares instead of one.

35  With the introduction of the imputation system it became clear that, in many cases, there were tax disadvantages to bonus issues.

For a large company, the administrative costs of such actions may run to $100 000 or more. Yet it does not affect in any other way the company's cash flows or the proportion of these cash flows attributable to each shareholder. You may think that you are better off, but that is an illusion. You just have more pieces of paper representing claims to the same amount of wealth.[36] As a senior manager of one of Australia's largest investment funds commented, 'At every company general meeting I attend two questions are always asked. The first is—will tea be served? The second is—will there be a bonus issue? The first question is the more important!'

Suppose that BHP shares are selling for $18 and BHP makes a 1-for-1 bonus issue. The shareholder ends up with two shares. After the bonus we would expect each share to sell for $18/2 = $9. Dividends per share, earnings per share and all other 'per share' variables would be one-half their previous levels.

A variety of justifications have been proposed for splits and bonus dividends. The most common justification given by firms is that it provides a reward for loyal shareholders. Another justification is that it gives shareholders a return while saving cash.[37] A disarmingly simple explanation was offered by a textbook which observed that shareholders like share splits because they expect them to be followed by more share splits. Claims such as these contrast strongly with the efficient-markets notion that investors are concerned solely with their share of the company's cash flows.

Another suggestion is that there is an optimal price range for a share. If the price is too high, it is argued, this inhibits liquidity and marketability of the shares. Of course, extremely high share prices are inconvenient for small investors. In September 1994 shares in Japan Telecom Company (NTT) were issued at ¥4.7 million each, or about $60 000. That is a nuisance if you only have a few thousand dollars to invest.[38] A bonus issue, or share split, might have benefit in this case. But it is difficult to believe that the same argument applies to shares in Australian companies, most of which are priced at less than $20.[39]

## *Calculating abnormal returns

We can check whether investors are fooled by share splits. If investors are fooled, we should find abnormal changes in the share price at the time of the split. First, however, we must explain how you can identify these abnormal price movements.[40] In Chapter 9 we introduced you to the concept of security alphas and betas. Alpha ($\alpha$) describes how much on average the share price moved when the market was unchanged. Beta ($\beta$) describes the average additional return for each 1 per cent change in the market index. For example, Table 9.1 showed that Fairfax's share price rose on average by about 3.04/12 per cent per month when the market was unchanged ($\alpha = 0.253$), and it rose a further 1.53 per cent for each 1 per cent change in the market index ($\beta = 1.53$).[41] Now

---

[36]   These days you do not even get the pieces of paper. There is just a change to the number of shares registered in your name in the shareholder database on a computer somewhere.

[37]   One company in which one of the authors held shares used this justification to cut out the cash dividend entirely and substituted a bonus dividend instead. The company went bust before the bonus shares were delivered.

[38]   Lakonishok and Lev provide some evidence that many companies do split their shares in order to keep the price in a desirable trading range. See J. Lakonishok and B. Lev, 'Share Splits and Share Dividends: Why, Who and When', *Journal of Finance*, 42: 913–32 (September 1987).

[39]   Compare this with the United States where a price of US$100 would not be considered exceptionally high. There are also some very high-priced American shares. Berkshire Hathaway shares, for example, have sold for $8600 each.

[40]   A little knowledge is a dangerous thing. If you want a good estimate of the abnormal return, you need to know more about how to calculate it than the brief overview that we provide. We suggest that you consult S. J. Brown and J. B. Warner, 'Measuring Security Price Performance', *Journal of Financial Economics*, 8: 205–58 (1980).

[41]   It is important when estimating alpha and beta that you choose a period in which you believe the share behaved normally. If its performance was abnormal, then estimates of alpha and beta cannot be used to measure the returns that investors expected. As a precaution ask yourself whether your estimates of expected returns *look* sensible.

suppose that you were interested in the performance of Fairfax shares in a month when the market rose 6.2 per cent. On past evidence you would judge that the expected percentage change in the share price that month was:

Expected return = 0.253 + (1.53 × market change) = 0.253 + (1.53 × 6.2) = 9.74%

Suppose the Fairfax share price actually rose by 10 per cent in that month. Its abnormal price change was therefore,

Abnormal price change = actual change − expected change = 10% − 9.74%
= +0.26%

This 0.26 per cent rise in the Fairfax share price is above the normal return in such market conditions.[42] Note that as long as Fairfax does not pay a dividend during the month, the *return* and the *percentage price change* are identical.

Because of the difficulty of accurately estimating alpha and beta, this method of calculating abnormal returns is not too reliable for individual firms. This is particularly the case in Australia where thin trading complicates the estimation process. Fortunately, the errors tend to average out when we estimate average abnormal returns across several companies.[43]

**Abnormal returns and share splits**     Now we can look at the abnormal price movements that generally take place around the time of a share split. Figure 13.7 summarises the results of an important study of splits during the period from 1926 to 1960.[44] It shows the cumulative abnormal performance of shares around the time of the split after adjustment for the increase in the number of shares.[45] The cumulative abnormal returns (percentage price changes) are calculated by successively adding together the abnormal returns from each of the periods. Notice the substantial rise in price that accumulates before the date of the split. The announcement of the split would have occurred in the last month or two of this period. That means the decision to split is both the consequence of a rise in price and the cause of a further but smaller rise.

It looks as if shareholders are not as hard-headed as we have been making out: They do seem to care about form as well as substance. However, during the subsequent year two-thirds of the splitting companies announced above-average increases in cash dividends. Usually such an announcement would cause an unusual rise in the share price, but in the case of the splitting companies there was no such occurrence at any time after the split. Indeed, the shares of those companies that did *not* increase their dividends by an above-average amount declined in value to levels prevailing well before the split. The apparent explanation is that the split was accompanied by an explicit or implicit promise of a subsequent dividend increase, and the rise

---

[42] You can also use the capital asset pricing model to measure abnormal returns. You will generally get an answer that is of a similar order of magnitude to that above, but it can differ. The CAPM states that the expected return for a share is

$$\text{Expected return} = r_f + \beta(\text{E}[r_m] - r_f)$$

With the benefit of hindsight we can plug in the actual market return for the month. We assumed this to be a 6.2 per cent change in the index but we must also add the 0.25 per cent monthly dividend yield. Suppose the interest rate ($r_f$) was 7.5 per cent a year, or about 0.625 per cent a month. Therefore,

Expected return = 0.625 + 1.53 (6.45 − 0.625) = 9.54%. Abnormal return = actual return − expected return = 10 − 9.54 = +0.46%

In this case the results of the two methods differ by about 0.2 per cent.

[43] An alternative procedure is simply to assume that alpha is 0 and beta is 1. This seems to work quite well if you are only interested in the average abnormal return across several companies.

[44] See E. F. Fama, L. Fisher, M. Jensen and R. Roll, 'The Adjustment of Share Prices to New Information', *International Economic Review*, 10: 1–21 (February 1969). Later researchers have discovered that shareholders make abnormal gains both when the split or share dividend is announced and when it takes place. Nobody has offered a convincing explanation for the latter phenomenon. See, for example, M. S. Grinblatt, R. W. Masulis and S. Titman, 'The Valuation Effects of Share Splits and Share Dividends', *Journal of Financial Economics*, 13: 461–90 (December 1984).

[45] By this we mean that the study looked at the change in the shareholders' wealth. A decline in the price of BHP shares from $18 to $9 at the time of a 1-for-1 bonus, or at the time of a 2-for-1 split, would not affect shareholders' wealth.

**figure 13.7**

Cumulative abnormal returns at the time of a share split. (Returns are adjusted for the increase in the number of shares.) Notice the rise before the split and the absence of abnormal changes after the split.

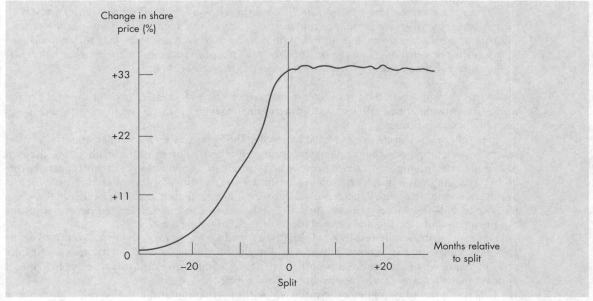

*Source*: E. Fama et al., op. cit., Footnote 44, Figure 2b, p.13. © Blackwell Publishers.

in price at the time of the split had nothing to do with a predilection for splits as such but with the information that it was thought to convey.[46]

A similar story applies to bonus issues. It was common for the managers of Australian companies making bonus issues to announce that the dividend rate would be maintained on the enlarged share capital. In other words, the promise was that total dividend payments would be increased. A bonus seems an expensive way to send this message, however.

## A second example—accounting changes

There are other occasions on which managers seem to assume that investors suffer from financial illusion. For example, some firms devote enormous ingenuity to the task of manipulating earnings reported to shareholders. This is done by 'creative accounting'—that is, by choosing accounting methods which stabilise and increase reported earnings. Presumably firms go to this trouble because management believes that shareholders take the figures at face value. Leonard Spacek, a leading accountant, echoed this belief in the following complaint.

> *Let us assume that you sincerely want to report the profits in the way you feel fairly presents the true results of your company's business. This is an admirable and objective motive; but when you do this, you find that your competitor shows a relatively more favourable profit result than you do. This creates a demand for the competitor's share,*

---

[46] This does not imply that investors like high-dividend payouts for their own sake. It could be that dividend increases are valued only because they are a sign of company prosperity. For example, Paul Healy and Krishna Palepu found that companies initiating dividends subsequently report higher than normal earnings increases. See 'Earnings Information Conveyed by Dividend Initiations and Omissions', *Journal of Financial Economics*, **21**: 149–75 (September 1988). We return to this point in Chapter 16.

*while yours lags behind. You put your analyst to work, and you find that if your competitor followed the same accounting practices you do, your results would be better than his. You show this analysis to your complaining shareholders. Naturally, they ask, 'If this is true, and if your competitor's accounting practices are generally accepted too, why not change your accounting practices and thus improve your profits?' At that point you try to explain why your accounting is much more factual and reliable than your competitor's. Your shareholders listen, but nothing you can say will convince them that they should give up a 20 per cent, 50 per cent or 100 per cent possible increase in the market value just because you like certain accounting practices better than others.*[47]

Is Spacek right? Can the firm increase its market value by creative accounting? Or are the firm's shares traded in an efficient, well-functioning market, in which investors can see through such financial illusions?

A number of researchers have tried to resolve this question by looking at how the market reacts when companies change their accounting methods. For example, Robert Holthausen has studied what happens to share prices when American companies boost their reported profits by switching from accelerated depreciation to straight-line depreciation.[48] This switch is purely cosmetic. It reduces the reported depreciation charge but it does not affect the company's tax bill—the American tax authorities allow firms to use accelerated depreciation for tax purposes and straight-line depreciation for reporting purposes.

Figure 13.8 shows the results of Holthausen's study. The average abnormal return over the two days following the announcement was a negligible −0.1 per cent. So it looks as if prices are not changed by cosmetic accounting changes.[49] *Some* investors may be fooled, but it appears that they are not the ones who determine prices.

This result not only suggests the futility of earnings manipulation. It also raises some more basic questions about the role of accounting conventions. Jack Treynor illustrates the problem with the fable of nail soup:

*There was once a band of itinerant soldiers who, when they had difficulty persuading townsmen to feed them, hit upon the following solution. They set a large pot of water to boiling and then, when all the townsmen were watching curiously, dropped in a nail and announced with much licking of lips that they were making nail soup. The townsmen were assured that there would be enough soup for everybody. When one of the soldiers allowed that a few carrots actually improved the flavour of nail soup, a townsman dashed off to fetch some carrots. When it was observed that tomatoes made a wonderful garnish for nail soup, another townsman quickly produced some tomatoes. Soon the nail soup contained beef stock, turnips and onions. Before the soup was served, the nail was removed. But the townsmen continued to regard the soup as nail soup.*[50]

Nail soup was nourishing, but not because of the nail. Earnings have information content, but not necessarily because of the ingredients that have been the main concern of accounting standards boards around the world. Accountants painstakingly put the nail into the soup; analysts painstakingly take it out, all the while believing they are really supping on nail soup. The

---

47  See L. Spacek, Business Success Requires an Understanding of Unsolved Problems of Accounting and Financial Reporting, address before the financial accounting class, Graduate School of Business Administration, Harvard University, 25 September 1959.

48  See R. W. Holthausen, 'Evidence on the Effect on Bond Covenants and Management Compensation Contracts on the Choice of Accounting Techniques: The Case of Depreciation Switch-Back', *Journal of Accounting and Economics*, 3: 73–109 (1981).

49  Sometimes apparently cosmetic changes can have economic substance. Suppose, for example, that the amount of debt a firm can issue is restricted to half the book value of its assets. Then any accounting change that increases book value also allows the firm to raise more debt.

50  See J. L. Treynor, 'Discussion: Changes in Accounting Techniques and Share Prices', *Empirical Research in Accounting: Selected Studies, 1972*, Institute for Professional Accounting, Graduate School of Business, University of Chicago, 1972, p. 43.

**figure 13.8**

Cumulative abnormal return on shares of firms switching from accelerated to straight-line depreciation, 1955–78.
Note: Returns are measured over 10-day periods, except during the 10 days on either side of the announcement, when they are measured daily.

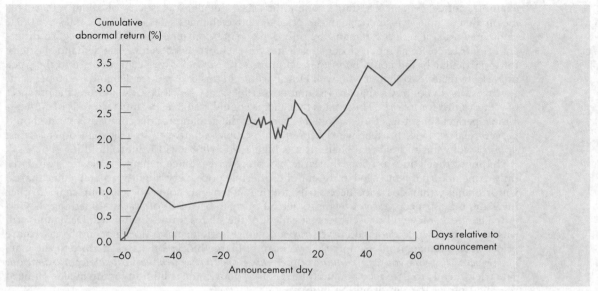

*Source*: Reprinted from R. W. Holthausen, 'Evidence on the Effect on Bond Covenants and Management Compensation Contracts on the Choice of Accounting Techniques: The Case of Depreciation Switch-Back', *Journal of Accounting and Economics*, **3**: 73–109, © 1981, with permission from Elsevier Science.

overall process may seem unnecessarily complicated since the same result could have been obtained without the nail.

## Lesson 5: The do-it-yourself alternative

In an efficient market investors will not pay others for what they can do equally well themselves. As we shall see, many of the controversies in corporate financing centre on how well individuals can replicate corporate financial decisions. For example, companies often justify mergers on the grounds that they produce a more diversified and hence more stable firm. But if investors can hold the shares of both companies, why should they thank the companies for diversifying? It is much easier and cheaper for them to diversify than it is for the firm.

The financial manager needs to ask the same question when considering whether it is better to issue debt or shares. If the firm issues debt, it will create financial leverage. As a result, the shares will be more risky and will offer a higher expected return. But shareholders can obtain financial leverage without the firm issuing debt. They can issue debt on their own account. The problem for the financial manager is therefore to decide whether the company can issue debt more cheaply than the individual shareholder.

Suppose the financial manager concludes that by issuing debt the company can do something for investors that the investors cannot do for themselves. The manager must ask another question: How many other financial managers have reached the same conclusion, and how many have acted on it? Perhaps the opportunity has already gone. In an efficient market securities for which there is a premium will not long remain in short supply. Another feature of an efficient market is that even when investors cannot do it themselves, they will not pay a premium for opportunities that are in plentiful supply.

# Lesson 6: Seen one share, seen them all

The elasticity of demand for any article measures the percentage change in the quantity demanded for each percentage addition to the price. If the article has close substitutes, the elasticity will be strongly negative; if there are no close substitutes, it will be near zero. For example, coffee, which is a staple commodity, has a demand elasticity of about $-0.2$. This means that a 5 per cent increase in the price of coffee changes sales by $-0.2 \times 0.05 = -0.01$; in other words, it reduces demand by only 1 per cent. Consumers are likely to regard different *brands* of coffee as much closer substitutes for each other. Therefore, the demand elasticity for a particular brand could be in the region of, say, $-2.0$. A 5 per cent increase in the price of Nescafé relative to that of Maxwell House would in this case reduce demand by 10 per cent.

Investors do not buy a share for its unique qualities; they buy it because it offers the prospect of a fair return for its risk. This means that shares should be like *very* similar brands of coffee— almost perfect substitutes for each other. Therefore, the demand for the company's share should be very elastic. If its prospective risk premium is lower relative to its risk than other shares, *nobody* will want to hold that share. If it is higher, *everybody* will want to hold it.

Suppose that you want to sell a large block of shares. Since demand is elastic, you naturally conclude that you need only cut the offering price very slightly to sell your shares. Unfortunately, that does not necessarily follow. When you come to sell your shares, other investors may suspect that you want to get rid of them because you know something they do not. Therefore, they will revise their assessment of the shares' value downward. Demand is still elastic but the whole demand curve moves down. Elastic demand does not imply that share prices never change; it *does* imply that you can sell large blocks of shares at close to the market price *as long as you can convince other investors that you have no private information.* The trick then is to convince potential buyers that your trade is **liquidity motivated** (you need the cash) rather than **information motivated**.

Here is one case that supports this view. In June 1977 the Bank of England offered its holding of BP shares for sale at £8.45 each. The bank owned nearly 67 million BP shares so that the total value of the holding was £564 million, or about $1150 million. It was a huge sum to ask the public to find.

Anyone who wished to apply for BP shares had nearly two weeks within which to do so.[51] Just before the bank's announcement the price of BP shares was £9.12. Over the next two weeks the price drifted down to £8.98, largely in line with the British equity market. Therefore, by the final application date, the discount being offered by the bank was only 6 per cent. In return for this discount, any applicant had to raise the necessary cash, taking the risk that the price of BP would decline before the result of the application was known, and had to pass over to the Bank of England the next dividend on BP.

If Nescafé coffee is offered at a discount of 6 per cent, the demand is unlikely to be overwhelming. But the discount on BP shares was enough to bring in applications for nearly $6 billion worth of shares, nearly five times the amount on offer.

We admit that this case was unusual in some respects, but an important study by Myron Scholes of a large sample of secondary offerings confirmed the ability of the market to absorb large blocks of share.[52] The average effect of the offerings was to reduce the share price slightly, but the decline was almost independent of the amount offered. Scholes' estimate of the demand elasticity for a company's share was $-3000$. Of course, this figure was not meant to be precise and some researchers have argued that demand is not as elastic as Scholes' study suggests.[53] However, there seems to be widespread agreement with the general point that you

---

51   However, applicants were required to put up only £3 per share on application and the remainder at a later date.

52   See M. Scholes, 'The Market for Securities: Substitution versus Price Pressure and the Effects of Information on Share Prices', *Journal of Business*, **45**: 179–211 (April 1972). A secondary distribution is a large block of shares sold off the floor of the exchange.

53   For example, see W. H. Mikkelson and M. M. Partch, 'Share Price Effects and Costs of Secondary Distributions', *Journal of Financial Economics*, **14**: 165–94 (1985).

can sell large quantities of shares at close to the market price as long as other investors do not deduce that you have some private information.

Here again we encounter an apparent contradiction with practice. Many corporations seem to believe that the demand elasticity is not only low, but that it varies with the share price, so that when the price is relatively low, new shares can be sold only at a substantial discount. The idea is that the expansion of supply creates downward price pressure. However, Paul Asquith and David Mullins, who searched for evidence of price pressure, found that new share issues by utilities drove down their share prices on average by only 0.9 per cent.[54] We will come back to the subject of price pressure when we discuss share issues in Chapter 15.

## 13.5 Summary

The patron saint of the Bolsa (stock exchange) in Barcelona, Spain, is Nuestra Senora de la Esperanza—Our Lady of Hope. She is the perfect patron, for we all hope for superior returns when we invest. But competition between investors will tend to produce an efficient market. In such a market, prices will rapidly impound any new information and it will be very difficult to make consistently superior returns. We may indeed *hope*, but all we can rationally *expect* in an efficient market is that we shall obtain a return that is just sufficient to compensate us for the time value of money and for the risks we bear. We must also understand that because of the effect of risk we will sometimes get more return than we expect and sometimes less. On average, over a sufficiently long period, the pleasant and unpleasant surprises should balance out.

The efficient-market hypothesis comes in three different flavours. The weak form of the hypothesis states that prices efficiently reflect all the information contained in the past series of share prices. In this case it is impossible to earn superior returns simply by looking for patterns in share prices—in other words, price changes are random. This means that today's price is the best predictor of tomorrow's price.

The semistrong form of the hypothesis states that prices reflect all published information. That means it is impossible to make consistently superior returns just by reading the newspaper, looking at the company's annual accounts, and so on.

The strong form of the hypothesis states that share prices effectively impound all available information. It tells us that inside information is hard to find because in pursuing it you are in competition with thousands, perhaps millions, of active, intelligent and greedy investors. The best you can do in this case is to assume that securities are fairly priced and to hope that one day Nuestra Senora will reward your humility.

The concept of an efficient market is astonishingly simple and remarkably well supported by the facts. Less than 30 years ago any suggestion that security investment is a fair game was generally regarded as bizarre. Today it is not only widely accepted in business schools, but it also permeates investment practice and government policy towards the security markets.

For the corporate treasurer who is concerned with issuing or purchasing securities the efficient-market theory has obvious implications. However, the existence of efficient markets does not mean that the financial manager can let financing 'take care of itself'. It provides only a starting point for analysis. It is time to get down to details about securities, issue procedures and financial institutions. We start in Chapter 14.

---

[54] See P. Asquith and D. W. Mullins, 'Equity Issues and Offering Dilution', *Journal of Financial Economics*, **15**: 61–89 (January–February 1986). In the United States state and federal regulatory commissions, which set the prices charged by local utilities, have sometimes allowed significantly higher earnings to compensate the firm for price pressure.

## FURTHER READING

The classic review article on market efficiency is:

> E. F. Fama, 'Efficient Capital Markets: A Review of Theory and Empirical Work', *Journal of Finance*, 25: 383–417 (May 1970).

The sequel is also worth reading. In the sequel Fama suggests that sequels are rarely as good as the original, nevertheless there is a sequel to the sequel which suggests that the evidence against market efficiency is less than compelling:

> E. F. Fama, 'Efficient Capital Markets II', *Journal of Finance*, 47: 1575–1617 (December 1991).
>
> E. F. Fama, 'Market Efficiency, Long-term Returns and Behavioral Finance', *Journal of Financial Economics*. 49: 283–306 (September 1998).

An interesting Australian test of technical analysis is:

> R. Ball, 'Filter Rules: Interpretation of Market Efficiency, Experimental Problems and Australian Evidence', *Accounting and Finance*, 5: 2–17 (November 1978).

The following book contains a selection of classic articles:

> P. H. Cootner (ed.), *The Random Character of Share Market Prices*, M.I.T. Press, Cambridge, Mass., 1964.

Possible exceptions to the efficient-market theory are contained in:

> G. Hawawini and D. B. Keim, 'On the Predictability of Common Stock Returns: World-Wide Evidence', in R. A. Jarrow, V. Maksimovic and W. T. Ziemba (eds.), *Finance*, North Holland, 1994.
>
> 'Symposium on Some Anomalous Evidence on Capital Market Efficiency', a special issue of the *Journal of Financial Economics*, 6 (June 1977).

A discussion of capital market anomalies that is quite easy to read is:

> R. W. Faff, 'Capital Market Anomalies: A Survey of the Evidence', *Accounting Research Journal*, pp. 3–22 (Spring 1992).

The following book contains an interesting collection of articles on the crash of 1987:

> R. W. Kamphuis, Jr et al. (eds.), *Black Monday and the Future of Financial Markets*, Dow Jones-Irwin, Inc., Homewood, Ill., 1989.

## QUIZ

**1.** Share prices appear to behave as though successive values:

a. Are random numbers.

b. Follow regular cycles.

c. Differ by a random number.

Which (if any) of these statements are true?

**2.** Supply the missing words:

'There are three forms of the efficient-market hypothesis. Tests of randomness in share prices provide evidence for the _____ form of the hypothesis. Tests of share price reaction to well-publicised news provide evidence for the _____ form and tests of the performance of professionally managed funds provide evidence for the _____ form. Market efficiency results from competition between investors. Many investors search for new information about the company's business that would help them to value the share more accurately. This is known as _____ research. Such research helps to ensure that prices reflect all available information: In other words, it helps to keep the market efficient in the _____ form. Other investors study past share prices for recurrent patterns that would allow them to make superior profits. This is known as _____ research. Such research helps to ensure that prices reflect all the information contained in past share prices: In other words, it helps to keep the market efficient in the _____ form.'

**3.** Which of the following statements (if any) are true? The efficient-market hypothesis assumes:
   a. That there are no taxes.
   b. That there is perfect foresight.
   c. That successive price changes are independent.
   d. That investors are irrational.
   e. That there are no transaction costs.
   f. That forecasts are unbiased.

**4.** The shares of United Boot are priced at $400 and offer a dividend yield of 2 per cent. The company has a 2-for-1 share split.
   a. Other things being equal, what would you expect to happen to the share price?
   b. In practice would you expect the share price to fall by more or less than this amount?
   c. Suppose a few months later United Boot announces a rise in dividends that is exactly in line with that of other companies. Would you expect the announcement to lead to a slight abnormal rise in the share price, a slight abnormal fall or no change?

**5.** True or false?
   a. Financing decisions are less easily reversed than investment decisions.
   b. Financing decisions do not affect the total size of the cash flows; they just affect who receives the flows.
   c. Tests have shown that there is almost perfect negative correlation between successive price changes.
   d. The semistrong form of the efficient-market hypothesis states that prices reflect all publicly available information.
   e. In efficient markets the expected return on each share is the same.
   f. Myron Scholes' study of the effect of secondary distributions provided evidence that the demand schedule for a single company's shares is highly elastic.

**6.** Analysis of 60 monthly rates of return on United Futon ordinary shares indicates $\beta = 1.45$ and $\alpha = -0.2$ per cent per month. A month later, the market is up by 5 per cent and United Futon is up by 6 per cent. What is Futon's abnormal rate of return?

**7.** True or false?
   a. Fundamental analysis by security analysts and investors helps keep markets efficient.
   b. Technical analysis concentrates on the covariances among security returns. Technical trading rules attempt to make money by purchasing shares with low covariances.
   c. If the efficient-market hypothesis is correct, managers will not be able to increase share prices by 'creative accounting', which boosts reported earnings.
   d. Research on share splits shows a strong tendency for the share price to rise before the split is announced. This evidence supports the semistrong and strong forms of the efficient-market hypothesis.
   e. Movements of the share market are helpful in predicting future performance of the national economy.

**8.** Geothermal has just received good news. Its earnings have increased by 20 per cent from last year's value. Most investors are anticipating an increase of 25 per cent. Will Geothermal's share price increase or decrease when the announcement is made?

## QUESTIONS AND PROBLEMS

**1.** How would you respond to the following comments?
   a. 'Efficient market, my eye! I know of lots of investors who do crazy things.'
   b. 'Efficient market? Balderdash! I know at least a dozen people who have made a bundle in the share market.'
   c. 'The trouble with the efficient-market theory is that it ignores investors' psychology.'
   d. 'Despite all the limitations, the best guide to a company's value is its written-down book value. It is much more stable than market value, which depends on temporary fashions.'

**2.** Respond to the following comments:
   a. 'The random walk theory with its implication that investing in shares is like playing roulette is a powerful indictment of our capital markets.'
   b. 'If everyone believes you can make money by charting share prices, then price changes will not be random.'
   c. 'The random walk theory implies that events are random but many events are not random—if there is drought today, there is a fair bet that the drought will continue tomorrow.'

**3.** Which of the following observations *appear* to indicate market inefficiency? Explain whether the inefficiency is weak, semistrong or strong. (*Note:* If the market is not weak-form-efficient, it is said to be *weak-form-inefficient*; if it is not semistrong-form-efficient, it is *semistrong-form-inefficient*, and so on.)
   a. Securities with tax concessions offer lower pre-tax returns than taxable government bonds.
   b. Managers make superior returns on their purchases of their company's share.
   c. There is a positive relationship between the return on the market in one quarter and the change in aggregate corporate profits in the next quarter.
   d. There is disputed evidence that shares which have appreciated unusually in the recent past continue to do so in the future.
   e. The shares of an acquired firm tend to appreciate in the period before the merger announcement.
   f. Shares of companies with unexpectedly high earnings *appear* to offer high returns for several months after the earnings announcement.
   g. Very risky shares on the average give higher returns than safe shares.

**4.** Look again at Figure 13.4.
   a. Is the steady rise in the share price before the split evidence of market inefficiency?
   b. How do you think those shares performed that did *not* increase their dividends by an above-average amount?

**5.** Share splits and bonus issues are important because they convey information. Can you suggest some other financial decisions that convey information?

**6.** Estimate the *abnormal* return in each of the past three months for a share of your choice.

**7.** Between April 1985 and April 1990 Rankenstein Laboratories' beta was $\beta = 1.02$. Rankenstein's alpha was $\alpha = -1.52$, reflecting sharp declines in Rankenstein's shares on news of a lightning strike in the R&D laboratories. Suppose in a later month the share market falls by 5 per cent and Rankenstein shares by 6 per cent.

a. What is Rankenstein's abnormal return for that month?

b. What is Rankenstein's abnormal return compared to a predicted return based on the capital asset pricing model? The risk-free rate of interest and the market risk premium are both 8 per cent per year.

c. Which measure of abnormal returns is more sensible in this case? (*Hint:* In an efficient market would you *forecast* $\alpha = -1.52$, looking forward from 1990?)

**8.** It is sometimes suggested that low price-earnings shares are generally underpriced. Describe a possible test of this view. Be as precise as possible.

**9.** 'If a project provides an unusually high rate of return in one year, it will probably do so again in the next year.' Does this statement make sense if you use the definition of economic rate of return that we gave in Chapter 12?

**10.** 'Long-term interest rates are at record highs. Most companies therefore find it cheaper to finance with shares or relatively inexpensive short-term bank loans.' Discuss.

**11.** 'If the efficient-market hypothesis is true, then it makes no difference what securities a company issues. All are fairly priced.' Does this follow?

**12.** 'If the efficient-market hypothesis is true, the pension fund manager might as well select a portfolio with a pin.' Explain why this is not so.

**13.** Bond dealers buy and sell bonds at very low spreads. In other words, they are willing to sell at a price only slightly higher than the price at which they buy. Used-car dealers buy and sell cars at very wide spreads. What has this got to do with the strong form of the efficient-market hypothesis?

**14.** In May 1987 Citicorp announced that it was bolstering its loan loss reserves by $3 billion in order to reflect its exposure to Third World borrowers. Consequently, second quarter earnings were transformed from a $0.5 billion profit to a $2.5 billion loss.

In after-hours trading the price of Citicorp shares fell sharply from their closing level of $50, but the next day when the market had had a chance to digest the news, the price recovered to $53. Other bank shares fared less well and *The Wall Street Journal* reported that Citicorp's decision 'triggered a big sell-off of international banking shares that roiled share markets around the world'.

Comment on the Citicorp action varied. The bank's chairman claimed that 'it significantly strengthens the institution' and analysts and bankers suggested that it was a notable step towards realism. For example, one argued that it was the recognition of the problem that made the difference, while another observed that the action 'is merely recognising what the share market has been saying for several months: that the value of the sovereign debt of the big US money centre banks is between 25 per cent and 50 per cent less than is carried in their books'. The London *Financial Times* made the more cautionary comment that Citicorp had 'simply rearranged its balance sheet, not strengthened its capital base' and one columnist described the move as an 'outsize piece of cosmetic self-indulgence rather than a great stride towards the reconstruction of Third World debt'. A lead article in one paper stated that 'even if all this means that Citicorp shareholders are $3 billion poorer today, the group as a whole is better placed to absorb whatever shocks lie ahead'.

There was also considerable discussion of the implications for other banks. As one analyst summed up, 'There's no question that the market will put higher confidence in those institutions that can reserve more fully.'

Discuss the general reaction to the Citicorp announcement. It is not often that a company announces a $2.5 billion loss in one quarter and its share price rises. Do you think that the share price reaction was consistent with an efficient market?

**15.** About two decades ago the reporting practices of Australian banks were changed so that the banks disclosed their hidden reserves. At the time of these disclosures the banks' share prices moved up. A student of one of the authors queried the price movement as follows: 'Everyone knew that the banks had hidden reserves, so if markets are efficient why have bank share prices increased?' Can you answer his query?

**16.** Refer to Figure 13.2 and identify the line that charts actual performance of the market index. Two corporate treasurers, Alpha and Beta, are contemplating this chart. Each needs to make an issue of shares at some time in the coming year.

Alpha: 'My company's going to issue right away. The stock market cycle is obviously close to topping out, and the next move is almost certainly down. Better to issue now and get a decent price for the shares.'

Beta: 'You're too nervous—we're waiting. The chart clearly shows a strong upward trend.'

What would you say to Alpha and Beta?

**17.** We suggested three possible interpretations of the small-firm effect—a required return for an unidentified risk factor, a coincidence or market inefficiency. Write three brief memos arguing each point of view.

**18.** 'It may be true that in an efficient market there *should* be no patterns in share prices, but if everyone believes they *do* exist, then this belief will be self-fulfilling.' Discuss.

**19.** Look at Table 13.3, which shows monthly returns on the market and for two shares. Both shares announced dividend increases in this period—Executive Cheese in April 1993 and Paddington Beer in July 1994. Calculate the average abnormal return of the two shares during the months when the dividend increase was announced.

**20.** Look at Table 13.2. Which of the predictions about the direction of the market movements is consistent with a belief in market efficiency?

**21.** If markets are really efficient then there is no profit to be made from security analysis. In that case such analysis cannot recover costs and so should not take place. But, if no security analysis took place then we would expect markets to be much less efficient. Discuss this paradox.

table 13.3 _____

| | (a)<br>Market<br>return | (b)<br>Executive<br>Cheese return | (c)<br>Paddington<br>Beer return |
|---|---|---|---|
| 1993: | | | |
| January | 0.7% | 4.6% | 4.4% |
| February | 1.4 | 10.5 | 2.3 |
| March | 2.2 | 8.8 | −5.6 |
| April | −2.5 | 13.5 | −12.5 |
| May | 2.7 | 15.3 | −4.5 |
| June | 0.3 | 0.1 | 0.8 |
| July | −0.5 | −1.2 | 2.6 |
| August | 3.8 | −2.4 | 7.7 |
| September | −0.7 | −12.7 | 5.4 |
| October | 2.0 | 3.5 | 12.9 |
| November | −0.9 | −14.5 | 10.1 |
| December | 1.2 | −19.2 | 12.7 |
| 1994: | | | |
| January | 3.4 | 12.0 | 9.8 |
| February | −2.7 | 10.8 | −8.1 |
| March | −4.4 | −15.9 | −0.8 |
| April | 1.3 | 0.0 | 14.5 |
| May | 1.6 | 13.8 | −0.4 |
| June | −2.5 | 12.3 | −9.2 |
| July | 3.3 | −8.4 | 14.5 |
| August | 4.1 | 4.6 | −0.1 |
| September | −2.4 | −4.9 | −4.5 |
| October | 2.3 | 9.3 | −5.5 |
| November | −3.7 | −4.1 | −2.0 |
| December | 1.5 | −10.7 | 8.9 |

# chapter 14

# AN OVERVIEW OF SOURCES OF CORPORATE FINANCING

This chapter begins our analysis of long-term financing decisions—a task we will not complete until Chapter 26. We will devote considerable space in these chapters to the classic finance problems of dividend policy and the use of debt versus equity financing. Yet to concentrate on these problems alone would miss the enormous *variety* of financing instruments that are used by companies today.

Generally, most securities issued by companies can be classified as either debt or equity securities. They differ in three primary ways:

1. Equity securities offer part ownership of the company to their shareholders, while debt securities only provide loan capital with no associated claim to ownership.

2. Holders of equity securities obtain their return from holding equity through capital appreciation (depreciation) caused by share price rises (falls) and through the receipt of dividends if they are distributed by the company from profits. In contrast, debtholders receive both interest and repayment of the principal amount of any monies on loan.

3. In the case of liquidation, debtholders have senior claims to the company's assets over equity holders.

For example, look at Table 14.1. It shows some of the many debt securities issued and used by Amcor Ltd.[1] The company has also issued ordinary shares to its shareholders. As at June

---

[1] As reported in Amcor Ltd Annual Report, 1998.

1998 Amcor had over $485 million in short-term debt and over $1588 million from banks and other lenders. It also had in excess of $426 million in undated subordinated convertible securities, which allow the conversions of debt to equity.

In 1998 the consolidated entity of Amcor had available a bank overdraft (both secured and unsecured) to a maximum of $80.2 million. Amcor also had bank bill facilities totalling $25.2 million, with expiry dates extending to November 1998;[2] a promissory note facility of $600 million, maturing in February 2001;[3] US$100 million drawn under a $550 million multi-currency facility, maturing in June 2000; a $150 million fully drawn advance maturing in 2004; $361.8 million drawn under a £225 syndicated multi-currency facility maturing in June 2002; and $13.3 million in term loans with scheduled repayments to 2009. In addition, the company had lease liabilities to the value of $29.4 million and US dollar debt totalling $312.0 million.[4] The company also reported that it had a policy to hedge all material foreign exchange transactions using forward foreign exchange contracts, and manage interest rate exposures by entering interest rate swaps and through the use of interest rate options.

At this stage you may not know what 'swaps', 'options', 'bank acceptance bills', 'promissory note facilities', 'a euronote facility', 'convertible notes' or 'ordinary shares' are. Relax—we will tell you in this chapter. Than we will go on to discuss a series of questions chosen to put corporate financing in perspective. Do companies rely too heavily on internal financing rather than new issues of debt or equity? Are debt ratios of Australian corporations dangerously high?

This chapter is an introductory survey of financing alternatives. It touches on many topics to be explored more carefully later in the book. But later in this chapter we will come to an extremely important general issue, the problem of corporate control or governance, and the agency costs incurred when control is imperfect. We close the chapter by comparing the systems of corporate control known as corporate governance in Australia with those of the United States, Germany and Japan.

## 14.1  Ordinary shares

In Chapter 15 we will deal in some detail with the manner in which firms issue shares and with the different types of shares that can be issued. For now we will focus on the most common type of equity on issue in the Australian share market. To give you some idea of the size of this market, in the 12 months to December 1996 there were in excess of 6.1 million transactions involving over 92 million shares that were traded on the Australian Stock Exchange.[5] New shares were issued during 1997 in a variety of manners with a total value in excess of $18.2 million. Major new share issues in 1997 included the floating of Colonial Ltd ($350 million), Stadium Australian Group ($365 million) and Telstra Corporation ($8578 million). Not all issues of shares were for newly listed companies—for example, Pasminco Ltd issued $500 million in new shares under a rights issue.[6]

The directors of a company have a number of choices when issuing shares—they can issue either ordinary or preference shares.[7] Obviously, if the price of the share at the time of issue is set too high, then the issue may be undersubscribed.

---

2    As at 30 June 1998, there were no bank accepted bills.

3    As at 30 June 1998, $555 million was outstanding under the facility.

4    Comprising US$125 million Sunclipse Inc. notes with a coupon of 6.75 per cent due 2003 and US$75 million Twinpak Inc. notes with a coupon of 6.375 per cent, due 2000.

5    Transactions totalled $231 billion. See the Australian Stock Exchange, *1998 Fact Book*, Australian Stock Exchange Ltd, Sydney, 1998.

6    We will have more to say about different types of share issues in Chapter 15.

7    To be discussed in Section 14.3.

**table 14.1** _____

Large firms typically issue many different securities. This table shows some of the debt securities on Amcor Ltd's balance sheet at 30 June 1998.

Bank overdraft facilities (both secured and unsecured)

Bill acceptance facilities

Promissory note facility

Eurocommercial paper/medium-term note program

Transferable loan certificate/euronote facility

American commercial paper program

Mortgage loans (secured)

Bank loans

Industrial revenue bonds supported by bank letters of credit

Loans from associated companies

US$ notes

Undated subordinated convertible securities

Leases

_Source_: Amcor Ltd Annual Report, 1998.

When issuing shares, companies invite applications from the public via a prospectus, or offer shares to existing shareholders via rights issues, bonus issues, dividend reinvestment schemes and employee shareholder plans, or place the shares via private placement with specified shareholders. It is also possible to issue convertible securities whereby debt securities subsequently are converted to equity. Shares can be issued payable in full at the time of application, by paying a deposit at the time of application and subsequently paying the remainder on allotment of shares, or by part payment at the time of application or allotment and subsequently either at call or by instalments.

In Australia, the total amount outstanding in equity capital at 30 June 1997[8] was $744.1 billion, of which $427.0 billion was issued by private trading corporate enterprises, $91.8 billion by banks and $128.3 by Commonwealth, state and local government public trading enterprises. The primary holders of this equity capital were life offices and superannuation funds (19.11 per cent), households and unincorporated businesses (19.15 per cent) and shareholders residing outside Australia (28.76 per cent).

But what is an ordinary share? Let us not get too technical or legalistic,[9] but essentially the holder of a share gets a set of rights and obligations to a specified amount of the cash flows generated by the business from its trading activities and at the time of winding up. Ordinary shares also confer a number of rights while the company is a going concern, including the ability to vote on key matters concerning the firm such as election of the board of directors, authorisation to issue new capital and granting of permission for corporate mergers.

Prior to the introduction of the _Company Law Review Act 1998_ on 1 July 1998, a company's memorandum of association set out the total amount of share capital and nominated the number and type of shares that could be issued by each company at a fixed amount known as par value. The amount of total share capital was previously known as 'authorised', 'nominal'

_____

8   Australian Bureau of Statistics, _Financial Accounts_, Cat. No. 5232.0, ABS, Canberra, September 1998, Table 35 'The Equities Market'.

9   Ordinary shares are defined in the Corporations Law, s. 9.

or 'registered' capital. The total amount of authorised capital did not have to be issued.[10] Since July 1998, companies no longer have a limit on the number of shares that can be issued or a requirement to state a par value for shares.[11] Since July 1998, companies can now have either replacement rules or a constitution, or some combination of both, which assists in the simplification of both the formation of companies and increases the uniformity of the internal operation of companies. A company can now issue more shares by a resolution passed at a general meeting.[12] Ordinary shares can be issued as fully paid, contributing or partly paid shares.[13] At the time of their issue, fully paid shares are paid for in full by those purchasing the shares. In the case of contributing shares, only a portion of the nominated issue price is paid with the balance on call at a specified future date, at the company's discretion, or at the time of insolvency. In Australia, as at June 1998 less than 20 companies had contributing shares on issue (such as Linden & Conway Ltd, which had $1.80 unpaid on some of its $2.00 shares).

## Shareholders' rights

Ordinary shareholders are the owners of the business. They hold the *equity interest* or *residual claim*, since they receive whatever assets or earnings are left over in the business after all its debts are paid. They have *limited liability*: the most shareholders can lose, if their company goes bust, is their investment in the shares. None of the shareholders' other assets is exposed to the company's troubles.

Under the Corporations Law (s. 209) every company is required to maintain a register of its shareholders. The register must contain details about shareholders, including:

■ Names and addresses of shareholders.
■ The number of shares held by each shareholder.
■ The identification number of each share held by each shareholder.
■ The number of share certificates on issue.
■ The amount that has been paid for each share or, in the case of partly paid shares, the amount agreed to be paid.
■ The date the shareholder entered the register.
■ The date the shareholder ceased to own shares in the company.

The share register takes on significant legal importance. Why? Because the ordinary shareholders are the owners of the company. They therefore have a general *pre-emptive right* to anything of value that the company may wish to distribute. They also have the ultimate control of the company's affairs. In practice, this control is limited to a right to vote, either in person or by proxy, on appointments to the board of directors and a number of other matters.

If the company's constitution specifies a *majority voting* system, each director is voted on separately and shareholders can cast one vote for each share that they own. If the articles permit *cumulative voting*, the directors are voted on jointly and the shareholders can, if they want, allot all their votes to just one candidate.[14] Cumulative voting makes it easier for a

---

[10] Prior to July 1998, the firm's memorandum of association and its articles of association were its primary legal documents. Each firm had its own documents, leading to substantively different documentation between firms.

[11] Following the introduction of the amendments, if 100 members or markets holding 5 per cent of votes served a notice on the company, the company was required to include a new provision in the company constitution that prevented it from issuing more shares than it was permitted to at 1 July 1998.

[12] Within one month of issuing the shares, the company must advise the Australian Securities and Investment Commission on: the number of shares issued; the amount to be paid for each share; unpaid amounts on any of the shares; the class or type of shares issued; and whether any shares were issued for non-cash consideration.

[13] In Australia, very few shares are issued as contributing shares. For discussion of the issues associated with their valuation see R. Brown and N. Hathaway, 'Valuing Contributing Shares', *Accounting and Finance*, **31** (2): 53–68 (1991).

[14] For example, suppose there are five directors to be elected and you own 1000 shares. You therefore have a total of $5 \times 1000 = 5000$ votes. Under the majority voting system, you can cast a maximum of 1000 votes for any one candidate. Under a cumulative voting system, you can cast all 5000 votes for your favourite candidate.

minority group among the shareholders to elect directors representing the group's interests. That is why minority groups devote so much of their efforts to campaigning for cumulative voting.

On many issues a simple majority of votes cast is sufficient to carry the day, but the company constitution will specify some decisions that require a supermajority of, say, 75 per cent of those eligible to vote. For example, a supermajority vote is sometimes needed to approve a merger. This requirement makes it difficult for the firm to be taken over and therefore helps to protect the incumbent management.

The issues on which shareholders are asked to vote are rarely contested, particularly in the case of large, publicly traded firms. Occasionally there are *proxy contests* in which the firm's existing management and directors compete with outsiders for control of the corporation. But the odds are stacked against the outsiders, for the insiders can get the firm to pay all the costs of presenting their case and obtaining votes.

Ordinary shares are, of course, issued by companies. But a few equity securities are issued by trustee companies. For example, in Australia it is also possible to invest in equity and property trusts. These trusts pool funds from a range of investors who invest in the trust via a prospectus. The trust then buys and sells shares in listed companies or properties that are managed by a property management company under the watchful eye of a trustee. Australian companies in this category include Colonial Industrial Property Trust, Colonial Retail Property Trust, Tasmanian Trustees and Westfield America Trust.

## 14.2 A first look at debt

When they borrow money, companies promise to make regular interest payments and repay the principal (i.e. the original amount borrowed) according to an agreed schedule. However, this liability is limited. Shareholders have the right to default on any debt obligation if they are willing to hand over the corporation's assets to the lenders. Clearly, they will choose to do this only if the value of the assets is less than the amount of the debt. In practice, this handover of assets is far from straightforward. Sometimes there may be hundreds of lenders with different claims on the firm.

Because lenders are not regarded as proprietors of the firm, they do not normally have any voting power. The company's payments of interest are regarded as a cost and are deducted from taxable income. Thus, interest is paid from *before-tax* income. In contrast, dividends on ordinary shares are paid out of *after-tax* income. Therefore, the government provides a tax subsidy on the use of debt, which it does not provide on equity. We will have more to say about taxes, including dividend imputation, in Chapter 18.

For many companies, debt finance is a more significant source of operating funds than equity finance. During the 1980s, due to the ease of raising debt and accessing further loans, many Australian corporations used debt finance for corporate expansion activity. As noted by Berns and Baron:[15]

> *Reliance upon debt rather than equity as a source of finance had a further attraction in the content of the entrepreneurship that flourished at this time. Whereas reliance upon equity finance tends to dilute control and thus to reduce the power of the individual entrepreneur, debt finance avoids this.*

From Table 14.2 it is obvious that the primary sources of debt finance for Australian companies involve the use of bills of exchange and bank loans. Bills of exchange are discussed in detail in Chapter 32. Loans are discussed in Chapter 24 and include borrowings that do not

---

[15]   S. Berns and P. Baron, *Company Law and Governance: An Australian Perspective*, Oxford University Press, Melbourne, 1998, p. 293.

**table 14.2**

Composition of the total amount of debt and equity outstanding by private corporate trading enterprises, 1991 to 1997 ($billion).

| Year | Loans | Long-term debt securities | Bills of exchange | Promissory notes | Equity market |
|---|---|---|---|---|---|
| 1991–92 | 161.4 | 13.2 | 49.2 | 14.9 | 235.8 |
| 1992–93 | 157.5 | 12.8 | 45.7 | 14.9 | 259.4 |
| 1993–94 | 153.5 | 11.1 | 46.9 | 9.7 | 321.5 |
| 1994–95 | 161.9 | 11.4 | 45.4 | 10.2 | 330.5 |
| 1995–96 | 179.8 | 16.6 | 52.8 | 13.6 | 372.4 |
| 1996–97 | 191.0 | 21.4 | 52.3 | 15.1 | 427.0 |

Source: Australian Bureau of Statistics, op. cit., Footnote 8, Tables 29, 30, 31, 34 and 35.

involve the issue of a debt security, and bank overdrafts, bank loans (secured and unsecured) and lease arrangements.[16]

In 1999 the Reserve Bank of Australia reported[17] that, although bank bills and certificates of deposit were still the major forms of short-term debt corporate finance in Australia, the use of promissory notes had increased by over 70 per cent since 1995 due to the Bank's encouragement of firms to issue paper in their own corporate name. The Reserve Bank attributed this shift to Australian banks attempting to decrease their exposure to bank capital charges[18] through direct lending to corporates. In the long-term debt market, the Reserve Bank identified that asset backed or securitised bonds and corporate bonds had increased since the early 1990s. This was attributed to positive prospects for Australian business, an increased demand for longer dated securities from the funds management area and a decrease in the supply of government debt. Table 14.3 shows the growth in short-term and long-term debt from December 1995 to December 1998:

**table 14.3**

The growth in short-term and long-term debt, December 1995–December 1998 ($billion).

| | December 1995 | December 1998 |
|---|---|---|
| Money market (short-term debt) | | |
| Bank bills and certificates of deposit | 96 | 132 |
| Promissory notes | 22 | 38 |
| Treasury notes | 17 | 11 |
| Bond market (long-term debt) | | |
| Commonwealth bonds | 90 | 80 |
| State government bonds | 43 | 40 |
| Corporate bonds | 10 | 20 |
| Asset backed bonds | 7 | 19 |

Source: Adapted from Reserve Bank of Australia, op. cit., Footnote 17, Table 1.

---

[16]  Leases are discussed in Chapter 26.

[17]  See Reserve Bank of Australia, 'Australian Financial Markets', *Reserve Bank of Australia Bulletin*, March 1999, pp. 1–12.

[18]  Australian banks are required under capital adequacy rules to risk-weight all loans and hold capital consistent with the risk-weighting.

# Debt comes in many forms

Some orderly scheme of classification is essential to cope with the almost infinite variety of corporate debt claims. We will spend several chapters in Part Seven examining the various features of debt. But here is a preliminary guide to the major distinguishing characteristics.

**Maturity**     *Long-term debt* is any obligation repayable more than one year from the date of issue. Debt due in less than one year is termed *short-term debt* and is carried on the balance sheet as a current liability. The most common short-term commercial debt security in Australia is the bill of exchange. Some large creditworthy companies also issue promissory notes. Usually companies back up their commercial security issues with a bank. That is, the bank agrees to lend money to repay the bill if some crisis or setback prevents the company from repaying or refinancing the bill directly. This agreement may be struck between the company and its bank to accept bills up to a threshold level, say $50 million, over a window of time, say 12 months, at which time the arrangement is reviewed. Of course, such facilities are not used just for bills. Financial managers arrange lines of credit to cover all kinds of seasonal or unexpected cash needs. Rather than renegotiate the term of borrowing at the maturity of each bill at promissory rate, companies set up a 'facility' with institutions which allows them to draw down or roll over amounts up to a set limit as their commercial needs arise. We will have more to say about this topic in Chapter 32.

**Repayment provision**     Long-term loans are commonly repaid in a steady, regular way, perhaps after an initial grace period. In Australia, most companies use bank and lease finance as opposed to the issuing of corporate bonds. However, from time to time for particular projects some firms will issue either foreign bonds or europroducts, which may require alternative repayment provisions in terms of both the timing and amount of any repayments. Discussion of these products can be found in Chapter 34.

**Seniority**     Some debt instruments are **subordinated**. In the event of default the subordinated lender gets in line behind the firm's general creditors. The subordinated lender holds a junior claim and is paid after all senior creditors are satisfied. When you lend money to a firm, you can assume that you hold a senior claim unless the debt agreement says otherwise. However, this does not always put you at the front of the line, for the firm may have set aside some of its assets specifically for the protection of other creditors. That brings us to our next classification.

**Security or collateral**     In establishing the terms of any debt agreement it is necessary to identify whether the raising of the debt will be on a secured or unsecured basis. If the debt is secured then this usually involves the mortgage[19] or issuing of a charge[20] against property or assets held by the corporation. In the event of default, the holders of secured loans have first claim on the mortgaged assets; investors holding unsecured debt have a general claim on the unmortgaged assets but only a subordinated claim on the mortgaged assets. An asset pledged to ensure payment of a debt security or loan is called **collateral**. Thus, a retailer might offer inventory or accounts receivable as collateral to obtain a short-term bank loan. If you start a small business and go to a bank for financing, the bank may ask you to put up your home as collateral until the business accumulates enough assets and earning power to support the loan on its own.

**Default risk**     Seniority and security do not guarantee payment. A bond can be senior and secured, but still can be as risky as a vertiginous tightrope walker—it depends on the value and risk of the issuing firm's assets. A debt security is **investment-grade** if it qualifies for one of the

---

[19]  When a mortgage is used as security the mortgage deed is transferred from the debtor to the creditor under the condition that the mortgage deed will be returned on the repayment of the debt.

[20]  The term charge is used to represent a transfer of rights with respect to the property that will be exercised only under certain specified conditions (usually called covenants). There is no direct interest in the property under charge as is the case with a mortgage.

top four ratings from the Moody's or Standard & Poor's rating services. (We describe the rating criteria in Chapter 23.) Other ratings are regarded as speculative grade.

**Public versus privately placed debt**    From time to time firms will issue debt instruments such as short-term notes, certificates or bonds. A *public issue* of debt is offered to anyone who wants to buy, and once issued, it can be freely traded by Australian and foreign investors in the secondary market for debt securities. In a private placement the issue is sold directly to a small number of qualified lenders, including banks, insurance companies and pension finds. The securities cannot be resold to individuals, only to qualified institutional investors. However, there is increasingly active trading *among* these investors. Companies in Australia along with those in Germany, Japan or France generally borrow directly from banks or other financial institutions. Bank debt is by definition privately placed. However many large American corporations look mostly to the public market for debt financing.

**Floating versus fixed rates**    Loan agreements negotiated with banks usually incorporate a **floating rate**. For example, your firm may be offered a loan at '1 per cent above prime'. The **prime rate**, or *indicator rate*, a benchmark interest rate charged by banks to creditworthy corporate customers, is adjusted up or down as interest rates on traded securities change.[21] Therefore, when the prime rate changes the interest on your floating-rate loan also changes. The prime rate is set with reference to short-term money market rates, which are very sensitive to changes in rates on cash deposits. In relation to *fixed rates*, lending rates are set with reference to securities available on similar terms in long-term capital markets. In relation to money market securities, floating-rate instruments have their payments linked to BBSW (the bank bill swap rate), which is an average interest rate available generally for maturities out to five years. Another common base is **LIBOR** (London interbank offered rate), which is the interest rate at which major international banks in London lend dollars to each other.

**Country and currency**    Many large firms in Australia, particularly those having significant overseas operations, borrow abroad. If such a firm wants long-term debt, it will probably borrow by an issue of **eurobonds** sold simultaneously in several countries; if it wants unfunded debt, it will probably obtain a *eurodollar loan* from a bank. Corporations in Australia sometimes issue notes or bonds denominated in foreign currencies. Often, foreign subsidiaries of Australian companies borrow directly from banks in the countries in which the subsidiaries are operating.[22] Cross-currency borrowing also occurs the other way around— that is, foreign corporations offer debt denominated in Australian dollars in Australia.

**A debt by any other name**    The word *debt* sounds straightforward, but companies enter into a number of financial arrangements that look suspiciously like debt but are treated differently in accounts. Some of these obligations are easily identifiable. For example, accounts payable are simply obligations to pay for goods that have already been delivered. Other arrangements are not so easily detected. For example, instead of borrowing money to buy equipment, many companies **lease** or rent it on a long-term basis. As we will show in Chapter 26, such arrangements are economically equivalent to secured long-term debt.

## 14.3 Preference shares

In the chapters that follow we shall have much more to say about ordinary shares and debt. **Preference shares**, on the other hand, account for only a small part of new issues, and so they

---

21   'Prime' can be misleading, because the *most* creditworthy corporations—large, blue-chip companies—can negotiate bank loans at interest rates *below* prime.

22   In such cases the parent company may get the added benefit of knowing that its foreign subsidiary is also being watched over by a bank that is familiar with local conditions.

will occupy less time later on. However, we shall see that they are a useful method of financing in mergers and certain other special situations.

Preference shares are legally an equity security but they display characteristics that are similar to debt securities. Despite the fact that they are a fixed rate dividend (like a fixed rate of interest on debt), payment of the dividend is almost invariably within the complete discretion of the directors. The only stipulation is that no dividends be paid on the ordinary shares until the preference share dividend has been paid. For some older issues, the firm could pay ordinary share dividends *without* making up preference share dividends that had been skipped in previous years. This gave an opportunity for considerable abuse. Therefore, almost all new issues specifically provide that the obligation should be cumulative, so the firm must pay *all* past preference share dividends as soon as circumstances allow before ordinary shareholders get a cent. In Australia, preference shares are usually issued on either a cumulative or non-cumulative basis.

Like ordinary shares, preference shares do not have a final repayment date. However, roughly half the issues make some provision for periodic retirement, and in many cases companies have an option to repurchase or call preference shares at a specified price. Such issues are called 'redeemable' in that they have a fixed maturity date. If the company goes out of business, the claim of the preference shares is junior to any debt but senior to ordinary shares. Australian preference shares are issued as either redeemable or non-redeemable.

Preference shares typically do not confer any voting privileges except in special class meetings. However, almost always the consent of two-thirds of the preference shareholders in a special class meeting must be obtained on all matters affecting the seniority of their claim. Most issues also provide the holder with some voting power if the dividend is skipped.

Unlike interest payments on debt, the preference share dividend is not an allowable deduction from taxable corporate income. Thus, the dividend is paid from after-tax income. For most industrial firms this is a serious deterrent to issuing preference shares.

# 14.4 Convertible securities

Corporations often issue securities with terms that can be altered subsequently at the option of the firm, the holder of the security, or both. A **convertible** note, bond or preference share gives its owner the option to exchange the bond or preference share for a predetermined number of ordinary shares. The convertible security holder hopes that the issuing company's share price will zoom up so that the bond can be converted for a big profit. But if the share price zooms down, there is no obligation to convert. A convertible is therefore like a package of a corporate bond and an option. There is, however, one principal difference. When the owners of a convertible wish to exercise their option to buy ordinary shares, they do not pay cash— they just give up the bond. The features that distinguish convertible notes or bonds from other bonds include:

- The ratio at which the convertible notes or bonds can be converted to ordinary shares is known as the conversion ratio. This can be expressed as the number of ordinary shares that will be exchanged or, alternatively, the conversion price at which the exchange will occur.
- The issuer usually sets a window of time during which conversion may occur. This is referred to as the conversion period.
- The contingent nature of convertible securities implies that they result in a dilution of shareholders' equity.

Chapter 22 will include a detailed discussion of convertible securities and their pricing. We will also see in Chapter 20 that *all* corporate securities can be analysed in terms of options. In fact, once you read that chapter and learn how to analyse options, you will find that they are all around you.

## 14.5 Variety is the very spice of life

We have indicated several dimensions along which corporate securities can be classified. The financial manager has at least that many alternatives in designing corporate securities. As long as you can convince investors of its attractions, you can issue a convertible, subordinated, floating-rate note denominated in any currency you choose to pick. Rather than combining features of existing securities, you may create an entirely new one. We can imagine a coal mining company issuing preference shares on which the dividend fluctuates with coal prices. We know of no such security, but it is perfectly legal to issue it and—who knows?—it might generate considerable interest among investors.[23] Alternatively, dividends could be paid with the issue of additional shares—as a form of dividend reinvestment.

Variety is intrinsically good. People have different tastes, levels of wealth, rates of tax, and so on. Why not offer them a choice? Of course, the problem is the expense of designing and marketing new securities. But if you can think of a new security that will appeal to investors, you may be able to issue it on especially favourable terms and thus increase the value of your company.

Financial market innovation in recent years has been unusually fast and extensive. New varieties of debt seem to appear almost daily. In addition, there has been a remarkable growth in the use of **derivatives**. These are side bets on interest rates, exchange rates, commodity prices, and so on. Firms do not issue derivatives to raise money; they buy or sell them to protect against adverse changes in various external factors. Here are five types of derivatives that have experienced rapid growth in the last decade.

**Exchange traded equity options**   An option gives the firm the right, but not the obligation, to buy or sell an asset in the future at a price that is agreed on today. We have already seen that firms sometimes issue options on their own or tacked on to other securities. But, in addition, there is a huge volume of dealing in options that are created by specialised options exchanges. Trading in share options commenced in 1976 on the Australian Options Market—this market is now known as the ASX Derivatives Market. It is now possible to buy or sell options on shares, indices, bonds, currencies and commodities on exchanges throughout the world. We describe options and their applications in Chapters 20 and 21.

**Third party warrants**   Since 1991, the Australian Stock Exchange has also traded in third party warrants. These derivative instruments are options issued by a financial institution or other approved warrant issuer over assets or instruments such as shares in a single company, several companies, an index or a commodity.[24] Warrants can be issued as either puts or calls, and usually at the time of issue have longer terms to maturity than exchange traded equity options. If the warrant is exercised, the warrant issuer is required to sell the underlying asset under call warrants, or buy the asset in the case of put warrants. Australian warrants differ from those in both the United States and Japan. In these countries the company issuing the shares also issues warrants over its own shares. Thus, if a call warrant is exercised, the company must issue more ordinary shares—hence there is a dilution effect on earnings per share. However, in Australia, the warrant issuer uses ordinary shares already on issue. There are several types of warrants[25] available to the market in Australia. In recent years, the warrant market has become a very popular market.[26]

---

23  However, our coal bond seems humdrum compared with some bonds that have been issued. For example, in 1990 the Swedish company Electrolux issued a bond whose final payment was linked to the event of an earthquake in Japan.

24  Definition adapted from the Australian Stock Exchange derivatives publication, *Understanding Warrants*, Australian Stock Exchange, Sydney, May 1997.

25  For a detailed overview of the different types of third party warrants available in the Australian market see the Australian Stock Exchange Web site: *http://www.asx.com.au/derivatives/DA12340.htm*.

26  See A. Hunter, 'Warrants Get Their Foothold on ASX', *JASSA* (*Journal of the Australian Society of Security Analysts and the Securities Institute of Australia*), September 1991, pp. 27–9; and S. Calder, 'The Time Has Come for Equity Warrants', *Stock Exchange Journal*, November 1995, pp. 12–15.

**Futures**    A futures contract is an order that you place in advance to buy or sell an asset or commodity. The price is fixed when you place the order, but you do not pay for the asset until the delivery date. Futures markets have existed for a long time in commodities such as wheat, soybeans and copper. The major development of the 1970s occurred when the futures exchanges began to trade contracts on financial assets, such as bonds, currencies and stock market indexes. Since then, the worldwide daily volume of transactions in these financial futures has grown to more than $1 trillion. In Australia, all futures trading is conducted at the Sydney Futures Exchange.

**Forwards**    Futures contracts are standardised products bought and sold on organised exchanges. A forward contract is a tailor-made futures contract that is not traded on an organised exchange. For example, firms that need to protect themselves against a change in the exchange rate usually have bought or sold forward currency through a bank. Since 1983, banks also have been prepared to enter into forward contracts to borrow or lend money. If you buy one of these forward rate agreements (FRAs), you agree to borrow in the future at a rate that is fixed today; if you sell an FRA, you agree to lend in the future at a preset rate.

**Swaps**    Suppose that you would like to swap your Australian dollar debt for yen denominated debt. In this case, you can arrange for a bank to pay you each year the dollars that are needed to service your dollar debt, and in exchange you agree to pay the bank the cost of servicing a Japanese yen loan. Such an arrangement is known as a *currency swap*. Companies also enter into *interest-rate swaps*. For example, the bank might agree to pay you each year the cost of servicing a fixed-rate loan, and in return you agree to pay the bank the cost of servicing a similar floating-rate loan.

We discuss swaps, as well as futures and forward contracts, in Chapter 25.

# Financial innovation

Developing a new financial instrument is like developing any other product. Initially, the emphasis is on creativity and experiment. Then, as the market develops, the focus switches to low-cost methods of volume production. Finally, it becomes economic to offer the customer optional extras.

For example, when swaps were invented, banks were unwilling to take one side of the swap for their own accounts. They acted solely as arrangers and looked about for another firm that was prepared to take on the other side of the bargain. No two swaps were alike, and they would take weeks to fix up. Within five years, banks were prepared to take on the risks of swaps themselves, documentation was standardised and you could arrange a swap within hours. Banks also were beginning to work on the problem of making it easy for one party to resell its side of the swap to someone else. Perhaps by the time you read this chapter, there will be a regular market for trading swaps. As swaps have become more standardised and cheaper to arrange, banks also have been able to offer extra features. For example, you can now buy a forward swap and even an option on a swap (known as a 'swaption').

What are the causes of financial innovation? One answer is taxes and regulation. In the following chapters, we shall come across a number of cases where taxes and government regulation have in effect subsidised innovation. But why do many new instruments survive long after the initial government stimulus has been removed? And why has so much innovation occurred in the last 20 years? Taxes and regulation have been around for much longer than that.

A second motive for innovation is to widen investor choice. In particular, the recent sharp fluctuations in exchange rates and interest rates have increased the demand by firms and investors for ways to hedge themselves against such hazards.

But this still cannot be the entire explanation. For example, firms have long been able to protect themselves against exchange-rate changes by buying or selling forward currency through a bank. So why are traded currency futures needed as well? The answer is that many of these new financial instruments are low-cost ways to mass-produce a particular service. These low production costs reflect improvements in telecommunications and computing which make it possible to disseminate prices and execute orders rapidly throughout the world.

## 14.6 Patterns of corporate financing

That completes our brief tour of corporate securities and derivative instruments. You may feel like the tourist in Europe who has just seen 12 cathedrals in four days. But there will be plenty of time in later chapters for reflection, detail and analysis.

In 1992 the Reserve Bank of Australia reported its findings from an extensive study of 224 Australian publicly listed firms over the period from 1973 to 1990.[27] The study investigated changes in the capital structure of the firms. The period of the study was one of significant regulatory change[28] and a period of increasing financial innovation. The study found that after remaining relatively constant throughout most of the 1970s, at between 50 and 55 per cent of total assets, the level of corporate debt relative to total assets increased substantially in the 1980s, to peak at almost 65 per cent in 1989. In the period from 1992 to 1995 this extreme level dropped back from approximately 60 per cent in 1992 to 55 per cent in 1995.[29] The major components of the total debt throughout the whole period from 1973 to 1995 were trade creditors and long-term debt. Trade creditors varied between 18 and 25 per cent through the period, while long-term debt regularly accounted for most of the balance.

Is there really a trend to heavier reliance on debt financing? This is a hard question to answer in general, because financing policy varies so much from industry to industry and firm to firm. But a few statistics will do no harm as long as you keep these difficulties in mind. The Reserve Bank extended its study by examining the corporate structure across industry groups broadly classified as mining, manufacturing, wholesale, retail and service companies. The Bank found that industry debt to asset ratios were relatively constant across the study period but were at their highest in the wholesale and service sectors. Furthermore, it found that mining and manufacturing appeared to have lower debt to asset ratios than the others. In relation to trade credit, retail and wholesale had higher ratios than service and manufacturing firms, with mining firms having the lowest. Given the production and distribution cycle for goods and services in an economy, there are not too many surprises here.

Look at Table 14.4, which shows the average balance sheet of all listed companies, industrial companies and resource-based companies trading on the Australian Stock Exchange in 1995. All figures are expressed as a percentage of total assets to facilitate comparisons between the figures. First, we note that consistent with the requirements of accounting, the total of the assets is equal to the total of equity plus liabilities. Our interest is mostly with the composition of equity and debt. Therefore, it is noted that for each of the profiles, shareholders' equity is substantively different to any individual grouping of debt. It should be noted that shareholders' equity is the largest component on each of the average balance sheets, followed by long-term debt and finally trade creditors and debt due within 12 months (money market debt). This result is consistent for each of the groupings. Comparing industrials to resource-based companies shows that equity capital is proportionally higher and long-term debt is lower for resource-based companies than for industrials. This would also be reflective of the higher risk attributed to resource companies, which may be either exploration or production based. From Table 14.4 it is also obvious that preference shares, convertible notes and overdrafts are much lower than other forms of capital expenditure.

---

27  P. Lowe and G. Shuetrim, *The Evolution of Corporate Financial Structure: 1973–1990*, Reserve Bank of Australia Research Discussion Paper Number 9216, Sydney, 1992.

28  The Australian dollar was floated and exchange controls were relaxed in December 1983, and interest rates were deregulated in 1986.

29  See Australian Stock Exchange, *Financial and Profitability Study*, Australian Stock Exchange, Sydney, 1996.

table 14.4 _____

The average balance sheet of all listed companies, industrial companies and resource-based companies trading on the Australian Stock Exchange, 1995 (%).

| | All companies | Industrial companies | Resource-based companies |
|---|---|---|---|
| Aggregate total assets ($million) | 274214.4 | 187793.0 | 86421.3 |
| **Assets:** | | | |
| Cash and liquid assets | 5.1 | 5.0 | 5.3 |
| Trade debtors | 8.2 | 9.8 | 4.8 |
| Stocks | 9.4 | 10.3 | 7.4 |
| Other current assets | 5.7 | 6.2 | 4.6 |
| Investments | 9.7 | 10.5 | 8.0 |
| Deferred assets | 14.6 | 13.6 | 16.7 |
| Net plant and property | 41.9 | 37.0 | 52.4 |
| Intangibles | 5.4 | 7.6 | 0.8 |
| **Shareholders' equity:** | | | |
| **Ordinary shareholders' equity** | **45.6** | **44.6** | **47.9** |
| Preference capital | 0.4 | 0.4 | 0.1 |
| Convertible notes | 1.6 | 1.9 | 1.0 |
| Minority interests | 3.7 | 2.5 | 6.1 |
| **Liabilities:** | | | |
| Bank overdraft | 0.5 | 0.5 | 0.6 |
| **Trade creditors** | **7.8** | **9.3** | **4.5** |
| Tax provisions | 1.3 | 1.2 | 1.4 |
| **Debt due (within one year)** | **4.2** | **5.0** | **2.4** |
| Other current liabilities | 7.5 | 8.0 | 6.6 |
| **Long-term debt** | **20.8** | **22.0** | **18.3** |
| Other deferred liabilities | 6.6 | 4.6 | 11.1 |

*Note:* Banks and finance, insurance, investment and financial services and property trusts are excluded.
*Source:* Australian Stock Exchange, op. cit., Footnote 29.

# Do firms rely too heavily on internal funds?

Not all profits obtained by companies are paid out in dividends to shareholders. Companies usually retain a portion of their earnings after interest and tax payments for future use by the firm. These funds can be used to facilitate further growth by the firm, or can be retained in reserves for future dividends or acquisitions or to cover the cost of future extraordinary items.

Some may argue that a firm that retains $1 million could have paid out the cash as dividends and then sold new ordinary shares to raise the same amount of additional capital. In the same way, any reinvestment of dollars labelled 'depreciation' amounts to investing dollars that could have been paid to investors. The opportunity cost of capital ought not to depend on whether the project is financed by depreciation, retained earnings or a new share issue.

Why, then, do managers have an apparent preference for financing by retained earnings? Some believe that managers are simply taking the line of least resistance, dodging the 'discipline of securities markets'.

But there are other reasons for relying on internally generated funds. The issue costs of new securities are avoided, for example. Moreover, the announcement of a new equity issue usually is bad news to investors, who worry that the decision to issue signals lower future profits or higher risk.[30] A firm with a shortage of internally generated cash may have to issue shares, incurring the costs of issue and sending a bad-news signal to investors, in order to fund capital investment.

## 14.7 Corporate governance in Australia, Germany and Japan

At the end of 1998, 641 575 114 fully paid ordinary shares of Amcor Ltd were issued and outstanding, with a total market capitalisation of over $4 billion. No single investor held more than 14.22 per cent of these shares. Of the 115 974 registered shareholders at Amcor Ltd as at 30 June 1998, more than 90 per cent held less than 5000 shares, and of these, directors held less than 1 per cent of the total shareholding of fully paid shares.

As shown in Table 14.5, as at 19 August 1998, the major proportion of the ownership of the firm was concentrated into the hands of only 20 shareholders, who held in excess of 50 per cent of the shares on issue.

In relation to its concentration of share ownership, Amcor is typical of most large Australian corporations. Ownership is dispersed, and there is no controlling block of shares held by managers or any single outside investor. In 1988 the median percentage ownership by chief executive officers (CEOs) of the largest public companies in the United States was less than 1 per cent, at only 0.037.[31] So there is separation of *ownership* (by many shareholders) and *control* (by professional managers).

Given this separation, it is natural to ask again[32] how managers are led to act in the owners' interests. Economists call this a *principal-agent problem*. Shareholders are the principals; managers are their agents. *Agency costs* are incurred when (1) agents depart from value-maximising decisions and (2) principals incur costs to monitor agents and influence their actions. Of course, there are no costs if the shareholders are also the managers; but separation of ownership and control is inescapable in modern economies, and some agency costs naturally follow.

As noted by Ramsay,[33] typical areas of conflict within a firm may exist between managers and directors regarding remuneration and between shareholders and directors/managers regarding issues of loyalty and effort. Conflict also exists between creditors and shareholders regarding the payment of excessive dividends, claim dilution by taking on senior debt rather than subordinated debt, asset substitution and excessive risk taking, and between employee and managers/directors/shareholders over wages and conditions of employment. Further areas

---

30  Managers do have insiders' insights and naturally are tempted to issue when share price looks good to them, that is, when they are less optimistic than outside investors. The outside investors realise this and will buy a new issue only at a discount from the pre-announcement price. More on share issues in Chapter 15.

31  This is the median ownership of CEOs of the 120 largest companies measured by market capitalisation. See M. C. Jensen and K. J. Murphy, 'CEO Incentives—It's Not How Much You Pay, But How', *Harvard Business Review*, **68**: 138–53 (May–June 1990).

32  Chapter 2 contains a preliminary discussion of corporate objectives and managers' interests.

33  I. M. Ramsay, 'The Corporate Governance Debate and the Role of Directors Duties', in *Corporate Governance and the Duties of Company Directors*, The Centre of Corporate Law and Securities Regulation, Faculty of Law, The University of Melbourne, Melbourne, 1997.

**table 14.5**

Top 20 holders of Amcor Ltd ordinary shares, as at 19 August 1998.

| Amcor's top 20 shareholders | Fully-paid ordinary shares | Percentage of total |
|---|---|---|
| Westpac Custodian Nominees Limited | 91 314 579 | 14.22 |
| National Nominees Limited | 29 999 326 | 4.67 |
| Chase Manhattan Nominees Limited | 26 652 755 | 4.15 |
| ANZ Nominees Limited | 18 554 564 | 2.89 |
| Permanent Trustee Company Limited | 16 214 263 | 2.53 |
| BT Custodial Services Pty Limited | 15 613 317 | 2.43 |
| SAS Trustee Corporation | 13 796 435 | 2.15 |
| Perpetual Trustees Nominees Limited | 13 681 237 | 2.13 |
| Queensland Investment Corporation | 13 477 037 | 2.10 |
| AMP Life Limited | 12 336 381 | 1.92 |
| Citicorp Nominees Limited | 11 079 236 | 1.73 |
| MLC Limited | 11 039 918 | 1.72 |
| Australian Foundation Investment Company Limited | 8 689 852 | 1.35 |
| NRMA Investments Pty Limited | 8 255 355 | 1.29 |
| Commonwealth Custodial Services Limited | 7 564 590 | 1.18 |
| Perpetual Trustees Australia Limited | 5 762 146 | 0.90 |
| IOOF Australia Trustees (NSW) Limited | 5 471 482 | 0.85 |
| Permanent Trustee Australia Limited | 4 904 386 | 0.76 |
| GIO Personal Investment Services Limited | 4 093 727 | 0.64 |
| Perpetual Trustee Company Limited | 3 556 154 | 0.55 |
| Total | 322 057 740 | 50.16 |

*Source*: Amcor Ltd Annual Report, 1998.

of conflict exist between individuals and institutional shareholders and between secured and unsecured creditors. Laws, institutions and business practice have evolved to mitigate these costs, though in different ways in different countries. Each major industrialised country has its own system of *corporate control* or *corporate governance*. Corporate governance is able to focus on these and related issues by applying mechanisms that seek to minimise the conflicts identified above.

Now, government is never perfect—do elected officials always do what their constituents want? Or for that matter, what they promise? A government that works reasonably well is something to be proud of. Does the Australian system of corporate governance work reasonably, or at least tolerably, well? Let us review how it operates.

A company's board of directors is elected by the shareholders and is supposed to represent the shareholders' interests. The board appoints top management and approves major investment and financing decisions. But the responsiveness of directors to shareholders' interests has been questioned. The nomination of new directors is usually made by existing directors, who include top management. These candidates are almost always approved in routine shareholder votes. Dissatisfied shareholders can propose a competing slate of candidates and launch a proxy fight,[34] in an attempt to vote them in, but this is expensive and usually unsuccessful. Thus, dissidents do not usually stand and fight but sell their shares instead.

Yet selling the shares also can send a powerful message. If enough shareholders bail out, the share price tumbles. This damages top management's reputation and compensation. Part of top managers' remuneration comes as bonuses tied to new earnings or from share options, which pay off if the share price rises but are worthless if the price falls below a stated threshold.[35] This should motivate managers to increase earnings and share price and therefore to act for shareholders. Whether the motivation is adequate in practice is controversial.[36]

But managers and directors do watch the share price, and they listen to security analysts and major institutional investors. Moreover, directors do act when the long-run health of their company is threatened.

For managers and directors who forget to act, there is always the threat of a hostile takeover. The further a company's share price falls, due to lax management or inappropriate financial policies, the easier it is for another company or group of investors to buy up a majority of the shares, take control and make the changes needed to realise the company's potential value.

Thus, in Australia the agency problems created by separation of ownership and control are offset by:

■ the right incentives for top management, particularly compensation tied to changes in earnings and share price;
■ the legal duty of managers and directors to act in shareholders' interests;
■ the threat of takeover.

The system of ownership and control in Australia is very similar to that of the United States.

Since 30 June 1996 all listed firms are required by the ASX listing rules[37] to disclose in their annual report the main corporate governance practices adopted by the organisation. A study by Ernst and Young[38] examined the disclosures of 112 listed firms and found that all firms had provided some form of corporate governance disclosure but had placed varying degrees of disclosure to issues such as executive/non-executive mix of the board, board membership criteria and appointments, procedures for seeking independent advice, compensation and remuneration, nomination and reviewing external auditors, major business risks, ethical policies and internal controls.

## Ownership and control in Germany

These principles of corporate governance do not apply worldwide. Australia, the United States, Canada, the United Kingdom and other English-speaking countries all have broadly similar systems, but other countries do not.

Germany is a good example. Figure 14.1 summarises the ownership of Daimler-Benz, one of the largest German companies, in 1990. The immediate owners were Deutsche Bank, the largest German bank, with 28 per cent; Mercedes Automobil Holding, with 25 per cent; and the Kuwait government, with 14 per cent. The remaining 32 per cent of shares were widely held by about 300 000 individual and institutional investors.

---

34 So-called because the dissident group contacts other shareholders and asks for proxies to vote their shares for the alternative slate. If enough proxies are collected, the dissidents win and through their directors take control of the company.
35 The threshold is called the *exercise price*. See Chapter 20.
36 Jensen and Murphy, op. cit., Footnote 31, argue that top managers of the largest corporations are 'paid like bureaucrats'; that is, their total compensation is not sufficiently responsive to shareholders' returns.
37 Australian Stock Exchange listing rule 4.10.3.
38 Ernst and Young, *Corporate Governance Survey: A Grade for Directors*, Corporate Governance Series, August 1997.

**figure 14.1**

Ownership of Daimler-Benz.

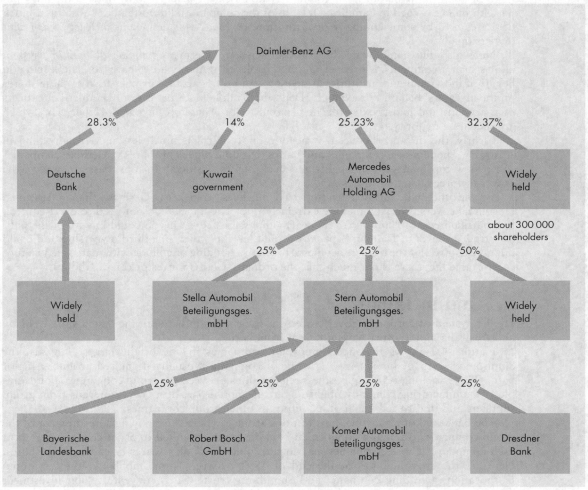

*Source:* Franks and Mayer, op. cit., Footnote 40, figures 2 and 3(a).

But this was only the top layer. Mercedes Automobil Holding was half-owned by two holding companies, 'Stella' and 'Stern' for short. The rest of its shares were widely held. Stern's shares were in turn split four ways between two banks, Robert Bosch (an industrial company) and another holding company, 'Komet'. Stella's ownership was split four ways too, but we ran out of space.[39]

The difference between German and Australian ownership patterns leaps out from Figure 14.1. Note the concentration of ownership of Daimler-Benz shares in large blocks and the several layers of owners. A similar figure for Amcor Ltd would just say, 'Amcor Ltd, 100 per cent widely held'.

---

[39] A five-layer ownership tree for Daimler-Benz is given in S. Prowse, 'Corporate Governance in an International Perspective: A Survey of Corporate Control Mechanisms Among Large Firms in the U.S., U.K., Japan and Germany', *Financial Markets, Institutions, and Instruments*, **4** (February 1995), Table 16.

In Germany, these blocks are often held by other companies—a *cross-holding* of shares—or by holding companies for families. Franks and Mayer, who examined the ownership of 171 large German companies in 1990, found 47 with blocks of shares held by other companies and 35 with blocks owned by families. Only 26 of the companies did *not* have a substantial block of shares held by some company or institution. (A block was defined as at least 25 per cent ownership.)[40]

Note also the bank ownership of Daimler-Benz. Germany's *universal banking* system allows such investments. Moreover, German banks customarily hold shares for safekeeping on behalf of individual and institutional investors and often acquire proxies to vote these shares on the investors' behalf. For example, Deutsche Bank held 28 per cent of Daimler-Benz for its own account and had proxies for 14 per cent more. Therefore, it *voted* 42 per cent, which approaches a majority.[41]

Clearly, the distance between ownership and control is much less in Germany than in Australia. The families, companies and banks that hold blocks of shares in German companies can review top management's plans and decisions as 'insiders'. In most cases they have the power to force changes if necessary.

On the other hand, outside investors have much less influence in Germany than in Australia. Hostile takeovers, for example, are extremely rare. The 'blocks' do not need to exert control, and outside investors find takeovers nearly impossible. (Even if you could buy all of the publicly traded shares of Daimler-Benz, you would have less than one-third ownership and could not take control.) If the insiders acquiesce to empire building or collude with managers in a too-comfortable life, there is not much that the ordinary German investor can do about it.

## . . . and in Japan

Japan's system of corporate governance is in some ways in between the systems of Germany and Australia and in other ways different from both.

Figure 14.2 shows the most important companies in one of the largest *kiretsus*, the Sumitomo group. A kiretsu is a network of companies, usually organised around a major bank. There are long-standing business relationships between the group companies. For example, a manufacturing company might buy a substantial part of its raw materials from group suppliers and in turn sell much of its output to other group companies.

The bank and other financial institutions at the kiretsu's centre own shares in most of the group companies (though a commercial bank in Japan is limited to 5 per cent ownership of each company). Those companies may in turn hold the bank's shares or each other's shares. Here are the cross-holdings at the end of 1991 between Sumitomo Bank; the Sumitomo Corporation, a trading company; and Sumitomo Trust, which concentrates on investment management:

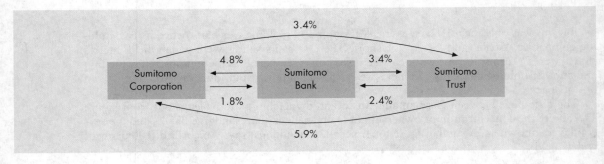

---

40  J. Franks and C. Mayer, The Ownership and Control of German Corporations, working paper, London Business School, September 1994, Table 1.

41  Franks and Mayer, op. cit., Footnote 40, Table 6.

**figure 14.2** _____

Some of the larger companies in the Sumitomo group. Over 40 smaller subsidiaries and affiliates are not shown.

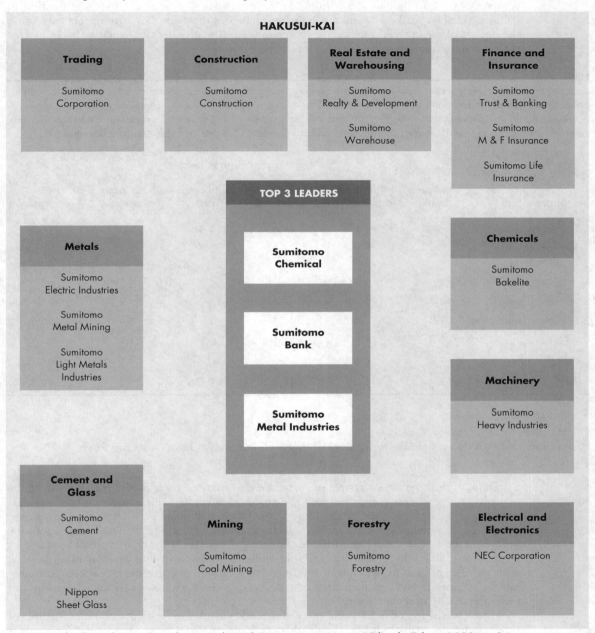

_Source_: Dodwell Marketing Consultants, _Industrial Groupings in Japan_, 10th ed., Tokyo, 1992, p. 84.

Thus, the bank owns 4.8 per cent of Sumitomo Corporation, which owns 1.8 per cent of the bank. Both own shares in Sumitomo Trust . . . and so on. Table 14.6 is a matrix of cross-holdings between these three companies and three additional ones. Although these companies' shares are publicly traded, because of the cross-holdings the supply of shares available for purchase by outside investors is much less than the total number outstanding.

The kiretsu is tied together in other ways. Most debt financing comes from the kiretsu's banks or from elsewhere in the group. (Until the mid-1980s, all but a handful of Japanese companies were forbidden access to public debt markets. By the mid-1990s, the fraction of debt provided by banks was still much greater than that in Australia.)[42] Managers may sit on the boards of directors of other group companies, and a 'presidents' council' of the CEOs of the most important group companies meets regularly.

table 14.6
_____

Cross-holdings of ordinary shares between six companies in the Sumitomo group. Read *down* the columns to see the holdings of each of the companies by the five others. Thus, 4.6 per cent of Sumitomo Chemical was owned by Sumitomo Bank, 4.4 per cent by Sumitomo Trust and 9.8 per cent by other Sumitomo companies. These figures were compiled by examining the 10 largest shareholders of each company. Smaller cross-holdings are not reflected.

| Shareholder | Percentage of shares held in: | | | | | |
| --- | --- | --- | --- | --- | --- | --- |
| | Sumitomo Bank | Sumitomo Metal Industries | Sumitomo Chemical | Sumitomo Trust | Sumitomo Corporation | NEC Corporation |
| Sumitomo Bank | — | 4.1 | 4.6 | 3.4 | 4.8 | 5.0 |
| Sumitomo Metal Industries | * | — | * | 2.5 | 2.8 | * |
| Sumitomo Chemical | * | * | — | * | * | * |
| Sumitomo Trust | 2.4 | 5.9 | 4.4 | — | 5.9 | 5.8 |
| Sumitomo Corporation | 1.8 | 1.6 | * | 3.4 | — | 2.2 |
| NEC Corporation | * | * | * | 2.9 | 3.7 | — |
| Other[†] | 9.7 | 4.8 | 9.8 | 10.4 | 9.5 | 11.6 |
| Total[†] | 13.9 | 16.4 | 18.8 | 22.6 | 26.7 | 24.6 |

*Notes:*
\* *Cross-holding does not appear in the 10 largest shareholdings.*
† *Based on the 10 largest shareholdings in 1991.*
*Source*: Compiled from Dodwell Marketing Consultants, *Industrial Groupings in Japan*, 10th ed., Tokyo, 1992.

Think of the kiretsu as a system of corporate governance, where power is split between the main bank, the largest companies and the group as a whole. This confers certain financial advantages. First, firms have access to additional 'internal' financing—internal to the group, that is. Thus, a company with capital budgets exceeding operating cash flows can turn to the main bank or other kiretsu companies for financing. This avoids the cost or possible bad-news signal of a public sale of securities. Second, when a kiretsu firm falls into financial distress, with insufficient cash to pay bills or fund necessary capital investments, a 'workout' can usually be arranged. New management can be brought in from elsewhere in the group and financing can be obtained, again 'internally'.

Hoshi, Kashyap and Scharfstein tracked capital expenditure programs of a large sample of Japanese firms—many, but not all, members of kiretsus. The kiretsu companies' investments were more stable and less exposed to the ups and downs of operating cash flows or to episodes of financial distress.[43] It seems that the financial support of the kiretsus enabled their members to invest 'for the long run'.

_____

42   German companies also rely heavily on bank debt, though public debt was never forbidden.
43   T. Hoshi, A. Kashyap and D. Scharfstein, 'Corporate Structure, Liquidity and Investment: Evidence From Japanese Industrial Groups', *Quarterly Journal of Economics*, 27: 67–88 (September 1990).

The Japanese system of corporate control has its disadvantages too, notably for outside investors, who have very little influence. Japanese managers' compensation is rarely tied to shareholders' returns. Takeovers are unthinkable. Japanese companies have been particularly stingy with cash dividends—hardly a concern when growth was rapid and share prices stratospheric, but a serious issue for the future.

# 14.8 Summary

Financing is principally a marketing problem. The company tries to split the cash flows generated by its assets into different streams that will appeal to investors with different tastes, wealth and tax rates. In this chapter we have introduced you to the principal sources of finance and outlined their relative importance.

The simplest and most important source of finance is shareholders' equity, raised by either share issues or retained earnings. The next most important source of finance is debt. Debtholders are entitled to a fixed regular payment of interest and the final repayment of principal. If the company cannot make the repayments, it can file for bankruptcy. The usual result is that the debtholders then take over and either sell off the company's assets or continue to operate them under new management.

Note that the tax authorities treat interest payments as a cost. That means the company can deduct interest when calculating its taxable income. Interest is paid from pre-tax income. Dividends and retained earnings come from after-tax income.

The variety of corporate debt instruments is almost endless. The instruments are classified by maturity, repayment provisions, seniority, security, default risk, interest rates (floating or fixed), issue procedures (public or private placement), and the country and currency of the debt.

Although limited in its use in Australia, the third source of finance is preference shares, which are like debt in that they promise a fixed dividend payment, but payment of this dividend is within the discretion of the directors. They must, however, pay the dividend on the preference shares before they are allowed to pay a dividend on the ordinary shares. Lawyers and tax experts treat preference shares as part of the company's equity. That means preference share dividends are not tax-deductible. This is one reason that this form of finance is less popular than debt.

The fourth source of finance consists of convertible notes and convertible preference shares. These securities give their holder the right to convert the notes or the preference shares to ordinary shares. They are therefore like a mixture of straight debt or a preference share and a longer dated option.

Companies also trade in derivative securities to hedge their exposure to external risks, including fluctuations in commodity prices, interest rates and foreign exchange rates. Derivative securities include exchange traded options, futures and forward contracts, and swaps. In some cases it is possible to tailor-make derivatives to the needs of a particular client. Such instruments are said to be traded in the over-the-counter market.

The large volume of trade in these derivative instruments reflects a wave of recent innovation in world financial markets. This innovation was stimulated by changes in taxes and government regulation; by demand from corporations and investors for new instruments to hedge against increasingly volatile interest and exchange rates; and by improvements in telecommunications and computing, which make it possible to execute transactions cheaply and quickly throughout the world.

We sketched the German and Japanese systems of corporate finance especially for readers in Australia, who may regard their system as natural. In some circumstances the German or Japanese system can work better. Here are two key differences.

First, corporate finance in the United Kingdom, the United States and many other English-speaking countries relies more on financial markets, and less on banks or other financial intermediaries, than is the case in most other countries. American corporations routinely issue publicly traded debt in situations where Australian, Japanese or European companies borrow extensively from banks.

Second, Australian corporate finance puts fewer buffers between managers and the share market. The block holdings and layered ownership structure of German companies are rare in Australia and the United States, and of course there is nothing remotely like a Japanese kiretsu. So CEOs and CFOs in Australia usually find their remuneration is tied to shareholders' returns. Negative returns may bring insomnia or bad dreams about takeovers.

These international comparisons illustrate different approaches to the problem of corporate governance—the problem of ensuring that managers act in shareholders' interests. Agency costs are incurred when managers pursue other objectives or when shareholders have to spend time and money monitoring or controlling managers' actions.

## FURTHER READING

For a comprehensive review of legal issues as they apply to debt and equity markets in Australia see:

> S. Berns and P. Baron, *Company Law and Governance: An Australian Perspective*, Oxford University Press, Melbourne, 1998.

For those who need a quick fix, Australian debt, equity and derivatives markets are reviewed in:

> E. Carew, *Fast Money 4*, Allen & Unwin, Sydney, 1998.
> M. McGrath and C. Viney, *Financial Institutions, Instruments and Markets*, 2nd ed., McGraw-Hill, Sydney, 1997.
> B. Warner, *Australia's Financial Markets: An Introduction*, Allen & Unwin, Sydney, 1989.

Donaldson surveys corporate attitudes to different sources of finance in:

> G. Donaldson, *Corporate Debt Capacity*, Division of Research, Graduate School of Business Administration, Harvard University, Boston, 1961.

Taggart describes long-term trends in corporate financing in:

> R. A. Taggart, 'Secular Patterns in the Financing of Corporations', in B. M. Friedman (ed.), *Corporate Capital Structures in the United States*, University of Chicago Press, 1985.

Kester's article is a useful comparison of financing in the United States and Japan:

> W. C. Kester, 'Capital and Ownership Structure: A Comparison of United States and Japanese Manufacturing Corporations', *Financial Management*, 15: 5–16 (Spring 1986).

For a discussion of corporate governance as it applies in Australia see:

> I. M. Ramsay, 'The Corporate Governance Debate and the Role of Directors Duties', in *Corporate Governance and the Duties of Company Directors*, The Centre of Corporate Law and Securities Regulation, Faculty of Law, The University of Melbourne, Melbourne, 1997.

The classic paper on agency issues is:

> M. C. Jensen and W. C. Meckling, 'Theory of the Firm: Managerial Behavior, Agency Costs and Capital Structure', *Journal of Financial Economics*, 3: 305–60 (1976).

The following, while not exciting reading, is a good, comprehensive survey of international differences in corporate governance:

> S. Prowse, 'Corporate Governance in an International Perspective: A Survey of Corporate Control Mechanisms Among Large Firms in the U.S., U.K., Japan and Germany', *Financial Markets, Institutions, and Investments*, 4: 1–63 (1995).

QUIZ

**1.** The share capital permitted under the constitution of the Alfred Cake Company
is 100 000 shares. The equity is currently shown in the company's books as
follows:

| | |
|---|---|
| ▌ Authorised value of ordinary shares | $40 000 |
| ▌ Additional paid-in capital | 10 000 |
| ▌ Retained earnings | 30 000 |
| ▌ Ordinary shares | 80 000 |
| ▌ Shares held in Treasury (2000 shares) | 5 000 |
| ▌ Net shareholders' equity | $75 000 |

   a. How many shares are issued?
   b. How many are outstanding?
   c. Explain the difference between your answers to Parts (a) and (b).
   d. How many more shares can be issued without the approval of the
      shareholders?
   e. Suppose that the company issues 10 000 shares at $2 a share. Which of the
      above figures would be changed?

**2.** If there are 10 directors to be elected and a shareholder owns 80 shares, indicate
the maximum number of votes that he or she can cast for a favourite candidate
under:
   a. Majority voting.
   b. Cumulative voting.

**3.** Fill in the blanks, using the terms listed at the end of this question.
   a. Debt maturing in more than one year is often called _____ debt.
   b. An issue of bonds that is sold simultaneously in several countries is called a(n)
      ____.
   c. If a lender ranks behind the firm's general creditors in the event of a default, his
      or her loan is said to be _____.
   d. Unsecured bonds are usually termed _____.
   e. In many cases, a firm is obliged to make regular contributions to a(n) _____.
   f. Most bonds give the firm the right to repurchase or _____ the bonds at
      specified prices.
   g. Interest on many bank loans is based on the _____ of interest.
   h. The interest rate on _____ loans is tied to the short-term interest rates.
   i. Where there is a(n) _____, securities are sold directly to a small group of
      institutional investors. These securities cannot be resold to individual investors.
      In the case of a(n) _____, debt can be freely bought and sold by
      individual investors.
   j. A long-term, non-cancellable rental agreement is called a(n) _____.
   k. A(n) _____ bond can be exchanged for shares of the issuing corporation.
   l. A(n) _____ gives its owner the right to buy shares in the issuing company at
      a predetermined _____.
Terms: lease, funded, floating-rate, eurobond, exercise price, commercial paper,
convertible, term loan, subordinated, call, sinking fund, prime rate, debentures,
mortgage bond, private placement, public issue, senior, unfunded, eurodollar rate,
warrant

**4.** The figures in the following table are in the wrong order. Place them in their correct
order.

|  | Per cent of total sources, 1998 |
|---|---|
| Internally generated cash | 17 |
| Financial deficit | −6 |
| Net share issues | 72 |
| Debt issues | 28 |

**5.** True or false?
   a. Firms sell forward contracts primarily to raise money for new capital investment.
   b. Firms trade in futures contracts to hedge their exposure to the unexpected changes in interest rates, foreign exchange rates or commodity prices.
   c. Financial innovation is partly caused by deregulation of financial markets.
   d. A large fraction of preference shares is held by corporations.
   e. In Japan, one finds extensive cross-holdings of shares within kiretsus.
   e. German universal banks may hold up to 5 per cent of the shares of German industrial companies.
   f. Investments in partnerships cannot be publicly traded.
   g. Hostile takeovers are extremely difficult and are therefore rare in Japan.
   h. Compared with companies in the United States, Australian companies are more likely to borrow from a bank than issue a debt security in public markets.

**6.** Agency costs are incurred when (a) _____ and (b) _____. Fill in the blanks.

**7.** What is meant by 'separation of ownership and control'? Why does this separation concern investors and financial analysts?

**8.** What are the chief differences in the roles of banks in corporate finance in Australia, Germany and Japan?

## QUESTIONS AND PROBLEMS

**1.** It is sometimes suggested that since retained earnings provide the bulk of industry's capital needs, the securities markets are largely redundant. Do you agree?

**2.** Can you think of any new kinds of security that might appeal to investors? Why do you think they have not been issued?

**3.** The shareholders of the Pickwick Paper Ltd need to elect five directors. There are 200 000 shares outstanding. How many shares do you need to own to *ensure* that you can elect at least one director if:
   a. The company has majority voting?
   b. The company has cumulative voting?

**4.** Compare the yields on convertible preference shares with those on convertible bonds. Can you explain the difference?

**5.** Who are the main holders and issuers of preference shares? Explain why.

**6.** Michael Jensen has pointed to the dangers of excessive free cash flow. These dangers stem from a principal-agent problem. Explain why.

7.  Work out the financing proportions for several listed Australian industrial and resource-based companies and compare the results to Table 14.4.

8.  What is a kiretsu? What are the main financial and business linkages that hold a kiretsu together?

9.  Some managers have argued that hostile takeovers are wasteful and that the Australian economy would be more efficient and competitive if takeovers were made more difficult. Can you identify arguments for and against this view?

10. The German and Japanese financial systems have certain advantages when a company falls into financial difficulty. What are these advantages?

# chapter 15

# HOW CORPORATIONS ISSUE SECURITIES

When entrepreneurs want to start a new business, buy an existing business or expand their current business with updated technology, enter into new markets or create new business segments, they need capital. This capital can be issued in the form of equity or debt or in some cases a combination of both.

In the first part of this chapter we are going to explain how new private companies can raise venture capital. Then we will review how these companies can transform to become public companies and finally how established public companies issue securities.

## 15.1 Venture capital

Let us suppose that since 1993 you and your friend have spent every spare weekend in a workshop at the back of your house trying to develop a battery-operated environmentally-friendly motor for lawn mowers. Until now you have relied solely on your own personal savings to fund all expenses. With each attempt you are both confident that the battery-operated motor is not far from completion. After two years of trial and error you now believe the motor is near to completion.

On 1 April 1995 you and your friend establish and register the small proprietary company Battery Mowers Pty Ltd. The company involves initial capital made up of personal savings, money from a joint ticket Lotto win and funds from the sale of a residential investment property. The company issues 500 000 shares at $1.00 each. The shares are distributed equally between you and your friend—or should we say, business partner.

At this stage Battery Mowers has assets of $500 000 and has issued equity of $500 000. The company also has the idea for a viable product and is close to the initial production of a prototype battery-operated motor.

Eureka! On 10 November 1995 Battery Mowers Pty Ltd finally identifies the right specification for the engine and by 30 November has produced the first operational prototype—the ENVIRO Mark I. Now you and your friend have not only the best lawns in the neighbourhood, but also the quietest and most energy efficient mower. Due to your success you and your partner decide that you should begin to make and sell the lawn mowers.

However, during 1995 the company's bank account has drained away due to expenses as design and testing proceeded. Your bankers were not interested in lending money for your project as a commercial venture and unfortunately neither of you had direct access to further funds, so a transfusion of capital from an alternative source was needed. A friend advises that you need **venture capital**. But what is venture capital?

Venture capital financing is the provision of equity and/or debt funding by wealthy individuals and/or companies to start up operations of small companies where the risk of business failure is considered to be high. The companies to which venture capital is provided are usually regarded as new, innovative and fast growing. In exchange for providing the finance the venture capitalists receive ordinary shares in the business, or preference shares, convertible debentures[1] or loans with warrants.[2] In Australia venture capital is generally distinguished from development capital as follows.[3]

Venture capital is regarded as capital invested in businesses that are unlisted companies, have a new or innovative product (just like the ENVIRO Mark I), process or service, usually cannot offer any collateral or other security and promise high rates of growth and above average rates of return. In contrast, **development capital** is regarded as capital that is invested in businesses that are more established, usually have a proven track record of operation, established markets, positive cash flow and usually require further funding to reach their full potential.

In Australia most venture capital is provided by a small number of companies and trusts, private superannuation funds and government bodies such as the Commonwealth Development Bank.[4] The *Australian Venture Capital Journal* reported in its March 1998 edition that the venture capital industry invested a total of $346.8 million in 201 deals in 1997. This followed a successful year in 1996 with 217 deals worth $442.1 million. The average deal size in 1997 was $1.7 million. The most popular industry segments receiving funding in 1997 were industrial and manufacturing, information technology and software, communications, health and biosciences and food and beverages.[5]

When venture capital is provided, the individuals and/or the companies providing the capital supply both capital and management expertise. As noted by Harper,[6] the aim of every venture capitalist is to bring the company into which funds are invested to the point where it

---

1    Convertible debentures involve a loan (debt) issued by the venture capital company that is convertible into ordinary shares in the company at a specified conversion rate and date.

2    Warrants provide the opportunity for the venture capital company to issue a loan (debt) while giving the opportunity but not the obligation to buy shares in the company equivalent to the amount of the loan if the venture capital company wishes to exercise the warrant and buy shares in the company at some future date.

3    See Department of Industry Technology and Regional Development, *Australian Development Capital Directory*, Australian Government Publishing Service, Canberra, 1992.

4    A comprehensive comparison of Australian and Japanese venture capital markets is detailed in A. Gray, 'Venture and Development Capital in Australia and Japan', *Economic Papers*, December 1994 Supplement.

5    The information in the journal was compiled from the *Australian Venture Capital Journal*/Price Waterhouse Venture Capital Survey.

6    See I. R. Harper, 'The Impact of Financial Deregulation on the Availability of Venture Capital in Australia', in *Issues in Business Finance*, Economic Planning Advisory Council Background Paper No. 15, Australian Government Publishing Service, Canberra, July 1991.

can be sold—to the management, to another company or via a public offering. The capital gain realised by the venture capitalist from either interest or dividends paid by the company represents the return for their investment for being involved in both the financing and the management of the business.

You research alternative funding possibilities and decide to approach a venture capitalist with a detailed **business plan**, which describes a wide range of information regarding the business including:

- The nature and history of the business and its future.[7]
- The management of the business.[8]
- A description of current and proposed financing arrangements.[9]
- Identification of operational and financial risk factors.
- The estimated return on the investment.
- The proposed exit process.
- Financial statements, historical information and projections.

Surveys of venture capitalists by Tyebjee and Bruno[10] in 1984 and another by Premus[11] in the same year showed that most venture capitalists were particularly interested in the management skills and history of the business, the size of the market into which the company was entering, the company's potential for growth, the proposed rate of return on the venture capitalists' investment and whether the investment would provide the funded company with a niche or unique position.

You and your friend approach a venture capitalist that is very interested in your business venture. It is proposed in the business plan that the venture capitalist will provide $500 000 in return for 500 000 preference shares of $1.00 each. As a result of this *start-up* funding,[12] Battery Mowers Pty Ltd has a projected market value balance sheet (after financing) that reads as follows:

**Battery Mowers Pty Ltd**
**First stage balance sheet**
**January 1996**
**(market value)**

| | | | |
|---|---|---|---|
| Cash from new equity | $500 000 | New equity from venture capitalist | $500 000 |
| Other assets, mostly intangible | $500 000 | Original equity held by original shareholders | $500 000 |
| Value | $1 000 000 | | $1 000 000 |

By accepting the $1 million valuation of the business at January 1996, the venture capitalist implicitly put $500 000 on the idea of the future potential of the ENVIRO Mark I and Battery Mowers Pty Ltd. In return for the capital provided, you and your friend give up half

---

7   This includes details of the product or service provided, existing and potential customers, marketing and operational strategies, identification of the corporate structure and identification of suppliers and the detailing of any litigation pending, government regulations or conflicts of interest.

8   It is necessary to identify directors, key employees, bankers, solicitors, accountants, consultants and any principal shareholders to the company.

9   Details are needed of the current and proposed capital structure, identification of any guarantees or available collateral, how funding is to be used and the proposed level of involvement of the venture capitalist in the business.

10  See T. T. Tyebjee and A. V. Bruno, 'A Model of Venture Capitalist Investment Activity', *Management Science*, **30** (1984).

11  See R. Premus, *Venture Capital and Innovation*, study prepared for the Joint Committee of the US Congress, US Government Printing Office, Washington, 1984.

12  This is also known as 'first stage' or 'ground floor' financing.

of the equity in the company[13] and accept representatives of the venture capitalist to the board of directors of Battery Mowers Pty Ltd.[14]

The success of a new business depends critically on the effort put in by the managers. So venture capital firms try to structure a deal so that management has a strong incentive to work hard. For example, an entrepreneur who demands a watertight employment contract and a fat salary is not going to find it easy to raise venture capital. You and your friend decide to put up with modest salaries and, therefore, you will cash in only from appreciation of your shares. If Battery Mowers Pty Ltd fails, you will get nothing. The venture capitalist's firm bought preference shares so it has priority in any claims on the business. The preference shares are designed to convert automatically to ordinary shares when and if Battery Mowers succeeds in an initial public offering, or if Battery Mowers consistently generates more than a target level of earnings. This raises even further the stakes for the company's management.[15]

Venture capitalists rarely give a young company all the money it will need all in one lump sum. Instead, they provide the funds in stages. At each stage they give enough to reach the next major checkpoint in the growth of the company. Thus, in December 1996, having tested the prototype extensively, Battery Mowers is back asking for more funds for pilot production and test marketing. Its *second stage* financing[16] is $1.5 million, of which another $500 000 comes from the original venture capitalist and the other $1 million from two other venture capital partners and wealthy individual investors. The balance sheet after the second stage is as follows:

**Battery Mowers Pty Ltd**
**Second stage balance sheet**
**December 1996**
**(market value in millions)**

| | | | |
|---|---|---|---|
| Cash from new equity | $1.5 | New equity second stage | $1.5 |
| Fixed assets | 0.20 | | |
| Other assets, mostly intangible | 0.80 | Equity from start-up capital | 0.75 |
| | | Original equity held by original shareholders | 0.75 |
| | ──── | | ──── |
| Value | $3.00 | | $3.00 |

The after the money valuation of the firm is now $3 million. The original venture capitalist increased its equity from the start-up capital investment to $0.75 million and you and your friend have added $2 million to the value of the company.

Is this starting to sound like a money machine? It may seem so with the benefit of hindsight. At the time of the start-up capital in January 1996 it was not clear whether Battery Mowers would ever get to second stage funding: if the prototype had not worked, the original venture capitalist firm could have refused to put up more funds and effectively closed the

---

13  For a formal analysis of how management's investment in the business can provide a reliable signal of the company's value see H. E. Leland and D. H. Pyle, 'Information Asymmetries, Financial Structure, and Financial Intermediation', *Journal of Finance*, **32**: 371–87 (May 1977).

14  Venture capital investors do not necessarily demand a majority on the board of directors. Whether they do depends, for example, on how mature the business is and on what fraction of it they own. A common compromise gives an equal number of seats to the founders and to outside investors; the two parties then agree to one or more additional directors to serve as tie breakers in case any conflicts should arise. Regardless of whether they have a majority of directors, venture capital companies are seldom silent partners; their judgement and contacts often can prove useful to a relatively inexperienced management team.

15  Notice there is a trade-off here. Battery Mowers' management is being asked to put all its eggs into one basket. That creates pressure for managers to work hard, but it also means that they take on risk that they could have diversified away. The problem of ensuring that managers act in the interests of investors is sometimes referred to as an *agency problem*. For a discussion of these issues see M. C. Jensen and W. H. Meckling, 'Theory of the Firm: Managerial Behavior, Agency Costs and Capital Structure', *Journal of Financial Economics*, **3**: 305–60 (1976).

16  Later stage financing is also called 'expansion', 'growth' or 'mezzanine' finance.

business down.[17] Alternatively, it could have advanced second stage funds in a smaller amount with less favourable terms. The board of directors could also have fired you and your friend and replaced both of you with someone else to try to redevelop the business.

It is well known that many new businesses do not survive and that only a minority go on to become publicly listed firms. Two rules for success can be drawn from these observations:

■ Do not shy away from uncertainty; accept a low probability of success. But do not buy into a business unless you see the chance of a profitable return.
■ Cut your losses; identify losers early, and if you cannot fix the problem—by replacing management, for example—there is no point in throwing more good money after bad.

Fortunately for Battery Mowers Pty Ltd, everything continues like clockwork. Third stage financing is arranged and full-scale production in new premises on an industrial estate near Brisbane begins on schedule in January 1998. Battery Mowers is acclaimed by horticulturists and environmentalists worldwide—the company even gets a mention on one of those lifestyle programs on television. Plans are developed for expansion into overseas markets and it is expected that in the near future Battery Mowers must decide whether to:

■ Allow a leveraged buy-out (LBO) by a competitor.[18]
■ Engage in a management buy-out (MBO).[19]
■ Offer shares publicly via an initial public offering.

An active venture capital market is regarded by many as being an integral part of the infrastructure of well-established capital markets. Due to the perceived high risk of many projects, venture capitalists are not able to provide capital for all projects. This has caused an apparent venture capital 'gap'.[20] In response to this perceived 'gap' the Australian government introduced the Management and Investment Company (MIC) program in 1984 with the objective of promoting the development of an Australian venture capital industry and encouraging management and financial support for young Australian enterprises that had potential for fast growth, were export orientated and used innovative technology. The Australian government provided considerable tax advantages to registered MICs. However, only low levels of funding were available to projects in their 'start-up' stage, with preference being given to more established businesses, and most funding being given in expansion and management buy-out stages instead of the much needed start-up stage. The MIC program was discontinued in June 1991.[21] The MIC scheme licensed 14 investment companies that raised over $350 million and funded over 150 businesses.

Due to the continuing need for access to venture capital, in particular for technology companies, the Australian government established the Small Business Innovation Fund (SBIF) in 1997. Under this scheme selected private sector venture capital managers applied to establish between four to six venture capital funds[22] to which the Australian government would commit $130 million on a two for one basis to raise a total capital pool of $195 million.

Do you need a new lawn mower? Have you ever considered buying one of the ENVIRO Mark I mowers?

---

[17]  If the venture capitalist refused to invest at the second stage, it would have been an exceptionally hard sell convincing another investor to step into the project in its place. The other outside investors knew they had less information about Battery Mowers than the venture capitalist and would have read the refusal of the venture capitalist to provide more funding as a bad omen for Battery Mowers' prospects.

[18]  Leveraged buy-out involves the acquisition of the firm through the use of debt financing. See Chapter 33.

[19]  Similar to a leveraged buy-out, but the purchase group is led by the management of the firm. See Chapter 33.

[20]  For discussion of the 'reality' of this perceived gap see Harper, op. cit., Footnote 6.

[21]  Gray, op. cit., Footnote 4, expressed concern that the cessation of the MIC program would cause an avoidance of funding for start-up and early stage funding, with priority being given to later stage funding and funding for management buy-outs.

[22]  Five management companies were eventually offered licences under the program. See the December 1997 issue of the *Australian Venture Capital Journal*.

## 15.2 The initial public offering

Very few businesses make it big. Probably 90 per cent of venture capitalists' investments will fail or offer poor returns. But venture capitalists keep sane by forgetting about the many failures and reminding themselves of the success stories. When the original venture capitalist invested start-up capital in Battery Mowers, it was not looking for a high income stream from the investment; instead, it was hoping for rapid growth in the value of the firm that would allow Battery Mowers to 'go public' and give it an opportunity to cash in on some of its gains.

If Battery Mowers continues to grow it will eventually require new capital to implement its second generation production technology. At this point it may decide to make an **initial public offering (IPO)**.[23] This involves issuing more shares that can be purchased by the public. Often, when companies go public, the issue is solely intended to raise new capital for the company. But there are also occasions when no new capital is raised and all the shares on offer are being sold by existing shareholders. Some of the biggest initial public offerings occur when governments sell off their public assets. Significant listings of government enterprises in Australia include the Commonwealth Bank (12 September 1991), GIO (23 July 1992), Tabcorp (15 August 1994) and Qantas (31 July 1995). Several significant well-known private sector IPOs in recent years include Woolworths (1993), Cable & Wireless Optus (1998) and AMP (1998).

In Australia, publicly issued shares are traded on the Australian Stock Exchange (ASX). Companies issuing shares in a public float seek quotation on the official list of traded shares. The ASX places certain demands on companies seeking to list on the exchange—these are called initial listing requirements. ASX listing requirements are intended to embrace the interests of listed entities, maintain investor protection and protect the reputation of the market. As stated in Ron Bennett's book on the Australian stock market,[24] the ASX listing requirements are based on four principles:

- *The listing and quotation principle*, whereby the company must meet certain requirements with respect to size, quality, operations, disclosure and investor interest.
- *The market information principle*, whereby the company must advise the share market, in a timely manner, of any information that may affect the value of its securities or influence investment decisions.
- *The regulatory principle*, whereby securities must have rights and obligations attached, security holders are consulted on matters of significance to the company and the company must operate to the highest standards of integrity, accountability and responsibility.
- *The trading and settlement principle*, whereby market transactions must be commercially certain.

Companies seeking to list on the ASX must meet the prerequisites for admission to the official list along with continuing obligations. The issue price of new shares must be at least 20 cents. To obtain entry on the official list of the ASX, a firm must be a going concern, have at least 500 shareholders each with a parcel of shares having a value of at least $2000,[25] have issued capital of $1 million and have a profitable trading record of $1 million cumulatively for the past three years with $400 000 operating profit in the past year.[26]

In the year to June 1996, the Australian Stock Exchange was used to raise just under $5 billion in new company initial public offerings or floats with 59 companies added to the

---

23  IPOs are also known as floats and unseasoned issues.

24  R. Bennett, *The Australian Stockmarket: A Guide for Players, Planners and Procrastinators*, ABC Books, Sydney, 1998.

25  Firms must operate an identifiable predominant business activity for at least the past three years and must provide unqualified audited accounts for the same period.

26  For more information regarding the listing requirements and the procedure for listing on the ASX refer to the Australian Stock Exchange publication *ASX Guide to Listing*, Melbourne, November 1997.

official Australian Stock Exchange list. In the previous year to June 1995, 66 companies were added with new equity capital amounting to just over $2 billion. New company IPOs in the year to December 1997 were in excess of $12.8 billion due to the floating of Telstra, which accounted for more than $8.5 billion. This contrasts significantly to the year ended June 1991 when less than $100 million was issued.[27]

# A short legal digression[28]

There are four general forms of business organisation—the sole trader, the partnership, the private or proprietary company and the public company. Company structures such as the proprietary and public company often are preferred to the sole trader and partnership structures where people are personally responsible for all the company's debts. Under the proprietary and public company structures it is possible to limit the liability of the shareholders of the business.

When shares are issued by a company, they are purchased by investors who wish to be joint owners of the company. Shareholders do not control the day to day operations of the firm directly but are afforded certain rights by virtue of being shareholders, such as the ability to participate in the election of a board of directors who appoint managers to run the company on behalf of the shareholders.

Broadly speaking, we often talk about companies as though they are all one and the same—in fact, they are quite different in terms of the size of their share ownership, in the obligations and liabilities of shareholders and in the modes of participation in share capital.[29]

In Australia, three types of company structure are permitted—the small proprietary company, the large proprietary company and the public company. The small proprietary companies[30] usually employ less than 50 employees, have gross operating revenue of less than or equal to $10 million, or gross assets less than or equal to $5 million. They differ from large proprietary companies in that large companies usually must not meet at least two of these criteria due to regulatory requirements. Large proprietary companies must have at least one but no more than 50 shareholders, cannot engage in any fundraising activity that would require the lodgment of a prospectus, need only one director who can also be the company secretary, do not have to prepare and distribute audited financial statements,[31] and do not have to hold an annual meeting. Proprietary companies usually contain the word *Proprietary* or the abbreviation *Pty* after their name.

Public companies, however, have greater capital needs than proprietary companies and can issue shares or raise debt finance from the general public. There is no upper limit on the number of shareholders. Audited financial statements must be prepared and distributed, they must have at least three directors and a company secretary, and must hold meetings with shareholders subject to regulatory requirements. Proprietary companies cannot be listed on the ASX and there are often restrictions in place on the trading of their shares, whereas public companies are listed on the ASX and their shares can be traded by investors.

The liability of shareholders can also be used to differentiate between companies. One of three categories of liability is usually adopted—limited liability, no liability and unlimited

---

[27] Refer to the Australian Stock Exchange Annual Reports 1995 and 1996 and the ASX *1998 Fact Book*, see *http://www.asx.com.au/asxir/pub310.htl.*

[28] For a very comprehensive survey of recent changes in Corporations Law and the regulatory structure affecting Australian companies see P. Jubb, S. Haswell and I. Langfield-Smith, 'Companies and Corporate Regulations', in *Company Accounting*, 2nd ed., Nelson ITP, Melbourne, 1998.

[29] Some companies are also formed under special purpose regulations, such as finance companies, life insurance companies and foreign companies.

[30] A minimum of two of the three criteria must apply in order for the company to be classified as a small proprietary company, otherwise it is classified as a large proprietary company.

[31] Unless required to do so by the Australian Securities and Investment Commission or by members holding 5 per cent of the company's shares, or it is a controlled foreign company not covered by consolidated accounts lodged with ASIC.

liability. In the case of limited liability, a company's shareholders' liability is limited to the amount of money owed to the company. In the case of fully paid shares, the shareholder has no further liability. In the case of partly paid shares, the shareholder is liable for the unpaid component of the share price. Limited liability companies have the word *Limited* or the letters *Ltd* after their name. Alternatively, no liability shares can be issued where the extent of the shareholders' liability does not exceed the amount already paid—such shares are typically issued by mining exploration companies. Such firms have the letters *NL* after their name. A final form of liability is that of unlimited liability, whereby the shareholders' liability is unlimited in the event of company liquidation.

As at 30 June 1997 there were in excess of one million companies registered in Australia. Of these companies more than 98 per cent were proprietary companies limited by shares. Despite this incredible proportion, the constraints on share ownership in proprietorships also potentially limits their access to capital—hence most attention is usually paid to public companies.

Companies can either have share capital, where shareholders purchase shares in the company with each share representing ownership in the company, or they can be limited by guarantee, where no shares are issued and the companies rely on donations, fund raising and grants for their capital needs. Alternatively, companies can be registered as limited both by shares and guarantee. As at 30 June 1997, there were almost 9400 companies registered in Australia that were limited either by guarantee or by shares and guarantee.

To set up a new company, a person must apply to the Australian Securities and Investment Commission for registration of the company. When it is registered, every Australian company receives a unique nine digit identification number known as the Australian Company Number (ACN). This number must appear on most documents issued by the company.[32] For example, the ACN of Woolworths Ltd is 000 014 675.

Prior to changes in the Corporations Law from 1 July 1998,[33] each company's memorandum of association specified in part the maximum amount of share capital and types of shares that the company was authorised to issue, known as authorised share capital. All shares were issued at a par value, which represents the minimum value at which shares could be issued. Shares issued above the par value were said to be issued at a premium. It was common practice by most companies not to issue all of the authorised capital, and most firms issued shares at a price above the par value. The number of authorised shares and their par values could only be altered by amending the memorandum of association.[34]

As we discussed in Chapter 14, the *Company Law Review Act 1998* abolished the concepts of memorandum of association and par value. Companies are no longer required to have a memorandum of association or articles of association. Instead, companies have a single set of rules known as a constitution, or they can opt to have no constitution but rely on rules of internal management which are set out in the law and are known as Replaceable Rules. Existing companies can continue to have their memorandum and articles as their constitution, they can repeal them and adopt the replaceable rules or alternatively substitute them with a new constitution. The concept of par value is replaced by the concept of nominal value, and companies are still allowed to issue shares at a premium. Companies may now include in their constitution a numerical limit on the number of shares that can be issued. The Corporations Law also places constraints on the type of shares that can be issued.[35]

---

32  This includes documents such as all documents lodged with the ASIC, statements of account, including invoices, receipts, orders for goods and services, business letterheads, official company notices, cheques, promissory notes and bills of exchange, brochures and leaflets advertising goods and services. For more information regarding the ACN refer to the ASIC Web site at *http://www.asc.gov.au/page-315-html*.

33  The Australian Corporations Law 1989 was amended on the 11 December 1995 by passing the *Corporate Law Simplification Act* and again on 1 July 1998 by passing the *Company Law Review Act 1998*. The impact of these amendments was to substantially ease the regulatory constraints imposed on small business in particular.

34  The memorandum of association could only be amended if such a provision existed in the articles of association.

35  For more details regarding the regulatory requirements of Australian companies see the Web sites of both the Australian Securities and Investment Commission (*http://www.asc.gov.au*) and the ASX (*http://www.asx.com.au*).

# Arranging a public issue

Any public company seeking to raise equity or debt capital from the public must issue a **prospectus**.[36] The public is invited to invest via the prospectus. The prospectus may be for the issue of shares or debt. The prospectus must provide details of the business of the company, including the board of directors, senior management and financial information about the company including historical profitability, forecasts, operating and financial risks and consolidated balance sheets. It should contain also details of the share issue offer, including its timetable and an application form. The prospectus is regarded as the company director's statement of the company's record and future prospects. The details contained therein must conform with the requirements of the Corporations Law and the ASX listing requirements. The prospectus must contain sufficient information for prospective investors to be able to make an informed investment decision regarding the financial position and prospects of the company as well as the rights attached to the securities.

Should Battery Mowers Pty Ltd decide to issue shares to the public and therefore go public in 2000, there are a series of regulatory constraints that it must consider. Prior to the issue of the shares, Battery Mowers will need to register as a public company and apply to the Australian Stock Exchange to become a listed company on the ASX, so that shares held by its existing and new investors can be quoted securities that can be traded on the share market conducted by the Exchange.

## example: Cable & Wireless Optus IPO in 1998

In November 1998 Cable & Wireless Optus (CWO)[37] commenced trading on the Australian Stock Exchange. The share issue involved an offer of 1026.9 million fully paid ordinary shares valued at $6653 million, with 375 million shares offered by Cable & Wireless Optus and 651.9 million shares offered by vendor shareholders—Mayne Nickless (556.9 million existing shares), AMP (70 million existing shares) and National Mutual (25 million existing shares). Under the offer, shares were available to:

■ The public under a retail offer.
■ Mayne Nickless investors under an entitlement offer.
■ Institutional investors.
■ Employees of Cable & Wireless Optus.

The application price under the retail and entitlement offers was set at $1.85. The price ultimately paid by applicants was set to be the lower of the $1.85 per share and the final price determined under the institutional offer. Retail investors could apply for a minimum of 1000 shares and thereafter in multiples of 100 shares. Entitlement investors could invest in Cable & Wireless Optus in a non-renounceable entitlement offer made to Mayne Nickless investors. These shareholders had to be registered in the books of Mayne Nickless at 16 October 1998. The entitlement offer was made at the rate of 1.6 CWO shares for each 1.0 Mayne Nickless share held together with an offer of approximately 4.5 CWO shares for Mayne Nickless option holders. The institutional offer was made on the basis of

---

[36]  A prospectus is also required when seeking money from the general public for a pooled or collective investment, a unit trust or any other managed investment scheme such as a property trust, equity trust, cash management trust and agricultural investment scheme.

[37]  Cable & Wireless Optus is the second largest provider of telecommunications services in Australia and provides a broad range of communications services, including mobile communications, national and international long distance services, local telephone services, business network services, Internet services and pay television. Its operating revenue exceeded $2.5 billion in 1997 and it employs more than 5000 staff. The company commenced trading on the ASX on 17 November 1998.

a book-building process, whereby institutional firms bid for shares both in terms of the number of shares required and the price at which they were willing to purchase the shares.

To offer the shares, Cable & Wireless Optus issued a prospectus dated 29 September 1998 and applied to the ASX for admission to the official list and for official quotation of its shares. The shares were listed on 17 November 1998 at a price of $2.61 per share.

The prospectus issued by Cable & Wireless Optus provided a detailed timetable indicating critical dates regarding the offer, details of CWO business, corporate structure, industry and operations, its board of directors and senior management. It also provided financial information including historical and pro-forma profitability, an assessment of risk factors and discussion of regulatory issues affecting the company. In addition, the prospectus detailed the share issue offer and included an independent accountant's report, a glossary of terms and, as you would expect, an application section.

## Pricing a new issue

Companies issuing shares for the first time are faced with the dilemma of deciding the appropriate number of shares to issue and the price at which to issue the shares. A company might seek the assistance of an underwriter, who will be responsible for the determination, in consultation with the issuing company, of an appropriate issue price and for the placement and sale of the newly issued shares. Factors to consider include:

▌ The number of shares available for issue as specified (if specified) under the company's constitution.
▌ The price-earnings ratio of competitors in similar or related industries.
▌ The future earnings and dividend potential of the firm.
▌ The capital structure of the firm.
▌ The market share of the firm.
▌ Operational and financial risks.
▌ The current and expected state of the economy and the market.
▌ The timing of the issue relative to other events.

We will return to the issue of share valuation in Chapter 27.

A further consideration at the time of issue is whether the issue price should be set as a fixed price, at an open price offer where the price is determined at the end of the offer period or as a constrained open price offer. The fixed price offer is the traditional method employed, whereby the price is fixed in advance and every subscriber to the offer knows exactly what the purchase price per share will be before making their decision to purchase shares. Under a fixed price offer, the share issue is then highly exposed to changes in market conditions. If market conditions downturn and the price is considered too high relative to the market, the issue may be undersubscribed.[38]

Under the open price offer subscribers place bids for the shares both in terms of quantity and price. This form of issue usually involves a *book-building* process, whereby institutional investors record all bids within certain price ranges. At the conclusion of the book-building offer stage a final price is determined and allocations are sold to the bidders. Usually only those bidders with prices above the final price are allocated shares. Open price offers can potentially result in a large range of potential bid prices for the shares. This is why a

---

[38] By also limiting the size of allocations to individual institutional clients, this form of issue can generate excess demand that ensures a liquid market for the shares at the time of their issue. Alternatively, a broader base of shareholders can be achieved at the time of issue by increasing the pool of shares available to retail clients.

constrained open price offer places an upper and lower price between which all bids will be considered. This form of offer, like the open book process, still involves a final price being determined and those with bids equal to or above the final price being allocated shares. The open price method ensures that when the shares are listed, the shares will have a liquid market due to unmet demand for the shares.

For example, when Austin Group Limited, a Geelong clothing group involved in marketing and distribution, issued shares in 1993 it had a fixed offer price of $1.50 per share. Cable & Wireless Optus used an open book offer in 1998[39] and Woolworths Ltd used a constrained open book in 1993, constraining bids between $2.15 and $2.45. As noted by Woolworths in its prospectus dated 19 May 1993,[40] the final price was to be determined on the basis of 'the bids and indications of interest received in the institutional offer, and having regard to (our) own objective of maximising the proceeds of the offer, the desire for an orderly secondary market in the shares and the creation of an ownership base of long-term shareholders'.

# The role of the underwriter

At the time of issuing shares, public companies usually seek the advice of investment banks, which assist by providing advice and helping with the preparation of all necessary documentation. A further role played by such firms is that of underwriting the issue. In the case of large share issues, underwriters often form a syndicate with other firms, including stockbrokers, to facilitate the distribution of the shares.

In Australia, underwriters receive a fee, usually set as a fixed amount or as a percentage of the amount to be raised under the share issue.[41] In return they provide financial and procedural advice and handle the sale of the shares. In this capacity, the underwriters directly participate in the application and subscription process. Usually they assist in a number of ways:

▪ The underwriter may guarantee that the issue will be fully subscribed. If the issue is not fully subscribed by the closing date of the offer, the underwriter agrees to purchase all unpurchased shares at the offer price. The fee charged will reflect the probability that the share issue may be undersubscribed.

▪ The underwriter may enter into a *stand-by* arrangement, whereby they agree to purchase any unpurchased shares if the offer should be undersubscribed.

▪ The underwriter may, due to the riskiness of the share issue, be unwilling to enter into the commitments above and may only be willing to underwrite the shares on a *best efforts* basis. Under this arrangement, the underwriter agrees to sell as many of the shares as possible but does not guarantee the sale of all shares on issue.

Once the shares are issued, the underwriter is allowed to support the market by repurchasing shares at the market price.[42] We have no information about the effects of such stabilising transactions. But, if capital markets are efficient, then transactions affect prices only

---

[39] As noted earlier, the retail and entitlement offers final price was determined by the lower of either the offer price of $1.85 or the final price determined by the institutional offer.

[40] Woolworths Ltd prospectus, 1993, p. 60.

[41] Usually set under 1 per cent of the value of the share issue. For example, at the time of the Woolworths' share issue in 1993, the managers of the Australian and New Zealand syndicate were paid a management fee of 0.75 per cent of the final price in respect of shares sold to Australian and New Zealand institutions pursuant to the institutional part of their offer. The joint lead managers of the offer were paid a fixed fee of $500 000 for performing the book-building process of the offer. Australian underwriters differ from those in the United States, where underwriters play an additional role to providing advice, buying the new issue from the company and then selling the shares to the public. In return for their participation, underwriters receive a spread—that is, they are allowed to purchase the shares for a price less than the price at which the shares are subsequently sold to the public.

[42] In such cases syndicate members could escape their obligation by selling their shares in the market to the principal underwriter. To prevent this, a record is kept so that syndicate members whose shares end up in the hands of the principal underwriter lose that part of their selling concession.

insofar as they are thought to convey information. In that case, the underwriters' efforts at stabilisation cannot have a lasting effect on prices.

In any case, if the issue obstinately remains unsold and the market price falls substantially below the offering price, the underwriters have no alternative but to break the syndicate. The members then dispose of their commitments individually as best they can.

Most companies raise new capital only occasionally, but underwriters are in the business all the time. Established underwriters are therefore careful of their reputation and will not handle a new issue unless they believe the facts have been presented fairly to investors. Thus, in addition to handling the sale of an issue, the underwriters in effect give their seal of approval to it. This implied endorsement might be worth quite a bit to a company that is coming to the market for the first time.

In a study of 340 industrial company IPOs in Australia between 1980 and 1990, How, Izan and Monroe[43] analysed the impact of the quality and quantity of information supplied by independent advisers such as accountants, independent experts and underwriters and how they influenced the degree of underpricing at the time of each IPO. They found significant evidence that the choice of underwriter had a significant direct impact on the level of underpricing. Why is this possible? It has been demonstrated that underwriter reputation has a significant role to play in mitigating the information asymmetries between investors and managers.[44]

Underwriting is not always fun. On 15 October 1987, the British government finalised arrangements to sell its holding of BP shares at £3.30 a share. This huge issue involving more than US$12 billion was the largest share offering in history. It was underwritten by an international group of underwriters and simultaneously marketed in a number of countries. Four days after the underwriting was agreed, the October crash caused share prices around the world to nosedive. The underwriters unsuccessfully appealed to the British government to cancel the issue.[45] By the closing date of the offer, the price of BP shares had fallen to £2.96, and the underwriters had lost more than a billion pounds.

## Costs of a public issue

In Australia, initial public offering fees are usually divided between administrative and underwriting fees. In the year ended December 1995, the average cost of issuing new shares was approximately 2.5 per cent of the value of issued shares. This was made up of 1.5 per cent in administrative fees and 1 per cent in underwriting fees. Administrative fees include the preparation of legal documentation and the prospectus and are payable to merchant banks, accountants and solicitors. They also include expert and management fees. In addition, administrative costs include the stock exchange listing fee, and the cost of printing, advertising and mailing the prospectus.

In a 1995 study, Fay[46] examined the fees paid to underwriters and in particular to the pricing of underwriting risk[47] in 87 Australian IPOs between 1991 and 1993. The average fee charged was usually a fee set as a fixed percentage of the offer price. The weighted average for industrial firms in 1994 was 2.6 per cent and 4 per cent for resource-based firms. The maximum fee permitted was set at 10 per cent of the offer price. The study showed that although the stand-by

---

43   See J. How, H. Izan and G. Monroe, 'Differential Information and Underpricing of IPOs: Australian Evidence', *Accounting and Finance*, 35 (**1**): 87–105 (May 1995).

44   See R. Ball, P. Brown and F. J. Finn, 'Share Capitalisation Changes, Information and the Australian Equity Market', *Australian Journal of Management*, **2**: 105–25 (1977); and R. Booth and R. Smith, 'Capital Raising, Underwriting and the Certification Hypothesis', *Journal of Financial Economics*, **13** (1984).

45   The government's only concession was to put a floor on the underwriters' losses by giving them the option to resell their shares to the government at £2.80 a share.

46   See N. Fay, The Pricing of Underwriting Risk in Initial Public Offerings: Australian Evidence, unpublished manuscript, Department of Accounting and Finance, The University of Melbourne, November 1995.

47   When a company undertakes a share issue, there is always a risk that the offer will not be fully subscribed due to insufficient demand. The purpose of underwriting is to transfer the risk of undersubscription from the company issuing the shares to the underwriter, such that the company will be guaranteed receipt of the full subscription value of the IPO. In return, the company pays a fee to the underwriter.

position taken by underwriters was similar to that of a put option held by the issuing company, underwriting risk was significantly overpriced relative to the offer price but was fairly priced relative to the initial share price on listing—especially in relation to resource over industrial companies.

## Underpricing of IPOs

Whenever a company goes public, it is very difficult to decide how much investors will be willing to pay for the shares. A number of researchers have tried to measure the success of gauging the value of such issues. With remarkable unanimity they have found that on average investors who buy at the issue price realise very high returns over the next few weeks. For example, a study by Ibbotson, Sindelar and Ritter[48] of nearly 10 600 new issues in the United States from 1960 to 1992 indicated average underpricing of 15.3 per cent. An Australian study by Finn and Higham[49] of 93 IPOs between 1966 and 1978 found average abnormal returns of 29.2 per cent. Another study by Taylor and Walter[50] of 139 IPOs between 1977 and 1986 found average abnormal returns of 13.4 per cent.

Let us consider the behaviour of the Cable & Wireless Optus share price in the months since its listing. As discussed above, the retail application price for CWO shares was $1.85 per share,[51] the final price for Australian and overseas institutions following the institutional bids was $2.61. The shares first traded for $2.61. The shares listed on Tuesday 17 November 1998. The closing price on that day for CWO shares was $2.65 per share after hitting a high of $2.74. By the Friday of the listing week (20 November 1998), the closing share price was $2.63. At 30 November 1998 the shares closed at $2.98; at 31 December 1998 they closed at $3.43; and by January 1999 they were at $3.77.

The literature has proposed a number of explanations for the underpricing anomaly.[52] These include:

- ■ underpricing serves as a form of insurance against legal liability;
- ■ incentives to underprice on the part of the underwriter due to information asymmetries about the value of the issuing company;
- ■ signalling that the issuing company is of a higher quality than other companies since only companies of high quality can be expected to recoup the loss of underpricing in the future;
- ■ incentives to keep uninformed investors in the market by underpricing;
- ■ signalling based on the existence of banking relationships, the presence of venture capitalists as shareholders, the use of underwriters and the use of a high quality auditor.

Do all issues result in underpricing? The obvious answer is no—while some issues are oversubscribed creating excess demand for the shares at the date of listing, some IPOs are also undersubscribed.[53] Hence simply subscribing an equal amount to every IPO will not result in handsome profits on average. If an issue is cheap, it is likely to be oversubscribed; if it is dear, it is likely to be undersubscribed. Hence you will receive a small proportion of the cheap (underpriced) issues and a large proportion of the dear (overpriced) issues.

---

48 R. Ibbotson, J. L. Sinclair and J. R. Ritter, 'The Market's Problem with the Pricing of Initial Public Offerings', *Journal of Applied Corporate Finance*, 7: 66–74 (1994).

49 F. J. Finn and R. Higham, 'The Performance of Unseasoned New Equity Issues in Cum-Stock Exchange Listings in Australia', *Journal of Banking and Finance*, 12: 333–51 (1988).

50 S. L. Taylor and T. S. Walter, Australian IPO Underpricing: Institutional Aspects and the Winner's Curse, working paper, Department of Accounting, University of Sydney, 1991.

51 In March 1999 CWO reported in a *Financial Performance Update* that retail shareholders subscribed for 11 per cent of issued capital at an initial offer price of $2.15 per share. This document is available at *http://www.optus.com.au/company/finperfup.pdf*.

52 For a comprehensive discussion of the explanations see I. M. Ramsay and B. K. Sidhu, 'Underpricing of Initial Public Offerings and Due Diligence Costs: An Empirical Investigation', *Company and Securities Law Journal*, 13: 186–201 (1995).

53 The problem faced by new issue investors is known as 'the winners curse'. See K. Rock, 'Why New Issues are Underpriced', *Journal of Financial Economics*, 15: 187–212 (January–February 1986).

## 15.3 Raising equity after the initial public offering

After its initial public offering, a company might continue to grow and, like most growing companies, it will from time to time make further issues of debt and/or equity finance. Any subsequent issue of securities within the limits of the company's constitution will need to be approved by the firm's board of directors. The primary methods used by companies in Australia to issue more shares include:

■ Rights issues.
■ Private placements.
■ Dividend reinvestment plans.
■ The floating of additional shares.

Table 15.1 displays the value of rights issues, private placements and dividend reinvestment plans in the years ended December 1987 to December 1997. Despite some record years in dollar value for rights issues and private placements, the only method to display sustained growth was dividend reinvestment plans.

**table 15.1**
Equity capital issues, December 1987 to December 1997 ($million)

| Year (to December) | Rights issues | Private placements | Dividend reinvestment plans |
|---|---|---|---|
| 1987 | 8005.8 | 4220.1 | 482.1 |
| 1988 | 6702.1 | 1694.4 | 568.9 |
| 1989 | 2314.2 | 1698.6 | 2418.0 |
| 1990 | 2347.1 | 1059.6 | 2514.0 |
| 1991 | 2724.5 | 1825.2 | 2017.1 |
| 1992 | 4415.5 | 2620.9 | 2645.3 |
| 1993 | 978.7 | 5450.3 | 2738.1 |
| 1994 | 3678.9 | 3344.6 | 3651.4 |
| 1995 | 2867.0 | 2103.8 | 3264.0 |
| 1996 | 1662.0 | 5423.0 | 3188.9 |
| 1997 | 4010.9 | 2861.4 | 3347.4 |

Source: ASX, *1998 Fact Book*, op. cit., Footnote 27, p. 8.

### Rights issues

In Australia, most companies seeking to raise further equity capital will make use of a rights issue. A rights issue involves the issue of securities to current shareholders who are given the right to purchase the securities, usually shares, in proportion to their holding of shares.[54]

---

[54] A rights issue that gives the shareholder one right for each share held is known as a 'New York right'. In the United States nearly all rights issues are conducted in this manner. In Australia you only need one right to purchase one new share. This is known as a 'Philadelphia right'. For example, assume that under a Philadelphia rights issue the owner of five shares received one right. This right would be correspondingly five times more valuable than under a New York right, where five shares would be issued on a one for one basis.

**How rights issues work**   The preliminary stages of a rights issue, regarding registration of the issue and the issue of a prospectus, are similar as for an IPO. Both the ASIC and ASX must be advised and a prospectus must be issued. Again, the advice of an investment bank may be obtained. However, given that the company is a known company at the time of the rights issue, the prospectus does not need to be as detailed as in the case of the IPO. The primary difference is in the selling procedures. Existing shareholders are advised that the company is conducting a rights issue, and that they are entitled to receive the right to an additional number of shares in proportion to the number of shares that they already hold.

Shareholders are advised of the purchase price or subscription price to purchase new shares and the calendar of critical dates for the rights issue. The rights issue will specify an ex-rights **date** and a subsequent date by which the right must be exercised. If shares are held by investors prior to the ex-rights date, they are said to be cum-rights, and any shares purchased on or after the ex-rights date are called ex-rights. Shares held cum-rights entitle the shareholder to participate in the rights issue. Shares held ex-rights do not give the same privilege. However, after the ex-rights date the rights can be traded independent to the shares up to the date specified for the exercise of the rights. In studying the impact of a rights issue, we are particularly interested in the impact of share prices at the time of the announcement of the rights issue and at the subsequent ex-rights date. But first we want to be able to value the rights attached to the shareholding.

If the rights issue is renounceable (which is the usual case in Australia), shareholders can accept the offer to buy the shares, let the offer lapse or sell their rights. In a renounceable rights issue, shareholders can sell the rights separately after the ex-rights date. If the issue is non-renounceable, holders of shares prior to the ex-rights date can either accept the offer to buy the shares or let the offer lapse.

Here is an example of how a rights issue works. In June 1998, Buttercup Engineering Ltd announced that it intended to issue $198 million of ordinary shares by a renounceable 'one for four rights issue'. Shareholders could exercise, sell or throw away their rights. The details of the rights issue are detailed in Table 15.2. The rights issue is a one for four issue, which means that shareholders have the right to purchase one share for each four shares currently held.

**table 15.2**

Details of Buttercup Engineering Ltd rights issue

| | |
|---|---|
| Rights issue | One for four issue |
| Ex-rights date | 31 July 1998 |
| Final acceptance date | 31 August 1998 |
| Cum-rights share price (28 July 1998) | $2.50 |
| Subscription or offer price | $2.00 |

How much is the right worth to the holder of four shares in Buttercup Engineering Ltd? The share price[55] in the cum-rights period should equal the theoretical price in the ex-rights period plus the value of the attached rights. In the ex-rights period the value of the share is equal to the price of the share less the subscription or offer price specified in the offer.

On 28 July 1998 the four shares are equal to the cum-rights price multiplied by the number of shares ($2.50 × 4 shares = $10.00). To calculate the theoretical ex-rights price, assume

---

[55]   In the United States this price is often referred to as the 'rights-on' price.

that the shareholder exercises the right and purchases one further share. The portfolio will now be worth the value of the cum-rights portfolio plus the cost of subscribing ($2.50 × 4 shares + $2.00 × 1 share = $12.00). At this time, the *theoretical ex-rights share price* is equal to $12.00/5 shares = $2.40. This price can be calculated as

$$\frac{(4 \times 2.50 + 1 \times 2.00)}{(4 + 1)} = \frac{12.00}{5} = \$2.40$$

The value of the right per share or the *theoretical rights price* in the cum-rights period is calculated as:

$$\frac{4 \times (2.50 - 2.00)}{(4 + 1)} = \frac{2.00}{5} = \$0.40$$

The difference between the cum-rights price and the theoretical ex-rights price ($2.50 − 2.40 = $0.10) represents the amount by which the price of the share can be expected to fall when trading goes ex-rights.

It can now be seen that the theoretical rights price of $2.40 is equal to the subscription price plus the cost of the right. That is, 2.00 + 0.40 = $2.40. Furthermore, the cum-rights price less the expected drop off in the price must equal the theoretical ex-rights share price. If this relationship did not hold, arbitrage profits could be obtained by shareholders.

In assessing whether shareholder wealth has been impacted by a rights issue, it is useful to assess the impact of the rights issue on the value of the portfolio held by a current and a potential investor. The wealth of a shareholder with four shares just prior to the one for four rights issue at the cum-rights price per share of $2.50 is $10.00. Ex-rights the investment is worth the value of the shares ex-rights plus the value of the rights equal to 4 × 2.40 + 0.40 = $10.00. It is obvious that the decline in the value of the shares is offset by the value of the rights. Consequently, the shareholder's wealth is unaffected.

It should be clear on reflection that Buttercup Engineering could have raised the same amount of money on a variety of rights terms. For example, instead of a one for four issue at $2.00, it could have used a one for two issue at $1.00 per share. If we work through the arithmetic again in Table 15.3 we can see that the issue price is irrelevant. In this case it would have sold twice as many shares at half the price. If we work through the calculations again we find that the issue price is irrelevant in a rights issue. Assume that we still hold four shares. Exercising of the one for two rights issue will entitle the shareholder to purchase two shares at $1.00 each. In this case the cum-rights price is $2.50 and the theoretical ex-rights share price is equal to:

$$\frac{(2 \times 2.50 + 1 \times 1.00)}{(2 + 1)} = \$2.00$$

and the expected fall in the share price when the shares go ex-rights is $0.50. The theoretical value of one right or theoretical rights price is

$$\frac{2 \times (2.50 - 1.00)}{(2 + 1)} = \frac{3}{3} = \$1.00$$

Hence, when trading goes ex-rights the price of the share is expected to equal the cum-rights price less the expected fall in the price (2.50 − 0.50 = $2.00), which is equal to the theoretical value of one right plus the subscription price (1.00 + 1.00 = $2.00).

The only factor that a firm needs to worry about in setting the terms of a rights issue is the possibility that the share price may fall below the subscription or offer price. If this does happen, assuming the rationality of the investors, the rights issue will be a disaster. Shareholders will not take up their rights. To avoid such a problem, for a fee it is again possible that the company holding the rights issue could obtain the services of an underwriter through a stand-by agreement, where the underwriter agrees to purchase the shares that have not been taken up under the rights issue.

**table 15.3**

Demonstration that the issue price in a rights issue does not affect the shareholders' wealth.

| | 1 for 4 at $2.00 | 1 for 2 at $1.00 |
|---|---|---|
| Number of shares held | 4 | 4 |
| Cum-rights price | 2.50 | 2.50 |
| Value of holding | 10.00 | 10.00 |
| Theoretical ex-rights share price (per share) | 2.40 | 2.00[a] |
| Value of one right when the share goes ex-rights (theoretical ex-rights price less the subscription price) | 0.40 | 1.00[b] |
| Number of new shares issued | 1 | 2 |
| **Amount of new investment** | 1 × 2.00 = $2.00 | 2 × 1.00 = $2.00 |
| Total number of shares | 5 | 6 |

Notes:

[a] Calculated as $(2 \times 2.50 + 1 \times 1.00)/(2 + 1) = 6/3 = 2.00$.

[b] Calculated as $2 \times (2.50 - 1.00)/(2 + 1) = 3/3 = 1.00$.

# The choice between the floating of new shares and the rights issue

You now know about the two principal forms of public issue—the floating of new shares and a rights issue. Under the floating offer all investors may subscribe, while the rights issue is restricted to existing shareholders. The former method is used for almost all debt issues and for equity IPOs. Rights issues are restricted to seasoned share issues.

Using arguments based on information asymmetry between the management of the company and the investors, some authors have argued that a rights issue can be viewed as a signal of negative information about the firm's ability to generate its own future cash flows.[56] However, such arguments ignore issues such as corporate governance and the regulatory requirements on firms at the time of issuing new shares.

One essential difference between the two methods is that in a rights issue the subscription price is largely irrelevant. Shareholders can sell their new shares or their rights at the ASX if they wish. In a float or new share issue, the issue price may be important. If the company sells shares for less than the market believes is a reasonable price, the buyer will make a profit at the expense of existing shareholders. Although this danger presents natural presumption in favour of the rights issue, it can be argued that underpricing is a serious problem only for unseasoned IPOs in which a rights issue is not a feasible alternative.[57]

---

[56] For a detailed presentation of these arguments in relation to information asymmetry see M. Miller and K. Rock, 'Dividend Policy Under Asymmetric Information', *Journal of Finance*, **40**: 1031–52 (1985); and S. Myers and N. Majluf, 'Corporate Investment and Financial Decisions When Firms Have Information That Investors Do Not Have', *Journal of Financial Economics*, **13**: 187–222 (1984).

[57] C. W. Smith, 'Alternative Methods of Raising Capital: Rights Issues Versus Underwritten Offerings', *Journal of Financial Economics*, **5**: 273–307 (December 1977).

## Private placements

When a firm makes a public offering it is obliged to register the issue with both the Australian Securities and Investment Commission and the Australian Stock Exchange. It can avoid this costly process if it can sell the securities privately to an institutional investor or to private investors as opposed to making a public offering. Typically, private placements are sold to institutions such as superannuation funds and fund managers at a discount to the current market price. ASX listing rules prohibit firms from privately placing more than 10 per cent of their capital in any one year to non-shareholders without shareholder approval. Placements do not require the issue of a prospectus. However, the announcement of the private placement regularly leads to a negative market price reaction and it may be viewed as a dilution of the voting power of existing holders of blocks of shares.[58]

## Dividend reinvestment plans

If existing shareholders elect, they can participate in dividend reinvestment plans (DRPs), where the company will automatically reinvest all, or part, of the shareholders' dividend payments into additional fully paid ordinary shares in the company. Dividend reinvestment plans became an important source of equity finance in the late 1980s and, as we noted in Table 15.1, have consistently grown as a source of funding since that time. These plans allow shareholders to reinvest their dividend receipts in shares in the company. They resolve an obvious conflict between companies and shareholders, in that firms would like to retain higher levels of earnings and pay out less in dividends. With dividend reinvestment plans, companies are able to recapture the dividends they pay out.

The reinvestment of dividends is a cost-effective way of raising new capital as it does not require a prospectus and has a ready-made market of existing shareholders. In 1994 DRPs accounted for 21 per cent of all ASX equity raisings, compared to only 2.5 per cent in 1987.

DRP shares are usually issued at a discount to the market price by between 2.5 and 10 per cent, with most companies at about 5 per cent. They are particularly attractive to small investors because of the lack of transaction costs. An investor's entitlement to shares under the DRP is usually calculated as follows:

$$\frac{\text{Cash dividend in cents per share} \times \text{number of participating shares}}{\text{Market price per share} - \text{discount}}$$

In June 1996 there were in excess of 70 listed firms in Australia having DRPs including BHP, Coles Myer Limited, GIO Australia Holdings Limited, MIM Holdings Limited and Qantas. Investors wishing to participate in DRPs must apply to each company on a prescribed application form. All shares issued via DRPs are regarded as dividends for tax purposes.

An alternative dividend retirement plan involves what are referred to as share election schemes or bonus share plans. Under these plans, shares are issued from a company's share premium reserve rather than from company profits. These shares are generally excluded from the definition of dividends for tax purposes but do attract capital gains tax. This type of investment is well suited to foreign investors who do not pay Australian income tax.

We will have more to say about DRPs in Chapter 16.

## 15.4 Market reaction to share issues

Because share issues usually throw a large additional supply onto the market, it is widely believed that they must temporarily depress the share price. If the proposed issue is very large, the price pressure may, it is thought, be so severe as to make it impossible to raise new money. If so, the firm effectively faces capital rationing.

---

58  For a comprehensive discussion see K. H. Wruck, 'Equity Ownership Concentration and Firm Value: Equity from Private Equity Financings', *Journal of Financial Economics*, **23**: 3–28 (1989).

Economists who have studied new issues of ordinary shares have generally found that announcement of the issue *does* result in a decline in the share price.[59] The fall in market value is equivalent, on average, to nearly a third of the new money raised by the issue.

What is going on here? Is the price of the share simply depressed by the prospect of the additional supply? It is possible, but there is a better explanation.

Suppose that a retailing fruit and vegetable chain's director is strongly optimistic about its prospects. From her point of view, the company's share price is too low. Yet the company wants to issue shares to finance expansion into Queensland. What is she to do? All of the choices have drawbacks. If the chain sells shares at too low a price, it will favour new investors at the expense of old shareholders. When investors come to share the director's optimism, the share price will rise, and the new investors' bargain price will be evident.

If the director could convince investors to accept her rosy view of the future, then new shares could be sold at a fair price. But this is not so easy. Directors always take care to *sound* upbeat, so just announcing 'I'm optimistic' has little effect. But supplying sufficiently detailed information about business plans and profit forecasts is costly, and also great assistance for competitors.

The director could scale back or delay the expansion until the company's share price recovers. That too is costly, but it may be rational if the share price is severely undervalued and a share issue is the only immediate source of financing.

If a director knows that the company's shares are *over*valued, the position is reversed. If the firm sells new shares at the high price, it will help its existing shareholders at the expense of the new ones. Managers might be prepared to issue shares even if the new cash were just put in the bank.

Of course, investors are not stupid. They can predict that managers are more likely to issue shares when they think the share price is overvalued, and that optimistic managers may cancel or defer issues. Therefore, when an equity issue is announced, they mark down the price of the shares accordingly. Thus, the decline in the price of the shares at the time of the new issue may have nothing to do with the increased supply, but simply with the information that the issue provides.[60]

Cornett and Tehranian devised a natural experiment that pretty much proves this point.[61] They examined a sample of share issues by commercial banks in the United States. Some of these issues were *involuntary*, that is, mandated by banking authorities to meet regulatory capital standards. The rest were ordinary, voluntary share issues designed to raise money for various corporate purposes. The involuntary issues caused a much smaller drop in share prices than the voluntary ones—which makes perfect sense. If the issue is outside the manager's discretion, announcement of the issue conveys no information about the manager's view of the company's prospects.[62]

Most financial economists now interpret the share price drop on equity issue announcements as an information effect, not a result of imperfect or inefficient markets.

There is, however, at least one big puzzle left. It appears that the long-run performance of companies that issue shares is substandard. Investors who bought these companies' shares *after* the share issue announcements earned lower returns than if they had bought into otherwise similar, non-issuing companies. This result holds for both IPOs and seasoned issues, and

---

[59]　See, for example, P. Asquith and D. W. Mullins, 'Equity Issues and Offering Dilution', *Journal of Financial Economics*, **15**: 61–90 (January–February 1986); R. W. Masulis and A. N. Korwar, 'Seasoned Equity Offerings: An Empirical Investigation', *Journal of Financial Economics*, **15**: 91–118 (January–February 1986); W. H. Mikkelson and M. M. Partch, 'Valuation Effects of Security Offerings and the Issuance Process', *Journal of Financial Economics*, **15**: 31–60 (January–February 1986). There appears to be a smaller price decline for utility issues. Also, Marsh observed a smaller decline for rights issues in the United Kingdom: see P. R. Marsh, 'Equity Rights Issues and the Efficiency of the UK Stock Market', *Journal of Finance*, **34**: 839–62 (September 1979).

[60]　This explanation was developed in Myers and Majluf, op. cit., Footnote 56.

[61]　M. M. Cornett and H. Tehranian, 'An Examination of Voluntary Versus Involuntary Issuances by Commercial Banks', *Journal of Economics*, **35**: 99–122 (1994).

[62]　The fact that regulators found it necessary to force a bank to raise additional capital is probably bad news too. Thus, it is no surprise that Cornett and Tehranian found some drop in share price even for the involuntary issues.

does not appear to reflect differences in risk.[63] It seems that the investors who bought the issues were overly optimistic, and failed to appreciate fully the issuing companies' information advantage. If so, we have an exception to the efficient market theory laid out in Chapter 13. It will be interesting to see whether the poor relative long-term performance of issuing companies' shares persists. We think the poor performance will disappear now that investors know about it.

## The dilution fallacy

The popular price-earnings fallacies were amply described in Chapter 4. But we have not yet dissected the dilution fallacy. We do so here because the fallacy sometimes confuses financial managers who are trying to decide whether to issue equity.

The imagined dangers of dilution are dramatised by the sad tale of Nonkuba Hats Ltd. Nonkuba's profitability is as follows:

- Book net worth — $100 000
- Number of shares — 10 000
- Book value per share — $100 000/10 000 = $10
- Net earnings — $8 000
- Earnings per share — $8 000/10 000 = $0.80
- Price-earnings ratio — 10
- Share price — 10 × $0.80 = $8.00
- Total market value — $80 000

The total amount of money that has been put up by Nonkuba's shareholders is $100 000—$10 per share. But that investment is earning only $0.80 per share—an 8 per cent book return. Investors evidently regard this return as inadequate, for they are willing to pay only $8 per share for Nonkuba shares.

Now suppose that Nonkuba raises $10 000 by issuing 1250 additional shares at the market price of $8 per share—suppose also that the $10 000 is invested to earn a return of 8 per cent. Now we have:

|  | Before the issue | After the issue |
|---|---|---|
| Book net worth | $100 000 | $110 000 |
| Number of shares | 10 000 | 11 250 |
| Book value per share | $100 000/10 000 = $10 | $110 000/11 250 = $9.78 |
| Net earnings | $8 000 | 8% of book net worth = $8 800 |
| Earnings per share | $8 000/10 000 = $0.80 | $8 800/11 250 = $0.7822 |
| Price-earnings ratio | 10 | 10 |
| Share price | 10 × $0.80 = $8.00 | 10 × $0.7822 = $7.82 |
| Total market value | $80 000 | $87 975 |

We note that selling shares below book value *does* decrease book value per share and the share price as well.

But there are two things wrong with our example. First, we assume investors could be tricked into paying $8 for shares shortly destined to be worth $7.82. Actually, if Nonkuba wishes to raise $10 000, it will have to offer shares *worth* $10 000. And since we know that

---

aggregate market value after the share issue is almost $88 000, the *original* 10 000 shares must end up with an aggregate value of $78 200. The price per share will therefore be $78 200/ 10 000 = $7.82, and the firm will have to issue $10 000/7.82 = 1279 shares to raise the capital it requires.

Many financial analysts would stop at this point, satisfied that they had 'proved' the folly of selling shares for less than book value. But there is a second thing wrong with our example: We never questioned Nonkuba's decision to expand. It is raising $10 000 and getting only $8000 in additional market value. In other words, the market's verdict is that expansion has an NPV of −$2000. Note that this is exactly the loss suffered by the original shareholders.

There is no harm whatsoever in selling shares at prices below book value per share, as long as investors know that you can earn an adequate rate of return on the new money. If the firm has good projects and needs equity capital to finance them, then 'dilution' should not bar it from going to the market.

## 15.5 Summary

In this chapter we have summarised the various procedures for issuing corporate securities. We first looked at how infant companies raised venture capital to carry them through to the point at which they can make their first public issue of shares. We then looked at how companies can make further public issues of securities by a general cash offer. It is always difficult to summarise a summary. Instead, we will attempt to state the most important implications for the financial manager who must decide how to raise capital.

1.  *Larger is cheaper.* There are always economies of scale in issuing securities. It is cheaper to go to the market once for $100 million than to make two trips for $50 million each. Consequently, firms 'bunch' security issues. That may often mean relying on short-term financing until a large issue is justified. Or it may mean issuing more than is needed at the moment in order to avoid another issue later.

2.  *There are no issue costs for retained earnings.* There are significant costs associated with any share issue. But share issues can be avoided to the extent that the firm can plough back its earnings. Why then do we observe firms paying generous cash dividends *and* issuing shares from time to time? Why don't they cut the dividend, reduce new issues and thereby avoid paying underwriters, solicitors and accountants? This is a question to which we will return in Chapter 16.

3.  *Private placements for the small, risky and unusual.* We do not mean that large, safe and conventional firms should rule out private placements. Enormous amounts of capital are sometimes raised by this method. For example, MIM Holdings raised over $400 million in 1984 in a private placement. But most placements are for parcels less than $100 000.

4.  *Watch out for underpricing.* Underpricing is a hidden cost to the existing shareholders. Fortunately, it is usually serious only for companies who are selling shares to the public for the first time.

5.  *New share issues may depress the price.* The extent of this price pressure varies, but for industrial issues in Australia the fall in the value of the existing shares may amount to a significant proportion of the money raised.

## FURTHER READING

A useful article on investment banking is:

C. W. Smith, 'Investment Banking and the Capital Acquisition Process', *Journal of Financial Economics*, **15**: 3–29 (January–February 1986).

The best sources of material on venture capital are the specialised journals. See, for example, recent issues of the *Australian Venture Capital Journal*. A very readable analysis of how venture capital financing is structured to provide the right incentives is contained in:

W. A. Sahlman, 'Aspects of Financial Contracting in Venture Capital', *Journal of Applied Corporate Finance*, **1**: 23–6 (Summer 1988).

Articles studying Australian IPOs include:

J. How, H. Izan and G. Monroe, 'Differential Information and Underpricing of IPOs: Australian Evidence', *Accounting and Finance*, **35** (1): 87–105 (May 1995).

S. L. Taylor and T. S. Walter, Australian IPO Underpricing: Institutional Aspects the Winner's Curse, working paper, Department of Accounting, University of Sydney, 1991.

There have been a number of studies of the market for unseasoned issues of ordinary shares. Good articles to start with are:

P. Asquith and D. W. Mullins, 'Equity Issues and Offering Dilution', *Journal of Financial Economics*, **15**: 61–90 (January–February 1986).

R. G. Ibbotson, J. L. Sindelar and J. R. Ritter, 'The Market's Problem with Initial Public Offerings', *Journal of Applied Corporate Finance*, **7**: 66–74 (Spring 1994).

P. R. Marsh, 'Equity Rights Issues and the Efficiency of the UK Stock Market', *Journal of Finance*, **34**: 839–62 (September 1979).

J. R. Ritter, 'The "Hot Issue" Market of 1980', *Journal of Business*, **57**: 215–41 (1984).

R. W. Masulis and A. N. Korwar, 'Seasoned Equity Offerings: An Empirical Investigation', *Journal of Financial Economics*, **15**: 91–118 (January–February 1986).

K. Rock, 'Why New Issues Are Underpriced', *Journal of Financial Economics*, **15**: 187–212 (January–February 1986).

Myers and Majluf analyse the information problems associated with security issues:

S. C. Myers and N. S. Majluf, 'Corporate Financing When Firms Have Information That Investors Do Not Have', *Journal of Financial Economics*, **13**: 187–222 (1984).

Very useful Web sites regarding issues discussed in this chapter include:

Australian Securities and Investment Commission (*http://www.asc.gov.au*)

Australian Stock Exchange (*http://www.asx.com.au*)

## QUIZ

**1.** Beside each of the following issue methods we have listed two issues. Choose the one more likely to employ that method:

   a. Rights issue (issue of seasoned shares/issue of unseasoned shares).

   b. Private placement (issue of seasoned shares/bond issue by industrial company).

**2.** State for each of the following pairs of issues which you would expect to involve the lower proportionate underwriting and administrative costs, other things being equal:

   a. A large issue/a small issue.

   b. A bond issue/an ordinary share.

**3.** You need to choose between issuing:

   ■ *A public issue of $10 million face value of 10-year debt.* The interest rate on the debt would be 8.5 per cent and the debt would be issued at face value. The underwriting fee would be 1.5 per cent and other expenses would be $80 000.

■ *A private placement of $10 million face value of 10-year debt.* The interest rate on the private placement would be 9 per cent and other expenses would only be $30 000.

a. What is the difference in the proceeds to the company net of expenses?
b. Other things being equal, which is the better deal?
c. What other factors beyond the interest rate and issue costs would you wish to consider before deciding between the two offers?

4. Allied and Associated Breweries Ltd is planning to market non-alcoholic beer. To finance the venture it proposes to make a rights issue at $10 of one new share for each two shares held. (The company currently has outstanding 100 000 shares priced at $20 a share.) Assuming that the new money is invested to earn a fair return, give values for the following:
a. Number of rights needed to purchase one share.
b. Number of new shares.
c. Amount of new investment.
d. Total value of company after issue.
e. Total number of shares after issue.
f. Cum-rights price.
g. Ex-rights price.
h. Price of a theoretical right.

5. True or false?
a. Venture capitalists typically provide start-up financing sufficient to cover all development expenses. Second stage financing is provided by shares issued in an initial public offering.
b. Large companies' shares may be listed and traded on several different international exchanges.
c. Share issues should be avoided if the increased number of shares reduces earnings per share.
d. Share price generally falls when the company announces a new issue of shares. This is attributable to the information released by the decision to issue.

## QUESTIONS AND PROBLEMS

1. In some countries initial public offerings of ordinary shares are sold by auction. Another procedure is for the underwriter to advertise the issue publicly and invite orders for shares at the issue price. If the applications exceed the number of shares on offer, then they are scaled down in proportion; if there are too few applications, any unsold shares are left with the underwriter. Compare these procedures with the initial public offering in Australia. Can you think of any better ways to sell new shares?

2. Why do venture capital companies prefer to advance money in stages?

3. 'For small issues of ordinary shares, the costs of flotation amount to about 5 per cent of the proceeds. This means that the opportunity cost of external equity capital is about 5 percentage points higher than that of retained earnings.' Does this follow?

4. Do you think that there could be a shortage of finance for new ventures? Should the government help to provide such finance and, if so, how?

**5.** Why are the issue costs for debt issues generally less than for equity issues? List the possible reasons.

**6.** In what circumstances is a private placement preferable to a public issue? Explain.

**7.** In 1998 Pandora Ltd makes a rights issue at $5 a share of one new share for every four shares held. Before the issue there were 10 million shares outstanding and the share price was $6.
a. What is the total amount of new money raised?
b. How many rights are needed to buy one new share?
c. What is the value of one right?
d. What is the ex-rights theoretical share price?
e. How far could the total value of the company fall before shareholders would be unwilling to take up their rights?

**8.** Question 7 contains details of a rights offering by Pandora Ltd. Suppose that the company had decided to issue new shares at $4. How many new shares would it have needed to raise the same sum of money? Recalculate the answers to Parts (b) to (e) in Question 7. Show that Pandora's shareholders are just as well off if it issues the shares at $4 a share rather than the $5 assumed in Question 7.

**9.** Construct a simple numerical example to show the following:
a. Existing shareholders are made worse off when a company makes a cash offer of new shares below the market price.
b. Existing shareholders are *not* made worse off when a company makes a rights issue of new shares below the market price even if the shareholders do not wish to take up their rights.

**10.** Here is recent financial data on Pisa Construction Ltd:

▪ Share price           = $40
▪ Number of shares      = 10 000
▪ Book net worth        = $500 000
▪ Market value of firm  = $400 000
▪ Earnings per share    = $4
▪ Return on investment  = 8 per cent

Pisa has not performed spectacularly to date. However, it wishes to issue new shares to obtain $80 000 to finance expansion into a promising market. Pisa's financial advisers think a share issue is a poor choice because, among other reasons, 'sale of shares at a price below book value per share can only depress the share price and decrease shareholders' wealth'. To prove the point they construct the following example:
   'Suppose 2000 new shares are issued at $40 and the proceeds invested. (Neglect issue costs.) Suppose return on investment does not change. Then:

$$\text{Book net worth} = \$580\,000$$
$$\text{Total earnings} = 0.08(580\,000) = \$46\,400$$

$$\text{Earnings per share} = \frac{46\,400}{12\,000} = \$3.87$$

Thus, the earnings per share declines, book value per share declines, and share price will decline proportionately to $38.70.'

Evaluate this argument with particular attention to the assumptions implicit in the numerical example.

**11.** There are three reasons that an ordinary share issue might cause a fall in price:
   a. Demand for the company's shares is inelastic.
   b. The issue causes price pressure until it has been digested.
   c. Management has information that shareholders do not have.
   Explain these reasons more fully. Which do you find most plausible? Is there any way that you could seek to test whether you are right?

# part 5

# DIVIDEND POLICY AND CAPITAL STRUCTURE

# chapter 16

# THE DIVIDEND CONTROVERSY

In this chapter we explain how companies set their dividend payments and we discuss the controversial question of how dividend policy affects value.

Why should you care about the answer to this question? Of course, if you are responsible for choosing your company's dividend payment, you will want to know how it affects value. But there is a more general reason than that. We have up to this point assumed that the company's investment decision is independent of its financing policy. In that case a good project is a good project is a good project, no matter who undertakes it or how it is ultimately financed. If dividend policy does not affect value, that is still true. But perhaps it *does* affect value. In that case the attractiveness of a new project may depend on where the money is coming from. For example, if investors prefer companies with high payouts, companies might be reluctant to take

on investments financed by retained earnings.

The first step towards understanding dividend policy is to recognise that the phrase means different things to different people. Therefore, we must start by defining what *we* mean by it.

A firm's decisions about dividends are often mixed up with other financing and investment decisions. Remember the cash flow identity in Chapter 1, where we showed how dividends, investment and financing decisions are linked together?

Some firms pay low dividends because management is optimistic about the firm's future and wishes to retain earnings for expansion. In this case the dividend is a by-product of the firm's capital budgeting decision. Suppose, however, that the future opportunities evaporate, that a dividend increase is announced and that the share price falls. How do we separate the impact of the dividend increase from the impact of investors' disappointment at the lost growth opportunities?

Another firm might finance capital expenditures largely by borrowing. This releases cash for dividends. In this case the firm's dividend is a by-product of the borrowing decision, and it is difficult to separate the valuation impact of borrowing from the impact of the dividend.

We must therefore isolate dividend policy from other problems of financial management. The precise question we should ask is: 'What is the effect of a change in cash dividends paid, *given the firm's capital budgeting and borrowing decisions*?' Of course, the cash used to finance a dividend increase has to come from somewhere. If we fix the firm's investment outlays and borrowing, there is only one possible source—an issue of shares. Thus, we define *dividend policy* as the trade-off between retaining earnings on the one hand and paying out cash and issuing new shares on the other. In terms of the cash flow identity we would write the relationship as follows:

$$\text{Investment} - \text{borrowing} - \text{cash operating income} = \text{share issue} - \text{dividends}$$

For example, assume that the firm has already decided to invest \$100 million and has set borrowing at \$50 million, and also that the cash operating income has been determined as \$40 million. The variables on the left-hand side of the equation are now fixed. The only decision left is to choose the trade-off between share issues and dividends on the right-hand side of the equation. If we pay no dividends we would have to make a \$10 million share issue in order to balance our cash flow. If we pay dividends of \$20 million, then we must make a \$30 million share issue. The higher the dividend the bigger the share issue.

This trade-off may seem artificial at first, for we do not observe firms scheduling a share issue with every dividend payment. But it is the only means to clearly separate the impact of the dividend decision from other financial decisions. Moreover, there are many firms that pay dividends and also issue shares from time to time. They could avoid the share issues by paying lower dividends. Many other firms restrict dividends so that they *do not* have to issue shares. They could issue shares occasionally and increase the dividend. Both groups of firms are facing the dividend policy trade-off.

## 16.1 How dividends are paid

Most companies in Australia make two dividend payments per year: an interim dividend and a final dividend. The dividends are set by recommendation of the company's board of directors. The interim dividend is normally at the discretion of the directors. Depending on the company's Articles of Association, the directors' recommendation for the final dividends may have to be ratified by shareholders at the company's annual general meeting. In general, the directors do not change dividends sharply from year to year. When dividends do change the bulk of the change will usually be made in the final dividend. A substantial increase in the interim dividend often signals particularly good profitability in the first half of the year that is expected to continue.

The dividend announcement states that the payment will be made to all those shareholders who are listed on the shareholder register at a particular 'books close date', or 'date of record'. After the books close dividend cheques are mailed to the registered shareholders. This mailing usually takes place between two weeks and two months after the books close date. Some companies may offer you the option of an electronic payment direct to your bank account.

Shares listed on the ASX are normally bought and sold 'cum (with) dividend' until a date specified by the exchange—the 'ex-dividend date'. For most of the 1990s this date was set seven business days before the books close date; in 1999 the ASX changed this back to five business days. For example, OPSM had a books close date of 6 April 1999 and an ex-dividend date of 29 March 1999. This is a calendar spread of nine days, but it spans the four-day Easter long-weekend—take that out and you are left with a difference of five business days.[1] This is

---

1   The circle is complete: before the seven business day rule was introduced the ex-date used to be five days before the books close date.

done so that investors who buy cum-dividend do not have to worry if their shares are not registered in time. The dividend must be paid over to them by the seller. Similarly, investors who
buy a share 'ex dividend' are obliged to return the dividend if they receive it.

The time taken to become a registered shareholder was sometimes excessive under the old
paper-based share transfer system. Now the ASX has moved to an electronic settlement system CHESS (Clearing House Electronic Subregister System) and transfers are accomplished
more quickly. Partly as a consequence of more rapid transfers, a new phenomenon has
emerged in the Australian share market. At the request of a broker, the ASX has in some cases
permitted cum-dividend trading in the ex-dividend period.

## Some legal limitations on dividends

Suppose that an unscrupulous board decided to sell all the firm's assets and distribute the money
as dividends. That would not leave anything in the kitty to pay the company's debts. Therefore,
debtholders often guard against this danger by placing a limit on dividend payments. They do
this by inserting a protective covenant in the debt contract that they agree with the firm.

The law also helps to protect the company's creditors against excessive dividend payments,
for example, preventing directors from paying a dividend if doing so would make the company insolvent.

There is a long legal tradition that dividends are to be paid out of profits not capital. Thus,
dividends may not normally be paid if this would cause a reduction in either the paid up capital
or share premium accounts. Effectively this means that there must be a credit entry in a profit
account at least equal to the proposed dividend. In 1992 an asset write-down by CSR of nearly
$700 million created an extraordinary loss that virtually wiped out the balance in the retained
profit account. In order to pay a dividend legally CSR sought approval from shareholders and the
courts to transfer over $500 million from its share premium reserve to its retained profit account.

The CSR example shows that although the principle of 'payment from profits' is clear, its
application is not straightforward. There has been extensive legal debate about what constitutes profit and capital. For example, in one case it was decided that a dividend could be paid
based on profit arising from the revaluation of an asset; in another case the reverse judgement
was reached; while in a third case it was judged that such a dividend could be paid but only
if all the company's assets were re-valued.

## Dividends come in many forms

There are many different forms of dividend. Their creation is often driven by attempts to minimise taxes and transactions costs and/or cater to different **shareholder clienteles**. For example,
an investor who is not resident in Australia and therefore not subject to Australian income tax
will prefer a different dividend policy to an Australian superannuation fund taxed at 15 per
cent. Subsequent to the introduction of the imputation system of taxation in 1987, the creation of alternative dividend schemes has become a growth industry in Australia.

In addition to the *regular* interim and final dividends companies may pay *special* or *extra*
dividends. By this labelling of the dividend the firm signals to investors that these are one-off
payments that they should not expect to continue. Despite the alternatives available, most dividends are regular dividends and are paid as cash.

### Dividends with franking credits
Under the imputation tax system the value of
the dividend received by the investor may be greater than its face value. We discuss imputation in detail later in this chapter. But we must introduce it here because you will need to
understand what is meant by statements such as 'the dividend is fully franked'. If an investor
receives a franked dividend this means the dividend is accompanied by a franking credit. *Some*
investors are able to use this credit to reduce their tax liability. The size of this credit largely
depends on how much Australian tax the company has paid on its profits. Tax legislation
requires the company to maintain a record of the franking credits obtained and the credits

distributed to shareholders. This record is maintained by keeping track of the fully franked dividends that a company can pay through a special account called the franking account.

Depending on the balance available in the franking account, the dividend may be fully or partially franked or not franked at all. This can have a substantial impact on the value of the package of dividends plus franking credits. With the corporate tax rate at 36 per cent, a $1 fully franked dividend is worth $1.56 to some shareholders. So the franking credit can be worth more than half the value of the dividend.

**Liquidating dividends**    Sometimes companies go into voluntary liquidation, and sometimes they are wound up by a liquidator representing debtholders. If there is anything left over for the shareholders this constitutes a *liquidating dividend*. To the extent that this dividend represents a distribution of income, or capital gains, previously earned by the company the liquidating dividend is taxed as an ordinary dividend. If the distribution is a return of capital then no income tax is payable. However, a capital gains tax liability may arise if the shares were purchased after 19 September 1985.

**Dividends in kind**    There are also non-cash dividends. For example, companies sometimes send shareholders a sample of their product or sell it to shareholders at a discount. Coles Myer, for example, offered shareholders a discount on purchases at Coles Myer stores. The British company Dundee Crematorium once offered its more substantial shareholders a discount cremation. Needless to say, you were not *required* to receive this dividend. Dividends in kind are generally liable to income tax, like ordinary cash dividends. We suspect, however, that they do not generate much tax revenue.

**Bonus dividends**    Between the time of writing and publication the law has changed. Shares no longer have a par value and therefore the share premium account no longer exists. The discussion below relates to bonus issues before these changes took place. We will provide an updated discussion on the publisher's Web site. But we predict an increase in stock splits in response to the abolition of the share premium account. Another form of non-cash dividend is the issue of bonus shares. Prior to imputation many companies used to regularly declare *bonus share dividends*, where extra share scrip was distributed to all shareholders. For example, in eight out of the 10 years prior to the introduction of the imputation system OPSM declared a bonus dividend. Suppose your company declares a 1-for-2 bonus—you will receive one extra share for every two shares that you own. In the company's books of account there will be a transfer from the share premium account, or possibly the retained earnings account, to the paid up capital account, equal to the par value of the shares issued. You end up with more shares, but the price per share falls.

As we discussed in Chapter 13, the bonus issue of itself does not make you any better off.[2] When bonus issues have a positive impact on company value it is because they are accompanied by an implicit or explicit promise of higher cash dividends. This in turn is a signal to investors that the company is now generating more cash. Of course, this makes the company more valuable.

Companies try to make sure that any bonus shares issued are charged against the share premium account rather than the retained earnings account. This might seem to be a triumph of form over substance. However, it has important tax consequences. If the bonus share issue is from the share premium account, the issue is treated as a distribution of capital and is not taxable in the hands of the investor. If the bonus issue is made from the retained earnings account, it is treated as a normal taxable dividend.

Nowadays Australian companies rarely make bonus issues to all shareholders. Instead, an increasing number offer **bonus share plans**. Under such plans the shareholder can elect to take bonus shares instead of a cash dividend.[3] These issues are not made pro rata to all

---

2  Because of tax effects it may make you worse off. However, as we discuss shortly, bonus shares can be valuable in cases where they are not distributed to all shareholders.

3  The rate of transformation of cash dividends into bonus shares is based on the market price after the existing shares go ex-dividend.

shareholders; therefore, the shareholders taking the bonus increase the proportion of the company that they own. These bonus shares have real value since they proportionately increase the holders' claims on the company's assets and cash flows.

As discussed above, the shares for the bonus share plan will usually be issued from the share premium reserve. This can be particularly attractive to those shareholders who originally purchased their shares before the capital gains tax was introduced in 1985. They receive the bonus issue tax-free and they also pay no capital gains tax when the bonus shares are sold.[4] Allowing shareholders to choose a tax-effective dividend in this way is known as dividend streaming.

In the past, a reason for streaming dividends through the creation of bonus share plans was that not all investors could use franking credits. Bonus shares issued from the share premium reserve do not involve the distribution of franking credits. So a bonus share plan allowed investors who could not use the franking credit to receive unfranked dividends, while allowing the investors who could use the franking credit to receive the normal franked dividends. This was an effective way of maximising the benefit of valuable franking credits. However, the government stepped in, and from 1 July 1990 bonus issues in place of dividends must be debited against the franking account at the same rate as the ordinary dividends. So now, although bonus share issues from the share premium account do not carry franking credits, they do use them up.

# Dividend reinvestment plans

Many companies have **dividend reinvestment plans** (DRPs or DRIPs).[5] For example, more than three-quarters of the top 50 Australian listed companies have DRPs, although some have suspended their DRP. The DRP allows shareholders to nominate that their dividend should be reinvested automatically in the company rather than received as cash.[6] Most companies that offer bonus share plans also offer DRPs. The distinction between the two is that in the DRP the investors are treated as though they have received the cash dividend and then reinvested it. So the investor is liable for tax on that dividend, but also receives any franking credit associated with the dividend.

Often the new shares are issued at a small discount (2 to 10 per cent) from the market price after the ex-dividend date. The firm offers this sweetener because it saves the underwriting costs of a regular share issue. Shareholders participating in the DRP further benefit in that they save the transactions cost involved in reinvesting on their own account.

In the United States shares for the DRP plan are often obtained by the company repurchasing some of its shares in the market. In Australia the shares are usually provided by the company issuing more scrip, which increases the paid up capital of the company.

DRPs have grown in number since the introduction of the imputation tax system. The DRP allows the company to distribute more of its franking credits by paying a larger dividend without too painful a drain on its cash flow. From 1990 to 1995 Australian listed companies raised of the order of $20 billion dollars from dividend reinvestment plans, which is about 20 per cent total equity raisings. So important have DRPs become as a source of equity capital that some companies have their DRPs underwritten. Of course, in times of recession the DRP can cause problems if more cash is coming in than the company can use. In some cases therefore companies have suspended their DRPs.

---

4   There is a drawback to this. The investor will not receive the franking credit associated with the normal dividend. Consequently, the bonus share plan is most attractive to those investors who either cannot use the franking credit or who have a marginal tax rate greater than the company tax rate.

5   K. Chan, D. McColough and M. Skully study the price effects of Australian dividend reinvestment plans in 'Australian Tax Changes and Dividend Reinvestment Announcement Effects: A Pre- and Post-Imputation Study', *Australian Journal of Management*, **18**: 41–62 (June 1993).

6   Sometimes companies do not restrict shareholders to reinvesting dividends but also allow them to buy additional shares at a discount. These are often known as share top up plans. For an amusing and true rags-to-riches story about these share purchase plans see M. S. Scholes and M. A. Wolfson, 'Decentralized Investment Banking: The Case of Dividend-Reinvestment and Share-Purchase Plans', *Journal of Financial Economics*, **24**: 7–36 (September 1989).

# Share repurchase and return of capital

When a firm wants to pay cash to its shareholders, it usually declares a cash dividend. But an alternative method is to repurchase its own shares. This has been a strong tradition in the United States. However, for many years Australian companies were not allowed to *directly* repurchase their shares. The alternative, a return of capital to shareholders, is a long, difficult and costly process involving the agreement of shareholders, creditors and confirmation by a court. Consequently, relatively few companies pursued this alternative. Some companies resorted to *indirect* share repurchase; for example, by creation of cross-shareholdings. Perhaps the best-known case occurred in 1986 when BHP was the subject of a takeover bid by Bell Group. As a consequence of the defence against the bid, BHP repurchased its own shares through a company that was originally a subsidiary of BHP.

Events such as the BHP incident and continuing criticism of the prohibition on direct repurchase led to new legislation in 1989. From November of that year companies were able to buy their own shares, subject to a number of conditions including the following:

- Directors must sign a declaration certifying that the company is expected to remain solvent for 12 months after the buyback offer.
- No more than 10 per cent of outstanding shares could be repurchased in any 12-month period.

In December 1995 buybacks were further simplified by the removal of these and other conditions. At first there was no great rush of Australian companies taking advantage of share buyback opportunities. However, managers and the market became more familiar with the process, and substantial buybacks took place in 1998.

Two forms of share repurchase are recognised. First, there is the on market offer, where the repurchase occurs in the ordinary course of trading on the share exchange. However, ASX listing rules restrict the price paid so that it is not more than 5 per cent in excess of the average closing price on the five days when the share was last traded. Second, there is the off market offer, which is any other repurchase. In the case of the off market offer the price is determined by the company. The off market offer can be made to all shareholders or to a particular group of shareholders.

Whether the repurchase is on market or off market has significant tax consequences. For on market repurchases the investor will be subject to a capital gains tax, in just the same way as if the share had been sold in the normal course of trading. In an off market offer the tax authorities treat the payment as in part consisting as a return of capital and in part a dividend. In late 1997 the Commonwealth Bank structured a buyback to take advantage of these provisions. They announced an offer to buy back $650 million worth of shares at a price of $16.65. The buyback was to be treated as a fully franked dividend, because the payment was classed as a distribution of retained earnings. This effectively made the $16.65 tax free in the hands of shareholders with tax rates of 36 per cent or less. The selling price for capital gains tax purposes was the $2 par value of the shares. Consequently, shareholders could record a large capital loss for tax purposes, which could subsequently be used to offset taxes on future capital gains.

In Australia when a return of capital takes place the shares have to be cancelled. In a share repurchase the shares are also cancelled, although this is under review and the law may change in the future. In contrast, in the United States when shares are repurchased the company may choose to retain them as **treasury stock** for reissue at some later date.

There are many motives for share repurchase.[7] For example, it may be a signal that managers believe the shares are undervalued; it may be a convenient way to increase leverage; it provides a way to shrink the firm; and it can also be used to buy out particular shareholders.

---

7    For a discussion of motives in Australia see J. D. Mitchell and P. Robinson, Motivations of Australian Listed Companies Effecting Share Buy-backs, working paper, University of Western Australia, 1997.

In some cases share repurchase may have tax advantages or may get round government regulations. In the period 1973–1974 the United States government imposed a limit on dividends, but it forgot to impose a limit on share repurchase. Many firms discovered share repurchase for the first time and the total value of repurchases swelled to about a fifth of the value of dividend payments.

Share repurchases also provide a convenient way to shrink companies when good investment opportunities are scarce. The American oil company Exxon provides the most dramatic example of this, having spent more than US$17 billion on share repurchases in the years up until the end of 1994.

Share repurchase plans were also big news in October 1987. On Monday 19 October share prices in the United States nose-dived more than 20 per cent. The next day the board of Citicorp approved a plan to repurchase $250 million of the company's shares. Citicorp was joined by a number of other corporations whose managers were equally concerned about the market crash. Altogether over a two-day period these firms announced plans to buy back a total of $6.2 billion of shares. News of these huge buying programs helped to stem the slide in prices.

Such repurchases are like bumper dividends; they cause large amounts of cash to be paid to shareholders. However, it does not seem that they substitute for dividends. Companies do not seem to cut their dividends when they undertake a large share repurchase.

One controversial Australian share repurchase was a deal between Coles Myer and the American Kmart Corporation. As part of the deal Coles Myer paid nearly $600 million to buy back 10 per cent of its shares held by the Kmart Corporation. Some shareholders were unhappy at the price paid of $4.55, which was about 10 per cent above the market price at that time.

Similar disquiet is sometimes expressed in regard to a form of repurchase known as *greenmail*. The target of a takeover attempt buys off the hostile bidder by repurchasing any shares that the bidder has acquired. 'Greenmail' means that these shares are repurchased by the target at a price that makes the bidder happy to agree to leave the target alone. This price does not always make the target's *shareholders* happy, as we point out in Chapter 33.

# 16.2 How do companies decide on dividend payments?

## Lintner's model

In the mid-1950s John Lintner conducted a classic series of interviews with company managers in the United States about their dividend policies.[8] His description of how dividends are determined can be summarised in four 'stylised facts':[9]

1. Firms have long-run target dividend payout ratios. Mature firms with stable earnings generally pay out a high proportion of earnings; growth companies have low payouts.
2. Managers focus more on dividend changes than on absolute levels. Thus, paying a $2.00 dividend is an important financial decision if last year's dividend was $1.00, but no big deal if last year's dividend was $2.00.
3. Dividend changes follow shifts in long-run, sustainable earnings. Managers 'smooth' dividends. Transitory earnings changes are unlikely to affect dividend payouts.
4. Managers are reluctant to make dividend changes that might have to be reversed. They are particularly worried about having to rescind a dividend increase.

---

8  J. Lintner, 'Distribution of Incomes of Corporations among Dividends, Retained Earnings and Taxes', *American Economic Review*, **46**: 97–113 (May 1956).

9  The stylised facts are given by Terry A. Marsh and Robert C. Merton, 'Dividend Behavior for the Aggregate Share Market', *Journal of Business*, **60**: 1–40 (January 1987). See pp. 5–6. We have paraphrased and embellished.

Lintner developed a simple model that is consistent with these facts and explains dividend payments well. Here it is: Suppose that a firm always stuck to its target payout ratio. Then the dividend payment in the coming year ($DIV_1$) would equal a constant proportion of earnings per share ($EPS_1$):

$$DIV_1 = \text{target dividend} = \text{target ratio} \times EPS_1$$

The dividend *change* would equal

$$DIV_1 - DIV_0 = \text{target change} = \text{target ratio} \times EPS_1 - DIV_0$$

A firm that always stuck to its payout ratio would have to change its dividend whenever earnings changed. But the managers in Lintner's survey were reluctant to do this. They believed that shareholders prefer a steady progression in dividends. Therefore, even if circumstances appeared to warrant a large increase in their company's dividend, they would move only partway towards their target payment. Their dividend changes therefore seemed to conform to the following model:

$$\begin{aligned} DIV_1 - DIV_0 &= \text{adjustment rate} \times \text{target change} \\ &= \text{adjustment rate} \times (\text{target ratio} \times EPS_1 - DIV_0) \end{aligned}$$

The more conservative the company, the more slowly it would move towards its target, and therefore the *lower* would be its adjustment rate.

Lintner's simple model suggests that the dividend depends in part on the firm's current earnings and in part on the dividend for the previous year, which in turn depends on that year's earnings and the dividend in the year before. Therefore, if Lintner is correct, we should be able to describe dividends in terms of a weighted average of current and past earnings.[10] The probability of an increase in the dividend rate should be greatest when *current* earnings have increased; it should be somewhat less when only the earnings from the previous year have increased, and so on. An extensive study of American companies by Eugene Fama and Harvey Babiak, and a smaller study of Australian companies by Terry Shevlin, confirmed this hypothesis and showed that the Lintner model explained dividends quite well.[11]

We can also tell you something about the magnitude of target payout ratios. In 1980 a survey of company managers by one of the authors revealed that a substantial majority of large public companies in Australia had explicit payout targets. Most of the targets were in the range 40 to 70 per cent, with 50 per cent being the most popular target.[12] About one-third of the firms had changed their target materially over a 10- to 15-year period.

---

[10]  This can be demonstrated as follows: Dividends per share in time $t$ are

$DIV_t = aT(EPS_t) + (1 - a)DIV_{t-1}$     (1)

where $a$ is the adjustment rate and $T$ the target payout ratio. But the same relationship holds in $t - 1$:

$DIV_{t-1} = aT(EPS_{t-1}) + (1 - a)DIV_{t-2}$     (2)

Substitute for $DIV_{t-1}$ in (1):

$DIV_t = aT(EPS_t) + aT(1 - a)(EPS_{t-1}) + (1 - a)^2 DIV_{t-2}$

We can make similar substitutions for $DIV_{t-2}$, $DIV_{t-3}$, etc, thereby obtaining

$DIV_t = aT(EPS_t) + aT(1 - a)(EPS_{t-1}) + aT(1 - a)^2(EPS_{t-2}) + \cdots + aT(1 - a)^n(EPS_{t-n})$

[11]  E. F. Fama and H. Babiak, 'Dividend Policy: An Empirical Analysis', *Journal of the American Statistical Association*, **63**: 1132–61 (December 1968), see p. 1134; and T. Shevlin, 'Australian Corporate Dividend Policy: Empirical Evidence', *Accounting and Finance*, 1–22 (May 1982). The Lintner model has been tested in many empirical studies over the last four decades and so far it has seen off all its potential competitors.

[12]  See G. H. Partington, 'Dividend Policy and Target Payout Ratios', *Accounting and Finance*, 63–74 (November 1984).

Some infrequent changes in payout targets are to be expected as a result of the business life cycle. In their initial growth phase firms may conserve cash for expansion by paying little or no dividends.[13] A low, or zero, payout target is used. This is a common strategy for growth shares; for example, it was followed by IBM for many years. A low-payout strategy is also to be expected for new companies with limited earnings that are struggling to survive and develop. As companies mature into 'cash cows' a higher payout target is likely. Finally, if business becomes more difficult in the company's old age, then declining or more volatile cash flows will dictate a lower target. A lower target means that dividends can be set at a level where dividend cuts can be avoided.

## Does the Lintner model apply under imputation?

The ideas we have just discussed are based on research conducted when companies were subject to the classical system of taxation. In a classical tax system companies pay tax on company income and individuals pay tax on the dividends they receive from the companies. Since 1987 Australia has had an imputation system. As we will subsequently discuss, this has led to pressure for higher but fluctuating payouts that vary according to the level of franked dividends the company has available. It is questionable therefore whether the Lintner model continues to be appropriate in Australia. However, in the early 1990s one of the authors supervised a follow-up to the study referenced in Footnote 12. This follow-up questionnaire study found that the use of target payout ratios was virtually unchanged compared to the early 1980s.[14]

It is clear that many companies have substantially overhauled their dividend policies. Evidence of this is provided by the increasing numbers of bonus share plans and DRPs. It is less clear whether actual dividend payouts have increased significantly. There is certainly evidence of a sharp rise in actual payout ratios in the early 1990s. However, this was also a period of depressed profits, and therefore the increase in payouts may be explained by firms' reluctance to cut dividends. A policy of holding dividends steady when profits are temporarily depressed results in higher payout ratios.

## The information content of dividends

We have suggested above that the dividend payment depends on both last year's dividend and this year's earnings. This simple model seems to provide a fairly good explanation of how companies decide on the dividend payment, but it is unlikely to be the whole story. We would also expect managers to take future prospects into account when setting the payment. And that is what we find.

For example, Healy and Palepu report that between 1970 and 1979 companies that made a dividend payment for the first time experienced relatively flat earnings growth until the year before the announcement.[15] In that year earnings grew by an average 43 per cent. If managers thought that this was a temporary windfall, they might have been cautious about committing themselves to paying out cash. But it looks as if they had good reason to be confident about prospects, for over the next four years earnings grew by a further 164 per cent.

Since dividends anticipate future earnings, it is no surprise to find that announcements of dividend cuts are usually taken as bad news (share price typically falls) and that dividend increases are good news (share price rises).[16] The market is taking the dividend as a signal of

---

13   Managers' preference to finance from internal funds makes sense if, because of information asymmetry, they are uncertain of being able to raise external finance at a fair price. They also save transactions costs.

14   See Stephanie Allen, Dividend Policy and Dividend Imputation, B.Bus. honours thesis, UTS, 1994.

15   See P. Healy and K. Palepu, 'Earnings Information Conveyed by Dividend Initiations and Omissions', *Journal of Financial Economics*, 21: 149–75 (1988).

16   For an Australian study see P. Brown, F. J. Finn and P. Hancock, 'Dividend Changes, Earnings Reports and Share Prices: Some Australian Findings', *Australian Journal of Management*, 2: 127–47 (October 1977). The problem in Australia is separating the effects of earnings and dividends as they are usually announced simultaneously.

the future sustainable cash flow of the business. Higher dividends are interpreted as a signal that managers are confident about the future cash flows of the business.

When interpreting the response of the market to announcements such as the dividend announcement remember that the price response does *not* depend on the announcement. It depends on the *difference* between the announcement and what the market expected it to be. In the case of dividends the market usually expects either a small increase or no increase, but of course there are exceptions to this.

In the case of the dividend initiations studied by Healy and Palepu the announcement of the dividend resulted in an abnormal rise of 4 per cent in the share price.[17] It is important not to jump to the conclusion that this shows that investors like higher dividends for their own sake. The dividend may be welcomed only as a sign of higher future earnings and cash flow.

Do you remember from Chapter 13 that share splits and bonus issues lead to share price increases? That is not because splits or bonuses create value, but because they signal future prosperity, specifically increased dividends. Now we see that dividend increases in turn may be important mostly as signals of future earnings. (Finally, we could say that *earnings* are important because they tell investors something about the *true* measures of corporate prosperity: cash flow and the extent of positive NPV capital investment opportunities.)

It is important to understand that the dividend signalling argument bypasses our earlier definition of dividend policy as the trade-off between dividends and share issues. Under the signalling argument investments and their performance are not fixed. You can have higher dividends without an increase in share issues because of unexpectedly better performance of your investments. In fact, higher dividends likely mean *fewer* share issues. If dividend increases signal bigger future cash flows then there will be more cash available to finance investments internally. Therefore, fewer share issues will be needed. Notice that the presumption in the signalling argument is that the bigger dividend has *not* been created simply by increasing your payout ratio. If you increase your payout ratio and your cash flow has not increased then you will have to have more share issues. Unless, instead, you issue debt or cut investment.

Of course, cash dividends, bonus issues and share splits are costly to the firm. Perhaps there might be cheaper ways to signal information to the market, but perhaps it is the cost of these signals that makes them believable. Words are cheap, but firms that do not expect to do well cannot afford to commit to generous cash dividends. They will either be forced to subsequently cut the dividend, or they will run out of cash. The evidence suggests that investors penalise dividend cuts by a severe price markdown. The penalty for the cut is greater than the price gain from a dividend increase of equivalent magnitude.

Dividend cuts do not always signal bad news. A company may find new and highly profitable investment opportunities that are best financed internally. The problem is for management to convince investors that a dividend cut means profitable investment rather than a decline in cash flow. This problem is compounded by the difficulty of informing investors without alerting competitors and thereby surrendering a competitive advantage. Conversely, dividend increases do not always signal good news. An unexpected increase in dividends from a growth share may mean that growth opportunities have unexpectedly diminished. Therefore, a dividend increase can be accompanied by a price decline even in cases where the increase is bigger than the market expects.

The importance of dividend signalling is like the chicken and the egg. Managers are concerned about the stability of dividends because they know investors expect dividend increases to be sustained and usually penalise dividend cuts. Investors rely on changes in dividends to convey information because they know that managers are concerned about dividend stability.

---

17  Share price changes were corrected for market movements by the methods explained in Chapter 13. Healy and Palepu also looked at companies that *stopped* paying a dividend. In this case the share price on average declined by an abnormal 9.5 per cent on the announcement, and earnings fell over the next four quarters.

Another force is now at work. For tax reasons there is pressure to immediately distribute any available franked dividends. The availability of franked dividends will fluctuate each year depending on company profitability and company tax payments. Thus, tax factors favour fluctuating dividends while signalling dictates stable dividends. It will be interesting to see where the balance is struck.

Market efficiency means that all information available to investors is quickly and accurately impounded in share prices. It does not imply that fundamental information about a company's operations or prospects is always cheaply or easily obtained. Investors therefore seize on any clue. That is why share prices respond to share splits, dividend changes and other actions or announcements that reveal managements' optimism or pessimism about their firms' futures. The more the asymmetry between the information held by managers and shareholders, the greater the impact of events that reveal managers' inside information.

## 16.3 Controversy about dividend policy

Now we turn to the controversial question of how dividend policy affects value. One endearing feature of economics is that it can always accommodate not just two but three opposing points of view. And so it is with the controversy about dividend policy. On the right there is a conservative group that believes that an increase in dividend payout increases firm value. On the left there is a radical group which believes that an increase in payout reduces value. And in the centre there is a middle-of-the-road party which claims that dividend policy makes no difference.

The middle-of-the-road party was founded in 1961 by Miller and Modigliani (nearly always referred to as 'MM' or 'M and M'), when they published a theoretical paper showing the irrelevance of dividend policy in a world without taxes, transaction costs or other market imperfections.[18] By the standards of 1961 MM were leftist radicals, because at that time most people believed that even under idealised assumptions increased dividends made shareholders better off.[19] But now MM's proof is generally accepted as correct, and the argument has shifted to whether taxes or other market imperfections alter the situation. In the process MM have been pushed towards the centre by a new leftist party which argues for *low* dividends. The leftists' position is based on MM's argument modified to take account of taxes and costs of issuing securities. The conservatives are still with us, relying on essentially the same arguments they used before 1961.

We begin our discussion of dividend policy with a presentation of MM's original argument. Then we undertake a critical appraisal of the positions of the three parties.

### Dividend policy is irrelevant in perfect capital markets

In their classic 1961 article MM argued as follows: Suppose your firm has settled on its investment program. You have worked out how much of this program can be financed from borrowing, and you plan to meet the remaining funds requirement from retained earnings. Any surplus money is to be paid out as dividends.

Now think what happens if you want to increase the dividend payment without changing the investment and borrowing policy. The extra money must come from somewhere. If the firm fixes its borrowing, the only way it can finance the extra dividend is to print some more shares

---

18   M. H. Miller and F. Modigliani, 'Dividend Policy, Growth and the Valuation of Shares', *Journal of Business*, **34**: 411–33 (October 1961).

19   Not everybody believed dividends made shareholders better off. MM's arguments were anticipated in 1938 in J. B. Williams, *The Theory of Investment Value*, Harvard University Press, Cambridge, Mass., 1938. Also, a proof very similar to MM's was developed by J. Lintner in 'Dividends, Earnings, Leverage, Share Prices and the Supply of Capital to Corporations', *Review of Economics and Statistics*, **44**: 243–69 (August 1962).

and sell them. The new shareholders are going to part with their money only if you can offer them shares that are worth as much as they cost. But how can the firm do this when its assets, earnings, investment opportunities and therefore market value are all unchanged? The answer is that there must be a *transfer of value* from the old to the new shareholders. The new ones get the newly printed shares, each one worth less than before the dividend change was announced, and the old ones suffer a capital loss on their shares. The capital loss borne by the old shareholders just offsets the extra cash dividend they receive.

Figure 16.1 shows how this transfer of value occurs. Our hypothetical company pays out a third of its total value as a dividend and it raises the money to do so by selling new shares. The capital loss suffered by the old shareholders is represented by the reduction in the size of the shaded boxes. But that capital loss is exactly offset by the fact that the new money raised (the white boxes) is paid over to them as dividends.

**figure 16.1** _____

This firm pays out a third of its worth as a dividend and raises the money by selling new shares. The transfer of value to the new shareholders is equal to the dividend payment. The total value of the firm is unaffected.

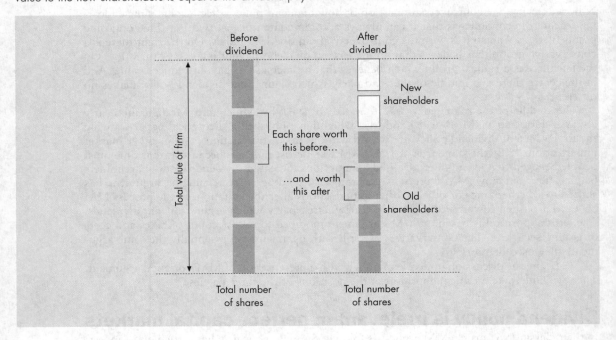

Does it make any difference to the old shareholders that they receive an extra dividend payment plus an offsetting capital loss? It might if that were the only way they could get their hands on cash. But as long as there are efficient capital markets, they can raise the cash by selling shares. Thus, the old shareholders can 'cash in' either by persuading the management to pay a higher dividend or by selling some of their shares. In either case there will be a transfer of value from old to new shareholders. The only difference is that in the former case this transfer is caused by a dilution in the value of each of the firm's shares, and in the latter case it is caused by a reduction in the number of shares held by the old shareholders. The two alternatives are compared in Figure 16.2.

Because investors do not need dividends to get their hands on cash, they will not pay higher prices for the shares of firms with high payouts. Therefore, firms ought not to worry about dividend policy. They should let dividends fluctuate as a by-product of their investment and financing decisions.

**figure 16.2** _____

Two ways of raising cash for the firm's original shareholders. In each case the cash received is offset by a decline in the value of the old shareholders' claim on the firm. If the firm pays a dividend, each share is worth less because more shares have to be issued against the firm's assets. If the old shareholders sell some of their shares, each share is worth the same but the old shareholders have fewer shares.

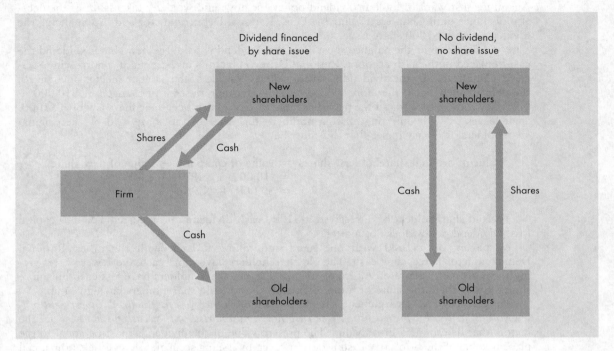

# Dividend irrelevance—an illustration

Consider the case of Rational Demiconductor, which at this moment has the following balance sheet:

| Rational Demiconductor's balance sheet (market values) | | | |
|---|---|---|---|
| Cash ($1 000 held for investment) | $1 000 | $0 | Debt |
| Fixed assets | $9 000 | $10 000 + NPV | Equity |
| Investment opportunity ($1 000 investment required) | NPV | | |
| Total asset value | $10 000 + NPV | $10 000 + NPV | Value of firm |

Rational Demiconductor has $1000 cash earmarked for a project requiring $1000 investment. We do not know how attractive the project is, and so we enter it at NPV; after the project is undertaken it will be worth $1000 + NPV. Note that the balance sheet is constructed with market values; equity equals the market value of the firm's outstanding shares (price per share multiplied by number of shares outstanding). It is not necessarily equal to book net worth.

Now Rational Demiconductor uses the cash to pay a $1000 dividend to its shareholders. The benefit to them is obvious: $1000 of spendable cash. It is also obvious that there must be a cost. The cash is not free.

Where does the money for the dividend come from? Of course, the immediate source of funds is Rational Demiconductor's cash account. But this cash was earmarked for the investment project. Since we want to isolate the effects of dividend policy on shareholders' wealth, we assume that the company *continues* with the investment project. That means that $1000 cash must be raised by new financing. This could consist of an issue of either debt or shares. Again, we just want to look at dividend policy for now, and we defer discussion of the debt-equity choice until Chapters 17 and 18. Thus, Rational Demiconductor ends up financing the dividend with a $1000 share issue.

Now we examine the balance sheet after the dividend is paid, the new shares sold and the cash replaced in the cash account. Rational Demiconductor's investment and borrowing policies are unaffected by the dividend payment. The assets side of the balance sheet is unchanged, the debt is unchanged, therefore its *overall* market value must be unchanged at $10 000 + NPV.[20] We know also that if the new shareholders pay a fair price, their share is worth $1000. That leaves us with only one missing number—the value of the share held by the original shareholders. It is easy to see that this must be

$$
\begin{aligned}
\text{Value of original shareholders' shares} &= \text{value of company} - \text{value of new shares} \\
&= (10\ 000 + \text{NPV}) - 1\ 000 \\
&= \$9\ 000 + \text{NPV}
\end{aligned}
$$

The old shareholders have received a $1000 cash dividend and incurred a $1000 capital loss. Dividend policy does not matter.

By paying out $1000 with one hand and taking it back with the other, Rational Demiconductor is recycling cash. The old shareholders have more cash and fewer shares giving them a smaller claim on future dividends. The new shareholders have less cash but more shares giving them the share of future dividends that the old shareholders have given up.

The essence of MM's argument is really very simple. *Once you fix the firm's investment policy, you fix its total expected future free cash flow and the risk of that cash flow.* These are the factors that determine a firm's value. The present value of the dividends must be equal to the present value of the firm's free cash flow. However, by issuing securities in an efficient financial market the firm can give you a dividend today that is higher than the firm's *current* free cash flow. You pay for this by giving up a share of the firm's free cash flow in the *future* which has a present value equal to the current dividend increase. What you cannot do by dividend changes is change the free cash flow or its risk. To do that you have to change investment policy.

## MM and the separation theorem

What we really have is an elaborate version of the separation theorem, which we discussed in Chapter 2. Remember how we showed you that you could use the capital market to convert cash flows to whatever pattern of consumption you desired, subject to the present value of your total consumption being equal to the present value of the cash flows? Dividend policy is much the same. Except that the firm creates on your behalf a pattern of dividends with a present value equal to the firm's underlying cash flow. By trading shares you can undo the firm's dividend pattern and create any alternative pattern you prefer. For example, you could have one big dividend today by selling all your shares. In perfect capital markets investors can costlessly create whatever pattern of homemade dividends they prefer. They have no reason to care what dividend pattern the firm provides and will pay neither more nor less for a particular dividend policy. They only care about the expected cash flows from the firm's investment.

Of course, our arguments ignore taxes, issue costs, information signalling and a variety of other complications. We will turn to these items in a moment. The really crucial assumption is that old

---

20  All other factors that might affect Rational Demiconductor's value are assumed constant. This is not a necessary assumption, but it simplifies the proof of MM's theory.

and new shares are sold at a fair price. The shares sold to raise $1000 by Rational Demiconductor must actually be *worth* $1000.[21] In other words, we have assumed efficient capital markets.

## Calculating share price

We have assumed that Rational Demiconductor's new shares can be sold at a fair price, but what is that price and how many new shares are issued?

Suppose that before this dividend payout the company had 1000 shares outstanding and that the project has an NPV of $2000. Then the old shares were worth in total $10 000 + NPV = $12 000, which works out at $12 000/1000 = $12 per share. After the company has paid the dividend and completed the financing the old shares are worth $9000 + NPV = $11 000. That works out at $11 000/1000 = $11 per share. In other words, the price of the old shares falls by the amount of the $1 per share dividend payment.

Now let us look at the new shares. Clearly, after the issue they must sell at the same price as the rest of the shares. In other words, they must be valued at $11. If the new shareholders get fair value, the company must issue $1000/$11 or 91 new shares in order to raise the $1000 that it needs.

## 16.4 The rightists

Much of traditional finance literature has advocated high-payout ratios. Here, for example, is a statement of the rightist position made by Graham and Dodd in 1951:

> . . . the considered and continuous verdict of the share market is overwhelmingly in favour of liberal dividends as against niggardly ones. The common share investor must take this judgement into account in the valuation of stock for purchase. It is now becoming standard practice to evaluate common stock by applying one multiplier to that portion of the earnings paid out in dividends and a much smaller multiplier to the undistributed balance.[22]

This belief in the importance of dividend policy is common in the business and investment communities. Shareholders and investment advisers continually pressure corporate treasurers for increased dividends. When there were wage-price controls in the United States and in the United Kingdom, it was deemed necessary to have dividend controls as well. As far as we know, no trade union objected that 'dividend policy is irrelevant'. After all, if wages are reduced, the employee is worse off. Dividends are the shareholders' wages and so, if the payout ratio is reduced, the shareholder is worse off. Therefore, fair play requires that wage controls be matched by dividend controls. Right?

Wrong! You should be able to see through that kind of argument by now. But let us turn to some of the more serious arguments for a high-payout policy.

## Do MM ignore risk?

One of the most common and immediate objections to MM's argument about the irrelevance of dividends is that dividends are cash in hand while future dividends are an uncertain expectation. However, if we forgo the current dividend in the expectation of thereby obtaining higher future dividends this will be reflected in a higher price for our shares. So the recipient of an extra cash

---

21    The 'old' shareholders get all the benefit of the positive-NPV project. The 'new' shareholders require only a fair rate of return. They are making a zero-NPV investment.

22    These authors later qualified this statement, recognising the willingness of investors to pay high price-earnings multiples for growth shares. But otherwise they have stuck to their position. We quoted their 1951 statement because of its historical importance. Compare B. Graham and D. L. Dodd, *Security Analysis: Principles and Techniques*, 3rd ed., McGraw-Hill Book Company, New York, 1951, p. 432, with B. Graham, D. L. Dodd and S. Cottle, *Security Analysis: Principles and Techniques*, 4th ed., McGraw-Hill Book Company, New York, 1962, p. 480.

dividend forgoes a capital gain. In an efficient market the cash dividend and the capital gain should have the same value. Even so, if the dividend is safe and the capital gain is risky, does not taking the dividend put the shareholder ahead?

It is true that dividends are more predictable than capital gains. Managers can stabilise dividends but they cannot control share price. From this it seems a small step to conclude that increased dividends make the firm less risky.[23] But the important point is, once again, that as long as investment policy and borrowing are held constant, a firm's *overall* cash flows are the same regardless of payout policy. The risks borne by *all* the firm's shareholders are likewise fixed by its investment and borrowing policies and unaffected by dividend policy.[24]

A dividend increase creates a transfer of ownership between 'old' and 'new' shareholders. The old shareholders—those who receive the extra dividend and do not buy their part of the share issue undertaken to finance the dividend—find their stake in the firm reduced. They have indeed traded an uncertain future cash flow for a safe receipt. But the reason their money is safe is not because it is special 'dividend money', but because it is in the bank. If the dividend had not been increased, the shareholders could have achieved an equally safe position just by selling shares to take the *current* capital gain and putting the money in the bank. The choice boils down to taking an extra dividend at the cost of an equal capital gain. We calculated a cum-dividend price for Rational Demiconductor of $12 and an ex-dividend price of $11. Which would you prefer: a $12 share or an $11 share and $1 cash? Suppose there was no dividend but you preferred to receive the cash, then you could sell one-twelfth of your shareholding. You would end up with the same investment in shares and the same amount of cash as if the firm had paid a $1 dividend.

If we really believed that the old shareholders are better off by converting a risky asset to dividend cash, then we would also have to argue that the new shareholders—those who traded cash for the newly issued shares—are worse off. But this does not make sense: the new shareholders are bearing risk, but they are getting paid for it. They are willing to buy a risky asset because the new shares are priced to offer a return adequate to cover the risk.

MM's argument for the irrelevance of dividend policy does not assume a world of certainty. It assumes an efficient capital market. Market efficiency means that the transfers of value created by shifts in dividend policy are carried out on fair terms. And since the *overall* value of (old and new) shareholders' equity is unaffected, nobody gains or loses.

## Market imperfections

We believe—and it is widely believed—that MM's conclusions follow from their assumption of perfect and efficient capital markets. Nobody claims that their model is an exact description of the so-called 'real world'. Thus, the dividend controversy finally boils down to arguments about imperfections, inefficiencies or whether shareholders are fully rational.[25] The factors likely to make dividend policy relevant are:

■ *Taxes*—If you can find a way to save tax, you can create extra value.
■ *Information asymmetries*—If managers have more information than investors, and investors infer some of this information from dividend announcements, then dividend signalling will affect value.

---

23  By analogy, one could presumably argue that interest payments are even more predictable, so that a company's risk would be diminished by increasing the proportion of receipts paid out as interest.

24  There are a number of variations of the 'bird-in-the-hand' argument. Perhaps the most persuasive is found in M. J. Gordon, 'Dividends, Earnings and Share Prices', *Review of Economics and Statistics*, **41**: 99–105 (May 1959). He reasoned that investors run less risk if the firm pays them cash now rather than retaining and reinvesting it in the hope of paying higher future dividends. But careful analysis of Gordon's argument—see M. J. Brennan, 'A Note on Dividend Irrelevance and the Gordon Valuation Model', *Journal of Finance*, **26**: 1115–22 (December 1971), for example—shows that he was really talking about changes in *investment* policy, not dividend policy.

25  Psychologists' experiments show that human beings are not 100 per cent rational decision makers. Shefrin and Statman use some of the psychologists' results to argue that investors may have an irrational preference for cash dividends. See H. Shefrin and M. Statman, 'Explaining Investor Preference for Cash Dividends', *Journal of Financial Economics*, **13**: 253–82 (June 1984).

▮ *Conflicts between managers, shareholders and bondholders*—There is nothing more difficult to control than a fistful of cash. Managers may misuse it, or shareholders may pocket it leaving nothing for the debtholders. Increasing the flow of dividends can mitigate the conflict between shareholders and managers but increase the conflict between shareholders and debtholders. This in turn can affect how the company's securities are priced.

▮ *Capital rationing*—Perhaps the firm cannot readily finance its dividends. Instead, dividends and investments may be competing uses for internally generated funds.[26] In this case dividend policy affects the value of the firm indirectly through its impact on investments.

▮ *Transactions costs*—Reducing total transactions costs for investors and the firm increases shareholder wealth.

Now we will look at some of these effects in more detail.

# Transaction costs and the clientele effect

There is a natural clientele for high-payout shares. For example, there are circumstances where some investors are legally restricted from holding shares lacking established dividend records. Trust funds may prefer high-dividend shares because dividends are regarded as spendable 'income', whereas capital gains are regarded as 'additions to principal', not to be spent.

There is also a natural clientele of investors ('widows and orphans') who rely on their share portfolios for a steady source of cash to live on. In principle this cash could be easily generated from shares paying no dividends at all; the investor could just sell off a small fraction of his or her holdings from time to time. But it is simpler and cheaper for BHP to send a half-yearly cheque than for its shareholders to sell, say, 100 shares every six months. BHP's regular dividends relieve many of its shareholders of transaction costs and considerable inconvenience.

On the other hand, there is also a natural clientele of investors for low-payout shares. Some investors are accumulating wealth for later consumption, or to support themselves in old age. For these investors the receipt of dividends gives rise to the transaction costs and inconvenience associated with reinvestment. It is to cater to these investors that firms have DRPs.

Finally there may be tax-based clienteles. Some investors are taxed more highly on dividends than on capital gains and naturally they prefer low payouts. For other investors the situation is exactly the reverse.

Where does the balance of such preferences lie: high payouts or low payouts? We do not know. We can, however, reach two important conclusions. First, identifying reasons why one group, such as 'widows and orphans', will prefer a particular dividend policy is not the same as demonstrating that there will be a *market wide* preference for such a policy. Second, *if* there is a particular dividend policy in short supply *and* investors are therefore prepared to pay a premium for such a policy, then smart corporate treasurers will move to supply that policy. In so doing they will eliminate the shortage of supply and thereby eliminate the valuation premium. This idea, attributable to MM, is known as the **clientele effect**. Simply stated, if policies adjust so that no unsatisfied clienteles remain in the market, then no policy will command a valuation premium.[27]

# Agency costs and free cash flow

High payouts can also help resolve the potential for conflict between managers and owners. Managers act as agents of the owners in controlling companies' assets. But managers' interests are

---

26 This is a relatively rare event for large Australian public companies. When internal funds are insufficient to finance desired dividends and investments the company will normally raise finance by issuing debt.

27 Research on the clientele effect has tended to concentrate on whether there are tax-induced clienteles. Although weak, there is some evidence of both tax- and transaction-cost clienteles. Australian companies' response to the imputation system seems to be an attempt to tailor dividend policies to the differing preferences among investors.

not always the same as owners' interests. Managers may pursue activities that are costly to owners such as consumption of unnecessary perquisites. Van Goghs in the boardroom and solid gold taps in the executive washroom probably do more for managers' egos than they do for shareholders' wealth. Perhaps even worse are unprofitable empire-building investments. Of course, investors try to monitor and control managers' behaviour, but this also is costly. The sum of the costs of undesirable activities and monitoring costs are known as agency costs. Reducing these costs can increase value. Managers recognise that it is in their own interest to commit to arrangements that will help control these costs. Otherwise, finance will become difficult to obtain and very expensive.

One important source of agency costs can be 'free cash flow'. This is the cash left over after all expense and debt payments have been made and (under some definitions) all positive NPV investments have been made. Since this cash cannot be invested at better than the required return it should be distributed to the shareholders.[28] However, managers may be tempted to use it for their own purposes. Committing to paying a substantial dividend that distributes a good proportion of the free cash flow reduces the free cash flow problem.

In this case the dividend decision has become mixed up with investment and operating decisions. The dividend increase may lead to a higher share price, not because investors particularly like dividends but because they want management to run a tighter ship.

An additional discipline from higher dividends is that the company makes more frequent trips to the capital market because less internal finance is available. Thus, greater care may be taken with investment funds since their use will need to be justified to the market.

## Issue costs and timing

The disadvantage of frequent trips to the capital market is that security issues are not cheap. Share issues may cost between 3 and 30 per cent of the amount raised.[29] Thus, high dividends impose significant issue costs on the firm. Also, as we discuss in Chapter 18, it may not always be possible to issue shares unless they are sold at *less* than a fair price. In which case lower payouts and more internal financing make sense.

Those advocating generous dividends counter with the argument that a regular cash dividend relieves shareholders of the risk of having to sell shares at 'temporarily depressed' prices. Of course, the firm will have to issue shares eventually to finance the dividend, but (the argument goes) the firm can pick the *right time* to sell. If firms really try to do this and if they are successful—two big *ifs*—then shareholders of high-payout firms do indeed get something for nothing.

## Information and confirmation effects

There is yet another line of argument that you can use to justify high payouts. Think of a market in which investors receive very little reliable information about a firm's earnings. Such markets exist in some European countries where a passion for secrecy and a tendency to construct many-layered corporate organisations produce asset and earnings figures that are next to meaningless. Some people say that, thanks to creative accounting, the situation is little better in Australia. How does an investor in such a world separate marginally profitable firms from the real money makers? One clue is dividends. A firm that reports good earnings and pays a generous dividend is putting its money where its mouth is.[30] We can understand why

---

[28] As an example, in 1994 Glaxo, an English company, had an accumulated surplus of cash in excess of $1 billion. Some shareholders were understandably nervous that managers might make a foolish acquisition.

[29] Costs at the top of the range would be rare.

[30] Of course, firms can cheat in the short run by overstating earnings and scraping up cash to pay a generous dividend. But it is hard to cheat in the long run, for a firm that is not making money will not have the cash flow to pay out. Financing dividends by issuing shares is self-defeating, for it ultimately reduces dividends per share and thereby reveals that the initial dividend was not supported by earnings.

investors would favour firms with established dividend records. We can also see how the information content of dividends would come about. Investors would refuse to believe a firm's reported earnings announcements unless they were backed up by an appropriate dividend policy.

MM regard the informational content of dividends as a temporary thing. A dividend increase signals management's optimism about future earnings, but investors will be able to *see for themselves* whether the optimism is justified. The jump in share price that accompanies an unexpected dividend increase *would have happened anyway* as information about future earnings came out through other channels. Therefore, MM expect to find changes in dividends associated with share price movements, but no permanent relationship between share price and the firm's long-run target payout ratio. MM believe management should be concerned with dividend *changes*, but not with the average *level* of payout.

## Maintaining dividend stability

If firms attract a particular clientele of investors and/or there are dividend information signalling effects, then the prescription for managers is clear—once you have settled on a dividend policy stick with it. Dividend instability will cause unnecessary transactions costs for investors as they rebalance their portfolios to achieve their desired cash flow for consumption. Instability will also complicate tax planning as investors try to arrange their portfolios to minimise their tax payments. Dividend instability can therefore result in the distribution of net cash flow to investors after taxes and transactions costs having a lower expected value and higher variance. There are also signalling effects to consider; volatile dividends may be perceived as signalling that the company's underlying cash flows are high variance.

There are therefore good reasons for management's traditional concern with dividend stability and their aversion to making sharp changes in dividend policy. Post-imputation, however, the game has changed. As we have mentioned, there are pressures for higher payouts and fluctuating dividends. Managements' response to the tax changes has been to structure their dividend policies with alternatives, such as dividend reinvestment, that allow individual investors to create a policy that suits them. This leads us to a big topic in the dividend literature—taxes.

## 16.5 Taxes and the radical left

The left-wing dividend creed is simple: Whenever dividends are taxed more heavily than capital gains, firms should pay the lowest cash dividend they can get away with. Available cash should be retained and reinvested or used to repurchase shares. For many years in Australia individuals paid *no* capital gains tax on assets that they held for more than a year. The apparently generous dividends of Australian companies during this period were therefore something of a challenge to the leftist camp.

The introduction of capital gains tax on assets acquired after 19 September 1985 undercut the leftists' argument in Australia. They were further battered by the introduction of the imputation system in 1987. In the United States the leftists' arguments were undercut by the *Tax Reform Act of 1986*, under which dividends and capital gains were taxed at the same rate.

The leftists' arguments nevertheless deserve a closer look. First, it is important to understand their historical contribution to the dividend controversy. Second, capital gains are taxed at relatively low rates in many countries (the United Kingdom, for example) and may one day regain their favoured tax treatment in Australia. Third, capital gains retain some tax advantages—for example, you are only taxed on real gains and you are only taxed when the gains are realised. So you can reduce the present value of taxes by deferring the realisation of the gain.[31] We must make the point, however, that you cannot easily enjoy both tax deferral and current consumption. If you want cash for consumption you either need the dividend or you need to sell part of your shareholding. In either event a tax liability arises.

## How taxes affect values

Corporations can transmute dividends into capital gains by shifting their dividend policies. When dividends are more heavily taxed than capital gains, such financial alchemy should be welcomed by any taxpaying investor. That is the basic point made by the leftist party when it argues for low-dividend payout.

If dividends are taxed more heavily than capital gains, investors should pay more for shares with low-dividend yields. In other words, they should accept a lower *pre-tax* rate of return from securities offering returns in the form of capital gains rather than dividends. Table 16.1 illustrates this. The shares of firms A and B are equally risky. Investors expect firm A to be worth $112.50 per share next year. The share price of firm B is expected to be only $102.50, but a $10 dividend is also forecast, and so the total pre-tax payoff is the same, $112.50.

**table 16.1**

Effects of a shift in dividend policy when dividends are taxed more heavily than capital gains. The high-payout share (firm B) must sell at a lower price in order to provide the same after-tax return.

| | Firm A (no dividend) | Firm B (high dividend) |
|---|---|---|
| Next year's price | $112.50 | $102.50 |
| Dividend | $0 | $10.00 |
| Total pre-tax payoff | $112.50 | $112.50 |
| Today's share price | $100 | $96.67 |
| Capital gain | $12.50 | $5.83 |
| Before-tax rate of return (%) | $\frac{12.5}{100} \times 100 = 12.5$ | $\frac{15.83}{96.67} \times 100 = 16.4$ |
| Tax on dividend at 50% | $0 | $0.50 \times 10 = \$5.00$ |
| Tax on capital gains at 20% | $0.20 \times 12.50 = \$2.50$ | $0.20 \times 5.83 = \$1.17$ |
| Total after-tax income (dividends plus capital gains less taxes) | $(0 + 12.50) - 2.50 = \$10.00$ | $(10.00 + 5.83) - (5.00 + 1.17) = \$9.66$ |
| After-tax rate of return (%) | $\frac{10}{100} \times 100 = 10.0$ | $\frac{9.66}{96.67} \times 100 = 10.0$ |

Yet we find B's share selling for less than A's and therefore offering a higher pre-tax rate of return. The reason is obvious: Investors prefer firm A because its return comes as capital gains. Table 16.1 shows that firms A and B are equally attractive to investors who pay a 50 per cent tax on dividends and a 20 per cent tax on capital. Each offers a 10 per cent return after all

---

31  When securities are sold, capital gains tax is paid on the difference between the selling price and the initial purchase price or basis, adjusted for inflation. Thus, shares purchased in 1992 for $20 and sold for $30 in 1995 would generate $10 per share in capital gains. If we assume that there is no inflation, this is a real gain and a tax of $2.80 is payable at say a 28 per cent tax marginal rate.
    Suppose the investor now decides to defer sale for one year. Then, if the interest rate is 8 per cent, the present value of the tax, viewed from 1995, falls to 2.80/1.08 = $2.59. That is, the effective capital gains rate is 25.9 per cent. The longer sale is deferred, the lower the effective rate (see Section 16.5).

taxes. The difference between the share prices of firms A and B is exactly the present value of the extra taxes the investors face if they buy B.[32]

The management of firm B could save these extra taxes by eliminating the $10 dividend and using the released funds to repurchase shares instead, or even retain the funds and invest them in a zero-NPV project. Firm B's current share price should rise to $100 as soon as the new policy is announced.

## Why pay any dividends at all?

Why then should *any* firm *ever* pay a cash dividend when dividends are taxed more heavily than capital gains? As long as it has appropriate investment opportunities, the firm should retain the cash to generate capital gains. If cash is to be distributed to shareholders, would not an on market share repurchase be better than a dividend? The leftist position seems to call not just for low payout by firm B, but for *zero* payout whenever capital gains have a tax advantage.

Few leftists would go quite that far. Firms sometimes run out of investment opportunities offering sufficient returns. A firm which eliminates dividends and starts repurchasing shares on a regular basis may find that the tax office would recognise the repurchase program for what it really is and would tax the payments accordingly.

The low-payout party has nevertheless maintained that the market rewards firms that have low-payout policies. They have claimed that firms that paid dividends and as a result had to issue shares from time to time were making a serious mistake. Any such firm was essentially financing its dividends by issuing shares; it should have cut its dividends at least to the point at which share issues were unnecessary. This would not only have saved taxes for share-holders; it would also have avoided the transaction costs of the share issues.

## Empirical evidence on dividends and taxes

It is hard to deny that taxes are important to investors. The Australian federal government used to issue bonds on which some of the interest was rebatable for tax purposes. These bonds sold at lower *pre-tax* yields than government bonds that were fully taxed. It does not seem likely that investors in bonds just forget about taxes when they enter the share market. Thus, we would expect to find an historical tendency for high-dividend shares to sell at lower prices and therefore to offer higher returns,[33] just as in Table 16.1.

Unfortunately, there are difficulties in measuring this effect. For example, suppose that share A is priced at $100 and is expected to pay a $5 dividend. Assuming no capital gains, the *expected* yield is therefore 5/100 = 0.05, or 5 per cent. The company now announces bumper earnings and a $10 dividend. Thus, with the benefit of hindsight, A's *actual* dividend yield is 10/100 = 0.10, or 10 per cent. If the unexpected increase in earnings causes a rise in share A's price, we will observe that a high actual yield is accompanied by a high actual return. But that would not tell us anything about whether a high *expected* yield was accompanied by a high *expected* return. In order to measure the effect of dividend policy, we need to estimate the dividends that investors expected.

A second problem is that nobody is quite sure what is meant by high-dividend yield. For example, bank shares have often offered high-dividend yields. But did they have a high-dividend yield all year, or only in months or on days that dividends were paid? Perhaps for most of the year they had zero dividend yields and were perfect holdings for the highly-taxed

---

32  Michael Brennan has modelled what happens when you introduce taxes into an otherwise perfect market and found that the capital asset pricing model continues to hold, but on an *after-tax* basis. Thus, if firms A and B have the same beta, they should offer the same after-tax rate of return. The spread between pre-tax and post-tax returns is determined by a weighted average of investors' tax rates. See M. J. Brennan, 'Taxes, Market Valuation and Corporate Financial Policy', *National Tax Journal*, **23**: 417–27 (December 1970).

33  Some researchers talk about high-dividend shares having to offer high yields. They are talking about a high total yield—dividends plus capital gains—not just about the dividend yield.

individuals.[34] Of course, high-tax investors did not want to hold a share on the days dividends were paid, but they could have sold their share temporarily to a share trader. Share traders were taxed equally on dividends and capital gains, and therefore should not have demanded any extra return for holding shares over the dividend period.[35] If shareholders could pass shares freely between each other at the time of the dividend payment, we should not observe any tax effects at all.

Finally, there is the question of what any measured dividend effect really means. Smart corporate treasurers are likely to take advantage of any profit opportunities that could be exploited by tailoring dividend policies to different tax clienteles. As supply of the desired policies expanded, this would tend to drive any dividend valuation premium towards zero. The process might stop before the premium reached zero, but only if the costs of adjusting dividends outweighed the benefits. In this case researchers run the risk of discovering more about the costs of adjusting dividend policy than about the value of tax effects.

Given these difficulties in measuring the relationship between expected dividend yield and return, it is not surprising that different researchers have come up with different results. Table 16.2 summarises some of the findings. Notice that in each of these tests the estimated tax rate was positive. In other words, high-yielding shares *appeared* to have lower prices and to offer higher returns. Notice, however, that in several cases the standard error is so large that estimated tax rate is not significantly different from zero. So, while the dividends-are-bad school can claim some weight of evidence on its side, the contest is by no means over.

Many respected scholars, including Merton Miller and Myron Scholes, were unconvinced. They stressed the difficulty of measuring dividend yield properly and proving the link between dividend yield and expected return.[36] Australian research by Ball, Brown, Finn and Officer highlighted the experimental difficulties.[37] They found an implied tax rate so large (146 per cent) that it is clearly absurd. They suggested the following explanation. If a share is high risk it is expected to offer a high return irrespective of its dividend yield. The question therefore is whether shares with high-dividend yields offer higher returns than low-dividend yield firms *after* controlling for differences in risk. This is well understood by the researchers doing modern dividend work, but what is not clear is whether the models they use to control for risk are adequate.[38] Suppose they are not adequate and the dividend yield is a proxy for risk factors omitted from the researchers' models. Then we cannot distinguish proxy effects due to misspecification of the models from the true price effect of the dividends.

## 16.6  The middle-of-the-roaders

The middle-of-the-road party, which is principally represented by Miller, Black and Scholes,[39] maintains that a company's value is not affected by its dividend policy. We have already seen

---

34  Suppose there are 250 trading days in a year. Think of a share paying half-yearly dividends. We could say that the share offers a high-dividend yield on two days, but a zero-dividend yield on the remaining 248 days.

35  The share could also be sold to a company which could 'capture' the dividend and then resell the shares. Companies are natural buyers of dividends because they effectively pay no tax on dividends. The dividends are taxable income but companies get a tax rebate based on the dividends received (section 46AAA rebate). This makes the dividends effectively tax-free.

36  Miller reviews several of the studies cited in Table 16.2 in 'Behavioral Rationality in Finance: The Case of Dividends', *Journal of Business*, 59: S451–68 (October 1986).

37  R. Ball, P. Brown, F.J. Finn and R R. Officer, 'Dividends and the Value of the Firm: Evidence from the Australian Equity Market', *Australian Journal of Management*, 4: 13–26 (April 1979).

38  Failure to control for risk is believed to explain the results of early dividend research, which claimed that investors preferred higher payouts. High-payout firms are typically less risky than low-payout firms; so what the early researchers had found was not a preference for higher dividends but a preference for less risk.

39  F. Black and M. S. Scholes, 'The Effects of Dividend Yield and Dividend Policy on Common Share Prices and Returns', *Journal of Financial Economics*, 1: 1–22 (May 1974); M. H. Miller and M. S. Scholes, 'Dividends and Taxes', *Journal of Financial Economics*, 6: 333–64 (December 1978); and M. H. Miller, 'Behavioral Rationality in Finance: The Case of Dividends', *Journal of Business*, 59: S451–68 (October 1986).

**table 16.2**

Some tests of the effect of yield on returns: A positive implied tax rate on dividends means that investors require a higher pre-tax return from high-dividend shares.

| Test | Test period | Implied tax rate (%) | Standard error of tax rate |
|------|-------------|----------------------|----------------------------|
| Brennan | 1946–65 | 34 | 12 |
| Black & Scholes (1974) | 1936–66 | 22 | 24 |
| Litzenberger & Ramaswamy (1979) | 1936–77 | 24 | 3 |
| Litzenberger & Ramaswamy (1982) | 1940–80 | 14–23 | 2–3 |
| Rosenberg & Marathe (1979) | 1931–66 | 40 | 21 |
| Bradford & Gordon (1980) | 1926–78 | 18 | 2 |
| Blume (1980) | 1936–76 | 52 | 25 |
| Miller & Scholes (1982) | 1940–78 | 4 | 3 |
| Stone & Bartter (1979) | 1947–70 | 56 | 28 |
| Morgan (1982) | 1946–77 | 21 | 2 |
| Ang & Peterson (1985) | 1973–83 | 57 | 27 |

*Source*: M. J. Brennan, Dividends and Valuation in Imperfect Markets: Some Empirical Tests, unpublished paper, not dated; F. Black and M. Scholes, 'The Effects of Dividend Yield and Dividend Policy on Common Share Prices and Returns', *Journal of Financial Economics*, **1**: 1–22 (May 1974); R. H. Litzenberger and K. Ramaswamy, 'The Effect of Personal Taxes and Dividends on Capital Asset Prices: Theory and Empirical Evidence', *Journal of Financial Economics*, **7**: 163–95 (June 1979); R. H. Litzenberger and K. Ramaswamy, 'The Effects of Dividends on Common Share Prices: Tax Effects or Information Effects', *Journal of Finance*, **37**: 429–43 (May 1982); B. Rosenberg and V. Marathe, 'Tests of Capital Asset Pricing Model Hypotheses', in H. Levy (ed.), *Research in Finance I*, JAI Press, Greenwich, Conn., 1979; D. F. Bradford and R. H. Gordon, 'Taxation and the Share Market Valuation of Capital Gains and Dividends', *Journal of Public Economics*, **14**: 109–36 (1980); M. E. Blume, 'Share Returns and Dividend Yields: Some More Evidence', *Review of Economics and Statistics*, **62**: 567–77 (November 1980); M. H. Miller and M. Scholes, 'Dividends and Taxes: Some Empirical Evidence', *Journal of Political Economy*, **90**: 1118–41 (1982); B. K. Stone and B. J. Bartter, 'The Effect of Dividend Yield on Share Returns: Empirical Evidence on the Relevance of Dividends', W.P.E.-76-78, Georgia Institute of Technology, Atlanta, Ga., 1979; I. G. Morgan: 'Dividends and Capital Asset Prices', *Journal of Finance*, **37**: 1071–86 (September 1982); J. S. Ang and D. K. Peterson, 'Return, Risk and Yield: Evidence from Ex-Ante Data', *Journal of Finance*, **40**: 537–48 (June 1985).

that this would be the case if there were no impediments such as transaction costs or taxes. The middle-of-the-roaders are aware of these phenomena, but nevertheless raise the following disarming question: If companies could increase their share price by distributing more or less cash dividends, why have they not already done so? Perhaps dividends are where they are because no company believes that it could increase its share price simply by changing its dividend policy. In other words, they invoke the tax clientele effect that we discussed earlier.

The adjustment of dividend supply to match demand is consistent with the existence of a clientele of investors who demand low-payout shares. Firms recognised that clientele long ago. Enough firms may have switched to low-payout policies to satisfy fully the clientele's demand. If so, there is no incentive for *additional* firms to switch to low-payout policies.

Miller, Black and Scholes similarly recognise possible 'high-payout clienteles', but argue that they are satisfied also. If all clienteles are satisfied, their demands for high or low dividends have no effects on prices or returns. It does not matter which clientele a particular firm chooses to appeal to. If the middle-of-the-road party were right, we should not expect to observe any general association between dividend policy and market values, and the value of any individual company would be independent of its choice of dividend policy.

The middle-of-the-roaders stress that companies would not have generous payout policies unless they believed that this was what investors wanted. But this does not answer the question, 'Why *should* so many investors want high payouts?'

Before the introduction of capital gains tax and dividend imputation this was the chink in the armour of the middle-of-the-roaders. If high dividends bring high taxes, it is difficult to believe that investors got what they wanted. The response of the middle-of-the-roaders was to argue that there were plenty of wrinkles in the tax system that determined shareholders could use to avoid paying taxes on dividends. For example, instead of investing directly in ordinary shares, they could do so through a pension fund or insurance company, which received more favourable tax treatment.

Remember Ms Kraft from Chapter 3? She never did find a real money machine, but she did discover lots of ways to shelter her dividends from taxes. Here is one way. Before 1985 she used to declare a substantial dividend income on her tax form, but she also borrowed against her shares and bought more. Elsewhere on her tax form she claimed a hefty deduction for interest incurred in gaining assessable income. In fact, she arranged her affairs so that the interest exactly offset her dividends and all her return came in tax-free capital gains.[40]

Even without tax avoidance it is not entirely clear that there was a market-wide tax disadvantage to dividends in Australia. While it may have been true that dividends had a tax disadvantage for individuals, this was not true for all investors. Life insurance funds, for example, received dividends tax-free but were taxed on capital gains. Indeed, pre-imputation as much as 70 per cent of dividends were tax-free in the hands of the initial recipients. These dividends were either going to tax-exempt investors such as charities or, as in the case of companies receiving dividends, the dividends were effectively tax-free.

Since the tax changes of the 1980s there is now an advantage to dividend receipts for many Australian investors. So it is easy to suppose that there is a substantial clientele of investors who are content to receive high dividends.

Has the 1980s tax reform led to a change in corporate and investor attitudes to dividends? There is a belief that it has led to a pressure for higher payouts, and there is some evidence, for example the work of Nicol,[41] that payouts have increased. But it is still early days. We need more data and evidence before we can be confident that there has been a shift in payouts or investors' required returns. We may also gain some clues from the experience of other countries that have changed tax rates on dividends relative to capital gains. In Canada, for example, dividend payouts did increase after a capital gains tax was introduced and dividend tax rates were cut for many investors.[42]

## Imputation and alternative tax systems

Prior to the introduction of the imputation system it *appeared* that shareholders' returns were taxed twice: once at the company level (corporate tax) and again in the hands of the shareholder (income tax). For example, if a company earned $100 and it was taxed at 36 per cent then this would leave $64 available for distribution as a dividend. Suppose all the $64 was distributed to shareholders. *If* the shareholders were taxed at 47 per cent, this only leaves $33.92 of the original $100. The balance, nearly $67, has gone in taxes. This is sometimes known as

40 Of course, the borrowing increased her risk, but more elaborate strategies could be devised that would not involve any increase in risk.

41 See R. E. Nicol, 'The Dividend Puzzle: An Australian Solution', *Australian Accounting Review*, 1: 42–55 (November 1992). However, remember our caution earlier in this chapter about the difficulty of interpreting the cause of increasing payouts in the early 1990s.

42 The Canadian experience is summarised in the Canadian edition, especially pp. 360–9 and 372–4. See R. Brealey, S. Myers, G. Sick and R. Whaley, *Principles of Corporate Finance*, McGraw-Hill Ryerson, Ltd., Toronto, 1986. Also see I. G. Morgan, 'Dividends and Share Price Behaviour in Canada', *Journal of Business Administration*, 12: 91–106 (Fall 1980).

a classical or **two-tier tax system**. Since dividends were taxed twice and capital gains were not taxed at the personal level prior to 1985, why did firms pay generous dividends? Perhaps, as we suggested above, many investors were not disadvantaged by a tax on dividends because they either had no tax liability or they avoided it.

Of course, dividends are paid regularly by companies that operate under very different tax systems. Indeed, outside the United States the classical system is now relatively rare. Some countries such as Germany tax investors at a higher rate on dividends than on capital gains, but they offset this by having a *split-rate system* of corporate taxes. Profits that are retained in the business attract a higher rate of corporate tax than profits that are distributed. Under this split-rate system, tax-exempt investors prefer the company to pay high dividends, whereas millionaires might vote to retain profits.

The claimed burden of double taxation under the classical system led to its replacement in Australia by the new imputation system.[43] Now, Australian shareholders are taxed on their share of profit received through dividends, but they may deduct from this tax bill their share of the corporate tax that the company has paid. The objective of the imputation system is that income derived from corporate sources should only be taxed at the investors' marginal tax rate. Thus, we could view the corporate tax as a form of tax paid for investors in advance, in much the same way as taxes are deducted from the wages of PAYE taxpayers. At the end of the year there is a settling up to determine whether there has been underpayment or overpayment of tax.

# Details of the imputation tax system and capital gains tax

## *Where franking credits come from

A company keeps track of its franking credits through a special account called the franking account.[44] This account provides a record of the quantity of retained earnings that can be paid out as franked dividends. Franking credits are primarily created by the payment of Australian corporate tax.[45] When a company pays its tax the value of the tax payment is converted to an equivalent value of fully franked dividends and this quantity is credited to the franking account. The conversion formula is:

$$\text{Franking account adjustment} = \text{tax paid} \times \frac{(1 - T_c)}{T_c},$$

where $T_c$ is the corporate tax rate.

For example, if the company had paid $1 million in tax at a corporate tax rate of 36 per cent, then the franking account balance would be increased by $1 million $\times (1 - 0.36)/0.36$, or $1.778 million. In other words, the company could pay $1.778 million of fully franked dividends.

If the company *receives* a fully franked dividend then the full value of the dividend is credited to the franking account. Therefore, in our example above, the receipt of $2 million of fully franked dividends would increase the franking account balance to $3.778 million. Thus, franking credits pass through the corporate structure to the non-corporate shareholders.

When the company *pays* a dividend it must frank the dividend by debiting the franking account with an amount equal to the dividend. This assumes that there is a sufficient franking balance available in the franking account to cover the dividend. Continuing our example above, if the company paid a $1.5 million dividend, the franking account balance would be reduced by $1.5 million. The dividend would be fully franked carrying a tax credit of $0.84

---

43    In fact the imputation system was not new. Australia has had variants on the imputation system in the past, and indeed there have been times when there were no corporate taxes.

44    This account does not form part of the company's double-entry accounting system.

45    Various adjustments to the franking account can also arise from tax office assessments, tax instalments paid against those assessments and the receipt of franked dividends from other Australian companies.

million ($1.5 million $\times$ (0.36/(1 − 0.36))). A balance of $2.278 million would remain in the franking account and would be carried forward to frank future dividend payments. If the company had paid a $4 million dividend then the franking account balance would be reduced to zero debiting it by $3.778 million and the dividend would only be 94.5 per cent (3.778/4) franked.[46]

Dividends may be unfranked or partially franked for two main reasons. The first is that the income has been earned offshore and has not been subject to Australian tax, in which case no franking credits are created. The second reason is that company profits have been taxed in Australia, but at an effective tax rate that is less than the statutory rate.

## Capital gains tax

As we discussed earlier in the chapter, investors' dividend policy preferences will largely be determined by the balance between payment of income taxes and gains taxes. We would expect that the introduction of the imputation system would tip the balance in favour of higher dividends. In order to check this out we should start by considering Australian capital gains tax arrangements. Capital gains taxes are only levied on assets acquired after 19 September 1995. The taxable gain is assessed as the difference between the net receipts from sale and the inflation-indexed cost base. This cost base is usually the purchase price of the asset plus costs incurred in its purchase. The cost base is indexed by the Consumer Price Index so that the tax is only levied on the real gain. One-fifth of the assessable gain is added to the taxpayer's income to determine the investor's marginal tax rate in the year the gain is realised.[47] This tax rate is then applied to the whole of the gain.[48] Gains tax is only levied on realisation, so the longer realisation of the gain is deferred, the lower the effective tax rate.

Although this system is often described as taxing capital gains as income, it is clear that the effective tax rate for many investors will be lower on gains than on income. However, there is an offsetting tax disadvantage to capital gains. Relief from corporate tax under the imputation system only applies to profits distributed as dividends. Profits retained within the firm face the prospect of double taxation through corporate taxes and gains taxes. The question is whether the investor would rather pay income tax on dividends or see profits retained and face both corporate tax and gains tax. This question can only be answered by looking at the particular imputation tax arrangements applying to particular classes of investors.

## How imputation works

To begin with we will consider a simple illustration of the imputation system. Table 16.3 shows how the imputation system works. Suppose that an Australian company earns pre-tax profits of $100 a share. After tax at 36 per cent the profit is 100 − 36 = $64 a share. The tax payment gives rise to a $36 franking credit and an entry in the company's franking account which records that the company can pay $64 of fully franked dividends. The company now declares a net dividend of $64 a share and sends shareholders a cheque for this amount. This dividend is accompanied by a statement of franking credits saying that the company has already paid $36 of tax on the shareholders' behalf. The tax authorities impute the full share of corporate income to the shareholder. Thus, shareholders are treated as if they received a total (grossed up) dividend of 64 + 36 = $100 and they are taxed on the full $100. But they are also allowed a tax credit of $36.[49] If all the

---

[46] It is possible to overfrank the dividend. In the above case this would mean debiting $4 million to the franking account and declaring the dividend to be fully franked. However, a penalty tax is payable, if at year-end the deficit in the franking account exceeds 10 per cent of the year's total franking credits.

[47] This treatment reduces the chance that a normally low-rate tax payer will be catapulted into the highest marginal tax bracket by a modest capital gain.

[48] Capital losses can be carried forward indefinitely to be used as offsets to future gains, but they are not subject to indexing.

[49] The general formula to convert fully franked dividends to the taxable share of profits, or grossed up dividend, is $D/(1 − T_c)$. Thus, $64/(1 − 0.36) = 100$. The tax liability is $[D/(1 − T_c)] \times T_d$, where $T_d$ is the investor's tax rate on dividends. The credit available is given by $[D/(1 − T_c)] \times T_c$, thus $[64/(1 − 0.36)] \times 0.36 = 36$. So the net tax payable is $[D/(1 − T_c)] \times [T_d − T_c]$.

shareholders were taxed at 36 per cent, there would be no more tax to pay.[50] Some investors, however, will have extra tax payments to make.

Consider a shareholder on the highest marginal tax rate 47 per cent (ignoring the Medicare levy), then he or she is required to pay an additional $11 of tax. On the other hand, if the shareholder is a superannuation fund, taxed at 15 per cent, then there is a surplus credit of $21. This $21 can be used as an offset against tax on other income in the current tax year. Unused credits cannot be carried forward to future years.

**table 16.3**

Tax payable by different classes of taxpayers under the imputation system. All of the $64 of after-tax income is paid as a dividend. The dividend after all taxes is the after-tax income less the balance of tax due.

|  | Investor tax rates | | | | |
|---|---|---|---|---|---|
|  | **Tax exempt 0%** | **Super fund 15%** | **Hypothetical 36%** | **High rate 47%** | **Overseas 25%** |
| Operating income | 100 | 100 | 100 | 100 | 100 |
| Corporate tax | 36 | 36 | 36 | 36 | 36 |
| After-tax income | 64 | 64 | 64 | 64 | 64 |
| Grossed up dividend | 100 | 100 | 100 | 100 | 64 |
| Income tax | 0 | 15 | 36 | 47 | 16 |
| Tax credit | 0 | 36 | 36 | 36 | 0* |
| Balance of tax due (rebateable) | 0 | (21) | 0 | 11 | 16 |
| Dividend after all taxes | 64 | 85 | 64 | 53 | 48 |

Note: * The overseas investor cannot claim the imputation credit, but since the dividend is franked there will be no Australian withholding tax liability. The investor simply pays their home country tax rate of 25 per cent.

Look once again at Table 16.3 and think what would happen if the corporate tax rate were zero. The shareholder with a 15 per cent tax rate would still end up with $85, the shareholder with a 47 per cent tax rate would still receive $53, and the shareholder with the 36 per cent rate will still receive $64. For these shareholders, under an imputation tax system, when a company pays out *all* its earnings there is effectively only one layer of tax—the tax on the shareholder. If a company pays unfranked dividends they have not been taxed at the corporate level so they too are only taxed at the shareholder's tax rate.

## Investors who cannot claim the franking credit
We hate to introduce complications when things seem so straightforward, but we have to point out that not all investors are subject to imputation; for example, the tax-exempt and overseas investors in Table 16.3. But first we will consider the tax arrangements that apply to Australian companies receiving dividends. For companies dividends are included as part of taxable income, but a tax rebate is allowed equal to the corporate tax rate multiplied by the dividends received. As a consequence of these arrangements dividends are effectively tax-free for most companies.[51] The imputation

---

[50] In Australia and New Zealand shareholders receive a credit for the full amount of corporate tax that has been paid on their behalf. In other countries, such as the United Kingdom and Spain, there is a partial imputation system; the tax credit is less than the corporate tax rate.

[51] There are exceptions. Unfranked dividends received by private companies are only eligible for the rebate if the dividend is a payment between companies within a wholly owned group of companies. Also, companies which have accumulated tax losses, or other tax shields, may have insufficient taxable income to take advantage of the tax rebate.

credits associated with the dividends received are not used up. As we discussed above, they pass through the company and ultimately end up in the hands of the non-corporate shareholders.

An important class of shareholders who are not able to claim imputation credits are the non-resident investors. Overseas investors are subject to a withholding tax on dividends from Australian companies. The withholding tax is paid direct to the tax office by the company paying the dividend. The tax is levied at a flat rate of 30 per cent or a lower rate of 15 per cent if Australia has a double tax agreement with the country in which the overseas investor resides. If the dividends are franked, however, no withholding tax is payable. This may seem like a significant benefit, but it is likely that the overseas investor could have claimed the withholding tax anyway, as an offset against income tax in their home country.

Now put yourself in the shoes of an overseas investor. You have just received fully franked dividends of $1 million. This means that you also have a franking credit of $562 500. You cannot use this credit, so would you chuck it in the bin? There are very few of us who can throw away half a million dollars without giving it another thought. As you might therefore expect, considerable thought and effort has gone into finding ways for such investors to obtain the value locked up in the franking credit. While on the other side of the fence the government busies itself trying to plug the loopholes.

There are also some resident investors who cannot claim imputation credits. These are investors who are tax-exempt, such as charities, and investors who do pay tax but have insufficient taxable income to utilise all their imputation credits. These unused credits do not give rise to a cash tax refund, and they cannot be carried forward to use in future tax years. So unused franking credits are lost.[52]

So where does all this leave us? Under an imputation tax system, high tax rate investors have to cough up the extra personal tax on dividends. If this is more than the tax they would pay on capital gains then they would prefer the company not to pay the dividend. Their choice will largely depend on how long they plan to hold the share. If their planned holding period is short the effective gains tax will be relatively high and they will prefer the dividend. For long holding periods they may prefer the capital gain. Low rate taxpayers, particularly super funds, have few doubts about the matter. If the company pays a dividend, these investors receive a tax credit for excess tax that the company has paid. Provided they can use this credit they prefer high dividend payout rates. Investors who cannot use the imputation credit, such as overseas investors, face taxes that look like a classical system, but with one important difference. Mechanisms exist for them to access some of the value from their imputation credits. However, no one can use the franking credits until the dividends to which they are attached are paid out by the company.

A clear conclusion flows from our analysis. If companies do not pay dividends sufficient to distribute the franking credits, this is likely to impose a cost on their shareholders.[53] Suppose we accept this argument and pay out sufficient dividends to exhaust our franking credits, should we then pay unfranked dividends?[54] Probably not. In this case the investors' incremental tax payment will be at their full personal tax rate, while the incremental tax on profit retained will be at the investors' gains tax rate. So investors will generally favour companies maximising franked dividends and minimising unfranked dividends.

## Dividends taxes and ex-dividend trading

A company with a positive balance in its franking account is making an interest-free loan to the government.[55] This hardly seems likely to be maximising shareholders' wealth. The corporate

---

52  In contrast with this companies can carry their imputation credits forward for later distribution to shareholders.

53  As always there are other factors to consider. Managers may be concerned, for example, that a policy of distributing all franking credits may lead to dividend instability and adverse information signalling effects.

54  Note that companies are not permitted to pay unfranked dividends while there is still a positive balance in the franking account. The mixture of franked and unfranked dividends will result in a combined dividend that is partially franked.

55  We are indebted to Bob Officer for this insight.

objective should be to get those franking credits into the hands of investors who can use them. Ingenious ways have been found to do this even though direct trading of imputation credits is prohibited. However, one simple way for shareholders to sell their credits is to trade them along with the dividend by selling the share cum-dividend and buying the shares back ex-dividend.[56]

Imagine a wallet containing $10. Next we take $2 out of the wallet. How much would the contents of the wallet sell for initially and after we remove the $2? We hope you said $10 and $8. Now a slightly more complex offer. When we initially offer you the wallet we tell you that you can buy all the contents of the wallet but we will levy a $0.50 tax. Alternatively, you can buy the contents of the wallet after we take and keep the $2. We hope you price this offer at $9.50 and $8. This is how we would expect the price of shares to behave on the ex-dividend day. Let us call the $2 a dividend. In the absence of taxes prices should drop by exactly the face value of the dividend ($10 − $8 = $2). If dividends are taxed, the price of the share should drop by less than the face value of the dividend ($9.50 − $8.00 = $1.50). The $1.50 drop is the after-tax value of the dividend.

One last alternative: we now tell you that the wallet contains $10 and a voucher for a small glass of beer. You can buy these contents of the wallet subject to a $0.50 tax, or you can buy the wallet's contents after we take out and keep the $2 and the beer voucher. The second part of the offer is still worth $8 but the first part is a more difficult offer to price. How much is the beer voucher worth? Let us suppose that a small glass of beer costs $1. Then you might value the voucher at $1; then again, you might not. It might be some time before you get round to using the voucher; if you are teetotal then you will never use it. For a teetotaller the voucher has no value at all unless it can be sold to someone else. So the value of the voucher might be anywhere from zero to $1. Let us suppose it is worth $0.70. In this case the value of our offer is $10 + $0.70 − $0.50 = $10.20, a value $2.20 greater than our offer of the $8 cash. The moral is that, if the dividend comes with a valuable imputation credit attached, the price drop off may be more than the face value of the dividend. However, the value of that credit may be difficult to establish.

Researchers in the United States and Australia have examined the ex-dividend drop-off ratio. This is the ratio of the decline in the share price on the ex-dividend day to the dividend per share. They have consistently found the average of this ratio to be less than one. In Australia, Philip Brown and Terry Walter[57] studied the drop-off ratio pre-imputation from 1974 to 1985, when the drop off averaged about 0.75.

Some researchers have been tempted to use the drop-off ratio to make inferences about the marginal tax rates of investors. The problem with this is that if the drop-off ratio is less than one, profitable trading opportunities exist for low to zero tax investors. For example, consider a share that sells for $10, pays a $1 dividend and its ex-dividend price drop follows the average at $0.75. For a $10 outlay a zero tax investor gets an asset worth $10.25, comprising a $1 dividend plus a share worth $9.25 ex-dividend. Some investors could also sell ex-dividend and claim a $0.75 capital loss to offset against other gains. They get an asset worth about $11.00 for a $10 outlay. Whether this is attractive depends on transaction costs and the risk of the strategy.

But most of this evidence has more historical than current interest, now that dividends and capital gains are taxed at the same rate and we have switched to the imputation system. Scott Walker and one of the authors[58] examined the value of dividends and franking credits by looking at shares trading cum-dividend in the ex-dividend period. This allowed them to isolate

---

[56] In the 1997 Australian Budget the Treasurer announced measures to try and curb this practice: it will be interesting to see if these measures succeed. The main requirement is that the shares have to be held for 45 days in order for shareholders to get the benefit of franking credits. There are also restrictions on using derivatives to reduce risk during this holding period.

[57] P. Brown and T. Walter, 'Ex-Dividend Behaviour of Australian Share Prices', *Australian Journal of Management*, **2**: 139–52 (December 1986). Philip Brown was also involved in a study of ex-dividend share prices after the introduction of imputation. Contrary to expectations the drop-off ratio appeared to decline, rather than increase, immediately after imputation was introduced. However, it seemed to increase over time, particularly after the 15 per cent tax was levied on superannuation funds. See P. Brown and A. Clarke, 'The Ex-Dividend Behaviour of Share Prices Before and After Dividend Imputation', *Australian Journal of Management*, **18**: 1–40 (June 1993).

[58] S. Walker and G. H. Partington, The Ex-Dividend Drop Off: Estimating the Value of Dividends from Cum-Dividend Trading in the Ex-Dividend Period, paper presented at the Accounting Association of Australia and New Zealand Conference, Hobart, 1997. An updated version of this paper can be found in *Accounting and Finance* (November 1999).

cases where shares were simultaneously being traded cum-dividend and ex-dividend. The difference in price should provide a good measure of the value of the dividends and the associated tax effects. On the basis of more than 1000 matched pairs of trades the researchers concluded that $1 face value of fully franked dividends is worth roughly $1.20, after transaction costs.[59] They pointed out that this is the value of a package consisting of the dividend, the franking credits and a potential tax loss from buying cum-dividend and selling ex-dividend. Untangling the value of the individual components of this package is not a simple task. It is clear, however, that if you can sell $1 of fully franked dividends for $1.20 during the ex-dividend period, you would be foolish to sell it for less than the present value of $1.20 at any other time. We can safely conclude therefore that a dollar of fully franked dividends is worth more than a dollar. The implication is that companies with undistributed franking credits should consider increasing their payout ratios.

## 16.7 Summary

Dividends come in many forms. The most common is the regular cash dividend, but sometimes companies pay an extra or special cash dividend, and sometimes they pay a dividend in the form of shares. A firm is not free to pay whatever dividends it likes. It may have promised its debtholders not to declare large dividends, and it is also prevented by law from paying dividends if it is insolvent, or if it has insufficient profit.

As an alternative to dividend payments, the company can repurchase its own shares. In an on market repurchase the tax office taxes shareholders only on the capital gains that they may realise as a result of the repurchase. However, repurchases are not yet common in Australia, although their use is growing.

When managers decide on the dividend, a primary concern seems to be to give shareholders a 'fair' level of dividends. Most managers have a conscious or subconscious long-term target payout rate. If firms simply applied the target payout rate to each year's earnings, dividends could fluctuate wildly. Managers therefore try to smooth dividend payments by moving only partway towards the target payout in each year. Also, they do not just look at past earnings performance: They try to look into the future when they set the payment. Investors are aware of this and they know that a dividend increase is often a sign of optimism on the part of management.

If we hold the company's investment policy constant, then dividend policy is a trade-off between cash dividends and the issue or repurchase of shares. Should firms retain whatever earnings are necessary to finance growth and pay out any residual as cash dividends? Or should they increase dividends and then (sooner or later) issue shares to make up the shortfall of equity capital? Or should they reduce dividends below the 'residual' level and use the released cash to repurchase shares?

If we lived in an ideally simple and perfect world, there would be no problem, for the choice would have no effect on market value. The controversy centres on the effects of dividend policy in our flawed world. A common—though by no means universal—view in the investment community is that high payout enhances share price. There are natural clienteles for high-payout shares. This is particularly the case under the imputation tax system. But under a classical tax system, we find it difficult to explain a *general* preference for dividends other than in terms of an irrational prejudice.

The most obvious and serious market imperfection has been the different tax treatment of dividends and capital gains. Before the tax reforms of the 1980s dividends received by

---

[59]  The face value of the dollar of dividends *plus* the franking credit is given by $1/(1 - T_c)$. With corporate tax at 36 per cent this makes the figure $1.56.

individuals were taxed at rates much higher than capital gains. Thus, investors should have required a higher before-tax return on high-payout shares to compensate for their tax disadvantage. High-income investors should have held mostly low-payout shares.

This view has a respectable theoretical basis and has some empirical support. The weak link is the theory's silence on the question of why companies continued to distribute such large sums contrary to the preferences of investors. Perhaps the explanation is that it was not contrary to their preferences after all. Maybe, the majority of investors suffered no tax disadvantage from the payment of dividends.

The third view of dividend policy starts with the notion that the actions of companies do reflect investors' preferences; the fact that companies pay substantial dividends is the best evidence that investors want them. If the supply of dividends exactly meets the demand, no single company could improve its market value by changing its dividend policy. Although this explains corporate behaviour, it is at a cost, for we cannot explain why dividends are what they are and not some other amount.

These theories are too incomplete and most of the evidence is too sensitive to minor changes in specification to warrant any dogmatism. Under a classical tax system, our natural sympathies lie with the third, middle-of-the-road view. Under an imputation system we lean towards higher payouts, at least to the extent that they distribute the available franking credits.

We conclude by making three points about dividend policy, which create a difficult choice for Australian companies. First, there is little doubt that sudden shifts in dividend policy can cause abrupt changes in share price. The principal reason is the information that investors read into the company's actions, although some casual evidence suggests that there may be other less rational explanations.[60] Given such problems, there is a case for smoothing dividends. If it is necessary to make a sharp dividend change, it makes sense for the company to provide as much forewarning as possible and to take care to ensure that the action is not misinterpreted.

Second, there is a case that a company should adopt a target payout that is sufficiently low as to minimise its reliance on external equity. So growth shares should have lower payouts. Why pay out cash to shareholders if that requires issuing new shares to get the cash back? In this context dividend reinvestment plans make good sense.

Third, the demand to distribute franking credits leads to pressure for higher and fluctuating payouts as profits and taxes vary over time. This conflicts with points one and two above. The difficult question facing financial managers is where to strike the balance.

## FURTHER READING

Lintner's classic analysis of how companies set their dividend payments is provided in:

J. Lintner, 'Distribution of Incomes of Corporations among Dividends, Retained Earnings and Taxes', *American Economic Review*, **46**: 97–113 (May 1956).

There have been a number of tests of how well Lintner's model describes dividend changes. One of the best known is:

E. F. Fama and H. Babiak, 'Dividend Policy: An Empirical Analysis', *Journal of the American Statistical Association*, **63**: 1132–61 (December 1968).

---

[60]  For example, in an article in *Fortune*, Carol Loomis tells the story of General Public Utilities ('A Case for Dropping Dividends', *Fortune*, 15 June 1968, pp. 181 ff.). In 1968 its management decided to reduce its cash dividend to avoid a share issue. Despite the company's assurances, it encountered considerable opposition. Individual shareholders advised the president to see a psychiatrist, institutional holders threatened to sell their shares, the share price fell nearly 10 per cent, and eventually GPU capitulated.

Australian evidence on the Lintner model is provided by:

> G. H. Partington, 'Dividend Policy and Target Payout Ratios', *Accounting and Finance*, 63–74 (November 1984).
>
> T. Shevlin, 'Australian Corporate Dividend Policy: Empirical Evidence', *Accounting and Finance*, 1–22 (May 1982).

Marsh and Merton have reinterpreted Lintner's findings and used them to explain the aggregate dividends paid by American corporations:

> T. A. Marsh and R. C. Merton, 'Dividend Behavior for the Aggregate Share Market', *Journal of Business*, **60**: 1–40 (January 1987).

The pioneering article on dividend policy in the context of a perfect capital market is:

> M. H. Miller and F. Modigliani, 'Dividend Policy, Growth and the Valuation of Shares', *Journal of Business*, **34**: 411–33 (October 1961).

There are several interesting models explaining the information content of dividends. Two influential examples are:

> S. Bhattacharya, 'Imperfect Information, Dividend Policy and the Bird in the Hand Fallacy', *Bell Journal of Economics and Management Science*, **10**: 259–70 (Spring 1979).
>
> M. H. Miller and K. Rock, 'Dividend Policy Under Asymmetric Information', *Journal of Finance*, **40**: 1031–52 (September 1985).

An Australian study that looks at the information conveyed by dividend announcements is:

> P. Brown, F. Finn and P. Hancock, 'Dividend Changes, Earnings Reports and Share Prices: Some Australian Findings', *Australian Journal of Management*, 127–47 (October 1977).

The most powerful advocacy of the 'dividends are good' case is Gordon. Brennan discusses the source of the differences between Gordon and MM:

> M. J. Gordon, 'Dividends, Earnings and Share Prices', *Review of Economics and Statistics*, **41**: 99–105 (May 1959).
>
> M. J. Brennan, 'A Note on Dividend Irrelevance and the Gordon Valuation Mode', *Journal of Finance*, **26**: 1115–22 (December 1971).

The effect of differential rates of tax on dividends and capital gains is analysed rigorously in the context of the capital asset pricing model in:

> M. J. Brennan, 'Taxes, Market Valuation and Corporate Financial Policy', *National Tax Journal*, **23**: 417–27 (December 1970).

An analysis of the effect of imputation on dividend policy is contained in:

> P. F. Howard and R. L. Brown, 'Dividend Policy and Capital Structure Under the Imputation Tax System: Some Clarifying Comments', *Accounting and Finance*, **32**: 51–61 (May 1992).

The argument that dividend policy is irrelevant even in the presence of taxes is presented in:

> F. Black and M. S. Scholes, 'The Effects of Dividend Yield and Dividend Policy on Common Share Prices and Returns', *Journal of Financial Economics*, **1**: 1–22 (May 1974).
>
> M. H. Miller and M. S. Scholes, 'Dividends and Taxes', *Journal of Financial Economics*, **6**: 333–64 (December 1978).

A brief review of some of the empirical evidence is contained in:

> R. H. Litzenberger and K. Ramaswamy, 'The Effects of Dividends on Common Share Prices: Tax Effects or Information Effects', *Journal of Finance*, **37**: 429–43 (May 1982).

The Australian evidence is presented in:

> R. Ball, P. Brown, F.J. Finn and R R. Officer, 'Dividends and the Value of the Firm: Evidence from the Australian Equity Market', *Australian Journal of Management*, **4**: 13–26 (April 1979).

Merton Miller reviews research on the dividend controversy in:

> M. H. Miller, 'Behavioral Rationality in Finance: The Case of Dividends', *Journal of Business*, **59**: S451–68 (October 1986).

The use of dividends as a device to control management's use of cash and thereby reduce the agency problems of free cash flow is discussed in:

> F. Easterbrook, 'Two agency cost explanations of Dividends', *American Economic Review*, **74**: 650–9 (September 1984).

A study of the ex-dividend behaviour of Australian shares can be found in:

> P. Brown and A. Clarke, 'The Ex-Dividend Day Behaviour of Australian Share Prices Before and After Dividend Imputation', *Australian Journal of Management*, **18**: 1–40 (1993).

An Australian study of the price effects of dividend re-investment plans can be found in:

> K. Chan, D. McColough and M. Skully, 'Australian Tax Changes and Dividend Reinvestment Announcement Effects: A Pre- and Post-Imputatation Study', *Australian Journal of Management*, **18**: 41–62 (June 1993).

## QUIZ

1. In 1997 St George Bank paid an interim dividend of $0.26 per share.
   a. Match each of the following sets of dates:
      | | |
      |---|---|
      | (A) 2 July 1997 | (a) Record date |
      | (B) 13 June 1997 | (b) Payment date |
      | (C) 4 June 1997 | (c) Ex-dividend date |
      | (D) 5 June 1997 | (d) Last with-dividend date |
   b. On one of these dates the share price is likely to fall by about the value of the dividend. Why?
   c. If the share price was about $7.60 in June, what was the prospective dividend yield?
   d. Suppose that in 1997 the company paid a 1-for-10 share dividend. What would be the expected fall in the share price?

2. Which of the following statements are false?
   a. A company may not generally pay a dividend out of legal capital.
   b. A company may not generally pay a dividend if it is insolvent.
   c. Realised long-term gains are taxed at the marginal rate of income tax.
   d. Nevertheless, the *effective* tax rate on capital gains can be less than the tax rate on dividends.
   e. Corporations are taxed on only 50 per cent of dividends received from other corporations.

3. Here are several 'facts' about typical corporate dividend policies. Which of the 'facts' are true and which false? Write out a corrected version of any false statements.
   a. Most companies set a target dividend payout ratio.
   b. They set each year's dividend equal to the target payout ratio multiplied by that year's earnings.
   c. Managers and investors seem more concerned with dividend changes than dividend levels.
   d. Managers often increase dividends temporarily when earnings are unexpectedly high for a year or two.

4. Between 1969 and 1988 one could explain about two-thirds of the variation in Classic Share's dividend changes by the following equation:

$$\text{DIV}_t - \text{DIV}_{t-1} = -0.90 + 0.54 \,(0.34 \,\text{EPS}_t - \text{DIV}_{t-1})$$

   What do you think was:
   a. Classic Share's target payout ratio?
   b. The rate at which dividends adjusted towards the target?

**5.** Share price usually rises when there is an unexpected dividend increase, and falls when there is an unexpected dividend cut. Why?

**6.** How did the tax reforms of the 1980s affect the taxation of dividends and capital gains? Are there any investors left who could have a rational tax reason to prefer capital gains? Other things being equal, how should the tax law changes affect prices and expected rates of return on high- versus low-payout shares? How is your answer affected by whether the dividends are fully franked, partially franked or unfranked?

**7.** How does the two-tier classical tax system in the United Sates differ from the imputation system?

**8.** Here is some key financial data for House of Herring Ltd:

| | |
|---|---|
| Earnings per share for 2006 | $5.50 |
| Number of shares outstanding | 40 million |
| Target payout ratio | 50% |
| Planned dividend per share | $2.75 |
| Share price, year-end 2006 | $130 |

House of Herring plans to pay the entire dividend early in January 2007. All corporate and personal taxes were repealed in 2005.

   a. Other things being equal, what will be House of Herring's share price after the planned dividend payment?
   b. Suppose the company cancels the dividend and announces that it will use the money saved to repurchase shares. What happens to the share price on the announcement date? Assume that investors learn nothing about the company's prospects from the announcement. How many shares will the company need to repurchase?
   c. Suppose the company announces that it will increase the dividends to $5.50 per share and then issues new shares to recoup the extra cash paid out as dividends. What happens to the cum-dividend and ex-dividend share prices? How many shares will need to be issued? Assume the announcement has no information content.

## QUESTIONS AND PROBLEMS

**1.** Look in a recent issue of the *Australian Financial Review* and choose a company reporting a regular dividend.
   a. How frequently does the company pay a regular dividend?
   b. What is the amount of the dividend?
   c. By what date must your share be registered for you to receive the dividend?
   d. How many weeks later is the dividend paid?
   e. Look up the share price and calculate the annual yield on the share.
   f. Work out the payout ratio.
   g. To what extent is the dividend franked?

**2.** Respond to the following comment: 'It's all very well saying that I can sell shares to cover cash needs, but that may mean selling at the bottom of the market. If the company pays a regular dividend, investors avoid that risk.'

**3.** 'Dividends are the shareholder's wages. Therefore, if a government adopts an income policy which restricts increases in wages, it should in all logic restrict increases in dividends.' Does this make sense?

**4.** Refer to the first balance sheet prepared for Rational Demiconductor in Section 16.3. Again, it uses cash to pay a $1000 cash dividend, planning to issue shares to recover the cash required for investment. But this time catastrophe hits before the shares can be issued. A new pollution control regulation increases manufacturing costs to the extent that the value of Rational Demiconductor's existing business is cut in half, to $4500. The NPV of the new investment opportunity is unaffected, however. Show that dividend policy is still irrelevant.

**5.** 'Risky companies tend to have lower target payout ratios and more gradual adjustment rates.' Explain what is meant by this statement. Why do you think it is so?

**6.** Consider the following two statements: 'Dividend policy is irrelevant' and 'Share price is the present value of expected future dividends' (see Chapter 4). They *sound* contradictory. This question is designed to show that they are fully consistent.

The current price of the shares of Charles River Mining Corporation is $50. Next year's earnings and dividends per share are $4 and $2, respectively. Investors expect perpetual growth at 8 per cent per year. The expected rate of return demanded by investors is $r = 12$ per cent.

We can use the perpetual-growth model

$$P_0 = \frac{DIV}{r - g} = \frac{2}{0.12 - 0.08} = 50$$

Suppose that Charles River Mining announces that it will switch to a 100 per cent payout policy, issuing shares as necessary to finance growth. Use the perpetual-growth model to show that current share price is unchanged.

**7.** The expected pre-tax return on three shares is divided between dividends and capital gains in the following way:

| Share | Expected dividend ($) | Expected capital gain ($) |
|-------|----------------------|---------------------------|
| A     | 0                    | 10                        |
| B     | 5                    | 5                         |
| C     | 10                   | 0                         |

a. If each share is priced at $100, what are the expected net returns on each share to (i) a superannuation fund, (ii) a corporation paying tax at 36 per cent, (iii) an individual paying tax at 20 per cent on income and 20 per cent on capital gains, (iv) a security trader paying tax at 47 per cent on investment income and capital gains and (v) an overseas investor taxed at 36 per cent on income, facing a 20 per cent tax rate on capital gains and subject to a 15 per cent withholding tax? In your calculations assume that the dividends are fully franked. Then repeat the calculation for unfranked dividends.

b. Suppose that before the 1987 introduction of imputation, shares A, B and C were priced to yield an 8 per cent *after-tax* return to individual investors paying 50 per cent tax on dividends and an effective 20 per cent tax on capital gains. What would A, B and C each sell for?

**8.** Answer the following question thrice, once assuming current tax law, once assuming tax law prior to the introduction of capital gains tax in 1985 and once assuming tax law prior to the introduction of imputation in 1987.

Suppose all investments offered the same expected return *before* tax. Consider two equally risky shares, Hi and Lo. Hi shares pay a generous dividend and offer low expected capital gains. Lo shares pay low dividends and offer high expected capital gains. Which of the following investors would prefer the Lo shares? Which would prefer the Hi shares? Which would not care? Explain.

a. A pension fund.
b. An individual.
c. A corporation.
d. A charitable endowment.
e. A security trader.
f. An overseas investor.

Assume that any share purchased will be sold after one year.

**9.** An article on share repurchase suggested: 'An increasing number of companies should recognise that the best investment they can make these days is in themselves.' Discuss this view. How is the desirability of repurchase affected by company prospects and the price of its shares?

**10.** Adherents of the 'dividends-are-good' school sometimes point to the fact that shares with high yields tend to have above-average price-earnings multiples. Is this evidence convincing? Discuss.

**11.** For each of the following four groups of companies, state whether you would expect them to distribute a relatively high or low proportion of current earnings and whether you would expect them to have a relatively high or low price-earnings ratio.

a. High-risk companies.
b. Companies that have recently experienced an unexpected decline in profits.
c. Companies that expect to experience a decline in profits.
d. 'Growth' companies with valuable future investment opportunities.

**12.** 'Many companies use share repurchase to increase earnings per share. For example, suppose that a company is in the following position:

| | |
|---|---|
| ▪ Net profit | $10 million |
| ▪ Number of shares before repurchase | 1 million |
| ▪ Earnings per share | $10 |
| ▪ Price-earnings ratio | 20 |
| ▪ Share price | $200 |

The company now repurchases 200 000 shares at $200 a share. The number of shares declines to 800 000 shares and the earnings per share increase to $12.50. Assuming the price-earnings ratio stays at 20, the share price must rise to $250.00.' Discuss.

**13.** a. The Horner Pie Company pays a twice-yearly dividend of $1. Suppose that the share price is expected to fall on the ex-dividend date by $0.90. Would you prefer to buy on the cum-dividend date or the ex-dividend date if you were (i) a tax-free investor, (ii) an investor with a marginal tax rate of 40 per cent on income and 16 per cent on capital gains or (iii) an investor taxed equally on dividends and capital gains at 47 per cent. Assume the dividends are fully franked and that transactions costs can be ignored.

b. In a study of ex-dividend behaviour under the classical tax system, Elton and Gruber estimated that the share price fell on the average by 85 per cent of the dividend. Assuming that the tax rate on capital gains was 40 per cent of the rate on income tax, what did Elton and Gruber's result imply about investors' marginal rate of income tax? (*Hint*: If you buy cum-dividend and sell ex-dividend, the return you get after taxes should be no greater than the extra cost of buying cum-dividend. Another way to think about the problem is that after allowing for the benefits obtained, it should be no more expensive to buy cum-dividend than to buy ex-dividend. If you really get stuck Elton and Gruber's formula was:

$$\frac{P_{Cum} - P_{Ex}}{DIV} = \frac{1 - T_p}{1 - T_G}$$

$P_{Cum}$ is the cum-dividend price, $P_{Ex}$ is the ex-dividend price, DIV is the dividend, $T_p$ is the personal tax rate on dividends, $T_G$ is the tax rate on capital gains.)
  c. Elton and Gruber also observed that the ex-dividend price fall was different for high-payout shares and for low-payout shares. Which group would you expect to show the larger price fall?
  d. Would the fact that investors in all tax brackets can trade shares freely around the ex-dividend date alter your interpretation of Elton and Gruber's study?
  e. Suppose Elton and Gruber conducted their test in Australia for the period 1988–92, after the 1987 introduction of the imputation tax system. How would you expect their results to change?

**14.** The middle-of-the-road party holds that dividend policy does not matter because the *supply* of high-, medium- and low-payout shares has already adjusted to satisfy investors' demands. Investors who like generous dividends hold shares that give them all they want. Investors who want capital gains see a surfeit of low-payout shares to choose from. Thus, high-payout firms cannot gain by transforming to low-payout firms, or vice versa.

Suppose this was the way it was just before the introduction of imputation in 1987. How would you expect the 1987 tax changes to affect the total cash dividends paid by Australian companies and the proportion of high- versus low-payout companies? Would dividend policy still be irrelevant after any dividend supply adjustments are completed? Explain.

**15.** How would you expect dividend policy to affect market value under (a) a split-rate tax system, (b) an imputation tax system and (c) a classical tax system? Construct simple examples to illustrate your arguments.

**16.** Comment briefly on each of the following statements:
  a. Unlike Australian firms, which are always being pressured by their shareholders to increase their dividends, Japanese companies pay out a much smaller portion of their earnings and so enjoy a lower cost of capital.
  b. Unlike new capital, which needs a stream of dividends to service it, retained earnings are essentially free capital.
  c. If a company repurchases shares instead of paying a dividend, the number of shares falls and earnings per share rise. Thus, share repurchase must always be preferred to paying a dividend.

**17.** Milly Mandy Ltd has one million shares outstanding, with a total market value of $20 million. The firm is expected to pay $1 million of dividends next year, and thereafter dividends are expected to grow at a rate of 5 per cent per year in perpetuity. The expected dividend in year 2 is therefore $1.05 million, and so on.

The company now announces that it will instead pay $2 million of dividends next year. The extra cash required will be raised simultaneously by an issue of shares. After that dividend payments will revert to the forecast, $1.05 million in year 2, and so on, with a 5 per cent growth rate. Assume no tax or information signalling effects.

a. At what price will the new shares be issued in year 1?
b. How many shares will the company need to issue?
c. What will be the expected dividend payments on these new shares and what therefore will be paid out to the *old* shareholders after year 1?
d. Show that the present value of cash flows to the current shareholders remains at $20 million.

**18.** We stated in Section 16.3 that MM's dividend irrelevance proposition assumes that new shares are sold at a fair price. Look back at Question 17. Assume that new shares are issued in year 1 at $10 a share. Show who gains and who loses. Is dividend policy still irrelevant? Why or why not?

**19.** In December 1995 Qantas paid a fully franked dividend of 3.5 cents, in April 1996 an interim dividend was paid of 6.5 cents 68 per cent franked, and in December 1996 a final dividend of 6.5 cents unfranked was paid. Assuming you owned 1000 shares and that 36 per cent is the corporate tax rate, calculate:

a. The total dividend received at each payment and the dollar value of the franked and unfranked components of the dividend.
b. The magnitude of the imputation tax credit.
c. How much tax you would pay on each dividend assuming a 47 per cent tax rate plus 1.5 per cent for the Medicare levy. What is the value of each dividend after personal tax?
d. What might account for the difference in franking?

**20.** At the end of the financial year a company has $40 million cash on hand with $35 million earmarked for an investment project offering an IRR of 14 per cent. The company is 100 per cent equity financed and shareholders have a required return on equity of 16 per cent. The dividend announcement date is approaching and last year's dividend was $10 million. How large a dividend should the company pay this year? How would your answer change if the company had an IRR on its project of 18 per cent?

**21.** It is 1996 and Ripper Bonus Ltd is about to pay a $0.50 dividend. Shareholders can elect to participate in the DRP. If they do so, the shares they receive will be priced at a 5 per cent discount to the average price on the five days following the ex-dividend date. Alternatively, shareholders can elect to participate in the bonus share plan and take bonus shares issued from the share premium reserve. The discount in this case is also 5 per cent. Assume shareholders owning 27 per cent of the shares take up the DRP and owners of 15 per cent of the shares take up the bonus share plan. The average share price over the five days following the ex-dividend date is $7.50.

Prior to the dividend the owners' equity section of the balance sheet is as follows:

| | |
|---|---|
| Paid up capital (20 million shares $1 par value) | $20 000 000 |
| Share premium reserve | $35 000 000 |
| Retained earnings | $30 000 000 |

a. How many shares will be issued under the bonus share plan and how many under the DRP?

   b.  Recompute the values for the owners' equity section of the balance sheet after the dividend has been paid.

   c.  Explain which type of investors will choose cash, which will choose the DRP and which the bonus share plan.

**22.** Select a company and collect its annual earnings and total dividend per year for several years. Try and collect at least 20 years of data. Then use regression to calculate the target payout ratio and the speed at which dividends adjust towards the target. Explain whether or not your estimates appear to make sense.

# chapter 17

# DOES DEBT POLICY MATTER?

A company's basic resource is the stream of cash flows produced by its assets. When the company is financed entirely by ordinary shares, all those cash flows belong to the shareholders. When it issues both debt and equity securities, it undertakes to split up the cash flows into two streams: a relatively safe stream that goes to the debtholders and a more risky one that goes to the shareholders.

The company's mix of different securities is known as its **capital structure.** The choice of capital structure is fundamentally a marketing problem. The company can issue dozens of distinct securities in countless combinations but it attempts to find the particular combination that will maximise its overall market value.

Are these attempts worthwhile? We must consider the possibility that *no* combination has any greater appeal than any other. Perhaps the really important decisions concern the company's assets, and decisions about capital structure are mere details—matters to be attended to but not worried about too much.

Modigliani and Miller (MM), who showed that dividend policy does not matter in perfect capital markets, also showed that financing decisions do not matter in perfect markets.[1] Their famous 'proposition I' states that a company cannot change the *total* value of its securities just by splitting its cash flows into different streams: the

1 MM's paper [F. Modigliani and M. H. Miller, 'The Cost of Capital, Corporation Finance and the Theory of Investment', *American Economic Review*, 48: 261–97 (June 1958)] was published in 1958, but their basic argument was anticipated in 1938 by J. B. Williams and to some extent by David Durand. See J. B. Williams, *The Theory of Investment Value*, Harvard University Press, Cambridge, Mass., 1938; and D. Durand, 'Cost of Debt and Equity Funds for Business: Trends and Problems of Measurement', in *Conference on Research in Business Finance*, National Bureau of Economic Research, New York, 1952.

company's value is determined by its real assets, not by the securities it issues. Thus, capital structure is irrelevant as long as the company's investment decisions are taken as given.

MM's proposition I allows complete separation of investment and financing decisions. It implies that any company could use the capital budgeting procedures presented in Chapters 2 to 12 without worrying about where the money for capital expenditures comes from. In those chapters, we assumed all equity financing without really thinking about it. If proposition I holds, that is exactly the right approach.

We believe that, because of market imperfections, capital structure *does* matter in practice. Nevertheless, we devote all of this chapter to MM's argument. If you do not fully understand the conditions under which MM's theory holds, you will not fully understand why one capital structure is better than another. The financial manager needs to know what kinds of market imperfection to look for.

In Chapter 18 we will undertake a detailed analysis of the imperfections that are most likely to make a difference, including taxes, the costs of bankruptcy and the costs of writing and enforcing complicated debt contracts. We will also argue that it is naive to suppose that investment and financing decisions can be completely separated.

But in this chapter we isolate the decision about capital structure by holding the decision about investment fixed. We also assume that dividend policy is irrelevant.

## 17.1 The effect of leverage in a competitive tax-free economy

We have referred to the company's choice of capital structure as a *marketing problem*. The financial manager's problem is to find the combination of securities that has the greatest overall appeal to investors—the combination that maximises the market value of the company. Before tackling this problem, we ought to make sure that a policy that maximises company value also maximises the wealth of the shareholders.

Let $D$ and $E$ denote the market values of the outstanding debt and equity of the Outback Mining Company. Outback's 1000 shares sell for $50 apiece. Thus

$$E = 1000 \times 50 = \$50\,000$$

Outback has also borrowed $25 000, and so $V$, the aggregate market value of all Outback's outstanding securities, is

$$V = D + E = \$75\,000$$

Outback's shares are known as *levered equity*. Its shareholders face the benefits and costs of *financial leverage,* or *gearing.* Suppose that Outback 'levers up' still further by borrowing an additional $10 000 and paying the proceeds out to shareholders as a special dividend of $10 per share. This substitutes debt for equity capital with no impact on Outback's assets.

What will Outback's equity be worth after the special dividend is paid? We have two unknowns, $E$ and $V$:

| | | | |
|---|---|---|---|
| Old debt plus | $25 000 | | |
| New debt | $10 000 | =$35 000 | =D |
| Equity | | ? | =E |
| Company value | | ? | =V |

If $V$ is \$75 000 as before, then $E$ must be $V - D = 75\,000 - 35\,000 = \$40\,000$. Shareholders have suffered a capital loss that exactly offsets the \$10 000 special dividend. But if $V$ *increases* to, say, \$80 000 as a result of the change in capital structure, then $E = \$45\,000$ and the shareholders are \$5000 ahead. In general, any increase or decrease in $V$ caused by a shift in capital structure accrues to the company's shareholders. We conclude that a policy that maximises the market value of the company is also best for the company's shareholders.[2]

This conclusion rests on two important assumptions: first, that Outback can ignore dividend policy and second, that after the change in capital structure the old and new debt is *worth* \$35 000.

Dividend policy may or may not be relevant, but there is no need to repeat the discussion of Chapter 16. We need only note that shifts in capital structure sometimes force important decisions about dividend policy. Perhaps Outback's cash dividend has costs or benefits that should be considered in addition to any benefits achieved by its increased financial leverage.

Our second assumption that old and new debt ends up worth \$35 000 seems innocuous. But it could be wrong. Perhaps the new borrowing has increased the risk of the old debt. If the holders of old debt cannot demand a higher rate of interest to compensate for the increased risk, the value of their investment is reduced. In this case Outback's shareholders gain at the expense of the holders of old debt even though the overall value of the debt plus equity is unchanged.

But this anticipates issues better left to Chapter 18. In this chapter we will assume that any issue of debt has no effect on the market value of existing debt.

# Enter Modigliani and Miller

Let us accept that the financial manager would like to find the combination of securities that maximise the value of the company. How is this done? MM's answer is that the financial manager should stop worrying: In a perfect market any combination of securities is as good as another. The value of the company is unaffected by its choice of capital structure. (Remember, in a perfect market there are no taxes.)

MM prove the irrelevance of capital structure using the *principle of no arbitrage*. Their proof is justifiably famous and the no arbitrage principle has become an important and powerful tool in finance. *The no arbitrage principle simply states that assets that offer the same cash flows must sell for the same price.* If not, astute investors will sell the higher priced asset and buy the lower priced asset. This action by arbitrageurs will cause a re-alignment of prices so that both assets sell for the same price. Equilibrium in a well-functioning capital market is characterised by an absence of arbitrage opportunities.

You can see the no arbitrage principle at work by imagining two companies that generate the same stream of operating income and differ only in their capital structure. Company U is unlevered. Therefore, the total value of its equity $E_U$ is the same as the total value of the company $V_U$. Company L, on the other hand, is levered. The value of its shares is therefore equal to the value of the company less the value of the debt:

$$E_L = V_L - D_L$$

Now think which of these companies you would prefer to invest in. If you do not want to take much risk, you can buy ordinary shares in the unlevered company U. For example, if you

---

2   This statement is usually true, but as we shall see in the next chapter there are some exceptions. See E. F. Fama, 'The Effects of a Company's Investment and Financing Decisions', *American Economic Review*, **68**: 272–84 (June 1978), for a rigorous analysis of the conditions under which a policy of maximising the value of the company is also best for the shareholders.

buy 1 per cent of company U's shares, your investment is $0.01V_U$ and you are entitled to 1 per cent of the gross profits:

| Dollar investment | Dollar return |
|---|---|
| $0.01V_U$ | $0.01$ profits |

Now compare this with an alternative strategy. This is to purchase the same fraction of both the debt and the equity of company L. Your investment and return would then be as follows:

| | Dollar investment | Dollar return |
|---|---|---|
| Debt | $0.01D_L$ | $0.01$ interest |
| Equity | $0.01E_L$ | $0.01$ (profits − interest) |
| Total | $0.01(D_L + E_L)$ | $0.01$ profits |
| | $= 0.01V_L$ | |

Both strategies offer the same payoff: 1 per cent of the company's profits. In well-functioning markets two investments that offer the same payoff must have the same price. Therefore, $0.01V_U$ must equal $0.01V_L$: the value of the unlevered company must equal the value of the levered company.

Suppose that you are willing to run a little more risk. You decide to buy 1 per cent of the outstanding shares in the *levered* company. Your investment and return are now as follows:

| Dollar investment | Dollar return |
|---|---|
| $0.01E_L$ | $0.01$ (profits − interest) |
| $= 0.01(V_L − D_L)$ | |

But there is an alternative strategy. This is to borrow $0.01D_L$ on your own account and purchase 1 per cent of the shares of the *unlevered* company. In this case, your borrowing gives you an immediate cash *inflow* of $0.01D$, but you have to pay interest on your loan equal to 1 per cent of the interest that is paid by company L. Your total investment and return are therefore as follows:

| | Dollar investment | Dollar return |
|---|---|---|
| Borrowing | $−0.01D_L$ | $−0.01$ interest |
| Equity | $0.01V_U$ | $0.01$ profits |
| Total | $0.01(V_U − D_L)$ | $0.01$ (profits − interest) |

Again, both strategies offer the same payoff: 1 per cent of profits after interest. Therefore, both investments must have the same cost. The quantity $0.01(V_L − D_L)$ must equal $0.01(V_U − D_L)$ and so $V_U$ must equal $V_L$.[3]

---

[3] You have not only seen the principle of no arbitrage in action but also some financial engineering—in this case creating different packages of securities to achieve the same cash flow.

It does not matter whether the world is full of cautious investors, incautious investors or a mixture of each. All would agree that the value of the unlevered company U must be equal to the value of the levered company L. As long as investors can borrow or lend on their own account on the same terms as the company, they can 'undo' the effect of any changes in the company's capital structure. This is the basis for MM's famous proposition I: 'The market value of any company is independent of its capital structure.' Note that this statement refers to the *total market value of the company not the total value of its equity*. Clearly, the more debt you have the less the total value of the equity.

# The law of the conservation of value

MM's argument that debt policy is irrelevant is an application of an astonishingly simple idea. If we have two streams of cash flow, A and B, then the present value of A + B is equal to the present value of A plus the present value of B. We met this principle of *value additivity* in our discussion of capital budgeting, where we saw that in perfect capital markets the present value of two assets combined is equal to the sum of their present values considered separately.

In the present context we are not combining assets, but splitting them up. But value additivity works just as well in reverse. We can slice a cash flow into as many parts as we like; the values of the parts will always sum back to the value of the unsliced stream. (Of course, we have to make sure that none of the stream is lost in the slicing. We cannot say, 'The value of a pie is independent of how it is sliced', if the slicer is also a nibbler.)

This is really a *law of conservation of value*. The value of an asset is preserved regardless of the nature of the claims against it. Thus, proposition I: Company value is determined on the *left-hand* side of the balance sheet by real assets—not by the proportions of debt and equity securities issued by the company.

The simplest ideas often have the widest application. For example, we could apply the law of conservation of value to the choice between issuing preferred shares, ordinary shares or some combination of both. The law implies that the choice is irrelevant, assuming perfect capital markets and providing that the choice does not affect the company's investment, borrowing and operating policies. If the total value of the equity 'pie' (preferred and ordinary shares combined) is fixed, the company's owners (its ordinary shareholders) do not care how this pie is sliced.

The law also applies to the *mix* of debt securities issued by the company. The choices of long-term versus short-term, secured versus unsecured, senior versus subordinated and convertible versus non-convertible debt all should have no effect on the overall value of the company.

Combining assets and splitting them up will not affect values as long as they do not affect an investor's choice. When we showed that capital structure does not affect choice, we implicitly assumed that both companies and individuals can borrow and lend at the same risk-free rate of interest. As long as this is so, individuals can 'undo' the effect of any changes in the company's capital structure.

In practice corporate debt is not risk-free and companies cannot escape with rates of interest appropriate to a government security. Some people's initial reaction is that this alone invalidates MM's proposition. It is a natural mistake, but capital structure can be irrelevant even when debt is risky.

If a company borrows money, it does not *guarantee* repayment: It repays the debt in full only if its assets are worth more than the debt obligation. The shareholders in the company therefore have limited liability.

Many individuals would like to borrow with limited liability. They might therefore be prepared to pay a small premium for levered shares *if the supply of levered shares was insufficient to meet their needs*.[4] But there are literally thousands of ordinary shares of companies that

---

4   Of course, individuals could *create* limited liability if they chose. In other words, the lender could agree that borrowers need repay their debt in full only if the assets of company X are worth more than a certain amount. Presumably, individuals do not enter into such arrangements because they can obtain limited liability more simply by investing in the shares of levered companies.

borrow. Therefore, it is unlikely that an issue of debt would induce investors to pay a premium for your shares.[5]

## An example of proposition I

Macbeth Spot Removers is reviewing its capital structure. Table 17.1 shows its current position. The company has no leverage and all the operating income is paid as dividends to the ordinary shareholders (we assume still that there are no taxes). The expected earnings and dividends per share are $1.50, but this figure is by no means certain—it could turn out to be more or less than $1.50. The price of each share is $10. Since the company expects to produce a level stream of earnings in perpetuity, the expected return on the share is equal to the earnings-price ratio, 1.50/10.00 = 0.15, or 15 per cent.[6]

**table 17.1**

Macbeth Spot Removers is entirely equity-financed. Although it *expects* to have an income of $1500 a year in perpetuity, this income is not certain. This table shows the return to the shareholder under different assumptions about operating income. The expected outcome is shown in heavy type. We assume no taxes.

| Data | | | | |
|---|---|---|---|---|
| Number of shares | | 1 000 | | |
| Price per share | | $10 | | |
| Market value of shares | | $10 000 | | |

| Outcomes | | | Expected | |
|---|---|---|---|---|
| Operating income ($) | 500 | 1 000 | **1 500** | 2 000 |
| Earnings per share ($) | 0.50 | 1.00 | **1.50** | 2.00 |
| Return on shares (%) | 5 | 10 | **15** | 20 |

Ms Macbeth, the company's chief executive, has come to the conclusion that shareholders would be better off if the company had equal proportions of debt and equity. She therefore proposes to issue $5000 of debt at an interest rate of 10 per cent and use the proceeds to repurchase 500 shares. To support her proposal, Ms Macbeth has analysed the situation under different assumptions about operating income. The results of her calculations are shown in Table 17.2.

In order to see more clearly how leverage would affect earnings per share, Ms Macbeth has also produced Figure 17.1. The solid line shows how earnings per share would vary with operating income under the company's current all equity financing. It is therefore simply a plot of the data in Table 17.1. The dotted line shows how earnings per share would vary given equal proportions of debt and equity. It is therefore a plot of the data in Table 17.2.

Ms Macbeth reasons as follows: 'It is clear that the effect of leverage depends on the company's income. If income is greater than $1000, the return to the equity holder is *increased* by leverage. If it is less than $1000, the return is *reduced* by leverage. The return is unaffected when operating income is exactly $1000. At this point the return on the market value of the

---

[5]  Capital structure is also irrelevant if each investor holds a fully-diversified portfolio. In that case he or she owns all the risky securities offered by a company (both debt and equity). But anybody who owns *all* the risky securities does not care about how the cash flows are divided between different securities.

[6]  See Section 4.4.

assets is 10 per cent, which is exactly equal to the interest rate on the debt. Our capital structure decision therefore boils down to what we think about income prospects. Since we expect operating income to be above the $1000 break-even point, I believe we can best help our shareholders by going ahead with the $5000 debt issue.'

As financial manager of Macbeth Spot Removers, you reply as follows: 'I agree that leverage will help the shareholder as long as our income is greater than $1000. But your argument ignores the fact that Macbeth's shareholders have the alternative of borrowing on their own account. For example, suppose that a person borrows $10 and then invests $20 in two unlevered Macbeth shares. This person has to put up only $10 of his or her own money. The payoff on the investment varies with Macbeth's operating income, as shown in Table 17.3. This is exactly the same set of payoffs as the investor would get by buying one share in the levered company. (Compare the last two lines of Tables 17.2 and 17.3.) Therefore, a share in the levered company must also sell for $10. If Macbeth goes ahead and borrows, it will not allow investors to do anything that they could not do already, and so it will not increase value.'

The argument that you are using is exactly the same as MM used to prove proposition I.

**table 17.2**

Macbeth Spot Removers is wondering whether to issue $5000 of debt at an interest rate of 10 per cent and repurchase 500 shares. This table shows the return to the shareholder under different assumptions about operating income.

| Data | | | | |
|---|---|---|---|---|
| Number of shares | | 500 | | |
| Price per share | | $10 | | |
| Market value of debt | | $5 000 | | |
| Interest at 10% | | $500 | | |

| Outcomes | | | Expected | |
|---|---|---|---|---|
| Operating income ($) | 500 | 1 000 | **1 500** | 2 000 |
| Interest ($) | 500 | 500 | **500** | 500 |
| Equity earnings ($) | 0 | 500 | **1 000** | 1 500 |
| Earnings per share ($) | 0 | 1 | **2** | 3 |
| Return on shares (%) | 0 | 10 | **20** | 30 |

**table 17.3**

Individual investors can replicate Macbeth's leverage

| Outcomes | | | Expected | |
|---|---|---|---|---|
| Operating income ($) | 500 | 1 000 | **1 500** | 2 000 |
| Earnings on two shares ($) | 1 | 2 | **3** | 4 |
| *Less* interest at 10% ($) | 1 | 1 | **1** | 1 |
| Net earnings on investment ($) | 0 | 1 | **2** | 3 |
| Return on $10 investment (%) | 0 | 10 | **20** | 30 |

**figure 17.1**

Borrowing increases Macbeth's EPS (earnings per share) when operating income is greater than $1000 and reduces EPS when operating income is less than $1000. Expected EPS rises from $1.50 to $2.

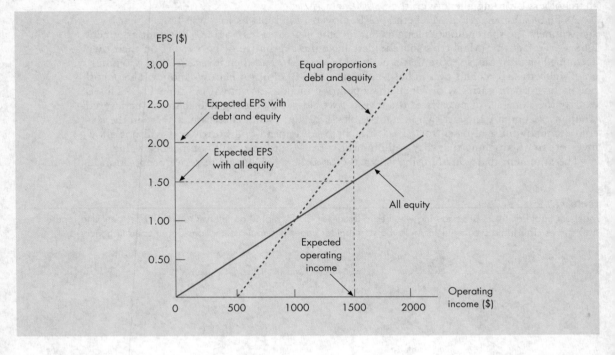

## 17.2 How leverage affects returns

### Implications of proposition I

Consider now the implications of proposition I for the expected returns on Macbeth shares:

|  | Current structure: all equity | Proposed structure: equal debt and equity |
|---|---|---|
| Expected earnings per share | $1.50 | $2.00 |
| Price per share | $10.00 | $10.00 |
| Expected return on share (%) | 15 | 20 |
| Required return on share (%) | 15 | 20 |

Leverage increases the expected stream of earnings per share, but *not* the share price. The reason is that the change in the expected earnings stream is exactly offset by a change in the rate at which the earnings are capitalised. The required return on the share (which for a perpetuity is equal to the earnings-price ratio) increases from 15 to 20 per cent to exactly match the change in expected returns. We now show how this comes about.

The expected return on a company's assets $r_A$ is equal to the ratio of expected operating income to the total market value of the company's securities, and if the market value is in equilibrium this ratio is equal to the required return on the assets.

Thus:

$$\text{Expected return on assets} = r_A = \frac{\text{expected operating income}}{\text{market value of all securities}}$$

$$= \text{required return on assets}$$

We have seen that in perfect capital markets the company's borrowing decision does not affect *either* the company's operating income *or* the total market value of its securities. Therefore, the borrowing decision does not affect either the expected return on the company's *assets* $r_A$ or the required return on those *assets*. As we shall see, however, it does affect the expected and required returns on *equity*.

Suppose that an investor holds all of a company's debt and all its equity. This investor would be entitled to all the company's operating income; therefore, the expected return on the portfolio would be equal to $r_A$.

The expected return on a portfolio is equal to a weighted average of the expected returns on the individual holdings. Therefore, the expected return on a portfolio consisting of *all* the company's securities is[7]

$$\text{Expected return on assets} = (\text{expected return on debt} \times \text{proportion in debt}) + (\text{expected}$$
$$\text{return on equity} \times \text{proportion in equity})$$

$$r_A = \left( r_D \times \frac{D}{D + E} \right) + \left( r_E \times \frac{E}{D + E} \right)$$

We can rearrange this equation to obtain an expression for $r_E$, the expected return on the equity of a levered company:

$$\text{Expected return on equity} = \text{expected return on assets} + \text{debt equity ratio} \times (\text{expected}$$
$$\text{return on assets} - \text{expected return on debt})$$

$$r_E = r_A + \frac{D}{E}(r_A - r_D)$$

If we assume equilibrium, this equation for the expected return on equity also gives us the required return on equity. Notice that if the company has no debt, $r_E = r_A$. Thus, for an unlevered firm the required return on equity depends only on the risk of the business, as measured by $r_A$. As leverage increases equity investors demand a financial risk premium $[(D/E)(r_A - r_D)]$. As you might guess this risk premium is higher the greater the level of leverage $(D/E)$. It is important to remember that the leverage ratio is expressed in terms of *market values* for debt and equity. The risk premium is also higher the greater the inherent risk of the business, as measured by the spread between the required return on assets and the required return on debt $(r_A - r_D)$.[8]

## Proposition II

The equation we have derived is MM's proposition II.

We can check out this formula for Macbeth Spot Removers. Before the decision to borrow

$$r_E = r_A = \frac{\text{expected operating income}}{\text{market value of all securities}}$$

$$= \frac{1\,500}{10\,000} = 0.15 \text{ or } 15\%$$

---

[7] This equation should look familiar. We introduced it in Section 9.2 when we showed that the company cost of capital is a weighted average of the expected returns on the debt and equity. (Company cost of capital is simply another term for the equilibrium expected return on assets, $r_A$.) We also stated in Section 9.2 that changing the capital structure does not change the company cost of capital. In other words, we implicitly assumed MM's proposition I.

[8] If we assume the debt is risk-free, then the spread between the required return on the assets and the cost of debt measures the risk premium for that asset.

If the company goes ahead with its plan to borrow, the expected return on assets $r_A$ is still 15 per cent. The expected return on equity is

$$r_E = r_A + \frac{D}{E}(r_A - r_D)$$

$$= 0.15 + \frac{5000}{5000}(0.15 - 0.10)$$

$$= 0.20, \text{ or } 20\%$$

The general implications of MM's proposition II are shown in Figure 17.2. The figure assumes that the company's bonds are essentially risk-free at low debt levels. Thus, $r_D$ is independent of $D/E$ and $r_E$ increases linearly as $D/E$ increases. As the company borrows more, the risk of default increases and the company is required to pay higher rates of interest. Proposition II predicts that when this occurs the rate of increase in $r_E$ slows down. This is also shown in Figure 17.2. The more debt the company has, the less sensitive $r_E$ is to further borrowing.

Why does the slope of the $r_E$ line in Figure 17.2 taper off as $D/E$ increases? Essentially because holders of *risky* debt bear some of the company's business risk. As the company borrows more, more of that risk is transferred from shareholders to debtholders. We will return to this issue in Chapter 18.

**figure 17.2**

MM's proposition II. The expected return on equity $r_E$ increases linearly with the debt-equity ratio so long as debt is risk-free. But if leverage increases the risk of the debt, debtholders demand a higher return on the debt. This causes the rate of increase in $r_E$ to slow down.

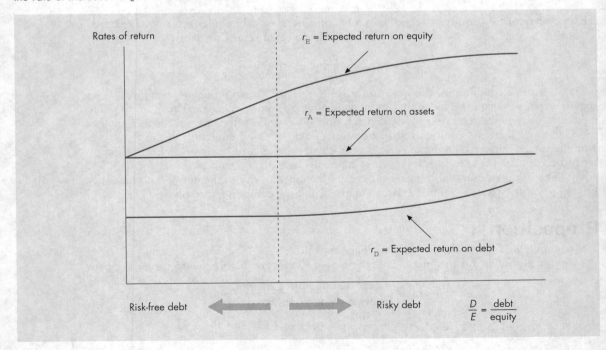

## The risk-return trade-off

Proposition I says that financial leverage has no effect on shareholders' wealth. Proposition II says that the rate of return they can expect to receive on their shares increases as the company's debt-equity ratio increases. How can shareholders be indifferent to increased leverage when it increases expected return? The answer is that any increase in expected return is exactly offset by an increase in shareholders' *required* rate of return due to the increased risk created by leverage.

Look at what happens to the risk of Macbeth shares if it moves to equal debt-equity proportions. Table 17.4 shows how a shortfall in operating income affects the payoff to the shareholders.

table 17.4 _____

Leverage increases the risk of Macbeth shares

|  | Operating income | $500 | $1500 |
|---|---|---|---|
| All equity: | Earnings per share ($) | 0.50 | 1.50 |
|  | Return on shares (%) | 5 | 15 |
| 50% debt: | Earnings per share ($) | 0 | 2 |
|  | Return on shares (%) | 0 | 20 |

The debt-equity proportion does not affect the *dollar* risk borne by equity holders. Suppose operating income drops from $1500 to $500. Under all equity financing, equity earnings drop by $1 per share. There are 1000 outstanding shares, and so *total* equity earnings fall by $1 × 1000 = $1000. With 50 per cent debt, the same drop in operating income reduces earnings per share by $2. But there are only 500 shares outstanding, and so total equity income drops by $2 × 500 = $1000, just as in the all equity case.

However, the debt-equity choice does amplify the spread of *percentage* returns. If the company is all equity financed, a decline of $1000 in the operating income reduces the return on the shares by 10 per cent. If the company issues risk-free debt with a fixed interest payment of $500 a year, then a decline of $1000 in the operating income reduces the return on the shares by 20 per cent. In other words, the effect of leverage is to double the amplitude of the swings in Macbeth's shares. Whatever the beta of the company's shares before the refinancing, it would be twice as high afterwards.

Just as the expected return on the company's assets is a weighted average of the expected return on the individual securities, so likewise is the beta of the company's assets a weighted average of the betas of the individual securities:[9]

Beta of assets = (proportion of debt × beta of debt) + (proportion of equity × beta of equity)

$$\beta_A = \left( \frac{D}{D + E} \times \beta_D \right) + \left( \frac{E}{D + E} \times \beta_E \right)$$

We can rearrange this equation also to give an expression for $\beta_E$, the beta of the equity of a levered company:

Beta of equity = beta of assets + debt to equity ratio × (beta of assets − beta of debt)

$$\beta_E = \beta_A + \frac{D}{E}(\beta_A - \beta_D)$$

Now you can see why investors require higher returns on levered equity. The required return simply rises to match the increased risk.

_____

[9]  This equation should also look old hat. We used it in Section 9.2, when we stated that changes in the capital structure change the beta of shares but not the asset beta.

In Figure 17.3 we have plotted the expected returns and the risk of Macbeth's securities, assuming that the interest on the debt is risk-free.[10]

**figure 17.3**

If Macbeth is unlevered, the expected return on its equity equals the expected return on its assets. Leverage increases both the expected return on equity ($r_E$) and the risk of equity ($\beta_E$).

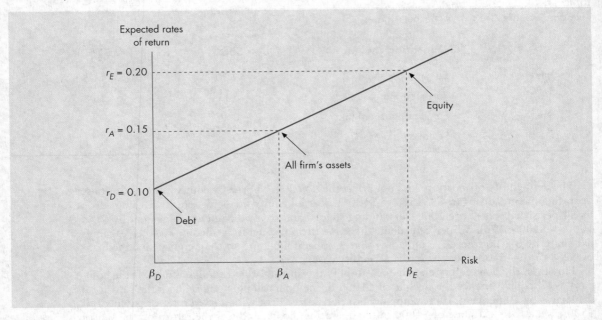

## 17.3 The traditional position

What did financial experts think about debt policy before MM? It is not easy to say because with hindsight we see that they did not think too clearly. However, a 'traditional' position has emerged in response to MM. In order to understand it, we have to discuss the **weighted average cost of capital**.

The required return on a portfolio of all the company's securities is often referred to as the *weighted average cost of capital*:[11]

$$\text{Weighted average cost of capital} = r_A = \left(\frac{D}{V} \times r_D\right) + \left(\frac{E}{V} \times r_E\right)$$

The weighted average cost of capital is used in capital budgeting decisions to find the net present value of projects that *would not change the business risk of the company*. All assets that have the same risk as the company have a required return equal to the weighted average cost of capital. Other assets with different risks have different required returns. Therefore, we *cannot* use the weighted average cost of capital to calculate the net present value of investments that have a different risk to the company. Why are we belabouring the obvious? Because

---

10    In this case $\beta_D = 0$ and $\beta_E = \beta_A + (D/E)\beta_A$.

11    Remember that in this chapter we ignore taxes. In Chapter 19 we shall see that the weighted average cost of capital formula needs to be amended when debt interest can be deducted from taxable profits.

people so often get it wrong! Note also that when we calculate the weighted average cost of capital we should use the market values for debt and equity.

For example, suppose that a company has $2 million of outstanding debt and 100 000 outstanding shares selling at $30 per share. Its current borrowing rate is 8 per cent and the financial manager thinks that the shares are priced to offer a 15 per cent return, therefore $r_E = 0.15$. (The hard part is estimating $r_E$, of course.) This is all we need to calculate the weighted average cost of capital:

$$D = \$2 \text{ million}$$
$$E = 100\ 000 \text{ shares} \times \$30 \text{ per share} = \$3 \text{ million}$$
$$V = D + E = 2 + 3 = \$5 \text{ million}$$

$$\text{Weighted average cost of capital} = \left(\frac{D}{V} \times r_D\right) + \left(\frac{E}{V} \times r_E\right)$$
$$= \left(\frac{2}{5} \times 0.08\right) + \left(\frac{3}{5} \times 0.15\right)$$
$$= 0.122, \text{ or } 12.2\%$$

Note that we are still assuming that proposition I holds. If it does not, we cannot use this simple weighted average as the discount rate even for projects that do not change the company's business 'risk class'. As we will see in Chapter 19, the weighted average cost of capital is at best a starting point for setting discount rates.

# Two warnings

Sometimes the objective in financing decisions is stated not as 'maximise overall market value' but as 'minimise the weighted average cost of capital'. These are equivalent objectives under the simplifying assumptions we have made so far. But what if MM's proposition I does *not* hold. Then the capital structure that maximises the value of the company *only* minimises the weighted average cost of capital, *provided* that operating income is independent of capital structure. Remember that in our perpetuity case the weighted average cost of capital equals the expected operating income divided by the market value of all securities. Anything that increases the value of the company reduces the weighted average cost of capital if operating income is constant. But if operating income is varying too, all bets are off.

In Chapter 18, where we examine some market imperfections, we will show that financial leverage can affect operating income in several ways. Therefore, maximising the value of the company is *not* always equivalent to minimising the weighted average cost of capital.

**Warning 1**    Shareholders want management to increase the company's value. They are more interested in being rich than in owning a company with a low weighted average cost of capital.

**Warning 2**    Trying to minimise the weighted average cost of capital seems to encourage logical short circuits like the following. Suppose that someone says, 'Shareholders demand—and deserve—higher required rates of return than debtholders do. Therefore, debt is the cheaper capital source. We can reduce the weighted average cost of capital by borrowing more.' But this does not follow if the extra borrowing leads shareholders to demand a still higher required rate of return. According to MM's proposition II the 'cost of equity capital' $r_E$ increases by just enough to keep the weighted average cost of capital constant. The moral is simple: as you increase the proportion of debt in the firm's capital structure, by substituting 'cheap' debt for 'expensive' equity, the 'expensive' equity becomes even more expensive. As a result you are no better off and the 'cheap' debt does not turn out to be such a bargain after all.

This is not the only logical short circuit that you are likely to encounter. We have cited two more in Question 5 at the end of this chapter.

# Rates of return on levered equity—the traditional position

You may ask why we have even mentioned the weighted average cost of capital at this point if it is often wrong or confusing as a financial objective. We had to because the traditionalists accept this objective and argue their case in terms of it.

The logical short circuit we just described rested on the assumption that $r_E$, the expected rate of return demanded by shareholders, does not rise as the company borrows more. Suppose, just for the sake of argument, that this is true. Then $r_A$, the weighted average cost of capital, must decline as the debt-equity ratio rises.

Take Figure 17.4, for example, which is drawn on the assumption that shareholders demand 12 per cent no matter how much debt the company has, and that debtholders always want 8 per cent. The weighted average cost of capital starts at 12 per cent and ends up at 8 per cent. Suppose that this company's operating income is a level, perpetual stream of $100 000 a year. Then company value starts at

$$V = \frac{100\,000}{0.12} = \$833\,333$$

and ends up at

$$V = \frac{100\,000}{0.08} = \$1\,250\,000$$

The gain of $416 667 falls into the shareholders' pockets.[12]

**figure 17.4**

If the expected rate of return demanded by shareholders $r_E$ is unaffected by financial leverage, then the weighted average cost of capital $r_A$ declines as the firm borrows more. At 100 per cent debt $r_A$ equals the borrowing rate $r_D$. Of course, this is an absurd and totally unrealistic case.

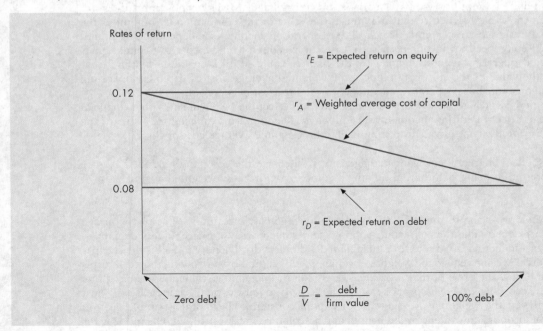

---

12  Note that Figure 17.4 relates $r_E$ and $r_D$ to $D/V$, the ratio of debt to company value, rather than to the debt-equity ratio $D/E$. In this figure we wanted to show what happens when the company is 100 per cent debt-financed. At that point $E = 0$ and $D/E$ is infinite.

Of course, this is absurd: A company that reaches 100 per cent debt *has to be bankrupt.* If there is *any* chance that the company could remain solvent, then the equity retains some value and the company cannot be 100 per cent debt-financed. (Remember that we are working with the *market* values of debt and equity.)

But if the company is bankrupt and its original shares are worthless pieces of paper, then its *lenders are its new shareholders.* The company is back to all equity financing! We assumed that the original shareholders demanded 12 per cent—why should the new ones demand any less? They have to bear all of the company's business risk.[13]

The situation described in Figure 17.4 is just impossible.[14] However, it is possible to stake out a position somewhere *between* Figures 17.3 and 17.4. That is exactly what the traditionalists have done. Their hypothesis is shown in Figure 17.5. They hold that a moderate degree of financial leverage may increase the expected equity return $r_E$ although not to the degree predicted by MM's proposition II. But irresponsible companies that borrow *excessively* find $r_E$ shooting up faster than MM predict. Consequently, the weighted average cost of capital $r_A$ declines at first, then rises. Its minimum point is the point of optimal capital structure. Remember that minimising $r_A$ is equivalent to maximising overall company value if, as the traditionalists assume, operating income is unaffected by borrowing.

**figure 17.5** _____

The dashed lines show MM's view of the effect of leverage on the expected return on equity $r_E$ and the weighted average cost of capital $r_A$. (See Figure 17.2.) The solid lines show the traditional view. Traditionalists say that borrowing at first increases $r_E$ more slowly than MM predict but that $r_E$ shoots up with excessive borrowing. If so, the weighted average cost of capital can be minimised if you use just the right amount of debt.

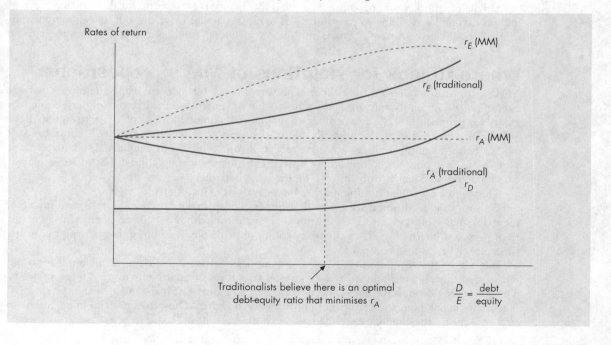

[13]  We ignore the costs, delays and other complications of bankruptcy. They are discussed in Chapter 18.

[14]  This case is often termed the net income (NI) approach because investors are assumed to capitalise income after interest at the same rate regardless of financial leverage. In contrast, MM's approach is a net operating-income (NOI) approach, because the value of the company is fundamentally determined by operating income, the total dollar return to both bondholders and shareholders. This distinction was emphasised by Durand in his important pre-MM paper (op. cit., Footnote 1).

Two arguments might be advanced in support of the traditional position. First, it could be that investors do not notice or appreciate the financial risk created by 'moderate' borrowing, although they wake up when debt is 'excessive'. If so, investors in moderately-leveraged companies may accept a lower rate of return than they really should.

That seems naive.[15] The second argument is better. It accepts MM's reasoning as applied to perfect capital markets, but holds that actual markets are imperfect. Imperfections may allow companies that borrow to provide a valuable service for investors. If so, levered shares might trade at premium prices compared to their theoretical values in perfect markets.

Suppose that corporations can borrow more cheaply than individuals. Then it would pay investors who want to borrow to do so indirectly by holding the shares of levered companies. They would be willing to live with expected rates of return that do not fully compensate them for the business and financial risk they bear.

Is corporate borrowing really cheaper? It is hard to say. Interest rates on home mortgages are often lower than rates on high-grade corporate debt. Rates on margin debt (borrowing from a stockbroker or bank with the investor's shares tendered as security) are not too different from the rates companies pay banks for short-term loans.

There are some individuals who face relatively high interest rates, largely because of the costs lenders incur in making and servicing small loans. There are economies of scale in borrowing. A group of small investors could do better by borrowing via a company, in effect pooling their loans and saving transaction costs.[16]

But suppose that this class of investors is large, both in number and in the aggregate wealth it brings to capital markets. Should not the investors' needs be fully satisfied by the thousands of levered companies already existing? Is there really an unsatisfied clientele of small investors standing ready to pay a premium for one more company that borrows?

Maybe the market for corporate leverage is like the market for cars. Australians need several million cars and are willing to pay thousands of dollars apiece for them. But that does not mean that you could strike it rich by going into the car business. You are at least 50 years too late.

## Where to look for violations of MM's propositions

MM's propositions depend on perfect capital markets. Here we are using the phrase *perfect capital markets* a bit loosely, for years scholars have argued about the *degree* of perfection necessary for proposition I. (We remember an off-the-cuff comment made many years ago by Ezra Solomon: 'A perfect capital market should be *defined* as one in which the MM theory holds.')

We believe capital markets are generally well-functioning, but they are not 100 per cent perfect 100 per cent of the time. Therefore, MM must be wrong some times in some places. The financial manager's problem is to figure out when and where.

That is not easy. Just finding market imperfections is insufficient.

Consider the traditionalists' claim that imperfections make borrowing costly and inconvenient for many individuals. That creates a clientele for whom corporate borrowing is better than personal borrowing. That clientele would, in principle, be willing to pay a premium for the shares of a levered company.

But maybe they do not *have* to pay a premium. Perhaps smart financial managers long ago recognised this clientele and shifted the capital structures of their companies to meet its needs. The shifts would not have been difficult or costly to make. But if the clientele is now satisfied it is no longer willing to pay a premium for levered shares. Only the financial managers who *first* recognised the clientele extracted any advantage from it.

---

15  This first argument may reflect confusion between financial risk and the risk of default. Default is not a serious threat when borrowing is moderate; shareholders worry about it only when the company goes 'too far'. But shareholders bear financial risk—in the form of increased volatility of rate of return and higher beta—even when the chance of default is nil. We demonstrated this in Figure 17.3.

16  Even here there are alternatives to borrowing on personal account. Investors can draw down their savings accounts or sell a portion of their investment in bonds. The impact of reductions in lending on the investor's balance sheet and risk position is exactly the same as increases in borrowing.

# Today's unsatisfied clienteles are probably interested in exotic securities

So far we have made little progress in identifying cases where company value might plausibly depend on financing. But our examples illustrate what smart financial managers look for. They look for an *unsatisfied* clientele, investors who want a particular kind of financial instrument but because of market imperfections cannot get it or cannot get it cheaply.

MM's proposition I is violated when the company, by imaginative design of its capital structure, can offer some *financial service* that meets the needs of such a clientele. Either the service must be new and unique, or the company must find a way to provide some old service more cheaply than other companies or financial intermediaries can.

Now, is there an unsatisfied clientele for garden-variety debt or levered equity? We doubt it. But perhaps you can invent an exotic security and uncover a latent demand for it.

# Pfizer's stillborn USUs

Inventing exotic securities is easy; finding investors who will rush to buy them is not. Here is an example of an unsuccessful attempt to launch a new security. This case is particularly interesting because it provides a direct challenge to MM's proposition I. In 1988 Pfizer, a company listed in the United States, announced that it would replace part of its ordinary shares with *unbundled shares units* (USUs).[17] Pfizer reasoned that when you buy shares you are effectively buying a package containing three components: (1) the current stream of dividend income, (2) possible *increases* in the dividend stream and (3) any capital appreciation. The idea of USUs was to allow you to buy any combination of these three components.

The plan worked as follows. Each shareholder could exchange his or her shares for three new securities:

1. A 30-year *base yield bond* which would pay the investor the equivalent of the current dividend on the share.
2. An *incremental dividend preferred share* which would give the holder any future increases in dividends on the share.

After 30 years the first two securities would have been paid off by Pfizer for a total of $152.50. If Pfizer's share price went above $152.50, the third part of the USU package would kick in:

3. An *equity appreciation certificate* would give the holder the option at any time during the next 30 years to buy an ordinary share at a fixed price of $152.50. Thus, the equity appreciation certificate would benefit from any appreciation in Pfizer's share price above $152.50.[18]

Unbundled shares units provided a real-world test of MM. If shareholders had rushed to convert their shares to USUs, then you would have found a counter example to MM's proposition I. Pfizer could have increased its overall market value by issuing a package of bonds, preferred shares and options rather than garden-variety ordinary shares.

But that was not the way things turned out. Shareholders were unimpressed. Two months later in an embarrassing and expensive U-turn it was announced that Pfizer had decided not to go ahead. MM's proposition I survived intact.[19]

---

[17] Other companies announcing USUs at the same time were Dow Chemical, American Express and Sara Lee. For an analysis of USUs see J. D. Finnerty and V. M. Borun, 'An Analysis of Unbundled Shares Units', *Global Finance Journal*, 1: 47–70 (Fall 1989).

[18] Suppose you hold the entire package for 30 years. You receive the current dividend on the shares plus any increases in the dividend. Then at the end of 30 years you can buy the shares with the $152.50 that you receive from repayment of the bond and the preferred shares. But you are not *obliged* to do so. If the share price is below $152.50, you can just hold onto the cash.

[19] There were a number of practical problems that had not been ironed out. For example, the American securities regulator, the Securities and Exchange Commission, objected to the loss of voting rights. There was also a tax wrinkle: shareholders who exchanged their shares for USUs would be considered to have sold the shares and therefore would be taxed on any capital gains.

# DINGOS

One Australian financing innovation that succeeded for a while was the DINGO (Discounted National Government Obligation). To create a DINGO interest-bearing government bonds were converted into non-interest bearing securities—bonds that sell at a deep discount.[20] This was achieved by stripping off the interest coupons and trading them separately. The advantage of the DINGO was that their return came as capital gains, not interest. Capital gains were not taxed at the time DINGOS were created and they experienced some success. It looked as though we were set to see corporate issuers of debt exploit the same opportunity. But then the government introduced a capital gains tax and the DINGO market went quiet.

# Imperfections and opportunities

The most serious capital market imperfections are often those created by government. In Chapter 18 we discuss at length the impact of taxes on capital structure. The effect of taxes is particularly important, but any government-created imperfection that supports a violation of MM's proposition I also creates a money-making opportunity. Companies and financial intermediaries will find some way to reach the clientele of investors frustrated by the imperfection.

For example, the Australian banking system was heavily regulated for many years. This regulation included limits placed on deposit and lending rates. One of the objectives of these limits was to protect the banks by limiting competition for depositors' money. As a consequence deposit rates offered by Australian banks were artificially low, and until 1984 the banks were prohibited from paying interest on cheque accounts.

These interest-rate regulations provided financial institutions with an opportunity to create value by offering cash management trusts. These are investment trusts which invest in Treasury notes, commercial paper and other high-grade, short-term debt instruments. Any saver with a few thousand dollars to invest can gain access to these instruments through the cash management trust, and can withdraw their money at very short notice, often at call. In more recent times some trusts have provided cheque-drawing facilities. Thus, the trusts resemble a cheque or savings account which pays close to market interest rates.[21] From their start in 1980, investment in these trusts had grown to more than $5 billion by 1992.

As cash management trusts and other non-bank financial institutions captured an increasing share of the banks' business, the protection given by government restrictions on bank interest rates became less and less helpful. Finally the restrictions were lifted, and banks met their competition head-on.

Long before interest-rate ceilings were finally removed, most of the gains had gone out of issuing higher-yielding securities to individual investors. Once the clientele was finally satisfied, MM's proposition I was restored (until the government created a new imperfection). The moral of the story is this: If you ever find an unsatisfied clientele, do something right away, or capital markets will evolve and steal it from you.

---

[20]  Such securities are also known as zero coupon bonds.

[21]  Money-market trusts offer rates slightly lower than those on the securities they invest in. This spread covers the fund's operating costs and management fees.

## 17.4 Summary

At the start of this chapter we characterised the company's financing decision as a marketing problem. Think of the financial manager as taking all the company's real assets and selling them to investors as a package of securities. Some financial managers choose the simplest package possible: all equity financing. Some end up issuing dozens of debt and equity securities. The problem is to find the particular combination that maximises the market value of the company.

Modigliani and Miller's (MM's) famous proposition I states that no combination is better than any other—the company's overall market value (the value of all its securities) is independent of capital structure. Their chain of logic may be summarised as follows—the *total* value of the company depends on the present value of the *total* expected cash flow (to debt and equity) for the business. In the absence of market imperfections *total* expected cash flow depends on the company's investments, not the way the investments are financed. So your financing package will not affect *total* value. Even if you do find some clever financing trick that exploits a market imperfection and somehow increases *total* cash flow, investors will only pay a premium for your company if you can exploit the imperfection more cheaply than they can, and the opportunity is in short supply.

Companies that borrow do offer investors a more complex menu of securities, but investors yawn in response. The menu is redundant. Any shift in capital structure can be duplicated or 'undone' by investors. Why should they pay extra for borrowing indirectly (by holding shares in a levered company) when they can borrow just as easily and cheaply on their own accounts?

MM agree that borrowing increases the expected rate of return on shareholders' investment. But it also increases the risk of the company's shares. MM show that the risk increase exactly offsets the increase in expected return, leaving shareholders no better or worse off.

Proposition I is an extremely general result. It applies not just to the debt-equity trade-off but to *any* choice of financing instruments. For example, MM would say that the choice between long-term and short-term debt has no effect on company value.

The formal proofs of proposition I all depend on the assumption of perfect capital markets.[22] MM's opponents, the 'traditionalists', argue that market imperfections make personal borrowing excessively costly, risky and inconvenient for some investors. This creates a natural clientele willing to pay a premium for shares of levered companies. The traditionalists say that companies should borrow to realise the premium.

But this argument is incomplete. There may be a clientele for levered equity, but that is not enough; the clientele has to be *unsatisfied*. There are already thousands of levered companies available for investment. Is there still an unsatiated clientele for garden-variety debt and equity? We doubt it.

Proposition I is violated when financial managers find an untapped demand and satisfy it by issuing something new and different. The argument between MM and the traditionalists finally boils down to whether this is difficult or easy. We lean towards MM's view: Finding unsatisfied clienteles and designing exotic securities to meet their needs is a game that is fun to play but hard to win.

---

[22] Proposition I can be proved umpteen different ways. The references at the end of this chapter include several more abstract and general proofs. Our formal proofs have been limited to MM's own arguments and (in the appendix to this chapter) a proof based on the capital asset pricing model.

# APPENDIX  MM and the capital asset pricing model

We showed in Section 17.2 that, as the company increases its leverage, the expected equity return goes up in lockstep with beta of the equity. Given this, it should be no surprise to find that we can use the capital asset pricing model to derive MM's proposition I. The following demonstration has been simplified by assuming that the company can issue risk-free debt.

The company is initially all equity financed. Its expected end-of-period value is $V_1$, which we take to include any operating income for the initial period. We now draw on the certainty-equivalent form of the capital asset pricing model, which we derived in the appendix to Chapter 9. This states that the present value of the company is

$$V = E = \frac{V_1 - \lambda \operatorname{Cov}(\tilde{V}_1, \tilde{r}_m)}{1 + r_f}$$

where $\lambda$ is the market price of risk $(r_m - r_f)/\sigma_m^2$.

Now suppose that the company borrows $D$ at the risk-free rate of interest and distributes the proceeds to shareholders. They get $D$ dollars now but next year they will have to repay the debt with interest. Therefore, instead of receiving $V_1$ at the end of the year, they can expect to receive only $V_1 - (1 + r_f)D$. The present value of their levered equity is therefore

$$E = \frac{V_1 - (1 + r_f)D - \lambda \operatorname{Cov}[\tilde{V}_1 - (1 + r_f)D, \tilde{r}_m]}{1 + r_f}$$

But since $(1 + r_f)D$ is known, it has no effect on the covariance. When debt is risk-free, shareholders have to bear *all* the risk associated with $V_1$. Therefore, we substitute $\operatorname{Cov}(V_1, r_m)$ for $\operatorname{Cov}[V_1 - (1 + r_f)D, r_m]$. This gives us

$$E = \frac{V_1 - (1 + r_f)D - \lambda \operatorname{Cov}[\tilde{V}_1, \tilde{r}_m]}{1 + r_f}$$

$$= \frac{V_1 - \lambda \operatorname{Cov}[\tilde{V}_1, \tilde{r}_m]}{1 + r_f} - D$$

To calculate the value of the company we add the value of the debt $D$. This gives

$$V = \frac{V_1 - \lambda \operatorname{Cov}[\tilde{V}_1, \tilde{r}_m]}{1 + r_f}$$

The value of the levered company is identical to the value of the unlevered company.

## FURTHER READING

The pioneering work on the theory of capital structure is:
> F. Modigliani and M. H. Miller, 'The Cost of Capital, Corporation Finance and the Theory of Investment', *American Economic Review*, 48: 261–97 (June 1958).

However, Durand deserves credit for setting out the issues that MM later solved:
> D. Durand, 'Cost of Debt and Equity Funds for Business: Trends and Problems in Measurement', in *Conference on Research in Business Finance*, National Bureau of Economic Research, New York, 1952, pp. 215–47.

MM provided a shorter and clearer proof of capital structure irrelevance in:
> F. Modigliani and M. H. Miller, 'Reply to Heins and Sprenkle', *American Economic Review*, 59: 592–5 (September 1969).

A somewhat difficult article, which analyses capital structure in the context of capital asset pricing theory, is:

R. S. Hamada, 'Portfolio Analysis, Market Equilibrium and Corporation Finance', *Journal of Finance*, **24**: 13–31 (March 1969).

More abstract and general theoretical treatments can be found in:

E. F. Fama, 'The Effects of a Company's Investment and Financing Decisions', *American Economic Review*, **68**: 272–84 (June 1978).

J. E. Stiglitz, 'On the Irrelevance of Corporate Financial Policy', *American Economic Review*, **64**: 851–66 (December 1974).

The Autumn 1988 issue of the *Journal of Economic Perspectives* contains an anniversary collection of articles, including one by Modigliani and Miller, which review and assess the MM propositions. The summer 1989 issue of *Financial Management* contains three more articles under the heading 'Reflections on the MM Propositions 30 Years Later'.

## QUIZ

**1.** Assume a perfectly competitive market with no corporate or personal taxes. Companies A and B each earn gross profits of P and differ only in their capital structure—A is wholly equity financed and B has debt outstanding on which it pays a certain $100 of interest each year. Investor X purchases 10 per cent of the equity of A.

  a. What profits does X obtain?
  b. What alternative strategy would provide the same result?
  c. Suppose investor Y purchases 10 per cent of the equity of B. What profits does Y obtain?
  d. What alternative strategy would provide the same result?

**2.** Ms Kraft owns 50 000 shares of the ordinary shares of Copperhead Corporation with a market value of $2 per share, or $100 000 overall. The company is currently financed as follows:

|  | Book value |
| --- | --- |
| Ordinary shares (8 million shares) | $2 000 000 |
| Short-term loans | $2 000 000 |

Copperhead now announces that it is replacing $1 million of short-term debt with an issue of ordinary shares. What action can Ms Kraft take to ensure that she is entitled to exactly the same proportion of profits as before? (Ignore taxes.)

**3.** The ordinary shares and debt of Northern Sludge are valued at $50 million and $30 million, respectively. Investors currently require a 16 per cent return on the ordinary shares and an 8 per cent return on the debt. If Northern Sludge issues an additional $10 million of ordinary shares and uses this money to retire debt, what happens to the expected return on the shares? Assume that the change in capital structure does not affect the risk of the debt and that there are no taxes. If the risk of the debt did change, would your answer underestimate or overestimate the expected return on the shares?

**4.** Company C is financed entirely by ordinary shares and has a beta of 1.0. The shares have a price-earnings multiple of 10 and are priced to offer a 10 per cent expected return. The company decides to repurchase half the ordinary shares and substitute an equal value of debt. If the debt yields a risk-free 5 per cent,
   a. Give:
      i.   The beta of the ordinary shares after the refinancing.
      ii.  The beta of the debt.
      iii. The beta of the company (i.e. shares and debt combined).
   b. Give:
      i.   The required return on the ordinary shares before the refinancing.
      ii.  The required return on the ordinary shares after the refinancing.
      iii. The required return on the debt.
      iv.  The required return on the company (i.e. shares and debt combined) after the refinancing.
   c. Assume that the operating profit of company C is expected to remain constant. Give:
      i.   The percentage increase in earnings per share.
      ii.  The new price-earnings multiple.

**5.** Suppose that Macbeth Spot Removers issues $2500 of debt and uses the proceeds to repurchase 250 shares.
   a. Rework Table 17.2 to show how earnings per share and share return now vary with operating income.
   b. If the beta of Macbeth's assets is 0.8 and its debt is risk-free, what would be the beta of the equity after the increased borrowing?

**6.** True or false? Explain briefly.
   a. Shareholders always benefit from an increase in company value.
   b. MM's proposition I assumes that actions which maximise company value also maximise shareholder wealth.
   c. The reason that borrowing increases equity risk is because it increases the probability of bankruptcy.
   d. If companies did not have limited liability, the risk of their assets would be increased.
   e. If companies did not have limited liability, the risk of their equity would be increased.
   f. Borrowing does not affect the return on equity if the return on the company's assets is equal to the interest rate.
   g. As long as the company is certain that the return on assets will be higher than the interest rate, an issue of debt makes the shareholders better off.
   h. MM's proposition I implies that an issue of debt increases expected earnings per share and leads to an offsetting fall in the price-earnings ratio.
   i. MM's proposition II assumes increased borrowing does not affect the interest rate on the company's debt.
   j. Borrowing increases company value if there is a clientele of investors with a reason to prefer debt.

**7.** Note the two blank graphs in Figure 17.6. On graph (a) assume MM are right, and plot the relationship between financial leverage and (i) the rates of return on debt and equity and (ii) the weighted average cost of capital. Then fill in graph (b) assuming the traditionalists are right.

**figure 17.6**

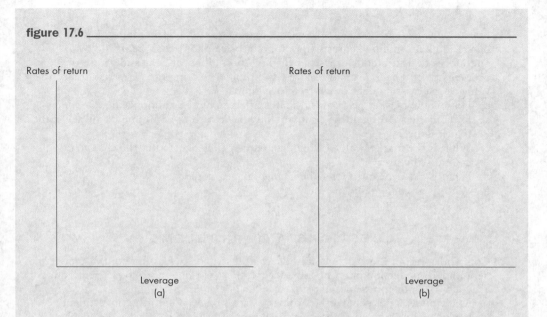

8.  Look at Figure 17.3. Suppose that Ms Macbeth's investment bankers have informed her that, since the new issue of debt is risky, debtholders will demand a return of 12.5 per cent, which is 2.5 per cent above the risk-free interest rate.
    a.  What are $r_A$ and $r_E$?
    b.  Suppose that the beta of the unlevered shares was 0.6. What will be $\beta_A$, $\beta_E$ and $\beta_D$ after the change to the capital structure?
    c.  Assuming that the capital asset pricing model is correct, what is the expected return on the market?

9.  Hopeful Mines Ltd is financed solely by ordinary shares, which offer an expected return of 13 per cent. Suppose now that the company issues debt and repurchase shares so that its debt ratio is 0.4. Investors note the extra risk and raise their required return on the shares to 15 per cent.
    a.  What is the interest rate on the debt?
    b.  If the debt is risk-free and the beta of the equity after the refinancing is 1.5, what is the expected return on the market?

10. Executive Chalk is financed solely by ordinary shares and has outstanding 25 million shares with a market price of $10 a share. It now announces that it intends to issue $160 million of debt and to use the proceeds to buy back ordinary shares.
    a.  How is the market price of the shares affected by the announcement?
    b.  How many shares can the company buy back with the $160 million of new debt that it issues?
    c.  What is the market value of the firm (equity plus debt) after the change in capital structure?
    d.  What is the debt ratio after the change in structure?
    e.  Who (if anyone) gains or loses?
    Now try the next question.

**11.** Executive Cheese has issued debt with a market value of $100 million and has outstanding 15 million shares with a market price of $10 a share. It now announces that it intends to issue a further $60 million of debt and to use the proceeds to buy back ordinary shares. Debtholders, seeing the extra risk, mark the value of the existing debt down to $70 million.

   a. How is the market price of the shares affected by the announcement?

   b. How many shares can the company buy back with the $50 million of new debt that it issues?

   c. What is the market value of the firm (equity plus debt) after the change in capital structure?

   d. What is the debt ratio after the change in structure?

   e. Who (if anyone) gains or loses?

## QUESTIONS AND PROBLEMS

**1.** Companies A and B differ only in their capital structure. A is financed 30 per cent debt and 70 per cent equity: B is financed 10 per cent debt and 90 per cent equity. The debt of both companies is risk-free.

   a. Mr X owns 1 per cent of the ordinary shares of A. What other investment package would produce identical cash flows for Mr X?

   b. Mrs Y owns 2 per cent of the ordinary shares of B. What other investment package would produce identical cash flows for Mrs Y?

   c. Show that neither Mr X nor Mrs Y would invest in the ordinary shares of company B if the total value of company A were less than that of B.

**2.** Hubbard's Pet Foods is financed 80 per cent by ordinary shares and 20 per cent by debt. The expected return on the ordinary shares is 12 per cent and the rate of interest on the bonds is 6 per cent. Assuming that the bonds are default-free, draw a graph that shows the expected return of Hubbard's ordinary shares $r_E$ and the expected return on the package of ordinary shares and bonds $r_A$ for different debt-equity ratios.

**3.** Here is a limerick:
There once was a man named Carruthers,
Who kept cows with miraculous udders.
He said, 'Isn't this neat?
They give cream from one teat,
And skim milk from each of the others!'

   What is the analogy between Mr Carruthers' cows and companies' financing decisions? What would MM's proposition I, suitably adapted, say about the value of Mr Carruthers' cows? Explain.

**4.** 'MM totally ignore the fact that as you borrow more, you have to pay higher rates of interest.' Explain carefully whether this is a valid objection.

**5.** Indicate what is wrong with the following arguments:

   a. 'As the company borrows more and debt becomes risky, both shareholders and debtholders demand higher rates of return. Thus, by *reducing* the debt ratio we can reduce *both* the cost of debt and the cost of equity, making everybody better off.'

   b. 'Moderate borrowing doesn't significantly affect the probability of financial distress or bankruptcy. Consequently moderate borrowing won't increase the expected rate of return demanded by shareholders.'

**6.** Each of the following statements is false or at least misleading. Explain why in each case.

  a. 'A capital investment opportunity offering a 10 per cent DCF rate of return is an attractive project if it can be 100 per cent debt-financed at an 8 per cent interest rate.'

  b. 'The more debt the company issues, the higher the interest rate it must pay. That is one important reason why companies should operate at conservative debt levels.'

**7.** Can you invent any new kinds of debt that might be attractive to investors? Why do you think they have not been issued?

**8.** It has been suggested that one disadvantage of ordinary share financing is that share prices tend to decline in recessions, thereby increasing the cost of capital and deterring investment. Discuss this view. Is it an argument for greater use of debt financing?

**9.** People often convey the idea behind MM's proposition I by various supermarket analogies. For example, 'The value of a pie should not depend on how it is sliced' or 'The cost of a whole chicken should equal the cost of assembling one by buying two drumsticks, two wings, two breasts, and so on'.

  Actually proposition I does not work in the supermarket. You will pay less for an uncut whole pie than for a pie assembled from pieces purchased separately. Supermarkets charge more for chickens after they are cut up.

  Why? What costs or imperfections cause proposition I to fail in the supermarket? Are these costs or imperfections likely to be important for corporations issuing securities on the Australian or world capital market? Explain.

**10.** Figure 17.5 shows that $r_D$ increases as the debt-equity ratio increases. In MM's world $r_E$ also increases but at a declining rate.

  a. Explain why.

  b. Redraw Figure 17.5, showing how $r_D$ and $r_E$ change for increasingly high debt-equity ratios. Can $r_D$ ever be higher than $r_A$? Can $r_E$ decline beyond a certain debt-equity ratio?

**11.** Imagine a company that is expected to produce a level stream of operating profits. As leverage is increased, what happens to:

  a. The ratio of the market value of the equity to income after interest?

  b. The ratio of the market value of the company to income before interest if (i) MM are right and (ii) the traditionalists are right?

**12.** The proposed unbundled share units of American Express would have allowed shareholders to exchange 25 per cent of their shares for USUs. Each share exchanged would give the shareholder a package of three securities:

  ■ *Part 1*: There was a 30-year base yield bond with a face value of $75. The American Express share price was about $28. The base yield bond would receive the then-current dividend of $0.84 per year.

  ■ *Part 2*: An incremental dividend depository preferred would receive any dividend increase over $0.84.

  ■ *Part 3*: An equity appreciation certificate would allow its holder to purchase one American Express share for $75—the face value of the base yield bond. This was to be an opportunity, not an obligation. One preferred share (Part 2 of the USU package) had to be turned in in order to buy the ordinary share.

The USUs would give no voting rights. However, they could be converted back to ordinary shares in the event of a takeover of American Express. Of course, the USUs were never issued. But suppose they had been.
a. Would one USU be worth more or less than one share?
b. Would you have accepted the exchange offer?
c. Why do you think USUs failed to excite investors' interest?

**13.** Archimedes Levers is financed by a mixture of debt and equity. You have the following information about its cost of capital:

$$r_E = \underline{\quad} \qquad r_D = 12\% \qquad r_A = \underline{\quad}$$
$$\beta_E = 1.5 \qquad \beta_D = \underline{\quad} \qquad \beta_A = \underline{\quad}$$
$$r_f = 10\% \qquad r_m = 18\% \qquad D/V = 0.5$$

Can you fill in the blanks?

**14.** Look back at Question 13. Suppose now that Archimedes repurchases debt and issues equity so that $D/V = 0.3$. The reduced borrowing causes $r_D$ to fall to 11 per cent. How do the other variables change?

**15.** Schuldenfrei A.G. pays no taxes and is financed entirely by ordinary shares. The shares have a beta of 0.8, a price-earnings ratio of 12.5 and are priced to offer an 8 per cent expected return. Schuldenfrei now decides to repurchase half the ordinary shares and substitute an equal value of debt. If the debt yields a *risk-free* 5 per cent, calculate:
a. The beta of the ordinary shares after the refinancing.
b. The required return and risk premium on the shares before the refinancing.
c. The required return and the risk premium on the shares after the refinancing.
d. The required return on the debt.
e. The required return on the company (i.e. shares and debt combined) after the refinancing.
   Assume that the operating profit of the firm is expected to remain constant in perpetuity. Give:
f. The percentage increase in earnings per share.
g. The new price-earnings multiple.

**16.** Gamma Airlines is currently all equity financed and its shares offer an expected return of 18 per cent. The risk-free interest rate is 10 per cent. Draw a graph with return on the vertical axis and debt-equity ratio ($D/E$) on the horizontal axis, and plot for different levels of leverage the expected return on assets ($r_A$), the expected return on equity ($r_E$) and the return on debt ($r_D$). Assume that the debt is risk-free. Now draw a similar graph with the debt ratio ($D/V$) on the horizontal axis.

**17.** Consider the following three tickets. Ticket A pays \$10 if _____ is elected as Prime Minister, ticket B pays \$10 if _____ is elected and ticket C pays \$10 if neither is elected. (Fill in the blanks yourself.) Could the three tickets sell for less than the present value of \$10? Could they sell for more? Try auctioning off the tickets. What are the implications for MM's proposition I?

**18.** Two firms, U and L, are identical except for their capital structure. Both will earn \$150 in a boom and \$50 in a slump. There is a 50 per cent chance of each event. U is entirely equity-financed and therefore shareholders receive the entire income. Its shares are valued at \$500. L has issued \$400 of risk-free debt at an interest rate of 10 per cent and therefore $40 of L's income is paid out as interest. There are no taxes or other market imperfections. Investors can borrow and lend at the risk-free rate of interest.

a. What is the value of L's shares?

b. Suppose that you invest $20 in U's shares. Is there an alternative investment in L that would give identical payoffs in boom and slump? What is the expected payoff from such a strategy?

c. Now suppose that you invest $20 in L's shares. Design an alternative strategy with identical payoffs.

d. Now show that MM's proposition II holds.

# chapter 18

# HOW MUCH SHOULD A FIRM BORROW?

In Chapter 17 we found that debt policy rarely matters in well-functioning capital markets. Few financial managers would accept that conclusion as a practical guideline. If debt policy does not matter, then they should not worry about it—financing decisions should be delegated to underlings. Yet financial managers do worry about debt policy. This chapter explains why.

If debt policy were *completely* irrelevant, then actual debt ratios should vary randomly from firm to firm and industry to industry. Yet almost all airlines, banks and real estate development companies rely heavily on debt. And so do many firms in capital-intensive industries like steel, aluminium, chemicals, petroleum and mining. On the other hand, it is rare to find a drug company

or advertising agency that is not predominantly equity-financed. Growth companies rarely use much debt despite rapid expansion and often heavy requirements for capital.

The explanation of these patterns lies partly in the things we left out of the last chapter. We ignored taxes. We assumed financial distress was cheap, quick and painless. It is not, and there are costs associated with financial distress even if liquidation or receivership is ultimately avoided.[1] We ignored potential conflicts of interest between the firm's security holders. For example, we did not consider what happens to the firm's 'old' creditors when new debt is issued or when a shift in investment strategy takes the firm into a riskier business. We ignored the information problems

---

[1] Much of the literature on financial distress talks about corporate bankruptcy. In Australia only people go bankrupt. For companies the final ignominy is either liquidation or receivership.

that favour debt over equity when cash must be raised from new security issues. We ignored the incentive effects of financial leverage on management's investment and payout decisions.

Now we will put all these things back in: taxes first, then the costs of financial distress. This will lead us to conflicts of interest and to information and incentive problems. In the end we will have to admit that debt policy *does* matter.

However, we will *not* throw away the MM theory we developed so carefully in Chapter 17. We are shooting for a theory combining MM's insights *plus* the effects of taxes, costs of financial distress and various other complications. We are not dropping back to the traditional view based on inefficiency in the capital market. Instead, we want to see how well-functioning capital markets

*respond* to taxes and the other things covered in this chapter.

After finishing with theory, we will have a look at the evidence. We will point out the variables that seem to explain differences in financial leverage from company to company and the instances in which increases in financial leverage seem to be good news to investors. Finally, we will attempt to draw the theory and evidence together in a checklist for financial managers to use when choosing their firms' debt-equity ratios.

This chapter assumes you have a reasonable working knowledge of the imputation tax system. If you do not have this knowledge you will probably find some sections of the chapter difficult to follow. If this proves to be a problem for you, then you should refer back to Chapter 16.

## 18.1 Corporate taxes

Debt financing has one important advantage—the interest that the company pays is a tax-deductible expense. Dividends and retained earnings are not. Thus, the return to debtholders escapes taxation at the corporate level. This can be a particular advantage under a classical system of taxation such as in the United States. It is less of an advantage under a full imputation tax system such as exists in Australia. The good news that tax has been saved at the corporate level is offset by the bad news that less corporate tax paid means less in imputation credits for shareholders. Thus, the tax advantage of debt at the corporate level is partially, and in some cases fully, offset by a tax disadvantage at the personal level. As we shall see this latter condition can sometimes arise under a classical tax system. But for the moment we will keep things simple by ignoring personal taxes. We start by considering only corporate taxes.

Table 18.1 shows simple income statements for firm U, which has no debt, and firm L, which has borrowed $1000 at 8 per cent. The tax bill of L is $28.80 less than that of U. This is the *tax shield* provided by the debt of L. In effect the government pays 36 per cent of the interest expense of L. The total income that L can pay out to its bondholders and shareholders increases by that amount.

Tax shields can be valuable assets. Suppose that the debt of L is fixed and permanent. (That is, the company commits to refinance its present debt obligations when they mature and to keep 'rolling over' its debt obligations indefinitely.) It looks forward to a permanent stream of cash flows in tax saved of $28.80 per year. The risk of these flows is likely to be less than the risk of the operating assets of L. The tax shields depend only on the corporate tax rate[2] and on the ability of L to earn enough to cover interest payments. Now the corporate tax rate can change, but in recent times the company tax rate has only been varied by about 3 per cent. So let us assume that dramatic changes to the corporate tax rate are unusual. The ability of L to earn its interest payments must be reasonably sure—otherwise it could not have borrowed at 8 per cent.[3] Therefore, we should discount the interest tax shields at a relatively low rate.

---

[2] Always use the marginal corporate tax rate, not the average rate. The marginal rate is the amount of tax being paid on the last dollar earned. For large corporations the marginal tax rate is 36 per cent at the time of going to press. Average rates are often much less than that because of accelerated depreciation and various other adjustments.

[3] If the income of L does not cover interest in some future year, the tax shield is not necessarily lost. Losses can be 'carried forward' and used to shield income in subsequent years. Of course, they have a lower present value.

table 18.1 _____

The tax deductibility of interest increases the total income that can be paid out to bondholders and shareholders.

|  | Income statement of firm U | Income statement of firm L |
|---|---|---|
| Earnings before interest and taxes | $1000.00 | $1000.00 |
| Interest paid to bondholders | 0 | 80.00 |
| Pre-tax income | 1000.00 | 920.00 |
| Tax at 36% | 360.00 | 331.20 |
| Net income to shareholders | $640.00 | $588.80 |
| Total income to both bondholders and shareholders | $0 + 640 = $640 | $80 + 588.80 = $668.80 |
| Interest tax shield (0.36 × interest) | $0 | $28.80 |

But what rate? The most common assumption is that the risk of the tax shields is the same as that of the interest payments generating them. Thus, we discount at 8 per cent, the expected rate of return demanded by investors who are holding the firm's debt:

$$\text{PV(tax shield in perpetuity)} = \frac{28.80}{0.08} = \$360$$

In effect, the government itself assumes 36 per cent of the $1000 debt obligation of L.

Given the assumptions above, the present value of the tax shield is independent of the return on the debt $r_D$. It equals the corporate tax rate $T_c$ multiplied by the amount borrowed $D$:

$$\text{Interest payment} = \text{return on debt} \times \text{amount borrowed} = r_D \times D$$

$$\text{PV(tax shield)} = \frac{(\text{corporate tax rate} \times \text{expected interest payment})}{\text{expected return on debt}}$$

$$= \frac{T_c(r_D \times D)}{r_D} = T_c D$$

Of course, the PV of the tax shield is less if the firm does not plan to borrow permanently or if it may not be able to use the tax shields in the future.

## How do interest tax shields contribute to the value of shareholders' equity?

MM's proposition I amounts to saying that 'the value of a pie does not depend on how it is sliced'. The pie is the firm's assets, and the slices are the debt and equity claims. If we hold the pie constant, then a dollar more of debt means a dollar less of equity value.

But there is really a third slice—the government's. Look at Table 18.2. It shows an *expanded* balance sheet with *pre-tax* asset value on the left and the value of the government's tax claim recognised as a liability on the right. MM would still say that the value of the pie—in this case *pre-tax* asset value—is not changed by slicing. But anything the firm can do to reduce the size of the government's slice obviously makes shareholders better off. One thing it can do is to borrow money, which reduces its tax bill and, as we saw in Table 18.1, increases the cash flows to debt and equity investors. The *after-tax* value of the firm (the sum of its debt and equity values as shown in a normal market value balance sheet) goes up by the PV of the tax shield. This increase in value is captured by the shareholders.

**table 18.2**

Normal and expanded market value balance sheets. In a normal balance sheet assets are valued after-tax. In the expanded balance sheet, assets are valued pre-tax and the value of the government's tax claim is recognised on the right-hand side. Interest tax shields are valuable because they reduce the government's claim.

| Normal balance sheet (market values) | |
|---|---|
| Asset value<br>(i.e. PV of after-tax cash flows)<br>Total assets | Debt<br>Equity<br>Total liabilities and equity |
| **Expanded balance sheet (market values)** | |
| Pre-tax asset value<br>(i.e. PV of *pre-tax* cash flows)<br>Total pre-tax assets | Debt<br>Government's claim (PV of future taxes)<br>Equity<br>Total liabilities and equity |

## Recasting News Corporation's capital structure

News Corporation is a large, successful firm that uses several billion dollars of long-term debt. Table 18.3a shows simplified book balance sheets for News Corporation. We assume that this represents a projection made in January for the position expected by financial year-end. We also assume that you are the chief financial officer of News Corporation. Casting off your hangover from the New Year celebrations, you are busy making plans for the company finances.

Suppose that as News Corporation's chief financial officer you have complete responsibility for its capital structure. Having projected the balance sheet values for the financial year-end you are wondering about the effect of borrowing an extra $1 billion. The borrowing would be on a permanent basis and you would use the money raised to repurchase shares.

Table 18.3b shows the new balance sheets assuming the $1 billion is raised. The book version simply has $1000 million more long-term debt and $1000 million less equity. But we know that News Corporation's assets must be worth more, for its tax bill has been reduced by 36 per cent of the interest on the new debt. In other words, News Corporation has an increase in PV(tax shield) which is worth $T_cD = 0.36 \times 1000 = \$360$ million. If the MM theory holds *except* for taxes, firm value must increase by $360 million to $23 716 million. News Corporation's shareholders get $1 billion cash and end up with equity worth $12 902 million.

Now you have repurchased $1000 million worth of shares, but News Corporation's equity value has dropped by only $640 million. Therefore, News Corporation's shareholders must be $360 million ahead. Not a bad day's work.[4]

## MM and taxes

We have just developed a version of MM's proposition I as 'corrected' by them to reflect corporate income taxes.[5] The new proposition is

$$\text{Value of firm} = \text{value if all equity financed} + \text{PV(tax shield)}$$

---

[4]  Notice that as long as the bonds are sold at a fair price, all the benefits from the tax shield go to the shareholders.

[5]  MM's original article [F. Modigliani and M. H. Miller, 'The Cost of Capital, Corporation Finance and the Theory of Investment', *American Economic Review*, 48: 261–97 (June 1958)] recognised interest tax shields, but did not value them properly. They put things right in their 1963 article 'Corporate Income Taxes and the Cost of Capital: A Correction', *American Economic Review*, 53: 433–43 (June 1963).

**table 18.3a** _____

Simplified balance sheets for News Corporation, January 1995 (figures in $million).

| | | | |
|---|---|---|---|
| **Book values[1]** | | | |
| Net working capital | 1 597 | 8 017 | Long-term debt |
| Long-term assets | 24 799 | 1 797 | Other long-term liabilities |
| | | 16 582 | Equity |
| Total assets | 26 396 | 26 396 | Total financing |
| **Market values[2]** | | | |
| Net working capital | 1 597 | 8 017 | Long-term debt |
| | | 1 797 | Other long-term liabilities |
| Market value of long-term assets[3] | 21 759 | 13 542 | Equity |
| Total assets | 23 356 | 23 356 | Total financing |

Notes:
1. Book values are assumed to be the same as the 1995 financial year-end.
2. Market value is assumed to equal the 1995 financial year-end book values for net working capital, long-term debt and other long-term liabilities. Equity is entered at actual market value in early January 1995 for ordinary shares and convertible preference shares (number of shares multiplied by share price). Non-convertible preference shares and special dividend shares are included at their book value. The market value of long-term assets is calculated as the balancing item.
3. The market value of the long-term assets includes the tax shield on the existing debt.

**table 18.3b** _____

Balance sheets for News Corporation with additional $1 billion of long-term debt substituted for shareholders' equity (figures in $million).[1]

| | | | |
|---|---|---|---|
| **Book values** | | | |
| Net working capital | 1 597 | 9 017 | Long-term debt |
| Long-term assets | 24 799 | 1 797 | Other long-term liabilities |
| | | 15 582 | Equity |
| Total assets | 26 396 | 26 396 | Total liabilities |
| **Market values** | | | |
| Net working capital | 1 597 | 9 017 | Long-term debt |
| Market value of long-term assets | 21 759 | 1 797 | Other long-term liabilities |
| Present value of additional tax shields[2] | 360 | 12 902 | Equity |
| Total assets | 23 716 | 23 716 | Total liabilities |

Notes:
1. The figures in Table 18.3b for net working capital, long-term assets and other long-term liabilities are identical to those in Table 18.3a.
2. The present value of tax shields is assumed equal to corporate tax rate (36 per cent) multiplied by the amount of additional debt obligation.

In the special case of permanent debt,

$$\text{Value of firm} = \text{value if all equity financed} + T_c D$$

Our imaginary financial surgery on News Corporation provides the perfect illustration of the problems inherent in this 'corrected' theory. That $360 million windfall came too easily; it seems to violate the law that 'there is no such thing as a money machine'. And if News Corporation's shareholders would be richer with an extra $1 billion of corporate debt, why not an extra $5 billion, or even an extra $15 billion?[6] Our formula implies that firm value and shareholders' wealth continue to go up as $D$ increases. The implied optimal debt policy is embarrassingly extreme: all firms should be 100 per cent debt-financed.

You rarely see companies adopt such an extreme debt policy, but there were some companies in Australia that came close. They were overseas-owned and were set up with a small quantity of share capital and a very large quantity of debt supplied by the overseas owners. The objective was to minimise Australian company tax. When the government woke up to what was happening they put in place 'thin capitalisation' rules under which the interest tax deduction for this type of company is disallowed. These cases were an exception; most companies have nothing like the extreme debt levels that MM's theory would suggest.

MM were not that fanatical about it. No one would expect their formula to apply at extreme debt ratios. But that does not explain why some companies not only exist but thrive with almost no debt at all. Nor does it explain why companies sometimes reduce their debt levels. In reality, News Corporation's debt was actually reduced by about $2 billion between 1993 and 1995. It is hard to believe that the management of News Corporation was simply missing the boat.

Therefore, we have argued ourselves into a corner. There are three ways out:

■ Perhaps a fuller examination of corporate *and personal* taxation will uncover a tax disadvantage of corporate borrowing, offsetting the present value of the corporate tax shield.
■ Perhaps the corporate tax benefit is smaller than we assume. For example, the marginal corporate tax rate may be lower than the statutory rate and the interest tax deduction may be riskier than we have assumed.
■ Perhaps firms that borrow incur other costs and risks—financial distress costs, for example— offsetting the present value of the tax shield.

We will now explore these escape routes.

## 18.2 Corporate and personal taxes

When personal taxes are introduced, the firm's objective is no longer to minimise the *corporate* tax bill; the firm should try to minimise the present value of *all* taxes paid on corporate income. 'All taxes' include *personal* taxes paid by bondholders and shareholders.

Figure 18.1 illustrates how corporate and personal taxes are affected by leverage. Depending on the firm's capital structure, a dollar of operating income will accrue to investors either as debt interest or equity income (dividends or capital gains). That is, the dollar can go down either branch of Figure 18.1.

Notice that Figure 18.1 distinguishes between $T_p$, the personal tax rate on interest, and $T_{pE}$, the *effective* personal rate on equity income.[7] The two rates are not necessarily equal. For

---

[6]    The last figure would result in an almost 100 per cent book-debt ratio. But News Corporation's *market* value would be $29 116 million according to our formula for firm value. News Corporation's shares would have an aggregate value of $3302 million, plus $15 billion would have been paid to shareholders.

[7]    It is traditional, natural and convenient to think of investors as people and hence talk about personal tax rates. We should remember, however, that the law recognises several types of 'legal persons' as having the capacity to act as investors, for example, superannuation funds and companies. This is important, because these investors may be subject to different taxes.

**figure 18.1**

The company's capital structure determines whether operating income is paid out as interest or equity income. Interest is taxed only at the personal level; while equity income is taxed at both the corporate and the personal levels. However, $T_{pE}$, the effective personal tax rate on equity income, can be less than $T_p$, the marginal personal tax rate, which is the rate paid on interest income.

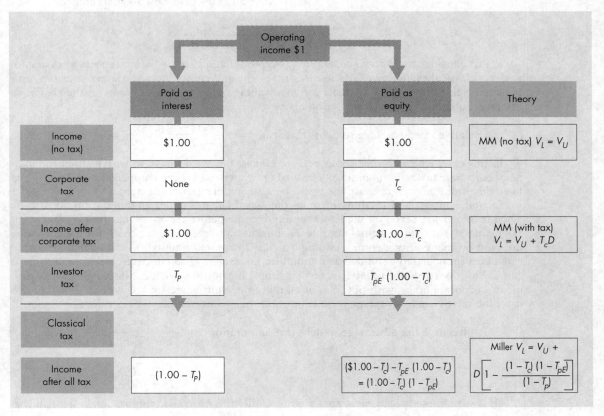

example, $T_{pE}$ can be effectively less than $T_p$ if equity income comes as capital gains. The tax rate on dividends and *realised* capital gains is the investor's marginal tax rate. However, capital gains taxes can be deferred until shares are sold, so the *effective* capital gains rate can be less than the tax rate on dividends.

As you study Figure 18.1 remember that effective tax rate on equity income, $T_{pE}$, is a weighted average of the tax rate on dividends and capital gains. We can use Figure 18.1 to analyse either the classical or the imputation tax system, but of course the weighting schemes used to calculate $T_{pE}$ differ. In the case of the imputation system the weighting scheme involves the corporate tax rate as well as the tax rate on dividends and capital gains.[8] This corporate tax adjustment allows for the effect of the imputation tax credit.

The firm's objective should be to arrange its capital structure so as to maximise investors' after-tax income. You can see from Figure 18.1 that corporate borrowing is better if $1 - T_p$ is more than $(1 - T_{pE})(1 - T_c)$; otherwise it is worse. If $(1 - T_p) = (1 - T_{pE})(1 - T_c)$ then it

---

[8]    The weighting scheme for the classical system is: $T_{pE} = \delta T_{\text{DIV}} + (1 - \delta)T_G$, where $\delta$ = the dividend payout ratio, $T_{\text{DIV}}$ = the tax rate on dividends and $T_G$ = the tax rate on capital gains.

The weighting scheme for the imputation system is: $T_{pE} = \dfrac{\delta(T_{\text{DIV}} - \gamma T_c)}{1 - T_c} + (1 - \delta)T_G$, where $\gamma$ = the proportion of corporate tax recovered by investors through imputation tax credits.

matters not whether we use debt or equity. This condition requires either that $T_{pE}$ and $T_c$ are both less than $T_p$, or that one of them is zero.

Notice that the *relative* tax advantage of debt over equity is:

$$\text{Relative tax advantage of debt} = \frac{\text{After all taxes cash flow to debtholder}}{\text{After all taxes cash flow to shareholder}}$$

$$= \frac{(1 - T_p)}{(1 - T_{pE})(1 - T_c)}$$

Let us consider two special cases. First, suppose that all equity income comes as dividends under a classical tax system. The result is that debt and equity income are taxed at the same personal rate. With $T_{pE} = T_p$, the relative advantage of debt depends only on the *corporate* tax rate. Substituting into the equation above gives:

$$\text{Relative tax advantage to debt (classical)} = \frac{(1 - T_p)}{(1 - T_p)(1 - T_c)} = \frac{1}{(1 - T_c)}$$

In this case, we can forget about personal taxes. But we do have to worry about the marginal corporate tax rate. Assuming a classical tax system where the companies consistently pay tax at the full marginal tax rate there will be a strong preference for debt.

Second, suppose all the equity income comes as dividends under an imputation tax system. Then investors are taxed on their total equity income before corporate tax (not just on after-tax dividends) at their marginal tax rate $T_p$. But they also receive a tax credit for the corporate tax paid on that equity income. Assuming a *fully integrated* imputation tax system all corporate tax is immediately refunded as imputation tax credits. The effective corporate tax rate is zero.[9] This does not mean that $T_c$ is zero; it simply means that when considering total tax payments corporate taxes wash out. Net of all taxes the equity investor receives $(1 - T_p)$. In this case, the relative tax advantage ratio is one and there is no reason to prefer debt or equity.[10]

$$\text{Relative tax advantage to debt (full imputation)} = \frac{(1 - T_p)}{(1 - T_{pE})(1 - T_c)}$$

$$= \frac{(1 - T_p)}{(1 - T_p)} = 1$$

Of course, these special cases are extreme. Under the Australian imputation system all corporate tax is not fully, or immediately, refunded.[11] While in countries such as the United States, which have a classical tax system, few companies will consistently pay taxes at a marginal rate that is equal to the statutory tax rate. The value of the tax advantage of debt therefore probably lies in the middle ground—greater than zero under imputation and less than the maximum under the classical system. We have more to say about this below.

---

9    Since the imputation system involves a refund of corporate tax we can think of that refund as effectively reducing the corporate tax rate. Since the refund is received by the shareholders we can alternatively think of the refund as reducing the personal tax payable. Sometimes it is more convenient to think in terms of effective corporate tax rates, and at other times it is more convenient to think in terms of the effective personal tax rates on equity.

10   The calculation is as follows. From Footnote 8:

$T_{pE} = \dfrac{\delta(T_{\text{DIV}} - \gamma T_c)}{1 - T_c} + (1 - \delta)T_G$, with $\delta = 1$ and $\gamma = 1$, this becomes $\dfrac{(T_{\text{DIV}} - T_c)}{1 - T_c}$. Setting $T_{\text{DIV}} = T_p$ and substituting

into the equation for the tax advantage of debt gives $\dfrac{(1 - T_p)}{\left[1 - \left(\dfrac{T_p - T_c}{1 - T_c}\right)\right](1 - T_c)} = \dfrac{(1 - T_p)}{(1 - T_c) - (T_p - T_c)} = 1$

11   Imputation credits are only available to investors for dividends paid, not total profits. Furthermore, some investors cannot fully utilise the credits that they receive.

One insight from the above analysis is that if we can forget about personal taxes, the advantage of corporate borrowing under the classical system is exactly as MM calculated it.[12] They do not have to assume away personal taxes. Their theory of debt and taxes requires only that debt and equity be taxed at the same rate. Consideration of a fully-integrated imputation system reminds us, however, that we should not blindly calculate the tax advantage of debt at the statutory corporate tax rate. When imputation reduces the effective corporate tax rate to zero, there is no value in the tax shield and we are back to MM's original theory, $V_L = V_U$.

In any event, we seem to have a simple, practical decision rule: Arrange the firm's capital structure to shunt operating income down that branch of Figure 18.1 where the tax is least. We will now try a couple of back-of-the-envelope calculations to see what that rule could imply.

# Debt policy before and after the 1980s tax reform

Before the Australian tax reforms of the mid-1980s the prevailing corporate tax rate had been 46 per cent. Tax rates on dividends and interest varied with investors, and some investors had personal tax rates higher than the corporate tax rate. However, the capital gains tax rate for a majority of investors was zero, provided the asset was held for more than a year.[13] Most corporate investors also got their dividends effectively tax-free.

You can see the two opposing tax effects. Corporate tax rates subsidised debt—the government in effect paid up to 46 cents for every dollar of interest. But the personal tax rules favoured equity because of the low tax rate on capital gains and low tax on dividends for some investors. Let us see how the two effects might almost cancel out.[14]

Consider a firm paying half its earnings as dividends. Suppose there is a zero rate on capital gains and this, combined with receipt of dividends by investors not liable for tax on dividends, cuts the effective tax rate on equity income to 7 per cent.[15] That is, $T_{pE} = 0.07$. If $T_p$, the tax rate on interest, is 0.47 then

| | Interest | Equity income |
|---|---|---|
| Income before tax | $1.00 | $1.00 |
| Less corporate tax at $T_t = 0.46$ | 0 | 0.46 |
| Income after corporate tax | 1.00 | 0.54 |
| Less tax at $T_p = 0.47$ and $T_{pE} = 0.07$ | 0.47 | 0.038 |
| Income after all taxes | $0.53 | $0.502 |

Advantage to debt = $0.028

---

[12] Of course, personal taxes reduce the dollar amount of corporate interest tax shields, but the appropriate discount rate for cash flows after personal tax is also lower. If investors are willing to lend at a prospective return *before* personal taxes of $r_p$, then they must also be willing to accept a return *after* personal taxes of $r_D(1 - T_p)$, where $T_p$ is the marginal rate of personal tax. Thus, we can compute the value after personal taxes of the tax shield on permanent debt:

$$PV \text{ tax shield} = \frac{T_c \times (r_D \times D) \times (1 - T_p)}{r_D \times (1 - T_p)} = T_c D$$

This brings us back to our previous formula for firm value:

$$\text{Value of firm} = \text{value if all equity finance} + T_t D$$

[13] For some investors the reverse was the case. For example, capital gains were taxed as income but dividends were tax-free for life insurance offices.

[14] For consistency in the analyses that follow we use 47 per cent as the investor tax rate. This was the highest personal tax rate at the time of writing. We ignore the Medicare levy.

[15] The 7 per cent is calculated as follows: Half the returns are untaxed capital gains. Of the dividends paid about 30 per cent were subject to tax, and let us assume the average rate of tax was 47 per cent. Then the effective tax rate on equity is $(0.5 \times 0) + (0.5 \times 0.3 \times 0.47) = 0.07$, or 7 per cent.

There is a small advantage to debt, but not a compelling one. For example, if we cut the corporate tax rate by 4 per cent, equity would edge ahead. In this example, the tax advantage of debt at the corporate level is largely balanced by the tax disadvantage to debt at the level of the investor. Of course, if the effective tax rate on equity income were larger, there would be a much bigger tax advantage to debt. If $T_{pE}$ were say 20 per cent, then the tax advantage to debt would grow to nearly 10 cents for each dollar of interest.

The Australian tax reforms of the mid-1980s have resulted in a widespread capital gains tax levied at the investor's income tax rate, a substantial reduction in the corporate tax rate (the rate is 36 per cent at the time of writing, but there are proposals to reduce it to 30 per cent) and the introduction of the imputation tax system. Corporate investors continue to get their dividends effectively tax-free. Here is a second numerical example, under the new tax regime. We assume a 100 per cent dividend payout and full use of imputation credits ($\gamma = 1$).

|  | Interest | Equity income |
|---|---|---|
| Income before tax | $1.00 | $1.00 |
| Less corporate tax at $T_c = 0.36$ | 0 | 0.36 |
| Income after corporate tax | 1.00 | 0.64 |
| Add corporate tax refunded as imputation credits | 0 | 0.36 |
| Less tax at $T_p = 0.47$ and $T_{pE} = 0.47^1$ | 0.47 | 0.47 |
| Income after all taxes | $ 0.53 | $0.53 |
|  | Advantage to debt = $0.00 | |

Note:
1. Under imputation, shareholder taxes are levied on the basis of the pre-tax profit represented by the dividend. In this case taxes are

$$\left[\left(\frac{0.64}{1 - 0.36}\right) \times 0.47\right] = \$1.00 \times 0.47.$$

In this example taxes provide no advantage to debt or equity. However, 100 per cent payout and full use of imputation credits are unrealistic assumptions. It is more realistic to assume that about 50 to 60 per cent of profits are paid out as dividends. Of the imputation credits attached to those dividends only about 50 to 60 per cent will be claimed by investors to offset their tax liabilities.

Let us see what happens when we take 50 per cent to be the dividend payout and 60 per cent to be the proportion of imputation credits used by investors. In this case, the effective value of the corporate tax refunded as imputation credits is $0.108 (60 per cent of half the corporate tax paid, i.e. $0.6 \times 0.5 \times 0.36$). In calculating the total tax liability of equity investors we must consider three components. First, half of the return comes as capital gains ($0.64 \times 0.5 = 0.32$). Because tax on these gains is not payable till the gains are realised this reduces the effective gains tax rate. We will take this tax rate to be 23.5 per cent[16] to give gains tax liability of $0.075, ($0.235 \times 0.32 = 0.075$). Next, there is the 40 per cent of the dividend on which no imputation credits are claimed. We will assume these dividends go to tax-exempt investors, so the tax liability here is zero. Finally, we have the 60 per cent of dividends on which the imputation credit is claimed. Here tax is levied on the dividend grossed up to the equivalent share of pre-tax profit. That is $[(0.32 \times 0.6)/(1 - 0.36) = 0.3]$ which we assume is

16   We have taken this to be half the assumed marginal rate of 47 per cent.

taxed at 47 per cent, to give a tax liability of $0.141. The total liability for equity investors therefore is $0.141 + $0.075 = $0.216.

|  | Interest | Equity income |
|---|---|---|
| Income before tax | $1.00 | $1.00 |
| Less corporate tax at $T_c = 0.36$ | 0 | 0.36 |
| Income after corporate tax | 1.00 | 0.64 |
| Add corporate tax refunded as imputation credits | 0 | 0.108 |
| Less tax at $T_p = 0.47$ and $T_{pE}$ as calculated above | 0.47 | 0.216 |
| Income after all taxes | $ 0.53 | $0.532 |

Advantage to equity = $0.002

Once again, debt and equity are neck and neck. However, this could easily change. For example, if the investors who cannot use imputation credits are not tax-exempt investors, but rather are overseas investors, then there will be taxes to be paid by these investors that will tip the balance in favour of debt. Conversely, if investors' capacity to use the imputation credits is greater than we assumed then the balance would tip in favour of equity. The important lesson to learn here is that the extent of any advantage that debt has under imputation depends on the dividend policy of the firm and the tax position of its investor clientele. We should be cautious about making general statements about the superiority of either debt or equity.

Another important lesson is that using reasonable numbers it is not difficult to construct examples where there is little to choose between debt and equity. In equilibrium, it would be no surprise to find that neither debt nor equity had much advantage. If debt is the better option then smart corporate treasurers will issue debt and will continue to do so until the advantage to debt has been eliminated, and vice versa if equity has the advantage.

However, as the back-of-the-envelope calculations show, it is difficult to provide definitive guidance about the relative merits of debt and equity. Which investors' tax rates should be used? What is $T_{pE}$, for example? We know it depends on tax rates on dividends and capital gains, and we have a formula for it in Footnote 8. That formula assumes one tax rate for dividends, but in the last example above we used two tax rates for dividends. We could have used more. The shareholder register of a large company may include tax-exempt investors (such as charities or universities) as well as millionaires, other companies and superannuation funds. All possible tax brackets will be mixed together. And it is the same with $T_p$, the personal tax rate on interest. Holding bonds is very attractive if you are a tax-exempt investor, but many taxpaying investors also hold corporate debt.

One way out is to use the tax rate of the marginal investor who is determining prices. But who is this investor? We do not really know. Perhaps in the Australian context it is an overseas investor. If so, the Australian domestic tax system may be largely irrelevant to prices and debt policy.

# *Merton Miller's 'Debt and Taxes'

How does capital structure affect firm value when investors have different tax rates? There is one model that may help us. It was put forward in 'Debt and Taxes', Merton Miller's 1976 Presidential Address to the American Finance Association.[17]

---

17  M. H. Miller, 'Debt and Taxes', *Journal of Finance*, **32**: 261–76 (May 1977).

Miller was considering debt policy under a classical tax system and provided us with a useful formula for the gain from leverage when tax rates on equity and debt income differ. In this case the value of a levered firm is given by:

$$V_L = V_U + D\left[1 - \frac{(1 - T_c)(1 - T_{pE})}{(1 - T_p)}\right]$$

The term following $V_U$ on the right-hand side of the equation is the value of the tax shield, or gain from leverage. Its interpretation is quite intuitive. Look back to our discussion of Figure 18.1 and you will see that the term $\frac{(1 - T_c)(1 - T_{pE})}{(1 - T_p)}$ is the relative tax advantage to equity. Suppose this ratio is one, in this case it does not matter whether you use debt or equity, so substituting debt for equity will not change the value of the firm. If the ratio were 0.8 then substituting $1 of debt for equity would, according to the formula, increase the value of the firm by $0.20. In the extreme case where all equity returns were taxed away ($T_{pE} = 100\%$), the ratio would be zero. Each dollar of debt substituted for equity would, in this case, increase the value of the firm by $1.00.

Miller then went on to examine the case where $T_{pE}$ is zero for all investors. This would apply, for example, if all equity income came as unrealised capital gains. The rate of tax on interest $T_p$ varies with the investor's tax bracket. Tax-exempt institutions do not pay any tax on interest; for them $T_p$ is zero. At the other extreme, millionaires might pay tax at a rate of 50 per cent on bond interest; for them $T_p$ is 0.50. Most investors fall somewhere between these two extremes.

Consider a simple world with these tax rates. Suppose that companies are initially financed entirely by equity. If financial managers are on their toes, this is unlikely to represent a stable situation. Think of it in terms of Figure 18.1. If every dollar goes down the equity branch, there are no taxes paid at the personal level (remember $T_{pE} = 0$). Thus, the financial manager need only consider whether the value of corporate taxes saved by creating an interest tax shield is greater than the extra personal taxes payable by the debtholders. If the effective corporate tax rate exceeds the personal tax rate on debt this creates an incentive for corporate borrowing. This incentive will be a strong one under the classical tax system. The same incentive will exist under the imputation system *if* you can hold $T_{pE}$ at zero, while at the same time reducing corporate tax by more than you increase debtholders' taxes. While this is feasible under certain conditions,[18] the analysis is complicated by the fact that under imputation corporate and personal taxes are usually linked. Under imputation, saving corporate tax can push up $T_{pE}$.[19] For the time being therefore let us confine our attention to the classical system.

As companies begin to borrow, some investors have to be persuaded to hold corporate debt rather than ordinary shares. There should be no problem in persuading tax-exempt investors to hold debt. They do not pay any personal taxes on bonds or shares. Thus, the initial impact of borrowing is to save corporate taxes and to leave personal taxes unchanged.

But as companies borrow more, they need to persuade taxpaying investors to migrate from shares to bonds. Therefore, they have to offer a higher interest rate on their bonds in order to compensate investors for the extra taxes they will have to pay. Companies can afford to keep increasing the interest rate that they offer as long as the corporate tax saving *is greater than* the extra personal tax. But there is no way that companies can afford to offer interest rates that will attract millionaires to hold their bonds. The corporate tax saving cannot compensate for the extra personal tax that those millionaires would need to pay. Thus, the migrations stop

---

[18] One special case, for example, is where all the return comes as capital gains which escapes personal tax through deferral of the gains. In this case, the investor gets no benefit from imputation credits and receives $(1 - T_c)$ after all tax. As long as $(1 - T_c)$ is greater than $(1 - T_p)$, then there is an incentive to borrow.

[19] Alternatively, you can think of the reduction in imputation credits as pushing up the effective corporate tax rate $T_c$.

when the corporate tax saving *equals* the personal tax loss. This point occurs when $T_p$, the personal tax rate of the migrating investor, equals the corporate tax rate $T_c$.

Let us put some numbers on this. The corporate tax rate $T_c$ was 46 per cent. We continue to assume that $T_{pE}$, the effective rate of tax on equity income, is zero for all investors. In this case, companies will offer higher and higher interest rates until they have persuaded all investors with tax rates below 46 per cent to hold bonds. But there is nothing to be gained (or lost) by persuading investors with tax rates *equal* to 46 per cent to hold bonds. In the case of these investors $1 of operating income will produce income after all taxes of $0.54, regardless of whether the dollar is interest or equity income:

|  | Income remaining after all taxes |
|---|---|
| Income paid out as interest | $1 - T_p = 1 - 0.46 = \$0.54$ |
| Income paid out as equity income | $(1 - T_{pE})(1 - T_c) = (1 - 0)(1 - 0.46) = \$0.54$ |

You can think of this another way. Suppose tax-free investors will accept a 10 per cent interest rate. This tells us that the equilibrium after tax return is 10 per cent. If so, what interest rate will an investor in the 46 per cent tax bracket require? Easy, $0.10/(1 - 0.46) = 0.1852$, or 18.52 per cent, the extra 8.52 per cent goes in tax leaving the investor with 10 per cent. What is the after-tax cost of debt to the company? It is $0.1852(1 - 0.46) = 0.10$, or 10 per cent. At this point the interest rate has been increased so much that the increase exactly offsets the tax saving from the interest tax deduction.

The resulting equilibrium is shown in Figure 18.2. This equilibrium is for the whole debt market, not for any particular firm. The extra interest demanded to pay additional taxes on debt income is shown by the upward sloping dotted line.[20] The tax saving for companies is shown by the solid horizontal line. The equilibrium is where the solid line and the dotted line intersect. At that point the extra personal tax paid on the marginal dollar of interest exactly matches the extra company tax saved. At the equilibrium point the distribution of an extra dollar of company cash flow as interest leaves total taxes unchanged. Going beyond that point will increase the total taxes paid. Below that point distributing more cash flow as interest will reduce total taxes.

In equilibrium taxes determine the aggregate amount of corporate debt in the economy,[21] but not the amount issued by any particular firm. The debt-equity ratio for companies as a whole depends on the corporate tax rate and the funds available to individual investors in the various tax brackets. If the corporate tax rate is increased, migration starts again, leading to a higher debt-equity ratio for companies as a whole. If personal tax rates are increased, the migration reverses, leading to a lower debt-equity ratio. If *both* personal and corporate tax rates are increased by the same amount—10 percentage points, say—there is no migration and no change.

The companies in our example that first sold bonds to tax-exempt investors may have gained an advantage. But once the 'low-tax' investors have bought bonds and the migrations have stopped, no single firm can gain an advantage by borrowing more, or suffer any penalty by borrowing less. Therefore, there is no such thing as an optimal debt-equity ratio *for any single firm*. The market equilibrium depends only on the *total* amount of debt. No single firm can influence that.

Here is an intriguing point about Miller's tax equilibrium: Because he assumes equity returns escape personal tax ($T_{pE} = 0$), investors are willing to accept lower rates of return on low-risk common shares than on debt. Consider a safe (zero-beta) share. The standard capital asset pricing model would give an expected return of $r = r_f$, the risk-free interest rate (see Section 7.4). But the investor migrating from equity to debt gives up $r$ and earns $r_f(1 - T_p)$,

---

[20]   We have arbitrarily shown this as a smooth curve. In practice it would probably look more like a series of steps.

[21]   That is the amount of debt such that the marginal debtholder in the economy has $T_p = T_c$.

**figure 18.2**

It pays companies to borrow as long as the corporate tax saving exceeds the extra personal tax paid by the marginal lender. MM and Miller disagree only about how the extra personal tax varies with total company borrowing.

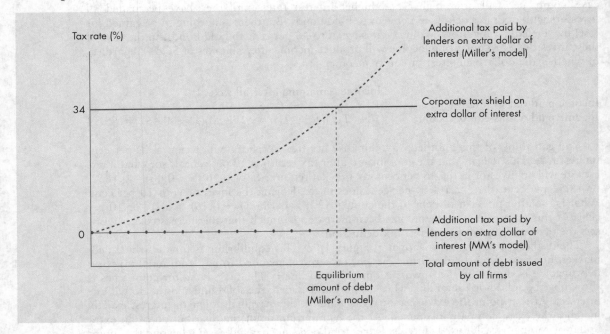

the *after-tax* interest rate. In equilibrium, the migrating investor is content with either debt or equity, so $r = r_f(1 - T_p)$. Moreover, that investor's $T_p$ equals the corporate rate $T_c$. Therefore, $r = r_f(1 - T_c)$. If we accept Miller's argument lock, stock and barrel, the security market line should pass through the after-tax risk-free interest rate.

The majority of financial managers and economists believe a classical tax system favours corporate borrowing. But it is easy to overestimate the advantage. Analyses like Tables 18.2a and 18.2b, which calculate the present value of a safe, perpetual stream of corporate interest tax shields, must overestimate debt's net value added. As Miller's paper shows, the aggregate supplies of corporate debt and equity should adjust to minimise the sum of corporate and personal taxes; and at the resulting equilibrium the higher personal tax rate on debt income should partially offset the tax deductibility of interest at the corporate level. The critical variable is the effective tax rate on equity: the more difficult it is to shield equity income from corporate tax, the greater the value of the debt tax shield.

## *Miller's model and imputation

Miller had a classical tax system in mind when he developed his model. However, Miller's model was not intended as a detailed description of the tax system operating in any particular country, but as a way of illustrating how corporate and personal taxes could cancel out and leave firm value independent of capital structure. It is therefore a fairly straightforward task to extend his approach to the imputation system.[22] First, let us redraw Figure 18.1. We do this

22   A good example of such analysis is Peter F. Howard and Robert L. Brown. 'Dividend Policy And Capital Structure Under The Imputation Tax System: Some Clarifying Comments', *Accounting and Finance*, **32(1)**: 51–61 (1992).

by separating out the effect of paying a dollar of equity income as dividends, or retaining a dollar to give rise to a dollar of capital gains. The result is Figure 18.3. We no longer use the effective tax rate $T_{pE}$, but separate out its components: the tax rate on capital gains $T_G$ and the tax rate on dividends, which we assume to be the investor's marginal tax rate $T_p$. We allow for the recovery of corporate tax on equity income paid as dividends, and we also allow that only some fraction $\gamma$ of the tax may be recovered. Of course, if $\gamma$ is equal to one then dividends and interest are taxed equivalently, and as Figure 18.3 shows, both would return $(1 - T_p)$ after all taxes.

**figure 18.3**

Figure 18.1 redrawn to show the effect under the imputation system of dividing equity income between dividends and retained earnings.

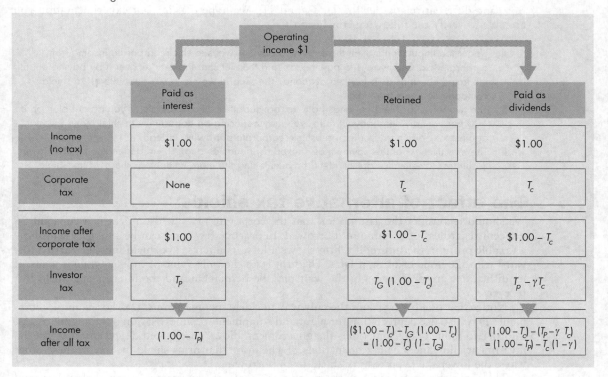

| | Paid as interest | Retained | Paid as dividends |
|---|---|---|---|
| Income (no tax) | $1.00 | $1.00 | $1.00 |
| Corporate tax | None | $T_c$ | $T_c$ |
| Income after corporate tax | $1.00 | $1.00 - T_c$ | $1.00 - T_c$ |
| Investor tax | $T_p$ | $T_G(1.00 - T_c)$ | $T_p - \gamma T_c$ |
| Income after all tax | $(1.00 - T_p)$ | $\begin{aligned}&(\$1.00 - T_c) - T_G(1.00 - T_c)\\ &= (1.00 - T_c)(1 - T_G)\end{aligned}$ | $\begin{aligned}&(1.00 - T_c) - (T_p - \gamma\ T_c)\\ &= (1.00 - T_p) - T_c(1 - \gamma)\end{aligned}$ |

The interesting and realistic case is where the firm pays some earnings as dividends and retains the balance to reinvest. Let us call the percentage paid out as dividends $\delta$, so $(1 - \delta)$ is retained. Then we can see from Figure 18.3 that one dollar of equity income will, after all taxes, return:

$$\delta[(1 - T_p) - T_c(1 - \gamma)] + (1 - \delta)[(1 - T_c)(1 - T_G)]$$

We can then write Miller's model as:

$$V_L = V_U + D\left[\frac{1 - \delta[(1 - T_p) - T_c(1 - \gamma)] + (1 - \delta)[(1 - T_c)(1 - T_G)]}{(1 - T_p)}\right]$$

You should be able to see that in the simple case where $\delta = 1$ and $\gamma = 1$, the equation simplifies to $V_L = V_U + D\left[1 - \dfrac{(1 - T_p)}{(1 - T_p)}\right]$. This can be further simplified to $V_L = V_U$.

However, this might not be true if *different* investors held the debt and the equity. In this case the $T_p$s could differ. For example, if tax exempt investors held all the debt their $T_p$ would be zero, and if taxable investors held all the equity their $T_p$ could be as high as 47 per cent. In that case there would be a strong incentive to issue more debt. As debt issues increased we would exhaust the capacity of tax-exempt investors to hold debt and we would then have to pay higher interest rates to attract taxable investors. As we continue issuing debt, both the tax rate of the marginal debtholder and the interest rate rise until we reach an equilibrium where $T_p$ is equal for both debt and equity holders. At this point we reach an equilibrium in which there is no tax advantage to debt.

In other words, Miller's equilibrium holds under the imputation system, provided companies pay out 100 per cent of their franked dividends ($\delta = 1$) and investors can use 100 per cent of their franking credits ($\gamma = 1$). You should experiment with the effects of different values for $\delta$, $\gamma$ and different relativities for $T_c$, $T_p$ and $T_G$. We hope that in your experimentation you are able to verify the following conclusions:

- Under the imputation system there are two obvious ways to shield corporate income from corporate tax. One way is to pay the tax and then let shareholders recover it by paying out all the taxed earnings as a franked dividend. The second way is to use debt interest to shield company earnings from tax.
- The two ways to shield earnings from tax are substitutes. For example, if you do not plan on a 100 per cent dividend payout ratio, you may be losing an opportunity to shield your investors against tax. However, you can substitute corporate borrowing instead.
- The effectiveness of the payment of franked dividends as a tax shield depends on $\gamma$. The lower $\gamma$, the less tax-effective are dividend payments and the more valuable is the debt tax shield.

## The effect of alternative tax shields

We should reconsider the assumption that the corporate tax shield on debt is a constant 36 per cent regardless of the amount borrowed. In practice few firms can be *sure* they will show a taxable profit in the future. If a firm shows a loss, its interest tax shield must be carried forward with the hope of using it later. The firm loses the time value of money while it waits. If its difficulties are deep enough, the wait may be permanent and the interest tax shield lost forever.

Notice that borrowing is not the only way to shield income against tax. For example, companies may also use depreciation for plant and equipment, or amortisation of intangible assets, in order to reduce tax. Sometimes the government allows accelerated depreciation or special investment allowances as tax deductions.[23] The more that firms shield income in these other ways, the lower the expected tax shield from borrowing.[24]

The more the firm borrows, the greater the total of interest and other deductions, and therefore the greater the chance that in some years there will be insufficient taxable income to absorb all the deductions. The greater the chance that the interest tax shield will not be fully utilised, the less it is worth.

Thus, corporate tax shields are worth more to some firms than to others.[25] Firms with plenty of non-interest tax shields and uncertain future prospects should borrow less than consistently profitable firms with lots of taxable profits to shield. Unprofitable firms with large accumulated tax loss carry-forwards should not borrow at all. When it cannot use interest tax

---

23  Note that these deductions are substitutes for interest, in that they reduce taxes without reducing the operating cash flow.

24  For a discussion of the effect of these other tax shields on company borrowing see H. DeAngelo and R. Masulis, 'Optimal Capital Structure Under Corporate and Personal Taxation', *Journal of Financial Economics*, 8: 5–29 (March 1980). Also see J. K. MacKie-Mason, 'Do Taxes Affect Corporate Financing Decisions?', *Journal of Finance*, 4: 1471–94 (December 1990).

25  Figure 18.2 no longer applies. The solid line representing the tax advantage to debt would have to slope down, and at different slopes for different firms.

shields, why should such a firm pay the higher interest rates that taxpaying investors demand to hold debt?

Under the imputation system we must also consider the opportunity for shareholders to utilise imputation credits. If the company distributes all available imputation credits to shareholders and all shareholders can use all their credits, then saving tax at the corporate level is of little or no value. In this case the tax shield is of little value to the firm. In framing its debt policy therefore the firm must consider both its dividend policy and the characteristics of its shareholders.

In practice firms may not distribute all available imputation credits, and even if they do, not all investors can fully use the credits to save personal tax. Therefore, we believe there can be a modest tax advantage to corporate borrowing, at least for companies that are reasonably sure that they can use the corporate tax shields and that some of their investors cannot fully use imputation credits. However, this advantage is likely to be smaller under an imputation tax system than under a classical tax system. For companies that do not expect to be able to use the corporate tax shields we believe there is likely to be a moderate tax disadvantage to borrowing.

## 18.3 Costs of financial distress

Financial distress occurs when promises to creditors are broken or honoured with difficulty. Sometimes financial distress leads to liquidation. Sometimes it only means skating on thin ice.

As we will see, financial distress is costly. Investors know that levered firms may fall into financial distress, and they worry about it. That worry is reflected in the current market value of the levered firm's securities. Thus, the value of the firm can be broken down into three parts:

$$\text{Value of firm} = \text{Value if all equity financed} + \text{PV tax shield} - \text{PV costs of financial distress}$$

The costs of financial distress depend on the probability of distress and the magnitude of costs encountered if distress occurs.

Figure 18.4 shows how the trade-off between the tax benefits and the costs of distress determines optimal capital structure. We assume that the PV of the tax shield initially increases as the firm borrows more. This provides the incentive to increase borrowing. At moderate debt levels the probability of financial distress is trivial, and so PV cost of financial distress is small and tax advantages dominate. But at some point the probability of financial distress increases rapidly with additional borrowing; the costs of distress begin to take a substantial bite out of firm value. Also, if the firm can't be sure of profiting from the corporate tax shield, the tax advantage of debt is likely to dwindle and eventually disappear. The theoretical optimum is reached when the present value of tax savings due to additional borrowing is just offset by increases in the present value of costs of distress.

## Financial distress costs

Let us get one thing clear from the start. Debt does not cause financial distress. What causes financial distress is a collapse in asset values below the value of the debt. This is often a result of operating problems leading to poor cash flow. In the absence of any debt in the firm shareholders would bear all the loss. In the presence of debt the shareholders and the debtholders share the loss. So when financial distress strikes the debtholders step in to try and salvage as much as they can from the wreckage. The resulting drama may make it appear that too much debt is the main culprit, whereas the real problem is too little cash flow. It is true, however, that higher levels of debt do increase the risk of financial distress. This is because a higher cash flow is required to service the debt.

You rarely hear anything nice said about corporate financial distress. But there is some good in almost everything. Corporate receiverships occur when shareholders exercise their

**figure 18.4**
The value of the firm is equal to its value if all equity financed plus the present value of the tax shield less the present value of the costs of financial distress.

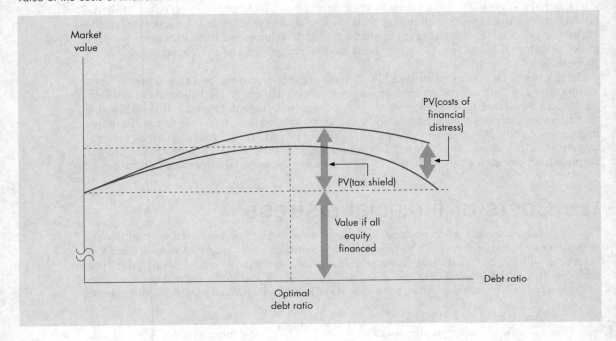

*right to default.* That right is valuable; when a firm gets into trouble, limited liability allows shareholders simply to walk away from it, leaving all its troubles to its creditors. They have the right to give the assets of the firm in full consideration for the outstanding debt. The former creditors become the new shareholders, and the old shareholders are left with nothing.

In our legal system all shareholders in companies automatically enjoy limited liability. But suppose that this were not so. Suppose that there are two firms with identical assets and operations. Each firm has debt outstanding and each has promised to repay $1000 (principal and interest) next year. But only one of the firms, Ace Limited, enjoys limited liability. The other firm, Ace Unlimited, does not; its shareholders are personally liable for its debt.

Figure 18.5 compares next year's possible payoffs to the creditors and shareholders of these two firms. The only differences occur when next year's asset value turns out to be less than $1000. Suppose that next year the assets of each company are worth only $500. In this case Ace Limited defaults. Its shareholders walk away; their payoff is zero. Bondholders get the assets worth $500. But Ace Unlimited's shareholders cannot walk away. They have to cough up $500, the difference between asset value and the bondholders' claim. The debt is paid whatever happens.

Suppose that Ace Limited does go into receivership. Of course, its shareholders are disappointed that their firm is worth so little. But they, and you, should clearly understand that the problem is not caused by the debt financing: it is caused by poor operating performance. Given poor operating performance, the right to the right to default is a valuable privilege. As Figure 18.5 shows, Ace Limited's shareholders are in better shape than Unlimited's.

The example illuminates a mistake people often make in thinking about the costs of financial distress. Receiverships are thought of as corporate funerals. The mourners (creditors and especially shareholders) look at their firm's present sad state. They think of how valuable their securities used to be and how little is left. Moreover, they think of the lost value as a cost of financial distress. That is the mistake. The financial distress is merely a legal mechanism for

**figure 18.5**

Comparison of limited and unlimited liability for two otherwise identical firms. If the two firms' asset values are less than $1000, Ace Limited shareholders default and its bondholders take over the assets. Ace Unlimited shareholders keep the assets, but they must reach into their own pockets to pay off its bondholders. The total payoff to both shareholders and bondholders (shown by the 45° line) is the same for the two firms.

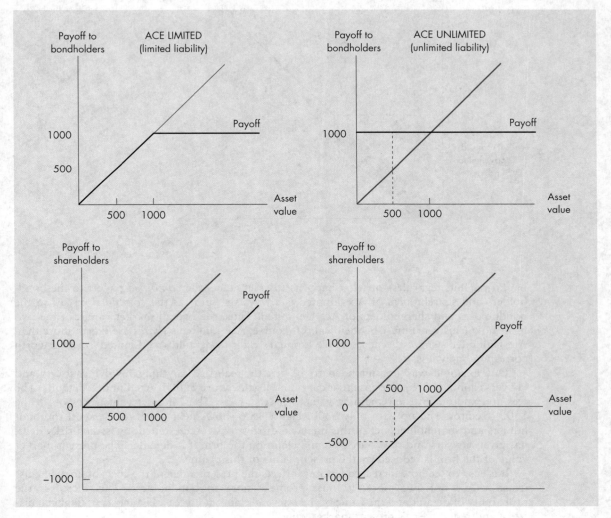

allowing creditors to take over when the decline in the value of assets triggers a default. Financial distress is not the *cause* of the decline in value.[26] It is the result.

Be careful not to get cause and effect reversed. When a person dies, we do not cite the implementation of his or her will as the cause of death (or the funeral).

We said that financial distress is a legal mechanism allowing creditors to take over when a firm defaults. Financial distress costs are the costs of using this mechanism. There are no financial distress costs at all shown in Figure 18.5. Note that only Ace Limited can default and go

---

[26]  Financial distress can, however, be the cause of further losses in value, for example when assets have to be sold quickly.

**figure 18.6**

Total payoff to Ace Limited security holders. There is a $200 bankruptcy cost in the event of default (shaded area).

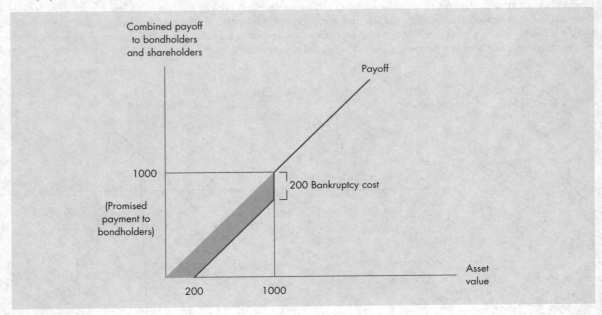

bankrupt. But, regardless of what happens to asset value, the *combined* payoff to the bondholders and shareholders of Ace Limited is always the same as the *combined* payoff to the bondholders and shareholders of Ace Unlimited. Thus, the overall market values of the two firms now (this year) must be identical. Of course, Ace Limited's *shares* are worth more than Ace Unlimited's shares because of Ace Limited's right to default. Ace Limited's *debt* is worth correspondingly less.

Our example was not intended to be strictly realistic. Anything involving courts and lawyers cannot be free. Suppose that court and legal fees are $200 if Ace Limited defaults. The fees are paid out of the remaining value of Ace's assets. Thus, if asset value turns out to be $500, creditors end up with only $300. Figure 18.6 shows next year's *total* payoff to bondholders and shareholders net of this financial distress cost. Ace Limited, by issuing risky debt, has given lawyers and the court system a claim on the firm if it defaults. The present market value of the firm is reduced by the present value of this claim.

It is easy to see how increased leverage affects the present value of the costs of financial distress. If Ace borrows more, it must promise more to bondholders. This increases the probability of default and the value of the lawyers' claim. It increases PV(costs of financial distress) and reduces Ace's present market value.

The costs of financial distress come out of the shareholders' pockets. Creditors foresee the costs and foresee that *they* will pay them if default occurs. For this they demand compensation in advance in the form of higher payoffs when the firm does *not* default. That is, they demand a higher promised interest rate. This reduces the possible payoffs to shareholders and reduces the present market value of their shares. Creditors also place restrictions on what the firm can do, as we will discuss later.

## Evidence on financial distress costs

Lawyers are generally well paid so the costs of legal action associated with financial distress can add up fast. Then there are the costs of the receiver/liquidator to cover. Sometimes the costs consume all the company's remaining assets, with the result that there is nothing left over for the creditors. On average, however, it appears that financial distress costs are not a large proportion of the pre-distress value of the company's assets. Lawrence Weiss, who studied 31 firms that went bankrupt between 1980 and 1986, found average costs of about 3 per cent of total assets. Similar results for Australia are reported by Pham and Chow, with the costs of bankruptcy at 3.6 per cent of company value. A study by Edward Altman found that costs were similar for retail companies but higher for industrial companies.[27] Also, financial distress eats up a larger fraction of asset value for small companies than for large ones.[28] There are significant economies of scale in going into liquidation.

If, on average, the actual cost of financial distress is a small fraction of asset value, then the expected cost is even smaller. This is because the actual cost must be weighted by the probability of financial distress. The probability of financial distress is less than 1 per cent for an average company, but let us assume it is 1 per cent. If we take 3.5 per cent to be the average distress cost, then the expected cost of financial distress is $0.01 \times 0.035 = 0.00035$. This is a trivial fraction of the asset value of a healthy firm, and the discounted present value will be less again. So why all the fuss about financial distress costs? There must be something more to the story.

# Direct versus indirect costs of financial distress

So far we have discussed the *direct* (i.e. legal and administrative) costs of financial distress. There are indirect costs too. The indirect costs reflect the difficulties of running a company while it is going through financial distress. Management's efforts to prevent further deterioration in the firm's business are often undermined by the delays and legal tangles that go with financial distress as a legal process. The creditors are primarily concerned with the quickest and least risky way of getting their money back, not maximising the value of the company. The creditors may therefore veto activities which are good for the company but are not directly in their interests. There are also costs associated with the response of customers and suppliers to the news that a company is in financial distress.

The indirect costs are nearly impossible to measure. But Altman, and Pham and Chow, have made a brave attempt to estimate them.[29] Their estimates were in excess of 20 per cent of the company's asset value. We also have circumstantial evidence indicating the importance of financial distress costs. For example, some years ago Chrysler shut down its Australian car operations and for several years Chrysler cars disappeared from Australian car sales yards. Why? Because the American parent company was in financial distress. Would you buy a car from a financially-distressed car manufacturer? You might, but your concern about quality standards and the availability of after-sales service and spare parts would probably lead you to demand a substantial price discount relative to similar cars produced by other manufacturers. If you were BHP would you have been allowing Chrysler plenty of credit to buy steel? Probably not; you might instead have demanded cash on delivery. The effect of such indirect costs for Chrysler was that the cost of doing business in Australia just became too great.

We do not know exactly what the sum of direct and indirect costs of financial distress amounts to. We suspect it is a significant number, particularly for large firms for which legal proceedings would be lengthy and complex. Perhaps the best evidence is the reluctance of creditors to force liquidation. In principle, they would be better off to end the agony and seize the

---

[27] The pioneering study of financial distress costs is J. B. Warner, 'Bankruptcy Costs: Some Evidence', *Journal of Finance*, **26**: 337–48 (May 1977). The Weiss and Altman papers are L. A. Weiss, 'Bankruptcy Resolution: Direct Costs and Violation of Priority of Claims', *Journal of Financial Economics*, **27**: 285–314 (October 1990) and E. I. Altman, 'A Further Investigation of the Bankruptcy Cost Question', *Journal of Finance*, **39**: 1067–89 (September 1984). Also see T. Pham and D. Chow, 'Some Estimates of Direct and Indirect Bankruptcy Costs in Australia: September 1978–May 1983', *Australian Journal of Management*, 75–95 (June 1987).

[28] D. K. Robertson and R. B. Tress ['Bankruptcy Costs: Evidence from Small-Firm Liquidations', *Australian Journal of Management*, 49–60 (June 1985)] show that for small firms in Australia the costs of liquidation consume most of the assets.

[29] See Footnote 27 for the references.

assets as soon as possible. Instead, creditors often overlook defaults in the hope of nursing the firm over a difficult period. They do this in part to avoid the costs of financial distress.[30] There is an old financial saying, 'Borrow $1000 and you've got a banker. Borrow $10 000 000 and you've got a partner.'

## Financial distress without liquidation

Not every firm that gets into trouble goes into receivership or liquidation. As long as the firm can scrape up enough cash to pay the interest on its debt, it may be able to postpone financial distress for many years. Eventually the firm may recover, pay off its debt and escape financial distress altogether.

When a firm is in trouble, both bondholders and shareholders want it to recover, but in other respects their interests may be in conflict. In times of financial distress the security holders are like many political parties—united on generalities but threatened by squabbling on any specific issue.

Financial distress is costly when these conflicts of interest get in the way of proper operating, investment and financing decisions. Shareholders are tempted to forsake the usual objective of maximising the overall market value of the firm and to pursue narrower self-interest instead. They are tempted to play games at the expense of their creditors. We will now illustrate how such games can lead to costs of financial distress.

Here is the Circular File Company's present book balance sheet:

| Circular File Company (book values) | | | |
|---|---|---|---|
| Net working capital | $20 | $50 | Bonds outstanding |
| Fixed assets | 80 | 50 | Ordinary shares |
| Total assets | $100 | $100 | Total liabilities |

We will assume there is only one share and one bond outstanding. The shareholder is also the manager. The bondholder is somebody else.

Here is its balance sheet in market values—a clear case of financial distress, since the face value of Circular's debt ($50) exceeds the firm's total market value ($30):

| Circular File Company (market values) | | | |
|---|---|---|---|
| Net working capital | $20 | $25 | Bonds outstanding |
| Fixed assets | 10 | 5 | Ordinary shares |
| Total assets | $30 | $30 | Total liabilities |

If the debt matured today, Circular's owner would default, leaving the firm to the debtholders. But suppose that the bond actually matures one year hence, that there is enough cash for Circular to limp along for one year and that the bondholder cannot 'call the question' and force liquidation before then.

---

[30] There is another reason. Creditors are not always given absolute priority in court approved reorganisations. Absolute priority means that creditors must be paid in full before shareholders receive a cent. Sometimes reorganisations are negotiated which provide 'something for everyone', even though creditors are *not* paid in full. Thus, creditors can never be sure how they will fare in the event that they attempt to force a liquidation.

The one-year grace period explains why the Circular share still has value. Its owner is betting on a stroke of luck that will rescue the firm, allowing it to pay off the debt with something left over. The bet is a long shot—the owner wins only if firm value increases from $30 to more than $50.[31] But the owner has a secret weapon: He controls investment and operating strategy.

# Risk shifting: the first game

Suppose that Circular has $10 cash. The following investment opportunity comes up:

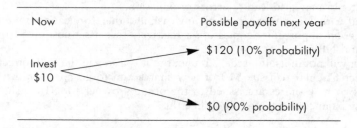

| Now | Possible payoffs next year |
|---|---|
| Invest $10 | $120 (10% probability) |
| | $0 (90% probability) |

This is a wild gamble and probably a lousy project. But you can see why the owner would be tempted to take it anyway. Why not go for broke? Circular will probably go under anyway, and so the owner is essentially betting with the bondholder's money. But the owner gets most of the loot if the project pays off. One example of this is when Bond Corporation spent more than a year fighting its creditors in the courts. There was little chance of success, but had Bond Corporation succeeded the payoff would have been enormous, while if they lost, it was really the creditors' money that had been used to pay the legal bills.

Suppose that the project's NPV is −$2 but that it is undertaken anyway, thus depressing firm value by $2. Circular's new balance sheet might look like this:

| Circular File Company (market values) | | | |
|---|---|---|---|
| Net working capital | $10 | $20 | Bonds outstanding |
| Fixed assets | 18 | 8 | Ordinary shares |
| Total assets | $28 | $28 | Total liabilities |

Firm value falls by $2, but the owner is $3 ahead because the bond's value has fallen by $5.[32] The $10 cash that used to stand behind the bond has been replaced by a very risky asset worth only $8. The more the value of the bond falls, the greater the gain to the owners. There was a suggestion, for example, that Bond Corporation should repurchase its debt at market value. This would have saved over a billion dollars compared to repaying the debt at face value. The problem, of course, is finding someone to finance such a transaction.

In our example above a game has been played at the expense of Circular's bondholder. The game illustrates the following general point. Shareholders of levered firms gain when business risk increases. Financial managers who act strictly in their shareholders' interests (and *against* the interests of creditors) will favour risky projects over safe ones. They may even take risky projects with negative NPVs.

---

[31]  We are not concerned here with how to work out whether $5 is a fair price for shareholders to pay for the bet. We will come to that in Chapter 20 when we discuss the valuation of options.

[32]  We are not calculating this $5 drop. We are simply using it as a plausible assumption. The tools necessary for calculation come in Chapter 20.

This warped strategy for capital budgeting clearly is costly to the firm and to the economy as a whole. Why do we associate the costs with financial distress? Because the temptation to play is strongest when the odds of default are high. National Australia Bank would never invest in our negative NPV gamble. Its creditors are not vulnerable to this type of game.

## Refusing to contribute equity capital: the second game

We have seen how shareholders, acting in their immediate, narrow self-interest, may take projects which reduce the overall market value of their firm. These are errors of commission. Conflicts of interest may also lead to errors of omission.

Assume that Circular cannot scrape up any cash and therefore cannot take that wild gamble. Instead a *good* opportunity comes up: a relatively safe asset costing $10 with a present value of $15 and NPV = +$5.

This project will not in itself rescue Circular, but it is a step in the right direction. We might therefore expect Circular to issue $10 of new shares and to go ahead with the investment. Suppose that two new shares are issued to the original owner for $10 cash. The project is taken. The new balance sheet might look like this:

| Circular File Company (market values) | | | |
| --- | --- | --- | --- |
| Net working capital | $20 | $33 | Bonds outstanding |
| Fixed assets | 25 | 12 | Ordinary shares |
| Total assets | $45 | $45 | Total liabilities |

The total value of the firm goes up by $15 ($10 of new capital and $5 NPV). Notice that the Circular bond is no longer worth $25, but $33. The bondholder receives a capital gain of $8 because the firm's assets include a new, safe asset worth $15. The probability of default is less and the payoff to the bondholder if default occurs is larger.

The shareholder loses what the bondholder gains. Equity value goes up not by $15, but by $15 − $8 = $7. The owner puts in $10 of fresh equity capital but gains only $7 in market value. Going ahead is in the firm's interest, but not the owner's.

Again, our example illustrates a general point. If we hold business risk constant, any increase in firm value is shared among bondholders and shareholders. The value of any investment opportunity *to the firm's shareholders* is reduced because project benefits must be shared with bondholders. Thus, it may not be in the shareholders' self-interest to contribute fresh equity capital even if that means forgoing positive NPV investment opportunities.

This problem theoretically affects all levered firms, but it is most serious when firms land in financial distress. The greater the probability of default, the more bondholders have to gain from investments which increase firm value.

## And three more games, briefly

As with other games, the temptation to play is particularly strong in financial distress:

1. *Cash in and run*: Shareholders may be reluctant to put money into a firm in financial distress, but they are happy to take the money out—in the form of a cash dividend, for example. The market value of the firm's shares goes down by less than the amount of the dividend paid, because the decline in *firm* value is shared with creditors. This game is just 'refusing to contribute equity capital' run in reverse.

2. *Playing for time*: When the firm is in financial distress, creditors would like to salvage what they can by forcing the firm to settle up. Naturally, shareholders want to delay this

as long as they can. There are various devious ways of doing this—for example, through accounting changes designed to conceal the true extent of trouble, by encouraging false hopes of spontaneous recovery or by cutting corners on maintenance, research and development, etc, in order to make this year's operating performance look better.

**3.** *Bait and switch*: This game is not always played in financial distress, but it is a quick way to get *into* distress. You start with a conservative policy, issuing a limited amount of relatively safe debt. Then you suddenly switch and issue a lot more. That makes all your debt risky, imposing a capital loss on the 'old' bondholders. Their capital loss is the shareholders' gain.

The most dramatic example of bait and switch occurred in October 1988, when the management of RJR Nabisco announced its intention to acquire the company in a *leveraged buy-out* (LBO). This put the company 'in play' for a transaction in which existing shareholders would be bought out and the company 'taken private'. The cost of the buy-out would be almost entirely debt-financed. The new private company would start life with an extremely high debt ratio.

RJR Nabisco had debt outstanding with a market value of about $2.4 billion. The announcement of the coming LBO drove down this market value by $298 million.[33]

# What the games cost

Why should anyone object to these games so long as they are played by consenting adults? Because playing them means poor decisions about investments and operations. These poor decisions are part of the agency costs of borrowing.

The more the firm borrows, the greater the temptation to play the games (assuming the financial manager acts in the shareholders' interest). The increased odds of poor decisions in the future prompt investors to mark down the present market value of the firm. The fall in value comes out of shareholders' pockets. Potential lenders, realising that games may be played at their expense, protect themselves by demanding better terms.

Therefore, it is ultimately in the shareholders' interest to avoid temptation. The easiest way to do this is to limit borrowing to levels at which the firm's debt is safe or close to it.

But suppose that the tax advantages of debt spur the firm on to a high debt ratio and a significant probability of default or financial distress. Is there any way to convince potential lenders that games will not be played? The obvious answer is to give lenders veto power over potentially dangerous decisions.

There we have the ultimate economic rationale for all that fine print, the debt covenants, backing up corporate debt. Debt contracts almost always limit dividends or equivalent transfers of wealth to shareholders; the firm may not be allowed to pay out more than it earns, for example. Additional borrowing is almost always limited. For example, many companies are prevented by existing bond indentures from issuing any additional long-term debt unless their ratio of earnings to interest charges exceeds 2.0. There is often a requirement that any new debt issued shall be subordinate to the existing debt. Sometimes companies will offer a negative pledge, where they promise that any debt issued will be unsecured.[34] By agreeing to debt covenants the company is bonding itself to behave in certain ways. Because the company's freedom of action is restricted additional costs are imposed on the company. These costs are a form of agency costs, known as bonding costs.

Sometimes firms are restricted from selling assets or making major investment outlays except with the lenders' consent. The risks of 'playing for time' are reduced by specifying accounting procedures and by giving lenders access to the firm's books and its financial forecasts.

---

[33] We thank Paul Asquith for these figures. RJR Nabisco was finally taken private not by its management but by another LBO partnership.

[34] RJR Nabisco bondholders might have done better if they had effective covenants to protect them against drastic increases in financial leverage. We discuss covenants and the rest of the fine print in debt contracts in Section 24.5.

Of course, fine print cannot be a complete solution for firms that insist on issuing risky debt. The fine print has its own costs; you have to spend money to save money. Obviously, a complex debt contract costs more to negotiate than a simple one. Afterwards it costs the lender more to monitor the firm's performance. Lenders anticipate monitoring costs and demand compensation in the form of higher interest rates; thus the monitoring costs—another agency cost of debt—are ultimately paid by shareholders.

Perhaps the most severe costs of the fine print stem from the constraints it places on operating and investment decisions. For example, an attempt to prevent the 'risk shifting' game may also prevent the firm from pursuing *good* investment opportunities. At the minimum there are delays in clearing major investments with lenders. In some cases lenders may veto high-risk investments even if NPV is positive. Lenders can lose from risk shifting even when the firm's overall market value increases. In fact, lenders may try to play a game of their own, forcing the firm to stay in cash or low-risk assets even if good projects are forgone.

Thus, debt contracts cannot cover every possible manifestation of the games we have just discussed. Any attempt to do so would be hopelessly expensive and doomed to failure in any event. Human imagination is insufficient to conceive of all the possible things that could go wrong. We will always find surprises coming at us on dimensions we never thought to think about.

We hope we have not left the impression that managers and shareholders always succumb to temptation unless restrained. Usually they refrain voluntarily, not only from a sense of fair play, but also on pragmatic grounds: A firm or individual that makes a killing today at the expense of a creditor will be coldly received when the time comes to borrow again. Aggressive game playing is done only by out-and-out crooks and by firms in extreme financial distress. Firms limit borrowing precisely because they do not wish to land in distress and be exposed to the temptation to play.

## Costs of distress vary with type of asset

Suppose your firm's only asset is a large downtown hotel, mortgaged to the hilt. The recession hits, occupancy rates fall and the mortgage payments cannot be met. The lender takes over and sells the hotel to a new owner and operator. You use your firm's share certificates for wallpaper.

What is the cost of financial distress? In this example, probably very little. The value of the hotel is, of course, much less than you hoped, but that is due to the lack of guests, not to the financial distress. Financial distress does not damage the hotel itself. The direct financial distress costs are restricted to items such as legal and court fees, real estate commissions and the time the lender spends sorting things out.

Suppose we repeat the story of Heartbreak Hotel for Fledgling Electronics. Everything is the same, except for the underlying real assets—not real estate but a high-tech going concern, a growth company whose most valuable assets are technology, investment opportunities and its employees' human capital.

If Fledgling gets into trouble, the shareholders may be reluctant to put up money to cash in on its growth opportunities. Failure to invest is likely to be much more serious for Fledgling than for a company like Heartbreak Hotel.

If Fledgling finally defaults on its debt, the lender would find it much more difficult to cash in by selling off the assets. Many of them are intangible assets which have value only as a part of a going concern. If the entity disappears, so do the intangibles.

Could Fledgling be kept as a going concern through default and reorganisation? It may not be hopeless, but there are a number of serious difficulties. The odds of defections by key employees are higher than if the firm had never got into financial trouble. Special guarantees may have to be given to customers who are doubtful whether the firm will be around to service its products. Aggressive investment in new products and technology will be difficult; each class of creditors will have to be convinced that it is in their interest for the firm to invest money in risky ventures. In short, it will not only be difficult to keep going, but also costly.

Some assets, like good commercial real estate, can pass through financial distress and reorganisation largely unscathed; the values of other assets are likely to be considerably diminished. The losses are greatest for the intangible assets that are linked to the health of the firm as a going concern—for example, technology, human capital and brand image. That may be why debt ratios are low in the pharmaceutical industry, where value depends on continued success in research and development, and in many service industries where value depends on human capital. We can also understand why highly profitable growth companies, such as Microsoft, use mostly equity finance.[35]

The moral of these examples is: *Do not think only about the probability that borrowing will bring trouble. Think also of the value that may be lost if trouble comes.*

# The trade-off theory of capital structure

Financial managers sometimes think of the firm's debt-equity decision as a trade-off between interest tax shields and the costs of financial distress. Of course, there is controversy about how valuable interest tax shields are and what kinds of financial trouble are most threatening, but these disagreements are only variations on a theme. Thus, Figure 18.4 illustrates the debt-equity trade-off.

This *trade-off theory* of capital structure recognises that target debt ratios may vary from firm to firm. Companies with safe, tangible assets and plenty of taxable income to shield ought to have high target ratios. Unprofitable companies with risky, intangible assets ought to rely primarily on equity financing.

If there were no costs of adjusting capital structure, then each firm should always be at its target debt ratio. However, there are costs, and therefore delays, in adjusting to the optimum. Firms cannot immediately offset the random events that bump them away from their capital structure targets, so we should see random differences in actual debt ratios among firms having the same target debt ratio.

All in all, this trade-off theory of capital structure choice tells a comforting story. Unlike MM's theory, which seemed to say that firms should take on as much debt as possible, it avoids extreme predictions and rationalises moderate debt ratios.

But what are the facts? Can the trade-off theory of capital structure explain how companies actually behave?

The answer is 'yes and no'. On the 'yes' side the trade-off theory successfully explains many industry differences in capital structure. High-tech growth companies, for example, whose assets are risky and mostly intangible, normally use relatively little debt. Airlines can and do borrow heavily because their assets are tangible and relatively safe.[36]

The trade-off theory also helps explain what kinds of companies 'go private' in leveraged buy-outs (LBOs). LBOs are acquisitions of public companies by private investors who finance a large fraction of the purchase price with debt. The target companies for LBO takeovers are usually mature 'cash cow' businesses with established markets for their products, but little in the way of high NPV growth opportunities. That makes sense by the trade-off theory, because these are exactly the kind of companies that *ought* to have high debt ratios.

The trade-off theory also says that companies saddled with extra heavy debt—too much to pay down with a couple of years internally generated cash—should issue shares, constrain dividends or sell off assets to raise cash to rebalance capital structure. Here again we can find confirming examples. Chrysler, when it emerged from near-financial distress in 1983, sold $432 million of new shares to help regain a conservative capital structure.[37] In 1991, after a

---

[35]  Recent empirical research confirms that firms holding largely intangible assets borrow less. See M. Long and I. Malitz, 'The Investment-Financing Nexus: Some Empirical Evidence', *Midland Corporate Finance Journal*, 3: 53–9 (Fall 1985).

[36]  We are not suggesting that all airline *companies* are safe; many are not. But air*craft* can support debt where air*lines* cannot. If Fly-by-Night Airlines fails, its aeroplanes retain their value in another airline's operations. There is a good secondary market in used aircraft, so a loan secured by aircraft can be well-protected even if made to an airline flying on thin ice (and in the dark).

[37]  Note that Chrysler issued shares *after* it emerged from financial distress. It did not *prevent* financial distress by raising equity money when trouble loomed on its horizon. Why not? Refer back to 'Refusing to contribute equity capital: the second game' in Section 18.3, or forward to the analysis of asymmetric information in Section 18.4.

second brush with financial distress, it again sold shares to replenish equity, this time for $350 million.[38]

On the 'no' side, there are other things the trade-off theory cannot explain. It cannot explain why some of the most successful companies thrive with little debt—pharmaceutical companies, for example. Granted their most valuable assets are intangible: the fruits of pharmaceutical research and development. We know that intangible assets and conservative capital structures tend to go together. But some pharmaceutical companies also have a very large corporate income tax bill and very high credit ratings. They could borrow enough to save tens of millions of tax dollars without raising a whisker of concern about possible financial distress.[39]

There is an odd fact about real-life capital structures: within an industry, the most profitable companies generally borrow the least.[40] Here the trade-off theory fails, for it predicts exactly the reverse. Under the trade-off theory, high profits should mean more debt-servicing capacity and more taxable income to shield and should give a *higher* target debt ratio.[41]

Two final points on the 'no' side for the trade-off theory. First, debt ratios in the early 1900s in the United States were just as high as in the 1990s. Yet in the early 1900s income tax rates were low (or zero). Second, debt ratios in several industrialised countries, such as Australia which has an imputation system, are equal to or higher than debt ratios in the United States. As we discussed earlier in the chapter an imputation system is likely to reduce, or eliminate, the value of the interest tax shields. Therefore, we would expect countries with an imputation system to have lower corporate debt ratios than the United States.

None of this disproves the trade-off theory. As George Stigler emphasised, theories are not rejected by circumstantial evidence; it takes a theory to beat a theory. So we now turn to a completely different theory of financing.

## 18.4 The pecking order of financing choices

The pecking order theory starts with *asymmetric information*—a fancy way of noting that managers know more about their companies' prospects, risks and values than outside investors.

Managers obviously know more than investors do. We can prove that by observing that share price changes are caused by managers' announcements. When a company announces an increased regular dividend, share price typically rises, because investors interpret the increase as a sign of management's confidence in future earnings. In other words, the dividend increase transfers information from managers to investors. This can only happen if managers know more in the first place.

Asymmetric information affects the choice between internal and external financing and between new issues of debt and equity securities. This leads to a *pecking order*, in which investment is financed first with internal funds, reinvested earnings primarily; then by new issues of debt; and finally with new issues of equity. New equity issues are a last resort when the company runs out of debt capacity, that is, when the threat of costs of financial distress brings regular insomnia to existing creditors and to the financial manager.

---

[38]  Chrysler simultaneously contributed US$300 million of newly-issued shares to its underfunded pension plans.

[39]  Research by Graham and Mackie-Mason has detected a tendency for tax-paying firms to prefer debt financing. See J. R. Graham, 'Debt and the Marginal Tax Rate', *Journal of Financial Economics*, 41: 41–73 (1996), and J. Mackie-Mason, 'Do Taxes Affect Corporate Financing Decisions?', *Journal of Finance*, 45: 1471–93 (December 1990). However, it seems clear that public companies rarely make major shifts in debt ratios just in pursuit of taxes.

[40]  For example, Carl Kester, in a study of the financing policies of firms in the United States and in Japan, found that in each country high book profitability was the most statistically significant variable distinguishing low- from high-debt companies. See 'Capital and Ownership Structure: A Comparison of United States and Japanese Manufacturing Corporations', *Financial Management*, 15: 5–16 (Spring 1986).

[41]  Here we mean debt as a fraction of the book or replacement value of the company's assets. Profitable companies might not borrow a greater fraction of their market value. Higher profits imply higher market value as well as stronger incentives to borrow.

We will take a closer look at the pecking order in a moment. First, you must appreciate how asymmetric information can force the financial manager to issue debt rather than shares.

## Debt and equity issues with asymmetric information

To the outside world Smith & Co and Jones & Boyo, our two example companies, have each had identical performance. Each runs a successful business with good growth opportunities. The two businesses are risky, however, and investors have learned from experience that current expectations are frequently bettered or disappoint.

Current expectations price each company's shares at $100 per share, but the true values could be higher or lower.

|  | Smith & Co | Jones & Boyo |
|---|---|---|
| True value could be higher, say | $120 | $120 |
| Best current estimate | 100 | 100 |
| True value could be lower, say | 80 | 80 |

Now suppose that both companies need to raise new money from investors to fund capital investment. There are two choices: issue bonds or issue new shares. How would the choice be made?

One financial manager—we will not tell you which one—might reason as follows: 'Sell shares for $100 per share? Ridiculous! They are worth at least $120. A share issue now would hand a free gift to new investors. I just wish those stupid, sceptical shareholders would appreciate the true value of this company. Our new factories will make us the world's lowest-cost producer. We've painted a rosy picture for the press and security analysts, but it just doesn't seem to be working. Oh well, the decision is obvious: we'll issue debt, not underpriced equity. A debt issue will save underwriting fees too.'

The other financial manager is in a different mood: 'Beefalo burgers were a hit for a while, but it looks like the fad is fading. The fast food division's got to find some good new products or it's all downhill from here. Export markets are OK for now, but how are we going to compete with those new Siberian ranches? Fortunately, the share price has held up pretty well—we've had some good short-run news for the press and security analysts. Now's the time to issue shares. We have major investments underway, and why add increased debt service to my other worries?'

Of course, outside investors cannot read the financial managers' minds. If they could, one share might trade at $120 and the other $80.

Why does not the optimistic financial manager simply educate investors? Then the company could sell shares on fair terms, and there would be no reason to favour debt over equity, or vice versa.

This is not so easy. (Note that both companies are issuing upbeat press releases.) Investors cannot be told what to think; they have to be convinced. That takes a detailed layout of the company's plans and prospects, including the inside scoop on new technology, product design, marketing plans, etc. Getting this across is expensive for the company and also helps its competitors. Why go to the trouble? Investors will learn soon enough as revenues and earnings evolve. In the meantime the optimistic financial manager can finance growth by issuing debt.

Now suppose there are two press releases.

▌ Jones & Boyo will issue $120 million of five-year senior notes.
▌ Smith & Co announced plans today to issue 120 million new shares of common share. The company expects to raise $120 million.

As a rational investor, you immediately learn two things. First, Jones' financial manager is optimistic and Smith's is pessimistic. Second, Smith's financial manager is also stupid to think that investors would pay $100 per share. The *attempt* to sell shares shows that it must be worth less. Smith might sell shares at $80 per share, but certainly not at $100.[42]

Smart financial managers think this through ahead of time. The end result? Both Smith and Jones end up issuing debt. Jones & Boyo issues debt because its financial manager is optimistic and does not want to issue undervalued equity. A smart, but pessimistic, financial manager at Smith & Co issues debt because an attempt to issue equity would force the share price down and eliminate any advantage from doing so. (Issuing equity also reveals the manager's pessimism immediately. Most managers prefer to wait. A debt issue lets bad news come out later through other channels.)

The story of Smith and Jones illustrates how asymmetric information favours debt issues over equity issues. If managers are better informed than investors and both are rational, then any company that can borrow will do so rather than issuing fresh equity. In other words, debt issues will be higher in the pecking order.

Taken literally, this reasoning seems to rule out any issue of equity. That is not right, because asymmetric information is not always important and there are other forces at work. For example, if Smith had already borrowed heavily, and would risk financial distress by borrowing more, then it would have a good reason to issue ordinary shares. In this case, announcement of a share issue would not be entirely bad news. The announcement would still depress share price—it would highlight managers' concerns about financial distress—but the fall in price would not necessarily make the issue unwise or infeasible.

High-tech, high-growth companies can also be credible issuers of ordinary shares. Such companies' assets are mostly intangible, and financial distress would be especially costly. This calls for conservative financing. The only way to grow rapidly and keep a conservative debt ratio is to issue equity. If investors see equity issued for these reasons, problems of the sort encountered by Jones' financial manager become much less serious.

With such exceptions noted, asymmetric information can explain the dominance of debt financing over new equity issues in practice.[43] Debt issues are frequent; equity issues rare. The bulk of external financing comes from debt, even in the countries with well-developed equity markets that are highly information-efficient. Equity issues are even more difficult in countries with less well-developed share markets.

An equity issue can be bad news in other ways as well. It is a signal that the company needs cash and is not confident of generating that cash from operations. This looks like bad news unless the cash is needed to finance an unexpected investment opportunity. Investors may start to wonder whether previous dividend increases were a reliable signal about firm value. Perhaps the equity issue is to recover the extra cash that was paid out.

All this reminds us of the difficulty in valuing equity. Which in turn is what makes us worry about opportunistic behaviour by managers trying to issue overvalued shares. If we could be confident in our equity valuation we would not be exposed to this risk. An advantage of debt is that it is much easier to value than equity, and so with debt issues we can worry less about the chance of a valuation error that can be exploited by opportunistic managers. Debt may even be a somewhat reassuring signal about cash flow. After all, we would not usually expect managers to commit to increased cash outflows for debt service if cash flow prospects look grim.[44]

None of this says that firms ought to strive for high debt ratios, just that it is better to raise equity by ploughing back earnings rather than issuing shares. In fact, a firm with ample internally-generated funds does not have to sell any kind of security and thus avoids issue costs and information problems completely.

---

[42]   Smith's share issue might not succeed even at $80. Persistence in trying to sell at $80 could convince investors that the share is worth even less!

[43]   For a rigorous explanation of the theory see S. C. Myers and N. S. Majluf, 'Corporate Financing and Investment Decisions When Firms Have Information Investors Do Not Have', *Journal of Financial Economics*, **13**: 187–222 (June 1984).

[44]   We have to note, however, that even debt issues can create information problems if the odds of default are significant. A pessimistic manager may try to issue debt quickly, before bad news gets out. An optimistic manager will delay pending good news, perhaps arranging a short-term bank loan in the meantime. Rational investors will take this behaviour into account in pricing the risky debt issue.

# Implications of the pecking order

The pecking order theory of corporate finance goes like this.[45]

1. Firms prefer internal finance.
2. They adapt their target dividend payout ratios to their investment opportunities, while trying to avoid sudden changes in dividends.
3. Sticky dividend policies, plus unpredictable fluctuations in profitability and investment opportunities, mean that internally-generated cash flow is sometimes more than capital expenditures and at other times less. If it is more, the firm pays off debt or invests in marketable securities. If it is less, the firm first draws down its cash balance or sells its marketable securities.
4. If external finance is required, firms issue the safest security first. That is, they start with debt, then possibly hybrid securities such as convertible bonds, then perhaps equity as a last resort.

In this story, there is no well-defined target debt-equity mix, because there are two kinds of equity, internal and external, one at the top of the pecking order and one at the bottom. Each firm's observed debt ratio reflects its cumulative requirements for external finance.

Notice that although the pecking order theory is based on asymmetric information the ranking (retained earnings, debt issue, equity issue) is exactly the pecking order that you would get if you wanted to minimise the transactions costs of the issue. The two effects tend to reinforce each other. If you want to minimise total costs—that is, transactions costs and the cost of adverse price response to the security issue—then you will follow the pecking order.[46]

The pecking order explains why the most profitable firms generally borrow less—not because they have low target debt ratios, but because they do not need outside money. Less profitable firms issue debt because they do not have internal funds sufficient for their capital investment program, and because debt financing is first on the pecking order of *external* financing.

In the pecking order theory, the attraction of interest tax shields is assumed to be a second-order effect. Debt ratios change when there is an imbalance of internal cash flow, net of dividends, and real investment opportunities. Highly profitable firms with limited investment opportunities work down to a low debt ratio. Firms whose investment opportunities outrun internally-generated funds are driven to borrow more and more.

This theory explains the inverse intra-industry relationship between profitability and financial leverage. Suppose firms generally invest to keep up with the growth of their industries. Then rates of investment will be similar within an industry. Given sticky dividend payouts, the least profitable firms will have less internal funds and will end up borrowing more.

The pecking order seems to do a good job in predicting changes in many mature firms' debt ratios. These companies' debt ratios increase when they have financial deficits and decline when they have surpluses. If asymmetric information makes major equity issues or retirements[47] rare, this behaviour is nearly inevitable.

The pecking order is less successful in explaining inter-industry differences in debt ratios. For example, debt ratios tend to be low in high-tech, high-growth industries, even when the need for external capital is great. There are also mature, stable industries—electric utilities, for example—in which ample cash flow is not used to pay down debt. High dividend payout ratios give the cash flow back to investors instead.

---

[45] The description is paraphrased from S. C. Myers, 'The Capital Structure Puzzle', *Journal of Finance*, **39**: 581–2 (July 1984). For the most part, this section follows Myers' arguments.

[46] The cost of the price effect can be large. Suppose you have a $1 billion firm issuing $100 million of equity and the news causes prices to fall by 3 per cent. Since the price fall is across the total value of the firm, the cost is $30 million, or 30 per cent of the equity raised.

[47] Companies with low debt ratios and surplus cash sometimes buy back shares, but ordinary buybacks rarely cause material increases in debt ratios.

# Financial slack

Other things being equal, it is better to be at the top of the pecking order than at the bottom. Firms which have worked down the pecking order and need external equity may end up living with excessive equity, or passing up good investments because shares cannot be sold at what managers consider a fair price.

In other words, *financial slack* is valuable. Financial slack means cash, marketable securities, readily saleable real assets and ready access to the debt markets or to bank financing. Ready access basically requires conservative financing, so that potential lenders see the company's debt as a safe investment.

In the long run, a company's value rests more on its capital investment and operating decisions than on financing. Therefore, you want to make sure your firm has sufficient financial slack, so that financing is quickly available for good investments. Financial slack is most valuable to firms with plenty of positive NPV growth opportunities. That is another reason why growth companies usually aspire to conservative capital structures.

David Allen, in a series of interviews with financial managers of large Australian companies, found that in more than 90 per cent of these companies there was a policy of maintaining spare debt capacity. He also found a preference for internal financing and a reluctance to make new share issues, with debt being preferred if external finance had to be raised.[48] All this lines up nicely with the pecking order theory. But David Allen also found that 85 per cent of his sample considered taxes to have a major influence in structuring financing, and that three-quarters of the companies had a target debt ratio. So perhaps reality is a blend of the trade-off and the pecking order theories of capital structure.[49]

# Free cash flow and the dark side of financial slack[50]

Both theory and practice suggest the use of financial slack, but it does have a dark side. Too much of it may encourage managers to take it easy, expand their perks or empire-build with cash that should be paid back to shareholders. This risk of undisciplined use is a disadvantage to financing with retained earnings. When you raise finance externally you have to convince the market that it will be put to good use.

Michael Jensen has stressed the tendency of managers with ample free cash flow (or unnecessary financial slack) to plough too much cash into mature businesses or ill-advised acquisitions. 'The problem', Jensen says, 'is how to motivate managers to disgorge the cash rather than investing it below the cost of capital or wasting it in organisational inefficiencies.'[51]

One solution is for the firm to commit to a dividend policy that distributes the excess cash. Of course, this will lack credibility if there are frequent dividend cuts. In this context, a policy of avoiding dividend cuts makes sense. However, the discipline that this imposes lacks teeth. At the end of the day, if managers do cut dividends there is not a lot that shareholders can do about it.

Maybe debt is the answer. Scheduled interest and principal payments are contractual obligations of the firm. Managers have no choice—debt forces the firm to pay out cash. Perhaps

---

48  See D. E. Allen, 'The Determinants of the Capital Structure of Listed Australian Companies: The Financial Managers Perspective', *Australian Journal of Management*, 16: 104–27 (December 1991). A similar result with regard to financing choices can be found in Graham H. Partington, 'Dividend Policy And Its Relationship To Investment And Financing Policies: Empirical Evidence', *Journal of Business Finance And Accounting*, 12: 531–42 (1985).

49  It is possible to interpret the results on tax and debt ratios in a way consistent with the pecking order theory. Many of the companies faced a restriction, imposed by lenders, that placed an upper limit on the proportion of debt in the company's capital structure. Faced with such a restriction, and wanting to maintain some spare debt capacity, it would be sensible to set a debt target some distance below the lender's limit. With regard to taxes, the question is whether the choice of capital structure is determined by taxes, or whether *given* a capital structure, financing deals are put together to maximise tax benefits for the current transaction.

50  Some of the following material is drawn from S. C. Myers, 'Still Searching for Optimal Capital Structure', *Journal of Applied Corporate Finance*, 6: 4–14 (Spring 1993).

51  M. C. Jensen, 'Agency Costs of Free Cash Flow, Corporate Finance and Takeovers', *American Economic Review*, 26: 323 (May 1986).

the best debt level would leave just enough cash in the bank, after debt service, to finance all positive NPV projects, with not a penny left over.

We do not recommend this degree of fine-tuning, but the idea is valid and important. Debt can discipline managers who are tempted to invest too much. It can also provide the pressure to force improvements in operating efficiency. Here is one very successful example.

### Sealed Air's leveraged recapitalisation[52]   In 1989 Sealed Air Corporation undertook a *leveraged recapitalisation*. It borrowed the money to pay a $328 million special cash dividend. In one stroke the company's debt increased ten-fold. Its book equity (accounting net worth) went from $162 million to minus $161 million. Debt went from 13 per cent of total book assets to 136 per cent.

Sealed Air was a profitable company. The problem was that its profits were coming too easily, because its main products were protected by patents. When the patents expired, strong competition was inevitable, and the company was not ready for it. In the meantime, there was too much financial slack:

> *. . . we didn't need to manufacture efficiently; we didn't need to worry about cash. At Sealed Air, capital tended to have limited value attached to it—cash was perceived as being free and abundant.*[53]

So the leveraged recap was used to 'disrupt the status quo, promote internal change' and simulate 'the pressures of Sealed Air's more competitive future'.[54] This shake-up was reinforced by new performance measures and incentives, including increases in share ownership by employees.

It worked. Sales and operating profits increased steadily without major new capital investments, and net working capital *fell* by half, releasing cash to help service the company's debt. The company's share price quadrupled in the five years after the recapitalisation.

Sealed Air's recapitalisation was not typical. It is an exemplar chosen with hindsight. It was also undertaken by a successful firm under no outside pressure. As we will see in Chapter 33, most leveraged recapitalisations are responses to takeover threats, or take the form of leveraged buy-outs or LBOs, where management and/or private investors borrow to make a takeover. But much of the value added in these cases has come from the same source as Sealed Air's. These are *diet deals* designed to force successful but overweight organisations to shed financial fat—that is, to disgorge cash, reduce operating costs and use assets more efficiently. The deals start with debt that would be imprudent for normal firms. But the debt is used to make sure the diet is adhered to.

## One last piece of empirical evidence

One of the reasons why issues like the debt controversy are so difficult to resolve is that we cannot run a scientific experiment to determine the facts of the case. If we could, we would take several companies and match each of them with another company *identical in every respect except for the level of debt*. So we would take BHP and create a second BHP but with a different debt level; we would then do the same to CSR, and so on. Finally, tired but satisfied with a good day's work, we would sit back and watch what happened to their share prices. Of course, this is fantasy, but there is something that comes close—**exchange offers**.

Exchange offers are deals where a company offers its security holders the opportunity to exchange the securities they hold for some other type of security. For example, BHP might offer its shareholders the opportunity to swap some of their shares for debt. The company's assets do

---

[52] See K .H. Wruck, 'Financial Policy As a Catalyst for Organizational Change: Sealed Air's Leveraged Special Dividend', *Journal of Applied Corporate Finance*, 7: 20–37 (Winter 1995).

[53] Ibid, p. 21.

[54] Ibid.

not change, just the way they are financed. Exchange offers are more common in the United States than in Australia, so most of the research has been done in the United States. Unfortunately for our purposes, this means that the research has been done under a classical tax system.

The results of the studies consistently show that leverage-increasing transactions (shares retired in exchange for debt) are accompanied by a positive price response when the exchange offer is announced.[55] When leverage-reducing exchange offers (debt retired in exchange for shares) are announced the share price goes down. The greater the leverage effect, the greater the share price response. For example, swapping ordinary shares for preference shares has a less positive price effect than swapping ordinary shares for debt.

While it is clear that the leverage-increasing transactions are good news, it is less clear why. Perhaps the investors believe there is a tax advantage to debt. However, this does not explain why there should be a positive response to swapping ordinary shares for preference shares. Perhaps investors are pleased that managers are committing to disgorging more cash, and since this commitment extends into the future, investors may see it as a confident signal from management about the strength of future cash flows. Perhaps also there is a wealth transfer from debtholders to shareholders, as the existing debt becomes more risky.

Of course, it is also possible that companies that make exchange offers differ from 'normal' companies. For example, it is quite common for companies approaching financial distress, or in it, to restructure by offering their creditors shares in exchange for the debt. It is not difficult to understand why this is bad news. Equally, it is not difficult to see why caution should be exercised in generalising the results of such cases to other firms.

## 18.5 Summary

Our task in this chapter was to show why capital structure matters. We did not throw away MM's proposition I that capital structure is irrelevant; we added to it. However, we did not arrive at any simple, satisfactory theory of optimal capital structure.

The traditional trade-off theory emphasises taxes and financial distress. The value of the firm is broken down as:

$$\text{Value if all equity financed } + \text{ PV(tax shield)} - \text{ PV(costs of financial distress)}$$

According to this theory, the firm should increase debt until the value from PV(tax shield) is just offset, at the margin, by increases in PV(costs of financial distress).

The cost of financial distress can be broken down as follows:

1. Financial distress costs
   a. Direct costs such as court fees.
   b. Indirect costs reflecting the difficulty of managing a company undergoing reorganisation.

2. Costs of financial distress short of financial distress
   a. Conflicts of interest between bondholders and shareholders of firms approaching financial distress may lead to poor operating performance and investment decisions. Shareholders acting in their narrow self-interest can gain at the expense of creditors by playing 'games' which reduce the overall value of the firm.
   b. The fine print in debt contracts is designed to prevent these games. But fine print increases the costs of writing, monitoring and enforcing the debt contract.

---

55    A comprehensive review of such studies can be found in C. W. Smith, 'Raising Capital: Theory and Evidence', *Midland Corporate Finance Journal*, 6–22 (Spring 1986)

The value of the tax shield is more controversial. It would be easy to compute if we had only corporate taxes to worry about. In that case the net tax saving from borrowing would be just the marginal corporate tax rate $T_c$ multiplied by $r_D D$, the interest payment. This tax shield is usually valued by discounting at the borrowing rate $r_D$. In the special case of fixed permanent debt

$$\text{PV(tax shield)} = \frac{T_c(r_D \times D)}{r_D} = T_c D$$

Some economists have become accustomed to thinking only of the corporate tax advantages of debt. But many firms seem to thrive with no debt at all despite the strong tax inducement to borrow. Maybe the tax shield is not worth as much as we think, and perhaps the explanation lies in the interaction of corporate and personal taxes.

Under the imputation tax system the good news that tax has been saved at the corporate level is offset by the bad news that this means less imputation credits for shareholders. In a fully-integrated imputation system, where shareholders recover all the corporate tax paid, there is no value in the interest tax shield. Reality is more complex. Not all firms distribute all the available imputation credits and not all investors can fully utilise the credits they receive. In some cases therefore saving tax at the corporate level via the interest tax shield still has some value.

Miller has presented a theory that may explain why debt tax shields may have little or no value under a classical tax system. He argued that the net tax saving from corporate borrowing can be zero when personal taxes as well as corporate taxes are considered. Interest income is not taxed at the corporate level but is taxed at the personal level. Equity income is taxed at the corporate level but may largely escape personal taxes if it comes in the form of capital gains. Thus $T_{pE}$, the effective personal rate on equity income, is usually less than $T_p$, the regular personal rate that applies to interest income. This reduces the relative tax advantage of debt:

$$\text{Relative advantage} = \frac{(1 - T_p)}{(1 - T_{pE})(1 - T_c)}$$

(Note that if interest and equity income are taxed at the same effective personal rates, then the relative advantage of debt under the classical tax system is $1/(1 - T_c)$ and it is 1 under a fully-integrated imputation tax system.)

In Miller's theory the supply of corporate debt expands as long as the corporate tax rate exceeds the personal tax rate of the investors absorbing the increased supply. The supply that equates these two tax rates establishes an optimal debt ratio for the aggregate of corporations. But, if the total supply of debt suits investors' needs, any single taxpaying firm must find that debt policy does not matter.

Although Miller's model was developed for a classical tax system we can use his framework for analysing the imputation tax system. We can also apply his proposition that, if debt has a tax advantage, then corporate treasurers attempting to exploit that advantage are going to bid up the interest rate. In that process they will trade away some, or all, of the tax advantage of debt.

The variety of tax situations faced by investors and firms prevents us advising one policy for all firms. Instead, we suggest that borrowing may make sense for some firms, but not for others. However, we do not generally expect the tax benefit to be large. If a firm can be fairly sure of earning a profit, and the investors will not fully recover the corporate taxes paid, then there is likely to be a net tax saving from borrowing. However, for firms that are unlikely to earn sufficient profits to benefit from the corporate tax shield, there is little or no tax advantage to borrowing. For these firms the net tax benefit could even be negative. This is because the interest rate is likely to be set by firms that can use the tax benefit of debt.

The trade-off theory balances the tax advantages of borrowing against the costs of financial distress. Corporations are supposed to pick a target capital structure that maximises firm value. Firms with safe, tangible assets and plenty of taxable income to shield ought to have high debt targets. Unprofitable companies with risky, intangible assets ought to rely primarily on equity financing.

This theory of capital structure successfully explains many industry differences in capital structure, but it does not explain why the most profitable firms *within* an industry generally have the most conservative capital structures. (Under the trade-off theory, high profitability should mean high debt capacity *and* a strong corporate tax incentive to use that capacity.)

There is a competing pecking order theory, which states that firms use internal financing when available, and choose debt over equity when external financing is required. This explains why the less profitable firms in an industry borrow more—not because they have higher target debt ratios, but because they need more external financing, and because debt is next on the pecking order when internal funds are exhausted.

The pecking order is a consequence of asymmetric information. Managers know more about their firms than outside investors do and are reluctant to issue shares when they believe the price is too low. They try to time issues when shares are fairly priced or overpriced. Investors understand this and interpret a decision to issue shares as bad news. That explains why share price usually falls when a share issue is announced.

Debt is better than equity when these information problems are important. Optimistic managers will prefer debt to undervalued equity, and pessimistic managers will be pressed to follow suit. The pecking order theory says that equity will be issued only when debt capacity is running out and there is a cash shortage.

The pecking order theory is clearly not 100 per cent right. There are many examples of equity issued by companies that could easily have borrowed. But the theory does explain why most external financing comes from debt, and it explains why changes in debt ratios tend to follow requirements for external financing.

The pecking order stresses the value of financial slack. Without sufficient slack, the firm may be caught at the bottom of the pecking order and be forced to choose between issuing undervalued shares, borrowing and risking financial distress, or passing up positive NPV investment opportunities.

There is, however, a dark side to financial slack. Surplus cash or credit tempts managers to overinvest or to indulge an easy and glamorous corporate lifestyle. When temptation wins, or threatens to win, a leveraged recapitalisation may be in order. A recap drastically increases debt service, forcing the company to disgorge cash and prodding managers and organisations to try harder to be more efficient.

## FURTHER READING

Modigliani and Miller's analysis of the present value of interest tax shields at the corporate level is in:

> F. Modigliani and M. H. Miller, 'Corporate Income Taxes and the Cost of Capital: A Correction', *American Economic Review*, 53: 433–43 (June 1963).

> F. Modigliani and M. H. Miller, 'Some Estimates of the Cost of Capital to the Electric Utility Industry, 1954–57', *American Economic Review*, 56: 333–91 (June 1966).

Miller extends the MM model to personal as well as corporate taxes; Brown and Howard extend Miller's analysis to the imputation tax system; DeAngelo and Masulis argue that firms with plenty of non-interest tax shields, e.g. shields from depreciation, should borrow less:

> M. H. Miller, 'Debt and Taxes', *Journal of Finance*, 32: 261–76 (May 1977).

> Peter F. Howard and Robert L. Brown, 'Dividend Policy And Capital Structure under the Imputation Tax System: Some Clarifying Comments', *Accounting and Finance*, 32: 51–61 (1992).

H. DeAngelo and R. Masulis, 'Optimal Capital Structure under Corporate Taxation', *Journal of Financial Economics*, **8**: 5–29 (March 1980).

The following articles analyse the conflicts of interest between bondholders and shareholders, and their implications for financing policy (do not read the last article until you have read Chapter 20):

M. C. Jensen and W. H. Meckling, 'Theory of the Firm: Managerial Behavior, Agency Costs and Ownership Structure', *Journal of Financial Economics*, **3**: 305–60 (October 1976).

S. C. Myers, 'Determinants of Corporate Borrowing', *Journal of Financial Economics*, **5**: 146–75 (1977).

D. Galai and R. W. Masulis, 'The Option Pricing Model and the Risk Factor of Stock', *Journal of Financial Economics*, **3**: 53–82 (January–March 1976).

Myers describes the pecking order theory, which is in turn based on work by Myers and Majluf; Baskin examines some of the evidence for that theory; Allen provides Australian evidence on the pecking order theory, based on interviews with financial managers:

S. C. Myers, 'The Capital Structure Puzzle', *Journal of Finance*, **39**: 575–92 (July 1984).

S. C. Myers and N. S. Majluf, 'Corporate Financing and Investment Decisions When Firms Have Information Investors Do Not Have', *Journal of Financial Economics*, **13**: 187–222 (June 1984).

J. Baskin, 'An Empirical Investigation of the Pecking Order Hypothesis', *Financial Management*, **18**: 26–35 (Spring 1989).

D. E. Allen, 'The Determinants of the Capital Structure of Listed Australian Companies: The Financial Manager's Perspective', *Australian Journal of Management*, **16**: 104–27 (December 1991).

Three useful reviews of theory and evidence on optimal capital structure are:

M. J. Barclay, C. W. Smith and R. L. Watts, 'The Determinants of Corporate Leverage and Dividend Policies', *Journal of Applied Corporate Finance*, **7**: 4–19 (Winter 1995).

M. Harris and A. Raviv, 'The Theory of Optimal Capital Structure', *Journal of Finance*, **48**: 297–356 (March 1991).

S. C. Myers, 'Still Searching for Optimal Capital Structure', *Journal of Applied Corporate Finance*, **6**: 4–14 (Spring 1993).

A review of the evidence from exchange offers can be found in:

C. W. Smith, 'Raising Capital: Theory and Evidence', *Midland Corporate Finance Journal*, 6–22 (Spring 1986).

The Spring 1993 and Winter 1995 issues of the *Journal of Applied Corporate Finance* contain several articles on the incentive effects of capital structure, including:

K. H. Wruck, 'Financial Policy As a Catalyst for Organizational Change: Sealed Air's Leveraged Special Dividend', *Journal of Applied Corporate Finance*, **7**: 20–37 (Winter 1995).

Altman's book is a general survey of the financial distress decision; there are also several good studies of the conflicting interests of different security holders and the costs and consequences of reorganisation:

E. A. Altman, *Corporate Financial Distress: A Complete Guide to Predicting, Avoiding and Dealing with Bankruptcy*, John Wiley & Sons, New York, 1983.

M. White, 'The Corporate Bankruptcy Decision', *Journal of Economic Perspectives*, **3**: 129–52 (Spring 1989).

J. R. Franks and W. N. Torous, 'An Empirical Analysis of US Firms in Reorganization', *Journal of Finance*, **44**: 747–70 (July 1980).

J. R. Franks and W. N. Torous, 'How Shareholders and Creditors Fare in Workouts and Chapter 11 Reorganizations', *Journal of Financial Economics*, **35**: 349–70 (May 1994).

L. A. Weiss, 'Bankruptcy Resolution: Direct Costs and Violation of Priority of Claims', *Journal of Financial Economics*, **27**: 285–314 (October 1990).

The Summer 1991 issue of the *Journal of Applied Corporate Finance* contains several articles on financial distress and reorganisations.

Australian evidence on the cost of financial distress can be found in:

T. Pham and D. Chow, 'Some Estimates of Direct and Indirect Bankruptcy Costs in Australia: September 1978–May 1983', *Australian Journal of Management*, 75–95 (June 1987).

D. K. Robertson and R. B. Tress, 'Bankruptcy Costs: Evidence from Small-Firm Liquidations', *Australian Journal of Management*, 49–60 (June 1985).

The January–February 1986 issue of the *Journal of Financial Economics* (vol. 15, no. 1/2) collects a series of empirical studies on the share price impacts of debt and equity issues and capital structure changes.

## QUIZ

**\*1.** Compute the present value of interest tax shields generated by these three debt issues. Consider corporate taxes only. The marginal tax rate is $T_c = 0.35$.
  a. A $1000, one-year loan at 8 per cent.
  b. A five-year loan of $1000 at 8 per cent. Assume no principal is repaid until maturity.
  c. A $1000 perpetuity at 7 per cent.

**\*2.** Here are book and market value balance sheets of the United Frypan Company (UF):

| Book | | | | Market | | | |
|---|---|---|---|---|---|---|---|
| Net working capital | $20 | Debt | $40 | Net working capital | $20 | Debt | $40 |
| Long-term assets | 80 | Equity | 60 | Long-term assets | 140 | Equity | 120 |
| | $100 | | $100 | | $160 | | $160 |

Assume that MM's theory holds with taxes. There is no growth and the $40 of debt is expected to be permanent. Assume a 40 per cent corporate tax rate.
  a. How much of the firm's value is accounted for by the debt-generated tax shield?
  b. How much better off will UF's shareholders be if the firm borrows $20 more and uses it to repurchase shares?
  c. Now suppose that government passes a law which eliminates the deductibility of interest for tax purposes after a grace period of five years. What will be the new value of the firm, other things being equal? (Assume an 8 per cent borrowing rate.)

**\*3.** What is the relative tax advantage of corporate debt if the corporate tax rate is $T_c = 0.34$? Assume a classical tax system where the personal tax rate is $T_p = 0.31$, but all equity income comes as capital gains and escapes tax entirely ($T_{pE} = 0$). How does the relative tax advantage change if the company decides to pay out all equity income as cash dividends? Now answer the question assuming the Australian imputation system. How does your answer under the imputation system change if the company pays out all its earnings as dividends and investors can use all the imputation credits that they receive?

**4.** This question tests your understanding of 'financial distress'.
  a. What are the costs of going bankrupt? Define these costs carefully.
  b. 'A company can incur costs of financial distress without ever going bankrupt.' Explain how this can happen.

c. Explain how conflicts of interest between bond- and shareholders can lead to costs of financial distress.

**5.** On 29 February 2003, when PDQ Computers announced financial distress, its share price fell from $3.00 to $0.50 per share. There were 10 million shares outstanding. Does that imply financial distress costs of $10 \times (3.00 - 0.50) = \$25$ million? Explain.

**\*6.** 'The firm can't use interest tax shields unless it has (taxable) income to shield.' What does this statement imply for the debt policy? Explain briefly.

**7.** Let us go back to Circular File's market value balance sheet:

| | | | |
|---|---|---|---|
| Net working capital | $20 | $25 | Bonds outstanding |
| Fixed assets | 10 | 5 | Ordinary shares |
| | | | |
| Total assets | $30 | $30 | Total liabilities |

Who gains and who loses from the following manoeuvres?
a. Circular scrapes up $5 in cash and pays a cash dividend.
b. Circular halts operations, sells its fixed assets and converts net working capital into $20 cash. Unfortunately, the fixed assets fetch only $6 on the second-hand market. The $26 cash is invested in Treasury notes.
c. Circular encounters an acceptable investment opportunity, NPV = 0, requiring an investment of $10. The firm borrows to finance the project. The new debt has the same security, seniority, etc, as the old.
d. Suppose that the new project has NPV = +$2 and is financed by an issue of preferred shares.
e. The lenders agree to extend the maturity of their loan from one year to two years in order to give Circular a chance to recover.

**\*8.** What types of firms would be likely to incur heavy costs in the event of bankruptcy or financial distress? What types would incur relatively light costs? Give a few examples of each type.

**\*9.** The conventional theory of optimal capital structure states that firms trade off corporate interest tax shields against the possible costs of financial distress due to borrowing. What does this theory predict about the relationship between book profitability and target book-debt ratios? Is the theory's prediction consistent with the facts?

**10.** What is meant by the 'pecking order' theory of capital structure? Could this theory explain the observed relationship between profitability and debt ratios? Explain briefly.

**11.** Why does asymmetric information push companies to raise external funds by borrowing rather than issuing shares?

**12.** 'A high debt ratio forces the company to pay out cash, thereby increasing value to investors.' Explain why, or in what circumstances, this is true.

**13.** For what kinds of companies is financial slack most valuable? Are there situations in which financial slack should be reduced by borrowing and paying out the proceeds to the shareholders? Explain.

**14.** Explain why equity can have a positive value when the company is in financial distress, and even when the company is in receivership.

## QUESTIONS AND PROBLEMS

**1.** Suppose that an Australian company has a dividend payout ratio of 50 per cent. The company's shareholders are all Australian residents taxed at 47 per cent, but because of deferral of realisation the effective tax rate on capital gains is only 30 per cent. The company's profits are fully taxed at 36 per cent. Assuming the company is consistently profitable and starts with no debt, show how adding debt to the capital structure can reduce investors' total taxes.

What other strategy might the company use instead of increasing debt?

**2.** 'The trouble with MM's argument is that it ignores the fact that individuals can deduct interest for personal income tax.' Analyse this statement under both the classical and imputation tax systems.

What difference would it make if individuals were not allowed to deduct interest for personal tax?

**3.** Look back at the News Corporation example in Section 18.1. Suppose that News Corporation moves to a 40 per cent book-debt ratio ($D/V$) by issuing debt and using the proceeds to repurchase shares. Consider only corporate taxes. Now reconstruct Table 18.3b to reflect the new capital structure.

**4.** Calculate the tax shield for an actual Australian company assuming:
   a. Debt is permanent.
   b. Personal tax rates on debt and equity income are the same.
   c. All corporate tax paid is recovered as imputation tax credits.

   How would the share price change if the company announced tomorrow that it intended to replace all its debt with equity?

   Repeat your analysis assuming that only 50 per cent of corporate tax paid is recovered as imputation credits.

**\*5.** Explain the implications of Miller's capital structure theory for the debt policy of:
   a. A company that pays corporate income tax.
   b. A company that is not in a taxpaying position.
   c. A company that is paying taxes now, but is unsure that it will have taxable income in the future.

   Assume the following tax rates: 46 per cent for corporations; personal rates of up to 50 per cent for dividends and interest; and effective personal rates of, say, 10 per cent on capital gains. Do your analysis first assuming a classical tax system, then an imputation tax system.

**\*6.** Imagine the following very simple world. There are three groups of investors with the following tax rates:

| Group | Tax rate (%) |
|-------|--------------|
| A | 60 |
| B | 40 |
| C | 0 |

They can choose from government bonds, perpetual corporate bonds and ordinary shares. The government bonds and shares attract no personal tax. Interest from corporate bonds attracts personal tax but is deductible for corporate tax. The corporate tax rate is 50 per cent. Interest payments on government bonds total $20 million. Cash flow (before interest and taxes) from corporations totals $300 million. Each group starts with the same amount of money. Regardless of what changes are made in capital structure, the three groups always invest the same amount, and they require a minimum return of 10 per cent after taxes on any security.

a. Suppose that companies are financed initially by shares. Company X now decides to allocate $1 million of its pre-tax cash flows to interest payments on debt. Which group or groups of investors will buy this debt? What will be the rate of interest? What will be the effect on the value of company X?

b. Other companies have followed the example of company X and interest payments now total $150 million. At this point company Y decides to allocate $1 million to interest payments on debt. Which group or groups will buy this debt? What will be the rate of interest? What will be the effect on the value of company Y?

c. Total interest payments have somehow risen to $250 million. Now company Z substitutes common share for debt, thereby *reducing* interest payments by $1 million. Which group or groups will sell their debt to company Z? At what rate of interest can company Z repurchase the debt? What will be the effect on the value of company Z?

d. What is the equilibrium capital structure? Which groups will hold which securities? What is the rate of interest? What is the total value of all companies? Show that in equilibrium even an unlevered company has no incentive to issue debt. Similarly show that even a company with above-average leverage has no incentive to reduce its debt.

**\*7.** Here is a difficult problem. Assume a classical tax system. What difference does the deduction for depreciation make to Miller's equilibrium? Try recalculating the equilibrium in Question 6, assuming that companies can deduct depreciation of:
a. $100 million.
b. $50 million.

**\*8.** The expected return on (risk-free) equity is 14 per cent, and the risk-free interest rate is 20 per cent. Assume Miller's model under a classical tax system.
a. What is the implied personal tax rate of the marginal lender? (Assume that equity income is free of personal tax.)
b. Company A has large depreciation tax shields and uncertain income. As a result, A's expected marginal rate of corporate tax is 40 per cent if it finances solely with equity. For every 5 per cent increase in A's debt ratio, A's marginal tax rate is expected to decline by 2 per cent. How much should A borrow?

**9.** Look at some real companies with different types of assets. What operating problems would each encounter in the event of financial distress? How well would the assets keep their value?

**10.** The Salad Oil Storage Company (SOS) has financed a large part of its facilities with long-term debt. There is a significant risk of default, but the company is not on the ropes yet. Explain:
a. Why SOS shareholders could lose by investing in a positive NPV project financed by an equity issue.

   b. Why SOS shareholders could gain by investing in a negative NPV project financed by cash.

   c. Why SOS shareholders could gain from paying out a large cash dividend.
How might the firm's adherence to a target debt ratio mitigate some or all of the problems noted above?

**11.** a. Who benefits from the 'fine print' in bond contracts when the firm gets into financial trouble? Give a one-sentence answer.

   b. Who benefits from the fine print when the bonds are issued? Suppose the firm is offered the choice of issuing (1) a bond with standard restrictions on dividend payout, additional borrowing, etc and (2) a bond with minimal restrictions, but a much higher interest rate? Suppose the interest rates on both (1) and (2) are fair from the viewpoint of lenders. Which bond would you expect the firm to issue? Why?

**12.** It becomes clear that Sadly Gone Ltd is going into receivership. Immediately before the shares are suspended from trading they are priced at \$5.25 per share, down from about \$20 earlier in the year. How much of this drop should be attributed to financial distress costs—all, part or none? Explain.

**13.** 'I was amazed to find that the announcement of a share issue drives down the value of the issuing firm by *30 per cent*, on average, of the proceeds of the issue. That issue cost dwarfs the underwriter's fee and the administrative costs of the issue. It makes share issues prohibitively expensive.'

   a. You are contemplating a \$100 million share issue. On past evidence, you anticipate that announcement of this issue will drive down share price by 3 per cent and that the market value of your firm will fall by 30 per cent of the amount to be raised. On the other hand, additional equity funds are necessary to fund an investment project which you believe has a positive NPV of \$40 million. Should you proceed with the issue?

   b. Is the fall in market value on announcement of a share issue an *issue cost* in the same sense as an underwriter's fee? Respond to the quote which begins this question.
Use your answer to Part (a) as a numerical example to explain your response to Part (b).

**14.** Ronald Masulis[56] has analysed the share price impact of *exchange offers* of debt for equity or vice versa. In an exchange offer the firm offers to trade freshly-issued securities for seasoned securities in the hands of investors. Thus, a firm that wanted to move to a higher debt ratio could offer to trade new debt for outstanding shares. A firm that wanted to move to a more conservative capital structure could offer to trade new shares for outstanding debt securities.

Masulis found that debt for equity exchanges were good news (share price increased on announcement) and equity for debt exchanges were bad news.

   a. Are these results consistent with the 'trade-off' theory of capital structure?

   b. Are the results consistent with the evidence that investors regard announcements of (i) share issues as bad news, (ii) share repurchases as good news and (iii) debt issues as no news, or at most trifling disappointments?

   c. How could Masulis' results be explained?

---

**15.** Leveraged recapitalisation usually increases the market value of the firm. In other words, the aggregate value of all the firm's debt and equity securities is higher after the recap than before. Is this inconsistent with MM's proposition I? Explain carefully.

**16.** You will often find arguments in the capital budgeting literature that external capital rationing is unlikely. Yet banks will often impose capital rationing (they will not lend at any interest rate) on highly levered companies. Can you explain this?

# chapter 19

# INTERACTIONS OF INVESTMENT AND FINANCING DECISIONS

We first addressed problems of capital budgeting in Chapter 2. At that point we had said hardly a word about financing decisions; we proceeded under the simplest possible assumption about financing, namely, all equity financing. We would get the same results in an idealised Modigliani and Miller (MM) world in which all financing decisions are irrelevant. In a strict MM world, firms can analyse real investments as if they are to be all equity financed; the actual financing plan is a mere detail to be worked out later.

Under MM assumptions, decisions to spend money can be separated from decisions to raise money. In this chapter we reconsider the capital budgeting decision when investment and financing decisions *interact* and cannot be wholly separated.

In the early chapters you learned how to value a capital investment opportunity by a four-step procedure:

1. Forecast the project's incremental cash flow after corporate tax, assuming the project is entirely equity-financed.
2. Assess the project's risk.
3. Estimate the opportunity cost of capital, that is, the expected rate of return offered to investors by the equivalent-risk investments traded in capital markets.
4. Calculate NPV, using the discounted cash flow formula.

In effect, we were thinking of each project as a mini-firm and asking, 'How much would that mini-firm be worth if we spun it off as a separate, all equity financed enterprise? How much would investors be willing to pay for shares in the project?'

Of course, this procedure rests on the concept of *value additivity*. In well-functioning capital markets the market value of the firm is the sum of the present value of all the assets held by the firm[1]—the whole equals the sum of the parts. If value additivity did *not* hold, then the value of the firm with the project could be more, or less, than the sum of the separate value of the project and the value of the firm without the project. We could not determine the project's contribution to firm value by evaluating it as a separate mini-firm.

In this chapter we stick with the value additivity principle but extend it to include value contributed by financing decisions. There are two ways of doing this:

1. *Adjust the discount rate.* The adjustment has traditionally been downwards, to account for the value of interest tax shields. Adjusting the discount rate is the most common approach to handling interactions between the investment and financing decisions. The adjustment has commonly been implemented via the after-tax weighted average cost of capital, or WACC for short.[2]

2. *Adjust the present value.* That is, start by estimating the project's 'base-case' value as an all equity financed mini-firm, and then adjust this base-case NPV to account for the project's impact on the firm's capital structure. Thus

Adjusted NPV (ANPV, or just APV for short) = base-case NPV + NPV of financing decision caused by project acceptance

Once you identify and value the side effects of financing a project, calculating its APV (adjusted net present value) is no more than addition or subtraction.

To keep things simple, we start by ignoring the effect of personal taxes. So initially, we consider the interaction of investment and financing

decisions in the presence of corporate taxes only. This is quite reasonable if we are only interested in investment and financing decisions under a classical tax system. We then extend our analysis to the imputation tax system. Under the imputation system there is an interaction of corporate and personal taxes. You need to understand how this affects the interaction of the investment and financing decisions.

We conclude the chapter by re-examining a basic and apparently simple issue: What should be the discount rate for a risk-free project? Once we recognise the tax deductibility of debt interest, we will find that all risk-free, or *debt-equivalent*, cash flows can be evaluated by discounting at the *after-tax* interest rate. We also remind you that the marginal effective corporate tax rate may differ from the statutory rate. Where this is the case, we need to take it into account when we adjust for tax effects.

This is a big chapter, which ties together a lot of important ideas. We suggest that you take it slowly.

**Some important advice.** The topics covered in this chapter are a common source of confusion among students and in practice. To avoid this confusion you need to understand that just as there is more than one way to skin a cat, there is more than one way to measure the discount rate (cost of capital) that you use in a DCF valuation of a project.[3] To see why, consider a simple project which yields a constant cash flow in perpetuity. The value of this project is $V$: let us call its cash flow $C$ and its discount rate $r^*$. The value of the project is given by:

$$V = \frac{C}{r^*}$$

Mathematically speaking it is quite clear that many combinations of values for $C$ and $r^*$ will give the same value for $V$.[4] Given the cash flow $C$

---

1    All assets means intangible as well as tangible assets. For example, a going concern is usually worth more than a haphazard pile of tangible assets. Thus, the aggregate value of a firm's tangible assets often falls short of its market value. The difference is accounted for by going-concern value or by other intangible assets such as accumulated technical expertise, an experienced sales force or valuable growth opportunities.

2    Although we talk about '*the*' WACC, in fact there are many possible variants of WACC. When *we* talk about WACC we mean the traditional WACC, that is: $r^* = r_D(1 - T_c)\frac{D}{V} + r_E\frac{E}{V} = \text{WACC}$.

3    Timothy Nantell and Robert Carlson provide a clear demonstration of this point in 'The Cost of Capital as a Weighted Average', *Journal of Finance*, 30: 1343–55 (December 1975). They also show that academics had been confused about this topic.

4    In fact, the number of possible combinations of $C$ and $r$ is infinite.

and the value $V$ we would define the discount rate as:

$$r^* = \frac{C}{V}$$

The moral is simple: the discount rate $r^*$ has to be defined consistently with the project cash flow $C$ in order to get the correct value for $V$. However, there are several ways the cash flow $C$ can be defined. For example, before corporate tax, after corporate tax assuming all equity finance, after corporate tax allowing for the tax deductibility of interest, after corporate tax allowing for the tax benefit of imputation, after all taxes both corporate and personal, and so on. For each definition of $C$ there is a corresponding definition of $r^*$ that will give the correct value for $V$. The trick is to match up the correct pairs of $C$ and $r^*$. Once you understand this you greatly reduce your chances of making a multi-million dollar valuation error.

The most common definition of cash flow is the after-corporate-tax cash flow generated by the project, assuming the project is entirely equity financed—commonly known as the unlevered cash flow. This is the usual starting point for both the traditional WACC and the APV methods of project evaluation.

There is a further idea that will help you avoid errors. In evaluating the project we are interested in its NPV. For our simple project with an investment $I$ the NPV is given by:

$$NPV = \frac{C}{r^*} - I$$

The question we are interested in is whether the cash flow $C$ is sufficient to service the investment $I$ and leave some cash over. Thus, the cash flow $C$ must be defined consistently with the definition of the investment. This takes us back to our discussion of Level 1 and Level 2 consistency, which we made a fuss about in Chapter 6. We made a fuss about it there and remind you here, because we find that failure to understand and apply these ideas is a very common source of error in project valuation.

## 19.1 The after (company) tax weighted average cost of capital

Think back to Chapter 17 and Modigliani and Miller's proposition I. MM showed that, in the absence of taxes or financial market imperfections, the cost of capital does not depend on financing.[5] In other words, the weighted average of the expected returns to debt and equity investors equals the opportunity cost of capital, regardless of the debt ratio:

$$\text{Weighted average return to debt and equity} = r_D \frac{D}{V} + r_E \frac{E}{V}$$

$$= r, \text{ a constant, independent of } \frac{D}{V}$$

Here $r$ is the opportunity cost of capital, the expected rate of return investors would demand if the firm had no debt at all; $r_D$ and $r_E$ are the expected rates of return on debt and levered equity, the 'cost of debt' and 'cost of equity'. The weights $D/V$ and $E/V$ are the fractions of debt and equity, based on *market values*; $V$, the total market value for the firm, is the sum of $D$ and $E$.

---

[5]   Since there are no taxes the problem of matching up the correct definitions of discount rate and cash flow are largely avoided.

But you cannot look up $r$, the opportunity cost of capital, in the *Australian Financial Review* or find it on the Internet. So financial managers turn the problem around: they start with the estimates of $r_D$ and $r_E$ and then infer $r$.[6] Under MM's assumptions,

$$r = r_D \frac{D}{V} + r_E \frac{E}{V}$$

We have discussed this weighted average cost of capital formula in Chapters 9 and 17. However, the formula misses a crucial difference between debt and equity: interest payments are tax deductible. Therefore, we move on to the *after-tax* weighted average cost of capital, nicknamed WACC:

$$r^* = r_D(1 - T_c)\frac{D}{V} + r_E \frac{E}{V} = \text{WACC}$$

Here $T_c$ is the marginal corporate tax rate.

The WACC has a long tradition of use under a classical tax system. When we use the WACC under a classical tax system, the cash flows that we discount are the project net cash flows assuming they are fully taxed at the corporate rate. This unlevered cash flow excludes the effect of the interest tax shield. The tax benefit of the debt is captured in the reduced discount rate. We can also use the traditional after-tax WACC under the imputation tax system, but we have to make some adjustments to the cash flow. These adjustments reflect two things: the tax benefit of the imputation tax credit and the reduced benefit of the debt tax shield under imputation. As we shall see later there are several ways that these effects can be accounted for.

But for the time being (until we reach Section 19.4) we will assume away the problem of personal taxes. This means that we can temporarily ignore the complications of the imputation tax system and worry only about the interaction of the financing decision and corporate taxes.

Notice that the after-tax WACC ($r^*$) is less than the opportunity cost of capital ($r$), because the 'cost of debt' is calculated after tax, as $r_D(1 - T_c)$. Thus, the tax advantages of debt financing are reflected in a lower discount rate. Notice too that all the variables in the weighted average formula refer to the firm as a whole. As a result, the formula gives the right discount rate only for projects that are just like the firm undertaking them. The formula works for the 'average' project. It is incorrect for projects that are safer or riskier than the average of the firm's existing assets. It is also incorrect for projects whose acceptance would lead to an increase or decrease in the firm's debt ratio.

The idea behind the weighted average formula is simple and intuitively appealing. If the new project is profitable enough to pay the (after-tax) interest on the debt used to finance it, and also to generate a superior expected rate of return on the equity invested in it, then it must be a good project. What is a 'superior' equity return? One that exceeds $r_E$, the expected rate of return required by investors in the firm's shares. Let us see how this idea leads to the weighted average formula.

Suppose that the firm invests in a new project that is expected to produce the same yearly income in perpetuity. If the firm maintains its debt ratio, the amount of debt used to finance the project is

$$\text{Firm's debt ratio} \times \text{investment} = \frac{D}{V} \times \text{investment}$$

Similarly, the equity used to finance the project is

$$\text{Firm's equity ratio} \times \text{investment} = \frac{E}{V} \times \text{investment}$$

---

6   There is a real danger in this process. People become confused about the direction of causality. They get so used to estimating $r$ by measuring $r_D$ and $r_E$ that they fall into the trap of thinking that the magnitude of $r_D$ and $r_E$ determines the magnitude of $r$. Of course, by now you know that it is the other way around.

If the project is worthwhile, the income must cover after-tax interest charges and provide an acceptable return to equityholders. The after-tax interest costs on the additional debt are equal to

$$\frac{\text{After-tax}}{\text{interest rate}} \times \frac{\text{value of}}{\text{debt}} = r_D(1 - T_c) \times \frac{D}{V} \times \text{investment}$$

The minimum acceptable income to equityholders is

$$\frac{\text{Expected return}}{\text{on equity}} \times \frac{\text{value of}}{\text{equity}} = r_E \times \frac{E}{V} \times \text{investment}$$

Therefore, for the project to be acceptable, its net cash flow $C$ *must exceed*

$$r_D(1 - T_c) \times \frac{D}{V} \times \text{investment} + r_E \times \frac{E}{V} \times \text{investment}$$

This brings us back to the weighted average formula. Just divide through by the initial investment:

$$\frac{\text{Net cash flow}}{\text{Investment}} \; \textit{must exceed} \; r_D(1 - T_c)\frac{D}{V} + r_E\frac{E}{V}$$

Note that the ratio of the project's annual net cash flow to investment is just the project's return. Therefore, our formula gives the minimum acceptable rate of return from the project.

We have derived the WACC only for firms and projects offering perpetual cash flows. In an important result, Miles and Ezzell have shown that the traditional after-tax WACC formula works for any cash flow pattern *if* the firm adjusts its borrowing to maintain a constant debt ratio $D/V$ (measured in *market values*), regardless of whether things turn out well or poorly. When the firm departs from this policy, the weighted average formula is only approximately correct.[7]

# Example: the Geothermal project

Geothermal Ltd has only one asset, a brand-new well and pumping station located near thermal springs in the North Island of New Zealand. The pumping station extracts geothermal energy to supply heat and airconditioning for a shopping centre. The company has $5 million of perpetual debt outstanding yielding 8 per cent. Equity investors put up the other $5 million of the $10 million required to build the geothermal project.

The project has turned out well. It is generating $2.085 million in earnings before interest and taxes, 25 per cent higher than originally forecast. The company's one million shares are now trading at $7.50, a 50 per cent capital gain on the shareholders' original outlay of $5 per share. The shares offer an expected future rate of return of 14.6 per cent. The marginal corporate tax rate is 35 per cent.[8]

---

7  J. Miles and R. Ezzell, 'The Weighted Average Cost of Capital, Perfect Capital Markets and Project Life: A Clarification', *Journal of Financial and Quantitative Analysis*, **15**: 719–30 (September 1980). This paper's result reminds us that cost of capital derivations, in a perpetuity framework, do not automatically carry through to projects with finite lives and varying cash flows.

8  At the time of writing the corporate tax rate in Australia is 36 per cent. This rate, however, has changed over recent years. At the time of writing tax reform is on the agenda, so there is a significant probability that the rate may change again in the near future. Recent history suggests a rate outside the bounds of 30 per cent to 40 per cent is unlikely, so the rate we have chosen, 35 per cent, seems a fair compromise for purposes of illustration. (At the time of going to press (after the recent election) 30 per cent seems to have emerged as the most likely rate.)

Geothermal's book and market value balance sheets are as follows:

| Geothermal Ltd (book values, $million) | | | |
| --- | --- | --- | --- |
| Project value | $10 | $5 | Debt |
| | | 5 | Equity |
| | $10 | $10 | |

| Geothermal Ltd (market values, $million) | | | |
| --- | --- | --- | --- |
| Project value | $12.5 | $5 | Debt (D) |
| | | 7.5 | Equity (E) |
| | $12.5 | $12.5 | Firm value (V) |

Of course, we cannot observe the market value of Geothermal's project directly, but we know what it is worth to debt and equity investors (5 + 7.5 = $12.5 million). This value is entered on the left of the market value balance sheet. The project's NPV is +$2.5 million, the difference between its market value and the $10 million investment.

Why did we show the book balance sheet? Only so you could draw a big X through it. Do so now. We hope this will help you remember that book values are not relevant to estimating the cost of capital.

When estimating the weighted average cost of capital, you are not interested in past investments but in current values and expectations for the future. Geothermal's true debt ratio is not 50 per cent, the book ratio, but 40 per cent, because its project is worth $12.5 million. The cost of equity, $r_E = 0.146$, is the expected rate of return from purchase of shares at $7.50 per share, the current market price. It is not the return on book value per share. You cannot buy shares in Geothermal for $5.00 any more. Similarly, the cost of debt is the current yield. The capital market is telling you that the opportunity cost of debt with the same risk as yours is 8 per cent before tax. You can always make at least an 8 per cent return pre-tax by buying back your own debt.

So we have the following inputs for Geothermal:

$$
\begin{aligned}
\text{Cost of debt } (r_D) &= 0.08 \\
\text{Cost of equity } (r_E) &= 14.6 \\
\text{Marginal tax rate } (T_c) &= 0.35 \\
\text{Debt ratio } (D/V) &= 0.4 \\
\text{Equity ratio } (E/V) &= 0.6
\end{aligned}
$$

The company's WACC is:

$$ r^* = 0.08(1 - 0.35)(0.4) + 0.146(0.6) = 0.1084, \text{ or } 10.84\% $$

That is how you calculate the weighted average cost of capital.[9]

---

[9]   In practice it is pointless to calculate discount rates to this many decimal places. We do so here to avoid confusion from rounding errors. Earnings and cash flows are carried to three decimal places for the same reason.

Let us now use it to value Geothermal's project. We undertake a standard discounted cash flow analysis, exactly as in Chapter 6. Since the project does not depreciate, after-tax earnings and cash flow are the same.

| | |
|---|---|
| Pre-tax earnings | $2.085 |
| Tax at 35% | 0.730 |
| After-tax earnings | $1.355 million |

This is a perpetual cash flow, $C = 1.355$, so

$$\text{PV} = \frac{C}{r^*} = \frac{1.355}{0.1084} = \$12.5 \text{ million}$$

which confirms that Geothermal's project is accurately valued by discounting its after-tax cash flows at the weighted average cost of capital.

Note that the interest tax shield on Geothermal's debt is not reflected in the $1.355 million annual cash flow. Standard capital budgeting practice calculates taxes *as if* all financing comes from equity. The value added by the tax shields is not forgotten; it is picked up in the discount rate $r^*$.[10]

Finally, we confirm that Geothermal's shareholders can actually expect to earn 14.6 per cent.

$$\begin{aligned}
\text{After tax interest (\$)} &= (1 - T_c)\, r_D D \\
&= (1 - 0.35)(0.08)\, 5 = 0.26
\end{aligned}$$

$$\begin{aligned}
\text{Expected equity income (\$)} &= C - (1 - T_c) r_D D \\
&= 1.355 - 0.26 = 1.095
\end{aligned}$$

Geothermal's earnings are level and perpetual, so the expected rate of return on equity is equal to the expected equity income divided by the equity value:

$$\text{Expected equity return} = r_E = \frac{\text{expected equity income}}{\text{equity value}}$$

$$= \frac{1.095}{7.5} = 0.146, \text{ or } 14.6\%$$

Because this project is Geothermal's only asset, its PV equals the total market value of Geothermal's debt and equity securities. But if Geothermal wants to expand the project, or undertake another one, it could use the same 10.84 per cent discount rate. Of course, this requires that:

**1.** The new investment has the same risk and therefore the same opportunity cost of capital as the existing project.
**2.** Geothermal will stick to a 40 per cent market value debt ratio.

---

[10]  In this example it would be easy to add the interest tax shields back to the project cash flow. This 'adjusted' cash flow could be discounted at a weighted average cost of capital calculated using the *pre-tax* cost of debt. But for most projects (not perpetuities) it is much easier to capture the value of interest tax shields in the discount rate.

# Some tricks of the trade

Geothermal had just one asset and two sources of financing. A real company's market value balance sheet has many more elements, for example.[11]

| | |
|---|---|
| Current assets, including cash, inventory and accounts receivable | Current liabilities, including accounts payable and short-term debt |
| Plant and equipment | Long-term debt $(D)$ |
| | Preferred shares $(P)$ |
| Growth opportunities | Equity $(E)$ |
| Firm value $(V)$ | Firm value $(V)$ |

Several questions immediately arise.

1. *How does the formula change when there are more than two sources of financing?* Easy: there is one cost for each element. The weight for each element is proportional to its market value. For example,

$$r^* = r_D(1 - T_c)\frac{D}{V} + r_P\frac{P}{V} + r_E\frac{E}{V},$$

   where $r_P$ is the investor's expected rate of return on preferred shares.

2. *What about short-term debt?* Many companies only consider long-term financing when calculating WACC. They leave out the cost of short-term debt. In principle this is incorrect, because we usually define the size of the investment as the finance provided by equity and debt. The lenders who hold short-term debt are investors who can claim their share of operating earnings. A company which ignores this claim will understate the required return on capital investments.

   But 'zeroing out' short-term debt is not a serious error if this debt is only temporary, seasonal or incidental financing, or if it is offset by holdings of cash and marketable securities.[12] Suppose, for example, that your company's British subsidiary takes out a six-month loan from a British bank to finance its inventory and accounts receivable. The dollar equivalent of this loan will show up as a short-term debt on the parent's balance sheet. At the same time head office may be lending money by investing surplus dollars in short-term securities. If lending and borrowing offset, there is no point in including the cost of short-term debt in the weighted average cost of capital, because the company is not a *net* short-term borrower.

3. *What about other current liabilities?* Current liabilities are often 'netted out' in project evaluation by subtracting them from current assets. The difference is entered as net working capital on the left-hand side of the balance sheet. So the current liabilities have been shifted from the right-hand side of the balance sheet to the left-hand side. The sum of long-term financing on the right is called *total capitalisation*.

---

[11] This balance sheet is for exposition and should not be confused with a real company's books. We include the value of growth opportunities, which accountants do not recognise, though investors do. It excludes certain accounting entries, for example deferred taxes.

Deferred taxes arise, for example, when a company uses faster depreciation for tax purposes than in reports to investors. That means the company reports more taxes than it pays. The difference is accumulated as a liability for deferred taxes. In a sense there is liability, because the tax office 'catches up', collecting extra taxes as assets age. But this is irrelevant in capital investment analysis, which focuses on actual after-tax cash flows and uses accelerated tax depreciation.

Deferred taxes should not be regarded as a source of financing or an element of the weighted average cost of capital formula. The liability for deferred taxes is not a security held by investors. It is a balance sheet entry created to serve the needs of accounting.

[12] Financial practitioners have rules of thumb for deciding whether short-term debt is worth including in the weighted average cost of capital. Suppose, for example, that short-term debt is 10 per cent of total assets and net working capital is small or negative. Then short-term debt is almost surely being used to finance long-term assets and should be explicitly included in WACC.

| Net working capital<br>  = current assets<br>  − current liabilities<br>Plant and equipment<br>Growth opportunities | Long-term debt   (D)<br>Preferred shares   (P)<br>Equity   (E) |
|---|---|
| Total assets − current liabilities | Total capitalisation   (V) |

When net working capital is treated as an asset, forecasts of cash flows for capital investment projects must treat increases in net working capital as a cash outflow and decreases as an inflow. This is standard practice, which we followed in Section 6.2.

Since current liabilities include short-term debt, netting them out against current assets excludes the cost of short-term debt from the weighted average cost of capital. We have just explained why this can be an acceptable approximation. But when short-term debt is an important source of financing—as is common for small firms and sometimes true for some large ones—it should be shown explicitly on the right side of the balance sheet, not netted out against current assets. The interest cost of short-term debt is then one element of the weighted average cost of capital.

There is one other area of difficulty with current liabilities. Let us paraphrase questions we have sometimes had from corporate treasurers together with our answers:

'What about non-interest bearing current liabilities such as accounts payable? Can't such spontaneously-generated liabilities be a cheap source of finance to the firm?'

'Yes, sometimes.'

'So shouldn't we include them in our cost of capital?'

'No.'

'Why not?'

'Level 1 consistency.'

'What?'

'Let us explain. When you work out the investment in a project you calculate how much debt and equity you need to start the project and provide working capital. So your cost of capital has to reflect the cash flows needed to service that debt and equity. When you calculated your working capital requirements you netted out the spontaneous finance that you would obtain. That reduced your working capital requirement. Spontaneous finance was therefore excluded from your required investment. If you also reduce your cost of capital for spontaneous finance you will be double counting the benefit.'[13]

**4.** *How are the costs of the financing elements calculated?* You can often use share market data to get an estimate of $r_E$, the expected rate of return demanded by investors in the company's shares. One way of doing this is to estimate the company's equity beta and use the CAPM to estimate the required return on the shares. Another way is to use the dividend growth model, but estimates of the growth rate $g$ are notoriously unreliable.

The next step is to estimate the borrowing rate $r_D$ and the debt and equity ratios $D/V$ and $E/V$. In some cases the values for these variables can be directly observed in the capital market. But most Australian corporate debt is not actively traded, so its market value and market yield cannot be observed directly. Instead you can sometimes value a non-traded debt security by looking to debt securities which *are* traded, or recently issued, and which have approximately the same default risk and maturity as the non-traded debt (see Chapter 23). For healthy firms the market value of debt is usually not too far from book value, so many managers and analysts use book value for $D$ in the weighted average cost of capital formula. This will work very well in cases where the default risk is not high and the debt has a variable interest rate. However, be sure to use *market*, not book, values for $E$ and make sure you use current market interest rates for $r_D$.

---

[13] The accounting for liabilities such as accounts payable is in the actual project cash flows. In the case of payables the cash flows for purchases extinguish the payables liability.

Estimating the required return on other security types can be troublesome. Estimating the value and required return for preferred shares is much the same as for debt and is usually not too complicated.[14] However, convertible preference shares are a different story.[15] For convertible preference shares, or convertible debt, the investor's return comes partly from an option to exchange the security for the company's shares. This raises problems that we will have to defer till our discussion of convertibles in Chapter 22.

Estimating the cost of junk debt, where the risk of default is high, is likewise difficult. The higher the odds of default, the lower the market price of the debt and the higher the *promised* rate of interest. But the weighted average cost of capital is an *expected* rate of return, not a promised one. This is bad news: there is no easy or tractable way of estimating the expected rate of return on most junk debt issues.[16] There is some good news: most Australian corporate debt is not junk debt—the odds of default are small. That means the promised and expected rates of return are close, and the promised rate can be used as an approximation in the weighted average cost of capital.

## Industry costs of capital

The WACC is a *company* cost of capital. Strictly speaking, it works only for projects that are carbon copies of the firm's existing assets, in both business risk and financing. Often it is used as a benchmark discount rate companywide; the benchmark is then adjusted upwards for unusually risky projects and downwards for unusually safe ones.

You can also calculate WACC for *industries*. Suppose that a pharmaceutical company has a subsidiary that produces specialty chemicals. What discount rate is better for the subsidiary's projects—the company WACC or a weighted average cost of capital for a portfolio of 'pure play' specialty chemical companies? The latter rate is better in principle and also in practice if good data are available for firms with operations and markets similar to the subsidiary's.

## Mistakes people make in using the weighted average formula

The weighted average formula is useful and widely used, but it is also dangerous. The danger lies in misuse and this can happen even in experienced hands. First, you need to make sure that you are discounting cash flows defined consistently with WACC. Second, the formula is only strictly correct if the project has exactly the same risk as the firm and supports a constant debt-to-equity ratio which is the same as the firm's. Third, by making the tax adjustment for debt in the discount rate we implicitly assume that we can get the full benefit of the tax deductibility of debt in each and every period.

Here is an example of the logical errors that people often make. Manager Q, who is campaigning for a pet project, might look at the formula

$$r^* = r_D(1 - T_c)\frac{D}{V} + r_E\frac{E}{V}$$

---

14 The estimates of yield and value are like those for debt, but you have more chance of finding that the preference shares are traded. You will probably also find that the preference shares are a very small proportion of the overall market value of the firm. In which case errors in your preference share estimates do not carry much weight in the WACC.

15 For a discussion of the use of these securities see Kevin Davis, 'Convertible Preference Shares: An Australian Capital Structure Innovation', *Accounting and Finance*, 36: 213–28 (November 1996).

16 In the unlikely event that betas can be estimated for the junk issue or for a sample of similar issues, the expected return can be calculated from the capital asset pricing model. Otherwise, an estimate of the annual probability of default should be subtracted from the promised yield. Evidence on historical default rates on junk bonds is described in Chapter 24.

and think, 'Aha! My firm has a good credit rating. It could borrow, say, 90 per cent of the project's cost if it likes. That means $D/V = 0.9$ and $E/V = 0.1$. My firm's borrowing rate $r_D$ is 8 per cent, and the required return on equity $r_E$ is 15 per cent. Therefore

$$r^* = 0.08(1 - 0.35)(0.9) + 0.15(0.1) = 0.062, \text{ or } 6.2\%$$

When I discount at that rate, my project looks great.'

Q is wrong on several counts. First, the weighted average formula works only for projects that are carbon copies of the firm. The firm is not 90 per cent debt-financed.

Second, the immediate source of funds for a project has no necessary connection with the hurdle rate for the project. What matters is the project's overall contribution to the firm's borrowing power. A dollar invested in Q's pet project will not increase the firm's debt capacity by $0.90. If it borrows 90 per cent of the project's cost, it is really borrowing in part against its *existing* assets.[17] Any advantage from financing the new project with more debt than normal should be attributed to the old projects, not to the new one.

Third, even if the firm were willing and able to lever up to 90 per cent debt, its cost of capital would not decline to 6.2 per cent (as Q's naive calculation predicts). You cannot increase the debt ratio without creating financial risk for shareholders and thereby increasing $r_E$, the expected rate of return they demand from the firm's ordinary shares. Going to 90 per cent debt would certainly increase the borrowing rate, too.

# 19.2 Adjusted present value

The weighted average cost of capital is a bit of a black box—when it works, it is great; when it does not, most managers do not know how to adjust it. Too much is rolled into a (deceptively simple) tax adjustment to the 'cost of debt'.

We now take a different tack. Instead of messing around with the discount rate, we explicitly adjust cash flows and present values for the costs or benefits of financing. This approach is called **adjusted present value (APV)**.

The adjusted present value rule is easiest to understand in the context of simple numerical examples. We start by analysing a project under base-case assumptions and then consider possible financing side effects of accepting the project.

## The base case

The APV method begins by valuing the project as if it were a mini-firm financed solely by equity. A firm in sunny Queensland is considering a project to produce solar water heaters. It requires a $10 million investment and offers a level after-tax cash flow of $1.8 million per year for 10 years. The opportunity cost of capital is 12 per cent, which reflects the project's business risk. Investors would demand a 12 per cent expected return to invest in the mini-firm's shares.

Thus, the mini-firm's base-case NPV is

$$\text{NPV} = -10 + \sum_{t=1}^{10} \frac{1.8}{(1.12)^t} = +\$0.17 \text{ million, or } \$170\,000$$

Considering the project's size, this figure is not substantially greater than zero. In a pure MM world where no financing decision matters, the financial manager would lean towards taking the project but would not be heartbroken if the project were discarded.

---

[17]  If the project fails, the firm will still have the debt which must be supported by the cash flows from the other assets. If, and only if, the financial claim disappears should the project fail, can we directly link the finance to the project.

## Issue costs

But suppose that the firm actually has to finance the $10 million investment by issuing shares (it will not have to issue shares if it rejects the project) and that issue costs soak up 5 per cent of the gross proceeds of the issue. That means the firm has to issue $10 526 000 (i.e. $10 million/(1 − 0.05)) in order to obtain $10 000 000 cash. The $526 000 difference goes to underwriters, lawyers and others involved in the issue process.

The project's APV is calculated by subtracting the issue cost from base-case NPV:[18]

$$\text{APV} = \text{base-case NPV} - \text{issue cost}$$
$$= +170\,000 - 526\,000 = -\$356\,000$$

The firm would reject the project because APV is negative.

## Additions to the firm's debt capacity

Consider a different financing scenario. Suppose that the firm has a 50 per cent target debt ratio. Its policy is to limit debt to 50 per cent of its assets. Thus, if it invests more, it borrows more; in this sense investment adds to the firm's debt capacity.[19]

Is debt capacity worth anything? The most widely accepted answer is 'yes' because of the tax shields generated by interest payments on corporate borrowing. (Look back to our discussion of debt and taxes in Chapter 18.) For example, MM's theory states that the value of the firm is independent of its capital structure *except* for the present value of interest tax shields:

$$\text{Firm value} = \text{value with all equity financing} + \text{PV(tax shield)}$$

This theory tells us to compute the value of the firm in two steps. First, compute its base-case value under all equity financing; then, add the present value of taxes saved due to a departure from all equity financing. This procedure is like an APV calculation for the firm as a whole.

We can repeat the calculation for a particular project. For example, suppose that the solar heater project increases the firm's assets by $10 million and therefore prompts it to borrow $5 million more. To keep things simple, we assume that this $5 million loan is repaid in equal instalments, so that the amount borrowed declines with the depreciating book value of the solar heater project. We also assume that the loan carries an interest rate of 8 per cent. Table 19.1 shows how the value of the interest tax shields is calculated. This is the value of the additional debt capacity contributed to the firm by the project. We obtain APV by adding this amount to the project's NPV:

$$\text{APV} = \text{base-case NPV} + \text{PV(tax shield)}$$
$$= +170\,000 + 576\,000 = \$746\,000$$

## The value of interest tax shields

In Table 19.1 we boldly assumed that the firm could fully capture interest tax shields of $0.35 on every dollar of interest. We also treated the interest tax shields as safe cash inflows and discounted them at a low 8 per cent rate.

---

18   Sometimes you will find people attempting to incorporate flotation costs into the discount rate; we strongly advise against this practice.

19   *Debt capacity* is potentially misleading because it seems to imply an absolute limit to the amount the firm is *able* to borrow. That is not what we mean. The firm limits borrowing to 50 per cent of assets as a rule of thumb for optimal capital structure. It could borrow more if it wanted to.

**table 19.1**

Calculating the present value of interest tax shields on debt supported by the solar heater project (figures in $'000).

| Year | Debt outstanding at start of year | Interest | Interest tax shield | Present value of tax shield |
|------|-----------------------------------|----------|---------------------|-----------------------------|
| 1 | $5000 | $400 | $140 | $129.6 |
| 2 | 4500 | 360 | 126 | 108.0 |
| 3 | 4000 | 320 | 112 | 88.9 |
| 4 | 3500 | 280 | 98 | 72.0 |
| 5 | 3000 | 240 | 84 | 57.2 |
| 6 | 2500 | 200 | 70 | 44.1 |
| 7 | 2000 | 160 | 56 | 32.6 |
| 8 | 1500 | 120 | 42 | 22.7 |
| 9 | 1000 | 80 | 28 | 14.0 |
| 10 | 500 | 40 | 14 | 6.5 |
| | | | Total | $576.0 |

*Assumptions:*
1. *Marginal tax rate = $T_c$ = 0.35; tax shield = 0.35 × interest.*
2. *Debt principal is repaid at the end of the year in 10 × $500 000 instalments.*
3. *Interest rate on debt is 8 per cent.*
4. *Present value is calculated at the 8 per cent borrowing rate. The assumption here is that the tax shields are just as risky as the interest payments generating them. (Later we will relax this assumption.)*

The true present value of the tax shields is almost surely less than $576 000:

**1.** You cannot use tax shields unless you pay taxes, and you do not pay taxes unless you make profits. Few firms can be *sure* that future profitability will be sufficient to use up the interest tax shields.

**2.** The government takes two bites out of corporate income: the corporate tax and the tax on bondholders' and shareholders' personal income. The corporate tax favours debt; the personal tax favours equity.

**3.** A project's debt capacity depends on how well it does. When profits exceed expectations the firm can borrow more; when the project fails it will not support any debt. If the future amount of debt is tied to project value, then the interest tax shields given in Table 19.1 are estimates, not fixed amounts.

In Chapter 18 we argued that the effective tax shield on interest was probably not the statutory corporate tax rate $T_c$ but some lower figure, call it $T^*$. We were unable to pin down an exact figure for $T^*$.

Suppose, for example, that we believe $T^* = 0.25$. We can easily recalculate the APV of the solar heater project. Just multiply the present value of the interest tax shields by 25/35. The bottom line of Table 19.1 drops from $576 000 to 576 000(25/35) = $411 000. APV drops to:

$$\text{APV} = \text{base-case NPV} + \text{PV(tax shield)}$$
$$= +170\,000 + 411\,000 = \$581\,000$$

PV(tax shield) drops still further if the tax shields are treated as uncertain forecasts and discounted at a higher rate. Suppose the firm ties the amount of debt to actual future project cash flows. Then the interest tax shields become just as risky as the project and should be discounted at the 12 per cent opportunity cost of capital.[20] PV(risky tax shield) drops to $362 000 at $T^* = 0.25$.

## Review of the APV approach

If the decision to invest in a capital project has important side effects on other financial decisions made by the firm, those side effects should be taken into account when the project is evaluated. They include interest tax shields on debt supported by the project (a plus), any issue costs of raising financing for the project (a minus), or perhaps other side effects such as the value of a government-subsidised loan tied to the project.

The idea behind APV is 'divide and conquer'. The approach does not attempt to capture all the side effects in a single calculation. A series of present value calculations is made instead. The first establishes a base-case value for the project: its value as a separate, all equity-financed mini-firm. Then, each side effect is traced out, and the present value of its cost or benefit to the firm is calculated. Finally, all the present values are added together to estimate the project's total contribution to the value of the firm. Thus, in general,

$$\text{Project APV} = \text{base-case NPV} + \text{sum of the present values of the side effects of accepting the project}$$

The wise financial manager will want to see not only the adjusted present value, but also where that value is coming from. For example, suppose that base-case NPV is positive but the benefits are outweighed by the costs of issuing shares to finance the project. That should prompt the manager to look around to see if the project can be rescued by an alternative financing plan.

# 19.3 Adjusted discount rates and adjusted present value

Calculating APV is not mathematically difficult, but tracing out and evaluating a project's financing side effects take financial sophistication. In particular, it is a difficult task to work out the equity discount rate for the base case. One way is to unlever the firm's existing equity beta, to get an asset beta, but this is not a trivial task.[21]

In the face of these difficulties, managers seem to find it simpler to use an adjusted discount rate than to use the APV method.[22] The after-tax weighted average cost of capital is one example of an adjusted discount rate, but there are other formulas. Let us take a closer look.

## APV for the Geothermal project

In Section 19.1 we evaluated the Geothermal project using the weighted average cost of capital. Let us revisit the hot springs of New Zealand and evaluate the Geothermal project using the APV method. Then we can see how the WACC and APV methods compare.

---

20  This is not quite right. Note, for example, that the first interest tax shield depends on the original debt amount of $5000, which is not uncertain. The second tax shield is in turn known in period 1. The exact discounting procedure is covered later.

21  In order to make this adjustment we need to know how the use of debt affects the value of the firm. For that we need a theory of capital structure. The problem is that there is no general agreement about what this theory should be. We provide some alternative beta adjustment formulas later in the chapter.

22  This is one case where the simple things in life are not necessarily the best.

We ignore any issue costs and concentrate on the value of interest tax shields supported by the project. To keep things simple, we assume throughout this section that the only financing side effect is the interest tax shields on debt supported by the project, and we consider corporate taxes only. (In other words, $T^* = T_c$.)

The base-case NPV is found by first discounting after-tax project cash flows of $1.355 million at the opportunity cost of capital of 12 per cent, and then subtracting the $10 million outlay. (We will explain later, when we introduce the Miles–Ezzell formula, how we know that Geothermal's opportunity cost of capital is 12 per cent.) The cash flows are perpetual, so

$$\text{Base-case NPV} = -10 + \frac{1.355}{0.12} = +\$1.29 \text{ million}$$

Thus, the project would be worthwhile even with all equity financing. But it actually supports debt of $5 million. At an 8 per cent borrowing rate ($r_D = 0.08$) and a 35 per cent tax rate ($T_c = 0.35$), annual interest tax shields are $0.35 \times 0.08 \times 5 = 0.14$ million, or $140\,000$.

What are those tax shields worth? It depends on the *financing rule* the company follows. There are two common rules.

■ Financing rule 1: *Debt fixed*. Borrow a fraction of *initial* project value and pay off the debt on a predetermined schedule. (We followed this rule for the solar heater project in Table 19.1.)
■ Financing rule 2: *Debt rebalanced*. Adjust the debt in each future period to keep it at a constant fraction of project value at that future date.

What do these rules mean for the Geothermal project? Under financing rule 1 for a perpetuity debt remains constant. So, debt stays at $5 million come hell or high water and interest tax shields stay at $140\,000 per year. The tax shields are tied to fixed interest payments, so the 8 per cent cost of debt is a reasonable discount rate.

$$\text{PV(tax shields, debt fixed)} = \frac{140\,000}{0.08} = \$1\,750\,000, \text{ or } \$1.75 \text{ million}$$

$$\text{APV} = \text{base-case NPV} + \text{PV(tax shield)} = +1.29 + 1.75 = +3.04, \text{ or about } \$3 \text{ million}$$

If Geothermal were financed solely by equity, firm value would be $11.29 million. With fixed debt of $5 million, firm value increases by PV(tax shield) to $11.29 + 1.75 = \$13.04$ million. Notice that this is higher than our earlier value of $12.5 million from Section 19.1, which implicitly assumed financing rule 2.

Under financing rule 2, debt is rebalanced to 40 per cent of actual project value. The means future debt levels are not known at the start of the project; they depend on the project's actual performance. That also means that future interest payments track changes in actual project cash flows and pick up the business risk of the project.

Figure 19.1 shows how the debt supported by the Geothermal project changes for three possible cash flows in year 1. If cash flows are below the $1.355 million forecast, project value falls, debt is reduced and interest tax shields in year 2 fall proportionately. You can see that interest tax shields are perfectly correlated with the surprises in project cash flows and have basically the same risk characteristics. The next period's interest tax shields are, however, known once this period's debt is determined.

Valuing these forecasted interest tax shields exactly is a bit of work, but it is worth it to demonstrate that everything comes out right. The first tax shield is not uncertain (it depends on the initial debt of $5 million),[23] so we discount at the borrowing rate of 8 per cent:

$$\text{PV} = \frac{0.14}{1.08} = 0.13, \text{ or } \$130\,000$$

---

[23]　We have finessed a technical problem here. In order to work out the starting quantity of debt $D$ we multiply the value of the firm $V$ by the target level of leverage $L$. But in order to work out $V$ we need to know the dollar value $D$ of the debt that we plan to start with. We could start with an approximate value for $D$, but an iterative process may be necessary to improve the approximation, depending on the level of precision required in our calculation of $V$.

The second tax shield is also forecasted at $0.14 million, but depends on the first year's cash flow and project value (as in Figure 19.1). It is uncertain for one year, *then* known when debt is rebalanced in year 1. Therefore, we discount for the first year at the opportunity cost of capital (12 per cent) and for the second year at 8 per cent:

$$PV = \frac{0.14}{(1.12)(1.08)} = 0.116, \text{ or } \$116\,000$$

The third tax shield is not known for two years, so there are two years discounting at 12 per cent and one at 8 per cent:

$$PV = \frac{0.14}{(1.12)^2(1.08)} = 0.103, \text{ or } \$103\,000, \text{ and so on.}$$

**figure 19.1** _____

Interest tax shields assuming debt is rebalanced to 40 per cent of the value of the Geothermal project. Cash flows may rise, fall or remain the same. Project value and debt adjust proportionally, so that debt is always 40 per cent of project value. The top decision tree starts at year 0, the bottom at year 1, and assumes that cash flows fall below forecasts in year 1. Note that interest tax shields are based on the previous year's debt (figures in $million).

| Start:<br>Year 0 | Year 1 | | | | Interest tax<br>shield year 1 |
|---|---|---|---|---|---|
| | Actual<br>cash flow | Updated<br>cash flow | Project<br>value | Rebalanced<br>debt | (Based on debt at<br>year 0) |
| Cash flow forecast = 1.355 | 1.49 | 1.49 | 13.75 | 5.5 | 0.14 |
| | 1.355 | 1.355 | 12.5 | 5.0 | 0.14 |
| | 1.23 | 1.23 | 11.36 | 4.55 | 0.14 |
| Project value = 12.5<br>Debt = 5.0 | | | | | |

| Continue:<br>Year 1 | Year 2 | | | | Interest tax<br>shield year 2* |
|---|---|---|---|---|---|
| | Actual<br>cash flow | Updated<br>cash flow | Project<br>value | Rebalanced<br>debt | (Based on debt at<br>year 1) |
| (Assuming cash flows drop<br>to 1.23) | 1.355 | 1.355 | 12.5 | 5.0 | 0.127 |
| | 1.23 | 1.23 | 11.36 | 4.55 | 0.127 |
| | 1.12 | 1.12 | 10.33 | 4.13 | 0.127 |
| Project value = 11.36<br>Debt = 4.55 | | | | | |

*Note:*  * *The forecasted tax shield is still $0.14 million, but the actual tax shield turns out to be $0.127 million.*

This may look complicated, but it is actually easy to remember. You can always *approximate* the value of interest tax shields generated under financing rule 2 just by discounting at the opportunity cost of capital. For the third tax shield, this would give

$$\text{Approximate PV} = \frac{0.14}{(1.12)^3} = 0.100, \text{ or } \$100\,000$$

For practical purposes you can usually stop here. But to correct the approximation, just multiply the approximate PV by 1.12/1.08, that is $(1 + r)/(1 + r_D)$. This cancels out one year's discounting at $r$ and adds one year at $r_D$; for the third tax shield,

$$PV = \frac{1.12}{1.08} \times 0.100 = 0.103 \text{ as before}$$

So the general rule for valuing interest tax shields under financing rule 2 is

1.  Discount at the opportunity cost of capital, because future tax shields are tied to actual cash flows.
2.  Multiply the resulting PV by $(1 + r)/(1 + r_D)$, because the tax shields are fixed one period before receipt. This is equivalent to using the valuation formula:

$$PV(\text{tax shield}) = \sum_{t=1}^{n} \frac{(\text{interest})T_c}{(1 + r)^t} \times \frac{(1 + r)}{(1 + r_D)} = \sum_{t=1}^{n} \frac{(\text{interest})T_c}{(1 + r_D)(1 + r)^{t-1}}$$

For the Geothermal project, the forecasted interest tax shields are $0.14 million in perpetuity. The opportunity cost of capital is 12 per cent.

$$\text{Approximate PV(tax shield)} = \frac{0.14}{0.12} = 1.17$$

$$\text{Exact PV(tax shield)} = \frac{1.12}{1.08} \times 1.17 = \$1.21 \text{ million}$$

The APV of the project, given these assumptions about future debt capacity, is

$$APV = \text{base-case NPV} + PV(\text{tax shield}) = 1.29 + 1.21 = \$2.5 \text{ million}$$

Firm value with debt rebalancing is

Firm value with all equity financing + PV(tax shield) = 11.29 + 1.21 = \$12.50 million

Notice that the value is less with financing rule 2 than with rule 1 because the tax shields are uncertain.

# APV and the weighted average cost of capital

We have now valued the Geothermal project three different ways:

1.  APV (debt fixed) = +$3.1 million
2.  APV (debt rebalanced) = +$2.5 million
3.  NPV (discounting at WACC) = +$2.5 million

The second and third calculations are identical because the underlying assumptions about financing are the same. It is worth repeating the point we made in Section 19.1: *discounting at WACC assumes that debt is rebalanced every period to maintain a constant ratio of debt to the market value of the firm.*[24]

This is certainly a more reasonable assumption than financing rule 1, which says that debt is paid off on an absolutely fixed schedule. Any capital budgeting procedure that assumes debt levels are fixed when a project is undertaken is grossly oversimplified. Should we assume that the Geothermal project contributes $5 million to the firm's debt capacity—not just when the project is undertaken, but 'from here to eternity'? That amounts to saying that the future value of the project will not change—a strong assumption indeed. Suppose the price of oil shoots up unexpectedly a year after the project is undertaken; since the Geothermal project *saves* oil, its

---

[24]  This point is emphasised by J. Miles and R. Ezzell, op. cit., Footnote 7.

cash flow and value shoot up too. Suppose the project's value doubles. In that case, will not its contribution to debt capacity also double, to $10 million? It works the other way too: if the oil price falls out of bed, the contribution to debt capacity tumbles.

The better rule is not 'Always borrow $5 million' but 'Always borrow 40 per cent of the Geothermal project's value'. Then if project value increases, the firm borrows more. If it decreases, it borrows less. Under this policy you can no longer discount future interest tax shields at the borrowing rate because the shields are no longer certain. Their size depends on the amount actually borrowed and therefore on the actual future value of the project.

## APV and hurdle rates

APV tells you whether a project makes a net contribution to the value of the firm. It can also tell you a project's *break-even* cash flow or internal rate of return. Let us check this for the Geothermal project. We first calculate the income at which APV = 0. We will then determine the project's minimum acceptable internal rate of return (IRR).

$$\text{APV} = \frac{\text{annual income}}{r} - \text{investment} + \text{PV(tax shield)}$$

$$= \frac{\text{annual income}}{0.12} - 10 + \text{PV(tax shield)} = 0$$

This equation sets APV = 0, but we must work out both the annual income and the PV of the tax shield. Let us calculate the PV of the tax shield. It will be less than the values calculated earlier, because if APV = 0 the project is only worth $10 million, not $12.5 million, and under financing rule 2 will support only $4 million (40% × 10), not $5 million, in debt. In other words, debt drops by 20 per cent, and so must the PV(tax shield).

Therefore, we reduce PV(tax shield) by 20 per cent, from $1.21 million to $0.97 million, and solve for annual income:

$$\text{APV} = \frac{\text{annual income}}{0.12} - 10 + 0.97 = 0$$

$$\text{Annual income} = \$1.084 \text{ million}$$

or 10.84 per cent of the $10 million outlay. In other words, the minimum acceptable IRR for the project is 10.84 per cent. At this IRR project APV is zero.

Suppose that we encounter another project with perpetual cash flows. Its opportunity cost of capital is also $r = 0.12$ and it also expands the firm's borrowing power by 40 per cent of project value. We know that if such a project offers an IRR greater than 10.84 per cent, it will have a positive APV. Therefore, we could shorten the analysis by just discounting the project's cash inflows at 10.84 per cent.[25] The 10.84 per cent adjusted cost of capital for the Geothermal project is (no surprise) identical to Geothermal's weighted average cost of capital calculated in Section 19.1. This discount rate is an *adjusted cost of capital r**. It reflects both the project's business risk and its contribution to the firm's debt capacity.

## A general definition of the adjusted cost of capital

We recapitulate the two concepts of cost of capital:

▌ *Concept 1. The opportunity cost of capital (r)*: the expected rate of return offered in capital markets by equivalent-risk assets. The opportunity cost of capital depends on the risk of the project's cash flows. This opportunity cost of capital is the correct discount rate for the project if it is all-equity-financed.

---

[25] Remember that forecasted project cash flows in this case do *not* reflect the tax shields generated by any debt the project may support. Project taxes are calculated assuming all equity financing. In other words, we use the unlevered cash flow.

■ *Concept 2. The adjusted cost of capital* (r*): an adjusted opportunity cost or hurdle rate that reflects the financing side effects of an investment project.

Some people just say 'cost of capital'. Sometimes their meaning is clear in context. At other times, they do not know which concept they are referring to and that can sow widespread confusion.

When financing side effects are important, you should accept projects with positive APVs. But if you know the adjusted discount rate, you do not have to calculate APV; you just calculate NPV at the adjusted rate. If we could find a simple, universally correct method for calculating $r^*$, we would be all set.

The weighted average cost of capital formula is one way to calculate the adjusted cost of capital, but it is not universally correct. Remember, WACC works when the project being valued has the same business risk and financing as the firm as a whole and you keep your leverage ratio constant. The WACC formula does not tell you what to do if a project is safer or riskier than the company average or if it is financed in a different way.

So when all projects are 'average', WACC works fine. When projects differ, their adjusted costs of capital differ, too. To understand these differences, we need a formula showing how WACC depends on financial leverage and the opportunity cost of capital. We will give two formulas which rest on somewhat different assumptions.

## The Miles–Ezzell formula
James Miles and Russell Ezzell came up with the following useful formula for adjusting WACC:[26]

$$r^* = \text{WACC} = r - Lr_D T^* \left( \frac{1 + r}{1 + r_D} \right),$$

where $L$ is the debt-to-value ratio and $T^*$ is the net tax value per dollar of interest paid. In practice $T^*$ is very hard to pin down, and the marginal corporate tax rate $T_c$ is used instead.

The formula assumes financing rule 2, that the firm adjusts its future borrowing to keep debt proportions constant. Therefore, it is consistent with the weighted average cost of capital formula and can be used to adjust WACC if, say, a new project has different debt capacity than the firm's other assets.

This is a common problem. Financial managers can usually get reasonable estimates of WACC, and for 'average' projects WACC is the only discount rate needed. But when financing or business risks change, the WACC formula does not tell the manager what to do.

Suppose, for example, that Geothermal's financial manager does not know what $r$, the opportunity cost of capital, is. However, the manager observes that Geothermal has $5 million of debt and that firm value with financing rule 2 is $12.5 million. Thus, the debt-to-value ratio $L$ is $5/12.5 = 0.4$. The manager also calculates the WACC at 10.84 per cent. Since the Miles–Ezzell $r^*$ equals WACC and all variables but $r$ are known (including $T^* = T_c = 0.35$),

$$r^* = r - Lr_D T_c \left[ \frac{1 + r}{1 + r_D} \right] = \text{WACC}$$

$$= r - 0.4(0.08)(0.35)\left( \frac{1 + r}{1.08} \right) = 0.1084$$

You can check that solving for $r$ gives $r = 0.12$, which is the same figure that we used to calculate the APV.

---

[26] J. Miles and R. Ezzell, op. cit., Footnote 7.

Now you know what return investors would demand if Geothermal were all equity financed, you can use the Miles–Ezzell formula to find the adjusted cost of capital at any debt level. If a new project's debt capacity is only, say, 30 per cent of project value, the financial manager could substitute in the formula to get the correct hurdle rate. With $L = 0.30$,

$$r^* = 0.12 - 0.3(0.08)(0.35)\left(\frac{1.12}{1.08}\right) = 0.111, \text{ or } 11.1\%$$

The adjusted cost of capital (equal to WACC in this case) is the downward sloping line in Figure 19.2.[27]

The financial manager can also calculate the cost of equity ($r_E$) at 30 per cent debt. (It will be lower than at Geothermal's 40 per cent debt ratio because financial risk is reduced.) If WACC $= 0.111$ at $L = 0.3$ and the cost of debt stays at $r_D = 0.08$,

$$\text{WACC} = r_D(1 - T_c)\frac{D}{V} + r_E\frac{E}{V} = r^*$$

$$= 0.08(1 - 0.35)(0.3) + r_E(0.7) = 0.111$$

$$r_E = 0.136, \text{ or } 13.6\%$$

We have plotted $r_E$ as the upward-sloping line in Figure 19.2.

The general formula for $r_E$ as a function of the opportunity cost of capital and financial leverage is a bit elaborate, but the following formula (familiar from Chapters 9 and 17—MM with no taxes) is an excellent approximation.

$$r_E = r + (r - r_D)\frac{D}{E}$$

For Geothermal, $D/V = 0.4$, so $D/E = 0.4/0.6 = 0.667$. That implies

$$r_E = 0.12 + (0.12 - 0.08)0.667 = 0.147, \text{ or } 14.7\%$$

a trifle higher than the true cost of equity of 14.6 per cent that we found back in Section 19.1. The true cost of equity is the upward-sloping line in Figure 19.2.

In drawing this figure, we have assumed the cost of debt is 8 per cent regardless of whether the debt ratio is 30 or 40 per cent. This assumption is not too bad if the risk of default is small, and it simplifies the figure because $r_E$ plots as a straight line so long as $r_D$ is constant. But at higher debt ratios life is more complicated. The cost of debt increases as the debt ratio increases, and the rate of increase in the cost of equity declines (compare with Figure 17.2). Moreover, the firm becomes less and less sure that it will generate enough future income to use all interest tax shields. Therefore, the curve for WACC 'bottoms out', as shown in Figure 19.2 for high debt ratios.

**MM's formula**    Another formula for adjusting WACC was suggested by Modigliani and Miller.[28] MM's formula is

$$r^* = \text{WACC} = r(1 - T^*L)$$

---

27   Note that the horizontal axis in Figures 19.2 and 19.3 is the debt-equity ratio, $D/E$. This is the format used in Figure 17.2. Debt-to-value ratios of 0.3 and 0.4 correspond to debt-equity ratios of $0.3/0.7 = 0.43$ and $0.4/0.6 = 0.67$.

28   The formula first appeared in F. Modigliani and M. H. Miller, 'Corporate Income Taxes and the Cost of Capital: A Correction', *American Economic Review*, 53: 433–43 (June 1963). It is explained more fully in M. H. Miller and F. Modigliani, 'Some Estimates of the Cost of Capital to the Electric Utility Industry: 1954–1957', *American Economic Review*, 56: 333–91 (June 1966). In these articles, MM assumed that $T^*$ equals the corporate tax rate $T_c$.

**figure 19.2**

Miles and Ezzell's formula shows how the weighted average cost of capital declines as a function of the debt ratio. The example shown here applies to the Geothermal project, with an opportunity cost of capital of 12 per cent and WACC of 10.84 per cent at a 40 per cent debt-to-value ratio.

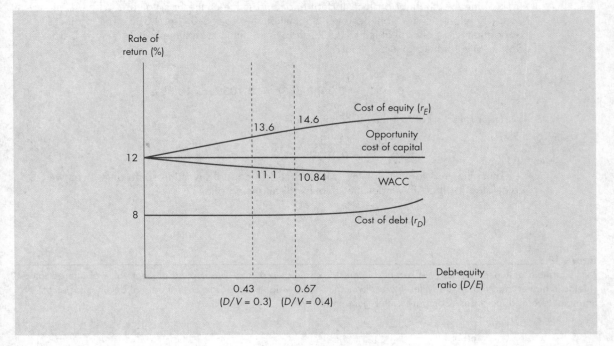

The MM formula assumes debt is fixed at the start of the project, not rebalanced. In practice $T^*$ is usually replaced with $T_c$, the marginal corporate tax rate.

The MM formula works for the Geothermal project or for any other project that is expected to (1) generate a level, perpetual cash flow and (2) support fixed permanent debt. The formula is exactly right only if these two assumptions are met. Assets offering perpetual cash flow streams are like abominable snowmen: often referred to but seldom seen. But MM's formula still works reasonably well for projects with limited lives or irregular cash flow streams if the fixed-debt assumption (financing rule 1) holds. Using the formula to calculate the present value of these projects typically results in an error of 2 to 6 per cent.[29] This is not too bad when you consider that a biased cash flow forecast could easily put project value off the mark by 20 to 60 per cent.

When MM's debt-fixed assumption is appropriate their formula can be used to calculate the opportunity cost of capital, given an estimate for WACC, or to see how WACC or $r_E$, the cost of equity, change at different debt ratios. WACC and $r_E$ for this case are plotted in Figure 19.3. By the way, MM's formula for $r_E$ is

$$r_E = r + (1 - T_c)(r - r_D)\frac{D}{E}$$

---

[29]    See S. C. Myers, 'Interactions of Corporate Financing and Investment Decisions—Implications for Capital Budgeting', *Journal of Finance*, **29**: 1–25 (March 1974).

## example

We illustrate the differences between the MM and Miles–Ezzell formulas with one last look at the Geothermal project. If debt financing is fixed, the firm value is $13.04 million. Therefore, if the firm borrows $5 million $L = 5/13.04 = 0.383$. The project's opportunity cost of capital is $r = 0.12$, and we continue to assume that $T^* = T_c = 0.35$. So the MM formula gives:

$$r^* = r(1 - T^*L)$$
$$= 0.12(1 - 0.35)(0.383) = 0.1039, \text{ or } 10.39\%$$

The project's NPV at this discount rate is

$$NPV = \frac{1.355}{0.1039} - 10 = \$3.04 \text{ million}$$

Thus, the MM formula for the adjusted cost of capital gives the same answer as we calculated for the APV under the 'debt-fixed' financing rule.

**figure 19.3**

MM's formula assumes that debt is fixed and interest tax shields are safe. The implied present value of interest tax shields is higher than that in the Miles–Ezzell formula, so the weighted average cost of capital declines faster as financial leverage increases. Compare with Figure 19.2.

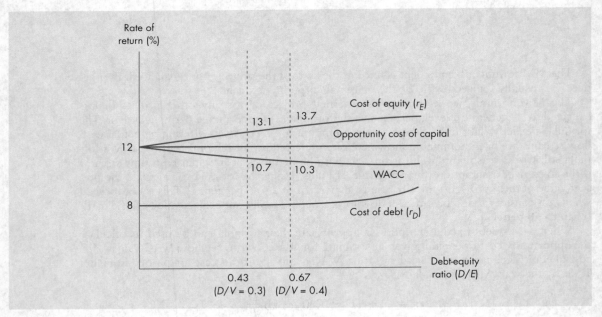

## 19.4 The interaction of corporate and personal taxes: effects of imputation[30]

Under the imputation tax system the shareholders recover, via imputation tax credits, some fraction of the corporate taxes paid (see Chapter 16). This has two effects relevant to the discussion here. First, it decreases the *effective* corporate tax rate and thereby increases the cash flow to shareholders. Second, the decrease in the effective corporate tax rate reduces the *effective* tax shield provided by debt (see Chapter 18). So how do we adjust for imputation? We have to allow for the increased cash flow to shareholders and the increased after-tax cost of debt. There are several ways we can do this,[31] but the adjustment is trivially simple *if* we can work out the imputation-adjusted corporate tax rate.

Given the effective corporate tax rate under imputation, we can use all the analysis for the APV and WACC that we have just worked through. All we have to do is substitute the effective corporate tax rate under imputation $T_{IC}$ wherever we earlier used the statutory corporate tax rate $T_c$.[32] For example, we can compute the base case for the APV as $C(1 - T_{IC})/r$,[33] and we could value a project by using the adjusted discount rate

$$r^{*1} = r_D(1 - T_{IC})\frac{D}{V} + r_E\frac{E}{V}$$

to discount the cash flow defined as $C(1 - T_{IC})$.

But there is something else we that we need to check. We must make sure that the opportunity cost of capital $r$ (the unlevered cost of equity used for the APV base case) and the levered cost of equity $r_E$ (used to calculate the adjusted discount rate $r^*$) are *measured* correctly. We are allowing for the imputation tax benefit by substituting $T_{IC}$ for $T_c$, and in so doing we calculate the cash flow as $C(1 - T_{IC})$.[34] This cash flow is after corporate tax and before personal tax, but it also includes allowance for the personal tax benefit of unlevered imputation credits. The cost of equity must therefore be measured before personal tax, and we must make sure that it has not been lowered to allow for the imputation tax benefit. That way we measure the equity discount rate and cash flow consistently, and we avoid double counting the benefit of the imputation credits.

What we need to know is the total return that the shareholders require from the capital gains yield, plus the dividend yield, plus the yield from imputation credits. We could write this as:

$$\text{Shareholders' required return} = \text{required}\left[\frac{P_1 - P_0 + D_1}{P_0} + \frac{IC_0}{P_0}\right]$$

where $P_0$ = last period's price; $P_1$ = the current price; $D_1$ = the current dividend; and $IC_0$ = the *value* of the imputation credit distributed with the dividend.

---

[30]   We acknowledge our debt to Bob Officer in developing this section, particularly his paper 'The Cost of Capital of a Company Under an Imputation Tax System', *Accounting and Finance*, 1–17 (May 1994).

[31]   The alternatives we discuss are exactly equivalent in a perpetuity framework. Some of these alternatives may not be strictly applicable in a multi-period framework. However, our first alternative is applicable in a multi-period framework as long as we make the usual assumptions, such as debt rebalancing to hold the leverage ratio constant.

[32]   A rigorous analysis which confirms this result can be found in a paper by Peter Monkhouse, 'Adapting the APV Valuation Methodology and the Beta Gearing Formula to the Dividend Imputation Tax System', *Accounting and Finance*, 37: 69–88 (May 1997). Using the effective corporate tax rate is also one of the alternatives derived by Bob Officer in his 1994 paper, op. cit., Footnote 30.

[33]   If we assume financing rule 2, the value of the debt tax shield is given by $\displaystyle\sum_{t=1}^{n} \frac{(\text{interest})T_{IC}}{(1 + r_D)(1 + r)^{t-1}}$

[34]   You can think of this as equivalent to the unlevered cash flow taxed at the statutory corporate rate, plus the value of imputation credits that would be distributed assuming the firm was unlevered.

For a levered firm the above equation gives the required value for $r_E$, while for an unlevered firm it gives $r$.

The first term of the equation poses no new problems; it gives the usual definition of return. The last term, which represents the imputation yield, is more difficult to deal with, because we cannot just assume that the credit is valued at its face value.

You may find adding in the imputation yield a bit confusing. Think of it this way; if we did not add in the imputation yield, we would have a lower discount rate applied to an increased cash flow. That would double count the imputation benefits. To explain this more fully we need to consider how the imputation system may change the cost of equity.[35]

## Changes in the cost of equity

We start by briefly considering the big picture. It is possible that major tax changes may cause a major disturbance in the equilibrium of capital markets such that the price of time and risk may change. In other words, the risk-free rate and the market risk premium may change. It is also possible that the risk characteristics of corporate cash flows may be changed and that the form of asset pricing models may change. These are interesting possibilities, but we will not pursue them here because we think this chapter is already difficult enough.[36] We have also seen no convincing empirical evidence that these effects have been significant. Until we do we are going to assume them away. So having opened the vista of the big picture we hastily close it, and return to the nitty gritty of tax at the level of the firm and its shareholders.

The first thing we need to remember is that the cost of equity that we observe in the share market is an after corporate tax, but before personal tax, required return.[37] This distinction is quite clear under a classical tax system, but the line gets blurred under imputation. So let us consider how a firm's cost of equity observed in the share market may change as we switch from a classical to an imputation tax system. Two polar cases suggest themselves. The first assumes that the marginal investor setting prices in Australia is an overseas investor[38] who gets no benefit from imputation tax credits. Imputation is of no value to such investors. In this case the switch to the imputation system will leave share prices unchanged and the cost of equity will likewise be unchanged.[39]

The second case assumes that the marginal investor gets the full benefit of the imputation credits, and we also assume that the return he/she requires after all taxes remains unchanged. In this case share prices will go up by the present value of the taxes saved. The after corporate tax, but before personal tax, required return will appear to fall. This fall will occur because the investors recover the corporate tax as a reduction in their personal tax liability. They end up paying less tax. So the return they demand in terms of dividends and capital gains before personal tax goes down.

The size of the apparent fall depends on what imputation does to effective tax rates. We believe that reality lies somewhere between our two polar cases. So effective tax rates under imputation are probably lower than under the classical system. Therefore, $r$ and $r_E$ measured before personal tax will be lower unless you make an explicit allowance for the 'hidden' component of returns represented by the extra tax saving or imputation yield.

If $r$ and $r_E$ vary according to how they are measured, this can be a source of ambiguity. So let us be clear: wherever $r$ and $r_E$ appear in our formulas for imputation, they are measured by adding the imputation yield to the dividend and capital gains yields. If we are to measure

---

[35]  As it turns out, the value we get for $r$ and $r_E$ will probably be much the same as we would get under the classical tax system.

[36]  For one example of the CAPM under imputation and a comparison with the traditional no-tax CAPM see Martin Lally, 'The CAPM Under Dividend Imputation', *Pacific Accounting Review*, 4: 31–44 (December 1992).

[37]  It represents the investor's after-all-taxes required return grossed up for the personal tax that the investor has to pay.

[38]  In other words, domestic share prices are set by international capital flows.

[39]  The argument for this is given in R. R. Officer, 'A Note on the Cost of Capital and Investment Evaluation for Companies Under the Imputation Tax', *Accounting and Finance*, 65–71 (November 1988).

the return on the market $(r_m)$ consistently, then it must also be measured including the imputation yield on the market index. If we continue to measure $r_m$ in the traditional way without the imputation yield, then the market risk premium $(r_m - r_f)$ will *appear* to drop under an imputation tax system.

### example

These ideas may be easier to grasp if we look at some numbers. Suppose that we are the marginal investors holding the shares of an unlevered company. Our required return after all taxes is 8 per cent. Our personal tax rate is 47 per cent. Then assuming a classical tax system, we want a return before personal tax of $r = 0.08/(1 - 0.47)$, or about 15 per cent. In order to satisfy us, the company would have to earn an after corporate tax return on equity of about 15 per cent. Now suppose we get an imputation credit. Let us say that the credit saves us tax equivalent to a 5 per cent increase in our return. We still want 8 per cent after all taxes. However, we will now accept an apparent 10 per cent before personal tax return, but only if we continue to get the imputation credit as well. The credit is less visible than the other components of our return—dividends and capital gains—so it is easily overlooked. In fact, it is not counted at all if we measure returns in the traditional way (dividend yield plus capital gain).

So it now appears that the company only has to earn a 10 per cent return after corporate tax. But it also has to pay sufficient corporate tax to keep supplying our imputation credits. We could use the 10 per cent as our base-case discount rate provided we apply it to the traditional unlevered cash flow $C(1 - T_c)$.[40] If we do this we are following the consistency principle and we will get the correct value.[41] But it is not difficult to see how this could run us into trouble if our corporate tax payments vary and the supply of imputation credits comes and goes.[42] Alternatively, we can use the adjusted tax rate and discount the cash flow $C(1 - T_{IC})$ at $r = 15$ per cent (10 per cent dividends and capital gains plus 5 per cent imputation credits).

# The effective corporate tax rate

Of course, it is one thing to talk about the effective corporate tax rate under imputation $T_{IC}$, but quite another to work out what it is. There are two main factors that determine how much the imputation credits reduce the corporate tax rate $T_c$. These are the fraction of current imputation credits that the firm distributes $f$, and the value of those credits to the company's shareholders. As a first *approximation* we can write:[43]

$$\text{Effective tax rate under imputation } T_{IC} = T_c\,[1 - (f \times \omega)] = T_c\,(1 - \gamma)$$

where $\omega$ = the value of the imputation credit as a per cent of the credit's face value when received by investors. In other words, $\omega$ is the value in cents of $1 face value of imputation

---

[40]  If we want to apply an adjusted discount rate to this cash flow we use $r^{*2} = r_D(1 - T_c)\dfrac{D}{V} + r_E\dfrac{(1 - T_c)}{(1 - T_{IC})}\dfrac{E}{V}$.

  Where $r_E$ is measured including the imputation yield, that would be $r_E = 15$ per cent in our example.

[41]  We are applying a before-personal-tax, but including imputation benefit, discount rate to a before-personal-tax, excluding imputation benefit, cash flow. That way we avoid double counting the imputation benefit.

[42]  Your valuation implicitly assumes the credits are there all the time.

[43]  To be entirely accurate we should allow for the fact that $f$ and $\omega$ may vary over time and that imputation credits not distributed now may be distributed later. However, we may justify our approximation as being similar in spirit to the convenience of using $r_D(1 - T_c)$ when computing the traditional after-tax cost of debt.

credits when distributed, while $\gamma$ is the value of imputation credits expressed as a proportion of currently created credits.[44] Notice that when firms pay out all their imputation credits $f = 1$, and if those credits are valued at 100 per cent of their face value $\omega = 1$, then $T_{IC} = 0$. In other words, we can ignore corporate taxes and capital structure entirely and discount the before corporate tax cash flows at the rate $r$. At the other extreme if $f$ or $\omega$ is zero, then $T_{IC} = T_c$, and we can forget about imputation because we get exactly the same results as under the classical tax system.

As we keep saying, reality probably lies somewhere in between these two extremes, perhaps about half way between them. If so, we might set $\gamma = 0.5$. This at least has the merit of simplicity, but perhaps it is too simple. In any event, we should expect some cross-sectional variation in $\gamma$ because $f$, and possibly $\omega$, will differ across firms.

## Alternative adjustments under imputation

Those of you with a good memory may be wondering about our statement made near the beginning of the chapter that you could use the traditional WACC under imputation provided you adjusted the cash flow. Remember our equation for the traditional WACC:

$$r^* = r_D(1 - T_c)\frac{D}{V} + r_E\frac{E}{V} = \text{WACC}$$

This discount rate is traditionally applied to the unlevered cash flow $C(1 - T_c)$. But under imputation we need to add the value of the *levered* imputation credit to the cash flow. This is determined by the tax the company actually pays, which in turn is the face value of the credit. This is given by $(C - \text{interest})T_c$. The face value of the credit is converted to a value for investors by multiplying with $\gamma$. Thus, under imputation the traditional WACC is used to discount the following cash flow:

Unlevered cash flow + value of imputation credit *after* leverage =
$$C(1 - T_c) + \gamma(C - \text{interest})T_c$$

Let us see if this makes sense. The traditional formula for WACC makes no allowance for the reduction in the effective debt tax shield under imputation—it assumes interest tax shields give a tax saving of $T_c$ per dollar of interest. Neither does the traditional WACC make any allowance for the value of imputation credits to shareholders. Therefore, we have to make both these adjustments in the cash flow. And that is exactly what we have done. If we paid no interest we would pay tax on all the operating cash flow and have an imputation credit of $CT_c$ with a value of $\gamma CT_c$. However, the interest payment reduces the tax payable by (interest) $\times T_c$ and so reduces the value of the imputation credit by $\gamma$(interest) $\times T_c$. Putting these adjustments together gives $\gamma(C - \text{interest})T_c$, which is exactly the adjustment above.

Bob Officer[45] also suggests a 'plain vanilla' alternative, where the adjusted discount rate is defined as:

$$r^{*3} = r_D\frac{D}{V} + r_E\frac{E}{V}$$

This has the merit of keeping corporate tax adjustments out of the discount rate. These adjustments are all made in the cash flow, which is defined as $C - T_{IC}(C - \text{interest})$. This is the levered cash flow available to service debt and equity, after allowing for the tax deductibility of interest and the value of the imputation tax credit.

---

[44]   We implicitly assume here that the proportion $(1 - f)$ of the credits remain locked up in the company forever, or at least for so long, or at such risk, that their present value is negligible. This will be the case if $f$ is held constant into the distant future.

[45]   See Bob Officer, op.cit., Footnote 30.

All these alternatives can be confusing, so for ease of reference we summarise the alternative adjustments for imputation in Table 19.2.

**table 19.2**

Alternative combinations of discount rate and cash flow that give consistent values under an imputation tax system.

| Description | Discount rate | Cash flow |
|---|---|---|
| Traditional discount rate and cash flow, both with an adjusted corporate tax rate | $r^{*1} = r_D(1 - T_{IC})\dfrac{D}{V} + r_E\dfrac{E}{V}$ | $C(1 - T_{IC})$ |
| Traditional cash flow with adjustment to the cost of equity | $r^{*2} = r_D(1 - T_c)\dfrac{D}{V} + r_E\dfrac{(1 - T_c)}{(1 - T_{IC})}\dfrac{E}{V}$ | $C(1 - T_c)$ |
| Traditional WACC with adjustment to the cash flow | $r^{*} = r_D(1 - T_c)\dfrac{D}{V} + r_E\dfrac{E}{V}$ | $C(1 - T_c) + \gamma(C - \text{interest})T_c$ |
| 'Plain vanilla' WACC with adjustment to the cash flow | $r^{*3} = r_D\dfrac{D}{V} + r_E\dfrac{E}{V}$ | $C - T_{IC}(C - \text{interest})$ |

Notes:
1. $T_{IC} = T_c[1 - (f \times \omega)] = T_c(1 - \gamma)$
2. The cost of equity $r_E$ is measured to include the component of return that investors receive in the form of imputation tax credits.

# 19.5 Discounting safe, nominal cash flows

Suppose you are considering purchase of a $100 000 machine. The manufacturer sweetens the deal by offering to finance the purchase by lending you $100 000 for five years, with annual interest payments of 5 per cent. You would have to pay 13 per cent to borrow from a bank. Your marginal tax rate is 35 per cent ($T_c = 0.35$).

How much is this loan worth? If you take it, the cash flows in thousands of dollars are:

| | | | Period | | | |
|---|---|---|---|---|---|---|
| | 0 | 1 | 2 | 3 | 4 | 5 |
| Cash flow | $100 | −5 | −5 | −5 | 5 | −105 |
| Tax shield | | +1.75 | +1.75 | +1.75 | +1.75 | +1.75 |
| After-tax cash flow | $100 | −3.25 | −3.25 | −3.25 | −3.25 | −103.25 |

What is the right discount rate?

Here you are discounting *safe, nominal* cash flows. Safe because your company must commit to pay if it takes the loan and we assume negligible default risk.[46] Nominal because the payments would be fixed regardless of future inflation. Now, the correct discount rate for safe,

---

[46] In theory, 'safe' means literally risk-free, like the cash returns on a Treasury bond. In practice it means that the risk of not paying or receiving a cash flow is small.

nominal cash flows is your company's *after-tax*, *un*subsidised borrowing rate.[47] In this case $r^* = r_D(1 - T_c) = 0.13(1 - 0.35) = 0.845$.[48] Therefore,

$$NPV = +100 - \frac{3.25}{(1.0845)} - \frac{3.25}{(1.0845)^2} - \frac{3.25}{(1.0845)^3} - \frac{3.25}{(1.0845)^4} - \frac{103.25}{(1.0845)^5}$$

$$= +20.52, \text{ or } \$20\,520$$

The manufacturer has effectively cut the machine's purchase price from $100 000 to $100 000 − $20 520. You can now go back and recalculate the machine's NPV using this fire-sale price, or you can use the NPV of the subsidised loan as one element of the machine's adjusted present value.

## A general rule

Clearly, we owe an explanation of why $r^* = r_D(1 - T_c)$ for safe, nominal cash flows.[49] It is no surprise that $r^*$ depends on $r_D$, the unsubsidised borrowing rate, for that is investors' opportunity cost of capital, the rate they would demand from your company's debt. But why should $r_D$ be converted to an *after-tax* figure?

Let us simplify by taking a *one-year* subsidised loan of $100 000 at 5 per cent. The cash flows, in thousands of dollars, are:

| Period | 0 | 1 |
|---|---|---|
| Cash flow | $100 | −105 |
| Tax shield | | +1.75 |
| After-tax cash flow | $100 | −103.25 |

Now ask, 'What is the maximum amount $X$ that could be borrowed for one year through regular channels if $103 250 is set aside to service the loan?'

'Regular channels' means borrowing at 13 per cent pre-tax and 8.45 per cent after tax. Therefore, you will need 108.45 per cent of the amount borrowed to pay back principal plus after-tax interest charges. If $1.0845X = 103\,250$, $X = \$95\,205$. Now if you can borrow $100 000 by a subsidised loan, but only $95 205 through normal channels, the difference ($4795) is money in the bank. Therefore, it must also be the NPV of this one-period subsidised loan.

When you discount a safe, nominal cash flow at an after-tax borrowing rate, you are implicitly calculating the *equivalent loan,* the amount you could borrow through normal channels, using the cash flow as debt service. Note that:

$$\text{Equivalent loan} = PV \begin{pmatrix} \text{cash flow} \\ \text{available for} \\ \text{debt service} \end{pmatrix} = \frac{103\,250}{1.845} = 95\,205$$

In some cases it may be easier to think of taking the lender's side of the equivalent loan rather than the borrower's. For example, you could ask, 'How much would my company have to invest today in order to cover next year's debt service on the subsidised loan?' The answer

---

[47]    In Section 13.1 we calculated the NPV of subsidised financing using the *pre-tax* borrowing rate. Now you can see that was a mistake. Using the pre-tax rate implicitly defines the loan in terms of its pre-tax cash flows, violating a rule promulgated way back in Section 6.1: *Always* estimate cash flows on an after-tax basis.

[48]    Of course, this assumes that the marginal tax saving is at the rate $T_c$.

[49]    Remember that under imputation we just substitute $T_{IC}$ for $T_c$.

is $95 205: If you lend that amount at 13 per cent, you will earn 8.45 per cent after tax, and therefore have 95 205(1.0845) = $103 250. By this transaction, you can in effect cancel, or 'zero out', the future obligation. If you can borrow $100 000 and then set aside only $95 205 to cover all the required debt service, you clearly have $4795 to spend as you please. That amount is the NPV of the subsidised loan.

Therefore, regardless of whether it is easier to think of borrowing or lending, the correct discount rate for safe, nominal cash flows is an after-tax interest rate.[50]

In some ways, this is an obvious result once you think about it. Companies are free to borrow or lend money. If they *lend,* they receive the after-tax interest rate on their investment; if they *borrow* in the capital market, they pay the after-tax interest rate. Thus, the opportunity cost to companies of investing in debt-equivalent cash flows is the after-tax interest rate. This is the adjusted cost of capital for debt-equivalent cash flows.

## Some further examples

Here are some further examples of debt-equivalent cash flows:

**Payout fixed by contract**   Suppose you sign a maintenance contract with a truck leasing firm, which agrees to keep your leased trucks in good working order for the next two years in exchange for 24 fixed monthly payments. These payments are debt-equivalent flows.[51]

**Depreciation tax shields**   Capital projects are normally valued by discounting the total after-tax cash flows they are expected to generate. Depreciation tax shields contribute to project cash flow, but they are not valued separately; they are just folded into project cash flows along with dozens, or hundreds, of other specific inflows and outflows. The project's opportunity cost of capital reflects the average risk of the resulting aggregate.

However, suppose we ask what depreciation tax shields are worth *by themselves.* For a firm that is *sure* to pay taxes, depreciation tax shields are a safe, nominal flow. Therefore, they should be discounted at the firm's after-tax borrowing rate.[52]

## 19.6 Your questions answered

*Question:* All these cost of capital formulas—which ones do financial managers actually use?
*Answer:* The after-tax weighted average cost of capital, most of the time. WACC is estimated for the company, or sometimes for an industry. We recommend industry WACCs when data is available for several comparable firms. The firms should have similar assets, operations, business risks and growth opportunities.

Of course, conglomerate companies, with divisions operating in two or more unrelated industries, should not use a single company or industry WACC. Such firms should try to estimate a different industry WACC for each operating division.
*Question:* But WACC is the correct discount rate only for 'average' projects. What if the project's financing differs from the company's or the industry's?
*Answer:* Remember that investment projects are usually not separately financed. Even when they are, you should focus on the project's contribution to the firm's overall debt capacity, not

---

[50]  Borrowing and lending rates should not differ by much if the cash flows are truly safe—that is, if the chance of default is small. Usually your decision will not hinge on the rate used. If it does, ask which offsetting transaction—borrowing or lending—seems most natural and reasonable for the problem at hand. Then use the corresponding interest rate.

[51]  We assume you are locked into the contract. If it can be cancelled without penalty, you may have a valuable option.

[52]  The depreciation tax shields are cash inflows, not outflows as for the contractual payout or the subsidised loan. For safe, nominal inflows, the relevant question is, 'How much could the firm borrow today if it uses the inflow for debt service?' You could also ask, 'How much would the firm have to lend today to generate the same future inflow?'

on its immediate financing. (Suppose it is convenient to raise all of the money for a particular project with a bank loan. That does not mean the project itself supports 100 per cent debt financing. The company is borrowing against its existing assets as well as the project.)

But if the project's debt capacity is materially different from the company's existing assets, or if the company's overall debt policy changes, WACC should be adjusted.

We recommend two nearly equivalent approaches. First, you can adjust WACC using the Miles–Ezzell formula. Second, you can estimate new costs of debt and equity and recalculate WACC at the new debt ratio.

*Question:* Could we do one more numerical example?

*Answer:* Sure. Suppose that WACC has been estimated as follows at a 30 per cent debt ratio:

$$\text{WACC} = r_D(1 - T_c)\frac{D}{V} + r_E\frac{E}{V}$$

$$= 0.09(1 - 0.35)(0.3) + 0.15(0.7) = 0.1226, \text{ or } 12.26\%$$

What is the correct discount rate at a 50 per cent debt ratio?

First, let us use the Miles–Ezzell formula:

$$r^* = \text{WACC} = r - Lr_DT^*\left[\frac{1 + r}{1 + r_D}\right],$$

where $r$ is the opportunity cost of capital, that is, investors' required rate of return under all equity financing. At a 30 per cent debt ratio ($L = 0.3$), the formula is:

$$r^* = \text{WACC} = r - 0.3(0.09)(0.35)\left[\frac{(1 + r)}{(1.09)}\right] = 0.1226$$

Solving for $r$ gives an opportunity cost of capital of $r = 0.1325$, or 13.25 per cent.

The opportunity cost of capital does not change with leverage. So at a 50 per cent debt ratio it will still be 13.25 per cent. But the cost of debt, $r_D$, will probably be higher. Say it is 9.5 per cent. Now, recalculate $r^*$ with $L = D/V = 0.50$. (We assume for simplicity that $T^*$, the net tax advantage of corporate borrowing, is the same as the marginal corporate rate, $T_c = 0.35$).

$$r^* = 0.1325 - 0.5(0.095)(0.35)\left[\frac{1.1325}{1.095}\right] = 0.1153, \text{ or about } 11.5\%$$

*Question:* Do we have to use Miles–Ezzell's formula? Why not just calculate a new WACC?

*Answer:* That is the second approach. It may look easier, but *you must change the cost of equity*, because $r_E$, shareholders' required rate of return, increases with financial risk. The formula for $r_E$ is MM's proposition II:

$$r_E = r + (r - r_D)\frac{D}{E}$$

Note that $r_E$ depends on the debt-equity ratio $D/E$, not on the ratio of debt to firm value. At 50 per cent debt, $D/E = 0.50/0.50 = 1.0$. The new cost of equity at this debt policy is

$$r_E = 0.1325 + (0.1325 - 0.095)(1.0) = 0.17$$

Now recalculate WACC:

$$\text{WACC} = 0.095(1 - 0.35)(0.5) + 0.17(0.5) = 11.59, \text{ again about } 11.5\%$$

This is a very close approximation to the $r^*$ obtained from the Miles–Ezzell formula.[53]

---

[53] The Miles–Ezzell formula implies a very similar, but more complicated, expression for $r_E$.

*Question:* How do I use the capital asset pricing model to calculate the after-tax weighted average cost of capital?

*Answer:* First, plug the equity beta into the capital asset pricing formula to calculate $r_E$, the expected return to equity. Then, use this figure, along with the after-tax cost of debt and the debt-to-value and equity-to-value ratios in the WACC formula. We covered this in Chapter 9. The only change here is use of the after-tax cost of debt, $r_D(1 - T_c)$.

*Question:* What if I have to recalculate the equity beta for a different debt ratio?

*Answer:* The formula for beta is

$$\beta_E = \beta_A + (\beta_A - \beta_D)\frac{D}{E},$$

where $\beta_E$ is the equity beta; $\beta_A$ the asset beta; and $\beta_D$ the beta of the company's debt.[54]

*Question:* Can I use the capital asset pricing model and the asset beta to calculate the opportunity cost of capital?

*Answer:* Sure. We covered this in Chapter 9. You can back out the asset beta from the preceding formula, or use the fact that the asset beta is a weighted average of the debt and equity betas:[55]

$$\beta_A = \beta_D\frac{D}{V} + \beta_E\frac{E}{V}$$

Suppose you needed the opportunity cost of capital as an input to the Miles–Ezzell formula. You could calculate $\beta_A$, then $r$ from the capital pricing model.

*Question:* Can you guarantee the accuracy of beta after these adjustments?

*Answer:* No. In the Australian context your beta estimate is likely to have a substantial standard error before you start making any adjustments. You then adjust it using an equation that rests on a small mountain of assumptions, which may or may not be appropriate. We suggest a sensitivity analysis to see whether the magnitude of the adjustment is critical to your project valuation.

*Question:* I think I understand how to adjust for differences in debt capacity or debt policy. How about differences in business risk?

*Answer:* If business risk is different, then $r$, the opportunity cost of capital, is different.

Figuring out the right $r$ for an unusually safe or risky project is never easy. Sometimes the financial manager can use estimates of risk and expected return for companies similar to the project. Suppose, for example, that a traditional pharmaceutical company is considering a major commitment to biotechnical research. The financial manager could pick a sample of biotech companies, estimate their average beta and cost of capital, and use these estimates as benchmarks for the biotechnical investment.

But in many cases it is difficult to find a good sample of matching companies for an unusually safe or risky project. Then the financial manager has to adjust the opportunity cost of capital by judgement.[56] Section 9.4 may be helpful in such cases.

*Question:* Let us go back to the cost of capital formulas. The tax rates are confusing. When should I use $T_c$ or $T_{IC}$ and when $T^*$?

*Answer:* Use $T_c$, the marginal corporate tax rate, when (1) calculating WACC as a weighted average of the costs of debt and equity and (2) when discounting safe, nominal cash flows. Under the

---

[54] Notice that this formula has exactly the same form as the equation for $r_E$ under MM's proposition II (see above). We have just substituted $\beta$ for $r$. We can use this adjustment formula for $\beta_E$ when there are no corporate taxes. Alternatively, we can use it when there is a fully integrated imputation system, since this is equivalent to no corporate taxes. We can also use it as an approximation in the Miles–Ezzell world of corporate taxes under financing rule 2.

[55] This formula assumes financing rule 2, or no corporate taxes. If debt is fixed, taxes complicate the formulas. For example, if debt is fixed and permanent, and only corporate taxes are considered, the formula for $\beta_E$ changes to:

$$\beta_E = \beta_A + (\beta_A - \beta_D)(1 - T_c)\frac{D}{E}$$

[56] The judgement is often implicit. That is, the manager will not necessarily announce that the discount rate for a high-risk project is, say, 2.5 percentage points above the standard rate. But the project will not be approved unless it offers a higher-than-standard rate of return.

classical tax system the discount rate is adjusted *only* for corporate taxes.[57] If you want to adjust for imputation then one way is to substitute $T_{IC}$ for $T_c$ in the discount rate and the cash flows.

The Miles–Ezzell and MM formulas, which show how the cost of capital depends on financing, in principle call for $T^*$, the net tax gain per dollar of interest paid by the firm. This does depend on the effective personal tax rates on debt and equity income. $T^*$ is almost surely less than $T_c$, but it is very difficult to pin down the numerical difference. Therefore, in practice $T_c$ is often used as an approximation, but under imputation we could substitute $T_{IC}$.

*Question:* When do I need adjusted present value (APV)?

*Answer:* The WACC and Miles–Ezzell formulas pick up only one financing 'side effect': the value of interest tax shields on debt supported by a project. If there are other side effects—subsidised financing tied to a project, for example—you should use APV.

You can also use APV to show the value of interest tax shields:

$$APV = \text{base-case NPV} + \text{PV(tax shield)},$$

where the base-case NPV assumes all equity financing. But it is usually easier to do this calculation in one step, by discounting project cash flows at an adjusted cost of capital (WACC or $r^*$). Remember, though, that discounting by WACC or the Miles–Ezzell $r^*$ assumes financing rule 2, that is, debt rebalanced to a constant fraction of future project value.

We also have to assume that $T_c$, $T^*$ or $T_{IC}$ is expected to be constant over time.

If either of these conditions is not right, you may need the APV to calculate the PV(tax shield), as we did for the solar heater project in Table 19.1.

Suppose for example, that you are analysing a company just after a leveraged recapitalisation. The company has a very high initial debt level but plans to pay down the debt as rapidly as possible. This would not match either financing rule 1 or financing rule 2. However, APV could be used to obtain an accurate valuation.

## 19.7 Summary

Investment decisions nearly always have side effects on financing: every dollar spent has to be raised somehow. Sometimes the side effects are irrelevant or at least unimportant. In an ideal world with no taxes, transaction costs or other market imperfections, only investment decisions would affect firm value. In such a world firms could analyse all investment opportunities as if they were all equity financed. Firms would decide which assets to buy and then worry about getting the money to pay for them. No one would worry where the money came from because debt policy, dividend policy and all other financing choices would have no impact on shareholders' wealth.

The side effects cannot be ignored in practice. There are two main ways to take them into account. You can calculate NPV by discounting at an adjusted discount rate, or you can discount at the opportunity cost of capital and then add or subtract the present value of financing side effects. The second approach is called adjusted present value (APV).

The most commonly used adjusted discount rate is the after-tax weighted average cost of capital (WACC):

$$r^* = r_D(1 - T_c)\frac{D}{V} + r_E\frac{E}{V}$$

Here $r_D$ and $r_E$ are the expected rates of return demanded by investors in the firm's debt and equity securities, respectively; $D$ and $E$ are the current market values of debt and

---

[57] The effects of personal income taxes are reflected in $r_D$ and $r_E$, the rates of return demanded by debt and equity investors. Under the imputation system, however, there is a hidden component of returns—the value of the imputation credits.

equity; and V is the total market value of the firm ($V = D + E$). If you use this traditional version of WACC under a classical tax system you should use it to discount the unlevered cash flow $C(1 - T_c)$. If you use it under an imputation tax system you should use it to discount the unlevered cash flow *plus* the value of the levered imputation credit

$$C(1 - T_c) + \gamma(C - \text{interest})T_c.$$

Alternatively, under imputation you can modify WACC by substituting the effective corporate tax rate under imputation $T_{IC}$ for the statutory rate $T_c$,

$$r^* = r_D(1 - T_{IC})\frac{D}{V} + r_E\frac{E}{V}$$

and then apply the modified WACC to $C(1 - T_{IC})$.

Strictly speaking, the WACC formula only works for projects that are carbon copies of the existing firm—projects with the same business risk that will be financed to maintain the firm's current market-debt ratio. But firms can use WACC as a benchmark rate, to be adjusted for differences in business risk or financing.

Miles and Ezzell have developed a formula relating WACC to financial leverage:

$$r^* = r - Lr_DT^*\left[\frac{1 + r}{1 + r_D}\right]$$

Here $r$ is the opportunity cost of capital, which depends on business risk, $T^*$ is the net tax saving per dollar of interest paid, and $L$ is the ratio of debt supported by the project to project value. For the firm as a whole, $L = D/V$.

The exact value of $T^*$ is extremely elusive, so most financial managers set it to $T_c$, the marginal corporate tax rate. Under imputation they could use $T_{IC}$. Then they can use the Miles–Ezzell formula to calculate how WACC varies with the debt ratio $D/V$. They can also calculate how $r_E$, the 'cost of equity', changes with financial leverage. The following formula is a very close approximation.

$$r_E = r + (r - r_D)\frac{D}{E}$$

Miles and Ezzell assumed the firm adjusts its borrowing to keep a constant debt-to-market value ratio. This assumption also underlies WACC. In cases where debt is paid off on a fixed schedule, MM's adjusted discount rate formula applies.

$$r^* = r(1 - T^*L)$$

Again, in practice $T^*$ is usually replaced with $T_c$.

Remember that all these formulas rest on special assumptions. For example, they assume financing matters only because of interest tax shields. When this or other assumptions are violated, only APV will give an absolutely correct answer.

APV is, in concept at least, simple. First, calculate the present value of the project as if there are no important side effects. Then, adjust present value to calculate the project's total impact on firm value. The rule is to accept the project if APV is positive:

$$\text{Accept project if APV} = \text{base-case NPV} + \begin{array}{c}\text{present value}\\ \text{of financing}\\ \text{side effects}\end{array} > 0$$

The base-case NPV is the project's NPV computed assuming all equity financing and perfect capital markets. Think of it as the project's value if it were set up as a separate mini-firm. You would compute the mini-firm's value by forecasting its cash flows and discounting at the opportunity cost of capital for the project. The cash flows should be net of the taxes that an all equity financed mini-firm would pay.

Financing side effects are evaluated one by one and their present values added to or subtracted from base-case NPV. We looked at several cases:

1. *Issue costs.* If accepting the project forces the firm to issue securities, then the present value of issue costs should be subtracted from base-case NPV.
2. *Interest tax shields.* Debt interest is a tax-deductible expense. Most people believe that interest tax shields contribute to firm value. Thus, a project that prompts the firm to borrow more generates additional value. The project's APV is increased by the present value of interest tax shields on debt the project supports.
3. *Special financing.* Sometimes special financing opportunities are tied to project acceptance. For example, the government might offer subsidised financing for socially desirable projects. You simply compute the present value of the financing opportunity and add it to base-case NPV.

Remember not to confuse *contribution to corporate debt capacity* with the immediate source of funds for investment. For example, a firm might, as a matter of convenience, borrow $1 million for a $1 million research program. But the research would be unlikely to contribute $1 million in debt capacity; a large part of the $1 million new debt would be supported by the firm's other assets.

Also remember that *debt capacity* is not meant to imply an absolute limit on how much the firm *can* borrow. The phrase refers to how much it *chooses* to borrow. Normally, the firm's optimal debt level increases as its assets expand; that is why we say that a new project contributes to corporate debt capacity.

Calculating APV may require several steps: one step for base-case NPV and one for each financing side effect. Many firms try to calculate APV in a single calculation. They do so by the following procedure. After-tax cash flows are forecast in the usual way—that is, as if the project is all equity financed. But the discount rate is adjusted to reflect the financing side effects. If the discount rate is adjusted correctly, the result is APV:

$$\begin{array}{c} \text{NPV at adjusted} \\ \text{discount rate} \end{array} = \text{APV} = \begin{array}{c} \text{NPV at opportunity} \\ \text{cost of capital} \end{array} + \begin{array}{c} \text{present value of} \\ \text{financing side effects} \end{array}$$

WACC and the Miles–Ezzell and MM formulas are, of course, examples of adjusted discount rates.

This chapter is almost 100 per cent theory. The theory is difficult. If you think you understand all the formulas, assumptions and relationships on the first reading, we suggest psychiatric assistance.

# APPENDIX *Adjusted discount rates for debt-equivalent cash flows

You may have wondered whether our procedure for valuing debt-equivalent cash flows is consistent with the adjusted discount rate approaches presented earlier in this chapter. Yes, it is consistent, as we will now illustrate.

Remember from Section 18.2 that the value of corporate interest tax shields depends on the personal tax rates paid by debt and equity investors. No one knows for sure what the relevant personal rates actually are. The polar views are those of Modigliani and Miller

(MM) on one hand, and Miller on the other. MM assume that investors face the same tax rate on debt and equity income, so that only corporate taxes need be considered; in that case, $T^* = T_c$. But Miller argues that debt investors pay higher effective tax rates than equity investors, so much so that any advantage of the corporate interest tax shield is entirely offset, and $T^* = 0$.

Let us look at a very simple numerical example from each viewpoint. Our problem is to value a \$1 million payment to be received from a blue-chip company one year hence. After taxes at 35 per cent, the cash inflow is \$650 000. The payment is fixed by contract.

Since the contract generates a debt-equivalent flow, the opportunity cost of capital is the rate investors would demand on a one-year note issued by the blue-chip company, which happens to be 8 per cent. For simplicity, we will assume this is your company's borrowing rate too. Our valuation rule for debt-equivalent flows is therefore to discount at $r^* = r_D (1 - T_c) = 0.08(1 - 0.35) = 0.052$:

$$PV = \frac{650\,000}{1.052} = \$617\,900$$

# Valuing debt-equivalent cash flows under MM assumptions

Now let us see how MM would address this same problem. The opportunity cost of capital is still $r_D = 0.08$, or 8 per cent. With $T^* = T_c$ the MM adjusted-cost-of-capital formula is $r^* = r_D(1 - T_c L)$.

What is $L$? In Section 19.2 we defined it as a project's 'marginal contribution to the firm's debt capacity', expressed as a fraction of project value, which is normally well below 1. But the debt capacity of a safe cash flow is 100 per cent of its value, because the firm could 'zero out' the cash flow by taking out an equivalent loan with the same after-tax debt service. Thus, we can think of 'debt capacity' as the offsetting equivalent loan. Since the equivalent loan has exactly the same present value as the debt-equivalent flow, $L = 1$.

The MM adjusted-cost-of-capital formula for debt-equivalent cash flows therefore boils down to the same after-tax borrowing rate we used to discount the \$650 000 inflow:

$$r^* = r(1 - T_c L) = r_D(1 - T_c) = 0.08(1 - 0.35) = 0.052$$

We get the same result from the Miles–Ezzell formula. With $r = r_D$ and $L = 1$:

$$r^* = r - L r_D T_c \left(\frac{1 + r}{1 + r_D}\right)$$

$$= r_D - 1 \times r_D T_c \left(\frac{1 + r_D}{1 + r_D}\right)$$

$$= r_D - r_D T_c = r_D(1 - T_c)$$

Let us also try an APV calculation under MM assumptions. This is a two-part calculation. First, the \$650 000 inflow is discounted at the opportunity cost of capital, 8 per cent. Second, we add the present value of interest tax shields on debt supported by the project. Since the firm can borrow 100 per cent of the cash flow's value, the tax shield is $(r_D)(T_c)(\text{APV})$, and APV is

$$APV = \frac{650\,000}{1.08} + \frac{0.08(0.35)APV}{1.08}$$

Solving for APV we get $617 900, the same answer we obtained by discounting at the after-tax borrowing rate.[58]

Thus, our valuation rule for debt-equivalent flows is a special case of the APV rule once we adopt MM's assumptions about debt and taxes.

## Valuing debt-equivalent cash flows under Miller's assumptions

But suppose that you share Miller's view that there is no tax advantage to debt, so that $T^* = 0$. That would seem to imply that debt-equivalent cash flows should be discounted at the *pre-tax* borrowing rate. For example, if we set $T^* = 0$ in the MM adjusted-cost-of-capital formula, $r^* = r(1 - T^*L) = r(1 - 0 \times L) = r$, the opportunity cost of capital. And we would normally set $r = r_D$ for debt-equivalent flows.

However, the reason why $T^* = 0$ in Miller's theory is that debt investors' personal tax rate equals the corporate rate $(T_p = T_c)$, while the effective tax rate on equity income is zero $(T_{pE} = 0)$ (see Section 18.2). Thus, debt investors demand a higher pre-tax rate of return on safe investments than equity investors do. For example, if the after-personal-tax return on debt is $0.08(1 - 0.34) = 0.053$, or 5.3 per cent, then equity investors will also be content with a 5.3 per cent rate of return on a safe, *untaxed* equity investment.

Therefore, equity investors' opportunity cost of capital for a safe cash flow is the *after-tax* interest rate: $r = r_D(1 - T_p) = r_D(1 - T_c)$.

Thus, although $T^* = 0$ in Miller's world, we nevertheless end up discounting debt-equivalent flows at $r_D(1 - T_c)$, because that is the rate the firm's shareholder's demand.

## FURTHER READING

The adjusted present value rule was developed in:

> S. C. Myers, 'Interactions of Corporate Financing and Investment Decisions: Implications for Capital Budgeting', *Journal of Finance*, **29**: 1–25 (March 1974).

Formulas for the adjusted discount rate are explained in:

> F. Modigliani and M. H. Miller, 'Corporate Income Taxes and the Cost of Capital: A Correction', *American Economic Review*, **53**: 433–43 (June 1963).

> M. H. Miller and F. Modigliani, 'Some Estimates of the Cost of Capital to the Electric Utility Industry: 1954–1957', *American Economic Review*, **56**: 333–91 (June 1966).

> J. Miles and R. Ezzell, 'The Weighted Average Cost of Capital, Perfect Capital Markets and Project Life: A Clarification', *Journal of Financial and Quantitative Analysis*, **15**: 719–30 (September 1980).

There have been dozens of articles on the weighted average cost of capital and other issues discussed in this chapter. Here are four representative ones:

> M. J. Brennan, 'A New Look at the Weighted-Average Cost of Capital', *Journal of Business Finance*, **5**: 24–30 (1973).

> D. R. Chambers, R. S. Harris and J. J. Pringle, 'Treatment of Financing Mix in Analyzing Investment Opportunities', *Financial Management*, **11**: 24–41 (Summer 1982).

> R. A. Taggart, Jr, 'Consistent Valuation and Cost of Capital Expressions with Corporate and Personal Taxes', *Financial Management*, **20**: 8–20 (Autumn 1991).

> R. Officer, 'The Measurement of a Firm's Cost of Capital', *Accounting and Finance*, 31–61 (November 1991).

---

[58]  Notice that in the APV calculation we did not use that after-tax discount rate to calculate the PVs. Had we done so we would have been double counting the tax shield benefits.

Discussions about how to adjust for imputation can be found in:

C. Cliffe and A. Marsden, 'The Effect of Dividend Imputation on Company Financing Decisions and Cost of Capital in New Zealand', *Pacific Accounting Review*, 4: 1–29 (December 1992).

R. R. Officer, 'The Cost of Capital of a Company Under an Imputation Tax System', *Accounting and Finance*, 34:1–17 (May 1994).

P. Monkhouse, 'Adapting the APV Valuation Methodology and the Beta Gearing Formula to the Dividend Imputation Tax System', *Accounting and Finance*, 37: 69–88 (May 1997).

The valuation rule for safe, nominal cash flows is developed in:

R. S. Ruback, 'Calculating the Market Value of Risk-Free Cash Flows', *Journal of Financial Economics*, 15: 323–39 (March 1986).

## QUIZ

1. Calculate the weighted average cost of capital (WACC) for Federated Junkyards of the World, using the following information.

   ▌ Debt: $75 000 000 book value outstanding. The debt is trading at 90 per cent of par. The yield to maturity is 9 per cent.

   ▌ Equity: 2 500 000 shares selling at $42 per share. Assume the expected rate of return on Federated's shares is 18 per cent.

   ▌ Taxes: Federated's marginal tax rate is $T_c = 0.35$.

   What are the key assumptions underlying your calculation? For what type of project would Federated's weighted average cost of capital be the right discount rate? Which cash flow should you discount using WACC under a classical tax system, and which cash flow under an imputation tax system?

2. Refer again to Question 1. Using the Miles–Ezzell formula calculate Federated's average opportunity cost of capital. Then calculate Federated's WACC at 25 per cent debt-to-value ratio. What would the expected rate of return on Federated's shares be at this ratio? Assume that Federated's borrowing rate stays at 9 per cent.

3. Table 19.3 shows a *book* balance sheet for the Wishing Well Motel chain. The company's long-term debt is secured by its real estate assets, but it also uses short-term bank financing. It pays 10 per cent interest on the bank debt and 9 per cent interest on the secured debt. Wishing Well has 10 million shares of outstanding trading at $90 per share.

   Calculate Wishing Well's WACC. Assume that the book and market value of Wishing Well's debt are the same. The marginal tax rate is 35 per cent.

**table 19.3**

Balance sheet for Wishing Well (figures in $million)

| Cash, marketable securities | 100 | Accounts payable | 120 |
|---|---|---|---|
| Inventory | 50 | Bank loan | 280 |
| Accounts receivable | 200 | Current liabilities | 400 |
| Current assets | 350 | Long-term debt | 1800 |
| Real estate | 2100 | | |
| Other assets | 150 | Equity | 400 |
| Total | 2600 | Total | 2600 |

**4.** Suppose Wishing Well is evaluating a new motel and resort on a romantic site near Alice Springs. Explain how you would forecast the after-tax cash flows for this project. (*Hint*: How would you treat taxes? Interest expense? Changes in working capital?)

**5.** In order to finance the Alice Springs project, Wishing Well will have to arrange an additional $80 million of long-term debt and make a $20 million equity issue. Underwriting fees and other costs of this financing will total $4 million. How would you take this into account in valuing the proposed investment?

**6.** A project costs $1 million and has a base-case NPV of exactly zero (NPV = 0). What is the project's APV in the following cases?
  a. If the firm invests, it has to raise $500 000 by share issue. Issue costs are 15 per cent of *net* proceeds.
  b. The firm has ample cash on hand. But if it invests, it will have access to $500 000 of debt financing at a subsidised interest rate. The present value of the subsidy is $175 000.
  c. If the firm invests, its debt capacity increases by $500 000. The present value of interest tax shields on this debt is $76 000.
  d. If the firm invests, it issues equity, as in Part (a), and borrows, as in Part (c).

**7.** Use the Miles–Ezzell and MM adjusted-discount-rate formulas to value the solar heater project analysed in Section 19.2. Assume 50 per cent debt financing ($L = 0.50$). Explain why the two formulas give different NPVs.

**8.** Whispering Pines Ltd is all equity financed. The expected rate of return on the company's shares is 12 per cent.
  a. What is the opportunity cost of capital for an average-risk Whispering Pines investment?
  b. Suppose the company issues debt, repurchases shares and moves to a 30 per cent debt-to-value ratio ($D/V = 0.30$). What will the company's weighted average cost of capital and expected return on equity be at the new capital structure? The borrowing rate is 7.5 per cent and the tax rate is 35 per cent. Use the Miles–Ezzell formula.

**9.** Consider the APV of the solar heater project, as calculated using Table 19.1. How would the APV change if the net tax shield per dollar of interest were not $T_c = 0.35$, but $T^* = 0.10$?

**10.** Consider a project lasting one year only. The initial outlay is $1000 and the expected inflow is $1200. The opportunity cost of capital is $r = 0.20$. The borrowing rate is $r_D = 0.10$, and the net tax shield per dollar of interest is $T_c = 0.35$.
  a. What is the project's base-case NPV?
  b. What is its APV if the firm borrows 30 per cent of the project's required investment?
  c. What is the project's APV under the imputation tax system with a 100 per cent payout ratio and imputation credits valued at 60 per cent of face value?

**11.** The WACC formula seems to imply that debt is 'cheaper' than equity—i.e. that a firm with more debt could use a lower discount rate $r^*$. Does this make sense? Explain briefly.

**12.** What discount rate should be used to value safe, nominal cash flows? Explain briefly.

**13.** You are considering a five-year lease of office space for R&D personnel. Once signed, the lease cannot be cancelled. It would commit your firm to six annual $100 000 payments, with the first payment due immediately. What is the present value of the lease if your company's borrowing rate is 9 per cent and its tax rate is 34 per cent? *Note*: The lease payments would be tax-deductible.

## QUESTIONS AND PROBLEMS

**1.** Consider another perpetual project like the Geothermal venture described in this chapter. Its initial investment is $1 000 000 and the expected cash inflow is $85 000 a year in perpetuity. The opportunity cost of capital with all equity financing is 10 per cent, and the project allows the firm to borrow an additional 40 per cent of project value at 7 per cent. Assume the net tax advantage to borrowing is $0.35 per dollar of interest paid ($T^* = T_c = 0.35$).
   a. What is the project's value if debt is adjusted each period to maintain the 40 per cent debt-to-value ratio? Use an adjusted discount rate for your calculation.
   b. Show that your answer to Part (a) is also the project's APV. (*Hint*: how much debt will the project support at the start?)
   c. What is the project's value if debt is *not* increased if the project does well or reduced if it does poorly? (Otherwise use the same assumptions as in Part (a).) Use an adjusted discount rate for your calculation.
   d. Show that your answer to Part (c) is the project's APV assuming fixed borrowing.

**2.** Suppose the project described in Question 1 is to be undertaken by a university. Funds for the project will be withdrawn from the university's endowment, which is invested in a widely-diversified portfolio of shares and bonds. However, the university can also borrow at 7 per cent.
   Suppose the university bursar proposes to finance the project by issuing $400 000 of perpetual bonds at 7 per cent, and by selling $600 000 worth of ordinary shares from the endowment. The expected return on the ordinary shares is 10 per cent. He therefore proposes to evaluate the project by discounting at a weighted average cost of capital, calculated as:

$$r^* = r_D \frac{D}{V} + r_E \frac{E}{V}$$
$$= 0.07 \left( \frac{400\,000}{1\,000\,000} \right) + 0.10 \left( \frac{600\,000}{1\,000\,000} \right)$$
$$= 0.088, \text{ or } 8.8\%$$

What is right or wrong with the bursar's approach? Should the university invest? Should it borrow?

**3.** Table 19.4 shows a simplified balance sheet for Bunny Felt. Calculate the company's weighted average cost of capital. The debt has just been refinanced at an interest rate of 6 per cent (short-term) and 8 per cent (long-term). The expected rate of return on the company's shares is 15 per cent. There are 7.46 million shares outstanding and the shares are trading at $46.00. The tax rate is 35 per cent.

**4.** How will Bunny Felt's WACC and cost of equity change if it issues $50 million in new equity and uses the proceeds to retire long-term debt? Assume the company's borrowing rates are unchanged.

**table 19.4**

Simplified book balance sheet Bunny Felt (figures in $'000)

| | | | |
|---|---|---|---|
| Cash, and marketable securities | 1 500 | Short-term debt | 75 600 |
| Accounts receivable | 120 000 | Accounts payable | 62 000 |
| Inventories | 125 000 | Current liabilities | 137 600 |
| Current assets | 246 500 | Long-term debt | 208 600 |
| Property, plant and equipment | 302 000 | Deferred taxes | 45 000 |
| Other assets | 89 000 | Shareholders' equity | 246 300 |
| Total | 637 500 | Total | 637 500 |

5. Short-term interest rates are frequently below long-term rates. Tax effects aside, does that mean that using more short-term debt reduces the overall cost of capital? (*Hint*: Think back to Chapter 17.)

6. Rapidly growing companies may have to issue shares to finance capital expenditures. In doing so they incur underwriting and other issue costs. Some analysts have tried to adjust WACC to account for these costs. For example, if issue costs are 8 per cent of equity issue proceeds, and equity issues account for all of equity financing, the cost of equity might be divided by $1 - 0.08 = 0.92$. This would increase a 15 per cent cost of equity to $15/0.92 = 16.3$ per cent.

    Explain why this sort of adjustment is *not* a smart idea. What is the correct way to take issue costs into account in project valuation?

7. Digital Organics (DO) has the opportunity to invest $1 million now ($t = 0$) and expects after-tax returns of $600 000 in $t = 1$ and $700 000 in $t = 2$. The project will last for two years only. The appropriate cost of capital is 12 per cent with all equity financing, the borrowing rate is 8 per cent and DO will borrow $300 000 against the project. This debt is to be repaid in two equal instalments. Assume debt tax shields have a net value of $0.30 per dollar of interest paid. Calculate the project's APV. Value the tax shields using the procedure followed in Table 19.1. Recompute the APV assuming an imputation tax system with $T_{IC}$ equal to 20 per cent.

8. Refer again to Quiz Question 10 for this chapter. Suppose the firm borrows 30 per cent of the project's *value*.
   a. What is the project's APV?
   b. What is the minimum acceptable rate of return for projects of this type?
   c. Show that your answer to Part (b) is consistent with the Miles–Ezzell formula.
   d. Recompute the APV under an imputation tax system assuming a 100 per cent payout ratio, and imputation credits valued at 50 per cent of their face value.
   e. If we assume a payout less than 100 per cent in this case, we create a problem in valuing the project under imputation. What is the problem?

9. List the assumptions underlying the MM adjusted-discount-rate formula. Derive the formula algebraically for a perpetual project. Then try to derive it for a one-period project like the one described in Quiz Question 10. Keep MM's other assumptions intact. (*Hint*: You will end up with the Miles–Ezzell formula. In other words, their formula works for one-period projects; MM's does not.)

**10.** The Bunsen Chemical Company is currently at its target debt ratio of 40 per cent. It is contemplating a $1 million expansion of its existing business. This expansion is expected to produce a cash inflow of $130 000 a year in perpetuity.

The company is uncertain whether to undertake this expansion and how to finance it. The two options are a $1 million issue of ordinary shares or a $1 million issue of 20-year debt. The flotation costs of a share issue would be around 5 per cent of the amount raised and the flotation costs of a debt issue would be around 1.5 per cent.

Bunsen's financial manager, Miss Polly Ethylene, estimates that the required return on the company's equity is 14 per cent, but she argues that the flotation costs increase the cost of new equity to 19 per cent. On this basis, the project does not appear viable.

On the other hand, she points out that the company can raise new debt on a 7 per cent yield which would make the cost of new debt 8.5 per cent. She therefore recommends that Bunsen should go ahead with the project and finance it with an issue of long-term debt.

Is Miss Ethylene right? How would you evaluate the project?

**11.** Curtis Bog, chief financial officer of Sphagnum Pulp and Paper Ltd, is reviewing a consultant's analysis of Sphagnum's weighted average cost of capital. The consultant proposes:

$$r^* = (1 - T_c)r_D\frac{D}{V} + r_E\frac{E}{V} = \text{WACC}$$

$$= (1 - 0.34)(0.103)(0.55) + 0.183(0.45)$$

$$= 0.1197, \text{ or about } 12\%$$

Mr Bog wants to check that this calculation is consistent with the capital asset pricing model. He has observed or estimated the following numbers:

- Betas: $\beta_{debt} = 0.15$, $\beta_{equity} = 1.09$.
- Expected market risk premium = $r_m - r_f = 0.085$.
- Risk-free rate of interest = $r_f = 9$ per cent.

Show Mr Bog how to calculate $\beta_{assets}$; the opportunity cost of capital for Sphagnum's assets; and the adjusted hurdle rate $r^*$. Does your $r^*$ match the consultant's weighted average cost of capital? (Expect some rounding errors.)

*Note:* We suggest you simplify by ignoring personal income taxes and assuming that the promised and expected rates of returns on Sphagnum debt are equal.

Somebody now tells Mr Bog that under the imputation system the effective tax rate for Sphagnum is only 40 per cent of the statutory rate. Explain to him what this means and how he can use this information in evaluating Sphagnum's projects.

**12.** Apple Isle Hydro is 40 per cent debt financed and has a weighted average cost of capital of 9.7 per cent:

$$r^* = (1 - T_c)r_D\frac{D}{V} + r_E\frac{E}{V} = \text{WACC}$$

$$= (1 - 0.35)(0.085)(0.40) + 0.125(0.60)$$

$$= 0.097$$

Banker's Tryst is advising Apple Isle Hydro to issue $75 million of preferred shares at a dividend yield of 9 per cent. The proceeds would be used to repurchase and retire ordinary shares. The preferred issue would account for 10 per cent of the pre-issue market value of the firm.

Banker's Tryst argues that these transactions would reduce the Hydro's WACC to 9.4 per cent:

$$\text{WACC} = r^* = (1 - 0.35)(0.085)(0.40) + 0.09(0.10) + 0.125(0.50)$$
$$= 0.094, \text{ or } 9.4\%$$

Do you agree with this calculation? Explain.

**13.** Look again at the Geothermal project in Section 19.1. Recompute its value under the imputation system assuming that the company distributes all its after-tax earnings as a dividend, and that investors in Geothermal value imputation credits at 80 per cent of their face value.

How does your valuation change if investors value the imputation credits:
a. At 100 per cent of face value?
b. At zero per cent of face value?

**14.** Consider a different financing scenario for the solar water heater project discussed in Section 19.1. The project requires $10 million and has a base-case NPV of $170 000. Suppose the firm happens to have $5 million in the bank which could be used for the project.

The government, eager to encourage solar energy, offers to help finance the project by lending $5 million at a subsidised rate of 5 per cent. The loan calls for the firm to pay the government $647 500 annually for 10 years (this amount includes both principal and interest).
a. What is the value of being able to borrow from the government at 5 per cent? Assume the company's normal borrowing rate is 8 per cent and the corporate tax rate is 35 per cent.
b. Suppose the company's normal debt policy is to borrow 50 per cent of the book value of its assets. It calculates the present value of interest tax shields by the procedure shown in Table 19.1 and includes this present value in APV. Should it do so here, given the government's offer of cheap financing?
c. Suppose instead that the firm normally borrows 30 per cent of the *market* value of its assets. Does this change your answer to Part (b)? (*Hint:* The Miles–Ezzell formula can be used to calculate project APV in this case. That formula does not capture the value of the subsidised loan, however.)

**15.** Table 19.5 is a simplified book balance sheet for Ample Petroleum at year-end 1998. Other information:

∎ Number of outstanding shares ($N$) = 261.6 million.
∎ Price per share end of year ($P$) = $33.
∎ Beta based on 60 monthly returns, against the Statex Accumulation Index, $\beta = 0.87$. Standard error of $\beta = 0.20$.
∎ Historical average market risk premium, 1926–98, 8.4 per cent.
∎ Interest rates, start of year 1999:
  ∎ Treasury notes, 6.5 per cent
  ∎ 20-year Treasury bonds, 7.9 per cent
  ∎ New issue rate for Ample assuming straight long-term debt, 9.5 per cent.

- ∎ Yield on preferred shares, 9.3 per cent (Can you remember why preferred shares offer a lower return than straight debt?)
- ∎ Excess return of Treasury bonds over bills, 1926–98, 1.4 per cent.
- ∎ Marginal tax rate, 35 per cent.

a. Calculate Ample's weighted average cost of capital. Use the capital asset pricing model and the data given above. Make additional assumptions and approximations as necessary.

b. With regard to imputation credits Ample's $\gamma = 0.6$. Recompute WACC using the effective corporate tax rate under imputation.

c. What would Ample's weighted average cost of capital be if it moved to *and maintained* a debt to market value ratio *(D/V)* of 25 per cent? Calculate both the traditional WACC and an imputation-adjusted WACC.

**table 19.5** _____

Simplified book balance sheet for Ample Petroleum, 1998 (figures in $million)

| Current assets | 2 645 | Current liabilities | 2 441 |
|---|---|---|---|
| Net property, plant and equipment | 8 042 | Long-term debt | 3 106 |
| Investments and other assets | 929 | Deferred taxes | 944 |
| | | Other liabilities | 1 992 |
| | | Shareholders' equity | 2 953 |
| Total | 11 436 | Total | 11 436 |

**16.** In Question 15 you calculated a WACC for Ample Petroleum. Ample could also use an industry WACC. Under what conditions would the industry WACC be the better choice? Explain. (*Hint*: See Section 9.2.)

# part 6

## OPTIONS

# chapter 20

# CORPORATE LIABILITIES AND THE VALUATION OF OPTIONS

We all love the great outdoors. You and your partner are considering the purchase of a second-hand GXL Landcruiser and have found the car you want, but would like a few days to think about it and to consider other choices. The purchase price has been agreed at $50 000. The seller has indicated that she also has a number of others interested in the car. You want some extra time. What are you going to do?

One choice would be to negotiate that you get first chance to purchase the car in three days time for $50 000 in return for paying a non-refundable amount of $1000 now. The $1000 is not a deposit for the car. If the seller agrees, in three days time you have two choices—you can purchase the Landcruiser for $50 000 or you can decide not to go ahead with the purchase. Either way, you will be out of pocket for the initial payment of $1000. From the seller's point of view, she will receive and keep the $1000 regardless of your choice—but

she is then obliged to sell the car to you in three days time at the agreed price of $50 000 regardless of any other offers. If you do not proceed with the purchase in three days time, the seller keeps the $1000 and can sell the Landcruiser to other interested parties. What you have negotiated is an option to purchase the Landcruiser.

Options contracts give the purchaser the right, but not the obligation, to buy or sell a parcel of assets at a predetermined price within a given time frame. In addition to options on physical assets, there are also options available on individual shares, foreign exchange, bonds, commodities, share market indices and futures contracts.

In Australia options are traded at the ASX Derivatives Market (formerly the Australian Options Market) (individual shares on listed companies and share market indices), the Sydney Futures Market (options on futures contracts) and **over-the-counter** (OTC) by banks and other financial institutions (options that are constructed to suit the requirements of individual clients).

Options trading is a specialised business and its devotees speak a language all of their own. They talk of calls, puts, straddles, butterflies, deep-in-the-money options, barriers and spreads. We will not tell you the meaning of all these terms but by the time you have finished this chapter you should know the principal kinds of options and how to value them.

Why should the financial manager of an industrial company be interested in such matters? Because managers routinely use currency, commodity and interest-rate options to reduce risk. For example, a company may tender for a capital project and, if it is successful, it may need to borrow extra funds. The company may take out an option to protect against any future increases in interest rates and to provide flexibility subject to the outcome of the tender. The option may be exercised if the tender is successful and interest rates at that time are greater than the agreed interest rate. In Chapter 25 we will explain further how firms use options and other derivative products to hedge against risk.

Many capital investment proposals include an option to buy additional equipment at some future date. For instance, a company may invest in a patent that allows it to exploit a new technology or it may purchase adjoining land that gives it an opportunity to expand. In each case the company is paying money today for the opportunity to make a further investment later. To put it another way, it is acquiring growth opportunities.

Here is another disguised option. You are considering the purchase of a tract of desert land that is known to contain gold deposits. Unfortunately, the cost of extraction is higher than the current price of gold. Does that mean that the land is almost worthless? Not at all. You are not obliged to mine the gold, but ownership of the land gives you the option to do so. Of course, if you know that the gold price will remain below the extraction cost, then the option is worthless. But if there is uncertainty about future gold prices, you could be lucky and make a killing.[1]

If the option to expand has value, what about the option to bail out? Projects do not usually go on until the equipment disintegrates. The decision to terminate a project is usually taken by management. Once the project is no longer profitable, the company will cut its losses and exercise an option to abandon the project. Some projects have higher abandonment value than others. Those that use standardised equipment may offer a valuable abandonment option. Others may actually cost money to discontinue. For example, it is very costly to decommission nuclear power plants or to reclaim land that has been strip-mined.

The other important reason why financial managers need to understand options is that they are often tacked on to an issue of corporate securities and so provide the investor or the company with the flexibility to change the terms of the issue. For example, in Chapter 22 we will show how warrants and convertibles give their holders an option to buy ordinary shares in exchange for cash, bonds notes or preference shares. Then in Chapter 24 we will see how bonds may give the issuer or the investor the option of early repayment or at call.

In fact, whenever a company borrows funds it creates an option. The reason is that the borrower is not compelled to repay the debt at maturity. If the value of the company's assets is less than the amount of the debt, the company will choose to default on the payment and the bondholders will get to keep the company's assets. Thus, when the firm borrows, the lender effectively acquires the company and the shareholders obtain the option to buy it back by paying off the debt. This is an extremely important insight. It means that anything that we can learn about traded call options applies equally to corporate liabilities.[2]

In this chapter we use traded share options to explain how options work and how they are valued. But we hope our brief survey has convinced you that the interest of financial managers in options goes far beyond traded share options. That is why we are asking you here to invest to acquire several important ideas. The return to this investment comes primarily in later chapters.

---

1    In Chapter 11 we valued Kingsley Solomon's gold mine by calculating the value of the gold in the ground and then subtracting the value of the extraction costs. That is strictly correct only if we *know* that the gold will be mined. Otherwise, the value of the mine is increased by the value of the option to leave the gold in the ground if its price is less than the extraction cost.

2    This relationship was first recognised by Fischer Black and Myron Scholes in 'The Pricing of Options and Corporate Liabilities', *Journal of Political* Economy, **81**: 637–54 (May–June 1973).

# 20.1 Calls, puts and shares

The ASX Derivatives Market was founded in 1976 as the Australian Options Market. Trading on this exchange provides the opportunity for options to be bought or sold on many listed companies, such as ANZ, CRA, MIM, News Corporation, CSR, PBL, Western Mining and Westpac. Options are also available on the All Ordinaries Share Market Index.

Liquidity in the market is sustained by standardisation of the contract size, the expiry date of the option and the exercise price. At the time of listing the option contract, the contract size is set at 1000 shares per option contract. Most options trade on a quarterly maturity or expiration cycle with the expiry date on the last Friday of the expiry month, provided that it is a business day. Exercise or strike prices of the options are set according to the underlying share price:

| Share price | Intervals |
|---|---|
| Up to $1.00 | $0.10 |
| $1.01 to $5.00 | $0.25 |
| $5.01 to $10.00 | $0.50 |
| $10.01 and over | $1.00 |

In the December quarter of 1995 approximately 1.4 million call options with a value in excess of $528 million and 670 000 put options with a value in excess of $213 million were traded at the ASX Derivatives Market. This included in excess of 34 000 contracts traded daily.[3]

Table 20.1 is an extract from the table of option prices in a daily newspaper in January 1996.[4] It shows the buying prices of two types of options on CSR Ltd shares—calls and puts. We will explain each of these below in turn.

**table 20.1**

The buying prices of call and put options on CSR Ltd shares in January 1996. The CSR Ltd share price was $4.50.

| Expiry date | Exercise price | Price of call option | Price of put option |
|---|---|---|---|
| March 96 | 4.50 | 0.15 | 0.09 |
| June 96 | 4.25 | 0.43 | 0.08 |
| June 96 | 4.50 | 0.26 | 0.18 |
| June 96 | 4.75 | 0.15 | 0.31 |

A **call option** gives its owner the right to buy shares at a specified *exercise* or *striking* price. In some cases the option can be exercised only on one particular day, and it is then conventionally known as a *European* call; in other cases it can be exercised on or at any time before that day, and it is then known as an *American* call. We shall concentrate initially on the conceptually simpler European option, but almost all our remarks apply equally well to its American cousin.

The third column of Table 20.1 sets out the prices of CSR call options with different exercise prices and exercise dates. The first entry shows that for $0.15 you can acquire an option to buy CSR shares for $4.50 on or before March 1996. Moving down to the highlighted row, you can see that for a price of $0.26 you could extend your option to buy CSR shares at $4.50 until June

3    ASX Derivatives Market, *ASXD Facts: December 1995 Quarter*, 1996.
4    *Australian Financial Review*, 3 January 1996.

1996. The second and fourth rows also show the price of a June 1996 option at the expiration price of $4.25 and $4.75. You should note that the prices of each of the call options differ.

In Chapter 13 we met Louis Bachelier, who in 1900 suggested that security prices follow a random walk process. Bachelier also devised a very convenient shorthand to illustrate the effects of investing in different options.[5] We will use this shorthand to compare three possible investments in CSR Ltd (hereafter, CSR)—a call option, a put option and the share itself.

**figure 20.1**

Payoffs to owners of calls, puts and shares (shown by the coloured lines) depend on the share price. (a) Result of buying a call exercisable at $4.50 (b) Result of buying a put exercisable at $4.50 (c) Result of buying a share (d) Result of buying a share and a put option exercisable at $4.50—this is equivalent to owning a call and having $4.50 in the bank.

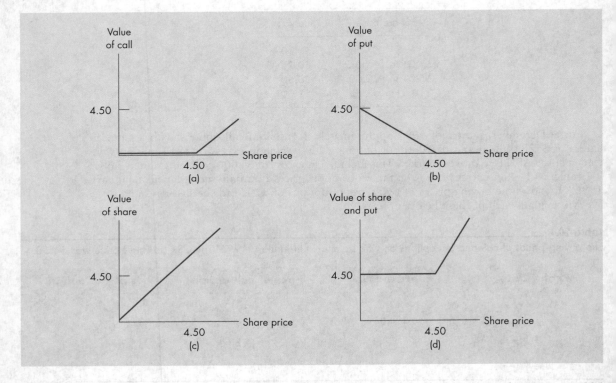

The *position* or *payoff* diagram in Figure 20.1(a) shows the possible values of a CSR June 1996 call option that is exercisable at $4.50. The outcome from investing in CSR calls depends on what happens to the share price between January and June 1996. If the share price at June 1996 turns out to be less than the $4.50 exercise price, no one will pay $4.50 to obtain the share via the call option. Our call option will in that case be valueless and we will not exercise it. On the other hand, if the share price turns out to be greater than $4.50, it will pay us to exercise our option to buy the share. In this case the option will be worth the market price of the share minus the $4.50 that we must pay to acquire it. For example, if the share is worth $6.00, the call is worth $1.50.

$$\text{Value of call option at expiration} = \text{market price of the share} - \text{exercise price}$$
$$= \$6.00 - \$4.50$$
$$= \$1.50$$

---

5  L. Bachelier, *Theorie de la Speculation*, Gauthier-Villars, Paris, 1900. Reprinted in English in P. H. Cootner (ed.), *The Random Character of Stock Market Prices*, MIT Press, Cambridge, Mass., 1964.

Now let us look at the CSR European **put option** with the same exercise price. Whereas the call gives us the right to *buy* a share for $4.50, the comparable put gives us the right to *sell* a share for $4.50. Therefore, the circumstances in which the put will be valuable are just the opposite of those in which the call will be valuable. We can see this from the position diagram in Figure 20.1(b). If CSR's share price immediately before expiration turns out to be *greater* than $4.50, no one will want to sell the share at that price. Our put option will be worthless. Conversely, if the share price turns out to be *less* than $4.50, it will pay to buy the share and then take advantage of the option to sell it for $4.50. In this case the value of the put option at expiration is the difference between the $4.50 proceeds of the sale and the market price of the share. For example, if the share is worth $3.50, the put is worth $1.00:

$$\text{Value of put option at expiration} = \text{exercise price} - \text{market price of the share}$$
$$= \$4.50 - \$3.50$$
$$= \$1.00$$

Our third investment consists of CSR shares. Figure 20.1(c) betrays few secrets when it shows that the value of this investment is always exactly equal to the market value of the share.

# Selling calls, puts and shares

Let us now look at the position of an investor who sells these investments. The individual who sells, or 'writes', a call promises to deliver shares if asked to do so by the call buyer. In other words, the buyer's asset is the seller's liability. If at expiration the share price is below the exercise price, the buyer will not exercise the call and the seller's liability will be zero. If it rises above the exercise price, the buyer will exercise and the seller must sell the shares at the agreed exercise price. If the seller holds the shares he or she must give up the shares. If the seller does not hold the shares he or she will need to purchase them at the current market price for sale to the buyer of the option. The seller loses the difference between the share price and the exercise price received from the buyer. Notice that it is the buyer who always has the option to exercise.

Suppose that at the expiry date the price of CSR shares turns out to be $6.00, which is above the option's exercise price of $4.50. In this case the buyer will exercise the call. The seller is forced to sell shares worth $6.00 for only $4.50 and therefore loses $1.50 per share. Of course, the $1.50 loss to the writer of the option is the buyer's gain.

Figure 20.2(a) shows how the payoffs to the seller of the CSR call option vary with the share price. Notice that Figure 20.2(a) is just a mirror image of Figure 20.1(a).

In just the same way we can depict the position of an investor who sells, or 'writes', a put by standing Figure 20.1(b) on its head. The seller of the put has agreed to pay $4.50 for the share if the put buyer should request it. Clearly the seller will be safe as long as the share price remains above $4.50, but will lose money if the share price falls below this figure. The worst thing that can happen is for the share to be worthless. The seller would then be obliged to pay $4.50 for a share worth $0. The 'value' of the option position would be −$4.50.

Finally, Figure 20.2(c) shows the position of someone who sells the share short. Short sellers sell shares which they do not yet own. As they say on Wall Street:

*He who sells what isn't his'n*
*Buys it back or goes to prison.*

Eventually, therefore, the short seller will have to buy the share back. The short seller will make a profit if it has fallen in price and a loss if it has risen.[6] You can see that Figure 20.2(c) is simply an upside-down Figure 20.1(c).

---

[6]  Selling short is not as simple as we have described it. For example, a short seller usually has to put up margin, that is, deposit cash or securities with the broker. This assures the broker that the short seller will be able to repurchase the stock when the time comes to do so.

**figure 20.2**

Payoffs to sellers of calls, puts and shares (shown by the coloured lines) depend on the share price. (a) Result of selling a call exercisable at $4.50 (b) Result of selling a put exercisable at $4.50 (c) Result of selling a share short.

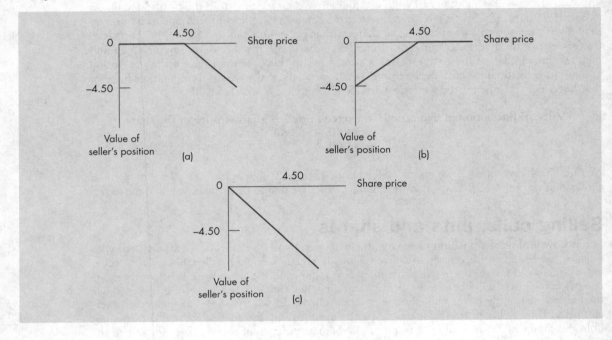

## 20.2 Holding calls, puts and shares in combination

We now return to the option buyer and see what happens when we add two investments together. Suppose, for example, that our portfolio contains both a CSR share and an option to sell (put) it for $4.50. We can read off the value of each of these holdings from panels (b) and (c) in Figure 20.1. Notice that if the CSR share price is higher than $4.50 when the option expires at the end of six months, the put option will be worthless and the value of our portfolio will be equal to the share price. Conversely, if the share price falls below $4.50, the decline in the value of the share will be offset exactly by the rise in that of the put. In Figure 20.1(d) we have plotted the total value of these two holdings.[7]

Figure 20.1(d) tells us something about the relationship between a call option and a put option. You can see why if we compare it with Figure 20.1(a). Regardless of the share price, the final value of our combined investment in the share and the put is exactly $4.50 greater than that of a simple investment in the call. In other words, if you (1) buy the share and (2) retain a put option to sell the share after six months for $4.50, you have the same payoff as you would if you had (1) bought a six-month call option and (2) set aside enough money to pay for the share at $4.50 in six months time on the expiration date. Therefore, if you are

---

[7]   You may find it helpful to check that Figure 20.1(d) is the sum of Figures 20.1(b) and 20.1(c). For example, for a share price equal to zero, the value of the package is value of share + value of put = 0 + 4.50 = $4.50. For a share price of $1.00, the value of the package is value of share + value of put = 1.00 + 3.50 = $4.50.

committed to holding the two packages until the end of six months, the two packages should sell for the same price. This gives us a fundamental relationship for European options:[8]

Value of call + present value of exercise price = value of put + share price

We call this relationship put call parity.

To repeat, this relationship holds because the payoff of

[Buy call, invest present value of exercise price in safe asset[9]]

is identical to the payoff of

[Buy share, buy put]

Here is a slightly different example. Suppose that in January 1996 you want to invest in one CSR share but do not have any cash on hand. However, you know you will receive $4.50 six months hence. Therefore, you borrow the present value of $4.50 from your bank and invest that amount in the share. At the end of six months your payoff is the share price less the $4.50 owed to the bank.

Now compare this with an alternative strategy to buy a six-month call option with an exercise price of $4.50 and to sell a six-month put option with an exercise price of $4.50. The final value of such a package would be equal to the sum of Figure 20.1(a) and 20.2(b). Figure 20.3 shows that this sum is always equal to the market price of the share less $4.50. It is not difficult to see why. If the share price rises, we would exercise our call and pay $4.50 to obtain the share; if it goes down, the other person would exercise his or her option and sell us a share for $4.50. In either case, we would pay $4.50 and acquire the share. Since our two investment strategies have exactly the same consequences, they should have exactly the same value.[10] In other words, we have the following rearrangement of our earlier equation:

Value of call − value of put = share price − present value of exercise price

which holds because

[Buy call, sell put]

is identical to

[Buy share, borrow present value of exercise price[11]]

Of course, there are many ways to express the basic relationship between share price, call and put values, and the present value of the exercise price. Each expression implies two investment strategies that give identical results.

One more example. Solve the basic relationship for the value of a put:

Value of put = value of call − value of share + present value of exercise price

---

8    This relationship holds only if you are committed to holding the options until the final exercise date. It does not hold for American options, where you can exercise before the final date. We discuss possible reasons for early exercise in Chapter 21.

9    This present value is calculated at the risk-free rate of interest. It is the amount you would have to invest today in Treasury notes to realise the exercise price on the option's expiration date.

10   Reminder: this relationship is strictly true for European options where you are committed to hold them until the final exercise date. Since the CSR options are American options, the relationship is only an approximation.

11   Again, present value is computed at the risk-free rate of interest. In other words, the comparison assumes that you are certain to pay off the loan.

**figure 20.3**

Result of buying a call and selling a put, each exercisable at $4.50. Whatever happens to the share price, you end up paying $4.50 and acquiring the share at the expiration date of the option. You could achieve the same outcome by buying the share and borrowing the present value of $4.50, to be repaid on the expiration date.

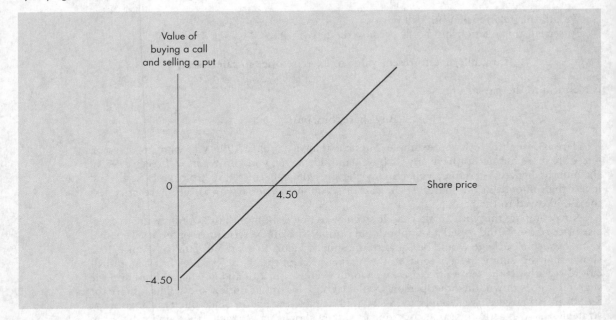

From this expression you can deduce that

[Buy put]

is identical to

[Buy call, sell share, invest present value of exercise price]

In other words, if puts were not available, you could create them by buying calls, selling shares and lending.

Manoeuvres such as these are called *option conversions*. Calls can be converted into puts, or vice versa, by taking the appropriate position in the share and borrowing or lending. As a result, we do not need calls, puts, shares *and* borrowing or lending in this world (and we hope not in the next). Given any three of these investment opportunities we can always construct the fourth.

## *The difference between safe and risky bonds

In Chapter 18[12] we discussed the plight of Circular File Company, which borrowed $50. Unfortunately, the firm fell on hard times and the market value of its assets fell to $30.

---

[12]  See Section 18.3.

Circular's bond and share prices fell to $25 and $5, respectively. Circular's market value balance sheet is now:

| Circular File Company (market values) | | | |
|---|---|---|---|
| Asset value | $30 | $25 | Bond value |
|  |  | $5 | Share value |
|  | $30 | $30 | Firm value |

If Circular's debt were due and payable now, the firm could not repay the $50 it originally borrowed. It would default, bondholders receiving assets worth $30 and shareholders receiving nothing. The reason Circular's shares are worth $5 is that the debt is not due now but rather a year from now. A stroke of good fortune could increase firm value enough to pay off the bondholders in full, with something left over for the shareholders.

Let us go back to a statement that we made at the start of the chapter. Whenever a firm borrows, the lender effectively acquires the company and the shareholders obtain the option to buy it back by paying off the debt. The shareholders have in effect purchased a call option on the assets of the firm. The bondholders have sold them this call option. Thus, the balance sheet of Circular File can be expressed as follows:

| Circular File Company (market values) | | | |
|---|---|---|---|
| Asset value | $30 | $25 | Bond value = asset value − value of call |
|  |  | $5 | Share value = value of call |
|  | $30 | $30 | Firm value |

If this still sounds like a strange idea to you, try drawing one of Bachelier's position diagrams for Circular File. It should look like Figure 20.4. If the future value of the assets is less than $50, Circular will default and the shares will be worthless. If the value of the assets exceeds $50, the shareholders will receive asset value less the $50 paid over to the bondholders. The payoffs in Figure 20.4 are identical to a call option on the firm's assets, with an exercise price of $50.

Now look again at the basic relationship between calls and puts:

**Value of call + present value of exercise = value of put + value of share**

To apply this to Circular File, we have to interpret 'value of share' as 'asset value', because the ordinary share is a call option on the firm's assets. Also, 'present value of exercise price' is the present value of receiving the promised payment of $50 to bondholders *for sure* next year. Thus:

**Value of call + present value of promised payment to bondholders = value of put + asset value**

Now we can solve for the value of Circular bonds. This is equal to the firm's asset value less the value of the shareholders' call option on these assets:

**Bond value = asset value − value of call**
**= present value of promised payment to bondholders − value of put**

**figure 20.4** _____

The value of Circular's ordinary share is the same as the value of the call option on the firm's assets with an exercise price of $50.

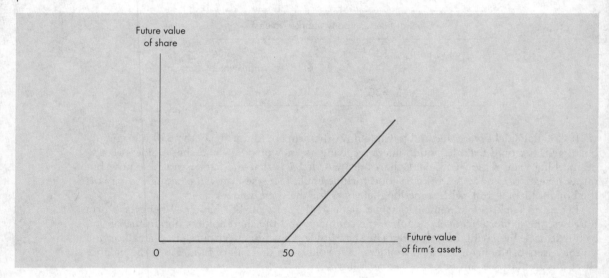

Circular's bondholders have in effect (1) bought a safe bond and (2) given the shareholders the option to sell them the firm's assets for the amount of the debt. You can think of the bondholders as receiving the $50 promised payment, but they have given the shareholders the option to take the $50 back in exchange for the assets of the company. If firm value turns out to be less than the $50 that is promised to bondholders, the shareholders will exercise their put option.

Circular's risky bond is equal to a safe bond less the value of the shareholders' option to default. To value this risky bond we need to value a safe bond and then subtract the value of the default option. The default option is equal to a put option on the firm's assets.

In the case of Circular File the option to default is extremely valuable because default is likely to occur. At the other extreme, the value of BHP's option to default is trivial compared to the value of BHP's assets. Default on BHP bonds is possible but extremely unlikely. Option traders would say that for Circular File the put option is 'deep in the money' because today's asset value ($30) is well below the exercise price ($50). For BHP the put option is well 'out of the money' because the value of BHP's assets substantially exceeds the value of BHP's debt.

We know that Circular's shares are equivalent to a call option on the firm's assets. They are also equal to (1) owning the firm's assets, (2) borrowing the present value of $50 with the obligation to repay regardless of what happens, as well as (3) buying a put on the firm's assets with an exercise price of $50.

We can sum up by presenting Circular's balance sheet in terms of asset value, put value and the present value of a sure $50 payment:

| Circular File Company (market values) | | |
|---|---|---|
| Asset value | $30 | $25 | Bond value = present value of promised payment − value of put |
| | | $5 | Share value = asset value − present value of promised payment + value of put |
| | $30 | $30 | Firm value = asset value |

**figure 20.5**

You can also think of Circular's bond (the coloured line) as equivalent to a risk-free bond (the upper black line) *less* a put option on the firm's assets with an exercise price of $50 (the lower black line).

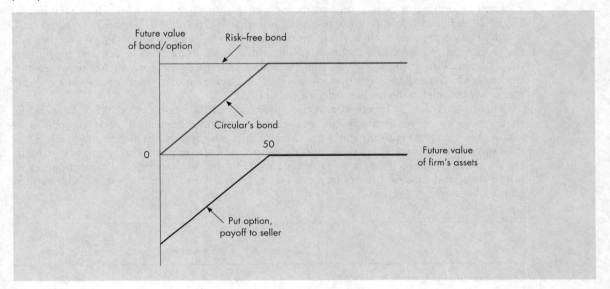

Again, you can check this with a position diagram. The coloured line in Figure 20.5 shows the payoffs to Circular's bondholders. If the firm's assets are worth more than $50, the bondholders are paid off in full; if the assets are worth less than $50, the firm defaults and the bondholders receive the value of the assets. You could get an identical payoff pattern by buying a safe bond (the upper black line) and selling a put option on the firm's assets (the lower black line).

## *Spotting the option

Options rarely come with a large label attached. Often the trickiest part of the problem is to identify the option. For example, we suspect that until it was pointed out, you did not realise that every risky bond contains a hidden option. Further examples of options are detailed in Chapter 21.

For now though the following general theorem can be applied whenever an event is contingent on other factors:

*Any set of contingent payoffs—that is, payoffs which depend on the value of some other asset—can be valued as a mixture of simple options on that asset.*

For instance, if you needed to value a capital project that would pay off $2 million if the price of copper was less than $1500 per tonne but only $1 million if the price was greater than $1500, you could use option theory to do so.

## 20.3  What determines option values?

So far we have said nothing about how the market value of options is determined. However, we do know what an option is worth when it matures. Consider, for example, our earlier case of an option to buy CSR shares at $4.50. If CSR's share price is below $4.50 at the expiration date, the call will be worthless; if the share price is above $4.50, the call will be worth the value of the share less $4.50. In terms of Bachelier's position diagram, the relationship is depicted by the heavy line in Figure 20.6.

Even before maturity the price of the option can never remain *below* the heavy line in Figure 20.6. For example, if our option were priced at $0.20 and CSR's share price was $7.50, it would pay any investor to buy the option, exercise it for an additional $4.50 and then sell the share. That would give a money machine with a profit of $2.80. The demand for options from investors using the money machine would quickly force the option price up at least to the heavy line in the figure. For options that still have some time to run, the heavy line is therefore a *lower* limit on the market price of the option.

The diagonal line in Figure 20.6 is the *upper* limit to the option price. Why? Because the share gives a higher ultimate payoff than the option, whatever happens. If at the option's expiration the share price ends up above the exercise price, the option is worth the share price *less* the exercise price. If the share price ends up below the exercise price, the option is worthless, but the share's owner still has a valuable security. Let $P$ be the share price at the option's expiration date, and assume the option's exercise price is $4.50. Then the extra dollar returns realised by shareholders are:

|  | Share payoff | Option payoff | Extra payoff from holding share |
|---|---|---|---|
| Option exercised ($P$ greater than $4.50) | $P$ | $P - \$4.50$ | $4.50 |
| Option expires unexercised ($P$ less than or equal to $4.50) | $P$ | 0 | $P$ |

**figure 20.6**

Value of a call before its expiration date (dashed line). The value depends on the share price. It is always worth more than its value if exercised now (heavy line). It is never worth more than the share price itself.

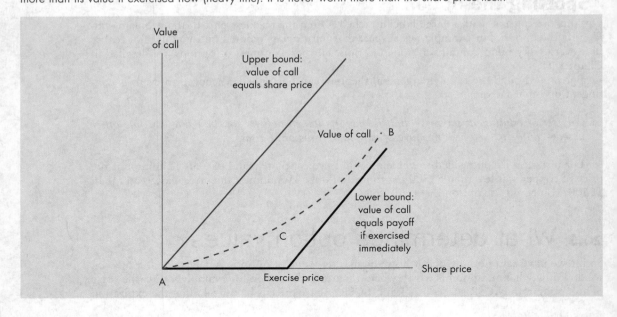

If the share and the option have the same price, everyone will rush to sell the option and buy the share. Therefore, the option price must be somewhere in the shaded region of Figure 20.6. In fact, it will lie on a curved, upward-sloping line like the dashed curve shown in the figure. This line begins its travels where the upper and lower bounds meet (at zero). Then it rises, gradually becoming parallel to the upward-sloping part of the lower bound. This line tells us an important fact about option values: *the value of an option increases as the share price increases*, if the exercise price is held constant.

That should be no surprise. Owners of call options clearly hope that the share price will rise and are happy when it does. But let us look more carefully at the shape and location of the dashed line. Three points, A, B and C, are marked on the dashed line. As we explain each point you will see why the option price has to behave as the dashed line predicts.

**Point A**     *When the share is worthless, the option is worthless.* A share price of zero means that there is no possibility the share will ever have any future value.[13] If so, the option is sure to expire unexercised and worthless, and it is worthless today.

**Point B**     *When the share price becomes high, the option price approaches the share price less the present value of the exercise price.* Notice that the dashed line representing the option price in Figure 20.6 eventually becomes parallel to the ascending heavy line representing the lower bound on the option price. The reason is as follows: the higher the share price, the higher the probability that the option will eventually be exercised. If the share price is high enough, exercise becomes a virtual certainty; the probability that the share price will fall below the exercise price before the option expires becomes trivially small.

If you own an option that you *know* will be exchanged for a portion of the share, you effectively own the share now. The only difference is that you do not have to pay for the share (by handing over the exercise price) until later, when formal exercise occurs. In these circumstances, buying the call is equivalent to buying the share but financing part of the purchase by borrowing. The amount implicitly borrowed is the present value of the exercise price. The value of the call is therefore equal to the share price less the present value of the exercise price.

This brings us to another important point about options. Investors who acquire shares by way of a call option are buying on instalment credit. They pay the purchase price of the option today, but they do not pay the exercise price until they actually take up the option. The delay in payment is particularly valuable if interest rates are high and the option has a long maturity. With an interest rate $r_f$ and the time to maturity $t$, then we would expect the value of the option to depend on the product[14] of $r_f$ and $t$: *The value of an option increases with both the rate of interest and the time to maturity.*[15]

**Point C**     *The option price always exceeds its minimum value* (except when share price is zero). We have seen that the dashed and heavy lines in Figure 20.6 coincide when share price is zero (point A), but elsewhere the lines diverge; that is, the option price must exceed the minimum value given by the heavy line. The reason for this can be understood by examining point C. At point C, the share price exactly equals the exercise price. The option is therefore worthless if exercised today. However, suppose that the option will not expire until three months hence. Of course, we do not know what the share price will be at the expiration date. There

---

[13]  If a share can be worth something in the future, then investors will pay *something* for it today, although possibly a very small amount.

[14]  Using continuous compounding, the present value of the exercise price is (exercise price $\times e^{-r_f t}$). The discount factor $e^{-r_f t}$ depends on the product of $r_f$ and $t$.

[15]  This is because the higher the risk-free rate, the lower will be the present value of the exercise price.

is a roughly 50 per cent chance that it will be higher than the exercise price and a 50 per cent chance that it will be lower. The possible payoffs to the option are therefore:

| Outcome | Payoff |
|---|---|
| Share price rises (50% probability) | Share price less exercise price (option is exercised) |
| Share price falls (50% probability) | Zero (option expires worthless) |

If there is a positive probability of a positive payoff, and if the worst payoff is zero, then the option must be valuable. That means the option price at point C exceeds its lower bound, which at point C is zero. In general, the option prices will exceed their lower-bound values as long as there is time left before expiration.

One of the most important determinants of the *height* of the dashed curve (i.e. of the difference between actual and lower-bound value) is the likelihood of substantial movements in the share price. An option on a share whose price is unlikely to change by more than 1 or 2 per cent is not worth much; an option on a share whose price may halve or double is very valuable.

Panels (a) and (b) in Figure 20.7 illustrate this point. The panels compare the payoffs at expiration of two options with the same exercise price and the same share price. The panels assume that the share price equals the exercise price (like point C in Figure 20.6), although this

**figure 20.7**
Call options are written against the shares of (a) firm X and (b) firm Y. In each case the current share price equals the exercise price, so that each option has a 50 per cent chance of ending up worthless (if the share price falls) and a 50 per cent chance of ending up 'in the money' (if the share price rises). However, the chance of a large payoff is greater for the option on firm Y's share, because Y's share price is more volatile and therefore has more 'upside potential'.

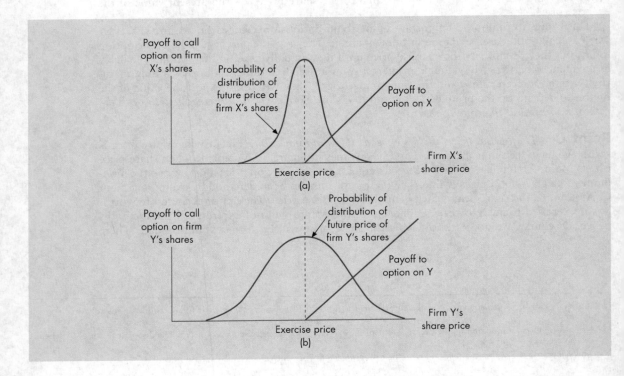

is not a necessary assumption. The only difference is that the price of share Y at its option's expiration date (Figure 20.7(b)) is much harder to predict than the price of share X at its option's expiration date. You can see this from the probability distributions superimposed on the figures.

In both cases there is roughly a 50 per cent chance that the share price will decline and make the options worthless, but if the prices of shares X and Y rise, the odds are that Y will rise more than X. Thus, there is a larger chance of a big payoff from the option on Y. Since the chance of a zero payoff is the same, the option on Y is worth more than the option on X. Figure 20.8 illustrates this: the higher curved line belongs to the option on Y.

**figure 20.8** _____

Value of calls on shares of firm X and shares of firm Y. The calls on Y's shares are worth more because Y's shares are more volatile (see Figure 20.7). The higher curved line describes the value of a call on Y's shares; the lower curved line describes the value of a call on X's shares.

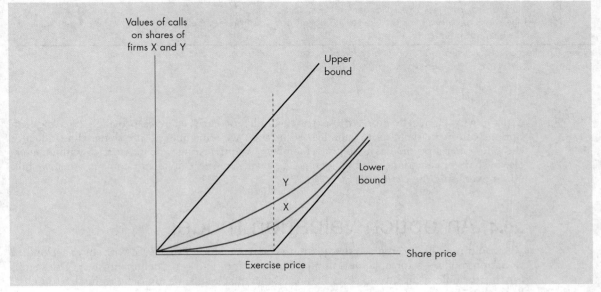

The probability of large share price changes during the remaining life of an option depends on two things: (1) the variance (i.e. volatility) of the share price *per period* and (2) the number of periods until the option expires. If there are $t$ remaining periods, and the variance per period is $\sigma^2$, the value of the option should depend on cumulative variability $\sigma^2 t$.[16] Other things being equal, you would like to hold an option on a volatile share (high $\sigma^2$). Given volatility, you would like to hold an option with a long life ahead of it (large $t$). Thus, the value of an option increases *with both the variability of the share and the time to maturity*.

It is a rare person who can keep all these properties straight at first reading. Therefore, we have summed them up in Table 20.2.

There are other things you need to know about the factors that influence the value of an option. Under some special conditions it can be desirable to exercise an option early. We

_____

16  Here is an intuitive explanation. If the share price follows a random walk (see Section 13.2), successive price changes are statistically independent. The cumulative price change before expiration is the sum of $t$ random variables. The variance of a sum of independent random variables is the sum of the variances of those variables. Thus, if $\sigma^2$ is the variance of the daily price change, and there are $t$ days until expiration, the variance of the cumulative price change is $\sigma^2 * t$.

**table 20.2**

What the price of a call option depends on

---

1. If the following variables *increase*      the changes in the call option price are:

   Share price ($P$)      positive

   Exercise price (EX)      negative

   Interest rate ($r_f$)      positive

   Time to expiration ($it$)      positive

   Volatility of share price ($\sigma$)      positive

2. Other properties:

   (a) Upper bound. The option price is always less than the share price.
   
   (b) Lower bound. The option price never falls below the payoff to immediate exercise ($P - $ EX or zero, whichever is larger).
   
   (c) If the share is worthless, the option is worthless.
   
   (d) As the share price becomes very large, the option price approaches the share price less the present value of the exercise price.

*Note: The direct effects of increases in $r_f$ or $\sigma$ on option price are positive. There may also be indirect effects. For example, an increase in $r_f$ could reduce share price P. This in turn could reduce option price.*

explain why later. Therefore, the extra flexibility of early exercise provided by American options can make them more valuable. So how do we remember all the things that influence the value of an option? Easy, we just remember: 'An interesting time in America with an exercise in share price variance and dividends.' You will see where dividends come in when we talk about exercising the option early.

## 20.4 An option valuation model

We would now like to replace the qualitative statements of Table 20.2 with an exact option valuation model—a formula we can plug numbers into and get a definite answer. The search for this formula went on for years before Fischer Black and Myron Scholes finally found it. Before we show you what they found, we should say a few words to explain why the search was so difficult.

## Why discounted cash flow will not work for options

Our standard operating procedure of (1) forecasting expected cash flow and (2) discounting at the opportunity cost of capital is not helpful for options. The first step is messy but feasible. Finding the opportunity cost of capital is impossible, because the risk of an option changes every time the share price moves,[17] and we know it *will* move along a random walk through the option's lifetime.

When you buy a call you are *taking a position* in the share but putting up less of your own money than if you had bought the share directly. Thus, an option is always riskier than the underlying share. It has a higher beta and a higher standard deviation of return.

---

[17] It also changes over time, even with the share price constant.

How much riskier the option is depends on the share price relative to the exercise price. An option that is in the money (share price greater than exercise price) is safer than one that is out of the money (share price less than exercise price). Thus, a share price increase raises the option's price *and* reduces its risk. When the share price falls, the option's price falls *and* its risk increases. That is why the expected rate of return that investors demand from an option changes day by day, or hour by hour, every time the share price moves.

We repeat the general rule: *The higher the share price relative to the exercise price, the safer the option, although the option is always riskier than the share. The option's risk changes every time the share price changes.*

## Constructing option equivalents from ordinary shares and borrowing

If you have digested what we have said so far, you can appreciate why options are hard to value by standard discounted cash flow formulas and why a rigorous option valuation technique eluded economists for many years. The breakthrough came when Black and Scholes exclaimed 'Eureka! We have found it![18] The trick is to set up an *option equivalent* by combining ordinary share investment and borrowing. The net cost of buying the option equivalent must equal the value of the option.'

We will show you how this works with a simple numerical example. In Table 20.1 we saw that in January 1996 you could have bought six-month call options on CSR shares with an exercise price of $4.50. CSR's share price at that time was also $4.50, so the option was at the money.[19] The interest rate was approximately 3.75 per cent for six months or just over 7.5 per cent a year. To keep matters simple, we will assume that CSR shares can do only two things during the period January to June 1996—either the price will fall by 10 per cent to $4.05 or it will rise by 20 per cent to $5.40.

If CSR's share price falls to $4.05, the call option will be worthless; but if the price rises to $5.40, the option will be worth $0.90.[20] The possible payoffs of the option are therefore:

| Share price = $4.05 | Share price $5.40 |
|---|---|
| $0 | $0.90 |

Now compare these payoffs with what you would get if you bought two-thirds of one share[21] and borrowed $2.60 from the bank:[22]

| | Share price = $4.05 | Share price = $5.40 |
|---|---|---|
| Two-thirds share of one share | $2.70 | $3.60 |
| Repayment of loan + interest | $2.70 | $2.70 |
| Total payoff | $0 | $0.90 |

---

[18]  We do not know whether Black and Scholes, like Archimedes, were sitting in their bathtubs at the time.

[19]  For the purpose of this analysis we will ignore the fact that CSR's shareholders receive dividends on their shares, while option holders do not. We will discuss how to handle dividends in Chapter 21.

[20]  Share price − exercise price = $5.40 − $4.50 = $0.90.

[21]  Although two-thirds of one share is used in this example, the example could also be used with the assumption that three options are bought for each of two shares (i.e. $2/3 \times 3 = 2$). This increases the borrowing from $2.60 to $8.10 and gives a payoff of $0.00 if the share price equals $4.05 and $2.70 if the share price equals $5.40.

[22]  The amount that you need to borrow from the bank is simply the present value of the difference between the payoffs from the options and the payoff from holding, in this case, two-thirds of a share. The total amount repayable after six months is $2.70. The principal of this loan is equal to $2.60.

Notice that the payoffs from the levered investment in the share are identical to the payoffs from the call option. Therefore, both investments must have the same value:

$$\text{Value of the calls} = \text{value of 2/3 of the share} - \$2.60 \text{ bank loan}$$

$$= 4.50 \times \frac{2}{3} - 2.60 = \$0.40$$

Presto! You have valued a call option.

To value the CSR option, we borrowed money and bought two-thirds of the share in such a way that we replicated exactly the payoff from a call option. The number of shares that are needed to replicate one call is often called the **hedge ratio** or the **option delta**. In our CSR example the call is replicated by a levered position in two-thirds of one share. The option delta is, therefore, two-thirds or 0.66. How did we know that CSR's call option was equivalent to a levered position in two-thirds of a share? We used a simple formula that says

$$\text{Option delta} = \frac{\text{Spread of possible option prices}}{\text{Spread of possible share prices}}$$

$$= \frac{(0.90 - 0)}{(5.40 - 4.05)}$$

$$= \frac{2}{3}, \text{ or } 0.66$$

You have learned not only to value a simple option, but also that you can replicate an investment in the option by a levered investment in the underlying asset. Thus, if you cannot buy or sell an option on an asset you can create a homemade option by a replicating strategy of buying or selling delta shares and borrowing or lending the balance.

# *The risk-neutral method

Notice why the CSR call option has to sell for $0.40. If the option price is higher than $0.40, using this method, you could make a certain profit by buying two-thirds of a share, selling a call option and borrowing $2.60. Similarly, if the option is less than $0.40, you could make an equally certain profit by selling two-thirds of a share, buying a call and lending the balance. In either case we may have a ready-made money machine.

If there is a money machine, everyone scurries to take advantage of it. So when we said that the option price must be $0.40 or there would be a money machine, we did not have to know anything about investor attitudes to risk. The price cannot depend on whether investors detest risk or could not care about risk.

This suggests an alternative way to calculate the value of the CSR option. We can pretend that all investors are *indifferent* about risk, work out the expected future value of the option in such a world and discount it back at the risk-free interest rate to give the current value. Let us check that this method gives the same answer.

If investors are indifferent to risk, the expected return on the share must be equal to the rate of interest:

$$\text{Expected return on CSR shares} = 3.75\% \text{ per six months}$$

We know that CSR shares can either rise by 20 per cent to $5.40 or fall by 10 per cent to $4.05. We can therefore calculate the probability of a price rise in this hypothetical risk-neutral world:

$$\text{Expected return} = (\text{probability of rise}) \times 20 + (1 - \text{probability of rise}) \times (-10) = 3.75\%$$

Therefore,

$$\text{Probability of rise} = 0.4583, \text{ or } 45.83\% [23]$$

Since we have assumed our investors are risk-neutral—that is, that they do not care about risk—these probabilities are often referred to as risk-neutral probabilities.

We know that if the share price rises by 20 per cent, the CSR call option will be worth $5.40; if it falls, the call will be worth nothing. Therefore, the expected value of the call option is:

$$
\begin{aligned}
\text{Expected value of call option} &= (\text{probability of rise} \times 0.90) + [(1 - \text{probability of rise}) \times 0] \\
&= (0.4583 \times 0.90) + (0.5417 \times 0) \\
&= \$0.41
\end{aligned}
$$

And the current value of the call is

$$
\frac{\text{Expected future value}}{(1 + \text{interest rate})} = \frac{0.41}{(1 + 0.0375)}
$$
$$
= 0.3951, \text{ or } \$0.40
$$

This is exactly the same answer that we got earlier!
We now have two ways to calculate the value of an option:

1. Find the combination of shares and loan that replicates an investment in the option. Since the two strategies give identical payoffs in the future, they must sell for the same price today.

2. Pretend that investors do not care about risk, so that the expected return on the share is equal to the interest rate. Next work out the risk-neutral probabilities, then calculate the expected future value of the option in this risk-neutral world and discount it at the interest rate.

## Valuing the CSR put option

Valuing the CSR call option may have seemed like pulling a rabbit out of a hat. To give you a further chance to see how to price options, we will use the same method to value another option, this time the six-month CSR June 1996 put option with a $4.50 exercise price.[24]

We will continue to assume that CSR's share price will either rise by 20 per cent to $5.40 or fall by 10 per cent to $4.05. If the share price rises to $5.40, the option to sell will be worthless. If the share price falls to $4.05, the option will be worth $0.45.[25] Thus, the payoffs to the put are:

| Share price = $4.05 | Share price = $5.40 |
| --- | --- |
| Payoff = $0.45 | Payoff = $0 |

---

[23] Note that this is not the true probability that CSR's shares will rise. Since investors dislike risk they will almost surely have a higher expected return than the risk-free interest rate from their investment in CSR shares. Therefore, the true probability of a price rise is greater than 0.4583.

[24] When valuing an American put option, you will need to recognise the possibility that it will pay to exercise early. We discuss this complication in the next chapter. It is important for valuing the CSR put, but we will ignore it at this point.

[25] Exercise price − share price = $4.50 − $4.05 = $0.45.

We start by calculating the option delta using the formula that we presented above:[26]

$$\text{Option delta} = \frac{(0 - 0.45)}{(5.40 - 4.05)}$$

$$= -\frac{1}{3}, \text{ or } -0.33$$

The delta of a put option is always negative—that is, you need to *sell* delta shares to replicate the put. In the case of the CSR put you can replicate the option payoffs by selling one-third of a CSR share and lending $1.73. Since you have sold the share short, you will need to pay out money at the end of six months to buy it back, but you will have money coming in from the loan. The net payoffs are exactly the same as if you bought the put option:

|  | Share price = $4.05 | Share price = $5.40 |
|---|---|---|
| Sale of one-third of a share | −$1.35 | −$1.80 |
| Repayment of loan + interest | +$1.80 | +$1.80 |
| Total payoff | $0.45 | $0 |

Since the two investments have the same payoffs, they must have the same value:

$$\text{Value of the put} = -(\text{value of } \tfrac{1}{3} \text{ of the share}) + \$1.73 \text{ bank loan}$$

$$= -(4.50 \times \frac{1}{3}) + 1.73$$

$$= \$0.23$$

## *Valuing the put option by the risk-neutral method

Valuing the CSR put option with the risk-neutral method is simple. We already know that the probability of a rise in the share price is 45.83 per cent. Therefore, the expected value of the put option in a risk-neutral world is:

$$\text{Expected value of put option} = (\text{probability of rise} \times 0) + [(1 - \text{probability of rise}) \times 0.45]$$
$$= (0.4583 \times 0) + (0.5417 \times 0.45)$$
$$= \$0.24$$

And the current value of the put is:

$$\frac{\text{Expected future value}}{(1 + \text{ interest rate})} = \frac{0.24}{(1 + 0.0375)}$$
$$= \$0.23$$

## *The relationship between call and put prices

We pointed out earlier that for European options there is a simple relationship between the value of the call and that of the put:[27]

$$\text{Value of a put} = \text{value of a call} - \text{share price} + \text{present value of exercise price}$$

---

[26]   The delta of a put option with the same exercise price and term to maturity as a call option is equal to the delta of the call option minus 1. In our example, delta of put = $(2/3) - 1 = -1/3$.

[27]   Reminder: this formula is only applicable when options have the same exercise price and exercise date.

Since we have already calculated the value of the CSR call, we could also have used this relationship to find the value of a put.

$$\text{Value of a put} = (0.40) - (4.50) + \left[ \frac{4.50}{(1 + 0.0375)} \right]$$

$$= \$0.23$$

Everything checks out with the above calculations.

# 20.5 The Black–Scholes formula

Let us summarise our discussion of option pricing thus far. The essential trick in pricing any option is to set up a package of investment in the share and a loan that will replicate exactly the payoffs from the option. If we can price the share and the loan, then we can also price the option.

Our example of the CSR call option is fanciful in one important respect: there will be more than two possible prices for CSR's shares at the end of six months. We could make the problem slightly more realistic by assuming that there are two possible changes in the share price in each three-month period. That would give a wider range of six-month prices. It would still be possible to construct a series of levered investments in the share that would give exactly the same prospects as the option.[28]

There is no reason to stop at three-month periods. We could go on to take shorter and shorter intervals, with each interval showing two possible changes in CSR's share price. Eventually we would reach a situation in which CSR's share price was changing continuously and generating a continuum of possible six-month prices. We could still replicate the call option by a levered investment in the share, but we would need to adjust the degree of leverage continuously as the year went by.

Calculating the value of this levered investment may sound like a hopelessly tedious business, but Black and Scholes derived a formula that does the trick. It is an unpleasant-looking formula, but its interpretation is as follows:

$$\text{Value of call option} = [\text{delta} \times \text{share price}] - [\text{bank loan}]$$
$$\uparrow \qquad\qquad \uparrow \qquad\qquad\qquad \uparrow$$
$$[N(d_1) \times P] - [N(d_2) \times \text{PV(EX)}]$$

where $d_1 = \log [P/\text{PV(EX)}] \, \sigma t + \sigma^2$; $d_2 = d_1 - \sigma t$; $N(d)$ = cumulative normal probability density function;[29] EX = exercise price of option; PV(EX) is calculated by discounting at the risk-free interest rate $r_f$, $\text{PV(EX)} = \text{EX} \, e^{-r_f t}$; $t$ = number of periods to exercise date; $P$ = price of share now; and $\sigma$ = standard deviation per period of (continuously compounded) rate of return on share.

Notice that the value of the call in the Black–Scholes formula has the same properties that we identified earlier. The willingness of investors to bear risk does not affect value, neither does the expected return on the share.[30] The value of the option increases with the level of the share price ($P$); it decreases with the present value of the exercise price (PV(EX)), which in turn depends on the interest rate and time to maturity; and it increases with the time to maturity multiplied by the share's variability ($\sigma \sqrt{t}$).

---

[28] We will work through a two-period example in Chapter 21.

[29] That is, $N(d)$ is the probability that a normally distributed random variable $\tilde{x}$ will be less than or equal to $d$. $N(d_1)$ in the Black–Scholes formula is the option delta. Thus, the formula tells us that the value of a call is equal to an investment of $N(d_1)$ in the ordinary shares less borrowing of $N(d_2) \times \text{PV(EX)}$.

[30] Although the expected return affects the price of the share, it does not affect the *relative* value of the share and option.

To derive the formula, Black and Scholes assumed that there is a continuum of share prices, so that to replicate an option investors must continuously adjust their holding in the share. Of course, this is not literally possible, but the formula performs remarkably well in the real world where shares trade only intermittently and prices jump from one level to another.

The Black–Scholes formula has also proved very flexible. It can be adapted to value a variety of options on a variety of assets with special features, such as foreign currency, bonds and futures. It is not surprising, therefore, that it has been hugely influential and has become the standard model for valuing options. Every day dealers on the options exchanges use this formula to make huge trades. These dealers are not for the most part trained in the formula's mathematical derivation; they just use a computer or a specially-programmed calculator to find the value of the option.

## Using the Black–Scholes formula

Appendix Tables 6 and 7 allow you to use the Black–Scholes formula to value a variety of simple options. To use the tables, follow these four steps:

**Step 1**  Multiply the standard deviation of the changes in the asset's value (the returns on the asset) by the square root of time to the option's expiration. For example, suppose that you wish to value the six-month call option on CSR shares and assume that the standard deviation of the continuously compounded share price changes is 15 per cent per year.

$$\text{Standard deviation} \times \text{time} = 0.15 \times \sqrt{0.5} = 0.11$$

**Step 2**  Calculate the ratio of the asset value to the present value of the option's exercise price. For example, if the CSR share price and the exercise price are both \$4.50 and the interest rate is 3.75 per cent for six months, then:

$$\frac{\text{Asset value}}{\text{PV(exercise price)}} = \frac{4.50}{\left[\dfrac{4.50}{(1 + 0.0375)}\right]}$$

$$= 1.04$$

**Step 3**  Now turn to Appendix Table 6 and look up the entry corresponding to the numbers that you calculated in Steps 1 and 2. There is no entry corresponding exactly to the figures that we just calculated—that is always a problem with tables. But we have highlighted the three entries that bracket the value of the CSR option. Interpolating for the 'standard deviation times square root of time' between the values for 0.10 and 0.15 tells us that the value of a CSR call option is about 6.5 per cent of the share price, or \$0.29. This is higher than the price of \$0.26 reported in Table 20.1. It would appear that we need a lower estimate of the variability of CSR shares to be consistent with market prices.[31] The *implied volatility*—that is, the standard deviation that would produce the market price of \$0.26—is 13.17 per cent.[32]

If you want to know the value of a put option with the same exercise price of \$4.50, then you can use the simple relationship that we derived in the previous section:

$$\text{Value of a put} = (0.26) - (4.50) + \left[\frac{4.50}{(1 + 0.0375)}\right]$$

$$= 0.10$$

---

[31]  Recall that as yet we have not included any provision for dividends or for the fact that the CSR call option is an American option.

[32]  The Black–Scholes formula is often used not to calculate the option value, but to forecast volatility. That is, investors assume that the quoted call price and the formula are correct and then solve for an implied volatility from the formula.

**Step 4**　Table 7 tells you the option delta. For example, if you look up the equivalent entry in Table 7, you see that the CSR call option has a delta of about 0.66. This means that instead of buying a call for $0.26, you could achieve the same result by buying 0.66 of a share (at a cost of 0.66 × $4.50 = $2.97) and borrowing the balance ($2.97 − $0.26 = $2.71).

To find the option delta for the put, you simply subtract 1 from the entry in Table 7. In our example

$$
\begin{aligned}
\text{Put option delta} &= \text{call option delta} - 1 \\
&= 0.66 - 1 \\
&= -0.34
\end{aligned}
$$

In other words, instead of *paying out* $0.10 to buy a CSR Ltd put option, you could sell 0.34 shares (for a cash inflow of 0.34 × $4.50 = $1.53) and buy a Treasury note with the available cash ($0.10 + $1.53 = $1.63).

## 20.6 Summary

If you have managed to reach this point, you are probably in need of a rest, so we will summarise what we have learned so far and take up the subject of options again in Chapter 21.

There are two basic types of option. An American call is an option to buy an asset at a specified exercise price on or before a specified exercise date. Similarly, an American put is an option to sell the asset at a specified price on or *before* a specified date. European calls and puts are exactly the same except that they cannot be exercised before the specified exercise date. Calls and puts are the basic building blocks that can be combined to give any pattern of payoffs.

What determines the value of a call option? Common sense tells us that it ought to depend on three things:

1. In order to exercise an option you have to pay the exercise price. Other things being equal, the less you are obliged to pay, the better. Therefore, the value of an option increases with the ratio of the asset price to the exercise price.
2. You do not have to pay the exercise price until you decide to exercise the option. Therefore, an option gives you a free loan. The higher the rate of interest and the longer the time to maturity, the more this free loan is worth. Therefore, the value of an option increases with the interest rate multiplied by the time to maturity.
3. If the price of the asset falls short of the exercise price, you will not exercise the option. You will therefore lose 100 per cent of your investment in the option no matter how far the asset depreciates below the exercise price. On the other hand, the more the price rises above the exercise price, the more profit you will make. Therefore, the option holder does not lose from increased variability if things go wrong, but gains if they go right. The value of an option increases with the variance per period of the share return multiplied by the number of periods to maturity.

We showed you how to value an option on a share when there are only two possible changes in the share price in each sub-period. Black and Scholes have also derived a formula that gives the value of an option when there is a continuum of possible future share prices. Tables in the Appendix should allow you to apply this formula to a number of simple option problems. Unfortunately, not all option problems are simple. Therefore, in Chapter 21 we will look at some of the complications and work through several examples of moderate complexity.

## FURTHER READING

The classic articles on option valuation are:

F. Black and M. Scholes, 'The Pricing of Options and Corporate Liabilities', *Journal of Political Economy*, **81**: 637–54 (May–June 1973).

R. C. Merton, 'Theory of Rational Option Pricing', *Bell Journal of Economics and Management Science*, **4**: 141–83 (Spring 1973).

There are also a number of good texts on option valuation. They include:

J. Cox and M. Rubinstein, *Options Markets*, Prentice-Hall, Inc., Englewood Cliffs, N.J., 1985.

J. Hull, *Options, Futures and Other Derivative Securities*, Prentice-Hall, Inc., Englewood Cliffs, N.J., 2nd ed., 1993.

R. Jarrow and A. Rudd, *Option Pricing*, Dow Jones-Irwin, Inc., Homewood, Ill., 1983.

The magazines *Risk*, *Journal of Derivatives* and *Derivatives Quarterly* contain regular articles on the valuation of more complex options. For example, in 1991 *Risk* published a series of articles by Mark Rubinstein on exotic options.

## QUIZ

**1.** Complete the following passage: A _____ option gives its owner the opportunity to buy a share at a specific price which is generally called the _____ price. A _____ option gives its owner the opportunity to sell shares at a specified price. Options that can be exercised only at maturity are called _____ options. The ordinary shares of firms that borrow are a _____ option. Shareholders effectively sell the firm's _____ to _____, but retain the option to buy the _____ back. The exercise price is the _____.

**2.** Fill in the blanks:
   a. A firm that issues warrants is selling a _____ option.
   b. A firm that enters a stand-by agreement, whereby the underwriter to a rights issue guarantees to take up any unwanted share, acquires a _____ option.
   c. Rights are _____ options on the issuing firm's share.
   d. An oil company acquires mining rights to a silver deposit. It is not obligated to mine the silver, however. The company has effectively acquired a _____ option, where the exercise price is the cost of opening the mine.
   e. Some preference shareholders have the right to redeem their shares at par value after a specified date. (If they hand over their shares, the firm sends them a cheque equal to the share's par value.) These shareholders have a _____ option.
   f. An executive who qualifies for a share option plan acquires a _____ option.
   g. An investor who buys shares in a levered firm acquires a _____ option on the firm's assets.
   h. A firm buys a standard machine with a ready second-hand market. The second-hand market gives the firm a _____ option.

**3.** Look at Figures 20.9(a) and (b). Match each figure with one of the following positions:
   a. Call buyer.
   b. Call seller.
   c. Put buyer.
   d. Put seller.

**figure 20.9**

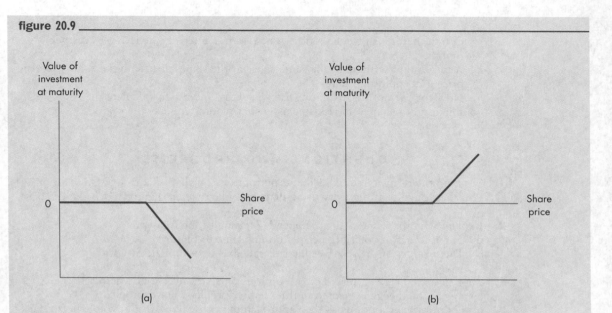

(a)    (b)

**4.** Suppose that you hold part of a share and a put option on that share. What is the payoff when the option expires if:
   a.  The share price is below the exercise price?
   b.  The share price is above the exercise price?

**5.** There is another strategy involving calls and borrowing and lending that gives the same payoffs as the strategy described in Question 4. What is the alternative strategy?

**6.** What is the lower bound to the price of a call option? What is the upper bound?

**7.** What is a call option worth if:
   a.  The share price is zero?
   b.  The share price is extremely high relative to the exercise price?

**8.** How does the price of a call option respond to the following changes, other things being equal? Does the call price go up or down?
   a.  Share price increases.
   b.  Exercise price is increased.
   c.  Risk-free interest rate increases.
   d.  Expiration date of the option is extended.
   e.  Volatility of share price falls.
   f.  Time passes, so the option's expiration date comes closer.

**9.** 'An option is always riskier than the share it is written on.' True or false? How does the risk of an option change when the share price changes?

**10.** Why can't you value options using a standard discounted cash flow formula?

**11.** Use Appendix Table 6 to value the following options.
   a.  A call option written on a parcel of shares that are selling for $6 per share with a $6 exercise price. The share's standard deviation is 6 per cent per month. The

option matures in three months. The risk-free interest rate is 1 per cent per month.

b. A put option written on the same share at the same time, with the same exercise price and expiration date.

Now for each of these options use Appendix Table 7 to calculate the combination of share and risk-free asset that would replicate the option.

## QUESTIONS AND PROBLEMS

1. Look up the terms of actual call and put options on shares, currencies, and so on. Plot their payoffs at maturity using diagrams like those in Figures 20.1 and 20.2.

2. Explain why the value of a call depends on each of the following:
   a. The *product* of volatility per period and time to maturity.
   b. The *product* of the risk-free interest rate and time to maturity.

3. Look at actual trading prices of call options on shares to check whether they behave as the theory presented in this chapter predicts. For example:
   a. Follow several options as they approach maturity. How would you expect their prices to behave? Do they actually behave that way?
   b. Compare two call options written on the same share with the same maturity but different exercise prices.
   c. Compare two call options written on the same share with the same exercise price but different maturities.

*4. How would the value of Circular File ordinary shares (see Section 20.2) change if:
   a. The value of the firm's assets increased?
   b. The maturity of its debt was extended?
   c. The assets became safer (less volatile)?
   d. The risk-free rate of interest increased (hold the value of the firm's assets constant)?

5. Rank and File Ltd is considering a rights issue to raise $50 million. An underwriter offers to 'stand-by' (i.e. to guarantee the success of the issue by buying any unwanted shares at the issue price). The underwriter's fee is $2 million.
   a. What kind of option does Rank and File acquire if it accepts the underwriter's offer?
   b. What determines the value of the option?
   c. How would you calculate whether the underwriter's offer is a fair deal?

6. Which *one* of the following statements is correct?
   a. Value of put + present value of exercise price = value of call + share price.
   b. Value of put + share price = value of call + present value of exercise price.
   c. Value of put − share price = present value of exercise price − value of call.
   d. Value of put + value of call = share price − present value of exercise price.
   
   The correct statement equates the value of two investment strategies. Plot the payoffs to each strategy as a function of the share price. Show that the two strategies give identical payoffs.

7. The price of Backwoods Chemical Ltd shares on 20 January is $9 per share. Three call options are trading on the shares, one maturing on 20 April, one on 20 July and one on 20 October. All three options have the same $10 exercise price.

The standard deviation of Backwoods' shares is 42 per cent per year. The risk-free interest rate is 11 per cent per year. What are the three call options worth?

**8.** The ordinary shares of Triangular File Ltd are selling at $9. A 26-week call option written on Triangular File's shares is selling for $0.80. The call's exercise price is $10. The risk-free interest rate is 10 per cent per year.

   a. Suppose that puts on Triangular's shares are not traded, but you want to buy one. How would you do it?

   b. Suppose that puts *are* traded. What should a 26-week put with an exercise price of $10 sell for?

**9.** Test the option conversion formula you used to answer Question 8 by using it to explain the relative prices of traded puts and calls.

**\*10.** Refer again to the Circular File balance sheet given in Section 20.2. Suppose that the government suddenly offers to guarantee the $50 principal payment due to bondholders next year and also to guarantee the interest payment due next year. (In other words, if firm value falls short of the promised interest and principal payment, the government will make up the difference.) This offer is a complete surprise to everyone. The government asks nothing in return, and so its offer is cheerfully accepted.

   a. Suppose that the promised interest rate on Circular's debt is 10 per cent. The rate on one-year government notes is 8 per cent. How will the guarantee affect bond value?

   b. The guarantee does *not* affect the value of Circular's shares. Why? *(Note: There could be some effect if the guarantee allows Circular to avoid costs of financial distress or bankruptcy. See Section 18.3.)*

   c. How will the value of the firm (debt plus equity) change?

   Now suppose that the government offers the same guarantee for *new* debt issued by *Rectangular File Company*. Rectangular's assets are identical to Circular's, but Rectangular has no existing debt. Rectangular accepts the offer and uses the proceeds of a $50 debt issue to repurchase or retire shares.

   Will Rectangular shareholders gain from the opportunity to issue the guaranteed debt? By how much, approximately? (Ignore taxes.)

**11.** How would you use Appendix Table 6 to estimate the volatility of ordinary shares on which call options are written and actively traded?

**12.** Show how the option delta changes as the share price rises relative to the exercise price. Explain intuitively why this is the case. What would happen to the option delta if the exercise price of an option were zero? What would happen if the exercise price became indefinitely large?

**13.** Is it more valuable to own an option to buy a portfolio of shares or a portfolio of options to buy each of the individual shares? Say briefly why.

**14.** Discuss briefly the relative risk of the following positions:

   a. Buy shares and a put option on the shares.

   b. Buy shares.

   c. Buy call.

   d. Buy shares and sell call option on the shares.

   e. Buy bond.

   f. Buy shares, buy put and sell call.

   g. Sell put.

**15.** A very difficult question: Use our conversion formula (see Section 20.2) and the one-period binomial model to show that the option delta for a put option is equal to the option delta for a call option minus 1.

**\*16.** Option traders often refer to straddles and butterflies. Here is an example of each:

■ *Straddle*   Buy call with exercise price of $10 and simultaneously buy put with exercise price of $10.
■ *Butterfly*   Simultaneously buy one call with exercise price of $10, sell two calls with exercise price of $11 and buy one call with exercise price of $12.

a. Draw position diagrams for the straddle and butterfly, showing the payoffs from the investor's net position. Each strategy is a bet on variability. Explain briefly the nature of each bet.
b. The profitability of a straddle or a butterfly depends on how much the share price has changed by the time the option matures and not on how the share price varies *before* maturity. If you believe that volatility *during* the option's life will be higher than expected, how can you construct a hedged position to take advantage of your belief? What if you believe that volatility will be lower than expected?

**17.** In 1988 the Australian firm Bond Corporation sold a share in some land that it owned near Rome for $110 million and as a result boosted its 1988 earnings by $74 million. In 1989 a television program revealed that the buyer was given a put option to sell its share in the land back to Bond for $110 million and that Bond had paid $20 million for a call option to repurchase the share in the land for the same price.[33]
a. What happens if the land is worth more than $110 million when the options expire? What if it is worth less than $110 million?
b. Use position diagrams to show the net effect of the land sale and the option transactions.
c. Assume a one-year maturity on the options. Can you deduce the interest rate?
d. The television program argued that it was misleading to record a profit on the sale of land. What do you think?

**\*18.** a. The Chase Manhattan Bank has offered its more wealthy customers an unusual type of time deposit known as the *guaranteed market investment account*. The account does not pay a fixed rate of interest, but instead the depositor receives a proportion of any rise in Standard & Poor's index. How should the bank invest the money in order to minimise its risk?
b. Suppose that the interest rate is 10 per cent, the standard deviation of returns on Standard & Poor's index is 20 per cent per year and the deposit has a maturity of three months. What proportion of any appreciation in the index could the bank afford to offer depositors?
c. You can also make a deposit with Chase Manhattan which does not pay interest if the market index rises, but which makes an increasingly large payment as the market index falls. How should the bank protect itself against the risk of offering this deposit?

---

33   See the *Sydney Morning Herald*, 14 March 1989, p. 27. The options were subsequently renegotiated.

**19.** Figure 20.10 shows some complicated position diagrams. Work out the combination of shares, bonds and options that produces each of these positions.

**figure 20.10**

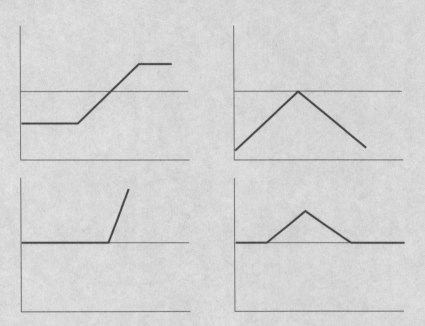

**20. a.** If you cannot sell a share short, you can achieve exactly the same final payoff by a combination of bonds and options. What is this combination?
  **b.** Now work out the mixture of shares and options that gives the same final payoff as a bond.

**21.** A difficult question: Three six-month call options are traded on Hogswill Ltd shares:

| Exercise price | Call option price |
| --- | --- |
| $90 | $5 |
| 100 | 11 |
| 110 | 15 |

How could you make money by trading in Hogswill options? (*Hint:* Draw a graph with the option price on the vertical axis and the ratio of share price to exercise price on the horizontal axis. Plot the three Hogswill call options on your graph. Does this fit with what you know about how option prices should vary with the ratio of share price to exercise price?) Now look in the newspaper at options with the same maturity date but different exercise prices. Can you find any money-making possibilities?

# chapter 21

# APPLICATIONS OF OPTION PRICING THEORY

This chapter brings the first reward to your investment in learning about options. We describe four common and important real options found in capital investment projects:

- The option to make follow-on investments if the immediate investment project succeeds.
- The option to abandon a project.
- The option to wait (and learn) before investing.
- Flexibility in production facilities.

Real options such as these allow managers to add value to their firm, by acting to amplify good fortune or to mitigate loss. Managers often do not use the term 'option' to describe these opportunities; for example, they may refer to 'intangibles' rather than to puts or calls. But when they review major investment proposals, these option 'intangibles' are often the key to their decisions.

We also will work through some simple numerical examples to show how real options can be valued. These examples ignore many complexities that are encountered in practice, however; think of them as back-of-the-envelope estimates of the value of more realistic but complex real options. These examples also provide an opportunity to learn more about the *technique* of option valuation. By the time you have worked through the examples in this chapter, you should know how to use the binomial method to value options on assets that last for more than one period, how to pick sensible figures for the upside and downside price changes, and how to value an option on an asset that pays dividends.

Since the only feasible way to solve most practical option problems is with a computer, why do we ask you to work through a number of option problems by hand? The reason is that unless you understand the basics of option valuation, you are likely to make mistakes in setting up an option problem, and you will not know how to interpret the computer's answers and explain them to others.

## 21.1 The value of follow-on investment opportunities

It is 1995. You are assistant to the chief financial officer (CFO) of Electronic Engines Ltd, an experimental engine manufacturer specialising in the development of turbo engines, located on the Gold Coast. You are helping the CFO evaluate the proposed introduction of the EE Mark I turbo engine.

The Mark I's forecasted cash flows and NPV are shown in Table 21.1. Unfortunately, the Mark I cannot meet Electronic Engines customary 20 per cent hurdle rate and has a $46 million negative NPV, contrary to top management's strong gut feeling that Electronic Engines ought to be in the turbo engine market.

**table 21.1**

Summary of cash flows and financial analysis of the EE Mark I turbo engine (figures in $million).

| Year | 1995 | 1996 | 1997 | 1998 | 1999 | 2000 |
|---|---|---|---|---|---|---|
| After-tax operating cash flow (1) | −200 | +110 | +159 | +295 | +185 | 0 |
| Capital investment (2) | 250 | 0 | 0 | 0 | 0 | 0 |
| Increase in working capital (3) | 0 | 50 | 100 | 100 | −125 | −125 |
| Net cash flow (1) − (2) − (3) | −450 | +60 | +59 | +195 | +310 | +125 |
| NPV at 20% = −$46.45, about −$46 million | | | | | | |

*Note: After-tax operating cash flow is negative in 1995 because of R&D costs.*

'The Mark I just can't make it on financial grounds', the CFO says, 'but we've got to do it for strategic reasons. I'm recommending we go ahead.'

'But you're missing the all-important financial advantage', you reply.

'What financial advantage is that?'

'If we don't launch the Mark I, it will probably be too expensive to enter the electric turbo engine market later, when Honda, Ferrari, Williams and others are firmly established. If we go ahead, we have the opportunity to make follow-on investments which could be extremely profitable. The Mark I gives not only its own cash flows, but also a call option to go on with a Mark II turbo. That call option is the real source of strategic value.'

'So it's strategic value by another name. That doesn't tell me what the Mark II investment's worth. The Mark II could be a great investment or a lousy one—we haven't got a clue.'

'That's exactly when a call option is worth the most', you point out perceptively. 'The call lets us invest in the Mark II if it's great and walk away from it if it's lousy.'

'So what's it worth?'

'Hard to say precisely, but I've done a back-of-the-envelope calculation which suggests that the value of the option to invest in the Mark II could more than offset the Mark I's $46 million negative NPV. [The calculations are shown in Table 21.2.] If the option to invest is worth $55 million, the total value of the Mark I is its own NPV, −$46 million, plus the $55 million option attached to it, or +$9 million.'

'You're just overestimating the Mark II', the CFO says gruffly. 'It's easy to be optimistic when an investment is three years away.'

'No, no', you reply patiently. 'The Mark II is expected to be no more profitable than the Mark I—just twice as big and therefore twice as bad in terms of discounted cash flow. I'm forecasting it to have a negative NPV of about $100 million. But there's a chance the Mark II could be extremely valuable. The call option allows Electronic Engines to cash in on those upside outcomes. The chance to cash in could be worth $55 million.'

**table 21.2** _____

Calculating what the option to invest in the EE Mark II turbo engine could be worth.

---

*Assumptions*

1. The decision to invest in the EE Mark II turbo engine must be made after three years, in 1998.

2. The Mark II investment is double the scale of the Mark I (note the expected rapid growth of the industry). Investment required is $900 million (the exercise price), which is taken as fixed.

3. Forecasted cash inflows of the Mark II are also double those of the Mark I, with present value of about $800 million in 1998 and $800/(1.2)^3 = $463 million in 1995.

4. The future value of the Mark II cash flows is highly uncertain. This value evolves as a share price does with a standard deviation of 35 per cent per year. (Many high-technology shares have standard deviations higher than 35 per cent.)

*Interpretation*

The opportunity to invest in the Mark II is a three-year call option on an asset worth $463 million with a $900 million exercise price.

*Valuation*

See Appendix Table 6:

Standard deviation $\times$ time $= 0.35 \sqrt{3} = 0.61$

$$\frac{\text{Asset value}}{\text{PV(exercise price)}} = 463 / \left[ \frac{900}{(1 + 0.10)^3} \right] = 0.68$$

Call value/asset value $= 0.119$ (closest figure from Appendix Table 6)

Call value $= 0.119 \times 463 = 55.1$, or about $55 million

---

'Of course, the $55 million is only a trial calculation, but it illustrates how valuable follow-on investment opportunities can be, especially when uncertainty is high and the product market is growing rapidly. Moreover, the Mark II will give us a call on the Mark III, the Mark III on the Mark IV, and so on. My calculations don't take subsequent calls into account.'

'I think I'm beginning to understand a little bit of corporate strategy', mumbles the CFO.

# Real options and the value of management

Discounted cash flow (DCF) implicitly assumes that firms hold real assets passively. It ignores the options found in real assets—options that sophisticated managers can act to take advantage of. You could say that DCF does not reflect the value of management.

Remember that the DCF valuation method was first developed for bonds and shares. Investors in these securities are necessarily passive: with rare exceptions, there is nothing investors can do to improve the interest rate they are paid or the dividends they receive. A bond or an ordinary share can be sold, of course, but that merely substitutes one passive investor for another.

Options and securities such as convertible bonds that contain options are fundamentally different. Investors who hold options do not have to be passive. They are given a right to make a decision, which they can exercise to capitalise on good fortune or to mitigate loss. This right clearly has value whenever there is uncertainty. However, calculating that value is not a simple matter of discounting. Option pricing theory tells us what the value is, but the necessary formulas do not look like DCF.

Now consider the firm as an investor in *real* assets. Management can *add value* to those assets by responding to changing circumstances—by taking advantage of good fortune or mitigating loss.

Management has the opportunity to act because many investment opportunities have real options embedded in them, options that management can exercise when it is in the firm's interest to do so. DCF misses this extra value because it implicitly treats the firm as a passive investor. Thus, the value of the Electronic Engines' project was the DCF value plus the value of the option to expand.

# 21.2 The option to abandon

In the case of Electronic Engines' turbo engine, we needed to value an option to expand. Sometimes we face the opposite problem and need to value an option to abandon a business. For example, suppose Electronic Engines Ltd must choose between two possible technologies for production of a new product—an electronic engine for a motor cycle.

1. Technology A uses computer-controlled machinery custom-designed to produce the complex shapes required for the engines in high volumes and at low cost. But if the engine does not sell, this equipment will be worthless.
2. Technology B uses standard machine tools. Labour costs are much higher, but the tools can be sold or shifted to another use if the motor does not sell.

Technology A looks better in a discounted cash flow analysis of the new product, because it was designed to have the lowest possible cost at the planned production volume. Yet you can sense the advantage of technology B's flexibility if you are unsure whether the new electronic engine will fire up or flop in the marketplace.

In such cases managers may ignore technology A's better DCF value and choose technology B instead for its 'intangible' flexibility advantage. But we can make the value of this flexibility more concrete by modelling it as a put option.

Just for simplicity, assume that the initial capital outlays for technologies A and B are the same. Technology A, with its low-cost customised machinery, will provide a payoff of $20 million if the motor cycle engine is popular and $5 million if it is not. Think of these payoffs as the project's cash flow in its first year of production plus the present value of all subsequent cash flows. The corresponding payoffs to technology B are $18 million and $3 million. These payoffs are shown in Table 21.3.

**table 21.3**
Payoffs from producing electronic motor cycle engines (millions of dollars).

|  | Technology A | Technology B |
| --- | --- | --- |
| Buoyant demand | $20 | $18 |
| Sluggish demand | $5 | $3 |

*If you are obliged to continue in production regardless of how unprofitable the project turns out to be,* then technology A is clearly the superior choice. But suppose that you can bail out of technology B for $8 million.[1] If the engine is not a success in the market, you would do better to sell off the plant and equipment for $8 million rather than continuing with a project

---

[1]   In practice, the abandonment value of technology B is unlikely to be certain. For example, suppose that it could be either $2 million or $14 million. In the former case, you would do better to continue with the project even if demand is sluggish. In the latter case, you would be better off by $11 million if you abandon when demand is sluggish.

with a present value of only $3 million. Thus, once we recognise the option to sell the assets, the payoffs to technology B change as follows:

| | | |
|---|---|---|
| Buoyant demand | continue production | own business worth $18 million |
| Sluggish demand | exercise option to sell assets | receive $8 million |

A put option on a share is an insurance policy that pays off when the share ends up below the put's exercise price. Technology B provides the same kind of insurance policy. If the electronic motor cycle engine sales are disappointing, you can abandon the machinery and realise its $8 million value. This abandonment option is a put option with an exercise price equal to the sale value of the machinery. The total value of the project using technology B is its DCF value, assuming that the company does not abandon, *plus* the value of the abandonment put.[2] When you value this put option, you are placing a value on flexibility.

## Valuing the abandonment put—an example

Dalby Airways Ltd, a commercial carrier in the Darling Downs region, is considering the purchase of a turboprop aeroplane for its business. Figure 21.1 summarises the possible payoffs from the aeroplane. If the airline gets off to a good start and demand is high, Dalby Airways calculates it will have a business worth $738 000 by the end of the first year. If things do not work out, it will be worth only $415 000. Dalby Airways estimates that there is a 60 per cent chance that the business will succeed and therefore calculates the expected value in year 1 as $(0.6 \times 738) + (0.4 \times 415) = 609$, or $609 000. The company discounts this at a 10 per cent cost of capital to give a present value of $609/1.1 = \$553\,000$.[3] Note that these calculations do not allow for the possibility of abandonment. If the business does not take off in the first year,[4] Dalby Airways would do better to sell the aeroplane for $500 000 rather than retain a business that is worth only $415 000.

What is the value of this option to bail out? We know now that you cannot use standard DCF where there is an option involved, because the discount rate changes as the value of the underlying asset changes. To value Dalby Airways option to abandon, you need to value a one-year put option on the turboprop with an exercise price of $500 000.

Dalby Airways will require the following information to value the put (dollar figures in thousands):

- Present value of business without option to abandon = $553
- Exercise price = $500
- Maturity = one year
- Interest rate = 5 per cent
- Future value of business with high demand = $738
- Future value with low demand = $415

---

2   Imagine a share that pays either $3 or $18. If you own both the share and a put option on the share with an exercise price of $8, the possible payoffs on your investment are:

   Share price $18   keep share      own share worth $18

   Share price $3    exercise put option   receive $8 exercise price

   Investing in technology B is exactly like owning both the share and the put option.

3   This is not assumed to be the *total* value of the business to Dalby Airways, since it also expects to earn some income during the first year. This income does not affect the value of the option to abandon at the end of the first year, and so we ignore it here.

4   This pun was (at first) unintentional.

**figure 21.1**

*The possible payoffs to Dalby Airways from investing in a turboprop. (The payoffs assume that the company continues to operate the aeroplane.)*

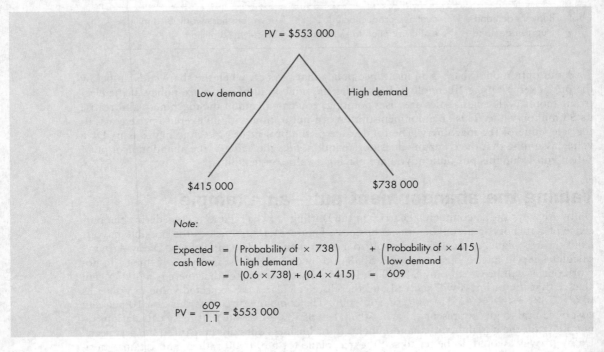

PV = $553 000

Low demand          High demand

$415 000                              $738 000

Note:

$$\text{Expected cash flow} = \binom{\text{Probability of} \times 738}{\text{high demand}} + \binom{\text{Probability of} \times 415}{\text{low demand}}$$

$$= (0.6 \times 738) + (0.4 \times 415) = 609$$

$$PV = \frac{609}{1.1} = \$553\,000$$

Since Dalby Airways can foresee only two outcomes, this problem is tailor-made for the binomial method that we used in Chapter 20 to value the CSR option. Here is a chance to show that you have not forgotten it.

Remember that there are two ways to use the binomial method:

▌ Construct a package of the underlying asset and a loan that would provide the same payoffs as the option.
▌ Pretend that individuals are risk-neutral and then value the expected payoffs from the option in this risk-neutral world.

We will use the risk-neutral approach.

We start the risk-neutral method by assuming that Dalby Airways is indifferent about risk. In this case it would be content if the business just offered the 5 per cent risk-free rate of interest. The company knows that either the value of the business will go from $553 000 to $738 000, a rise of 33 per cent, or it will go down to $415 000, a fall of 25 per cent. It is possible, therefore, to calculate the probability that value will rise in our hypothetical risk-neutral world:

$$\text{Expected return} = (\text{probability of rise}) \times (33) + (1 - \text{probability of rise}) \times (-25)$$
$$= 5\%$$

Therefore, the *probability of rise* equals 52 per cent.[5]

---

[5]    Notice that the *true* probability of rise in value is 60 per cent. However, we do not need to know this in order to value the option (though we needed the true probability to calculate the present value of the business *without* the abandonment option).

We know that if the business is successful, the option to abandon will be worthless. If Dalby Airways is unsuccessful, it will sell the turboprop and save $500 - 415 = 85$, or $85 000. Therefore, the expected future value of the option to abandon is:

$$
\begin{aligned}
\text{Expected return} &= (\text{probability of rise}) \times (0) + (1 - \text{probability of rise}) \times (85) \\
&= (0.52) \times (0) + (0.48) \times (85) \\
&= 41, \text{ or } \$41\,000
\end{aligned}
$$

And the current value of the option to abandon is:

$$
\frac{\text{Expected future value}}{(1 + \text{interest rate})} = \frac{41}{(1 + 0.05)}
$$
$$
= 39, \text{ or } \$39\,000
$$

Thus, recognising the option to abandon increases the value of Dalby Airways' business by $39 000:

$$
\begin{aligned}
\text{Value of business with abandonment option} &= \text{value of business without abandonment} \\
&\quad \text{option } + \text{ value of option} \\
&= 553 + 39 \\
&= 592, \text{ or } \$592\,000
\end{aligned}
$$

# *What happens to the Dalby Airways option if there are more than two possible outcomes?

The Dalby Airways option provides a good opportunity to extend our understanding of the binomial model. Notice that Dalby Airways considered only two possible changes to the value of its business—a rise of 33 per cent if demand is high or a fall of 25 per cent if demand is low. As an alternative, suppose that in each six-month period the value of Dalby Airways could either rise by 22.6 per cent or fall by 18.4 per cent (we will tell you shortly how we picked these figures). Figure 21.2 shows the possible firm values by the year's end. You can see that there are now three possible outcomes. Firm value could rise to $832 000, it could remain unchanged or it could decline to $368 000. That might be somewhat more realistic than Dalby Airways initial 'boom or bust' scenario.

We continue to assume that Dalby Airways has the option to sell the aeroplane at the end of the year for $500 000. In Figure 21.2 we show the associated value of this option in brackets underneath the possible year-end values.[6] Thus, if the value of the firm turns out to be $832 000, the abandonment option will be worthless. At the other extreme, if the firm's value is $368 000, the option will be worth

$$
\text{Exercise price} - \text{firm value} = 500 - 368 = 132, \text{ or } \$132\,000
$$

## Option values after six months

We first use the risk-neutral trick to work out option values at the end of six months. If investors are risk-neutral, the expected return on the firm must be equal to the interest rate,

---

6   We assume the aeroplane cannot be sold at the end of six months. In other words, we assume that the abandonment option is European.

**figure 21.2**

*The possible future values of Dalby Airlines. Figures in parentheses show the values of an option to sell the airline's assets for $500 000.*

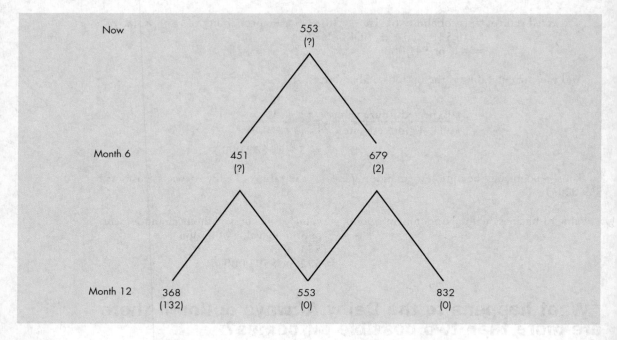

which is 5 per cent a year, or 2.5 per cent for six months. So the probability of a rise is calculated as follows:[7]

$$\text{Expected return} = (\text{probability of rise}) \times 22.6 + (1 - \text{probability of rise}) \times 18.4 = 2.5\%$$

Hence,

$$\text{Probability of rise} = 0.51, \text{ or } 51\%$$

Therefore, the *probability of rise* equals 51 per cent.

Suppose that we are in month 6 and the firm value is $456. In that case there is a 51 per cent chance that at the end of the year the option will be worthless and there will be a 49 per cent chance that it will be worth $132. Thus, the expected value of the option at the end of the year will be equal to $65.[8] With an interest rate of 2.5 per cent every six months,

$$\text{Value at month 6} = \frac{65}{(1 + 0.025)} = \$63$$

---

[7]    The general formula for calculating the probability of a rise is:

$$p = \frac{(\text{interest rate} - \text{downside change})}{(\text{upside change} - \text{downside change})}$$

Thus, in the case of Dalby Airways

$$p = \frac{(2.5 - (-18.4))}{(22.6 - (-18.4))} = 0.51$$

[8]    Expected value of option at end of the year:

$$\text{Expected value} = (0.51) \times (0) + (0.49) \times (132) = \$65$$

If the value of Dalby Airways is $679 at the end of six months, the option is certain to be worthless at the year end, and therefore its value at month 6 is zero.

## Option value now

We can now get rid of two of the question marks in Figure 21.2. Figure 21.3 shows that if firm value in month 6 is $451, the option value is $63; and if firm value is $679, the option value is zero. Now all we have to do is to work back to the value of the option today.

**figure 21.3** _____

*We have worked back from the month 12 values to calculate the value of the Dalby Airlines abandonment option in month 6.*

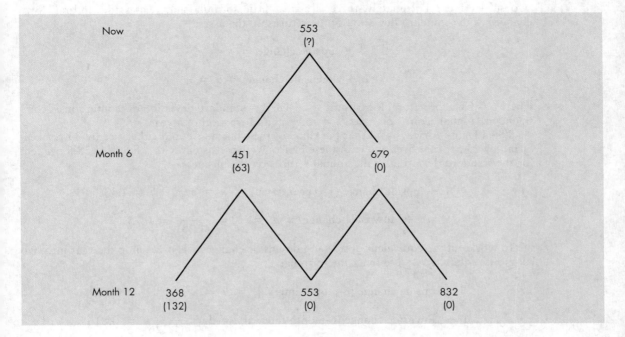

The expected value of the option in month 6 is

Expected return = (probability of rise) × (22.6) + (1 − probability of rise) × (18.4)
　　　　　　　 = (0.51) × (0) + (0.49) × (63)
　　　　　　　 = 31, or $31 000

Therefore, the value today is

$$\frac{\text{(Expected value of option at month 6)}}{(1 + \text{interest rate})} = \frac{31}{(1 + 0.025)} = 30, \text{ or } \$30\,000$$

In the one-step example we assumed that demand could be only high or low, and that gave us an option value of $39 000. The two-step calculation allowed us to recognise that demand could take on three possible values, and that changed our estimate of the option value to $30 000. It took us longer to value the option in the two-step case, but the principle was exactly the same and it did not require any mathematics more advanced than multiplication and division.

# The general binomial method

Moving to two steps when valuing the Dalby Airways option probably added extra realism. But there is no reason to stop there. We could go on to take shorter and shorter intervals in each of which there are only two possible changes in the value of the enterprise. For example, we could divide the year into 12 sub-intervals of one month each. That would give 13 possible year-end values. We could still use the binomial method to work back from the final date to the present. Of course, it would be tedious to do such a calculation by hand, but with a computer you can whiz through options with many periods to run.

Since an asset can usually take on an almost limitless number of future values, the binomial method is likely to give a more realistic and accurate measure of the option's value if we work with a large number of sub-periods. But that raises an important question: How do we pick sensible figures for the up and down changes in value? For example, why did we pick figures of 22.6 per cent and −18.4 per cent when we revalued the Dalby Airways option by using two sub-periods? Fortunately, there is a neat little formula that relates the up and down changes to the standard deviation of the returns on the asset:

$$1 + \text{upside change} = u = e^{\sigma h}$$

$$1 + \text{downside change} = d = \frac{1}{u}$$

where $e$ = base for natural logarithms = 2.718; $\sigma$ = standard deviation of (continuously compounded) annual returns on asset; $h$ = interval as a fraction of a year.

When Dalby Airways said that the value of their business could either rise by 33 per cent or fall by 25 per cent over one year, these figures were consistent with a figure of 28.8 per cent for the standard deviation of the annual returns on the business:

$$1 + \text{upside change (1-year interval)} = u = e^{.288 \times 1} = 1.33$$

$$1 + \text{downside change} = d = \frac{1}{u} = \frac{1}{(1.33)} = 0.75$$

To work out the equivalent upside and downside changes when we chop the year into two six-month intervals, we use the same formula:

$$1 + \text{upside change (6-month interval)} = u = e^{.288 \times 0.5} = 1.226$$

$$1 + \text{downside change (6-month interval)} = d = \frac{1}{(1.226)} = 0.816$$

The left-hand columns in Table 21.4 also show the equivalent up and down moves in the value of the firm if we chop the year into monthly or weekly sub-periods.

As the number of intervals is increased, the values that you obtain from the binomial method should get closer and closer to the Black–Scholes value. In fact, you can think of the Black–Scholes formula as a shortcut alternative to the binomial method as the number of intervals gets very large. For the Dalby Airways option the Black–Scholes formula gives a value of $28 200. The right-hand column of Table 21.4 shows that if you divide the year into 52 weekly sub-periods, the binomial method gives a good approximation to the Black–Scholes formula. Why do the option values change as we chop time into ever smaller pieces? Figure 21.4 shows the answer. A one-step binomial assumes that only two things can happen—a very good outcome or a very bad one. The Black–Scholes formula is more realistic: it recognises a continuum of outcomes.

If the Black–Scholes formula is more accurate and quicker to use than the binomial method, why bother with the binomial method at all? The answer is that there are circumstances in which you cannot use the Black–Scholes formula, but where the binomial method will still give you a good measure of the option's value. We will come across one such case in the next section.

**table 21.4**

As the number of intervals is increased, you must adjust the range of possible share price changes to keep the same standard deviation. But you will get increasingly close to the Black–Scholes measure of the Dalby Airways option. (Note that sometimes you may move away from the Black–Scholes value temporarily. For example, this happens when the number of intervals is increased from 3 to 4.)

| Intervals in a year (1/h) | Change in interval (per cent) | | Estimated option value |
| --- | --- | --- | --- |
| | Upside (thousands) | Downside (thousands) | |
| 1 | +33.3 | −25 | $39.4 |
| 2 | +22.6 | −18.4 | $30.2 |
| 3 | +18.2 | −15.3 | $29.8 |
| 4 | +15.5 | −13.4 | $30.4 |
| 12 | +8.7 | −8.0 | $29.1 |
| 52 | +4.1 | −3.9 | $28.3 |
| | | Black–Scholes value | $28.2 |

*Note:* The standard deviation is $\sigma = 0.288$.

**figure 21.4**

In the left-hand histogram we assume that only two things can happen to Dalby Airway's venture—high demand or low demand. The histogram shows present values at year 1, assuming no abandonment. The lognormal distribution on the right is more realistic because it recognises a continuum of possible present values and does not ignore intermediate outcomes. The Black–Scholes model is based on the lognormal distribution.

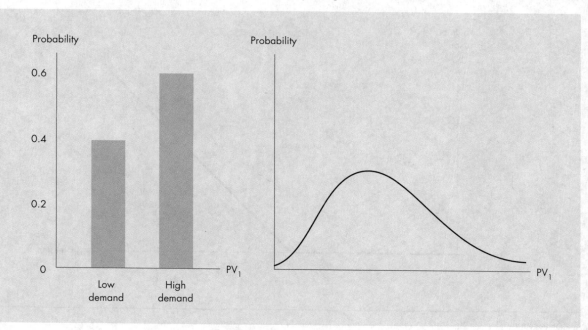

## 21.3 The timing option

Optimal investment timing is easy when there is no uncertainty. You just calculate project NPV at various future investment dates and pick the date that gives the highest current value.[9] Unfortunately, this simple rule breaks down in the face of uncertainty.

Suppose that you have a project which could be a big winner or a big loser. The project's upside outweighs its downside, and it has a positive NPV if undertaken today. However, the project is not 'now or never'. Should you invest right away or wait? It is hard to say. If the project is truly a winner, waiting means loss or deferral of its early cash flows. But if it turns out to be a loser, waiting could prevent a bad mistake.

In Chapter 6 we sidestepped this problem of optimal investment timing under uncertainty. Now we have the tools to confront it head-on, because the opportunity to invest in a positive NPV project is equivalent to an in the money call option. Optimal investment timing means exercising that call at the best time.

### Example of timing option

We will suppose that the project we have been discussing involves construction of a wood-chipping factory in Tasmania for $180 million. Due to fluctuations in the building sector, the demand for woodchipping fluctuates widely, depending on the price of competing suppliers.

Assume first that construction of the plant is a now-or-never opportunity. That is the same as having an about-to-expire call option on the factory with an exercise price equal to the $180 million investment required to build it. If the present value of the plant's forecasted cash flows exceeds $180 million, the call option's payoff is the project's NPV. But if project NPV is negative, the call option's payoff is zero, because in that case the firm will not make the investment. We have plotted these payoffs as the solid coloured line in Figure 21.5.

**figure 21.5**

*The opportunity to invest in the woodchipping factory amounts to a call option. If investment is now or never, the call's payoffs are shown by the solid coloured line. If investment can be postponed, the call option is valuable even if the project NPV is zero or negative.*

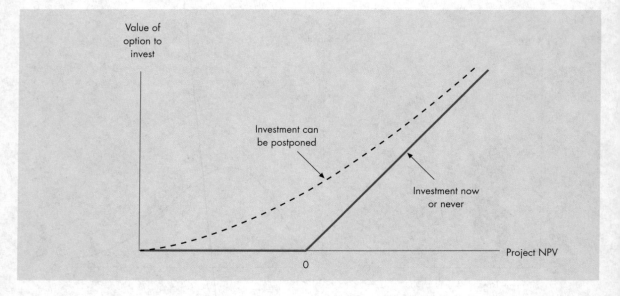

Now suppose that you could choose to delay construction of the plant for up to two years. Even though the project may have a zero or negative NPV if undertaken today, your call option has value because two years time gives room for hope that the volatile and sensitive woodchipping market will take off. We have shown a possible range of option values as the curved line in Figure 21.5.

The decision to launch or defer investment in the woodchipping factory amounts to deciding whether to exercise the call option immediately or to wait and possibly exercise later.[10] Naturally this involves a trade-off. You are reluctant to exercise, because despite today's rosy forecasts, investment in the woodchipping factory may still turn out to be a mistake. When you give up your option to wait, you can no longer take advantage of the volatility of the project's future value. Remember, option holders like volatility because it generates upside potential and the option contract limits loss. On the other hand, as long as the project has a positive NPV, you are eager to exercise in order to get your hands on the cash inflows. If the cash flows (and NPV) are high enough, you will gladly exercise your call before its time is up.

The cash flows from an investment project play the same role as dividend payments on an ordinary share. When a share does not pay dividends, an American call option is always worth more alive than dead and should never be exercised early.[11] But payment of a dividend before the option matures reduces the ex-dividend price and the possible payoffs to the call option at maturity. Think of the extreme case: if a company pays out all its assets in one bumper dividend, then afterwards the share price must be zero and the call is worthless. Therefore, any in the money call would be exercised just before this liquidating dividend.

Dividends do not always prompt early exercise, but if they are sufficiently large, call option holders capture them by exercising just before the ex-dividend date. We see managers acting in the same way: when a project's forecasted cash flows are sufficiently large, managers 'capture' the cash flows by investing right away.[12] But when forecasted cash flows are small, managers are inclined to hold on to their call rather than investing, even when project NPV is positive. This explains why managers are sometimes reluctant to commit to positive NPV projects. This caution is rational as long as the option to wait is open and sufficiently valuable.

# *Valuing the woodchipping option

We will put some numbers on the woodchipping factory and then show how to calculate option values when there are cash flows on the asset. Figure 21.6 shows the possible cash flows and end-of-year values for the woodchipping project. You can see that the current value of the project is $200 million. If demand turns out to be low in year 1, the cash flow is only $16 million and the remaining value of the project falls to $160 million. But if demand is high in year 1, the cash flow is $25 million and value rises to $250 million. A second year of low demand would cause cash flow to fall to $12.8 million and project value to fall to $128 million, and so on.[13]

---

10  European options cannot be exercised immediately. American options permit the holder to exercise the option prior to its expiry date.

11  Prior to maturity all options have both intrinsic value (often referred to as the moneyness of the option) and extrinsic or time value. When there are no distributions available from the underlying asset there is no incentive to exercise early and the value of an American option equals that of a European option. Exercising early would result in the taking of any intrinsic value but not obtaining any speculative value from holding till maturity. The investor would be better off to sell the option rather than to kill it. See R. C. Merton, 'Theory of Rational Option Pricing', *Bell Journal of Economics and Management Science*, 4: 141–83 (1973).

12  In this case the call's value equals its lower bond value because it is exercised immediately: the two lines in Figure 21.5 touch where project PV is high enough to trigger immediate investment. At this and higher PVs the value of a European call option, which could not be exercised immediately, would lie below the value of a now-or-never investment.

13  We have been a bit vague about 'forecasted project cash flows'. If competitors can enter and take away cash that you have earned, the meaning is clear. But what about the decision to, say, develop an oil well? In this case, a delay will not waste barrels of oil in the ground; it simply postpones their production and the associated cash flow. The cost of waiting is the decline in today's *present value* of revenues from production. Present value declines if the future rate of increase in oil prices is not sufficiently high, that is, if the discounted price of oil is less than the current price. See Chapters 11 and 25.

**figure 21.6**

*The possible cash flows and end-of-period values for the first year of the woodchipping factory.*

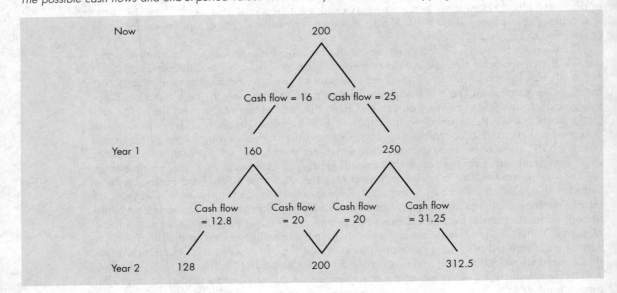

Although the project lasts indefinitely, we assume that investment cannot be postponed beyond the end of the second year, and therefore we show only the cash flows for the first two years and the possible values at the end of two years. Notice that if you undertake the investment right away, you capture the first year's cash flow ($16 million or $25 million); if you delay, you miss out on this cash flow, but you have more information on how the project is likely to work out.

If demand is high in the first year, the woodchipping factory has a cash flow of $25 million and a year-end value of $250 million. The total return is $(25 + 250)/200 − 1 = 0.375$, or 37.5 per cent. If demand is low, the plant has a cash flow of $16 million and a year-end value of $160 million. Total return is $(16 + 160)/200 − 1 = −0.12$, or −12 per cent. In a risk-neutral world, the expected return would be equal to the interest rate, which we assume is 5 per cent:

$$\text{Expected return} = 5\%$$
$$= (\text{probability of rise}) \times 37.5 + (1 - \text{probability of rise}) \times -12$$

Therefore, the probability of a high demand is 34.3 per cent.

We want to value a call option on the woodchipping project with an exercise price of $180 million. We begin as usual at the end and work backwards. The bottom row of Figure 21.7 shows the possible values of this option at the end of year 2. If project value is $160 million, the option to invest is worthless. At the other extreme, if project value is $250 million, option value is $250 − 180 = \$70$ million.

To calculate option values at year 1, we work out the expected payoffs in a risk-neutral world and discount at the interest rate of 5 per cent. Thus, if project value in year 1 is $160 million, option value is:

$$\frac{[(0.343 \times 70) + (0.657 \times 0)]}{(1 + 0.05)} = 22.9$$

Hence, the value of the option is $22.9 million.

But here is where we need to recognise the opportunity to exercise the option early. The option is worth $22.9 million if we keep it open, but it is worth $200 − 180 = \$20$ million if exercised now.

**figure 21.7**

*The values of the option to build a woodchipping factory. The option to build the factory in the future is worth more than the NPV of the factory if built today.*

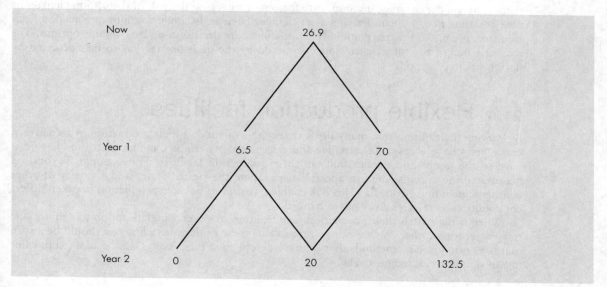

Thus, the fact that the woodchipping project has a positive NPV is not sufficient for investing. Other factors also might need to be considered including government regulations regarding environmental issues, and, some might argue, public opinion.

Notice how we worked this out. We worked backwards from the final period in the usual way, but at each step we checked whether the option was worth more dead than alive and we used the higher of the two values. Suppose that construction of the woodchipping factory could be delayed until the end of the second year. In this case we would have two steps to the binomial tree. Again we would start from the final exercise date and work back through the tree. However, at each step we should always remember to check whether the option is worth more dead than alive and use the higher of the two values as we work back to the current time. The same technique can be used whenever you need to value an American option on a dividend-paying share.

# Option valuation and decision trees

Calculating option values by the binomial method is basically a process of solving decision trees. You start at some future date and work back through the tree to the present, checking at each decision point to determine the best future action. Eventually the possible cash flows generated by future events and actions are folded back to a present value.

Is the binomial method merely another application of decision trees, a tool of analysis that you learned about in Chapter 10? The answer is no, for at least two reasons. First, option theory gives us a simple, powerful framework for describing complex decision trees. If you could delay construction of the woodchipping factory for many years, the complete decision tree would overflow the largest classroom chalkboard. Now that you know about options, we can just refer to the opportunity to invest in the woodchipping factory as 'an American call on a perpetuity with a constant dividend yield'. Of course, not all real problems have such easy option analogues, but we can often approximate complex decision trees by some simple package of assets and options. A custom decision tree may get closer to 'reality', but the time and expense may not be worth it. Most business people buy their suits off the rack even though a custom-made suit would fit better and look nicer.

Second, and more important, option pricing theory is absolutely essential for discounting within decision trees. Standard discounted cash flow does not work within decision trees for the same reason that it does not work for puts and calls. As we pointed out in Section 20.4, there is no single, constant discount rate for options because the risk of the option changes as time and the price of the underlying asset change. There is no single discount rate inside a decision tree, because if the tree contains meaningful future decisions, it also contains options. The market value of the future cash flows described by the decision tree has to be calculated by option pricing methods.

## 21.4  Flexible production facilities

By varying their output mix many firms are capable of varying their production. Alternatively, many firms have access to alternative sources of raw materials. Car manufacturers have discovered the importance of flexibility in their production facilities. For example, Toyota has manufacturing and distribution operations in Japan, the United States and a variety of other countries including Australia. This has enabled Toyota to balance production between different countries as relative costs have changed.[14]

When firms switch their production facilities they are exercising an option to acquire one risky asset for another. We are not going to value these options here but you should be aware that the option pricing methods that we have described in this chapter can be adapted to valuing an option to exchange assets.

## 21.5  A checklist

When we introduced option valuation in the last chapter, we focused on the valuation of European calls. In the course of this chapter we have encountered European and American options, calls and puts, and options on assets that pay dividends and on those that do not. You may find it useful to have the following checklist of how different combinations of features affect option value.

**American calls—no dividends**
We know that in the absence of dividends the value of a call option increases with time to maturity. So if you exercised an American call option early, you would needlessly reduce its value. Since an American call should not be exercised before maturity, its value is the same as that of a European call, and the Black–Scholes formula applies to both options.

**European puts—no dividends**
If we wish to value a European put, we can use a formula that we developed in Chapter 20:

$$\text{Value of put} = \text{value of call} - \text{value of share} + \text{PV(exercise price)}$$

**American puts—no dividends**
It can sometimes pay to exercise an American put before maturity in order to reinvest the exercise price. For example, suppose that immediately after you buy an American put, the share price falls to zero. In this case there is no advantage to holding on to the option since it cannot become more valuable. It is better to exercise the put and invest the exercise money. Thus, an American put is always more valuable than a European put. In our extreme example, the difference is equal to the present value of the interest that you could earn on the exercise price. In all other cases the difference is less.

---

14    See J. Perlez, 'Japanese Mix and Match Auto Plans and Markets', *The New York Times*, 26 March 1993.

Because the Black–Scholes formula does not allow for early exercise, it cannot be used to value an American put exactly. But you can use the step-by-step binomial method as long as you check at each point whether the option is worth more dead than alive and then use the higher of these two values.

### European calls on dividend-paying shares

Part of the share value is composed of the present value of dividends to which the option holder is not entitled. Therefore, when using the Black–Scholes model to value a European call on a dividend-paying share, you should reduce the price of the share by the present value of dividends that are paid before the option's maturity.[15]

---

#### example

Dividends do not always come with a label attached; so look out for instances where the asset holder gets a benefit and the option holder does not. For example, when you buy foreign currency, you can invest it to earn interest; but if you own an option to buy foreign currency, you miss out on this income.

Suppose that in May 1996 you are offered a one-year option to buy sterling at the current exchange rate of $2.00 per pound; that is, $2.00 = £1. You have the following information:

- Maturity of option　　　　　　　　　　　　　$t = 1$
- Exercise price　　　　　　　　　　　　　　　$E = \$2.00$
- Current price of sterling　　　　　　　　　　$P = \$2.00$
- Standard deviation of exchange rate changes　$\sigma = 10$ per cent
- Australian dollar interest rate　　　　　　　　$r_\$ = 9.5$ per cent
- Sterling interest rate　　　　　　　　　　　　$r_£ = 6.75$ per cent

If you buy sterling, you can invest it to earn interest at 6.75 per cent. By buying the option rather than sterling itself you miss out on this 'dividend'. Therefore, to value the call option, you must first reduce the current price of sterling by the amount of the lost interest:[16]

$$\text{Adjusted price of sterling} = P^*$$

$$= \frac{\text{current price}}{(1 + r_£)}$$

$$= \frac{\$2.00}{(1 + 0.0675)}$$

$$= \$1.87$$

Now you can apply the Black–Scholes formula:

$$\text{Standard deviation} \times \text{time} = 0.10\sqrt{1} = 0.10$$

---

15　For real options the 'dividends' are cash flows generated by some real assets. The present value of these cash flows would be excluded from the asset's present values when you value an option on the asset. For example, our valuation of the abandonment option for Dalby Airways turboprop ignored the income that the aeroplane would generate in year 1, before the option to sell the aeroplane could be exercised.

16　Note that:
$$\text{Current price} - \text{PV(interest)} = P - \left[\frac{r_£ * P}{(1 + r_£)}\right] = \frac{P}{(1 + r_£)}$$

$$\frac{\text{Price}}{\text{PV(exercise price)}} = P^* / \left[ \frac{E}{(1 + r_\$)} \right]$$

$$= 1.87 / \left[ \frac{2.00}{(1 + 0.095)} \right]$$

$$= 1.02$$

Using the call option tables in Appendix Table 6 gives

$$\text{Value of call} = 0.05 \times P^*$$
$$= 0.05 \times 1.87$$
$$= \$0.0935$$
$$= \$0.09$$

that is, 9 cents per pound. An option to purchase £1 million on these terms would be worth $90 000.

### American calls on dividend-paying shares

We have seen that when the shares do not pay dividends, an American call option is *always* worth more alive than dead. That way, you not only keep your option open, but also earn interest on the exercise money. Even when there are dividends, you should never exercise early if the dividend you gain is less than the interest that you lose by having to pay the exercise price early. However, if the dividend is sufficiently large, you might want to capture it by exercising the option just before the ex-dividend date.

The only general method for valuing an American call on a dividend-paying share is to use the step-by-step binomial method. In this case you must check at each stage whether the option is more valuable if exercised just before the ex-dividend date or whether you should hold it for at least one more period.

### example

Here is a last chance to practise your option valuation skills by valuing an American call on a dividend-paying share. Figure 21.8 summarises the possible price movements in Austral Industries Ltd shares. The share price is currently assumed to be $10.00, but over the next year it could either fall by 20 per cent to $8.00 or rise by 25 per cent to $12.50. In either case the company will then pay its regular dividend of $2.00. Immediately after payment of this dividend the share price will fall to 8 − 2 = $6.00 or 12.50 − 2.00 = $10.50. Over the second year the price will again either fall by 20 per cent from the ex-dividend price or rise by 25 per cent.[17]

Suppose that you wish to value a two-year American call option on an Austral Industries Ltd ordinary share. Figure 21.9 shows the possible option values at each point, assuming an exercise price of $7.00 and an interest rate of 12 per cent. We will

---

17  Notice that the payment of a fixed dividend in year 1 results in four possible share prices at the end of year 2. In other words, 6 × 1.25 does not equal 10.50 × 0.8. Do not let that put you off. You still start from the end and work back one step at a time to find the possible option values at each date.

**figure 21.8**
*Possible values of Austral Industries shares.*

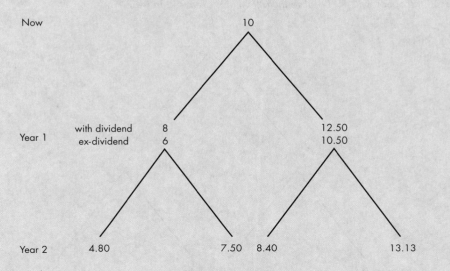

not go through all the calculations behind these figures, but we will focus on the option values at the end of year 1.

Suppose that the share price has fallen in the first year. What is the option worth if you hold on to it for a further period? You should be used to this problem by now. First, pretend that investors are risk-neutral and calculate the probability that the shares will rise in price. This probability turns out to be 71 per cent.[18] Now calculate the expected payoff on the option and discount at 12 per cent.

$$\text{Option value if not exercised} = \frac{[(0.71) \times (0.50) + (0.29) \times (0)]}{(1 + 0.12)}$$

$$= \$0.32$$

Thus, if you hold on to the option, it is worth $0.32. However, if you exercise the option just before the ex-dividend date, you pay an exercise price of $7.00 for shares worth $8.00. This $1.00 value from exercising is greater than the $0.32 from holding on to the option. Therefore, in Figure 21.9 we put in an option value of $1.00 if the share price falls in year 1.

You will also want to exercise if the share price rises in year 1. The option is worth $4.25 if you hold on to it but $5.50 if you exercise. Therefore, in Figure 21.9 we put in a value of $5.50 if the share price rises.

The rest of the calculation is routine. Calculate the expected option payoff in year 1 and discount by 12 per cent to give the option value today:

$$\text{Option value today} = \frac{[(0.71 \times 5.50) + (0.29 \times 1.00)]}{(1 + 0.12)}$$

$$= \$3.75$$

---

[18]   Using the formula in Footnote 8 gives:

$$p = \frac{(r - d)}{(u - d)} = \frac{[12 - (-20)]}{[25 - (-20)]} = 0.71$$

**figure 21.9**

*Values of a two-year call option on Austral Industries shares. Exercise price is $7.00. Although we show option values for year 2, the option will not be alive then. It will be exercised in year 1.*

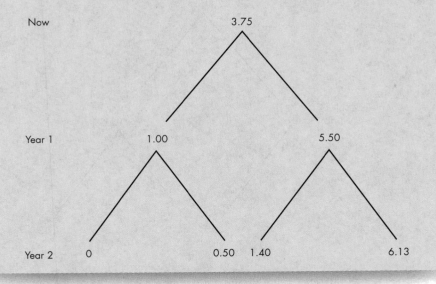

## A conceptual problem

This checklist obviously applied to traded puts and calls. But do the valuation techniques developed for these financial options work for *real* options?

When we introduced option pricing models in Chapter 20 we suggested that it is possible to construct a package of the underlying asset and a loan that would give exactly the same payoffs as the option. If the two investments do not sell for the same price, then there are arbitrage possibilities. But many assets are not liquidly traded. This means that we can no longer rely on arbitrage arguments to justify the use of option pricing models.

The risk-neutral method still makes practical sense, however. It is really just an application of the *certainty equivalent* method introduced in Chapter 9. The key assumption is that the company's shareholders have access to assets with the same risk characteristics (the same beta) as the capital investments being evaluated by the firm.

Think of each security as having a *double*—a security or portfolio with identical risk. Then the expected rate of return offered by the double is also the cost of capital for the real investment and the discount rate for a DCF valuation of the investment project. Now what would investors pay for a *real option* based on the project? The same as for an identical traded option written on the double. This traded option does not have to exist. It is enough to know that it would be valued by investors who could employ either the arbitrage or the risk-neutral method. The two methods give the same answer.

When we value a *real option* by the risk-neutral method we are calculating the option's value if it could be traded. This exactly parallels standard capital budgeting. As we stressed way back in Chapters 2 and 5, a DCF calculation of a project NPV is an estimate of the project's market value if it could be set up as a mini-firm with shares traded on the share market. The certainty-equivalent (risk-neutral) value of a real option is likewise an estimate of the option's market value if it were traded.

# 21.6 Summary

In Chapter 20 you learned the basics of option valuation. In this chapter we described four important real options.

**1.** *The option to make follow-on investments.* Companies often cite 'strategic' value when taking on negative NPV projects. A close look at the projects' payoffs reveals a call option on follow-on projects in addition to the immediate projects' cash flows. Today's investments can generate tomorrow's opportunities.

**2.** *The option to abandon.* The option to abandon a project provides partial insurance against failure. This is a put option; the put's exercise price is the value of the project's assets if sold or shifted to a more valuable use.

**3.** *The option to wait (and learn) before investing.* This is equivalent to owning a call option on the investment project. The call is exercised when the firm commits to the project. But often it is better to defer a positive NPV project in order to keep the call alive. Deferral is most attractive when uncertainty is great and immediate project cash flows—which are lost or postponed by waiting—are small.

**4.** *Flexible production facilities.* Firms often build flexibility into their production facilities, so that they can use the cheapest raw materials or produce the most valuable set of outputs. In this case they effectively acquire the option to exchange one asset for another.

We should offer here a healthy warning. The real options encountered in practice are usually considerably more complex than the simple examples that we examined in this chapter. For instance, you may be able to bail out from a project at any time rather than simply on the single occasion that we assumed for the Dalby Airways example. The price at which you can bail out is likely to change over time and will rarely be known in advance. Also, once you have abandoned, you may be able to reinstate the project if business improves. Handling such complexities typically requires financial modelling skills and on some occasions a large number-crunching computer.

Modelling the problem also requires informed judgement. For example, when we discussed the option to postpone investment, we assumed that postponement causes you to miss out on the first year's cash flow, but that you learn what this flow would have been if you had undertaken the project. That may not always be the case. Sometimes you may learn nothing by waiting, so that at the end of the year you are at exactly the same position as when you started. Obviously, how much you learn by waiting makes a considerable difference to your estimate of option value.

Our examples provided an opportunity to review and extend the option valuation methods introduced in Chapter 20.

The binomial method assumes that the time to the option's maturity can be divided into a number of sub-intervals in each of which there are only two possible price changes. In Chapter 20 we valued an option with only one period to expiration. Here we showed you how to value an option with many periods to expiration. The advantage of chopping the life of the option into many sub-periods is that it allows you to recognise that the asset may take on many future values. You can think of the Black–Scholes formula as a shortcut solution when there are an indefinite number of these sub-periods and therefore an indefinite number of possible future asset prices. Regardless of the number of sub-periods, the basic idea behind the binomial method is the same. You start at the option's maturity and work back one step at a time to find the option's initial value. But that raises a question: How do we pick sensible numbers for the up and down moves in the asset values? We introduced a formula that allows you to derive the up and down moves consistent with a given standard deviation of asset returns.

One of the advantages of holding the asset is that you may receive dividends: the option holder generally does not get these dividends. If there are no dividends, you would never want to exercise a call option before maturity. (Even if you *knew* that you were going to exercise it, you would prefer to pay the exercise money later rather than sooner.) But when the asset does pay a dividend, it may pay to exercise a call option early in order to capture the dividend. You can still use the binomial method to value the option, but at each point you need to check whether the option is worth more dead than alive.

## FURTHER READING

The Spring 1987 issue of the *Midland Corporate Finance Journal* contains articles on real options and capital investment decisions. See also Dixit and Pindyck for a discussion of the role of options in capital investment decisions:

A. K. Dixit and R. S. Pindyck, 'The Options Approach to Capital Investment', *Harvard Business Review*, 73: 105–15 (May–June 1995).

In 1998 *The Quarterly Review of Economics and Finance* had a special issue titled 'Real Options: Developments and Applications'.

The standard text for the valuation of real options is:

A. K. Dixit and R. S. Pindyck, *Investment Under Uncertainty*, Princeton University Press, Princeton, N.J., 1994.

Mason and Merton review a range of option applications to corporate finance:

S. P. Mason and R. C. Merton, 'The Role of Contingent Claims Analysis in Corporate Finance', in E. I. Altman and M. G. Subrahmanyan (eds.), *Recent Advances in Corporate Finance*, Irwin, Inc., Homewood, Ill., 1985.

Brennan and Schwartz have worked out an interesting application to natural resource investments:

M. J. Brennan and E. S. Schwartz, 'Evaluating Natural Resource Investments', *Journal of Business*, 58: 135–57 (April 1985).

A further application of valuing strategic options using the real option approach as discussed in this chapter can be found in Chapter 11 of Grinblatt and Titman. They apply the approach to a mining company and consider: a mine with no strategic options; a mine with an abandonment option; vacant land; the option to delay the start of a project; the option to expand capacity; and flexibility in production technology.

M. Grinblatt and S. Titman, *Financial Markets and Corporate Strategy*, McGraw-Hill, Boston, 1998.

The texts given under the heading of Further Reading in Chapter 20 can be referred to for further discussion of the binomial method and the practical complications of applying option pricing theory.

## QUIZ

1. Describe the real option in each of the following cases.
   a. Backwoods Chemical postpones a major plant expansion. The expansion has positive NPV on a discounted cash flow basis, but top management wants to get a better fix on product demand before proceeding.
   b. Telstra commits to production of digital switching equipment specially designed for the European market. The project has a negative DCF NPV, but is justified by the need for a strong market position in the rapidly growing, and potentially very profitable, market.
   c. Cable & Wireless Optus vetos a fully integrated, automated production line for the new digital switches. It relies on standard, less expensive equipment. The automated production line is more efficient overall, according to a discounted cash flow calculation.

d. Qantas buys a jumbo jet with special equipment allowing the aeroplane to be switched quickly from passenger to freight use.

**2.** Wombat Ltd shares are thinly traded and therefore the price changes only once a month: either it goes up by 20 per cent, or it falls by 16.7 per cent. Its price now is $4.00. The interest rate is 12 per cent per year, or about 1 per cent per month.
   a. What is the value of a one-month call option with an exercise price of $4.00?
   b. What is the option delta?
   c. Show how the payoffs of this call option can be replicated by buying Wombat shares and borrowing.
   d. What is the value of a two-month call option with an exercise price of $4.00?
   e. What is the option delta of the two-month call over the first one-month period?

**3.** 'The Black–Scholes formula gives the same answer as the binomial method when _____.' Complete the sentence and briefly explain.

**4.** For which of these options *might* it be rational to exercise before maturity? Say briefly why or why not.
   a. American put on a non-dividend-paying share.
   b. American call—the dividend payment is $0.50 per annum, the exercise price is $10 and the interest rate is 10 per cent.
   c. American call—the interest rate is 10 per cent and the dividend payment is 5 per cent of future share price. (*Hint*: The dividend depends on the share price which could either rise or fall in the future.)

**5.** Suppose a share price can go up by 15 per cent or down by 13 per cent over the next period. You own a one-period put on the share. The interest rate is 10 per cent and the current share price is $6.00.
   a. What exercise price leaves you indifferent between holding the put or exercising it now?
   b. How does this 'break-even' exercise price change if the interest rate is increased?

**6.** Dr Livingstone I. Presume holds £600 000 in East African gold shares. Bullish as he is on gold mining, he requires absolute assurance that at least £500 000 will be available in six months to fund an expedition. Describe two ways for Dr Presume to achieve this goal. There is an active market for puts and calls on East African gold shares, and the sterling rate of interest is 12.4 per cent per year.

## QUESTIONS AND PROBLEMS

**1.** Describe each of the following situations in the language of options.
   a. Drilling rights are held by your company to undeveloped heavy crude oil in Western Queensland. Development and production of the oil now is a negative NPV endeavour. (The break-even oil price is $28 per barrel, versus a spot price of $22.) However, the decision to develop can be put off for up to five years. Development costs are expected to increase by 5 per cent per year.
   b. A restaurant is producing net cash flows, after all out-of-pocket expenses, of $70 000 per year. There is no upward or downward trend in the cash flows, but they fluctuate, with an annual standard deviation of 15 per cent. The real estate occupied by the restaurant is owned, not leased, and could be sold for $500 000. Ignore taxes.

c. A variation on Part (b): Assume the restaurant faces known fixed costs of $30 000 per year incurred so long as the restaurant is operating. Thus

$$\text{Net cash flow} = \text{revenue less variable costs} - \text{fixed costs}$$
$$\$70\,000 = 100\,000 - 30\,000$$

The annual standard deviation of the forecast error of revenue less variable costs is 10.5 per cent. The interest rate is 10 per cent. Ignore taxes.

d. The British–French treaty giving a concession to build a railroad link under the English Channel also requires the concessionaire to propose by the year 2000 to build a 'drive-through link' if 'technical and economic conditions permit . . . and the increase in traffic shall justify it without undermining the expected return on the first [rail] link'. Other companies will not be permitted to build a link before the year 2020.

**2.** Perform a sensitivity analysis on Table 21.1. The CFO would like to know how the present value of the option on the Mark II depends on:
   a. The degree of uncertainty (standard deviation).
   b. The forecasted NPV of the Mark II.
   c. The rate of growth of the micro market (which determines the possible scale of the Mark II project).

**3.** You own a one-year call option on one acre of prime Melbourne real estate. The exercise price is $2 million and the current, appraised market value of the land is $1.7 million. The land is currently used as a parking lot, generating just enough money to cover government taxes. Over the last five years similar properties have appreciated by 20 per cent per year. The annual standard deviation is 15 per cent and the interest rate is 12 per cent. How much is your call worth? Use the Black–Scholes formula and Appendix Table 6.

**4.** A variation on Question 3: Suppose the land is occupied by a warehouse, generating rents of $150 000 after real estate taxes and all other out-of-pocket costs. The value of the land plus warehouse is again $1.7 million. Other facts are as in Question 3. You have a *European* call option. What is it worth?

**5.** The price of Fremantle Ltd shares is $10. During each of the next two six-month periods the price may either rise by 25 per cent or fall by 20 per cent (equivalent to a standard deviation of 31.5 per cent a year). At month 6 the company will pay a dividend of $2. The interest rate is 10 per cent per six-month period. What is the value of a one-year American call option with an exercise price of $8? Now recalculate option value, assuming that the dividend is equal to 20 per cent of the with-dividend share price.

**6.** Plasterboard Ltd's share price is $2.20 and could halve or double in each six-month period (equivalent to an annual standard deviation of 98 per cent). A one-year call option on Plasterboard shares has an exercise price of $16.50. The interest rate is 21 per cent a year.
   a. What is the value of the Plasterboard call?
   b. Now calculate the option delta for the second six months if: (i) the share price rises to $440 and (ii) the share price falls to $110.
   c. How does the call option delta vary with the level of the share price? Explain, intuitively, why.
   d. Suppose that in month 6 the Plasterboard share price is $1.10. How at that

point could you replicate an investment in the company's shares by a combination of call options and risk-free lending? Show that your strategy does indeed produce the same returns as an investment in the shares.

**7.** Suppose that you own an American put option on Plasterboard shares (see Question 6) with an exercise price of $2.20.
   a. Would you ever want to exercise the put early?
   b. Calculate the value of the put.
   c. Now compare the value with that of an equivalent European put option.

**8.** Recalculate the value of the Plasterboard option (see Question 6) assuming that the option is American and that at the end of the first six months the company pays a dividend of $0.25. How would your answer change if the option were European?

**9.** Suppose that you have an option which allows you to sell Plasterboard shares in month 6 for $16.50 or to buy one or more shares in month 12 for $16.50 (see Question 6). What is the value of this unusual option?

**10.** The current price of North Queensland Airlines shares is $10. During each six-month period it will either rise by 11.1 per cent or fall by 10 per cent (equivalent to an annual standard deviation of 14.9 per cent). The interest rate is 5 per cent per six-month period.
   a. Calculate the value of a one-year European put option on North Queensland Airlines shares with an exercise price of $10.20.
   b. Recalculate the value of the North Queensland Airlines put option, assuming that it is an American option.

**11.** The current price of United Manufacturing Ltd (UML) shares is $2.00. The standard deviation is 22.3 per cent a year and the interest rate is 21 per cent a year. A one-year call option on UML has an exercise price of $1.80.
   a. Use the Black–Scholes model to value the call option on UML.
   b. Use the formula given in Section 21.2 to calculate the up and down moves that you would use if you valued the UML option with the one-period binomial method. Now value the option by using that method.
   c. Recalculate the up and down moves and revalue the option by using the two-period binomial method.
   d. Use your answer to Part (c) to calculate the option delta
      i. today,
      ii. next period if the share price rises and
      iii. next period if the share price falls.
         Show at each point how you would replicate a call option with a levered investment in the company's shares.

**12.** Options have many uses. They allow you (a) to take a levered position in the asset, (b) to sell the asset short, (c) to ensure against a fall in the value of the asset, (d) to hedge against any changes in the asset value and (e) to bet on the asset's variability.
      Explain how you can use options in these ways. Are there other means to achieve the same ends?

**13.** Suppose you construct an option hedge by buying a levered position in delta shares and selling one call option. As the share price changes, the option delta changes and you will need to adjust your hedge. You can minimise the cost of adjustments if changes in the share price have only a small effect on the option delta. Construct an example to show whether the option delta is likely to vary more if you hedge with an option where:

a. The exercise price is less than the share price.
b. The exercise price is equal to the share price.
c. The exercise price is greater than the share price.

**14.** Suppose you expect to need a new plant ready to produce turbo engines in 36 months. If design A is chosen, construction must begin immediately. Design B is more expensive, but you can wait 12 months before breaking ground. Figure 21.10 shows the cumulative present value of construction costs for the two designs up to the 36-month deadline. Assume that the designs, once built, are equally efficient and have equal production capacity.

**figure 21.10**

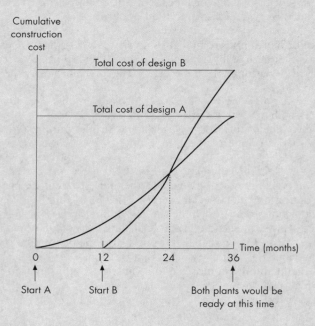

A standard discounted cash flow analysis ranks design A ahead of design B. But suppose the demand for turbo engines falls and the new factory is not needed; then, as Figure 21.6 shows, the firm is better off with design B, provided the project is abandoned before month 24. Describe this situation as the choice between two (complex) call options. Then describe the same situation in terms of (complex) abandonment put options. The two descriptions should imply identical payoffs to each design, given optimal exercise strategies.

**15.** In August 1986 Salomon Brothers issued four-year Standard & Poor's 500 Index Subordinated Notes (SPINS). These pay no interest, but at maturity the investor receives the face value plus a possible bonus. This bonus is equal to $1000 times the proportionate appreciation in the market index.

a. What would be the value of SPINS if issued today?

b. If Salomon Brothers wished to hedge itself against a rise in the market index, how should it do so?

**16.** Other things being equal, which of these American options are you most likely to want to exercise early?
   a. A put option on a share with a large dividend or a call on the same share.
   b. A put option on a share that is selling well below exercise price or a call on the same share.
   c. A put option when the interest rate is high or the same put option when the interest rate is low.
   Illustrate your answer with examples, using the two-step binomial method.

**17.** Is it better to exercise a call option on the with-dividend date or on the ex-dividend date? How about a put option? Explain.

**18.** Reconcile the following statements:
   a. 'The option pricing model assumes that price depends on variance rather than beta. It is therefore inconsistent with the CAPM.'
   b. 'DCF models of company value state that higher dividends increase share value. This is inconsistent with the option pricing model, which states that higher dividends reduce option values.'
   c. 'An increase in interest rates leads investors to demand higher return and therefore leads to a fall in share prices. This is inconsistent with the option pricing model, which states that higher interest rates lead to a rise in option values.'
   d. 'It's crazy to say that the value of a call option does not depend on the probability that the share price will rise. It is clear that the greater the likelihood of a rise in the share price, the more it makes sense to buy a call.'

**19.** Suppose that investment in the woodchipping factory (see Section 21.3) is deferred until the end of two years due to a change in government. Discuss how the deferral affects the project's NPV. Would the project's NPV change if you could undertake the project only at years 0 and 2?

**20.** You can buy each of the following items of information about an American call option for $10 each: share price; present value (exercise price); standard deviation × square root of the time to maturity; interest rate (per annum); time to maturity; value of a European put; and expected return on the share. How much would you need to spend to value the option?

# chapter 22

# WARRANTS AND CONVERTIBLES

As we discussed in Chapters 20 and 21, the holder of a call (put) option has the right but not the obligation to purchase (sell) an agreed number of shares at a later date at an agreed exercise price. Up to this point, our attention has been directed towards discussion of exchange traded options, whereby the exercise of the option simply involves the transfer of existing shares that have previously been issued between the parties to the option. The company named in the option is not required to issue more shares.

However, companies do write options that allow the holder to purchase new shares in the future at an agreed exercise price. In the United States and Japan, such issues are often referred to as **warrants**. In Australia, we distinguish between company issued options (or warrants) and third party warrants. Company issued options are generally regarded as long-term options to purchase

ordinary shares at a specified exercise price in the future. The exercise may be either European (at the final date of the option) or American (at any time through the life of the option), or during selected dates or windows during the life of the option. As we discussed in Chapter 14, third party warrants are longer dated options usually issued by financial institutions involving put or call options over existing shares.

In this chapter, we are principally interested in company issued options. But why would a company issue options? Initially it could be for the purpose of raising capital—recall that each option purchased by the option holders for future exercise has an option premium. Subsequently, if the share price exceeds the exercise price, the holders will exercise and the company will receive a cash inflow equal to the number of shares multiplied by the exercise price. Hence, options provide a distinct opportunity to raise capital both now and in the future.[1] Alternatively, the options may have no premium cost (such as executive options as part of a remuneration package or employee options), or they may form part of a dividend issued to existing shareholders.

A company also could elect to issue securities that convert to ordinary shares at predetermined future dates. Such instruments are referred to as convertible securities. Convertible bonds give their owners the right to exchange the bonds for other securities. Convertible preference shares give their owners the right to exchange the preference shares for other securities. In both cases, the decision to convert, or to exercise the embedded option, rests with the holder of the convertible security. As at June 1998 several Australian companies (such as Amcor Ltd, Bendigo Bank Ltd, JB Were Capital Markets Ltd and Pacific Mining NL) had convertible notes on issue. Convertible preference shares have been issued by companies such as Arrowfield Group Ltd and Greens Foods Ltd. All of the above issues are publicly traded on the Australian Stock Exchange.

In recent years in Australia a number of firms have issued converting securities as opposed to convertible securities. Converting securities differ from convertible securities in two major ways. First, for converting securities conversion is mandatory. For example, during the year to June 1998, Oil Search Ltd issued 1.189 million 9.50 per cent converting preference shares of $100 each. The shares were convertible into ordinary shares, at the discretion of Oil Search Ltd, at a 10 per cent discount to the share price at the time of conversion. The shares expired in May 2000.[2] Second, the conversion rate can vary over time and is determined by the interaction between the value of currently traded shares and a predetermined threshold level.[3] Converting preference shares have been issued by companies such as Colonial Limited, News Corporation Ltd, Suncorp Metway Ltd and SPC Ltd. Converting preference shares are also traded on the Australian Stock Exchange.[4]

When considering why convertible securities are less popular now to investors and issuers, relative to other forms of capital raising,[5] it should be noted that taxation considerations in the form of capital gains tax since 1985 and dividend imputation since 1987 have both affected the view of investors to debt and equity securities.[6] Both forms of taxation were discussed in Chapter 15. Also, prior to the late 1980s and the introduction of capital gains tax and franking credits, many convertible securities were privately placed with superannuation companies. Changes in the taxation of superannuation firms has made such private placements less attractive.

What are these strange securities—warrants and convertibles? How should you value them? Why are they issued? We will answer each of these questions in turn.

---

[1]   Provided the options are call options and the share price is greater than the exercise price.

[2]   See 'Notes to the Accounts—20: Share Capital' in Oil Search Ltd annual report, 1998.

[3]   Although all converting shares have these features, each security issued into the Australian market is designed separately and therefore possesses design features unique to that issue. See K. Davis, 'Converting Preference Shares: An Australian Capital Structure Innovation', *Accounting and Finance*, **36** (**2**): 213–28 (November 1996).

[4]   For a comprehensive list of traded convertibles and converting shares—including last dates to convert, redemption dates and share conversion ratios—see *ASX Journal*, which is included in each issue of *Shares*.

[5]   See Chapter 14 and the discussion about recent changes in debt equity capital structure. For the 'average' Australian listed company, the level of convertible securities has declined from around 4 per cent of total assets in 1987 to only 2 per cent of total assets in 1995.

[6]   See C. Armitage, 'Taxation Aspects of Corporate Finance', in R. Bruce et al., *Handbook of Australian Corporate Finance*, Butterworths, Sydney, 1997. These include restrictions on convertible note structures that allow deductibility of interest payments, and in the case of converting preference shares, restrictions as to what constitutes a 'debt dividend' as opposed to a dividend on a share. Debt dividends are regarded as the dividends paid to an investor that are regarded as the equivalent of interest on a loan. Refer to Chapter 16 for discussion of taxation of dividends and implications for corporate decision making.

## 22.1 What is a company issued option or warrant?

A warrant gives the right, but not the obligation, to buy a pre-specified number of shares at a predetermined exercise price. Company issued options and warrants usually have a term to maturity of three to 10 years. Exercise of the warrant results in the firm having to issue new shares to the holder of the warrant.

Let us consider an example. In April 1998 Melba Technologies Ltd, a small company producing font cartridges for laser printers, raised $6.2 million by selling one million shares at $6 each and one million company issued options at $0.20 each. Each of these warrants allowed the holder to buy one share for $7.20 at any time before April 2001. This meant that the share price needed to rise by at least 20 per cent over the three-year period to make it worthwhile to exercise the warrants. Let us assume that, one year after the issue, the share price of Melba shares nearly doubled to $11.50 and the price of the warrants multiplied over 20 times to $4.25.

The warrant holders are not entitled to vote or to receive dividends. But the exercise price of the warrant is automatically adjusted for any share dividends or share splits. For example, if Melba splits its share 2 for 1, it must also split the options 2 for 1 and reduce the exercise price per warrant to $7.20/2 = $3.60.[7]

## Valuing warrants

As a trained option spotter (having read Chapters 20 and 21), you have probably already classified the Melba Technologies Ltd warrant as a three-year American call option exercisable at $7.20. You can depict the relationship between the value of the warrant and the value of the ordinary shares with our standard option shorthand, as in Figure 22.1. The lower limit on the value of the warrant is the heavy line in the figure.[8] If the price of Melba shares is less than $7.20, the lower limit on the warrant price is zero; if the price of the shares is greater than $7.20, the lower limit is equal to the share price minus $7.20. Investors in warrants sometimes refer to this lower limit as the *theoretical* value of the warrant. It is a misleading term because both theory and practice tell us that before the final exercise date the value of the warrant should lie *above* the lower limit, on a curve like the one shown in Figure 22.1.

The height of this curve depends on two things. As we explained in Chapter 20, it depends on the variance of the share returns per period ($\sigma^2$) multiplied by the number of periods before the option expires ($\sigma^2 t$). It also depends on the rate of interest multiplied by the length of the option period ($r_f t$). Of course, as time runs out on a warrant, its price snuggles closer and closer to the lower bound. On the final day of its life, its price hits the lower bound.

## Two complications: dividends and dilution

If the warrant has no unusual features and the share pays no dividends, then the value of the option can be estimated from the Black–Scholes formula described in Chapter 20.

But there is a problem when warrants are issued against dividend-paying shares. The warrant holder is not entitled to dividends. In fact, the warrant holder loses every time a cash dividend is paid, because the dividend reduces share price and thus reduces the value of the warrant. It may pay to exercise the warranty before maturity in order to capture the extra income.[9]

---

7    The Melba Technologies Ltd warrant is fairly standard, but you do occasionally encounter 'funnies'. For example, the American firm Emerson Electric has issued a warrant in which the owner gets some money back if the warrant is *not* exercised. There are also 'income warrants' that make a regular interest payment.

8    Do you remember why this is a lower limit? What would happen if, by some accident, the warrant price were *less* than the share price minus $7.20?

9    This cannot make sense unless the dividend payment is larger than the interest that could be earned on the exercise price. By *not* exercising, the warrant holder keeps the exercise price and can put this money to work.

**figure 22.1**

Relationship between the warrant and the share price. The heavy line is the lower limit for warrant value. Warrant value falls to the lower limit just before the option expires. Before expiration, warrant value lies on a curve like the one shown here.

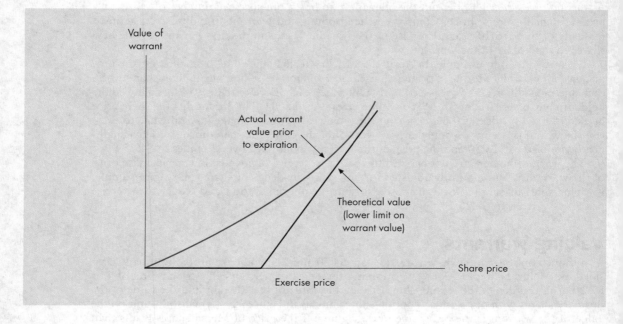

Remember that the Black–Scholes option valuation formula assumes that the share pays no dividends. Thus, it will not give the theoretically correct value for a warrant issued by a dividend-paying company. However, we showed in Chapter 21 how you can use the one-step-at-a-time binomial method to value options on dividend-paying shares.

Another complication is that exercising the warrants increases the number of shares. Therefore, exercise means that the company's assets and profits are spread over a larger number of shares. For example, Melba's net income in the first quarter of 1998 was $141 000, and the company had 3.1 million shares outstanding. So earnings per share were 141/3100 = $0.05. If the warrants are exercised, there will be 3.1 + 1 = 4.1 million shares outstanding. Unless net income is increased by the influx of cash from exercise, earnings per share will fall to 141/4100 = $0.03. Companies with significant amounts of warrants or convertible issues outstanding are required to report earnings on a 'fully diluted' basis.

This problem of *dilution* never arises with exchange traded call options or third party warrants. If you buy or sell one of these options, there is no effect on the number of shares outstanding.

## An alternative example: valuing Exotic Solutions' warrants

Assume Exotic Solutions Ltd, a company specialising in the provision of consulting advice in the area of financial engineering, has just issued a $2 million package of debt and warrants. Here are some basic data that we can use to value the warrants:

- Number of shares outstanding (N):                1 million
- Current share price (P):                          $12

- Number of warrants issued per share outstanding ($q$): 0.10
- Total number of warrants issued ($Nq$): 100 000
- Exercise price of warrants (EX): $10
- Time to expiration of warrants ($t$): 4 years
- Annual standard deviation of share price changes ($\sigma$): 0.40
- Rate of interest ($r$): 10%

Suppose that without the warrants the debt is worth $1.5 million. Then investors must be paying $0.5 million for the warrants:

Cost of warrants = total amount of financing − value of loan without warrants
500 000 = 2 000 000 − 1 500 000

$$\text{Each warrant costs investors } \frac{500\ 000}{100\ 000} = \$5$$

Table 22.1 shows the market value of Exotic Solutions' assets and liabilities both before and after the issue.

**table 22.1**

Exotic Solutions' market value balance sheet ($million)

| | | | |
|---|---|---|---|
| **Before the issue** | | | |
| Existing assets | $16 | $4 | Existing loans |
| | | 12 | Ordinary shares (1 million shares at $12 a share) |
| Total | $16 | $16 | Total |
| **After the issue** | | | |
| Existing assets | $16 | $4 | Existing loans |
| New assets financed by debt and warrants | 2 | 1.5 | New loans without warrants |
| Total | $18 | 5.5 | Total debt |
| | | 0.5 | Warrants |
| | | $12 | Ordinary shares |
| | | 12.5 | Total equity |
| | | $18.0 | Total |

Now let us take a stab at checking whether the warrants are really worth the $500 000 that investors are paying for them. Remember that the warrant is a call option to buy Exotic Solutions' shares. The shares do not pay a dividend. Therefore, we can use the call option data in Appendix Table 6 to value the warrants. First we need two inputs:

Standard deviation × square root of time
= $\sigma\sqrt{t} = 0.40\sqrt{4} = 0.80$

and

$$\text{Share price divided by the present value of the exercise money} = \frac{P}{PV(EX)}$$

$$= \frac{12}{10/(1 + 0.10)^4}$$

$$= 1.75$$

From Appendix Table 6 we find

$$\frac{\text{Call option value}}{\text{Share price}} = \frac{C}{P} = 0.511$$

Therefore,

$$\text{Call option value} = 0.511 \times \text{share price} = 0.511 \times \$12 = 6.132, \text{ or } \$6.13$$

Thus, the warrant issue looks like a good deal for investors and a bad deal for Exotic Solutions. Investors are paying only $5 a share for warrants that are worth $6.13.

## *How the value of Exotic Solutions is affected by dilution

Unfortunately, our calculations for Exotic Solutions' warrants do not tell the whole story. Remember that when investors exercise a traded call or put option, there is no change in either the company's assets or the number of shares outstanding. But, if Exotic Solutions' warrants are exercised, the number of shares outstanding will increase by $Nq = 100\,000$. Also, the assets will increase by the amount of the exercise money ($Nq \times EX = 100\,000 \times \$10 = \$1$ million). In other words, there will be dilution. We need to allow for this dilution when we value the warrants.

Let us call the value of Exotic Solutions' equity $V$:

$$\text{Value of equity} = V = \text{value of Exotic Solutions' assets} - \text{value of debt}$$

If the warrants are exercised, equity value will increase by the amount of the exercise money to $V + NqEX$. At the same time the number of shares will increase to $N + Nq$. So the share price after the warrants are exercised will be

$$\text{Share price after exercise} = \frac{V + NqEX}{N + Nq}$$

At maturity, the warrant holder can choose to let the warrants lapse or exercise them and receive the share price less the exercise price. Thus, the value of the warrants will be the share price minus the exercise price or zero, whichever is the higher. Another way to write this is

$$\text{Warrant value at maturity} = \text{maximum (share price} - \text{exercise price, 0)}$$

$$= \max\left(\frac{V + NqEX}{N/Nq} - EX, 0\right)$$

$$= \max\left(\frac{V/N - EX}{1 + q}, 0\right)$$

$$= \frac{1}{(1 + q)}\max\left(\frac{V}{N} - EX, 0\right)$$

This tells us the effect of dilution on the value of Exotic Solutions' warrants. The warrant value is the value of $1/(1 + q)$ call options written on the shares of an alternative company with the same total equity value V, *but with no outstanding warrants*. The alternative company's share price would be equal to $V/N$—that is, the total value of Exotic Solutions' equity (V) divided by the number of shares outstanding (N).[10] The share price of this alternative company is more variable than Exotic Solutions' share price. So when we value the call option on the alternative company, we must remember to use the standard deviation of the changes in $V/N$.

Now we can recalculate the value of Exotic Solutions' warrants allowing for dilution. First, we find the value of one call option on the shares of an alternative company with a share price of $V/N$.

Current equity value of alternative company

$$= V$$
$$= \text{value of Exotic Solutions' assets} - \text{value of loans}$$
$$= 18 - 5.5 = \$12.5 \text{ million}$$

$$\text{Current share price of alternative company} = \frac{V}{N}$$
$$= \frac{12.5 \text{ million}}{1 \text{ million}}$$
$$= \$12.50$$

To use the option calculator we calculate

$$\text{Share price divided by PV(exercise price)} = \frac{12.50}{10/(1 + 0.10)^4}$$
$$= 1.83$$

Also, suppose the standard deviation of the share price changes of the alternative company is $\sigma^* = 0.41$.[11] Then

$$\text{Standard deviation of alternative company} \times \text{square root of time}$$
$$= \sigma^*\sqrt{t} = 0.41\sqrt{4} = 0.82$$

---

10  The modifications to allow for dilution when valuing warrants were originally proposed in F. Black and M. Scholes, 'The Pricing of Options and Corporate Liabilities', *Journal of Political Economy*, **81**: 637–54 (May–June 1973). Our exposition follows a discussion in D. Galai and M. I. Schneller, 'Pricing of Warrants and the Valuation of the Firm', *Journal of Finance*, **33**: 1333–42 (December 1978).

11  How in practice could we compute $\sigma^*$? It would be easy if we could wait until the warrants had been trading for some time. In that case, $\sigma^*$ could be computed from the returns on a package of *all* the firm's share and warrants. In the present case we need to value the warrants *before* they start trading. We argue as follows: the standard deviation of the *assets* before the issue is equal to the standard deviation of a package of the ordinary shares and the existing loans. For example, suppose that the firm's debt is risk-free and that the standard deviation of the share returns *before* the bond-warrant issue is 38 per cent. Then we calculate the standard deviation of the initial assets as follows:

Standard deviation of initial assets = proportion in ordinary shares × standard deviation of ordinary shares

$$= \frac{12}{16} \times 38 = 28.5\%.$$

Now suppose that the assets after the issue are equally risky. Then,

Standard deviation of assets after issue = proportion of equity after issue × standard deviation of equity ($\sigma^*$).

Hence,

$$28.5 = \frac{12.5}{18} \times \text{standard deviation of equity } (\sigma^*)$$

Standard deviation of equity ($\sigma^*$) = 41.04, or 41%.

Notice that in our example the standard deviation of the share returns *before* the warrant issue was slightly lower than the standard deviation of the package of shares and warrants. However, the warrant holders bear proportionately more of this risk than do the shareholders; so the bond/warrant package could either increase or reduce the risk of the share.

Using a little interpolation in Appendix Table 6 we find

$$\frac{\text{Call option value}}{\text{Share price}} = \frac{C}{P} = 0.53$$

Therefore, the value of the call on the alternative company is equal to

$$\frac{C}{P} \times \frac{V}{N} = 0.53 \times 12.50 = \$6.63$$

The value of the Exotic Solutions' warrants are equal to

$$= \frac{1}{(1 + q)} \times \text{value of call on an alternative firm}$$

$$= \frac{1}{(1 + 0.10)} \times 6.63$$

$$= \$6.02$$

This is a somewhat lower value than the one we computed when we ignored dilution, but it is still a bad deal for Exotic Solutions.

It might sound from all this as if you need to know the value of Exotic Solutions' warrants to compute their value. This is not so. The formula does not call for warrant value for $V$, the value of Exotic Solutions' equity (i.e. the shares *plus* warrants). Given equity value, the formula calculates how the overall value of equity should be split up between shares and warrants. Thus, suppose that Exotic Solutions' underwriter advises that \$500 000 extra can be raised by issuing a package of bonds and warrants rather than bonds alone. Is this a fair price? You can check using the Black–Scholes formula with the adjustment for dilution.

Finally, notice that these modifications are necessary to apply the Black–Scholes formula to value a warrant. They are not needed by the warrant holder, who must decide whether to exercise at maturity. If at maturity the price of the share exceeds the exercise price of the warrant, the warrant holder will of course exercise.

## 22.2 What is a convertible bond?

The convertible bond is a close relative of the bond-warrant package. Also, many companies choose to issue convertible preference shares or converting preference shares as an alternative to issuing packages of preference shares and warrants. We will concentrate on convertible bonds. But almost all our comments apply to convertible preference share issues.

Consider, for example, the convertible notes issued by Amcor Ltd.[12] In 1994 Amcor issued 16.1 million 6.5 per cent subordinated convertible unsecured notes of \$9.35 each.[13] The notes were convertible into 16.1 million ordinary shares at any time between 1 July 1995 and 31 October 2003. Prior to conversion the notes paid interest to the holders of 6.50 per cent per annum paid semiannually in April and October. The notes were undated but could not be redeemed until after 31 October 2003. In other words, an original holder of the convertible notes had a nine-year option to return the bond to the company and receive one share per note in exchange. In the financial year ending 30 June 1998, notes with a face value of \$34 595 were converted into 3700 shares. A quick calculation shows that each note was converted at its face value of \$9.35. The number of shares into which each bond can be converted is called the bond's *conversion ratio*. The conversion ratio of Amcor's convertible notes was 1.00. In order to receive one Amcor share, the owner of the convertible note had to surrender a note

---

12  For details regarding the convertible note discussed here, see the Amcor Ltd annual report, 1998.
13  The issue was first listed on the Australian Stock Exchange on 7 February 1994.

with a face value of $9.35. This figure is called the *conversion price*. Anybody who bought the bond at $9.35 in order to convert it into one share paid the equivalent of $9.35 per share.

# The convertible menagerie

The Amcor convertible issue is fairly typical, but you may come across more complicated cases. One of the most unusual types of convertible is the *LYON* (liquid yield option note). This is a callable and putable, convertible zero coupon bond (and you cannot get much more complicated than that). LYONs have been issued by a number of large American companies, including Eastman Kodak, American Airlines and Motorola. Eurodisney once raised almost US$1 billion through an issue of LYONs.

Let us look at an example. In 1990 Chemical Waste Management issued a LYON at a price of 30.7 per cent. It was a 20-year zero coupon bond that was convertible at any time into a fixed number of shares, although the company could instead pay out the cash equivalent of these shares. Notice that if investors converted immediately, they would be giving up a bond worth $307. If they waited 20 years to convert, they would be relinquishing a bond worth $1000. So the cost of buying shares through the convertible increased each year.

The Chemical Waste LYON contained two other options. The company had the option to *call* the bond for cash, and the bondholders had an annual option to *put* the bond back to the company for cash. The exercise price of each of these options increased each year.[14] The put option on the LYON provided a more solid floor for investors. Even if interest rates rose and prices of other bonds fell, LYON holders had a guaranteed price at which they could sell their bonds.[15] Obviously, investors who exercised the put would be giving up the opportunity to convert their bonds into shares: it would be worth taking advantage of the guarantee only if the conversion price of the bond was well below the exercise price of the put.[16]

# Valuing convertible bonds[17]

The owner of a convertible bond owns a bond and a call option on the company's shares. So does the owner of a bond-warrant package. There are differences, of course, the most important being the requirement that a convertible owner give up the bond in order to exercise the call option. The owner of a bond-warrant package can (generally) exercise the warrant for cash and keep the bond. Nevertheless, understanding convertibles is easier if you analyse them first as bonds and then as call options.

Imagine that Southern Star Bank (SSB) Ltd has issued convertible bonds with a total face value of $1 million and that these can be converted at any stage to one million ordinary shares. The price of SSB's convertible bond depends on its *bond value* and its *conversion value*. The bond value is what each bond would sell for if it could *not* be converted. The conversion value is what the bond would sell for if it had to be converted immediately.

**Value at maturity**    Figure 22.2(a) shows the possible *bond values* when the SSB convertible matures. As long as the value of the company's assets is *less* than $1 million, there will not be enough to pay off the bondholders. In the extreme case that the assets are worthless, the bondholders will receive nothing. Thus, the horizontal line in Figure 22.2(a) shows the

---

14   To further confuse matters, the firm could exercise its call option immediately, but investors could not exercise their put option until 1993. Thereafter, both options had the same exercise price. However, in the first two years the firm could not call the bond if the price of the ordinary shares was below a specified minimum. If the bond was called, investors had a final chance to convert to ordinary shares.

15   Of course, this guarantee would not be worth much if the firm was in financial distress and *could not* buy the bonds back.

16   The reasons for issuing LYONs are discussed in J. J. McConnell and E. S Schwartz, 'The Origin of LYONs: A Case Study in Financial Innovation', *Journal of Applied Corporate Finance*, 41: 561–76 (July 1986).

17   A comprehensive review of different convertible securities markets throughout the world is discussed in L. A. Zubulake, *The Complete Guide to Convertible Securities Worldwide*, John Wiley & Sons, New York, 1991.

payoff if the bond is repaid in full, and the sloping line shows the payoffs if the company defaults.[18]

You can think of the bond values as a lower bound, or 'floor', to the price of the convertible. But remember, if the company falls on hard times, the bonds may not be worth very much. So the 'floor' has a nasty slope.

Figure 22.2(b) shows the possible *conversion values* at maturity. We assume that SSB already has one million ordinary shares outstanding, so the convertible holders will be entitled to half the value of the company. For example, if the company is worth $2 million,[19] the one million shares obtained by conversion would be worth $1 each. Each convertible bond can be exchanged for 1000 shares and therefore would have a conversion value of 1000 × 1 = $1000.

SSB's convertible also cannot sell for less than its conversion value. If it did, smart investors would buy the convertible, exchange it rapidly for shares, and sell the shares. Their profit would be equal to the difference between the conversion value and the price of the convertible.

Therefore, there are *two* lower bounds to the price of the convertible: its bond value and its conversion value. Investors will not convert if bond value exceeds conversion value; they will do so if conversion value exceeds bond value. In other words, the price of the convertible at maturity is represented by the higher of the two lines in Figure 22.2(a) and (b). This is shown in Figure 22.2(c).

**figure 22.2** _____

(a) The bond value when SSB's convertible bond matures. If company value is at least $1 million, the bond is paid off in full; if it is less than $1 million, the bondholders receive the value of the company's assets. (b) The conversion value at maturity. If converted, the value of the convertible bond rises in proportion to company value. (c) At maturity the convertible bondholder can choose to receive the principal repayment on the bond or convert to ordinary shares. The value of the convertible bond is therefore the higher of its bond value and its conversion value.

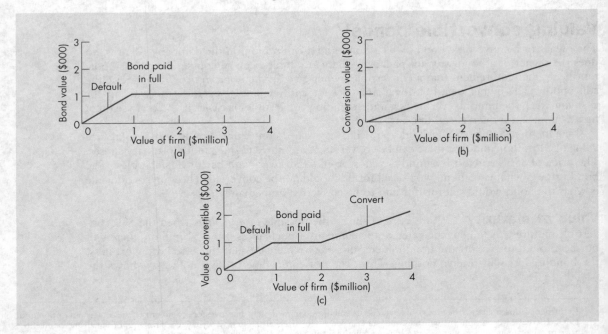

---

18   You may recognise this as the position diagram for a default-free bond *minus* a put option on the assets with an exercise price equal to the face value of the bonds. See Section 20.1.

19   Firm value is equal to the value of SSB's ordinary shares *plus* the value of its convertible bonds.

**Value before maturity**    We also can draw a similar picture to Figure 22.2 when the convertible is *not* about to mature. Because even healthy companies may subsequently fall sick and default on their bonds, other things being equal, the bond value will be lower when the bond has some time to run. Thus, bond value before maturity is represented by the curved line in Figure 22.3(a).[20]

Figure 22.3(c) shows that the lower bound to the price of a convertible before maturity is again the lower of the bond value and conversion value. However, before maturity the convertible bondholders *do not have to make a now-or-never choice for or against conversion.* They can wait and then, with the benefit of hindsight, take whatever course turns out to give them the highest payoff. Thus, before maturity a convertible is always worth more than its lower bound value. Its actual selling price will behave as shown by the top line in Figure 22.3(d). The difference between the top line and the lower bound is the value of a call option on the company. Remember, however, that this option can be exercised only by giving up the bond. In other words, the option to convert is a call option with an exercise price equal to the bond value.

**figure 22.3**

(a) Before maturity, the bond value of SSB's convertible bond is close to that of a similar default-free bond when company value is high, but it falls sharply if company value falls to a very low level. (b) The conversion value at maturity. If converted, the value of the convertible rises in proportion to company value. (c) If investors were obliged to make an immediate decision for or against conversion, the value of the convertible would be equal to the higher of bond value or conversion value. (d) Since convertible bondholders do not have to make a decision until maturity, (c) represents a lower limit. The value of the convertible bond is worth *more* than either bond value or conversion value.

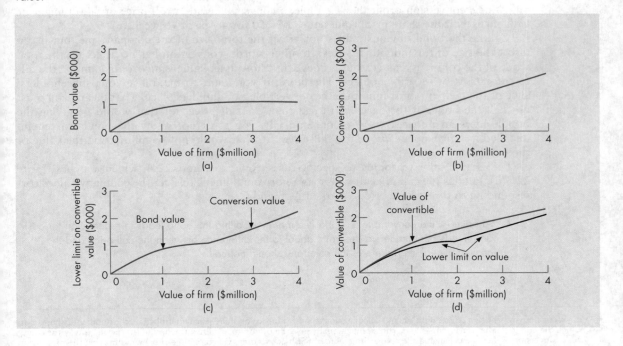

---

[20]    Remember, the value of a risky bond is the value of a safe bond *less* the value of a put option on the firm's assets. The value of this option increases with maturity.

# Dilution and dividends revisited

If you want to value a convertible, it is easiest to break down the problem into two parts. First estimate bond value; then add the value of the conversion option.

When you value the conversion option, you need to look out for the same things that make warrants more tricky to value than traded options. For example, dilution may be important. If the bonds are converted, the company saves on its interest payments and is relieved of having to eventually repay the loan; on the other hand, net profits have to be divided among a larger number of shares.[21]

Companies are obliged to show in their financial statements how earnings would be affected by conversion.[22]

Also, you must remember that the convertible owner is missing out on the dividends on the ordinary shares. If these dividends are higher than the interest on the bonds, it may pay to convert before the final exercise date in order to pick up the extra cash income.

# Forcing conversion

Companies usually retain an option to buy back or 'call' the convertible bond at a preset price. If the company calls the bond, the owner has a brief period, usually about 30 days, within which to convert the bond or surrender it.[23] If a bond is surrendered, the investor receives the call price in cash. But if the share price is higher than the call price, the investor will convert the bond instead of surrendering it. Thus, a call can *force conversion* if the share price is high enough.

Most convertible bonds provide for two or more years of *call protection*. During this period the company is not permitted to call the bonds. However, many convertibles can be called 'early', before the end of the call protection, if the share price has risen enough to provide a nice conversion profit. For example, a convertible with a call price of $4.00 might be callable early if the share price trades above $6.50 for at least two weeks.

Calling the bond obviously does not affect the total size of the company pie, but it can affect the size of the individual slices. In other words, conversion has no affect on the total value of the company's assets, but it does affect how asset value is *distributed* among the different classes of security holders. Therefore, if you want to maximise your shareholders' slice of the pie, you must minimise the convertible bondholders' slice. That means you must not call the bonds if they are worth *less* than the call price, for that would be giving the bondholders an unnecessary present. Similarly, you must not allow the bonds to remain uncalled if their value is *above* the call price, for that would not be minimising the value of the bonds.

Let us apply this reasoning to specific cases. Refer to Figure 22.4, which matches Figure 22.3(d), but has the call price drawn in as a horizontal line. Consider the company values corresponding to three share prices, marked A, B and C:

▮ At price A, the convertible is 'out of the money'. Calling the bond leads to redemption for cash and hands bondholders a 'free gift' equal to the difference between the call price and the convertible value. Therefore, the company should not call.

---

[21] In practice, investors often ignore dilution and calculate conversion value as the share price multiplied by the number of shares into which the bonds can be converted. A convertible bond actually gives an option to acquire a fraction of the 'new equity'—the equity *after* conversion. When we calculated the conversion value of SSB's convertible, we recognised this by multiplying the proportion of ordinary shares that the convertible bondholders would receive by the total value of the firm's assets (i.e. the value of the ordinary shares plus the value of the convertible).

[22] These 'diluted' earnings take into account the extra shares but not the savings in interest payments.

[23] Companies may also reserve the right to force conversion of warrants. For example, Melba Technologies has the right to redeem its warrants for $4.20 each provided that the market price of the share is at least $9 for 10 consecutive days. Obviously, in these circumstances holders will exercise their warrants if Melba announces its intention to redeem.

■ Suppose call protection ends with price at level C. Then the financial manager should call immediately, forcing the convertible value down to the call price.[24]

■ What if call protection ends with price at level B, barely above the call price? In this case the financial manager will probably wait. Remember, if a call is announced, bondholders have a 30-day period in which to decide whether to convert or redeem. The share price could easily fall below the call price during this period, forcing the company to redeem for cash. Usually calls are not announced until the share price is about 20 per cent above the call price. This provides a safety margin to ensure conversion.[25]

Do companies follow these simple guidelines? On the surface they do not, for there are many instances of convertible bonds selling well above the call price. But the explanation seems to lie in the call-protection period, during which companies are not allowed to call their bonds. Paul Asquith found that most convertible bonds that are worth calling are called as soon as possible after this period ends.[26] The typical delay for bonds that can be called is slightly less than four months after the conversion value first exceeds the call price.

**figure 22.4** _____

The decision to call a convertible. The financial manager should call at price C but wait at prices A and B. (*Note:* The conversion price is the straight upward-sloping line.)

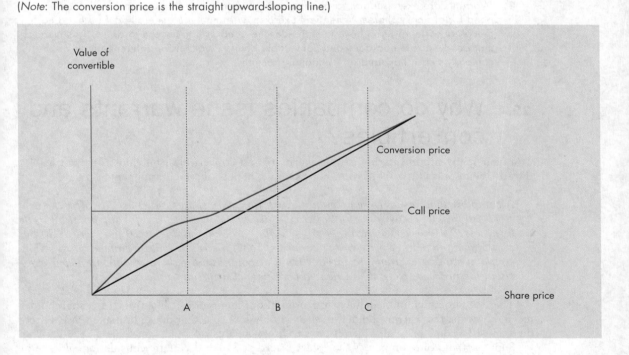

----

[24] The financial manager might delay calling for a time at price C if interest payments on the convertible debt are less than the extra dividends that would be paid after conversion. This delay would reduce cash payments to bondholders. Nothing is lost if the financial manager always calls 'on the way down' if share price subsequently falls towards level B. Note that investors may convert voluntarily if dividends after conversion exceed interest on the convertible bond.

[25] See P. Asquith and D. Mullins, 'Convertible Debt: Corporate Call Policy', *Journal of Finance*, **46**: 1273–90 (September 1991).

[26] See P. Asquith, 'Convertible Bonds Are Not Called Late', *Journal of Finance*, **50**: 1275–89 (September 1995).

## 22.3 The difference between warrants and convertibles

We have dwelt on the basic similarity between warrants and convertibles. Now let us look at some of the differences:

1. *Warrants are usually issued privately.* Packages of bonds with warrants, preference shares with warrants, employee options and executive options tend to be more common in private placements. By contrast, most convertible bonds are issued publicly.
2. *Warrants can be detached.* When you buy a convertible, the bond and the option are bundled up together. You cannot sell them separately. This may be inconvenient. If your tax position or attitude to risk inclines you to bonds, you may not want to hold options as well. Sometimes warrants are also 'non-detachable', but usually you can keep the bond and sell the warrant.
3. *Warrants may be issued on their own.* Warrants do not have to be issued in conjunction with other securities. Many companies also give their executives long-term options to buy shares. These executive share options are not usually called warrants, but that is exactly what they are. Companies can also sell warranties on their own directly to investors, though they rarely do so.
4. *Warrants are exercised for cash.* When you convert a bond, you simply exchange your bond for ordinary shares. When you exercise warrants, you generally put up extra cash, though occasionally you have to surrender the bond or can choose to do so. This means that bond-warrant packages and convertible bonds usually have different effects on the company's cash flow and on its capital structure.

## 22.4 Why do companies issue warrants and convertibles?

You hear many arguments for issuing warrants and convertibles, but most of them have a 'Heads I win, tails you lose' flavour. For example, here is one such argument:[27]

> *A company that wishes to sell common stock (ordinary shares) must usually offer the new stock (shares) at 10 per cent to 20 per cent below the market price for the flotation to be a success.[28] However, if warrants are sold for cash, exercisable at 20 per cent to 50 per cent above the market price of the common stock, the result will be equivalent to selling common stock at a premium rather than a discount; and if the warrants are never exercised, the proceeds from their sale will become a clear profit to the company.*

There is something immediately suspicious about an argument like this. If the shareholder inevitably wins, the warrant holder must inevitably lose. But that does not make sense. Surely there must be some price at which it pays to buy warrants.

Suppose that your company's shares are priced at $10 and you are considering an issue of warrants exercisable at $12. You believe that you can sell these warrants at $1. If the share price subsequently fails to reach $12, the warrants will not be exercised. You will have sold warrants for $1 each, which with the benefit of hindsight proved to be worthless to the buyer. If the share price reaches $13, say, the warrants will be exercised. Your company will have

---

[27]   See S. T. Kassouf: *Evaluation of Convertible Securities*, Analytical Investors, New York, p. 6. We hasten to add that Kassouf's lapse is *not* characteristic of him. He is a respected scholar who has made important contributions to finance.
[28]   This is an overestimate of the discount associated with seasoned issues. See Chapter 15.

received the initial payment of $1 *plus* the exercise price of $12. On the other hand, it will have issued to the warrant holders shares worth $13 per share. The net result is a standoff. You have received a payment of $13 in exchange for a liability worth $13.

Think now what happens if the share price rises above $13. Perhaps it goes to $20. In this case, the warrant issue will end up producing a loss of $7. This is not a cash outflow but an opportunity loss. The company receives $13, but in this case it could have sold shares for $20. On the other hand, the warrant holders gain $7: they invest $13 in cash to acquire shares that they can sell, if they like, for $20.

Our example is oversimplified—for instance, we have kept quiet about the time value of money and risk—but we hope it has made the basic point. When you sell warrants, you are selling options and getting cash in exchange. Options are valuable securities. If they are properly priced, this is a fair trade—in other words, it is a zero NPV transaction.

You can see why the quotation is misleading. When it refers to 'selling shares at a premium', the implicit comparison is with the market value of the shares today. The relevant comparison is with what they may be worth tomorrow.

Managers often use similar arguments to justify the sale of convertibles. For example, several surveys have revealed two main motives for their use. A large number of managers look on convertibles as 'cheap dirt'. A somewhat higher proportion regard them as a deferred sale of shares at an attractive price.[29]

We have seen that a convertible is like a package of a straight bond and an option. The difference between the market value of the convertible and that of the straight bond is therefore the price investors place on the call option. The convertible is 'cheap' only if this price overvalues the options.

What then of the other managers—those who regard the issue as a deferred sale of ordinary shares? A convertible bond gives you the right to buy shares by giving up a bond.[30] Bondholders may decide to do this, but then again they may not. Thus, issue of a convertible bond *might* amount to a deferred share issue. But if the company *needs* equity capital, a convertible issue is an unreliable way of getting it.

Taken at their face value, the motives of these managers are irrational. Convertibles are not just cheap debt, nor are they a deferred sale of shares. But we suspect that these simple phrases encapsulate some more complex and rational motives.

In 1996, a comprehensive survey in the United States by Billingsley and Smith[31] of firms issuing convertible securities found that the primary motives for issuing convertibles were that the shares on issue at the time of the convertible issue were undervalued, the coupon rate on the convertible debt was generally cheaper than the coupon required on corporate debt and the firm expected that the convertibles would be converted to equity and therefore provide a form of 'delayed equity' financing.

Convertibles tend to be issued by the smaller and more speculative companies. They are almost invariably unsecured and generally subordinated. Now put yourself in the position of a potential investor. You are approached by a small company with an untried product line that wants to issue some junior unsecured debt. You know that if things go well, you will get your money back; but if they do not, you could easily be left with nothing. Since the company is in a new line of business, it is difficult to assess the chances of trouble. Therefore, you do not know what the fair rate of interest is. Also, you may be worried that once you have made the loan, management will be tempted to run extra risks. It may take on additional senior debt,

---

29   See, for example, E. F. Brigham, 'An Analysis of Convertible Debentures: Theory and Some Empirical Evidence', *Journal of Finance*, **21**: 35–54 (March 1966).

30   That is much the same as already having the share together with the right to sell it for the convertible's bond value. In other words, instead of thinking of a convertible as a bond plus a call option, you could think of it as the share plus a put option. Now you see why it is wrong to think of a convertible as equivalent to the sale of shares; it is equivalent to the sale of both shares *and* a put option. If there is any possibility that investors will want to hold on to their bond, the put option will have some value.

31   See R. Billingsley and D. Smith, 'Why Do Firms Issue Convertible Debt?', *Financial Management*, **25** (2): 93–9 (Summer 1996).

or it may decide to expand its operations and go for broke on your money. In fact, if you charge a very high rate of interest, you could be encouraging this to happen.

What can management do to protect you against a wrong estimate of the risk and to assure that its intentions are honourable? In crude terms, it can give you a piece of the action. You do not mind the company running unanticipated risks as long as you share in the gains as well as the losses.[32]

Convertible securities and warrants make sense whenever it is unusually costly to assess the risk of debt or whenever investors are worried that management may not act in the bondholders' interest.[33]

You can also think of a convertible issue as a *contingent* issue of equity. If a company's investment opportunities expand, its share price is likely to increase, allowing the financial manager to call and force conversion of a convertible bond into equity. Thus, the company gets fresh equity when it is most needed for expansion. Of course, it is also stuck with debt if the company does not prosper.[34]

The relatively low coupon rate on convertible bonds may also be a convenience for rapidly growing companies facing heavy capital expenditures. They may be willing to give up the conversion option to reduce immediate cash requirements for debt service. Without the conversion option, lenders might demand extremely high (promised) interest rates to compensate for the probability of default. This would not only force the company to raise still more capital for debt service but also increase the risk of financial distress. Paradoxically, lenders' attempts to protect themselves against default may actually increase the probability of financial distress by increasing the burden of debt service on the company.[35]

## 22.5 Summary

Instead of issuing straight bonds, companies may either sell packages of bonds with warrants or alternatively issue convertible bonds.

A warrant is just a long-term call option issued by the company. You already know a good deal about valuing call options. You know from Chapter 20 that call options must be worth at least as much as the share price less the exercise price. You know that their value is greatest when they have a long time to expiration, when the underlying share is risky and when the interest rate is high.

As we have seen, warrants are somewhat trickier to value than call options traded on the options exchanges. First, because they are long-term options, it is important to recognise that the warrant holder does not receive any dividends. Second, dilution must be allowed for.

---

[32]  See M. J. Brennan and E. S. Schwartz, 'The Case for Convertibles', *Journal of Applied Corporate Finance*, **1**: 55–64 (Summer 1988).

[33]  Changes in risk ought to be more likely when the firm is small and its debt is low grade. If so, we should find that the convertible bonds of such firms offer their owners a larger potential ownership share. This is indeed the case. See C. M Lewis, R. J. Rogalski and J. K. Seward, An Empirical Analysis of Convertible Debt Financing by NYSE/AMEX and NASDAQ Firms, unpublished paper, Amos Tuck School of Business Administration, Dartmouth College, August 1994.

[34]  Jeremy Stein points out that an issue of a convertible sends a better signal to investors than a straight equity issue. As we explained in Chapter 15, announcement of an ordinary share issue prompts worries of overvaluation and usually depresses share price. Convertibles are hybrids of debt and equity and send a less negative signal. Also, if the firm is likely to need equity, its willingness to issue a convertible, and to take the chance that share price will rise enough to allow forced conversion, also signals management's confidence. See J. Stein, 'Convertible Bonds as Backdoor Equity Financing', *Journal of Financial Economics*, **32**: 3–21 (1992).

[35]  This fact led to an extensive body of literature on 'credit rationing'. A lender rations credit if it is irrational to lend more to a firm regardless of the interest rate the firm is willing to *promise* to pay. Whether this can happen in efficient, competitive capital markets is controversial. We give an example of credit rationing in Chapter 32. For a review of this literature, see E. Baltensperger, 'Credit Rationing: Issues and Questions', *Journal of Money, Credit and Banking*, **10**: 170–83 (May 1978).

A convertible bond gives its holder the right to swap the bond for ordinary shares. The rate of exchange is usually measured by the *conversion ratio*—that is, the number of shares that the investor gets for each bond. Sometimes the rate of exchange is expressed in terms of the *conversion price*—that is, the face value of the bond that must be given up in order to receive one share.

Convertibles are like a package of a bond and a call option. When you evaluate the conversion option, you must again remember that the convertible holder does not receive dividends and that conversion results in dilution of the ordinary shares. There are two other things to watch out for. One is the problem of default risk. If the company runs into trouble, you may have not only a worthless conversion option but also a worthless bond. Second, the company may be able to force conversion by calling the bond. It should do this when the market price of the convertible exceeds the call price.

You hear a variety of arguments for issuing warrants or convertibles. Convertible bonds and bonds with warrants are almost always junior bonds and are frequently issued by risky companies. We think that this says something about the reasons for their issue. Suppose that you are lending to an untried company. You are worried that the company may turn out to be riskier than you thought or that it may issue additional senior bonds. You can try to protect yourself against such eventualities by imposing very restrictive conditions on the debt, but it is often simpler to allow some extra risk as long as you get a piece of the action. The convertible and bond-warrant package give you a chance to participate in the company's successes as well as its failures. They diminish the possible conflicts of interest between bondholder and shareholder.

## FURTHER READING

The items listed in Chapter 20 under 'Further Reading' are also relevant to this chapter, in particular Black and Scholes' discussion of warrant evaluation.

Ingersoll's work represents the 'state-of-the-art' in valuing convertibles:

> J. E. Ingersoll, 'A Contingent Claims Valuation of Convertible Securities', *Journal of Financial Economics*, 4: 289–322 (May 1977).

Ingersoll also examines corporate call policies on convertible bonds in:

> J. E. Ingersoll, 'An Examination of Corporate Call Policies on Convertible Securities', *Journal of Finance*, 32: 463–78 (May 1977).

Brennan and Schwartz's paper was written about the same time as Ingersoll's and reaches essentially the same conclusions; they also present a general procedure for valuing convertibles:

> M. J. Brennan and E. S. Schwartz, 'Convertible Bonds: Valuation and Optimal Strategies for Call and Conversion', *Journal of Finance*, 32: 1699–715 (December 1977).

Two useful articles on warrants are:

> D. Galai and M. A. Schneller, 'Pricing of Warrants and the Value of the Company', *Journal of Finance*, 33: 1333–42 (December 1978).

> E. S. Schwartz, 'The Valuation of Warrants: Implementing a New Approach', *Journal of Financial Economics*, 4: 79–93 (January 1977).

Asquith's analysis of the effect of call protection provides evidence that companies' decisions on calling convertibles are more efficient than was previously believed:

> P. Asquith, 'Convertible Bonds Are Not Called Late', *Journal of Finance*, 50: 1275–89 (September 1995).

For a non-technical discussion of the pricing of convertibles and the reasons for their use see:

> M. J. Brennan and E. S. Schwartz, 'The Case for Convertibles', *Journal of Applied Corporate Finance*, 1: 55–64 (Summer 1988).

# QUIZ

1. Wattle Ltd warrants entitle the owner to buy one share at $4.00.
   a. What is the 'theoretical' value of the warrant if the share price is:
      i. $2.00?
      ii. $3.00?
      iii. $4.00?
      iv. $5.00?
      v. $6.00?
   b. Plot the theoretical value of the warrant against the share price.
   c. Suppose the share price is $6.00 and the warrant price is $0.50. What would you do?

2. In 1999 Bigcom Ltd issued warrants. Each warrant can be exercised before 2004 at a price of $7.00 per share. The Bigcom share price is currently $4.60.
   a. Does the warrant holder have a vote?
   b. Does the warrant holder receive dividends?
   c. If the shares were split 3 for 1, how would the exercise price be adjusted?
   d. Suppose that, instead of reducing the exercise price after a 3-for-1 split, the company gives each warrant holder the right to buy *three* shares at $7.00 apiece. Would this have the same effect?
   e. What is the 'theoretical' value of the warrant?
   f. Prior to maturity, is the warrant worth more or less than the 'theoretical' value?
   g. Other things being equal, would the warrant be more or less valuable if:
      i. The company increased its rate of dividend payout?
      ii. The interest rate declined?
      iii. The shares became riskier?
      iv. The company extended the exercise period?
      v. The company reduced the exercise period?
   h. A few companies issue perpetual warrants (i.e. warrants with no final exercise date). Suppose that the Bigcom warrants were perpetual. In what circumstances might it make sense for investors to exercise their warrants?

3. Amalgamated Sludge Ltd has 10 million warrants outstanding, each of which may be converted into one ordinary share. Assume that net income is $40 million and that there are 20 million shares outstanding.
   a. Calculate earnings per share.
   b. Calculate earnings per share on a fully diluted basis.

4. Suppose that Biota Aircraft has issued a 4.75 per cent convertible subordinated debenture due 2005. The conversion price is $50, and the price of ordinary shares is $4.15. The market price of the convertible is 91 per cent of the face value and the debenture is callable at $102.75. Assume the value of the bond in the absence of a conversion feature is about 65 per cent of face value.
   a. What is the conversion ratio of the debenture?
   b. If the conversion ratio were 5, what would be the conversion price?
   c. What is the conversion value?
   d. At what share price is the conversion value equal to the bond value?
   e. Can the market price be less than the conversion value?
   f. How much is the convertible holder paying for the option to buy one ordinary share?
   g. By how much do the ordinary shares have to rise by 2005 to justify conversion?
   h. When should Biota call the debenture?

**5.** Financing with convertible debt is especially appropriate for small, rapidly growing or risky companies. Briefly explain why.

## QUESTIONS AND PROBLEMS

**1.** Refer again to the Melba Technologies warrant discussed in Section 22.1. Immediately after the issue Melba had three million shares and one million warrants outstanding. Suppose Melba split its shares 3 for 1 (i.e. each share is split into three shares).
   a. After the shares were split how many shares and warrants were outstanding?
   b. What was the exercise price of the warrants after the split? Would this also have been adjusted?
   c. Suppose that when the warrants expired in April 2001, the share price was $10. What was the value of the warrants?
   d. Suppose that one year *before* expiration the share price was $10. Would the warrants have sold for more or less than your answer to Part (c)? Would they have sold for their theoretical value? Explain.
   e. In 1998 Melba's net income was $464 000, and at year-end there were three million shares outstanding. Calculate its undiluted and diluted earnings per share.

**\*2.** Use the Black–Scholes formula to compute the value of the Melba Technologies warrant immediately after its issue, assuming a share price of $6 and a warrant price of $0.20. Begin by ignoring the problem of dilution. Then go on to describe how dilution would affect your calculations.

**3.** Occasionally companies extend the life of warrants that would otherwise expire unexercised. What is the cost of doing this?

**\*4.** Here is a question on dilution: Electric Conductors Ltd has outstanding 2000 ordinary shares with a total market value of $20 000, *plus* 1000 warrants with a total market value of $5000. Each warrant gives its holder the option to buy one share at $20.
   a. To value the warrants, you first need to value a call option on an alternative share. What is the current price of this alternative share? How might you calculate its standard of deviation?
   b. Suppose that the value of a call option on this alternative share was $6. Calculate whether the Electric Conductors warrants were undervalued or overvalued.

**5.** Surplus Value Ltd has $10 million (face value) of convertible bonds outstanding in 2000. Each bond has the following features:

| | | |
|---|---|---|
| ▮ | Conversion price: | $2.50 |
| ▮ | Current call price: | 105 (per cent of face value) |
| ▮ | Current trading price: | 130 (per cent of face value) |
| ▮ | Maturity: | 2010 |
| ▮ | Current share price: | $3.00 (per share) |
| ▮ | Interest rate: | 10 (coupon as per cent of face value) |

   a. What is the bond's conversion value?
   b. Can you explain why the bond is selling above the conversion value?
   c. Should Surplus call? What will happen if it does call?

**6.** Growth-Tech has issued $10 million of a 10 per cent subordinated convertible debenture. Assume:

- ■ Net income:                        $50 million
- ■ Number of shares outstanding:      2.5 million
- ■ Conversion ratio:                  50
- ■ Tax rate:                          50 per cent
  a. Calculate earnings per share.
  b. Calculate earnings per share on a fully diluted basis.

**7.** Gum Tree Ltd warrants have an exercise price of $4.00. The share price is $5.00. The dividend on the share is $0.30, and the interest rate is 10 per cent.
  a. Would you exercise your warrants now or later? State why.
  b. If the dividend increased to $0.50, it could pay to exercise now if the share price had low variability and it could be better to exercise later if the share price had high variability. Explain why.

**8.** 'The company's decision to issue warrants should depend on the management's forecast of likely returns on the share.' Do you agree?

**9.** In each case, state which of the two securities is likely to provide the higher return:
  a. When the share price rises—share *or* convertible bond?
  b. When interest rates fall—zero coupon bond *or* convertible bond?
  c. When the specific risk of the share decreases—zero coupon bond *or* convertible bond?
  d. When the dividend on the share increases—share *or* convertible bond?

**10.** Towncorp Ltd has issued three-year warrants to buy 12 per cent perpetual debentures at a price of 120 per cent. The current interest rate is 12 per cent, and the standard deviation of returns on the bond is 20 per cent. Use the Black–Scholes model to obtain a rough estimate of the value of Towncorp warrants.

**11.** Emu Stores has outstanding one million ordinary shares with a total market value of $40 million. It now announces an issue of one million warrants at $5 each. Each warrant entitles the owner to buy one Emu share for a price of $30 at any time within the next five years. Emu Stores has stated that it will not pay a dividend within this period. The standard deviation of the returns on Emu's equity is 20 per cent a year, and the interest rate is 8 per cent.
  a. What is the market value of each warrant?
  b. What is the market value of each share after the warrant issue? (*Hint*: The value of the share is equal to the total value of the equity less the value of the warrants.)

**12.** Look again at Question 11. Suppose that Emu now forecasts the following dividend payments:

| End of year | Dividend (cents) |
| --- | --- |
| 1 | 20 |
| 2 | 30 |
| 3 | 40 |
| 4 | 50 |
| 5 | 60 |

Re-estimate the market values of the warrant and shares.

**13.** Occasionally, it is said that issuing convertible bonds is better than issuing shares when the company's shares are undervalued. Suppose that the financial managers of the Butternut Furniture Company does, in fact, have inside information indicating that the Butternut share price is too low. Butternut's future earnings will in fact be higher than investors expect. Suppose further that the inside information cannot be released without giving away a valuable competitive secret. Clearly, selling shares at the present low price would harm Butternut's existing shareholders. Will they also lose if convertible bonds are issued? If they do lose in this case, is the loss more or less than it would be if ordinary shares are issued?

Now suppose that investors forecast earnings accurately, but still undervalue the shares because they overestimate Butternut's actual business risk. Does this change your answers to the questions posed above? Explain.

**14.** This question illustrates that when there is scope for the company to vary its risk, lenders may be more prepared to lend if they are offered a piece of the action through the issue of a convertible bond.

Ms Brown is proposing to form a new company with initial assets of $10 million. She can invest this money in one of two projects. Each has the same expected payoff, but one has more risk than the other. The relatively safe project offers a 40 per cent chance of a $12.5 million payoff and a 60 per cent chance of an $8 million payoff. The risky project offers a 40 per cent chance of a $20 million payoff and a 60 per cent chance of a $5 million payoff.

Ms Brown initially proposes to finance the company by an issue of straight debt with a promised payoff of $7 million. Ms Brown will receive any remaining payoff. Show the possible payoffs to the lender and to Ms Brown (a) if she chooses to invest in the safe project and (b) if she chooses to invest in the risky project. Which project is Ms Brown likely to choose? Which will the lender want her to choose?

Suppose now that Ms Brown offers to make the debt convertible into 50 per cent of the value of the company. Show that in this case the lender receives the same expected payoff from the two projects.

**15.** Piglet Pie Company has issued a zero coupon 10-year bond, which can be converted into one Piglet ordinary share. Comparable straight bonds are yielding 8 per cent. Piglet shares are priced at $5.00 a share.
a. Suppose that you had to make a now-or-never decision on whether to convert or stay with the bond. Which would you do?
b. If the convertible bond is priced at $550, how much are investors paying for the option to buy Piglet shares?

**16.** Barry Thompson, the autocratic CEO of Thompson Oil, was found dead this morning in a pool of blood on his office floor. He had been shot. Yesterday, Thompson had flatly rejected an offer by Tom Dickens to buy all Thompson Oil's assets for $1 billion cash, effective 1 January 2000. With Thompson out of the way, Dickens' offer will be accepted immediately.

The immediate suspects are Thompson's two nieces, Daisy and Mary, and his nephew John.

Thompson Oil's capital structure is as follows:

▪ *Debt*: $250 million face value, issued in 1995 at a coupon rate of 6 per cent, with market value of 60 per cent of face value. This debt will be paid off at par if Dickens' offer goes through.

▪ *Shares*: 30 million shares closing yesterday at $10 per share.

■ *Warrants*: Warrants to buy an additional 20 million shares at $10 per share, expiring 31 December 1999. The last trade of the warrants was at $1 per warrant.

Here are Daisy, John and Mary's stakes in Thompson Oil:

|  | Debt (market value) | Shares (number of shares) | Warrants (number of warrants) |
|---|---|---|---|
| Daisy | $6 million | 1.0 million | 0 |
| John | 0 | 0.5 million | 2 million |
| Mary | 0 | 1.5 million | 1 million |

Which niece or nephew stands to gain most (in portfolio value) by eliminating old Thompson and allowing Dickens' offer to succeed? Explain. Make additional assumptions if you find them necessary.

# part 7

# DEBT FINANCING

# chapter 23

# VALUING RISKY DEBT

How do you estimate the present value of a bond? The answer is simple. You take the cash flows and discount them at the opportunity cost of capital or the yield to maturity. Therefore, if a bond produces cash flows of $C$ dollars per period for $N$ periods and is then repaid at its face value (per $100), the present value is

$$PV = \frac{C}{(1 + r_1)^1} + \frac{C}{(1 + r_2)^2} + \ldots + \frac{C}{(1 + r_N)^N} + \frac{100}{(1 + r_N)^N}$$

where $r_1, r_2, \ldots, r_N$ are the appropriate discount rates for the cash flows to be received by the bond's owner in periods $1, 2, \ldots, N$. This is correct as far as it goes, but it does not tell us anything about what *determines* the discount rates. For example:

1. In 1963, Australian Treasury notes offered a return of 3.23 per cent; in 1989 they offered a return of 17.17 per cent. Why does the same security offer radically different yields at different times?

2. In 1988 the Reserve Bank of Australia acting on behalf of the Australian government could borrow for 26 weeks at an interest rate of about 17 per cent; but it only had to pay a rate of about 11.95 per cent for 10-year loans. Why do bonds maturing at different dates offer different rates of interest? In other words, why is there a *term structure* of interest rates?

3. In March 1999 Australian government bonds with 10 years to maturity were trading at 5.50 per cent. At that time, you could not have borrowed from a bank at that rate. Why not? What explains the premium you have to pay?

These questions lead to deep issues that will keep economists simmering for years. But we can give general answers and at the same time present some fundamental ideas.

Why should the financial manager care about these ideas? Who needs to know how bonds are priced as long as the bond market is active and efficient? Efficient markets protect the ignorant trader. If it is necessary to check whether the price is right for a proposed bond issue, you can check the prices of similar bonds. There is no need to worry about the historical behaviour of interest rates, the term structure or other issues discussed in this chapter.

We do not believe that ignorance is desirable even when it is harmless. At least you ought to be able to read the *Australian Financial Review* and talk to investment bankers. More importantly, you will encounter many problems of bond pricing where there are no similar instruments already traded. How do you evaluate a private placement with a custom-tailored repayment schedule? How about financial leases? In Chapter 26 we will see that they are essentially debt contracts, but often extremely complicated ones, for which traded bonds are not close substitutes. You will find that the terms, concepts and facts presented in this chapter are essential to the analysis of these and other practical problems in financing covered in later chapters. We start, therefore, with our first question: 'Why does the general level of interest rates change over time?'

## 23.1 The classical theory of interest

### Real interest rates

Suppose that everyone knows that there is not going to be any inflation. If so, all interest rates are *real* rates—they include no premium for anticipated inflation. What are the essential determinants of the rate of interest in such a world? The classical economist's answer to this question is summed up in the title of Irving Fisher's great book: *The Theory of Interest: As Determined by Impatience to Spend Income and Opportunity to Invest It*.[1]

The real interest rate, according to Fisher, is the price that equates the supply and demand for capital. The supply depends on people's longer-term willingness to save—that is, to postpone consumption.[2] The demand depends on the longer-term opportunities for productive investment. Real interest rates are believed to affect business spending, housing investment in the retail sector and the level of consumption of durable goods. As such, real interest rates directly affect the business cycle and the transmission of macroeconomic monetary policy by governments.

For example, suppose that investment opportunities generally improve. Firms have more good projects, and so are willing to invest more at any interest rate. Therefore, the rate has to rise to induce individuals to save the additional amount that firms want to invest.[3] Conversely, if investment opportunities deteriorate, there will be a fall in the real interest rate.

Fisher's theory emphasises that the real rate of interest depends on real phenomena. A high aggregate willingness to save may be associated with such factors as high aggregate wealth

---

[1]   Irving Fisher, *The Theory of Interest: As Determined by Impatience to Spend Income and Opportunity to Invest It*, Augustus M. Kelley, Publishers, New York, 1965; originally published in 1930.

[2]   Some of this saving is done indirectly. For example, if you hold 1000 BHP shares, and BHP retains earnings of $1 per share, BHP is saving $1000 on your behalf.

[3]   We assume that investors save more as interest rates rise. It does not *have* to be that way—here is an example of how a higher interest rate could mean *less* saving. Suppose that 20 years hence you need $10 000 for your children's university expenses. How much will you have to set aside today to cover this obligation? The answer is the present value of $10 000 after 20 years, or $10\ 000/(1 + r)^{20}$. The higher $r$, the lower the present value and the less you have to set aside.

(because wealthy people usually save more), an uneven distribution of wealth (an even distribution would mean few rich people, who do most of the saving), and a high proportion of middle-aged people (the young do not need to save and the old do not want to—'You cannot take it with you'). Correspondingly, a high propensity to invest may be associated with a high level of industrial activity or major technological advances.

More recently, in 1995, a study by the OECD[4] investigated the determinants of real long-term rates in 17 countries and found that real interest rates were influenced by the rate of return on business capital, portfolio risk, inflation uncertainty, indicators of future savings and investments such as current account deficits and government deficits, monetary policy and inflation shocks.

## Inflation and interest rates

Now let us see what Irving Fisher had to say about the effect of inflation on interest rates. Suppose that consumers are equally happy with 100 pineapples today or 105 pineapples in a year's time. In this case, the real, or 'pineapple', rate of interest is 5 per cent. Suppose also that I know the price of pineapples will increase over the year by 10 per cent. Then I will part with $100 today if I am repaid $115 at the end of the year. That $115 is needed to buy me 5 per cent more pineapples than I can get from my $100 today. In other words, the nominal, or 'money', rate of interest must equal the real, or 'pineapple', rate plus the prospective rate of inflation. A change of one percentage point in the expected inflation rate produces a change of one percentage point in the nominal interest rate. That is Fisher's theory: A change in the expected inflation will cause the same change in the nominal interest rate.[5]

In principle, there is no upper limit to the real rate of interest. But is there any lower limit? For example, is it possible for the money rate of interest to be 5 per cent and the expected rate of inflation to be 10 per cent, thus giving a negative real interest rate? If this happens, you may be able to make money in the following way. You borrow $100 at an interest rate of 5 per cent and you use the money to buy pineapples. You store the pineapples and sell them at the end of the year for $110, which leaves you enough to pay off your loan plus $5 for yourself.

Since easy ways to make money are rare, we can conclude that, if it does not cost anything to store goods, the money rate of interest is unlikely to be less than the expected rise in prices. But many goods are even more expensive to store than pineapples, and others cannot be stored at all (you cannot store haircuts, for example). For these goods, the money interest rate can be less than the expected price rise.

**Comment**    If you look back to our discussion of inflation and discount rates in Chapter 3, you will see that our pineapple example is a bit oversimplified. If pineapples cost $1.00 a piece today and $1.10 next year, you need $1.10 × 105 = $115.50 next year to buy 105 pineapples. The money interest rate is 15.5 per cent, not 15.

The exact formula relating real and money rates is

$$1 + r_{money} = (1 + r_{real})(1 + i)$$

where $i$ is the expected inflation rate. Thus

$$r_{money} = r_{real} + i + i(r_{real})$$

4    The study involved countries such as the United States, Japan, Germany, the United Kingdom, Canada, Australia and New Zealand. See A. Orr, M. Edey and M. Kennedy, The Determinants of Real Long-Term Interest Rates: 17 Country Pooled Time Series Evidence, Working Paper No. 155, Organisation for Economic Cooperation and Development, Paris, 1995.

5    The pineapple example is derived from R. Roll, 'Interest Rates on Monetary Assets and Commodity Price Index Changes', *Journal of Finance*, **27**: 251–78 (May 1972).

In our example, the money rate should be

$$r_{\text{money}} = 0.05 + 0.10 + 0.10(0.05)$$
$$= 0.155$$

When we said the money rate should be 15 per cent, we ignored the 'cross-product' term $i(r_{\text{real}})$. This is a common rule of thumb, because the cross-product is usually small. But there are countries where $i$ is large (sometimes 100 per cent per year or more). In such cases it pays to use the full formula.

**Back to Fisher's theory**    Not all economists would agree with Fisher that the real rate of interest is unaffected by the inflation rate. For example, if changes in prices are associated with changes in the level of industrial activity, then in inflationary conditions I might want more or less than 105 pineapples in a year's time to compensate me for the loss of 100 today.

We wish we could show you the past behaviour of interest rates and expected inflation. Unfortunately, there is no absolute consensus of what constitutes expected inflation—is it better measured using survey data, time series models using past inflation data or modelled using factors known to influence the level of inflation?[6] Instead, we have done the next best thing and plotted in Figure 23.1 Australian 90-day bank accepted bill interest rates against actual inflation between 1984 and 1997. The average real rate of interest as measured by the difference between the two series was 6.30 per cent with a peak of 11.38 per cent in December 1985 and a low of 2.59 per cent in September 1995. The average level of inflation was 4.52 per cent. The plot reflects a systematic transition in the level of inflation in Australia following a shift in monetary policy in the period after 1989.[7] Prior to this time, inflation was on average much higher (6.58 per cent) than in the post 1991 period (1.97 per cent).

Fisher's theory states that changes in anticipated inflation produce corresponding changes in the rate of interest. Eugene Fama has suggested that one way to test Fisher's theory is to twist it around and measure whether the inflation rate cannot be forecasted by subtracting a constant real rate from the observed nominal rate. That is, if Fisher's theory is right:

Nominal interest rate = real interest rate + inflation rate forecasted by investors

can be represented as:

Inflation rate forecasted by investors = nominal interest rate − real interest rate

Of course, investors cannot predict the actual inflation rate perfectly—there will be a random forecast error. But in an efficient market, we expect them to be right on average. Thus, the forecast error should be zero on average.[8]

Suppose we observe the nominal returns on Treasury notes and the actual rates of inflation. We can fit the following regression equation to the data:

Actual inflation rate = $a$ + $b$(nominal interest rate) + random forecasting error

If Fisher is correct, the coefficient $b$ should be close to 1.0 and the constant $a$ should be equal to minus the real rate of interest. Fama fitted this equation to American data for the

---

6    It is possible to decompose the actual level of inflation (at the time of an economic announcement) into both an expected an unexpected component. Market participants form their expectations, and if their forecasts are correct, the unexpected component will be equal to zero.

7    For a discussion of the Reserve Bank of Australia's rhetoric and action regarding its use of monetary policy to achieve and maintain low inflation see Reserve Bank of Australia, 'Six Years of Inflation Targeting', *Reserve Bank of Australia Bulletin*, May 1999.

8    See E. F. Fama, 'Short-Term Interest Rates as Predictors of Inflation', *American Economic Review*, 65: 269–82 (June 1975).

**figure 23.1**

Australian 90-day bank accepted bill interest rates and inflation, 1984–97.

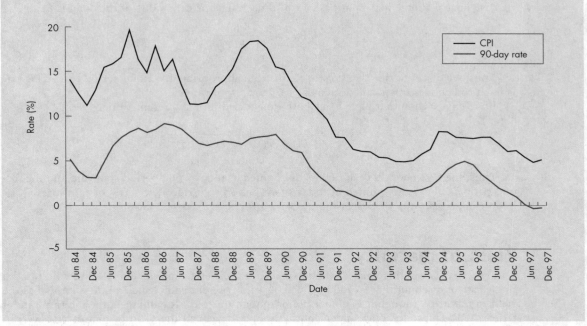

*Source*: Equinet database.

period 1953 to 1971 assuming that that the real rate of interest was constant and found *b* to be very close to 1.0.[9]

Before leaving this topic, we must add two qualifications. First, the real interest rate is really an *expected* rate. When you buy a Treasury note and hold it to maturity, you know what the dollar payoff will be, but the *real* payoff is uncertain because future inflation is not wholly predictable. Thus, to be perfectly precise, we should define the real interest rate as follows:

Real interest rate  =  *expected* real rate of return from Treasury notes
                    =  nominal rate of return on Treasury notes  −  *expected* rate of inflation

Second, Nelson and Schwert, and Hess and Bicksler, have pointed out that the (expected) real interest rate *does* vary over time. Indeed, we have seen that the real rate appears to have been unusually high since 1981. If that is so, Fama's test may be inappropriate.[10] Until these problems have been resolved, we recommend that you look on Fisher's theory simply as a rule of thumb. Thus, if the expected inflation rate changes, your best bet is that there will be a corresponding change in the interest rate.

---

9    Fama's estimate of *b* was 0.98, which is almost identical to the figure that Fisher would predict. See Fama, op. cit., Footnote 8.

10   C .R. Nelson and G. Schwert, 'Short-Term Interest Rates and Predictors of Inflation: On Testing the Hypothesis that the Real Rate of Interest Is Constant', *American Economic Review*, 67: 478–86 (June 1977); P. Hess and J. Bicksler, 'Capital Asset Prices Versus Time Series Models as Predictors of Inflation', *Journal of Financial Economics*, 2: 341–60 (December 1975).

## 23.2 Term structure and yields to maturity

We turn now to the relationship between short-term and long-term rates of interest. Suppose that we have a simple loan that pays $1 at time 1. The present value of this loan is

$$PV = \frac{1}{(1 + r_1)^1}$$

Thus, we discount the cash flow at $r_1$, the rate appropriate for a one-period loan. This rate is fixed today; it is often called today's one-period **spot rate**.[11]

If we have a loan that pays $1 at both time 1 and time 2, present value is

$$PV = \frac{1}{(1 + r_1)^1} + \frac{1}{(1 + r_2)^2}$$

Thus, the first period's cash flow is discounted at today's one-period spot rate and the second period's flow is discounted at today's two-period spot rate. The series of spot rates $r_1$, $r_2$, and so on, is one way of expressing the *term structure of interest rates*.

## Yield to maturity

Rather than discounting each of the payments at a different rate of interest, we could find a single rate of discount that would produce the same present value. Such a rate is known as the **yield to maturity**, though it is in fact no more than our old acquaintance, the internal rate of return (IRR), masquerading under another name. If we call the yield to maturity $y$, we can write the present value as

$$PV = \frac{1}{(1 + y)^1} + \frac{1}{(1 + y)^2}$$

All you need to calculate $y$ is the price of a bond, its annual payment and its maturity. You can then rapidly work out the yield with the aid of a pre-programmed calculator or you can find it in a set of bond tables.

Look at Table 23.1, which contains two panels from a mini-book of bond tables. Each panel shows yields for bonds with a particular coupon. For example, suppose that you have an 8 per cent bond maturing in 10 years and priced at 85. (In bond tables, bond prices are quoted as percentages of the bond's face value.) Look at the second panel of our mini-book of bond tables. This shows yields for bonds with an 8 per cent coupon. If you run your eye down the column for 10 years, you will see that a bond priced at 87.54 yields 10 per cent and a bond priced at 82.07 yields 11 per cent. Obviously, the yield on your bond lies somewhere in between, about 10.5 per cent.

Real books of bond tables contain several hundred pages, each crammed with bond prices, for different combinations of coupon, yield and maturity, but in all other respects, they are the same as our mini-book of Table 23.1.

---

[11] Spot rates can be defined as the rate of interest on an investment that is made for a period of time starting today and lasting for a specified period of time—for example, 90 days, 180 days, one year, three years, five years, seven years or 10 years.

**table 23.1**

Each page of this mini-book of bond tables shows bond prices for a different coupon level.

| Coupon = 7% | Years | | | | |
|---|---|---|---|---|---|
| Yield | 6 | 8 | 10 | 12 | 14 |
| 6.00% | 104.98 | 106.28 | 107.44 | 108.47 | 109.38 |
| 7.00 | 100.00 | 100.00 | 100.00 | 100.00 | 100.00 |
| 8.00 | 95.31 | 94.17 | 93.20 | 92.38 | 91.67 |
| 9.00 | 90.88 | 88.77 | 86.99 | 85.50 | 84.26 |
| 10.00 | 86.71 | 83.74 | 81.31 | 79.30 | 77.65 |
| 11.00 | 82.76 | 79.08 | 76.10 | 73.70 | 71.76 |
| 12.00 | 79.04 | 74.74 | 71.33 | 68.62 | 66.48 |
| 13.00 | 75.52 | 70.70 | 66.94 | 64.03 | 61.76 |
| 14.00 | 72.20 | 66.94 | 62.92 | 59.86 | 57.52 |

| Coupon = 8% | Years | | | | |
|---|---|---|---|---|---|
| Yield | 6 | 8 | 10 | 12 | 14 |
| 6.00% | 109.95 | 112.56 | 114.88 | 116.94 | 118.76 |
| 7.00 | 104.83 | 106.05 | 107.11 | 108.03 | 108.83 |
| 8.00 | 100.00 | 100.00 | 100.00 | 100.00 | 100.00 |
| 9.00 | 95.44 | 94.38 | 93.50 | 92.75 | 92.13 |
| 10.00 | 91.14 | 89.16 | 87.54 | 86.20 | 85.10 |
| 11.00 | 87.07 | 84.31 | 82.07 | 80.27 | 78.82 |
| 12.00 | 83.23 | 79.79 | 77.06 | 74.90 | 73.19 |
| 13.00 | 79.60 | 75.58 | 72.45 | 70.02 | 68.13 |
| 14.00 | 76.17 | 71.66 | 68.22 | 65.59 | 63.59 |

## example

The yield to maturity is unambiguous and easy to calculate. An understanding of this concept is essential for any bond dealer. By now, however, you should have learned to treat any internal rate of return with suspicion.[12] The more closely we examine the yield to maturity, the less informative it is seen to be. Here is an example.

Assume it is July 1998. You are contemplating an investment in the Australian Commonwealth Treasury bond market and come across the following quotations for two bonds:

---

12    See Chapter 5.

| Bond series | Price | Yield to maturity (IRR) |
|---|---|---|
| 7% July 2002 | $99.29 | 7.21% |
| 13% July 2002 | $119.63 | 7.18% |

The phrase '7 per cent July 2002' means a bond maturing in July 2002 paying annual interest amounting to 7 per cent of the bond's face value. The interest payment is called a *coupon* payment. Bond investors would say that these bonds have a 7 per cent coupon. Face value plus interest is paid back at maturity, 2002. If the face value of the bond is $100, you would have to pay $99.29 to buy the bond and your yield would be 7.21 per cent.

Letting 1998 be $t = 0$, 1999 be $t = 1$, and so on, we have the following calculation:[13]

| | Cash flows | | | | | |
|---|---|---|---|---|---|---|
| Bond | $C_0$ | $C_1$ | $C_2$ | $C_3$ | $C_4$ | Yield in per cent |
| 7% July 2002 | −$99.29 | +7 | +7 | +7 | +107 | 7.21 |
| 13% July 2002 | $119.63 | +13 | +13 | +13 | +113 | 7.18 |

Although the two bonds mature at the same date, they presumably were issued at different times, the 7 per cent coupon bonds when interest rates were low, and the 13 per cent coupon bonds when interest rates were high.

Are the 7 per cent July 2002 a better buy? Is the market making a mistake by pricing these two issues at different yields? The only way you will know for sure is to calculate the bonds' present values by using spot rates of interest $r_1$ for 1999, $r_2$ for 2000, and so on. This is done in Table 23.2.

The important assumption in Table 23.2 is that long-term interest rates are higher than short-term interest rates. We have assumed that the one-year interest rate is $r_1 = 6.5$ per cent, the two-year rate is $r_2 = 6.75$ per cent, and so on. When each year's cash flow is discounted at the rate appropriate to that year, we see that each bond's present value is exactly equal to the quoted price. Thus, each bond is *fairly priced*.

Alternatively, the 7 per cent July 2002 bond could be priced using the yield to maturity of 7.21 per cent as follows:[14]

$$\text{Bond price} = \frac{7}{(1 + 0.0721)^1} + \frac{7}{(1 + 0.0721)^2} + \frac{7}{(1 + 0.0721)^3}$$
$$+ \frac{7}{(1 + 0.0721)^4}$$

$$\text{Bond price} = \$99.292$$

Why do the 7 per cent July 2002 bonds have a higher yield than the 13 per cent coupon bonds maturing at the same time? Because for each dollar that you invest in the

---

[13]  Coupon payments are actually made semiannually on Commonwealth government securities—the owners of the 7 per cent July 2000 bonds would receive $35 every six months. Thus, our calculations are a little bit off what you would get from using bond tables like Table 23.1. Also, the yields are rounded, not exact.

[14]  The one cent difference is induced through rounding because the true IRR is not 7.21 per cent but rather 7.2073 per cent.

**table 23.2** _____

Calculating present value of two bonds when long-term interest rates are higher than short-term rates.

| Period | Interest rate | 7% July 2002 | | 13% July 2002 | |
| | | $C_t$ | $PV@r_t$ | $C_t$ | $PV@r_t$ |
|--------|---------------|--------|----------|--------|----------|
| $t = 1$ | $r_1 = 0.0650$ | 7 | 6.573 | 13 | 12.207 |
| $t = 2$ | $r_2 = 0.0675$ | 7 | 6.143 | 13 | 11.408 |
| $t = 3$ | $r_3 = 0.0700$ | 7 | 5.714 | 13 | 10.612 |
| $t = 4$ | $r_4 = 0.0725$ | 107 | 80.871 | 113 | 85.406 |
| Totals | | 128 | 99.301 | 152 | 119.633 |
| Implied (IRR) yield to maturity | | 7.207331% | | 7.180191% | |
| Rounded yield to maturity | | 7.21% | | 7.18% | |

7 per cent coupon bonds you receive relatively little cash inflow in the first three years and a relatively high cash inflow in the final year. Therefore, although the two bonds have identical maturity dates, the 7 per cent coupon bonds provide a greater proportion of their cash flows in 2002. In this sense, the 7 per cent coupon bonds are a longer-term investment than the 13 per cent coupon bonds. Their higher yield to maturity just reflects the fact that long-term interest rates are higher than short-term rates.

The price of a bond and its yield to maturity have an inverse relationship. If the yield increases, the price of the bond will decrease. Similarly, if the yield decreases, the price of the bond will increase. Consider the prices of 7 per cent July 2002 bond if yields were to take on different values across the range 6.0 to 8.0 per cent:

| Yield to maturity (%) | Price ($) |
|-----------------------|-----------|
| 6.00 | 103.4651 |
| 6.25 | 102.5840 |
| 6.50 | 101.7129 |
| 6.75 | 100.8516 |
| 7.00 | 100.0000 |
| 7.25 | 99.1580 |
| 7.50 | 98.3253 |
| 7.75 | 97.5020 |
| 8.00 | 96.6879 |

These calculations also highlight a bond pricing relationship between the coupon and the yield:

■ If the yield to maturity is less than the coupon (i.e. the yield is less than 7 per cent in the above example), the purchase price of the bond will be greater than the bond's face value. The bond is said to be trading at a premium to the face value.

- If the yield to maturity is equal to the coupon (i.e. the yield equals 7 per cent in the above example), the price of the bond is equal to the face value. The bond is said to be trading at par.
- If the yield to maturity is greater than the coupon (i.e. the yield is greater than 7 per cent in the above example), the purchase price will be less than the face value. The bond is said to be trading at a discount to the face value.

## Problems with yield to maturity

With this in mind, we can sum up the problems with the yield to maturity.

First, when a bond's yield to maturity is calculated, the *same* rate is used to discount *all* payments to the bondholder. The bondholder may actually demand different rates of return ($r_1$, $r_2$, and so on) for different periods. Unless two bonds offer exactly the same pattern of cash flows, they are likely to have different yields to maturity. Therefore, the yield to maturity on one bond can offer only a rough guide to the appropriate yield on another.

Second, yields to maturity do not determine bond prices. It is the other way around. The demand by companies for capital and the supply of savings by individuals combine to determine the spot rates $r_1$, $r_2$, and so on. These rates then determine the value of any package of future cash flows. Finally, *given* the value, we can compute the yield to maturity. We cannot, however, derive the appropriate yield to maturity *without* first knowing the value. We cannot, for example, assume that the yield should be the same for two bonds with the same maturity unless they also happen to have the same coupon.

The yield to maturity is a complicated average of spot rates of interest. Suppose that $r_2$ is greater than $r_1$. Then the yield on a two-year coupon bond must lie between $r_1$ and $r_2$. In this case, the yield on the two-year bond provides an underestimate of the two-year spot rate. Of course, if $r_2$ is less than $r_1$, it would be the other way around—the yield on the two-year bond would overestimate the two-year spot rate. Sometimes these differences can be dramatic. For example, in the United Kingdom in 1977 the 20-year spot rate of interest $r_{20}$ was nearly 20 per cent. But this *yield* on high coupon bonds maturing in 20 years was only about 13 per cent. The reason was that short-term spot rates of interest were much lower than 20 per cent. The yield on 20-year bonds was an average of short-term and long-term rates.[15]

In Chapter 5, we asserted that one problem with internal rates of return is that they do not add up. In other words, even if you know the return on A and the return on B, you cannot generally work out the return on A + B. Let us illustrate. Suppose your portfolio is evenly divided between two bonds both priced at 100. Bond A is a one-year bond with a 10 per cent coupon and therefore yields 10 per cent. Bond B is a two-year bond with an 8 per cent coupon and therefore yields 8 per cent. You might think that the yield on your portfolio would be halfway between, at 9 per cent. You would be wrong. The yield is 8.68 per cent. In other words

$$\text{PV bond 1} + \text{PV bond 2} = \text{cash flows from bond 1 discounted} +$$
$$\text{cash flows from bond 2 discounted}$$
$$100 + 100 = 200$$
$$= \left[ \frac{10}{(1 + 0.0868)^1} + \frac{100}{(1 + 0.0868)^2} \right] +$$
$$\left[ \frac{8}{(1 + 0.0868)^1} + \frac{8}{(1 + 0.0868)^2} + \frac{100}{(1 + 0.0868)^2} \right]$$

Thus, it is dangerous to rely on the yield to maturity. Like most averages, it hides much of the interesting information.

---

[15] For a good analysis of the relationship between the yield to maturity and spot rates see S. M. Shaefer, 'The Problem with Redemption Yields', *Financial Analysts Journal*, 33: 59–67 (July–August 1977).

# Measuring the term structure

Financial managers who just want a quick, summary measure of interest rates look in the financial press at the yields to maturity on government bonds. For example, the yield to maturity on Commonwealth Treasury bonds reported in the *Australian Financial Review* on 15 August 1996 included:

| Series | Yield per year (%) | (14 August 1996) |
|---|---|---|
| 12.50% | March 1997 | 6.81 |
| 12.50% | September 1997 | 6.84 |
| 12.50% | January 1998 | 6.96 |
| 7.00% | August 1998 | 7.07 |
| 6.25% | March 1999 | 7.19 |
| 12.00% | July 1999 | 7.25 |
| 7.00% | April 2000 | 7.39 |
| 13.00% | July 2000 | 7.43 |
| 8.75% | January 2001 | 7.53 |
| 12.00% | November 2001 | 7.65 |
| 9.75% | March 2002 | 7.75 |
| 10.00% | October 2002 | 7.82 |

Managers will often make broad generalisations such as 'If we borrow money today, we will have to pay an interest rate of 6.50 per cent.' But if you want to understand why different bonds sell at different prices, you need to dig deeper and estimate the spot rates of interest.

Look back at Table 23.2, which shows how investors value the 7 per cent coupon bonds. Four years before maturity each bond is like a package of four mini-bonds. The package contains one mini-bond paying $7 at $t = 1$, another $7 at $t = 1$, another $7 at $t = 2$, and so on up to the fourth mini-bond, which pays $107 at $t = 4$.

To calculate the spot rates of interest, we must first work out the price of each mini-bond. For example, assume that in 1998 you could buy the following packages:

**1.** Invest $1290.80 to buy *thirteen* 7 per cent July 2002 bonds.
　or
**2.** Invest $837.44 to buy *seven* 13 per cent July 2002 bonds.

Each package provides a $91 cash flow each year for three years. But in year 4, when both bonds mature, the first package gives $13 \times 107 = \$1391$, and the second package gives $7 \times 113 = \$791$. Thus, the only cash flow advantage of package 1 occurs in year 4. It costs $453.36 more to buy package 1 ($1290.80 - 837.44 = \$453.36$), but you gain $600 in year 4 ($1391 - 791 = \$600$). Investors must be indifferent between the two packages—if they were not, they would dump one bond and buy the other, and the bond prices would change. Thus, an extra $100 received in year 4 must be worth $75.58 now:

$$PV(\$100 \text{ in year } 4) = \$75.58$$

But this present value depends on the four-year spot rate $r_4$

$$PV = \frac{100}{(1 + r_4)^4} = \frac{100}{(1 + 0.0725)^4} = 75.58$$

Solving for $r_4$, we find that it equals 0.072499, or 7.25 per cent.

In this example, we had two bonds with the same four-year maturity, but different coupons. This allowed us to work out the price of a bond that made a payment only in year

4 and this in turn gave us the four-year spot rate. In order to work out the exact prices of bonds and spot prices for all other periods, we would need to complete series of matching bonds. In practice, we are never so fortunate, but as long as we have a fair spread of coupons and maturities, we can get quite satisfactory estimates of the spot rates.

In 1982, in the United States, several investment bankers came up with a novel idea. They reasoned that many investors would welcome the opportunity to buy individual bonds rather than the complete package. So the banks bought Treasury bonds and reissued their own separate bonds, each of which made only one payment.[16] If you have got a smart idea, you can be sure that others will soon clamber on to your bandwagon. It was therefore not long before the Treasury issued its own bonds, known as 'stripped' bonds.[17] The stripped bond yields give another measure of spot interest rates.

## Pricing bonds of different maturity

Do you remember how we valued options? The profit or loss on an option depends only on what happens to the underlying share. You can therefore create a mixture of a risk-free loan and the share, which gives exactly the same payoffs as the option. If both packages give the same payoffs, they must sell for the same price. The principle of no arbitrage can also be applied to the calculation of the spot yield curve from the observed yields to maturity of bonds.

### example

Assume it is currently March 1999 and we observe the yields to maturity coupon rates and prices for bonds with maturities at six-monthly intervals, as shown in Table 23.3.[18] From this information it is possible to calculate implied spot rates for each of the maturities.[19] Let us have a go at calculating the first three maturities.[20]

The bond with six months (0.5 years) to maturity is presently yielding 4.65 per cent at a price of $97.7531 per $100 face value.

The implied spot rate for longer maturities can be calculated by recalling that firstly, a bond's cash flow can be stripped into a number of bonds, each with its own implied spot rate for each maturity. Secondly, the purchase price of each bond is equal to the accumulated amounts of all the cash flows discounted by their respective spot rates.

The 1.0-year bond will have two coupon payments—one at 0.5 years and the other after 1.0 years when the face value will also be paid. From the above calculations we know that the spot rate for the first coupon (0.5 years) is equal to 10.75 per cent, but the spot rate for the second payment is unknown.

The 1.0-year spot rate is calculated as follows:

---

16 These mini-bonds had a variety of exotic names. The Merrill Lynch issues were known as TIGRs (Treasury Investment Growth Receipts). Those issued by Salomon Brothers were known as CATS (Certificate of Accrual on Treasury Securities).

17 The Treasury continued to auction coupon bonds in the normal way but investors could exchange them at the Federal Reserve Bank for stripped bonds.

18 The rates quoted are approximate rates as at 31 March 1999.

19 The method used here is similar to examples given using the 'bootstrapping' approach detailed in J. Hull, *Introduction to Futures and Options*, Prentice-Hall, Englewood Cliffs, N.J., 1995; and by D. Daugaard, *The Swaps Market*, Financial Training and Analysis Services Pty Ltd, Sydney, 1991.

20 Assume the face value of the bonds is equal to $100.

## table 23.3

Yields to maturity and coupon rates for bonds maturing 0.5 to five years[21]

| Term to maturity | Coupon rate (% p.a.) | Yield to maturity (% compounded p.a.) | Price per $100 face value ($) |
|---|---|---|---|
| 0.5 | — | 4.65 | 97.7531 |
| 1.0 | 12.00 | 4.70 | 107.1054 |
| 1.5 | 7.00 | 4.70 | 103.3730 |
| 2.0 | 13.00 | 4.75 | 115.6794 |
| 2.5 | 8.70 | 4.90 | 108.9837 |
| 3.0 | 12.00 | 4.95 | 119.6168 |
| 3.5 | 9.70 | 5.00 | 115.1322 |
| 4.0 | 10.00 | 5.05 | 117.9737 |
| 4.5 | 9.50 | 5.10 | 117.7733 |
| 5.0 | 9.00 | 5.20 | 116.8588 |

**Step 1    Identify all relevant cash flows:**

| After 0.5 years | Coupon | = | 6.00 | = $CF_{0.5}$ |
|---|---|---|---|---|
| After 1.0 years | Coupon | = | 6.00 | |
| | Face value | = | 100.00 | |
| | | | 106.00 | = $CF_{1.0}$ |

**Step 2    Set the cash flows to be discounted equal to the purchase price:**

$$PV\ (bond) = \frac{CF_{0.50}}{(1 + 0.0465)^{0.50}} + \frac{CF_{1.00}}{(1 + SR_{1.00})^{1.00}}$$

where $SR_{1.00}$ is the one year spot rate.

$$PV\ (bond) = \frac{6}{(1 + 0.0465)^{0.50}} + \frac{106}{(1 + SR_{1.00})^{1.00}}$$

**Step 3    Solve for $SR_{1.00}$:**

$$PV\ (bond) = \frac{6}{(1 + 0.0465)^{0.50}} + \frac{106}{(1 + SR_{1.00})^{1.00}}$$

$$PV\ (bond) = 107.1054$$

$$107.1054 = 5.8652 + \frac{106}{(1 + SR_{1.00})^{1.00}}$$

$$107.1054 - 5.8652 = \frac{106}{(1 + SR_{1.00})^{1.00}}$$

[21]    For the sake of simplicity all calculations are conducted assuming equal intervals for each half year. The calculations could be adjusted by using the actual days to maturity rather than years to maturity. For example, see Daugaard, op. cit., Footnote 19, pp. 51–6.

$$101.2402^*(1 + SR_{1.00})^{1.00} = 106$$

$$SR_{1.00} = \frac{106}{101.2402} - 1$$

$$SR_{1.00} = 0.047015, \text{ or } 4.70\%$$

The procedure is repeated for calculating the implied spot rate for the bond with a term to maturity of 1.5 years.

**Step 1   Identify all relevant cash flows:**

| After 0.5 years | Coupon | = | 3.50 | = | $CF_{0.5}$ |
|---|---|---|---|---|---|
| After 1.0 years | Coupon | = | 3.50 | = | $CF_{1.0}$ |
| After 1.5 years | Coupon | = | 3.50 | | |
| | Face value | = | 100.00 | | |
| | | | 103.50 | = | $CF_{1.5}$ |

**Step 2   Set the cash flow to be discounted equal to the purchase price:**

$$PV \text{ (bond)} = \frac{CF_{0.50}}{(1 + 0.0465)^{0.50}} + \frac{CF_{1.00}}{(1 + 0.0470)^{1.00}} + \frac{CF_{1.50}}{(1 + SR_{1.50})^{1.50}}$$

where $SR_{1.50}$ is the 1.5 year spot rate.

$$PV \text{ (bond)} = \frac{3.50}{(1 + 0.0465)^{0.50}} + \frac{3.50}{(1 + 0.0470)^{1.00}} + \frac{103.50}{(1 + SR_{1.50})^{1.50}}$$

**Step 3   Solve for $SR_{1.50}$:**

$$PV \text{ (bond)} = \frac{3.50}{(1 + 0.0465)^{0.50}} + \frac{3.50}{(1 + 0.0470)^{1.00}} + \frac{103.50}{(1 + SR_{1.50})^{1.50}}$$

$$PV \text{ (bond)} = 103.3730$$

$$103.3730 = 3.4214 + 3.3429 + \frac{103.50}{(1 + SR_{1.50})^{1.50}}$$

$$96.6089 = \frac{103.50}{(1 + SR_{1.50})^{1.50}}$$

$$96.6089^*(1 + SR_{1.50})^{1.50} = 103.50$$

$$(1 + SR_{1.50})^{1.50} = \frac{103.50}{96.6089} = 1.071332$$

$$SR_{1.50} = (1.071332)^{(1/1.50)} - 1 = 0.047007, \text{ or } 4.70\%$$

This three-step process is repeated for all other terms to maturity. It is then possible to construct an implied spot rate yield curve. Table 23.4 details all the implied spot rates calculated from the data in Table 23.3.

In Figure 23.2 we have plotted the term structure of the spot rates for maturities from 0.5 to five years. You can see from the plot that investors required a return of 4.65 per cent for a half-year investment, 4.98 per cent for a three-year investment and 5.25 per cent for a five-year investment.

We can use a similar idea to check that bonds of different maturity are consistently priced. For example, suppose that the price of each bond depends only on what happens to the short-term rate of interest. Then you could exactly duplicate the payoffs on any bond by holding a mixture of two other bonds. If both investments give the same payoff, you know that they should sell for the same price. If they do not, you unload the expensive investment and buy the cheap one. We will have more to say about these new theories later.

**table 23.4**

Spot yields for maturities 0.50 to five years

| Terms to maturity | Spot rate |
| :---: | :---: |
| 0.5 | 4.65 |
| 1.0 | 4.70 |
| 1.5 | 4.70 |
| 2.0 | 4.76 |
| 2.5 | 4.92 |
| 3.0 | 4.98 |
| 3.5 | 5.02 |
| 4.0 | 5.08 |
| 4.5 | 5.14 |
| 5.0 | 5.25 |

**figure 23.2**

Australian spot yield curve for maturities of 0.5 to five years, March 1999.

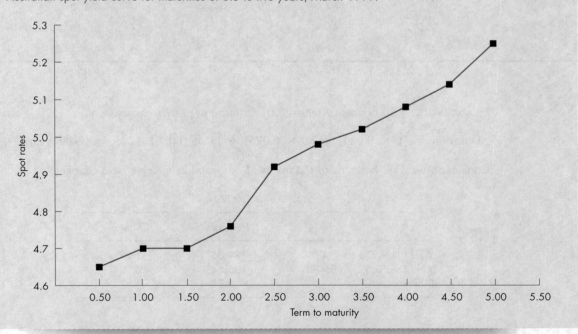

## 23.3 Duration and volatility

We now need to look more carefully at the variability of long-term and short-term bonds. But what do we mean by these phrases? For example, a bond that matures in year 6 also makes interest payments in each of years 1 through to 5. Therefore, it is somewhat misleading to describe the bond as a six-year bond; the average time to each cash flow is less than six years.

Assume that in August 1995, Commonwealth Treasury 9.50 August 2002 bonds had a present value of 108.25 and yielded 7.92 per cent. Table 23.5 shows where this present value comes from. Notice that the cash flow in year 7 accounts for only 59.30 per cent of value. About 40 per cent of the value comes from earlier cash flows.

Bond analysts often use the term **duration** to describe the average time to each payment. If we call the total value of the bond $V$, then duration is calculated as follows:[22]

$$\text{Duration} = \left[\frac{1 \times \text{PV}(C_1)}{V}\right] + \left[\frac{2 \times \text{PV}(C_2)}{V}\right] + \left[\frac{3 \times \text{PV}(C_3)}{V}\right] + \ldots$$

**table 23.5**

The first four columns show that the cash flow in year 7 accounts for only 59.30 per cent value of the 9.50 per cent August 2003 bond. The final column shows how to calculate a weighted average of the time to each cash flow. This average is the bond's duration.

| Year | C | PV(C) at 7.92 | Proportion of total value PV(C)/V | Proportion of total value × time |
|------|------|---------------|-----------------------------------|----------------------------------|
| 1 | 95 | 88.03 | 0.081 | 0.081 |
| 2 | 95 | 81.57 | 0.075 | 0.150 |
| 3 | 95 | 75.58 | 0.070 | 0.210 |
| 4 | 95 | 70.04 | 0.065 | 0.260 |
| 5 | 95 | 64.90 | 0.060 | 0.300 |
| 6 | 95 | 60.13 | 0.056 | 0.336 |
| 7 | 1095 | 642.24 | 0.593 | 4.151 |
| | | $V = 1082.59$ | 1.000 | Duration = 5.488 years |

Hence, for the 9.50 per cent August 2002 Commonwealth Treasury bond,

$$\text{Duration} = [1 \times 0.081] + [2 \times 0.075] + [3 \times 0.070] + \ldots = 5.488 \text{ years}$$

Consider now what happens to the prices of our bond as interest rates change:

9.5% August 2002 bond

| | New price | Change |
|---|-----------|--------|
| Yield falls 0.5% (to 7.42%) | 111.05 | +2.59% |
| Yield rises 0.5% (to 8.42%) | 105.54 | −2.50% |
| Difference | 5.51 | |

---

[22] We assume annual interest payments. Actual payments are semiannual.

Thus, a 100 basis point variation in yield causes the price of the 9.5 per cent coupon bonds to change by 5.09 per cent. We can say that the bond has a volatility of 5.09 per cent.

Bond analysts are able to use this measure to provide summary information regarding the sensitivity of bonds to yield and price changes. This is useful when attempting to assess the impact of yield changes on a portfolio and if attempting to choose between available bonds.

A further measure used by bond analysts to assess the relationship between the bond's volatility and its duration is a measurement known as modified duration. This measure captures the positive relationship between the bond's duration and its volatility:[23]

$$\text{Modified duration} = \text{volatility (per cent)} = \frac{\text{duration}}{(1 + \text{yield})}$$

In the case of the 9.5 per cent coupon bond,

$$\text{Volatility (per cent)} = \frac{5.488}{(1 + 0.0792)} = 5.085248$$

$$= 5.09\%$$

Volatility is a useful summary measure of the likely effect of a change in interest rates on the value of a bond. The longer a bond's duration and/or the lower the coupon rate, the greater its volatility. In Chapter 25 we will make use of this relationship between duration and volatility to describe how firms can protect themselves against interest rate changes. Here is an example that should give you a flavour of things to come.

Suppose your firm has promised to make retirement pension payments to retired employees. The discounted value of these pension payments is $1 million and therefore the firm puts aside $1 million in the pension fund and invests that money in government bonds. So, the firm has a liability of $1 million and (through the pension fund) an offsetting asset of $1 million.

But, as interest rates fluctuate, the value of the pension liability will change and so will the value of the bonds in the pension fund. How can the firm ensure that the value of the bonds is always sufficient to meet the liabilities? Answer: By making sure that the duration of the government bonds is the same as the duration of the pension liability.

## 23.4 Explaining the term structure

The term structure of interest rates and the yield curve are terms that are often used synonymously to describe the relationship between interest rates and the time to maturity.

When investors speak of the yield curve they are generally referring to the curve that links the yield to maturity of available government securities. From time to time, short-dated securities may trade at lower rates than longer-dated securities (ascending yield curve); short-dated securities may trade at higher yields than longer-dated securities (descending yield curve); short-, medium- and long-term rates may be the same (flat yield curve); or medium-term rates may be higher than both short- and long-term rates (humped back yield curve).

---

[23] Modified duration is related to the approximate percentage change in price for a given change in yield:

$$\frac{\Delta}{\Delta y} \times \frac{1}{P} = \frac{1}{(1 + y)} duration$$

$$\frac{\Delta P}{\Delta y} \times \frac{1}{P} = -modified\ duration$$

$$\frac{\Delta P}{P} = -modified\ duration \times \Delta yield$$

Modified duration is also related to the appropriate dollar change in yield:

$$\frac{\Delta P}{\Delta y} \times \frac{1}{P} = -modified\ duration$$

$$\Delta P = -modified\ duration \times P \times \Delta y$$

Over time, the shape of the yield curve will shift. Figure 23.3 shows a plot of monthly data for overnight cash rates and 10-year government bonds from January 1984 to December 1998. The plot highlights that at different times the longer dated 10-year bond rate is either above, near or below the short-term cash rate. A clearer assessment of the relationship, which also gives some insight into the changes in the shape of the yield curve, is given in Figure 23.4, which plots the differences in the rate (10-year cash rate). A positive number indicates an ascending yield curve, while a negative number indicates a descending yield curve. If the rates are equal it is very likely that the yield curve is either flat or humped during this period.

Analysis of the two figures reveals that the yield curve was ascending (indicating the long-term rates were higher than the short-term rates) in the periods January 1984 to March 1985, May 1987 to June 1988 and from May 1991 to December 1998. The yield curve was descending in the periods April 1985 to April 1986, August 1986 to May 1987 and July 1988 to August 1990. In the other periods the yield curve was going through periods of transition and was either flat or humped.

Why do we see these shifts in the term structure over time? The changes are mostly driven by changes in the demand and supply of funds at different maturities along the yield curve and by arbitrage constraints that prevent rates from erratically fluctuating over time.

Let us demonstrate with the following simple example involving two investors—Ms Long and Mr Short.

## Ms Long's problem

Ms Long wants to invest $1000 for two years. Two strategies open to her are described in Table 23.6. Strategy L1 is to put the money in a one-year bond at an interest rate of $r_1$. At the end of the year she must then take her money and find another one-year bond. Let us call the rate of interest on this second bond $_1r_2$—that is, the spot rate of interest at time 1 on a loan maturing at time 2.[24] As Table 23.6 shows, the final payoff to this strategy is $1000(1 + r_1)(1 + _1r_2)$.

**table 23.6**

Two investment strategies for Ms Long, who wants to invest $1000 for two years.

| Strategy | Now | Year 1 | Year 2 (final payoff) |
|---|---|---|---|
| L1: Invest in two 1-year bonds | $1000 ⟶ | $1000 (1 + $r_1$) ⟶ Invest in first bond yielding $r_1$ | $1000 (1 + $r_1$)(1 + $_1r_2$) Invest in second bond yielding $_1r_2$ |
| L2: Invest in one 2-year bond | $1000 ⟶ | | $1000 (1 + $r_2$)$^2$ Invest in bond yielding $r_2$ |
| Strategy L2 can be expressed as | $1000 ⟶ | $1000 (1 + $r_1$) ⟶ Invest for 1 year at $r_1$ | $1000 (1 + $r_1$)(1 + $_1f_2$) Invest for second year at implicit forward rate $_1f_2$ |

Of course, Ms Long cannot know for sure what the one-year spot rate of interest $_1r_2$ will be at the start of the second year. Suppose that she *expects* it to be 11 per cent. That is, $E(_1r_2) = 0.11$. The current one-period spot rate is 10 per cent. The expected final payoff is

$$1000(1 + r_1)[1 + E(_1r_2)] = 1000(1 + 0.10)(1 + 0.11)$$
$$= \$1221$$

---

[24]   Be careful to distinguish $_1r_2$ from $r_2$, the spot rate on a two-year bond held from time 0 to time 2. The quantity $_1r_2$ is a *one-year* spot rate established today for a one-year bond held from time 1 to time 2.

**figure 23.3**
Cash rates and 10-year bond rates, 1984–98.

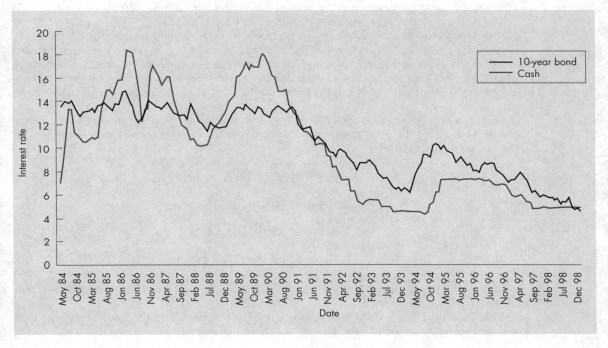

**figure 23.4**
Difference between cash rates and 10-year bond rates, 1984–98.

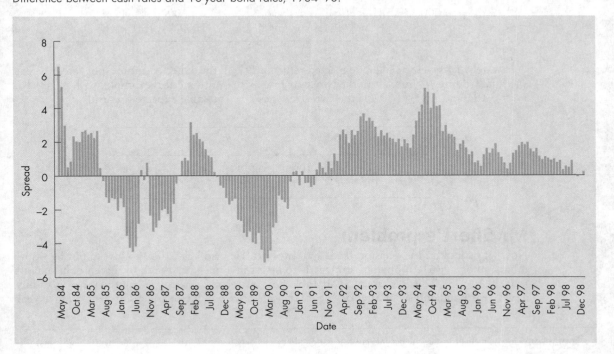

Instead of making two separate investments of one year each, Ms Long could invest her money today in a bond that pays off in year 2 (strategy L2 in Table 23.6). That is, she would invest the *two-year* spot rate $r_2$, and receive a final payoff of $1000 (1 + r_2)^2$.

If $r_2 = 10.5$ per cent, the payoff is $1000(1 + 0.105)^2 = \$1221$

Now look below the dashed line in Table 23.6. The table shows that strategy L2 can be re-interpreted as investing for one year at the spot rate $r_1$ and for the second year at a **forward rate** $_1f_2$.[25] The forward rate is the extra return that Ms Long gets by lending for two years rather than one. This forward rate is *implicit* in the two-year spot rate $r_2$. It is also *guaranteed*: by buying the two-year bond, Ms Long can 'lock in' an interest rate of $_1f_2$ for the second year.

Suppose that the two-year spot rate is 10.5 per cent as before. Then the forward rate $_1f_2$ must be 11 per cent. By definition, this forward rate is the implicit interest rate in the second year of the two-year loan:

$$(1 + r_2)^2 = (1 + r_1)(1 + {}_1f_2)$$

$$(1.105)^2 = (1.10)(1 + {}_1f_2)$$

$${}_1f_2 = \frac{(1.105)^2}{1.10} - 1$$

$${}_1f_2 = 0.110023, \text{ or } 11\%$$

The two-year spot rate of 10.5 per cent is an average of the 10 per cent one-year spot rate and the 11 per cent forward rate.

What should Ms Long do? One possible answer is that she should follow the strategy that gives the highest *expected* payoff. That is, she should compare:

| Expected payoff to strategy L1 | To | (Certain) payoff to strategy L2 |
|---|---|---|
| $1000(1 + r_1)[1 + E({}_1r_2)]$ | to<br>or to | $1000(1 + r_2)^2$<br>$1000(1 + r_1)(1 + {}_1f_2)$ |

Strategy L1 gives the higher expected return if $E({}_1r_2)$, the expected future spot rate, exceeds the forward rate $_1f_2$ implicit in the two-year rate $r_2$. In our numerical example, with $r_1 = 0.10$, $r_2 = 0.105$ and $E({}_1r_2) = 0.11$, the two strategies give the same expected return:

| Strategy | Payoff |
|---|---|
| L1 | $1000(1.10)(1.11) = \$1221$ (expected) |
| L2 | $1000(1.105)^2 = \$1221$ (certain) |

## Mr Short's problem

Now let us look at the decision faced by Mr Short. He also has $1000 to invest, but he wants it back in one year. An obvious strategy is to invest in a one-year bond. In this case, his payoff is $1000(1 + r_1)$. This is strategy S1 in Table 23.7. A second strategy (S2 in the table) is to buy a two-year bond and sell it after one year. The sale price will be the bond's present value in year

---

[25]  Forward rates are equivalent to the one-period spot rate expected at some date in the future.

1. At that time, the bond will have one year to maturity. Its present value will be equal to its year 2 payoff $1000(1 + r_2)^2$ discounted at $_1r_2$, the one-period spot rate prevailing in year 1:

$$\text{PV of 2-year bond at year 1} = \frac{1000(1 + r_2)^2}{(1 + {}_1r_2)}$$

**table 23.7**

Two investment strategies for Mr Short, who wants to invest $1000 for one year.

| Strategy | Now | | Year 1 (final payoff) |
|---|---|---|---|
| S1: Invest in 1-year bond | $1000 | Invest at $r_1$ | $1000(1 + r_1)$ |
| S2: Invest in 2-year bond, but sell in 1 year | $1000 | Invest, sell for PV at year 1 | $\dfrac{\$1000(1 + r_2)^2}{1 + {}_1r_2}$ |

We know from Ms Long's problem that the two-period rate $r_2$ can be expressed in terms of the one-period spot rate $r_1$ and the forward rate $_1f_2$. Thus

$$\text{PV of 2-year bond at year 1} = \frac{1000(1 + r_1)(1 + {}_1f_2)}{(1 + {}_1r_2)}$$

Of course, Mr Short cannot predict the future spot rate, and therefore he cannot predict the price at year 1 of the two-year bond. But if $r_2 = 0.105$, and he expects the spot rate to be $_1r_2 = 0.11$, then the expected price is:

$$\frac{1000(1.105)^2}{1.11} = \frac{1221}{1.11} = \$1100$$

What should Mr Short do? Suppose that he prefers the strategy that gives the highest expected payoff. Then he should compare:[26]

| (Certain) payoff to strategy S1 | To | Expected payoff to strategy S2 |
|---|---|---|
| $1000(1 + r_1)$ | to | $\dfrac{1000(1 + r_1)^2}{1 + E({}_1r_2)}$ |

---

[26] Here we are making an approximation because the expected payoff of S2 in $t = 1$ is not exactly equal to
$$\frac{1000(1 + r_2)^2}{(1 + E({}_1r_2))}$$
We should calculate the expected price of the two-year bond at $t = 1$. Call this $\widetilde{P}$. By definition:
$$\widetilde{P} = \frac{1000(1 + r_2)^2}{1 + {}_1\tilde{r}_2} \quad \text{where } {}_1\tilde{r}_2 \text{ denotes that the interest rate is random}$$
and
$$E(\widetilde{P}) = E\left[\frac{1000(1 + r_2)^2}{1 + {}_1\tilde{r}_2}\right]$$
but
$$E\left[\frac{1000(1 + r_2)^2}{1 + {}_1\tilde{r}_2}\right] \text{ is only approximately equal to } \frac{1000(1 + r_2)^2}{(1 + E({}_1r_2))}$$
In general for any positive random variable $\tilde{x}$, $E\left[\dfrac{1}{\tilde{x}}\right]$ is greater than $\dfrac{1}{E(\tilde{x})}$.
This is called *Jensen's inequality*. Ignoring Jensen's inequality can be dangerous if the variance of $\tilde{x}$ is large.

Strategy S2 is better if the forward rate $f_2$ exceeds the expected future spot rate $E(_1r_2)$. If Mr Short faces the same interest rates as Ms Long [$r_1 = 0.10$, $r_2 = 0.105$, $E(_1r_2) = 0.11$, $_1f_2 = 0.11$], the two strategies give the same expected return:

| Strategy | Payoff |
|---|---|
| S1 | $1000(1.10) = \$1100$ (certain) |
| S2 | $\dfrac{[1000(1.105)^2]}{1.11} = \dfrac{[1000(1.10)(1.11)]}{1.11} = \$1100$ (expected) |

## The expectations hypothesis

You can see that if the world is made up of people like Ms Long and Mr Short, all trying to maximise their expected return, then one-year and two-year bonds can exist side by side only if

$$_1f_2 = E(_1r_2)$$

This condition was satisfied in our numerical example—both $_1f_2$ and $E(_1r_2)$ equalled 11 per cent. But what happens if the forward rate exceeds the expected future spot rate? Then both Ms Long and Mr Short prefer investing in two-year bonds. If the world were made up entirely of expected return maximisers, and $_1f_2$ exceeds $E(_1r_2)$, no one would be willing to hold one-year bonds. On the other hand, if the forward rate were less than the expected future spot rate, no one would be willing to hold two-year bonds. Since investors *do* hold both one- and two-year bonds, it follows that forward rates of interest must equal expected future spot rates (providing that investors are interested only in expected return).

This is the *expectations hypothesis* of the term structure.[27] It says that the *only* reason for an upward-sloping term structure is that investors expect future spot rates to be higher than current spot rates; and the *only* reason for a declining term structure is that investors expect spot rates to fall below current levels. The expectations hypothesis also implies that investing in short-term bonds (as in strategies L1 and S1) gives exactly the same expected return as investing in long-term bonds (as in strategies L2 and S2).

## The liquidity-preference theory

Unfortunately, the expectations theory says nothing about risk. Look back for a moment at our two simple cases. Ms Long wants to invest for two years. If she buys a two-year bond, she can nail down her final payoff today. If she buys a one-year bond, she knows her return for the first year but she does not know at what rate she will be able to re-invest her money. If she does not like this uncertainty, she will tend to prefer the two-year bond, and she will hold the one-year bond only if

$$E(_1r_2) \text{ is greater than } _1f_2$$

What about Mr Short? He wants to invest for one year. If he invests in a one-year bond, he can nail down his payoff today. If he buys the two-year bond, he will have to sell it next

---

27    The expectations hypothesis is usually attributed to Lutz and Lutz. See F. A. Lutz and V. C. Lutz, *The Theory of Investment in the Firm*, Princeton University Press, Princeton, N.J., 1951.

year at an unknown price. If he does not like this uncertainty, he will prefer the one-year investment, and he will hold two-year bonds only if

$$E(_1r_2) \text{ is less than } _1f_2$$

Here we have the basis for the *liquidity-preference theory* of term structure.[28] Other things being equal, Ms Long will prefer to invest in two-year bonds and Mr Short in one-year bonds. If more companies want to issue two-year bonds than there are Ms Longs to hold them, they will need to offer a bonus to tempt some of the Mr Shorts to hold them. Conversely, if more companies want to issue one-year bonds than there are Mr Shorts to hold them, they will need to offer a bonus to tempt some of the Ms Longs to hold them.

Any bonus shows up as a difference between forward rates and expected future spot rates. This difference is usually called the *liquidity premium*.

Advocates of the liquidity-preference theory believe that for the most part there is a shortage of lenders like Ms Long. In this case, the liquidity premium is positive and the forward rate will exceed the expected spot rate. A positive liquidity premium rewards investors for lending long by offering them higher long-term rates of interest. Thus, if this view is right, the term structure should be upward sloping more often than not. Of course, if future spot rates are expected to fall, the term structure could be downward sloping and *still* reward investors for lending long. But the liquidity-preference theory would predict a less dramatic downward slope than the expectations hypothesis would.

# Introducing inflation

We argued above that Ms Long could nail down her return by investing in two-year bonds. What do we mean by that? If the bonds are issued by the Australian government, she can be virtually certain that she will be paid the promised number of dollars. But she cannot be certain what that money will buy. The expectations hypothesis and the liquidity-preference theory of term structure implicitly assume that future inflation rates are known. Let us consider the opposite case in which the *only* uncertainty about interest rates stems from uncertainty about inflation.[29]

Suppose that Irving Fisher is right, and short rates of interest always incorporate fully the market's latest views about inflation. Suppose also that the market learns more as time passes about the likely inflation rate in a particular year. Perhaps today it has only a very hazy idea about inflation in year 2, but in a year's time it expects to be able to make a much better prediction.

Because future inflation rates are never known with certainty, neither Ms Long nor Mr Short can make a completely risk-free investment. But since they expect to learn a good deal about the inflation rate in year 2 from experience in year 1, next year they will be in a much better position to judge the appropriate interest rate in year 2. It is therefore more risky for either of them to make a forward commitment to lend in year 2. Even Ms Long, who wants to invest for two years, would be incurring unnecessary risk by buying a two-year bond. Her least risky strategy is to invest in successive one-year bonds. She does not know what her reinvestment rate will be, but at least she knows that it will incorporate the latest information about inflation in year 2.

Of course, this means that borrowers must offer some incentive if they want investors to lend long. Therefore, the forward rate of interest $f_2$ must be greater than the expected spot rate $E(_1r_2)$ by an amount that compensates investors for the extra inflation risk.

---

28  The liquidity-preference theory is usually attributed to Hicks. See J. R. Hicks, *Value and Capital: An Inquiry into Some Fundamental Principles of Economic Theory*, 2nd ed., Oxford University Press, Oxford, 1946. For a theoretical development see R. Roll, *The Behaviour of Interest Rates: An Application of the Efficient Market Model to U.S. Treasury Bills*, Basic Books, Inc., New York, 1979.

29  The following is adapted from R. A. Brealey and S. M. Schaefer, 'Term Structure and Uncertain Inflation', *Journal of Finance*, **32**: 277–90 (May 1977).

## example

Suppose that the real interest rate is always 2 per cent. Nominal interest rates therefore equal 2 per cent plus the expected rate of inflation. Suppose that the *expected* inflation rate is 8 per cent for both year 1 and year 2. However, inflation may accelerate to 10 per cent in year 1, or it may decrease to 6 per cent. To keep things simple, assume that the actual inflation rate for year 1 continues for year 2:

|  | Actual inflation in year 1 | Actual inflation in year 2 |
|---|---|---|
| Expected inflation rate = 0.08 | 0.10 | 0.10 |
|  | 0.08 | 0.08 |
|  | 0.06 | 0.06 |

Each outcome has a probability of 1/3.

Now reconsider Ms Long's problem. Suppose that she can lend for either one or two years at 10 per cent (the 2 per cent real rate plus the 8 per cent inflation rate). If she invests in a one-year bond, she will get 1000(1.1) = $1100 in year 1. This amount is re-invested, but at what rate? The answer is that the future spot rate $_1r_2$ will be 2 per cent plus the inflation rate experience in year 1 and projected for year 2:

| Actual inflation rate | Spot interest rate in year 1 |
|---|---|
| 0.10 | 0.12 |
| 0.08 | 0.10 |
| 0.06 | 0.08 |

Thus, the final payoffs to lending short are:

|  | Year 1 | Re-invest at | Final payoff in year 2 |
|---|---|---|---|
|  | 1100 | $_1r_2 = 0.12$ | 1232 |
| Invest for first year | 1100 | $_1r_2 = 0.10$ | 1210 |
| At $r_1 = 0.10$ | 1100 | $_1r_2 = 0.08$ | 1188 |

Now Ms Long could lock in a $1210 payoff in year 2 by purchasing a two-year bond at 10 per cent $[1000(1 + r_2)^2 = 1000(1 + 0.10)^2 = \$1210]$. But this would not lock in her *real* return. In fact, lending short is the *safer* strategy when the final payoffs are converted back to current dollars:

| Strategy | Final payoffs | Inflation rate | Inflation-adjusted payoffs[a] |
|---|---|---|---|
| Buy 2-year bond | 1210 | 0.10 | 1000 |
|  | 1210 | 0.08 | 1037 |
|  | 1210 | 0.06 | 1077 |

| Strategy | Final payoffs | Inflation rate | Inflation-adjusted payoffs[a] |
|----------|---------------|----------------|-------------------------------|
| Buy 1-year bond | 1232 | 0.10 | 1018 |
|          | 1210 | 0.08 | 1037 |
|          | 1188 | 0.06 | 1057 |

*Note:*

[a] *The inflation-adjusted payoffs are calculated by dividing by* $(1 + i)^2$. *In this case i is the actual inflation rate.*

# A comparison of theories of the term structure

We have described three views about why changes to long and short interest rates differ—the expectations hypothesis, the liquidity-premium theory and the inflation-premium theory. The first view, the expectations hypothesis, is somewhat extreme and not fully supported by the facts. Empirical testing in Australia has found very mixed results. For example, studies by Juttner, Tuckwell and Luedecke,[30] and by Kearney, MacDonald and Hillier,[31] using data from the 1980s, found little support for the expectations hypothesis. However, a study by Tease[32] and another by Alles[33] using data from both the 1980s and 1990s found some support for the hypothesis. A study by Yip[34] in 1991 using New Zealand data also found support for the hypothesis.[35]

The expectations hypothesis has few strict adherents, but Fama's study in 1984 confirms that long-term interest rates do reflect, in part, investors' expectations about future short-term rates. Our other two theories both suggest that long-term bonds ought to offer some additional return to compensate for their additional risk. The liquidity-preference theory supposes that risk comes solely from uncertainty about the underlying real rates. This may be a fair approximation in periods of price stability such as the 1960s and 1990s. The inflation-premium theory supposes that the risk comes solely from uncertainty about the inflation rate, which may be a fair approximation in periods of fluctuating inflation such as the 1970s and 1980s.

If short-term rates of interest are significantly lower than long-term rates, it is often tempting to borrow short term rather than long term. Our discussion of term structure theories should serve to warn against naïve strategies. One reason for higher long rates could be that short rates are expected to rise in the future. Also, investors who buy long bonds may be accepting liquidity or inflation risks for which they correctly want compensation. You should borrow short when the term structure is upward sloping only if you feel that investors are *overestimating* the risks of lending long.

---

30   See J. Juttner, R. Tuckwell and D. Luedecke, 'Are Expectations of Short-Term Interest Rates Rational?', *Australian Economic Papers*, pp. 356–69 (December 1985).

31   See C. Kearney, R. MacDonald and J. Hillier, 'The Efficiency of the Market for Bank Accepted Bills', *The Economic Record*, pp. 225–33 (September 1989).

32   See W. J. Tease, 'The Expectations Theory of the Term Structure of Interest Rates in Australia', *The Economic Record*, pp. 120–7 (June 1988).

33   See L. A. Alles, 'Time Varying Risk Premium and the Predictive Power of the Term Structure of Interest Rates', *Accounting and Finance*, 35 (2): 77–96 (1995).

34   See H. Yip, 'The Information Content and Usefulness of the Term Structure of the New Zealand Bank Bill Market', *Accounting and Finance*, 31 (2): 1–12 (1991).

35   The expectations hypothesis states that if the forward rate of interest is 1 per cent above the spot rate of interest, then your best estimate is that the spot rate of interest will rise by 1 per cent. In a study of the American Treasury bill market between 1959 and 1982, Eugene Fama found that a forward premium *does* on average precede a rise in the spot rate, but the rise is less than the expectations hypothesis would predict. See E. F. Fama, 'The Information in the Term Structure', *Journal of Financial Economics*, 13: 509–28 (December 1984).

If the risk of bond investment comes primarily from uncertainty about the real rate, then the safest strategy for investors is to hold bonds that match their liabilities. For example, the firm's pension fund generally has long-term liabilities. The liquidity-preference theory, therefore, implies that the pension fund should favour long-term bonds. If the risk comes from uncertainty about the inflation rate, then the safest strategy is to hold short bonds. For example, most pension funds have real liabilities that depend on the level of wage inflation. The inflation-premium theory implies that, if a superannuation fund wants to minimise risk, it should favour short-term bonds.

## *Some new theories of the term structure

These term structure theories tell us how bond prices may be determined at a point in time. More recently, financial economists have proposed some important theories of how price *movements* of different bonds are related.

The basic idea underlying these new theories is that the returns on bonds with different maturities tend to move together. For example, if short-term interest rates are high, it is a good bet that long-term rates will be high also. If short-term rates fall, long-term rates usually keep them company.

These linkages between interest-rate movements can tell us something about consistent relationships between bond prices. Let us illustrate.[36]

**figure 23.5**

The current one-year interest rate is 8 per cent. We assume that in each future year the rate will either halve or increase 1.5 times.

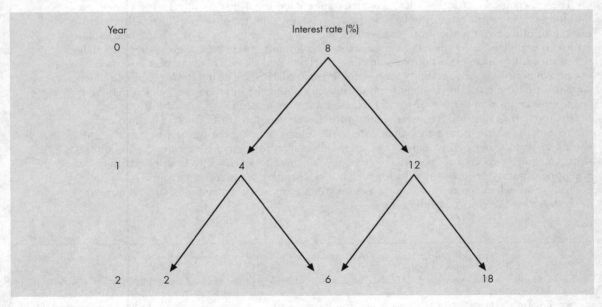

Each branch in Figure 23.5 shows what could happen to the short-term rate of interest. The rate is currently 8 per cent, but next period we assume that it could either halve to 4 per cent or rise to 12 per cent. Then in period 2 it could again either halve or rise 1.5 times, giving possible interest rates of 2, 6 or 18 per cent.

---

[36]  We are grateful to John Cox, from whom we have borrowed and adapted the following example.

**figure 23.6**

We show here how the yield to maturity and the price of three bonds might vary with the short-term rate of interest (shown in Figure 23.5). These bonds offer the same expected reward per unit of risk.

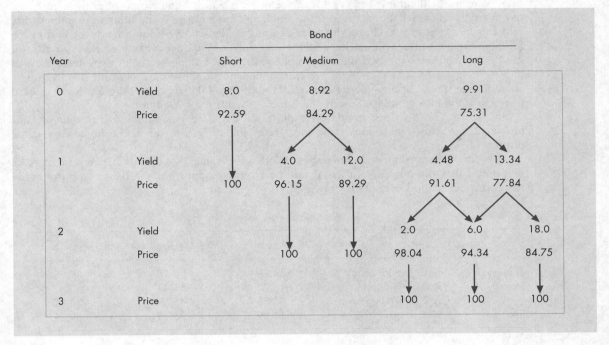

Figure 23.6 shows the prices of two zero coupon bonds, which we have called *Short* and *Medium* (for the moment ignore the third bond, *Long*). Each branch in the diagram shows how the price for the two bonds and their yield to maturity will vary, depending on what happens to the short-term interest rate:

1.  Short is a one-year bond that pays off 100 in period 1. It offers the one-year interest rate of 8 per cent and is therefore priced at 100/1.08 = $92.59.
2.  Medium is a two-year bond. We know that next year the one-year interest rate is equally likely to be 4 per cent or 12 per cent. So in year 1 there is a 50 per cent chance that Medium will be priced at 100/1.04 = $96.15 or 100/1.12 = $89.29. The expected price is (0.5 × 96.15) + (0.5 × 89.29) = 92.72.

The return from Short is a sure fire 8 per cent. But the return from Medium is uncertain. Since investors do not like this uncertainty, they will require a higher expected return to compensate. Suppose that they demand a premium to invest in Medium of 2 per cent over the 8 per cent risk-free rate and therefore price it at 92.72/1.10 = $84.29. At this price they stand to make a return of 14.07 per cent if interest rates fall and 5.93 per cent if they rise. The spread of possible returns is 14.07 – 5.93 = 8.14 per cent. So we can say that the ratio of reward to risk on Medium is:

$$\frac{\text{Expected risk premium (\%)}}{\text{Spread of possible returns (\%)}} = \frac{2}{8.14} = 0.246^{37}$$

---

37　Where there are only two possible outcomes, it is acceptable to measure risk by the range of outcomes. If there were many possible outcomes, this would not be the case.

In a well-functioning market all bonds must be priced to offer the same ratio of expected reward to risk. So we can now use this information about the price of the medium bond to value any other bond. The third bond shown in Figure 23.6 is a three-year bond, Long. At each point in the diagram we have added the price at which Long would offer the same ratio of reward to risk as Medium. For example, look at what happens if the short-term interest rate falls to 4 per cent in year 1 and the price of Long is $91.61. We know that at the end of the following year its price will be either $94.04 (a return of 7.01 per cent) or $94.34 (a return of 2.98 per cent). Since the two outcomes are equally likely, Long offers an expected return of $(0.5 \times 7.01) + (0.5 \times 2.97) = 4.99$ per cent, 0.99 per cent above the 4 per cent risk-free interest rate. The spread of possible returns is $7.01 - 2.98 = 4.04$ per cent and the ratio of reward to risk is $0.99/4.04 = 0.246$, exactly the same as the ratio for Medium.

In Figure 23.6 all three bonds offer the same expected risk premium per unit of risk. However, the three-year bond is the most risky and therefore offers the highest expected return.[38]

Why do we say that each bond has to offer the same risk premium per unit of risk? Because, if they did not do so, there would be arbitrage opportunities. To see why this is the case, consider the following two strategies:

|  |  | Cash flow today | Cash flow year 1 Interest rate = 4% | Interest rate = 12% |
|---|---|---|---|---|
| Strategy 1: | Buy 1 Medium bond | −84.29 | +96.15 | +89.29 |
| Strategy 2: | Buy 0.5047 Short bonds | −46.73 | +50.47 | +50.47 |
|  | Buy 0.4887 Long bonds | −37.56 | +45.68 | +38.82 |
| Total |  | −84.29 | +96.15 | +89.29 |

Notice that, regardless of whether interest rates rise or fall, Medium provides exactly the same payoff as a mixture of Short and Long. Since the two investments provide the same payoffs, they must cost the same today—that is, they must cost $84.29.

Suppose that the price of Medium is greater than $84.29 and all other prices are unchanged. Then Medium would offer a lower reward for risk than the other two bonds and you could make an arbitrage by selling one Medium bond and buying a package of the other two.

If you read about options in Chapter 20, you may remember that we were able to price an option by designing a package of the risk-free asset and an ordinary share that would give the same payoffs as the option. We are using the same idea here. To value the medium bond we constructed a package of a risk-free short-term bond and a long-term bond that provided identical payoffs.

We can also borrow another idea from Chapter 20. We have seen that, if the medium bond does not sell for the same price as the equivalent package of short and long bonds, then there are arbitrage opportunities. Regardless of investors' attitudes to risk, such arbitrage opportunities cannot exist if securities are fairly priced. So, even if investors are totally indifferent to risk, the two equivalent packages must sell for the same price. This suggests an alternative way to value the medium bond. We can *pretend* that investors are indifferent to risk, work out the expected bond payoffs in such a world and discount at the risk-free interest rate. Let us check that this gives the same set of bond values.

Look, for example, at the returns that are offered by the long bond in year 1. If interest rates fall, the bond provides a return of $(91.61/75.31) - 1 = 21.64$ per cent; if rates rise, it

---

[38]  Notice that Long has the longest duration and therefore the greatest volatility.

provides a return of $(77.84/75.31) - 1 = 3.36$ per cent. If investors are indifferent to risk and the expected return is equal to the 8 per cent risk-free interest rate, then:

(Probability of interest rate fall × 21.64) + [(1 − probability of interest fall × 3.36] = 8%

Therefore:

$$\text{Probability of interest rate fall} = 0.254$$

Now we can use this (pretend) probability to price the medium bond. We know that if interest rates fall, Medium will be worth $96.15 and that if they rise it will be worth $89.29. So, if investors are indifferent to risk, the expected value of Medium in year 1 is:

$$(0.254 \times 96.15) + (0.746 \times 89.29) = \$91.03$$

The current value of Medium is therefore

$$\frac{\text{Expected future value}}{1 + \text{interest rate}} = \frac{91.03}{1.08} = \$84.29$$

the same value that we obtained by constructing a replicating portfolio.

Our simple example should give you a flavour for these modern theories of term structure, but you can probably think of a number of improvements that would make the example more realistic. First, short-term interest rates have more built-in suitability than we implied. If they rise this year, they are more likely to fall back to a 'normal' level next year. If they fall next year, they are more likely to bounce back later. Second, short-term interest rates fluctuate more than long-term rates. Third, short-term and long-term rates do not move in perfect lockstep, as our example implied. Sometimes, for example, short-term rates rise, but the spread between short-term and long-term rates falls. In this case, it might be more realistic to assume that the return on each bond depends on the change in both the short-term interest rate and the spread between the long and short rates. Making the model more realistic also makes it more complex, but if we know how interest rates can change and how the returns on different bonds are linked, we can still say something about consistent patterns of bond prices.

## 23.5 Allowing for the risk of default

You should by now be familiar with some of the basic ideas about the two questions 'Why do interest rates change?' and 'Why short rates may differ from long rates'. It only remains to consider our third question: 'Why do some borrowers have to pay a higher rate of interest than others?'

The answer is obvious: 'Bond prices go down, and interest rates go up, when the probability of default increases.' But when we say 'interest rates go up', we mean *promised* interest rates. If the borrower defaults, the *actual* interest rate paid to the lender is less than the promised rate. The *expected* interest rate may go up with increasing probability of default, but this is not a logical necessity.

These points can be illustrated by a simple numerical example. Suppose that the interest rate on one-year, *risk-free* bonds is 9 per cent. Back-a-Bourke Chemicals Ltd (BBCL) has issued 9 per cent notes with face values of $100, maturing in one year. What will the BBCL notes sell for?

The answer is easy—if the notes are risk-free, just discount principal ($100) and interest ($9) at 9 per cent:

$$\text{PV of notes} = \frac{(\$100 + 9)}{1.09} = \$100$$

Suppose, instead, that there is a 20 per cent chance that BBCL will default. If default does occur, holders of its notes receive nothing. In this case, the possible payoffs to the noteholder are:

|  | Payoff | Probability |
| --- | --- | --- |
| Full payment | $109 | 0.80 |
| No payment | 0 | 0.20 |

The expected payment is 0.8($109) + 0.2($0) = $87.20

We can value the BBCL notes like any other risky asset, by discounting their expected payoffs ($87.20) at the appropriate opportunity cost of capital. We might discount at the risk-free interest rate (9 per cent) if BBCL's possible default is totally unrelated to other events in the economy. In this case the default risk is wholly diversifiable, and the beta of the notes is zero. The notes would sell for

$$\text{PV of notes} = \frac{\$87.20}{1.09} = \$80$$

An investor who purchased these notes for $80 would receive a *promised* yield of about 36 per cent:

$$\text{Promised yield} = \frac{\$109}{\$80} - 1 = 0.363, \text{ or } 36.30\%$$

That is, an investor who purchased the notes for $80 would earn a 36.30 per cent rate of return *if* BBCL does not default. Bond traders therefore might say that the BBCL notes 'yield 36 per cent'. But the smart investor would realise that the notes' *expected* yield is only 9 per cent, the same as on risk-free bonds.

This, of course, assumes that risk of default with these notes is wholly diversifiable, so that they have no market risk. In general, risky bonds do have market risk (i.e. positive betas) because default is more likely to occur in recessions when all businesses are doing poorly. Suppose that investors demand a 2 per cent risk premium and an 11 per cent expected rate of return. Then the BBCL notes will sell for 87.20/1.11 = $78.559 and offer a promised yield of (109/78.559) − 1 = 0.388, or about 39%.

You rarely see traded bonds offering 39 per cent yields, although we will soon encounter an example of one company's bonds that had a promised yield of 50 per cent.

## Bond ratings

The relative quality of most traded bonds can be judged from bond ratings given by Moody's and Standard & Poor's. For example, Moody's classifies several thousand bond issues into the categories described in Table 23.8.

Bonds rated Baa or above are known as *investment-grade* bonds. Banks and many superannuation funds and other financial institutions will not invest in bonds unless they are investment-grade. Bonds below this grade are known as *speculative-grade* bonds. Bond ratings are judgements about firms' financial and business prospects. If there is insufficient information to permit a judgement, the bond will not be rated. There is no fixed formula by which ratings are calculated. Nevertheless, investment bankers, bond portfolio managers and others who follow the bond market closely can get a fairly good idea of how a bond will be rated by looking at a few key numbers, such as the firm's debt-equity ratio, the ratio or earnings to interest and the return on assets.[39]

---

39   See, for example, R. S. Kaplan and G. Urwitz, 'Statistical Models of Bond Ratings: A Methodological Inquiry', *Journal of Business*, 52: 231–61 (April 1979).

**table 23.8**

Key to Moody's bond ratings

### Aaa

Bonds which are rated **Aaa** are judged to be of the best quality. They carry the smallest degree of investment risk and are generally referred to as 'gilt edged'. Interest payments are protected by a large or by an exceptionally stable margin, and principal is secure. While the various protective elements are likely to change, such changes as can be visualised are most unlikely to impair the fundamentally strong position of such issues.

### Aa

Bonds which are rated **Aa** are judged to be of high quality by all standards. Together with the **Aaa** group they comprise what are generally known as high grade bonds. They are rated lower than the best bonds because margins of protection may not be as large as in **Aaa** securities, or fluctuation of protective elements may be of greater amplitude, or there may be other elements present which make the long-term risk appear somewhat larger than the **Aaa** securities.

### A

Bonds which are rated **A** possess many favourable investment attributes and are to be considered as upper-medium-grade obligations. Factors giving security to principal and interest are considered adequate, but elements may be present which suggest a susceptibility to impairment some time in the future.

### Baa

Bonds which are rated **Baa** are considered as medium-grade obligations (i.e. they are neither highly protected nor poorly secured). Interest payments and principal security appear adequate for the present but certain protective elements may be lacking or may be characteristically unreliable over any great length of time. Such bonds lack outstanding investment characteristics and in fact have speculative characteristics as well.

### Ba

Bonds which are rated **Ba** are judged to have speculative elements; their future cannot be considered as well-assured. Often the protection of interest and principal payments may be very moderate and thereby not well safeguarded during both good and bad times over the future. Uncertainty of position characterises bonds in this class.

### B

Bonds which are rated **B** generally lack characteristics of the desirable investment. Assurance of interest and principal payments or of maintenance of other terms of the contract over any long period of time may be small.

### Caa

Bonds which are rated **Caa** are of poor standing. Such issues may be in default or there may be present elements of danger with respect to principal or interest.

### Ca

Bonds which are rated **Ca** represent obligations which are speculative in a high degree. Such issues are often in default or have other marked shortcomings.

### C

Bonds which are rated **C** are the lowest-rated class of bonds, and issues so rated can be regarded as having extremely poor prospects of ever attaining any real investment standing.

Moody's bond ratings, where specified, are applicable to financial contracts, senior bank obligations and insurance company senior policy holder and claims obligations with an original maturity in excess of one year. Obligations relying on support mechanisms such as letters of credit and bonds of indemnity are excluded unless explicitly rated. Obligations of a branch of a bank are considered to be domiciled in the country in which the branch is located.

Unless noted as an exception, Moody's rating on a bank's liability to repay senior obligations extends only to branches located in countries which carry a Moody's Sovereign Rating for Bank Deposits. Such branch obligations are rated at the lower of the bank's rating or Moody's Sovereign Rating for Bank Deposits for the country in which the branch is located. When the currency in which an obligation is denominated is not the same as the currency of the country in which the obligation is domiciled, Moody's ratings do not incorporate an opinion as to whether payment of the obligation will be affected by the actions of the government controlling the currency of denomination. In addition, risks associated with bilateral conflicts between an investor's home country and either the issuer's home country or the country where an issuer branch is located are not incorporated into Moody's ratings.

Moody's makes no representation that rated bank obligations or insurance company obligations are exempt from registration under the *U.S. Securities Act of 1933* or issued in conformity with any other applicable law or regulation. Nor does Moody's represent that any specific bank or insurance company obligation is legally enforceable or a valid senior obligation of a rated issuer.

*Source*: Moody's Investor Services.

*Note*: *Moody's applies numerical modifiers 1, 2 and 3 in each generic rating classification from Aa through to Caa. The modifier 1 indicates that the obligation ranks in the higher end of its generic rating category; the modifier 2 indicates a mid-range ranking; and the modifier 3 indicates a ranking in the lower end of that generic rating category.*

Since bond ratings reflect the probability of default, it is not surprising that there is usually a close correspondence between a bond's rating and its promised yield.

Once Moody's or Standard & Poor's rate a bond, the rating is not changed unless there is a significant shift in the company's financing or prospects. But the rating agencies do change their minds when conditions warrant it.

In the United States, bonds rated below Baa are often known as **junk bonds**. Until recently most junk bonds were 'fallen angels', that is, they were bonds of companies that had fallen on hard times. But during the 1980s new issues of junk bonds multiplied tenfold as more and more companies issued large quantities of low grade debt to finance takeovers or to defend themselves against being taken over. Many junk bonds have defaulted, while some of the more successful issuers have called their bonds, thus depriving their holders of the prospect of a continuing stream of high coupon payments.[40]

In Australia, very few companies have chosen to issue fixed interest loan securities—examples include St George Bank Ltd, ANZ Banking Group Ltd, Telstra Corporation Ltd, Crown Ltd, Orica Ltd and Seven Network Ltd. The most liquid markets in Australia are for bonds issued by the Commonwealth government, state government centralised borrowing authorities known as semigovernment bonds,[41] a number of other government statutory authorities,[42] and mortgage and asset backed securities and commercial paper programs.[43]

## Option pricing and risky debt

In Section 20.2 we showed that holding a corporate bond is equivalent to lending money with no chance of default *but* at the same time giving shareholders a put option on the firm's assets. When a firm defaults, its shareholders are in effect exercising their put. The put's value is the value of limited liability—of the shareholders' right to walk away from their firm's debts in exchange for handing over the firm's assets to its creditors. To summarise,

Bond value = bond value assuming no chance of default − value of put

Thus, valuing bonds should be a two-step process. This first step is easy: Calculate the bond's value assuming no default risk. (Discount promised interest and principal payments at the yield on comparable Australian government issues.) Second, calculate the value of a put written on the firm's assets, where the maturity of the put equals the maturity of the bond, and the exercise price of the put equals the promised payments to bondholders.

Owning a corporate bond is *also* equivalent to owning the firm's assets *but* giving a call option on these assets to the firm's shareholders.

Bond value = asset value − value of call on assets

Thus, you can also calculate a bond's value, given the true value of the firm's assets, by valuing a call on these assets, and subtracting the call value from the asset value. (The call value is just the value of the firm's ordinary shares.)

---

[40] The development of this market for low grade corporate bonds was largely the brainchild of the investment banking firm Drexel Burnham Lambert. The result was that for the first time corporate midgets were able to take control of corporate giants, and they could finance this activity by issues of debt. However, issuers of junk bonds often had debt ratios of 90 or 95 per cent. In the United States many worried that these high levels of leverage resulted in undue risk and pressed for legislation to ban junk bonds. Junk bonds promise a higher yield than American Treasury bonds but, of course, companies cannot always keep their promises.

[41] Such as the Queensland Treasury Corporation (QTC), New South Wales Treasury Corporation (NSWTC) and the South Australian Government Financing Authority (SAFA).

[42] Such as the Queensland Electricity Commission, the Mount Gambier Hospital Ltd and the Australian Barley Board.

[43] Such as RAMS Mortgage Corporation Ltd, Macquarie Securitisation Ltd (formerly PUMA Management Ltd) and Fanmac Ltd.

Therefore, if you can value puts and call on a firm's assets, you can value its debt.[44]

In practice, this is a good bit more difficult than it sounds. The put or call you have to value is usually not the simple option described in Chapter 20, but a much more complex one. Suppose, for example, that Gosford Industrials Ltd (GI) issues a 10-year bond that pays interest annually. We can still think of GI bonds as a call option that can be exercised by making the promised payments. But in this case there are 10 payments rather than just one.

To value GI bonds we would have to value 10 sequential call options. The first option can be exercised by making the first interest payment when it comes due. By exercise the shareholders obtain a second call option, which can be exercised by making the second interest payment. The reward to exercising is that the shareholders get a third call option, and so on. Finally, in year 10 the shareholders can exercise the tenth option. By paying off both the principal and the last year's interest the shareholders regain unencumbered ownership of GI's assets.

Of course, if the firm does not make any of these payments when due, bondholders take over and shareholders are left with nothing. In other words, by not exercising one call option, shareholders give up all subsequent call options.

Valuing GI's shares when the 10-year bond is issued is equivalent to valuing the first of the 10 call options. But you cannot value the first option without valuing the nine following ones.[45] Even this example understates the practical difficulties, because large firms may have dozens of outstanding debt issues with different interest rates and maturities, and before the current debt matures they may make further issues. But do not lose heart. Computers can solve these problems, more or less by brute force, even in the absence of simple, exact valuation formulas.

**figure 23.7**

How the interest rate on risky corporate debt changes with leverage and maturity. These curves are calculated using option pricing theory under the following simplifying assumptions: (1) The risk-free interest rate is constant for all maturities. (2) The standard deviation of the return on the company's assets is 25 per cent per annum. (3) No dividends are paid. (4) Debt is in the form of discount bonds (i.e. only one payment is made, at maturity). (5) Leverage is the ratio of the *market* value of the debt plus equity.

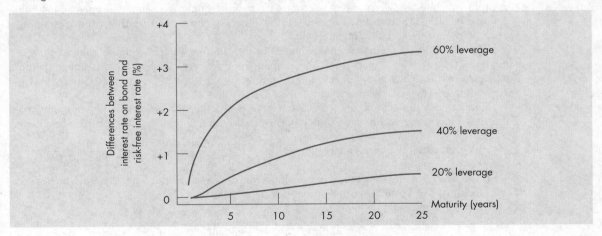

Figure 23.7 shows a simple application. The figure is designed to give you some feel for the effect of default risk on (promised) bond yields. It takes a company with average operating risk and shows how the interest rate should increase with the amount of bonds that are issued and

---

44   However, option valuation procedures cannot value the *assets* of the firm. Puts and calls must be valued as a proportion of asset value. For example, note that the Black–Scholes formula (discussed in Chapter 20) requires a share price in order to compute the value of the option.

45   The other approach to valuing GIL's debt (subtracting put value from risk-free bond value) is no easier. The analyst would be confronted by not one simple put, but a package of 10 sequential puts.

their maturity. You can see, for example, that if the company raises 20 per cent of its capital in the form of 20-year bonds, it should pay about one-half of a percentage point above the government borrowing rate to compensate for the default risk. Companies with more leverage or with longer-maturity bonds ought to pay higher premiums.[46]

In practice, interest-rate differentials tend to be greater than those shown in Figure 23.7. Does this mean that companies are paying too much for their debt? Probably not; there are a number of other possible explanations. For example, notice that Figure 23.7 makes several artificial assumptions. One assumption is that the company does not pay dividends. If it does regularly pay out part of its assets to shareholders, there may be substantially fewer assets to protect the bondholders in the event of trouble. In this case, the market may be quite justified in requiring a higher yield on the company's bonds. Also, most publicly issued corporate and mortgage or asset backed bonds are less easily marketable than Commonwealth Treasury and semigovernment bonds, which trade every day in huge quantities.

## 23.6 Summary

Efficient debt management presupposes that you understand how bonds are valued. That means you need to consider three problems:

1. What determines the general level on interest rates?
2. What determines the difference between long-term and short-term rates?
3. What determines the difference between the interest rates on company and government debt?

Here are some things to remember.

In Section 23.1 we saw that the level or rate of interest depends on the demand for savings and the supply. The *demand* comes from firms who wish to invest in new plant and equipment. The *supply* of savings comes from individuals who are willing to consume tomorrow rather than today. The equilibrium interest rate is the rate that produces a *balance* between the demand and supply.

The best-known theory about the effect of inflation on interest rates is that suggested by Irving Fisher. He argued that the nominal, or money, rate of interest is equal to the expected real rate plus the expected inflation rate. If the expected inflation rate increases by 1 per cent, so too will the money rate of interest.

The value of any bond is equal to the cash payments discounted at the spot rates of interest. For example, the value of a 10-year bond with a 5 per cent coupon equals:

$$PV(\text{percentage of face value}) = \frac{5}{(1 + r_1)} + \frac{5}{(1 + r_2)^2} + \dots + \frac{105}{(1 + r_{10})^{10}}$$

Bond dealers generally look at the yield to maturity on a bond. This is simply the internal rate of return $y$, the discount rate at which

$$\text{Bond price} = \frac{5}{(1 + y)} + \frac{5}{(1 + y)^2} + \dots + \frac{105}{(1 + y)^{10}}$$

The yield to maturity $y$ is a complex average of the spot interest rates $r_1$, $r_2$, and so on. Like most averages it can be a useful summary measure, but it can also hide a lot of interesting information.

When you invest in a bond you usually receive a regular interest payment and then the final principal payment. Duration measures the *average* time to each payment. It is a useful summary measure of the length of a loan. It is also important because there is a direct

---

[46]  But beyond a certain point (not shown in Figure 23.7), the yield premiums begin to decline with increasing maturity.

relationship between the duration of a bond and its volatility. A change in interest rates has a greater effect on the price of the bond with a long duration.

We saw that the short-term and long-term rates may differ. The one-period spot rate $r_1$ may be very different from the two-period spot rate $r_2$. In other words, investors often want a different annual rate of interest for lending for one year than for two years. Why is this? The *expectations hypothesis* says that bonds are priced so that the expected rate of return from investing in bonds over any period is independent of the maturity of the bonds held by the investor. The expectations hypothesis predicts that $r_2$ will exceed $r_1$ *only* if *next* year's one-period interest rate is expected to rise.

The *liquidity-preference theory* points out that you are not exposed to risks of changing interest rates and changing bond prices if you buy a bond that matures exactly when you need the money. However, if you buy a bond that matures *before* you need the money, you face the risk that you may have to reinvest your savings at a low rate of interest. And if you buy a bond that matures *after* you need the money, you face the risk that the price will be low when you come to sell it. Investors do not like risk and they need some compensation for taking it. Therefore, when we find that $r_2$ is generally higher than $r_1$, it may mean that investors have relatively short horizons and have to be offered an inducement to hold long bonds.

No bonds are risk-free in real terms. If inflation rates are uncertain, the safest strategy for an investor is to keep investing in short bonds and to trust that the rate of interest on the bonds will vary as inflation varies. Therefore, another reason why $r_2$ may be higher than $r_1$ is that investors have to be offered an inducement to accept additional inflation risk.

Finally, we come to our third question: 'What determines the difference between interest rates on company and government debt?' Company debt sells at a lower price that government debt. This discount represents the value of the company's option to default. We showed you how the value of this option varies with the degree of leverage and the time to maturity. Moody's and Standard & Poor's rate company bonds according to their default risk, and the price of the bonds is closely related to these ratings.

## FURTHER READING

The classic work on interest rates is:

> Iriving Fisher, *The Theory of Interest: As Determined by Impatience to Spend Income and Opportunity to Invest It*, Augustus M. Kelley, Publishers, New York, 1965. Originally published in 1930.

Fisher's work also anticipated Lutz and Lutz's expectations hypothesis of the term structure of interest rates:

> F. A. Lutz and V. C. Lutz, *The Theory of Investment of the Firm*, Princeton University Press, Princeton, N.J., 1951.

The liquidity-premium hypothesis is due to Hicks and our description of the effect of inflation on term structure is taken from Brealey and Schaefer:

> J. R. Hicks, *Value and Capital: An Inquiry into Some Fundamental Principles of Economic Theory*, 2nd ed., Oxford University Press, Oxford, 1946.

> R. A. Brealey and S. M. Schaefer, 'Term Structure and Uncertain Inflation', *Journal of Finance*, **32**: 277–90 (May 1977).

Good reviews of the term structure literature may be found in Nelson and Roll:

> C. R. Nelson, 'The Term Structure of Interest Rates: Theories and Evidence', in J. L. Bicksler (ed.), *Handbook of Financial Economics*, North-Holland Publishing Company, Amsterdam, 1980.

> R. Roll, *The Behaviour of Interest Rates: An Application of the Efficient Market Model to U.S. Treasury Bills*, Basic Books, Inc., Publishers, New York, 1970.

Dobson, Sutch and Vanderford review empirical tests of term structure theories. Two more recent tests of term structure theories are provided by Fama:

S. Dobson, R. Sutch and D. Vanderford, 'An Evaluation of Alternative Empirical Models of the Term Structure of Interest Rates', *Journal of Finance*, **31**: 1035–66 (September 1976).

E. F. Fama, 'The Information in the Term Structure', *Journal of Financial Economics*, **13**: 509–28 (December 1984).

E. F. Fama, 'Term Premiums in Bond Returns', *Journal of Financial Economics*, **13**: 529–46 (December 1984).

When there are no zero coupon bonds or strips, measuring term structure is more complicated. See, for example:

S. M. Schaefer, 'Measuring a Tax Specific Term Structure of Interest Rates in the Market for British Government Securities', *Economic Journal*, **91**: 415–38 (June 1981).

The following paper by Schaefer is a good review of the concept of duration and how it is used to hedge fixed liabilities:

S. M. Schaefer, 'Immunisation and Duration: A Review of Theory, Performance and Applications', *Midland Corporate Finance Journal*, **3**: 41–58 (Autumn 1984).

The Cox, Ingersoll and Ross paper uses no-arbitrage conditions to derive a rigorous model of the term structure. The Brennan and Schwartz paper is a readable description of a model that links each bond's return to both the short-term and long-term interest rates and then derives consistent bond prices:

J. C. Cox, J. E. Ingersoll and S. A. Ross, 'A Theory of the Term Structure of Interest Rates', *Econometrica*, **53**: 385–407 (May 1985).

M. J. Brennan and E. S. Schwartz, 'Bond Pricing and Market Efficiency', *Financial Analysts Journal*, **38**: 49–56 (September–October 1982).

Fama's tests indicate that the expected real rate of interest was essentially constant between 1953 and 1971. However, if you read Fama's paper, you should also read the replies by Hess and Bicksler and by Nelson and Schwert:

E. F. Fama, 'Short-Term Interest Rates as Predictors of Inflation', *American Economic Review*, **65**: 269–82 (June 1975).

P. Hess and J. Bicksler, 'Capital Asset Prices Versus Time Series Models as Predictors of Inflation', *Journal of Financial Economics*, **2**: 341–60 (December 1975).

C. R. Nelson and G. Schwert, 'Short-Term Interest Rates as Predictors of Inflation: On Testing the Hypothesis that the Real Rate of Interest is Constant', *American Economic Review*, **67**: 478–86 (June 1977).

Empirical testing of the expectations hypothesis using Australian and New Zealand data can be found in the following studies:

L. A. Alles, 'Time Varying Risk Premium and the Predictive Power of the Term Structure of Interest Rates', *Accounting and Finance*, **35** (2): 77–96 (1995).

J. Juttner, R. Tuckwell and D. Luedecke, 'Are Expectations of Short-Term Interest Rates Rational?', *Australian Economic Papers*, pp. 356–69 (December 1985).

C. Kearney, R. MacDonald and J. Hillier, 'The Efficiency of the Market for Bank Accepted Bills', *The Economic Record*, pp. 225–33 (September 1989).

W. J. Tease, 'The Expectations Theory of the Term Structure of Interest Rates in Australia', *The Economic Record*, pp. 120–7 (June 1988).

H. Yip, 'The Information Content and Usefulness of the Term Structure of the New Zealand Bank Bill Market', *Accounting and Finance*, **31** (2): 1–12 (1991).

Robert Merton has shown how option pricing theory can be applied to risky debt:

R. Merton, 'On the Pricing of Corporate Debt: The Risk Structure of Interest Rates', *Journal of Finance*, **29**: 449–70 (May 1974).

The following papers take a detailed look at the default experience of junk debt in the 1980s:

E. Altman, 'Measuring Corporate Bond Mortality and Performance', *Journal of Finance*, **44**: 909–22 (September 1989).

P. Asquith, D. W. Mullins and E. D. Wolff, 'Original Issue High Yield Bonds: Aging Analyses of Defaults, Exchanges and Calls', *Journal of Finance*, **44**: 923–52 (September 1989).

## QUIZ

**1.** The real interest rate is determined by the demand and supply for capital. Draw a diagram showing how the demand by companies for capital and the supply of capital by investors vary with the interest rate. Use this diagram to show:
   a. What will happen to the amount of investment and saving if firms' investment prospects improve? How will the equilibrium interest rate change?
   b. What will happen to the amount of investment and saving if individuals' willingness to save increases at each possible interest rate? How will the equilibrium interest rate change? Assume firms' investment opportunities do not change.

**2.** a. What is the formula for the value of a two-year, 5 per cent bond in terms of spot rates?
   b. What is the formula for its value in terms of yield to maturity?
   c. If the two-year spot rate is higher that the one-year rate, is the yield to maturity greater or less than the two-year spot rate?
   d. In each of the following sentences choose the correct term from within the parentheses:
        'The (yield-to-maturity/spot-rate) formula discounts all cash flows from one bond at the same rate even though they occur at different points in time.'
        'The (yield-to-maturity/spot-rate) formula discounts all cash flows received at the same point in time at the same rate even though the cash flows may come from different bonds.'

**3.** Use Table 23.1 to check your answers to the following:
   a. If interest rates rise, do bond prices rise or fall?
   b. If the bond yield is greater than the coupon, is the price of the bond greater or less than 100?
   c. If the price of a bond exceeds 100, is the yield greater or less than the coupon?
   d. Do high coupon bonds sell at higher or lower prices than low coupon bonds?

**4.** Use Table 23.1 to answer the following questions:
   a. What is the yield to maturity on a 7 per cent, eight-year bond selling at $74.86?
   b. What is the approximate price of a 5 per cent, nine-year bond yielding 10 per cent?
   c. A 9 per cent, 12-year bond yields 14 per cent. If the yield remains unchanged, what will be its price two years hence? What will the price be if the yield falls to 10 per cent?

**5.** a. Suppose that the one-year spot rate of interest at time 0 is 1 per cent and the two-year spot rate is 3 per cent. What is the forward rate of interest for year 2?
   b. What does the expectations hypothesis of term structure say about the relationship between this forward rate and the one-year spot rate at time 1?
   c. Over a very long period of time, the term structure in Australia has been, on average, upward sloping. Is this evidence for or against the expectations hypothesis?
   d. What does liquidity-preference theory say about the relationship between the forward rate and the one-year spot rate at time 1?
   e. If the liquidity-preference theory is a good approximation and you have to meet long-term liabilities (school fees for your children, for example) is it safer to invest in long-term or short-term bonds? Assume inflation is predictable.
   f. If the inflation-premium theory is a good approximation and you have to meet long-term real liabilities, is it safer to invest in long-term or short-term bonds?

**6.** What does the inflation-premium theory say about the relationship between the forward rate and the one-year spot rate at time 1?
   a. State the four Moody's ratings that are generally known as 'investment-grade' ratings.
   b. Other things being equal, would you expect the yield to maturity on a corporate bond to increase or decrease with:
   i. The company's business risk?
   ii. The expected rate of inflation?
   iii. The risk-free rate of interest?
   iv. The degree of leverage?

**7.** True or False? Explain.
   a. Longer maturity bonds necessarily have longer durations.
   b. The longer a bond's duration, the lower is its volatility.
   c. Other things being equal, the lower the bond coupon the higher its volatility.
   d. If interest rates rise, bond durations rise also.

**8.** Calculate the durations and volatilities of securities A, B and C. Their cash flows are shown below. The interest rate is 8 per cent.

| | Period | | |
|---|---|---|---|
| | 1 | 2 | 3 |
| A | 40 | 40 | 40 |
| B | 20 | 20 | 120 |
| C | 10 | 110 | |

**9.** In May 1995 the 10.75 per cent May 2003 bonds offered a semiannually compounded yield of 6.65 per cent. Recognising that coupons are paid semiannually, calculate the bond's price.

## QUESTIONS AND PROBLEMS

**1.** Why might Fisher's theory about inflation and interest rates *not* be true?

**2.** You have estimated spot interest rates as follows:

| Year | Spot rate (%) |
|---|---|
| 1 | $r_1 = 5.00$ |
| 2 | $r_2 = 5.40$ |
| 3 | $r_3 = 5.70$ |
| 4 | $r_4 = 5.90$ |
| 5 | $r_5 = 6.00$ |

    a.  What are the discount factors for each date (i.e. the present value of $1 paid in year $t$)?

    b.  What are the forward rates for each period?

    c.  Calculate the PV of the following Treasury notes.

       i.  5 per cent, two-year note.

      ii.  5 per cent, five-year note.

     iii.  10 per cent, five-year note.

     iv.  Explain intuitively why the yield to maturity on the 10 per cent bond is less than on the 5 per cent bond.

**3.** Look at the spot interest rates shown in Question 2. Suppose that someone told you that the six-year spot interest rate was 4.80 per cent. Why would you not believe them? How could you make money if they were right? What is the minimum sensible value for the six-year spot rate?

**4.** Look just one more time at the spot interest rates shown in Question 2. What can you deduce about the one-year spot interest rate in four years if:

    a.  The expectations hypothesis of term structure is right?

    b.  The liquidity-preference theory of term structure is right?

    c.  The term structure contains an inflation uncertainty premium?

**5.** Assume the term structure of interest rates is upward sloping. How would you respond to the following comment? 'The present term structure of interest rates makes short-term debt more attractive to corporate treasurers. Firms should avoid new long-term debt issues.'

**6.** It has been suggested that the Fisher theory is a tautology. If the real rate of interest is defined as the difference between the nominal rate and the expected inflation rate, then the nominal rate *must* equal the real rate plus the expected inflation rate. In what sense is Fisher's theory *not* a tautology?

**7.** Look up the prices of five Australian Commonwealth Treasury bonds with different coupons and different maturities. Use bond tables to calculate how their prices would change if their yields to maturity increased by one percentage point. Are long-term bonds or short-term bonds most affected by the change in yields? Are high coupon bonds or low coupon bonds most affected?

**8.** Under what conditions can the expected real interest rate be negative?

**9.** Bond-rating services usually charge corporations for rating their bonds.

    a.  Why do they do this, rather than charge those investors who use the information?

    b.  Why will a company pay to have its bonds rated even when it knows that the service is likely to assign a below-average rating?

    c.  A few companies are not willing to pay for their bonds to be rated. What can investors deduce about the quality of these bonds?

**10.** A 6 per cent, six-year bond yields 12 per cent and a 10 per cent, six-year bond yields 8 per cent. Calculate the six-year spot rate. (Assume annual coupon payments.)

**11.** In July 1998 a series of risk-free zero coupon bonds were priced as follows:

| Maturity | Price |
|----------|-------|
| 1999 | 92.8 |
| 2000 | 86.4 |
| 2001 | 80.3 |
| 2002 | 74.6 |
| 2003 | 69.2 |
| 2004 | 64.1 |
| 2005 | 59.3 |

   a. Estimate the spot rates of interest.
   b. Estimate the forward rates of interest.
   c. If the expectations hypothesis of term structure is correct, what is the expected one-year rate of interest in 2003?

**12.** Are high coupon bonds more likely to yield more than low coupon bonds when the term structure is upward sloping or when it is downward sloping?

**13.** Look back to the Gosford Industrials Ltd example at the start of Section 23.5. Suppose that the firm's book balance sheet is:

| Gosford Industrials Ltd (book values) | | | |
|---|---|---|---|
| Net working capital | $400 | $1000 | Debts |
| Net fixed assets | 1600 | 1000 | Equity |
| Total assets | $2000 | $2000 | Total liabilities and net worth |

The debt has a one-year maturity and a promised interest rate of 9 per cent. Thus, the promised payment to GIL's creditors is $1090. The market value of the assets is $1200 and the standard deviation of asset value is 45 per cent per year. The risk-free interest rate is 9 per cent. Use Appendix Table 6 to value the GIL's debt and equity.

**14.** Assume that Figure 23.5 correctly describes the path of short-term interest rates. The prices and yields of the three bonds that we described in Section 23.4 have changed. The yield to maturity of Medium is 8.18 per cent. The yield to maturity on Long is currently 7.80 per cent. Next period it will fall to 3.98 per cent if the short-term interest rate falls and will rise to 11.84 per cent if the short-term rate rises.
   a. Are these yields consistent, or are there arbitrage profits to be made?
   b. How would your answer change if the yield of Medium is currently 7.93 per cent and all other yields are unchanged?
   c. Suppose that short-term rates are equally likely to rise or fall. What can you deduce about the expected return on the three bonds and investors' attitude to risk?

**15.** In Section 23.4, we stated that the duration of the 9.5 per cent August 2002 bond was 5.488 years. Construct a table like Table 23.5 to show that this is so.

**16.** Look back at the example of the short, medium and long bonds in Section 23.4. Assume that to invest in Medium investors require an expected return of 11 per cent in year 1 (i.e. a risk premium of 3 per cent).

a. Recalculate the value of Medium and the ratio of its expected reward to risk.
b. Now find out the value of Long at each point in time. Remember that it must offer the same expected reward per unit of risk as Medium.
c. Show now how you could replicate the Medium bond with a package of the Short and Long bonds. (*Hint:* If the spread of possible returns on Medium is $x$ per cent of the spread on Long, then your investment in Long should be $x$ per cent of your investment in Medium.)
d. Finally, pretend that investors are risk-neutral and show that the prices that you have estimated are neutral world discounted at the risk-free interest rate.

**17.** The formula for the duration of a perpetual bond that makes an equal payment each year in perpetuity is $(1 + \text{yield})/\text{yield}$. If bonds yield 5 per cent, which has the longer duration—a perpetual bond or a 15-year zero coupon bond? What if the yield is 10 per cent?

**18.** Here is a difficult question. We stated in Question 17 that the duration of a perpetual bond that makes an equal payment each year in perpetuity is $(1 + \text{yield})/\text{yield}$. Can you prove this result?

**19.** You have just been fired as finance manager. As consolation the board of directors gives you a five-year consulting contract at $150 000 per year. What is the duration of this contract if your personal borrowing rate is 9 per cent? Use duration to calculate the change in the contract's present value for a half a per cent (0.50 per cent or 0.0050) increase in your borrowing rate.

**20.** The one-year spot rate is $r_1 = 6$ per cent and the forward rate for a one-year loan maturing in year 2 is $_1f_2 = 6.4$ per cent. Similarly, $_2f_3 = 7.3$ per cent and $_4f_5 = 8.2$ per cent. What are the spot rates $r_2$, $r_3$, $r_4$ and $r_5$? If the expectations hypothesis holds, what can you say about expected future interest rates?

**21.** Suppose your company will receive $100 million at $t = 4$ but must make a $107 million payment at $t = 5$. Assume the spot and forward rates from Question 20. Show how the company can lock in the interest rate at which it can invest at $t = 4$. Will the $100 million, invested at this locked-in rate, be sufficient to cover the $107 million liability?

# chapter 24

# THE MANY DIFFERENT KINDS OF DEBT

In Chapters 17 and 18 we discussed how much a company should borrow. But companies also need to think what type of debt to issue. They must decide whether to issue short-term or long-term debt; whether the debt should involve a bank loan, money raised from the public, or a private placement, debenture or a straight, convertible or some other structured bond; whether the exposure should be at a fixed or floating rate of interest; whether the debt should be secured or unsecured; whether the debt can be repaid or called prior to maturing or not; whether they must consider the impact of regulatory constraints; and whether to issue the debt in the Australian market, an overseas or foreign market or in the euromarkets.

Firms looking to increase their capital are faced with a very significant decision—they may seek to minimise their internal expenses as well as to maximise their revenue from operations. However, for large capital injections internal financing may not be sufficient—it usually comes down to a decision about debt versus equity external financing. As we discussed in Chapter 14, equity financing results in continuous part ownership of the firm from being a shareholder. In return, shareholders are guaranteed receipt of a stream of dividends over time (if the firm pays dividends) and a claim over the assets of the firm if the firm is liquidated. This contrasts with debt, which provides no such claim of ownership to creditors or lenders,[1] and where interest

---

[1] It is important to differentiate between ownership and a claim over assets if the assets of the firm are offered as security to a debt contract. In the case of liquidation, creditors and lenders with security are given higher priority than ordinary shareholders in making any claim against the firm's assets.

payments are made on outstanding debt and the debt securities usually have only a limited life or maturity.

Debt securities are issued by the Commonwealth government, state governments, semigovernment bodies authorised to issue debt and corporates. In this chapter we are principally interested in discussing the long-term debt market—we will return to the short-term debt market in Chapter 32. The major types of long-term debt instrument used in Australia include:

- Bank loans—secured and unsecured
- Commonwealth Treasury bonds
- Semigovernment securities
- Debentures
- Unsecured bonds or notes
- Convertible bonds or notes
- Securitised or asset-backed bonds or notes
- Infrastructure bonds or notes

As at June 1998 there was over $859 billion[2] outstanding in loans ($524 billion) and other long-term debt instruments ($335.4 billion) in the Australian long-term debt securities market. Of the outstanding loan capital, almost 40 per cent was to private corporates. Between them, financial institutions accounted for almost 40 per cent of the outstanding loans, with life offices borrowing more than 26 per cent. In relation to the long-term debt securities, private corporates accounted for only 7.5 per cent, financial institutions for about 37 per cent and Commonwealth and state governments and their authorities accounted for about 55 per cent. It is obvious from these statistics that Australian private companies have a preference for raising debt via loans, while the government principally uses long-term debt instruments such as bonds.

We begin our discussion by looking at the different markets for obtaining long-term debt securities *used by corporates*. We examine the domestic, foreign and euromarkets as sources of corporate debt, placing most emphasis on the Australian domestic market.

As our focus is principally on corporate debt, we examine the alternative types of long-term debt instruments that are issued by companies in the Australian market—including loans, debentures, unsecured notes, convertible securities and specially structured securities. We also examine the differences between secured and unsecured debt and the use of restrictive provisions, known as debt covenants, that seek to prevent companies from doing anything that would endanger their ability to repay their debt.

Debt may be sold to the public or placed privately with larger financial institutions. Because privately placed debt is broadly similar to public issues, we will not discuss this at length.

We discuss financial innovation in the long-term debt market and discuss a few unusual bonds, thinking about the reasons for innovation in the debt market. Such innovations may result in possibly only a few basis points reduction in yield, but on a large issue this can translate into a saving of several million dollars. You will see in an example involving the world's largest ever asset-backed bond issue (involving the Irish aircraft leasing company GPA, which raised over US$4 billion in 1996) that opportunities may present themselves to structure debt agreements so as to remove long-term debt from the consolidated balance sheet of a company. While discussing innovation we also turn our attention to two areas of bond market innovation where Australia has developed a strong competitive advantage—securitised or asset-backed bonds and infrastructure bonds.

We conclude the chapter by looking at a particular form of private debt, known as project finance. This is the glamorous part of the debt market. The words 'project finance' usually conjure up images of multimillion-dollar loans to finance mining ventures in exotic parts of the world. You will find there is something to the popular image, but it is not the whole story.

---

2   See Australian Bureau of Statistics, *Australian National Accounts, Financial Accounts*, Catalogue No. 5232.0, ABS, Canberra, September 1998. The amount of $859.4 billion does not include $352.9 billion of loans to households and unincorporated enterprises.

## 24.1 Domestic bonds, foreign bonds and eurobonds

A firm looking to borrow for the long term can do so in its own domestic or home country, it can raise funds by borrowing overseas, or it can borrow via a euroloan or eurobond issue through the euromarket. By examining the geographical location of the issuing company, the currency in which the debt is raised and the country in which the debt is issued, it is possible to differentiate between domestic, foreign and eurocurrency loans and bonds.

A domestic loan can be borrowed or a bond issued in the home country of the firm in that country's currency. For example, a Sydney-based firm can raise funds by borrowing in Australian dollars in Australia from an Australian bank. Since the mid-1990s the Australian long-term debt market has been experiencing a period of increased demand for long-term debt securities, which some argue cannot be met by the supply of the domestic market alone.[3] This is partially due to the Commonwealth government's change in budgetary policy to surplus budgeting and debt reduction through a reduction of the public sector borrowing requirement, a reduction in debt issued by state government centralised borrowing authorities, and the introduction of compulsory superannuation contributions.

A foreign loan can be borrowed or a foreign bond issued by a firm that is not domiciled in the country where the loan or the bond issue takes place. The debt is issued in the currency of the country where the debt instrument is issued and foreign bonds can only trade in that market. Therefore, they will be subject to the rules and regulations of the foreign market. For example, a Sydney firm may elect to issue its debt securities in deutschmarks in Germany and then have them trade in the German long-term debt market. The United States is by far the largest market for foreign bonds, but Japan and Switzerland are also important. Bonds issued in these markets have a variety of nicknames. For example, a bond sold by a foreign company in the United States is known as a *yankee bond*, one sold by a foreign firm in Japan is a *samurai*, and so on.[4]

Firms can raise funds in the euromarkets either by borrowing using a eurocurrency loan or by issuing eurobonds. The eurocurrency loans are usually issued at a floating rate of interest at a fixed spread above LIBOR (the London interbank offered rate) or another reference rate, have maturities up to 10 years and are made available via eurobanks. A eurocurrency is a currency on deposit in a bank outside of the country of origin for the currency. For example, if a large British multinational firm operating in Australia deposits sterling into an account in an Australian bank, the deposit is known as a eurodeposit. These funds can then be loaned out to another bank, which then lends the funds to a firm as a long-term eurocurrency loan.

Eurobonds are bonds that are sold outside of the country in whose currency the bond has been issued. They are usually sold simultaneously in a number of foreign countries by an international syndicate of underwriters. Although eurobonds may be sold throughout the world, eurobond writers and dealers are mainly located in London. They primarily include the London branches of American, European and Japanese commercial and investment banks. As barriers to the movement of capital have come down, the distinction between eurobonds and domestic bonds has become less clear-cut. For example, an Australian firm may offer its bonds simultaneously both in Australia and internationally.

Eurobond issues are generally made in currencies that are actively traded, fully convertible and relatively stable. The American dollar has been the most popular choice, followed by the yen, the deutschmark, the British pound, the French franc and the Australian dollar. There is also a sizeable market in ECU bonds. An ECU, or European currency unit, is simply a basket of European currencies. Occasionally, companies issue dual-currency bonds that pay interest in one currency and principal in another.

---

[3]　See C. Wood, 'Fixed-Interest Gap to Widen', *Business Review Weekly*, 18 May 1998.

[4]　Other currency sectors of the foreign bond market having special names include British sterling (bulldog), Dutch guilder (Rembrandt) and Spanish peseta (matador).

## 24.2 The long-term corporate debt market[5]

As discussed in Chapter 14, in Australia the primary long-term corporate domestic debt markets include the domestic loan market and the bond markets for debentures, unsecured notes, corporate bonds, convertible securities and structured debt financing, including securitised or asset-backed bonds and infrastructure bonds.

In Amcor Ltd's 1998 annual report,[6] the company reported having $1588.9 million in non-current borrowings. Of this amount, less than 4 per cent was reported as secured borrowing, with 96 per cent being unsecured. The long-term debt was also a mix of bank loans and long-term debt market securities. This total amount of non-current borrowing was made up as follows:

| Secured borrowings ($million) | |
| --- | --- |
| Mortgage loans | 5.0 |
| Bank loans | 8.4 |
| Bonds | 45.3 |

| Unsecured borrowings ($million) | |
| --- | --- |
| Commercial paper | 555.0 |
| Bank loans | 625.0 |
| US$ notes | 312.0 |
| Other loans | 8.8 |
| Lease liabilities ($million) | 29.4 |

From this point forward we will examine the corporate loan market in detail. Then we will return to discuss the other corporate debt markets.

## Corporate loan market

As shown in Table 24.1, the Australian corporate loan market for private corporate trading enterprises has remained relatively constant at around 40 per cent of all loans and placements[7] through the period 1994 to 1998. If we examine the sources of the loans, it can be seen that the primary sources of loan capital included banks, non-bank deposit taking institutions and the rest of the world. However, it should also be noted that since 1995 the rest of the world has declined quite significantly as a source of funds to Australian corporates. This is partially due to three significant changes in the Australian market. First, the period since 1995 has been one of declining domestic interest rates (you might want to review Figure 23.1 and Figure 23.3 again). Second, the depreciation of the Australian dollar through this period has made payments to service overseas debt less attractive. Third, due to changes in superannuation rules there has been an increase in the demand for long-term assets by firms with longer-dated portfolios such as superannuation and insurance companies.

Traditionally, prior to the deregulation of the banking system in the 1980s, banks loaned funds to corporates for the long term up to 10 years, but required high levels of security including mortgages over buildings and land and charges over assets including equipment. Furthermore, the loan was usually in the form of either a fully-drawn advance or a term loan involving the repayment of principal and interest at a fixed rate of interest, and a strong relationship had generally developed over many years between the bank and the corporate borrower. Australian banks encountered significant competition in the 1970s as non-bank

---

5   For discussion of the government debt market see Chapter 14.

6   For specific details of the various borrowings indicated see Amcor Ltd's 1998 annual report.

7   After excluding loans to households and unincorporated businesses.

**table 24.1**

The Australian corporate loans market, 1994–98

|  | 1994 | 1995 | 1996 | 1997 | 1998 |
|---|---|---|---|---|---|
| Total loans and placements to private corporate trading enterprises ($ billion) | 153.5 | 161.9 | 179.8 | 191.0 | 207.7 |
| Expressed as a percentage of all loans and placements[a] (%) | 35.98 | 36.72 | 41.61 | 39.50 | 39.64 |
| Sources of funds ($billion): | | | | | |
| Private trading corporate enterprises | 9.5 | 8.8 | 10.2 | 9.8 | 8.5 |
| Banks | 63.5 | 67.7 | 80.5 | 87.5 | 106.9 |
| Non-bank deposit taking institutions | 35.7 | 38.9 | 46.0 | 49.2 | 52.2 |
| Life offices and superannuation funds | 3.7 | 3.6 | 4.3 | 5.4 | 5.2 |
| Other financial institutions | 5.9 | 8.1 | 6.9 | 7.0 | 6.9 |
| State and local general government | 0.5 | 0.3 | 0.3 | 0.2 | 0.1 |
| Rest of the world | 34.6 | 34.3 | 31.6 | 31.8 | 28.0 |

*Note:*

(a) *Excludes loans to households and unincorporated enterprises.*

*Source*: Australian Bureau of Statistics, *Australian National Accounts, Financial Accounts*, Catalogue No. 5232, ABS, Canberra, Table 29: The loan market.

financial institutions entered the corporate loan market and several corporates chose to raise funds directly from the financial markets through short-term instruments such as bills of exchange and promissory notes and through the issuing of corporate bonds and debentures.

Fully-drawn advances (FDAs) are arrangements whereby the bank lends up to a maximum pre-specified loan principal amount. The loan is drawn down in full by the borrower and both principal and interest are repaid in regular payments over time. Such arrangements could be set in place on either a revolving on non-revolving basis. Under a revolving arrangement, as the funds are repaid by the borrower, this amount can be drawn down again by the borrower up to the pre-specified limit. This is similar to an overdraft facility. Such arrangements are subject to regular review. Under the more typical, non-revolving arrangement—you guessed it—the flexibility of the revolving FDA is not present and the firm must repay the loan and any interest without any subsequent draw downs. FDAs can be either secured or unsecured.

Term loans are typically amortising loans or balloon payment loans. Amortising term loans involve the payment of an initial principal amount to the borrower, which is then repaid over a period of time along with interest at regular intervals—monthly, quarterly or semiannually. Balloon payment loans are similar in that they involve an initial draw down of the principal amount and then can be interest only or only partially amortising over the life of the loan. At the end of the agreed loan period the loan principal has not been fully amortised and the residual amount is then due and payable as a balloon payment. The terms and conditions of the loan are agreed to via a loan agreement. Term loans can be secured or unsecured. If the loan is secured via a mortgage over property the loan is often referred to as a mortgage loan. Other forms of security include charges or liens over real or personal property, which authorise the bank to sell the assets if the loan should default. As a source of finance, term loans are very important for the purchase and construction of new or replacement major assets. Interest only loans also are available where the borrower draws down the principal, only pays interest and then repays the principal in full at maturity. There is no amortisation of the principal.

With deregulation of the banking system came a relaxation of the security requirements and flexibility in the form by which FDAs and term loans could be offered to corporates. The banks became increasingly fixated on gaining market share and therefore sought to lend more funds to the corporate sector as a proportion of total funds loaned than had traditionally been the practice. A government inquiry in 1991[8] into the deregulation of the Australian banking system found that banks had inadequate infrastructure to handle high volume large loan business, and that banks had replaced traditional banking relationships with an acceptance of multiple relationships resulting in a relaxation of borrower–lender relationship. It also found that the banks had introduced new lending techniques such as 'name' lending where the perceived credibility of the borrower was the principal factor in the decision to advance credit. The experiences of lending money without appropriate security, problems in the area of security valuation and a dramatic increase in interest rates in the late 1980s and early 1990s led to a series of significant corporate loan defaults resulting in significant changes in the prudentiality requirements of Australian financial institutions. The experience from this period has led to a very well-structured and competitive banking environment.

With the deregulation of the Australian banking system, and due to the increased competitiveness of institutions, Australian banks are now regarded as being far more prudent, while also providing the flexibility needed to provide an adequate lending infrastructure to Australian corporates. It is now possible to obtain corporate loans either as FDAs or as term loans, and at either fixed or floating rates, or a combination of the two.[9] Loans can be negotiated as principal and interest, interest only, or as a combination of both and balloon payment loans. Furthermore, loan security is now viewed as an important requirement in bank lending management and many loan agreements now also dictate loan covenants. We will have more to say about these shortly. To some extent, the line between short-, medium- and long-term debt market bank financing is becoming increasingly blurred, as it is also now possible to establish overdraft and bank bill lending facilities up to five years, whereby the debt is rolled over every three or six months at the prevailing market rate.

## Corporate debentures and unsecured notes

The Australian Corporations Law (ss. 9 and 1045) differentiates between three methods available for firms wishing to undertake long-term borrowing:

■ Mortgage debenture or certificates of mortgage stock
■ Debenture or certificates of debenture stock
■ Unsecured notes or unsecured deposit notes

In Australia the term *debenture* is generally used to describe any document that acknowledges the debt of a firm in respect of money that is or may be deposited with or lent to the firm. The debt is usually secured by a charge over specific company assets or a floating charge over the company's unpledged assets. If no security is taken, the issue is known as an *unsecured note*. The firm is permitted to pay interest on funds deposited or lent to it and in exchange the investor or lender receives a debenture that acknowledges the company's debt. However, in recent years Australian firms have decreased their use of debentures as a form of capital raising and instead use unsecured notes. Both securities are typically issued in units of $100 face value and pay interest either half-yearly or quarterly.

---

[8]    See House of Representatives Standing Committee on Finance and Public Administration, *A Pocket Full of Change: Banking and Deregulation*, Australian Government Publishing Service, Canberra, 1991.

[9]    Interest is charged against a nominated percentage of the principal of the loan at a fixed rate of interest, while the remainder is paid at a floating rate of interest. A fixed rate of interest implies that the rate of interest is fixed for the term of the loan agreement or until the end of a review period. Restrictions and penalties usually apply for early repayment of fixed rate debt by the borrower. Floating rates of interest imply the prevailing market prime lending rate plus a margin to reflect the default risk of the company borrowing the funds. The floating rate can vary during the term of the loan. There are usually no restrictions on early debt repayment.

Table 24.2 shows the primary issuers of long-term debt securities during the period 1994 to 1998. The major issuers of corporate debt in Australia are financial rather than non-financial institutions. Of the long-term debt securities issued by private trading corporate enterprises most are held by Australian financial institutions and by overseas investors. Obviously, the major issuer of long-term debt in Australia is the government, including its trading enterprises.

**table 24.2**

The Australian long-term debt securities market, 1994–98 ($billion)

|  | 1994 | 1995 | 1996 | 1997 | 1998 |
|---|---|---|---|---|---|
| Issued by: | | | | | |
| Government including trading enterprises | 168.7 | 188.6 | 185.3 | 196.2 | 185.5 |
| **Private sector trading enterprises** | **11.1** | **11.4** | **16.6** | **21.4** | **25.2** |
| Banks | 37.7 | 33.6 | 37.2 | 48.6 | 59.3 |
| Non-bank financial institutions | 16.3 | 20.8 | 24.6 | 28.5 | 31.2 |
| Other financial institutions | 12.6 | 15.1 | 17.5 | 26.8 | 34.2 |
| Total | 246.4 | 269.5 | 281.2 | 321.4 | 335.4 |

*Source*: Australian Bureau of Statistics, op. cit., Footnote 2, Table 34: The long-term debt securities market.

When a firm wishes to borrow funds by issuing debentures to a large number of potential lenders it would be administratively inconvenient if each debenture had to be issued separately. Therefore, borrowers issue a single fund of debenture stock and issue to each subscriber a certificate of debenture stock or unsecured notes. A firm wishing to issue a certificate of debenture stock[10] or unsecured notes must provide to potential investors a prospectus (which has been lodged with the Australian Securities and Investment Commission), any application forms, details in a trust deed of the trustee[11] and the terms for the issue.[12]

The trust company or trustee represents the interests of the bondholder. It must see that the terms of the trust deed are observed, that the prospectus is consistent with the trust deed, that the secured property is sufficient to discharge the principal of the debt when it falls due, and it must look after the bondholders' interests in the event of default.[13]

Almost all debenture issues in Australia are issued in registered form. This means that the company's register records the ownership of each debenture and the firm pays the interest and final principal amount directly to each owner.

In many countries, bonds and debentures may be issued in *bearer* form. In this case, the certificate constitutes the primary evidence of ownership, so that the bondholder must send in

---

[10] For discussion of the legal aspects of issuing debentures refer to R. B. Vermeesch and K. E. Lindgren, *Business Law of Australia*, Butterworths, Sydney, 1995.

[11] As noted in P. Lipton and A. Herzberg, *Understanding Company Law*, The Law Book Company, Sydney, 1991, the trust deed must contain the following information, as detailed in s. 1054 of the Corporations Law:

- Limitations on the total amount that can be borrowed.
- Details of the operational and financial history and current position of the organisation.
- Details of any covenants, positive and/or negative.

[12] Exclusions are detailed in s. 66 of the Corporations Law.

[13] H. A. J. Ford and P. P. Austin, *Principles of Corporations Law*, Butterworths, Sydney, 1995, identified that the advantages of having a trustee to act on behalf of the lenders under the trust deed include:

- A concentration of supervision of the borrowing.
- Legal title of the security is held by the trustee on behalf of all lenders.
- There is no need to reassign the title of the security as the identity of the lenders changes with each trade.
- Legal enforcement and realisation of the security can be done on behalf of all investors.

coupons to claim interest and must send the certificate itself to claim the final repayment of principal. Eurobonds almost invariably allow the owner to hold them in bearer form.

# Major features of a debenture or an unsecured note

Table 24.3 provides a summary of the major features that should be included in the documentation of a debenture or an unsecured note.

**table 24.3**
Summary of the details for inclusion in a certificate of debenture or an unsecured note.

| |
|:---:|
| Title of the company |
| Program size |
| Instrument |
| Minimum denominations |
| Rating |
| Status as to whether the debt is secured or unsecured |
| Trustee |
| Lead manager |
| Managers |
| Issue method |
| Listing |
| Marketability of the debt |
| Method of transfer |
| Guarantor |
| Covenants |
| Amount issued |
| Maturity date of the issue |
| Coupon rate of the issue |
| Issue date |
| Issue yield to maturity |

The *program size* details the total amount of the borrowing to be undertaken under the trust deed. It is possible that the total amount may not be issued all at the one time. Hence a firm may establish, for example, an $800 million program but only issue $150 million initially and then issue the remainder at a future date. In this case, the section *amount issued* would show $150 million. The trust deed would detail the total amount to be issued under the program and the final date by which the bonds will be issued.

The *instrument* would detail the type of debt instrument to be issued. It would also identify the date of the relevant trust deed and the final term to maturity of all debt instruments to be issued under the program. If the instruments have any special features, such as being convertible or linked to the performance of inflation, equity indexes or commodities, this would be detailed here.

The *bond rating* is also identified, including the issuer of the rating and the date of the rating. It is also important to identify whether the debt is *secured* or *unsecured*.

When the debt is issued, investors are advised of the *minimum denominations* of the issue.

This amount represents the minimum face value at which the debt is available and can be traded. Depending on whether the debt is for private placement or for public issue this may vary from $1 million to $1000.[14]

When issuing the debt, the firm will often seek financial advice from financial intermediaries including banks and capital market firms. It is therefore necessary to identify the *lead manager* and *other managers* of the issue. These firms play an important role in the structuring, and in some cases in the underwriting and distribution, of the debt. They are responsible for the marketing of the debt and are required to maintain its liquidity. They are required to always be prepared to offer to buy and/or sell quotations for the debt to facilitate market transactions in the debt. A statement as to the requirements of the lead manager and other managers is often included in the section *marketability of the debt*.

Any *guarantors* for the debt are identified and the nature of the guarantee is stated along with any significant *covenants*. All negative and positive covenants are detailed in the trust deed. Also included are the *maturity date of the issue* from the program that is currently on issue, the *issue date, the issue yield* and *the coupon rate* identifying the frequency of the coupon payments. In Australia most coupons are paid semiannually.

The regular coupon or interest payment on a debenture is a hurdle that the firm must keep jumping.[15] If the company ever fails to pay the interest, lenders may demand their money back or realise the security in the case of secured debt, rather than waiting for conditions to deteriorate further. Thus, the coupon payments provide added protection for lenders.[16]

# Corporate bonds

As discussed above, debentures have been the traditional method in Australia via which firms obtain long-term debt financing. In the late 1980s, following the share market crash and a brief period in which the Commonwealth government undertook surplus budgeting and the states were required to rationalise their funding needs, large Australian corporates began to issue corporate bonds as an alternative to other forms of debt market securities. Unlike debentures, corporate bonds have less restrictive covenants than bank loans or debentures, are typically issued by high-quality public companies with high credit ratings as unsecured notes and are placed privately with large institutional investors. Because they are privately placed they often do not require the issue of a prospectus, which results in a saving to the company making the bond issue.

Examples of companies that have issued corporate bonds include Amcor Ltd, Seven Network Limited, Fairfax Holdings Limited, Commonwealth Bank of Australia and Telstra.

# Structured debt finance

For most debt instruments the coupon or interest payments are fixed for the life of the debenture. But in some issues the payment varies with the general level of interest rates or is linked to some other commodity or economic indicator. For example, the payment may be tied to LIBOR (London interbank offered rate), SIBOR (Singapore interbank offered rate) or in Australia, to BBSW (banks bill swap rate).

We will have more to say about structured finance when we discuss financial innovation later in this chapter. For now here is an example to get you thinking out of the box or perhaps even pushing the edge of your envelope.

---

[14]   The Melbourne City Link Project issued equity infrastructure bonds valued at $1.00 each. But to invest in the Project is was necessary to purchase a minimum of two parcels of 499 bonds.

[15]   There is one type of bond where the borrower is obliged to pay interest only if it is covered by the year's earnings. These are the so-called *income bonds*. For a discussion of the attractions of income bonds see J. J. McConnell and G. G. Schlarbaum, 'Returns, Risks, and Pricing Income Bonds, 1956–1976 (Does Money Have an Odour?)', *Journal of Business*, 54: 33–64 (January 1981).

[16]   See F. Black and J. C. Cox, 'Valuing Corporate Securities: Some Effects of Bond Indenture Provisions', *Journal of Finance*, 31: 351–67 (May 1976). Black and Cox point out that the interest payment would be a trivial hurdle if the company could sell assets to make the payment. Such sales are therefore restricted.

In recent years, some firms have been structuring their debt differently from traditional debentures. Companies tailor not only the debt to the size and maturity requirements of the investors, but also the return and risk on coupons to investors' needs. For example, an investor may prefer a debt instrument to have a coupon payment that varies with changes in the West Texas oil price. A fund manager may hold a portfolio of industrial shares, the dividends of which are likely to be decreased if oil prices increase sharply—as firms will retain a higher proportion of their earnings. Such investors would like the opportunity to invest in a debt instrument where the cash flows increase as oil prices rise so as to offset the decrease in value in the equity portion of their portfolio. The coupon payments of the debt instrument could be structured such that if at the time of the coupon payment the West Texas oil price is at or below the average price level for the past 12 months, the investor will obtain a fixed rate of return. However, if the West Texas oil price is above this average price, the usual fixed level coupon is supplemented with an increase that reflects the growth in the oil price.

For example, assume the average price of West Texas oil over the past 12 months has been $21 per barrel and that if prices at the coupon date are not above this level, then the semi-annual coupon will be paid at a fixed rate of 5 per cent (10 per cent p.a.). Let us look at two scenarios:

1. If the West Texas oil price is ≤ $21.00, the coupon rate will be 5 per cent.
2. If the West Texas oil price is > $21.00, then the semiannual coupon will equal:

$$0.05 + 0.05 \times \frac{P_{WT} - 21}{100}$$

So if the West Texas oil price at the coupon date is $25, the coupon will increase from 5 per cent to 7 per cent.[17]

Often, floating rate notes (FRNs) specify a minimum (or *floor*) interest rate, or they may specify a maximum (or *cap*) on the rate.[18] You may also come across *collars* that stipulate both a maximum and minimum payment or *drop-lock*, which provide that, if the rate falls to a specified trigger point, the payment is then fixed for the remainder of the bond's life. FRNs are particularly popular with banks and finance companies. Since the interest that these companies earn on their assets varies with the level of interest rates, they can offset some of these fluctuations by simultaneously issuing FRNs. If short-term rates fall, then banks *receive* lower interest on their loans to customers, but they also *pay* less interest on their floating rate debt.

As detailed in Table 24.4, in December 1998 structured finance took on many forms in the Australian market. Over 80 per cent of the securities on issue were floating rate securities, and under 7 per cent of the securities were fixed rate, while the balance were either zero coupon bonds or indexed securities. Of the structured securities on issue, more than 50 per cent could be classified as pass-through asset-backed securities.[19]

# 24.3 Private versus public placements of long-term debt

The firm's choice between private bank lending and the issuing of debt in the form of bonds, debentures and notes to the public has been the subject of a wide literature, which suggests

---

[17] For detailed discussion of structured financing techniques see C. Turner, 'How to Cut Funding Costs and Please Investors', *Corporate Finance*, pp. 46–9 (September 1994).

[18] Instead of issuing a straight (uncapped) FRN, a company will sometimes issue a capped FRN and at the same time sell the cap to another investor. The first investor receives a coupon payment up to the specified maximum and the second investor receives any interest in excess of this maximum.

[19] For a very detailed overview of the structured finance market in Australia refer to Standard & Poor's, 'Australian Structured Finance Market Review', in *Structured Finance: Australia & New Zealand*, Melbourne, 1998.

**table 24.4**

Market share of structured securities on issue at December 1998

| Instrument (types of security on issue) | Market share (%) |
| --- | --- |
| Floating rate pass-through bonds | 48.8 |
| Commercial paper | 36.6 |
| Fixed-reverting to floating rate pass-through bonds | 4.8 |
| Medium-term notes | 2.8 |
| Floating rate notes | 2.2 |
| Fixed rate pass-through bonds | 1.3 |
| Inflation indexed bonds | 1.4 |
| Transferable investment certificates | 0.8 |
| Interest only bonds | 0.3 |
| Index replication notes | 0.3 |
| Fixed rate bonds and notes | 0.3 |
| Zero coupon bonds | 0.2 |
| Fixed rate amortising bonds | 0.2 |
| Total | 100.0 |

*Source*: Standard & Poor's Rating Services. Statistics based on rated securities outstanding as at 31 December 1998.

that the covenants required in private lending agreements are more restrictive than those required for public debt issues and are therefore value enhancing due to their impact. The monitoring and contractual debt restrictions imposed by covenants are argued, by agency theorists, to increase managers' incentives to follow value-maximising policies and the covenants are believed to constrain them from taking actions that reduce firm value. The counterargument suggests that the use of bank debt can be value reducing as it may prevent managers from investing in positive NPV projects, decrease financial flexibility and give monopoly power to the bank over borrowers in any further negotiations.

Long-term debt securities are also often placed privately at the time of issue with a small number of financial institutions. The placements can be in the form of a *family issue* to current holders of the company's shares, debentures, notes and bonds or as an *institutional private placement* where offers are made to institutions that deal in this form of security. The placements often result from direct negotiation between the issuer, or an investment banker acting on their behalf as an arranger of the issue, and institutional investors. Whether you decide to make a public issue or a private placement will depend partly on the relative issue costs, for a public issue involves much higher issue costs but permits a lower rate of interest for borrowing. But your choice should not depend solely on these costs. There are three other ways in which the private placement bond may differ from its publicly issued counterpart.

First, if you place an issue privately with one or two financial institutions, it may be necessary to sign only a simple promissory note. This is just an IOU which lays down certain conditions that the borrower must observe. However, when you make a public issue of debt, apart from the registration requirements and cost of issuing a prospectus, you must worry about who is to represent the debtholders in any subsequent negotiations and what procedures are needed for paying interest and principal. Therefore, the contractual arrangement has to be that much more complicated.

The second characteristic of publicly issued bonds is that they are highly standardised products. They have to be—investors are constantly buying and selling them without checking the fine print in the agreement. This is not so necessary in private placements. They are not regularly traded; they are bought and held by large institutions that are well-equipped to evaluate any unusual features. Furthermore, because private placements involve lower fixed issue costs, they tend to be issued by smaller companies. These are just the companies that most need custom-tailored debts.

All bond agreements seek to protect the lender by imposing a number of conditions or covenants on the borrower. In the case of private placements of debt these restrictions may be severe.[20] For example, if the borrower wishes to issue any more bonds or make operational changes, the firm may need the permission of the existing debtholders. Because there are only one or two lenders involved, this permission is usually obtained easily. That would not be possible with publicly issued debt. Therefore, the limitations tend to be less stringent in the case of public issues. This is the third difference between public and most private debt.

## 24.4 Debt covenants

All public and private issued debt contain covenants in the trust deed that serve to protect the interests of the lenders and increase the value of the firm by reducing the need for monitoring by lenders.[21]

Debt covenants may be either negative or positive. Any breach of these covenants may be considered a default, providing the lenders, via the trustee, with the right to take action associated with a default. Shanmugan and his coauthors in their text on bank management note that the objectives of imposing covenants are to obtain control over the firm's cash flows and balance sheet and to act as a means to call or trigger restructuring of the borrowing.[22]

Negative covenants may include limiting access to further debt, restricting all borrowing by the parent or subsidiary companies, restricting the holding of investments, restricting the payment of dividends or other cash payouts such as share buybacks, and restricting the disposition of assets and the payment of rentals or leases or making asset disposition transactions. Further negative covenants may place restrictions with respect to the firm's operating activities and preservation of the lender's collateral, and may impose restrictions on changes in management, control and ownership of the company.

Positive covenants may include maintaining the firm's corporate presence in certain markets, maintaining its assets, paying taxes, paying its indebtedness, attending to administrative and accounting reporting requirements, and complying with all applicable laws, regulations and commercial contracts.

Before 1980 most debentures had covenants limiting further issues of debt and changes in the level of payment of dividends. But then large institutions relaxed their requirements for large public companies and undertook a wide range of unsecured lending with very little or no such restrictions. However, over time restrictions on debt issues and dividend payments quietly returned to fashion. Debt market analysts and lawyers began to look more closely at 'event risks' like debt-financed corporate takeovers and acquisitions.[23] Some companies offer *poison put* clauses that oblige the borrower to repay the bonds if a large quantity of shares is bought by a single investor and the firm's debt is down-rated.

---

20   The covenants may be both negative and positive in nature.

21   See C. W. Smith and J. B. Warner, 'On Financial Contracting: An Analysis of Bond Covenants', *Journal of Financial Economics*, 7: 117–61 (1979).

22   See B. Shanmugan, C. Turton and G. Hempel, *Bank Management*, John Wiley & Sons, Brisbane, 1992.

23   P. Asquith and T. A. Wizman, Event Risk, Bond Covenants, and the Return to Existing Bondholders in Corporate Buyouts, unpublished paper, Sloan School of Management, M.I.T., Cambridge, Mass., June 1990.

A recent Australian study by Cotter[24] in 1998 of the use and restrictions imposed by covenants in private bank lending provided a useful insight into the world of corporate banking and its use of covenants by providing information regarding interviews held with bankers responsible for loans to listed companies. It was reported that the bankers 'indicated that the diversity in covenants included in loan contracts is large and determined on a firm-by-firm basis, depending on individual firm circumstances. However, some systematic relations are expected to exist with regard to borrower industry, size and credit rating, and which party is in the strongest negotiating position, the bank or the borrower'. The study found that the most frequently used accounting (or financial information) based covenants in Australian bank loan agreements are leverage,[25] interest coverage,[26] prior charges as a percentage of total tangible assets and current ratios.[27] The restrictiveness of the covenants was found to vary with firm size and between industries. Larger firms were found to have fewer restrictions than smaller firms and industrial firms had fewer restrictions than mineral producers.

The inclusion of restrictions on new debt issues or dividend payments prevents the company from doing things that would benefit the shareholders at the expense of the debtholders, but the restrictions do not make the debt securities safe. Therefore, lenders also seek to protect themselves by arrangements that give them the chance to demand repayment at the first sign of trouble. For example, bank loans sometimes specify that the bank can demand repayment if there is a 'material adverse change' that impairs the borrower's ability to repay the loan.[28]

We have already seen that lenders impose a number of hurdles that the company must keep jumping. The most obvious of these hurdles are the regular interest payments and sinking fund contributions. If these obligations are not met, the loan becomes repayable immediately. That is why the company will always try to make the payment if it possibly can. Another, rather different, hurdle is the repayment of other outstanding debt.

Many issues contain a *cross-default* clause. This says that the company is in default if it fails to meet its obligations on any of its debt issues. Thus, a cross-default clause may enable the lender to get out before the firm has missed a payment on that particular loan.

Most trust deeds also include so-called *positive* or *affirmative* covenants, which impose certain duties on the borrower. In the case of public bond issues many of these affirmative covenants are innocuous. For example, the company may be obliged to furnish bondholders with a copy of its annual accounts. If it does not do so, it is in default on the bonds.

Many privately placed issues impose much more onerous affirmative covenants. The most common of these are covenants to maintain at all times some minimum level of working capital or net worth. If the amount of working capital or net worth is a good guide to the value of the company, the lenders are putting a ceiling on the amount they can lose.

We do not want to give the impression that the lenders are constantly seeking an opportunity to cry 'default' and then demand their money back. If the company does default, the lenders have the *right* to claim repayment but they will not generally do so. The more usual result is that the lenders or the trustee will seek a detailed explanation from the company and

---

24  See J. Cotter, 'Utilisation and Restrictiveness of Covenants in Australian Private Debt Contracts', *Accounting and Finance*, **38** (2): 181–96 (1998). Related studies can be found in P. Mather, The Use of Financial Covenants in Australian Bank Loan Contracts, Monash University Working Paper, 1997, which compiles descriptions of accounting-based covenants used in Australia in private debt agreements through the use of a survey and interviews with bank officers; and I. Ramsay and B. K. Sidhu, 'Accounting and Non-Accounting Based Information in the Market for Debt: Evidence From Australian Private Debt Contracts', *Accounting and Finance*, **38** (2): 197–221 (1998).

25  Expressed as the ratio of total liabilities to total tangible assets.

26  Expressed as the ratio of earnings before interest and tax (EBIT) to gross interest expense.

27  Expressed as current assets to current liabilities.

28  'Material adverse change' is usually not specifically defined—the clause protects the lender in scenarios where the borrower falls into default without triggering specific covenants. Of course, this clause might be a dangerous weapon in the hands of a short-sighted and unscrupulous lender, who could pretend to see an adverse change and try to extort a higher interest rate by threatening to demand immediate repayment. Fortunately, few if any financial institutions play this game. They would be sued for trying it, and their reputation for *not* taking unfair advantage of their customers is a valuable business asset.

discuss possible changes in its operating policy. It is only as a last resort that lenders demand early repayment and force the company into liquidation.

## 24.5 Security and seniority of corporate debt

Many domestic long-term debt instruments in Australia, whether they are loans or other debt securities, are secured obligations. This means that if the company defaults on the debt, the trustee or lender (in the case of bank loans) may take possession of the relevant or secured assets. If there are insufficient funds on the sale of the assets to satisfy the claim, the remaining debt will have a general claim alongside any unsecured debt against the other assets of the firm.

As such, unsecured debt is regarded as being subordinate or junior to secured debt. Secured debt is often also regarded as unsubordinate or senior debt. Holders of subordinate debt will want to be compensated with a higher rate of return for bearing the additional risk relative to unsubordinated debt. How do banks and trustees make decisions whether security is required? Generally, large Australian firms have strong equity support in their capital structure and stability in their cash flows—this makes the decision pretty easy.

The difference between a corporate debt security and a comparable Commonwealth Treasury bond is that the company has an option to default—the government supposedly does not. That is a valuable option. If you do not believe us, think about whether (other things being equal) you would prefer to be a shareholder in a company with limited liability or in a company with unlimited liability. Of course, you would prefer to have the option to walk away from your debts. Unfortunately, every silver lining has its cloud, and the drawback to having a default option is that investors expect to be compensated for giving it to the issuer of the debt. That is why corporate bonds sell at lower prices and therefore higher yields than government bonds.[29] For example, in 1996, five-year AA rated corporate bonds were issued in Australia at between 27 to 29 basis points above the equivalent maturity Commonwealth Treasury bonds; A rated corporate bonds at 34 to 36 basis points; and BBB+ corporate bonds at 42 to 47 basis points.

Investors know that there is a risk of default when they buy a corporate debenture. But they still want to make sure that the company plays fair. They do not want it to gamble with their money or take unreasonable risks. Therefore, the trust agreement may include a number of restrictive covenants to prevent the company from purposely increasing the value of its default option.[30] For example, a new issue of debt hurts the original debenture holders by increasing the *ratio* of senior debt to company value. They would not object to the issue if the company kept the ratio the same by simultaneously issuing more ordinary shares. Therefore, the bond agreement often states that the company may issue more senior debt only if the ratio of senior debt to the net asset value is within a specified limit.

Why don't senior lenders demand limits on *subordinated* debt? The answer is that the subordinated lender does not get *any* money until the senior debtholders have been paid in full.[31] The senior bondholders therefore view subordinated bonds in much the same way that they view equity: They would be happy to see an issue of either.

Of course, the converse is not true. Holders of subordinated debt *do* care about both the total amount of debt and the proportion that is senior to their claim. As a result, the indenture for an issue of subordinated debt generally includes a restriction on both total debt and senior debt.

All bondholders worry that the company may issue more secured debt. An issue of mortgage bonds usually imposes a limit on the amount of secured debt. This is not necessary when

---

[29]  In Chapters 20 and 23 we showed that this option to default is equivalent to a put option on the assets of the firm.

[30]  We described in Section 18.3 some of the games that managers could play at the expense of the bondholders.

[31]  For discussion of debt subordination practices in Australia see B. Johnston, 'Debt Subordination: The Australian Perspective', *Australian Business Law Review*, **15** (2): 80–146 (April 1987).

you are issuing unsecured debentures. As long as the debenture holders are given equal protection, they do not care how much you mortgage your assets. Therefore, the bond agreement for a debenture issue usually includes a so-called **negative pledge clause**, in which the debenture holders imply, 'Me too'.[32]

During the 1950s and 1960s many companies found that they could circumvent some of these restrictions if instead of borrowing money to buy an asset, they entered into a long-term agreement to rent or lease it. For the debtholder this arrangement is very similar to secured borrowing. Therefore, trust deeds began to also include limitations on leasing.

Leases are an example of a hidden debt. After their fingers had been burned, bondholders began to impose restrictions on leases. But you want to shut the stable door *before* your fingers have been burned. We will have more to say about lease in Chapter 26.

An unscrupulous borrower can try to increase the value of the default option by issuing more debt. But that is not the only way that it can exploit its existing debtholders. For example, we know that the value of an option is affected by dividend payments. If the company pays out large dividends to its shareholders and does not replace the cash by an issue of more shares, there is less asset value available to cover the debt. Therefore, many debenture issues restrict the amount of dividends that the company may pay.[33]

## 24.6 Repayment provisions

### Debt defeasance

In the 1980s a number of Australian companies operated under restrictive trust deeds that had been written in the 1960s and 1970s. These trust deeds generally reflected the conservative nature of banking at the time and resulted in high levels of security for debt with strict gearing limitations that limited the capacity for corporate expansion. Attempts to negotiate early redemption of debt often required the payment of substantial premiums to lenders that made the practice prohibitive.[34]

Australian firms wanted to raise further debt but were restricted due to their existing trust deeds. A solution was found in the practice of **debt defeasance**.[35]

Debt defeasance is described in Australian Taxation Ruling IT 2495 as an arrangement where a borrower liable to repay a loan at a future date pays a third party an amount approximating the present value of the debt in consideration for the third party agreeing to pay the amount owed by the borrower when it comes due. Two kinds of arrangements are recognised—'legal' defeasance[36] and 'in substance' defeasance.[37]

---

[32] 'Me too' is not acceptable legal jargon. Instead, the bond agreement usually says something like, 'The company will not issue, assume or guarantee any debt secured by a line on any principal property without providing that the (existing) securities shall be secured equally and rateably'. If the firm *does* subsequently issue secured debt, this negative pledge clause allows the debenture holders to demand repayment. But is does not invalidate the security given to the other debtholders.

[33] Usually, these restrictions prohibit the company from paying dividends if their cumulative amount would exceed the sum of (1) cumulative net income, (2) the proceeds from the sale of stock or conversion of debt and (3) a dollar amount equal to about one year's dividend.

[34] Strategic acquisitions, mergers, disinvestments and internal reorganisations often required trustee consent under the terms of the trust deed—this consent was rarely granted.

[35] Recent reviews of the practice of debt defeasance in Australia include B. Marks, 'Corporate Finance—Revisiting Debt Defeasance', *CCH Journal of Australian Taxation*, pp. 43–5 (April–May 1990); R. G. Nenna and M. A. Clough, 'Debt Defeasance: A Corporate Perspective', *CCH Journal of Australian Taxation*, pp. 14–25 (October–November 1990); and S. Barkoczy and N. Bellamy, 'Debt Defeasance: Unilever and ICI Compared', *CCH Journal of Australian Taxation*, pp. 2– 19 (February–March 1996).

[36] This involves a tripartite agreement involving the lender, borrower and third party. The borrower pays an amount equal to the present value of the debt to the third party. The lender immediately releases the borrower from the contractual obligation to repay the loan in consideration of the third party agreeing to pay the lender the amount of the debt when it is due.

[37] Under the agreement, the lender is not a party to the agreement and the borrower's contractual obligation to repay the lender is therefore unaltered. The borrower pays an amount equal to the present value of the debt to the third party. However, the borrower remains primarily liable for the debt, although they do have a contractual right to demand the third party to make payments on their behalf.

Firms using the practice of debt defeasance increase their reported income and in the case of 'legal' defeasance remove the debt from their balance sheet. To release themselves from the obligations of their trust deeds, some firms would repurchase their own debt at a discount using a subsidiary company or alternatively actively seek a third party to purchase the debt.

The Australian Tax Office ruling had the impact that the difference between the amount of the principal and the interest due at a future date, and the amount paid to the lender to release the debt or to the third party to take over the obligation to pay the full amount of the principal or interest at the due date, was deemed to be assessable income to the borrower company.[38] Hence debt defeasance lost some of its initial appeal.

## Call provisions and debenture redemption

Corporate debenture issues often include a call option that allows the company to pay back or redeem the debt early. Occasionally also you come across debentures that give the *investor* the repayment option. Retractable (or putable) debentures give investors the option to demand early repayment, and extendible debentures give them the option to extend the bond's life.

Call provisions are fairly typical of long-term debentures and unsecured notes. Most such issues are callable at a premium that is initially roughly equal to the coupon, and are 'non-refundable' (NR) for 5 to 10 basis points 'below interest cost'. Medium-term loans are either wholly non-callable (NC) or are non-refundable below interest cost for most of their lives.

The option to call the debenture is obviously attractive to the issuer. If interest rates decline and bond prices rise, the issuer has the opportunity to repurchase the bonds below their potential value.

How does a company know when to call its debt securities? The answer is simple. Other things being equal, if it wishes to maximise the value of its shares, it must minimise the value of its debt. Therefore, it should never call the debt if its market value is less than the call price. Equally, it *should* call the debt if it is worth *more* than the call price.

Of course, investors take the call option into account when they buy or sell the debt instrument. They know that the company may call the debenture as soon as it is worth more than the call price. Therefore, no investor will be willing to pay more than the call price for the debt instrument. The market price of the debt may therefore reach the call price but it will not rise above it. This gives the company the following rule for calling its debt obligations: *Call the debt when, and only when, the market price reaches the call price.*[39]

If we know how bond prices behave over time, we can modify our basic option valuation model of Chapter 20 to give us the value of the callable debenture *given* that investors know the company will call the issue as soon as the market price reaches the call price. For example, look at Figure 24.1. It illustrates the relationship between the value of a non-redeemable 8 per cent five-year debenture and the value of a callable 8 per cent five-year debenture. Suppose that the value of the non-redeemable debenture is very low. In this case there is little likelihood that the company will ever wish to call its debentures. (Remember that it will call the debt only if they are worth more than the call price.) Therefore, the value of the callable debenture will be almost identical to the value of the non-redeemable debenture. Now suppose that this debenture is worth exactly 100. In this case there is a good chance that the company will wish at some time to call its debenture. Therefore, the value of our callable debenture will be slightly less than that of the non-redeemable debenture. If interest rates decline further, the price of the straight will move above 100. But no one will ever pay *more* than 100 for the callable debenture.

---

[38] See Marks, op. cit., Footnote 35.

[39] See M. J. Brennan and E. S. Schwartz, 'Savings Bonds, Retractable Bonds, and Callable Bonds', *Journal of Financial Economics*, 5: 67–88 (1977). Of course, this assumes that the debenture is correctly priced, that investors are acting rationally and that investors expect the *firm* to act rationally. Also, we ignore some complications. First, you may not wish to call a debenture if you are prevented by a non-refunding clause from issuing new debt. Second, the call premium is a tax-deductible expense for the company but is taxed as a capital gain to the debtholder. Third, there are other possible tax consequences to both the company and the investor from replacing a low coupon debenture with a higher coupon debenture. Fourth, there are costs to calling and reissuing debt.

**figure 24.1**

Relationship between the value of a callable debenture and that of a straight (non-callable) debenture. Assumptions: (1) Both debentures have an 8 per cent coupon and a five-year maturity. (2) The callable debenture may be called at any time before maturity. (3) The short-term interest rate follows a random walk, and the expected returns on debentures of all maturities are equal.

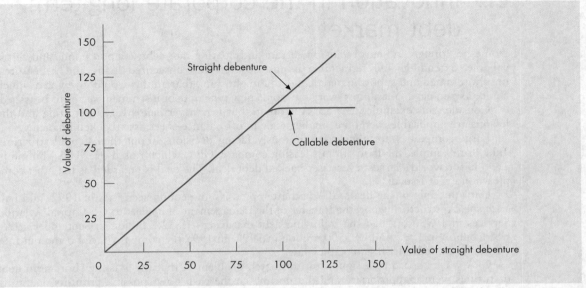

*Source*: Brennan and Schwartz, op. cit., Footnote 39. Reprinted from M. J. Brennan and E. S. Schwartz, 'Savings Bonds, Retractable Bonds, and Callable Bonds', *Journal of Financial Economics*, **5**: 67–88, ©1977, with permission of Elsevier Science.

A call provision is not a free lunch. It provides the issuer with a valuable option but that is recognised in a lower issue price. So why do companies bother with call provisions? One reason is that trust deeds often place a number of restrictions on what the company can do. Companies are happy to agree to these restrictions as long as they can escape from them if they subsequently prove too inhibiting. The call provision provides the escape route.

## Sinking fund provisions

Some debt securities include a *sinking fund provision*, or a requirement that the firm must pay back or retire a certain amount of the debt security face value on issue in each year. To do this the company makes a regular payment into a sinking fund. The funds are then used by the trustee to select and retire debt prior to maturity. As an alternative, the company can repurchase bonds on issue and place them into the fund. This provision is regarded as an advantage to remaining debtholders as it reduces the total face value on the debt security due at maturity.

However, a sinking fund provision is only a weak test for solvency *if the company is allowed to repurchase bonds in the marketplace*. Since the market value of the debt securities must always be less than the value of the firm, financial distress reduces the cost of repurchasing debt in the market. So the sinking fund actually gets progressively lower as the hurdler gets progressively weaker.

## Extendible and retractable bonds

Occasionally you may come across debt securities that give the *investor* as opposed to the borrower the repayment option. Extendible bonds give investors the option to extend the life of the securities, and retractable securities give them the option to demand early repayment. The Belgian government once issued a bond that gave both borrower *and* lender the right to demand early repayment at the bond's face value.

## 24.7 Innovation in the corporate long-term debt market

Domestic, foreign and eurobonds; fixed-rate and floating-rate debt; coupon bonds and zeros; callable, extendible and retractable bonds; secured and unsecured loans and debentures; unsubordinated and subordinated debt—you might think that all this would give you as much choice as you need. Yet almost every day some new type of debt instrument seems to be issued.

Consider this example. It is not Australian, but it is nevertheless very interesting and the lessons are applicable even on a smaller scale in off-balance-sheet asset-backed financing.

Large companies are almost continuously facing decisions about their capital structure. Take, for example, the Irish aircraft leasing company GPA, which raised over US$4 billion in 1996 in the world's largest ever asset-backed debt deal. The deal is regarded as the most complex bond ever issued.[40]

Until the time of the deal, GPA had attempted issuing equity securities in 1992, and balance sheet restructuring and the transfer of the management of its fleet to GE Capital Aviation Services in 1993, and had the following debt maturing—US$2.7 billion in September 1996, US$1 billion in 1997 and US$500 million in 1998. In 1995 the company faced being put into examination under Irish bankruptcy law.

GPA was exposed to a significant mismatch problem in that the existing short-term debt maturities were inappropriate and did not match the cash flows possible from its operating leases. The debt financing deal put in place for GPA by Morgan Stanley has been commended for its problem solving, innovation, execution and distribution.

The debt structure works as follows: A special purpose trust was established in the United States. This trust purchased notes issued by two special purpose companies. The special purpose trust issued various classes of certificates at both floating and fixed rates of interest with maturities between two and 16 years.[41] The proceeds of the issues were used to buy 201 commercial jet and 28 turboprop aircraft from GPA together with related leases and receivables. The money received by GPA was used to refinance most of its secured debt obligations.

Transfer of the aircraft from GPA took place either by direct sale to one of the American companies or by sale of 100 per cent equity of a number of aircraft owning companies. Cash flows for the special purpose trust were obtained from leasing the aircraft.[42] When issued the

---

[40]  GPA's deal is described in greater detail in M. Fisher, 'The $4 Billion Bond That Saved GPA', *Corporate Finance*, pp. 16–19 (April 1996).

[41]  The certificates issued were for the following amounts, interest rates and terms to maturity:

| Certificate principal ($m) | Interest rate (%) | Expected final payment date |
| --- | --- | --- |
| 650 | LIBOR + 0.25 | March 1998 |
| 600 | LIBOR + 0.32 | March 1999 |
| 648 | LIBOR + 0.35 | March 1999 |
| 500 | LIBOR + 0.47 | March 2001 |
| 500 | LIBOR + 0.62 | March 2003 |
| 375 | LIBOR + 1.10 | March 2009 |
| 375 | 8.150 | March 2011 |
| 400 | 10.875 | March 2012 |

[42]  The ability to service the debt is contingent on the global aircraft leasing market and the ability of GE Capital Aviation Services (GECAS) who will manage the aircraft and service the portfolio. The certificates are not secured by the aircraft or the leases. GECAS held an option to purchase GPA that has now been extended and its cost decreased.

debt certificates were bought by 150 institutions mostly in the United States and Europe. The deal permitted GPA to repay most of its secured debt and provided a solution that was consistent with American aviation requirements.

If we had to award a prize for the most unusual bond, it would probably go to a eurobond issued in 1990 by the Swedish company Electrolux. The principal repayment in this bond depends on whether an earthquake occurs in Japan. But there are many other bonds that are only a little less exotic. For example, in 1989 the Norwegian Christania Bank issued a three-year bond that came in two tranches. Tranche A paid interest equal to the long-term prime rate but subject to a maximum (or 'cap') of 12.8 per cent. Tranche B paid interest of 12.8 per cent *less* the long-term prime rate. Thus, if the general level of interest rose, the interest payment on Tranche B fell.[43] However, it was not allowed to fall below zero. You may like to check for yourself that if you invested an equal amount in each tranche, the average interest rate on your two holdings was 6.4 per cent, which was well above the going interest rate for Japanese domestic bonds.

This was not the end of the complications of Tranche B, since the principal repayment was not fixed at 100 per cent. Instead, it declined if the Japanese stock market index fell. If the index fell by about 50 per cent, the bondholder did not receive any principal repayment at all. You can think of the investor in tranche B as buying an unusual variable rate note and also selling a put option on the Japanese stock market. The high yield on the bonds was therefore offset by the possible capital loss. For many years the majority of public euroyen issues involved some option such as this. Why?

One reason is that life insurance companies in Japan cannot distribute capital gains to policy holders and therefore have a powerful appetite for high yielding bonds even if it means taking on the risk of a capital loss. Christania Bank paid a high interest rate on the package, but it got a put option in exchange. If it did not want to hold onto this put option, it could easily have sold it to foreign investors who were worried that the Japanese equity market might be overpriced and who wanted to protect themselves against a fall in the Japanese equity market.

Here are a couple more examples of bonds with quite unusual characteristics.

*Pay-in-kind* bonds (PIKs) make regular interest payments, but in the early years of the bond's life the issuer can choose to pay interest in the form of either cash or more bonds with the equivalent face value.[44] That can be a valuable option. If the company falls on hard times and bond prices fall, it can hand over low-priced bonds instead of hard cash.[45] Many of the companies that have issued PIKs have been taken over in a leveraged buy-out. These firms are often very short of cash in the initial years and therefore find the option to pay interest in the form of bonds particularly attractive.

A *liquid yield option note* (LYON) is a callable and retractable, convertible, zero coupon bond (and you cannot get much more complicated than that). In August 1990 Chemical Waste Management issued a LYON at a price of 30.7 per cent. It was a 20-year zero coupon bond that was convertible at any time into a fixed number of shares, although the company could instead pay out the cash equivalent of these shares. In addition, the bondholder had an annual option to sell the bond back to the company for cash, and Chemical Waste Management had the option to *call* the bond for cash. The exercise price of these two options increased each year.[46]

---

43    Bonds whose interest payments move in the opposite direction to the general level are called *reverse floaters* or *yield-curve notes*. Our favourite example of a reverse floater is an issue in 1986 by Hong Kong Mass Transit Railway, which offered a five-year American dollar floater with warrants. The warrants had a maturity of one year and gave the holder the right to buy a five-year Hong Kong dollar reverse floater paying 15.15 per cent less than the short-term Hong Kong interest rate (HIBOR).

44    For a discussion of PIKs see L. S. Goodman and A. H. Cohen, 'Pay-in-Kind Debentures: An Innovation', *Journal of Portfolio Management*, 15: 9–16 (Winter 1989).

45    To complicate matters, most PIKs are callable. So, if interest rates fall and bond prices rise, the firm may buy the bonds back at their call price.

46    To complicate matters, the company could exercise its call option immediately, but investors could not exercise their put option until 1993. Thereafter, both options had the same exercise price. However, in the first two years the company could not call the bond if the price of ordinary shares was below a specified minimum. If the bond is called, investors have a final chance to decide whether to convert to ordinary shares. For an interesting discussion of an earlier LYON issue by Chemical Waste Management's parent company see J. McConnell and E. S. Schwartz, 'Taming LYONS', *Journal of Finance*, 41: 561–76 (July 1986).

# The causes of innovation

It is often difficult to foresee which new securities will become popular and which will never get off the ground. However, Merton Miller believes that government often has a crucial role to play in the process of financial innovation. He compares government regulation and tax with the grain of sand that irritates the oyster and produces the pearl.[47] This would suggest that the wave of innovation that has swept capital markets in recent years may be prompted by the increasing strains of a tax and regulatory system that dates back to the 1930s and 1940s. As noted by Finnerty[48] and Van Horne among others,[49] most financial innovation is driven by a range of factors such as tax advantages or taxation differences or asymmetries between the effective tax rates of companies, reduced transaction costs, reduced agency costs, risk reallocation, incentives to increase liquidity, regulatory and legislative factors, the level and volatility of interest rates, the globalisation of markets, academic research, accounting reporting benefits such as off-balance-sheet financing and technological advancements.

# The gains from innovation

Often an idea starts as a one-off deal between a bank and its customer. As demand for a particular debt security grows, the tailor-made product is replaced by tradable securities that perform a similar function. In an environment of global competition, industry acquisitions, divestitures and corporate restructuring, borrowers and lenders continue to innovate new debt security structures to match their respective funding and investment needs. There are economies of scale in the debt securities market just as in other lines of business, and this creates a continuing pressure for standardisation of products. In Chapter 25 we will see how increased volatility in interest rate, exchange rate and commodity markets brought about low-cost methods to hedge these risks.[50]

Innovations survive if it is possible to standardise the product and if they widen investor choice. When economists smile in their sleep, they are probably dreaming of a complete capital market in which there are as many different securities as there are possible future states of the world. Such a market would give investors the widest possible choice and allow them to select portfolios that would protect them against any combination of hazards.

# Indexed bonds

Of course, complete markets are just make-believe, but we do observe a constant demand for new securities to protect against new dangers. For example, in countries such as Israel or Brazil that suffer from persistent inflation, investors do not want bonds that offer a fixed money return from coupons; they want ones that give a fixed *real* return. Therefore, in these countries payments on most debt are indexed to the rate of inflation.

Inflation indexed bonds were first issued in Australia by the Commonwealth government in July 1985 under the name of Treasury indexed bonds. The bonds were issued either with their capital value indexed to inflation or their coupon payments linked to inflation. For example, the bond might have been issued with a coupon of 5 per cent plus the rate of inflation for the coupon period. So if inflation were at 3 per cent, the coupon would be paid at 8 per cent. Subsequently, several corporates issuing bonds for long-term infrastructure projects such as the Sydney Hills Motorway (M2) have also used this type of bond issue. In Australia, there is approximately $10 billion in inflation-linked securities available—including capital index Commonwealth bonds, indexed annuities and infrastructure bonds.[51]

---

47  See M. H. Miller, 'Financial Innovation: The Last Twenty Years and the Next', *Journal of Financial and Quantitative Analysis*, 21: 459–71 (December 1986).

48  J. D. Finnerty, 'Financial Engineering in Corporate Finance: An Overview', *Financial Management*, pp. 14–33 (Winter 1988).

49  See J. C. Van Horne, 'Of Financial Innovation and Excesses', *Journal of Finance*, pp. 621–31 (July 1985).

50  For a general discussion of the way that market innovations have stemmed from a drive for more efficient ways to provide financial services see I. A. Cooper, 'Innovations: New Market Instruments', *Oxford Review of Economic Policy*, 2(1): 1–17 (1986).

51  For a discussion of the differences between payments on conventional bonds and indexed bonds see J. M. Wrase, 'Inflation Indexed Bonds: How Do They Work?', in *Business Review*, Federal Reserve Bank of Philadelphia, July–August 1997.

# Convertibles

Another innovation popular in the Australian market has been the development of convertible bonds. We discussed this type of debt security back in Chapter 22. These bonds combine both debt and equity characteristics. Conventional or 'plain vanilla' convertibles are fixed income securities that pay a straight debt coupon but include an embedded option that gives the investor the right but not the obligation to exchange the bond for a fixed number of shares. The exercise price of the option—known as the *conversion price*—is struck out of the money (i.e. the conversion price is greater than the share price at the time the bond is issued), thereby ensuring the issuer is selling equity on a deferred basis at a premium to the prevailing share price. Convertible bonds provide the opportunity to raise cheap debt and to sell equity on a deferred basis at a price that is at a premium to the current share price. However, as there is no obligation to exercise the embedded option, the ultimate choice of the conversion price is subject to the issuer's assessment of the future value of its equity.

By allowing the inputs to the plain vanilla convertible to vary—such as the coupon rate, the conversion premium, the term to maturity and any call provisions of the bond—it is possible to engineer other structures. These include deep discount or low coupon, premium redemption and putable convertible debt securities.

# Securitisation and asset-backed bonds

A significant amount of innovation has occurred with the increasing popularity of asset-backed securities. These bonds have undergone a process of *securitisation*, whereby generally liquid assets such as retail and commercial mortgages, credit card receivables, consumer loans, leases and accounts receivable are sold to a trust, which then issues securities backed by the underlying assets. In considering what type of assets can be securitised, some may argue that provided there is a revenue stream from the assets, they can be securitised. In 1996, British singer David Bowie securitised royalty payments from his records and issued bonds to the value of US$55 million. In Australia there is in excess of $8 billion in asset-backed bonds on issue. These bonds are generally AAA rated and those with five years to maturity were issued at about 26 basis points above Commonwealth Treasury bonds of similar maturity.

Typically in Australia the structure of the asset securitisation is a single tier structure, as shown in Figure 24.2. Securitisation involves the pooling and repackaging of assets into securities financed through the capital markets. The process of securitisation involves the following steps. First, create pools of assets with clearly identifiable cash flows. Second, transfer the assets to a bankruptcy-remote entity generally known as a special purpose vehicle (SPV) such as a trust to insulate the pool from the credit risk of the organisation pooling the assets. Cash flow from the assets is collected by the SPV and used to repay any issued debt securities. Third, structure asset-backed bonds so as to create a reliable cash flow stream that is credit enhanced via external or internal credit enhancements. External credit enhancements include corporate guarantees, surety bonds and insurance. Internal credit enhancements include senior or unsubordinated debt structures, in which a portion of the cash flows may still be designated as junior or subordinated debt, and overcollateralisation. Finally, issue the asset-backed bonds as either a pass through or collateralised asset-backed security.[52]

# An Australian example of financial innovation: infrastructure bonds

In the period between 1960 and 1990 Australian Commonwealth, state and local governments significantly decreased their expenditure on public infrastructure projects. This decrease was caused by a number of factors: governments' change in priorities from longer-dated projects to

---

[52]  A comprehensive review of the securitisation process, including discussion of the role of credit enhancement and the role of the trustee, can be found in *Corporate Finance Guide to Securitisation*, Euromoney Publications, London, 1994.

**figure 24.2**

A single-tier asset securitisation process.

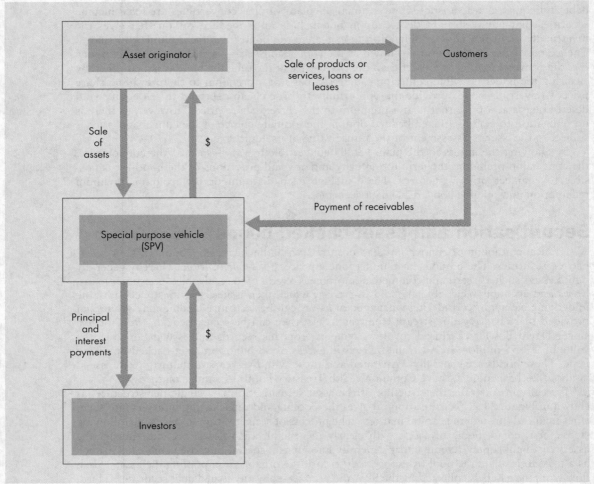

*Source*: ANZ Investment Bank, *Securitisation: A Guide for Companies*, ANZ, Melbourne, 1998.

debt reduction and user pay principles; the use of government business enterprises to manage the operation of projects on a cost recovery basis or by applying efficient pricing principles;[53] and the increasing cost of infrastructure projects relative to other government priorities.

The Commonwealth Treasury reported in 1992[54] that the private sector should be encouraged to undertake a greater proportion of the financing, management and construction of infrastructure projects. The 'One Nation' economic statement in 1992 saw the introduction of taxation concessions that generated tax advantages in the establishment of infrastructure bond facilities. Each facility could issue infrastructure borrowing securities, also known as

53   See Bureau of Industry Economics Report, *Issues in Infrastructure Pricing*, Australian Government Publishing Service, Canberra, August 1995.

54   Alison Smith, *Economic Infrastructure in Australia*, Treasury Research Paper No. 4, The Treasury, Canberra, September 1992.

infrastructure notes and Develop Australia bonds. These bonds offered tax incentives to encourage the private sector to participate in infrastructure projects.[55]

Issuers of infrastructure bonds issue their borrowing instruments after obtaining authority from the Develop Allowance Authority known as 'Invest Australia'. Once this authority is obtained, the borrowing facility allows borrowers to issue bonds or enter into borrowing agreements in which interest payments are non-deductable to the issuer, but the investor either does not pay tax on interest earned or at its election can obtain a 33 per cent tax rebate in respect of interest. Furthermore, lenders can deduct interest paid on debt raised to finance the purchase of the bonds.

To date, major projects have been initiated in the areas of transport, electricity, gas, water and sewerage. In 1996, the market for infrastructure bonds in Australia was estimated to be potentially in excess of $28 billion, making it the third largest market behind Commonwealth Treasury bonds ($80 billion) and semigovernment bonds ($70 billion).[56]

As noted by Martini and Lee,[57] securities issued to finance infrastructure projects can be classified as belonging to one or more of the following types:

■ *Infrastructure bonds*, which are subject to special tax treatment.
■ *Index-linked infrastructure bonds*, where interest payments and/or capital are based on a prescribed fixed rate above the consumer price index.
■ *Equity infrastructure securities*, which behave similar to debt instruments with an option on the residual value of the project.
■ *Hybrid securities*, which have payoff features similar to debt in the early phases of the project and later convert to equity.

How do the authorised projects operate? Well, let us have a closer look at two projects, one in Sydney and the other in Melbourne.

The M2 Motorway Project in Sydney is supervised by Hills Motorway Limited and the majority of the funds to complete the project were procured by Hills Motorway Management Limited who manage Hills Motorway Trust. Investors were permitted to invest in the Trust via application forms with the prospectus dated November 1994, which identified the following debt instruments to be used in the project:[58]

■ An infrastructure loan of approximately $153 million.
■ A term debt facility of approximately $111 million, repayable over a term ending in 2009.
■ A CPI bond facility of approximately $200 million linked to increases in CPI, repayable over a term ending in 2021.

To extend the period over which concessions could potentially be used, the CPI bondholders voted in September 1996 to refinance the borrowing in the form of a direct infrastructure bond using a refinancing infrastructure borrowing[59] that allows for the project to receive positive cash flows on the basis of the sale of tax deductions to retail customers at amounts in excess of the corporate tax rate.

---

[55] As noted by G. Harris and D. Clifford, 'Infrastructure Bonds—A New Dawn', *Journal of Banking and Finance Law and Practice*, 5 (4): 298–304 (December 1994), initial interest in the issue of infrastructure bonds was negligible until the lack of interest promoted a review by the government and changes were announced in the 'Working Nation' statement in 1994.

[56] Many current and potential projects were identified in an 'Infrastructure' special feature in the *Australian Financial Review*, 7 February 1996, including the Smithfield Power Project ($172 million), Sydney's M2 Motorway Project ($496 million) and the Melbourne City Link Project ($1.7 billion).

[57] C. Martini and D. Lee, 'Difficulties in Infrastructure Financing', *Journal of Applied Finance and Investment*, 1: 24–7 (March–April 1996).

[58] This information was obtained from the M2 Motorway prospectus dated November 1994, which allowed for the issue of 1 326 000 units in Hills Motorway Trust and 1 326 000 shares in Hills Motorway Limited at a combined application price of $1.00 for one unit and one share.

[59] For details see Macquarie Bank Debt Markets, 'The Hills Motorway Limited (M2)—Refinancing of the Infrastructure Bond', *Debt Markets Perspective*, pp. 16–19 (October 1996).

The Melbourne City Link Project has been undertaken within a legal structure comprising Transurban City Link Limited, who will oversee the construction of the project by two firms in a joint venture, and City Link Management Limited, who will manage the City Link Unit Trust. Investors invested in the Project via the application form in the prospectus dated February 1996. Funding for the project is required in two phases—the construction phase and the operations phase. The debt funding structure for the project comprises a core project debt facility supported by a CPI bond facility, an infrastructure loan facility, an equity infrastructure note facility and a subordinated facility.[60]

## 24.8  Project finance

Privately placed loans are usually direct obligations of the parent or one of its principal subsidiaries. In recent years there has been considerable interest in a new type of private loan that is tied as far as possible to the fortunes of a particular project and that minimises the exposure of the parent. Such a loan is usually referred to as *project finance* and is a specialty of large international banks.

### Project finance: some common features

Project financing packages often feature high debt-to-equity ratios due to the high capital costs associated with development of the project; funding techniques vary from project to project; the financial returns to investors are reliant on the income of the project; and there often is only limited recourse to the project promoters by segregating the project from the sponsor's other assets so as to quarantine the project from the risks of the sponsor's other assets. The structure of project financing involves allocating the risks of the project among the funding partners.[61]

Project finance is often provided in the form of a straight loan. However, an alternative arrangement known as a *production payment* exists where the banks do not lend directly to the parent or operating company organising the project. Instead, they lend to an intermediate company that is controlled by them. This company then uses the money to make an advance payment to the project's owner against future delivery of the product. When the product is delivered, the intermediate company can sell it and use the proceeds to repay the banks.

We can classify project financing according to the contractual obligations of the project's owners. The purest, but least common, method of financing offers the lender *no recourse* against the owners at any stage. This notion of no recourse is somewhat imprecise, for the banks may well require a general assurance from the parent that it will do its best to ensure the success of the project. Although these 'comfort letters' are usually too general to be sued upon, they do represent a potentially embarrassing commitment on the part of the parent.

Once of the most common threats to a successful project loan is a serious delay in completion. Occasionally, the project may even turn out to be technically infeasible. Our second class of loans therefore consists of those that are supported by a *completion guarantee*. Such a guarantee may be provided by the parent company or by an insurance company in the form of *completion bonding*.

---

60   This information was obtained from the Melbourne City Link prospectus dated 20 February 1996. The prospectus allowed for the issue of up to 127 000 parcels of securities at an issue price of $500 per parcel (with a minimum of two parcels per application). Each parcel comprised 499 equity infrastructure bonds issued by Transurban City Link Limited, one share in Transurban City Link Limited and one unit in the City Link Unit Trust.

61   P. D. Slattery, 'Project Finance—An Overview', *Corporate and Business Law Journal*, 6: 61–116 (1993), examines those features that distinguish project financing from traditional forms of corporate funding and identifies the following risks that the project will have to confront: completion risk, raw material risk, operating risk, market risk, political risk, reserves risk, foreign currency risk, interest rate risk, environmental risk, tax risk, force majeure risk and delivery risk.

Most project loans provide lenders with more recourse against the parent. Here are three other examples of how the parent companies may provide some limited guarantees:

▌ *The throughput agreement.* Many oil pipeline loans involve a throughput agreement. This states that if other companies do not make sufficient use of the pipeline, the owners themselves will ship enough oil through it to provide the pipeline company with the cash that it needs to service the loan.

▌ *The cost company arrangement.* Under a cost company arrangement, the project's owners receive all the project's output free of charge. In exchange, they agree to pay all operating costs including loan service. Thus, the project has no net income, and each parent firm simply deducts from its own profits its share of the project's expenses.

▌ *The cash deficiency arrangement.* Under this arrangement, the project's owners agree to provide the operating company with enough funds to maintain a certain level of working capital.

In any project financing, the payments on the loan should correspond as closely as possible to the ability of the project to generate cash. For example, if the project's completion date is uncertain, the first payment date might simply be set at a specified number of months after completion. If the loan involves a large final payment, it is common to include an *earnings recapture* clause under which a proportion of any surplus earnings is applied to reduce the final payment. A lender who bears the risk of inadequate reserves will wish to ensure that the reserves are not depleted too rapidly. In these cases, therefore, it is common to assign a *proportion* of revenues to loan repayments rather than a fixed sum.

# The benefits of project finance

Various motives have been suggested for the use of project finance rather than direct borrowing by the parent company. It is tempting to believe that the value of a project to the parent is enhanced if it can be made to stand alone as a self-financing entity, or that the parent benefits from its success and is isolated from its failure. Such a result is improbable. When we look at actual project loans, we find that not only is the parent rarely isolated from the vicissitudes of the project, but the rate of interest on the project loan is directly related to the degree of support that the parent provides.

However, project finance does allow the parent to transfer specific risks to the lenders. Correspondingly, with many loans for projects in politically unstable countries, the lenders are taking on the risk of adverse government action. Many companies believe that expropriation by a foreign government is *less likely* when they raise money by project financing.

Project financing may not be shown as debt on the company's balance sheet and in some cases the owner's guarantees may not be shown on the balance sheet at all. In this case the financing is said to be 'off-balance-sheet'. This attracts some financial managers—but lenders or shareholders usually recognise these hidden liabilities.

Project financing can be costly to arrange, but sometimes the arrangement is simpler than a direct loan. Projects are often jointly owned, and it may be easier to negotiate one project loan than separate financing to each of several parents. Also, security for project lenders commonly derives as much from contractual arrangements as from tangible assets. For example, a bank's security for a pipeline loan depends on throughput agreements, and its security for a tanker loan depends on charter agreements. In such instances it may be simplest to tie the loan directly to these contracts.

## 24.9 Summary

Now that you have read this chapter, you should have a fair idea of what you are letting yourself in for when companies seek to borrow long-term debt.

A company can make an issue of debt in the domestic Australian market or it can do so in foreign markets or in the euromarket. Furthermore, the company must assess whether it wishes to borrow funds from a bank or issue securities under its own name as debentures, unsecured notes or corporate bonds.

The significant changes in the regulatory requirements on banks have liberalised the market for fully-drawn advances and long-term loans. However, some still believe that the requirements imposed by providing security and by negative covenants make this form of lending less attractive.

The detailed agreement for issuing corporate long-term debt securities is set out in the trust deed between your company and a trustee. The main provisions are summarised in the prospectus at the time of issue if the debt securities are to be issued publicly. The trust deed states whether the bonds are unsubordinated or subordinated and whether they are secured or unsecured. Most long-term corporate debt securities issued in Australia are unsecured debentures or notes. This means that they are general claims on the corporation. In the event of a default when the issue is secured, the trustee to these issues can repossess the specified company's assets in order to pay off the debt.

Many long-term debt issues have a *sinking fund*. This means that the company must set aside enough money each year to retire a specified amount of the debt. A sinking fund reduces the average life of the debt, and as long as the company is not allowed to repurchase debt in the marketplace, it provides a yearly test of the company's ability to service its debt. It therefore protects the debtholders against the risk of default.

Many long-dated bonds may have call provisions by which the debt can be called at a premium, which is initially equal to the coupon and which declines progressively to zero. There is one common limitation to this right—companies are generally prohibited from calling the bond in the first few years if they intend to replace it with another bond at a lower rate of interest. The option to call the bond may be very valuable: If interest rates decline and bond values rise, you may be able to call a bond that would be worth substantially more than the call price. Of course, if investors know that you may call the bond, the call price will act as a ceiling on the market price. Your best strategy, therefore, is to call the debt as soon as the market price hits the call price. You are unlikely to do better than that. The trust deed also lays down certain conditions. Here are some examples of things the company must *not* do:

1. Issues of unsubordinated debt or loans prohibit the company from issuing further junior debt instruments if the ratio of chargeable debt to net tangible assets exceeds a specified maximum.
2. Issues of subordinated debt or loans may also prohibit the company from issuing further debt if the ratio of *all* debt to net tangible assets exceeds a specified maximum.
3. Unsecured debt securities and loans incorporate a *negative pledge* clause, which prohibits the company from securing additional debt without giving equal treatment to the existing unsecured debt securities.
4. Many debt securities and loans place a limit on the company's dividend payments.

Conditions that require the company to take positive steps to protect the bondholders are known as *positive covenants*. In public bond issues these conditions are generally innocuous. The really important positive covenants are those that give the bondholder the chance to claim a default and get money out while the company still has a substantial value. For example, some contracts require the company to maintain a minimum level of working capital or net worth. Since a deficiency in either is a good indication of financial weakness, this condition is tantamount to giving the bondholders the right to demand their money back as soon as life appears hazardous.

There is an enormous variety of long-term corporate debt securities, and new forms are spawned almost daily. By a principle of natural selection some of these new instruments become popular and may even replace existing species. Others are ephemeral curiosities. We do not know all the reasons for the success of some innovations but we suggest that many new securities owe their origin to tax rules and government regulation. The lasting innovations are those that reduce costs or widen investor choice.

## FURTHER READING

For a detailed overview of the long-term debt market and project finance in Australia see the articles by Julian Perch and Chris Williams on 'Bank Finance', Robert Barry and Cliff Standout on 'Domestic Sources of Long-Term Corporate Debt' and Michael Skull and Richard Fernando on 'Project Finance' in:

> R. Bruce, B. McKern, I. Pollard and M. Skully, *Handbook of Australian Corporate Finance*, 5th ed., Butterworths, Sydney, 1997.

For an overview of the products available in Australian long-term debt markets see:

> B. Hunt and C. Terry, *Financial Instruments and Markets*, Thomas Nelson, Melbourne, 1993.
>
> M. McGrath and C. Viney, *Financial Institutions, Instruments and Markets in Australia*, 2nd ed., McGraw-Hill, Sydney, 1997.
>
> G. Pierson, R. Brown, S. Easton and P. Howard, *Business Finance*, 7th ed., McGraw-Hill, Sydney, 1998.

For discussion of up-to-date developments in the long-term debt market see the journals *Euromoney, Risk* and *Corporate Finance*.

Recent reviews of the practice of debt defeasance in Australia include:

> S. Barkoczy and N. Bellamy, 'Debt Defeasance: Unilever and ICI Compared', *CCH Journal of Australian Taxation*, pp. 2–19 (February–March 1996).
>
> B. Marks, 'Corporate Finance: Revisiting Debt Defeasance', *CCH Journal of Australian Taxation*, pp. 43–5 (April–May 1990).
>
> R. G. Nenna and M. A. Clough, 'Debt Defeasance: A Corporate Perspective', *CCH Journal of Australian Taxation*, pp. 14–25 (October–November 1990).

Johnston provides a detailed discussion of debt subordination practices in Australia:

> B. Johnston, 'Debt Subordination: The Australian Perspective', *Australian Business Law Review*, **15** (**2**): 80–146 (April 1987).

The articles by Brennan and Schwartz and by Kraus provide a general discussion of call provisions:

> M. J. Brennan and E. S. Schwartz, 'Savings Bonds, Retractable Bonds and Callable Bonds', *Journal of Financial Economics*, **5**: 67–8 (1977).
>
> A. Kraus, 'An Analysis of Call Provisions and the Corporate Refunding Decision', *Midland Corporate Finance Journal*, **1**: 46–60 (Spring 1983).

Smith and Warner provide an extensive survey and analysis of covenants:

> C. W. Smith and J. B. Warner, 'On Financial Contracting: An Analysis of Bond Covenants', *Journal of Financial Economics*, **7**: 117–61 (June 1979).

The use of covenants in Australian public and private debt contracts is discussed in:

> J. Cotter, 'Utilisation and Restrictiveness of Covenants in Australian Private Debt Contracts', *Accounting and Finance*, **38** (**2**): 181–96 (1998).
>
> I. Ramsay and B. K. Sidhu, 'Accounting and Non-Accounting Based Information in the Market for Debt: Evidence from Australian Private Debt Contracts', *Accounting and Finance*, **38** (**2**): 197–221 (1998).

D. Stokes and K. L. Tay, 'Restrictive Covenants and Accounting Information in the Market for Convertible Notes: Further Analysis', *Accounting and Finance*, **28** (2): 57–73 (1988).

G. Whittred and I. Zimmer, 'Accounting Information in the Market for Debt', *Accounting and Finance*, **26** (2): 19–33 (1986).

A very detailed overview of factors promoting the innovation of financial instruments is given in:

J. D. Finnerty, 'Financial Engineering in Corporate Finance: An Overview', *Financial Management*, Winter 1988.

Three very useful books on structured securities:

F. J. Fabozzi and I. M. Pollack (eds.), *Handbook of Fixed Income Securities*, 2nd ed., Dow Jones-Irwin, Homewood, Ill., 1987.

J. F. Marshall and V. K. Bansal, *Financial Engineering*, 2nd ed., Kolb Publishing Company, Miami, 1992.

J. Walmsley, *The New Financial Instruments*, John Wiley & Sons, New York, 1988.

For further discussion of project finance see:

J. W. Kensinger and J. D. Martin, 'Project Finance: Raising Money the Old-Fashioned Way', *Journal of Applied Corporate Finance*, **1**: 69–81 (Fall 1988).

## QUIZ

**1.** Select the most appropriate term from within the parentheses:
   a. (Interest only bank loans/amortising bank loans) require payment of both principal and interest throughout the term of the loan.
   b. (Short-dated notes/long-dated debentures) are often non-callable.
   c. (Sinking fund provisions/call provisions) allow the trustee to retire debt prior to maturity by holding elections among debtholders.
   d. (Large industrial firms/small mining firms) usually have high levels of unsecured debt.
   e. (Term loans/debentures) require authorisation from the trustee before any amendments can be made to the trust deed.

**2.** a. If interest rates rise, will callable or non-callable bonds fall more in price?
   b. The Belgian government has issued bonds that may be repaid after a specified date at the option of either the government or the bondholder. If each side acts rationally, what will happen on that date?

**3.** Identify the factors that have prompted debt market innovation in the 1990s and into the new millennium.

**4.** a. As a senior debtholder would you like the company to issue more junior debt, would you prefer it not to do so, or would you not care?
   b. You hold debt secured on the company's existing property. Would you like the company to issue more unsecured debt, would you prefer it not to do so, or would you not care?

## QUESTIONS AND PROBLEMS

1.  After a sharp change in interest rates, newly issued bonds generally sell at yields different to outstanding bonds of the same quality. One suggested explanation is that there is a difference in the value of the call provision. Explain how this could arise.

2.  Obtain a prospectus for a recent debenture issue and identify the terms and conditions of the issue.

3.  What restrictions are imposed on a company's freedom to issue further debt? Be as precise as possible.

4.  Explain carefully why senior debt covenants place different restrictions on a company's freedom to issue additional debt.

5.  A retractable bond is a bond that may be repaid before maturity at the investor's option. Sketch a diagram similar to Figure 24.1 showing the relationship between the value of an ordinary bond and a retractable bond.

6.  What determines the value of an indexed bond? Should the rate of interest on an indexed bond be higher or lower than the expected real rate on a nominal bond?

7.  Explain carefully why bond indentures place limitations on the following actions:
    a.  Sale of the company's assets.
    b.  Payment of dividends to shareholders.
    c.  Issue of additional senior debt.

8.  Look up the terms of an asset-backed bond. A common problem with many securitised bonds is that the repayments from the customers may occur in advance of the term to maturity, leading to a pre-payment risk. How is this managed in the asset-backed bond selected? Has this bond increased the shareholders' risk or reduced it?

9.  Does the issue of additional junior debt harm senior bondholders? Would your answer be the same if the junior debt matured *before* the senior debt? Explain.

10. In Section 24.7 we referred to Christania Bank's exotic bond. Explain how you would value Tranche B. Assume that the principal repayment is fixed at 100 per cent of par. (*Hint*: Find a package of other securities that would produce identical cash flows.) What does this tell you about the riskiness of Hong Kong Mass Transit Railway's warrants?

11. Dorlcote Milling Ltd has outstanding a $1 million corporate bond with a coupon set at 3 per cent maturing in 10 years. The coupon on any new debt issued by the company is 10 per cent. The finance director, Mr Tulliver, cannot decide whether there is a tax benefit to repurchasing the existing bonds in the marketplace and replacing them with new 10 per cent bonds. What do you think? Start by assuming that all bondholders are tax-exempt. Then introduce Miller's idea that higher-rate taxpayers will gravitate to tax efficient securities and force up their prices.

**12.** Look up a recent issue of an unusual bond in, say, a recent issue of the periodicals *Euromoney*, *Risk* or *Corporate Finance*. Why do you think this bond was issued? What investors do you think it would appeal to? How would you value the unusual features?

**13.** In a number of countries such as France it is not uncommon for firms to band together to make a debt issue. A portion of the receipts is put aside in a safe government bond and the remainder is parcelled out among the different issuers. Each firm is responsible for its portion of the total debt, but in the event of default by any one firm the lenders can draw on the money invested in the government bond. Do you think this is a good idea? How would you value this debt?

**14.** Some eurobonds involve payments in more than one currency. For example, in 1985 Anheuser-Busch issued a 10-year yen bond at a price of US$101 per $100 face value. The coupon payment was to be made in yen but the final repayment of principal was to be made in dollars at an exchange rate of 208 yen to the dollar. How would you value such a bond? When the bond matured in 1995 the exchange rate was approximately 99 yen to the dollar. Would Anheuser-Busch have done better to have issued a straight yen bond?

**15.** Bond prices can fall either because of a change in the general level of interest rates or because of an increased risk of default. To what extent do floating rate bonds and putable bonds protect the investor against each of these risks?

**16.** Corporate term loans may stipulate either a fixed rate or a variable rate. As a borrower, what considerations might cause you to prefer one rather than the other? Would your answer differ if you could swap from fixed to floating or floating to fixed at will?

**17.** Suppose that a company simultaneously issues a zero coupon bond and a coupon bond with identical maturity. Both are callable at any time at their face value. Other things being equal, which bond is likely to offer the higher yield? Why?

# chapter 25

# HEDGING FINANCIAL RISK

Most of the time we take risk as God-given. An asset or business has its beta, and that is that. Its cash flow is exposed to unpredictable changes in raw material costs, tax rates, technology and a long list of other variables. There is nothing the manager can do about it.

That is not wholly true. To some extent, managers can choose the risks that the business takes. We have already come across one way that they can do so. In our discussion of real options in Chapter 21 we described how companies reduce risk by building flexibility into their operations. A company that uses standardised machine tools rather than specialised equipment lowers the cost of bailing out if things go wrong.

A petrochemical plant that is designed to use either oil or natural gas as a feedstock reduces the impact of an unfavourable shift in relative fuel prices. And so on.

In this chapter we shall explain how companies also enter into financial contracts that insure against or hedge (i.e. offset) a variety of business hazards. But first we should give some reasons *why* they do so.

Insurance and hedging are seldom free: At best they are zero NPV transactions.[1] Most businesses insure or hedge to reduce risk, not to make money. Why, then, bother to reduce risk in this way? For one thing, it makes financial planning easier and reduces the odds of an

---

[1] Hedging transactions are zero NPV when trading is costless and markets are completely efficient. In practice, the firm has to pay small trading costs at least.

embarrassing cash shortfall. A shortfall might mean only an unexpected trip to the bank, but if financing is hard to obtain on short notice, the company might need to cut back its capital expenditure program. In extreme cases an unhedged setback could trigger financial distress or even liquidation. Banks and bondholders are aware of this possibility and, before lending to your firm, they often will insist that it be properly insured.

In some cases, hedging also makes it easier to decide whether an operating manager deserves a stern lecture or a pat on the back. Suppose your confectionery division shows a 60 per cent profit increase in a period when cocoa prices decline by 12 per cent. How much of the increase is due to the change in cocoa prices and how much to good management? If cocoa prices were hedged, it is probably good management. If they were not, things have to be sorted out with hindsight by asking, 'What would profits have been *if* cocoa prices had been hedged?'[2]

Finally, hedging extraneous events can help focus the operating manager's attention. It is naïve to expect the manager of the confectionery division *not* to worry about cocoa prices if her bottom line and bonus depend on them. That worrying time would be better spent if the prices were hedged.[3]

Of course, managers are not paid to avoid all risks, but if they can reduce their exposure to risks for which there are no compensating rewards, they can afford to place larger bets when the odds are in their favour. Many financial decisions involve a package of bets. For example, when BMW decides to launch a modified model aimed at the Australian market—a three- or five-year commitment—it is betting on, among other things, the exchange rate between Australian dollars and deutschmarks (since BMW costs are in deutschmarks and its revenues are in Australian dollars). It is also betting on the exchange rate between Australian dollars and pounds (since this affects the competitive position of Jaguar). Perhaps BMW is optimistic about everything except the short-run dollar–deutschmark exchange rate—it fears that the deutschmark will appreciate, making German cars expensive in Australia. Should that pessimism stop BMW from going ahead with the new model? It might if there were no way to hedge out the exchange-rate bet. But BMW can use the currency forward markets to eliminate the bet on the exchange rate.[4] Therefore, management should ask two questions:

1. Should we go ahead with the new model, assuming that the company hedges the currency risk?
2. What bets, if any, should be placed on the currency?[5]

Unpredictable changes in commodity prices, interest rates and exchange rates can all adversely affect the earning capacity of any firm. However, as noted by Smithson, Smith and Wilford[6] and Grinblatt and Titman[7], if a firm manages its price risk it will decrease the volatility of the value of the firm's future earnings and cash flows. Through risk management the firm also can decrease transaction costs associated with increased probability of

---

2   Many large firms insure or hedge away operating divisions' risk exposures by setting up internal, make-believe markets between each division and the treasurer's office. Trades in the internal markets are at real (external) market prices. The object is to relieve the operating managers of risks outside their control. The treasurer makes a separate decision on whether to offset the *firm's* exposure.

3   A Texas oil producer who lost hundreds of millions in ill-fated deals protested, 'Why should I worry? Worry is for strong minds and weak characters.' If there are any financial managers with weak minds and strong characters, we especially advise them to hedge whenever they can.

4   We explain later how currency forward markets work.

5   One final point: If BMW's worries about the exchange rate are confirmed, is the company in a stronger competitive position if it has hedged against a change in the exchange rate? It is certainly true that BMW will make more money if it has hedged. But there is a general maxim that you should not let the profits in one part of your business (currency hedging) cross-subsidise losses in another part (making cars). If, for example, the deutschmark should appreciate to the point where BMW would do better to stop exporting to Australia, it should do just that. It should *not* go on selling cars at a loss just because it is making large profits on its currency position.

6   See C. W. Smithson, C. W. Smith and D. S. Wilfred, *Managing Financial Risks*, McGraw-Hill, Chicago, 1995.

7   See M. Grinblatt and S. Titman, *Financial Markets and Corporate Strategy*, Irwin/McGraw-Hill, Boston, 1998.

financial distress and avoid investment decision errors caused by underinvestment in positive NPV projects caused by volatility in the firm's earnings. It also can help to improve the planning of future capital needs by reducing the need to gain access to outside capital markets and improve the design of management compensation contracts.

We start the chapter by looking briefly at how firms use insurance to reduce risk. We then turn to hedging: We first introduce you to some of the basic tools of hedging, including how to identify exposures and potential risk and the characteristics of some hedging instruments such as forward and futures contracts swaps. Finally, we explain how to set up a hedge.

# 25.1 Insurance

Most businesses buy insurance against a variety of hazards—the risk that their plant will be damaged by fire; that their ships, aeroplanes or vehicles will be involved in accidents; that the firm will be held liable for environmental damage; and so on.

When a firm takes out insurance, it is simply transferring the risk to the insurance company. Insurance companies have some advantages in bearing risk. First, they may have considerable experience in insuring similar risks, so they are well placed to estimate the probability of loss and price the risk accurately. Second, they may be skilled at providing advice on measures that the firm can take to reduce the risk, and they may offer lower premiums to firms that take this advice. Third, an insurance company can *pool* risk by holding a large diversified portfolio of policies. The claims on any individual policy can be highly uncertain, yet the claims on a portfolio of policies may be very stable. Of course, insurance companies cannot diversify away macroeconomic risks; firms use insurance policies to reduce their specific risk, and they find other ways to avoid macro risks.

Insurance companies also suffer some *disadvantages* in bearing risk, and these are reflected in the prices they charge. Suppose your firm owns a $1 billion offshore oil platform. A meteorologist has advised you that there is a 1-in-10 000 chance that in any year the platform will be destroyed as a result of a storm. Thus, the *expected* loss from storm damage is $1 billion/ 10 000 = $100 000.

The risk of storm damage is almost certainly not a macroeconomic risk and can potentially be diversified away.[8] So you might expect that an insurance company would be prepared to insure the platform against such destruction as long as the premium was sufficient to cover the expected loss. In other words, a fair premium for insuring the platform should be $100 000 a year.[9] Such a premium would make insurance a zero NPV deal for your company. Unfortunately, no insurance company would offer a policy for only $100 000. Why not?

▮ *Reason 1: Administrative costs.* An insurance company, like any other business, incurs a variety of costs in arranging the insurance and handling any claims. For example, disputes about the liability for environmental damage can eat up millions of dollars in legal fees. Insurance companies need to recognise these costs when they set their premiums.

▮ *Reason 2: Adverse selection.* Suppose that an insurer offers life insurance policies with 'no medical needed, no questions asked'. There are no prizes for guessing who will be most tempted to buy this insurance. Our example is an extreme case of the problem of *adverse*

---

[8]  If the potential liability is large, insurance companies often spread the risk among themselves. But the consequences of major catastrophes—such as earthquakes, hurricanes and other environmental disasters—can be so huge that it is difficult even for a group of insurers to diversify the risk. For example, claims for asbestosis against members of Lloyd's of London alone have already amounted to over $5 billion and could eventually reach several times that figure.

[9]  This is imprecise. If the premium is paid at the beginning of the year and the claim is not settled until the end, then the zero NPV premium equals the discounted value of the expected claim or $100 000/(1 + r)$.

*selection*. Unless the insurance company can distinguish between good and bad risks, the latter will always be most eager to take out insurance. The premium to insure your oil platform will need to recognise this fact.

■ *Reason 3: Moral hazard*. Two farmers met on the road to town. 'Fred', said one, ' I was sorry to hear about your shed burning down.' 'Shh', replied the other, 'that's tomorrow night.' The story is an example of another problem for insurers, known as *moral hazard*. Once a risk has been insured, the owner may be less careful to take proper precautions against damage. Insurance companies are aware of this and factor it into their pricing.

When these extra costs are small, insurance may be close to a zero NPV transaction. When they are large, insurance may be a costly way to protect against risk.

Major public companies typically buy insurance against large potential losses and self-insurance against routine ones. The idea is that large losses can trigger financial distress. On the other hand, routine losses for a corporation are predictable, so there is little point paying premiums to an insurance company and receiving back a fairly constant proportion as claims.

BP has challenged the conventional wisdom. Like all oil companies, BP is exposed to a variety of potential losses. Some arise from routine events such as vehicle accidents and industrial injuries. At the other extreme, they may result from catastrophes such as a major oil spill or the loss of an offshore oil platform. In the past BP purchased considerable external insurance.[10] During the 1980s it paid out an average of $115 million a year in insurance premiums and recovered $25 million a year in claims.

Recently BP took a hard look at its insurance strategy. It reasoned that it made sense to allow local managers to insure against relatively routine risks, for in those cases insurance companies have an advantage in assessing and pricing risk and compete vigorously against one another. However, it decided that for the most part it would no longer insure externally against losses above US$10 million. For these larger, more specialised risks BP felt that insurance companies had less ability to assess the risk and were less well placed to advise on safety measures. As a result, BP concluded, insurance against large risks was not competitively priced.

How much extra risk does BP assume by its decision not to insure against major losses? BP estimated that large losses of above $500 million could be expected to occur once in 30 years. But BP is a huge company with equity worth about $35 billion. So even a $500 million loss, which could throw most companies into bankruptcy, would translate after tax into a fall of only 1 per cent in the value of BP's equity. BP concluded that this was a risk worth taking. In other words, it concluded that for large, low-probability risks the share market was a more efficient risk-absorber than the insurance industry.

# Homemade insurance

The insurance policies that we have been discussing are offered by specialist insurance companies. But sometimes you can construct your own policies by using exchange traded options. For example, assume that it is July 1998 and you are an investor holding a large parcel of Commonwealth Bank shares valued at $20.08 each.[11] You are concerned that recent news regarding the Asian economic crisis might cause the Bank's shares to fall below $19.00. You can insure your holding against loss by acquiring Commonwealth Bank put options[12] for exercise at an exercise price of $19.00 and at a premium cost of $0.40. If the price of Commonwealth Bank shares falls below $19.00, the investor can exercise the option and sell the shares for $19.00.

---

[10]  Our description of BP's insurance strategy draws heavily on N. A. Doherty and C. W. Smith Jr, 'Corporate Insurance Strategy: The Case of British Petroleum', *Journal of Applied Corporate Finance*, 6: 4–15 (Fall 1993). However, with one or two exceptions, insurance has not been available for the very largest losses of $500 million or more.

[11]  Details obtained from the *Australian Financial Review*, 21 July 1998.

[12]  Put options give the holder the right, but not the obligation, to *sell* the asset at a predetermined price at or by a set exercise date.

Here is another example: Imagine that you have just bid on a large construction project in France. Payment will be in French francs, but many of the costs will be in Australian dollars. By the time that you will find out whether you have been awarded the contract, the value of the franc might have declined and the project might no longer be profitable. In that case you can insure yourself against currency loss by taking out an option to sell francs. If you get the contract and the franc depreciates, the value of the option should offset the reduction in the dollar value of the contract. If you *do not* get the contract, you simply have an option which will be profitable if the franc depreciates and is valueless otherwise.

Of course, such insurance does not come free; the price you pay for the option is the insurance premium. If the franc appreciates, you have with the benefit of hindsight bought unnecessary insurance.

## 25.2 Exposure identification

A critical step in the process of managing risk is in the identification and quantification of potential exposures. For example, an investor holding a share portfolio is exposed to share price decreases, a corporate treasury investing in bonds is exposed to interest rate decreases and a jeweller is exposed to price increases in the price of precious metals and stones.

How can we get started in managing these or similar exposures?

A good starting point is always to identify the type of any potential exposure and then quantify the exposure to evaluate the project or investment's sensitivity. To identify the type of exposure it is important to clearly understand whether the firm is a buyer or seller of the goods or financial assets. A buyer is exposed to any unexpected future price increase (yield decrease), while a seller is exposed to any unexpected future price decrease (yield increase). Next, the exact specifications of the commodity or asset to be traded in the future should be identified. Then, time series, regression-based, simulation or scenario analysis can be used to identify possible future outcomes for the future price relative to the current price. A comparison can then be made between the expected price and the current price as well as an examination of the impacts on cash flows to the firm. The firm now has a view of the direction and possibly the magnitude of future price changes. Hence, it is now in a position to assess its hedging needs subject to whether it is a buyer or seller of goods in the future.

A decision can now be made as to whether:

■ No hedge should be implemented.
■ A partial hedge should be implemented.
■ The exposure should be fully hedged.

## 25.3 Hedging with futures[13]

Hedging involves taking on one risk to offset another. We will explain shortly how to set up a hedge, but first we will give some examples and describe some tools that are specially designed for hedging. These are futures, forwards and swaps. Together with options, they are known as derivative instruments or derivatives because their value depends on the value of another asset. You can think of them as side bets on the value of the underlying asset.[14]

We start with the oldest actively traded derivative instruments, **futures contracts**. Futures were originally developed for agricultural and other commodities. For example, assume it is

---

13　For a comprehensive discussion of futures contract pricing and theoretical issues see R. Heaney, 'Futures Contract Pricing and Hedging: A Review of Theory and Evidence', *Accounting Research Journal*, 8 (1): 48–65 (1995).

14　'Side bet' conjures up an image of wicked speculators. Derivatives attract their share of speculators, some of whom might be wicked, but they are also used by sober and prudent business people to reduce risk.

currently March 1998 and suppose that a wheat farmer expects to have 1000 tonnes of wheat to sell in September this year. If he is worried that the price may decline in the interim, he can hedge by selling 1000 tonnes of September wheat futures. As a futures seller of wheat the farmer is fearful of any price decrease. Hence, the farmer will sell futures contracts. The hedge will involve selling 20 futures contracts—each contract is for 50 tonnes of Australian standard white wheat. In this case he agrees to deliver 1000 tonnes of wheat in September at a price that is set today. Do not confuse this futures contract with the option, in which the holder has a choice whether or not to make the delivery; the farmer's futures contract is a firm promise to deliver wheat.

A miller is in the opposite position. She needs to *buy* wheat after the harvest. The miller is exposed to any unhedged price increase in the price of wheat between March and September. If she would like to fix the price of this wheat ahead of time, she can do so by *buying* wheat futures. In other words, she agrees to take delivery of wheat in the future at a price that is fixed today. The miller also does not have an option; if she holds the contract to maturity, she is obliged to take delivery.

Both the farmer and the miller have less risk than before.[15] The farmer has hedged risk by *selling* wheat futures; this is termed a **short hedge**. The miller has hedged risk by *buying* wheat futures; this is known as a **long hedge**.

The price of wheat for immediate delivery is known as the **spot price**. When the farmer sells wheat futures, the price that he agrees to take for his wheat may be very different from the spot price. But as the date for delivery approaches, a futures contract becomes more and more like a spot contract and the price of the future snuggles up to the spot price. The difference between the futures price and the spot price can be estimated at any point in time during the life of the futures contract and is known as the *basis*.[16]

The farmer may decide to wait until his futures contract matures and then deliver wheat to the buyer. In practice, such delivery is very rare, for it is more convenient for the farmer to buy back the wheat futures just before maturity.[17] If he is properly hedged, any loss on his wheat crop will be exactly offset by the profit on his sale and subsequent repurchase of wheat futures.

## Commodity and financial futures

Futures contracts are bought and sold on organised exchanges throughout the world. Table 25.1 details the major exchanges.

Each of the exchanges offers contracts that can be classified as either commodity or financial futures contracts. Prior to the 1970s and the deregulation of financial markets throughout the world, most exchanges only traded commodity futures. Financial futures have been a remarkably successful innovation. They were invented in 1972; within a few years, trading in financial futures significantly exceeded trading in commodity futures.

Commodity futures differ from financial futures in that their value is derived from a physical commodity such as wheat, whereas financial futures derive their value from a financial asset or financial index.

---

[15] We oversimplify. For example, the miller will not reduce risk if bread prices vary in proportion to the post-harvest wheat price. In this case, the miller is in a hazardous position of having fixed her cost but not her selling price. This point is discussed in A. C. Shapiro and S. Titman, 'An Integrated Approach to Corporate Risk Management', *Midland Corporate Finance Journal*, 3: 41–56 (Summer 1985).

[16] At the time of maturity of the futures contract, the basis should equal zero. During the life of the contract the basis (expressed as futures – spot) can be either positive or negative. For a comprehensive discussion of the basis see J. Hull, *Options, Futures and other Derivative Securities*, 3rd ed., Prentice-Hall, Englewood Cliffs, N.J., 1997.

[17] In the case of some of the financial futures described below, you *cannot* deliver the asset. At maturity, the buyer simply receives (or pays) the difference between the spot price and the price at which he or she agreed to purchase the asset.

**table 25.1**
Major worldwide futures exchanges

### United States and Canada
Chicago Board of Trade

Chicago Mercantile Exchange

Kansas City Board of Trade

Montreal Exchange

New York Mercantile Exchange

### United Kingdom and Europe
DeutscheTerminboorse

International Petroleum Exchange of London

London International Financial Futures Exchange

London Metal Exchange

Marchea Terme International de France

OM Stockholm

### Australasian region
Hong Kong Futures Exchange

New Zealand Futures at Options Exchange

Osaka Securities Exchange

Singapore International Monetary Exchange

Sydney Futures Exchange

Tokyo International Financial Futures Exchange

Commodity futures include contracts on agricultural products as well as metals, natural resources and, more recently, electricity. The commodities against which commodity futures are written usually have varying degrees of seasonability, storability and quality. Hence, the standardisation of these contracts requires the identification of precisely which type and quality of the commodity is being traded.

Financial futures, however, offer the opportunity to hedge or protect against movements in equity markets, interest rates and currencies. For many firms the wide fluctuations in these rates have become at least as important a source of risk as changes in commodity prices. Financial futures are similar to commodity futures, but instead of placing an order to buy or sell a commodity at a future date, you place an order to buy or sell a financial asset at a future date.

In Australia, futures contracts are traded at the Sydney Futures Exchange (SFE). The primary futures contracts are detailed in Table 25.2. Most trading on the Australian Exchange occurs in the area of financial rather than commodity futures.

Unlike over-the-counter markets where financial institutions can tailor-make financial instruments to the amount, maturity and term to maturity, as mentioned above, all futures contracts are standardised with respect to the maturity dates available, the size of individual contracts and the units by which price is quoted. For example, Table 25.3 shows the features of the four major financial futures contracts traded at the Sydney Futures Exchange.

table 25.2 _____

Futures contracts traded at the Sydney Futures Exchange[18]

### Commodity futures

Fine wool

Greasy wool

Broad wool

Wheat

New South Wales electricity

Victorian electricity

### Financial futures

90-day bank accepted bills

3-year Commonwealth government bonds

10-year Commonwealth government bonds

All ordinaries share price index

### Individual share futures

| | | |
|---|---|---|
| ANZ | MIM | Telstra instalment receipts |
| BHP | NAB | Telstra |
| RIO | NCP | WBC |
| FBG | PDP | WMC |

table 25.3 _____

Financial futures—contract specifications

| Contract | Contract unit | Inception date | Contract months | Quotes and minimum price movements | Trading halt at maturity of contract | Settlement day |
|---|---|---|---|---|---|---|
| All ordinaries share price index | $25 per index point Australian Stock Exchange all ordinaries index | 16 February 1983 | March, June, September and December up to six quarters ahead | Quoted in index points Minimum movement is 1 point = $25 | 4.20 p.m. on the last business day of the contract month unless otherwise determined by the board | Second business day following the last trading day |
| 90-day bank accepted bills | $1 million face value of 90-day bank accepted bills | 17 October 1979 | March, June, September and December up to 20 quarters ahead | Quoted as 100 − yield % p.a. to two decimal places; minimum price movement 0.01% | 12.00 p.m. on the business day immediately prior to the settlement day | Second Friday of the delivery month

*continues* |

[18] Contracts traded at 31 July 1998.

| Contract | Contract unit | Inception date | Contract months | Quotes and minimum price movements | Trading halt at maturity of contract | Settlement day |
|---|---|---|---|---|---|---|
| *continued* | | | | | | |
| 3-year Treasury bonds | $100 000 face value, 12% p.a. coupon rate, 3-year term government Treasury bond | 17 May 1988 | March, June, September and December up to two quarters ahead | Quoted as 100 − yield % p.a. to two decimal places; minimum price movement 0.01% | 12.00 p.m. on the 15th day of the contract month (or next business day) | First business day following the last trading day |
| 10-year Treasury bonds | $100 000 face value, 12% p.a. coupon rate, 10-year term government Treasury bond | 5 December 1984 | March, June, September and December up to two quarters ahead | Quoted as 100 − yield % p.a. to three decimal places; minimum price movement 0.005% | 12.00 p.m. on the 15th day of the contract month (or next business day) | First business day following the last trading day |

# The mechanics of future trading[19]

To facilitate a trade on the Sydney Futures Exchange, a company will contact a floor member of the Exchange who will trade on their client's behalf. Next, the buy or sell order is relayed to the staff on the trading floor who execute the trade. Once the contracts are bought or sold the Exchange's clearing house is advised. When trading futures contracts, even though the price is agreed to on the floor of the Exchange between two parties, the actual contract is in fact with the Exchange's clearing house. This allows two features to futures contracts:

▪ As both parties to the contract may not necessarily know each other, the clearing house[20] provides a mechanism which gives the two parties a guarantee that the contract will be honoured.

▪ Not all contracts are held to maturity. In fact, less than 2 per cent of all futures contracts are held this long. So, rather than requiring the company to search out the original contract buyer or seller, the company can reverse its original position (e.g. by selling futures contracts if it already holds buy positions) by simply taking an offsetting contract with the same delivery month as the original contract with another available buyer or seller on the floor of the Exchange.[21] The net effect will be that the number of contracts held by the company can go to zero even if the original counterparty still has an open position. This process is known as *novation*, and you are said to have novated your contract. This is possible because the contract is not actually with the counterparty but with the Exchange's clearing house.[22]

---

19  For a very comprehensive overview of the obligations of futures market participants in Australia see M. Markovic, 'The Legal Status of Futures Market Participants in Australia', *Company and Securities Law Journal*, pp. 82–100 (April 1989).

20  A very useful overview of the role of the SFE clearing house, its operations and the duties of market participants can be found in M. G. Hains, 'Reflections on the Sydney Futures Exchange Clearing House: The Rise of the Mirrored Contract Theory', *Journal of Banking and Finance Law and Practice*, 5 (4): 257–80 (December 1994).

21  In some contracts, such as the bank accepted bill futures contract, it is also possible for the position to be offset using a procedure called *exchange for physical*, whereby a position can be offset by delivering the bank bills prior to maturity.

22  For a very detailed discussion of trading on the SFE and information regarding the available contracts refer to the SFE Internet site at *http:\\www.sfe.com.au*.

When you buy or sell a futures contract, the price is fixed today but payment is not made until later. You will, however, be asked to put up an initial margin for each contract bought or sold in the form of either cash or bank bills to demonstrate that you have the money to honour your side of the bargain. This money is maintained in a margin account on your behalf by a floor member of the Exchange. The initial margin is determined by the Exchange's clearing house.

In addition, futures contracts are *marked to market daily*. This means each day any profits or losses on the contract are calculated; you pay the Exchange any losses and receive any profits. For example, suppose that our farmer agreed to sell 1000 tonnes of wheat at $2.50 a tonne. The next day the price of wheat futures declines to $2.00 a tonne. The farmer now has a profit on his sale of $1000 \times \$0.50 = \$500$. The Exchange's clearing house therefore pays this $500 to the farmer via his margin account. You can think of the farmer as closing out his position every day and then opening up a new position. Thus, after the first day the farmer has realised a profit of $500 on his trade and now has an obligation to deliver wheat for $2.00 a tonne. The 50 cents that the farmer has already been paid *plus* the $2.00 that remains to be paid equals the $2.50 selling price at which the farmer originally agreed to deliver wheat.

Of course, our miller is in the opposite position. The fall in the futures price leaves her with a *loss* of 50 cents a tonne. She must therefore pay over this loss to the Exchange's clearing house. In effect, the miller closes out her initial purchase at a 50 cent loss and opens a new contract to take delivery at $2.00 a tonne.[23]

## Spot and futures prices—commodities

The difference between buying *commodities* today and buying commodity futures is more complicated. First, because payment is again delayed, the buyer of the futures earns interest on her money. Second, she does not need to store the commodities and therefore saves warehouse costs, wastage, and so on. On the other hand, the futures contract gives no **convenience yield**, which is the value of being able to get your hands on the real thing. The manager of a clothing store is unlikely to sell his broad wool futures contracts if Hobart is hit by a sudden cold snap, in the same way that a grocery store owner cannot stock the shelves with wheat futures if he runs out of bread. All this means that for commodities,

$$\frac{\text{Futures price}}{(1 + r_f)^t} = \text{spot price} + \text{PV(storage costs)} - \text{PV(convenience yield)}$$

where $r_f$ is the risk-free rate of interest and $t$ is the time to the maturity of the contract.

No one would be willing to hold the futures contract at a higher futures price or to hold the commodity at a lower futures price.[24]

You cannot observe PV(convenience yield) or PV(storage costs) separately, but you can infer the difference between them by comparing the spot price to the discounted futures price. This difference—that is, convenience yield less storage cost—is called *net convenience yield*.

Here is an example using the broad wool futures contract. Let us assume that in April 1997 the price of merino combing fleece 23-micron broad wool was $13.70 per kilogram and that the futures price for delivery in October 1997 was $13.80. Of course, if you bought and held the futures, you paid after six months. The present value of this outlay assuming a risk-free rate of 7.0 per cent in April 1997 was:

$$\frac{13.80}{(1 + 0.07)^{0.50}} = \$13.34$$

---

[23] Notice that neither the farmer nor the miller need be concerned about whether the other party will honour his or her side of the bargain. The Futures Exchange guarantees the contract and protects itself by settling up profits and losses each day.

[24] Our formula could overstate the futures price if no one is willing to hold the commodity, that is, if inventories fall to zero or some absolute minimum.

So PV(net convenience yield) was positive, about 0.36 cents per kilogram.

$$\text{PV(net convenience yield)} = \text{spot prices} - \frac{\text{future price}}{(1 + r_f)^t}$$
$$= 13.70 - 13.34$$
$$= 0.36, \text{ or 36 cents}$$

Sometimes the net convenience yield is expressed as a percentage of the spot price or, in this case, as 0.36/13.70, or 2.63 per cent. Figure 25.1 plots percentage net convenience yields for other commodities such as gold, copper and heating oil. Notice that the convenience of holding gold rather than a future entitlement to gold is very small. However, the spread between the spot and future prices of oil bounces around and can rise to very high levels when troubles in the Middle East revive fears of an interruption of supply.[25]

## Spot and futures prices—financial futures

If you want to buy a security, you have a choice. You can buy it for immediate delivery at the spot price. Alternatively, you can place an order for later delivery; in this case you buy at the futures price. When you buy a financial future, you end up with exactly the same security that you would have if you bought in the spot market. However, there are two differences. First, you do not pay for the security up front, and so you can earn interest on its purchase price. Second, you miss out on any dividend or interest that is paid in the interim. This tells us something about the relationship between the spot and futures prices:[26]

$$\frac{\text{Futures price}}{(1 + r_f)^t} = \text{spot price} - \text{PV(dividends or interest payments forgone)}$$

where $r_f$ is the risk-free rate of interest and $t$ is the time to the maturity of the contract.

It is interesting to compare the formulas for futures prices of commodities with the formulas for securities. PV(convenience yield) plays the same role as PV(dividends or interest payments forgone). But financial assets cost nothing to store, so PV(storage costs) does not appear in the formula for financial futures.

Let us consider an example and show how the above formula works using the all ordinaries share price index futures contract. Suppose six-month all ordinaries share price index futures trade at 2814 when the index is at 2788. The six-month interest rate is 5.15 per cent per annum and the average dividend yield on shares is 3.22 per cent per annum. The all ordinaries share price index trades at the price of $25 multiplied by the index per contract. Are these numbers consistent?

Suppose you buy the futures contract and set aside the money needed under the agreement. You need to invest approximately $68 606:

$$\frac{\text{Futures price}}{(1 + r_f)^t} = \frac{2814 \times 25}{(1 + 0.0515)^{0.5}}$$
$$= \$68\,605.58, \text{ or } \$68\,606$$

What do you get in return?

25  For evidence that the net convenience yield is related to the level of inventories see M. J. Brennan, 'The Price of Convenience and the Valuation of Commodity Contingent Claims', in D. Lund and B. Oksendal (eds.), *Stochastic Models and Option Values*, North-Holland Publishing Company, Amsterdam, 1991.

26  This relationship is strictly true only if the contract is not marked to market. Otherwise, the value of the futures depends on the path of interest rates up to the delivery date. In practice, this qualification is usually unimportant. See J. C. Cox, J. E. Ingersoll, and S. A. Ross, 'The Relationship Between Forward and Future Prices', *Journal of Financial Economics*, 9: 321–46 (1981).

**figure 25.1** _____

*Monthly* percentage net convenience yields (convenience yield *less* storage costs) for three commodities. Note the different vertical scales.

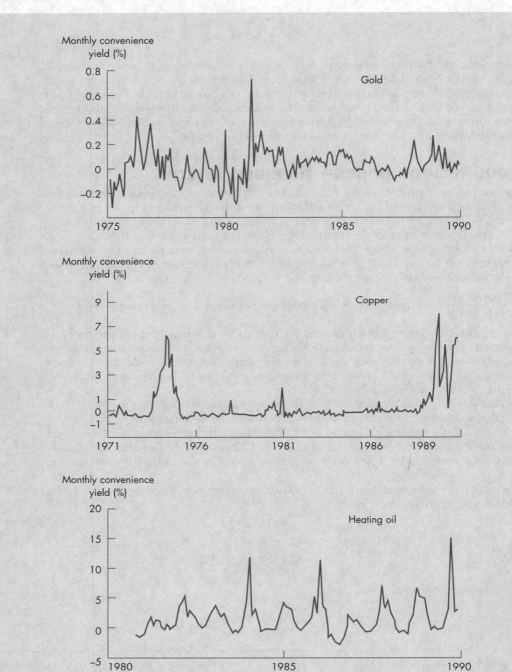

*Source*: R. S. Pindyck, 'The Present Value Model of Rational Commodity Pricing', *Economic Journal*, **103**: 511–30 (May 1993). © Royal Economic Society.

Everything you would have got by buying the index now at the spot price, except for the dividends paid over the next six months. If we assume, for simplicity, that a half-year's dividends are paid in six months (rather than evenly over the six months):

$$\text{Spot price} - \text{PV(dividends)} = 2788 - \left( \frac{2788 \times 0.0161}{(1 + 0.0515)^{0.50}} \right) \times 25$$

$$= 68\,605.66, \text{ or } \$68\,606$$

Hence the payoff is approximately $68 606.
You get what you pay for.

## A couple of examples—BAB and SPI futures

It is time to put all you have learnt to this point to use. Let us have a closer look at two examples—one involving hedging short-term borrowing with bank accepted bill futures and one involving hedging the value of a portfolio of shares.[27]

Assume it is currently December 1998 and 90-day bank bills are yielding 6 per cent in the physical or spot market. In your role as corporate treasurer you know that your company will need to borrow $2 million using bill financing in early September 1999. In December 1998, 90-day bank accepted bill futures for delivery in September 1999 are trading at 5.75 per cent. You could remain unhedged but you are concerned about the possibility of an upward movement in short-term rates in the new year, driven by renewed fears of inflation. What is the nature of your exposure? Obviously, to remain unhedged you will be exposed to any subsequent yield increases. You decide to hedge using the BAB futures contract. Let us assume a naïve hedge is appropriate.

In December 1998 you sell two 90-day BAB September 1999 delivery futures contracts at a yield of 5.75 per cent. The selling price is calculated as follows:

$$SP = 2 \times \left[ \frac{1\,000\,000}{1 + \dfrac{5.75}{100} \times \dfrac{90}{365}} \right]$$

$$= 2 \times 986\,020$$

$$= 1\,972\,040$$

The selling price is $1 972 040.
Now, let us assume the clock has rolled forward and it is now September 1999. Let us assume that 90-day bank bill interest rates rise by September 1999 to 5.90 per cent. You decide to offset your original contract and novate your original position. You therefore purchase two 90-day BAB September 1999 futures contracts on 1 September 1999 at a yield of 5.90 per cent. The price of the two contracts at the time of the trade is $2 \times 985\,661 = \$1\,971\,322$. Given that you sold the contracts for $1 972 040 and then offset the trade at $1 971 322, you have generated a profit from the futures market of $718.

What is your effective borrowing rate? Obviously, you will still need to borrow at the market rate of 5.90 per cent, but you can offset the interest cost with the profits from the futures trade. Here is the calculation.

The price of the physical market borrowing based on two bank bills each with a face value of $1 million at a yield of 5.90 over 90 days is equal to $1 971 322. Remember that in 90 days time in December 1999 you will need to repay the face value of $2 million. The effective borrowing cost is equal to:

---

[27] Numerous other examples are available from the SFE Internet site (see Footnote 22) and in the book by W. Slatyer and E. Carew, *Trading Asia-Pacific Financial Futures Markets*, Allen and Unwin, Sydney, 1993.

$$\text{Effective yield} = \frac{2\,000\,000 - (1\,971\,322 + 718)}{1\,971\,040} \times \frac{365}{90} \times \frac{100}{1}$$

$$= \frac{2\,000\,000 - 1\,972\,040}{1\,971\,040} \times \frac{365}{90} \times \frac{100}{1}$$

$$= 5.75\%$$

The bottom line is simple: the effective yield of your company's borrowing will be 5.75 per cent. Alternatively, if the borrowing could have been delayed till mid-September, then the contract to sell two bank accepted bills could have been settled at the rate of 5.75 per cent as agreed to in December 1998.

Consider an alternative example. Assume that you hold the portfolio below, which has a current value of $1 million. Assume that all ordinaries share price index futures for delivery in December 2002 are currently trading at around 2385.

| Share | Beta | Number of shares | Price | Value of shares |
|-------|------|------------------|-------|-----------------|
| A | 1.05 | 400 000 | 0.50 | 200 000 |
| B | 1.40 | 200 000 | 2.00 | 400 000 |
| C | 1.80 | 400 000 | 1.00 | 400 000 |
| | | | | $1 000 000 |

The weighted beta of this portfolio[28] is equal to:

$$\beta_p = 1.05 \times \frac{200\,000}{1\,000\,000} + 1.40 \times \frac{400\,000}{1\,000\,000} + 1.80 \times \frac{400\,000}{1\,000\,000}$$

$$= 1.49$$

Your exposure in holding the portfolio is that the value of the portfolio might fall if the value of the all ordinaries should fall—recall that beta is regarded as a measure of the relationship of the individual shares to movements in the value of the market portfolio. Hence a short hedge would be the appropriate hedge. Having established that you need to sell futures contracts in order to protect the value of your portfolio, next you need to identify how many futures contracts are required.

If a naïve hedge were applied, then 16.77,[29] or 17, contracts would be needed. However, a naïve hedge would be inappropriate because the variability of the portfolio is different to the variability of the all ordinaries index.[30] The correct hedge would reflect an adjustment for the beta of the portfolio:

$$\text{Number of contracts required} = 1.49 \times \frac{1\,000\,000}{2385 \times 25}$$

$$= 24.9895, \text{ or } 25 \text{ contracts}$$

You decide to sell 25 all ordinaries share price index futures contracts. The total value of the 25 contracts is $2385 \times 25 \times 25 = \$1\,490\,625$.

---

[28]  The portfolio's weighted beta represents betas for each share adjusted to represent each share's contribution to the value of the portfolio. Hence, for share A, its contribution is 20 per cent to the value of the portfolio.

[29]  Calculated as $\dfrac{\$ \text{ value of the portfolio}}{\$ \text{ value of each futures contract}} = \dfrac{1\,000\,000}{2385 \times 25} = 16.77$

[30]  Recall that a beta equal to 1 is consistent with the beta of the market index.

Let us assume the value of the all ordinaries falls by 4 per cent. The value of the portfolio, given the weighted beta of 1.49, falls to $940 400.[31] If the portfolio was unhedged then its value would have fallen by 1 000 000 − 940 400 = $59 600.

If we assume the futures market also fell by about 4 per cent to 2289, the hedged position can be offset by buying 25 contracts for a price of $1 430 625. The futures trading generates a profit of $60 000. This profit can be added back into the portfolio to give a total portfolio value of $1 000 400. Alternatively, the funds could have been used to purchase more shares for the portfolio at their decreased prices.[32]

# 25.4 Forward contracts

Each day, millions of dollars of futures contracts are bought and sold at futures exchanges throughout the world. This liquidity is possible only because futures contracts are standardised and mature on a limited number of dates each year.

Fortunately, there is usually more than one way to skin a financial cat. If the terms of futures contracts do not suit your particular needs, you may be able to buy or sell a forward contract. Forward contracts are simply tailor-made futures contracts. The main forward market is in foreign currency. Banks quote prices at which they will buy and sell forward currency for periods up to one year ahead, and in the case of the major currencies they are prepared to fix a price for five years or more. There is a huge volume of business in forward currency.[33]

It is also possible to enter into a forward interest-rate contract. For example, suppose that you know that at the end of six months you are going to need a three-month loan. You can lock in the interest rate on that loan by buying a **forward rate agreement** (**FRA**) from a bank.[34] For example, the bank might offer to sell you a six-month forward rate agreement on three-month BBSW against 7 per cent. If at the end of six months the three-month BBSW rate is greater than 7 per cent, the bank will pay you the difference in interest based on a notional principal; if the three-month BBSW is less than 7 per cent, you pay the difference. Obviously, if the BBSW rate is 7 per cent there will be no cash transfer between the parties.[35]

## Homemade forward contracts

Suppose that you borrow $90.91 for one year at 10 per cent and lend $90.91 for two years at 12 per cent. These interest rates are for loans made today; therefore, they are spot interest rates. The cash flows on your transactions are as follows:

|  | Year 0 | Year 1 | Year 2 |
|---|---|---|---|
| Borrow for one year at 10% | +90.91 | −100 | |
| Lend for two years at 12% | −90.91 | | +114.04 |
| Net cash flow | 0 | −100 | +114.04 |

---

31 Calculated as 1 000 000 × (1 − (0.04 × 1.49)) = 940 400.

32 The analysis and its interpretation assumes the stability of beta both for the individual shares and also for the portfolio. In reality, the individual share betas and hence the portfolio beta will most likely change over time, requiring a constant monitoring of the futures market position.

33 For a theoretical discussion of the differences between futures and forward contracts see J. Cox, J. Ingersoll and S. Ross, 'The Relation Between Forward Prices and Futures Prices', *Journal of Financial Economics*, pp. 321–46 (December 1981); and K. R. French, 'A Comparison of Futures and Forward Prices', *Journal of Financial Economics*, pp. 311–42 (November 1983).

34 Note that the party which profits from a rise in rates is described as the 'buyer'. In our example, you would be said to 'buy six against nine months money', meaning that the forward rate agreement is for a three-month loan in six months time. For a comprehensive discussion of the Australian FRA market see M. McGrath and C. Viney, *Financial Institutions, Instruments and Markets*, 2nd ed., McGraw-Hill, Sydney, 1997; or E. Carew, *Derivatives Decoded*, Allen and Unwin, Sydney, 1997.

35 Unlike futures contracts, forwards are not marked to market. Thus, all profits or losses are settled when the contract matures.

Notice that you do not have any net cash outflow today, but you have contracted to pay out money in year 1. The interest rate on this forward commitment is 14.04 per cent. To calculate this forward interest rate, we simply worked out the extra return for lending for two years rather than one:

$$\text{Forward interest rate} = \frac{(1 + \text{2-year spot rate})^2}{(1 + \text{1-year spot rate})} - 1$$

$$= \frac{(1 + 0.12)^2}{(1 + 0.10)} - 1$$

$$= 0.1404, \text{ or } 14.04\%$$

In our example, you manufactured a forward loan by borrowing short-term and lending long. But you can also run the process in reverse. If you wish to fix today the rate at which you borrow next year, you borrow long and lend the money until you need it next year.

You can also construct a do-it-yourself forward contract to buy or sell foreign exchange. For example, suppose that you want to place an order today to buy US dollars in one year. Assume that the current (or spot) exchange rate is $1 = 0.6520, the one-year Australian interest rate is 5.40 per cent, and the one-year US interest rate is 6 per cent. You now borrow A\$500 for one year, exchange these dollars into US dollars and lend your US dollars for a year. Your cash flows are as follows:

|  | Now | | After one year | |
| --- | --- | --- | --- | --- |
|  | Australian dollars | US dollars | Australian dollars | US dollars |
| Borrow Australian dollars at 5.40% | +500 | | −527 | |
| Change to US dollars | −500 | +327 | | |
| Lend US dollars at 6% | | −327 | | +345.56 |
| Net cash flow | 0 | 0 | −527 | +345.56 |

Your net cash flow today is zero, but you have committed to pay out A\$527 at the end of the year and receive US\$345.56. Thus you have constructed a homemade forward contract to buy US dollars at an exchange rate of $1 = 345.56/527 = 0.6557$.

This homemade forward contract tells us the fair price for a forward (or futures) contract to buy US dollars:

$$\text{Forward price} = \text{spot price} \times \frac{1 + \text{US dollar interest rate}}{1 + \text{Australian dollar interest rate}}$$

$$= 0.6520 \times \frac{1 + 0.06}{1 + 0.0540} = \text{US\$0.6557}$$

What would happen if the price of futures was higher than this figure, say US\$0.6800 per dollar? Then everyone would rush to buy forward, thereby generating extra US dollars at year 1. The forward commitment could be covered by borrowing US dollars, changing to Australian dollars at the spot rate and lending Australian dollars. If the futures price was lower, everyone would do the reverse. Sharp-eyed arbitrageurs with families to support (and/or expensive lifestyles) are constantly on the lookout for such discrepancies.

If you can make your own forward contracts for interest rates or currencies, why does anyone bother to trade on the financial futures exchanges? The answer: Convenience and cost.

Some of the most popular futures contracts are the interest rate and currency futures contracts that are closest to maturity. In principle these are the easiest to replicate, but the huge volume of business in financial futures makes them a very low cost tool for hedging (or speculation).

## 25.5 Swaps

Suppose that Possum Ltd wishes to borrow deutschmarks to help finance its European operations. Since Possum is better known in Australia, the financial manager believes that the company can obtain more attractive terms on an Australian dollar loan than on a deutschmark loan. Therefore, the company issues $10 million for five years with interest fixed at 12 per cent per annum in Australia. At the same time, Possum arranges with a bank to **swap** its future dollar liability for deutschmarks. Under this arrangement, the bank agrees to pay Possum sufficient dollars to service its dollar loan; in exchange, Possum agrees to make a series of annual payments in deutschmarks to the bank. Possum and the bank are referred to as *counterparties*.

Here are Possum's cash flows (in millions):

|  | Year 0 | | Years 1–4 | | Year 5 | |
|---|---|---|---|---|---|---|
|  | Dollars | Deutschmarks | Dollars | Deutschmarks | Dollars | Deutschmarks |
| 1. Issue dollar loan | +10 | | −1.2 | | −11.2 | |
| 2. Swap dollars for deutschmarks | −10 | +20 | +1.2 | −1.6 | +11.2 | −21.6 |
| 3. Net cash flow | 0 | +20 | 0 | −1.6 | 0 | −21.6 |

The combined effect of Possum's two steps (line 3) is to convert a 12 per cent dollar loan into an 8 per cent deutschmark loan. The device that makes this possible is the *currency swap*. You can think of the cash flows for the swap (line 2) as a series of forward currency contracts. In each of years 1 through to 4 Possum agrees to purchase $1.2 million at a cost of 1.6 million deutschmarks; in year 5 it agrees to buy $11.2 million at a cost of 21.6 million deutschmarks.[36]

The bank's cash flows from the swap are the reverse of Possum's. It has undertaken to pay out dollars in the future and receive deutschmarks. Since the bank is now exposed to the risk that the deutschmark will weaken unexpectedly against the dollar, it will try to hedge the risk by engaging in a series of futures or forward contracts or by swapping deutschmarks for dollars with another counterparty. As long as Possum and the other counterparty honour their promises, the bank is fully protected against risk. The recurring nightmare for swap managers is that one party will default, leaving the bank with a large unmatched position.

Swaps are not new. For many years the British government limited purchases of foreign currency to invest abroad. These restrictions led many British firms to arrange so-called back-to-back loans. The firms would lend sterling to a company in the United States and simultaneously borrow dollars, which could then be used for foreign investment. In taking out the back-to-back loan, the British firms agreed to make a series of future dollar payments in exchange for receiving a flow of sterling income.

In 1979 these limits on overseas investment were removed, and British firms no longer needed to take out back-to-back loans. However, during the 1980s the banks did a respray job on the back-to-back loan and relaunched it as a swap. Swaps turned out to be very popular with corporate customers; in recent years some two-thirds of dollar eurobond issues have been accompanied by a swap.

---

[36] Usually in a currency swap the two parties make an initial payment to each other (i.e. Possum pays the bank $10 million and receives 20 million deutschmarks). However, this is not necessary, and in the case of interest-rate swaps that are in the *same* currency, no initial payments occur and there are no financial principal repayments. Interest-rate swaps are explained below.

Swaps are not limited to future exchanges of currency. The most common form of swap is actually an *interest-rate swap*, in which counterparties swap fixed interest-rate loans for floating-rate loans. In this case, one party promises to make a series of fixed annual payments in return for receiving a series of payments that are linked to the level of short-term interest rates. Sometimes swaps are used to convert between floating-rate loans that are tied to different base rates. For example, a firm might wish to swap a series of payments that are linked to the prime rate for a series of payments that are linked to the bank accepted bill rate.

For example, Cadbury Schweppes uses both currency swaps and interest-rate swaps. It has access to an active US dollar commercial paper program, which it estimates reduces its interest costs by 30 basis points (i.e. 0.30 percentage points). But Cadbury does not want all its funding to be variable-rate and denominated in US dollars. So it swaps the dollars raised from its commercial paper program for fixed-rate pesetas, Australian dollars, and so on.

It is also possible to swap commodities using *commodity swaps*. In this case you do not need to deliver the commodities; you just settle up any differences in their value. For example, Cadbury Schweppes could lock in the price at which it buys sugar by agreeing to pay an amount that goes up and down with sugar prices; the counterparty pays Cadbury a fixed stream of payments. In contrast, a sugar producer could lock in the price at which it *sells* sugar by paying a fixed cash amount, while its counterparty pays an amount that is linked to sugar prices.

Figure 25.2 provides a summary of the different kinds of swaps.

**figure 25.2**

Some examples of swaps. A swap is an agreement by two counterparties (A and B) to exchange currencies, interest payments or commodities on a series of future dates.

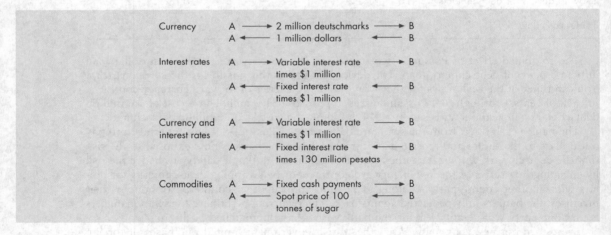

## Do-it-yourself rate swaps

Before we leave swaps, one more example may be helpful. We begin with a homemade fixed-to-floating interest-rate swap.

Bancorp has made a five-year, $50 million loan to fund part of the construction cost of a large electricity generation project. The loan carries a fixed interest payment of 8 per cent. Annual interest payments are therefore $4 million. Interest payments are made annually, and all the principal will be repaid at year 5. The bank wants to swap the $4 million, five-year annuity (the fixed interest payments) into a floating-rate annuity.

The bank could borrow at a 6 per cent fixed rate for five years.[37] Therefore, the $4 million interest it receives could support a fixed-rate loan of 4/0.06 = $66.67 million. This will be the *notional principal* amount of the swap.

---

[37]  The spread between the bank's 6 per cent borrowing rate and the 8 per cent lending rate is the bank's profit on the project financing.

The bank can construct the homemade swap as follows: It borrows $66.67 million at a fixed interest rate of 6 per cent for five years and simultaneously lends the same amount at LIBOR. We assume that LIBOR is now 5 per cent.[38] LIBOR is a short-term interest rate, so future interest receipts will fluctuate as the bank's investment is rolled over.

The net cash flows to this strategy are shown in the top panel of Table 25.4. Notice that there is no net cash flow in year 0 and that in year 5 the principal amount of the short-term investment is used to pay off the $66.67 million loan. What is left? A cash flow equal to the *difference* between the interest earned (LIBOR × 66.67) and the $4 million outlay on the fixed loan. The bank also has $4 million per year coming in from the project financing, so it has transformed that fixed payment into a floating payment keyed to LIBOR.

**table 25.4**

The top part shows the cash flows to a homemade fixed-to-floating interest-rate swap. The bottom part shows the cash flows to a standard swap transaction.

| | | | Year | | | |
|---|---|---|---|---|---|---|
| | **0** | **1** | **2** | **3** | **4** | **5** |
| 1. Borrow $66.67 at 6% fixed rate | +66.67 | −4 | −4 | −4 | −4 | −(4 + 66.67) |
| 2. Lend $66.67 at LIBOR floating rate (initially 5%) | −66.67 | +0.05 × 66.67 | + $LIBOR_1$ × 66.67 | + $LIBOR_2$ × 66.67 | + $LIBOR_3$ × 66.67 | + $LIBOR_4$ × 66.67 + 66.67 |
| Net cash flow | 0 | −4 + 0.05 × 66.67 | −4 + $LIBOR_1$ × 66.67 | −4 + $LIBOR_2$ × 66.67 | −4 + $LIBOR_3$ × 66.67 | −4 + $LIBOR_4$ × 66.67 |
| Net cash flow | 0 | −4 + 0.05 × 66.67 | −4₁ + LIBOR × 66.67 | −4 + $LIBOR_2$ × 66.67 | −4 + $LIBOR_3$ × 66.67 | −4 + $LIBOR_4$ × 66.67 |

Of course, there is an easier way to do this, as shown in the bottom panel of Table 25.4. The bank can just call a swap dealer and agree to a five-year, fixed-to-LIBOR swap on a notional principal of $66.67 million.[39] Naturally, Bancorp takes the easier route and enters the swap. Let us see what happens.

The starting payment is based on the starting LIBOR rate of 5 per cent:

Bank ⟶ $4 ⟶ Counterparty
Bank ⟵ 0.05 × $66.67 = $3.33 ⟵ Counterparty
Bank ⟶ Net = $0.67 ⟶ Counterparty

The second payment is based on LIBOR at year 1. Suppose it increases to 6 per cent:

Bank ⟶ $4 ⟶ Counterparty
Bank ⟵ 0.06 × $66.67 = $4 ⟵ Counterparty
Bank         Net = 0         Counterparty

---

[38]  Maybe the short-term interest rate is below the five-year interest rate because investors expect interest rates to rise.
[39]  Both strategies are equivalent to a series of forward contracts on LIBOR. The forward prices are $4 million each for $LIBOR_1$ × 66.67, and so on. Separately negotiated forward prices would not be $4 million for any one year, but the PVs of the 'annuities' of forward prices would be identical.

What about the *value* of the swap at year 2? That depends on long-term interest rates. First, suppose that they do not move, so a 6 per cent note issued by the bank would still trade at par. In this case the swap still has zero value. (You can confirm this by checking that the NPV of a new three-year homemade swap is zero.) But if long-term interest rates increase, say, to 7 per cent, the value of a three-year note falls to

$$PV = \frac{4}{1.07} + \frac{4}{(1.07)^2} + \frac{4 + 66.67}{(1.07)^3} = \$64.92 \text{ million}$$

Now the swap is worth $66.67 - 64.92 = \$1.75$ million.

How do we know the swap is worth $1.75 million? Consider the following strategy:

**1.** The bank can enter a new three-year swap deal in which it agrees to *pay* LIBOR on the same notional principal of $66.67 million.
**2.** In return it receives fixed payments at the new 7 per cent interest rate, that is, $0.07 \times 66.67 = \$4.67$ per year.

The new swap cancels the cash flows of the old one, but it generates an extra $0.67 million for three years. This extra cash flow is worth

$$PV = \sum_{1}^{3} \frac{0.67}{(1.07)^t} = \$1.75 \text{ million}$$

Remember, ordinary interest-rate swaps have no initial cost or value (PV = 0), but their value drifts away from zero as time passes and long-term interest rates change. One counterparty wins as the other loses.

## 25.6 How to set up a hedge

In each of our examples of hedging the firm has offset the risk by buying one asset and selling an equal amount of another asset. For example, our farmer owned 1000 tonnes of wheat and sold 20 contracts equivalent to 1000 tonnes of wheat futures. As long as the wheat that the farmer owns is identical to the wheat that he promises to deliver, this strategy minimises risk. However, the hedge described above assumes a one-for-one price movement in both the price of the wheat and the price of the futures contract—consequently this type of hedge is often referred to as a naïve hedge.

In practice, the wheat that the farmer owns and the wheat that he agrees to sell under the futures markets are unlikely to be identical. For example, if he sells wheat futures on the Sydney Futures Exchange, he agrees to deliver Australian standard white wheat at a range of possible locations, including Moree in northern New South Wales, in September. But perhaps he is growing a different type of wheat many kilometres from Moree; in this case the prices of the two wheats will not move exactly together. However, knowledge of the correlation between the price movements of the two types of wheat can be used to adjust any subsequently calculated price movements.

A plot similar to Figure 25.3 shows hypothetically how changes in the prices of both the spot wheat and futures wheat may have been related in the past. Notice two things about this figure: First, the scatter of points suggests that the price changes are imperfectly related. If so, it is not possible to construct a hedge that eliminates all risk. Some residual, or *basis*, risk will remain. Second, the slope of the fitted line shows that a 1 per cent change in the price of the futures price was on average associated with a 0.8 per cent change in the price of the farmer's wheat price. Because the price of the farmer's wheat is relatively insensitive to changes in Australian white wheat prices, he needs to sell $0.8 \times 1000$ tonnes or 16 contracts of wheat futures to minimise risk.

Let us generalise. Suppose that you already own an asset, A (e.g. wheat), and that you wish to hedge against changes in the value of A by making an offsetting sale of another asset, B (e.g.

**figure 25.3**

Hypothetical plot of past changes in the price of the farmer's wheat against changes in the price of wheat futures.

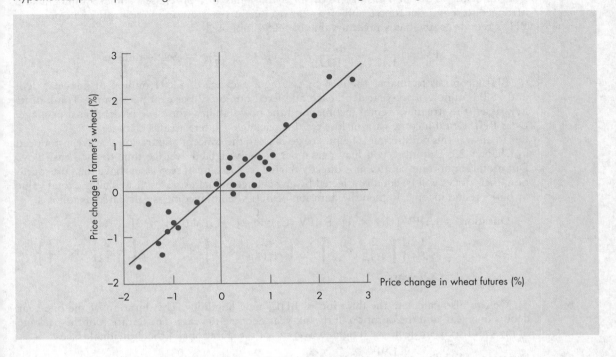

wheat futures). Suppose also that percentage changes in the value of A are related in the following way to percentage changes in the value of B:

$$\text{Expected change in A} = a + \delta \,(\text{expected change in B})$$

Delta ($\delta$) measures the sensitivity of A to changes in the value of B. It is also equal to the *hedge ratio*—that is, the number of units of B which should be sold to hedge the purchase of A. You minimise risk if you offset your position in A by the sale of delta units of B.[40]

The trick in setting up a hedge is to estimate the delta or hedge ratio. This sometimes calls for a strong dose of judgement. For example, we referred earlier to the fact that BMW is exposed to fluctuations in the exchange rate between Australian dollars and deutschmarks. But how much would the value of the company fall if the deutschmark appreciated? The answer depends on how demand for BMW cars in Australia would be affected by a rise in price, whether BMW could shift production to lower-cost countries, how competitors would react, and so on.

Sometimes, as in our example of the wheat farmer, a little history may help to estimate the sensitivity of the value of asset A to fluctuations in the value of B. It also might be possible to call on a little theory to set up the hedge.

---

[40] Notice that A, the item that you wish to hedge, is the dependent variable. Delta measures the sensitivity of A to changes in B.

# Using theory to set up the hedge

Bottom-of-the-Harbour Leasing (BHL) in Sydney has just purchased some equipment and arranged to rent it out for $2 million a year over eight years. At an interest rate of 12 per cent, BHL's rental income has a present value of $9.94 million:[41]

$$PV = \frac{2}{1.12} + \frac{2}{(1.12)^2} + \ldots + \frac{2}{(1.12)^8} = \$9.94 \text{ million}$$

BHL proposes to finance the deal by issuing a package of $1.91 million of one-year debt and $8.03 million of six-year debt, each at a fixed rate of 12 per cent per annum. Think of its new asset (the stream of rental income) and the new liability (the issue of debt) as a package. Does BHL rental income gain or lose on this package if interest rates change?

To answer this question, it is helpful to go back to the concept of duration that we introduced in Chapter 23. Duration, you may remember, is the weighted average time to each cash flow. Duration is important because it is directly related to volatility. If two assets have the same duration, their prices will be equally affected by any change in interest rates. If we call the total value of BHL's rental income $V$, then the duration of BHL's rental income is calculated as follows:

$$\text{Duration} = \frac{1}{V}[PV\ (C_1) \times 1] + [PV\ (C_2) \times 2] + [PV\ (C_3) \times 3] + \ldots$$

$$= \frac{1}{9.94}\left\{\left[\frac{2}{1.12} \times 1\right] + \left[\frac{2}{(1.12)^2} \times 2\right] + \ldots + \left[\frac{2}{(1.12)^8} \times 8\right]\right\}$$

$$= 3.9 \text{ years}$$

We can also calculate the duration of BHL's new liabilities. The duration of the one-year debt is one year, and the duration of the six-year debt is 4.6 years. The duration of the package of one- and six-year debt is a weighted average of the durations of the individual issues:

$$\text{Duration of liability} = \frac{1.91}{9.94} \times \text{duration of one-year debt} + \frac{8.03}{9.94} \times \text{duration of six-year debt}$$

$$= (0.192 \times 1) + (0.808 \times 4.6)$$
$$= 3.9 \text{ years}$$

Thus, both the asset (the lease) and the liability (the debt package) have a duration of 3.9 years. Therefore, both are affected equally by a change in interest rates. If rates rise, the present value of BHL's rental income will decline, but the value of its debt obligation will also decline by the same amount. By equalising the duration of the asset and that of the liability, BHL has *immunised* itself against any change in interest rates. It looks as if BHL's financial manager knows a thing or two about hedging.

When BHL set up the hedge, it needed to find a package of loans that had a present value of $9.94 million and a duration of 3.9 years. Call the proportion of the proceeds raised by the six-year loan $x$ and the proportion raised by the one-year loan $(1 - x)$. Then

$$\text{Duration of package} = (x \times \text{duration of six-year loan}) + [(1 - x) \times \text{duration of one-year loan}]$$
$$3.9 \text{ years} = (x \times 4.6 \text{ years}) + [(1 - x) \times 1 \text{ year}]$$
$$x = 0.808$$

Since the package of loans must raise $9.94 million, BHL needs to issue $0.808 \times 9.94 = \$8.03$ million of the six-year loan.

An important feature of this hedge is that it is dynamic. As interest rates change and time passes, the duration of BHL's asset may no longer be the same as that of its liability. Thus, to remain hedged against interest rate changes, BHL must be prepared to keep adjusting the duration of its debt.

---

[41] We ignore tax in this example.

**table 25.5**

BHL can hedge by issuing this sinking fund bond that pays out $2 million each year. Cash flows ($million)

| | Year | | | | | | | |
|---|---|---|---|---|---|---|---|---|
| | **1** | **2** | **3** | **4** | **5** | **6** | **7** | **8** |
| Balance at start of year | 9.94 | 9.13 | 8.23 | 7.22 | 6.08 | 4.81 | 3.39 | 1.79 |
| Interest at 12% | 1.19 | 1.10 | 0.99 | 0.87 | 0.73 | 0.58 | 0.40 | 0.21 |
| Sinking fund payment | 0.81 | 0.90 | 1.01 | 1.13 | 1.27 | 1.42 | 1.60 | 1.79 |
| Interest plus sinking fund payment | 2.00 | 2.00 | 2.00 | 2.00 | 2.00 | 2.00 | 2.00 | 2.00 |

If BHL is not disposed to follow this dynamic hedging strategy, it has an alternative. It can devise a debt issue whose cash flows exactly match the rental income from the lease. For example, suppose that it issues an eight-year sinking fund bond; the amount of the sinking fund is $810 000 in year 1, and the payment increases by 12 per cent annually. Table 25.5 shows that the bond payments (interest plus sinking fund) are $2 million in each year.

Since the cash flows on the asset exactly match those on the liability, BHL's financial manager can now relax. Each year the manager simply collects the $2 million rental income and hands it to the bondholders. Whatever happens to interest rates, the firm is always perfectly hedged.

Why wouldn't BHL's financial manager *always* prefer to construct matching assets and liabilities? One reason is that it may be relatively costly to devise a bond with a specially tailored pattern of cash flows. Another may be that BHL is continually entering into new lease agreements and issuing new debt. In this case the manager can never relax; it may be simpler to keep the durations of the assets and liabilities equal than to maintain an exact match between the cash flows.

Here is another case where some theory can help you set up a hedge. In Chapter 20 we came across options. These give you the right, but not the obligation, to buy or sell an asset. Options are derivatives; their value depends only on what happens to the price of the underlying asset.

As discussed in Chapter 21, the *option delta* summarises the link between the option and the asset. For example, if you own an option to buy BHP shares, the change in the value of your investment will be the same as it would be if you held delta shares of BHP.

Since the option price is tied to the asset price, options can be used for hedging. Thus, if you own an option to buy BHP shares and at the same time you sell delta shares of BHP, any change in the value of your position in the shares will be exactly offset by the change in the value of your option position.[42] In other words, you will be perfectly hedged—hedged, that is, for the next short period of time. Option deltas change as the share price changes and time passes. Therefore, option-based hedges need to be adjusted frequently.

Options can be used to hedge commodities too. The miller could offset changes in the cost of future wheat purchases by buying call options on wheat (or on wheat futures). But this is not the simplest strategy if the miller is trying to lock in the future cost of wheat. She would have to check the option delta to determine how many options to buy, and she would have to keep track of changes in the option delta and reset the hedge as necessary.[43]

It is the same for financial assets. Suppose you hold a well-diversified portfolio of shares with a beta of 1.0 and near-perfect correlation with the market return. You want to lock in the portfolio's value at year-end. You could accomplish this by selling call options on the index,

---

[42] We are assuming that you hold one option and hedge by selling δ shares. If you owned one share and wanted to hedge by selling options, you would need to sell 1/δ options.

[43] *Quiz:* What is the miller's position if she buys call options on wheat and simply holds them to maturity?

but to maintain the hedge, the option position would have to be adjusted frequently. It is simpler just to sell index futures maturing at year-end. If you wish to lock in the price of an individual share, you will probably hedge with options, but it is also possible to use individual share futures contracts.

Speaking of betas . . . what if your portfolio has a beta of 0.60, instead of 1.0? Then your hedge will require 40 per cent fewer index futures contracts. And since your low-beta portfolio is probably not perfectly correlated with the market, there will be some basis risk as well. In this context our old friend beta ($\beta$) and the hedge ratio ($\delta$) are one and the same. Remember, to hedge A with B, you need to know $\delta$ because

$$\text{Expected change in value of A} = a + \delta \text{ (change in value of B)}$$

When A is a share or portfolio, and B the market, we estimate beta from the same relationship:

$$\text{Expected change in share or portfolio value} = a + \beta \text{ (change in market index)}$$

## 25.7 Is 'derivative' a four-letter word?

Our earlier example of the farmer and the miller showed how futures might be used to reduce business risk. However, if you were to copy the farmer and sell wheat futures without an off-setting holding of wheat, you would not be *reducing* risk. You would be *speculating*.

Speculators in search of large profits (and prepared to tolerate large losses) are attracted by the leverage that derivatives provide. By this we mean that it is not necessary to lay out much money up front and the profits or losses may be many times the initial outlay.[44] 'Speculation' has an ugly ring, but a successful derivatives market needs speculators who are prepared to take on risk and provide more cautious people like our farmer and miller with the protection they need. For example, if there is an excess of farmers wishing to sell wheat futures, the price of futures will be forced down until enough speculators are tempted to buy in the hope of a profit. If there is a surplus of millers wishing to buy wheat futures, the reverse will happen. The price of wheat futures will be forced *up* until speculators are drawn to sell.

Speculation may be necessary to a thriving derivatives market, but it can get companies into serious trouble. For example, the Japanese company Showa Shell reported a loss of $1.5 billion on positions in foreign exchange futures. The German metals and oil trading company Metallgesellschaft took a loss of about $1.3 billion from oil futures and Proctor & Gamble lost $157 million on swap positions.[45]

Australia has not been isolated from its own derivatives-related disaster. In 1987 management at AWA uncovered significant 'irregularities' in its foreign exchange operations involving Japanese yen/US dollar forward contracts and announced a loss of $30 million which eliminated its expected profit for the 1986/87 financial year.[46]

---

[44] For example, if you buy or sell forward, no money changes hands until the contract matures, though you might be required to put up margin to show that you can honour your commitment. This margin does not need to be cash; it can be in the form of safe securities.

[45] We should be cautious, however, not to fall into the trap of assuming that losses on derivatives positions always indicate speculation. If those derivatives form part of a hedge, there should be offsetting profits from other assets. For example, it is not clear how far Metallgesellschaft (MG) was hedging or speculating. The company had agreed to deliver oil to customers in the future at a fixed price and, since it stood to take a large loss if oil prices rose, the firm's policy was to hedge this risk by buying oil futures. Culp and Miller argue that the company was following a reasonable hedging strategy and would not have incurred serious losses had it stuck to its policy. But MG's top management bailed out when oil prices fell and large losses were recorded on its futures contracts. (MG's management may have been misled by its accounting system, which recorded the losses on the futures positions but not the profits on the contracts to deliver oil.) Unfortunately, the managers bailed out at the worst possible time, since they had to renegotiate delivery contracts in a period of *rising* oil prices. See C. Culp and M. H. Miller, 'Metallgesellschaft and the Economics of Synthetic Storage', *Journal of Applied Corporate Finance*, 7: 62–72 (Winter 1995).

[46] For a detailed discussion of the events surrounding the AWA case see J. A. Batten, 'AWA: Internal Control and Foreign Exchange Trading' in *International Finance in Australia: A Case Study Approach*, Butterworths, Sydney, 1993.

These tales of woe have some cautionary messages for corporations. During the 1970s and the 1980s many firms turned their treasury operations into profit centres and proudly announced their profits from trading in financial instruments. But it is not possible to make large profits in financial markets without also taking large risks, so these profits should have served as a warning rather than a matter for congratulation.

A Boeing 747 weighs 400 tonnes, flies at about 1000 kilometres per hour and is inherently very dangerous. But we do not ground 747s; we just take precautions to ensure that they are flown with care. Similarly, it is foolish to suggest that firms should ban the use of derivatives, but it makes obvious sense to take precautions against their misuse. Here are two bits of horse sense:

- *Precaution 1.* Do not be taken by surprise. By this we mean that senior management needs to monitor regularly the value of the firm's derivatives positions and know what bets the firm has placed. At its simplest, this might involve asking what would happen if interest rates or exchange rates were to change by 1 per cent. But large banks and consultants also have developed sophisticated models for measuring the risk of derivatives positions. J.P. Morgan, for example, offers corporate clients its RiskMetrics software to keep track of their risk.
- *Precaution 2.* Place bets only when you have some comparative advantage that ensures the odds are in your favour. If a bank were to announce that it was drilling for oil or launching a new soap powder, you would rightly be suspicious about whether it had what it takes to succeed. Conversely, when an industrial corporation places large bets on interest rates or exchange rates, it is competing against some highly paid pros in banks and other financial institutions. Unless it is better informed than they are about future interest rates or exchange rates, it should use derivatives for hedging, not for speculation.

Imprudent speculation in derivatives is undoubtedly an issue of concern for the company's shareholders, but is it a matter for more general concern? Some people believe so. They point to the huge volume of trading in derivatives and argue that speculative losses could lead to major defaults that might threaten the whole financial system. These worries have led to calls for increased regulation, but we should warn you about careless measures of the size of the derivatives markets and the possible losses. In 1992 the total principal amount of derivatives outstanding in the world was estimated at $17.6 trillion (i.e. $17.6 thousand billion).[47] This is a very large sum, but it tells you *nothing* about the amount of money at risk. For example, suppose that a bank enters into a $10 million interest-rate swap and the other party goes bankrupt the next day. How much has the bank lost? Nothing. It has not paid anything up front; the two parties simply promised to pay sums to each other in the future. Now the deal is off.

Suppose that the other party does not go insolvent until a year after the bank entered into the swap. In the meantime interest rates have moved in the bank's favour, so it should be receiving more money from the swap than it is paying out. When the other side defaults on the deal, the bank loses the difference between the interest that it is due to receive and the interest that it should pay. But it does not lose the principal of $10 million.[48] The only meaningful measure of the potential loss from default is the amount that it would cost firms showing a profit to replace their swap positions.

---

[47]  United States General Accounting Office, Financial Derivatives: Action Needed to Protect the Financial System, report to congressional requesters, May 1994.

[48]  This does not mean that firms do not worry about the possibility of default, and there are a variety of ways that they try to protect themselves. In the case of swaps, firms are reluctant to deal with banks that do not have the highest credit rating.

## 25.8 Summary

As a manager, you are paid to take risks, but you are not paid to take *any* risks. Some are simply bad bets, and others could jeopardise the success of the firm. In these cases you should look for ways to insure or hedge.

Most businesses take out insurance against a variety of risks. Insurance companies have considerable expertise in assessing risk and may be able to pool risks by holding a diversified portfolio. Insurance works less well when the insurance policy attracts only the worst risk (*adverse selection*) or when the insured firm is tempted to skip on maintenance and safety procedures (*moral hazard*).

Insurance is generally purchased from specialist insurance companies, but there are also occasions when the firm can use financial options to insure against a decline in an asset's value.

The idea behind hedging is straightforward. You find two closely related assets. You then buy one and sell the other in proportions that minimise the risk of your net position. If the assets are *perfectly* correlated, you can make the net position risk-free.

The trick is to find the hedge ratio or delta—that is, the number of units of one asset that is needed to offset changes in the value of the other asset. Sometimes the best solution is to look at how the prices of the two assets have moved together in the past. For example, suppose you observe that a 1 per cent change in the value of B has been accompanied on average by a 2 per cent change in the value of A. The delta equals 2.0; to hedge each dollar invested in A, you need to sell two dollars of B.

On other occasions a little theory can help to set up the hedge. For example, the effect of a change in interest rates on an asset's value depends on the asset's duration. If two assets have the same duration, they will be equally affected by fluctuations in interest rates.

Many of the hedges described in this chapter are static. Once you have set up the hedge, you can take a long vacation, confident that the firm is well protected. However, some hedges, such as those that match durations, are dynamic. As time passes and prices change, you may need to rebalance your position to maintain the hedge.

Firms use a number of tools to hedge:

1. Futures contracts are advance orders to buy or sell an asset. The price is fixed today, but the final payment does not occur until the delivery date. The futures markets allow firms to place advance orders for dozens of different commodities, securities and currencies.

2. Futures contracts are highly standardised and are traded in huge volume on the futures exchanges. Instead of buying or selling a standardised futures contract, you may be able to arrange a tailor-made contract with a bank. These tailor-made futures contracts are called forward contracts. Firms regularly protect themselves against exchange-rate changes by buying or selling forward currency contracts.

3. It is also sometimes possible to construct homemade forward contracts. For example, as an alternative to buying forward currency, you could borrow Australian dollars, exchange them for foreign currency and then lend the foreign currency until it is needed. This has exactly the same cash flow consequences as a purchase of forward currency.

4. In recent years firms have entered into a variety of swap arrangements. For example, a firm may arrange for the bank to make all the future payments on its Australian dollar debt in exchange for paying the bank the cost of servicing a deutschmark loan.

Instead of using derivatives for hedging, some companies have decided that speculation is more fun, and this has sometimes got them into serious trouble. We do not believe that such speculation makes sense for an industrial company, but we caution against the view that derivatives are a threat to the financial system.

# FURTHER READING

Two general articles on corporate risk management are:

C. W. Smith and R. M. Stultz, 'The Determinants of Firms' Hedging Policies', *Journal of Financial and Quantitative Analysis*, **20**: 391–405 (December 1985).

K. A. Froot, D. Scharfstein and J. C. Stein, 'A Framework for Risk Management', *Journal of Applied Corporate Finance*, 7: 22–32 (Autumn 1994).

Useful material on the ways that companies use derivatives and on regulation of derivatives is provided by:

Global Derivatives Study Group, *Derivatives: Practices and Principles*, The Group of Thirty, Washington, D.C., July 1993.

Unites States General Accounting Office, Financial Derivatives: Actions Needed to Protect the Financial System, report to congressional requesters, May 1994.

For a detailed discussion of the use of derivatives securities in the Australian market refer to:

E. Carew, *Derivatives Decoded*, Allen and Unwin, Sydney, 1995.

D. Davagaard and T. Valentine, *Financial Risk Management*, Harper Educational (Australia), Sydney, 1995.

W. Slatyer and E. Carew, *Trading Asia-Pacific Financial Futures Markets*, Allen and Unwin, Sydney, 1993.

For a comprehensive discussion of theoretical aspects of futures pricing including discussion of the cost of carry model, basis risk and the implications for hedging refer to:

R. Heaney, 'Futures Contract Pricing and Hedging: A Review of Theory and Evidence', *Accounting Research Journal*, 8 (**1**): 48–65 (1995).

For further material on futures and swaps see:

D. Duffie, *Futures Markets*, Prentice-Hall, Inc., Englewood Cliffs, N.J., 1989.

S. Figlewski, K. John and J. Merrick, *Hedging with Financial Futures for Institutional Investors: From Theory to Practice*, Ballinger Publishing Company, Cambridge, Mass., 1986.

J. C. Hull, *Options, Futures and Other Derivative Securities*, 2nd ed., Prentice-Hall, Inc., Englewood Cliffs, N.J., 1993.

D. R. Siegel and D. F. Siegel, *Futures Markets*, Dryden Press, Chicago, 1989.

Schaefer's paper is a useful review of how duration measures are used to immunise fixed liabilities:

S. M. Schaefer, 'Immunisation and Duration: A Review of Theory, Performance and Applications', *Midland Corporate Finance Journal*, 3: 41–58 (Autumn 1984).

The Metallgesellschaft debacle makes fascinating reading. The following three papers cover all sides of the ensuing debate:

C. Culp and M. H. Miller, 'Metallgesellschaft and the Economics of Synthetic Storage', *Journal of Applied Corporate Finance*, 7: 62–76 (Winter 1995).

F. Edwards, 'The Collapse of Metallgesellschaft: Unhedgeable Risks, Poor Hedging Strategy, or Just Bad Luck?', *Journal of Future Markets*, 15 (May 1995).

A. Mello and J. Parsons, 'Maturity Structure of a Hedge Matters: Lessons from the Metallgesellschaft Debacle', *Journal of Applied Corporate Finance*, 7 (Spring 1995).

# QUIZ

**1.** True or false?

a. A perfect hedge of asset A requires an asset B that is perfectly correlated with A.

b. Hedging transactions in an active futures market have zero or slightly negative NPVs.

c. Longer maturity bonds necessarily have longer durations.

d. The longer a bond's duration, the lower is its volatility.
e. When you buy a futures contract, you pay now for delivery at a future date.
f. The holder of a futures contract receives the convenience yield on the underlying commodity.
g. The holder of a financial futures contract misses out on any dividend or interest payments made on the underlying security.

**2.** You own a $1 million portfolio of Aerospace Ltd shares with a beta of 1.2. You are enthusiastic about aerospace but uncertain about the prospects for the overall share market. Explain how you could 'hedge out' your market exposure by selling the market short. How much would you sell? How in practice would you go about 'selling the market'?

**3.** Securities A, B and C have the following cash flows:

|   | Period 1 | Period 2 | Period 3 |
|---|---|---|---|
| A | 40 | 40 | 40 |
| B | 120 | — | — |
| C | 10 | 10 | 110 |

a. Calculate their durations if the interest rate is 8 per cent.
b. Suppose that you have an investment of $10 million in A. What combination of B and C would immunise this investment against interest-rate changes?
c. Now suppose that you have a $10 million investment in B. How would you immunise? (*Hint*: Try selling A or B and borrowing short term.)

**4.** Calculate the value of a six-month forward contract on the All Ordinaries SPI forward contract. You have the following information:

■ Spot All Ordinaries Index          3045
■ Dividend yield                     2.5 per cent per year
■ Risk-free rate                     5.5 per cent per year

**5.** Calculate PV(convenience yield) for magnesium scrap from the following information:

■ Spot price:          $2550 per tonne
■ Futures price:       $2408 for a one-year contract
■ Interest rate:       12 per cent
■ PV(storage costs):   $100 per year

**6.** What is a currency swap? An interest-rate swap? Give an example of how swaps might be used.

**7.** Assume that residents of northeastern Victoria suffered record-setting low temperatures throughout June and July 1997. Spot prices of heating oil rose 25 per cent, to over $2 a litre.
a. What effect would this have had on the net convenience yield and on the relationship between forward and spot prices?
b. In mid-1988 refiners and distributors were surprised by record-setting high temperatures. What would have been the effect on net convenience yield and spot and forward prices for heating oil?

**8.** What is basis risk? In which of the following cases would you expect basis risk to be more serious?
  a. A broker owning a large block of BHP Ltd ordinary shares hedges by selling index futures.
  b. A Darling Downs corn farmer hedges the selling prices of her crop by selling Chicago corn futures.
  c. An importer must pay 900 million Italian lire in six months. He hedges by buying lire forward.

**9.** Why might a large, multinational company choose to insure against common events, such as vehicle accidents, but not against rare events which could cause large losses? Explain briefly.

**10.** What is meant by 'moral hazard' and 'adverse selection'? Explain why these effects tend to increase insurance premiums.

## QUESTIONS AND PROBLEMS

**1.** Les Diamond owns shares in a mutual fund worth $1 million on July 15. (This is an index fund that tracks Standard & Poor's 500.) He wants to cash in now, but his accountant advises him to wait six months so as to defer a large capital gains tax. Explain to Les how he can use share index futures to hedge out his exposure to market movements over the next six months. Could Les 'cash in' without actually selling his shares?

**2.** Refer back to Question 1. Suppose that the nearest index futures contract matures in seven months rather than six. Show how Les Diamond can still use index futures to hedge his position. How would the maturity date affect the hedge ratio?

**3.** Price changes on two gold mining shares have shown strong positive correlation. Their historical relationship is:

Average percentage change in A $= 0.001 + 0.75$(percentage change in B)

Changes in B explain 60 per cent of the variation of the changes in A ($R^2 = 0.6$).
  a. Suppose you own $100 000 of A. How much of B should you sell to minimise the risk of your net position?
  b. What is the hedge ratio?
  c. How would you construct a zero value hedge?
  d. Here is the historical relationship between A and gold prices:

Average percentage change in A $= -0.002 + 1.2$(percentage change in the gold price)

If $R^2 = 0.5$, can you lower the risk of your net position by hedging with gold (or gold futures) rather than with share B? Explain.

**4.** What is meant by 'delta' in the context of hedging? Give examples of how delta can be estimated or calculated.

**5.** In Section 25.5 we stated that the duration of BHL's lease equals the duration of its debt.
  a. Show that this is so.

b. Now suppose that the interest rate falls to 3 per cent. Show how the value of the lease and the debt package are now affected by a 0.5 per cent rise or fall in the interest rate. What would BHL need to do to re-establish the interest-rate hedge?

**6.** Line 1 of the following table shows cash outflows that your company has just promised to make. Below that are the cash flows on a blue-chip corporate note. The interest rate is 10 per cent. Your company can borrow at this rate if it wishes.

|  | Year 1 | Year 2 | Year 3 | Year 4 |
|---|---|---|---|---|
| Liability, millions | 0 | 0 | −$20 | −$20 |
| Note's cash payments as per cent of face value | 12 | 12 | 12 | 112 |

a. What is the present value of your liability?
b. Calculate the durations of the liability and the note.
c. Suppose you wish to hedge the liability by investing in a combination of the note and a short-term bank deposit with a duration of zero. How much must you invest in each?
d. Would this hedge continue to protect your company:
   i.  If interest rates dropped by 3 per cent?
   ii. If short-term interest rates fluctuate while longer-term rates remain basically constant?
   iii. If interest rates remain the same but two years pass?
e. Can you set up a hedge portfolio that relieves the financial manager of all the worries mentioned in Part (d)? Describe that portfolio.

**7.** Explain the chief differences between futures and forward contracts, for example for foreign exchange.

**8.** Table 25.6 contains spot and six-month futures prices for several commodities and financial instruments. There may be some money-making opportunities. See if you

**table 25.6**

Spot and six-month futures prices for selected commodities and securities

| Commodity | Spot price | Futures price | Comments |
|---|---|---|---|
| Magnesium | $2 550 per tonne | $2 728.50 per tonne | PV(storage costs) = PV(convenience yield) |
| Frozen quiche | $0.50 per kilo | $0.514 per kilo | PV(storage costs) = $0.10 per kilo; PV(convenience yield) = $0.05 per kilo |
| Nevada Hydro 8s of 2002 | 77 | 78.39 | 4% semiannual coupon payment is due just before futures contract expires |
| Costaguanan pulgas (currency) | 9 300 pulgas = $1 | 6 900 pulgas = $1 | Costaguanan interest rate is 95% per year |
| Establishment Industries ordinary shares | $95 | $97.54 | Establishment pays dividends of $2 per quarter; next dividend is paid two months from now |
| Cheap white wine | $12 500 per 10 000-litre tank | $14 200 per 10 000-litre tank | PV(convenience yield) = $250 per tank. Your company unexpectedly has surplus storage and can store 50 000 litres at no cost |

can find them, and explain how you would trade to take advantage of them. The interest rate is 14.5 per cent, or 7 per cent over the six-month life of the contracts.

**9.** The following table shows gold futures prices for varying contract lengths. Gold is predominantly an investment good, not an industrial commodity. Investors hold gold because it diversifies their portfolios and because they hope its price will rise. They do not hold it for its convenience yield.

Calculate the interest rate faced by traders in gold futures for each of the contract lengths shown below. The spot price is $456.90 per ounce.

|  | Contract length (months) | | | | |
| --- | --- | --- | --- | --- | --- |
|  | 1 | 2 | 3 | 4 | 5 |
| Futures price | $458.90 | $464.50 | $483.30 | $503.90 | $525.70 |

**10.** The Sydney Futures Exchange needs to be assured that new futures contracts serve the public interest. One of the tests that it applies is that the contract should provide price discovery—that is, the futures price should provide the public with new information on investors' forecasts of changes in spot prices. In justifying their proposals to trade index futures, the exchanges have argued that index futures provide information about investor views on futures prices. Evaluate this claim.

**11.** Firms A and B face the following borrowing rates for making a five-year fixed rate debt issue in Australian dollars or Swiss francs:

|  | Australian dollars | Swiss francs |
| --- | --- | --- |
| Firm A | 10% | 7% |
| Firm B | 8% | 6% |

Suppose that A wishes to borrow Australian dollars and B wishes to borrow Swiss francs. Show how a swap could be used to reduce the borrowing costs of each company. Assume a spot exchange rate of two Swiss francs per dollar.

**12.** 'Last year we had a substantial income in sterling, which we hedged by selling sterling forward. In the event sterling rose, and our decision to sell forward cost us a lot of money. I think that in future we should either stop hedging our currency exposure or just hedge when we think sterling is overvalued.' As financial manager, how would you respond to this chief executive's comment?

**13.** 'Speculators want futures contracts to be incorrectly priced; hedgers want them to be correctly priced.' Why?

**14.** Hoopoe Ltd wants to borrow 100 million Australian dollars at a fixed rate with a maturity of five years. It calculates that it can make a eurobond issue with the following terms:

- Interest:      10.625 per cent payable annually
- Maturity:      5 years
- Commissions    1.125 per cent

■ Agency fees:      0.15 per cent on coupon
                    0.075 per cent on principal
■ Issue expenses:   0.2 per cent

A bank has presented Hoopoe with a proposal for a Swiss franc issue combined with a currency swap in Australian dollars. The proposed terms for the Swiss franc issue are:

■ Amount:        200 million Swiss francs
■ Interest:      10.375 per cent annually
■ Maturity:      5 years
■ Commissions:   2.8 per cent
■ Agency fees:   0.75 per cent on coupon
                 0.30 per cent on principal
■ Issue expenses: 0.2 per cent

The counterparty of the swap would raise fixed dollars on the following terms:

■ Amount:          100 million Australian dollars (equivalent to 200 million Swiss francs)
■ Interest:        10.625 per cent annually
■ Maturity:        5 years
■ Commissions:     1.8 per cent
■ Agency expenses: 0.15 per cent of coupon
                   0.075 per cent on principal
■ Issue expenses:  0.2 per cent

The counterparty would be happy with an all-in cost in Swiss francs of 6.4 per cent.
a. Which alternative should Hoopoe undertake? (Ignore credit risk in your analysis.)
b. Suppose that you are the finance manager of Hoopoe. Discuss the credit risk issues involved in the alternatives.

**15.** If you buy a nine-month bank bill futures contract, you undertake to buy a 90-day bank accepted bill in nine months time. Suppose that bank accepted bills currently offer the following yields:

| Days to maturity | Annual yield |
| --- | --- |
| 90 | 6% |
| 180 | 6.5% |
| 270 | 7% |
| 365 | 8% |

What is the value of a nine-month bill futures contract?

**16.** In 1985 a German corporation bought $250 million forward to cover a future purchase of goods from the United States. However, the dollar subsequently depreciated, and the company found that if it had waited and then bought spot dollars, it would have paid 225 million deutschmarks less. One financial manager pointed out that the company could have waited to buy the dollars and meanwhile covered its exposure by using options. In that case it would have saved itself

225 million deutschmarks.[49] Evaluate the company's decision and the financial manager's criticism.

**17.** Large businesses spend millions of dollars annually on insurance. Why? Should they insure against all risks or does insurance make more sense for some risks than others?

**18. a.** An investor currently holding $1 million in long-term Treasury bonds becomes concerned about increasing volatility in interest rates. She decides to hedge her risk using Treasury-bond futures contracts. Should she buy or sell such contracts?

    **b.** The treasurer of a corporation that will be issuing bonds in three months also is concerned about interest-rate volatility and wants to lock in the price at which he could sell 8 per cent coupon bonds. How would he use Treasury-bond futures contracts to hedge his firm's position?

**19.** A gold-mining firm is concerned about short-term volatility in its revenues. Gold currently sells for $300 an ounce, but the price is extremely volatile and could fall as low as $280 or rise as high as $320 in the next month. The company will bring 1000 ounces to the market next month.

    **a.** What will be total revenues if the firm remains unhedged for gold prices of $280, $300 and $320 an ounce?

    **b.** The futures price of gold for one-month-ahead delivery is $301. What will be the firm's total revenues at each gold price if the firm enters a one-month futures contract to deliver 1000 ounces of gold?

    **c.** What will total revenues be if the firm buys a one-month put option to sell gold for $300 an ounce? The put option costs $2 per ounce.

**20.** Your firm has just tendered for a contract in Japan. You will not know for three months whether you get the contract, but if you do, you will receive a payment of 10 million yen one year from now. You are worried that if the yen declines in value, the dollar value of this payment will be less than you expect and the project could even show a loss. Discuss the possible ways that you could protect the firm against a decline in the value of the yen. Illustrate the possible outcomes if you do get the contract and if you do not.

**21.** Petrochemical Parfum (PP) is concerned about possible increases in the price of heavy fuel oil, which is one of its major inputs. Show how PP can use either options or futures contracts to protect itself against a rise in the price of crude oil. Show how the payoffs in each case would vary if the oil price is $18, $20 or $22 a barrel. What are the advantages and disadvantages for PP of using futures rather than options to reduce risk?

**22.** 'The farmer does not avoid risk by selling wheat futures. If wheat prices stay about $2.80 a tonne, then he will actually have lost by selling wheat futures at $2.50.' Is this a fair comment?

**23.** Explain the difference between insurance and hedging. Give an example of how options can be used for each.

---

[49] Example cited in *Managing Risks and Costs Through Financial Innovation*, Business International Corporation, New York, 1987.

**24.** Your investment bank has an investment of $100 million in the shares of the Swiss Roll Corporation and a short position in the shares of the Frankfurter Sausage Company. Here is the recent price history of the two shares:

| | Percentage price change | |
| Month | Frankfurter Sausage | Swiss Roll |
| --- | --- | --- |
| January | −10 | −10 |
| February | −10 | −5 |
| March | −10 | 0 |
| April | +10 | 0 |
| May | +10 | +5 |
| June | +10 | +10 |

On the evidence of these six months, how large would your short position in Frankfurter Sausage need to be to hedge you as far as possible against movements in the price of Swiss Roll?

**25.** A year ago your bank entered into a $50 million five-year interest-rate swap. It agreed to pay company A each year a fixed rate of 6 per cent and to receive in return LIBOR plus 1 per cent. When the bank entered into this swap, LIBOR was 5 per cent, but now interest rates have risen, so on a four-year interest-rate swap the bank could expect to pay 6.5 per cent and receive LIBOR plus 1 per cent.
a. Is the swap showing a profit or a loss to the bank?
b. Suppose that at this point company A approaches your bank and asks to terminate the swap. If there are four annual payments still remaining, how much should the bank charge A to terminate?

**26.** At the time of the 1992 sterling crisis the London *Financial Times* commented, 'Many treasurers said yesterday that the direction of exchange rates was still too uncertain to justify [hedging by] locking in now.' Does this make sense?

**27.** Todd's Screwdriver Company has borrowed $20 million from a bank at a floating interest rate of 2 percentage points above three-month bank bills, which now yield 5 per cent. Assume that interest payments are made quarterly and that the entire principal of the loan is repaid after five years. Todd wants to convert the bank loan to fixed-rate debt. It could issue a five-year note at a fixed yield to maturity of 9 per cent. Such a note would now trade at par. The five-year risk free rate yield to maturity is 7 per cent.
a. Is Todd stupid to want long-term debt at an interest rate of 9 per cent? It is borrowing from the bank at 7 per cent.
b. Explain how the conversion could be carried out by an interest-rate swap. What will be the initial terms of the swap? (Ignore transaction costs and the swap dealer's profit.)
   One year from now medium-term and long-term Treasury yields have *decreased* to 6 per cent. Treasury note rates have *increased* to 6 per cent, so the term structure is now flat. (The changes actually occurred in month 5.) Todd's credit standing is unchanged; it could still borrow at 2 percentage points over Treasury rates.
c. What net swap payment will Todd make or receive?
d. Suppose that Todd now wants to cancel the swap. How much would it need to pay the swap dealer? Or would the dealer pay Todd? Explain.

**28.** Consider the commodities and financial assets listed in Table 25.7. The risk-free interest rate is 6 per cent a year, and the term structure is flat.

table 25.7 _____

Spot prices for selected commodities and financial assets

| Asset | Spot price | Comments |
|-------|------------|----------|
| Magnesium | $2800 per tonne | Net convenience yield = 4% per year |
| Oat bran | $0.44 per kilo | Net convenience yield = 0.5% per month |
| Biotech share index | 140.2 | Dividend yield = 0 |
| Allen Wrench Co. | $58.00 | Cash dividend = $2.40 per year |
| Five-year Treasury note | 108.93 | 8% coupon |
| Westonian ruple | 3.1 ruples = $1 | 12% interest rate in ruples |

a. Calculate the six-month futures price for each case.
b. Explain how a magnesium producer would use a futures market to 'lock in' the selling price of a planned shipment of 1000 tonnes of magnesium six months from now.
c. Suppose the producer takes the actions recommended in your answer to (b), but after one month magnesium prices have fallen to $2200. What happens? Will the producer have to undertake additional futures market trades to restore its hedged position?
d. Does the Biotech index futures price provide useful information about the expected future performance of Biotech shares?
e. Suppose Allen Wrench shares fall suddenly by $10 per share. Investors are confident that the cash dividend will not be reduced. What happens to the futures price?
f. Suppose interest rates suddenly fall. The spot rate for cash flows six months from now is 4 per cent (per year); it is 4.5 per cent for cash flows 12 months from now, 4.8 per cent for cash flows 18 months from now, and 5 per cent for all subsequent cash flows. What happens to the six-month futures price on the five-year Treasury note? What happens to a trader who shorted 100 notes at the futures price calculated in Part (a)?
g. An importer must make a payment of one million ruples three months from now. Explain *two* strategies the importer could use to hedge against unfavourable shifts in the ruple–dollar exchange rate.

# chapter 26

# LEASING

Most of us occasionally rent a car, bicycle or a holiday unit at the beach. Usually such personal rentals are short-lived—we may rent a car for a day or week. But in corporate finance longer-term rentals are common. A rental agreement that extends for six months or more and involves a series of periodic payments is called a **lease**.

Every lease involves two parties. The *user* of the asset is called the *lessee*. The lessee makes periodic payments to the *owner* of the asset, who is called the *lessor*. For example, if you sign an agreement to rent a unit for a year, you are the lessee and the owner is the lessor. Under the conditions of a lease, the lessee is granted exclusive right to use the asset by the lessor.

Firms lease as an alternative to buying capital equipment. Computers are often leased; so are cars, trucks, aircraft and ships. Just about every kind of asset has been leased sometime by somebody, including units, houses, tennis courts and zoo animals.

Hence, a lease is an agreement between the lessor and the lessee concerning the use and payment for an asset over a specific period of time.

You often see references to the *leasing industry*. This refers to lessors. (Almost all firms are lessees to at least a minor extent.) Who are the lessors?

Some of the largest lessors are equipment manufacturers. For example, IBM is the largest lessor of computers, and Xerox is the largest lessor of copiers. The other major groups of lessors are banks, finance companies and independent leasing companies. The latter offer a variety of services. Some act as lease brokers (arranging lease deals) as well as being lessors. Others specialise in leasing cars, trucks and standardised industrial equipment; they succeed because they can buy equipment in quantity, service it efficiently and if necessary resell it at a good price.

We began this chapter by cataloguing the different kinds of leases and some of the reasons for their use. Then we show how short-term, or cancellable, lease payments can be interpreted as equivalent annual costs. The remainder of the chapter analyses long-term leases used as alternatives to debt financing.

## 26.1 What is a lease?

Leases come in many forms, but in all cases the lessee (user) promises to make a series of payments to the lessor (owner) in return for the use of the asset. The lease contract specifies the monthly or semiannual payments, with the first payment usually due 'in advance' as soon as the contract is signed. The payments are usually level, but their time pattern can be tailored to the user's needs. For example, suppose that a manufacturer leases a machine to produce a complex new product. There will be a year's 'shakedown' period before volume production starts. In this case, it might be possible to arrange for lower payments during the first year of the lease. Any lease agreement will clearly state:

1. A concise identification of the asset to be leased.
2. The period of the lease.
3. The amount and timing of the periodic lease payments, including provisions for default.
4. The obligations of both the lessee and lessor under the agreement including details regarding responsibilities for insurance and maintenance.
5. The conditions applicable at the termination of the lease including the clear statement of obligations of the parties to the lease and stating the agreed residual value of the asset.
6. Provisions, if applicable, for cancellation of the lease.

Some leases are short-term and cancellable during the contract period at the option of the lessee. These are generally known as *operating leases*. Operating leases usually have a term to expiration for a time period less than the economic life of the asset and are cancellable if the lessee gives proper notice or the assets can be updated or replaced during the period of the lease. These leases sometimes have a separate or inclusive maintenance contract whereby the lessor assumes responsibility for the repair of the leased assets. Hence, operating leases are often also referred to as service or maintenance leases. When an operating lease is terminated, the leased equipment reverts back to the lessor.[1]

Other leases extend over most of the estimated economic life of the asset and cannot be cancelled or can be cancelled only if the lessor is reimbursed for any losses. These are called *financial*, *capital* or *full-payout leases*.[2]

Financial leases are a *source of financing*. Signing a financial lease contract is like borrowing money. There is an immediate cash inflow because the lessee is relieved of having to pay for the asset. But the lessee also assumes a binding obligation to make the payments specified in the lease contract. The user could have borrowed the full purchase price of the asset by accepting a binding obligation to make interest and principal payments to the lender. Thus, the cash flow consequences of leasing and borrowing are similar. In either case, the firm raises cash now and pays it back later. Hence, the lease term and the asset's useful life are usually identical or very similar and leases are often used as a direct substitute for long-term borrowing. A

---

[1]    However, in some cases a 'gentleman's agreement' may exist whereby at the expiration of the lease the lessee can purchase the goods for the residual value—such agreements are not formalised as such formality would affect the taxation status of any lease expense deductions. Such agreements are sometimes referred to as bargain purchase options where the lessee can either purchase the goods or enter into a new lease contract. The purchase price of the asset is usually below its fair market value.

[2]    In the shipping industry, a financial lease is called a *bareboat charter* or a *demise hire*.

large part of this chapter will be devoted to comparing leasing and borrowing as financial alternatives.[3]

Leases also differ in services provided by the lessor. Under a *full-service*, or *rental*, lease, the lessor promises to maintain and insure the equipment and to pay any taxes due on it. In a *net* lease, the lessee agrees to maintain the asset, insure it and pay any property taxes. Financial leases are usually net leases.

Most financial leases are arranged for brand new assets. The lessee identifies the equipment, arranges for the leasing company to buy it from the manufacturer and signs a contract with the leasing company. This is called a *direct* lease. In other cases, the firm sells an asset it already owns and leases it back from the buyer. These *sale and lease-back* arrangements are common in real estate. For example, firm X may wish to raise cash by selling a factory but still retain use of the factory. It could do this by selling the factory for cash to a leasing company and simultaneously signing a long-term lease contract for the factory. Legal ownership of the factory passes to the leasing company, but the right to use it stays with firm X.[4]

You may also encounter *leveraged* leases. These are financial leases in which the lessor borrows part of the purchase price of the leased asset, using the lease contract as security for the loan. This does not change the lessee's obligations, but it can complicate the lessor's analysis considerably. Typically, there are at least three parties to a leveraged lease agreement—the lessee, the lessor (who also acts as lease manager by structuring, negotiating and arranging the finance used to purchase the goods to be leased) and the providers of debt and/or equity finance to the lessor. We have more to say about leveraged leases later in this chapter.

## 26.2 Why lease?

Leasing involves numerous considerations including asking two critical questions:

1. Is the asset needed until its economic life expires?
2. How should the asset be financed?

You hear many suggestions about why companies should lease equipment rather than buy it. Let us look at some sensible reasons and then at four that are more dubious.

## Sensible reasons for leasing

### Short-term leases are convenient
Suppose you want the use of a car for a week. You could buy one and sell it seven days later, but that would be silly. Quite apart from the fact that registering ownership is a nuisance, you would spend some time selecting a car, negotiating purchase and arranging insurance. Then at the end of the week you would negotiate resale and cancel or transfer the registration and insurance. When you need a car only for a short time, it clearly makes sense to rent it. You save the trouble of registering ownership and you know the effective cost. In the same way, it pays a company to lease equipment that it needs for only a year or two. Of course, this kind of lease is always an operating lease.

Sometimes, the cost of short-term rentals may seem prohibitively high, or you may find it difficult to rent at any price. This can happen for equipment that is easily damaged by careless

---

3   In Australia, Accounting Standard AASB1008 classifies leases based on economic substance and classifies leases as financial leases if substantially all the risks and benefits of ownership pass to the lessee. For a comprehensive discussion of taxation and accounting issues associated with leasing in Australia refer to G. Whittred, I. Zimmer and S. Taylor, *Financial Accounting: Incentive Effects and Economic Consequences*, Harcourt Brace, Sydney, 1996; or P. Jubb, S. Haswell and I. Langfield-Smith, *Company Accounting*, 2nd ed., Nelson ITP, Melbourne, 1999.

4   This strategy was used by Australian banks during the 1980s as a means of divesting themselves of the ownership of numerous properties.

use. The owner knows that short-term users are unlikely to take the same care they would with their own equipment. When the danger of abuse becomes too high, short-term rental markets do not survive. Thus, it is easy enough to buy a Lamborghini Diablo, provided your pockets are deep enough, but nearly impossible to rent one.

**Asset life considerations**　In assessing the economic life of an asset it is critical that, among others, two primary issues be considered—obsolescence and salvage value. If the probability of obsolescence is high and obtaining a high salvage value is low then leasing should be considered a viable alternative.

**Cancellation options are valuable**　Some leases that *appear* expensive really are fairly priced once the option to cancel is recognised. We return to this point in the next section.

**Maintenance is provided**　Under a full-service lease, the user receives maintenance and other services. Many lessors are well equipped to provide efficient maintenance. However, bear in mind that these benefits will be reflected in higher lease payments.

**Standardisation leads to low administrative and transaction costs**
Suppose that you operate a leasing company which specialises in financial leases for trucks. You are effectively lending money to a large number of firms (the lessees) which may differ considerably in size and risk. But, because the underlying asset is in each case the same saleable item (a truck), you can safely 'lend' the money (lease the truck) without conducting a detailed analysis of each firm's business. You can also use a simple, standard lease contract. This standardisation makes it possible to 'lend' small sums of money without incurring large investigative, administrative or legal costs.

For these reasons leasing is often a relatively cheap source of cash for the small company. It offers financing on a flexible, piecemeal basis, with lower transaction costs than in a private placement or a public share issue.

**Tax deductions can be used**　The lessor owns the leased asset and deducts its depreciation from taxable income. If the lessor can make better use of depreciation tax deductions than an asset's user can, it may make sense for the leasing company to own the equipment and pass on some of the tax benefits to the lessee in the form of low lease payments.

# Some dubious reasons for leasing

## Leasing avoids capital expenditure controls
In many companies lease proposals are scrutinised as carefully as capital expenditure proposals, but in others leasing may enable an operating manager to avoid the elaborate approval procedures needed to buy an asset.

**Leasing preserves capital**　Leasing companies provide '100 per cent financing'; they advance the full cost of the leased asset. Consequently, they often claim that leasing preserves capital, allowing the firm to save its cash for other things.

But the firm can also 'preserve capital' by borrowing money. If Toowoomba Bus Lines leases a $500 000 bus rather than buying it, it does conserve $500 000 cash. It could also (1) buy the bus for cash and (2) borrow $500 000, using the bus as security. Its bank balance ends up the same whether it leases or buys or borrows. It has the bus in either case, and it incurs a $500 000 liability in either case. What is so special about leasing?

**Leases may be off-balance-sheet financing**　Until the end of 1986 financial leases were regarded as *off-balance-sheet financing*. That is, a firm could acquire an asset, finance it through a financial lease and show neither the asset nor the lease contract on its balance sheet. The firm was required only to add a brief footnote to its accounts describing its lease obligation. Accounting standards now require that all *capital* (financial) leases be *capitalised*.[5] That is, the present value of the lease payments must be calculated and shown alongside debt on the right-hand side of the balance sheet.[6]

In order to implement this new requirement, the Australian Accounting Standards Board (AASB) had to come up with objective rules for distinguishing between operating and financial (capital) leases. The AASB defines financial leases as leases which meet *any one* of the following requirements:

1. The lease agreement transfers all the benefits and risks of ownership to the lessee without transferring legal ownership during the period of the lease.
2. The lessee can purchase the asset for a bargain price when the lease expires.
3. The lease is non-cancellable and lasts for at least 75 per cent of the asset's estimated economic life, or the present value of the lease payments is at least 90 per cent of the asset's value.
4. The lease is relatively long term and for assets that are not easily moveable and saleable.

All other leases are operating leases as far as the accountants are concerned.

Many financial managers have tried to take advantage of this arbitrary boundary between operating and financial leases. Suppose that you wanted to finance a computer-controlled machine tool costing $1 million. The machine tool's life is expected to be 12 years. You could sign a lease contract for eight years, 11 months with lease payments having a present value of $899 000 (just missing requirement 3). You would also make sure the lease contract avoids requirements 1 and 2. Result? You have off-balance-sheet financing. This lease would not have to be capitalised, although it is clearly a long-term, fixed obligation.

Now we come to the $64 000 question: Why should anyone *care* whether financing is off-balance sheet or on-balance sheet? Shouldn't the financial manager worry about substance rather than appearance?

When a firm obtains off-balance-sheet financing, the conventional measures of financial leverage, such as the debt-equity ratio, understate the true degree of financial leverage. Some believe that financial analysts do not always notice off-balance-sheet lease obligations (which are still referred to in footnotes) or the greater volatility of earnings that results from the fixed lease payments. They may be right, but we would not expect such an imperfection to be widespread.

When a company borrows money, it must usually consent to certain restrictions on future borrowing. Early bond indentures did not include any restrictions on financial leases. Therefore, leasing was seen as a way to circumvent restrictive covenants. Loopholes such as these are easily stopped, and most bond indentures now include limits on leasing.

Long-term lease obligations ought to be regarded as debt whether or not they appear on the balance sheet. Financial analysts may overlook moderate leasing activity, just as they overlook minor debts. But major lease obligations are generally recognised and taken into account.

## Leasing affects income

Leasing can make the firm's balance sheet and income statement *look* better by increasing income or decreasing asset value, or both.

A lease which qualifies as off-balance-sheet financing affects income in only one way: the lease payments are an expense. If the firm buys the asset instead and borrows to finance it, both depreciation and interest expense are deducted. Leases are usually set up so that payments in the early years are less than depreciation plus interest under the buy-and-borrow alternative. Consequently, leasing increases income in the early years of an asset's life. The rate

---

5   See AAS17 (1984) and AASB1008 (1986) and Exposure Draft 82.
6   This 'asset' is then amortised over the life of the lease. The amortisation is deducted from book income, just as depreciation is deducted for a purchased asset.

of return can increase even more dramatically, because the value of assets (the denominator in the rate-of-return calculation) is understated if the leased asset never appears on the firm's balance sheet.

Leasing's impact on income should in itself have no effect on firm value. In efficient capital markets investors will look through the firm's accounting results to the true value of the asset and the liability incurred to finance it.

## 26.3 Operating leases

Remember our discussion of *equivalent annual costs* in Chapter 6? We defined the equivalent annual cost of, say, a machine as the annual rental payment sufficient to cover the present value of all the costs of owning and operating it.

In Chapter 6's examples, the rental payments were hypothetical—just a way of converting a present value to an annual cost. But in the leasing business the payments are real. Suppose you decide to lease a machine tool for one year. What will the rental payment be in a competitive leasing industry? The lessor's equivalent annual cost, of course.

### Example of an operating lease

The boyfriend of the daughter of the managing director of Entertainment Industries takes her to the Year 12 dance in a pearly white stretch limo. The managing director is very impressed by the car. He decides Entertainment Industries ought to have one for VIP transportation. Entertainment's managing director considers a one-year operating lease and approaches Diamond Limolease for a quote.

Table 26.1 shows Diamond's analysis. Diamond Limolease will be the lessor in any agreement with Entertainment Industries. Suppose it buys a new limo for $80 000 which it plans to lease out for five years (years 0 to 4). The table gives Diamond's forecasts of operating, maintenance and administrative costs, the latter including the costs for negotiating the lease, keeping track of payments and paperwork, and finding a replacement lessee when Entertainment's year is up. For simplicity we assume zero inflation and use a 7 per cent real cost of capital. Depreciation is assumed to be 25 per cent of the new limo, giving an annual depreciation of $20 000 or an after-tax saving of $7000. We also assume that the limo will have zero salvage value at the end of year 4. The present value of all costs, partially offset by the value of depreciation, is $85 090. Now, how much does Diamond have to charge in order to break even?

Diamond can afford to buy and lease out the limo only if the rental payments forecasted over four years have a present value of at least $85 090. The problem, then, is to calculate a four-year annuity with a present value of $85 090. We will follow common leasing practice and assume rental payments in advance.[7]

As Table 26.1 shows, the required annuity is $29 839, that is, about $30 000.[8] This annuity's present value (after taxes) exactly equals the present value of the after-tax costs of owning and operating the limo. In this case Diamond is keen to set the rent of the limo at an after-tax rate of return of 7 per cent. This involves solving for after-tax lease payments (ATLP) in the following present value equation:

$$\$85.09 = \sum_{n=0}^{4} \frac{\text{ATLP}}{(1 + 0.07)^n}$$

---

[7]   In Section 6.3 the hypothetical rentals were paid *in arrears*.

[8]   This is a level of annuity because we are assuming that (1) there is no inflation and (2) the services of a four-year-old limo are no different than a brand new limo. If users of ageing limos see them as obsolete or unfashionable, or if new limos are cheaper, then lease rates for older limos would have to be cut. This would give a *declining* annuity: initial users would pay more than the amount shown in Table 26.1; later users would pay less.

**table 26.1**
Calculating the zero NPV rental rate (or equivalent annual cost) for Entertainment Industries' pearly white stretch limo (figures in $000).

| | Year | | | | |
|---|---|---|---|---|---|
| | **0** | **1** | **2** | **3** | **4** |
| Initial cost | −80 | | | | |
| Maintenance, insurance, selling and administrative costs | −12 | −12 | −12 | −12 | −12 |
| Tax rebate on costs | +4.2 | +4.2 | +4.2 | +4.2 | +4.2 |
| Depreciation (after tax) | | +7 | +7 | +7 | +7 |
| Total | −87.80 | +0.80 | +0.80 | +0.80 | +0.80 |
| NPV at 7% = −85.09[a] | | | | | |
| Break-even rent (level) | 29.839 | 29.839 | 29.839 | 29.839 | 29.839 |
| Tax | 10.444 | 10.444 | 10.444 | 10.444 | 10.444 |
| Break-even rent after tax | 19.395 | 19.395 | 19.395 | 19.395 | 19.395 |
| NPV at 7% = $85.09[a] | | | | | |

*Note:* We assume no inflation and a 7 per cent real cost of capital. The tax rate is 35 per cent.
[a]　Note that the first payment of these annuities comes immediately. The standard annuity formula must be multiplied by $1 + r = 1.07$.

To Diamond, the interest rate implicit in the lease equates to the present value of the after-tax lease payments and any residual value with the fair value of the asset being leased. The lease payments form an annuity and are equivalent to the sum of the initial payment at the start of the lease (at $t = 0$) plus the present value of an annuity in advance. This can be expressed as follows:

$$\$85.09 = 19.395(A_{\overline{0}|0.07} + A_{\overline{4}|0.07})$$

$$\$85.09 = 19.395\left[1 + \left(\frac{1 - (1 + 0.07)^{-(5-1)}}{0.07}\right)\right]$$

The annuity provides Diamond with a competitive expected rate of return (7 per cent) on its investment. Diamond could try to charge Entertainment Industries more than $30 000, but if the managing director is smart enough to ask for bids from Diamond's competitors, the winning lessor will end up receiving this amount.

Remember that Entertainment Industries is not obligated to continue using the limo for more than one year. Diamond may have to find several new lessees over the limo's economic life. Even if Entertainment continues, it can renegotiate a new lease at whatever rates prevail in the future. Thus, Diamond does not know what it can charge in year 1 or afterwards. If pearly white limos fall out of favour with teenagers and managing directors, Diamond is probably out of luck.

In real life Diamond would have several further things to worry about. For example, how long will the limo stand idle when it is returned at year 1? If idle time is likely before a new lessee is found, then lease rates have to be higher to compensate.[9]

---

[9]　If, say, limos were off lease and idle 20 per cent of the time, lease rates would have to be 25 per cent above those shown in Table 26.1.

In an operating lease, the *lessor* absorbs these risks, not the lessee. The discount rate used by the lessor must include a premium sufficient to compensate its shareholders for the risks of buying and holding the leased asset. In other words, Diamond's 7 per cent real discount rate must cover the risks of investing in stretch limos. (As we will see in the next section, risk bearing in *financial* leases is fundamentally different.)

## Lease or buy?

If you need a car or limo for only a day or a week you will surely hire or rent it (perhaps from Avis, Hertz, Thrifty or another of your favourites); if you need one for five years you will probably buy it. In between there is a grey region in which the choice of lease or buy is not so obvious. The decision rule should be clear in concept, however: If you need an asset for your business, *buy it if the equivalent annual cost of ownership and operation is less than the best lease rate you can get from an outsider*. In other words, buy if you can 'rent to yourself' cheaper than you can rent from others. (Again, we stress that this rule applies to *operating* leases.)

If you plan to use the asset for an extended period, your equivalent annual cost of owning the asset will usually be less than the operating lease rate. The lessor has to mark up the lease rate to cover the costs of negotiating and administering the lease, the forgone revenues when the asset is off lease and idle, and so on. These costs are avoided when the company buys and rents to itself.

There are two cases in which operating leases may make sense even when the company plans to use an asset for an extended period. First, the lessor may be able to buy and manage the asset at less expense than the lessee. For example, the major motor vehicle leasing companies buy thousands of new vehicles every year. That puts them in an excellent bargaining position with motor vehicle manufacturers. These companies also run very efficient service operations, and they know how to extract the most salvage value when motor vehicles wear out and it is time to sell them. A small business, or a small division of a larger one, cannot achieve these economies and often finds it cheaper to lease than to buy.

Second, operating leases often contain useful options. Suppose Diamond offers Entertainment Industries the following two leases:

1. Lease 1: A one-year lease for $30 000.
2. Lease 2: A six-year lease for $32 000 *with the option to cancel the lease* at any time from year 1 on.[10]

The second lease has obvious attractions. Suppose Entertainment's managing director becomes fond of the limo and wants to use it for a second year. If rates increase, lease 2 allows Entertainment to continue at the old rate. If rates decrease, Entertainment can cancel lease 2 and negotiate a lower rate with Diamond or one of its competitors.

Of course, lease 2 is a more costly proposition for Diamond: in effect, it gives Entertainment an insurance policy protecting it from increases in future lease rates. The difference between the costs of leases 1 and 2 is the annual insurance premium. But lessees may happily pay for insurance if they have no special knowledge of future asset values or lease rates. A leasing company acquires such knowledge in the course of its business and can generally sell such insurance as profit.

Computers are frequently leased on a short-term cancellable basis. It is difficult to estimate how soon such equipment will become obsolete, because the technology of computers is advancing rapidly and somewhat unpredictably. Leasing with an option to cancel passes the

---

10   Diamond might also offer a one-year lease for $32 000 but give the lessee an option to *extend* the lease on the same terms for up to five additional years. This is, of course, identical to lease 2. It does not matter whether the lessee has the (put) option to cancel or the (call) option to continue.

risk of premature obsolescence from the user to the lessor. Usually the lessor is a computer manufacturer or a computer leasing specialist and therefore knows more about the risks of obsolescence than the user does. Thus, the lessor is better equipped than the user to bear these risks. It makes sense for the user to pay the lessor for the option to cancel.

Be sure to check out the options before you sign (or reject) an operating lease.[11]

## 26.4 Valuing financial leases

For operating leases, the decision centres on 'lease versus buy'. For *financial* leases, the decision amounts to 'lease versus borrow'. Financial leases extend over most of the economic life of the leased equipment. They are *not* cancellable. The lease payments are fixed obligations equivalent to debt service.

Financial leases make sense when the company is prepared to take on the business risks of owning and operating the leased asset. If Entertainment Industries signs a *financial* lease for the stretch limo, it is stuck with that asset. The financial lease is just another way of borrowing money to pay for the limo.

Financial leases do offer special advantages to some firms in some circumstances. However, there is no point in further discussion of these advantages until you know how to value financial lease contracts.

## Example of a financial lease

Imagine yourself in the position of Bill Smith, manager of Toowoomba Bus Lines (TBL). Your firm was established by your grandfather, who was quick to capitalise on the growing demand for transportation between Toowoomba and nearby townships like Oakey, Gatton and Dalby. The company has owned all its vehicles from the time the company was formed; you are now reconsidering that policy. Your operating manager wants to buy a new bus costing $500 000. It is expected that the bus will last only eight years before going to the scrap yard with no salvage value. You are convinced that investment in the additional equipment is worthwhile. However, the representative of the bus manufacturer has pointed out that her firm would also be willing to lease the bus to you for eight annual in-advance payments of $80 000 each. TBL would remain responsible for all maintenance, insurance and operating expenses.

Table 26.2 shows the direct cash flow consequences of signing the lease contract. (An important indirect effect is considered later.) The consequences are:

1. TBL does not have to pay for the bus. This is equivalent to a cash inflow of $500 000.
2. TBL no longer owns the bus, and so it cannot depreciate it. Therefore, it gives up a valuable depreciation tax benefit. Assuming straight-line depreciation at 20 per cent over five years, this amounts to $100 000 × 0.35 = $35 000 per annum.
3. TBL must pay $80 000 per year at the start of the next eight years to the lessor. The first payment is due immediately.
4. However, these lease payments are fully tax-deductible. At a 35 per cent marginal tax rate, the lease payments generate a tax shield of $28 000 per annum. You could say that the after-tax cost of the lease payment is $80 000 − $28 000 = $52 000.

We must emphasise that Table 26.2 assumes that TBL will pay taxes at the full 35 per cent marginal rate. If the firm were sure to lose money, and therefore pay no taxes, lines 2 and 4 would be left blank. The depreciation benefits are worth nothing to a firm that pays no taxes, for example.

---

11   McConnell and Schallheim calculate the value of options in operating leases under various assumptions about asset risk, depreciation rates, and so on. See J. J. McConnell and J. S. Schallheim, 'Valuation of Asset Leasing Contracts', *Journal of Financial Economics*, 12: 237–61 (August 1983).

Table 26.2 also assumes the bus will be worthless when it goes to the scrap yard at the end of year 7. Otherwise, there would be an entry for salvage value lost.

**table 26.2**

Cash flow consequences of the lease contract offered to Toowoomba Bus Lines (figures in $000).

| | Year | | | | | | | |
|---|---|---|---|---|---|---|---|---|
| | 0 | 1 | 2 | 3 | 4 | 5 | 6 | 7 |
| Cost of new bus | +500 | | | | | | | |
| Lost depreciation tax benefit | | −35.0 | −35.0 | −35.0 | −35.0 | −35.0 | 0.0 | 0.0 |
| Lease payment | −80.0 | −80.0 | −80.0 | −80.0 | −80.0 | −80.0 | −80.0 | −80.0 |
| Tax benefit of lease payment | +28.0 | +28.0 | +28.0 | +28.0 | +28.0 | +28.0 | +28.0 | +28.0 |
| Cash flow of lease | +448.0 | −87.0 | −87.0 | −87.0 | −87.0 | −87.0 | −52.0 | −52.0 |

## Who *really* owns the leased asset?

To a solicitor or a tax accountant, that would be a silly question: the lessor is clearly the *legal* owner of the leased asset. That is why the lessor is allowed to deduct depreciation from taxable income.

From an *economic* point of view, you might say that the *user* is the real owner, because in a *financial* lease, the user faces the risks and receives the benefits of ownership. TBL cannot cancel a financial lease. If the new bus turns out to be hopelessly costly and unsuited for TBL's routes, that is TBL's problem, not the lessor's. If it turns out to be a great success, the profit goes to TBL, not the lessor. The success or failure of the firm's business operations does not depend on whether the buses are financed by leasing or some other financial instrument.

In many respects, a financial lease is equivalent to a secured loan. The lessee must make a series of fixed payments; if the lessee fails to do so, the lessor can repossess the asset. Thus, we can think of a balance sheet like this:

| Toowoomba Bus Lines (figures in $000) | | | |
|---|---|---|---|
| Bus | 500 | 500 | Loan secured by bus |
| All other assets | 1000 | 450 | Other loans |
| | | 550 | Equity |
| Total assets | 1500 | 1500 | Total liabilities |

as being economically equivalent to a balance sheet like this:

| Toowoomba Bus Lines (figures in $000) | | | |
|---|---|---|---|
| Bus | 500 | 500 | Financial lease |
| All other assets | 1000 | 450 | Other loans |
| | | 550 | Equity |
| Total assets | 1500 | 1500 | Total liabilities |

Having said this, we must immediately add this qualification: Legal ownership can make a big difference when a financial lease expires, because the lessor gets the salvage value of the asset. Once a secured loan is paid off, the user owns the asset free and clear.

# Leasing and Australian tax

We have already noted that the lessee loses the tax depreciation of the leased asset but can deduct the lease payment in full. The *lessor*, as legal owner, uses the depreciation tax shield but must report the lease payments as taxable rental income.

However, the Australian Tax Office (ATO) will not allow the lessee to deduct the entire lease payment unless it is satisfied that the arrangement is a genuine lease and not a disguised instalment purchase or secured loan agreement. Here are examples of lease provisions that will arouse its suspicion:

1. Designating any part of the lease payment as 'interest'.
2. Giving the lessee the option to acquire the asset for, say, $1 when the lease expires. Such a provision would effectively give the asset's salvage value to the lessee.
3. Adopting a schedule of payments such that the lessee pays a large proportion of the cost over a short period and thereafter is able to use the asset for a nominal rent.
4. Including a so-called hell-or-high-water clause that obliges the lessee to make payments regardless of what subsequently happens to the lessor or the equipment.
5. Limiting the lessee's right to issue debt or pay dividends while the lease is in force.
6. Leasing 'limited use' property—for example, leasing a machine or production facility which is custom-designed for the lessee's operations and which therefore will have scant second-hand value.

Some leases are designed *not* to qualify as a true lease for tax purposes. Suppose a manufacturer finds it convenient to lease a new computer but wants to keep the depreciation tax shields. This is easily accomplished by giving the manufacturer the option to purchase the computer for $1 at the end of the lease. Then the ATO treats the lease as an instalment sale or hire purchase agreement, and the manufacturer can deduct depreciation and the interest component of the lease payment for tax purposes. But the lease is still a lease for all other purposes.

# A first pass at valuing a financial lease contract

When we left Bill Smith, manager of Toowoomba Bus Lines, he had just set down in Table 26.2 the cash flows of the financial lease proposed by the bus manufacturer.

These cash flows are typically assumed to be about as safe as the interest and principal payments on a secured loan issue by the lessee. This assumption is reasonable for the lease payments because the lessor is effectively lending money to the lessee. But the various tax benefits might carry enough risk to deserve a higher discount rate. For example, TBL might be confident that it could make the lease payments but not confident that it could earn enough taxable income to use these tax benefits. In that case, the cash flows generated by the tax benefits would probably deserve a higher discount rate than the borrowing rate used for the lease payments.

A lessee might, in principle, end up using a separate discount rate for each line of Table 26.2, each rate chosen to fit the risk of that line's cash flow. But established, profitable firms usually find it reasonable to simplify by discounting the types of flows shown in Table 26.2 at a single rate based on the rate of interest the firm would pay if it borrowed rather than leased. We will assume TBL's borrowing rate is 8 per cent.

At this point we must go back to our discussion in Chapter 19 of debt-equivalent flows. When a company lends money, it pays tax on the interest it receives. Its net return is the after-tax interest rate. When a company borrows money, it can *deduct* interest payments from its taxable income. The net cost of borrowing is the after-tax interest rate. Thus, the after-tax interest rate is the effective rate at which a company can transfer debt-equivalent flows from one time period to another. Therefore, to value the incremental cash flows stemming from the lease, we need to discount them at the after-tax interest rate.

To conduct the analysis on an after-tax basis, since TBL can borrow at 8 per cent, we should discount the lease cash flows at $r^* = 0.08(1 - 0.35) = 0.052$, or 5.2 per cent.[12]

This gives

$$\text{NPV lease} = +448.0 - \frac{87.0}{1.052} - \frac{87.0}{(1.052)^2} - \frac{87.0}{(1.052)^3} - \frac{87.0}{(1.052)^4} - \frac{87.0}{(1.052)^5}$$
$$- \frac{56.0}{(1.052)^6} - \frac{56.0}{(1.052)^7}$$
$$= -1.420, \text{ or } -\$1420$$

Since the lease has a negative NPV, TBL is better off buying the bus.

A positive or negative NPV is not an abstract concept; in this case, TBL's shareholders really are $1420 poorer if the company leases. Since the lease has a negative NPV, TBL is better off buying the bus. Let us now check how this situation comes about.

Look once more at Table 26.2. The lease cash flows are:

|  | Year | | | | | | | |
|---|---|---|---|---|---|---|---|---|
|  | 0 | 1 | 2 | 3 | 4 | 5 | 6 | 7 |
| Lease cash flows ($000) | +448.0 | −87.0 | −87.0 | −87.0 | −87.0 | −87.0 | −87.0 | −87.0 |

The lease payments are contractual obligations like the principal and interest payments on secured debt. Thus, you can think of the incremental lease cash flows in years 1 to 7 as the 'debt service' of the lease. Table 26.3 shows a loan with *exactly* the same debt service as the lease. The initial amount of the loan is $449 420. If TBL borrowed this sum, it would need to pay interest in the first year of $0.08 × 449 420 = -\$35 954$ and would *receive* a tax benefit on this interest of $0.35 × 35 954 = +\$12 584$. TBL could then repay $63 630 off the loan, leaving a net cash outflow of $87 000 (exactly the same as for the lease) in year 1 and an outstanding debt at the start of year 2 of $385 790.

As you look through the calculations in Table 26.3, you see that it costs exactly the same to service a loan that brings an immediate inflow of $449 420 as it does to service the lease, which brings in only $448 000. That is why we say that the lease has a net present value of $448 000 - 449 420 = -\$1420$. If TBL leases the bus rather than raising an equivalent loan,[13] there will be $1420 less in TBL's bank account.

Our example illustrates two general points about leases and equivalent loans. First, if you can devise a borrowing plan that gives the same cash flow as the lease in every future period but a higher immediate cash flow, then you should not lease. If, however, the equivalent loan provides the same future cash outflows as the lease but a lower immediate inflow, then leasing is the better choice.

Second, our example suggests two ways to value a lease:

1. *Hard way.* Construct a table like Table 26.3 showing the equivalent loan.
2. *Easy way.* Discount the lease cash flows at the *after-tax* interest rate that the firm would pay on an equivalent loan. Both methods give the same answer—in our case, an NPV of −$1420.

---

[12]  If TBL were affected by imputation credits, this would affect the discount rate to be used, as discussed in Chapter 19. Here we assume TBL is not affected by imputation credits.

[13]  When we compare the lease to its equivalent loan, we do not mean to imply that the bus alone could support all of that loan. Some part of the loan would be supported by TBL's other assets. Some part of the lease would likewise be supported by the other assets.

**table 26.3**

Details of the equivalent loan to the lease offered to TBL (figures in $; cash outflows shown with negative sign).

| | Year | | | | | | | |
|---|---|---|---|---|---|---|---|---|
| | **0** | **1** | **2** | **3** | **4** | **5** | **6** | **7** |
| Amount borrowed at year-end | 449 420 | 385 790 | 318 851 | 248 431 | 174 349 | 96 415 | 49 428 | 0 |
| Interest paid at 10% | | −35 954 | −30 863 | −25 508 | −19 874 | −13 948 | −7 713 | −3 954 |
| Interest tax shield at 35% | | 12 584 | 10 802 | 8 928 | 6 956 | 4 882 | 2 700 | 1 384 |
| Interest paid after tax | | −23 370 | −20 061 | −16 580 | −12 918 | −9 066 | −5 013 | −2 570 |
| Principal repaid | | −63 630 | −66 939 | −70 420 | −74 082 | −77 934 | −46 987 | −49 428 |
| Net cash flow of equivalent loan | | −87 000 | −87 000 | −87 000 | −87 000 | −87 000 | −52 000 | −52 000[a] |

*Note:* [a] *The actual cash payment at this point in time was only $51 998.*

# The story so far

We concluded that the lease contract offered to TBL was *not* attractive because the lease provided $1420 less financing than the equivalent loan. The underlying principle is as follows: *A financial lease is superior to buying and borrowing if the financing provided by the lease exceeds the financing generated by the equivalent loan.*

The principle implies this formula:

$$\text{Net value of lease} = \text{Initial financing provided} - \sum_{t=1}^{N} \frac{\text{LCF}_t}{[1 + r(1 - T_c)]^t}$$

where $\text{LCF}_t$ is the cash outflow attributable to the lease in period $t$ and $N$ is the length of the lease. Initial financing provided equals the cost of the leased asset *minus any immediate lease payment or other cash outflow* attributable to the lease.

Notice that the value of the lease is its incremental value relative to borrowing via an equivalent loan. A positive lease value means that *if* you acquire the asset, lease financing is advantageous. It does not prove you should acquire the asset.

However, sometimes favourable lease terms rescue a capital investment project. Suppose that TBL had decided *against* buying a new bus because the NPV of the $500 000 investment was −$2000 assuming normal financing. The bus manufacturer could rescue the deal by offering a lease with a value of, say, +$5000. By offering such a lease, the manufacturer would in effect cut the price of the bus to $495 000, giving the bus-lease package a positive value to TBL. We could express this more formally by treating the lease's NPV as a favourable financing side effect which adds to the project's adjusted present value (APV):[14]

$$\text{APV} = \text{NPV of project} + \text{NPV of lease}$$
$$= -2000 + 5000 = +\$3000$$

Notice also that our formula applies to net financial leases. Any insurance, maintenance and other operating costs picked up by the lessor have to be evaluated separately and added to the value of the lease. If the asset has salvage value at the end of the lease, that value should be taken into account also.

Suppose, for example, that the bus manufacturer offers to provide routine maintenance that would otherwise cost $2000 per year after tax. However, Mr Smith reconsiders and decides that

---

[14] See Chapter 19 for the general definition and discussion of APV.

the bus will probably be worth $10 000 after eight years. (Previously he assumed the bus would be worthless at the end of the lease.) Then the value of the lease increases by the present value of the maintenance savings and decreases by the present value of the lost salvage value.

Maintenance and salvage value are harder to predict than the cash flows shown in Table 26.2, and so they normally deserve a higher discount rate. Suppose that Mr Smith uses 10 per cent. Then the maintenance savings are worth

$$\sum_{t=0}^{7} \frac{2000}{(1 + 0.10)^t} = 11\ 736.84,\ \text{or}\ \$11\ 737$$

The lost salvage value is worth $\$10\ 000/(1.10)^8 = \$4665$.[15] Remember that we previously calculated the value of the lease as $-\$1420$. The revised value is therefore $-1420 + 11\ 737 - 4665 = 5652$, or $\$5652$. Suddenly, now the lease looks like a good deal.

## 26.5 When do financial leases pay?

We have examined the value of a lease from the viewpoint of the lessee. However, the lessor's criterion is simply the reverse. As long as lessor and lessee are in the same tax bracket, every cash outflow to the lessee is an inflow to the lessor, and vice versa. In our numerical example, the bus manufacturer would project cash flows in a table like Table 26.2, but with the signs reversed. The value of the lease to the bus manufacturer would be

$$
\begin{aligned}
\text{Value of lease to lessor} &= -448.0 + \frac{87.0}{1.065} + \frac{87.0}{(1.065)^2} + \frac{87.0}{(1.065)^3} + \frac{87.0}{(1.065)^4} \\
&\quad + \frac{87.0}{(1.065)^5} + \frac{56.0}{(1.065)^6} + \frac{56.0}{(1.065)^7} \\
&= +1.420,\ \text{or}\ +\$1420
\end{aligned}
$$

In this case, the values to lessee and lessor exactly offset $(-\$1420 + \$1420 = 0)$. The lessor can win only at the lessee's expense.

But both lessee and lessor can win if their tax rates differ. Suppose that TBL paid no tax $(T_c = 0)$. Then, the only cash flows of the bus lease would be:

| | Year | | | | | | | |
|---|---|---|---|---|---|---|---|---|
| | 0 | 1 | 2 | 3 | 4 | 5 | 6 | 7 |
| Cost of new bus | +500 | | | | | | | |
| Lease payment | −80.0 | −80.0 | −80.0 | −80.0 | −80.0 | −80.0 | −80.0 | −80.0 |

These flows would be discounted at 10 per cent, because $r_D(1 - T_c) = r_D$ when $T_c = 0$. The value of the lease is

$$
\begin{aligned}
\text{Value of lease} &= +500 - \sum_{t=0}^{7} \frac{80}{(1 + 0.10)^t} \\
&= +500 - 496.5096 \\
&= +3.4904,\ \text{or}\ \$3490
\end{aligned}
$$

---

[15]   For simplicity, we have assumed that maintenance expenses are paid at the start of the year and that salvage value is measured at the *end* of year 8.

In this case, there is a net gain of $1420 to the lessor (who has the 35 per cent tax rate) *and* a net gain of $3490 to the lessee (who pays zero tax). This mutual gain is at the expense of the government. On the one hand, the government gains from the lease contract because it can tax the lease payments. On the other hand, the contract allows the lessor to take advantage of depreciation and interest tax benefits which are of no use to the lessee. However, the government suffers a net loss in the present value of its tax receipts as a result of the lease.

Now you should begin to understand the circumstances in which the government incurs a loss on the lease and the other two parties gain. Other things being equal, the potential gains to lessor and lessee are highest when:

- The lessor's tax rate is substantially higher than the lessee's.
- The depreciation tax shield is received early in the lease period.
- The lease period is long and the lease payments are concentrated towards the end of the period.
- The interest rate $r_D$ is high—if it were zero, there would be no advantage in present value terms to postponing tax.

## 26.6 Evaluating a large, leveraged lease

Recall from Section 26.1 that leveraged leases are financial leases in which the lessor borrows part of the purchase price of the asset to be leased, using the lease contract as security for the loan. Usually, the lessor borrows up to 80 per cent of the purchase price of the asset. For the lessor, they get the advantage of 100 per cent of the tax benefits associated with owning the asset due to the leverage, while they incur only a fraction of the costs associated with purchasing the asset. From the perspective of the lessee, there is no difference between their obligations under a leveraged as opposed to a non-leveraged lease. However, lessors are able to reduce their lease payment requirements while still obtaining a suitable rate of return.

Leveraged leases are particularly attractive to companies with substantial capital expenditure requirements—especially if they are unable immediately to use the tax deductions associated with buying and owning the asset such as depreciation and interest costs. Such deductions can be passed directly to the lessor who can then pass the benefits to the lessee through cheaper lease payments. Typically, leveraged leases are for large capital assets in excess of $15 million, such as aeroplanes, ships, manufacturing and mining equipment and even power stations.[16]

Now let us try using our new found knowledge to evaluate a very large leasing deal made in the United States. In 1971 Anaconda began to build a US$138 million aluminium reduction mill at Sebree, Kentucky. The company's original intention was to finance the project largely by a private placement of debt, but before it could do so, the Allende government expropriated Anaconda's Chilean copper mines and so provided the company with a US$356 million tax-deductible loss.

Anaconda clearly was unlikely to pay taxes for a number of years. If it went ahead and bought the mill, it could not make immediate use of depreciation tax shields or the 7 per cent investment tax credit which was then available. By leasing the mill, however, Anaconda could pass on these benefits to someone who could use them.[17] It therefore decided to purchase only the real estate at Sebree and to pay US$1.1 million to a leasing broker, U.S. Leasing International, to put together a *leveraged* lease for the US$110.7 million of plant and equipment. Figure 26.1 shows how this was arranged. First Kentucky Trust Company issued US$39 million of equity to a group of banks and finance companies and US$72 million of debt to a group of

---

16   See S. Das, 'Leveraged Leasing: Recent Developments', *Rydges,* pp. 112–14 (February 1982) for discussion of how Qantas has used leveraged leases. A comprehensive discussion of the obligations and risks faced by lessees and lessors can be found in C. Kortge and J. Caldicott, 'The Dangers of Leveraged Leasing', *Australian Accountant*, pp. 29–33 (December 1994).

17   The Anaconda lease was described in P. Vanderwicken, 'Powerful Logic of the Leasing Boom', *Fortune*, 87: 132–61 (November 1973). Our analysis of its present value is taken from S. C. Myers, D. A. Dill and A. J. Bautista, 'Valuation of Financial Lease Contracts', *Journal of Finance*, 33: 647–69 (May 1978).

insurance companies. It then used this money to purchase the mill and lease it to Anaconda. Anaconda agreed to make 40 lease payments, pre-paid semiannually, over a 20-year period. The first 21 payments were set at US$3.99 million each and the last 19 at US$5.46 million each.

The US$72 million loan was secured by a first claim on Anaconda's lease payments and by a mortgage on the plant. It was *not* guaranteed by First Kentucky or the equity investors. It was a *non-recourse* loan: if Anaconda defaulted on the lease payments, the insurance companies' only protection would be the value of the mill and a general claim against Anaconda.

This is called a *leveraged* lease because part of the cost of the plant was raised by a loan secured by the asset and the lease payments. The lessor, First Kentucky Trust, really acted as an intermediary, receiving the lease payments from Anaconda, paying the debt service and distributing what was left over to the equity investors. First Kentucky in effect financed the lease contract by selling off debt and equity claims against it.

But let us look at the lease contract itself from the lessor's viewpoint. The initial outlay was US$110.7 million less the investment tax credit of US$7.75 million[18] and the initial pre-paid lease payment. The major subsequent cash inflows were the 39 semiannual lease payments, the depreciation tax shields and the salvage value in 1993.

**figure 26.1**

How Anaconda arranged a lease on its aluminium reduction mill. This is a leveraged lease because part of the cost of the plant was raised by borrowing.

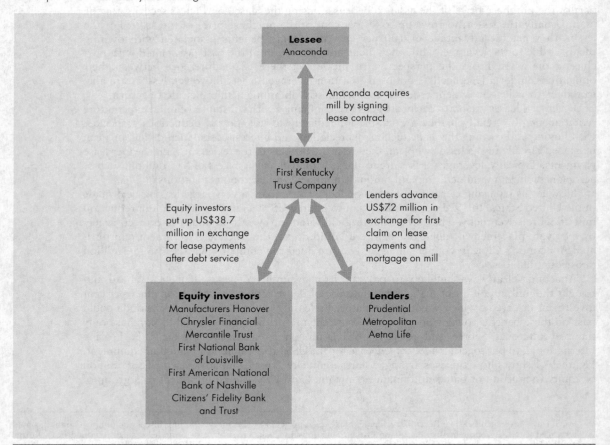

---

[18]    The investment tax credit (ITC) no longer exists. American companies used to be able to deduct 7 per cent of capital investment outlays directly from their corporate income taxes. Note that the ITC was not a deduction from taxable income but a *credit* against taxes.

As frequently happens in financial analysis, the hardest problem is to choose the right discount rate. Here is one way to look at it: The interest rate on the insurance companies' loan was 9.125 per cent. Because this debt is also protected by the lessor's equity, the lease payments must be *riskier* than the debt. On the other hand, the depreciation tax shield must be *safer* than the lease payments, for once the contract is signed, the size of the shields is independent of Anaconda's fortunes. Since our formula calls for a single rate of discount for both the after-tax lease payments and the depreciation tax shield, we will compromise on a discount rate of 9.125 per cent. The adjusted discount rate is 4.5625 per cent. (The marginal tax rate at the time was approximately 50 per cent.)

The present value calculations are set out in Table 26.4, along with a list of the other assumptions we have made. You can see that for the lessor the lease was moderately profitable: its net value was roughly 3 per cent of the plant's cost.

table 26.4 _____

Value of Anaconda lease to lessor (figures in US$million)

| Item | Present value |
|---|:---:|
| 1. Price | −110.7 |
| 2. Investment tax credit | +7.7 |
| 3. Depreciation tax shield | +44.3 |
| 4. After-tax lease payments | +60.8 |
| 5. Salvage value | +0.9 |
| Total value to *lessor* | +3.0 |

*Notes:*

1. Assumed tax rate is $T_c = 0.5$.

2. The adjusted discount rate for items 3 and 4 is 4.5625 per cent. (The present values were actually calculated assuming semi-annual cash flows and an equivalent semiannual rate.)

3. The discount rate for item 5 is 15 per cent, our guesstimate of the average cost of capital for Anaconda's assets.

4. The depreciation schedule was based on an 11-year depreciable life and a 5 per cent book salvage value. The double-declining-balance method was used for the first two years and then a switch was made to sum-of-the-years' digits. This appears to be the fastest write-off available under 1973 regulations.

5. The lessor's estimate of the plant's after-tax salvage value appears to be US$10.9 million. This is not from the horse's mouth; it is inferred from other information.

6. In principle, ownership of the salvage value also creates debt capacity. We have not included an estimate of the NPV of this capacity to the lessors. It is in any event a small number.

*Source:* S. C. Myers, D. A. Dill, and A. J. Bautista, op. cit., Footnote 17. © Blackwell Publishers.

Table 26.4 is a practical application of the procedures we worked out in the previous section of this chapter. As such it takes no notice of the US$72 million partial debt financing for the purchase of the Anaconda mill. The calculation does not look to the sources of the up-front money required of the lessors. It looks at the alternative *uses* of this money: it compares the lease to an equivalent loan to Anaconda.[19]

_____

[19]  For lessors, the equivalent-loan method compares leasing and lending. Suppose we add all the after-tax cash flows of the proposed lease, including lease payments, depreciation tax shields, investment tax credit and salvage value. How much debt would these cash flows support? Table 26.4 tells us the answer: about US$3 million more than the US$110.7 million cost of the mill. That is why we say the lease has a NPV of US$3 million to the lessors.

Did the availability of the US$72 million loan add anything to the US$3 million NPV calculated in Table 26.4? Not if the loan was issued at a fair rate of interest. If it was, the present value of the loan immediately after issue was US$72 million, and the balance sheet for the Anaconda lease looked like this:

| | | | |
|---|---|---|---|
| Present value of lease cash flows[20] | 113.7 | Present value of the loan | 72.0 |
| | | Present value of equity | 41.7 |
| | 113.7 | | 113.7 |

The equity lessors put up US$38.7 million, so their NPV was $41.7 - 38.7 = +$US$3 million. (If the loan had been issued at an especially favourable rate, its present value would have been less than US$72 million, and the lessor's value would have been correspondingly higher.)

All this analysis is from the lessor's point of view. It is not so easy to evaluate the lease from Anaconda's side because we do not know when the company expected to resume paying taxes. If the 'tax holiday' extended for 15 years, the lease was worth about $36 million to Anaconda.[21]

## 26.7 Summary

A lease is just an extended rental agreement. The owner of the equipment (the *lessor*) allows the user (the *lessee*) to operate the equipment in exchange for regular lease payments.

There are a wide variety of possible arrangements. Short-term, cancellable leases are known as *operating leases*. In these leases, the lessor bears the risks of ownership. Long-term, non-cancellable leases are called *financial, capital,* or *full-payout* leases. In these leases, the lessee bears the risks. Financial leases are *sources of financing* for assets the firm wishes to acquire and use for an extended period.

Many vehicle or office equipment leases include insurance and maintenance. They are *full-service* leases. If the lessee is responsible for insurance and maintenance, the lease is a *net* lease.

Frequently, the lessor acquires the asset directly from the manufacturer. This is a *direct* lease. Sometimes the lessor acquires the asset from the user and then leases it back to the user. This is a *sale and lease-back* lease.

Most leases involve only the lessee and the lessor. But if the asset is very costly, it may be convenient to arrange a *leveraged* lease, in which the cost of the leased asset is financed by issuing debt and equity claims against the asset and the future lease payments.

The key to understanding operating leases is equivalent annual cost. In a competitive leasing market, the annual operating lease payment will be forced down to the lessor's equivalent annual cost. Operating leases are attractive to equipment users if the lease payment is less than the *user's* equivalent annual cost of buying the equipment. Operating leases make sense when the user needs the equipment only for a short time, when the lessor is better able to bear the risks of obsolescence, or when the lessor can offer a good deal on maintenance. Remember too that operating leases often have valuable options attached.

A financial lease extends over most of the economic life of the leased asset and cannot be cancelled by the lessee. Signing a financial lease is like signing a secured loan to finance purchase of the leased asset. With financial leases, the choice is not 'lease versus buy' but 'lease versus borrow'.

---

[20]  This is the sum of lines 2 to 5 in Table 26.4.

[21]  See J. R. Franks and S. Hodges, 'Valuation of Financial Lease Contracts: A Note', *Journal of Finance*, **33** (May 1983), Table 3, p. 667.

Many companies have sound reasons for financing via leases. For example, companies that are not paying taxes can usually strike a favourable deal with a taxpaying lessor. Also, it may be less costly and time-consuming to sign a standardised lease contract than to negotiate a long-term secured loan.

When a firm borrows money, it pays the after-tax rate of interest on its debt. Therefore, the opportunity cost of lease financing is the after-tax rate of interest on the firm's bonds. To value a financial lease, we need to discount the incremental cash flows from leasing by the after-tax interest rate.

An equivalent loan to a lease is one that commits the firm to exactly the same future cash flows. When we calculate the net present value of the lease, we are measuring the difference between the amount of financing provided by the lease and the financing provided by the equivalent loan:

$$\text{Value of lease} = \text{financing provided by lease} - \text{value of equivalent loan}$$

We can also analyse leases from the lessor's side of the transaction, using the same approaches we developed for the lessee. If lessee and lessor are in the same tax bracket, they will receive exactly the same cash flows but with signs reversed. Thus, the lessee can gain only at the lessor's expense, and vice versa. However, if the lessee's tax rate is lower than the lessor's, then both can gain at the government's expense.

## FURTHER READING

The approach to valuing financial leases presented in this chapter is based on:

S. C. Myers, D. A. Dill and A. J. Bautista, 'Valuation of Financial Lease Contracts', *Journal of Finance*, **31**: 799–819 (June 1976).

J. R. Franks and S. D. Hodges, 'Valuation of Financial Lease Contracts: A Note', *Journal of Finance*, **33**: 647–69 (May 1978).

Other useful works include Nevitt and Fabozzi's book and the theoretical discussions of Miller and Upton and Lewellen, Long and McConnell:

P. K. Nevitt and F. J. Fabozzi, *Equipment Leasing*, 3rd ed., Dow Jones-Irwin, Inc., Homewood, Ill., 1988.

M. H. Miller and C. W. Upton, 'Leasing, Buying and the Cost of Capital Services', *Journal of Finance*, **31**: 761–86 (June 1976).

W. G. Lewellen, M. S. Long and J. J. McConnell, 'Asset Leasing in Competitive Capital Markets', *Journal of Finance*, **31**: 787–98 (June 1976).

The options embedded in many operating leases are discussed in:

T. E. Copeland and J. F. Weston, 'A Note on the Evaluation of Cancelable Operating Leases', *Financial Management*, **11**: 68–72 (Summer 1982).

J. J. McConnell and J. S. Schallheim, 'Valuation of Asset Leasing Contracts', *Journal of Financial Economics*, **12**: 237–61 (August 1983).

For a comprehensive discussion of taxation and accounting issues associated with leasing in Australia see:

G. Whittred, I. Zimmer and S. Taylor, *Financial Accounting: Incentive Effects and Economic Consequences*, Harcourt Brace, Sydney, 1996.

P. Jubb, S. Haswell and I. Langfield-Smith, *Company Accounting*, 2nd ed., Nelson ITP, Melbourne, 1999.

## QUIZ

1. The following terms are often used to describe leases:
   a. Direct
   b. Full-service
   c. Operating
   d. Financial
   e. Rental
   f. Net
   g. Leveraged
   h. Sale and lease-back
   i. Full-payout
   Match each of these terms with one of the following statements. (*Note*: Some statements may match more than one term.)
   A. The initial lease period is shorter than the economic life of the asset.
   B. The initial lease period is long enough for the lessor to recover the cost of the asset.
   C. The lessor provides maintenance and insurance.
   D. The lessee provides maintenance and insurance.
   E. The lessor buys the equipment from the manufacturer.
   F. The lessor buys the equipment from the prospective lessee.
   G. The lessor finances the lease contract by issuing debt and equity claims against it.

2. Some of the following reasons for leasing are rational. Others are irrational or assume imperfect or inefficient capital markets. Which of the following reasons are the rational ones?
   a. The lessee's need for the leased asset is only temporary.
   b. Specialised lessors are better able to bear the risk of obsolescence.
   c. Leasing provides 100 per cent financing and thus preserves capital.
   d. Leasing allows firms with low marginal tax rates to 'sell' depreciation tax shields.
   e. Leasing increases earnings per share.
   f. Leasing reduces the transaction cost of obtaining external financing.
   g. Leasing avoids restrictions on capital expenditures.
   h. Leasing can reduce the alternative minimum tax.

3. Explain why the following statements are true.
   a. In a competitive leasing market, the annual operating lease payment equals the lessor's equivalent annual cost.
   b. Operating leases are attractive to equipment users if the lease payment is less than the *user's* equivalent annual cost.

4. True or false?
   a. Lease payments are usually made at the start of each period. Thus, the first payment is usually made as soon as the lease contract is signed.
   b. Financial leases can still provide off-balance-sheet financing.
   c. The cost of capital for a financial lease is the interest rate the company would pay on a bank loan.
   d. An equivalent loan's principal plus after-tax interest payments exactly match the after-tax cash flows of the lease.
   e. A financial lease should not be undertaken unless it provides more financing than the equivalent loan.
   f. It makes sense for firms that pay no taxes to lease from firms that do.

g. Other things being equal, the net tax advantage of leasing increases as nominal interest rates increase.

5. Diamond has branched out to rentals of office furniture to start-up companies. Consider a $3000 desk. Desks last for six years and can be depreciated on a five-year straight-line method. What is the break-even operating lease rate for a new desk? Assume that lease rates for old and new desks are the same and that Diamond's pre-tax administrative costs are $400 per desk per year. The cost of capital is 9 per cent and the tax rate is 35 per cent. Lease payments are made in advance, that is, at the start of each year. The inflation rate is zero.

6. Refer again to Question 5. Suppose a blue-chip company requests a six-year *financial* lease for a $3000 desk. The company has just issued five-year notes at an interest rate of 6 per cent per year. What is the break-even lease rate in this case? Assume administrative costs drop to $200 per year. Explain why your answer to Question 5 and this question differ.

7. Suppose that National Waferonics has before it a proposal for a four-year financial lease. The firm constructs a table like Table 26.2. The bottom line of its table shows the lease cash flows:

|  | Year 0 | Year 1 | Year 2 | Year 3 |
|---|---|---|---|---|
| Lease cash flow | +62 000 | −26 800 | −22 200 | −17 600 |

These flows reflect the cost of the machine, depreciation tax shields and the after-tax lease payments. Ignore salvage value. Assume the firm could borrow at 10 per cent and faces a 35 per cent marginal tax rate.
a. What is the value of the equivalent loan?
b. What is the value of the lease?
c. Suppose the machine's NPV under normal financing is −$5000. Should National Waferonics invest? Should it sign the lease?

## QUESTIONS AND PROBLEMS

1. A lessee does not have to pay to buy the leased asset. Thus, it is said that 'leases provide 100 per cent financing'. Explain why this is *not* a true advantage to the lessee.

2. In Quiz Question 5 we assumed identical lease rates for old and new desks.
a. How does the initial break-even lease rate change if the expected inflation rate is 5 per cent per year? Assume that the *real* cost of capital does not change. (*Hint*: Look at the discussion of equivalent annual costs in Chapter 6.)
b. How does your answer to Part (a) change if wear and tear force Diamond to cut lease rates by 10 per cent in real terms for every year of a desk's age?

3. Why do you think that leasing of cars, trucks, aeroplanes, ships and computers is such big business? What efficiencies offset the costs of running these leasing operations?

**4.** Look at Table 26.1. How would the initial break-even operating lease rate change if rapid technological change in limo manufacturing reduces the costs of new limos by 5 per cent per year? (*Hint:* We discussed technological change and equivalent annual costs in Chapter 6.)

**5.** Financial leases make sense when the lessee faces a lower marginal tax rate than the lessor. Does this tax advantage carry over to *operating* leases?

**6.** Magna Charter has been asked to operate an aeroplane for a mining company exploring north and west of Kalgoorlie. Magna will have a firm one-year contract with the mining company and expects that the contract will be renewed for the five-year duration of the exploration program. If the mining company renews at year 1, it will commit to use the aeroplane for four more years.
   Magna Charter has the following choices.

   ▮  Buy the aeroplane for $500 000.
   ▮  Take a one-year operating lease for the aeroplane. The lease rate is $118 000, paid in advance.
   ▮  Arrange a five-year, non-cancellable financial lease at a rate of $75 000 per year, paid in advance.

   These are net leases: all operating costs are absorbed by Magna Charter.
   How would you advise Agnes Magna, the charter company's finance manager?
   For simplicity, assume five-year, straight-line depreciation for tax purposes. The company's tax rate is 35 per cent. The weighted average cost of capital for the aeroplane business is 14 per cent, but Magna can borrow at 9 per cent. The expected inflation rate is 4 per cent.
   Ms Magna thinks the aeroplane will be worth $300 000 after five years. But if the contract with the mining company is not renewed (there is a 20 per cent probability of this outcome at year 1), the aeroplane will have to be sold on short notice for $400 000.
   If Magna Charter takes the five-year financial lease and the mining company cancels at year 1, Magna can sublet the aeroplane, that is, rent it out to another user.
   Make additional assumptions as necessary.

**7.** Here is a variation on Question 6. Suppose Magna Charter is offered a five-year *cancellable* lease at an annual rate of $125 000, paid in advance. How would you go about analysing this lease? You do not have enough information to do a full option pricing analysis, but you can calculate costs and present values for different scenarios.

*The following questions all apply to financial leases.*

**8.** Look again at the bus lease described in Table 26.2.
   a.  What is the value of the lease if TBL's marginal tax rate is $T_c = 0.20$?
   b.  What would the lease value be if TBL had to use diminishing balance depreciation for tax purposes?

**9.** In Section 26.4 we showed that the lease offered to Toowoomba Bus Lines had a positive NPV of $820 if TBL paid no tax *and* a +$700 NPV to a lessor paying 35 per cent tax. What is the minimum lease payment the lessor could accept under these assumptions? What is the maximum amount that TBL could pay?

**10.** Recalculate the value of the lease to Toowoomba Bus Lines if the company pays no taxes until year 3. Calculate the lease cash flows by modifying Table 26.2. Remember that the after-tax borrowing rate for periods 1 and 2 differs from the rate for periods 3 to 7.

**11.** Nerdhead College needs a new computer system. It can either buy it for $250 000 or lease it from Compulease. The lease terms require Nerdhead to make six annual payments (pre-paid) of $62 000. Nerdhead pays no tax. Compulease pays tax at 35 per cent. Compulease can depreciate the computer for tax purposes over five years. The computer will have no residual value at the end of year 5. The interest rate is 8 per cent.
   a. What is the NPV of the lease for Nerdhead College?
   b. What is the NPV for Compulease?
   c. What is the overall gain from leasing?

**12.** Many companies calculate the internal rate of return (IRR) of the incremental after-tax cash flows from financial leases. What problems do you think this may give rise to? To what rate should the IRR be compared?

**13.** The overall gain from leasing is the sum of the lease's value to the lessee and its value to the lessor. Construct simple numerical examples showing how this gain is affected by:
   a. The rate of interest.
   b. The choice of depreciation schedule.
   c. The difference between the tax rates of the lessor and lessee.
   d. The length of the lease.

**14.** Discuss the following two opposite statements. Which do you think makes more sense?
   a. 'Leasing is tax avoidance and should be legislated against.'
   b. 'Leasing ensures that the government's investment incentives work. It does so by allowing companies in non-taxpaying positions to take advantage of depreciation allowances.'

**15.** The Safety Razor Company has a large tax-loss carry-forward and does not expect to pay taxes for another 10 years. The company is therefore proposing to lease $100 000 of new machinery. The lease terms consist of eight equal lease payments pre-paid annually. The lessor can write off the machinery over seven years using the tax depreciation schedules given in Table 6.5. There is no salvage value at the end of the machinery's economic life. The tax rate is 35 per cent, and the rate of interest is 10 per cent. Wilbur Occam, the president of Safety Razor, wants to know the maximum lease payment that his company should be willing to make and the minimum payment that the lessor is likely to accept. Can you help him? How would your answer differ if the lessor was obliged to use straight-line depreciation?

**16.** In Section 26.5 we listed four circumstances in which there are potential gains from leasing. Check them out by conducting a sensitivity analysis on the Toowoomba Bus Lines lease, assuming that TBL does not pay tax. Try, in turn:
   a. A lessor tax rate of 50 per cent (rather than 35 per cent).
   b. Immediate 100 per cent depreciation in year 0 (rather than five-year ACRS).
   c. A three-year lease with four annual rentals (rather than an eight-year lease).
   d. An interest rate of 20 per cent (rather than 10 per cent).

In each case, find the minimum rental that would satisfy the lessor and calculate the NPV to the lessee.

**17.** In Section 26.5 we stated that if the interest rate was zero, there would be no advantage in postponing tax and therefore no advantage in leasing. Value the Toowoomba Bus Lines lease with an interest rate of zero. Assume that TBL does not pay tax. Can you devise any lease terms that would make both a lessee and a lessor happy? (If you can, we would like to hear from you.)

**18.** A lease with a varying rental schedule is known as a *structured lease*. Try structuring the Toowoomba Bus Lines lease to increase value to the lessee while preserving the value to the lessor. Assume that TBL does not pay tax. (*Note:* In practice, the tax authorities will allow some structuring of rental payments but might be unhappy with some of the schemes you devise.)

# part 8

# FINANCIAL PLANNING

# chapter 27

# ANALYSING FINANCIAL PERFORMANCE

Financial management is best understood by considering each aspect incrementally. Thus far we have broken down the financial manager's job into a series of clearly defined topics, such as capital budgeting, dividend policy, share issue procedures, debt policy and leasing. But in the end the financial manager has to consider the combined effects of these decisions on the firm as a whole.

In this chapter we look at how you can use financial data to analyse a firm's overall performance and assess its current financial standing. For example, you may need to check whether your own firm's financial performance is in the ballpark of standard practice. Or you may wish to understand the policies of a competitor or to check on the financial health of a customer.

Understanding the past performance of the company is a necessary prelude to contemplating the future. Therefore, the other chapters in Part Eight are devoted to financial planning. Chapter 28 shows how managers use long-term financial plans to establish concrete goals and to anticipate surprises. Chapter 29 then discusses short-term planning, in which the emphasis is on ensuring that the firm has enough cash to pay its bills and put any spare cash to good use. Chapter 29 also serves as an introduction to Part Nine, which covers the management of the firm's short-term assets and liabilities.

But all that comes later. The business at hand is to analyse financial performance. At the centre of this analysis is the company annual report. Hence we start our inquiry of financial performance by identifying the core aspects of the annual report. The analysis and interpretation of the information contained in the annual report is critical to assessing each company's performance. We then use the time-honoured method of financial ratio analysis. We discuss how ratios are used, and we note the limitations of the accounting data which most of the ratios are based on. We also take the opportunity to refer back to earlier chapters in which we discuss the firm's long-term financial decisions, and we look ahead to the later chapters on short-term financial decisions.

# 27.1 Annual reports

The public company's annual report performs many functions, some regulatory and others public relations based. The regulatory requirements[1] include the provision of financial statements, declarations of accounting policies and the provision of a director's report and an auditor's report. The primary statements reported by companies are the profit and loss statement, the balance sheet and a statement of cash flows.[2] Most publicly listed companies are consolidated entities—where the listed company comprises the parent company, after which the listed company is named and a number of smaller controlled companies operating in most cases in related markets. For example, in 1998 the consolidated company Amcor Ltd[3] had the single entity of the parent company, Amcor Ltd, and also included in excess of 180 controlled entities. From the perspective of the investor, and when assessing company performance, it is most important that the consolidated figures are reported, rather than just the parent company figures.

The information included in financial reports is useful for making performance, investment and credit-related decisions. Annual reports provide information about the assets, liabilities and equity of companies, as well as information regarding substantive transactions, and identify events that affected performance and profitability.

The financial reports must contain information in accordance with AASB 1001, 'Accounting Policies Disclosure', which requires a summary of the accounting policies applied by the company, including any changes to previously applied accounting policy. The purpose of this reporting function is to ensure that the financial information reported is consistent with the required accounting standards, that the concepts of relevance and reliability are satisfied and that the financial reports are comparable with previous years and across companies.

The directors are also required to prepare a detailed report that must contain information such as their names, qualifications and contractual interests, the principal activities and review of the company's operations (including any significant changes during the financial year), the reported profit and loss after income tax, dividends paid or declared and details of share options and directors' benefits.[4]

The annual report also acts as a public relations vehicle for the firm, providing a window through which the public can view and understand the primary operations of the company. It also provides the opportunity to detail the company's primary objectives and organisational structure. Consider the contents of the 1998 Annual Report of Amcor Ltd. The report is 72 pages long (excluding the front and back covers) and has the following items detailed in the table of contents:

---

[1] See the Australian Corporations Law Part 2M, which specifies the reports that must be produced, their timing and minimum content.

[2] The financial statements are required to give a 'true and fair view' of the company for the financial year and comply with Australian Accounting Standards issued by the Australian Accounting Standards Board.

[3] Amcor Ltd is an Australian listed company specialising in packaging and paper activities. Other activities include merchanting and substantial investment interests in Kimberley-Clark Australia Pty Ltd and Spicers Paper Limited. Amcor Ltd operates over 300 plants and offices in 25 countries and employs more than 22 900 staff. The company's capitalisation places it as a member of the Australian Stock Exchange 20 Leaders Index, the Australian Stock Exchange Paper and Packaging Index and the Australian Stock Exchange All Ordinaries Index.

[4] Directors must also provide a statement stating whether in their opinion the profit and loss statement and balance sheet represent a true and fair view of the company and whether they are reasonable grounds to believe that the company will be able to pay its debts when they fall due.

| Contents | Page |
|---|---|

The Amcor Annual Report provides both the required regulatory information and also significantly detailed information that gives an insight into the operations and organisation of the company. However, for us, the financial performance is best reflected via examination of the financial statements.

# The profit and loss statement

If they are to survive, companies must eventually make profits. These profits, and at times losses, are reported in the profit and loss statement, which is also referred to as the income statement or the statement of profit. The contents of profit and loss statements are regulated by AASB 1018, 'Profit and Loss Accounts', which requires that companies must take into account all items of revenue and expenses arising in the financial year and the operating profit or loss both before and after income tax, the level of income tax, the level of income tax paid, abnormal items, extraordinary items and transfers to and from reserves and distributions to shareholders.

Until 30 June 1997, the Australian Corporations Law specified that the profit and loss account was required to adhere strictly to the following format. Despite the removal of this requirement, the requirements of AASB 1018 and AASB 1034, 'Information to be Disclosed in Financial Reports',[5] still require reports to follow a similar format (see over).

The operating profit of the firm is a direct function of the revenue and expenses incurred in generating those revenues. An extract from the 1998 profit and loss statement of Amcor Ltd is shown in Table 27.1.[6] Total net sales equalled $6056.1 million and other revenues including interest and dividends received and revenues from the sale of assets and business and controlled entities amounted to $323.4 million. After deducting the expenses incurred in the operation of the business we are left with operating profit before depreciation, amortisation, interest, abnormal items and income tax of $767.1 million. After deducting depreciation and

---

[5]   For a detailed discussion of the application of accounting standards to the preparation of financial reports see P. Jubb, S. Haswell and I. Langfield-Smith, *Company Accounting*, 2nd ed, Nelson, Melbourne, 1999.

---

### Profit and loss statement format requirements

Income tax attributable to operating profit or loss
Operating profit or loss after income tax
Profit or loss on extraordinary items
Income tax attributable to operating profit and loss on extraordinary items
Profit or loss on extraordinary items after income tax
Operating profit or loss and extraordinary items after income tax
Outside equity interests in operating profit or loss and extraordinary items after income tax
Operating profit or loss and extraordinary items after income tax attributable to members of the chief entity
Retained profits or accumulated reserves at the beginning of the financial year
Aggregate of amounts transferred from reserves
Total available for appropriation
Dividends provided for or paid
Aggregate of amounts transferred to reserves
Other appropriations
Retained profits or accumulated losses at the end of the financial year

---

amortisation ($256.4 million) and net interest ($112.4 million) we are left with operating profit before abnormal items and income tax.

Abnormal items include revenues and expenses that are part of the ordinary business of the company but are regarded as abnormal because of their size or their effect on operating profit.[7] AASB 1018 provides examples of abnormal items as bad debt write-offs, inventory write-downs, differences arising due to movements in foreign exchange rates, write-offs of research and development expenditure, depreciation adjustments or proceeds from the sale of investment properties. For Amcor Ltd, abnormal items in 1998 amounted to $291.6 million due to plant closure and rationalisation costs, write-downs of current assets and goodwill and profits on disposal of businesses and controlled entities.

From the operating profit before tax ($106.7 million), we subtract income tax expenses ($51.1 million) and outside equity interests in operating profit after income tax ($5.1 million) to obtain the net operating profit (loss) attributable to members of the parent entity (before extraordinary items). In some years items of revenue or expense may occur that are outside the ordinary operations of the business and are not recurring in nature—such items are known as extraordinary items. AASB 1018 provides examples such as the sale or abandonment of a significant business or the expropriation or unintended destruction of property. In 1998 Amcor Ltd did not report any extraordinary items.

Once extraordinary items have been identified and included it is possible to identify the operating profit (loss) after income tax. From Table 27.1 this equals $50.5 million. To this amount we add the amount of retained profits or accumulated losses of the company as reported at the beginning of the financial year ($582.4 million). Next, we identify the total amount available for appropriation ($654.6) after making adjustments for reserves, which include both capital and revenue reserves ($21.7 million).[8] From the total amount available for appropriation the board

---

6   See Amcor Ltd Annual Report 1998.

7   For example, in 1997 Amcor had abnormal items totalling $371.1 million, which resulted in a net operating loss after tax of $80.1 million compared with a net operating profit after tax before abnormals of $243.3 million.

8   Reserves are regarded as a component of shareholders' equity and include the capital reserves such as share premium reserves, forfeited shares reserves and asset revaluation reserves (which are not normally made available for cash distribution to shareholders) and the revenue reserves including retained profits, the general reserve and reserves for plant expansions which are made available for distribution.

**table 27.1**

Extract from profit and loss accounts of Amcor Ltd and its controlled entities, for the year ended 30 June 1998.

| Item | Consolidated ($000) |
|---|---|
| Operating revenue: | |
| Net sales | 6056.1 |
| Other revenue | 323.4 |
| Operating profit before depreciation, amortisation, interest, abnormal items and income tax | 767.1 |
| Depreciation and amortisation | (256.4) |
| Operating profit before interest, abnormal items and income tax | 510.7 |
| Net interest | (112.4) |
| Operating profit before abnormal items and income tax | 398.3 |
| Abnormal items | (291.6) |
| Operating profit before income tax | 106.7 |
| Income tax expense attributable to operating profit | (51.1) |
| Operating profit (loss) after income tax | 55.6 |
| Outside equity interests in operating profit after income tax | (5.1) |
| Net operating profit attributable to members of the parent entity | 50.5 |
| Retained profit at 1 July | 582.4 |
| Aggregate of amounts transferred from reserves | 21.7 |
| Total available for appropriation | 654.6 |
| Dividends | (243.8) |
| Aggregate of amounts transferred to reserves | (24.4) |
| Retained profit at 30 June | 386.4 |

of directors identifies the amount to be paid to shareholders as dividends ($243.8 million), transferred to reserves ($24.4 million) and to be held as retained profits ($386.4 million).

# Balance sheet

Whilst the profit and loss statement provides a review of the operations of the company over the whole year, the balance sheet provides a single snapshot of the assets, liabilities and shareholders' equity of the company on a nominated balance day (normally 30 June each year).

The balance sheet is normally presented in such a manner as to reflect the accounting convention that assets (A) equals liabilities (L) plus shareholders' equity (S).[9] Hence, any impact, good or bad, to these components will inevitably cause change to one or both of the other

---

[9]   This convention facilitates the opportunity to draw conclusions regarding assets, liabilities and shareholders' equity. Hence, while $A = L + S$ it also implies $L = A - S$ and $S = A - L$.

parts of the equation. Until 1997 the Australian Corporations Law required that balance sheets should be presented in the following format:

| Balance sheet format requirements |
| --- |
| **Current assets** |
| Cash |
| Receivables |
| Investments |
| Inventories |
| Other |
| **Total current assets** |
| Receivables |
| Investments |
| Inventories |
| Property, plant and equipment |
| Intangibles |
| Other |
| **Total current liabilities** |
| **Non current liabilities** |
| Creditors and borrowings |
| Provisions |
| Other |
| **Total non-current liabilities** |
| **Total liabilities** |
| **Net assets** |
| **Shareholders' equity** |
| Share capital |
| Reserves |
| Retained profits or accumulated losses |
| Shareholders' equity attributable to members of the chief entity |
| Outside equity interests in controlled entities |
| **Total shareholders' equity** |

Accounting standard AASB 1034, 'Information to be Disclosed in Financial Reports' specifies certain reporting obligations that must be adhered to in reporting. The net result is that many balance sheets now report consistent with the above structure. For example, AASB 1034.4.1 specifies that:

*Information presented in the balance sheet and the notes must be condensed into relevant and comparable categories. Assets must be classified according to their nature or function (see paragraph 4.1.2) and liabilities (see paragraph 4.1.3) and equity items (see paragraph 4.1.4) must be classified according to their nature. The classification of assets, liabilities and equity in this manner assists users in identifying significant characteristics of the performance, financial position, and financing and investing activities of the entity.*

Table 27.2 reports an extract from Amcor's 1998 balance sheet.[10] The assets of the company are recorded as both current and non-current. Current assets include cash and those items that can reasonably be consumed or converted to cash within one year, such as marketable securities,

---

10    See Amcor Ltd Annual Report 1998.

**table 27.2**

Balance sheet for Amcor Ltd and its controlled entities, as at 30 June 1998.

|  | ($000) |
|---|---|
| **Assets** | |
| **Current assets** | |
| Cash | 264.2 |
| Receivables | 1038.3 |
| Inventories | 967.0 |
| Total current assets | 2269.5 |
| **Non-current assets** | |
| Receivables | 103.2 |
| Investments | 279.0 |
| Property, plant and equipment | 3820.7 |
| Intangibles | 510.9 |
| Other | 196.9 |
| Total non-current assets | 4910.7 |
| **Total assets** | **7180.2** |
| **Liabilities** | |
| Current liabilities | |
| Accounts payable | 838.2 |
| Borrowings | 485.9 |
| Provisions | 448.2 |
| Total current liabilities | 1772.3 |
| **Non-current liabilities** | |
| Accounts payable | 10.4 |
| Borrowings | 1588.9 |
| Provisions | 493.4 |
| Total non-current liabilities | 2092.7 |
| **Total liabilities** | **4291.2** |
| **Shareholders' equity** | |
| Share capital | 641.9 |
| Reserves | 1813.4 |
| Retained profits | 386.4 |
| Shareholders' equity attributable to members of the parent entity | 2841.7 |
| Outside equity interests | 47.3 |
| **Total shareholders' equity** | **2889.0** |

receivables and inventories. Non-current assets include items such as land, buildings, leasehold, plant, equipment, long-term investments and intangible assets.[11] These assets are assumed to be used in the continuing operation of the business.[12] For Amcor in 1998, current assets amounted to $2269.5 million, non-current assets $4910.7 million and total assets $7180.2 million.

Liabilities are also categorised as current and non-current. Current liabilities as the name implies are short-term liabilities and include bank loans and overdrafts, trade credit, payables to associated entities, dividends payable and provisions[13] that are likely to be paid or performed within the next 12 months. Non-current liabilities should include longer dated debt and provisions. For Amcor in 1998, total liabilities amounted to $4291.2 million, made up of $1772.3 million in current liabilities and $2092.7 million in non-current liabilities.

Shareholders' equity[14] should detail share capital for different classes of equity—for example, ordinary and preference shares, retained earnings of the company and reserves.

From Table 27.2 it should be noted how the accounting convention of A = L + S holds.[15] Due to the double-entry nature of accounting, if Amcor were to purchase major plant and equipment valued at $500 million and financed by short-term debt, this would have the impact of increasing the company's total assets while also increasing the total liabilities.

## Statement of cash flows

Since 1992 Australian companies have been required to produce a statement of cash flows in accordance with AASB 1026, 'Statement of Cash Flows'. This financial statement discloses the gross cash inflows and outflows of the company and thereby represents a sources and uses of funds statement. The statement is usually divided into three major functional areas involving cash flows from operating activities, investing activities and financing activities. Table 27.3 shows the statement of cash flows for Amcor Ltd for the year ended 30 June 1998.

The statement of cash flows summarises how the firm raised and applied funds during the financial year. In particular, it is useful as a supplement to the profit and loss account and the balance sheet to demonstrate how funds have been used. As noted by Sharma,[16] the information provided by the statement of cash flows when read in conjunction with other financial statements helps decision makers to assess the firm's ability to generate future cash flows, meet its financial commitments, fund changes in the nature or scope of its operations and obtain external finance.

## 27.2 Financial ratios

The figures reported in a company's financial reports, while providing relevant financial information, do not reveal as much in isolation as financial ratios. As noted by Luplau:[17]

> A company's accounting records only provide a record of the past and investors are concerned with the future performance of companies. Decision making using financial statements is made possible via ratio analysis and trend interpretation.

---

[11] Intangible assets include non-physical assets such as goodwill, licences, patents, trademarks and mining rights. Their valuation is usually the subject of great debate due to their non-tangible nature.

[12] Non-current assets are also known as operating assets, fixed assets, tangible assets or the long-lived assets of the company.

[13] Provisions include carrying forward balances for accumulated sick leave or annual leave for staff, taxation, or specific commitments or contingencies.

[14] Also known as owners' equity, proprietorship, capital or net worth.

[15] Total assets = liabilities plus shareholders' equity.
$5\,978\,550\,000 = 3\,101\,080\,000 + 2\,877\,470\,000$.

[16] See D. Sharma, 'Analysing the Statement of Cashflows', *Australian Accounting Review*, **6** (2): 37–44 (1996). Sharma's article also develops a series of cash flow ratios useful to assess liquidity, financial structure and returns, and applies these ratios to analysis of Brash Holdings Ltd between 1991 and 1993.

[17] D. Luplau, 'The Fine Art of Financial Analysis', *ASX Journal*, May 1997.

**table 27.3**

Extract from statement of cash flows for Amcor Ltd and its controlled entities, for the year ended 30 June 1998.

|  | **($000)** |
|---|---|
| **Cash flows from operating activities** |  |
| Receipts from customers | 5944.4 |
| Payments to suppliers and employees | (5364.8) |
| Dividends received | 38.5 |
| Interest received | 12.8 |
| Interest paid | (151.4) |
| Income taxes refunds (paid) | (42.7) |
| Other income received | 47.8 |
| **Net cash provided by operating activities** | **484.6** |
| **Cash flows from investing activities** |  |
| Loans repaid—controlled entities | — |
| Loans to associated companies | (0.6) |
| Loans repaid by associated companies and other persons | 30.2 |
| Acquisition of: |  |
|   Controlled entities and businesses | (157.6) |
|   Property, plant and equipment | (427.8) |
| Proceeds on disposal of: |  |
|   Controlled entities and businesses | 197.0 |
|   Investments | 0.5 |
|   Property, plant and equipment | 22.6 |
| **Net cash used in investing activities** | **(335.7)** |
| **Cash flows from financing activities** |  |
| Dividends paid | (240.9) |
| Proceeds from issue and call on partly paid shares | 10.5 |
| Proceeds from issue of notes | — |
| Loans from associated companies and other persons | 10.6 |
| Loans repaid to associated companies and other persons | — |
| Proceeds from borrowings | 528.9 |
| Repayment of borrowings | (410.6) |
| Principal lease repayments | (17.1) |
| **Net cash (used in)/provided by financing activities** | **(118.6)** |
| **Net increase (decrease) in cash held** | **30.3** |
| **Cash at the beginning of the year** | **154.8** |
| Exchange rate changes on foreign currency cash flows and cash balances | 74.3 |
| **Cash at end of the year** | **259.4** |

We have all heard stories of financial whizzes who in minutes can take a company's accounts apart and find its innermost secrets in financial ratios. The truth, however, is that financial ratios are no substitute for a crystal ball. They are just a convenient way to summarise large quantities of financial data and to compare firms' performances. Ratios help you to ask the right questions; they seldom answer them.

We will describe and calculate five types of financial ratios:

- *Leverage ratios* show how heavily the company is in debt.
- *Liquidity ratios* measure how easily the firm can obtain cash to pay its debts as they come due.
- *Activity ratios* measure how different asset groups contribute to profitability.
- *Profitability (or performance) ratios* are used to judge how efficiently the firm is using its assets.
- *Market value ratios* show how the firm is valued by investors.

## Brambles Industries Ltd

Brambles Industries Ltd is an Australian listed company specialising in equipment hire (35.2 per cent of revenue), transport and logistics (23.1 per cent of revenue) and specialised services such as industrial services, waste and records management (41.7 per cent of revenue). Well-known Australian businesses operated by Brambles Industries Ltd include Chep pallet management, Wreckair industrial equipment hiring and Cleanaway industrial and municipal waste management.[18] The company is managed on a geographical basis corresponding to three major regions—Australia/New Zealand (40.8 per cent of revenue), Europe (41.8 per cent of revenue) and America/rest of the world (18.1 per cent of revenue). The company's capitalisation places the company as a member of the Australian Stock Exchange 20 Leaders Index (approximately 3.02 per cent), the Australian Stock Exchange Transport Index (approximately 66.70 per cent) and the Australian Stock Exchange All Ordinaries Index (approximately 1.86 per cent).

Tables 27.4, 27.5 and 27.6 contain information that you need to calculate the primary financial ratios for Brambles Industries Ltd for the financial years 1997 and 1998.[19] The company had a declared dividend of $0.74 in 1998 and $0.71 in 1997. The company had 224.417 million shares on issue in 1998 and 222.447 million on issue in 1997.

The profit and loss statement in Table 27.4 shows the amount that the company earned during the years 1996, 1997 and 1998. In 1998, Brambles total sales revenue equalled $4013.9 million, other revenue equalled $483.6 million,[20] and total earnings before abnormals ($28.6 million) and taxation ($157.3 million) amounted to $414.5 million. Although not directly reported in the profit and loss statement, the net interest for Brambles was $61.8 million in 1998 and $48.2 million in 1997.[21] After adjusting for abnormals, taxation and outside equity interests ($7.2 million in 1998) the net operating profit attributable to members of the parent entity in 1998 was $284.2 million. Of this amount, $165.8 million was distributed to shareholders and the balance was retained by the company.

Many analysts consider a firm's performance both with abnormals included and also with abnormals excluded. This helps to facilitate both intertemporal and interfirm comparisons. Furthermore, while the operating profit after tax gives a good guide to profitability, the earnings capacity of the firm is also measured using the measure of earnings before interest and tax (EBIT), or earnings before tax (EBT). Consider Brambles in 1998 and 1997. In 1998, Brambles reported abnormal items of $28.6 million and tax on abnormal items as

---

18  Brambles also operates rail wagon rental in Europe and marine towage/barge shipping in coastal Australia.

19  Includes Brambles Industries Ltd and its controlled entities: from Brambles Industries Ltd annual reports 1997 and 1998.

20  Includes interest and dividends received from controlled entities and the proceeds from the disposal of non-current assets.

21  Net interest can be calculated from the entries for interest received and interest paid in the notes to the accounts.

$27.7 million, giving an after-tax figure for abnormals of $0.9 million. No abnormals were reported in 1997. On page 834 we show EBIT, EBT, operating profit after income tax, and operating profit after income tax attributable to members of the chief entity, both including and excluding abnormal items.

**table 27.4**

Profit and loss accounts for Brambles Industries Ltd, for the years ended 30 June 1998, 30 June 1997 and 30 June 1996

| Consolidated | 1998 ($million) | 1997 ($million) | 1996 ($million) |
| --- | --- | --- | --- |
| **Sales revenue** | | | |
| Controlled entities | 2938.4 | 2668 | 2969.2 |
| Equity share of associated (including Chep USA) | 1075.5 | 740.7 | |
| **Total sales revenue** | 4013.9 | 3408.7 | 2969.2 |
| Share of associates | | | |
| Net profit attributable to members | 78.1 | — | |
| Dividends received | — | 73.2 | |
| Other revenue | 405.5 | 165.4 | 194.6 |
| **Operating profit before abnormal items and income tax** | 414.5 | 376.2 | 331.7 |
| Abnormal items before income tax | 28.6 | — | (15.1) |
| **Operating profit before income tax** | 443.1 | 376.2 | 316.6 |
| Income tax attributable to operating profit before abnormal items | (129.6) | (127.8) | (111.5) |
| Income tax attributable to abnormal items | (27.7) | — | 15.4 |
| **Operating profit after income tax** | 285.8 | 248.4 | 220.5 |
| Outside equity interests in operating after income tax | (1.6) | (5.2) | (5.4) |
| **Operating profit after income tax attributable to members of the chief entity** | 284.2 | 243.2 | 176.1 |
| Retained profits at the beginning of the financial year | 400.5 | 321.5 | 258.6 |
| Equity accounting adjustment | (25.5) | — | — |
| Aggregate of amounts transferred from reserves | 55.6 | 0.6 | 0.3 |
| Total available for appropriation | 714.8 | 565.3 | 474.0 |
| Dividends provided for or paid | (165.8) | (157.8) | (152.5) |
| Aggregate of amounts transferred to reserves | — | (6.8) | — |
| **Retained profits at the end of the financial year** | 548.9 | 400.5 | 321.5 |

| | 1998 | | 1997 | |
|---|---|---|---|---|
| | Including abnormals ($million) | Excluding abnormals ($million) | Including abnormals ($million) | Excluding abnormals ($million) |
| EBIT | 476.3 | 476.3 | 424.4 | 424.4 |
| Net interest | 61.8 | 61.8 | 48.2 | 48.2 |
| Abnormals | 28.6 | — | 0.0 | — |
| EBT | 443.1 | 414.5 | 376.2 | 376.2 |
| Tax expense | 157.3 | 129.6 | 127.8 | 127.8 |
| Operating profit after income tax | 285.8 | 284.9 | 248.4 | 248.4 |
| Outside equity interests | 1.6 | 1.6 | 5.2 | 5.2 |
| Operating profit after income tax attributable to members of chief entity | 284.2 | 283.3 | 243.2 | 243.2 |
| Abnormals (after tax) | 0.0 | 28.6 − 27.7 = 0.9 | 0.0 | 0.0 |
| Net profit before extraordinary items | 284.2 | 284.2 | 243.2 | 243.2 |

Brambles' 1996, 1997 and 1998 balance sheets are shown in Table 27.5. Both Brambles' assets and liabilities are listed in declining order of liquidity. Current assets include cash, accounts receivable, inventories and other short-term assets. Non-current assets include longer dated receivables, investments, plant, property and equipment, intangibles such as goodwill, and other non-current assets such as future income tax benefits, prepayments and deferred expenditure. Both current and non-current liabilities are reported for creditors and borrowers and provisions such as employee entitlements, repairs and maintenance, and deferred income tax. Shareholders' equity is simply equivalent to the total value of the assets less the current and long-term liabilities ($1691.3 million in 1998; $1463.6 million in 1997). It is also equal to ordinary shares plus retained profits—that is, the net amount that the firm has received from shareholders or reinvested on their behalf, reserves and outside equity interests in controlled entities.

Brambles' 1996, 1997 and 1998 statements of cash flows are shown in Table 27.6. The information reported shows a 23 per cent increase in cash flows from operations from 1997 to 1998, an almost 48 per cent increase in net investing cash outflows, and a net increase of $73.7 million in cash flows from financing operations.

## Leverage ratios

Companies finance their capital structure and short-term financial requirements through equity and debt. When a firm borrows money, it promises to make a series of fixed payments. Because the shareholders get only what is left after the debtholders have been paid, debt is said to create *financial leverage*. Our first set of ratios measures this leverage. Table 27.7 reports leverage ratios for Brambles for 1998 and 1997.

table 27.5
Balance sheets for Brambles Industries Ltd, as at 30 June 1998, 30 June 1997 and 30 June 1996

| Consolidated | 1998 ($million) | 1997 ($million) | 1996 ($million) |
|---|---|---|---|
| **Current assets** | | | |
| Cash | 58.9 | 69.7 | 67.8 |
| Receivables | 713.4 | 488.0 | 519.2 |
| Inventories | 99.1 | 83.7 | 78.0 |
| Other | 23.9 | 17.7 | 17.3 |
| **Total current assets** | 895.3 | 659.1 | 684.3 |
| **Non-current assets** | | | |
| Receivables | 21.6 | 26.1 | 39.2 |
| Investments in associates | 340.3 | 222.0 | 251.0 |
| Other investments | 129.4 | 93.4 | |
| Inventories | 2.0 | 2.0 | 1.6 |
| Property, plant and equipment | 2184.8 | 1857.2 | 1738.3 |
| Intangibles | 326.9 | 209.5 | 169.6 |
| Other | 55.3 | 68.2 | 83.2 |
| **Total non-current assets** | 3060.3 | 2478.4 | 2282.9 |
| **Total assets** | 3955.6 | 3137.5 | 2967.2 |
| **Current liabilities** | | | |
| Accounts payable | 406.3 | 338.0 | 346.8 |
| Borrowings | 46.6 | 24.1 | 23.2 |
| Provisions | 311.6 | 230.4 | 249.9 |
| **Total current liabilities** | 764.5 | 592.5 | 618.9 |
| **Non-current liabilities** | | | |
| Accounts payable | 7.7 | 1.4 | 1.4 |
| Borrowings | 1300.2 | 912.7 | 780.0 |
| Provisions | 191.9 | 167.3 | 147.9 |
| **Total non-current liabilities** | 1499.8 | 1081.4 | 929.3 |
| **Total liabilities** | 2264.3 | 1673.9 | 1548.2 |
| **Net assets** | 1691.3 | 1463.6 | 1419.0 |
| **Shareholders' equity** | | | |
| Share capital | 112.2 | 111.2 | 110.4 |
| Reserves | 1015.5 | 932.8 | 952.0 |
| Retained profits | 548.9 | 400.5 | 321.5 |
| Shareholders' equity attributable to members of the chief entity | 1676.6 | 1444.5 | 1383.9 |
| Outside equity interests in controlled entities | 14.7 | 19.1 | 35.1 |
| **Total shareholders' equity** | 1691.3 | 1463.6 | 1419.0 |

**table 27.6**

Cash flow sheets for Brambles Industries Ltd, for the years ended 30 June 1998, 30 June 1997 and 30 June 1996

| Consolidated | 1998 ($million) | 1997 ($million) | 1996 ($million) |
|---|---|---|---|
| **Cash flows operating activities** | | | |
| Receipts in the course of operations | 2935.3 | 2755.8 | 3069.8 |
| Payments in the course of operations | (2231.2) | (2162.5) | (2403.0) |
| Dividends received from associates | 77.7 | 65.2 | 45.4 |
| Other dividends received | 0.1 | | |
| Interest received | 6.1 | 7.5 | 4.6 |
| Interest paid | (71.5) | (50.3) | (69.4) |
| Income taxes paid | (93.5) | (109.9) | (99.0) |
| **Net operating cash inflows/outflows** | 623.0 | 505.8 | 548.4 |
| **Cash flows from investing activities** | | | |
| Purchase of property, plant and equipment | (651.4) | (437.7) | (419.7) |
| Proceeds from sales of property, plant and equipment | 121.3 | 74.5 | 76.3 |
| Acquisition of entities | (189.6) | (152.0) | (53.3) |
| Purchase of other investments | (85.8) | (29.4) | (16.3) |
| Proceeds from sale of entities | 107.0 | 61.7 | 57.2 |
| Proceeds from sale of other investments | 12.1 | 26.7 | 1.2 |
| Loans and associates | (29.4) | (51.3) | (15.5) |
| Loans repaid by associates | 21.0 | 37.8 | 10.7 |
| **Net investing cash inflows/outflows** | (694.8) | (469.7) | (359.4) |
| **Cash flows from financing activities** | | | |
| Proceeds from issues of shares | 29.8 | 21.8 | 21.2 |
| Borrowings: | | | |
|   Proceeds | 2924.1 | 1484.8 | 1670.6 |
|   **Repayments** | (2744.9) | (1378.2) | (1763.1) |
| Dividends paid: | | | |
|   Shareholders of chief entity | (160.7) | (155.2) | (147.5) |
|   Outside equity interests | (1.6) | (4.7) | (8.0) |
|   Other cash inflows | 10.3 | — | 1.3 |
|   Other cash outflows | (15.8) | (1.0) | (6.3) |
| **Net financing cash inflows (outflows)** | 41.2 | (32.5) | (231.8) |
| **Net increase/decrease in cash held** | (30.6) | 3.6 | (42.8) |
| Cash at beginning of year | 61.7 | 59.4 | 122.9 |
| Loans from controlled entities | — | — | — |
| Exchange rate adjustment | 11.9 | (1.3) | (20.7) |
| **Cash at end of year** | 43.0 | 61.7 | 59.4 |

**table 27.7**

Leverage ratios for Brambles Industries Ltd, 1998 and 1997

| Ratio | Formula | 1998 | 1997 |
|---|---|---|---|
| Debt ratio | $\dfrac{\text{Long-term debt}}{\text{long-term debt + equity}}$ | $\dfrac{1300.2}{1300.2 + 1691.3} = 43.46\%$ | $\dfrac{912.7}{912.7 + 1463.6} = 38.41\%$ |
| Debt to equity ratio | $\dfrac{\text{Long-term debt}}{\text{equity}}$ | $\dfrac{1300.2}{1691.3} = 76.88\%$ | $\dfrac{912.7}{1463.6} = 62.36\%$ |
| Debt to total capitalisation ratio | $\dfrac{\text{Long-term debt}}{\text{total capitalisation}}$ | $\dfrac{1300.2}{1300.2 + 199.6 + 1691.3} = 40.74\%$ | $\dfrac{912.7}{912.7 + 168.7 + 1463.6} = 35.86\%$ |
| Times interest earned | $\dfrac{\text{EBIT}}{\text{interest}}$ | $\dfrac{476.3}{61.1} = 7.79$ times | $\dfrac{424.4}{48.2} = 8.81$ times |
| Equity ratio | $\dfrac{\text{Total shareholders' equity}}{\text{total assets}}$ | $\dfrac{1691.3}{3955.6} = 42.76\%$ | $\dfrac{1463.6}{3137.5} = 46.65\%$ |

## Debt ratios

Financial leverage is usually measured by the ratio of long-term debt to long-term capital. The ratio can be expressed as:[22]

$$\text{Debt ratio} = \frac{\text{Long-term debt}}{\text{Long-term debt} + \text{equity}}$$

## Debt to equity ratios

A more frequently used measure of financial leverage is the ratio of debt to equity.[23] The higher the ratio, the greater the possibility that the company may experience difficulties repaying debts, especially if interest rates rise.[24]

$$\text{Debt to equity ratio} = \frac{\text{Long-term debt}}{\text{equity}}$$

Notice that both the debt ratio and the debt to equity ratio make use of book (or accounting) values rather than market values.[25] The market value of the company finally determines whether debtholders get their money back, so you can expect analysts to look at the face amount of the debt as a proportion of the total market value of debt and equity. The main reason that they do not do this is that the market values are often not readily available. Does it matter much? Perhaps not; after all, the market value includes the value of intangible assets generated by research and development, advertising, staff training, and so on. These assets are not readily saleable, and if the company falls on hard times, the value of these assets may disappear altogether. For some purposes, it may be just as good to follow the accountant and ignore these intangible assets. As we saw in Chapter 24, this is just what lenders do when they insist that the borrower should not allow the book ratio to exceed a specified limit.

Debt ratios can be calculated in several different ways. Suppose the analysts 'net out' current liabilities against current assets, leaving only long-term financing on the right-hand side of the balance sheet. The sum of the long-term debt, other liabilities and equity is called total capitalisation. For Brambles in 1998:

| | | | |
|---|---|---|---|
| Net working capital (current assets – current liabilities) | 130.8 | Long-term debt | 1300.2 |
| | | Other liabilities | 166.6 |
| Long-term assets | 3060.3 | Equity | 1691.3 |
| | 3191.1 | Total capitalisation | 3191.1 |

The ratio of debt to total capitalisation is

$$\text{Debt to total capitalisation} = \frac{\text{Long-term debt}}{\text{Total capitalisation}}$$

If other liabilities are treated as debt equivalent, the ratio increases to

$$\frac{\text{Long-term debt} + \text{other liabilities}}{\text{Total capitalisation}}$$

---

22  Some analysts treat long-term financial leases as a commitment by the firm to a series of fixed future payments and therefore include financial leases in both the denominator and numerator of the formula. In Australia most companies classify non-current lease liabilities as part of their non-current borrowings on their balance sheet.

23  This ratio is also reported as the ratio of long-term debt to equity.

24  Companies can structure their debt as either short term or long term or some combination of both. The maturity structure of a company's debt is usually a function of several factors such as interest-rate expectations, project life and the company policy with respect to asset/liability management. The ratio of long-term debt to total debt can be used to show the proportion of long-term debt.

25  In the case of leased assets accountants try to estimate the present value of the lease commitments. In the case of long-term debt they simply show face value. This can sometimes be very different from present value. For example, the present value of low coupon debt may be only a fraction of its face value. The difference between the book value of equity and its market value can be even more dramatic.

**Times interest earned (or interest cover)**    Another measure of financial leverage is the extent to which interest is covered by EBIT:

$$\text{Times interest earned} = \frac{\text{EBIT}}{\text{interest}}$$

This ratio highlights whether the company is obtaining a healthy level of profit to protect against a fall in business activity or to meet increases in interest rates. The regular interest payment is a hurdle that companies must keep jumping if they are to avoid default. The times-interest-earned ratio measures how much clear air there is between hurdle and hurdler. However, always bear in mind that such summary measures tell only part of the story. For example, it might make sense to measure whether the firm is generating enough cash to cover other fixed charges such as regular repayments of existing debt or long-term lease payments.

# Liquidity ratios

Liquidity ratios provide information regarding the ability of the company to gain access to cash. The continued viability of any company is a function of its ability to meet debt repayments as they come due. If you are extending credit or lending to a company for a short period, you are interested not only in the amount of the company's debts, but also whether the company will be able to lay its hands on the cash to repay you. That is why credit managers and bankers look at several measures of *liquidity*. Another reason that managers focus on liquid assets is that the figures are more reliable. The book value of a catalytic cracker may be a poor guide to its true value, but at least you know what cash in the bank is worth.

Liquidity ratios also have some *less* desirable characteristics. Because short-term assets and liabilities are easily changed, measures of liquidity can rapidly become out of date. You might not know what that catalytic cracker is worth, but you can be fairly sure that it will not disappear overnight. Also, companies often choose a slack period for the end of their financial year. For example, retailers may end their financial year in January, after the Christmas boom. At such times the companies are likely to have more cash and less short-term debt than is the case during the busier seasons. Table 27.8 reports liquidity ratios for Brambles for 1998 and 1997.

**Net working capital to total assets**    Current assets are those assets that the company expects to turn into cash in the near future. The difference between current assets and current liabilities is known as *net working capital*. Net working capital roughly measures the company's potential reservoir of cash. Managers often express net working capital as a proportion of total assets.

$$\text{Net working capital to total assets} = \frac{\text{net working capital}}{\text{total assets}}$$

**Current ratio**    The current ratio measures the ability of a company to repay its short-term debt using short-term assets.

$$\text{Current ratio} = \frac{\text{current assets}}{\text{current liabilities}}$$

Changes in the current ratio can sometimes mislead. For example, suppose that a company borrows a large sum from the bank and invests it in short-term securities. If nothing else changes, net working capital is unaffected, but the current ratio changes. For this reason it might be preferable to net off the short-term investments and the short-term debt when calculating the current ratio.

**Quick (liquidity or acid test) ratio**    Some assets are closer to cash than others. If trouble comes, inventories may not sell at anything above fire-sale prices. (Trouble comes typically because customers are not buying and the firm's warehouse is stuffed full of unwanted

**table 27.8**

Liquidity ratios for Brambles Industries Ltd, 1998 and 1997

| Ratio | Formula | 1998 | 1997 |
|---|---|---|---|
| Net working capital | Current assets − current liabilities | $895.3 - 764.5 = 130.8$ | $659.1 - 592.5 = 66.6$ |
| Net working capital to total assets | $\dfrac{\text{Net working capital}}{\text{total assets}}$ | $\dfrac{130.8}{3955.6} = 3.31\%$ | $\dfrac{66.6}{3137.5} = 2.12\%$ |
| Current ratio | $\dfrac{\text{Current assets}}{\text{current liabilities}}$ | $\dfrac{895.3}{764.5} = 1.17 \text{ times}$ | $\dfrac{659.1}{592.5} = 1.11 \text{ times}$ |
| Quick ratio[a] | $\dfrac{\text{Cash} + \text{short-term securities} + \text{receivables}}{\text{current liabilities}}$ | $\dfrac{36.3 + 22.6 + 456.4}{764.5} = 67.40\%$ | $\dfrac{58.0 + 11.7 + 400.0}{592.5} = 79.27\%$ |
| Cash ratio | $\dfrac{\text{Cash} + \text{short-term securities}}{\text{current liabilities}}$ | $\dfrac{36.3 + 22.6}{764.5} = 7.70\%$ | $\dfrac{58.0 + 11.7}{592.5} = 11.76\%$ |
| Times interest earned | $\dfrac{\text{EBIT}}{\text{interest}}$ | $\dfrac{476.3}{61.1} = 7.79 \text{ times}$ | $\dfrac{424.4}{48.2} = 8.81 \text{ times}$ |

Note: (a) Total receivables is $735.0 million in 1998 and $514.1 million in 1997. This amount represents both trade debtors ($456.4 million in 1998 and $400 million in 1997) and other debtors from transactions outside the usual operating activities of the group involving controlled entities. Hence the receivables figure used reflects the trade debtors figures.

goods.) Thus, managers often focus only on cash, short-term securities, and bills that customers have not yet paid.

$$\text{Quick ratio} = \frac{\text{cash} + \text{short-term securities} + \text{receivables}}{\text{current liabilities}}$$

**Cash ratio**    The most conservative of the liquidity ratios is the cash ratio, which only uses cash and cash equivalent balances. For Brambles,

$$\text{Cash ratio} = \frac{\text{cash} + \text{short-term securities}}{\text{current liabilities}}$$

**Interest cover**    Interest expense must be paid from operating profit. Hence, it is useful to know the relationship between EBIT and interest expense. The higher the cover, the better the prospects of the company to repay its interest on debt.

$$\text{Interest cover} = \frac{\text{EBIT}}{\text{interest expense}}$$

# Activity ratios

Activity ratios examine how different asset groups, such as sales, inventory, accounts receivable and fixed assets, contribute to profitability. Examination of these ratios also allows some control by financial managers over areas such as working capital, inventory and accounts receivable. Firms need to invest in both short-term and long-term assets. Hence, the higher the ratio, the more efficient the firm's operations, as fewer assets are required to maintain a given level of operations (usually proxied by sales). Table 27.9 shows the activity ratios for Brambles for 1998 and 1997.

**Asset turnover**    To measure the overall investment activity of companies incorporating short-term and long-term assets, asset turnover can be used to measure the relationship between sales and average total assets. It measures the efficiency in generating sales from the assets.

$$\text{Total asset turnover} = \frac{\text{sales}}{\text{average total assets}}$$

A high ratio could indicate that the firm is working close to capacity. It may also prove difficult to generate further business without an increase in invested capital. Notice that since the assets are likely to change over the course of a year, we use the *average* of the assets at the beginning and the end of the year. Averages are usually used whenever a *flow* figure (in this case, sales) is compared with a *stock* or snapshot figure (in this case, total assets).

**Sales to net working capital**    Net working capital can be measured more accurately than other assets. Also, the level of net working capital can be adjusted more rapidly to reflect temporary fluctuations in sales. Thus, managers sometimes focus on how hard working capital has been put to use.

$$\text{Sales to net working capital} = \frac{\text{sales}}{\text{average net working capital}}$$

**Working capital turnover**    Net working capital is best proxied as current assets minus current liabilities. The amount of working capital turnover provides a measure of how

**table 27.9**

Activity ratios for Brambles Industries Ltd, 1998 and 1997

| Ratio | Formula | 1998 | 1997 |
|---|---|---|---|
| Assets turnover | $\dfrac{\text{Sales}}{\text{average total assets}}$ | $\dfrac{4013.9}{(3955.6 + 3137.5)/2} = 1.13$ times | $\dfrac{3408.7}{(3137.5 + 2967.2)/2} = 1.12$ times |
| Sales to net working capital | $\dfrac{\text{Sales}}{\text{average net working capital}}$ | $\dfrac{4013.9}{(130.8 + 66.6)/2} = 40.67$ times | $\dfrac{3408.7}{(66.6 + 65.4)/2} = 51.65$ times |
| Working capital outstanding | $\dfrac{\text{Net working capital}}{\text{sales}} \times 365$ | $\dfrac{130.8}{4013.9} \times 365 = 11.89$ days | $\dfrac{66.6}{3137.5} \times 365 = 7.75$ days |
| Working capital turnover | $\dfrac{365}{\text{working capital outstanding}}$ | $\dfrac{365}{11.89} = 30.70$ times | $\dfrac{365}{7.75} = 47.10$ times |
| Days inventory held | $\dfrac{\text{Inventory}}{\text{sales}} \times 365$ | $\dfrac{101.1}{4013.9} \times 365 = 9.19$ days | $\dfrac{85.70}{3408.7} \times 365 = 9.18$ days |
| Inventory turnover | $\dfrac{365}{\text{days inventory held}}$ | $\dfrac{365}{9.19} = 39.72$ times | $\dfrac{365}{9.18} = 39.76$ times |
| Days receivable outstanding[a] | $\dfrac{\text{Receivables}}{\text{sales}} \times 365$ | $\dfrac{456.4}{4013.9} \times 365 = 41.50$ days | $\dfrac{400.0}{3408.7} \times 365 = 42.83$ days |
| Inventory turnover | $\dfrac{365}{\text{days receivable outstanding}}$ | $\dfrac{365}{41.50} = 8.80$ times | $\dfrac{365}{42.83} = 8.52$ times |

Note: [a] Total receivables is $735.0 million in 1998 and $514.1 million in 1997. This amount represents both trade debtors ($456.4 million in 1998 and $400 million in 1997) and other debtors from transactions outside the usual operating activities of the group involving controlled entities. Hence the receivables figure used reflects the trade debtors figures.

much working capital is necessary to maintain the level of sales and the average frequency that it is turned over in any year.

$$\text{Working capital outstanding} = \frac{\text{working capital}}{\text{sales}} \times 365$$

To measure the rate at which Brambles turns over its working capital during any year:

$$\text{Working capital turnover} = \frac{365}{\text{working capital outstanding}}$$

**Inventory turnover**   Managers sometimes look at the rate at which companies turn over their inventory. To measure the effectiveness of the firm's inventory policy they consider the ratio of the company's inventory to total sales.

$$\text{Days inventory held} = \frac{\text{inventory}}{\text{sales}} \times 365$$

To measure how frequently Brambles turns over its inventory during any year:

$$\text{Inventory turnover} = \frac{365}{\text{days inventory held}}$$

**Receivables turnover**   Understanding accounts receivable turnover provides information regarding the credit management skills of the company and indicates the level of investment of receivables[26] from trade debtors to maintain the firm's level of sales. Relevant ratios include the receivables outstanding, which gives the average number of days receivables are outstanding, and the receivables turnover.

$$\text{Receivables outstanding} = \frac{\text{receivables}}{\text{sales}}$$

The rate of receivables turnover is measured as:

$$\text{Receivables turnover} = \frac{365}{\text{receivables outstanding}}$$

# Profitability ratios

Profitability ratios are used to assess how well the company has made use of its assets in the operation of the business. Several aspects confuse the measurement of profitability, including the role of abnormal items, extraordinary items, taxation expense and interest expense. The two most important measures in assessing profitability are EBIT (earnings before interest and tax), which is often referred to as the operating profit of the firm, and EBT (earnings before tax). EBIT's importance is highlighted by understanding that firms finance their operations differently, some using equity and others using debt. By not including the costs of interest and tax the reported earnings figure can be compared between companies and trends can be assessed over time. For Brambles, EBIT (before abnormals of $28.6 million) was reported as $476.3 million in 1998 and $424.4 million in 1997. EBT (before abnormals) was $414.5 in 1998 and $376.2 in 1997. Table 27.10 shows the profitability ratios for Brambles for 1998 and 1997.

---

26   Receivables include trade debtors after accounting for provision for doubtful debts for both the chief entity and all controlled entities.

**table 27.10**

Profitability ratios for Brambles Industries Ltd, 1998 and 1997

| Ratio | Formula | 1998 | 1997 |
|---|---|---|---|
| Gross profit margin ratio | $\dfrac{\text{EBIT}}{\text{total sales}}$ | $\dfrac{476.6}{4013.9} = 11.87\%$ | $\dfrac{424.2}{3408.7} = 12.44\%$ |
| Net profit margin (including abnormals) | $\dfrac{\text{Operating profit after tax}}{\text{total sales}}$ | $\dfrac{284.2}{4013.9} = 7.08\%$ | $\dfrac{243.2}{3408.7} = 7.13\%$ |
| Return on total assets (including abnormals) | $\dfrac{\text{Operating profit after tax}}{\text{average total assets}}$ | $\dfrac{284.2}{(3955.6 + 3137.5)/2} = 8.01\%$ | $\dfrac{243.2}{(3137.5 + 2967.2)/2} = 7.97\%$ |
| Return on total sales | $\dfrac{\text{EBIT}}{\text{average total sales}}$ | $\dfrac{476.3}{(4013.9 + 3408.7)/2} = 12.83\%$ | $\dfrac{424.4}{(3408.7 + 3163.8)/2} = 12.91\%$ |
| Return on shareholders' equity (including abnormals) | $\dfrac{\text{Operating profit after tax}}{\text{average shareholders' equity}}$ | $\dfrac{284.2}{(1691.3 + 1463.6)/2} = 18.02\%$ | $\dfrac{243.2}{(1463.6 + 1419.0)/2} = 16.87\%$ |
| Effective tax rate (including abnormals) | $\dfrac{\text{Tax expense}}{\text{operating profit before tax}}$ | $\dfrac{157.3}{443.1} = 35.50\%$ | $\dfrac{127.8}{376.2} = 33.97\%$ |
| Payout ratio[a] | $\dfrac{\text{Total dividends}}{\text{operating profit after tax}}$ | $\dfrac{165.8}{284.2} = 58.34\%$ | $\dfrac{157.8}{243.2} = 64.88\%$ |

Note: [a] While the total dividends paid in 1998 are recorded as $165.9 million in the profit and loss statement, the actual dividends paid were only $165.8 million. The balance of $0.1 million represents an adjustment to the final dividend in 1997. Similarly, while the total dividends paid in 1997 are recorded as $158.0 million, the actual dividends paid in 1997 amounted to $157.8 million, with the balance of $0.2 million being an adjustment for 1996 final dividends.

**Net operating profit after tax**    While EBIT reflects the operating profit of the company, net operating profit (including abnormals) after tax reflects the profit available to shareholders after adjusting for net interest, tax and outside equity interests in operating profit but before extraordinary items. For Brambles, net operating profit was $284.2 million in 1998 and $243.2 million in 1997.

**Net profit margin (pre-tax profit to sales ratio)**    If you want to know the proportion of sales that finds its way into profits, you look at the profit margin:

$$\text{Net profit margin} = \frac{\text{EBIT} - \text{tax}}{\text{sales}}$$

Net profit margin is sometimes measured as net income/sales. This measure ignores the profits that are paid out to debtholders as interest and therefore should not be used to compare firms with different capital structures. When making comparisons between firms, it makes sense to recognise that firms that pay more interest pay less tax. We suggest that you calculate the taxes that the firm would pay if it were all-equity-financed. To do this you need to adjust taxes by adding back interest-rate shields (interest payments $\times$ marginal tax rate). The revised formula becomes:

$$\text{Net profit margin (adjusted)} = \frac{\text{EBIT} - (\text{tax} + \text{interest-rate shield})}{\text{sales}}$$

**Return on total assets**    Managers often measure the performance of a firm by the ratio of operating profit before tax to total assets.[27]

$$\text{Return on assets} = \frac{\text{operating profit before income tax}}{\text{average total assets}}$$

Some profitability or efficiency ratios can be linked in useful ways. For example, the return on assets depends on the firm's sales-to-assets ratio and profit margin:

$$\frac{\text{Income}}{\text{Assets}} = \frac{\text{sales}}{\text{assets}} \times \frac{\text{income}}{\text{sales}}$$

All firms would like to earn a higher return on assets, but their ability to do so is limited by competition. If the expected return on assets is fixed by competition, firms face a trade-off between the sales-to-assets ratio and the profit margin. Thus, we find that fast food chains, which turn over their capital frequently, also tend to operate on low profit margins. Classy hotels have relatively high margins, but this is offset by lower sales-to-assets ratios.

Firms often seek to increase their profit margins by becoming more vertically integrated— for example, they may acquire a supplier or one of their sales outlets. Unfortunately, unless they have some special skill in running these new businesses, they are likely to find that any gain in profit margin is offset by a decline in the sales-to-assets ratio.

---

[27]    When comparing the returns on total assets for firms with different capital structures, it makes sense to add back interest shields. This adjusted ratio then measures the return that the company would have earned if it were all-equity-financed. One other point about return on assets: since profits are a flow figure and assets are a snapshot figure, analysts commonly divide profits by the average of assets at the start and end of the year. The reason they do this is that the firm may raise large amounts of new capital during the year and then put it to work. Therefore, part of the year's earnings is a return on the new capital. However, this measure is potentially misleading; be careful not to compare it with the cost of capital. After all, when we defined the return that shareholders require from investing in the capital market, we divided expected profit by the initial outlay, not by an average of starting and ending values.

$$\text{Return on assets} = \frac{\text{EBIT} - \text{tax}}{\text{assets at start of year} + (\text{new capital raised}/2)}$$

### EBIT/sales

By examining the ratio of EBIT to sales revenue the company can identify the operating profit earned (in cents) per dollar of sales.

$$\text{Return to sales} = \frac{\text{EBIT}}{\text{Sales}}$$

### Return on shareholders' equity

This ratio focuses on the return to shareholders on their equity interest in the company.[28]

$$\text{Return on shareholders' equity} = \frac{\text{operating profit after tax}}{\text{average total shareholders equity}}$$

### Effective tax rate

The effective tax rate reflects the ratio between the tax expense incurred and the level of operating profit before tax.

$$\text{Effective tax rate} = \frac{\text{tax expense}}{\text{operating income before tax}}$$

### Payout ratio

The payout ratio measures the proportion of after-tax earnings that is paid out as dividends. Thus,

$$\text{Payout ratio} = \frac{\text{dividend per share}}{\text{earnings per share}}$$

We saw in Section 16.2 that managers do not like to cut dividends and that they try to maintain them despite temporary shortfalls in earnings. Therefore, if a company's earnings are particularly variable, management is likely to play it safe by setting a low average payout ratio. When earnings fall unexpectedly, the payout ratio is likely to rise temporarily. Likewise, if earnings are expected to rise next year, management may feel that it can pay slightly more generous dividends, and this year's payout ratio will be higher.

Earnings not paid out as dividends are ploughed back into the business as retained earnings.[29]

$$\text{Proportion of earnings ploughed back} = 1 - \text{payout ratio}$$
$$= \frac{\text{earnings} - \text{dividend}}{\text{earnings}}$$

## Market value ratios

Provided regulatory requirements are met, there are no restrictions prohibiting the financial manager from introducing industry-specific data into the company accounts or elsewhere in the annual report. For example, BHP could report the cost per tonne of steel produced, Qantas could report revenues per passenger mile flown throughout the year, a private hospital could report costs in terms of per bed occupancy day, and so on. Managers find it helpful to look at ratios that combine accounting and share market data. Here we consider several market-based measures. Table 27.11 shows the market-based ratios for Brambles for 1998 and 1997.

---

[28]  Due to the different classes of shares on issue and the respective rights afforded to the holders of such shares, ordinary shareholders need a measure to assess the rate of return on ordinary shareholders' equity:

$$\frac{\text{Net profit} - \text{dividends paid or due on preference shares}}{\text{total shareholders' equity} - \text{preference shareholder contributions}}$$

[29]  If you multiply this figure by the return on equity, you can see roughly how rapidly the shareholders' investment is growing as a result of ploughback.

**table 27.11**
Market value based ratios for Brambles Industries Ltd, 1998 and 1997

| Ratio | Formula | 1998 | 1997 |
|---|---|---|---|
| Weighted average number of shares | | 223 167 047 | 221 681 164 |
| Actual number of shares at year-end | | 224.417 million | 222.447 million |
| Earnings per share (after abnormals) | $\dfrac{\text{Operating profit after tax (after abnormals)}}{\text{average number of ordinary shares}}$ | $\dfrac{284.2}{223\ 167\ 047} = 127.3$ cents | $\dfrac{243.2}{221\ 681\ 164} = 109.7$ cents |
| Earnings per share (before abnormals) | $\dfrac{\text{Operating profit after tax (before abnormals)}}{\text{average number of ordinary shares}}$ | $\dfrac{283.3}{223\ 167\ 047} = 126.9$ cents | $\dfrac{243.2}{221\ 681\ 164} = 109.7$ cents |
| Price earnings ratio (after abnormals) | $\dfrac{\text{Market value per share}}{\text{earnings per share}}$ | $\dfrac{31.69}{1.273} = 24.89$ | $\dfrac{26.191}{1.097} = 23.86$ |
| Share price (30 June) | | $31.69 | $26.191 |
| Dividend yield | $\dfrac{\text{Dividend per share}}{\text{market value per share}}$ | $\dfrac{0.74}{31.69} = 2.34\%$ | $\dfrac{0.71}{26.191} = 2.71\%$ |
| Dividend cover (after abnormals) | $\dfrac{\text{Operating profit after tax} - \text{preference shares}}{\text{total dividends}}$ | $\dfrac{284.2}{165.8} = 1.71$ times | $\dfrac{243.2}{157.8} = 1.54$ times |
| Net tangible asset backing per share | $\dfrac{\text{Shareholders' equity} - \text{outside interests} - \text{interest}}{\text{number of shares}}$ | $\dfrac{1691.3 - 14.7 - 326.9}{224.417} = 6.014$ | $\dfrac{1463.6 - 19.1 - 209.5}{222.447} = 5.552$ |

## Earnings per share

The measure of earnings per share (EPS) is a commonly applied measure to establish the value of the net profit per ordinary share.

$$\text{EPS} = \frac{\text{operating profit after tax}}{\text{number of ordinary shares on issue}}$$

However, as noted by Kenley,[30] this measure does not capture many features, including the different classes of shares on issue, the gains (or losses) from extraordinary items, any new share issues during the year, and the role played by convertible notes, options, bonus issues from existing reserves and shares subject to cancellation.

The most common adjustment occurs due to changes in the number of shares on issue during the year. This can be achieved by calculating the average number of shares on issue either as an arithmetic or a weighted average. For example, assume there were 6 000 000 ordinary shares outstanding at the commencement of the year and 7 000 000 by year-end. The arithmetic average number of shares on issue for the year would be 6 500 000 shares. If the additional shares were issued in August, a weighted average could be calculated as follows.

$$6\ 000\ 000 + \frac{4}{12}(1\ 000\ 000) = 6\ 400\ 000$$

Brambles reported the weighted average number of shares in 1998 to be 223 167 047 and in 1997 to be 221 681 164. The earnings per share can be estimated as follows:

$$\text{EPS before abnormals} = \frac{\text{operating profit before abnormals}}{\text{average number of ordinary shares}}$$

$$\text{EPS after abnormals} = \frac{\text{net operating profit after abnormals}}{\text{average number of ordinary shares}}$$

## Price-earnings ratio

Earnings per share is an important measure due to the role it plays in calculating the earnings yield and the price-earnings ratio (P/E ratio).

$$\text{Earnings yield} = \frac{\text{EPS}}{\text{market value per share}}$$

$$\text{Price-earnings ratio} = \frac{\text{market value per share}}{\text{EPS}}$$

The price-earnings ratio measures the price that investors are prepared to pay for each dollar of earnings. If we assume Brambles' EPS before abnormals was $1.269 and its share price was $31.69 at the end of June 1998, the P/E ratio would equal:

$$\text{P/E ratio} = \frac{31.69}{1.269} = 24.97$$

Hence, at the close of share trading on 30 June 1998, it cost approximately $24.97 to buy one dollar of Brambles' after-tax earnings before abnormals. In Chapter 4 we explained that a high P/E ratio might indicate that investors think the firm has good growth opportunities or that its earnings are relatively safe and therefore more valuable. Of course, it might also mean temporarily depressed earnings. If a company just breaks even, reporting zero earnings, its P/E ratio is infinite.

---

30   W. J. Kenley, *Using Financial Statements*, CCH, Sydney, 1989.

**Dividend yield**    The shares' dividend yield is simply the expected dividend as a proportion of the share price.[31] Thus, for Brambles:

$$\text{Dividend yield} = \frac{\text{dividend per share}}{\text{market value per share}}$$

Remember that the return to an investor comes in two forms—dividend yield and capital appreciation. If a share has a low dividend yield, it might indicate that investors are content with a relatively low rate of return or that they are looking for the compensation of a rapid growth in dividends and consequent capital gains.

**Dividend cover (times covered)**    This ratio measures how much of the tax profit is being used to finance dividends.[32]

$$\text{Dividend cover} = \frac{\text{net operating profit after tax} - \text{preference dividends}}{\text{total dividends to shareholders}}$$

Most companies do not issue preference shares, but when they do, preference shares rank above ordinary shares and their dividends are therefore deducted from net profit after tax before calculating the dividend cover for ordinary shares. If the dividend cover is less than one, this implies that the company is paying out more in dividends than it is earning in profits. Hence, to maintain the dividend payout ratio it must pay dividends from past years' retained earnings. The company cannot sustain this indefinitely and it is possible that the firm may decrease the size of future dividends if it is unlikely to significantly increase future earnings.

**Net tangible assets backing per share (net asset backing)**    This ratio provides a value for the tangible assets of the company. This measure provides a useful tool for comparison to market share prices. If the net tangible assets (NTA) per share is less than the market price, then the company is undervalued and would be attractive to take over.[33]

$$\text{NTA per share} = \frac{\text{shareholders' equity} - \text{outside interests} - \text{intangibles}}{\text{number of shares}}$$

The ratio of net tangible assets to the share price provides a relative measure of NTA to market value.

**Tobin's $q$ ratio**    Tobin's[34] $q$ ratio measures the relationship between the market value of a company's debt and equity to the current replacement cost of its assets.

$$\text{Tobin's } q \text{ ratio} = \frac{\text{market value of assets}}{\text{estimated replacement cost}}$$

Tobin argued that firms have an incentive to invest when $q$ is greater than 1 (i.e. when capital equipment is worth more than the cost of replacing it) and that they will stop investing only when $q$ is less than 1 (i.e. when equipment is worth less than its replacement cost). When $q$ is less than 1, it may be cheaper to acquire assets through merger rather than to buy new assets. Of course, it is possible to think of cases where the existing assets are worth much more

---

[31]    The analysis of the dividend yield is complicated under dividend imputation as the value of the yield will vary from investor to investor, contingent on whether all or part of the dividend has been franked and whether the investor is eligible to claim imputation credits.

[32]    Dividend cover can also be calculated as:

$$\frac{\text{EPS}}{\text{dividend per share}}$$

[33]    This assumes that assets will obtain their recorded 'book' value if sold in the market.

[34]    J. Tobin, 'A General Equilibrium Approach to Monetary Policy', *Journal of Money, Credit, and Banking*, **1**: 15–29 (February 1969). For estimates of $q$ see G. von Furstenberg, 'Corporate Investment: Does Market Valuation Really Matter?', *Brookings Papers on Economic Activity*, **2**: 347–97 (1977).

than they cost but there is no scope for further profitable investment. Nevertheless, a high value for $q$ is usually a sign of valuable growth opportunities. The reverse is also true. Just because an asset is worth *less* than what it would cost if bought today, do not conclude that it can be better employed elsewhere. But companies whose assets are valued below replacement cost ought to look over their shoulders to see whether predators are threatening to take them over and redeploy the assets.

We should also expect $q$ to be higher for firms with a strong competitive advantage, and so it turns out. The companies with the highest values for $q$ tend to be those with very strong brand images or know-how. Those with low values have generally been found to be in highly competitive and shrinking industries.[35]

Takeover target firms have generally been found in the finance literature to have low $q$ ratios. In a study of takeover activity, Hasbrouck[36] found that well-managed firms had high $q$ ratios, while firms with low $q$ ratios were found to have poor management. Target company shares were often found to be selling at a value below their replacement cost. Other studies examining the competence of management to use the firm's assets most productively have generally found similar results.[37]

## Choosing a benchmark

We have shown you how to calculate the principal financial ratios for Brambles Ltd. But we still need some way of judging whether a ratio is too high or low.

A good starting point is to compare the current year's ratios with equivalent figures for earlier years. For example, you can see from the first two columns of Table 27.12 that in 1998 Brambles improved its profitability despite increases in activity leverage.

It is also helpful to compare a company's financial position with that of other firms in the same industry. However, when conducting such an analysis it is important to remember the size of the firm relative to others in the industry and the possibility that outlier firms will dominate any average statistics. For example, as shown in Table 27.12, Brambles dominates both the equally weighted and weighted averages for companies in the transport index. Overall, we find that the ratios for Brambles indicate higher leverage, liquidity and profitability than other companies in the transport index—Qantas Ltd, Toll Holdings Ltd and Finemores Holdings Ltd. In relation to liquidity the ratios are not greatly different between the firms. However, when examining asset turnover, an activity ratio, we find that the smaller firms, Toll Holdings Ltd and Finemores Holdings Ltd, outperform both Brambles and Qantas.[38]

Financial ratios are also available for other industries and provide a mechanism to compare between industries. Table 27.13 gives the principal ratios for major industry groups. The data should give you a feel for some of the differences between industries.

Be selective in your choice of financial ratios, because many ratios tell you similar things. For example, as sure as pigs have tails, a firm with a high debt ratio will also have a high debt-equity ratio. So, it is pointless to calculate both these measures. Conversely, there is almost no relationship between changes in a firm's current ratio and its return on equity. You can get additional information by looking at both figures.[39]

---

[35] See E. B. Lindberg and S. A. Ross, ' Tobin's $q$ Ratio and Industrial Organisation', *Journal of Business*, **54**: 1–33 (January 1981).

[36] See J. Hasbrouck, 'The Characteristics of Takeover Targets', *Journal of Banking and Finance*, **9** (3): 351–62 (1985).

[37] See L. Lang and R. M. Stulz, 'Tobin's $q$, Corporate Diversification and Firm Performance', *Journal of Political Economy*, **102**: 1248–80 (1994).

[38] The increases in sales for each of the companies are Brambles (17.76 per cent to $4013.9 million), Qantas (3.79 per cent to $8131.5 million), Toll (81.80 per cent to $854.44 million) and Finemores (15.05 per cent to $297.74 million). However, the size of the average assets for Finemores ($246.145 million) and Toll ($157.585 million) are significantly less than the average assets for Brambles ($3546.55 million) and Qantas ($10 105.45 million).

[39] For evidence on the correlations between financial ratios see G. Foster, *Financial Statement Analysis*, 2nd ed., Prentice-Hall, Englewood Cliffs, N.J., 1986.

**table 27.12**

Financial ratios for Brambles Industries Ltd and companies in the transport industry

| Ratio | Brambles Industries Ltd | | Qantas Ltd | Toll Holdings Ltd | Finemore Holdings Ltd | Average ratio[a] | Weighted average ratio[b] |
|---|---|---|---|---|---|---|---|
| | 1997 | 1998 | 1998 | 1998 | 1998 | 1998 | 1998 |
| **Leverage** | | | | | | | |
| Debt ratio (%) | 38.41 | 43.46 | 41.61 | 27.93 | 18.92 | 32.98 | 42.47 |
| Times interest earned (times) | 8.81 | 7.79 | 2.88 | 4.08 | 7.43 | 5.55 | 6.04 |
| Equity ratio (%) | 46.65 | 42.76 | 28.60 | 32.08 | 47.00 | 37.61 | 37.74 |
| **Liquidity** | | | | | | | |
| Current ratio (%) | 1.11 | 1.17 | 1.07 | 1.01 | 0.66 | 0.98 | 1.13 |
| **Activity** | | | | | | | |
| Asset turnover (times) | 1.12 | 1.13 | 0.80 | 3.47 | 1.89 | 1.82 | 1.06 |
| **Profitability** | | | | | | | |
| Net profit margin (%) | 7.13 | 7.08 | 3.75 | 1.72 | 2.98 | 3.88 | 5.83 |
| Return on assets (%) | 7.97 | 8.01 | 3.02 | 5.99 | 5.63 | 5.66 | 6.25 |
| Payout ratio (%) | 64.88 | 58.34 | 51.87 | 47.86 | 58.58 | 54.16 | 55.95 |
| **Market** | | | | | | | |
| Number of shares (million) | 222.447 | 224.417 | 1177.33 | 44.73 | 39.79 | | |
| Share price (June 30) ($) | 26.191 | 31.69 | 2.43 | 2.19 | 2.07 | | |
| EPS (before abnormals) (cents) | 109.7 | 126.9 | 26.8 | 28.3 | 21.5 | | |
| EPS (after abnormals) (cents) | 109.7 | 127.3 | 26.8 | 30.6 | 22.5 | | |
| Price-earnings ratio (after abnormals) (%) | 23.88 | 24.89 | 10.45 | 7.16 | 9.20 | 12.93 | 19.56 |

Note: [a] Equally weighted for each company.

[b] Weighting based on approximate participation in transport index—Brambles (63.50%), Qantas (34.50%), Toll Holdings (1.50%) and Finemores (0.50%).

# A cautionary tale

Financial ratios provide information for a wide range of users including management, both existing and potential creditors and debtors, employees, customers, investors, government and regulators. While this information is contingent on the accounting numbers reported in financial statements, the financial ratios should be interpreted in such a way as to take account of the accounting methods employed and the possibility of timing and window-dressing in financial statements. Furthermore, while ratio analysis helps to eliminate size differences across

**table 27.13**

Average financial ratios for several industry groups, 1994[a]

| | Gold | Building materials | Food and household | Chemicals | Engineering | Retail | Transport | Diversified industrial | Tourism and leisure | Resources | Industrials | All companies |
|---|---|---|---|---|---|---|---|---|---|---|---|---|
| EBIT/total assets (%) | 10.97 | 7.3 | 9.08 | 12.5 | 9.64 | −7.24 | 3.79 | 9.68 | 7.67 | 8.43 | 7.76[b] | 7.97[b] |
| EBIT/sales (%) | 23.59 | 7.92 | 8.86 | 9.82 | 7.51 | 3.46 | 3.5 | 9.999 | 15.16 | 16.29 | 8.56[b] | 10.26[b] |
| Effective tax rate (%) | 22.36 | 32.78 | 26.23 | 31.72 | 28.73 | 42.54 | 195.96 | 33.66 | 29.34 | 29.58 | 26.09[b] | 27.4[b] |
| Days shares held (days) | 54.44 | 39.82 | 44.41 | 68.16 | 65.69 | 47.16 | 5.48 | 62.95 | 4.66 | 51.55 | 44.45[b] | 46.01[b] |
| Days receivables outstanding (days) | 26.06 | 51.78 | 38.72 | 40.91 | 59.61 | 8.21 | 49.09 | 48.08 | 23.98 | 34.52 | 39.78[b] | 38.63[b] |
| Debt/equity (%) | 32.53 | 58.34 | 92.49 | 25.18 | 56.31 | 92.47 | 76.67 | 68.95 | 32.93 | 50.68 | 71.11 | 64.07 |
| Interest cover (times) | 15.51 | 3.86 | 3.14 | 7.54 | 5.58 | 2.68 | 1.47 | 5.00 | 6.16 | 5.36 | 3.24[b] | 3.74[b] |
| Current ratio (times) | 1.54 | 1.48 | 1.32 | 1.22 | 1.86 | 1.70 | 1.21 | 1.23 | 0.80 | 1.46 | 1.35[b] | 1.38[b] |

*Note:* (a) *Banks, insurance and property trusts excluded.*
(b) *These figures exclude banks and other financial institutions.*

*Source:* 1995 Stock Exchange Financial and Profitability Study.

firms and over time it ignores the existence of fixed costs and suggests that the relationship between numerator and denominator is proportional and linear. Negative accounting numbers when used in ratios produce positive ratios, which can be misleading. Hence, the ratios should only be considered after first analysing the 'raw' accounting numbers. Time series factors, discussed below, also need to be considered.

# What role for earnings?

Earnings reflect the capacity of the firm to produce income from the firm's available assets using both debt and equity. Any growth in earnings will reflect not only the performance of the firm itself, but also industry-wide, economy-wide and global influences. The importance of these external influences on a company's income is shown in Table 27.14. On average, an estimated 17 per cent of the yearly variation in income is due to changes in the aggregate income of all corporations. A further 26 per cent is explained by changes in the industry's income.

table 27.14 _____

Percentage of changes in net income due to economy-wide and industry-wide influences (measured for 315 firms, 1964–83)

| | Economy-wide influences (%) | Industry-wide influences (%) |
|---|:---:|:---:|
| Crude petroleum and natural gas | 14 | 23 |
| Paper and allied products | 49 | 12 |
| Drugs | 14 | 26 |
| Petroleum refining | 37 | 23 |
| Steel and blast furnaces | 35 | 23 |
| General industrial machinery | 23 | 21 |
| Radio and TV transmitting equipment | 14 | 15 |
| Electronic components | 32 | 12 |
| Trucking | 21 | 27 |
| Air transportation | 12 | 13 |
| Electric services | 8 | 39 |
| Natural gas distribution | 13 | 8 |
| Electric and other services combinations | 6 | 45 |
| Retail/grocery stores | 9 | 17 |
| State banks, Federal Reserve System | 5 | 25 |
| Average | 17 | 26 |

*Source*: Foster, op. cit., Footnote 39.

Does growth in earnings bode well for the future? Not necessarily. Statisticians who have studied the time path of firms' reported earnings conclude that earnings behave much like share prices—that is, they follow a random walk.[40] There is very little relationship between a

_____

[40]  See, for example, R. Ball and R. Watts, 'Some Time Series Properties of Accounting Income', *Journal of Finance*, **27**: 663–82 (June 1972).

company's earnings growth in one period and that in the next. Therefore, do not extrapolate growth mechanically. A firm with above-average earnings growth might sustain it, but such growth is equally likely to be followed by below-average growth.[41]

Since earnings changes are unrelated from one year to the next, your best measure of past growth is the simple average of past annual percentage growth rates. There is little point in fitting a trend line to past earnings, and such a trend line tells you little about likely future earnings.

Of course, there are many sources of information that may help you forecast earnings. For example, when a firm enjoys a high P/E ratio despite disappointing earnings, this suggests that investors expect an earnings rebound. Or suppose a firm announces a significant technological jump ahead of its competitors; you do not need a PhD to figure out the likely impact on earnings.

## The meaning of accounting earnings

In Chapter 12 we discussed the distinction between economic earnings and accounting earnings. Economists often define *earnings* as cash flow plus the change in value of the company's assets. But we know from the behaviour of share prices that changes in asset values are fundamentally unpredictable and very volatile. A company's published earnings follow a much smoother path than economic earnings.

Accountants do not really try to track year-to-year economic earnings and accounting earnings. They seem to be more interested in showing the long-run average profitability of the firm's assets. For example, they do not try to record actual yearly changes in the value of the firm's plant and equipment. Instead, they set up a depreciation schedule ahead of time and, except in abnormal circumstances, they stick to it. Thus, the company's income statement reflects partly what actually happened (the operating cash flow) and partly what was forecasted to happen (the depreciation in asset value).

## How inflation affects book returns

We will steer clear of 'inflation accounting' because the subject is so complex when one gets down to practical proposals. We will simply remind you of how inflation bears on standard book earnings.

First, inflation increases the nominal value of work in process and finished inventory. Suppose you are a clothing manufacturer. In January, you make up 1000 men's suits worth $300 a piece, but you do not sell the suits until June. During this time your competitors have raised their prices by 6 per cent, and you have quite literally followed suit. Thus, the goods are finally sold for $300 \times 1.06 = \$318$. Part of your profit on this batch of suits can be attributed to inflation while the suits sat in inventory. You receive an *inventory profit* of $18 per suit.

Inventory profits are indeed profits. You are better off with them than without. They are properly included in nominal income. However, they are not part of real income, except to the extent that the inventories appreciate faster than the general price level.

There is a second problem. As inflation progresses, the net book value of fixed assets becomes more and more out of date—that is, book value understates current value or replacement cost. Reported income is also affected in two ways. First, income is overstated because depreciation is understated. Second, nominal income is understated because appreciation of asset value due to inflation is ignored. (A calculation of real, that is, inflation-adjusted, economic income would not include the second effect.)

---

[41] In fact, it is slightly *more* likely to be followed by below-average growth. This is particularly true when there has been a sharp jump in earnings. See, for example, L. D. Brooks and D. A. Buckmaster, 'First-Difference Signals and Accounting Income Time-Series Properties', *Journal of Business Finance and Accounting*, 7: 437–54 (Autumn 1980).

Inflation has a third effect on the book profits of firms that borrow. Lenders are paid back in inflated future dollars, so they demand a higher interest rate to compensate for the declining real value of their loan. The part of the interest rate that compensates for expected inflation is called the *inflation premium*. The full interest payment, including the inflation premium, is deducted from the firm's net book income. But book income does not recognise the compensating gain that the shareholders make at the expense of lenders. Remember, lenders gain from the inflation premium but lose as inflation drives down the real value of their asset. Shareholders lose by paying the inflation premium but gain because inflation drives down the real value of their obligation. Book income recognises shareholders' loss but not the offsetting gain.[42]

## 27.3 Applications of financial analysis

We have discussed how to calculate and interpret summary measures of a company's financial position. We conclude this chapter with a glimpse at some of the ways that these measures can help the financial manager.

Suppose that you are a credit analyst or bank lending officer with the job of deciding whether a particular company is likely to repay its debt. What can you learn from the company's financial statements?

To answer this question, William Beaver compared the financial ratios of 79 firms that subsequently failed with the ratios of 79 that remained solvent.[43] Beaver's sample failed firms behaved much as you would expect. They had more debt than the surviving firms, and they had a lower return on sales and assets. They had less cash but more receivables. As a result, they had somewhat lower current ratios and dramatically lower cash ratios. Contrary to popular belief, the failed firms had less, rather than more, inventory.

Figure 27.1 provides some idea of the predictive power of these financial ratios. You can see that five years before failure, the group of failed firms appeared to be consistently less healthy. As we move progressively closer to the date of collapse, the difference between the two groups becomes even more marked.

Instead of looking at a number of separate clues, it may be more useful to combine the different bits of information into a single measure of the likelihood of bankruptcy. We will describe in Chapter 30 how companies construct such a measure.

## Using financial ratios to estimate market risk

Chapter 9 describes how the return that investors require from a company's shares depends on its market risk, or beta. If you have sufficient history of share price data, you can estimate beta by looking at the extent to which the price was affected by fluctuations in the market. But share price data are not always available, so economists have examined whether accounting data can be used to estimate beta. For example, we know that as the firm issues more debt, the market risk of the equity increases. So, it is no surprise that there is a strong relationship between a firm's debt ratio and its equity beta.

In addition to looking at these standard ratios, financial managers sometimes calculate an 'accounting beta'. In other words, they estimate the sensitivity of each company's earnings' changes to changes in the aggregate earnings of all companies. An accounting beta of less than 1.0 means that on average the company's earnings changed by less than 1 per cent for each 1 per cent change in aggregate earnings. Conversely, an accounting beta of more than 1.0 implies

---

42  For a provocative discussion on inflationary biases in book income see F. Modigliani and R. A. Cohn, 'Inflation, Rational Valuation and the Market', *Financial Analysts Journal*, 35: 24–44 (March–April 1979).

43  See W. H. Beaver, 'Financial Ratios and Predictors of Failure', *Empirical Research in Accounting: Selected Studies*, supplement to *Journal of Accounting Research*, pp. 77–111 (1966). Several later studies have come up with similar (but pictorially less eye-catching) findings. For a review of these studies see Foster, op. cit., Footnote 39.

**figure 27.1** _____

Beaver's study showed that the financial ratios of firms that subsequently fail are different from those of firms that survive. Note that the horizontal axis measures the number of years *before* failure; thus moving from right to left brings the failed firms *closer* to failure.

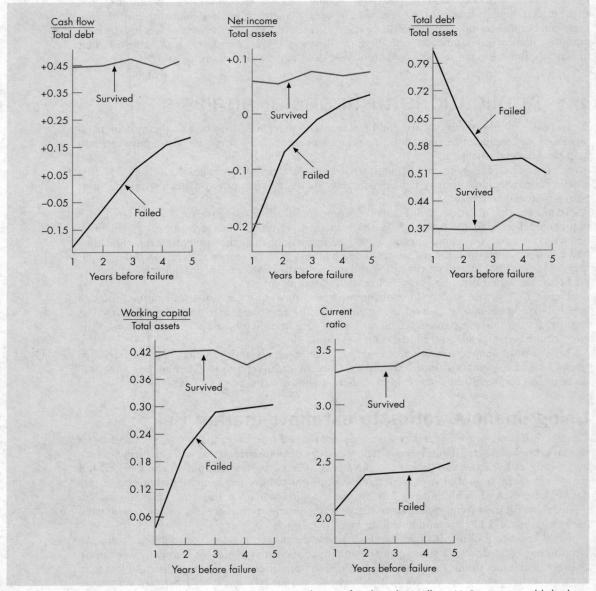

*Source:* Figure 1 (Profile Analysis) of 'Financial Ratios as Predictors of Failure' by William H. Beaver as published in the *Journal of Accounting Research* supplement 1996, Empirical Research in Accounting, Selected Studies, page 82.

that the firm's earnings changed by more than 1 per cent for each 1 per cent change in aggregate earnings.

Instead of looking at these measures one by one, it makes sense to combine them into a single measure of risk. Hochman found that the debt ratio, dividend yield and accounting beta could together provide about as good a prediction of a share's beta as an estimate based on past share price data.[44]

# Using financial ratios to predict bond ratings

Moody's bond ratings are widely used as a yardstick of bond quality. Therefore, they indicate which investors are likely to buy your company's bonds and what interest rate they will require. Financial managers pay considerable attention to their company's bond ratings and would like to know in advance how a new issue of bonds would be rated or how a change in circumstances would affect the ratings on existing debt.

Financial ratios can help to predict bond ratings. For example, one study found that issuers of the more highly rated bonds generally had lower debt ratios, a higher ratio of earnings to interest, a higher return on assets and a long history of dividend payments.[45] The bond issues were also more likely to be senior and to be large in value. The study also combined these variables into a single measure of bond quality and looked at how well it could forecast Moody's ratings for a sample of newly issued bonds in 1984.

Table 27.15 shows that the forecast was spot on almost 60 per cent of the time and was out by more than one category on only four occasions.

**table 27.15**

Moody's bond ratings for a sample of new issues were similar to the predicted ratings (e.g. a total of 31 bonds were predicted to have A ratings, and of these, 18 actually received an A rating).

| Actual ratings | Predicted ratings | | | | | |
| --- | --- | --- | --- | --- | --- | --- |
| | Aa | A | Baa | Ba | B | Total |
| Aa | 7 | 8 | | | | 15 |
| A | 4 | 18 | 2 | | 1 | 25 |
| Baa | | 4 | 4 | | | 8 |
| Ba | | 1 | 2 | 1 | 1 | 5 |
| B | | | 2 | 1 | 5 | 8 |
| Total | 11 | 31 | 10 | 2 | 7 | 61 |

*Source*: J. A. Gentry, D. T Whitford and P. Newbold, 'Predicting Industrial Bond Ratings with a Profit Model and Fund Flow Components', *Financial Review*, **23**: 269–86 (August 1988).

Of course, lenders also are interested in bond quality; they do not want to lend to a triple-A borrower only to find a few years later that they now own a junk bond. That is why lenders will often specify key financial ratios that the borrower must maintain. For example, firms are often obliged to observe a maximum debt ratio or a minimum current ratio. We discussed these restrictions in Chapter 24.

---

44  S. Hochman, 'The Beta Coefficient: An Instrumental Variables Approach', *Research in Finance*, Vol. 4, JAI Press, Greenwich, Conn., 1983. The pioneering study in the use of accounting data to measure risk was W. H. Beaver, P. Kettler and M. Scholes, 'The Association Between Market-Determined and Accounting-Determined Risk Measures', *Accounting Review*, 45: 654–82 (October 1970).

45  J. A. Gentry, D. T. Whitford and P. Newbold, 'Predicting Industrial Bond Ratings with a Profit Mode and Fund Flow Components', *Financial Review*, 23: 269–86 (August 1988).

## 27.4 Summary

If you are analysing a company's financial statements, there is a danger of being overwhelmed by the sheer volume of data. That is why managers use a few salient ratios and summarise the firm's leverage, liquidity, activity, profitability and market value. We have described some of the more popular financial ratios.

We offer the following general advice to users of these ratios:

- Financial ratios seldom provide answers, but they do help you ask the right questions.
- There is no international standard for financial ratios. A little thought and common sense are worth far more than blind application of formulas.
- Be selective in your choice of ratios. Different ratios often tell you similar things.
- You need a benchmark for assessing a company's financial position. Compare financial ratios with the company's ratios in earlier years and with the ratios of other firms in the same business.
- Be careful not to extrapolate past rates of earnings growth—earnings follow approximately a random walk.
- Accounting earnings do not incorporate the year-by-year fluctuations in the true values of the company's assets. Instead, accountants try to provide a picture of long-run sustainable earnings.

Financial statement analysis helps you understand what makes the firm tick. We looked briefly at three particular applications. First, healthy firms have different financial ratios than firms that are heading for insolvency. Second, financial ratios provide valuable clues about a firm's market risk. Finally, we saw that a company's financial ratios can be used to predict the rating on a new issue of bonds.

### FURTHER READING

There are some good general texts on financial statements analysis. See, for example:

G. Foster, *Financial Statement Analysis*, 2nd ed., Prentice-Hall, Englewood Cliffs, N.J., 1986.

Fischer Black's provocative paper argues that the true object of accounting rules is to produce earnings proportional to value, not changes in value:

F. Black, 'The Magic in Earnings: Economic Earnings Versus Accounting Earnings', *Financial Analysts Journal*, 36: 3–8 (November–December 1980).

Three classic articles on the application of financial ratios to specific problems are:

W. H. Beaver, 'Financial Ratios and Predictors of Failure', *Empirical Research in Accounting: Selected Studies*, supplement to *Journal of Accounting Research*, pp. 77–111 (1966).

W. H. Beaver, P. Kettler and M. Scholes, 'The Association Between Market-Determined and Accounting-Determined Risk Measures', *Accounting Review*, 45: 654–82 (October 1970).

J. O. Horrigan, 'The Determination of Long Term Credit Standing with Financial Ratios', *Empirical Research in Accounting: Selected Studies*, supplement to *Journal of Accounting Research*, pp. 44–62 (1966).

### QUIZ

1. Table 27.16 gives abbreviated sheets and income statements for Georgia-Pacific Ltd. Calculate the following financial ratios:
   a. Debt ratio
   b. Times interest earned
   c. Current ratios

    d.  Quick ratio
    e.  Net profit margin
    f.  Inventory turnover
    g.  Return on equity
    h.  Payout ratio

**table 27.16**

Income statement and balance sheet for Georgia-Pacific Ltd, 1994 ($million)

| Income statement | |
|---|---|
| Net sales | $12 738 |
| Cost of goods sold | 9 881 |
| Other expenses | 1 086 |
| Depreciation | 746 |
| Earnings before interest and tax (EBIT) | 1 025 |
| Net interest | 453 |
| Tax | 246 |
| Earnings | 326 |
| Dividends | 145 |

| Balance sheet | | |
|---|---|---|
| | **End of year** | **Start of year** |
| Cash and short-term securities | $53 | $41 |
| Receivables | 566 | 377 |
| Inventories | 1 209 | 1 202 |
| Other current assets | 34 | 26 |
| Total current assets | 1 862 | 1 646 |
| Timberland, plant and equipment | 6 851 | 6 829 |
| Other long-term assets | 2 015 | 2 070 |
| Total assets | $10 728 | $10 545 |
| | | |
| Short-term debt | $11 117 | $880 |
| Payables | 603 | 582 |
| Other current liabilities | 605 | 602 |
| Total current liabilities | 2 325 | 2 064 |
| Long-term debt and capital leases | 3 904 | 4 157 |
| Other long-term liabilities | 1 879 | 1 922 |
| Ordinary shareholders' equity | 2 620 | 2 402 |
| Total liabilities | $10 728 | $10 545 |

*Source*: Georgia-Pacific Ltd Annual Report 1994.

**2.** There are no universally accepted definitions of financial ratios, but five of the following ratios make no sense at all. Substitute the correct definitions.

a. Return on equity $= \dfrac{\text{EBIT} - \text{tax}}{\text{average equity}}$

b. Profit margin $= \dfrac{\text{dividend}}{\text{share price}}$

c. Profit margin $= \dfrac{\text{EBIT} - \text{tax}}{\text{sales}}$

d. Inventory turnover $= \dfrac{\text{sales}}{\text{average inventory}}$

e. Current ratio $= \dfrac{\text{current liabilities}}{\text{current assets}}$

f. Sales to net working capital $= \dfrac{\text{average sales}}{\text{net working capital}}$

g. Interval measure $= \dfrac{\text{current assets} - \text{inventories}}{\text{average daily expenditure from operations}}$

h. Average collection period $= \dfrac{\text{sales}}{\text{average receivables}/365}$

i. Quick ratio $= \dfrac{\text{current assets} - \text{inventories}}{\text{current liabilities}}$

j. Tobin's $q = \dfrac{\text{market value of assets}}{\text{replacement cost of assets}}$

**3.** True or false?
a. A company's debt-equity ratio is always less than 1.
b. The quick ratio is always less than the current ratio.
c. The return on equity is always less than the return on assets.
d. Successive earnings levels are unrelated to each other.
e. Successive earnings changes are unrelated to each other.
f. Earnings follow roughly a random walk. This means that if earnings turn out to be higher than expected, you should revise upwards your forecast of future earnings by a similar proportion.
g. Accounting earnings follow a less smooth path than economic earnings.
h. If a project is slow to reach full profitability, straight-line depreciation is likely to produce an overstatement of profits in the early years.
i. A substantial new advertising campaign by a cosmetics company will tend to depress earnings and cause the shares to sell at a low price-earnings multiple.

**4.** In each of the following cases, explain briefly which of the two companies is likely to be characterised by the higher ratio:
a. Debt-equity ratio: a shipping company or a computer software company.
b. Payout ratio: United Foods Inc or Computer Graphics Inc.

c. Ratio of sales to assets: an integrated pulp and paper manufacturer or a paper mill.
d. Average collection period: a supermarket chain or a mail-order company.
e. Price-earnings multiple: Basic Sludge Company or Fledgling Electronics.
f. Tobin's $q$: an iron foundry or a pharmaceutical company with strong patent protection.

**5.** A firm has $30 000 of inventories. If this represents 30 days sales, what is the annual cost of goods sold? What is the inventory turnover ratio?

**6.** Keller Cosmetics Ltd maintains a profit margin of 4 per cent and a sales-to-assets ratio of 3.
a. What is its return on assets?
b. If its debt-equity ratio is 1.0, its interest payments and taxes are each $10 000, and EBIT is $40 000, what is the return on equity?

**7.** A firm has a long-term debt-equity ratio of 0.4. Shareholders' equity is $1 million. Current assets are $200 000, and the current ratio is 2.0. Long-term assets total $1.5 million. What is the ratio of debt to total capitalisation?

**8.** Magic Flutes has total receivables of $3000, which represents 20 days sales. Average total assets are $75 000. The firm's profit margin is 5 per cent. Find the firm's return on assets and sales-to-assets ratio.

**9.** Consider this simplified balance sheet for Geomorph Trading Ltd:

| | | | |
|---|---|---|---|
| Current assets | 100 | 60 | Current liabilities |
| | | 280 | Long-term debt |
| Long-term assets | 500 | 70 | Other liabilities |
| | | 190 | Equity |
| | 600 | 600 | |

a. Calculate the ratio of debt to equity.
b. What are Geomorph's net working capital and total capitalisation?
c. Calculate the ratio of debt to total capitalisation.

**10.** Airlux Antarctica Ltd has current liabilities of $200 million and a crash—sorry, *cash*—ratio of 0.05. How much cash and marketable securities does it hold?

**11.** On average, it takes Microlimp Ltd's customers 60 days to pay their bills. If Microlimp Ltd has annual sales of $500 million, what is the average value of unpaid bills?

**12.** This question reviews some of the difficulties encountered in interpreting accounting numbers.
a. Give four examples of important assets, liabilities or transactions that may not be shown on the company's books.
b. How does investment in intangible assets, such as research and development, distort accounting ratios? Give at least two examples.
*c. Explain the three ways in which accelerating inflation affects earnings and profitability ratios based on historical-cost accounting.

## QUESTIONS AND PROBLEMS

**1.** Discuss alternative measures of financial leverage. Should the market value of equity be used or the book value? Is it better to use the market value of debt, the book value or the book value discounted at the risk-free interest rate?

How should you treat off-balance-sheet obligations such as pension liabilities? How would you treat preferred shares, deferred tax reserves and minority interests?

**2.** As you can see, someone has spilt ink over some of the entries in the balance sheet and income statement of Kimberley's Railways Ltd in Western Australia (Table 27.17). Can you use the following information to work out the missing entries?

- Financial leverage: 0.4
- Times interest earned: 8

**table 27.17**
Balance sheet and income statement of Kimberley's Railways Ltd ($million)

| Balance sheet | | |
|---|---|---|
| | **December 1996** | **December 1995** |
| Cash | ▢▢▢ | 30 |
| Accounts receivable | ▢▢▢ | 34 |
| Inventory | ▢▢▢ | 26 |
| Total current assets | ▢▢▢ | 80 |
| Fixed assets, net | ▢▢▢ | 25 |
| Total | ▢▢▢ | 105 |
| Notes payable | 30 | 35 |
| Accounts payable | 25 | 20 |
| Total current liabilities | ▢▢▢ | 55 |
| Long-term debt | ▢▢▢ | 20 |
| Equity | ▢▢▢ | 30 |
| Total | 115 | 105 |
| **Income statement** | | |
| Sales | ▢▢▢ | |
| Costs of goods sold | ▢▢▢ | |
| Selling, general and administrative expenses | 10 | |
| Depreciation | 20 | |
| EBIT | ▢▢▢ | |
| Interest | ▢▢▢ | |
| Earnings before tax | ▢▢▢ | |
| Earnings available for ordinary shareholders | ▢▢▢ | |

- ▮ Current ratio:                           1.4
- ▮ Quick ratio:                             1.0
- ▮ Cash ratio:                              0.2
- ▮ Return on total assets:                  0.18
- ▮ Return on equity:                        0.41
- ▮ Inventory turnover:                      5.0
- ▮ Receivables' collection period:          71.2 days

**3.** Use financial ratio analysis to compare two companies chosen from the same industry.

**4.** Read and discuss Fischer Black's paper 'The Magic in Earnings' (see Further Reading list).

**5.** Describe some of the ways that the choice of accounting technique can temporarily depress or inflate earnings.

**6.** Suppose that at year-end 1998 Brambles Industries Ltd had unused lines of credit that would have allowed it to borrow a further $300 million. Suppose also that it used this line of credit to raise short-term loans of $300 million and invested the proceeds in marketable securities. Would the company have appeared to be:
   a. more or less liquid?
   b. more or less highly levered?
   Calculate the appropriate ratios.

**7.** Recalculate Brambles Industries Ltd's financial ratios at the end of 1999. What problems arise in ensuring figures comparable with those of 1998?

|                                    | Company code |       |       |     |       |
|------------------------------------|:------------:|:-----:|:-----:|:---:|:-----:|
|                                    | A            | B     | C     | D   | E     |
| Net income ($million)              | 10           | 0.5   | 6.67  | −1  | 6.67  |
| Total book assets ($million)       | 300          | 30    | 120   | 50  | 120   |
| Shares outstanding ($million)      | 3            | 4     | 2     | 4   | 10    |
| Share price ($)                    | 100          | 5     | 50    | 8   | 10    |

**8.** You have been asked to calculate a measure of the industry price-earnings ratio. Discuss the possible ways that you might calculate such a measure. Does changing the method of calculation make a significant difference in the end result?

**9.** a. 'When calculating times interest earned, we average earnings over the past five years. This gives a better measure of the company's typical earnings.'
   b. 'For simplicity we just divide current earnings by interest payments.'
   c. 'We also fit a trend line to earnings and then measure times interest earned using the current trend value.'
   d. 'We also fit a trend line to earnings and then use that trend to forecast earnings. We then measure times interest earned using forecasted earnings. After all, it is the future, not the past, that any credit analyst is concerned with.'
   What assumption is each of these speakers making? If you wish to measure the credit worthiness of a business, what would be the best way to compute times

interest earned? (Perhaps there are alternatives that none of the speakers has considered?)

**10.** Suppose you wish to use financial ratios to estimate the risk of a company's shares. Which of those that we have described in this chapter are likely to be helpful? Can you think of other accounting measures of risk?

**11.** In 1970 United Airlines bought four new jumbos for $21.8 million each. These aeroplanes were written down straight-line over 16 years to a residual value of $0.2 million each.[46] How would the company's financial ratios have changed if it had used a depreciation schedule that more clearly reflected the actual decline in aircraft values?

**12.** The British food company Ranks Hovis McDougall (RHM) believes that some of its most valuable assets are its brand names. Yet these assets have usually not been shown on the balance sheet. In 1988 RHM changed its accounting policy to include the value of brand names and thereby added £678 million (about $1.3 billion) to the balance sheet.[47] Do you think this change would facilitate comparisons between firms?

**13.** Sara Togas sells all its output to Cleopatra Stores. The following table shows selected financial data, in millions, for the two firms:

|  | Sales | Profits | Assets |
|---|---|---|---|
| Cleopatra Stores | $100 | $10 | $50 |
| Sara Togas | 20 | 4 | 20 |

Calculate the sales-to-assets ratio, the profit margin and the return on assets for the two firms. Now assume that the two companies merge. If Cleopatra continues to sell goods worth $100 million, how will the three financial ratios change?

**14.** Take another look at Geomorph Trading's balance sheet in Quiz Question 9, and consider the following additional information:

| Current assets | | Current liabilities | | Other liabilities | |
|---|---|---|---|---|---|
| Cash | 15 | Payables | 35 | Deferred tax | 32 |
| Inventories | 35 | Taxes due | 10 | Unfunded pensions | 22 |
| Receivables | 50 | Bank loan | 15 | R&R reserve | 16 |
|  | 100 |  | 60 |  | 70 |

The 'R&R reserve' covers the future costs of removal of an oil pipeline and environmental restoration of the pipeline route.

---

46  See M. D. Staunton, Pricing of Airline Assets and Their Valuation by Securities Markets, unpublished PhD dissertation, London Business School, 1992.

47  RHM reasoned that the omission of these assets could lead investors to undervalue the firm and could attract predators.

There are many ways to calculate a debt ratio for Geomorph. Suppose you are evaluating the safety of Geomorph's debt and want a debt ratio for comparison with the ratios of other companies in the same industry. Would you calculate the ratios in terms of total liabilities or total capitalisation? What would you include in debt——the bank loan, the deferred tax account, the R&R reserve, the unfunded pension liability? Explain the pros and cons of these choices.

**15.** How would rapid inflation affect the accuracy and relevance of a manufacturing company's balance sheet and income statement? Does your answer depend on how much debt the company has issued?

**16.** United Rations ordinary shares have a dividend yield of 4 per cent. Its dividend per share is $2, and it has 10 million shares outstanding. If the market-to-book ratio is 1.5, what is the total book value of the equity?

**17.** Look up some firms that have been in trouble. Plot the changes over the preceding years in the principal financial ratios. Are there any problems?

# chapter 28

# APPROACHES TO CORPORATE FINANCIAL PLANNING

If a firm made all its financial decisions in a piecemeal manner, the result would probably spell disaster for the future profitability and performance of the firm. Effective financial managers consider the overall effect of financing and investment decisions. Corporate financial planning is necessary because investment and financing decisions interact and should not be made independently. This process of considering the impact of these joint decisions is called corporate financial planning, and the end result is a financial plan.

Planning also helps financial managers avoid surprises and think ahead about how they should react to surprises that *cannot* be avoided. In Chapter 10 we stressed that financial managers are unwilling to treat capital investment proposals as 'black boxes'. They insist on understanding what makes projects work and what could go wrong with them. They attempt to trace out the possible impact of today's decisions on tomorrow's opportunities. The same approach is, or should be, taken when financing and investment decisions are considered in the aggregate. Without financial planning, the firm itself becomes a black box.

Finally, financial planning helps establish concrete goals to motivate managers and provide standards for measuring performance.

Planning should never be the exclusive preserve of the planners. Unless management is widely involved in the process, it will lack faith in the output. Also, financial plans should be tied in closely to the firm's business plans. A series of financial forecasts has little operational value unless management has thought about the production and marketing decisions which are needed to make those forecasts come about.

Financial planning is not easy to write about—it is the sort of topic that attracts empty generalities or ponderous detail. A full, formal treatment is beyond the scope of this book and probably beyond the capability of its authors. But there are a few specific helpful points we can make. First, we will summarise what corporate financial planning involves. Then we will describe the contents of a typical completed financial plan. Finally, we will discuss the use of *financial models* in the planning process.

## 28.1 What is corporate financial planning?

Corporate financial planning is a *process* of:

1. Analysing the financing and investment choices open to the firm.
2. Projecting the future consequences of present decisions, in order to avoid surprises and understand the link between present and future decisions.
3. Deciding which alternatives to undertake. (These decisions are embodied in the final financial plan.)
4. Measuring subsequent performance against the goals set in the financial plan.

Of course, there are different kinds of planning. Short-term corporate financial planning is discussed in Chapter 29. In short-term planning the *planning horizon* is rarely longer than the next 12 months. The firm wants to make sure that it has enough cash to pay its bills and that short-term borrowing and lending are arranged to the best advantage.

Here we are more concerned with long-term planning, in which a typical horizon is five years, although some firms look ahead 10 years or more.[1] For example, it can take at least 10 years for an electric utility to design, obtain approval for, finance, build and test a major generating plant.

### Financial planning focuses on the big picture

Many of the firm's capital expenditures are proposed by plant managers. But the expenditure decisions must also reflect strategic plans made by senior management. These strategic plans attempt to identify the businesses in which the firm has a real competitive advantage and which should be expanded. They also seek to identify businesses to sell or liquidate as well as those that should be allowed to run down.

Strategic planning involves capital budgeting on a grand scale. Financial planners try to look at the aggregate investment by each line of business and avoid getting bogged down in details. Of course, some projects are large enough to have significant individual impact. For example, Ford committed US$6 billion to the development of its self-proclaimed 'world car', the Mondeo, and you can safely bet that this project was explicitly analysed as part of Ford's long-range financial plan.

Financial planners also need to consider the following:

▌ The corporate structure of the organisation.
▌ Any acquisition or divestment strategies.
▌ The financial effects of any changes in the firm's operation.
▌ Issues relating to foreign exchange and interest-rate exposure.
▌ The availability of alternative funding sources.
▌ The relationship of the business with financial institutions.

---

[1] The planning horizon for the management of oak forests in France is 200 years! Even for Australian conifer forests it is 30 years.

At the beginning of the planning process the corporate staff might ask each division to submit three alternative business plans covering the next five years:

1. A *best-case* or aggressive growth plan, calling for heavy capital investment and new products, increased share of existing markets or entry into new markets.
2. A *normal growth* plan, in which the division grows with its markets but not significantly at the expense of its competitors.
3. A plan of *retrenchment* and specialisation, designed to minimise required capital outlays. This is planning for lean economic times.

Of course, the planners might also look at the opportunities and costs of moving into a wholly new area where the company may be able to exploit its existing strengths. Often they may recommend entering a market for 'strategic' reasons—that is, not because the *immediate* investment has positive net present value, but because it establishes the firm in the market and creates *options* for possibly valuable follow-up investments. In other words, there is a two-stage decision. At the second stage (the follow-up project) the financial manager faces a standard capital budgeting problem. But at the first stage projects may be valuable primarily for the options they bring with them. A financial manager could value a first-stage project's 'strategic value' by using options pricing theory.[2]

Sometimes there are three or more stages. Think of the progress of a technological innovation from its inception in basic research to product development to pilot production and market testing and finally to full-scale commercial production. The decision to produce at commercial scale is a standard capital budgeting problem. The decision to proceed with pilot production and test marketing is like purchasing an option to produce at commercial scale. The commitment of funds to development is like purchasing an option for pilot production and test marketing: the firm acquires an option to purchase an option. The investment in research at the very first stage is like acquiring an option to purchase an option to purchase an option.

Here we will stick our necks out by predicting the increasing use of options pricing theory for formal analysis of these sequential investment decisions. Financial planning eventually will be thought of not as a search for a single investment plan but rather as the management of the portfolio of options held by the firm. This portfolio consists not of traded puts and calls but of *real* options (options to purchase real assets on possibly favourable terms) or options to purchase other real options.[3] Because the firm's long-term future is likely to depend on the options that it acquires today, we would expect planners to take a particular interest in these options.

Most plans contain a summary of planned financing. This part of the plan should logically include a discussion of dividend policy, because the more the firm pays out, the more capital it will need to find from sources other than retained earnings.

Growing firms will need to pay for investments in plant, equipment and working capital. A commitment to pay interest on debt may also absorb large amounts of cash. For example, in 1995 Eurotunnel needed to lay its hands on more than $3 million a day simply to pay debt interest. If cash flows from operations do not cover these outflows, the firm will have to raise additional funds.

Some firms need to worry much more than others about raising money. A firm with limited investment opportunities, ample operating cash flow and a moderate dividend payout accumulates considerable 'financial slack' in the form of liquid assets and unused borrowing power. Life is relatively easy for the managers of such firms, and their financing plans are routine. Whether that easy life is in the interests of their shareholders is another matter.

Other firms have to raise capital by selling securities. Naturally, they give careful attention to planning what kinds of securities are to be sold and when. Such firms may also find their

---

2   See Section 21.1.
3   The importance of real options to strategic decisions is emphasised in S. C. Myers, 'Finance Theory and Financial Strategy', *Interfaces*, **14**: 126–37 (January–February 1984).

financing plans complicated by covenants on their existing debt. For example, debt covenants can impact on the credit ratings attributed to firms—as noted by Emery and Finnerty,[4] limitations or covenants such as restrictions against the sale of assets and debt restrictions such as prohibiting firms from taking on more debt if interest cover drops below a pre-specified level can result in a lowering of borrowing costs, by protecting debtholders from wealth expropriation and by limiting management's bargaining power in debt negotiations.

## Financial planning is not just forecasting

Forecasting concentrates on the most likely future outcome. But financial planners are not concerned solely with forecasting. They need to worry about unlikely events as well as likely ones. If you think ahead about what could go wrong, then you might be able to build flexibility into the plan and react faster to trouble if it occurs. Also, financial planning does not attempt to *minimise* risk. Instead, it is a process of deciding which risks to take and which are necessary or not worth taking.

Companies have developed a number of ways of looking at these 'what if' questions. Some work through the consequences of the plan under the most likely set of circumstances and then use *sensitivity analysis* to vary the assumptions one at a time. For example, they might look at how badly the company would be hit if a policy of aggressive growth coincided with a recession. Other companies might look at the consequences of each business plan under several plausible scenarios.[5] For example, one scenario might envisage high interest rates leading to a slowdown in world economic growth and lower commodity prices. The second scenario might involve a buoyant domestic economy, high inflation and a weak currency.

## The contents of a completed financial plan

A completed financial plan for a large company is a substantial document. A smaller firm's plan would have the same elements but less detail and documentation. For the smallest, youngest businesses, the financial plan may be entirely in the financial manager's head. The basic elements of the plans will be similar, however, for firms of any size.

The plan will present pro-forma (i.e. forecasted) balance sheets, income or profit and loss statements, and statements describing sources and uses of cash or the statement of cash flows. Because these statements embody the firm's financial goals, they may not be strictly unbiased forecasts. The earnings figure in the plan may be somewhere between an honest forecast and the earnings that management *hopes* to achieve.

The plan will also describe planned capital expenditures, usually broken down by category (e.g. investments for replacement, expansion or new products for mandated expenditures such as pollution control equipment) and by division or line of business. There will be narrative description of why these amounts are needed for investment and of the business strategies to be used to reach these financial goals. The descriptions might cover areas such as research and development efforts, steps to improve productivity, design and marketing of new products, pricing strategy, and so on.

These written descriptions record the end result of discussions and negotiations between operating managers, corporate staff and top management. They ensure that everyone involved in implementing the plan understands what is to be done.[6]

---

4   See D. R. Emery and J. D. Finnerty, 'A Review of Recent Research Concerning Corporate Debt Provisions', *Financial Markets, Institutions and Instruments,* 1(5): 23–40 (1992).

5   For a description of the use of different planning scenarios in the Royal Dutch/Shell group see P. Wack, 'Scenarios: Uncharted Waters Ahead', *Harvard Business Review,* 63 (September–October 1985), and 'Scenarios: Shooting the Rapids', *Harvard Business Review,* 63 (November–December 1985).

6   Managers come up with better strategies when they are forced to present them formally and expose them to criticism. Haven't you often found that you did not *really* understand an issue until you were forced to explain it to someone else?

## 28.2 Three requirements for effective planning

The requirements for effective planning follow from the purposes of planning and the desired end result. Clearly the process of financial planning involves:

- Analysis of the current situation.
- Development of financial goals for the firm.
- Creation of a financial plan.
- Implementation of the plan.
- Evaluation and, if necessary, revision of the plan.

Thus, effective planning relies on three critical areas of analysis:

1. Identification of the current scenario and forecasting the future economic, financial and social change conditional on information available at the time of doing the analysis.
2. Finding the optimal financial plan.
3. Monitoring the financial plan as it unfolds.

### Current scenario analysis and forecasting

By developing an understanding of the current financial position of the firm it is possible to then consider a base against which different courses of action can be evaluated and the benefits or consequences of maintaining or changing the current situation can be assessed. Similarly, financial goals should be developed which are realistic and consistent with the current situation and future proposed developments.

The firm will never have perfectly accurate forecasts. If it did, there would be less need for planning. Still, the firm must do the best it can.

Forecasting should not be reduced to a mechanical exercise. For example, earnings follow roughly a random walk, so naïve extrapolation of past earnings growth will not work.

To supplement their judgement, forecasters rely on a variety of data sources and forecasting methods. For example, forecasts of the economic and industry environment may involve use of econometric models which take account of interactions between economic variables. Forecasts of demand will partly reflect these projections of the economic environment, but they might also be based on formal models that marketing specialists have developed for predicting buyer behaviour or on recent consumer surveys to which the firm has access.[7]

Because information and expertise may be inconveniently scattered throughout the firm, effective planning requires administrative procedures to ensure that this information is not passed by. Also, many planners reach outside for help. There is a thriving industry of firms that specialise in preparing macroeconomic and industry forecasts for use by companies.

Inconsistency of forecasts is a potential problem because planners draw on information from many sources. Forecasted sales may be the sum of separate forecasts made by managers of several business units. Left to their own devices, these managers may make different assumptions about inflation, growth of the national economy, availability of raw materials, and so on. Achieving consistency is particularly hard for vertically integrated firms, where the

---

[7]   For an interesting example of how forecasting is organised in one company see R. N. Dino, R. E. Riley and P. G. Yatrakis, 'The Role of Forecasting in Corporate Strategy: The Xerox Experience', *Journal of Forecasting*, **1**: 335–48 (October–December 1982).

raw material for one business unit is the output of another. For example, an oil company's refining division might plan to produce more petrol than the marketing division plans to sell. The oil company's planners would be expected to uncover this inconsistency and align the plans of the two divisions.

It is tempting to conduct planning in a vacuum and to ignore the fact that the firm's competitors are developing their own plans. For example, your ability to implement an aggressive growth plan and increase market share depends on what the competition is likely to do. In fact, we can generalise by rephrasing a recommendation from Chapter 11: *When you are presented with a set of corporate forecasts, do not accept them at face value. Probe behind the forecasts and try to identify the economic model on which they are based.*

## Finding the optimal financial plan

In the end the financial manager has to judge which plan is best. We would like to tell you exactly how to make this choice, but we cannot. There is no model or procedure that encompasses all the complexity and intangibles encountered in financial planning. As a matter of fact, there never will be one. This bold statement is based on our third law:

▌ *Axiom*: The supply of unsolved problems is infinite.
▌ *Axiom*: The number of unsolved problems that humans can hold in their minds is at any time limited to 10.
▌ *Law*: Therefore, in any field there will always be 10 unsolved problems which can be addressed but which have no formal solution.

You will note that the last chapter of this book discusses 10 unsolved problems in finance.

Financial planners have to face the unsolved issues and cope as best they can by judgement. Take dividend policy, for example. At the end of Chapter 16 we were unable to say for sure whether a generous dividend policy was a good or bad thing, though we were able to identify some of the issues that managers need to consider. Nevertheless, financial planners have to *decide* on the dividend policy.

You sometimes hear managers stating corporate goals in terms of accounting numbers. They might say, 'Our objective is to achieve an annual sales growth of 20 per cent', or 'We want a 25 per cent return on book equity and a profit margin of 10 per cent'. On the surface such objectives do not make sense. Shareholders want to be richer, not to have the satisfaction of a 10 per cent profit margin. Also, a goal that is stated in terms of accounting ratios is non-operational unless it is translated back into what the statement means for business decisions. For example, what does a 10 per cent profit margin imply—higher prices, lower costs, a move into new, high-margin products, or increased vertical integration?

So why do managers define objectives in this way? In part such goals may be a mutual exhortation to try harder, like singing the company song before work. But we suspect that managers are often using a code to communicate real concerns. For example, the goal to increase sales rapidly may reflect managers' beliefs that increased market share is needed to achieve scale economies, or a target profit margin may be a way of saying that the firm has been pursuing sales growth at the expense of margins.

The danger is that everyone may forget the code and the accounting targets may be seen as goals in themselves.

## Watching the financial plan unfold

Long-term plans have an annoying habit of falling out of date almost as soon as they are made. They are then left to gather dust. Of course, you can always restart the planning process from scratch, but it may help if you can think ahead of time about how to revise your forecasts in the light of unexpected events. For example, suppose that profits in the first six months turn out to be 10 per cent below forecast. Since profits follow roughly a random walk, they do not generally bounce back after a fall. Unless you know that there were some temporary influences at work, you should revise your profit forecasts for later years by reducing them 10 per cent.

We have mentioned that long-term plans are also used as a benchmark to judge subsequent performance. But performance appraisals have little value unless you also take into account the business background against which they were achieved. If you know how a downturn in the economy is likely to throw you off plan, then you have a standard against which to judge your performance during such a downturn.

## 28.3 Financial planning models

Financial planners often use a financial planning model to help them explore the consequences of alternative financial strategies. These models range from general purpose ones, not much more complicated than the illustration presented later in this section, to models containing literally hundreds of equations and interacting variables.

Most large firms have a financial model or have access to one. Sometimes they may use more than one—perhaps a detailed model integrating capital budgeting and operational planning, a simpler model focusing on the aggregate impacts of financial strategy and a special model for evaluating mergers.

The reason for the popularity of such models is a simple and practical one. They support the financial planning process by making it easier and cheaper to construct pro-forma financial statements. The models automate an important part of planning that used to be boring, time-consuming and labour-intensive.

Programming these financial planning models used to consume large amounts of computer time and high-priced talent. These days standard spreadsheet programs are regularly used to solve quite complex financial planning problems.

Table 28.1 shows the year-end 1997 financial statements for Big Banana Fruit & Vege Supplies from the central coast of New South Wales.

In 1997, earnings before interest and taxes (EBIT) was 10 per cent of sales revenue. Net earnings were $117 000 after payment of taxes and 9 per cent interest on $400 000 outstanding debt. The company paid out approximately 65 per cent of its earnings as dividends. Big Banana Fruit & Vege Supplies' operating cash flow was not sufficient to pay the dividend and also to provide the cash needed for investment and expand net working capital. Therefore, $59 000 of ordinary shares was issued. The firm ended the year with debt equal to 40 per cent of total capitalisation (i.e. debt and equity).

Now suppose that you are asked to prepare pro-forma statements for Big Banana Fruit & Vege Supplies for 1998. You are told to assume business as usual *except* that (1) sales and operating costs are expected to be up 30 per cent over 1997 and (2) ordinary shares are not to be issued again. You interpret 'business as usual' to mean that (3) interest rates will remain at 9 per cent, (4) the firm will stick to its traditional 65 per cent dividend payout and (5) net working capital and fixed assets will increase by 30 per cent to support the larger sales volume.

These assumptions lead to the pro-forma statements shown in Table 28.2. Note that projected net income is up by almost 24 per cent,[8] to $145 000, which is heartening. But a glance at the sources and uses of funds statement shows that $404 000 has to be raised for additional working capital and for replacement and expansion of fixed capital.[9]

---

8    The actual growth in net income is 23.93 per cent, from $117 000 to $145 000.

9    Big Banana Fruit & Vege Supplies' existing fixed capital is assumed to depreciate by $104 000 in 1998. Thus, it has to invest $104 000 simply to maintain the net book value of its fixed assets. Total investment is $104 000 plus the growth in net fixed assets required by the increased sales volume. Incidentally, we realise that requiring the net book value of fixed assets to grow in lockstep with sales volume is an arbitrary and probably unrealistic assumption. We adopt it only to keep things simple.

**table 28.1**

1997 financial statements for Big Banana Fruit & Vege Supplies (figures in $000)

| Income statement | |
|---|---:|
| Revenue (REV) | 2160 |
| Cost of goods sold (CGS) | 1944 |
| Earnings before interest and taxes | 216 |
| Interest (INT)[a] | 36 |
| Earnings before taxes | 180 |
| Tax at 35% (TAX) | 63 |
| Net income (NET) | 117 |

| Sources and uses of funds | |
|---|---:|
| Sources: | |
| Net income (NET) | 117 |
| Depreciation (DEP)[b] | 80 |
| Operating cash flow | 197 |
| Borrowing (ΔD) | 0 |
| Share issues (SI) | 59 |
| Total sources | 256 |
| Uses: | |
| Increase in net working capital (ΔNWC) | 41 |
| Investment (INV) | 139 |
| Dividends (DIV) | 76 |
| Total uses | 256 |

| Balance sheet | | | |
|---|---:|---:|---:|
| | **1997** | **1996** | **Change** |
| Assets: | | | |
| Net working capital (NWC)[c] | 201 | 160 | +41 |
| Fixed assets (FA) | 799 | 740 | +59[d] |
| Total assets | 1000 | 900 | +100 |
| Liabilities: | | | |
| Debt (D) | 400 | 400 | 0 |
| Equity (E) | 600 | 500 | +100[e] |
| Total liabilities | 1027 | 900 | +100 |

Notes:

[a] Interest is 9 per cent of the $400 000 in outstanding debt.

[b] Depreciation is a non-cash expense. Therefore, we add it back to net income to find operating cash flow.

[c] Net working capital is defined as current assets less current liabilities.

[d] The increase in the book value of fixed assets equals investment less depreciation. Change in FA = $\Delta FA$ = INV − DEP = 139 − 80 = 59.

[e] Book equity increases by retained earnings less dividends plus share issues. Change in E = $\Delta E$ = NET − DIV + SI = 117 − 76 + 59 = 100.

**table 28.2**

1998 Pro-forma financial statements for Big Banana Fruit & Vege Supplies (figures in $000)

| Income statement | |
|---|---|
| Revenue (REV) | 2808 |
| Cost of goods sold (CGS) | 2527 |
| Earnings before interest and taxes | 281 |
| Interest (INT) | 58 |
| Earnings before taxes | 223 |
| Tax at 35% (TAX) | 78 |
| Net income (NET) | 145 |

| Sources and uses of funds | |
|---|---|
| Sources: | |
| Net income (NET) | 145 |
| Depreciation (DEP) | 104 |
| Operating cash flow | 249 |
| Borrowing (ΔD) | 249 |
| Share issues (SI) | 0 |
| Total sources | 498 |
| Uses: | |
| Increase in net working capital (ΔNWC) | 60 |
| Investment (INV) | 344 |
| Dividends (DIV) | 94 |
| Total uses | 498 |

| Balance sheet | | | |
|---|---|---|---|
| | **1998** | **1997** | **Change** |
| Assets: | | | |
| Net working capital (NWC) | 261 | 201 | +60 |
| Fixed assets (FA) | 1039 | 799 | +240 |
| Total assets | 1300 | 1000 | +300 |
| Liabilities: | | | |
| Debt (D) | 649 | 400 | +249 |
| Book Equity (E) | 651 | 600 | +51 |
| Total liabilities | 1300 | 1000 | +300 |

*Assumptions:*

*CGS   Assumed to remain at 90 per cent of REV.*

*INT    9 per cent of debt (D). This assumes all new debt is taken out early in 1998 so that a full year's interest must be paid.*

*TAX   Tax rate remains at 35 per cent.*

*DEP   Remains at 10 per cent of FA. This assumes all new investment is made early in 1998 so that a full year's depreciation is taken.*

*ΔD     Balancing item. Big Banana Fruit & Vege Supplies must borrow $249 000 to cover planned expenditure.*

*continues*

SI         *Big Banana Fruit & Vege Supplies' management has decided not to issue shares in 1998, therefore SI = 0.*
ΔNWC       *Net working capital expands in proportion to the increase in REV (30 per cent increase).*
INV, FA    *Required fixed assets FA are assumed to expand in proportion to the growth in REV. Investment must therefore cover depreciation plus the increase in FA.*
DIV        *Payout stays at 65 per cent of NET.*
E          *The increase in equity retained earnings (NET − DIV) plus share issues (SI).*
           *NET − DIV + SI = 145 − 94 + 0 = 51*

Big Banana Fruit & Vege Supplies' decision against another share issue means that $249 000 has to be raised by additional borrowing. This results in an increase in the debt to equity ratio from 0.6667 to 0.9969 and a reduction in the interest coverage from 8.22 to 6.64 (earnings before interest and taxes divided by interest).

To produce Table 28.2, you forecasted sales, costs and the capital needed to generate the increased sales. Given the payout ratio, these forecasts determined the amount of external finance that the firm needs. Finally, the decision not to issue new equity ensured that the need for funds had to be satisfied by an issue of debt. Thus, debt was the *balancing item*. This did not have to be the case. For example, we could have limited the amount of external financing and asked how much Big Banana Fruit & Vege Supplies needed to retain in order to finance its growth plan. In this case, the dividend payment would have been the balancing item. Or we could have specified the amount of external financing and the dividend policy and then looked at how rapidly Big Banana Fruit & Vege Supplies could grow.

We have spared you the trouble of actually calculating the figures necessary for Table 28.2. The calculations do not take more than a few minutes for this simple example, *provided* you set up the calculations correctly and make no arithmetic mistakes. If that time requirement seems trivial, remember that in reality you probably would be asked for four similar sets of statements covering each year from 1999 to 2002. Probably you would be asked for alternative projections under different assumptions (e.g. a 20 instead of a 30 per cent growth rate of revenue) or different financial strategies (e.g. freezing dividends at their 1997 level of $76 000). This would require lots of work. Building a model and letting the computer toil in your place have obvious attractions.

Table 28.3 shows a 15-equation model for Big Banana Fruit & Vege Supplies. There is one equation for each variable needed to construct pro-forma statements like Tables 28.1 and 28.2. Of the equations, six are accounting identities ensuring that the income statement adds up, the balance sheet balances and sources of funds match uses. The functions of the equations are as follows: (1) and (8) set revenues and share issues equal to values specified by the model user. Equations (2), (12) and (13) specify cost of goods sold, net working capital and fixed assets as constant proportions of sales. The remaining equations relate interest to debt outstanding (3), taxes to income (4), depreciation to fixed assets (6) and dividends to net income (11).

The *input* for our model comprises nine items: a sales forecast (REV); a decision on the amount of shares to be issued (SI); and seven coefficients, $a_1$ through to $a_7$, tying cost of goods sold to revenue, interest payments to borrowing, and so on. Take the coefficient $a_5$, for example. In developing Table 28.2, we assumed dividends to be 65 per cent of net income. In the model this would be expressed as $a_5 = 0.65$.

Table 28.4 shows that our model works. In the table we insert the values for REV, SI, and $a_1$ through to $a_7$ that correspond to the assumptions underlying Table 28.2. And we get the right answers, confirming that the model can be used to forecast Big Banana Fruit & Vege Supplies' financial results. All we would have to do is give the computer the nine input items, tell it to solve the 15 simultaneous equations, and instruct it to print out the results in the format of Table 28.2.

**table 28.3**

Financial model for Big Banana Fruit & Vege Supplies

| | | Income statement equations | |
|---|---|---|---|
| (1) | REV | = forecast by model user | |
| (2) | CGS | = $a_1$ REV | $(a_1 = 0.90)$ |
| (3) | INT | = $a_2$ D | $(a_2 = $ interest rate$)$ |
| (4) | TAX | = $a_3$ (REV − CGS − INT) | $(a_3 = $ tax rate$)$ |
| (5) | NET | = REV − CGS − INT − TAX | (accounting identity) |
| | | **Sources and uses statement equations** | |
| (6) | DEP | = $a_4$ FA | $(a_4 = 0.10)$ |
| (7) | ΔD | = ΔNWC + INV + DIV − NET − DEP − SI | (accounting identity) |
| (8) | SI | = value specified by model user | |
| (9) | ΔNWC | = NWC − NWC (−1) | (accounting identity) |
| (10) | INV | = DEP + FA − FA (−1) | (accounting identity) |
| (11) | DIV | = $a_5$ NET | $(a_5 = $ dividend payout ratio$)$ |
| | | **Balance sheet equations** | |
| (12) | NWC | = $a_6$ REV[a] | $(a_6 = 0.093)$ |
| (13) | FA | = $a_7$ REV[b] | $(a_7 = 0.37)$ |
| (14) | D | = ΔD + D (−1) | (accounting identity) |
| (15) | E | = E (−1) + NET − DIV + SI | (accounting identity) |

Notes:

'(−1)' means a number taken from the previous year's balance sheet. These numbers are constants, not variables.

(a) Alternatively, NWC could be set equal at NWC = NWC(−1) × (1+$a_6$), where $a_6$ is equal to growth rate of REV.

(b) Alternatively, FA could be set equal at FA = FA(−1) × (1+$a_7$), where $a_7$ is equal to growth rate of REV.

The Big Banana Fruit & Vege Supplies model is too simple for practical application. You probably have already thought of several ways to improve it—by keeping track of the number of outstanding shares, for example, and printing out earnings and dividends per share.

Or you might want to distinguish short-term lending and borrowing opportunities, now buried in net working capital.

But beware: There is always the temptation to make a model bigger and even more detailed. You may end up with an exhaustive model that is too cumbersome for routine use. Exhaustive detail gets in the way of the intended use of corporate planning models, namely, to project the financial consequences of a variety of strategies and assumptions. The fascination of detail, if you give in to it, distracts attention from crucial decisions like share issues and dividend policy and allocation of capital by business area. Sometimes decisions like these end up being 'wired into' the model, just as the Big Banana Fruit & Vege Supplies model arbitrarily sets dividends equal to a constant proportion of net income.

**table 28.4**

Model forecast for Table 28.2

| | | Income statement equations | |
|---|---|---|---|
| (1) | REV | = forecast = 2808 | |
| (2) | CGS | = 0.9 REV | $(a_1 = 0.9)$ |
| | | = 0.9 (2808) = 2527 | |
| (3) | INT | = 0.09 D | $(a_2 = 0.09)$ |
| | | = 0.09 (649.3) = 58 | |
| (4) | TAX | = 0.35 (REV − CGS − INT) | $(a_3 = 0.35)$ |
| | | = 0.35 (2808 − 2527 − 58) = 78 | |
| (5) | NET | = REV − CGS − INT − TAX | |
| | | = 2808 − 2527 − 58 − 78 = 145 | |
| | | **Sources and uses statement equations** | |
| (6) | DEP | = 0.1 FA | $(a_4 = 0.1)$ |
| | | = 0.1 (1039) = 104 | |
| (7) | ΔD | = ΔNWC + INV + DIV − NET − DEP − SI | |
| | | = 60 + 344 + 94 − 145 − 104 − 0 = 249 | |
| (8) | SI | = specified as 0 | |
| (9) | ΔNWC | = NWC − NWC (−1) | |
| | | = 261 − 201 = 60 | |
| (10) | INV | = DEP + FA − FA (−1) | |
| | | = 104 + 1039 − 799 = 344 | |
| (11) | DIV | = 0.65 NET | $(a_5 = 0.65)$ |
| | | = 0.65 (145) = 94 | |
| | | **Balance sheet equations** | |
| (12) | NWC | = 0.093 REV | $(a_6 = 0.093)$ |
| | | = 0.093 (2808) = 261 | |
| (13) | FA | = 0.37 REV | $(a_7 = 0.37)$ |
| | | = 0.37 (2808) = 1039 | |
| (14) | D | = ΔD + D (−1) | |
| | | = 249 + 400 = 649 | |
| (15) | E | = E (−1) + NET − DIV + SI | |
| | | = 600 + 145 − 94 + 0 = 651 | |

# There is no finance in corporate finance models

Why do we say that there is no finance in corporate financial models? The first reason is that most such models incorporate an accountant's view of the world. They are designed to forecast accounting statements, and their equations naturally embody the accounting conventions employed by the firm. Consequently, the models do not emphasise the tools of financial analysis: incremental cash flow, present value, market risk, and so on.[10]

Second, corporate financial models produce no signposts pointing towards optimal financial decisions. They do not even tell which alternatives are worth examining. All this is left to their users.

Our third law implies that no model can find the best of all financial strategies. However, it is possible to build linear programming models that help search for the best financial strategy subject to specified assumptions and constraints. These 'intelligent' financial planning models should prove more flexible for sensitivity analysis and more effective in screening alternative financial strategies. Ideally they will suggest strategies that would never occur to the unaided financial manager.

The appendix to this chapter sketches a linear programming model based on the modern finance theory presented in this book.

# 28.4  External financing and growth

We started this chapter by noting that financial plans force managers to be consistent in their goals for growth, investment and financing. Before leaving the topic of financial planning therefore we should look at the relationship between a firm's growth objectives and its requirements for external financing.

Recall that in 1997 Big Banana Fruit & Vege Supplies starts the year with $1 000 000 of fixed assets and working capital. It forecasts sales growth of 30 per cent during 1997, which will result in retentions of:

$$\text{Net income} - \text{dividends} = \$145\,000 - \$94\,000 = \$51\,000$$

However, the higher sales volume also requires a 30 per cent addition to assets. Thus:

$$\text{New investment} = \text{growth rate} \times \text{initial assets}$$
$$\$300\,000 = 0.30 \times \$1\,000\,000$$

Part of the funds needed to pay for the new assets is provided by the retained earnings. The remainder must come from external financing. Therefore,

$$\text{Required external financing} = \text{new investment} - \text{retained earnings}$$
$$= \$300\,000 - \$51\,000 = \$249\,000$$

The amount of external financing that Big Banana Fruit & Vege Supplies requires depends on the projected growth. The faster the firm grows, the more it needs to invest and therefore the more it needs to raise new capital. This is illustrated by the sloping line in Figure 28.1. At low growth rates, Big Banana Fruit & Vege Supplies generates more funds than necessary for expansion. In this sense, its requirement for further external funds is negative. It may choose to use its surplus to pay off some of its debt or buy back its shares. In fact, the vertical intercept

---

[10]  Of course, there is no reason why the manager cannot use the output to calculate the present value of the firm (given some assumptions about growth beyond the planning period), and this is sometimes done.

**figure 28.1**

Big Banana Fruit & Vege Supplies' required external financing increases with the projected growth rate. Forecast growth of 30 per cent requires external financing of $249 000. With no external financing Big Banana Fruit & Vege Supplies can grow by only 4.3 per cent. This is the internal growth rate.

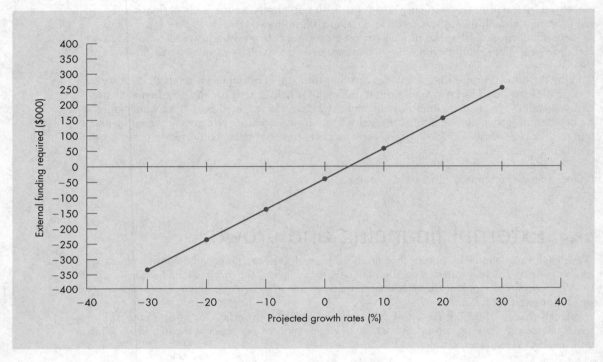

in Figure 28.1, at zero growth, is the negative of retained earnings. When growth is zero, no funds are needed for expansion, so all retained earnings are surplus.

As the projected growth rate increases, more funds are needed to pay for the necessary investments. Therefore, the plot in Figure 28.1 is upward-sloping. For high rates of growth Big Banana Fruit & Vege Supplies must issue new securities to pay for the investments. The sloping line crosses the horizontal axis at a growth rate of 4.3 per cent. At this point external financing is zero; Big Banana Fruit & Vege Supplies is growing as fast as possible without raising new capital. This is called the *internal growth rate*. The growth rate is internal in the sense that it can be maintained without resort to additional sources of capital.

If we set required external financing to zero, we can solve for the internal growth rate as:

$$\text{Internal growth rate} = \frac{\text{retained earnings}}{\text{assets}} = \frac{\text{NET} - \text{DIV}}{\text{assets}}$$

Hence the internal growth rate can be calculated as follows:

$$\text{Internal growth rate} = \frac{123\,000 - 80\,000}{1\,000\,000}$$

$$= 0.043, \text{ or } 4.3 \text{ per cent}$$

Thus the firm's rate of growth without additional sources of capital will equal the ratio of retained earnings to assets.

We can gain more insight into what determines the internal growth rate by multiplying the top and bottom of the expression for internal growth by *net income* and *equity*, as follows:

$$\text{Internal growth rate} = \frac{\text{retained earnings}}{\text{net income}} \times \frac{\text{net income}}{\text{equity}} \times \frac{\text{equity}}{\text{assets}}$$

$$= \text{ploughback ratio} \times \text{return on equity} \times \frac{\text{equity}}{\text{assets}}$$

A firm can achieve a higher growth rate without raising external capital if (1) it ploughs back a high proportion of its earnings, (2) it has a high return on equity (ROE) and (3) it has a low debt-to-asset ratio.[11]

Instead of focusing on the maximum growth rate that can be supported without *any* external financing, firms may be interested in the growth rate that can be sustained without additional *equity* issues. Of course, if the firm is able to issue enough debt, virtually any growth rate can be financed. It makes more sense to assume that the firm has settled on an optimal capital structure which it will maintain even as equity is augmented by retained earnings. The firm issues only enough debt to keep its debt ratio constant. The *sustainable growth rate* is the highest growth rate the firm can maintain without increasing its financial leverage. It turns out that the sustainable growth rate depends only on the ploughback rate and the return on equity.[12]

$$\text{Sustainable growth rate} = \text{ploughback ratio} \times \text{return on equity}$$

We first encountered this formula in Chapter 4, where we used it to help value the firm's equity.

These simple formulas remind us that financial plans need to be consistent. Firms can grow rapidly in the short term by relying on debt finance, but such growth cannot be maintained without incurring excessive debt levels.

---

[11]  Notice that the internal growth rate does not stay constant over time. If the proportion of debt in the balance sheet declines, retained earnings make proportionately larger additions to the firm's assets and the internal growth rate increases.

[12]  Here is proof:

$$\text{Required equity issues} = \text{growth rate} \times \text{assets} - \text{retained earnings} - \text{new debt issues}$$

We find the sustainable growth rate by setting required new equity issues to zero and solving for growth:

$$\text{Sustainable growth rate} = \frac{\text{retained earnings} + \text{new debt issues}}{\text{assets}}$$

$$= \frac{\text{retained earnings} + \text{new debt issues}}{\text{debt} + \text{equity}}$$

However, because both debt and equity are growing at the same rate, new debt issues must equal retained earnings multiplied by the ratio of debt to equity, $D/E$. Therefore, we can write the sustainable growth as:

$$\text{Sustainable growth rate} = \frac{\text{retained earnings} \times (1 + D/E)}{\text{debt} + \text{equity}}$$

$$= \frac{\text{retained earnings} \times (1 + D/E)}{\text{equity} \times (1 + D/E)} = \frac{\text{retained earnings}}{\text{equity}}$$

$$= \frac{\text{retained earnings}}{\text{net income}} \times \frac{\text{net income}}{\text{equity}} = \text{ploughback} \times \text{ROE}$$

## 28.5 Summary

Most firms take financial planning seriously and devote considerable resources to it. What do they get for this effort?

The tangible product of the planning process is a financial plan describing the firm's financial strategy and projecting its future consequences by means of pro-forma balance sheets, income statements and statements of sources and uses of funds. The plan establishes financial goals and is a benchmark for evaluating subsequent performance. Usually it also describes why that strategy was chosen and how the plan's financial goals are to be achieved.

The plan is the end result. The process that produces the plan is valuable in its own right. First, planning forces the financial manager to consider the combined effects of all the firm's investment and financing decisions. This is important because these decisions interact and should not be made independently.

Second, planning, if it is done right, forces the financial manager to think about events that could upset the firm's progress and to devise strategies to be held in reserve for counterattack when unhappy surprises occur. Planning is more than forecasting, because forecasting deals with the most likely outcome. Planners also have to think about events that may occur even though they are unlikely.

To repeat, financial planning is a *process* of:

1. Analysing the interactions of the financing and investment choices open to the firm.
2. Projecting the future consequences of present decisions, in order to avoid surprises and understand the links between present and future decisions.
3. Deciding which alternatives to undertake. (These decisions are embodied in the final financial plan.)
4. Measuring subsequent performance against the goals set in the financial plan.

In this chapter we discussed long-range or 'strategic' planning, in which the *planning horizon* is usually five years or more. This kind of planning deals with aggregate decisions; for example, the planner would worry about whether a division should go for heavy capital investment and rapid growth, but not whether the division should choose machine tool A versus tool B. In fact, planners must be constantly on guard against the fascination of detail, because giving in to it means slighting crucial issues like investment strategy, debt policy and the choice of a target dividend payout ratio.

There is no theory or model that leads straight to *the* optimal financial strategy. Consequently, financial planning proceeds by trial and error. Many different strategies may be projected under a range of assumptions about the future before one strategy is finally chosen.

The dozens of separate projections that may be made during this trial and error process generate a heavy load of arithmetic and paperwork. Firms have responded by developing corporate planning models to forecast the financial consequences of specified strategies and assumptions about the future. These models are efficient and widely used. But remember that there is no finance in them. Their primary purpose is to produce accounting statements. The models do not search for the best financial strategy but only trace out the consequences of a strategy specified by the model user.

One of the most difficult aspects of deciding which strategies to examine closely is that the best strategy may not be an obvious one. In the appendix to this chapter we describe a linear program model which is based on the concepts of finance rather than accounting and which does help the financial manager search for the best financial plan.

# APPENDIX: LONGER

This appendix is a brief introduction to LONGER, a linear programming model devised by Myers and Pogue to support financial planners.[13] Other applications of linear programming to financial planning are described in the articles listed in 'Further Reading' below.

LONGER differs from the typical corporate financial model described in this chapter in two important respects. First, it *optimises*: it calculates the *best* financial plan, given specified assumptions and constraints. The typical planning model merely *projects* the consequences of a financial strategy chosen by the model user. Second, the model is based on finance theory rather than accounting. It assumes well-functioning capital markets. Consequently, its objective is to maximise the firm's net present value. It relies on value additivity and the Modigliani–Miller theory that the chief advantage of debt is the tax shields created by debt interest payments.

LONGER is introduced by a simple numerical example. Then extensions of the model are briefly described. The final part of this appendix shows how the shadow prices generated as part of LONGER's solution are interpreted. The shadow prices are an easy way to understand *adjusted present value* (APV), which measures the value of capital projects which have important financing side effects. APV and its practical implications were covered more fully in Chapter 19. This appendix should give a deeper appreciation of the APV method and the assumptions underlying it.

# Example[14]

Consider a firm which has to decide how much to invest or borrow in the coming year. Let:

$x$ = new investment, in millions of dollars (we assume for simplicity that the firm has only one project)

$y$ = new borrowing, in millions of dollars

Also, assume that:

1. Available investment opportunities can absorb $1 million at most. The investments generate a perpetual stream of after-tax cash flows. Let the expected average value of these flows be $C$. In this case $C = 0.09x$, thus the project offers a 9 per cent internal rate of return.
2. Assume that the market will capitalise the returns at the rate $r = 0.10$. Thus, if all-equity financing is used, these assets generate a net present value of $-\$0.10$ per dollar invested $(-x + 0.09x/0.10 = -0.1x)$.
3. The firm's policy is to limit new debt to 40 per cent of new investment.
4. The firm has $800\,000$ in cash available.
5. Any excess cash is paid out in dividends.
6. The additions to debt and equity are expected to be permanent.

For simplicity, we begin with the Modigliani–Miller valuation formula for the firm.[15] If the firm does nothing ($x$ and $y = 0$), then $V$ will be given by:

$$V = V_0 + T_C D$$

---

[13]  S. C. Myers and G. A. Pogue, 'A Programming Approach to Corporate Financial Management', *Journal of Finance*, **29**: 579–99 (May 1974). © Blackwell Publishers.

[14]  This example is based on one presented by Myers and Pogue, op. cit., Footnote 13.

[15]  See Section 18.1.

Where   $V_0$ = market value of the firm's *existing* assets if they were all-equity-financed
$T_C$ = marginal corporate income tax rate (0.5 in this example)
$D$ = amount of debt *already* outstanding, excluding any borrowing for new investments.

The amount $T_C D$ is the present value of the tax shields generated by the outstanding debt, assuming the debt is fixed and permanent.

For our example,

$$V = V_0 + 0.5D - 0.1x + 0.5y$$

Now $V_0$ and $D$ are fixed and therefore not relevant to the choice of $x$ and $y$. Therefore, we can just maximise the quantity $-0.1x + 0.5y$, subject to constraints on the amount invested ($x \le 1$), the amount of debt issued ($y \le 0.4x$), and the balance of sources and uses of funds ($x \le y + 0.8$).

## The solution

This is the linear programming problem depicted in Figure 28.2. First look at the shaded area representing the set of feasible solutions. The feasible region is below the line $x = 1$ because the firm's investment opportunity will absorb $1 million at most. It is below the line $x = 0.8 + y$ because the amount invested is limited to cash on hand ($0.8 million) plus additional borrowing. It is above and to the left of the line $y = 0.4x$ because new debt is limited to 40 per cent of new investment.

**figure 28.2**

In this example, the firm can invest at most $1 million and borrow 40 per cent of new investment. Funds for the new investment must come from existing cash ($0.8 million) or new borrowings. The investment is not attractive in its own right (NPV = $-$0.1x), but the firm is willing to invest in order to borrow because the tax shields created by borrowing outweigh the net loss in value attributable to the new investment.

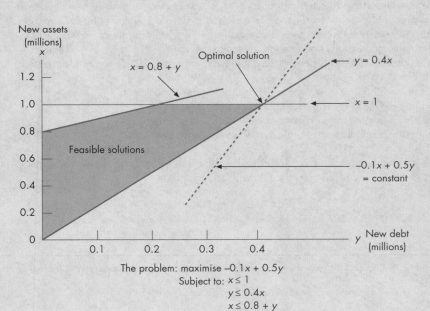

The problem: maximise $-0.1x + 0.5y$
Subject to: $x \le 1$
$y \le 0.4x$
$x \le 0.8 + y$

Now look at the dashed line in Figure 28.2. It shows different combinations of $x$ and $y$ that would produce the same increase in firm value (i.e. they give the same value for $-0.1x + 0.5y$). We could also have drawn a series of parallel dashed lines. Those to the left would represent lower increases in firm value (i.e. lower values of $-0.1x + 0.5y$). Those to the right would represent higher increases in firm value. The dashed line in Figure 28.2 shows the greatest feasible increase in firm value, given the constraints.

The firm does not want to invest (because NPV $= -\$0.10$ per dollar invested), but it does want to borrow, and in order to borrow it has to invest. Thus, firm value is maximised when $x = 1$, $y = 0.4$. The firm invests and borrows as much as it can.

However, note that the constraint $x \leq 0.8 + y$ is not binding at the optimal solution. The firm borrows $200\,000 more than it needs for investment. Thus, it has $200\,000 available for dividends.

Why does the optimal solution call for investing in a project with a negative net present value? The reason is that the project allows the firm to issue more debt, and the value of tax savings generated by the debt more than offsets the investment's inadequate return. (In fact, the optimal solution remains $x = 1.0$, $y = 0.4$ so long as the investment generates more than $-\$0.20$ per dollar invested. If it generates less than that, $-\$0.30$ for example, the solution becomes $x = y = 0$.) The debt capacity constraint thus makes financing and investment decisions interdependent.

## Effects of dividend policy

The sources–uses constraint is not binding in the example, and therefore does not create an interaction of financing and investment decisions. However, what if it is binding? What if the firm has, say, only $500\,000 cash on hand?

At first glance the effect is to change the sources–uses constraint to $x \leq 0.5 + y$, which changes the optimal solution to $x = \frac{5}{6}$, $y = \frac{1}{3}$.

However, if we consider dividend policy, then we should also allow new issues of equity. The constraint should really be

$$x = \text{DIV} \leq 0.5 + y + \text{SI}$$

where DIV and SI are dividends paid and equity issued in millions. If dividend policy is irrelevant, then DIV and SI have no effect in the objective function, and the constraint itself is irrelevant. Thus, the optimal solution remains at $x = 1$, $y = 0.4$. The firm must make a $100\,000 share issue, but this is a mere detail once the investment and borrowing decisions are made.

However, in practice there would be transaction costs associated with the share issue. These costs would have to be subtracted from the objective function, and the sources–uses constraint would become relevant and binding. The solution values for $x$ and $y$ will clearly be affected if the transaction cost is large enough.

Thus, the sources–uses constraint becomes important only if there are transaction costs to security issues or if dividend policy matters for other reasons.

## Extending the model

The example we have just examined was limited to two variables by our goal of presenting it graphically on the two dimensions of the printed page. But the computer does not need a picture like Figure 28.2 to solve a linear program. We can extend LONGER to a practical level of detail by adding variables and constraints.

We have already referred to one extension. Suppose that the firm can pay dividends or issue ordinary shares but that cash available is cut to $0.5 million. The linear program becomes:

- Maximise:     $-0.1x + 0.5y + a\text{DIV} + b\text{SI}$
- Subject to:   $x \le 1$
              $y \le 0.4x$
              $x + \text{DIV} \le 0.5 + y + \text{SI}$

If dividend policy is irrelevant, then both $a$ and $b$ are set at zero. But in practice $b$ would have to be negative to reflect the transaction costs of a share issue. And $a$ might be positive, negative or zero depending on your position on the dividend controversy (see Chapter 16).

Now suppose that there is a second investment opportunity to invest up to \$2 million in a project offering \$0.12 of NPV per dollar invested. However, the performance of project 2 is less predictable than project 1's performance, and so the firm is willing to borrow only 20 per cent of the amount invested in project 2. Our model now becomes:

- Maximise     $-0.1x_1 + 0.12x_2 + 0.5y + a\text{DIV} + b\text{SI}$
- Subject to:  $x_1 \le 1$
             $x_2 \le 2$
             $y \le 0.4x_1 + 0.2x_2$
             $x_1 + x_2 + \text{DIV} \le 0.5 + y + \text{SI}$

Because present values add, we can include as many projects as we like without upsetting the linear form of the objective. Moreover, there is no need for included projects to have the same risk or time pattern of cash flows. There is nothing wrong with setting an office building alongside a wildcat oil well, so long as you can come up with a net present value for each.

If we introduce projects with irregular patterns of cash flow over time, we would naturally want to allow borrowing to vary period by period. Suppose that the firm has a five-year planning horizon. Then we could replace the debt variable $y$ with five new variables $y_1, y_2 \ldots y_5$, where $y_t$ is planned total borrowing for year $t$. This naturally suggests that dividends and share issues should be allowed to vary over time also. Our objective function becomes:

- Maximise:     $-0.1x_1 + 0.12x_2$
              $+ c_1y_1 + c_2y_2 + \ldots + c_5y_5$
              $+ a_1\text{DIV}_1 + a_2\text{DIV}_2 + \ldots + a_5\text{DIV}_5$
              $+ b_1\text{SI}_1 + b_2\text{SI}_2 + \ldots + b_5\text{SI}_5$

Also, we will now need 12 constraints: two limiting the amount that can be invested in each project, five limiting the amount that can be borrowed in each of the five years covered by the financial plan, and five constraints ensuring that planned uses of funds do not exceed planned sources in any year.

Still more constraints might be added. The financial manager might wish to try to avoid any planned cut in dividends, for example. This would call for five more constraints:

- $\text{DIV}_1 \ge$ dividends in period 0
- $\text{DIV}_2 \ge \text{DIV}_1$
- $\text{DIV}_3 \ge \text{DIV}_2$
- $\text{DIV}_4 \ge \text{DIV}_3$
- $\text{DIV}_5 \ge \text{DIV}_4$

Some firms might require that their financial plan generate a steady growth in reported (book) earnings. Suppose that the target growth rate is $g$. Then we would need five more constraints of the form $Z_t \ge (1 + g) Z_{t-1}$, where $Z_t$ represents forecasted earnings in year $t$. The variable $Z_t$ would be determined by the other decision variables in the programming model.

But we must immediately add a caveat: Any constraint on acceptable *book* earnings, as opposed to economic earnings, raises difficult issues. Should the firm be willing to sacrifice present value just to achieve regular growth in reported earnings? If capital markets are efficient, investors ought to be able to look through any fluctuation of short-run earnings to the true, underlying value of the firm. If so, any constraint on earnings is superfluous at best.

Constraints on the growth of book earnings might perhaps be useful for keeping track of how pursuit of present value affects reported earnings. It may be that the financial plan can be changed to generate a pretty earnings pattern. If there is real conflict between value and book earnings, comparing solutions with and without this constraint will at least awaken managers to the cost of that pretty pattern.[16]

There are several other items of optional equipment that most might wish to add to LONGER, but we will stop at this point. You may wish to refer to Myers and Pogue's paper and the other suggested readings for the full story.

## Comparison of LONGER with the typical corporate planning model

A full-scale linear programming model for financial planning would become formidably complex, but no more so than a typical simulation model.[17] The two models applied to the same firm would have approximately the same number of variables, and the number of constraints included in LONGER would about match the number of equations in the simulation model. But the input requirements for LONGER would be greater because an objective function must be specified. In return, LONGER allows the planner to screen all feasible strategies, to reject the inferior ones automatically, and to identify the best strategy consistent with the assumptions and constraints embodied in the model.

However, linear programming models do not automate the *decisions* required by the financial plan. No model can capture all the issues that the financial manager must face. Nor would access to an optimisation model change the trial and error process of developing a financial plan; it only promises to make the process somewhat more efficient. *The optimum plan generated by any run of LONGER does no more than reflect the assumptions and constraints specified by the model user, who will naturally explore a variety of assumptions and constraints before reaching a final decision.*[18]

## Shadow prices, or marginal costs

The solution to any linear program includes a shadow price, or marginal cost, for each constraint. There are three constraints in the simple numerical example introduced at the start of this appendix, and therefore three shadow prices:

| Constraint | Shadow price | Explanation |
|---|---|---|
| Limit on investment ($x \leq 1$) | 0.1 | Project NPV is $-0.1x$. But investment supports $0.4x$ in debt worth $0.50 per dollar borrowed: $-0.1x + 0.4(0.5x) = +0.1x$ |
| Limit on debt ($y \leq 0.4x$) | 0.5 | $1 of additional debt generates tax shields worth $0.50 |
| Limit on available cash ($x \leq 0.8 + y$) | 0 | Firm has surplus cash at optimal solution. Additional cash has NPV of zero |

16  Eugene Lerner and Arnold Rappaport demonstrate the conflicts between pursuit of value and short-run earnings in 'Limit DCF in Capital Budgeting', *Harvard Business Review*, 46: 133–9 (September–October 1968).

17  Note our warning on the temptation to go into excessive detail. See Section 28.3.

18  Willard T. Carleton, Charles L. Dick, Jr and David H. Downes give a comprehensive and insightful discussion of the differences in design and use of the two model types, and argue that optimisation models are potentially more useful, in 'Financial Policy Models: Theory and Practice', *Journal of Financial and Quantitative Analysis*, 8: 691–709 (December 1973).

A *shadow price* is defined as the change in the objective per unit change in the constraint.[19] In our example the objective is to increase net present value. Therefore, the shadow price of 0.1 on the investment limit means that if the firm were allowed to invest $1 000 001 instead of $1 million, net present value would increase by $0.10.

The shadow price of 0.5 on the debt limit means that if the firm were allowed to borrow $400 001 instead of $400 000, holding investment fixed at $1 million, value would increase by $0.50.

The limit on available cash is not binding at the optimal solution. The firm borrows $200 000 more than it needs, and so the shadow price on that constraint is zero. That is, extra cash would have a *net* present value of zero.

Consider a slightly more complex example. Cash on hand is reduced to $500 000. Equity issues and dividend payments are allowed, but transaction costs absorb 10 per cent of the net proceeds of any issue. The linear programming problem changes to:

- Maximise:  $-0.1x + 0.5y + (0)\text{DIV} - 0.1\text{SI}$
- Subject to:  $x \le 1$
  $y \le 0.4x$
  $x + \text{DIV} \le 0.5 + y + \text{SI}$

The solution is $x = 1$, $y = 0.4$, $\text{DIV} = 0$ and $\text{SI} = 0.1$. The firm invests and borrows as before but has to issue $100 000 of equity to raise the necessary cash for investment.

The shadow prices for this problem are as follows:

| Constraint | Shadow price | Explanation |
|---|---|---|
| Limit on investment ($x \le 1$) | 0.04 | (See below) |
| Limit on debt ($y \le 0.4x$) | 0.6 | $1 of additional debt generates tax shields worth $0.50 *and* reduces equity issued by $1, saving $0.10 issue costs |
| Limit on available cash ($x + \text{DIV} \le 0.5 + \text{SI}$) | 0.1 | Extra cash reduces equity issued and saves $0.10 per $1 |

The shadow price on project investment goes down by 0.06, from $0.10 to $0.04 per dollar invested. This occurs because additional investment can be only 40 per cent debt-financed. The remainder must come from issuing new equity. Therefore, the value of the opportunity to invest an additional dollar increases by $0.6 \times 0.1 = 0.06$.

The shadow prices on the investment limits are particularly interesting because they show the project's net marginal contribution to firm value, when all of the project's financing side effects are accounted for. In this example, the project's marginal contribution is $0.04 per dollar invested. Remember that the project has negative NPV separately considered. But it has one favourable side effect (investment allows the firm to borrow) and one unfavourable side effect (investment requires equity issues and generates issue costs).

The shadow price for the project can be calculated by starting with its base case NPV of $-0.1$, adding the value of its marginal contribution to corporate borrowing and subtracting the marginal cost of the equity issue needed to finance it:

Net contribution to firm value = base-case NPV + value of project's marginal contribution to borrowing power − marginal cost of equity issue needed to finance project

---

[19] Shadow prices are valid only for marginal shifts in the constraints. The range over which shifts qualify as marginal varies from problem to problem.

Investing \$1 more effectively loosens the debt constraint by \$0.40 and tightens the cash constraint by \$1. Therefore, we can 'price out' the project's financing side effects by noting the shadow prices on these two constraints. Extra borrowing power is worth \$0.60 per dollar, and cash used up costs \$0.10 per dollar. Therefore:

$$\text{Net contribution to firm value} = -0.1 + 0.40\,(0.6) - (1.00)\,(0.1) = 0.04$$

'Net contribution to firm value' is no more or less than *adjusted present value*, or APV. APV is calculated automatically as a by-product of LONGER. But, as you saw in Chapter 19, for simple problems you can calculate APV by hand. You need APV because it is the only generally reliable approach to capital budgeting when investment decisions have important financing side effects.

## FURTHER READING

Corporate planning has an extensive literature of its own. Good books and articles include:

G. Donaldson, 'Financial Goals and Strategic Consequences', *Harvard Business Review*, **63**: 57–66 (May–June 1985).

G. Donaldson, *Strategy for Financial Mobility*, Harvard Business School Press, Boston, 1986.

A. C. Hax and N. S. Majluf, *The Strategy Concept and Process—A Pragmatic Approach*, 2nd ed., Prentice-Hall, Englewood Cliffs, N.J., 1984.

P. Lorange and R. F. Vancil, *Strategic Planning Systems*, Prentice-Hall, Englewood Cliffs, N.J., 1977.

Our description of what planning is and is not was influenced by:

P. Drucker, 'Long-Range Planning: Challenge to Management Science', *Management Science*, **5**: 238–49 (April 1959).

The links between capital budgeting, strategy and financial planning are discussed in:

S. C. Myers, 'Finance Theory and Financial Strategy', *Interfaces*, **14**: 126–37 (January–February 1984).

Here are two references on corporate planning models:

W. T. Carleton, C. L. Dick, Jr and D. H. Downes, 'Financial Policy Models: Theory and Practice', *Journal of Financial and Quantitative Analysis*, **8**: 691–709 (December 1973).

W. T. Carleton and J. M. McInnes, 'Theory, Models and Implementation in Financial Management', *Management Science*, **28**: 957–78 (September 1982).

LONGER is presented in:

S. C. Myers and G. A. Pogue, 'A Programming Approach to Corporate Financial Management', *Journal of Finance*, **29**: 579–99 (May 1974).

## QUIZ

**1.** True or false?
   a. Financial planning should attempt to minimise risk.
   b. The primary aim of financial planning is to obtain better forecasts of future cash flows and earnings.
   c. Financial planning is necessary because financing and investment decisions interact and should not be made independently.
   d. Firms' planning horizons rarely exceed three years.
   e. Individual capital investment projects are not considered in a financial plan unless they are very large.
   f. Financial planning requires accurate and consistent forecasting.
   g. Financial planning models should include as much detail as possible.

**2.** List the major elements of a completed financial plan.

**3.** 'There is no finance in financial planning models.' Explain.

**4.** Table 28.5 summarises the 1997 income statement and year-end balance sheet of Drake's Bowling Alleys. Drake's financial manager forecasts a 10 per cent increase in sales and costs in 1998. The ratio of sales to *average* assets is expected to remain at 0.40. Interest is forecast at 5 per cent of debt at start of year.
   a. What is the implied level of assets at the end of 1998?
   b. If the company pays out 50 per cent of net income as dividends, how much cash will Drake's need to raise in the capital markets in 1998?
   c. If Drake's is unwilling to make an equity issue, what will be the debt ratio at the end of 1998?

**table 28.5**
1997 financial statements for Drake's Bowling Alleys (figures in $000)

| Income statement | | |
|---|---|---|
| Sales | $1000 | (40% of *average* assets)[a] |
| Costs | 750 | (75% of sales) |
| Interest | 25 | (5% of debt at start of year)[b] |
| Pre-tax profit | 225 | |
| Tax | 90 | (40% of pre-tax profit) |
| Net income | $135 | |

| Balance sheet | | | |
|---|---|---|---|
| Assets | $2600 | Debt | $500 |
| | | Equity | 2100 |
| Total | $2600 | Total | $2600 |

*Notes:* [a] Assets at end-1997 were $2 400 000.
        [b] Debt at end-1997 was $500 000.

**5.** Abbreviated financial statements for Archimedes Levers are shown in Table 28.6. If sales increase by 10 per cent in 1998 and all other items, including debt, increase correspondingly, what must be the balancing item? What will be its value?

**table 28.6**

1997 financial statements for Archimedes Levers

| Income statement | | | | |
|---|---|---|---|---|
| Sales | | $4000 | | |
| Costs, including interest | | 3500 | | |
| Net income | | $500 | | |

| Balance sheet, year-end | | | | |
|---|---|---|---|---|
| | **1996** | **1997** | | **1996** | **1997** |

| | 1996 | 1997 | | 1996 | 1997 |
|---|---|---|---|---|---|
| Assets | $2700 | $3200 | Debt | $1033 | $1200 |
| | | | Equity | 1667 | 2000 |
| Total | $2700 | $3200 | Total | $2700 | $3200 |

**6.** What is the maximum possible growth rate for Archimedes (see Question 5) if the payout ratio is set at 50 per cent and:
  a. No external debt or equity is to be issued?
  b. The firm maintains a fixed debt ratio but issues no equity?

## QUESTIONS AND PROBLEMS

**1.** What are the dangers and disadvantages of using a financial model? Discuss.

**2.** Should a financial plan be considered an unbiased forecast of future cash flows, earnings and other financial variables? Why or why not?

**3.** How would Big Banana Fruit & Vege Supplies' financial model change if dividends were cut to zero in 1998? Use the revised model to generate a new financial plan for 1998. Show how the financial statements given in Table 28.2 would change. Do you think the new plan is an improvement on the old one? Discuss.

**4.** The balancing item in the Big Banana Fruit & Vege Supplies model is borrowing. What is meant by *balancing item*? How would the model change if dividends were made the balancing item instead? In that case how would you suggest that planned borrowing be determined?

**5.** Construct a new model for Big Banana Fruit & Vege Supplies based on your answer to Question 4. Does your model generate a feasible financial plan for 1998? (*Hint*: If it does not, you may have to allow the firm to issue shares.)

**6.** Big Banana Fruit & Vege Supplies' financial manager believes that revenues in 1998 could rise by as much as 50 per cent or by as little as 10 per cent. Recalculate the pro-forma financial statements under these two assumptions. How does the rate of growth in revenues affect the firm's borrowing requirement?

**7. a.** Use the Big Banana Fruit & Vege Supplies model (Table 28.3) to produce pro-forma income statements, balance sheets, and sources and uses of funds statements for 1999 and 2000. Assume 'business as usual', except that sales and costs expand by 30 per cent per year, as do fixed assets and net working capital. The interest rate is forecasted to remain at 9 per cent, and share issues are ruled out. Big Banana Fruit & Vege Supplies also plans to stick to its 46 per cent dividend payout ratio. (*Hint*: Interest expense depends on additional borrowing, which in turn depends on profit after interest and taxes. You may find it helpful to rearrange the equations so that you can calculate interest first.)
  **b.** What are the firm's debt ratio and interest coverage under this plan?
  **c.** Can the company continue to finance expansion by borrowing?

**8.** Discuss the relative merits of descriptive financial models, such as the Big Banana Fruit & Vege Supplies model, and optimising models such as LONGER. Descriptive models are much more commonly used in practice. Why do you think this is so?

**9.** Table 28.7 shows the 1998 financial statement for the Executive Computer Supplies Company. Annual depreciation is 10 per cent of fixed assets at the beginning of this year, plus 10 per cent of new investment. The company plans to invest a further $200 per year in fixed assets for the next five years and forecasts that the ratio of revenues to total assets at the start of each year will remain at 1.75. Fixed costs are expected to remain at $53 and variable costs at 80 per cent of revenue. The company's policy is to pay out two-thirds of net income as dividends and to maintain a book debt ratio of 20 per cent.
  **a.** Construct a model like the one in Table 28.3 for Executive Computer Supplies.
  **b.** Use your model to produce a set of financial statements for 1999.

**10.** Our model for Big Banana Fruit & Vege Supplies is an example of a 'top-down' planning model. Some firms use a 'bottom-up' financial planning model, which incorporates forecasts of revenues and costs for particular products, advertising plans, major investment projects, and so on. What are the advantages and disadvantages of the two model types? What sort of firms would you expect to use each type, and what would they use them for?

**11.** Corporate financial plans are often used as a basis for judging subsequent performance. What do you think can be learned from such comparisons? What problems are likely to arise, and how might you cope with these problems?

**12.** What problems are likely to be encountered in keeping the corporate financial plan up to date?

**13.** The financial statements of Eagle Sport Supply are shown in Table 28.8. For simplicity, 'Costs' includes interest. Assume that Eagle's assets are proportional to its sales.
  **a.** Find Eagle's required external funds if it maintains a dividend payout ratio of 60 per cent and plans a growth rate of 15 per cent in 1999.
  **b.** If Eagle chooses not to issue new shares, what variable must be the balancing item? What will its value be?

c. Now suppose that the firm plans instead to increase long-term debt only to $1100 and does not wish to issue any new shares. Why must the dividend payment now be the balancing item? What will its value be?

**14.** a. What is the internal growth rate of Eagle Sport Supply (see Question 13) if the dividend payout ratio is fixed at 60 per cent and the equity-to-asset ratio is fixed at two-thirds?

   b. What is the sustainable growth rate?

table 28.7 _____

1998 financial statements for Executive Computer Supplies (figures in $000)

| Income statement | |
|---|---:|
| Revenue | $1785 |
| Fixed costs | 53 |
| Variable costs (80% of revenue) | 1428 |
| Depreciation | 80 |
| Interest (at 8%) | 24 |
| Taxes (at 40%) | 80 |
| Net income | $120 |

| Sources and uses of funds | |
|---|---:|
| Sources: | |
| Operating cash flow | $200 |
| Borrowing | 36 |
| Share issues | 104 |
| | $340 |
| Uses: | |
| Increase in net working capital | $60 |
| Investment | 200 |
| Dividends | 80 |
| Total uses | $340 |

| Balance sheet, year-end | 1998 | 1997 |
|---|---:|---:|
| Assets: | | |
| Net working capital | $400 | $340 |
| Fixed assets | 800 | 680 |
| Total assets | $1200 | $1020 |
| Liabilities: | | |
| Debt | $240 | $204 |
| Book equity | 960 | 816 |
| Total liabilities | $1200 | $1020 |

**table 28.8**
1998 financial statements for Eagle Sport Supply

| **Income statement** | |
|---|---|
| Sales | $950 |
| Costs | 250 |
| EBIT | 700 |
| Taxes | 200 |
| Net income | $500 |

**Balance sheet, year-end**

| | 1997 | 1998 | | 1997 | 1998 |
|---|---|---|---|---|---|
| Assets | $2700 | $3000 | Debt | $900 | $1000 |
| | | | Equity | 1800 | 2000 |
| Total | $2700 | $3000 | Total | $2700 | $3000 |

**15.** Table 28.9 contains financial statements for Dynastatics Ltd. Although the company has not been growing, it now plans to expand and will increase net fixed assets (i.e. assets net of depreciation) by $200 per year for the next five years. It forecasts that the ratio of revenues to total assets will remain at 1.50. Annual depreciation is 10 per cent of fixed assets at the start of the year. Fixed costs are expected to remain at $56 and variable costs at 80 per cent of revenue. The company's policy is to pay out two-thirds of net income as dividends and to maintain a book debt ratio of 25 per cent of total capital.
   a. Produce a set of financial statements for 1998. Assume that net working capital will equal 50 per cent of fixed assets.
   b. Now assume that the balancing item is debt and that no equity is to be issued. Prepare a completed pro-forma balance sheet for 1998. What is the projected debt ratio for 1998?

**16.** Go Go Industries is growing at 30 per cent per year. It is all-equity financed and has total assets of $1 million. Its return on equity is 20 per cent. Its ploughback ratio is 40 per cent.
   a. What is the internal growth rate?
   b. What is the firm's need for external financing this year?
   c. By how much would the firm increase its internal growth rate if it reduced its payout ratio to zero?
   d. By how much would such a move reduce the need for external financing? What do you conclude about the relationship between dividend policy and requirements for external financing?

**table 28.9**

1997 financial statements for Dynastatics Ltd (figures in $000)

### Income statement

| | |
|---|---:|
| Revenue | $1800 |
| Fixed costs | 56 |
| Variable costs (80% of revenue) | 1440 |
| Depreciation | 80 |
| Interest (8% of beginning-of-year debt) | 24 |
| Taxable income | 200 |
| Taxes (at 40%) | 80 |
| Net income | $120 |
| Dividends | $80 |
| Retained earnings | $40 |

### Balance sheet, year-end

| | 1997 | 1996 |
|---|---:|---:|
| Assets: | | |
|   Net working capital | $400 | $400 |
|   Fixed assets | 800 | 800 |
| | $1200 | $1200 |
| Liabilities and shareholders' equity: | | |
|   Debt | $300 | $300 |
|   Equity | 900 | 900 |
| Total liabilities and shareholders' equity | $1200 | $1200 |

# chapter 29

# SHORT-TERM FINANCIAL PLANNING

**M**ost of this book is devoted to long-term financial decisions such as capital budgeting and the choice of capital structure. Such decisions are called *long term* for two reasons. First, they usually involve long-lived assets or liabilities. Second, they are not easily reversed, and therefore may commit the firm to a particular course of action for several years.

Short-term financial decisions generally involve short-lived assets and liabilities, and usually they *are* easily reversed. Compare, for example, a 180-day bank loan for $50 million with a $50 million issue of 20-year bonds. The bank loan is clearly a short-term decision. The firm can repay it six months later and be right back where it started. A firm might conceivably issue a 20-year bond in January and retire it in June, but it would be extremely inconvenient and expensive to do so. In practice, such a bond issue is a long-term decision, not only because of the

bond's 20-year maturity, but because the decision to issue it cannot be reversed at short notice.

A financial manager responsible for short-term financial decisions does not have to look far into the future. The decision to take the 180-day bank loan could properly be based on cash flow forecasts for the next few months only. The bond issue decision will normally reflect forecasted cash requirements five, 10 or more years into the future.

Managers concerned with short-term financial decisions can avoid many of the difficult conceptual issues encountered elsewhere in this book. In a sense, short-term decisions are easier than long-term decisions, but they are not less important. A firm can identify extremely valuable capital investment opportunities, find the precise optimal debt ratio, follow the perfect dividend policy, and yet founder because no one bothers to raise the cash to pay this year's bills. Hence the need for short-term planning.

In this chapter we review the major classes of short-term assets and liabilities, show how long-term financing decisions affect the firm's short-term financial planning problem, and describe how financial managers trace changes in cash and working capital. We also describe how managers forecast month-by-month cash requirements or surpluses and how they develop short-term investment and financing strategies.

Part Nine of the book takes a more detailed look at working capital management. Chapter 30 examines the decision to extend credit to the firm's customers. Chapter 31 describes the decisions to hold cash (instead of investing cash to earn interest) and the relationship between firms and commercial banks. Chapter 32 describes the many channels firms can use to invest or raise funds for short periods.

## 29.1 The components of working capital

Short-term or *current* assets and liabilities are collectively known as **working capital**. The difference between current assets and current liabilities is known as **net working capital**. However, most people just refer to net working capital as working capital. In the period 1992 to 1995, the average Australian firm listed on the Australian Stock Exchange held working capital at between 5 to 7 per cent of total assets, with current assets between 28 and 31 per cent of total assets and current liabilities between 22 and 25 per cent of total assets. Cash, liquid assets and accounts receivable remained relatively steady at around 14 per cent of total assets.[1]

One important current asset is *accounts receivable*. When one company sells goods to another company or to the government, it does not usually expect to be paid immediately. These unpaid bills, or *trade credit*, make up the bulk of accounts receivable. Companies also sell some goods on credit to the final consumer. This *consumer credit* makes up the remainder of accounts receivable. We will discuss the management of receivables in Chapter 30. You will learn how companies decide which customers are good or bad credit risks and when it makes sense to offer credit.

Another important current asset is *inventory*. Inventories may consist of raw materials, work in process or finished goods awaiting sale and shipment. Firms *invest* in inventory. The cost of holding inventory includes not only storage cost and the risk of spoilage or obsolescence, but also the opportunity cost of capital—that is, the rate of return offered by other equivalent-risk investment opportunities.[2] The benefits to holding inventory are often indirect. For example, a large inventory of finished goods (large relative to expected sales) reduces the chance of 'running out of stock' if demand is unexpectedly high. A producer holding a small finished goods inventory is more likely to be caught short, unable to fill orders promptly. Similarly, large inventories of raw materials reduce the chance that an unexpected shortage would force the firm to shut down production or use a more costly substitute material.

Bulk orders for raw materials lead to large average inventories, but may be worthwhile if the firm can obtain lower prices from suppliers. (That is, bulk orders may yield quantity discounts.) Firms are often willing to hold large inventories of finished goods, for similar reasons. A large inventory of finished goods allows longer, more economical production runs. In effect, the production manager gives the firm a quantity discount.

The task of inventory management is to assess these benefits and costs and to strike a sensible balance. In manufacturing companies the production manager is best placed to make this judgement. Since the financial manager is not usually directly involved in inventory management, we will not discuss the inventory problem in detail.

---

[1]  Refer to Australian Stock Exchange, *1996 Australian Stock Exchange Financial and Profitability Study*, Sydney, 1996.

[2]  How risky are inventories? It is hard to generalise. Many firms just assume inventories have the same risk as typical capital investments and therefore calculate the cost of holding inventories using the firm's average opportunity cost of capital. You can think of many exceptions to this rule of thumb, however. For example, some electronics components are made with gold connections. Should an electronics firm apply its average cost of capital to its inventory of gold? (See Section 11.3.)

The remaining current assets are cash and marketable securities. The cash consists of currency, demand deposits (funds in cheque accounts) and time deposits. The principal marketable security is commercial paper (short-term, unsecured notes sold by other firms) and bank accepted bills. Other securities include Treasury notes and Commonwealth and semi-government securities.

In choosing between cash and marketable securities, the financial manager faces a task like that of the production manager. There are always advantages to holding large 'inventories' of cash—they reduce the risk of running out of cash and having to raise more on short notice. On the other hand, there is a cost to holding idle cash balances rather than putting the money to work in marketable securities. In Chapter 31 we will tell you how the financial manager collects and pays out cash and decides on an optimal cash balance.

We have seen that a company's principal current asset consists of unpaid bills from other companies. One firm's credit must be another's debit. Therefore, it is not surprising that a company's principal current liability consists of *accounts payable*—that is, outstanding payments to other companies.

To finance its investment in current assets, a company may rely on a variety of short-term loans. Commercial banks are by far the largest source of such loans, but an industrial firm may also borrow from other sources. Another way of borrowing is to sell commercial paper in the form of bills of exchange or promissory notes.

Many short-term loans are unsecured, but sometimes the company may offer its inventory or receivables as security. For example, a firm may decide to borrow short-term money secured by its accounts receivable. When its customers have paid their bills, it can use the cash to repay the loan. An alternative procedure is to *sell* the receivables to a financial institution and let it collect the money. In other words, some companies solve their financing problem by borrowing on the strength of their current assets; others solve it by selling their current assets. In Chapter 32 we will look at the varied and ingenious methods of financing current assets.

# 29.2 Links between long-term and short-term financing decisions

All businesses require capital—that is, money invested in plant, machinery, inventories, accounts receivable and all the other assets it takes to run a business efficiently. Typically, these assets are not purchased all at once but obtained gradually over time. Let us call the total cost of these assets the firm's *cumulative capital requirement.*

Most firms' cumulative capital requirement grows irregularly, like the wavy line in Figure 29.1. This line shows a clear upward trend, as the firm's business grows. But there is also seasonal variation around the trend: In the figure the capital requirements peak late in each year. Finally, there would be unpredictable week-to-week and month-to-month fluctuations, but we have not attempted to show these in Figure 29.1.

The cumulative capital requirement can be met from either long-term or short-term financing. When long-term financing does not cover the cumulative capital requirement, the firm must raise short-term capital to make up the difference. When long-term financing *more* than covers the cumulative capital requirement, the firm has surplus cash available for short-term investment. Thus, the amount of long-term financing raised, given the cumulative capital requirement, determines whether the firm is a short-term borrower or lender.

Lines *A*, *B* and *C* in Figure 29.1 illustrate this. Each depicts a different long-term financing strategy. Strategy *A* always implies a short-term cash surplus. Strategy *C* implies a permanent need for short-term borrowing. Under *B*, which is probably the most common strategy, the firm is a short-term lender during part of the year and a borrower during the rest.

What is the *best* level of long-term financing relative to the cumulative capital requirement? It is hard to say. There is no convincing theoretical analysis of this question. We can make several practical observations, however. First, most financial managers attempt to 'match

**figure 29.1**

The firm's cumulative capital requirement (heavy line) is the cumulative investment in plant, equipment, inventory and all other assets needed for business. In this case the requirement grows year by year, but there is seasonal fluctuation within each year. The requirement for short-term financing is the difference between long-term financing (lines $A^+$, $A$, $B$ and $C$) and the cumulative capital requirement. If long-term financing follows line $C$, the firm *always* needs short-term financing. At line $B$ the need is seasonal. At lines $A$ and $A^+$ the firm never needs short-term financing. There is always extra cash to invest.

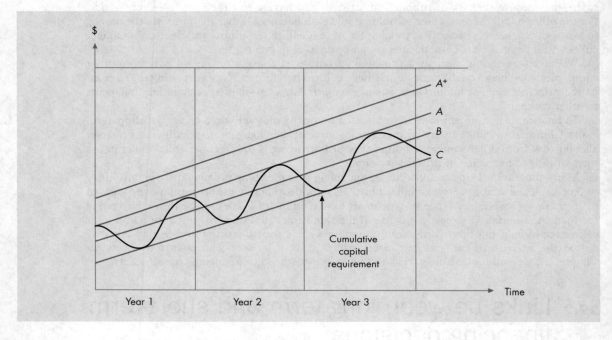

maturities' of assets and liabilities. That is, they finance long-lived assets like plant and machinery with long-term borrowing and equity. Second, most firms make a permanent investment in networking capital (current assets less current liabilities). They finance this investment from long-term sources.[3]

## The comforts of surplus cash

Many financial managers would feel more comfortable under strategy $A$ than strategy $C$. Strategy $A^+$ (the highest line) would be still more relaxing. A firm with a surplus of long-term financing never has to worry about borrowing to pay next month's bills. But is the financial manager paid to be comfortable? Finns usually put surplus cash to work in Treasury notes or other marketable securities. This is at best a zero NPV investment for a tax-paying firm.[4] Thus, we think that firms with a *permanent* cash surplus ought to go on a diet, retiring long-term securities to reduce long-term financing to a level at or below the firm's cumulative capital requirement. That is, if the firm is on line $A^+$, it ought to move down to line $A$, or perhaps even lower.

---

[3]   In a sense, this statement is true by definition. If net working capital (current assets less current liabilities) is positive, it must be financed by long-term debt or equity. Our point is that firms *plan* it in that way.

[4]   If there is a tax advantage to borrowing, as most people believe, there must be a corresponding tax disadvantage to lending, and investment in Treasury notes has a negative NPV (see Section 18.2).

## 29.3 Tracing changes in cash and working capital

Table 29.1 compares 1996 and 1997 year-end balance sheets for Swan Bedding and Blankets, a bedding distributor in Western Australia. Table 29.2 shows the firm's income statement for 1997. Note that Swan's cash balance increased by $10 000 during 1997. What caused this increase? Did the extra cash come from Swan's additional long-term borrowing, from reinvested earnings, from cash released by reducing inventory or from extra credit extended by Swan's suppliers? (Note the increase in accounts payable.)

The correct answer is 'all the above', as well as many other activities and actions taken by the firm during the year. All we can say is that sources of cash exceeded uses by $10 000.

In Australia, published financial statements must include a statement of cash flows prepared in accordance with AASB 1026.[5] This statement replaced the former flow of funds statement[6]—both are similar, but the statement of cash flows emphasises the cash inflows and outflows attributable to the operating activities, investment activities and financing activities of the firm. As noted by Van Horne et al.,[7] the statement of cash flows is very useful to analysts in identifying the firm's cash receipts and disbursements, but has a major deficiency in that by focusing solely on cash transactions it omits current period non-cash transactions which may also be of use to the analyst. Hence, financial analysts often still use flow of funds statements like the one shown in Table 29.3 to investigate the sources and uses of funds in the business and to prepare cash budgets and forecasts. The flow of funds statement in Table 29.3 shows that Swan *generated* cash from the following sources:

1. It issued $70 000 of long-term debt.
2. It reduced inventory, releasing $10 000.
3. It increased its accounts payable, in effect borrowing an additional $70 000 from its suppliers.
4. By far the largest source of cash was Swan's operations, which generated $160 000. See Table 29.2 and note: income ($120 000) understates cash flow because depreciation is deducted in calculating income. Depreciation is *not* a cash outlay. Thus, it must be added back in order to obtain operating cash flow.

Swan *used* cash for the following purposes:

1. It paid a $10 000 dividend. (Note: The $110 000 increase in Swan's equity is due to retained earnings: $120 000 of equity income, less the $10 000 dividend.)
2. It repaid a $50 000 short-term bank loan.[8]
3. It invested $140 000. This shows up as the increase in gross fixed assets in Table 29.1.
4. It purchased $50 000 of marketable securities.
5. It allowed accounts receivable to expand by $50 000. In effect, it lent this additional amount to its customers.

---

[5]  The statement of cash flows is required to be included in a company's financial report in accordance with the *Commonwealth Law Review Act 1998*. See Chapter 27.

[6]  Flow of funds statements had been required with balance sheets and income statements since 1983.

[7]  See Chapter 7 in J. Van Horne, J. Wachowicz, K. Davis and M. Lawriwsky, *Financial Management and Policy in Australia*, 4th ed., Prentice-Hall, Sydney, 1995.

[8]  This is principal repayment, not interest. Sometimes interest payments are explicitly recognised as a use of funds. If so, operating cash flow would be defined *before* interest—that is, as net income plus interest plus depreciation.

**table 29.1**
Year-end balance sheets for 1996 and 1997 for Swan Bedding and Blankets (figures in $000)

|  | 1996 | 1997 |
|---|---|---|
| Current assets |  |  |
| Cash | 40 | 50 |
| Marketable securities | 0 | 50 |
| Inventory | 260 | 250 |
| Accounts receivable | 250 | 300 |
| Total current assets | 550 | 650 |
| Fixed assets |  |  |
| Gross investment | 560 | 700 |
| Less depreciation | −160 | −200 |
| Net fixed assets | 400 | 500 |
| Total assets | 950 | 1150 |
| Current liabilities |  |  |
| Bank loans | 50 | 0 |
| Accounts payable | 200 | 270 |
| Total current liabilities | 250 | 270 |
| Long-term debt | 50 | 120 |
| Net worth (equity and retained earnings) | 650 | 760 |
| Total liabilities and net worth | 950 | 1150 |

**table 29.2**
Income statement for 1997 for Swan Bedding and Blankets (figures in $000)

| Sales | 3500 |
|---|---|
| Operating costs | −3210 |
|  | 290 |
| Depreciation | −40 |
|  | 250 |
| Interest | 10 |
| Pre-tax income | 240 |
| Tax at 50% | −120 |
| Net income | 120 |

**Note:** Dividend = $10 000; retained earnings = $110 000.

**table 29.3**
Sources and uses of cash for 1997 for Swan Bedding and Blankets (figures in $000)

| | |
|---|---:|
| Sources | |
| Issued long-term debt | 70 |
| Reduced inventories | 10 |
| Increased accounts payable | 70 |
| Cash from operations: | |
| Net income | 120 |
| Depreciation | 40 |
| Total sources | 310 |
| Uses | |
| Repaid short-term bank loan | 50 |
| Invested in fixed assets | 140 |
| Purchased marketable securities | 50 |
| Increased accounts receivable | 50 |
| Dividend | 10 |
| Total uses | 300 |
| Increase in cash balance | 10 |

# Tracing changes in net working capital

Financial analysts often find it useful to collapse all current assets and liabilities into a single figure for net working capital. Swan's net working capital balances were (in thousands):

| | Current assets | Less | Current liabilities | Equals | Net working capital |
|---|---|---|---|---|---|
| Year-end 1996 | $550 | − | $250 | = | $300 |
| Year-end 1997 | $650 | − | $270 | = | $380 |

Table 29.4 gives balance sheets which report only net working capital, not individual current asset or liability items.

'Sources and uses' statements can likewise be simplified by defining 'sources' as activities which contribute to net working capital, and 'uses' as activities which use up working capital. In this context working capital is usually referred to as *funds* and a '*sources and uses of funds*' statement is presented.

In 1997 Swan contributed to net working capital by:

1. Issuing $70 000 of long-term debt.
2. Generating $160 000 from operations.

It used up net working capital by:

1. Investing $140 000.
2. Paying a $10 000 dividend

**table 29.4**

Condensed year-end balance sheets for 1996 and 1997 for Swan Bedding and Blankets (figures in $000)

|  | 1989 | 1997 |
|---|---|---|
| Net working capital | 300 | 380 |
| Fixed assets |  |  |
|   Gross investment | 560 | 700 |
|   Less depreciation | −160 | 200 |
|   Net fixed assets | 400 | 500 |
| Total assets | 700 | 880 |
| Long-term debt | 50 | 120 |
| Net worth | 650 | 760 |
| Long-term liabilities and net worth[a] | 700 | 880 |

Note: [a]  When only net working capital appears on a firm's balance sheet, this figure (the sum of long-term liabilities and net worth) is often referred to as total capitalisation.

The year's changes in net working capital are thus summarised by Swan Bedding and Blankets' 'sources and uses of funds' statement, given in Table 29.5.

**table 29.5**

Sources and uses of funds (net working capital) for 1997 for Swan Bedding and Blankets (figures in $000)

| Sources |  |
|---|---|
|   Issued long-term debt | 70 |
|   Cash from operations |  |
|     Net income | 120 |
|     Depreciation | 40 |
|       Total sources | 230 |
| Uses |  |
|   Invested in fixed assets | 140 |
|   Dividend | 10 |
|     Total uses | 150 |
| Increase in net working capital | 80 |

# Profits and cash flow

Now look back to Table 29.3, which shows sources and uses of *cash*. We want to register two warnings about the entry called *cash from operations*. It may not actually represent real dollars—dollars you can buy beer with.

First, depreciation may not be the only non-cash expense deducted in calculating income. For example, most firms use different accounting procedures in their tax books than in their reports to shareholders. The point of special tax accounts is to minimise current taxable income. The effect is that the shareholder books overstate the firm's current cash tax liability,[9] and after-tax cash flow from operations is therefore understated.

Second, income statements record sales when made, not when the customer's payment is received. Think of what happens when Swan sells goods on credit. The company records a profit at the time of sale but there is no cash inflow until the accounts payable are paid. Since there is no cash inflow, there is no change in the company's cash balance, although there is an increase in working capital in the form of an increase in accounts receivable. No net addition to cash would be shown in a 'sources and uses' statement like Table 29.3. The increase in cash from operations would be offset by an increase in accounts receivable.

Later, when the bills are paid, there is an increase in the cash balance. However, there is no further profit at this point and no increase in working capital. The increase in the cash balance is exactly matched by a decrease in accounts receivable.

That brings up interesting characteristics of working capital. Imagine a company that conducts a very simple business. It buys raw materials for cash, processes them into finished goods and then sells these goods on credit. The whole cycle looks like this:

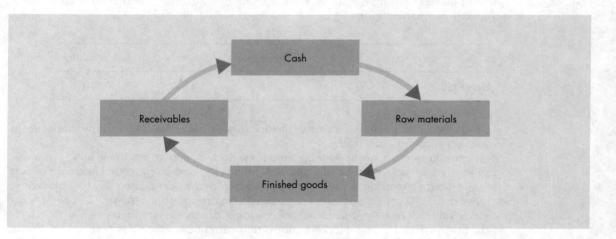

If you draw up a balance sheet at the beginning of the process, you see cash. If you delay a little, you find the cash replaced by inventories of raw materials and, still later, by inventories of finished goods. When the goods are sold, the inventories give way to accounts receivable and finally, when the customers pay their bills, the firm draws out its profit and replenishes the cash balance.

There is only one constant in this process—namely, working capital. The components of working capital are constantly changing. That is one reason why (net) working capital is a useful summary measure of current assets or liabilities.

---

9   The difference between taxes reported and paid to the Australian Tax Office shows up on the balance sheet as an increased deferred tax liability. The reason why a liability is recognised is that accelerated depreciation and other devices used to reduce current taxable income do not eliminate taxes, they only delay them. Of course, this reduces the present value of the firm's tax liability, but still the ultimate liability has to be recognised. In the 'sources and uses' statements an increase in deferred taxes would be treated as a source of funds. In the Swan Bedding and Blankets example we ignore deferred taxes.

The strength of the working capital measure is that it is unaffected by seasonal or other temporary movements between different current assets or liabilities. But the strength is also its weakness, for the working capital figure hides a lot of interesting information. In our example cash was transformed into inventory, then into receivables and back into cash again. But these assets have different degrees of risk and liquidity. You cannot pay bills with inventory or with receivables—you must pay with cash.

## 29.4  Cash budgeting

The past is interesting only for what one can learn from it. The financial manager's problem is to forecast *future* sources and uses of cash. These forecasts serve two purposes. First, they alert the financial manager to future cash needs. Second, the cash flow forecasts provide a standard, or budget, against which subsequent performance can be judged.

### Preparing the cash budget: expected cash inflow

There are at least as many ways to produce a monthly or quarterly cash budget as there are to skin a cat. Many large firms have developed elaborate 'corporate models'; others use a spreadsheet program to plan their cash needs. The procedures of smaller firms may be less formal. But there are common issues that all firms must face when they forecast. We will illustrate these issues by continuing the example of Swan Bedding and Blankets.

Most of Swan's cash inflow comes from the sale of mattresses. We therefore start with a sales forecast by quarter[10] for 1998:

|  | First quarter | Second quarter | Third quarter | Fourth quarter |
|---|---|---|---|---|
| Sales ($000) | 875 | 785 | 1160 | 1310 |

But sales become accounts receivable before they become cash. Cash flow comes from *collections* on accounts receivable.

Most firms keep track of the average time it takes customers to pay their bills. From this they can forecast what proportion of a quarter's sales is likely to be converted into cash in that quarter, and what proportion is likely to be carried over to the next quarter as accounts receivable. Suppose that 80 per cent of sales are 'cashed in' in the immediate quarter and 20 per cent in the next. Table 29.6 shows forecasted collections under this assumption.

In the first quarter, for example, collections from current sales are 80 per cent of $875 000, or $700 000. But the firm also collects 20 per cent of the previous quarter's sales, or 0.2(750) = $150 000. Therefore, total collections are $700 + $150 = $850 000.

Swan started the first quarter with $300 000 of accounts receivable. The quarter's sales of $875 000 were *added* to accounts receivable, but $850 000 of collections were *subtracted*. Therefore, as Table 29.6 shows, Swan ended the quarter with accounts receivable of $300 + 875 − 850 = $325 000. The general formula is

Ending accounts receivable = beginning accounts receivable + sales − collections

---

[10] Most firms would forecast by month instead of quarter. Sometimes weekly or even daily forecasts are made. But presenting a monthly forecast would triple the number of entries in Table 29.6 and subsequent tables. We wanted to keep the examples as simple as possible.

**table 29.6**

To forecast Swan Bedding and Blankets' collections on accounts receivable in 1998 you have to forecast sales and collection rates (figures in $000).

| | First quarter | Second quarter | Third quarter | Fourth quarter |
|---|---|---|---|---|
| 1. Receivables at start of period | 30 | 32.5 | 30.7 | 38.2 |
| 2. Sales | 87.5 | 78.5 | 116 | 131 |
| 3. Collections | | | | |
|     Sales in current period (80%) | 70 | 62.8 | 92.8 | 104.8 |
|     Sales in last period (20%) | 15[a] | 17.5 | 15.7 | 23.2 |
|        Total collections | 85 | 80.3 | 108.5 | 128.0 |
| 4. Receivables at end of period[b] | 32.5 | 30.7 | 38.2 | 41.2 |

*Notes:*

[a] *Sales in the fourth quarter of the previous year were $750 000.*

[b] $4 = 1 + 2 - 3$

The top section of Table 29.7 shows forecasted sources of cash for Swan Bedding. Collection of receivables is the main source but it is not the only one. Perhaps the firm plans to dispose of some land, or expects a tax refund or payment of an insurance claim. All such items are included as 'other' sources. It is also possible that you may raise additional capital by borrowing or selling shares, but we do not want to prejudge that question. Therefore, for the moment we just assume that Swan will not raise further long-term finance.

# Preparing the cash budget: expected cash outflow

So much for the incoming cash. Now for the outgoing cash. There always seem to be many more uses for cash than there are sources. For simplicity, we have condensed the uses into four categories in Table 29.7.

1. *Payments on accounts payable*. You have to pay your bills for raw materials, parts, electricity, and so on. The cash flow forecast assumes all these bills are paid on time, although Swan could probably delay payment to some extent. Delayed payment is sometimes called *stretching your payables*. Stretching is one source of short-term financing, but for most firms it is an expensive source, because by stretching they lose discounts given to firms that pay promptly. This is discussed in more detail in Section 30.1.
2. *Labour, administrative and other expenses*. This category includes all other regular business expenses.
3. *Capital expenditures*. Note that Swan Bedding and Blankets plans a major capital outlay in the first quarter.
4. *Taxes, interest and dividend payments*. This includes interest on presently outstanding long-term debt, but does not include interest on any additional borrowing to meet cash requirements in 1998. At this stage in the analysis, Swan does not know how much it will have to borrow, or whether it will have to borrow at all.

The forecasted net inflow of cash (sources minus uses) is shown in the box in Table 29.7. Note the large negative figure for the first quarter: a $465 000 forecasted outflow. There is a smaller forecasted outflow in the second quarter, and then substantial cash inflows in the second half of the year.

The bottom part of Table 29.7 (below the shaded line) calculates how much financing Swan will have to raise if its cash flow forecasts are right. It starts the year with $50 000 in cash. There is a $465 000 cash outflow in the first quarter, and so Swan will have to obtain at least $465 − $50 = $415 000 of additional financing. This would leave the firm with a forecasted cash balance of exactly zero at the start of the second quarter.

**table 29.7**
Swan Bedding and Blankets' cash budget for 1998 (figures in $000)

|  | First quarter | Second quarter | Third quarter | Fourth quarter |
|---|---|---|---|---|
| **Sources of cash** | | | | |
| Collections on accounts receivable | 850 | 803 | 1085 | 1280 |
| Other | 0 | 0 | 125 | 0 |
| **Uses of cash** | | | | |
| Payments on accounts payable | 650 | 600 | 550 | 500 |
| Labour, administrative and other expenses | 300 | 300 | 300 | 300 |
| Capital expenditures | 325 | 13 | 55 | 80 |
| Taxes, interest and dividends | 40 | 40 | 45 | 50 |
| Total uses | 1315 | 953 | 950 | 930 |
| **Sources minus uses** | −465 | −150 | +260 | +350 |
| **Calculation of short-term financing requirement** | | | | |
| 1. Cash at start of period | 50 | −415 | 565 | −305 |
| 2. Change in cash balance (source less uses) | −465 | −150 | +260 | +350 |
| 3. Cash at end of period[a] 1 + 2 = 3 | −415 | −565 | −305 | +45 |
| 4. Minimum operating cash balance | 50 | 50 | 50 | 50 |
| 5. Cumulative short-term financing required[b] 5 = 4 − 3 | 465 | 615 | 355 | 55 |

Notes:
[a] Of course, firms cannot literally hold a regular amount of cash. This is the amount the firm will have to raise to pay its bills.
[b] A negative sign would indicate a cash surplus. But in this example the firm must raise cash for all quarters.

Most financial managers regard a planned cash balance of zero as driving too close to the edge of the cliff. They establish a *minimum operating cash balance* to absorb unexpected cash inflows and outflows. We will assume that Swan's minimum operating cash balance is $50 000. That means it will have to raise the full $465 000 cash outflow in the first quarter and $150 000 more in the second quarter. Thus, its cumulative financing requirement is $615 000 in the second quarter. This is the peak, fortunately: The cumulative requirement declines in the third quarter by $260 000 to $355 000. In the final quarter Swan is almost out of the woods: Its cash balance is $45 000, just $5000 shy of its minimum operating balance.

The next step is to develop a *short-term financing plan* that covers the forecasted requirements in the most economical way possible. We will move on to that topic after two general observations:

**1.** The large cash outflows in the first two quarters do not necessarily spell trouble for Swan Bedding. In part, they reflect the capital investment made in the first quarter: Swan is spending $325 000, but it should be acquiring an asset worth that much or more. In part, the cash outflows reflect low sales in the first half of the year; sales recover in the second half. If this is a predictable seasonal pattern, the firm should have no trouble borrowing to tide it over the slow months.

**2.** Table 29.7 is only a best guess about future cash flows. It is a good idea to think about the *uncertainty* in your estimates. For example, you could undertake a sensitivity analysis, in which you inspect how Swan's cash requirements would be affected by a shortfall in sales or by a delay in collections. The trouble with such sensitivity analyses is that you are only changing one item at a time, whereas in practice a downturn in the economy might affect, say, sales levels *and* collection rates. An alternative but more complicated solution is to build a model of the cash budget and then simulate to determine the probability of cash requirements significantly above or below the forecasts shown in Table 29.7.[11] If cash requirements are difficult to predict, you may wish to hold additional cash or marketable securities to cover a possible unexpected cash outflow.

## 29.5 The short-term financing plan

Swan Bedding and Blankets' cash budget defines its problem: Its financial manager must find short-term financing to cover the firm's forecasted cash requirements. There are dozens of sources of short-term financing, but for simplicity we start by assuming that there are just two options.

## Options for short-term financing

**1.** *Unsecured bank borrowing.* Swan has an existing arrangement with its bank allowing it to borrow up to $410 000 at an interest cost of 11.5 per cent per year or 2.875 per cent per quarter. The firm can borrow and repay whenever it wants so long as it does not exceed the credit limit. Swan does not have to pledge any specific assets as security for the loan. This kind of arrangement is generally called a line of credit.[12]

When a company borrows on an unsecured line of credit, it is generally required by the bank to maintain collateral, which may be in the form of a deposit at the bank.[13] In our example, Swan has to maintain a balance of 20 per cent of the amount of the loan. In other words, if the firm wants to raise $100, it must actually borrow $125, because $25 (20 per cent of $125) must be left on deposit in the bank.

**2.** *Stretching payables.* Swan can also raise capital by putting off paying its bills. The financial manager believes that Swan can defer the following amounts in each quarter:

|  | Quarter 1 | Quarter 2 | Quarter 3 | Quarter 4 |
|---|---|---|---|---|
| Amount deferrable ($000) | 520 | 480 | 440 | 400 |

---

[11]  In other words, you could use Monte Carlo simulation. See Section 10.2.

[12]  Lines of credit are discussed in more detail in Chapter 32.

[13]  This requirement is not mandatory in Australia. In the United States firms are required by their banks to hold compensatory balances for services provided by the bank to the firm.

That is, $520 000 can be saved in the first quarter by *not* paying bills in that quarter. (Table 29.7 assumes these bills *are* paid in the first quarter.) If deferred, these payments *must* be made in the second quarter. Similarly, $480 000 of the second quarter's bills can be deferred to the third quarter, and so on.

Stretching payables is often costly, however, even if no ill will is incurred. The reason is that suppliers often offer discounts for prompt payment. Swan loses this discount if it pays late. In this example we assume the lost discount is 5 per cent of the amount deferred. In other words, if a $100 payment is delayed, the firm must pay $105 in the next quarter.

## The first financing plan

With these two options, the short-term financing strategy is obvious: Use the line of credit first, if necessary up to the $410 000 credit limit. If cash requirements exceed the credit limit, stretch payables.

Table 29.8 shows the resulting financing plan. In the first quarter the plan calls for borrowing the full amount available under the line of credit ($410 000) and stretching $36 000 of payables (see lines 1 and 2 in the table). In addition, the firm sells the $50 000 of marketable securities it held at the end of 1997 (line 8). Thus, under this plan it raises $496 000 in the first quarter (line 10).

Why raise $496 000 when Table 29.7 shows a cash requirement of only $465 000? The major reason is that the $410 000 borrowed under the line of credit requires a bank deposit of 20 per cent of $410 000, or $82 000. Swan can cover part of this with its $50 000 minimum balance, but $32 000 still has to be raised (line 15).

In the second quarter, the plan calls for Swan to maintain line of credit borrowing at the upper limit and stretch $200 000 in payables. This raises $164 000 after the $36 000 of payables stretched in the first quarter are paid.

Again, the amount of cash raised exceeds the amount required for operations ($164 000 versus $150 000). In this case, the difference is the interest cost of the first quarter's borrowing: $12 000 for the line of credit and $2000 for the stretched payables (lines 11 and 12).[14] In the third and fourth quarters the plan calls for Swan to pay off its debt. In turn, this releases cash tied up by the compensating balance requirement of the line of credit.

## Evaluating the first plan

Does the plan shown in Table 29.8 solve Swan's short-term financing problem? No: The plan is feasible, but Swan can probably do better. The most glaring weakness of this first plan is its reliance on stretching payables, an extremely expensive financing device. Remember that it costs Swan 5 per cent *per quarter* to delay paying bills—20 per cent per year at simple interest. The first plan would merely stimulate the financial manager to search for cheaper sources of short-term borrowing. Perhaps the $410 000 limit on the line of credit could be increased, for example.

The financial manager would ask several other questions as well. For example:

1. Does the plan yield satisfactory current and quick ratios?[15] Its bankers may be worried if these ratios deteriorate.[16]

---

[14] The interest rate on the line of credit is 11.5 per cent per year, or 11.5/4 = 2.875 per cent per quarter. Thus, the interest due is 0.02875(410) = 12, or $12 000. The 'interest' cost of the stretched payables is actually the 5 per cent discount lost by delaying payment. Five per cent of $36 000 is $1800, or about $2000.

[15] These ratios are discussed in Chapter 27.

[16] We have not worked out these ratios explicitly, although you can infer from Table 29.8 that they would be fine at the end of the year, but relatively low mid-year, when Swan's borrowing is high.

**table 29.8**

Swan Bedding and Blankets' first financing plan (figures in $000)

| | First quarter | Second quarter | Third quarter | Fourth quarter |
|---|---|---|---|---|
| New borrowing | | | | |
| 1. Line of credit | 410 | 0 | 0 | 0 |
| 2. Stretching payables | 36 | 20 | 0 | 0 |
| 3. Total repayments | 446 | 20 | 0 | 0 |
| 4. Line of credit | 0 | 0 | 48 | 362 |
| 5. Stretched payables | 0 | 36 | 200 | 0 |
| 6. Total | 0 | 36 | 248 | 362 |
| 7. Net new borrowing | 446 | 164 | −248 | −362 |
| 8. Plus securities sold | 50[a] | 0 | 0 | 0 |
| 9. Plus securities bought | 0 | 0 | 0 | 0 |
| 10. Total cash raised | 496 | 164 | −248 | −362 |
| Interest payments | | | | |
| 11. Line of credit | 0 | 12 | 12 | 10 |
| 12. Stretching payables | 0 | 2 | 10 | 0 |
| 13. Less interest on marketable securities | −1[a] | 0 | 0 | 0 |
| 14. Net interest paid | −1 | 14 | 22 | 10 |
| 15. Additional funds for compensating balance[b] | 32 | 0 | −10 | −22 |
| 16. Cash required for operations[c] | 465 | 15 | −26 | −35 |
| 17. Total cash required | 496 | 164 | −248 | −362 |

Notes:

[a] Swan held $50 000 in marketable securities at the end of 1997. The yield is assumed to be 2.4 per cent per quarter.

[b] 20 per cent of the amount borrowed on the line of credit in excess of $250 000. Swan's $50 000 minimum operating cash balance serves as compensating balance for loans up to $250 000.

[c] From Table 29.7.

**2.** Are there intangible costs of stretching payables? Will suppliers begin to doubt Swan's creditworthiness?

**3.** Does the plan for 1998 leave Swan in good financial shape for 1999? (Here the answer is yes, since Swan will have paid off all short-term borrowing by the end of the year.)

**4.** Should Swan try to arrange long-term financing for the major capital expenditure in the first quarter? This seems sensible, following the rule of thumb that long-term assets deserve long-term financing. It would also reduce the need for short-term borrowing dramatically. A counterargument is that Swan is financing the capital investment *only temporarily* by short-term borrowing. By year-end the investment is paid for by cash from operations. Thus, Swan's initial decision not to seek immediate long-term financing may reflect a preference for ultimately financing the investment with retained earnings.

**5.** Perhaps the firm's operating and investment plans can be adjusted to make the short-term financing problem easier. Is there any easy way of deferring the first quarter's large cash outflow? For example, suppose that the large capital investment in the first quarter is for new mattress-stuffing machines to be delivered and installed in the first half of the year. The new machines are not scheduled to be ready for full-scale use until August. Perhaps the machine manufacturer could be persuaded to accept 60 per cent of the purchase price on delivery and 40 per cent when the machines are installed and operating satisfactorily.

**6.** Swan may also be able to release cash by reducing the level of other current assets. For example, it could reduce receivables by getting tough with customers who are late paying their bills. (The cost is that in future they may take their business elsewhere.) Or it may be able to get by with lower inventories of beds. (The cost is that it may lose business if there is a rush of orders that it cannot supply.)

Short-term financing plans are developed by trial and error. You lay out one plan, think about it, then try again with different assumptions on financing and investment alternatives. You continue until you can think of no further improvements.

Trial and error is important because it helps you understand the real nature of the problem the firm faces. Here we can draw a useful analogy between the *process* of planning and our discussion in Chapter 10 that a project is not a black box. In Chapter 10 we described sensitivity analysis and other tools used by firms to find out what makes capital investment projects tick and what can go wrong with them.

Swan's financial manager faces the same kind of task: not just to choose a plan, but to understand what can go wrong with it and what will be done if conditions change unexpectedly.[17]

We cannot trace through each trial and error in Swan Bedding and Blankets' search for the best short-term financing plan. You may be buried in numbers already. Instead, we will wrap up this chapter by looking at Swan's second try.

# The second financing plan

The second financing plan, shown in Table 29.9, reflects two significant new assumptions:

**1.** A finance company[18] has offered to lend Swan up to 80 per cent of its accounts receivable at an interest rate of 15 per cent per year, or 3.75 per cent per quarter. In return, Swan is to pledge accounts receivable as security for the loan. This is clearly cheaper than stretching payables. It appears much more expensive than the bank line of credit—but remember that the line of credit requires a 20 per cent compensating balance, whereas every dollar borrowed against receivables can be spent.

**2.** The financial manager is uncomfortable with the first plan, which includes no cushion of marketable securities. The second plan calls for $25 000 in marketable securities to be held in a portfolio throughout the year.

A comparison of Tables 29.8 and Table 29.9 shows that the second plan is broadly similar to the first, except that borrowing against receivables replaces stretching payables, and the firm holds $25 000 of marketable securities. The second plan is also cheaper than the first. This can be seen by comparing net interest paid (line 14) under the two plans.

---

17   This point is even more important in *long-term* financial planning. See Chapter 28.
18   Finance companies are non-bank financial institutions that specialise in lending to businesses.

|  | Quarter 1 | Quarter 2 | Quarter 3 | Quarter 4 | Total |
|---|---|---|---|---|---|
| First plan | −1 | 14 | 22 | 10 | 45 |
| Second plan | −1 | 13 | 20 | 10 | 42 |

Over the year the second plan saves $45 000 − 42 000 = $3000 of interest.[19]

**table 29.9**

Swan Bedding and Blankets' second financing plan (figures in $000)

|  | First quarter | Second quarter | Third quarter | Fourth quarter |
|---|---|---|---|---|
| **New borrowing** |  |  |  |  |
| 1.  Line of credit | 410 | 0 | 0 | 0 |
| 2.  Stretching payables | 61 | 164 | 0 | 0 |
| 3.  Total repayments | 471 | 164 | 0 | 0 |
| 4.  Line of credit | 0 | 0 | 20 | 367 |
| 5.  Stretched payables | 0 | 0 | 224 | 0 |
| 6.  Total | 0 | 0 | 224 | 367 |
| 7.  Net new borrowing | 471 | 164 | −244 | −367 |
| 8.  Plus securities sold | 25[a] | 0 | 0 | 0 |
| 9.  Plus securities bought | 0 | 0 | 0 | 0 |
| 10.  Total cash raised | 496 | 164 | −244 | −367 |
| **Interest payments** |  |  |  |  |
| 11.  Line of credit | 0 | 12 | 12 | 11 |
| 12.  Stretching payables | 0 | 2 | 8 | 0 |
| 13.  Less interest on marketable securities | −1[a] | −1 | −1 | −1 |
| 14.  Net interest paid | −1 | 14 | 20 | 10 |
| 15.  Additional funds for compensating balance[b] | 32 | 0 | −4 | −28 |
| 16.  Cash required for operations[c] | 465 | 15 | −26 | −35 |
| 17.  Total cash required | 496 | 164 | −244 | −367 |

*Notes:*

*There are minor inconsistencies in this table because of rounding.*

[a] *Swan held $50 000 in marketable securities at the end of 1997. The yield is assumed to be 2.4 per cent per quarter.*

[b] *20 per cent of the amount borrowed on the line of credit in excess of $250 000. Swan's $50 000 minimum operating cash balance serves as compensating balance for loans up to $250 000.*

[c] *From Table 29.7.*

---

[19]  These are pre-tax figures. We simplified this example by forgetting that each dollar of interest paid is a tax-deductible expense.

# A note on short-term financial planning models

Working out a consistent short-term plan requires burdensome calculations.[20] Fortunately, much of the arithmetic can be delegated to a computer. Many large firms have built *short-term financial planning models* to do this. Smaller companies like Swan Bedding and Blankets do not face as much detail and complexity and find it easier to work with a spreadsheet program on a personal computer. In either case, the financial manager specifies forecasted cash requirements or surpluses, interest rates and credit limits, and the model grinds out a plan like those shown in Tables 29.8 and 29.9. The computer also produces balance sheets, income statements and whatever special reports the financial manager may require.

Smaller firms that do not want custom-built models can rent general-purpose models offered by banks, accounting firms, management consultants or specialised computer software firms. Most of these models are *simulation* programs.[21] They simply work out the consequences of the assumptions and policies specified by the financial manager. *Optimisation* models for short-term financial planning are also available. These models are usually linear programming models. They search for the *best* plan from a range of alternative policies identified by the financial manager.

As a matter of fact, we used a linear programming model developed by Pogue and Bussard[22] to generate Swan Bedding and Blankets' financial plans. Of course, in that simple example we hardly needed a linear programming model to identify the best strategy: It was obvious that Swan should always use the line of credit first, turning to the second-best alternative (stretching payables or borrowing against receivables) only when the limit on the line of credit was reached. The Pogue–Bussard model nevertheless did the arithmetic quickly and easily.

Optimisation helps when the firm faces complex problems with many interdependent alternatives and restrictions for which trial and error might never identify the *best* combination of alternatives.

Of course, the best plan for one set of assumptions may prove disastrous if the assumptions are wrong. Thus, the financial manager has to explore the implications of alternative assumptions about future cash flows, interest rates, and so on. Linear programming can help identify good strategies, but even with an optimisation model the financial plan is still sought by trial and error.

---

[20] If you doubt that, look again at Table 29.8 or Table 29.9. Notice that the cash requirements in each quarter depend on borrowing in the previous quarter, because borrowing creates an obligation to pay interest. Also, borrowing under a line of credit may require additional cash to meet compensating balance requirements; if so, that means still more borrowing and still higher interest charges in the next quarter. Moreover, the problem's complexity would have been tripled had we not simplified by forecasting per quarter rather than by month.

[21] Like the simulation models described in Section 10.2, except that the short-term planning models rarely include uncertainty explicitly. The models referred to here are built and used in the same way as the long-term financial planning models described in Section 28.3.

[22] G. A. Pogue and R. N. Bussard, 'A Linear Programming Model for Short-Term Financial Planning Under Uncertainty', *Sloan Management Review*, **13**: 69–88 (Spring 1972).

## 29.6 Summary

Short-term financial planning is concerned with the management of the firm's short-term, or *current*, assets and liabilities. The most important current assets are cash, marketable securities, inventory and accounts receivable. The most important current liabilities are bank loans and accounts payable. The difference between current assets and current liabilities is called *(net) working capital*.

Current assets and liabilities are turned over much more rapidly than the other items on the balance sheet. Short-term financing and investment decisions are more quickly and easily reversed than long-term decisions. Consequently, the financial manager does not need to look so far into the future when making them.

The nature of the firm's short-term financial planning problem is determined by the amount of long-term capital it raises. A firm that issues large amounts of long-term debt or ordinary shares, or which retains a large part of its earnings, may find that it has permanent excess cash. In such cases there is never any problem paying bills, and short-term financial planning consists of managing the firm's portfolio of marketable securities. We think that firms with permanent cash surpluses ought to return the excess cash to their shareholders.

Other firms raise relatively little long-term capital and end up as permanent short-term debtors. Most firms attempt to find a golden mean by financing all fixed assets and part of current assets with equity and long-term debt. Such firms may invest cash surpluses during part of the year and borrow during the rest of the year.

The starting point for short-term financial planning is an understanding of sources and uses of cash.[23] Firms forecast their net cash requirements by forecasting collections on accounts receivable, adding other cash inflows and subtracting all forecasted cash outlays.

If the forecasted cash balance is insufficient to cover day-to-day operations and to provide a buffer against contingencies, you will need to find additional finance. It may make sense to raise long-term finance if the deficiency is permanent and large. Otherwise, you may choose from a variety of sources of short-term finance. For example, you may be able to borrow from a bank on an unsecured line of credit, you may borrow on the security of your receivables or inventory, or you may be able to finance the deficit by not paying your accounts payable for a while. In addition to the explicit interest costs of short-term financing, there are often implicit costs. For example, the firm may be required to maintain a compensating balance at the bank, or it may lose its reputation as a prompt payer if it raises cash by delaying payment on its bills. The financial manager must choose the financing package that has lowest total cost (explicit and implicit costs combined) and yet leaves the firm with sufficient flexibility to cover contingencies.

The search for the best short-term financial plan inevitably proceeds by trial and error. The financial manager must explore the consequences of different assumptions about cash requirements, interest rates, limits on financing from particular sources, and so on. Firms are increasingly using computerised financial models to help in this process. The models range from simple spreadsheet programs that merely help with the arithmetic to linear programming models that help find the best financial plan.

---

[23] We pointed out in Section 29.3 that sources and uses of *funds* are often analysed rather than sources and uses of cash: Anything that contributes to working capital is called *source of funds*; anything that diminishes working capital is called a *use of funds*. 'Sources and uses of funds' statements are relatively simple because many sources and uses of cash are buried in changes in working capital. However, in forecasting, the emphasis is on cash flow: You pay bills with cash, not working capital.

**FURTHER READING**

Here are some general textbooks on working capital management:

G. W. Gallinger and P. B. Healey, *Liquidity Analysis and Management*, 2nd. ed., Addison-Wesley Publishing Company, Reading, Mass., 1991.

K. V. Smith and G. W. Gallinger, *Readings on the Management of Working Capital*, 3rd. ed., West Publishing Company, New York, 1988.

J. H. Van der Weide and S. F. Maier, *Managing Corporate Liquidity: An Introduction to Working Capital Management*, John Wiley & Sons, New York, 1985.

J. D. Wilson and J. F. Duston, *Financial Information Systems Manual*, Warren, Gorham and Lamont, Inc., Boston, 1986.

Pogue and Bussard present a linear programming model for short-term financial planning in:

G. A. Pogue and R. N. Bussard, 'A Linear Programming Model for Short-Term Financial Planning under Uncertainty', *Sloan Management Review*, **13**: 69–99 (Spring 1972).

**QUIZ**

**1.** Listed below are six different transactions that Swan Bedding and Blankets might make. Indicate how each transaction would affect:
a. Cash
b. Working capital
   The transactions are:
   i.   Pay out $20 000 cash dividend.
   ii.  A customer pays a $25 bill resulting from a previous sale.
   iii. Swan pays $50 previously owed to one of its suppliers.
   iv.  Borrow $10 000 long-term and invest the proceeds in inventory.
   v.   Borrow $10 000 short-term and invest the proceeds in inventory.
   vi.  Sell $50 000 of marketable securities for cash.

**2.** Here is a forecast of sales by National Bromide for the first four months of 1997 (figures in $000):

|  | Month | | | |
|---|---|---|---|---|
|  | 1 | 2 | 3 | 4 |
| Cash sales | 150 | 240 | 180 | 140 |
| Sales on credit | 1000 | 1200 | 900 | 700 |

On average, 50 per cent of credit sales are paid for in the current month, 30 per cent in the next month and the remainder in the month after that. What is the expected cash inflow from operations in months 3 and 4?

**3.** Fill in the blanks in the following statements:
a. A firm has a cash surplus when its _____ exceeds its _____. The surplus is normally invested in _____.
b. In developing the short-term financial plan, the financial manager starts with a _____ budget for the next year. This budget shows the _____ generated or absorbed by the _____ firm's operations, and also the minimum _____ needed to support these operations. The financial manager may also wish to invest in _____ as a reserve for unexpected cash requirements.

c. Short-term financing plans are developed by _____ and _____, often aided by computerised _____.

**4.** State how each of the following events would affect the firm's balance sheet. State whether each change is a source or use of cash and whether it is a source or use of funds.
a. A car manufacturer increases production in response to a forecasted increase in demand. Unfortunately, the demand does not increase.
b. Competition forces the firm to give customers more time to pay for their purchases.
c. Inflation increases the value of raw material inventories by 20 per cent.
d. The firm sells a parcel of land for $100 000. The land was purchased five years earlier for $200 000.
e. The firm repurchases its own ordinary shares.
f. The firm doubles its quarterly dividend.
g. The firm issues $1000 of long-term debt and uses the proceeds to repay a short-term bank loan.

**5.** Adjust the relevant tables in the chapter for each of the following events:
a. Swan repays only $20 000 of the short-term debt in 1997 (Tables 29.1, 29.3, 29.4 and 29.5).
b. Swan issues an additional $100 000 of long-term debt in 1997 and invests $120 000 in a new warehouse (Tables 29.1, 29.3, 29.4 and 29.5).
c. In 1997, Swan reduces the quantity of stuffing in each mattress. Customers do not notice but operating costs fall by 10 per cent (Tables 29.1, 29.2, 29.3, 29.4 and 29.5).
d. Starting in the fourth quarter of 1997, Swan employs some new staff who prove very effective in persuading customers to pay promptly. As a result, 90 per cent of sales are paid for immediately and 10 per cent are paid in the following quarter (Tables 29.6 and 29.7).
e. Starting in the first quarter of 1997, Swan cuts wages by $40 000 a quarter (Table 29.7).
f. In the second quarter of 1997, a disused warehouse mysteriously catches fire. Swan receives a $100 000 cheque from the insurance company (Table 29.7).
g. Swan's treasurer decides he can operate with an operating cash balance of $20 000 (Table 29.7).

## QUESTIONS AND PROBLEMS

**1.** Table 29.10 shows Swan Bedding and Blankets' year-end 1995 balance sheet, and Table 29.11 shows its income statement for 1996. Work out statements of sources and uses of cash and sources and uses of funds for 1996.

**2.** Work out a short-term financing plan for Swan Bedding and Blankets, assuming the limit on the line of credit is raised from $410 000 to $500 000. Otherwise adhere to the assumptions used in developing Table 29.9.

**3.** Look again at Swan Bedding and Blankets' second plan in Table 29.9. Note that the line of credit is cheaper than borrowing against accounts receivable. Would you expect this to be true in practice? Why or why not?

**table 29.10**
Year-end balance sheet for 1995 (figures in $000)

| Current assets | | Current Liabilities | |
|---|---|---|---|
| Cash | 40 | Bank loans | 40 |
| Marketable securities | 20 | Accounts payable | 150 |
| Inventory | 200 | | |
| Accounts receivable | 220 | | |
| Total current assets | 480 | Total current liabilities | 190 |
| Fixed assets | | | |
| Gross investment | 500 | | |
| Less depreciation | −140 | Long-term debt | 50 |
| Net fixed assets | 360 | Net worth (equity and retained earnings) | 600 |
| Total assets | 840 | Total liabilities and net worth | 840 |

**table 29.11**
Income statement for 1996 (figures in $000)

| | |
|---|---|
| Sales | 3000 |
| Operating costs | −2850 |
| | 150 |
| Depreciation | −20 |
| | 130 |
| Interest | −10 |
| Pre-tax income | 120 |
| Tax at 50% | −60 |
| Net income | 60 |

**4.** Suppose that Swan's bank offers to forget about the deposit requirement if the firm pays interest at a rate of 3.375 per cent per quarter. Should the firm accept this offer? Why or why not? (Except for this change, follow the assumptions underlying Table 29.9.) Would your answer change if Swan's cash requirements in the first and second quarters were much smaller—say, only $200 000 and $100 000, respectively?

**5.** In some countries the market for long-term corporate debt is limited and firms turn to short-term bank loans to finance long-term investments in plant and machinery. When a short-term loan comes due, it is replaced by another one, so that the firm is always a short-term debtor. What are the disadvantages of such an arrangement? Does it have any advantages?

**6.** Suppose a firm has surplus cash, but is *not* paying taxes. Would you advise it to invest in Treasury notes or other safe, marketable securities? How about investment in the preferred or ordinary shares of other companies?

**7.** Swan decides to lease its mattress-stuffing machines rather than to buy them. As a result, capital expenditure in the first quarter is reduced by $300 000, but the company must make lease payments of $15 000 for each of the four quarters. Assume that the lease has no effect on tax payments until after the fourth quarter. Construct two tables like Table 29.7 and Table 29.9 showing Swan's cumulative financing requirement and a new financing plan.

**8.** If a firm pays its bills with a 30-day delay, what fraction of its purchases will be paid in the current quarter? In the following quarter? What if the delay is 60 days?

**9.** What items in Table 29.8 would be affected by the following events?
  a. There is a rise in interest rates.
  b. The bank eliminates the requirement for a deposit.
  c. Suppliers demand interest for late payment.
  d. Swan receives an unexpected bill in the third quarter from the Australian Tax Office for underpayment of taxes in previous years.

# part 9

# SHORT-TERM FINANCIAL DECISIONS

# chapter 30

# CREDIT MANAGEMENT

**C**hapter 29 provided an overall idea of what is involved in short-term financial management. It is now time to get down to detail.

When companies sell their products, they sometimes demand cash on or before delivery, but in most cases they allow some delay in payment. Accounts receivable constitute on average about 20 per cent of a firm's current assets. These receivables include both domestic and export trade credit and consumer credit. Trade credit is by far the larger and will therefore be the main focus of this chapter.

In making the decision to offer credit, firms are effectively taking on the role of financial intermediaries. They are not only supplying the goods but also offering loans to their clients. The supply of finance is linked directly to the purchase of the firm's goods. But why do firms offer credit (supply of credit) and why do firms purchase goods on credit rather than raising funding directly from a bank (demand for credit)?

Studies by Crawford[1] and by Elliehausen and Wolken[2] suggest that the demand and supply of trade credit is affected by a range of economic and financial motives such as the relationship between the firm and its clients, competition, transaction costs, informational asymmetries between the parties, credit rationing by banks to certain client groups and convenience.

---

[1] A comprehensive review of theories as to why firms issue credit is given in P. Crawford, A Survey of the Trade Credit Literature, Discussion Paper No. 92/324, Department of Economics, University of Bristol, March 1992.

[2] See G. E. Elliehausen and J. D. Wolken, An Investigation of Motives for Trade Credit Use by Small Businesses, Board of Governors of the Federal Reserve System Staff Studies Paper No. 165, September 1993.

However, little attention has been given in the literature regarding the management of accounts receivable, which is often simply referred to as credit management. The process of credit management is of particular interest in finance as it is directly linked to the concept of risk and return. The firm must evaluate the risk of granting credit to its clients while considering the potential returns obtained from engaging in the activity of granting credit.[3]

Management of accounts receivable involves five major steps:

1. **Setting the terms of the sale**
   Your firm must consider the terms on which you are prepared to sell goods and services. How long are you willing to allow customers to pay their accounts? Are you prepared to offer a cash discount for early or prompt payment? What is the appropriate discount rate that you should offer? Which financial instruments should be used to ensure a clear commitment from the customer in relation to payment? The firm also needs to consider the costs involved in operating an accounts receivable section and should consider the benefits of reducing processing costs through bulk billing, netting of transactions and by using automated payment of standard items.

2. **Credit risk assessment**
   Your firm must consider which customers are likely to pay their accounts by evaluating their credit risk. You will need to consider aspects such as the perceived integrity of the officers of the firm being granted the credit, the customer's resources that are available to pay the obligation including an assessment of both short-term and long-term liquidity, the assets available to satisfy the obligation if payment is not made and general economic conditions.

   You will need to ask questions such as what evidence do you need of indebtedness? Which customers are likely to pay their accounts? To find out, should you rely on references, financial statements or numerical scoring techniques?

3. **Credit collection practices**
   After you have granted the credit, you then have the potential problem of collecting money from accounts as they become due. You need to consider how you intend to collect the money as it comes due. You need to consider how you are going to keep track of the payments. How will accounts be forwarded? What will you do when accounts become overdue?

4. **Identification and management of defaulters**
   Not all payments will be made in accordance with the agreed terms and conditions. From time to time despite your best efforts to obtain payment it will not be made and customers will default on their payments. You need to identify if there are payment problems—both real and potential. And you need to establish a corporate policy as to what to do about reluctant payers.

5. **Accounts receivable financing**
   When credit is granted, your firm faces a period of time while it does not have direct access to these funds. This obviously will affect the availability of short-term cash flow. Decisions therefore have to be made to identify how this 'receivables gap' can be managed and financed.

We will discuss each of these steps in turn.

---

[3]    A recent review of credit management practices and the many organisational and institutional structures involved is included in S. L. Mian and C. W. Smith Jr, 'Accounts Receivable Management Policy: Theory and Evidence', *Journal of Finance*, **47** (1): 169–200 (March 1992).

## 30.1 Setting the terms of the sale

Not all business transactions involve credit. For example, if you are producing goods to the customer's specification or incurring substantial delivery costs, then it may be sensible to ask for a cash sale or cash before delivery (CBD).[4] If you are providing goods or services to a wide variety of irregular customers, especially if this involves perishable goods, you may require cash on delivery (COD). Other possibilities include:

- CBD—cash before delivery.
- Net—payment due on delivery.
- Net 7 (10)—payment due seven (10) days after delivery.
- CND—cash next delivery.

If your product is expensive, custom designed or involves a lot of intellectual property in the provision of services then a formal sales contract should be signed. Often such contracts provide for *progress or stage payments* as work is carried out. For example, a large, extended consulting contract might call for 30 per cent payment after completion of field research, 30 per cent on submission of a draft report and the remaining 40 per cent when the project is finally completed. In some cases a firm may make sales to the same firm from which it makes purchases—the firms could decide to periodically reconcile their balances and make any necessary settlements—such terms are known as *contra terms*.

When we look at transactions that do involve credit, we encounter a wide variety of arrangements and considerable jargon. In fact, each industry seems to have its own particular usage with regard to payment terms. These norms have a rough logic. The seller will naturally demand earlier payment if its customers are in a high-risk business, if their accounts are small, or if the goods are perishable or quickly resold.

In order to induce customers to pay before the final date, it is common to offer a cash discount for prompt settlement.[5] For example, a manufacturer may require payment within 30 days but offer a 5 per cent discount to customers who pay within 10 days. These terms are referred to as 5/10, net 30. If a firm sells goods on terms of 2/30, net 60, customers receive a 2 per cent discount for payment within 30 days and must pay in full within 60 days.

Cash discounts are often very large. For example, a customer who buys on terms of 5/10, net 30 may decide to forgo the cash discount and pay on day 30. This means that the customer obtains an extra 20 days credit but pays about 5 per cent more for the goods. This is equivalent to borrowing money at a rate of 155 per cent per annum.[6] It is possible to calculate an implicit borrowing rate when terms are $d/t_1$, net $t_2$ as follows:

$$\text{Implicit borrowing cost} = \frac{d}{(1 - d)} \times \frac{365}{(t_1 - t_2)}$$

In order to increase the implicit borrowing costs, firms issuing trade credit could increase the discount rate or decrease the number of days between $t_1$ and $t_2$. Of course, any firm which delays payment beyond the due date gains a cheaper loan but damages its reputation for creditworthiness.

You can think of the terms of sale as fixing both the price for the cash buyer and the rate of interest charged for credit. For example, suppose that a firm reduces the cash discount from 5 to 4 per cent. That would represent an *increase* in the price for the cash buyer of 1 per cent, but a *reduction* in the implicit rate of interest charged the credit buyer from just over 5 per cent per 20 days to just over 4 per cent per 20 days.

---

[4] Sometimes referred to as cash in advance (CIA).

[5] In addition, many companies allow an 'anticipation rate'—that is, a discount calculated to give a normal rate of interest to those customers who miss the cash discount but pay before the final date. Some firms also add a service charge for late payment.

[6] The cash discount allows you to pay $95 rather than $100. If you do not take the discount, you take a 20-day loan, but you pay 5/95 = 5.26 per cent more for the goods. There are 365/20 = 18.25 20-day periods in a year. A dollar invested for 18.25 periods at 5.26 per cent grows to $(1 + 0.0526)^{18.25} = \$2.55$, a 155 per cent return on the original investment.

For many items that are bought on a recurrent basis, it is inconvenient to require separate payment for each delivery. A common solution is to pretend that all sales during the month in fact occur at the end of the month (EOM). Thus, goods may be sold on terms of 8/10, EOM, net 60. This allows the customer a cash discount of 8 per cent if the bill is paid within 10 days of the end of month; otherwise, the full payment is due within 60 days of the invoice date.[7] When purchases are subject to seasonal fluctuations, manufacturers often encourage customers to take early delivery by allowing them to delay payment until the usual order season. This practice is known as 'season dating'.

When setting the cash discount rate, the firm should consider the relative financing costs saved by the seller versus the cost of the discount, the seller's need for prompt payment to assist cash flows and that some customers who are granted the discount may always be prompt payers. A recurrent problem that can occur is that some customers will deduct the discount even when they pay late—a prompt follow-up procedure should be implemented in such cases as the unpaid amount will be due and payable.

## Commercial credit instruments

The terms of sale define the amount of any credit but not the nature of the contract. Repetitive sales to domestic customers are almost always made on **open account** and involve only an implicit contract. There is simply a record in the seller's books and a receipt signed by the buyer.

Apart from open accounts for credit, firms will also offer credit to their clients such as documentary credit, instalment credit and revolving credit.

Documentary credit involves the provision of some form of documentary undertaking that the funds will be repaid before the goods are released or the service provided. These may include promissory notes, bills of exchange or letters of credit.

If an order is very large and there is no complicating cash discount, the customer may be asked to sign a **promissory note**. This is just a straightforward IOU, worded along the following lines:

*Sydney*
*1 December 1998*
*Sixty days after date I promise to pay to the order of the XYZ Company one hundred thousand dollars ($100 000.00) for value received.*
*Signature*

Such an arrangement is not common, but it has two advantages. First, as long as it is payable to 'order' or to 'bearer', the holder may sell this note or use it as security for a loan. Second, the note eliminates the possibility of any subsequent disputes about the existence of the debt; the customer knows that he or she may be sued immediately for failure to pay on the due date.

If you want a clear commitment from the buyer, it is more useful to have it *before* you deliver the goods. In this case, the simplest procedure is to arrange a **commercial draft**. It works as follows. The seller draws a draft ordering payment by the customer and sends this draft to the customer's bank together with the shipping or transportation documents. If immediate payment is required, the draft is termed a **sight draft**,[8] otherwise it is known as a **time draft**. Depending on whether it is a sight or a time draft, the customer either pays up or acknowledges the debt by adding the word *accepted* and his or her signature. The bank then

---

7    Terms of 8/10, prox., net 60 would entitle the customer to a discount if the account was paid within 10 days of the end of the following (or 'proximo') month.

8    A sight draft enables the seller to obtain payment from the buyer before releasing control of the goods. On payment being made, the documents are passed over to the purchaser to obtain physical possession of the goods.

hands the shipping documents to the customer and forwards the money or the **trade acceptance** to the seller. The latter may hold the trade acceptance to maturity or may use it as security for a loan.

If the customer's credit is for any reason suspect, the seller may ask the customer to arrange for his or her bank to accept the time draft. In this case, the bank guarantees the customer's debt. These **bank acceptances** are often used in overseas trade; they have a higher standing and greater negotiability than trade acceptances.

The exporter who requires greater certainty of payment can ask the customer to arrange for an *irrevocable letter of credit*. In this case, the customer's bank sends the exporter a letter stating that it has established a credit in their favour at a bank in Australia. The client's bank gives the exporter its undertaking to pay, provided the conditions of the credit are met. Hence, customer risk is minimised—but the primary risk is that the foreign bank will not be able to pay or may delay payment when the time comes due. The exporter then draws a draft on the customer's bank and presents it to the bank in Australia together with the letter of credit and the shipping documents. The bank in Australia arranges for this draft to be accepted or paid and forwards the documents to the customer's bank. The country risk involved can be removed through the use of a confirmed irrevocable letter of credit. Here, another bank in Australia gives its commitment to the letter of credit payment.

If you sell goods to a customer who proves unable to pay, you often cannot get your goods back. You simply become a general creditor of the company, in common with other unfortunates. You can avoid this situation by making a *conditional sale*, so that title to the goods remains with the seller until full payment is made. The conditional sale is common practice in Europe and is also used by firms in Australia to purchase goods on an instalment basis. In this case, if the customer fails to make the agreed number of payments, then the equipment can be immediately repossessed by the seller.

# 30.2 Credit risk assessment

The objective of assessing credit risk is to evaluate applicants to determine whether credit should be granted. When assessing the credit risk of a firm it is necessary to consider the previous credit history of the client, the information supplied by the firm in a credit application, any information collected, evaluated and reported by credit reporting agencies, any bank or trade references and the financial statements of the organisation.

Firms are not allowed to discriminate between customers by charging them different prices. Neither may they discriminate by offering the same prices but different credit terms. However, it is possible to offer different terms of sale to different *classes* of buyer. You can offer volume discounts, for example, or discounts to customers willing to accept long-term purchase contracts. But as a rule, if you have a customer of doubtful standing, you keep to your regular terms of sale for that customer class. You protect yourself by restricting the volume of goods that the customer may buy on credit.

There are a number of ways in which you can find out whether customers are likely to pay their debts. The most obvious indication is whether they have paid promptly in the past. Prompt payment is generally a good omen, but beware of the customer who establishes a high credit limit on the basis of a series of small payments and then disappears, leaving you with a large unpaid bill.

If you are dealing with a new customer, you will probably check with a credit agency. Dun and Bradstreet is perhaps by far the most well known of these agencies throughout the world.[9] In addition to its rating service, Dun and Bradstreet provides on request a full credit report on

---

[9]   Alternative providers of credit information used extensively in Australia include the Credit Reference Association of Australia, Australian Business Research and Australian Corporate Reporting, all of which also provide credit reports and risk assessments among other services.

a potential customer. Credit agencies usually report the experience that other firms have had with your customer. You can also get this information by contacting the firms directly or through a credit bureau.

In addition to checking with your customer's bank, it might make sense to check what everybody else in the financial community thinks about your customer's credit standing. Does that sound expensive? Not if your customer is a public company. You just look at the Moody's or Standard & Poor's rating for the customer's outstanding debt. You can also compare the interest rates paid on the client's debt—of particular interest is the premium paid above the prime rate—these additional basis points reflect an assessment of the firm's default risk. Finally, you can look at how the customer's share price has been behaving recently. A sharp fall in price does not mean that the company is in trouble, but it does suggest that prospects are less bright than formerly.

# Quantitative approaches to credit risk analysis

Quantitative approaches involve the use of financial ratio analysis as we discussed in Chapter 27 and/or numerical credit scoring techniques through the use of either probability-based expert systems or statistical analysis. Quantitative approaches automate the analysis of credit risk and thereby remove any potential bias imposed by individual credit analysts with differing levels of expertise and experience.

**Financial ratio analysis**   We have suggested a number of ways to check whether your customer is a good risk. You can ask your collection manager, a specialised credit agency, a credit bureau, a banker or the financial community at large. But, if you do not like relying on the judgement of others, you can do your own homework. Ideally, this would involve a detailed analysis of the company's business prospects and financing, but this is usually too expensive. Therefore, credit analysts concentrate on the company's financial statements, using rough rules of thumb to judge whether the firm is a good credit risk. The rules of thumb are based on *financial ratios*. Chapter 27 described how these ratios are calculated and interpreted.

**Numerical credit scoring**   When the firm has a small regular clientele, the credit manager can easily handle the investigation process informally. But when the company is dealing directly with consumers or with a large number of small trade accounts, some streamlining is essential. In these cases, it may make sense to use a quantitative or mechanical scoring system to pre-screen credit applicants. In fact, computerised loan assessment is increasingly becoming commonplace. How does it work? The applicant applies for a loan by completing details on a loan application form. The details are then entered into a computer program, which scores or assigns a numerical value to the responses to individual questions. An aggregate score is then compiled from all of the scores and if you exceed a predetermined threshold you are on your way to being deemed a suitable applicant for the loan or trade credit.

When using a numerical scoring approach, the credit analyst asks a series of predetermined questions of the borrower with a view to comparing the borrower's characteristics with the known characteristics of clients that indicate the probability of default.[10] If you apply for a credit card or bank loan you will be asked a series of questions about your job, home and financial position. All applicants are requested to answer a standard questionnaire. Based on the previous experience of the bank with other customers it can calculate the probability of default associated with each characteristic. From this information, the bank is able to calculate an overall risk index for each applicant.[11]

---

10   See A. K. Reichert, C. C. Cho and G. M. Wagner, 'An Examination of the Conceptual Issues Involved in Developing Credit Scoring Models', *Journal of Business and Economic Statistics*, **1** (2): 101–14 (April 1983).

11   See P. F. Smith, 'Measuring Risk on Consumer Installment Credit', *Management Science*, **11**: 327–40 (November 1964).

Consider the questions detailed in Table 30.1. These questions are somewhat typical of the questions asked if you apply for consumer credit. However, due to anti-discrimination laws there are several indicators that cannot be used in the calculation of the risk index or in any credit evaluation—factors such as sex, race, age and religion. In a study of the default risk characteristics of bank loan customers, it was revealed that in total only 1.2 per cent of the borrowers subsequently defaulted. Some categories of borrowers with particular characteristics were more likely to default and therefore were greater credit risks than others. We have added the actual default rates for each category on the right-hand side of Table 30.1. For example, you can see that 7 per cent of the borrowers that had no telephone subsequently defaulted. Similarly, borrowers who lived in rented rooms, had no bank account, needed the loan to pay medical bills, and so on, were much worse credit risks than the average. We would encourage caution in the interpretation of these statistics—although such groups have a higher probability of default, this does not imply that they will default.

**table 30.1** _____

A condensed version of a questionnaire used by a bank for personal loan applicants. We have added in parentheses the percentage of borrowers in each category who subsequently defaulted.

| | |
|---|---|
| 1. Do you have: | |
| 1 or more telephones? | (0.7) |
| No telephone? | (7.0) |
| 2. Do you: | |
| Own your home? | (0.7) |
| Rent a house? | (2.2) |
| Rent an apartment? | (3.3) |
| Rent a room? | (7.3) |
| 3. Do you: | |
| Have 1 or more bank accounts? | (0.8) |
| No bank account? | (2.6) |
| 4. Is the purpose of the loan: | |
| To buy a car? | (0.8) |
| To buy household goods? | (0.6) |
| To pay medical expenses? | (2.5) |
| Other? | (1.3) |
| 5. How long did you spend in your last residence: | |
| 6 months or less? | (3.1) |
| 7 to 60 months? | (1.4) |
| More than 60 months? | (0.8) |
| 6. How long did you spend in your last job: | |
| 6 months? | (3.2) |
| 7 to 60 months? | (1.5) |
| More than 60 months? | (0.9) |

*continues*

*continued*

7.  What is your marital status:

    Single?                                             (1.6)

    Married?                                            (1.0)

    Divorced?                                           (2.9)

8.  What is your postal code?                           (0.1 to 11.4)

9.  For how long do you require the loan:

    12 months or less?                                  (1.6)

    More than 12 months?                                (1.0)

10. What is your occupation?                            (0.4 to 3.5)

11. What is your monthly income:

    $200 or less?                                       (2.3)

    $200 to $1000                                       (1.1)

    More than $1000?                                    (0.7)

12. What is your age:

    25 or under?                                        (1.5)

    26 to 30?                                           (1.8)

    More than 30?                                       (1.0)

13. How many are there in your family:

    One?                                                (1.6)

    Two to seven?                                       (1.1)

    Eight or more?                                      (2.6)

*Source*: Reprinted by permission from P. F. Smith, 'Measuring Risk on Consumer Installment Credit', *Management Science*, 11: 327–340 (November 1964). Copyright 1964 The Institute of Management Science.

Using the detailed probabilities in Table 30.1, or through an analysis of the characteristics of their own customer base, banks can calculate an overall risk index for each applicant for credit. For example, you could construct a rough and ready index based on the probabilities in Table 30.1. The person who had the characteristics of the worst performer, the person most likely to default, would have a credit risk index of:

$$7.0 + 7.3 + 2.6 + \ldots + 2.6 = 51.8$$

Compare this with the least risky client, the person least likely to default:

$$0.7 + 0.7 + 0.8 + \ldots + 1.1 = 7.8$$

The questionnaire in Table 30.1 is very dated—not too many loan applicants have a monthly income below $200. We wish we could give you an up-to-date and current version—but the financial institutions using this form of evaluation (we think it is most institutions) treat this information as though it is top secret. In reality, a bank that has a superior method of identifying good and bad credit risk customers has a significant advantage over its competition. In fact, when a British bank recently laid off a number of its employees, one unhappy staff member decided to leak details of the bank's credit scoring system to the press.[12]

Banks and the credit departments of industrial firms also have found that similar mechanical scoring systems can help them cut the costs of assessing credit applications from small businesses.[13] Typically, in the case of trade credit, firms are particularly interested in knowing the legal status of the firm, identifying the directors of the firm, details of outstanding debt by type and amount and the names of business referees with whom the firm has had prior credit arrangements.

One bank claimed that credit scoring reduced the cost of loan appraisal by two-thirds. It cited the case of an application for a $5000 credit line from an accounting firm. A clerk entered the information from the loan application into a computer and checked the firm's deposit balances with the bank together with the owner's personal and business credit files. Immediately, the loan officer could see the applicant's score was within the acceptable range. He could then go about checking that there was nothing obviously suspicious about the application.[14]

A significant word of caution is needed at this time—a credit score alone is insufficient in the credit-granting process—other factors for consideration must also be looked at, such as the capacity of the firm to repay, any collateral offered or available for the period of the credit, and the economic climate.

## Constructing better risk indexes

Many lenders that use credit scoring systems employ ad hoc formulas. You should be able to do better than that.

An inevitable problem of using credit scoring techniques is that it is possible for credit to be granted to firms that may still default or for firms that may not default to be refused credit. Obviously, a simple addition of separate probabilities representing different characteristics of clients ignores any possible interactions between the different characteristics. Consider that it might seem to be more alarming when a single applicant lives in a rented room as opposed to a married applicant living in their own house—but the single applicant may have an income in excess of $250 000, whereas the family has an income of only $60 000.

Suppose that you take just two factors—time spent in last residence and time spent in last job. You then plot a scatter diagram like Figure 30.1. The x's represent customers that subsequently paid their debts; the o's represent customers that defaulted. Now try to draw a straight line dividing the two groups. You cannot wholly separate them, but the line in our diagram keeps the two groups as far apart as possible. (Note that there are only three x's below the line and three o's above the line.) This line tells us that, if we wish to *discriminate* between the good and bad risks, we should give only half as much weight to job stability as we give to home stability. The index of creditworthiness in this case is given by:

$$Z = 2 \text{ (months in last residence)} + 1 \text{ (months in last job)}$$

You minimise the degree of misclassification if you predict that applicants with Z scores over 60 will pay their bills and that those with Z scores below 60 will not pay.[15]

---

12   See V. Orvice, 'Would You Get a Loan?', *Daily Mail,* 16 March 1994, p. 29.

13   See E. I. Altman, 'Commercial Bank Lending: Process, Credit Scoring, and Costs of Errors in Lending', *Journal of Financial and Quantitative Analysis,* 15 (4): 813–32 (November 1980).

14   See S. Hansell, 'Need a Loan? Ask a Computer: "Credit Scoring" Changes Small-Business Lending', *New York Times,* 18 April 1995, Section D, p. 1.

15   The figure 60 is an arbitrary constant. We could just as well have used 6. In this case the Z score is

$$Z = 0.20 \text{ (months in last residence)} + 0.10 \text{ (months in last job)}$$

**figure 30.1**

The x's represent a hypothetical group of bank borrowers who subsequently repaid their loans; the o's represent those who defaulted. The sloping line discriminates between the two groups on the basis of time spent in last home and time spent in last job. The line represents the equation

$$Z = 2 \text{ (months in last residence)} + 1 \text{ (months in last job)} = 60$$

Borrowers who plot above the line have Z scores greater than 60.

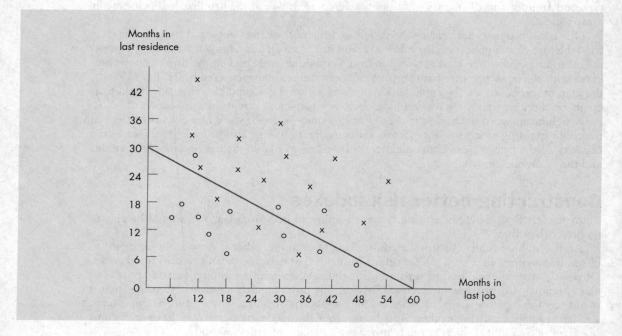

In practice, we do not need to confine our attention to just two variables nor do we need to estimate the equation by eye. *Multiple-discriminant analysis* (MDA) is a straightforward statistical technique for calculating how much weight to put on each variable in order to separate the sheep from the goats.[16]

Edward Altman has used MDA to predict bad business risks. Altman's objective was to see how well financial ratios could be used to distinguish which firms would go bankrupt during the period 1946–65. MDA gave him the following index of creditworthiness:[17]

$$Z = 3.3 \left( \frac{\text{EBIT}}{\text{total assets}} \right) + 1.0 \left( \frac{\text{sales}}{\text{total assets}} \right) + 0.6 \left( \frac{\text{market value equity}}{\text{book value of debt}} \right)$$

$$+ 1.4 \left( \frac{\text{retained earnings}}{\text{total assets}} \right) + 1.2 \left( \frac{\text{working capital}}{\text{total assets}} \right)$$

This equation did a good job at distinguishing the bankrupt and non-bankrupt firms. Of the former, 94 per cent had Z scores of *less* than 2.7 the year before they went bankrupt. In contrast, 97 per cent of the non-bankrupt firms had Z scores *above* this level.[18] At present,

---

[16]   MDA is not the only statistical technique that you can use for this purpose. Probit and logit analysis are two other potentially useful techniques. These estimate the probability of some event, for example default, as a function of observable firm-specific financial ratios.

[17]   EBIT is earnings before interest and taxes. E. I. Altman, 'Financial Ratios, Discriminant Analysis and the Prediction of Corporate Bankruptcy', *Journal of Finance*, 23: 589–609 (September 1968).

[18]   This equation was fitted with the benefit of hindsight. The equation did slightly less well when used to *predict* bankruptcies after 1965.

updated, refined (and secret) versions of Altman's original Z-score model are used by a number of institutions.

A comprehensive survey of worldwide use of the model in different countries is contained in a recent publication by Altman and Narayanan.[19] The purpose of the Altman model is to provide some indicator of business success—subsequent studies reviewed by Altman and Narayanan highlight the myriad different techniques used, the problems of data availability and, most importantly, the methods used to classify the firms as failed and non-failed firms. For example, whether a firm is categorised as having failed is subject to the definition used to describe failure. It can mean bankruptcy, filing by a company for bankruptcy either by the company or its creditors, bond default, bank loan default, delisting or liquidation.

Studies in Australia using MDA analysis[20] to examine corporate failure have found that the following financial ratios are very useful in predicting corporate distress:

- EBIT/total assets
- EBIT/interest
- Current assets/current liabilities
- Funded debt/shareholder funds
- Market value of equity/total liabilities

Furthermore, in the empirical testing undertaken using Australian data, the model has been shown to have a 90 per cent success rate in classifying failed firms as failed firms and similarly a 90 per cent success rate in classifying non-failed firms as non-failed firms.[21]

Credit scoring systems should carry a warning. When you construct a risk index, it is tempting to experiment with many different combinations of variables until you find the equation that would have worked best in the past. Unfortunately, if you 'mine' the data in this way, you are likely to find that the system works less well in the future than it did previously. If you are misled by these past successes into placing too much faith in your model, you may refuse credit to a number of potentially good customers. The profits that you lose by turning away customers could more than offset the gains that you make from avoiding a few bad eggs. As a result you could be worse off than if you had pretended that you could not tell one customer from another and extended credit to all of them.

Does this mean that you should not use credit scoring systems? Not a bit. It simply implies that it is not sufficient to have a good credit scoring system; you also need to know how much to rely on it. That is the topic of the next section.

# The credit decision

Let us suppose that you have taken the major step of establishing the procedure to be used by your institution to assess credit risk. Your next step is to apply the credit risk assessment and identify which customers should be offered credit.

If there is no possibility of repeat orders, the decision is relatively simple. Figure 30.2 summarises your choice. On the one hand, you can refuse credit. In this case you make neither a profit nor a loss. The alternative is to offer credit. Suppose that the probability that the customer will pay up is $p$. If the customer does pay, you receive additional revenues (REV) and you incur additional costs; your net gain is the present value of REV − COST. Unfortunately,

---

19    See E. I. Altman and P. Narayanan, 'An International Survey of Business Failure Classification Models', *Financial Markets, Institutions & Instruments*, 6 (2): 1–57 (1997). The *Journal of Banking and Finance* also contained numerous studies related to corporate distress in 1984 and 1988.

20    See studies by Castagna and Matolcsy (1985), Altman and Izan (1983) and Izan (1984). Details are given in the Further Reading section at the end of this chapter.

21    For a comprehensive review of credit scoring models and their application in the identification of credit risk see E. I. Altman and A. Saunders, 'Credit Risk Measurement: Developments over the Last 20 Years', *Journal of Banking and Finance*, Vol. 20 and 21 (1997).

you cannot be certain that the customer will pay; there is a probability $(1 - p)$ of default. Default means you receive nothing and incur the additional costs. The *expected* profit from the two courses of action is therefore as follows:

|  | Expected profit |
| --- | --- |
| Refuse credit | 0 |
| Grant credit | $p\text{PV}(\text{REV} - \text{COST}) - (1 - p)\text{PV}(\text{COST})$ |

You should grant credit if the expected profit from doing so is greater than the expected profit from refusing.

**figure 30.2**

If you refuse credit, you make neither a profit nor a loss. If you offer credit, there is a probability $p$ that the customer will pay and you will make REV − COST; there is also a probability $(1 - p)$ that the customer will default and you will lose COST.

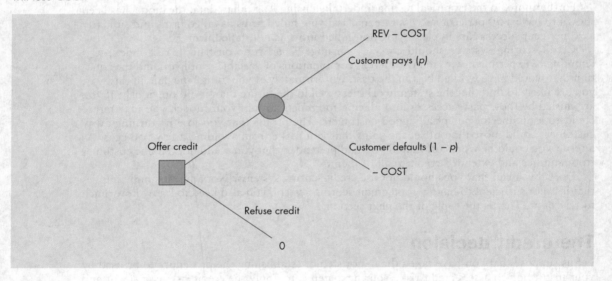

Consider for example the case of the Cast Iron Company. On each non-delinquent sale Cast Iron receives revenues with a present value of $1200 and incurs costs with a value of $1000. Therefore, the company's expected profit if it offers credit is

$$p\text{PV}(\text{REV} - \text{COST}) - (1 - p)\text{PV}(\text{COST}) = p \times 200 - (1 - p) \times 1000$$

If the probability of collection is 5/6 (83.33 per cent), Cast Iron can expect to break even:

$$\text{Expected profit} = \frac{5}{6} \times 200 - \left(1 - \frac{5}{6}\right) \times 1000$$

$$= 0$$

Therefore, Cast Iron's policy should be to grant credit whenever the chances of collection are better than 5 out of 6 (or greater than 83.33 per cent).

## When to stop looking for clues

We told you earlier where to *start* looking for clues about a customer's creditworthiness, but we never said anything about when to *stop*. Now we can work out how your profits would be affected by more detailed credit analysis.

Suppose that Cast Iron Company's credit department undertakes a study to determine which customers are most likely to default. It appears that 95 per cent of its customers have been prompt payers and 5 per cent have been slow payers. However, customers with a record of slow payment are much more likely to default on the next order than those with a record of prompt payment. On average, 20 per cent of the slow payers subsequently default, but only 2 per cent of the prompt payers do so.

In other words, consider a sample of 1000 customers, none of which has defaulted yet. Of these, 950 have a record of prompt payment and 50 have a record of slow payment. On the basis of past experience, Cast Iron should expect 19 of the prompt payers to default in the future and 10 of the slow payers to do so:

| Category | Number of customers | Probability of default | Expected number of defaults |
|---|---|---|---|
| Prompt payers | 950 | 0.02 | 19 |
| Slow payers | 50 | 0.20 | 10 |
| All customers | 1000 | 0.029 | 29 |

Now the credit manager faces the following decision: Should the company refuse to give any more credit to customers that have been slow payers in the past?

If you are aware that a customer has been a slow payer, the answer is clearly 'yes'. Every sale to slow payers has only an 80 per cent chance of payment ($p = 0.8$). Selling to a *slow* payer therefore gives an expected *loss* of $40:

$$\text{Expected profit} = p\text{PV}(\text{REV} - \text{COST}) - (1 - p)\text{PV}(\text{COST})$$
$$= 0.8(200) - 0.2(1000) = -\$40$$

But suppose that it costs $10 to search through Cast Iron's records to determine whether a customer has been a prompt or slow payer. Is it worth doing so? The expected payoff to such a check is

$$\text{Expected payoff to credit check} = (\text{probability of identifying a slow payer} \times \text{gain from not extending credit}) - \text{cost of credit check}$$
$$= (0.05 \times 40) - 10 = -\$8$$

In this case, checking is not worthwhile. You are paying $10 to avoid a $40 loss 5 per cent of the time. But suppose that a customer order 10 units at once. Then checking is worthwhile because you are paying $10 to avoid a *$400* loss 5 per cent of the time:

$$\text{Expected payoff to credit check} = (0.05 \times 400) - 10$$
$$= \$10$$

The credit manager therefore decides to check a customer's past payment records only on orders of more than five units. You can verify that a credit check on a five-unit order just pays for itself.

Our illustration is simplistic, but you have probably grasped the message. You do not want to subject each order to the same credit analysis. You want to concentrate your efforts on the large and doubtful orders.

### Credit decisions with repeat orders
So far we have ignored the possibility of repeat orders. But one of the reasons for offering credit today is that you may get yourself a good, regular customer.

Figure 30.3 illustrates the problem.[22] Cast Iron has been asked to extend credit to a new customer. You can find little information on the firm and you believe that the probability of payment is no better than 0.80. If you grant credit, the expected profit on this order is

$$\text{Expected profit on initial order} = p_1 \times \text{PV(REV} - \text{COST)} - (1 - p_1) \times \text{PV(COST)}$$
$$= (0.8 \times 200) - (0.2 \times 1000)$$
$$= -\$40$$

You decide to refuse credit.

**figure 30.3** _____

In this example, there is only a 0.8 probability that your customer will pay in period 1; but if payment is made, there will be another order in period 2. The probability that the customer will pay for the second order is 0.95. The possibility of this good repeat order more than compensates for the expected loss in period 1.

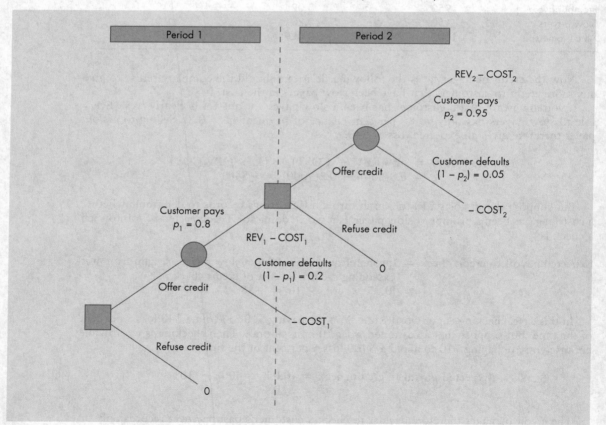

22   Our example is adapted from H. Bierman Jr and W. H. Hausman, 'The Credit Granting Process', *Management Science*, **16**: B519–32 (April 1970).

This is the correct decision if there is no chance of a repeat order. But look again at the example shown in the decision tree in Figure 30.3. If the customer does pay up, there will be a reorder next year. Because the customer has paid once, you can be 95 per cent sure that he or she will pay again. For this reason any repeat order is very profitable:

$$\text{Next year's expected profit on repeat order} = p_2 PV(REV_2 - COST_2) - (1 - p_2)PV(COST_2)$$
$$= (0.95 \times 200) - (0.05 \times 1000)$$
$$= \$140$$

Now you can re-examine today's credit decision. If you grant credit today, you receive the expected profit on the initial order *plus* the possible opportunity to extend credit next year:

$$\text{Total expected profit} = \text{expected profit on initial order} + \text{probability of payment and}$$
$$\text{repeat order} \times PV(\text{next year's expected profit on repeat order})$$
$$= -40 + 0.80 \times PV(140)$$

At any reasonable discount rate, you ought to extend credit. For example, if the discount rate is 20 per cent,

$$\text{Total expected profit (present value)} = -40 + \frac{0.8(140)}{1.2} = \$53.33$$

In this example you should grant credit even though you expect to make a loss on the order. The expected loss is more than outweighed by the possibility that you will secure a reliable and regular customer.

# Some general principles

Sometimes the credit manager faces clear-cut choices. In these circumstances it may be possible to estimate fairly precisely the consequences of a more liberal or a more stringent credit policy. But real-life situations are generally far more complex than our simple examples. Customers are not all good or bad. Many of them pay consistently late; you get your money, but it costs more to collect and you lose a few months interest. Then there is the question of risk. You may be able to measure the revenues and costs, but at what rate do you discount them?

Like almost all financial decisions, credit allocation involves a strong dose of judgement. Our examples are intended as reminders of the issues involved rather than as cookbook formulas. Here are the basic things to remember.

1. *Maximise profit.* As credit manager your job is not to minimise the number of bad accounts; it is to maximise expected profit. You must therefore recognise that you are concerned with a trade-off. The best that can happen is that the customer pays promptly; the worst is default. In the one case, the firm receives the full additional revenues from the sale less the additional costs; in the other, it receives nothing and loses the costs. You must weigh the chances of these alternative outcomes. If the margin of profit is high, you are justified in a liberal credit policy; if it is low, you cannot afford many bad debts.

2. *Concentrate on the dangerous accounts.* You should not expend the same effort on analysing all credit applications. If an application is small or clear-cut, your decision should be largely routine; if it is large or doubtful, you may do better to move straight to a detailed credit appraisal. Most credit managers do not make credit decisions on an order-by-order basis. Instead, they set a credit limit for each customer. The sales representative is required to refer the order for approval only if the customer exceeds this limit.

3. *Look beyond the immediate order.* The credit decision is a dynamic problem. You cannot look only at the immediate future. Sometimes it may be worth accepting a relatively poor risk as long as there is a likelihood that the customer will grow into a regular and reliable

buyer. New businesses must therefore be prepared to incur more bad debts than established businesses. This is part of the cost of building up a good customer list.

## 30.3 Credit collection practices

All firms employ differing collection policies with substantial diversity in their application. As noted by Mian and Smith,[23] firm size, existing distribution channels, industry concentration and the credit standing of the firm issuing the credit all influence the approach used in credit collection. Firms need to choose whether to manage the credit process internally, establish a financial subsidiary responsible for managing accounts receivable or outsource their credit operations to a credit collection agency to collect accounts.

It would be nice if all customers paid their bills by the due date. But they do not, and since you may also occasionally 'stretch' your payables, you cannot altogether blame them. A general rule of thumb is that there are four general types of customers:

▪ Those that pay when they should.
▪ Those that pay when they are reminded.
▪ Those that pay when threatened with legal action.
▪ Those that go insolvent before they pay.

With these in mind, a firm seeking to implement its own collection procedures should include procedures for the sending of invoices and follow up, including sending statements of account, written and telephone contact, and the use of personal visits, third party collection techniques and the sales force to give reminders to clients.

The credit manager keeps a record of payment experiences with each customer. The manager therefore knows that company A always takes the discount and that company Z is generally slow and takes 90 days to pay. In addition, the manager monitors overdue payments by drawing up a schedule of the ageing of receivables. This may look roughly like Table 30.2.

**table 30.2** _____
Schedule of the ageing of receivables (figures in $000)

| Customer's name | Amount not yet due | 1 month overdue | More than 1 month overdue | Total owed |
|---|---|---|---|---|
| A | 10 000 | 0 | 0 | 10 000 |
| B | 0 | 0 | 5 000 | 5 000 |
| : | : | : | : | : |
| Z | 5 000 | 4 000 | 21 000 | 30 000 |
| Total | 200 000 | 40 000 | 58 000 | 298 000 |

As noted in Table 30.2, the two firms B and Z both have accounts that are more than one month overdue with almost 19.46 per cent of all accounts in a similar position. As these accounts are in arrears, they will need follow up action as potentially defaulting accounts.

_____

23   See Mian and Smith, op. cit., Footnote 3.

# 30.4 Identification and management of defaulters

When a customer is in arrears, the usual procedure is to send a statement of account and to follow this at intervals with increasingly insistent letters, telephone calls or fax messages. If none of these has any effect, most companies turn the debt over to a collection agency or a solicitor. The fee for such services is usually between 15 and 40 per cent of the amount collected. An insolvent customer may seek relief by petitioning for bankruptcy or the liquidation of the company.

There is always a potential conflict of interest between the collection department and the sales department. Sales representatives commonly complain that they no sooner win new customers than the collection department frightens them off with threatening letters. The collection manager, on the other hand, bemoans the fact that the sales force is concerned only with winning orders and does not care whether the goods are subsequently paid for.

There are also many instances of cooperation between sales managers and the financial managers who worry about collections. For example, the specialty chemicals division of a major pharmaceutical company actually made a business loan to an important customer which had been suddenly cut off by its bank. The pharmaceutical company bet that it knew its customer better than the customer's bank did—and the pharmaceutical company was right. The customer arranged alternative bank financing, paid back the pharmaceutical company and became an even more loyal customer. It was a nice example of financial management supporting sales. In some companies sales commissions are linked to the collection of money rather than just to the 'point of sale'—this also has helped to elicit the cooperation of the sales staff in the collection process.

It is not common for suppliers to make business loans to customers in this way, but they lend money indirectly whenever they allow a delay in payment. Trade credit can be an important source of short-term funds for customers that cannot obtain a bank loan. But this raises an important question: If the bank is unwilling to lend or to provide an overdraft facility, does it make sense for you as the supplier to continue to extend trade credit? Here are two possible reasons why it may make sense. As in the case of our pharmaceutical company, you may have more information than the bank does about the customer's business—this is referred to as having an advantage due to asymmetric information. Second, you may be looking beyond the immediate transaction and recognise that your firm may stand to lose some profitable future sales if the customer goes out of business.[24]

# 30.5 Accounts receivable financing

When credit is granted, your firm faces a period where you do not have direct access to these funds until such time as they are repaid. The firm therefore needs to regard credit management as an essential aspect of the firm's short-term liquidity management.

Through careful consideration of the decision to grant credit, the discount rate to be applied, the terms of any discount and the commercial instruments available, through prudent credit risk assessment and the early identification of potential defaulters and through appropriate credit collection policies that strike a balance between risk management and continued sales, the firm can minimise the impact of a gap in funding caused by delayed or non-payment of credit.

Any identified liquidity gap should be examined in terms of its size and maturity and treated in terms of a short-term liquidity problem as discussed in Chapter 31. Two strategies gaining increasing prominence in Australia include the use of factoring and the use of credit insurance.

---

[24]    Of course, banks also need to recognise future opportunities to make profitable loans to the firm. The question is therefore whether suppliers have a greater stake in the continued prosperity of the firm.

# Factoring

A large firm has some advantages in managing its accounts receivable. First, it may be possible for divisions to pool information on the creditworthiness of its customers. Second, there are potential economies of scale in record keeping, billing, and so on, especially if the process can be computerised. Third, debt collection is a specialised business that calls for experience and judgement. The small firm may not be able to hire or train a specialised credit manager. However, it may be able to obtain some of these economies by farming part of the job out to a **factor**.

Factoring works as follows. Factoring allows the conversion of accounts receivable to cash prior to the customer paying the invoice. Following an examination of the accounts receivable of a firm by the factor, including analysis of the types of customers and the average period to payment as in Table 31.2, the factor and the company agree on credit limits for each customer and on particular customer types who they are allowed to factor. Accounts are usually accepted by the factor on either a recourse or non-recourse basis. Recourse accounts are customer accounts acceptable to the factor on the condition that the company agrees to pay the factor within a specified period for monies advanced by the factor if the factored accounts fail to pay their account. In the case of non-recourse factoring, the factor assumes full responsibility for collecting all outstanding amounts. Usually the factoring agreement will provide that the factor will advance 70 to 80 per cent of the value of the invoiced accounts at an interest cost of 2 or 3 per cent above the prime rate. Therefore, factoring can generate immediate cash flow to the company when the company invoices its customers. There are, of course, costs to such an operation, and the factor typically charges a fee of 1 to 2 per cent of the value of the invoice.[25]

In the case of *notification factoring*,[26] the company notifies each customer that the factor has purchased the debt. Thereafter, for any sale the company sends a copy of the invoice to the factor, the customer makes payment directly to the factor and the factor pays the company on the basis of the agreed arrangement regardless of whether the customer has paid. Notification factoring arrangements also usually provide assistance with collection and insurance against bad debts.

In addition to these services, the factoring company may also provide screening and credit assessment of new accounts, collection, insurance and finance. This is generally termed *on-line or full service factoring*.

As noted by Meagher,[27] factoring is available to firms in Australia with annual turnover of accounts receivable as low as $250 000. It allows firms to recover outstanding cash flows within 24 to 48 hours of issuing the credit rather than waiting 30, 60 or 90 days or even longer for payment.

Alternatively, firms may elect to use a technique called *invoice discounting*, which involves the company collecting the monies directly from the customer itself rather than via the factoring firm. The invoice discounter still retains title to the funds and the company collects the money as its agent. The customer is often unaware that the accounts have been discounted. The cash flow benefits to the company are similar to those of factoring—the company receives 80 to 85 per cent of the invoice value up front as a prepayment from the discounter, who then sends an invoice for the total amount of the invoices plus its charges to the company for payment at some time in the future.

# Credit insurance

Alternatively, if you do not want help with collection but do want protection against bad debts, you can obtain credit insurance. The credit insurance company obviously wants to be certain that you do not throw caution to the winds by extending boundless credit to the most

---

25  Many factoring firms are subsidiaries of banks. Their typical client is a relatively small manufacturing company selling on a repetitive basis to a large number of industrial or retail customers.

26  In the case of non-notification factoring, the customer is unaware that the company has entered into a factoring arrangement.

27  A comprehensive discussion of the benefits and practice of factoring for small business is included in a special feature on factoring in *Charter* (November 1995).

speculative accounts. It therefore generally imposes a maximum amount that it will cover for accounts with a particular credit rating. Thus, it may agree to insure up to a total of $100 000 of sales to customers with the highest Dun and Bradstreet rating, up to $50 000 to those with the next highest rating, and so on. You may claim not only if the customer actually becomes insolvent but also if an account is overdue. Such a delinquent account is then turned over to the insurance company, which makes vigorous efforts to collect.

International transactions can be protected by obtaining insurance through the Australian Export Finance and Insurance Corporation (EFIC), which can provide export payment protection (also known as export credit insurance)—this is insurance to protect the payments owed to Australian businesses for their exports. EFIC's role is to provide insurance products and financial services which assist exporters to manage the payment risks and finance risks associated with exporting. Payment risks relates to the risks of not being paid for exported goods or services because of possible commercial, political or economic problems in the country where the trade is occurring. Financial risks involve barriers that exporters face that present them with difficulties in winning export contracts. Such problems include having insufficient working capital to complete the export contract, having poor access to competitive funding or having insufficient collateral.

The credit insurance policies available through EFIC can provide cover for non-payment arising from either country or political risk (up to 100 per cent compensation), such as currency transfer blockages, wars, riots or civil unrest, or for commercial risk (up to 90 per cent compensation). In the year 1997–98 the Export Finance and Insurance Corporation provided credit insurance against non-payment up to $6.9 billion in exports and paid claims totalling $12.2 million from 139 claims under policies. Asian markets alone accounted for $2.3 billion of protection.[28]

## 30.6 Summary

Credit management involves five steps. The first task is to establish the normal terms on which goods will be sold and whether the firm will issue credit. This means that you must decide the length of the payment period and the size of any cash discounts. In most industries these conditions are standardised.

Most domestic sales are made on open account. In this case, the only evidence that the customer owes you money is the entry in your ledger and a receipt signed by the customer. Particularly if the customer is foreign, you may require a more formal contract. We looked at three such devices—the promissory note, the bill of exchange and the letter of credit.

The second task is to assess each customer's creditworthiness. There are a variety of sources of information—your own experience with the customer, the experience of other creditors, the assessment of a credit agency, a check with the customer's bank, the market value of the customer's securities, and an analysis of the customer's financial statements. Firms that handle a large volume of credit information often use a formal system for combining the various sources into an overall credit score. These numerical scoring systems help to separate the borderline cases from the obvious sheep or goats. We showed how you can use statistical techniques such as multiple-discriminant analysis to give an efficient measure of default risk.

When you have made an assessment of the customer's credit risk, you can move to the third step, which is to establish sensible credit limits. The job of the credit manager is not to minimise the number of bad debts; it is to maximise profits. This means that you should increase the customer's credit limit as long as the probability of payment multiplied by the expected profit is greater than the probability of default multiplied by the cost of the goods.

---

[28] Refer to EFIC's Web page at *www.efic.gov.au* for further information regarding the breadth of EFIC's operations.

Remember not to be too short-sighted in reckoning the expected profit. It is often worth accepting the marginal applicant if there is a chance the applicant may grow into a regular and reliable customer.

The fourth step is to establish the collection procedures to be used by the firm and be able to identify the size and maturity structure of all overdue accounts. Then, it is essential that the firm has in place procedures for dealing with the management of defaulters. This requires tact and judgement. You want to be firm with the truly delinquent customer, but you do not want to offend the good one by writing demanding letters just because a cheque has been delayed in the mail. You will find it easier to spot troublesome accounts if you keep a careful record of the ageing of receivables. The firm should also consider the potential benefits of factoring and credit insurance.

Finally, your firm must manage the liquidity gap generated from the issue of credit. This involves an understanding of liquidity management techniques to fund the size and maturity of any liquidity gap.

## FURTHER READING

Two standard texts on the practice and institutional background of credit management are:

N. Beckman and R. S. Foster, *Credits and Collections: Management and Theory*, 8th ed., McGraw-Hill, New York, 1969.

R. H. Cole, *Consumer and Commercial Credit Management*, 8th ed., Richard D. Irwin, Homewood, Ill., 1987.

Much more analytical discussions of the credit granting decision are contained in:

H. Bierman Jr and W. H. Hausman, 'The Credit Granting Decision', *Management Science*, **16**: B519–32 (April 1970).

J. J. Hampton and C. L. Wagner, *Working Capital Management*, John Wiley & Sons, New York, 1989.

D. R. Mehta, *Working Capital Management*, Prentice-Hall, Englewood Cliffs, N.J., 1974.

Altman's paper is the classic on numerical credit scoring:

E. I. Altman, 'Financial Ratios, Discriminant Analysis and the Prediction of Corporate Bankruptcy', *Journal of Finance*, **23**: 589–609 (September 1968).

Altman's book provides a general survey of the bankruptcy decision. The other three studies listed below are principally concerned with an analysis of the conflicting interests of different security holders and the costs and consequences of reorganisation:

E. I. Altman, *Corporate Financial Distress: A Complete Guide to Predicting, Avoiding and Dealing with Bankruptcy*, John Wiley & Sons, New York, 1983.

J. R. Franks and W. N. Torous, 'An Empirical Investigation of US Firms in Reorganization', *Journal of Finance*, **44**: 747–70 (July 1989).

M. Waite, 'The Corporate Bankruptcy Decision', *Journal of Economic Perspectives*, **3**: 129–52 (Spring 1989).

J. B. Warner, 'Bankruptcy, Absolute Priority, and the Pricing of Risky Debt Claims', *Journal of Financial Economics*, **4**: 239–76 (May 1977).

Australian applications of the Altman technique include:

E. I. Altman and H. Y. Izan, Identifying Corporate Distress in Australia: An Industry Relative Analysis, Australian Graduate School of Management, Sydney, Working Paper Series, 1983.

A. D. Castagna and Z. P. Matolcsy, 'The Prediction of Corporate Failure: Testing the Australian Experience', *Australian Journal of Management*, **10** (1) (June 1985).

H. Y. Izan, 'Corporate Distress in Australia', *Journal of Banking and Finance*, **8** (2): 303–20 (1984).

## QUIZ

**1.** Company X sells on a 1/30, net 60, basis. Customer Y buys goods with an invoice of $1000.

   a. How much can Y deduct from the bill if he or she pays on day 30?

   b. What is the effective annual rate of interest if Y pays on the due date rather than day 30?

   c. Indicate if you would expect company X to require shorter or longer payment if each of the following were true:

     i.   The goods are perishable.

     ii.  The goods are not rapidly resold.

     iii. The goods are sold to high-risk firms.

**2.** The lag between purchase date and the date at which payment is due is known as the 'terms lag'. The lag between the due date and the date on which the buyer actually pays is termed the 'due lag', and the lag between the purchase and actual payment dates is the 'pay lag'. Thus,

$$\text{Pay lag} = \text{terms lag} + \text{due lag}$$

State how you would expect the following events to affect each type of lag.

   a. The company imposes a service charge on late payers.

   b. A recession causes customers to be short of cash.

   c. The company changes its terms from net 10 to net 20.

**3.** Complete the following passage by selecting the appropriate terms from the following list (some terms may be used more than once): bill of exchange, open, commercial, trade, an Australian, his or her own, note, draft, account, promissory, bank, the customer's, letter of credit, shipping documents.

    Most goods are sold on ____. In this case the only evidence of the debt is a record in the seller's books and a signed receipt. When the order is very large, the customer may be asked to sign a(n) ____, which is just a simple IOU. An alternative is for the seller to arrange a(n) ____ ordering payment by the customer. In order to obtain the ____, the customer must acknowledge this order and sign the document. This signed acknowledgement is known as a(n) ____. Sometimes the seller may also ask ____ bank to sign the document. In this case it is known as a(n) ____. The fourth form of contract is used principally in overseas trade. The customer's bank sends the exporter a(n) ____ stating that it has established a credit in his or her favour at a bank in Australia. The exporter then draws a draft on ____ bank and presents it to ____ bank together with the ____ and ____. The bank then arranges for this draft to be accepted and forwards the ____ to the customer's bank.

**4.** The Branding Iron Company sells its irons for $50 apiece wholesale. Production cost is $40 per iron. There is a 25 per cent chance that wholesaler Q will go bankrupt within the next year. Q orders 1000 irons and asks for six months credit. Should you accept the order? Assume a 10 per cent per year discount rate, no chance of a repeat order and that Q will pay either in full or not at all.

**5.** Look back at Section 30.2. Cast Iron's costs have increased from $1000 to $1050. Assuming there is no possibility of repeat orders, answer the following:

   a. When should Cast Iron grant or refuse credit?

   b. If it costs $12 to determine whether a customer has been a prompt or slow payer in the past, when should Cast Iron undertake such a check?

**6.** Look back at the discussion in Section 30.2 of credit decisions with repeat orders. If $p_1 = 0.8$, what is the minimum level of $p_2$ at which Cast Iron is justified in extending credit?

**7.** True or false?
   a. Multiple-discriminant analysis is often used to construct an index of creditworthiness. This index is generally called a 'Z score'.
   b. It makes sense to monitor the credit manager's performance by looking at the proportion of bad debts.
   c. If a customer refuses to pay despite repeated reminders, the company will usually turn the debt over to a factor or a solicitor.

## QUESTIONS AND PROBLEMS

**1.** Here are some common terms of sale. Can you explain what they mean?
   a. 2/30, net 60.
   b. Net 10.
   c. 2/5, net 30, EOM.
   d. 2/10 prox., net 60.

**2.** Some of the items in Question 1 involve a cash discount. Calculate the rates of interest paid by customers who pay on the due date instead of taking the cash discount.

**3.** As treasurer of Universal Strategies Ltd, Aristotle Procrustes is worried about his bad-debt ratio, which is currently running at 6 per cent. He believes that imposing a more stringent credit policy might reduce sales by 5 per cent and reduce the bad-debt ratio to 4 per cent. If the cost of goods sold is 80 per cent of the selling price, should Mr Procrustes adopt the more stringent policy?

**4.** Jim Khana, the credit manager of Velcro Saddles, is reappraising the company's credit policy. Velcro sells on terms of net 30. Cost of goods sold is 85 per cent of sales and fixed costs are a further 5 per cent of sales. Velcro classifies customers on a scale of 1 to 4. During the past five years, the collection experience was as follows:

| Classification | Defaults as % of sales | Average collection period in days for non-defaulting accounts |
|:---:|:---:|:---:|
| 1 | 0.0 | 45 |
| 2 | 2.0 | 42 |
| 3 | 10.0 | 40 |
| 4 | 20.0 | 80 |

The average interest rate was 15 per cent. What conclusions (if any) can you draw about Velcro's credit policy? What other factors should be taken into account before changing this policy?

**5.** Look again at Question 4. Suppose (a) that it costs $95 to classify each new credit applicant and (b) that an almost equal proportion of new applicants falls into each of the four categories. In what circumstances should Mr Khana not bother to undertake a credit check?

**6.** Until recently, Bob's Cleaning Products sold its products on terms of net 60, with an average collection period of 75 days. In an attempt to induce customers to pay more promptly, it has changed its terms to 2/10, EOM, net 60. The initial effect of the changed terms is as follows:

| | Average collection period (days) | |
|---|---|---|
| Per cent of sales with cash discount | Cash discount | Net |
| 60 | 30[a] | 80 |

[a] *Some customers deduct the cash discount even though they pay after the specified date.*

Calculate the effect of the changed terms. Assume:
a. Sales volume is unchanged.
b. The interest rate is 12 per cent.
c. There are no defaults.
d. Cost of goods sold is 80 per cent of sales.

**7.** Look back at Question 6. Assume that the change in credit terms results in a 2 per cent increase in sales. Recalculate the effect of the changed credit terms.

**8.** Financial ratios were described in Chapter 27. If you were the credit manager, to which financial ratios would you pay most attention? Which do you think would be the least informative?

**9.** Discuss in which ways real-life decisions are more complex than the decision illustrated in Figure 30.3. How do you think these differences ought to affect the credit decision?

**10.** Discuss the problems with developing a numerical credit scoring system for evaluating personal loans.

**11.** If a company experiences a sudden decrease in sales, the ageing schedule in Table 30.2 will suggest that an abnormally high proportion of payments is overdue. Show why this happens. Can you suggest an alternative form of presentation that would make it easier to recognise a change in customer payment patterns?

**12.** Why do firms grant 'free' credit? Would it be more efficient if all sales were for cash and late payers were charged interest?

**13.** Sometimes a firm sells its receivables at a discount to a wholly owned 'captive finance company'. This captive finance company is financed partly by the parent, but it also issues substantial amounts of debt. What are the possible advantages to such an arrangement?

**14.** Explain why equity can sometimes have a positive value even when companies petition for bankruptcy.

**15.** Reliant Umbrellas has been approached by Tully FNQ Supplies of Tully in North Queensland. Tully FNQ Supplies has expressed interest in an initial purchase of 5000 umbrellas at $10 each on Reliant's standard terms of 2/30, net 60. Tully FNQ Supplies estimates that if the umbrellas prove popular with customers, its purchases in the North Queensland region could be 30 000 umbrellas a year. After deducting variable costs, this would provide an addition of $47 000 to Reliant's profits.

Reliant has been anxious for some time to break into the North Queensland market, but its credit manager has some doubts about Tully FNQ Supplies. For five years Tully FNQ Supplies had embarked on an aggressive program of store openings. In 1997, however, it went into reverse. A slowdown in tourism combined with aggressive price competition caused a cash shortage. Tully FNQ Supplies laid off employees, closed one store and deferred store openings. The company's Dun and Bradstreet rating is only fair and a check with Tully FNQ Supplies' other suppliers reveals that, although the company has traditionally taken cash discounts, it has recently been paying 30 days slow. Tully FNQ supplies has unused credit lines of $350 000 but has entered into discussions with the banks for a renewal of a $1 500 000 term loan due at the end of the year.

Table 30.3 summarises Tully FNQ Supplies' latest financial statements.

**table 30.3**

Tully FNQ Supplies: summary of financial statements (figures in $million)

|  | 1997 | 1996 |  | 1997 | 1996 |  | 1997 | 1996 |
|---|---|---|---|---|---|---|---|---|
| Cash | 1.0 | 1.2 | Payables | 2.3 | 2.5 | Sales | 55.0 | 59.0 |
| Receivables | 1.5 | 1.6 | Short-term loans | 3.9 | 1.9 | Cost of goods sold | 32.6 | 35.9 |
| Inventory | 10.9 | 11.6 | Long-term debt | 1.8 | 2.6 | Selling, general and administrative expenses | 20.8 | 20.2 |
| Fixed assets | 5.1 | 4.3 | Equity | 10.5 | 11.7 | Interest | 0.5 | 0.5 |
| Total assets | 18.5 | 18.7 | Total liabilities and equity | 18.5 | 18.7 | Tax | 0.5 | 0.5 |
|  |  |  |  |  |  | Net income | 0.6 | 0.6 |

As credit manager of Reliant, what is your attitude to extending credit to Tully FNQ Supplies?

16. Galenic Ltd. is a wholesaler for a range of pharmaceutical products. Before deducting any losses from bad debts, Galenic operates on a profit margin of 5 per cent. For a long time the firm has employed a numerical credit scoring system based on a small number of key ratios. This has resulted in a bad-debt ratio of 1 per cent.

Galenic has recently commissioned a detailed statistical study of the payment record of its customers over the past eight years and, after considerable experimentation, has identified five variables that could form the basis of a new credit scoring system. On the evidence of the past eight years, Galenic calculates that for every 10 000 accounts it would have experienced the following default rates:

| Credit score under proposed system | Number of accounts | | |
|---|---|---|---|
|  | Defaulting | Paying | Total |
| Greater than 80 | 60 | 9 100 | 9 160 |
| Less than 80 | 40 | 800 | 840 |
| Total | 100 | 9 900 | 10 000 |

By refusing credit to firms with a low credit score (less than 80) Galenic calculates that it would reduce its bad-debt ratio to 60/9160, or just under 0.7 per cent. While this may not seem like a big deal, Galenic's credit manager reasons that this is equivalent to a decrease of one-third in the bad-debt ratio and would result in a significant improvement in the profit margin.

a. What is Galenic's current profit margin, allowing for bad debts?

b. Assuming that the firm's estimates of default rates are right, how would the new credit scoring system affect profits?

c. Why might you suspect that Galenic's estimates of default rates would not be realised in practice? What are the likely consequences of overestimating the accuracy of such a credit scoring scheme?

d. Suppose that one of the variables in the proposed new scoring system is whether the customer has an existing account with Galenic (new customers are more likely to default). How would this affect your assessment of the proposal?

# chapter 31

# CASH MANAGEMENT

In December 1995, individuals and corporations in Australia held approximately $286 billion in cash. This included about $19 billion of currency and $267 billion of demand deposits with banks and other financial institutions. Cash pays no interest. Why, then, do sensible people hold it? Why, for example, don't you take all your cash and invest it in interest-bearing securities? The answer, of course, is that cash gives you more *liquidity* than securities. You can use it to buy things. It is hard enough getting Sydney taxi drivers to give you change for a $100 note for a short trip, but try asking them to give change from a bank accepted bill.

In equilibrium, all assets in the same risk class are priced to give the same expected marginal benefit. The benefit from holding bank accepted bills is the interest that you receive; the benefit from holding cash is that it gives you a convenient store of liquidity. In equilibrium, the marginal value of this liquidity is equal to the marginal value of the interest on an equivalent investment in bank accepted bills. This is just another way of saying that bank accepted bills are investments with zero net present value— they are fair value relative to cash.

Does this mean that it does not matter how much cash you hold? Of course not. The marginal value of liquidity declines as you hold increasing amounts of cash. When you have only a small proportion of your assets in cash, a little extra can be extremely useful; when you have a substantial holding, any additional liquidity is not worth much. Therefore, as financial manager you want to hold cash balances up to the point where the marginal value of the liquidity is equal to the value of the interest forgone.

If that seems more easily said than done, you might be comforted to know that production managers must make a similar trade-off. Ask yourself why they carry inventories of raw materials. They are not obliged to do so; they could simply buy materials day by day, as needed. But then they would pay higher prices for ordering in small lots, and they would risk production delays if the materials were not delivered on time. That is why they order more than the firm's immediate needs.[1]

But there is a cost to holding inventories. Interest is lost on the money that is tied up in inventories, storage must be paid for and often there is spoilage and deterioration. Therefore, production managers try to strike a sensible balance between the costs of holding too little inventory and those of holding too much.

That is all we are saying you need to do with cash. Cash is just another raw material that you require to carry on production. If you keep too small a proportion of your funds in the bank, you will need to make repeated small sales of securities every time you want to pay your bills.

On the other hand, if you keep excessive cash in the bank, you are losing interest. The trick is to hit a sensible balance.

Cash management involves planning and controlling the timing and amounts of cash receipts and payments by individuals and firms and ensuring surplus cash is invested in assets to provide a balance between liquidity and the maximisation of profits.

The trade-off between the benefits and costs of liquidity is one essential part of cash management. The other part is making sure that the collection and disbursement of cash are as efficient as possible. To understand this we will have to look closely at the relationships between firms and their banks. Most of the latter part of this chapter is devoted to the mechanics of cash collection and disbursement and the services offered by banks to assist firms in cash management.

## 31.1 Inventories and cash balances

Let us take a look at what economists have had to say about managing inventories and then see whether some of these ideas may help us to manage cash balances. Here is a simple inventory problem.

Everyman's Bookstore experiences a steady demand for the Australian edition of *Principles of Corporate Finance* from customers who find that it makes a serviceable bookend. Suppose that the bookstore sells 100 copies of the book a year and that it orders $Q$ books at a time from the publisher. Then it will need to place $100/Q$ orders per year:

$$\text{Number of orders per year} = \frac{\text{sales}}{Q} = \frac{100}{Q}$$

Just before each delivery, the bookstore has effectively no inventory of *Principles of Corporate Finance*. Just *after* each delivery it has an inventory of $Q$ books. Therefore, its *average* inventory is midway between 0 books and $Q$ books:

$$\text{Average inventory} = \frac{Q}{2} \text{ books}$$

For example, if the store increases its regular order by one book, the average inventory increases by 0.5 or half a book.

There are two costs to holding this inventory. First, there is the carrying cost. This includes the cost of the capital that is tied up in inventory, the cost of shelf space, and so on. Let us suppose that these costs work out to a dollar per book per year. Adding one more book to each

---

[1] Not much more, in many manufacturing operations. 'Just-in-time' assembly systems provide for a continuous stream of parts deliveries, with no more than two or three hours worth of parts inventory on hand. Financial managers likewise strive for just-in-time cash management systems, in which no cash lies idle anywhere in the company's business. This ideal is never quite reached because of the costs and delays discussed in this chapter. Large corporations get close, however.

**table 31.1**

How order cost varies with order size

| Order size, number of books | Number of orders per year | Total order costs ($) |
|:---:|:---:|:---:|
| 1 | 100 | 200 |
| 2 | 50 | 100 |
| 3 | 33 | 66 |
| 4 | 25 | 50 |
| 10 | 10 | 20 |
| 100 | 1 | 2 |

order therefore increases the average inventory by book and the carrying cost by $0.5 \times \$1.00$ = \$0.50. Thus, the marginal carrying cost is a constant \$0.50:

$$\text{Marginal carrying cost} = \frac{\text{carrying cost per book}}{2} = \$0.50$$

The second type of cost is the order cost. Imagine that each order placed with the publisher involves a fixed clerical and handling expense of \$2. Table 31.1 illustrates what happens to order costs as you increase the size of each order. You can see that the bookstore gets a large reduction in costs when it orders two books at a time rather than one, but thereafter the savings from increases in order size steadily diminish. In fact, the *marginal* reduction in order cost depends on the *square* of the order size:[2]

$$\text{Marginal reduction in order cost} = \frac{(\text{sales} \times \text{cost per order})}{Q^2}$$

$$= \frac{\$200}{Q^2}$$

Here, then, is the kernel of the inventory problem:

As the bookstore increases its order size, the number of orders falls but the average inventory rises. Costs that are related to the number of orders decline; those that are related to inventory size increase. It is worth increasing order size as long as the decline in order cost outweighs the increase in carrying cost. The optimal order size is the point at which these two effects exactly offset each other. In our example this occurs when $Q = 20$:

$$\text{Marginal reduction in order cost} = \frac{(\text{sales} \times \text{cost per order})}{Q^2}$$

$$= \frac{\$200}{20^2}$$

$$= \$0.50$$

---

2  Let $T$ = total order cost, $S$ = sales per year and $C$ = cost per order. Then

$$T = \frac{SC}{Q}$$

Differentiate with respect to $Q$:

$$\frac{dT}{dQ} = -\frac{SC}{Q^2}$$

Thus, an *increase* of $dQ$ reduces $T$ by $SC/Q^2$.

$$\text{Marginal carrying cost} = \frac{\text{carrying cost per book}}{2}$$

$$= \$0.50$$

The optimal order size is 20 books. Five times a year the bookstore should place an order for 20 books, and it should work off this inventory over the following 10 weeks. Its inventory of *Principles of Corporate Finance* will therefore follow the sawtoothed pattern in Figure 31.1.

**figure 31.1** _____

Everyman's Bookstore minimises inventory costs by placing five orders per year for 20 books per order. That is, it places orders at about 10-week intervals.

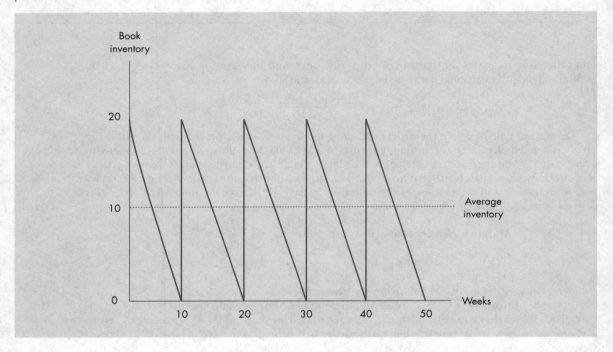

The general formula for optimum order size is found by setting marginal reduction in order cost equal to the marginal carrying cost and solving for $Q$:

$$\text{Marginal reduction in order cost} = \text{marginal carrying cost}$$

$$\frac{\text{Sales} \times \text{cost per order}}{Q^2} = \frac{\text{carrying cost}}{2}$$

$$Q^2 = \frac{(2 \times \text{sales} \times \text{cost per order})}{\text{carrying cost}}$$

$$Q = \sqrt{\frac{2 \times \text{sales} \times \text{cost per order}}{\text{carrying cost}}}$$

In our example,

$$Q = \sqrt{\frac{2 \times 100 \times 2}{1}} = \sqrt{400} = 20$$

## The extension to cash balances

William Baumol was the first to notice that this simple inventory model can tell us something about the management of cash balances.[3] Suppose that you keep a reservoir of cash that is steadily drawn down to pay accounts as they come due. When it runs out you replenish the cash balance by borrowing against an overdraft facility with your bank. The main carrying cost of holding this cash is the interest that you are losing. The order cost is the fixed administrative expense of each drawdown of borrowed funds. In these circumstances your inventory of cash also follows a sawtoothed pattern as in Figure 31.1.

In other words, your cash management problem is exactly analogous to the problem of optimum order size faced by Everyman's Bookstore. You just have to redefine variables. Instead of books per order, $Q$ becomes the amount of funds borrowed via the overdraft each time the cash balance is replenished. Cost per order becomes cost per drawdown of borrowed funds. Carrying cost is just the interest rate. Total cash disbursements take the place of books sold. The optimum $Q$ is

$$Q = \sqrt{\frac{2 \times \text{annual cash disbursements} \times \text{cost per drawdown of borrowed funds}}{\text{interest rate}}}$$

Suppose that the interest rate on the overdraft facility is 8 per cent, but every drawdown attracts a bank fee of \$20. Your firm pays out cash at a rate of \$105 000 per month or \$1 260 000 per year. Therefore, the optimum $Q$ is

$$Q = \sqrt{\frac{2 \times 1\,260\,000 \times 20}{0.08}}$$

$$= \$25\,100, \text{ or about } \$25\,000$$

Thus, your firm would drawdown approximately \$25 000 four times a month—about once a week. Its average cash balance would be \$25 000/2, or \$12 500.

In Baumol's model a higher interest rate implies a lower $Q$.[4] In general, when interest rates are high, you want to hold small average cash balances. On the other hand, if you use up cash at a high rate or if there are high costs to selling securities, you want to hold large average cash balances. Think about that for a moment. *You can hold too little cash.* Many financial managers point with pride to the tight control that they exercise over cash and to the extra interest that they have earned. These benefits are highly visible. The costs are less visible, but they can be very large. When you allow for the time that the manager spends in monitoring their cash balance, it may make sense to forgo some of that extra interest.

## The Miller–Orr model

Baumol's model works well as long as the firm is steadily using up its cash inventory. But that is not what usually happens. In some weeks the firm may collect a number of large unpaid bills and therefore receive a net *inflow* of cash. In other weeks it may pay its suppliers and so incur a net *outflow* of cash.

---

3    W. J. Baumol, 'The Transactions Demand for Cash: An Inventory Theoretic Approach', *Quarterly Journal of Economics*, **66**: 545–56 (November 1952).

4    Note that the interest rate is in the denominator of the expression for optimal $Q$. Thus, increasing the interest rate reduces the optimal $Q$.

Economists and management scientists have developed a variety of more elaborate and realistic models that allow for the possibility of both cash inflows and outflows. Let us look briefly at a model developed by Miller and Orr.[5] It represents a nice compromise between simplicity and realism.

Miller and Orr consider how the firm should manage its cash balance if it cannot predict day-to-day cash inflows and outflows. Their answer is shown in Figure 31.2. You can see that the cash balance meanders unpredictably until it reaches an upper limit. At this point the firm buys enough securities to return the cash balance to a more normal level. Once again the cash balance is allowed to meander until this time it hits a lower limit. When it does, the firm sells enough securities to restore the balance to its normal level. Thus, the rule is to allow the cash holding to wander freely until it hits an upper or lower limit. When this happens, the firm buys or sells securities to regain the desired balance.

**figure 31.2** _____

In Miller and Orr's model the cash balance is allowed to meander until it hits an upper or lower limit. At this point the firm buys or sells securities to restore the balance to the return point, which is the lower limit plus one-third of the spread between the upper and lower limits.

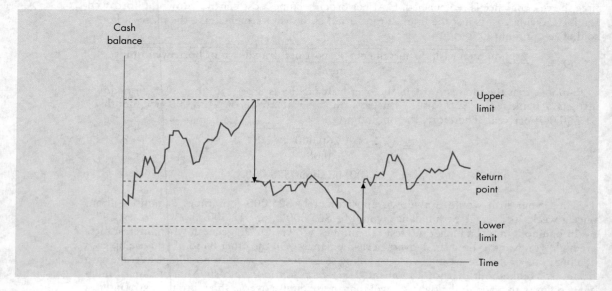

How far should the firm allow its cash balance to wander? Miller and Orr show that the answer depends on three factors. If the day-to-day variability in cash flows is large or if the fixed cost of buying and selling securities is high, then the firm should set the control limits far apart. Conversely, if the rate of interest is high, it should set the limits close together. The formula for the distance between barriers is[6]

$$\text{Spread between upper and lower cash balance limits} = 3\left(\frac{3/4 \times \text{transaction cost} \times \text{variance of cash flows}}{\text{interest rate}}\right)^{1/3}$$

---

[5]  M. H. Miller and D. Orr, 'A Model of the Demand for Money by Firms', *Quarterly Journal of Economics*, 80: 413–35 (August 1966).

[6]  This formula assumes the expected daily change in the cash balance is zero. Thus, it assumes that there are no systematic upward or downward trends in the cash balance. If the Miller–Orr model is applicable, you need only know the variance of the daily cash flows, that is, the variance of the daily *changes* in the cash balance.

Have you noticed one odd feature about Figure 31.2? The firm does not return to a point halfway between the lower and upper limits. The firm always returns to a point one-third of the distance from the lower limit to the upper limit. In other words, the return point is

$$\text{Return point} = \frac{\text{lower limit} + \text{spread}}{3}$$

Always starting at this return point means the firm hits the lower limit more often than the upper limit. This does not minimise the number of transactions—that would require always starting exactly in the middle of the spread. However, always starting in the middle would mean a larger average cash balance and larger interest costs. The Miller–Orr return point minimises the sum of transaction costs and interest costs.

# Using the Miller–Orr model

The Miller–Orr model is easy to use. The first step is to set the lower limit for the cash balance. This may be zero, some minimum safety margin above zero or a balance necessary to keep the bank happy—more on bank requirements later in the chapter. The second step is to estimate the variance of cash flows. For example, you might record net cash inflows or outflows for each of the last 100 days and compute the variance of those 100 sample observations. More sophisticated measurement techniques could be applied if there were, say, seasonal fluctuations in the volatility of cash flows. The third step is to observe the interest rate and the transaction cost of each purchase or sale of securities. The final step is to compute the upper limit and the return point and to give this information to a clerk with instructions to follow the 'control limit' strategy built into the Miller–Orr model. Table 31.2 gives a numerical example.

**table 31.2**

Numerical example of the Miller–Orr model

A. Assumptions:

   1. Minimum cash balance = $10 000

   2. Variance of daily cash flows = 6 250 000 (equivalent to a standard deviation of $2500 per day)

   3. Interest rate = 0.025 per cent per day

   4. Transaction cost for each sale of purchase of securities = $20

B. Calculation of spread between upper and lower cash balance limits:

$$\text{Spread} = 3\left(\frac{3/4 \times \text{transaction cost} \times \text{variance of cash flows}}{\text{interest rate}}\right)^{1/3}$$

$$= 3\left(\frac{3/4 \times 20 \times 6\,250\,000}{0.00025}\right)^{1/3}$$

$$= 21\,634, \text{ or about } \$21\,600$$

C. Calculate upper limit and return point:

   Upper limit = lower limit + 21 600 = $31 600

   $\text{Return point} = \text{lower limit} + \dfrac{\text{spread}}{3} = 10\,000 + \dfrac{21\,600}{3} = \$17\,200$

D. Decision rule:

   If cash balance rises to $31 600, invest $31 600 − 17 200 = $14 400 in marketable securities.

   If cash balance falls to $10 000, sell $7200 of marketable securities and replenish cash.

This model's practical usefulness is limited by the assumptions it rests on. For example, few managers would agree that cash inflows and outflows are entirely unpredictable, as Miller and Orr assume. The manager of a toy store knows that there will be substantial cash inflows around Christmas time. Financial managers know when dividends will be paid and when income taxes will be due. In Chapter 29 we described how firms forecast cash inflows and outflows and how they arrange short-term investment and financing decisions to supply cash when needed and put cash to work earning interest when it is not needed.

This kind of short-term financial plan is usually designed to produce a cash balance that is stable at some lower limit. But there are always fluctuations that financial managers cannot plan for, certainly not on a day-to-day basis. You can think of the Miller–Orr policies as responding to the cash inflows and outflows which cannot be predicted, or which are not *worth* predicting. Trying to predict *all* cash flows would take up enormous amounts of management time.

The Miller–Orr model has been tested on daily cash flow data for several firms. It performed as well as or better than the intuitive policies followed by these firms' cash managers. However, the model was not an unqualified success; in particular, simple rules of thumb seem to perform just as well.[7] The Miller–Orr model may improve our *understanding* of the problem of cash management, but it probably will not yield substantial savings compared with policies based on a manager's judgement, providing, of course, that the manager understands the trade-offs we have discussed.

# Raising cash by borrowing

So far we have assumed that surplus cash is invested in securities such as bank accepted bills and that cash is replenished when necessary by drawing down against an overdraft. The alternative may be to replenish cash by borrowing—for example, by drawing on a bank line of credit, or selling bank accepted bills or promissory notes.

Borrowing funds raises another problem. The interest rate that you pay to the bank is likely to be higher than the rate that you receive on securities. As financial manager, you therefore face a trade-off. To earn the maximum interest on your funds, you want to hold low cash balances, but this means that you are more likely to have to borrow to cover an unexpected cash outflow. For example, suppose either you can hold cash that pays no interest or you can invest in securities that pay interest at 10 per cent. The cost of keeping cash balances is the interest forgone by not investing the money in securities.

$$\text{Cost of cash balances} = 10\%$$

If you need more cash at short notice, it may be difficult or costly to sell securities, but you can borrow from the bank at 12 per cent. In this case, there is a simple rule for maximising expected return. You should adjust the cash balances until the probability that you will need to borrow from the bank equals[8]

$$\frac{\text{Cost of cash balances}}{\text{cost of borrowing}} = \frac{10}{12} = 0.83$$

---

[7]    For a review of tests of the Miller–Orr model see D. Mullins and R. Homonoff, 'Applications of Inventory Cash Management Models', in S. C. Myers (ed.), *Modern Developments in Financial Management*, Frederick A. Praeger, Inc., New York, 1976.

[8]    See, for example, J. H. W. Gosling, One-Period Optimal Cash Balances, unpublished paper presented to the European Finance Association, Scheviningen, Holland, 1981. Instead of keeping the money in cash you may be able to keep it in very liquid securities that are therefore easily sold but pay only a low rate of interest. The model works in this case also. For example, suppose that the interest rate on these liquid balances is 4 per cent. Then the cost of investing in liquid balances is the interest that you forgo by not investing in the less marketble securities:

$$\text{Cost of liquid balances} = 10 - 4 = 6\%$$

Our rule states that you should adjust the liquid balances until the probability that you will need to borrow equals:

$$\frac{\text{Cost of liquid balances}}{\text{cost of borrowing}} = \frac{6}{8} = 0.75.$$

When we look at the problem this way, the best cash balance depends on the cost of borrowing and the extent of uncertainty about future cash flow. If the cost of borrowing is high relative to the interest rate on securities, you should make sure that there is only a low probability that you will be obliged to borrow. If you are very uncertain about the future cash flow, you may need to keep a large cash balance in order to be confident that you will not have to borrow. If you are fairly sure about cash flow, you can keep a lower cash balance.

## Cash management in the largest corporations

For very large firms, the transaction costs of buying and selling securities become trivial compared with the opportunity cost of holding idle cash balances. Suppose that the interest rate is 8 per cent per year, or roughly $8/365 = 0.022$ per cent per day. Then the daily interest earned by $1 million is $0.00022 \times 1\,000\,000 = \$220$. Even at a cost of $50 per transaction, which is generously high, it pays to buy bank accepted bills today and sell them tomorrow rather than to leave $1 million idle overnight.

A corporation with $500 million of annual sales has an average daily cash flow of $500\,000\,000/365$, about $1.35 million. Firms of this size end up buying or selling securities once a day, every day, unless by chance they have only a small positive cash balance at the end of the day.

Why do such firms hold any significant amounts of cash? There are basically two reasons. First, cash may be left in non-interest-bearing accounts ready for immediate use. Second, large corporations may have many accounts with different banks in different locations. It is often better to leave idle cash in some of these accounts than to monitor each account daily and make daily transfers between them.

One major reason for the proliferation of bank accounts is decentralised management. You cannot give a subsidiary operating autonomy without giving its managers the right to spend and receive cash.

Good cash management nevertheless implies some degree of centralisation. You cannot maintain your desired inventory of cash if all the subsidiaries in the group are responsible for their own private pools of cash. And you certainly want to avoid situations in which one subsidiary is investing its spare cash at 8 per cent while another is borrowing at 10 per cent. It is not surprising therefore that even in highly decentralised companies there is generally central control over cash balances and bank relations.

## 31.2 Cash collection and disbursement systems

We have talked loosely about a firm's cash balance; it is now time to be more precise about how cash enters and exits the corporation and how the available cash balance is computed. The first necessary step is understanding **float**.

## Float

Suppose that CRA Ltd has $1 million on demand deposit with its bank. It now pays one of its suppliers by writing and mailing a cheque for $200 000. The company's ledgers are immediately adjusted to show a cash balance of $800 000. But the company's bank will not learn anything about this cheque until it has been received by the supplier, deposited at the supplier's bank and finally presented to CRA's bank for payment.[9] During this time CRA's bank continues to show

---

9    Cheques deposited with a bank are cleared through the Reserve Bank of Australia's clearing system, through a correspondent bank or through a clearing house of local banks.

in its ledger that the company has a balance of $1 million. The company obtains the benefit of an extra $200 000 in the bank while the cheque is clearing. This sum is often called **payment**, or **disbursement, float**:

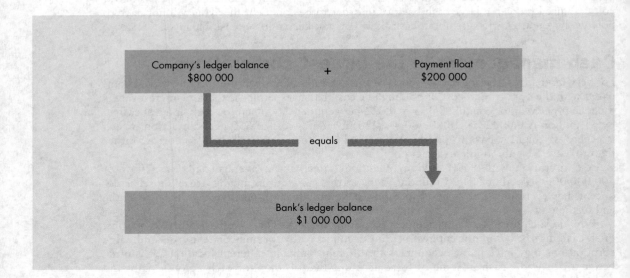

Float sounds like a marvellous invention, but unfortunately it can also work in reverse. Suppose that in addition to paying its supplier, CRA *receives* a cheque for $100 000 from a customer. It deposits the cheque, and both the company and the bank increase the ledger balance by $100 000:

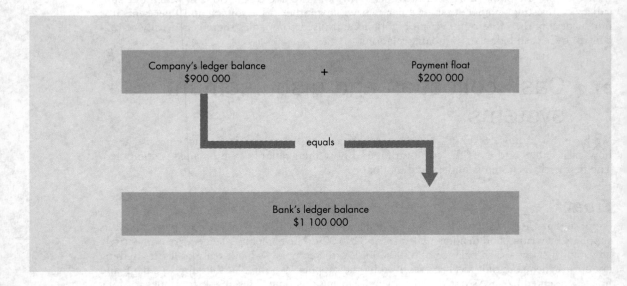

But this money is not available to CRA immediately. The bank does not actually have the money in hand until it has sent the cheque to, and received payment from, the customer's bank. Since the bank has to wait, it makes CRA wait too—usually one or two business days.

In the meantime, the bank will show that CRA has an *available balance* of $1 million and an **availability float** of $100 000:

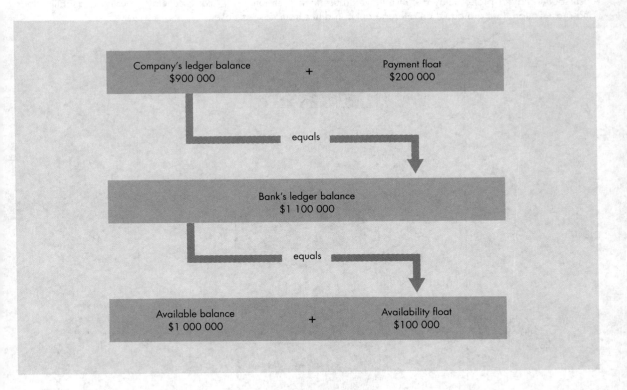

Notice that the company gains as a result of the payment float and loses as a result of the availability float. The difference is often termed the *net float*. In our example, the net float is $100 000. The company's available balance is therefore $100 000 greater than the balance shown in its ledger.

As financial manager you are concerned with the available balance, not with the company's ledger balance. If you know that it is going to be a week or two before some of your cheques are presented for payment, you may be able to get by on a smaller cash balance. This game is often called *playing the float*.

You can increase your available cash balance by increasing your net float. This means that you want to ensure that cheques paid in by customers are cleared rapidly and those paid to suppliers are cleared slowly. Be warned, though: the practice of playing 'float' may in some circumstances lead to legal penalties.[10]

# Managing float

Float is the child of delay. Actually, there are several kinds of delay, and so people in the cash management business refer to several kinds of float. Figure 31.3 summarises.

Of course, the delays that help the payer hurt the recipient. Recipients try to speed up collections. Payers try to slow down disbursements.

---

10  One such practice, known as 'kite flying', occurs when firms draw down one debt instrument to pay off another and then, when it is time to pay off the secondary debt, draw down on the original debt yet again. This continues over time with a net effect that the debt is not paid and interest and other charges accumulate over time.

**figure 31.3**

Delays create float. Each heavy arrow represents a source of delay. Recipients try to reduce delay to get available cash sooner. Payers prefer delay because they can use their cash longer. (*Note:* The delays causing availability float and presentation float are equal on average but can differ from case to case.)

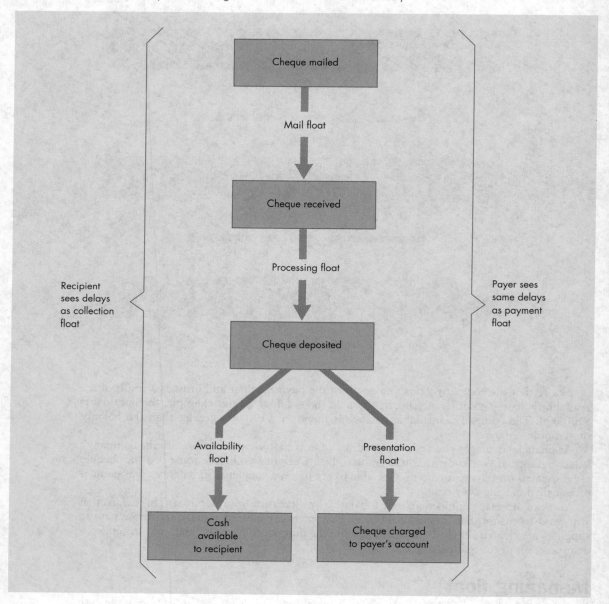

## Speeding up collections

In Australia, some companies use a form of **cash concentration** to speed up collections and to manage cash balances. In this case customers in a particular area make payment to a local branch office of the company rather than directly to company headquarters. The local branch office then deposits the cash and cheques into a local bank account. Surplus funds are periodically transferred or 'swept' into an account at one of the company's principal banks. This can occur on a daily basis at the close of business, resulting in surplus funds above a pre-determined amount being 'swept' from regional accounts to a centralised corporate account or, alternatively, if such accounts are below certain levels, being 'topped up' from the cen-tralised account.

A further facility allows for the 'netting' of the amounts in all the regional accounts with the central accounts of the company, which allows for centralised cash management. Some accounts have the facility for payments made in regional centres (either by the regional office of the firm or by its customers) to be made directly to the centralised account. Such accounts allocate iden-tification numerical codes that appear on the deposit slips used by each depositor. These codes then appear on the bank statements of the firm along with the amount of the deposits. This tech-nique brings many small balances together in one large, central balance, which then can be invested in interest-paying assets through a single transaction. This reduces float in two ways. First, because the branch office is nearer to the customer, mailing time is reduced. Second, since the customer's cheque is likely to be drawn on a local bank, the time taken to clear the cheque is also reduced. By concentrating the cash flows into a single account, cash management tech-niques can be applied to reduce the possibility of idle balances and to manage the periodicity of cash flows in different parts of the business.

Alternatively, many firms with high volume standardised payments, such as telecommuni-cations, electricity and water suppliers, insurance companies and charitable organisations, are now using **lockbox facilities** with their banks. This method of collection involves customers of the firm sending their payments to a single collection post box at a post office. Representatives from the bank collect the payments and for a fee deposit the payments directly to the firm's account. Any non-standard payments are treated as exceptions and referred directly to the firm. The bank then remits a detailed report of payments received and sends the invoices directly to the firm. This method of speeding up collections and remittance processing reduces the capital and operating expenses of the firm, results in economies of scale in the processing of accounts receivable, increases security and speeds up cash flow by reducing the processing time for pay-ments. On the downside, firms have to pay a fee for the lockbox facility and overdue accounts will not be as speedily recognised due to the time difference between when payment is expected and when the company is advised by the bank as to who has actually paid.

## Controlling disbursements

Speeding up collections is not the only way to increase the net float. You can also do so by slowing down disbursements. One tempting strategy is to increase mail time. For example, CRA could pay its Sydney suppliers with cheques mailed from Darwin and its Brisbane sup-pliers with cheques mailed from Perth.

But on second thought you will realise that these kinds of post office tricks are unlikely to give more than a short-run payoff. Suppose you have promised to pay a Sydney supplier on 30 June. Does it matter whether you mail the cheque from Darwin on 27 June or from Sydney on 29 June? Of course, you could use a remote mailing address as an excuse to pay late, but that is a trick easily seen through. If you have to pay late, you may as well mail late.

There are effective ways of increasing presentation float, however. For example, suppose that CRA pays its suppliers with cheques written on a Sydney bank. From the time that the cheque has been deposited by the supplier, there will be an average lapse of little more than a day before it is presented to CRA's bank for payment. The alternative is for CRA to pay its Sydney suppliers with cheques mailed to *arrive* on time, but written on a bank in Perth. In this case it may take three or four days before each cheque is presented for payment. CRA there-fore gains several days of additional float.[11]

---

11   Remote disbursement accounts are described in I. Ross, 'The Race is to the Slow Payer', *Fortune*, pp. 75–80 (April 1983).

For cash management purposes it is also useful to understand the operation of the system by which cheques are cleared in Australia. Historically, financial institutions collecting cheques deposited by their clients, such as CRA, would provisionally credit the customer's account with the amount of the cheque deposited. It is possible that the cheque may be drawn on either the same or perhaps another bank. At the time of processing the transaction, the drawee's[12] bank provisionally debits the account of the drawer[13] of the cheque. Banks do not normally allow customers to withdraw the deposited funds until such time as the cheque has been 'cleared' or not dishonoured by the other institution. If the cheque is not cleared, the initial transaction, the deposit, is reversed and the cheque returned dishonoured. To facilitate this clearing system, the banks and other financial institutions operate under the domestic payments system.

The Reserve Bank of Australia is responsible for the domestic payments system which operates between financial institutions. The payments system is at the core of the distribution of payments and receipts between companies such as CRA and others. Before 1998 a deferred multilateral netting arrangement[14] operated for the settlement of payment obligations in Australia between financial institutions. Under this system, after the close of each business day, the multilateral net positions for each financial institution who was a member of the payments system was determined and the settlement of net positions was achieved via the settlement of exchange settlement accounts with the Reserve Bank of Australia by early the next morning.

From the perspective of the Reserve Bank of Australia, international best practice would demand that all payments be made on a real time basis. In reality, not all payments, especially low value payments, can be accommodated in this manner. By April 1998 high value payments between participants were settled on a real time gross settlement (or RTGS) basis.[15] Under this system transactions are settled immediately and irrevocably on a transaction by transaction basis at the time the cheque is presented, rather than being deferred via the exchange settlement account system.

## Information technology and cash management

Cash collection and disbursement have traditionally involved the creation, transportation, recording and filing of cheques and other paper documents. In the early 1980s cheques accounted for about 85 per cent of all non-cash payments. By 1991 cheques still accounted for approximately 60 per cent of the total value of non-cash payments made in Australia. But by 1995 cheques accounted for just under 40 per cent of the total of non-cash payments in the economy. Where are all the cheques going and what caused the change? Increasingly, cheques are being replaced as a means of non-cash payment by electronic-based funds transfer which in 1995 accounted for over 60 per cent of the value of non-cash payments.[16]

By using electronic commerce[17] facilities, firms can now speed up collections and disbursements. Electronic commerce can decrease the speed of turnaround on cheque

---

12  The one being paid by the cheque and who obtains the credit to their account.

13  The party that wrote the cheque. This is the account from where the payment will be debited.

14  This involved the replacement of gross payment obligations between parties by a single net payment between the parties. Obviously, at the time of initial processing the drawer's account was not debited, but rather a series of suspense or administrative accounts were generated detailing all payments expected from other institutions.

15  For a detailed discussion of the payments system and RTGS see Part C of Commonwealth of Australia, *Settlement in the Payments System: Proposed Bills to Enhance The Stability Of The Payments System*, Business Law Division, The Treasury, AGPS, Canberra, 1998.

16  This data is reported in an Australian Attorney General Department paper, *Trends in the Payment System*, available at *http://law.gov.au/aghome/commprot/olec/ectftre.html*.

17  Electronic commerce, or e-commerce, is a term broadly used to describe business transactions, communications and data management either on, or using, electronic networks. This form of commerce replaces the exchange of paper-based documentation and permits short- and long-distance transactions to be completed at the push of a button at a computer terminal. Its primary benefit is found in the advantage of reducing the costs of completing transactions. For more detail regarding e-commerce refer to Commonwealth of Australia, *Electronic Commerce: Cutting Cybertape—Building Business' Corporate Law Economic Reform Program, Proposals for Reform, Paper No. 5*, AGPS, Canberra, 1997. Alternatively, a recent invention has been the idea of storing money on cards known as e-money. A report on this technique and its implications for financial markets can be found in Bank of International Settlements, *Implications for Central Banks of the Development of Electronic Money*, Bank of International Settlements, Basle, 1996.

processing—firms can use Electronic Funds Transfer at Point of Sale (EFTPOS), they can accept payments via credit cards such as VISA, American Express or Diners Club, or they can use electronic direct debit facilities such as Electronic Bill Pay Services (often referred to as B-Pay). Firms can also use electronic technology to facilitate and speed up transactions at both the national and international levels. Numerous large Australian firms now perform their cash receipts and disbursements electronically.

The chief barrier to the use of paperless cash management systems is that most customers and small- to medium-size businesses are not set up to use them, and in some instances the set up costs may be prohibitive. But for companies that are 'wired' to their banks, customers and suppliers, such a system has three distinct advantages:

▌ The marginal cost of transactions is very low.[18]
▌ Float is drastically reduced as wire transfers generate no float at all.
▌ Record keeping and routine transactions are easy to automate when money moves electronically.[19]

## International cash management

Cash management in domestic firms is relatively simple compared to that in large multinational firms operating in several countries, each with its own currency, banking system and legal structure. A single centralised cash management system is currently impossible for these companies, although they are moving towards it. A multinational typically sets up regional concentration accounts to prevent each of its operations from accumulating cash. The principal company is able to sweep any cash from its multicurrency accounts and then draw on these accounts to invest in marketable securities or to finance any subsidiaries that have a cash shortage.

There are many possible ways of pooling funds. For example, a multinational can open several accounts with the same bank but in different countries. In return, the bank agrees to lump all the accounts together when it calculates the interest that it pays on overall positive balances or charges on any shortfalls.

Electronic transfers and computer-based cash management systems are especially valuable in international business. The costs and delays involved in paper transactions can be very significant.

## 31.3 Bank relations

Much of the work of cash management—processing cheques, transferring funds, running lock-boxes, helping keep track of the company's accounts—is done by banks. Banks also provide many other services not so directly linked to cash management, for example handling payments and receipts in foreign currency, executing the purchase or sale of Treasury and other securities, or acting as a custodian for securities. Of course, banks also lend money, or give firms the *option* to borrow under a *line of credit*, a *revolving credit arrangement* or a *bank overdraft*.

A line of credit is a short-term arrangement between the bank and its customer that specifies the amount of unsecured credit that the bank will be willing to permit the company to borrow at any time. The company can draw against this line of credit at any time during the term of the agreement until such time as it has fully drawn its available amount. This arrangement is somewhat informal and no charges are made to the company until such time as it draws funds using the line of credit.

---

18   James D. Moss, 'Campbell Soup's Cutting Edge Cash Management', *Financial Executive*, 18: 39–42 (September–October 1992).

19   Robert J. Pisapia, 'The Cash Manager's Expanding Role: Working Capital', *Journal of Cash Management*, 10: 11–14 (November–December 1990).

This form of short-term funding arrangement differs from a revolving credit arrangement, which is a legal commitment on the part of the bank to extend credit to a maximum amount for a period of time. The arrangement is binding on the bank. Companies using such a facility are required to pay interest on all outstanding amounts and a commitment fee to the bank on any unused portions of the credit available. This differs from the line of credit where no charge is made for unused credit. Both of these credit facilities usually involve the company in borrowing using bank accepted bills.

These methods of short-term borrowing compare directly with bank overdrafts, which usually involve the company overdrawing its cheque account up to a predetermined limit. Once the overdraft limit is in place the company has complete discretion regarding its ability to overdraw its account and use the facility. Bank overdrafts are generally unsecured but some firms are asked to lodge a security deposit, or they can be secured against assets owned by the firm or by the directors of the company. Bank overdrafts are usually granted at call, which therefore means the bank can withdraw the facility and require the repayment of the outstanding balance as a loan.

Regardless of the borrowing type, the level at which the limits are imposed is conditional on the bank's discretion regarding the current and future creditworthiness of the firm based on the financial position of the company (if any security is offered), the bargaining power of the company and the lending capacity of the bank.

Other forms of short-term borrowing are discussed in Chapter 32.

The banks would argue that all these services must be paid for. Banks demand fees for account keeping administration, for processing cheques, for operating lockboxes or for standing by ready to lend. These fees are usually charged directly to customers' accounts. Furthermore, both federal and state governments levy taxes on either withdrawals or deposits, or both.

Banks like deposits as they can re-lend these deposits and earn interest on them. Banks are therefore prepared to pay interest to attract deposits.

# 31.4 Summary

Cash provides liquidity, but it does not pay interest. Securities pay interest, but you cannot use them to buy things. As financial manager you want to hold cash up to the point where the marginal value of liquidity is equal to the interest that you could earn on securities.

Cash is just one of the raw materials that you need to do business. It is expensive keeping your capital tied up in large inventories of raw materials when it could be earning interest. Why do you hold inventories at all? Why not order materials as and when you need them? The answer is that it is also expensive to keep placing many small orders. You need to strike a balance between holding too large an inventory of cash (and losing interest on the money) and making too many small adjustments to your inventory (and incurring additional administrative costs). If interest rates are high, you want to hold relatively small inventories of cash. If your cash needs are variable and your administrative costs are high, you want to hold relatively large inventories.

If the securities are not easily sold, you have the alternative of borrowing to cover a cash deficiency. Again, you face a trade-off. Since banks charge a high interest rate on borrowing, you want to keep sufficiently large liquid funds to prevent you having to keep borrowing. On the other hand, by having large liquid balances, you are also not earning the maximum return on your cash.

The cash shown in the company ledger is not the same as the available balance in your bank account. The difference is the net float. When you have written a large number of cheques awaiting clearance, the available balance will be larger than the ledger balance. When you have just deposited a large number of cheques which have not yet been collected by the bank, the available balance will be smaller. If you can predict how long it will take cheques to clear, you may be able to *play the float* and get by on a smaller cash balance.

You can also *manage* the float by speeding up collections and slowing down payments. One way to speed collections is to use *concentration banking*. Customers make payments to a regional office which then pays the cheques into a local bank account. Surplus funds are transferred or swept from the local account to an account at easy access to the firm via instructions under a periodic payment order. An alternative technique is *lockbox banking*. In this case customers send their payments to a local post office box. A bank empties the box at regular intervals and clears the cheques. Concentration banking and lockbox banking reduce mailing time and the time required to clear cheques.

In many cases you will want to keep somewhat larger balances in cash than are needed for everyday liquidity. One reason is that the bank may be a valuable source of ideas and business connections. Another reason is that you may use the bank as a source of short-term funds. Leaving idle cash at your bank may be implicit compensation for the willingness of the bank to stand ready to advance credit when needed under either a line of credit or a bank overdraft facility. A large cash balance may therefore be good insurance against a rainy day.

## FURTHER READING

Baumol and Miller and Orr were the pioneers in applying inventory models to cash management:

   W. J. Baumol, 'The Transactions Demand for Cash: An Inventory Theoretic Approach', *Quarterly Journal of Economics*, **66**: 545–56 (November 1952).

   M. H. Miller and D. Orr, 'A Model of the Demand for Money by Firms', *Quarterly Journal of Economics*, **80**: 413–35 (August 1966).

Mullins and Homonoff review tests of inventory models for cash management:

   D. Mullins and R. Homonoff, 'Applications of Inventory Cash Management Models', in S. C. Myers (ed.), *Modern Developments in Financial Management*, Frederick A. Praeger, Inc., New York, 1976.

The next article analyses concentration banking systems. The other article by Bernell Stone gives an overview of banking and cash management:

   G. Cornuejols, M. L. Fisher and G. L. Nemhauser, 'Location of Bank Accounts to Optimize Float: An Analytic Study of Exact and Approximate Algorithms', *Management Science*, **23**: 789–910 (April 1977).

   B. K. Stone, 'The Design of a Company's Banking System', *Journal of Finance*, **37**: 373–85 (May 1983).

The *Journal of Cash Management*, published by the National Corporate Cash Management Association, is a good reference for recent developments. Specialised texts include:

   J. E. Finnerty, *How to Manage Corporate Cash Effectively*, American Management Association, New York, 1990.

   N. C. Hill and W. L. Sartoris, *Short-Term Financial Management*, Macmillan Publishing Company, New York, 1988.

   J. G. Kallberg, K. L. Parkinson and J. K Ochs (eds.), *Essentials of Cash Management*, National Corporate Cash Management Association, Newtown, CT, 1989.

   J. Van der Weide and S. F. Maier, *Managing Corporate Liquidity: An Introduction to Working Capital Management*, John Wiley & Sons, New York, 1985.

# QUIZ

1. Everyman's Bookstore has experienced an increase in demand for the Australian edition of *Principles of Corporate Finance*. It now expects to sell 200 books a year. Unfortunately, inventory carrying costs have increased to $2 per book per year, whereas order costs have remained steady at $2 per order.
   a. What is the marginal carrying cost (for a unit increase in order size)?
   b. At what point does the marginal carrying cost equal the marginal reduction in order cost?
   c. How many orders should the store place per year?
   d. What is its average inventory?

2. Now assume that Everyman's Bookstore uses up cash at a steady rate of $20 000 a year. The interest rate is 2 per cent and each sale of securities costs $2.
   a. What is the marginal carrying cost of the cash (for a $1 increase in order size)?
   b. At what point does the marginal carrying cost equal the marginal reduction in order costs?
   c. How many times a year should the store sell securities?
   d. What is its average cash balance?

3. In the Miller and Orr cash balance model the firm should allow the cash balance to move within limits.
   a. What three factors determine how far apart these limits are?
   b. How far should the firm adjust its cash balance when it reaches the upper or lower limit?
   c. Why does it not restore the cash balance to the halfway point?

4. Suppose that you can hold cash that pays no interest or invest in securities paying interest of 8 per cent. The securities are not easily sold on short notice. Therefore, you must make up any cash deficiency by drawing on a bank line of credit which charges interest at 10 per cent. Should you invest more or less in securities under each of the following circumstances?
   a. You are unusually uncertain about future cash flows.
   b. The interest rate on bank loans rises to 11 per cent.
   c. The interest rates on securities and on bank loans both rise by the same proportion.
   d. You revise downward your forecast of future cash needs.

5. A company has the following cash balances:

   ▪ Company's ledger balance = $600 000
   ▪ Bank's ledger balance = $625 000
   ▪ Available balance = $550 000

   a. Calculate the payment float and availability float.
   b. Why does the company gain from the payment float?
   c. Suppose the company adopts a policy of writing cheques on a remote bank. How is this likely to affect the three measures of cash balance?

6. Explain why companies use zero-balance accounts to make disbursements.

## QUESTIONS AND PROBLEMS

**1.** How would you expect a firm's cash balance to respond to the following changes?
  a. Interest rates increase.
  b. The volatility of daily cash flow decreases.
  c. The transaction cost of buying or selling marketable securities goes up.

**2.** A firm maintains a separate account for cash disbursements. Total disbursements are $100 000 per month spread evenly over the month. Administrative and transaction costs of transferring cash to the disbursement account are $10 per transfer. Marketable securities yield 1 per cent per month. Determine the size and number of transfers that will minimise the cost of maintaining the special account.

**3.** Refer to Table 31.2. Calculate the optimal strategy under the following alternative assumptions:

  ■ Minimum cash balance = $20 000.
  ■ Standard deviation of daily cash flows = $5000.
  ■ Interest rate = 0.03 per cent per day.
  ■ Transaction cost of each purchase or sale of securities = $25.

**4.** Suppose that the rate of inflation accelerates from 5 to 10 per cent per year. Would firms' cash balances go up or down relative to sales? Explain.

**5.** A parent company settles the collection account balances of its subsidiaries once a week. (That is, each week it transfers any balances in the accounts to a central account.) The cost of a wire transfer is $10. A depository transfer cheque costs $0.80. Cash transferred by wire is available the same day, but the parent company must wait three days for depository transfer cheques to clear. Cash can be invested at 12 per cent per year. How much money must be in a collection account before it pays to use a wire transfer?

**6.** On 25 January Coot Company has $250 000 deposited with a local bank. On 27 January the company writes and mails cheques of $20 000 and $60 000 to suppliers. At the end of the month Coot's financial manager deposits a $45 000 cheque received from a customer in the morning mail and picks up the end-of-month account summary from the bank. The manager notes that only the $20 000 payment of the 27 January has cleared the bank. What are the company's ledger balance and payment float? What is the company's net float?

**7.** Every day, Shoes Are Us, a national retailer of leisure shoes, writes cheques to the value of $75 000. These cheques take an average of five days to clear. The company also receives payments of $125 000 every day. These receipts take three days to clear.
  a. Calculate the payment float, the availability float and the net float.
  b. What would be the company's annual savings if it could reduce its availability float to one day? Assume the interest rate is 8 per cent per annum. What would be the present value of these savings?

**8.** Pine Hut is a nationwide distributor of furniture hardware. The company now uses a central billing system for credit sales of $180 million annually. Pine Hut's principal bank offers to establish a new concentration banking system for a flat fee of $100 000 per year. The bank estimates that mailing and collection time can be reduced by three days. By how much will Pine Hut's availability float be reduced under the new system? How much extra interest income will the new system generate if the extra funds are used to reduce borrowing under Pine Hut's line of credit with its bank? Assume the borrowing rate is 12 per cent. Finally, should Pine Hut accept its bank's offer if collection costs under the old system are $40 000 per year?

**9.** A few years ago in the United States, Merrill Lynch increased its float by mailing cheques drawn on west coast banks to customers in the east and cheques drawn on east coast banks to customers in the west. A subsequent class action suit against Merrill Lynch revealed that in 28 months from September 1976 Merrill Lynch disbursed $1.25 billion in 365 000 cheques to New York State customers alone. The plaintiff's lawyer calculated that by using a remote bank Merrill Lynch had increased its average float by one day.[20]

   a. How much did Merrill Lynch disburse per day to New York State customers?
   b. What was the total gain to Merrill Lynch over the 28 months, assuming an interest rate of 8 per cent?
   c. What was the present value of the increase in float if the benefits were expected to be permanent?
   d. Suppose that the use of remote banks had involved Merrill Lynch in extra expenses. What was the maximum extra cost per cheque that Merrill Lynch would have been prepared to pay?

**10.** Suppose that interest rates were to double.

   a. What, according to the Baumol model, would happen to the firm's average cash balances?
   b. Recalculate the gain from operating the lockbox system (described in Section 31.2) given the new level of interest rates.

---

[20] See, for example, I. Ross, op. cit., Footnote 11.

# chapter 32

# SHORT-TERM LENDING AND BORROWING

I f a company has a temporary cash surplus, it can invest in short-term securities. If it has a temporary deficiency, it can replenish cash by selling securities or by borrowing on a short-term basis. Chapter 31 discussed when to make such changes. But you need to know more than that. There is an elaborate menu of short-term securities; you should be familiar with the most popular entrees. Similarly, there are many kinds of short-term debt, and you should know their distinguishing characteristics. That is why we have included the present chapter on short-term lending and borrowing. You will encounter little in the way of new theory, but there is a good deal of interesting institutional material.

## 32.1 Short-term lending

The market for short-term investments is generally known as the **money market**. The money market is not a physical marketplace. It consists of a loose agglomeration of banks and dealers linked together by computers, fax, e-mail and telephones. But a huge volume of securities is regularly traded on the money market, and competition is vigorous.

Most large companies manage their own money-market investments, buying and selling through banks or dealers. Small companies sometimes find it more convenient to hire a professional investment-management firm or to put their cash into a cash management fund. This is a mutual fund that invests only in short-term securities. In return for a fee, cash management funds provide professional management and a diversified portfolio of high quality, short-term securities.

In Chapter 24 we pointed out that there are three main markets for long-term dollar bonds. There is the small domestic bond market in Australia dominated by Commonwealth and semi-government bond issues. There is also an international market for eurobonds and a market for foreign bonds. Similarly in this chapter we shall see that in addition to the domestic money market, there is also an international market for short-term eurodollar and foreign debt investments.

A *euro-aussie dollar* is not some strange bank note—it is simply a deposit or loan that is transacted via a bank with eurobank facilities. For example, a bank in the United Kingdom can make a $5 million Australian dollar euro-aussie dollar loan to an Australian company by transferring the $5 million to the borrowing party as a $5 million dollar deposit in an Australian bank. The account of the Australian company increases by the $5 million and the loan is repaid in Australian dollars.

We will describe the principal domestic and eurodollar investments shortly, but bear in mind that there is also a market for investments in other eurocurrencies. For example, if an Australian company wishes to make a short-term investment in deutschmarks, it can do so directly in the Frankfurt money market or it can make a euromark deposit with a bank in London.

If we lived in a world without regulation and taxes, the interest rate on a eurodollar loan would have to be the same as that on an equivalent domestic dollar loan, the rate on a euro-aussie dollar loan would have to be the same as that on a domestic Australian dollar loan, and so on. However, the eurocurrency markets developed due to an ability to circumvent regulatory controls and due to an ability to provide cheaper finance.

The term eurodollar indicates that most of the business is conducted in Europe and principally in London, but there is also a growing market for dollar deposits in Singapore and other Asian centres. Currencies regularly traded in euro-lending or deposits include the Austrian shilling, Belgian franc, Canadian dollar, Danish krone, French franc, German mark, Italian lira, Japanese yen, Dutch guilder, American dollar, British pound sterling and Swiss francs.

Typically, banks use a reference rate to conduct their short-term interbank business. In lending money to clients they charge a lending margin over the reference rate. The reference rate is chosen so as to reflect the movements that occur in the rates paid on the banks' liabilities. Thus, if the cost of funds to banks has increased so too does the associated reference rate. The most commonly known reference rate is the London interbank offered rate (LIBOR). LIBOR is often referred to as a benchmark for pricing many types of short-term loans. For example, a company in Australia may issue a floating-rate note with interest payments tied to LIBOR. Alternatively, they may tie their deposit or short-term lending needs to the Australian bank bill swap rate (BBSW), or if funds are linked to a project in Asia, to the Singapore interbank offered rate (SIBOR) or Hong Kong interbank offered rate (HIBOR).

## Valuing money-market investments

When we value long-term debt, it is important to take default risk into account. Almost anything may happen in 10 years; even today's most respectable company may get into trouble eventually. This is the basic reason why semigovernment bonds, mortgage backed bonds and Australian corporate bonds offer higher yields than Commonwealth Treasury bonds. However, short-term debt is not risk-free either.

In general, the danger of default is less for money-market securities issued by companies than for longer-term securities and loans. There are two reasons for this. First, the range of possible outcomes is smaller for short-term investments. Even though the distant future may be clouded, you can usually be confident that a particular company will survive for at least the next month. Second, for the most part only well-established companies can borrow in the money market. If you are going to lend money for only one day, you cannot afford to spend too much time in evaluating the loan. Thus, you will consider only blue-chip borrowers.

Despite the high quality of money-market investments, there are often significant differences in yield between corporate and Australian government securities. For example, in June 1998 the rate of interest on three-month bank accepted bills was about 0.33 per cent higher than the rate on Treasury notes. Why is this? One answer is the risk of default on bank accepted bills. Furthermore, the yield is also a function of the demand and supply of the bills available, and the cash flow needs of borrowers and investors.

# Calculating the price of money-market investments

Typical money-market securities, such as bank bills, promissory notes, Treasury notes, certificates of deposit and bonds with maturities less than six months to maturity are priced as though they are pure discount securities or zero coupon bonds using a *simple interest* formula. In the United States and the United Kingdom similar instruments are regularly priced differently as a *discount* security. In simple interest, interest is actually calculated on the principal amount (the money invested or the loan taken), while in discount pricing there is no interest but rather a percentage discount from the face value (or accumulated value) of the instrument. Let us look at an example to highlight the difference.[1]

In June 1998, 180-day bank accepted bills were available at a simple interest yield of 5.40 per cent per annum. Let us assume an Australian firm, Kanga Ltd, wishes to borrow a total of $100 000 (including interest) over the 180-day period till December 1998. How would we calculate the price of this security?

First, let us examine the timing of all the cash flows connected to this security. As shown below, at Point A Kanga Ltd can borrow the present value of the face value ($100 000). In 180 days, at Point B, Kanga Ltd repays both the principal amount borrowed at Point A and the interest over the 180-day period between points A and B. The total amount repaid at Point B is the face value of $100 000.

| A | B |
|---|---|
| Kanga Ltd borrows the present value of $100 000 over 180 days at 5.40% p.a. | Kanga Ltd repays the face value of $100 000. |

Next we need to calculate the present value of the $100 000 at Point A. You may recall that in a simple interest calculation the present value (or principal) of an accumulated value is expressed as:

$$PV = \frac{AV}{(1 + r \times t)}$$

where PV is the present vale or principal; AV is the accumulated value (PV + interest); $r$ is the rate of interest; $t$ is the time to maturity.

We can use this simple interest relationship to price the bank bill for Kanga Ltd as follows:

$$PV = \frac{100\,000}{\left(1 + \dfrac{5.40}{100} \times \dfrac{180}{365}\right)}$$

$$= 97\,406.06, \text{ or } \$97\,406$$

This is a rather complicated way of saying that the price of a 180-day bank accepted bill which pays $100 000 in 180 days (in December 1998) could be purchased in June 1998 for

---

1   Many people in Australian financial markets regularly incorrectly refer to the price of a bank bill as being at a discount to the face value. This is because to calculate the principal or PV of the face value one can discount the face value by the rate of interest over the term to maturity. However, the face value actually represents the accumulated value of both the principal and the interest paid on the principal.

$97 406. Interest based on the principal is equal to $2594,[2] and the total amount repaid in December 1998 is $100 000. The following relationship must hold:

$$\text{Face value} = \text{principal} + \text{interest based on the principal}$$
$$100\,000 = 97\,406 + 2594$$

If an instrument is a pure discount security such as the above, then the return on the instrument consists of the difference between the amount you pay and the amount you receive at maturity—this means the security does not pay interest as per above.

When securities are discounted there is no interest payable. The price of the security is found by deducting the discount for the 'n' days from the face value. The discount is calculated as a percentage of the face value. Hence,

$$\text{Principal} = \text{face value} - \text{discount}$$

If the discount rate is assumed to be 5.26 per cent, then the purchase price is calculated as follows:

$$\text{Principal} = 100\,000 - 100\,000 \times \frac{5.26}{100} \times \frac{180}{365}$$

$$= 100\,000 - 2593.97$$
$$= 97\,406.03, \text{ or } \$97\,406$$

The discount is equal to $2593.97, or $2594. The yield over 180 days on this discounted security is equal to $(100\,000 - 97\,406)/97\,406 = 2.6631$ per cent, which is equivalent over a 365-day year to 5.40 per cent simple interest. No magic tricks here—clearly there is a relationship between yields and discounts. As noted by Sherris,[3] the discount rate is equal to the present value of the simple interest yield and can be calculated as:

$$d = \frac{r}{\left(1 + \dfrac{r}{100} \times \dfrac{n}{365}\right)}$$

$$d = \frac{5.40}{\left(1 + \dfrac{5.40}{100} \times \dfrac{180}{365}\right)}$$

$$d = 5.25997, \text{ or } 5.26\%$$

Furthermore, the 5.26 per cent discount rate, which is equivalent to a simple interest of 5.40 per cent,[4] is also equal to 5.47 per cent compounded annually.[5] Note that the simple interest yield is higher than the discount rate and that the compounded rate is higher than the simple interest yield. An important point to note here then is that when you read the yields on money-market securities it is important to know how the rate is expressed—in Australia, unless otherwise stated,

---

[2]  The interest figure of $2594 can be confirmed using simple interest calculations, where

$$\text{Interest} = \text{principal} \times \text{rate} \times \text{time}$$

In this case,

$$\text{Interest} = 97\,406 \times \frac{5.40}{100} \times \frac{180}{365} = 2593.94, \text{ or } \$2594.$$

[3]  For comprehensive discussion of the valuation of money-market securities see M. Sherris, *Money and Capital Markets: Pricing, Yield and Analysis*, Allen and Unwin, Sydney, 1991; and H. Crapp and J. Marshall, *Money Market Maths*, Allen and Unwin, Sydney, 1986.

[4]  To calculate the annualised yield, multiply the 180-day yield by 365/180.

[5]  The compounded rate is calculated as $[(1.026631)$ to the power of $365/180] - 1$.

the rate is a simple interest rate. In addition, the interest rate is based on a 365-day year—in the United States and in several other countries interest rates are based on a 360-day year.

## 32.2 Money-market investments

Table 32.1 summarises the principal money-market securities. We will describe each in turn, but you should note that in Australia the volume of business in three of these investments is much larger than in the others. These three are bills of exchange, promissory notes and negotiable certificates of deposit.

**table 32.1** _____

Money-market securities in Australia

| Investment | Borrower | Maturities when issued | Marketability | Basis for calculating interest | Comments |
|---|---|---|---|---|---|
| 11 a.m. cash | Banks, deposits industrial firms | Overnight renegotiated by 11 a.m. | No secondary market | Simple interest | Used to fund Treasury operations and for cash flow management |
| Cash— 24-hour call | Banks, industrial firms | 7 days then on 24-hour call | No secondary market | Simple interest | As per 11 a.m. cash |
| Treasury notes | Australian government | 5, 13 and 26 weeks | Secondary market mostly among banks | Simple interest | Notes are auctioned weekly |
| Bills of exchange (bank accepted or endorsed bills) | Industrial firms, banks | 1 to 9 months with most issued at 3 and 6 months | Strong secondary market | Simple interest | Demands to pay that have been accepted by a bank |
| Commercial paper (CP) (promissory notes) | Industrial firms, finance companies and banks | Maximum 180 days; usually 90 days or less | Usually via dealers or the issuer will repurchase paper | Simple interest | Unsecured promissory note, may be placed through dealer or directly with investor |
| Negotiable certificates of deposit (CDs) | Banks, savings and loans | Usually 1 to 6 months; also longer-maturity variable-rate CDs | Poor secondary market | Interest-bearing with interest at maturity | Receipt for time deposit |
| Repurchase agreements (repos) | Dealers in Australian government securities | Overnight to about 3 months; also open repos (continuing contracts) | No secondary market | Repurchase price set higher than selling price; difference quoted as repo interest rate | Sales of government securities by dealing with simultaneous agreement to repurchase |
| Medium-term notes (MTNs) | Largely finance companies and banks; also industrial firms | Minimum 270 days; usually less than 10 years | Dealers will repurchase notes | Interest-bearing; usually fixed rate | Unsecured promissory notes; usually placed through dealer |

# Cash and overnight deposits

The first two items in Table 32.1 are 11 a.m. cash and cash—24-hour call. These instruments are very similar in that they cater for very short-term deposits. The 11 a.m. cash allows financial intermediaries and firms to invest surplus funds on an overnight basis such that money is deposited for periods of 24 hours with the interest rate renegotiated each trading day at 11 a.m. For deposits out to seven days firms can use cash on 24-hour call. Here the firm can only withdraw deposited funds after providing 24 hours notice. Neither of these products has a secondary market and both are used by financial institutions and large companies for cash flow management purposes or to fund short-term corporate treasury operations.

# Treasury notes

Treasury notes are Commonwealth government securities that mature at short term of five, 13 and 26 weeks. They are issued (sold) in weekly tenders with the major buyers or investors being financial intermediaries.[6] At June 1997 there were $13.4 billion outstanding, of which 45 per cent were held by banks and 10 per cent were held by other financial intermediaries. Tender participants can enter a competitive bid and take the chance of receiving an allotment at their bid price. You do not have to participate in the auction in order to invest in Treasury notes. There is also a limited secondary market in which millions of dollars are bought and sold every day.

In Australia, Treasury notes pay their face value on maturity and the difference between the purchase price and the face value (the interest) represents the return from holding the security. The equivalent security in the United States is an American Treasury bill (T-bill), which has a very active secondary market.[7]

# Bills of exchange

The most liquid of the securities traded in the Australian domestic money market are **bills of exchange**. At June 1997 approximately $61.3 billion in bills was outstanding, of which 85 per cent were issued by private corporate trading enterprises. What are bills of exchange and why are they so popular with both borrowers and investors in Australia?

According to the *Bill of Exchange Act (1909)* a bill of exchange is defined as:

> *an unconditional order in writing, addressed by one person to another, signed by the person giving it, requiring the person to whom it is addressed to pay on demand, or at a fixed or determinable future time, a sum certain in money to or to the order of a specified person, or to bearer.*

In practice, a company wishing to borrow funds issues a bill of exchange to pay an amount specified on the bill (the face value), at a date specified on the bill (the due date), to the payee specified on the bill. The bill is then presented to its bankers for acceptance. If accepted, the company then sells the bill to the market. The bill is usually sold to a bank and the firm receives an amount equal to the purchase price of the bill at a simple interest yield to maturity appropriate for the term to maturity. The bank subsequently sells the bill in the secondary market to investors who buy these bank bills.

Bills of exchange can be either accepted or endorsed for payment by a bank. If the bill is *accepted for payment*, this implies that the bank agrees to pay the face value of the bill on the due date to the holder of the bill, whoever that may be. As acceptor of the bill, the bank therefore accepts from the issuer of the bill the responsibility for payment of the face value on the due date. Such bills are known as bank accepted bills (BABs), banker's acceptances or, more commonly, just bank bills.

---

6    Holdings of Commonwealth government securities are used by financial intermediaries to meet their capital adequacy obligations.

7    In the United States, Treasury bills are actually longer dated securities issued by the government with maturities out to 10 years.

The secondary market for bills of exchange is a very liquid market. Hence, the ultimate payee may not be the original payee named on the original bill, as bills can be transferred from one party to another. On the sale of the bill, the seller *endorses* the back of the bill with the name of the new payee and signs to signify the transfer has occurred.

If the firm's bank has not accepted the bill for payment but has been a payee, such bills are known as *bank endorsed* bills of exchange. Bills of exchange that are neither accepted nor endorsed by a bank are in the minority and are referred to as commercial bills of exchange.

At March 1998, of the $65.7 billion face value in bills outstanding, $65.2 billion were bank accepted bills. Why are BABs so popular?

As the bank accepting the bill is taking responsibility for the bill's payment at maturity, the default risk shifts from that of the originating firm to the bank—hence they are more attractive to investors than other forms of commercial paper and present an opportunity for credit enhancement for borrowers when banks act as endorser or acceptor.[8]

Bank bills are regularly used to manage seasonal and working capital requirements or for short-term investment or funding requirements. They are normally issued with maturities of 30, 60, 90 or 180 days, with most issues occurring at the 90-day and 180-day maturities. They are usually issued with a minimum face value of $100 000 in multiples of $100 000 face value. Furthermore, many corporates establish lines of credit with their banks known as a bill facility, or a bill acceptance facility,[9] whereby the bank guarantees to allow the corporates to present their bills of exchange up to a predetermined amount for acceptance by the bank and to borrow funds periodically or to roll over their lending requirements using bank bills over a period usually reviewed at the end of each year.

For example, let us assume Kanga Ltd had a bill facility arranged with its bank whereby it could borrow up to $100 000 face value each six months over the 12 months from June 1998 to June 1999. How would such a facility work in practice? Again, let us consider the timing of the cash flows by referring to the diagram below. At Point A, in June 1998, Kanga Ltd borrows for 180 days at 5.40 per cent at a price of $97 406. At Point B, in December 1998, Kanga Ltd repays the $100 000 face value and then borrows again under the bill facility for a further 180 days to June 1999 at the prevailing 180-day bank bill rate. At Point C, in June 1999, Kanga Ltd repays the face value of the second bank bill. If only life were this simple: a life without any bank fees. Obviously, the bank would be keen to collect its fee for establishing or setting up the bill acceptance facility, for the acceptance of Kanga Ltd's bills of exchange, and for maintaining and committing to the bill acceptance facility over the 12 months.

| A | B | C |
|---|---|---|
| June 1998 | December 1998 | June 1999 |
| Borrow principal amount under bank bill facility or 180 days at 5.40% | Repay face value of $100 000 from 180-day bill from Point A. Then, borrow principal amount under bank bill facility for 180 days at prevailing market rate | Repay face value of $100 000 from 180-day bill from Point B |

Furthermore, it is worth noting that *borrowers of funds sell bank bills, while investors buy bank bills.*

---

8   An additional feature of bank bills is that investors in need of funds before the due date can sell the bank bill at the prevailing interest rate.
9   Such facilities can also be referred to as bill rollover facilities.

# Commercial paper or promissory notes

A bank is an intermediary that borrows short-term funds from one group of firms or individuals and re-lends the money to another group. It makes the profit by charging the borrower a higher rate of interest than it offers the lender.

Sometimes it is convenient to have a bank in the middle. It saves lenders the trouble of looking for borrowers and assessing their creditworthiness, and it saves borrowers the trouble of looking for lenders. Depositors do not care whom the bank lends to: they need only satisfy themselves that the bank as a whole is safe.

There are also occasions on which it is *not* worth paying the intermediary to perform these functions. Larger, safe and well-known companies and semigovernment authorities can bypass the banking system by issuing their own short-term unsecured notes. These notes are known as commercial paper or promissory notes. These securities provide a written promise to pay a specified sum of money to the bearer on an agreed future date.

Promissory notes usually have a maximum maturity of 180 days, though most paper is for 90 days or less. Most buyers of promissory notes hold them to maturity, but the company or dealer that sells the paper is usually prepared to repurchase it earlier. This paper is also generally known as 'one-name paper', as the seller of the security does not endorse the back of the security at the time of sale. These securities are rarely credit enhanced and rely on the issuer's credit standing for their liquidity. Only nationally-known companies can find a market for their commercial paper, and even then dealers are reluctant to handle a company's paper if there is any uncertainty about its financial position.[10] Companies generally support their issue of commercial paper by arranging a backup line of credit with a bank, which guarantees that they can find the money to repay the paper. The risk of default is therefore small.[11]

At June 1997, $53 billion in promissory notes were outstanding in Australia. Of these, 28.5 per cent were issued by private corporate trading enterprises[12] and approximately 16 per cent by government authorities.[13]

Promissory notes issued in Australia are usually bearer securities issued at a discount to their face value. They are often unsecured obligations and the minimum denomination is usually $100 000.[14] The rate of interest paid on promissory notes is usually linked to BBSW plus a premium to reflect the default risk assigned by Moody's or Standard & Poor's at the time the paper is issued.

# Certificates of deposit

When you make a time deposit with a bank, you are lending money to the bank for a fixed period. If you need the money before maturity, the bank will usually allow you to withdraw it but will exact a penalty in the form of a reduced rate of interest.

Wouldn't it be nice if you could avoid that penalty by selling your loan to another would-be lender? You can if you have $50 000 or more to invest for less than one year. In this case, when the bank borrows, it issues a negotiable certificate of deposit (CD). A CD is simply evidence of a time deposit with a bank.

---

10  Moody's and Standard & Poor's publish quality ratings for commercial paper. For example, Moody's provides three ratings, from P-1 (denoting Prime 1, the highest grade paper) to P-3. Investors rely on these ratings, along with other information, when they compare the quality of different firms' paper. Most are reluctant to buy low-rated paper.

11  Firms may also issue *asset-backed paper*. For example, General Motors Acceptance Corporation (GMAC) has set up a special purpose company which buys up to $5 billion of GMAC's receivables at a discount and finances the purchase by selling commercial paper. The cash flows from the receivables are then used to repay the paper. This form of arrangement removes both the receivables and the debt from the firm's balance sheet. See I. Picke, 'GM's Monster Loan', *International Investor*, **27**: 37–9 (May 1993).

12  Such as BHP, CSR and Amcor Ltd.

13  Such as the Australian Wheat Board and the Australian Broadcasting Corporation.

14  Promissory notes are defined under the *Bills of Exchange Act (1909)*.

CDs typically have a maturity of between seven and 180 days, but banks also issue longer-term CDs, up to five years, with a variable interest rate. Most issues greater than one year are transferable. If you decide that you need the money before maturity, you do not have to ask the bank: you just sell your CD, if it is a transferable CD, to another investor. When the loan matures, the new owner of this type of CD presents it to the bank and receives payment.

We pointed out earlier that, instead of depositing dollars with a bank in Australia, a company can deposit them overseas with a foreign bank or the foreign branch of an Australian bank. Unlike domestic banking, such eurocurrency banking is a wholesale rather than a retail business. The customers are companies and governments, not individuals. They do not want cheque accounts; they want to earn interest on their money. Therefore, eurodollar bank deposits pay a fixed rate of interest, and they are for either a fixed term that may vary from one day to several years or an undefined term that may be called at one or more day's notice. Since a time deposit is an illiquid investment, the London branches of the major banks also issue negotiable eurodollar CDs.

Certificates of deposit are very similar to promissory notes except that the drawer is a bank as opposed to an industrial company. At June 1997 there was $58.1 billion outstanding in bank issued CDs. Of these, 46 per cent were held by other financial institutions and 33 per cent by market participants not located in Australia.

## Repurchase agreements

Repurchase agreements (repos or reciprocal purchase agreements) are effectively secured loans in which securities are transferred in exchange for cash, on the agreement that the deal will be reversed at a future date and at an agreed price. They work as follows. The investor buys part of the dealer's holding of Treasury securities and simultaneously arranges to sell them back again at a later date at a specified higher price.

Repos sometimes run for several months, but more frequently are just overnight (24-hour) agreements. No other domestic money-market investment offers such liquidity. Corporations can treat overnight repos almost as if they were interest-bearing demand deposits.

Suppose that you decide to invest cash in repos for several days or weeks. You do not want to keep renegotiating agreements every day. One solution is to enter into an *open repo* with a security dealer. In this case there is no fixed maturity to the agreement; either side is free to withdraw at one day's notice. Alternatively, you may arrange with your bank to transfer any excess cash automatically into repos.[15]

## Euronotes and medium-term notes

Firms may need to finance operations over the medium term of one to five years. This medium-term maturity has been filled by companies issuing unsecured *euronotes* and medium-term notes (MTNs).

Numerous Australian firms (banks and industrial companies) and semigovernment authorities make or have made use of euronote facilities under a *note issue facility* (or *NIF*). Euronotes are short-term, tradable debt instruments that are very similar to promissory notes in that they are drawn in the borrower's name. They are issued at a discount to the face value. Under euronote facilities, a syndicate of banks usually commit themselves to purchase the borrower's notes at a predetermined rate, at a spread over a predetermined reference rate such as LIBOR or to provide standby credit if required. Typically, such facilities are put in place for five to seven years with individual issues of paper being usually short term at around three to six months. If the notes are issued at periodic intervals the facility is referred to as a *revolving underwriting facility* (or *RUF*).

---

15  See 'Federal Funds and Repurchase Agreements', *Federal Reserve Bank of New York Quarterly Review*, 2: 33–48 (Summer 1997).

Apart from the interest rate margin paid above the reference rate which may vary from company to company, borrowers under a euronote facility face an establishment fee paid to the bank organising the facility and a maintenance fee paid either quarterly or semiannually.[16]

If a facility is not underwritten, then the issued paper is usually just known as eurocommercial paper.[17] The security of eurocommercial paper relies on the credit standing of the issuers and differs from euronote facilities in two primary ways:

■ The paper is not backed under a standby or underwriting commitment.

■ The paper is distributed by the issuer appointing dealers, who then place the paper with investors. The paper can be distributed by competitive bidding or by allotment.

You can think of medium-term notes as a hybrid between bonds and promissory notes. Like bonds, they are relatively long-term instruments; their maturity is never less than 270 days and may be as long as five years. On the other hand, like promissory notes, MTNs are not underwritten but are sold on a regular basis either through dealers or, occasionally, directly to investors.[18] Borrowers such as finance companies that are always needing cash welcome the flexibility of MTNs. For example, a company may tell its dealers the amount of money that it needs to raise that week, the range of maturities that it can offer and the maximum interest rate that it is prepared to pay. It is then up to the dealers to find the buyers. MTNs have been used extensively by Australian banks and semigovernment authorities—but the secondary market is very illiquid.

## 32.3 Short-term borrowing

You now know where to invest your surplus cash. But suppose that you have the opposite problem and face a temporary cash deficit. Where can you find the short-term funds?

We have in part already answered that question. Remember that all those money-market investments that we discussed above must be *issued* by someone. So your firm may be able to raise short-term money by issuing a bill of exchange, commercial paper or (in the case of a bank) issuing CDs. But there are also other possible sources of cash that we have not yet discussed. In particular, you may also take out a loan from a bank or finance company.

Obviously, if you approach a bank for a loan, the bank's lending officer is likely to ask searching questions about your firm's financial position and its plans for the future. Also, the bank will want to monitor the firm's subsequent progress. There is a good side to this. Other investors know that banks are hard to convince and, therefore, when a company announces that it has arranged a large banking facility, the share price tends to rise.

### Credit rationing

Before we discuss the different types of bank loans, we should note an interesting general point. The more that you borrow from the bank, the higher the rate of interest that you will be required to pay. However, there may come a stage at which the bank will refuse to lend you more, no matter how high an interest rate you are prepared to pay.

---

[16]  For a recent discussion of firms making use of offshore borrowing facilities refer to Reserve Bank of Australia, 'Recent Developments in the Australian Dollar Offshore Bond Market', *Bulletin*, 1–4 March 1996; and A. Ramsay, 'Funding from Offshore Sources', in R. Bruce et al. (eds.), *Handbook of Australian Corporate Finance*, 5th ed., Butterworths, Sydney, 1997.

[17]  A comprehensive example of the use of eurocommercial paper by the Australian Wheat Board is contained in J. A. Batten, 'Financing the Australian Wheat Harvest', in *International Finance in Australia: A Case Study Approach*, Butterworths, Sydney, 1993.

[18]  For discussion of the evolution and use of MTNs refer to E. L. James, 'Here Come Medium-Term Notes', *Institutional Investor*, 103–11 (March 1985).

This takes us back to our discussion in Chapter 18 of the games that borrowers can play with lenders. Suppose that Doris Brown is a budding entrepreneur with two possible investment projects offering the following payoffs:

|           | Investment | Payoff | Probability of payoff |
|-----------|-----------|--------|----------------------|
| Project 1 | −12       | +15    | 1.0                  |
| Project 2 | −12       | +24    | 0.5                  |
|           |           | 0      | 0.5                  |

Project 1 is sure fire and very profitable; project 2 is risky and a rotten project. Ms Brown now approaches her bank and asks to borrow the present value of $10 (the remaining money she will find out of her own purse). The bank calculates that the payoff will be split as follows:

|           | Expected payoff to bank                | Expected payoff to Ms Brown  |
|-----------|----------------------------------------|------------------------------|
| Project 1 | 10                                     | 15                           |
| Project 2 | $(0.5 \times 10) + (0.5 \times 0) = +5$ | $0.5 \times (24 - 10) = +7$  |

If Ms Brown accepts project 1, the bank's debt is certain to be paid in full; if she accepts project 2, there is only a 50 per cent chance of payment and the expected payoff to the bank is only $5. Unfortunately, Ms Brown will prefer to take project 2, for if things go well, she gets most of the profit, and if they go badly, the bank bears most of the loss. Unless the bank can specify in the fine print which project must be undertaken, it will not lend to Ms Brown the present value of $10. Suppose, however, that the bank agrees to lend the present value of $5. Then the payoffs would be:

|           | Expected payoff to bank                 | Expected payoff to Ms Brown   |
|-----------|-----------------------------------------|-------------------------------|
| Project 1 | +5                                      | +10                           |
| Project 2 | $(0.5 \times 5) + (0.5 \times 0) = +2.5$ | $0.5 \times (24 - 5) = +9.5$  |

By rationing Ms Brown to a smaller loan, the bank has now made sure that she will not be tempted to speculate with its money.[19]

# Unsecured loans

We have so far referred to bank loans as if they are a standard product, but in practice they come in a variety of flavours. The simplest and most common solution is to arrange a loan from your bank.[20] For example, many companies rely on bank loans to finance a temporary increase in inventories. Such loans are described as **self-liquidating loans**—in other words, the sale of the goods provides the cash to repay the loan. Another popular use of bank loans is for construction or 'bridging' finance. In this case, the loan serves as interim financing until a project is completed and long-term financing is arranged.

---

[19]  One must be careful in the interpretation of this credit rationing example, as default risk has not been taken into consideration, nor has the risk of the current or other projects.

[20]  Banks generally prefer that all loans be secured either via a charge over assets or via a mortgage facility.

Companies that frequently require short-term bank loans often ask their banks for a line of credit. This allows them to borrow at any time up to an established limit. A line of credit usually extends for a year and is then subject to review by the bank. Banks are anxious that companies do not use a line of credit to cover their need for long-term finance. Thus, they often require the company to 'clean up' its short-term bank loans for at least one month during the year.

The interest rate on a line of credit is usually tied either to the bank's prime rate of interest or to the CD rate—that is, the rate at which the bank can raise additional funds. In addition to the interest charge, banks often insist that in return for the line of credit the firm must maintain funds on deposit at the bank. For example, the firm might be asked to maintain a deposit equal to 10 per cent of funds potentially available under the line of credit. If as a result the firm maintains a higher cash balance than it otherwise would, the interest forgone on the additional deposit represents an extra cost to the loan.

Earlier in the chapter we noted that large companies often bypass the banking system and issue their own short-term unsecured debt—that is, commercial paper. Even after allowing for the issue expenses and the cost of backup lines of credit, commercial paper is generally substantially cheaper than a bank loan. Remember, however, that when times are hard and money is tight, the bank will give priority to its regular customers. Thus, few firms bypass the banking system entirely, even in good times when commercial paper is cheap and easy to sell.

## Loans secured by receivables

Banks often ask firms to provide security for loans. Since the bank is lending on a short-term basis, the security generally consists of liquid assets such as receivables, inventories or securities. Sometimes the bank will accept a 'floating lien' or 'charge' against receivables and inventories. This gives it a general claim against these assets, but it does not specify them in detail, and it sets few restrictions on what the company can do with the assets. More commonly, banks will require specific collateral.

If the bank is satisfied with the credit standing of your customers and the soundness of your product, it may be willing to lend you as much as 80 per cent of accounts receivable. In return, you pledge your receivables as collateral for the loan. If you fail to repay your debt, the bank can collect the receivables and apply the proceeds to repaying the debt. If the proceeds are insufficient, you are liable for any deficiency. The loan is therefore said to be *with recourse*.

When you pledge receivables, you must keep the bank up-to-date on credit sales and collections. When you deliver goods to your customers, you send the bank a copy of the invoice, together with a form of assignment, which gives the bank the right to the money your customers owe you. Then the firm can borrow up to the agreed proportion of this collateral.

Each day, as you make new sales, your collateral increases and you can borrow more money. Each day, customers pay their bills. This money is placed in a special collateral account under the bank's control and is periodically used to reduce the size of the loan. Therefore, as the firm's business fluctuates, so does the amount of collateral and the size of the loan.

A few receivables loans are on a notification basis. In this case the bank informs your customer of the lending arrangement and asks that the money be paid directly to the bank. Firms generally do not like their customers to know they are in debt, and therefore such loans are made more frequently without notification.

Receivables loans can be obtained not only from commercial banks, but also from finance companies which specialise in lending to businesses.

Loans against receivables are flexible and they provide a continuous source of funds. Also, banks are willing to lend the firm more with collateral than without it. However, it can be costly for borrower and lender alike to supervise and record changes in the collateral. Therefore, the rate of interest on receivables financing is usually high, and there may be an additional service charge on the loan.

We discussed factoring in Chapter 30. Do not confuse factoring with lending against receivables. Factors *buy* your receivables and, if you wish, advance a portion of the money. They are therefore subject to the agreements in place, are responsible for collecting the debt and suffer any losses if the customers do not pay. When you pledge your receivables as collateral for a loan, *you* remain responsible for collecting the debt and *you* suffer if a customer is delinquent.

If it moves, an investment banker will try to turn it into a security. In recent years receivables have sometimes been repackaged into securities. For instance, in 1986 First Boston Corporation set up a special purpose subsidiary, which bought 367 000 vehicle loans from General Motors Acceptance Corporation (GMAC). It then bundled these loans into three packages, each with a different maturity, and resold the packages to investors in the form of notes with the huge total value of $4 billion. GMAC provided a limited guarantee on these notes, but if a large number of car buyers defaulted on their payments, the noteholders would suffer a loss.

The GMAC notes are known as CARs (Certificates for Automobile Receivables). Other companies have bundled together a large number of credit card loans and sold the packages to investors. As you might guess, these packages are called CARDs (Certificates for Amortizing Revolving Debts).

Suppose that you are a car dealer who needs to finance an inventory of new cars. You cannot put the cars in a warehouse; you need to keep them in the showroom under your control. The common solution is to enter into a floor-planning arrangement. Under this arrangement, the finance company buys the cars from the manufacturer and you hold them in trust for the finance company. As evidence of this, you sign a trust receipt that identifies the cars involved. You are free to sell the cars, but when you do so, the proceeds are used to redeem the trust receipt. To make sure that the collateral is properly maintained, the finance company will make periodic inspections of the inventory.

Banks and finance companies also lend on the security of inventory, but they are choosy about the collateral they will accept. They want to make sure that they can identify and sell the inventory if you default. Cars and other standardised non-perishable commodities are good collateral for a loan; work in process and ripe bananas are poor collateral.

Although not widely used in Australia, it is also possible to lend money using inventories stored in warehouses as collateral. The procedure for lending against inventories depends on where the goods are stored. If you place goods in a public warehouse, the warehouse company gives you a warehouse receipt and will then release the goods only on the instructions of the holder of the receipt. Because the holder of the receipt controls the inventory, the receipt can be used as collateral for a loan. Notice, however, that the warehouse receipt only identifies the goods and where they are stored. It does not guarantee the grade of the goods or your claim to the goods, and it does not provide insurance against fire, theft and other hazards. Therefore, the lender will also need to be satisfied on all these matters.

*Warehouse loans* involve a somewhat more complicated arrangement than a standard loan agreement. In exchange for your loan agreement, the bank signs a banker's acceptance that matures on the same date. In other words, in exchange for your obligations under the loan agreement the bank gives you not cash but *its* agreement to lend you the funds. The advantage of this strange procedure is that the banker's acceptance is marketable whereas your promissory note is not. Therefore, you can sell your acceptance to the bank whenever you want the cash, and the bank can, if it chooses, resell the acceptance to another institution. The important feature of warehouse loans is that goods are physically segregated and under the control of an independent warehouse company.

The fact that liquid assets are easily saleable does not always make them good collateral. It also means the lender has to make sure that the borrower does not suddenly sell the assets and run off with the money. If you want to make your hair stand on end, read this little snippet from the United States, which we call the story of the great salad oil swindle. Fifty-one banks and companies made loans of nearly US$200 million to the Allied Crude Vegetable Oil Refining Corporation. Warehouse receipts issued by a field warehousing company were taken as security. Unfortunately, the cursory inspections by the employees of the field warehousing company failed to uncover the fact that, instead of containing salad oil, Allied's storage tanks were filled mainly with soap stock, sea water and unidentifiable sludge. When the fraud was discovered, the president of Allied went to jail, the field warehousing company went into bankruptcy and the 51 lenders were left out in the cold, looking for the US$200 million.

Lenders have been more careful since then, but no doubt they will be caught by some new scam sooner or later. Australia is not isolated from such controversy. In the early 1990s Australian banks involved in funding the equipment and assets for the National Health and Safety Council—who were regularly involved in rescue activity—were found to have been shown empty crates that were assumed to have been holding purchased goods.

## 32.4 Medium-term lending—term loans

When firms need medium-term financing they can raise it directly from investors by selling medium-term notes or short-dated bonds. Alternatively, they can take out a term loan from a bank. Banks typically make term loans of one to eight years.

Instead of arranging a term loan with a bank in Australia, you may take out a eurodollar term loan. If the sums involved are very large, these eurodollar loans may be arranged by a lead bank and then syndicated among a group of banks.

Term loans are usually repaid in level amounts over the period of the loan, although often there may be a large final 'balloon' payment or just a single 'bullet' payment at maturity. Banks can accommodate repayment patterns to the anticipated cash flows of the borrowing firm. For example, the first principal repayment might be delayed for a year pending completion of a new factory. Often term loans are renegotiated in midstream—that is, before maturity. Banks are usually willing to do this if the borrowing firm is an established customer, remains credit-worthy and has a sound business reason for making the change.

The rate of interest on the term loan is sometimes fixed for the life of the loan. But usually it is linked to the prime rate or to the bank bill swap rate. Thus, if the rate is set at '1 per cent over prime', the borrower may pay 8 per cent in the first year when prime is 7 per cent, 6 per cent in the second year when prime is 5 per cent, and so on. Occasionally, these variable-rate loans include a 'collar', which sets upper and lower limits on the interest that can be charged, or a 'cap', which sets an upper limit only.

Term loans are for the most part secured debt. Companies are required to provide security either in the form of a charge or lien over fixed and/or floating assets. Such loans also may include the very restrictive negative conditions of private placement bonds, and stipulate minimum levels of net worth and working capital. Term loans that are made to small companies often impose conditions on senior management. For example, the bank may require the company to insure the lives of senior managers, may place limits on management's remuneration, and may require personal guarantees for the loan. Term loans are usually subject to annual review by the participating banks.

A variant on the straight loan is the revolving credit or *credit facility*. This is a legally assured line of credit with a maturity of up to three years. The borrower may be allowed at the end of the period to convert the credit into a straight term loan. Alternatively, the borrower can use an *overdraft*, which is a revolving credit without maturity that the *bank* may in any year convert into a straight loan. For both revolving credit and overdrafts the company pays interest on any borrowings plus an 'insurance premium' on the unused amount, and it may also be required to maintain a compensating balance with the bank.

Revolving credit agreements are relatively expensive compared to straight lines of credit or short-term bank loans. But in exchange for the extra cost, the firm receives a valuable option: It has guaranteed access to the bank's money at a fixed spread above the prime rate. This amounts to a put option, because the firm can sell its debt to the bank on fixed terms even if its own creditworthiness deteriorates.

## Loan participations and assignments

The large Australian banks have more demand for loans than they can satisfy; for smaller banks it is the other way around. As a result, a lead bank may arrange a loan and then sell a large portion of it to other institutions. This has led to an increasingly active secondary market in bank loans.

These loan sales generally take one of two forms: *assignments* or *participants*. In the first case, a portion of the loan is transferred to the new lenders with the agreement of the borrower. In the second case, the lead bank provides a 'certificate of participation' which states that it will pay over a proportion of the cash flows from the loan. In such cases the borrower may not be aware that the sale has occurred. These loan participations differ from the syndicated loans that we described earlier; with a syndicated loan each bank has a separate loan agreement with the borrower.

## 32.5 Summary

If you have more cash than you currently need, you can invest the surplus in the money market. The principal money-market investments in Australia are:

- 11 a.m. cash
- Certificates of deposit
- Treasury notes
- Bank accepted bills
- Promissory notes
- Repurchase agreements

If none of these catches your fancy, you can make a short-term eurocurrency investment. For example, you can make an Australian dollar deposit with a bank in Japan.

No two of these securities are exactly the same. If you want to make effective use of your cash, you need to be aware of the differences in their liquidity, risk and yield. Table 32.1 summarises the main features of money-market instruments.

For many companies, surplus cash is not a worry; their problem is how to finance a temporary cash deficiency. One of the main sources of short-term funds is the unsecured bank loan. This is often taken out under a bank line of credit or facility, which entitles the firm to borrow up to an agreed limit. The interest rate that banks charge on unsecured loans must be sufficient to cover not only the opportunity cost of capital for the loans but also the costs of running a loan department. As a result, large regular borrowers have found it cheaper to issue their own short-term unsecured debt in the form of bills of exchange, which they arrange to be either accepted or endorsed by a bank for payment.

Bank loans with maturities exceeding one year are called *term loans*. These may be arranged with a bank in Australia, or the firm may take out a eurodollar term loan with a bank overseas. Large eurodollar term loans may be syndicated among a group of banks.

Another form of medium-term bank finance is the *revolving credit*, which guarantees the firm access to a line of credit. Revolving credits can often be converted into regular term loans.

If you ask to borrow more and more from a bank, you will eventually be asked to provide security for the loan. Sometimes this security consists of a floating lien on receivables and inventories. But usually you will be asked to pledge specific assets. The bank or finance company will take precautions to make sure that the collateral is properly identified and within its control. For example, when you borrow against receivables, the bank must be informed of all sales of goods and the resulting accounts receivable must be pledged to the bank. As customers pay their bills, the money is paid into a special collateral account under the bank's control. Similarly, when you borrow against stocks of raw materials, the bank may insist that the goods be held by an independent warehouse company. As long as the bank holds the warehouse receipt for these goods, they cannot be released without the bank's permission. Loans secured on finished goods are usually made under a floor-planning arrangement. In this case, you will be required to sign a trust receipt promising that your are merely holding the specified goods in trust for the lender, and the lender will make periodic inspections to see that you are keeping your promise.

You may also find that there comes a point at which the bank will not increase its lending no matter how high a rate of interest you are prepared to pay. Banks know that the more they lend, the more they are encouraging you to gamble with the money. Your aims and the bank's are more likely to coincide if your borrowing is kept to a responsible level.

## FURTHER READING

For a detailed description of the money market and short-term lending opportunities see:

F. J. Fabozzi (ed.), *The Handbook of Treasury and Agency Securities*, Probus Publishing, Chicago, 1990.

M. Stigum, *The Money Market: Myth, Reality and Practice*, 3rd ed., Richard D. Irwin, Homewood, Ill., 1990.

Examples of money-market instruments and their application as they apply to Australia can be found in:

B. Hunt and C. Terry, *Financial Instruments and Markets*, Thomas Nelson, South Melbourne, 1993.

M. McGrath and C. Viney, *Financial Institutions, Instruments and Markets in Australia*, 2nd ed., McGraw-Hill, Sydney, 1997.

R. W. Peters, *The Commercial Bill Market in Australia*, Longman Cheshire, Melbourne, 1987.

G. Pierson, R. Brown, S. Easton and P. Howard, *Business Finance,* 7th ed., McGraw-Hill, Sydney, 1998.

For a comprehensive overview of the mathematics of money-market securities see:

H. Crapp and J. Marshall, *Money Market Maths*, Allen and Unwin, Sydney, 1986.

M. Sherris, *Money and Capital Markets: Pricing, Yields and Analysis*, Allen and Unwin, Sydney, 1991.

Here is a practically-oriented book on sources of short-term and medium-term financing:

W. J. Korvuik and C. O. Maiburg, *The Loan Officer's Handbook*, Dow Jones-Irwin, Homewood, Ill., 1986.

## QUIZ

1. For each item below, choose the investment that best fits the accompanying description:
   a. Maturity often overnight (repurchase agreements *or* 11 a.m. cash)
   b. Maturity never more than 270 days (promissory notes *or* medium-term notes)
   c. Often directly placed (bank endorsed bills *or* promissory notes)
   d. Issued by the Commonwealth Treasury (bank accepted bills *or* Treasury notes)
   e. Sold by auction (cash—24-hour call *or* Treasury notes)

2. Complete the passage below by selecting the most appropriate terms from the following list: floating lien, field warehouse, clean-up provision, promissory notes, floor planning, line of credit, prime rate, public warehouse, compensating balance, trust receipt, warehouse receipt, collateral, medium-term notes, with recourse
   Companies with fluctuating capital needs often arrange a _____ with their bank. To make sure that this facility is not used to provide permanent funds, the bank usually incorporates a _____. The interest on any borrowing is tied to the bank's _____. In addition the bank generally requires that the company keep a _____ on deposit at the bank.

Secured short-term loans are sometimes covered by a _____ on all receivables and inventory. Generally, however, the borrower pledges specific assets as _____. If these assets are insufficient to repay the debt, the borrower is liable for the deficiency. Therefore, such loans are said to be _____. Warehouse loans are examples of secured short-term loans. The goods may be stored in a _____ or in a _____ that is established by the warehouse company on the borrower's premises. The warehouse company issues a _____ to the lender and releases the goods only on instructions. Loans to car dealers are usually made on a different basis. The dealer holds the inventory on behalf of the lender and issues a _____. This arrangement is known as a _____.

Banks are not the only source of short-term debt. Many large companies issue their own unsecured debt directly to investors, often on a regular basis. If the maturity is less than 270 days, it is known as _____ and does not need to be registered with the Australian securities Commission. Companies also sell debt to investors with maturities over 270 days. This is called _____.

3. Here are six questions about term loans:
   a. What is the usual minimum maturity of a term loan?
   b. Are compensating balances required?
   c. Are term loans usually secured loans? That is, are they usually backed up by specific collateral?
   d. How is the interest rate usually determined?
   e. What is a balloon payment?
   f. What is a revolving credit?

## QUESTIONS AND PROBLEMS

1. Look up current interest rates offered by short-term investment alternatives. Suppose that your firm has $1 million excess cash to invest for the next two months. How would you invest this excess cash? How would your answer change if the excess cash were $5000, $20 000, $100 000 or $100 million?

2. Interest rates on bank loans exceed rates on bank accepted bills. Why don't all firms issue bills of exchange rather than borrow directly from banks?

3. Do you think you could make money by setting up a firm which would (a) issue promissory notes and (b) relend money to businesses at a rate slightly higher than the promissory note rate but still less than the rate charged by banks?

4. Roy's Toys needs an extra $1 million in October to build up inventory for the Christmas season. First National Bank has offered to lend at 9 per cent subject to a 20 per cent compensation balance. A competitor, Second National, will lend at 11 per cent with no strings attached. Which bank is offering the better deal? Why? Would your answer change if Roy's Toys already had a $100 000 normal working balance at First National Bank?

5. Axle Chemical Ltd's treasurer has forecast a $1 million cash deficit for the next quarter. However, there is only a 50 per cent chance this deficit will actually occur. The treasurer estimates that there is a 20 per cent probability the company will have no deficit at all and a 30 per cent probability that it will actually need $2 million in short-term financing. The company can either take out a 90-day

unsecured loan at 1 per cent per month or establish a line of credit, costing 1 per cent per month on the amount borrowed plus a commitment fee of $20 000. Both alternatives also require a 20 per cent compensating balance for outstanding loans. If excess cash can be reinvested at 9 per cent, which source of financing gives the lower expected cost?

**6.** Suppose that you are a banker responsible for approving corporate loans. Nine firms are seeking secured loans. They offer the following assets as collateral:

a. Firm A, a heating oil distributor, offers a tanker load of fuel oil in transit from the Middle East.

b. Firm B, a wine wholesaler, offers 1000 cases of Yarra Valley chardonnay, located in a field warehouse.

c. Firm C, a stationer, offers an accounts receivable for office supplies sold to a company in Newcastle.

d. Firm D, a bookstore, offers its entire inventory of 15 000 used books.

e. Firm E, a wholesale grocer, offers a crate full of bananas.

f. Firm F, a computer retailer, offers its inventory of computers and computer software.

g. Firm G, a jeweller, offers 100 ounces of gold.

h. Firm H, a government securities dealer, offers its portfolio of Treasury notes.

i. Firm I, a boat builder, offers a half-completed luxury yacht. The yacht will take four months more to complete.

Which of these assets are most likely to be good collateral? Which are likely to be poor collateral? Explain.

**7.** Any one of the assets mentioned in Question 6 *could* be acceptable collateral under certain circumstances if appropriate safeguards were taken. What circumstances? What safeguards? Explain.

**8.** Term loans usually require firms to pay a floating interest rate. For example, the interest rate may be set at '1 per cent above prime'. The prime rate sometimes varies by several percentage points within a single year.

Suppose that your firm has decided to borrow $40 million for five years. It has three alternatives:

a. Borrow from a bank at the prime rate, currently 10 per cent. The proposed loan agreement requires no principal repayments until the loan matures in five years.

b. Issue a 180-day promissory note, currently yielding 9 per cent. Since funds are required for five years, the promissory note will have to be 'rolled ever' semiannually. That is, financing the $40 million requirement for five years will require 10 successive promissory note issues.

c. Borrow from an alternative financial institution at a fixed rate of 11 per cent. As in the bank loan, no principal has to be repaid until the end of the five-year period.

What factors would you consider in analysing these alternatives? Under what circumstances would you choose (a)? Under what circumstances would you choose (b) or (c)? (*Hint*: Do not forget Chapter 23.)

**9.** In Section 32.1 we described a 180-day bill of exchange that was issued on a yield of 5.40 per cent. Suppose that one month (30 days) has passed and the bill still offers the same annually compounded return. What is the percentage discount? What was your return over the month?

**10.** Look again at Question 9. Suppose another month has passed, so the bill has only 31 days left to run. It is now selling at a yield of 5 per cent. What is the yield calculated on a simple interest basis over a 365-day year? What was your realised return over the 12 months?

**11.** A 90-day bank accepted bill and a 180-day bank accepted bill both sell at a yield of 10 per cent. Which offers the higher annual yield? Would your answer differ if a discount rate were applied?

# part 10

# TAKEOVERS AND INTERNATIONAL FINANCE

# chapter 33

# TAKEOVERS

There is nothing like a battle for control over a company to spark public interest and set the corporate pulse racing. Control over another company can be acquired in several ways. The most common way of acquiring control of Australian public companies is the takeover bid. Takeovers of public companies attract the headlines, but in the Australian context private companies play an important role in takeover activity as both bidders and targets of bids. Foreign bidders also play a significant role in the Australian takeover market.

Later in the chapter we discuss some of the different forms an acquisition can take. But for the time being we will use the term **takeover** as a general description of all attempts to gain control over a company. Sometimes you will find the term **merger** used instead of takeover. In Australia a merger usually means a friendly takeover where one company issues shares as

payment for the bid. As a consequence shareholders of both the merging firms become owners of the new combined entity.

The scope and pace of takeover activity in Australia has been remarkable, particularly during the late 1980s. In the five years from 1986 to 1990 the number of bids was 912, with a combined value of $69.3 billion. You can see that takeovers involve big money. They are a substantial part of the corporate *investment* decision.

Bid success rates vary over time. Typically between 60 and 70 per cent of takeover bids are successful in acquiring control of the target company. However, the chances of success are greatly reduced, likely by more than half, if the target's management defend against the bid. Conversely, if the target's directors recommend in favour of the bid you are almost certain to succeed. The premium paid over the target's pre-bid value varies considerably across firms, and the average level of that premium changes over time. However, you can generally expect the premium to be between 20 and 40 per cent for successful bids. One other general feature of takeovers is that the bidder is usually much bigger than the target.[1]

**Waves managers and motives** Takeovers come in waves, and the rising wave of takeover activity is generally associated with buoyant share prices. During periods of intense takeover activity financial managers spend significant amounts of time either searching for firms to acquire, or worrying whether some other firm will acquire them. The behaviour of managers is particularly important in understanding takeover activity. Managers of a takeover target may be less than delighted by the prospect of a takeover bid, particularly if there is a risk that they are going to lose their job. It is not surprising then to see that managers often defend against an unwanted bid. This may just be naked self-interest on their part, but as we shall see later, it may also be in the interest of their shareholders. Managers may become carried away in the excitement of the hunt, or may be overconfident about their ability to spot bargains and turn round corporate cot cases. To reduce the chance that you will be sucked in by such activity we discuss some motives for mergers that make sense and some that are almost silly.

When you buy another company, you are making an investment, and the basic principles of capital investment decisions apply. You should go ahead with the purchase if it makes a net contribution to shareholders' wealth. But takeovers are often awkward transactions to evaluate. First, you have to be careful to define benefits and costs properly. Second, buying a company is more complicated than buying a new machine; special tax, legal and accounting issues must often be addressed. Third, you must be aware of the offensive and defensive tactics used in hostile takeovers, just in case a friendly deal cannot be consummated. Finally, you need to have a general understanding of why takeovers occur and who typically gains or loses as a result.

Takeovers are one of the most common forms of corporate restructuring, but there are others. If you look at the top 500 companies listed on the ASX, it is a reasonable bet that at least half will be restructured in a significant way over the next 10 years. A small number of companies will fade away into financial distress, some others will elect to be delisted being privatised in various ways, some will undergo financial reconstruction, some will be taken over or merged, some will be broken up and some will change their line of business and their names.

In addition to normal takeovers, we discuss reconstructions involving going private by **leveraged buy-outs** (LBOs), and we also discuss divestitures and spin offs. We attempt to explain why these deals can generate rewards for investors. We close with a look at the public policy issues raised by takeovers, and whether they create wealth.

# 33.1 Estimating the economic gains and costs from takeovers[2]

Suppose that you are the financial manager of firm A and that you wish to analyse the possible purchase of firm B, the takeover target. The first thing to think about is whether there is an economic gain from the takeover that will make your shareholders better off. There is an economic gain only if the two firms are worth more together than apart. For example, if you

---

[1]   There are exceptions. For example, when Robert Holmes a Court's Bell Group made a bid for BHP, it was akin to a trout chasing a whale. In this case the trout took a lot of fending off.

[2]   This chapter's approach to evaluating mergers follows that set out in S. C. Myers, 'A Framework for Evaluating Takeovers', in S. C. Myers (ed.), *Modern Developments in Financial Management*, Frederick A. Praeger, New York, 1976. However, we make one change in terminology: what we have called 'purchase premium' Myers calls 'cost'.

think that the combined firm would be worth PV$_{AB}$ and the separate firms are worth PV$_A$ and PV$_B$ then

$$\text{Gain} = \text{PV}_{AB} - (\text{PV}_A + \text{PV}_B)$$

If this gain is positive, there is an economic justification for takeover. But you also have to think about the cost of acquiring firm B. How much you have to pay will determine how the gain is shared between your shareholders and firm B. Take the easy case in which payment is made in cash. The premium that you have to pay as part of the cost of acquiring B is equal to the cash payment minus B's value as a separate entity. Thus

$$\text{Purchase premium} = \text{cash} - \text{PV}_B$$

You are likely to have to pay a positive premium to acquire B, because B's shareholders are in a monopolistic position. Notice that this is one of the rare cases where we should not substitute the current price for the PV of the share. This is because investors often anticipate the bid, and therefore the current share price may already impound the expected value of the bid premium.[3] The net present value to A of a takeover of B is measured by the difference between the gain and the premium. Therefore, you should go ahead with the takeover if its net present value, defined as

$$\text{NPV} = \text{gain} - \text{premium} = \text{PV}_{AB} - (\text{PV}_A + \text{PV}_B) - (\text{cash} - \text{PV}_B)$$

is positive.

We like to write the takeover criterion in this way because it focuses attention on two distinct questions. When you estimate the benefit, you concentrate on whether there are any gains to be made from the takeover. When you estimate cost, you are concerned with the division of these gains between the two companies.

An example may help make this clear. Firm A has a value of $200 million, and firm B has a value of $50 million. Merging the two would allow cost savings with a present value of $25 million. This is the gain from the takeover. Thus

$$
\begin{aligned}
\text{PV}_A &= \$200 \text{ million} \\
\text{PV}_B &= \$50 \text{ million} \\
\text{Gain} &= +\$25 \text{ million} \\
\text{PV}_{AB} &= \$275 \text{ million}
\end{aligned}
$$

Suppose that B is bought for cash, say, for $65 million. The premium for the acquisition is

$$\text{Premium} = \text{cash} - \text{PV}_B = 65 - 50 = \$15 \text{ million}$$

Note that the shareholders of firm B—the people on the other side of the transaction—are ahead by $15 million. Their gain is your cost.[4] They have captured $15 million of the $25 million takeover gain. Thus, when we write down the NPV of the takeover from A's viewpoint, we are really calculating that part of the gain which A's shareholders get to keep. The NPV to A's shareholders equals the overall gain to the takeover less that part of gain captured by B's shareholders:

$$\text{NPV} = 25 - 15 = +\$10 \text{ million}$$

---

[3]   Financial journalists often ignore this nicety and take the difference between the offer price of the bid and the target's share price just before the bid is announced. The premium reported in the financial press therefore tends to understate the true premium.

[4]   In practice, B's gain may be *less than* A's cost because money leaks out in fees for investment bankers, lawyers and accountants. For example, in the famous leveraged buy-out of RJR Nabisco, total fees for banks, investment banks, lawyers and accountants were an enormous US$1.1 billion, out of a US$25 billion purchase price.

Just as a check, let us confirm that A's shareholders really come out $10 million ahead. They start with a firm worth $PV_A$ = $200 million. They pay out $65 million in cash to B's shareholders and end up with a firm worth $275 million. Thus, their net gain is

$$NPV = \text{wealth with takeover} - \text{wealth without takeover}$$
$$= (PV_{AB} - \text{cash}) - PV_A = (\$275 - \$65) - \$200 = +\$10 \text{ million}$$

Suppose investors do not anticipate the takeover between A and B. The announcement will cause the value of B's shares to rise from $50 to $65 million, a 30 per cent increase. If investors agree with management's assessment of the takeover gains, the market value of A's shares will increase by $10 million, only a 5 per cent increase.

It makes sense to keep an eye on what investors think the gains from merging are. If A's share price falls when the deal is announced, then investors are sending the message that either the takeover benefits are doubtful, or that A is paying too much for them.

# Right and wrong ways to estimate the benefits of takeovers

Some companies begin their takeover analyses with a forecast of the target firm's future cash flows. Any revenue increases or cost reductions attributable to the takeover are included in the forecasts, which are then discounted back to the present and compared with the purchase price:

$$\text{Estimated net gain} = \text{DCF valuation of target, including takeover benefits}$$
$$- \text{cash required for acquisition}$$

In principle this is OK, but in practice it is a dangerous procedure. Even the brightest and best-trained analyst can make large errors in valuing a business. The estimated net gain may come up positive not because the takeover makes sense, but simply because the analyst's cash flow forecasts are too optimistic. On the other hand, a good takeover may not be pursued if the analyst fails to recognise the target's potential as a stand-alone business.

Our procedure *starts* with the target's stand-alone market value ($PV_B$) and concentrates on the *changes* in cash flow that would result from the takeover. *Ask yourself why the two firms should be worth more together than apart.*

The same advice holds when you are contemplating the *sale* of part of your business. There is no point in saying to yourself, 'This is an unprofitable business and should be sold.' Unless the buyer can run the business better than you can, the price you receive will reflect the poor prospects.

Sometimes you may come across managers who believe that there are simple rules for identifying good acquisitions. For example, they may say that they always seek to buy into growth industries or that they have a policy of acquiring companies that are selling below book value. But our comments in Chapter 11 about the characteristics of a good investment decision also hold true when you are buying a whole company. *You add value only if you can generate additional economic rents*—some competitive edge that other firms cannot match and the target firm's managers cannot achieve on their own.

One final piece of common sense: Often two companies bid against each other to acquire the same target firm. In effect, the target firm puts itself up for auction. In these cases ask yourself whether the target is worth more to you than to the other bidder. If the answer is no, you should be cautious about getting into a bidding contest. Winning such a contest may be more expensive than losing it. If you lose, you have simply wasted your time; if you win, you have probably paid too much.[5]

---

5   Corporate raiders who make a business of taking over other companies appear to earn better returns on takeovers than bidders in general. One probable reason for this is that they are prepared to walk away from the bid if the cost of winning starts to rise.

# 33.2 Sensible motives for takeovers

As we said at the start of the chapter takeovers are an investment, and just as there are many reasons for investments there are many and diverse reasons for takeovers. However, some are more sensible, and some more common, than others. Some motives are quite intriguing, for example the backdoor listing. In this case you have a private company and want to go public and list on the ASX. You could have a public float, but this can be costly and time consuming, and you would need to comply with ASX listing requirements. One way to bypass all this is to make a partial bid for a controlling interest[6] in a company without many assets that is already listed on the exchange. You now have a public listed company (a shell company) which acquires the assets of your private company and thus completes a backdoor listing.

The magic word in the motivation for takeovers is **synergy**. This is just a fancy way of saying $2 + 2 = 5$, or the value of the merged entity is greater than the sum of the parts. If you cannot identify the synergy in the takeover, you need to be sceptical about the benefit of the takeover. In some cases, of course, breakup rather than takeover is the objective. This is the case for asset strippers who hope to buy the company at a discount to asset value and then sell the parts for a price greater than the whole. In an efficient market, such opportunities are difficult to find.

## Types of mergers

Takeovers are often categorised as *horizontal*, *vertical* or *conglomerate*. A **horizontal** takeover is one that takes place between two firms in the same line of business. Such takeovers have long been popular and are still common today. For example, following deregulation of the financial system in the mid-1980s the Australian banking industry has experienced extensive horizontal takeovers, which were still continuing in 1997. The large banks have been active in the takeover market in attempts to maintain market dominance and greater economies of scale. Meanwhile the smaller regional banks have used takeovers for economies of scale and as a way of capturing market share.

A **vertical** takeover is one in which the buyer expands backwards towards the source of raw materials, or forwards in the direction of the ultimate consumer. This happens, for example, when a paper company buys a forestry company.

A **conglomerate** takeover involves companies in unrelated lines of business. Conglomerate takeovers became common in the 1970s and early 1980s. However, some of the action in the late 1980s and early 1990s came from breaking up the large conglomerates, such as Adsteam group[7] and Bond Corporation that had been formed a decade or so earlier.

With these distinctions in mind, we now consider motives for takeovers, that is, reasons why two firms may be worth more together than apart. But, first, a caveat. It would be nice if we could say that certain types of takeovers are generally successful and other types fail. Unfortunately, we know of no such simple generalisations. Many takeovers which seem to make economic sense fail because they are badly implemented. Others fail because the buyer misestimates the value of assets or fails to notice hidden liabilities. For example, the buyer may overestimate the value of stale inventory or the costs of renovating elderly plant and equipment, or may overlook the warranties on a defective product, or may forget environmental liabilities.

When takeovers fail the costs can be enormous, as was the case for Bond Corporation. The company expanded rapidly, largely through debt-financed conglomerate takeovers, buying breweries, a telephone company, a television station and building airships. Bond paid too much for companies it acquired, and consequently reached a point where it was no longer able to service its debts. For example, Bond purchased Channel 9 for about $1.1 billion, and a few

---

6   You do not want to acquire all the shares because if you do, there will not be a sufficient spread of ownership and the company will be de-listed in accordance with ASX rules. This strategy is less easy to pursue now because partial bids are more heavily regulated.

7   Companies spun off from the Adsteam group include Yates Seeds, Woolworths and David Jones.

years later was forced to sell it back to the original vendor for about half that price. Eventually Bond Corporation collapsed and creditors lost many hundreds of millions of dollars.

Sometimes takeovers fail because managers cannot handle the complex task of integrating two firms with different production processes, accounting methods and corporate cultures. It is always easier to buy another business than it is to integrate it with yours afterwards. This problem bedevilled Novell's acquisition of Wordperfect. That takeover at first seemed a perfect fit between Novell's strength in personal computers and Wordperfect's applications software. But Wordperfect's post-acquisition sales were horrible, partly due to competition from other word processing systems, but also because of a series of battles over turf and strategy:

> *Wordperfect executives came to view Novell executives as rude invaders of the corporate equivalent of Camelot. They repeatedly fought with . . . Novell's staff over everything from expenses and management assignments to Christmas bonuses. [This led to] a strategic mistake: dismantling a Wordperfect sales team . . . needed to push a long awaited set of office software products.*[8]

The value of most businesses depends on *human* assets—managers, skilled workers, scientists and engineers. If these people are not happy in their new roles in the acquiring firm, the best of them will leave. One Portuguese bank (BCP) learned this lesson the hard way when it bought an investment management firm against the wishes of the firm's employees. The entire workforce immediately quit and set up a rival investment management firm with a similar name. Beware of paying too much for assets that go down the lift and out to the parking area at the close of each business day. They may drive into the sunset never to return.

## Economies of scale

Just as most of us believe that we would be happier if only we were a little richer, so every manager seems to believe that his or her firm would be more competitive if only it were just a little bigger.

These **economies of scale** are the natural goal of horizontal takeovers.[9] In horizontal takeovers there may also be the benefits in having a larger market share and eliminating some of the competition. Economies of scale have also been claimed in conglomerate takeovers. The architects of these takeovers have pointed to the economies that come from sharing central services such as head office management, accounting and financial control, and being large enough to tap the global capital market.

A good example of takeovers in pursuit of economies of scale comes from the banking industry. Australia entered the 1980s with too many bank branches. This was a product of an industry where prices had been regulated and therefore competition had been in terms of service provision. This lead to an over-expansion of the branch network. With the advent of deregulation came an opportunity for takeovers and rationalisation of the branches. Two branch offices of different banks in the same location could be collapsed into one if the banks merged. For example, the merger between St George Bank and Advance Bank promised economies equivalent to 30 per cent of Advance Bank's costs. This was to be achieved by closing more than 150 branches and making a staff cut of about 1000 employees.

## Economies of vertical integration

Vertical takeovers seek economies in vertical integration. Large industrial companies commonly like to gain as much control as possible over the production process by expanding back

---

[8]   D. Clark, 'Software Firm Fights to Remake Firm After Ill-Fated Takeover', *The Wall Street Journal*, 12 January 1996, p. A1.

[9]   Economies of scale are enjoyed when the average unit cost of production goes down as production increases. One way to achieve economies of scale is to spread fixed costs over a larger volume of production.

towards the output of the raw material and forwards to the ultimate consumer. One way to achieve this is to merge with a supplier or a customer.

One reason for vertical integration is that it facilitates coordination and administration. Backward integration may also ensure the quality and security of supply. This is why wine companies take over vineyards. Forward integration ensures an outlet for the company's products. This is why breweries buy pubs.

Do not assume that more vertical integration is better than less. Carried to extremes it is absurdly inefficient, as in the case of LOT, the Polish state airline, which in the late 1980s found itself raising pigs to make sure that its employees had fresh meat on their tables.

# Combining complementary resources

Many small firms are acquired by large ones which can provide the missing ingredients necessary for the firm's success. The small firm may have a unique product but lack the engineering and sales organisation necessary to produce and market it on a large scale. The firm could develop engineering and sales talent from scratch, but it may be quicker and cheaper to merge with a firm that already has ample talent.[10] The two firms have *complementary resources*—each has what the other needs—and so it may make sense for them to merge. The two firms are worth more together than apart because each acquires something it does not have and gets it cheaper than by acting on its own. Also, the takeover may open up opportunities that neither firm would pursue otherwise. Of course, two *large* firms may also merge because they have complementary resources, as in the case of Novell and Wordperfect, but this is less common.

# Unused tax shields

Sometimes a firm may have potential tax shields, such as accumulated losses, but not have the profits to take advantage of them. It makes sense for such a company to acquire another company that has profits and a capacity to utilise more tax shields. Alternatively, the profitable company might acquire the company with tax losses. In either event the result will be less tax paid, and therefore less cash in the hands of the government and more cash in the hands of investors.[11] At least, that is the way it was before the imputation tax system was introduced to Australia.

Under the imputation system a reduction in tax paid at the corporate level may just mean more tax paid at the personal level. Under some circumstances the result may be no net tax benefit at all. In general, however, there will be a benefit from saving corporate tax. First, not all investors are able to utilise imputation credits for corporate tax paid. Second, there is usually a time lag between payment of corporate tax and the reduction in personal tax arising from the imputation credit. The time value of money makes it better to save tax earlier rather than later.

# Takeovers as a use for surplus funds

Here is another argument for takeovers. Suppose that your firm is in a mature industry. It is generating a substantial amount of cash, but it has few profitable investment opportunities. Ideally such a firm should distribute the surplus cash to shareholders by increasing its dividend payment, by a share repurchase or a return of capital. Unfortunately, energetic managers are often reluctant to adopt a policy of shrinking their firm in this way.

If the firm is not willing to purchase its own shares, it can instead purchase someone else's. Thus, firms with a surplus of cash and a shortage of good investment opportunities often turn

---

10  Of course, there are other mechanisms for achieving the same result. For example, a joint venture, where the companies pool the required resources, but do not merge their firms.

11  Takeovers blatantly undertaken *just* to use tax-loss carry-forwards may be challenged by the tax office. The use of the tax-loss carry-forwards is risky, unless you can meet a continuity test. Either the company must be continuing in the same line of business, or at least 51 per cent of the shareholders in the loss-making company must remain shareholders after the takeover.

to takeovers *financed by cash* as a way of redeploying their capital. There is no guarantee, of course, that such acquisitions will be wise ones. Conversely, firms which are short of cash may bid for companies with strong cash flow, and this led to brewery and TV companies being popular targets in the Australian 1980s takeover boom.

Some firms have excess cash and do not pay it out to shareholders or redeploy it by acquisition; it just piles up in the company. Shareholders may become nervous about how the cash is to be used and the firms often find themselves targets for takeover.[12] During the oil price slump of the early 1980s many cash-rich American oil companies found themselves threatened by takeover. This was not because their cash was a unique asset. The acquirers wanted to capture the companies' cash flow to make sure it was not frittered away on negative NPV oil exploration projects. We return to this *free cash flow* motive for takeovers later in this chapter.

## Eliminating inefficiencies

Cash is not the only asset that can be wasted by poor management. There are always firms with unexploited opportunities to cut costs and increase sales and earnings. Such firms are natural candidates for acquisition by other firms with better management. In some cases 'better management' may simply mean the determination to force painful cuts or realignment of the company's operations. Notice that the motive for such takeovers has nothing to do with benefits from combining two firms. Acquisition is simply the mechanism by which a new management team replaces the old one.

If this motive is important, one would expect that firms that perform *poorly* would tend to be targets for acquisition. This seems to be the case. Palepu, for example, found that investors in firms that were subsequently acquired earned relatively low rates of return over several years before the takeover.[13] We would also expect to find that acquisitions are often associated with a change in management of the target firm. And this is what Martin and McConnell found—the chief executive is four times more likely to be replaced in the year after the takeover than in earlier years, and the firms had generally been poor performers.[14] Apparently, many of these firms fell on bad times and were rescued, or reformed, by takeover.

Certainly, a takeover is not the only way to improve management. But sometimes it is the only simple and practical way. Managers are naturally reluctant to fire or demote themselves, and shareholders of large public firms do not usually have much *direct* influence on how their firm is run or who runs it.[15]

Of course, it is easy to criticise another firm's management and not so easy to do better. Some of the self-appointed scourges of poor management turn out to be less competent than those they replace. Here is how Warren Buffet, the Chairman of Berkshire Hathaway, summarises the matter:[16]

*Many managers were apparently over-exposed in impressionable childhood years to the story in which the imprisoned, handsome prince is released from the toad's body by a kiss from the beautiful princess. Consequently, they are certain that the managerial kiss will do wonders for the profitability of the target company. Such optimism is essential. Absent that rosy view, why else should the shareholders of company A want to own an interest in B at*

---

12  Takeovers in this case may take the form of leveraged buy-outs.

13  K. Palepu, 'Predicting Takeover Targets: A Methodological and Empirical Analysis', *Journal of Accounting and Economics*, 8: 3–36 (March 1986).

14  K. J. Martin and J. J. McConnell, 'Corporate Performance, Corporate Takeovers and Management Turnover', *Journal of Finance*, 46: 671–87 (June 1991).

15  It is difficult to assemble a large enough block of shareholders to effectively challenge management and the incumbent board of directors. Shareholders can have enormous indirect influence, however. Their displeasure shows up in the firm's share price. A low share price may encourage a takeover bid by another firm.

16  Berkshire Hathaway Annual Report, 1981, cited in G. Foster, 'Comments on M&A Analysis and the Role of Investment Bankers', *Midland Corporate Finance Journal*, 1: 36–8 (Winter 1983).

*a takeover cost that is two times the market price they'd pay if they made direct purchases on their own? In other words investors can always buy toads at the going price for toads. If investors instead bankroll princesses who wish to pay double for the right to kiss the toad, those kisses better pack some real dynamite. We've observed many kisses, but very few miracles. Nevertheless, many managerial princesses remain serenely confident about the future potency of their kisses, even after their corporate backyards are knee-deep in unresponsive toads.*[17]

## Expansion

Your company is doing well, so well in fact that you need to expand. You could build a new factory on a green field site, or you could take over another firm in the industry. A takeover would usually be quicker. Speed is important if the opportunity cost of sales lost through delay is high. Speed is also important if you are currently exploiting a competitive advantage that your competitors will erode with the passage of time. In such cases, expansion through takeover makes sense. A takeover also makes sense if, perhaps because of poor management of the target firm, you can acquire the assets more cheaply than it would cost to build your own facilities.

There is little doubt that many takeovers are concerned with expanding company revenue. Often this is achieved by access to new markets or through increasing market share. However, if the expansion by takeover is just about increasing sales and getting bigger without creating value, then think again. Such expansions may be good for empire-building managers, but they do nothing for shareholders.

## Cleanups[18]

Suppose you hold 70 per cent of the issued shares of a listed company, perhaps as a consequence of a previous takeover bid. It is not difficult to imagine that you might want to buy out the minority interest. Such minority interests often restrict your freedom of action, and by eliminating them you also save ASX listing fees and the costs associated with maintaining the share register.

## 33.3 Some dubious reasons for takeover

The benefits that we have described so far all make some economic sense. Other arguments that are sometimes given for takeovers are more dubious. Here are a few of the dubious ones.

## Diversification

We have suggested that the managers of a cash-rich company may prefer to see it use that cash for acquisitions rather than distribute it as extra dividends. That is why we often see cash-rich firms in stagnant industries diversifying their way into fresh woods and pastures new. But what about diversification as an end in itself? It is obvious that diversification reduces risk. Is not that a gain from merging?

The trouble with this argument is that diversification is easier and cheaper for the shareholder than for the corporation. No one has shown that investors pay a premium for diversified firms—in fact, some sell at a discount. A good example is the case of the American

---

17    Richard Roll calls this hubris, literally meaning pride against the gods. Roll argues that overconfident managers get caught up in the heat of the chase and in their determination to make the acquisition lose sight of what is a sensible price to pay. See 'The Hubris Hypothesis of Corporate Takeovers', *Journal of Business*, **59**: 197–216 (April 1986).

18    We are indebted to Elaine Hutson for suggesting this classification.

company Kaiser Industries. Kaiser Industries was dissolved as a holding company in 1977 because its diversification apparently *subtracted* from its value. Kaiser Industries' main assets were shares of Kaiser Steel, Kaiser Aluminum and Kaiser Cement. These were independent companies, and the shares of each were publicly traded. Thus, you could value Kaiser Industries by looking at the share prices of Kaiser Steel, Kaiser Aluminum and Kaiser Cement. But Kaiser Industries' shares were selling at a price reflecting a significant *discount* from the value of its investment in these companies. The discount vanished when Kaiser Industries revealed its plan to sell its holdings and distribute the proceeds to its shareholders.

Why the discount existed in the first place is a puzzle.[19] But the example at least shows that diversification does not *increase* value. Corporate diversification does not generally affect value in perfect markets as long as investors' diversification opportunities are unrestricted.[20] This is a consequence of the *value-additivity* principle introduced in Chapter 7. Suppose investors wanted to hold a portfolio diversified across two firms that eventually merged; they could simply have held those firms in their own portfolio. The merger buys investors no advantage in terms of diversification.

If diversified firms sold for a price that differed from an equivalent portfolio of individual securities, then arbitrageurs would have a profit opportunity. Suppose the diversified firm sold for a higher price than a portfolio which replicated the characteristics of the diversified firm. The arbitrageur would sell the diversified firm short and purchase the securities to construct the replicating portfolio. Clearly such activities would drive down the price of the diversified firm until it sold for the same price as the replicating portfolio.

There is one case in which merger diversification can actually harm investors. If one of the companies being merged has some unique characteristic that is very costly, or impossible to replicate, then the merger reduces the investors' opportunity set. This, however, is a rare event.

## The bootstrap game: takeovers and earnings per share

From the 1970s through to the mid-1980s some conglomerate companies made acquisitions which offered no evident economic gains. Nevertheless, the conglomerates' aggressive strategy produced several years of rising earnings per share. To see how this can happen, let us look at the acquisition of Muck and Slurry by the well-known conglomerate World Enterprises.

The position before the takeover is set out in the first two columns of Table 33.1. Notice that because Muck and Slurry has relatively poor growth prospects, its shares sell at a lower price-earnings ratio than World Enterprises (line 3). The takeover, we assume, produces no economic benefits, and so the firms should be worth exactly the same together as apart. The market value of World Enterprises after the takeover should be equal to the sum of the separate values of the two firms (line 6).

Since World Enterprises' shares are selling for double the price of Muck and Slurry's shares (line 2), World Enterprises can acquire the 100 000 Muck and Slurry shares for 50 000 of its own shares. Thus, World will have 150 000 shares outstanding after the takeover.

Total earnings double as a result of the takeover (line 5), but the number of shares increases by only 50 per cent. Earnings *per share* rise from $2.00 to $2.67. We call this a *bootstrap effect* because there is no real gain created by the takeover and no increase in the two firms' combined value. Since the share price is unchanged, the price-earnings ratio falls (line 3).

---

[19]  Perhaps it was partially due to management overheads of the holding company structure.

[20]  Where opportunities for investors to diversify are restricted, there may be benefit in the company diversifying for them. Suppose, for example, that you are the chairperson and majority shareholder of a company. You may be wealthy, but you have all your eggs in one corporate basket. You could sell off a substantial part of your shares in order to diversify, but this could result in a large capital gains tax. It may be better to merge with a firm in another line of business and hold on to the shares of the new entity. If the deal is properly structured, you can defer the capital gains tax, and you will have your eggs in two baskets rather than one.

**table 33.1** _____

Impact of takeover on market value and earnings per share of World Enterprises

|  | **World Enterprises (before takeover)** | **Muck and Slurry** | **World Enterprises (after acquiring Muck and Slurry)** |
|---|---|---|---|
| 1. Earnings per share | $2.00 | $2.00 | $2.67 |
| 2. Price per share | $40.00 | $20.00 | $40.00 |
| 3. Price-earnings ratio | 20 | 10 | 15 |
| 4. Number of shares | 100 000 | 100 000 | 150 000 |
| 5. Total earnings | $200 000 | $200 000 | $400 000 |
| 6. Total market value | $4 000 000 | $2 000 000 | $6 000 000 |
| 7. Current earnings per dollar invested in shares (line 1 divided by line 2) | $0.05 | $0.10 | $0.067 |

*Note: When World Enterprises purchases Muck and Slurry, there are no gains. Therefore, total earnings and total market value should be unaffected by the takeover. But earnings per share increase. World Enterprises only issues 50 000 of its shares (priced at $40) to acquire the 100 000 Muck and Slurry shares (priced at $20).*

Figure 33.1 illustrates what is going on here. Before the takeover $1 invested in World Enterprises bought 5 cents of current earnings and rapid growth prospects. On the other hand, $1 invested in Muck and Slurry bought 10 cents of current earnings but slower growth prospects. If the *total* market value is not altered by the takeover, then $1 invested in the merged firm gives 6.7 cents of immediate earnings but slower growth, and the Muck and Slurry shareholders get lower immediate earnings but faster growth. Neither side gains or loses provided everybody understands the deal.

Financial manipulators sometimes try to ensure that the market does *not* understand the deal. Suppose that investors are fooled by the exuberance of the president of World Enterprises and by plans to introduce modern management techniques into the Earth Sciences Division (formerly known as Muck and Slurry). They could easily mistake the 33 per cent post-takeover increase in earnings per share for real growth. If they do, the price of World Enterprises' shares rises and the shareholders of both companies receive something for nothing.

You should now see how to play the bootstrap, or 'chain letter', game. Suppose that you manage a company enjoying a high price-earnings ratio. The reason why it is high is that investors anticipate rapid growth in future earnings. You achieve this growth not by capital investment, product improvement or increased operating efficiency, but by purchasing slow-growing firms with low price-earnings ratios. The long-run result will be slower growth and a depressed price-earnings ratio, but in the short run earnings per share can increase dramatically. If this fools investors, you may be able to achieve the higher earnings per share without suffering a decline in your price-earnings ratio. But in order to *keep* fooling investors, you must continue to expand by takeover *at the same compound rate*. Obviously, you cannot do this forever; one day expansion must slow down or stop. Then earnings growth will cease, and your house of cards will fall.

This kind of game is not played so much in the 1990s, after investors' bitter experience with it in past decades. But there is still a widespread belief that you should not acquire companies with higher price-earnings ratios than your own. Of course, you know better than to believe that low-P/E shares are cheap and high-P/E shares are dear. If life were as simple as that, we should all be wealthy by now. Beware of false prophets who suggest that you can appraise takeovers on the basis of their immediate impact on earnings per share.

**figure 33.1** _____

*Effects of merger on earnings growth. By merging with Muck and Slurry, World Enterprises increases current earnings but accepts a slower rate of future growth. Its shareholders should be no better or worse off unless investors are fooled by the bootstrap effect.*

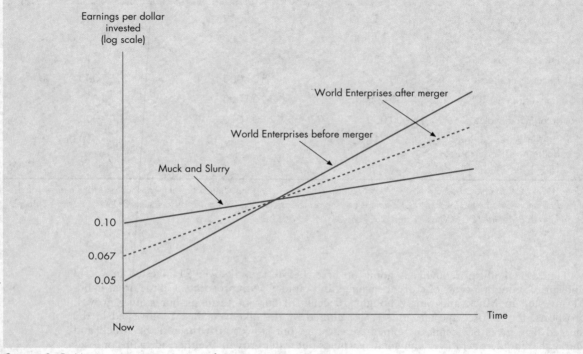

*Source*: S. C. Myers, op. cit., Footnote 2, fig. 1, p. 639.

## Lower financing costs

You often hear it said that merged firms are able to borrow more cheaply than the separate units. In part this is true. We have already seen (in Chapter 15) that there are significant economies of scale in making new issues. Therefore, if firms can make fewer, larger security issues by merging, there is a genuine saving. This is a particular benefit if the takeover means that the new entity is now large enough to tap financial markets overseas, particularly the Eurocurrency market.

But when people say that borrowing costs are lower for the merged firm, they usually mean something more than lower issue costs. They mean that when two firms merge, they can borrow at lower interest rates than they could separately. This, of course, is exactly what we should expect in a well-functioning bond market. While the two firms are separate, they do not guarantee each other's debt; if one fails, the bondholder cannot ask the other for money. But after the takeover each enterprise effectively does guarantee the other's debt—if one part of the business fails, the bondholders can still take their money out of the other part. Because these mutual guarantees usually make the debt less risky, lenders will accept a lower interest rate.[21]

_____

21  Of course, this is not always the case. For example, the demise of the State Bank of Victoria was largely due to its disastrous association with Tri-Continental. Similarly, debtholders in companies acquired by Bond Corporation may have felt less than comfortable.

Does the lower interest rate mean a net gain to the takeover? Not necessarily. Compare the following two situations:

▌ *Separate issues:* Firm A and firm B each make a $50 million bond issue.
▌ *Single issue:* Firms A and B merge and the new firm AB makes a single $100 million issue.

Of course, AB would pay a lower interest rate, other things being equal. But it does not make sense for A and B to merge just to get that lower rate. The firms' shareholders do gain from the lower rate, but they lose by having to guarantee each other's debt. In other words, they get the lower interest rate only by giving bondholders better protection. There is no *net* gain.

In Chapters 20 and 23 we showed that

$$\text{Bond value} = \text{bond value (assuming no chance of default)} \\ - \text{value of shareholders' (put) option to default}$$

Takeover increases bond value (or reduces the interest payments necessary to support a *given* bond value) only by reducing the value of shareholders' options to default. In other words, the value of the default option for AB's $100 million issue is less than the combined value of the two default options on A and B's separate $50 million issues.

Now suppose that A and B each borrow $50 million and *then* merge. If the takeover is a surprise, it will be a happy one for the bondholders. The bonds they thought were guaranteed by one of the two firms end up guaranteed by both. The shareholders lose, other things being equal, because they have given bondholders better protection but have received nothing for it.

There is one situation in which takeovers can create value by making debt safer. In Section 18.3 we described the choice of an optimal debt ratio as a trade-off of the value of tax shields on interest payments made by the firm against the present value of possible costs of financial distress due to borrowing too much. Merging decreases the probability of financial distress, other things being equal. If this allows increased borrowing, and increased value from the interest tax shields, there will be a net gain to the takeover.[22] This is an important point, because a lot of takeovers have been financed with debt, particularly during the 1980s. And the use of the associated debt tax shields has been suggested as the reason for the takeovers.[23] If the firms could increase their debt without the takeover, this is not a suggestion that would make much sense. The suggestion only makes sense if the takeover increases the debt capacity of the combined entities.

There is one other leverage-related motive for takeovers and that is to reduce leverage by raising equity. To do this a highly levered company makes a bid for a company with low leverage, using its own shares as consideration for the bid. If the bid succeeds, assets and equity go up and the leverage ratio comes down.

# 33.4 Estimating the cost of a takeover

To recapitulate: You should go ahead with a takeover if the gain exceeds the cost. The gain is the difference between the value of the merged firm and the value of the separate entities:

$$\text{Gain} = PV_{AB} - (PV_A + PV_B)$$

---

22   This takeover rationale was first suggested by W. G. Lewellen, 'A Pure Financial Rationale for the Conglomerate Takeover', *Journal of Finance*, 26: 521–37 (May 1971). If you want to see some of the controversy and discussion that this idea led to, look at R. C. Higgins and L. D. Schall, 'Corporate Bankruptcy and Conglomerate Takeover', *Journal of Finance*, 30: 93–114 (March 1975); and D. Galai and R. W. Masulis, 'The Option Pricing Model and the Risk Factor of Stock', *Journal of Financial Economics*, 3: 53–81(January–March 1976), especially pp. 66–9.

23   Indeed, several Australian politicians were vocal in calling for debt tax deductions associated with takeovers to be disallowed.

We have looked at where these gains may come from and how to estimate them. It is now time to focus on the costs. The real cost of a takeover is the premium that the buyer pays for the target firm over its value as a separate entity.

There are two main ways to pay for a bid: in cash or in shares. The method for estimating the premium varies according to the method of payment. Let us start with the simplest case, the cash bid.

## Estimating the premium in a cash bid

It is a straightforward problem to estimate the premium as long as the **consideration** (payment) for the target's shares is cash. However, it is important to bear in mind that if investors *expect* A to acquire B, the market value of B may be a poor measure of its value as a separate entity. Thus, it may help to rewrite our formula for premium as

$$\text{Premium} = (\text{cash} - MV_B) + (MV_B - PV_B)$$
$$= \text{observed premium paid over market value of B} + \text{difference between market value of B and its value as a separate entity}$$

This is one of the few places in this book where we have drawn an important distinction between market value (MV) and the true, or 'intrinsic', value (PV) of the firm as a separate entity. The problem here is not that the market value of B is wrong, but that it may not be the value of firm B as a separate entity. Potential investors in B's shares will see two possible outcomes and two possible values:

| Outcome | Value of B's shares |
|---------|---------------------|
| No takeover | $PV_B$: value of B as a separate firm |
| Takeover occurs | $PV_B$ *plus* some part of the benefits of the takeover |

If the second outcome is possible, $MV_B$, the share market value we observe for B, will overstate $PV_B$. This is exactly what *should* happen in a competitive capital market. Unfortunately, it complicates the task of a financial manager who is evaluating a takeover.

Here is an example. Suppose that just before the takeover announcement we observe the following:

|  | Firm A | Firm B |
|---|---|---|
| Market price per share | $7.50 | $1.50 |
| Number of shares | 10 000 000 | 6 000 000 |
| Market value of firm | $75 million | $9 million |

Firm A intends to pay $12 million cash for B. If B's market price reflects only its value as a separate entity, then

$$\text{Premium} = (\text{cash} - MV_B) + (MV_B - PV_B) = (12 - 9) + (9 - 9) = \$3 \text{ million}$$

However, suppose that B's share price has already risen $0.20 because of rumours of a favourable takeover offer. That means $MV_B$ overstates $PV_B$ by $0.2 \times 6\,000\,000 = 1\,200\,000$, or $1.2 million. The true value $PV_B$ is only $7.8 million. Then

$$\text{Premium} = (\text{cash} - MV_B) + (MV_B - PV_B) = (12 - 9) + (9 - 7.8) = \$4.2 \text{ million}$$

Notice that if the market made a mistake and the market value of B were *less* than its true value as a separate entity, say B was really worth $13 million, then the premium would be negative. In other words, B would be a *bargain* and the takeover would be worthwhile from A's point of view, even if the two firms were worth no more together than apart. Of course, A's shareholders' gain would be B's shareholders' loss because B would be sold for less than its true value.

Firms have made acquisitions just because their managers believed they had spotted a company whose intrinsic value was not fully appreciated by the share market. However, we know from the evidence on market efficiency that often 'cheap' shares turn out to be expensive. It is not easy for outsiders, whether investors or managers, to find firms that are truly undervalued by the market. (Of course, if the shares are bargain-priced, A does not need a takeover to profit by its special knowledge. It can just buy up B's shares on the open market and hold them passively, waiting for other investors to wake up to B's true value.[24])

If firm A is wise, it will not go ahead with a takeover if the premium exceeds the gain. Conversely, firm B will not consent to a takeover if it thinks the premium is negative, for a negative premium to A means a loss to shareholders in B. This gives us a range of possible cash payments that would allow the takeover to take place. Whether the payment is at the top or the bottom of this range depends on the relative bargaining power of the two participants. For example, if A makes an acquisition solely to use a tax-loss carry-forward, then it could equally well merge with B, C or D. Firm B has nothing special to offer, and its management is in no position to demand a large fraction of the gains. In this case, the premium paid by A is likely to be relatively low.

# Estimating the premium in a share bid

Estimating the premium is more complicated when a takeover is financed by an exchange of shares. Suppose that firm A offers 1 600 000 shares instead of $12 million in cash. Since A's share price before the announcement is $7.50 and B's market value is $9 million,[25] the premium *appears* to be

$$\text{Apparent premium} = 1\ 600\ 000 \times \$7.50 - \$9\ 000\ 000 = \$3\ 000\ 000$$

However, the apparent premium may not equal the true premium. Are A's shares really worth $7.50 each?

These shares may be worth $7.50 before the takeover is announced but not afterwards. Suppose the takeover is expected to generate cost savings worth $4.75 million:

$$\text{Gain} = PV_{AB} - (PV_A + PV_B) = 88.75 - (75 + 9) = \$4.75\ \text{million}$$

Given the gain and the terms of the deal, we can calculate share prices and market values *after* the takeover is negotiated and announced. Note that the new firm will have 11 600 000 shares outstanding. Therefore,

$$\text{New share price} = P_{AB} = \frac{88\ 750\ 000}{11\ 600\ 000} = \$7.65$$

The true premium is:

$$\text{Premium} = (1\ 600\ 000 \times \$7.65) - \$9\ 000\ 000 = \$3\ 240\ 000$$

---

24  However, it is hard to buy a substantial number of shares without tipping your hand. The market watches the volume of trades closely. Furthermore, when you acquire more than 5 per cent of a company's shares, the law requires you to lodge a substantial shareholder notice with the company and the Stock Exchange.

25  In this case we assume that B's market value reflects only its value as a separate firm.

The true premium can also be calculated by figuring out the gain to B's shareholders. They end up with 1 600 000 shares, or 13.8 per cent of the new firm AB. Their gain is

$$0.138(88\,750\,000) - 9\,000\,000 = \$3\,240\,000$$

In general, if B's shareholders are given the fraction $x$ of the combined firms,

$$\text{Premium} = x\text{PV}_{AB} - \text{PV}_{B}$$

We can now understand the first key distinction between cash and shares as financing instruments. If *cash* is offered, the *price paid is unaffected by the takeover gains.* If *shares* are offered, *the price paid depends on the gains* because the gains show up in the post-takeover share price. Shareholders in the target firm become shareholders of the bidder firm and thus benefit from any increase in the bidder's share price.

Paying the consideration in shares mitigates the effect of overvaluation or undervaluation of either firm. Suppose, for example, that A overestimates B's value as a separate entity, perhaps because it has overlooked some hidden liability. Thus, A makes too generous an offer. Other things being equal, A's shareholders are better off if it is a share offer, rather than a cash offer. With a share offer, the inevitable bad news about B's value will fall partly on the shoulders of B's shareholders.

## Asymmetric information

There is another key difference between cash and share financing for takeovers. A's managers will usually have access to information about A's prospects that is not available to outsiders. Economists call this *asymmetric information*.

Suppose A's managers are more optimistic than outside investors. They may think that A's shares will really be worth $8.00 after the takeover, rather than the $7.65 market price we just calculated. If they are right, the true premium for a share-financed takeover with B is

$$\text{Premium} = 1\,600\,000 \times \$8.00 - \$9\,000\,000 = \$3\,800\,000$$

B's shareholders would get a 'free gift' of $0.35 for every A share they receive—an extra gain of $0.35 × 1 600 000, or $560 000 in all.

Of course, if A's managers were really this optimistic, they would strongly prefer to finance the takeover with cash. Financing with shares would be favoured by *pessimistic* managers who think their company's shares are *over*valued.

Does this sound like 'win–win' for A—just issue shares when overvalued, cash otherwise? No, it is not that easy, because B's shareholders, and outside investors generally, understand what is going on. Suppose you are negotiating on behalf of B. You find that A's managers keep suggesting share rather than cash financing. You quickly infer A's managers' pessimism, mark down your own opinion of what the shares they offer are worth and drive a harder bargain. Investors who would value A's shares for $7.65 after a cash deal might value the shares at, say, only $7.40 if A insists on share financing. A would have to hand over more than 1 600 000 shares to get the deal done.

This asymmetric information story explains why buying firms' share prices generally fall when share-financed takeovers are announced.[26] In a study of Australian firms Bellamy and Lewin found that bidders experience a positive share price response to cash bids and a negative price response to share-financed bids.[27] In the light of the foregoing discussion, it is not

---

[26] The same reasoning applies to rights issues to raise cash. See Sections 15.4 and 18.4.

[27] See D. Bellamy and W. Lewin, 'Corporate Takeovers, Method of Payment and Bidding Firms' Shareholder Returns: Australian Evidence', *Asia Pacific Journal of Management*, 137–49 (October 1992). Similar results are found in the United States. See J. R. Franks, R. S. Harris and S. Titman, 'The Post-takeover Share-Price Performance of Acquiring Firms', *Journal of Financial Economics*, **29**: 81–96 (March 1991). This paper confirms the results of earlier research by Nickolaos Travlos. See 'Corporate Takeover Bids, Methods of Payment and Bidding Firms' Stock Returns', *Journal of Finance*, **42**: 943–63 (September 1987).

surprising to find that a majority of takeover bids in Australia are for cash and that cash bids are more likely to be successful.

## 33.5 The mechanics of a takeover

Buying a company is a much more complicated affair than buying a piece of machinery. Thus, we should look at some of the problems encountered in arranging takeovers. In practice these problems are often *extremely* complex, and specialists must be consulted. We are not trying to replace those specialists; we simply want to alert you to the kinds of legal, tax and accounting issues they deal with.

### Takeovers and the law

As bidder and target slug it out in a hostile bid, the excitement and drama is frequently heightened by appeals to the ASIC (Australian Securities and Investments Commission) and the courts.[28] The *Corporations Law*, Ch. 6 'Acquisition of Shares', is the most important source of law about takeovers. It sets out the law regarding the acquisition of shares and the form of takeover bids that are allowed. It also regulates the information that must be disclosed to the target's shareholders and the share market. The objective of this legislation is to ensure that shareholders in the target get a fair go and that the market is informed about the bid. In particular the legislation tries to ensure that not only are all target shareholders fully informed, but also that they have an equal opportunity to participate in the benefits of the bid. The day-to-day administration and policing of the legislation is in the hands of the ASIC. The ASIC has the power to grant exemptions from compliance with Ch. 6 requirements, or alternatively can modify the way in which Ch. 6 applies to particular bids. The ASIC can also apply to the Corporations and Securities Panel for an order that conduct in relation to a bid is unacceptable. If the panel makes such a declaration, it may also issue remedial orders, for example freezing transactions in the target's shares and cancelling agreements relating to the bid.

Other legislation that has an important impact on takeovers includes the *Trade Practices Act* and the *Foreign Acquisitions and Takeovers Act*. There is also legislation which restricts takeovers in particular industries, such as broadcasting, banking and insurance. ASX regulations provide an additional source of control in relation to bids involving public listed companies.

If you are a 'foreign person' then any bid you make is subject to the *Foreign Acquisitions and Takeovers Act*. If in your own right, or with associates, you seek to acquire 15 per cent, or more, of a company's shares you must seek the prior approval of the Treasurer. In practice this is done through the Foreign Investment Review Board. You may, however, launch a *conditional* bid without prior approval. In this case the offer to the target's shareholders must be made conditional on obtaining subsequent approval from the Foreign Investment Review Board. Small value transactions are exempt from these requirements.

Particularly, but not exclusively, in the case of horizontal takeovers the bidder needs to consider whether the bid might be judged anti-competitive, in which case the bid may fall foul of Section 50 of the *Trade Practices Act*. The result may be an injunction to prevent the bid proceeding or, in the case of a completed bid, an order from the Federal Court requiring the bidder to divest the assets acquired. To reduce these risks the bidder can ask the Australian Competition and Consumer Commission for an informal clearance. However, informal clearances do not prevent the Commission changing its mind and this has happened in the past. The safest course of action is to obtain from the Commission an authorisation to proceed despite anti-competitive consequences of the bid. The problem with this latter course of action is that the bid is delayed and the element of surprise is lost.

---

[28]  Sometimes the appeal is to state or federal governments, with a request to change the law.

# The form of the acquisition

If you think you can clear the legal hurdles, the next question is whether you can get the target's management onside. If you can get directors of the target to agree to the acquisition, your task will be much simpler. Such agreement is a more common event in the United States than in Australia, although two mining giants, Australia's CRA and Britain's RTZ, agreed to a multi-billion dollar merger that created the world's largest mining company.[29]

Whether the acquisition is friendly or hostile, you have two important decisions to make. First, the form in which the acquisition is to be undertaken. Second, what you will do with the acquired company if your takeover succeeds. You will also need to decide whether the consideration will be in cash, securities (usually shares) or a mixture of the two.

You may make the acquisition in the following ways:

- *By acquisition of assets*. The target's assets are purchased by the acquirer. In this case ownership of the assets needs to be transferred, and payment is made to the selling firm rather than directly to its shareholders.
- *By acquisition of shares*. The bidder acquires the target's shares and also perhaps quasi equity securities such as convertible notes. The acquisition of shares may take place through a scheme of arrangement. However, this is not common in Australia.[30] To succeed, a scheme of arrangement requires the support of management and the consent of shareholders and the courts. Alternatively, the bidder may make a direct offer to purchase shares from the shareholders of the target company. In the United States this is known as a tender offer.[31] In this case, the target's managers may not be involved at all. Their approval and cooperation are generally sought, but if they resist, the buyer will attempt to acquire an effective majority of the outstanding shares. If successful, the buyer has control and can, if necessary, complete the takeover and toss out incumbent management.
- *By a proxy contest*. In this case the bidder acquires control, but not ownership, of the target. To do this the bidder seeks the support of the target firm's shareholders to replace the company's board at the next annual meeting. This is called a *proxy fight* because the right to vote someone else's share is called a proxy. Such proxy fights are difficult to win and are not common in Australia.

What you do with the acquired company depends in part on the form of the acquisition and whether you got complete control. The alternatives are:

- *Merger*. The assets and liabilities of the target are completely absorbed by the bidder and the target ceases to exist as a separate company. Alternatively, the target and bidder may be combined to form a new company.
- *Unlisted company*. After a successful 100 per cent bid for a public company the target is delisted, but its corporate identity is maintained. For example, it may become a wholly-owned subsidiary of a corporate bidder, or a private company perhaps created by a management buy-out.
- *Listed company*. In the case of a partial bid, or a 100 per cent bid that is only partially successful, there may remain a sufficient spread of ownership so that the company can retain its ASX listing. This may particularly apply where a private company has made a partial bid for a public company.
- *Break up*. The acquired company is split up and some or all of the parts sold off.
- *Reverse takeover*. A bidder, which is smaller than the target, makes an offer using its own shares as consideration. Because the bidder is smaller than the target, the bidder's shareholders end up with a minority interest, and the target's shareholders end up with a controlling interest in the bidder.

---

[29]  A most unusual feature of this 'merger' was that both firms would continue to be listed as separate entities.

[30]  It was used, however, when St George Bank made an offer to take over Advance Bank.

[31]  In Australia, a tender offer generally refers to an offer to purchase a *limited* number of shares, so that the purchaser ends up controlling no more than 20 per cent of the target's voting shares.

# Restrictions on the acquisition of shares

Suppose you plan to take over a company. You might want to build up a toehold before you launch the bid. If so, you can quietly acquire up to 5 per cent of a company's shares. Once you reach the 5 per cent level you have to issue a substantial shareholding notice by the next trading day. This alerts the target company and the market to the presence of a possible bidder. From that point on the level of your shareholding will be a matter of considerable interest. You can continue to acquire shares until you hold 20 per cent of the voting shares of the company. Once you reach this point you are legally prohibited from increasing your holding beyond 20 per cent, but there are exceptions to this rule. The three most important exceptions allow:

- Creeping acquisitions.
- Acquisitions approved by independent shareholders.
- Formal takeover bids.

If you are in no hurry you might contemplate a creeping acquisition. In this case you can increase your holdings in the target by a maximum of 3 per cent every six months. This was the strategy that Campbell (soups) followed in its bid for Arnotts (biscuits). After a takeover bid early in 1993 Campbell held 53 per cent of Arnotts' shares, but because of an earlier agreement they were restricted to voting rights of about 15 per cent. Over the next four years Campbell followed a creeping acquisition strategy, lifting its shareholding to 70 per cent. At the end of 1997 Campbell took complete control, buying out the remaining shareholders in a scheme of arrangement.

If a creeping acquisition is too slow you might be able to persuade independent shareholders to vote to approve the acquisition. They can approve an allotment of shares, or allow you to buy out a few large shareholders, giving you sufficient shares to gain control. However, since this process means voting away their right to participate equally in the bid, such a vote may be opposed by many shareholders. Most likely therefore you would make a formal takeover bid.

Two types of formal takeover bid are permissible.

1. *Takeover scheme*, often called a Part A bid. You make a formal written offer to acquire shares direct from shareholders.
2. *Takeover announcement*, often called a Part C or on market bid. A stockbroker announces on your behalf that for a specified period and at a specified price the broking firm will stand in the market to purchase the target's shares.

# Part A bids

When the bid is a takeover scheme the offer document has to be accompanied by additional information known as a Part A statement which must be registered with the ASIC. The Part A statement requires disclosure of all information known to the bidder that is material to the target shareholders' decision whether to accept the offer. There are also specific disclosure requirements, such as details of the bidder, the bidder's toehold in the target and the period the bid will remain open. The offer period must be for a minimum of one month and a maximum of six months. However, the six-month limit can subsequently be extended to a full year.

The offer document together with an acceptance form is the basis for the purchase contract and specifies matters such as the form of the consideration and the price offered. If, as occurs quite frequently, the bid price is subsequently increased, the increase must be offered to all the target's shareholders, including those that have already accepted the bid. If the consideration is for cash then the *minimum* price that can be offered is the highest price at which shares were purchased by the bidder in the four months preceding the bid. Under certain conditions, the bidder may purchase shares in the market, concurrently with the bid. However, if the price paid in the market is higher than that offered in the formal bid, the bidder must raise the bid price to match that paid in the market.

An important part of the offer is the conditions that are attached. These are usually of two types. The first type prescribes conditions that will invalidate the offer. Many of these prescribed occurrences are standard conditions defined in the legislation. They include the target going into liquidation, or selling off major assets, or substantially changing its capital structure. The second type is a requirement for a minimum level of acceptances, usually set at either 50 or 90 per cent of the issued shares. If these conditions are not satisfied, the bid may be withdrawn. The bidder usually reserves the right to waive the conditions and declare the bid unconditional.

In a takeover scheme you make an offer to *each and all* shareholders to acquire 100 per cent or some lesser *but fixed* proportion of their shares. This creates a problem if you wish to launch a partial bid. To understand why it is easiest to consider an example. Suppose you hold 20 per cent of the target's shares and want to take your holding to 60 per cent. This means that you want to buy another 40 per cent, or half of the shares belonging to other shareholders. So you make an offer to buy 50 per cent of the shares of each shareholder. Unfortunately, only 70 per cent of the shareholders accept your offer and they hold only 60 per cent of the outstanding shares. As a consequence you only get to increase your shareholding by 30 per cent, not the 40 per cent you wanted. If you could increase the proportion of shares purchased from the shareholders who accept the bid you could solve your problem. However, you are not allowed to do so. Clearly, it is going to be very difficult to set the right proportion in advance. For this reason partial bids are now quite infrequent.

## Part C bids

An on market, or Part C, bid can only be launched by a bidder who holds less than 30 per cent of the target's shares. In some cases, however, this condition can be waived by the ASIC. The bid can only be for cash. It must also be unconditional except for the prescribed conditions in the legislation. The offer must be open for one month and can be extended for further one-month periods. The price can be increased, and there is no requirement to pay this higher price to target shareholders who have already accepted the lower price. The Part C statement that accompanies an on market bid is much the same as a Part A statement. However, since there is no formal written offer document, the Part C statement must include full particulars of the on market offer.

## Compulsory acquisition and sale

When the battle is over and the dust has settled, a few stragglers from the target may be left defiant on the battlefield. Provided the bidder has acquired at least 90 per cent of the issued shares, representing acceptances by at least 75 per cent of the shareholders, a mop up of the rest of the shares can proceed by a compulsory acquisition.[32] Conversely, where a bidder has acquired at least 90 per cent of the shares, remaining minority shareholders can require the bidder to purchase their shares. Holders of options and convertible notes can also require the bidder to purchase their securities if the acquisition of shares reaches 90 per cent or more.

## A note on takeover accounting

Takeovers sometimes raise complex accounting issues. The two main methods of accounting for takeovers are the *purchase of assets method* and the *pooling of interests method*. In efficient capital markets the choice between these two methods should make little difference, but managers and accountants agonise over the choice anyway.

In Australia the accounting profession has come down on the side of purchase method. So provided you stay in Australia you may never need to worry about pooling. Under the

[32] If the bidder's toehold was less than 10 per cent prior to the bid, then only the acquisition of 90 per cent of the target's shares is required in order to proceed to a compulsory acquisition.

purchase method the acquisition is treated as an investment in an asset and the book value equals the purchase price. The essential differences between pooling and purchase are illustrated in Table 33.2. The table shows what happens when A Company buys B Company, leading to a new AB Company. The two firms' initial (book) balance sheets are shown at the top of the table. The next balance sheet is AB Company's under pooling of interest. Note that this is nothing more than the two firms' separate balance sheets added together at their original book values. The final balance sheet shows what happens when purchase accounting is used. We assume that B Company has been purchased for $1.8 million, 180 per cent of book value.

**table 33.2** _____

Purchasing versus pooling in the merger of A Company with B Company (figures in $million).

| A Company | | | | B Company | | | |
|---|---|---|---|---|---|---|---|
| NWC | 2.0 | 3.0 | D | NWC | 0.1 | 0 | D |
| FA | 8.0 | 7.0 | E | FA | 0.9 | 1.0 | E |
| | 10.0 | 10.0 | | | 1.0 | 1.0 | |

| Balance sheets of AB Company | | | | | | | |
|---|---|---|---|---|---|---|---|
| | | | | **AB Company** | | | |
| Under pooling of interests | | | | NWC | 2.1 | 3.0 | D |
| | | | | FA | 8.9 | 8.0 | E |
| | | | | | 11.0 | 11.0 | |
| | | | | **AB Company** | | | |
| Under purchase accounting, assuming that | | | | NWC | 2.1 | 3.0 | D |
| A Company pays $1.8 million for B Company | | | | FA | 9.1 | 8.8 | E |
| | | | | Goodwill | 0.6 | | |
| | | | | | 11.8 | 11.8 | |

Note:

NWC = net working capital; FA = net book value of fixed assets; D = debt; E = book value of equity.

Why did A Company pay an $800 000 premium over book value? There are two possible reasons. First, the true values of B's *tangible* assets—its working capital, plant and equipment—may be greater than $1 million. Second, A Company may be paying for *intangible* assets that are not listed on B Company's balance sheet. The intangible asset may be a promising product or technology developed by B Company, for example. Or it may be no more than B Company's share of the economic gains from the takeover.

Under the purchase method of accounting, A Company is viewed as buying an asset worth $1.8 million—as indeed it is. The problem is how to show that asset on the left-hand side of AB Company's balance sheet. B Company's tangible assets have a book value of only $1 million. The Australian Accounting Standard requires this problem to be solved in two steps. First, the assets of the acquisition must be revalued to their fair market value. Generally, the revaluation only applies to tangible assets, but sometimes identifiable intangibles such as brand names are included in the asset valuation. In the case of B Company let us say that fixed assets are worth $1.1 million, rather than their $0.9 million book value. The total of B's assets are now worth $1.2 million. This leaves $0.6 million to account for. The accountant takes care of this in the second step, by creating a new asset category called **goodwill** and assigning $0.6 million to it. The goodwill must subsequently be amortised against future income. The company can choose the period over which the goodwill is charged against income, but the period may not exceed 20 years.

All this is somewhat arbitrary, but reasonable enough. Intangible assets do have value, and so there is no reason why such assets should not be shown on the balance sheet when a firm buys them. Nevertheless, most managers would prefer to pool if they could. The reason is that the amortisation of goodwill reduces reported income. Thus, AB Company's reported income will be reduced by at least $600\ 000/20 = \$30\ 000$ each year. Under pooling, goodwill never appears, and so reported income is at least $30\ 000 higher.

Now all this has absolutely no cash consequences. The amortisation charges are *not* cash outflows and they are not tax-deductible expenses. Thus, the choice between purchase and pooling should have no effect on the value of the merged firms.

Hong, Mandelker and Kaplan tested this proposition by looking at a sample of 159 acquisitions made between 1954 and 1964 in the United States. In the United States the pooling method is allowed under some circumstances. During the period studied there were fewer restrictions on pooling than there are now.[33] They found no evidence that shareholders of acquiring firms did better under pooling than under purchase accounting.

## Some tax considerations

Takeovers are both good news and bad news for shareholders in the target company. On the one hand, they are generally being offered a price substantially higher than the prevailing market price; on the other hand, they are going to be exposed to capital gains tax on any gain they make on disposal of their shares.[34] The tax to be paid may be considerable if shareholders originally purchased their shares at substantially below the current market price. However, if the company's shareholders are able to utilise imputation credits there is a way to reduce some of the pain. In a friendly takeover it may be possible to arrange that the target pay a big franked dividend to its shareholders, with a corresponding reduction in the bid consideration. Thus, part of the taxable gain is transformed to a rebatable dividend. This contrivance was used when St George Bank took over Advance Bank. Of course, if you play this game too hard you run the risk that the tax office may strike the arrangement down as a tax avoidance scheme.

There is also bad news in relation to the costs of a takeover defence. These costs are generally not tax deductible expenses for the target. This is because it is difficult to demonstrate that they are necessarily incurred in earning taxable income.

The bidder is in a more favourable position in that the transactions costs of mounting the bid will usually be tax deductible. If the purchase of the shares is financed by borrowing, then the interest paid will also be tax deductible. However, the actual payment for the target's shares will generally be considered a capital transaction, and therefore will not be tax deductible.

## 33.6 Responding to the bid and mounting a defence

Having received a bid the directors of the target must respond within 14 days by supplying a Part B statement in response to a Part A statement, and a Part D statement in response to a Part C statement. The objective of the Part B, or Part D, statements is to provide the target's

---

[33]  H. Hong, G. Mandelker and R. S. Kaplan, 'Pooling vs Purchase: The Effects of Accounting for Takeovers on Stock Prices', *Accounting Review*, 53: 31–47 (January 1978).

[34]  There are three exceptions to this:
- For share traders any gain will be taxed as income.
- If the shares were acquired before 20 September 1995, they are exempt from capital gains tax.
- If the takeover was by a scheme of arrangement and the consideration was in the form of shares, there are limited circumstances where it may be possible to rollover the gains liability.

It is currently proposed to exempt investors from capital gains tax when the consideration is in the form of shares in the bidder.

shareholders with information known to the directors of the target that is material to the bid. There will usually be a recommendation from the directors either for or against acceptance of the bid. If the directors do not wish to make such a recommendation they are required to explain why. There must also be disclosure of shares that directors hold in the target and the bidder, and whether or not the directors intend to accept the bidder's offer. Usually the directors' response to the bid will be accompanied by an independent expert's report on the value of the target's shares.[35]

## Defences subsequent to a bid

If the directors of the target decide to defend against the bid they have several alternative defences available.[36] They will usually start by criticising the bid as inadequate. Of course, this criticism will carry greater weight if supported by the independent expert's report. Directors may also criticise the bidder, particularly if consideration for the bid is in the form of securities issued by the bidder.[37] Another popular defence is the disclosure of favourable information about the target, such as a forecast of increased profits. This might also be accompanied by a promise of increased dividends. Legal action or the acquisition of shares by parties other than the bidder are also common defences. Less common defences are the pacman defence, where you make a counter-bid for shares of the bidder, or the selling off of assets that the bidder wants. This latter course of action is known as selling off the crown jewels. Appeals to patriotism, shareholder loyalty and requests for protection by state or federal governments have also been used as takeover defences. For example, Arnotts used the SAO defence—Stay Australian Owned—but in the end it was unsuccessful.

The acquisition of shares by parties friendly to the target management is often known as a **white knight** defence. The white knight can either make a competing bid or, more usually, obtain a strategic shareholding of a size sufficient to block the bid. This latter defence was used when Elder's obtained a large number of shares in BHP in order to help block a bid for BHP made by Bell Group. One problem with the white knight defence is that the white knight may turn out to be a predator and subsequently launch an unwanted bid.

Managers sometimes worry that a shareholder with a large block of shares represents the risk of a hostile bid. They may offer to buy out the shareholder at a favourable price to eliminate this threat. Such payments were often made to corporate raiders who were left with a substantial shareholding after a failed bid. Thus, the payments for share repurchase became known as **greenmail**. An alternative to the share repurchase is a standstill agreement where a major shareholder agrees not to increase their shareholding for some period of time. However, this does not always work. Campbell Investments was the white knight when Bond Corporation made a bid for Arnotts in about 1985. Campbell entered into a standstill agreement in which it undertook not to use its voting rights to control Arnotts' board. In the end, however, Campbell successfully acquired 100 per cent of Arnotts.

An obvious question is whether defending against a bid is in the shareholders' interest. The first point to be made is that the directors have a fiduciary responsibility to their shareholders. Therefore, they risk legal action by the ASIC, or disgruntled shareholders, if in frustrating a bid they are acting against the shareholders' interest. Casey and Eddey found that directors are more likely to recommend acceptance of a bid when the premium is high and are more likely to defend when the premium is low. This appears to be in the shareholders' interest, particularly as a bid defence quite often results in a higher offer, or a counter bid from another bidder.[38]

---

35  In the case of Part B statements, a valuer's report is required by law where the bidder owns 30 per cent or more of the target's voting shares, or if the bidder has a representative on the target's board.

36  An extensive analysis of takeover defences can be found in Roger S. Casey and Peter H. Eddey, 'Defence Strategies of Listed Companies Under the Takeover Code', *Australian Journal of Management*, 153–71 (December 1986).

37  Such criticism can be very effective. The demise of Bond Corporation probably began with a failed attempt to take over the British company Lonhro. Lonhro's Tiny Rowland produced a devastating report on Bond Corporation as part of Lonhro's takeover defence.

38  Casey and Eddey, op. cit., Footnote 36.

Why do managers contest takeover bids? One reason is to extract a higher price from the bidder. Another possible reason is that managers believe their jobs may be at risk in the merged company. These managers are not trying to obtain a better price; they want to stop the bid altogether. Some companies reduce these conflicts of interest by offering their managers **golden parachutes**, that is, generous payoffs if they lose their jobs as the result of a takeover. Sometimes these payoffs can be very large; for example, the American company Revlon offered its president $35 million. It may seem odd to reward managers for being taken over. However, if it overcomes their opposition to takeover bids, even $35 million may be a small price to pay.[39]

## Takeover defences before a bid

Frequently, managers do not wait for a bid before taking defensive action. Instead, they deter potential bidders by persuading shareholders to agree to '**shark-repellent**' changes to the company's articles of association. These may include restrictions on the appointment of directors, restrictions on share acquisitions and plebiscite provisions which require a vote of shareholders to approve any partial bid. Restrictions on share acquisition are very effective for private companies; however, for listed companies such restrictions are prohibited under ASX listing rules. Private companies can also create shares with differential voting rights, but listed companies are unable to do this except for issues of preference shares. Golden parachutes may also deter bidders. However, for listed companies the only form of golden parachute permissible is a very long period of notice, or pay in lieu, before a manager can be retrenched. Arrangements may also be made that trigger a change in ownership or control of the 'crown jewels' in the event of the takeover.

A popular defence in the United States is the **poison pill**. Existing shareholders are issued rights that, in the event of a bid, can be used to purchase the company's ordinary shares or convertible notes at a bargain price.[40] However, ASX listing rules generally prevent this sort of poison pill for Australian listed companies. New anti-takeover devices will keep cropping up. All we can say is, 'Stay tuned'. However, there is one further takeover defence that we have not yet stressed. Here is the story of how the American company Phillips Petroleum restructured its balance sheet in order to keep its independence.

## Phillips restructures to stave off takeover

In 1982 Mesa Petroleum had been involved in a battle for General American Oil Co (GAO) but had dropped its bid when GAO agreed to sell out to Phillips Petroleum. Two years later Mesa bought 6 per cent of Phillips' shares at an average price of $38 a share and then bid for a further 15 per cent at $60 a share.

Phillips responded in three ways.[41] First, it agreed to buy back Mesa's holding, giving Mesa a profit on the deal of $89 million.[42] Second, it raised its dividend by 25 per cent, reduced capital spending and announced a program to sell $2 billion of assets. Third, it agreed to repurchase about 50 per cent of its shares and to issue instead $4.5 billion of debt. Table 33.3

---

[39] Of course, excessively lavish parachutes may have the opposite effect and cause managers to throw themselves into the arms of almost any suitor.

[40] Often the price is set about half the market price.

[41] Phillips also devised a poison pill that would make it a less appetising morsel for future predators. This poison pill gave shareholders the right to exchange their shares for notes worth $62 a share if anyone bought 30 per cent or more of Phillips' shares. (The purchaser who triggered this provision would not be entitled to any of the notes.)

[42] Phillips' move to deter Mesa by buying out its holding at a premium is another example of greenmail. But giving in to greenmail can be dangerous, as Phillips soon discovered. Just six weeks later a group led by another corporate raider, Carl Icahn, acquired nearly 5 per cent of Phillips' shares and made an offer to buy the remainder. Phillips responded with a second greenmail payment: It bought out Icahn and his pals, giving them a profit of about $35 million.

shows how this leveraged repurchase changed Phillips' balance sheet. The new debt ratio was about 80 per cent, and book equity shrank by $5 billion to $1.6 billion.

**table 33.3**

Phillips' balance sheet was dramatically changed by its leveraged repurchase (figures in $billion).

|  | 1985 | 1984 |  | 1985 | 1984 |
|---|---|---|---|---|---|
| Current assets | $3.1 | $4.6 | Current liabilities | $3.1 | $5.3 |
| Fixed assets | 10.3 | 11.2 | Long-term debt | 6.5 | 2.8 |
| Other | 0.6 | 1.2 | Other long-term liabilities | 2.8 | 2.3 |
|  |  |  | Equity | 1.6 | 6.6 |
| Total assets | $14.0 | $17.0 | Total liabilities | $14.0 | $17.0 |

This massive debt burden put Phillips on a strict cash diet. It was forced to sell assets and pinch pennies wherever possible. Capital expenditures were cut back from $1065 million in 1985 to $646 million in 1986. In the same years the number of employees fell from 25 300 to 21 800.

Austerity continued through the late 1980s. By the end of the decade, long-term debt was reduced to $3.9 billion, and Phillips had regained an investment-grade debt rating. Employment was steady, and capital expenditures were gradually increasing, although not to the levels of the early 1980s.

How did this restructuring shield Phillips from takeover? Certainly not by making purchase of the company more expensive. On the contrary, restructuring drastically reduced the total market value of Phillips' outstanding shares and therefore reduced the likely cost of buying out its remaining shareholders.

But restructuring removed the chief *motive* for takeover, which was to force Phillips to generate and pay out more cash to investors. Before the restructuring investors sensed that Phillips was not running a tight ship and worried that it would plough back its ample operating cash flow into mediocre capital investments or ill-advised expansion. They wanted Phillips to pay out its free cash flow rather than let it be soaked up by a too-comfortable organisation or ploughed into negative NPV investments. Consequently, Phillips' share price did not reflect the potential value of its assets and operations. *That* created the opportunity for a takeover. One can almost hear the potential raider thinking:

So what if I have to pay a 30 or 40 per cent premium to take over Phillips? I can borrow most of the purchase price and then pay off the loan by selling surplus assets, cutting out all but the best capital investments and wringing out slack in the organisation. It'll be a rough few years, but if surgery's necessary, I might as well be the doctor and get paid for doing it.

Phillips' managers did not agree that the company was slack or prone to overinvestment. Nevertheless, they bowed to pressure from the share market and undertook the surgery themselves. They paid out billions to repurchase shares and to service the $6.5 billion in long-term debt. They sold assets, cut back capital investment and put their organisation on the diet investors were calling for.

When the takeover motive is to eliminate inefficiency or distribute excess cash, the target's best defence is to do what the bidder would do, and thus avoid the cost, confusion and random casualties of a takeover battle.

## 33.7 Other forms of reconstruction

### Divestitures—sell-offs, spin-offs and tracking stocks

Firms not only acquire businesses; they also sell them. Sell-offs are often the consequence of takeovers. New management may have planned to sell off part of the acquisition, or sell-offs may result from takeovers that did not work out as planned.[43] Other sell-offs occur because a company decides to rid itself of poorly performing divisions, or wants to refocus its activities on core businesses, or needs to reduce borrowings.

Sell-offs of non-core business became quite common in the 1980s. For example, CSR sold off its interests in mineral resources and energy. Burns Philp reduced its activities from nearly a dozen divergent business areas to two—hardware and food, particularly yeasts and spices. This reconstruction involved selling off more than 25 underperforming businesses during 1982 to 1986. In the period from shortly after the start of the sell-off up to 1986, Burns Philp's share price more than trebled.[44] We should not overconclude about the merits of sell-offs from a single example. However, the aim of sell-offs should be to increase shareholder wealth, and there is more substantial evidence from the United States that share prices do respond positively to sell-offs.[45]

Sell-offs usually involve the sale of major assets, lines of business or complete subsidiary companies. It sometimes happens, but rarely, that all the assets of the company are sold off in a voluntary liquidation. Sell-offs are usually made to another company, but sometimes the sale is made to managers of that part of the business being sold. But there is another alternative which we consider next.

Instead of selling a business to another firm, companies may spin off a subsidiary by distributing its shares to the shareholders of the parent company.[46] Some spin-offs may have tax advantages. This was the case when Westfield Limited transferred six of its shopping centres to the Westfield Property Trust, issuing units in the trust to Westfield Limited's shareholders.[47] There may also be regulatory advantages or the creation of an opportunity to renegotiate debt covenants. Spin-offs may widen investor choice by allowing them to invest directly in just one part of the business. Sometimes managers believe that the market is not fully valuing the components of a company and that splitting the whole into its parts will increase total value. For example, when BHP spun off its gold-producing activities into a separate company, one reason advanced for this was a belief that the market was not fully valuing the tax exempt status that gold producers enjoyed at that time. In New Zealand Fletcher Challenge split itself into four companies with separately traded shares. The objective was to give an identity to its energy and building divisions separate from its main image of forests, pulp and paper.

Another motive for spin-offs is that they can improve efficiency. Companies sometimes refer to a business as being a 'poor fit'. By spinning it off, the management of the parent company can concentrate on its main activity. If each business must stand on its own feet, there is no risk that funds will be siphoned off from one in order to support unprofitable investments in the other. In the extreme case where one business defaults on its debt, it does not drag the other business down with it. Moreover, if the two parts of the business are independent, it is easy to see the value of each and to reward managers accordingly. This is starting to sound as if spin-offs are a free lunch, therefore we need to remember that there are also additional costs involved in having two companies rather than one.

---

[43] One study concluded that over 30 per cent of assets acquired in a sample of hostile merger contests were subsequently sold. See S. Bhagat, A. Schleifer and R. Vishny, 'Hostile Takeovers in the 1980s: The Return to Corporate Specialisation', in *Brookings Papers on Economic Activity: Microeconomics*, 1990.

[44] This performance was not sustained. Burns Philp's performance in the 1990s can be most kindly described as only modest.

[45] See P. C. Jain, 'The Effect of Voluntary Sell-Off Announcements on Shareholder Wealth', *Journal of Finance*, pp. 207–24 (March 1985).

[46] Sometimes the shareholders have to make a small cash payment.

[47] This innovation was copied by a number of companies until the tax advantages were eliminated by subsequent changes to the tax law.

A third alternative to sell-offs and spin-offs has recently emerged in the United States—tracking stocks.[48] When a company issues a tracking stock, it is issuing an equity security where holders of the security have a claim to the income, but not the assets, of a particular segment of the business. For example, the telecommunications company AT&T recently announced its plans to issue a tracking stock for a newly created AT&T consumer services unit. This tracking stock will be listed on the New York Stock Exchange. Purchasers of the stock will have purchased a 'pure-play' in AT&T's consumer service business without being exposed to the risk of any of AT&T's other business activities. This means that AT&T shareholders will effectively sell off their claim to part of the company's income stream, while retaining ownership of all the assets. AT&T's shareholders will not lose their entire claim to consumer services income because AT&T will retain a substantial shareholding in the tracking stock.

## Leveraged buy-outs

Leveraged buy-outs, or LBOs, differ from ordinary takeovers in two ways. First, a large fraction of the purchase price is debt-financed. This debt financing may represent more than 90 per cent of the value of the assets. Some, perhaps all, of this debt has a low bond rating.[49] Second, the remaining equity in the LBO is privately held by a small group of (usually institutional) investors. When this group is led by the company's management, the acquisition is called a **management buy-out** (**MBO**).

The momentum for LBOs and MBOs was generated in the United States. There, in the 1970s many management buy-outs were arranged for unwanted divisions of large, diversified companies. Smaller divisions outside the companies' main lines of business often lacked top management's interest and commitment, and divisional management chafed under corporate bureaucracy. Many such divisions flowered when spun off as MBOs. Their managers, pushed by the need to generate cash for debt service and encouraged by a substantial personal stake in the business, found ways to cut costs and compete more effectively. In the 1980s MBO/LBO activity extended to buy-outs of entire businesses, including large, mature public corporations.

The growth of LBO/MBO activity in Australia has been much less dramatic.[50] The number and scale of transactions have been relatively small and even the *larger* Australian MBOs of the 1980s were typically smaller than the *average* takeover. Of course, there are exceptions. One of the most notable was Warwick Fairfax's failed privatisation of John Fairfax Ltd in 1987. The privatisation of this newspaper empire involved debt in excess of $1.5 billion. It was not long before the newly privatised company was experiencing difficulty servicing its debt, and in December 1990 it was placed in receivership. The company was subsequently sold to Tourang Ltd and the struggle for control by various media moguls has continued to the present day.

Most of our lessons on LBOs come from the USA.[51] The saga is best told through the most dramatic and best-documented LBO of them all: the $25 billion takeover of RJR Nabisco in 1988 by Kohlberg, Kravis and Roberts (KKR). The players, tactics and controversies of LBOs are writ large in this case.

---

48  The creation of tracking stocks addresses two issues that we raised earlier in the book. They are an example of the creation of securities to better meet investor needs. They also address the problem of reduced choice, and possible destruction of value, when firms diversify.

49  In the United States much of the LBO activity was financed with junk bonds, that is, bonds with a rating below Baa.

50  There are probably several reasons for this. There was hardly a corporate bond market in Australia for investment grade bonds, let alone a junk bond market. The introduction of the imputation system lessened the tax advantages of highly-levered transactions. There was also the opportunity to observe the problems that some LBOs were experiencing in the United States.

51  You may reasonably ask if LBOs are primarily an American phenomenon, why do we need to study them? The answer is simple—finance is an international activity. Australian companies have American subsidiaries; they also raise finance for Australian and overseas activities in American markets. We also need to learn about financial innovations overseas: which work, which do not, which to copy and which to avoid.

# RJR Nabisco

On 28 October 1988 the board of directors of RJR Nabisco revealed that Ross Johnson, the company's chief executive officer, had formed a group of investors prepared to buy all RJR's shares for US$75 per share in cash and take the company private. Johnson's group was backed up and advised by Shearson Lehman Hutton, the investment bank subsidiary of American Express.

RJR's share price immediately moved to about US$75, handing shareholders a one-day 36 per cent gain over the previous day's price of US$56. At the same time RJR's bonds fell, since it was clear that existing bondholders would soon have a lot more company.[52]

Johnson's offer lifted RJR onto the auction block. Once the company was in play, its board of directors was obliged to consider other offers, which were not long coming. Four days later Kohlberg, Kravis and Roberts bid US$90 per share, US$79 in cash plus PIK preferred shares valued at US$11. (PIK means 'pay in kind'. The preferred dividends would be paid not in cash, but in more preferred shares.[53])

The resulting bidding contest had as many turns and surprises as a Dickens novel. RJR's board set up the Committee of Independent Directors, advised by the investment bank Lazard Freres, to set rules for the bidding. Financial projections for RJR were made available to KKR and another bidding group put together by First Boston.

The bidding finally closed on 30 November, some 32 days after the initial offer was revealed. In the end it was Johnson's group against KKR. KKR offered US$109 per share, after adding US$1 per share (roughly US$230 million) in the last hour.[54] The KKR bid was US$81 in cash, convertible subordinated debentures valued at about US$10 and PIK preferred shares valued at about US$18. Johnson's group bid US$112 in cash and securities.

But the RJR board chose KKR. True, Johnson's group had offered US$3 per share more, but its security valuations were viewed as 'softer' and perhaps overstated. Also, KKR's planned asset sales were less drastic; perhaps their plans for managing the business inspired more confidence. Finally, the Johnson group's proposal contained a management compensation package that seemed extremely generous and had generated an avalanche of bad press.

But where did the takeover benefits come from? What could justify offering US$109 per share, about US$25 billion in all, for a company that only 33 days previously was selling for US$56 per share?

KKR and the other bidders were betting on two things. First, they expected to generate billions of additional cash from interest tax shields, reduced capital expenditures and sales of assets not strictly necessary to RJR's core businesses. Asset sales alone were projected to generate US$5 billion. Second, they expected to make those core businesses significantly more profitable, mainly by cutting back on expenses and bureaucracy. Apparently there was plenty to cut, including the RJR 'Air Force', which at one point included 10 corporate jets.

In the year after KKR took over, new management was installed that sold assets and cut back operating expenses and capital spending. There were also layoffs. As expected, high interest charges meant a net loss of US$976 million for 1989, but pre-tax operating income actually increased, despite extensive asset sales, including the sale of RJR's European food operations.

Inside the firm, things were going well. But outside there was confusion, and prices in the junk bond market were rapidly declining, implying much higher future interest charges for RJR and stricter terms on any refinancing. In mid-1990 KKR made an additional equity investment, and in December 1990 it announced an offer of cash and new shares in exchange for US$753 million of junk bonds. RJR's chief financial officer described the exchange offer as 'one further step in the deleveraging of the company'.[55] For RJR, the world's largest LBO, it seemed that high debt was a temporary, not permanent, virtue.

---

52  N. Mohan and C. R. Chen track the abnormal returns of RJR securities in 'A Review of the RJR Nabisco Buyout', *Journal of Applied Corporate Finance*, 3: 102–8 (Summer 1990).

53  See Section 24.7.

54  The whole story is reconstructed by B. Burrough and J. Helyar in *Barbarians at the Gate: The Fall of RJR Nabisco*, Harper & Row, New York, 1990. See especially Chapter 18.

55  G. Andress, 'RJR Swallows Hard, Offers $5-a-Share Stock', *The Wall Street Journal*, 18 December 1990, pp. C1–2.

# Barbarians at the gate?

The RJR LBO crystallised views on LBOs, the American junk bond market and the takeover business. For many it exemplified all that was wrong worldwide with finance in the 1980s, especially the willingness of 'raiders' to carve up established companies, leaving them with enormous debt burdens, basically in order to get rich quick.

There was plenty of confusion, stupidity and greed in the LBO and takeover business. Not all the people involved were nice. On the other hand, LBOs and takeovers generated enormous increases in market value, and most of the gains went to selling shareholders, not the raiders. For example, the biggest winners in the RJR Nabisco LBO were the company's shareholders.

We should therefore consider briefly where these gains may have come from before we try to pass judgement on LBOs and takeovers in general. There are several possibilities.

**The junk bond markets**     LBOs and debt-financed takeovers may have been driven by artificially cheap funding from the junk bond markets. With hindsight it seems that investors in junk bonds underestimated the risks of default in junk bonds. Default rates climbed painfully in 1989 and 1990; for example, Edward Altman reported $4.8 billion in defaults in the first six months of 1990.[56] At the same time the junk bond market became much less liquid after the demise of Drexel Burnham, the chief market maker. Yields climbed dramatically, and new issues dried up. Suddenly junk-financed LBOs became as scarce as great blind dates.

If junk bond investors in 1985 had appreciated the risk of what actually happened in 1990, junk finance would have been dearer. That would have slowed down LBOs and other highly-leveraged transactions.

**Leverage and taxes**     As we explained in Chapter 18, borrowing money can save taxes, particularly under the classical tax system of the United States. But taxes were not the main driving force behind LBOs. The value of interest tax shields was just not big enough to explain the observed gains in market value.[57] For example, Richard Ruback has estimated the present value of additional interest tax shields generated by the RJR LBO at $1.8 billion.[58] But the gain in market value to RJR shareholders was about $8 billion.

Of course, if interest tax shields were the main motive for LBOs' high debt, then LBO managers would not be so concerned to pay off debt. We saw that this was one of the first tasks facing RJR Nabisco's new management as well as the management of Phillips Petroleum after its leveraged recapitalisation.

**Other stakeholders**     We should look at the total gain to *all* investors in an LBO, not just the selling shareholders. It is possible that their gain is just someone else's loss and that no value is generated overall.

Bondholders are the obvious losers. The debt they thought was well secured may turn into junk when the borrower goes through an LBO. We noted how market prices of RJR Nabisco debt fell sharply when Ross Johnson's first LBO offer was announced. But again, the value losses suffered by bondholders in LBOs are not nearly large enough to explain shareholder gains. For example, Mohan and Chen's estimate[59] of losses to RJR bondholders was at most $575 million—painful to the bondholders, but far below shareholders' gain.

**Leverage and incentives**     Managers and employees of LBOs work harder and often smarter. They have to generate cash for debt service. Moreover, managers' personal fortunes are riding on the LBO's success. They become owners rather than organisation people.

---

56  E. I. Altman, 'Setting the Record Straight on Junk Bonds: A Review of Research on Default Rates and Returns', *Journal of Applied Corporate Finance*, **3**: 82–95 (Summer 1990). See also Section 23.4.

57  Moreover, there are some tax costs to LBOs. For example, selling shareholders realise capital gains and pay taxes that otherwise could be deferred.

58  R. S. Ruback, RJR Nabisco, case study, Harvard Business School, Cambridge, Mass., 1989.

59  Mohan and Chen, op. cit., Footnote 52.

It is hard to measure the payoff from better incentives, but there is some preliminary evidence of improved operating efficiency in LBOs. Kaplan, who studied 48 MBOs between 1980 and 1986, found average increases in operating income of 24 per cent three years after the LBO. Ratios of operating income and net cash flow to assets and sales increased dramatically. He observed cutbacks in capital expenditures but not in employment. Kaplan suggests that these 'operating changes are due to improved incentives rather than layoffs or managerial exploitation of shareholders through inside information'.[60]

**Cost savings from going private**    When a company goes private there are cost savings. There are no longer listing fees to pay, nor are there the costs of maintaining a large share register, producing glossy annual reports and the like.

Reporting and regulatory requirements may be simplified and management no longer faces the worry and restraints on action that dissident shareholders can cause. Set against these savings, however, are the substantial transaction costs that usually accompany going private. It is difficult to believe that the magnitude of net savings justifies going private in most cases.

**Free cash flow**    The free cash flow theory of takeovers is basically that mature firms with a surplus of cash will tend to waste it. This contrasts with standard finance theory, which says that firms with more cash than positive NPV investment opportunities should give the cash back to investors through higher dividends, share repurchases or other devices. But we see firms like RJR Nabisco spending on corporate luxuries and questionable capital investments. One benefit of LBOs is to put such companies on a diet and force them to pay out cash to service debt.

The free cash flow theory predicts that mature, 'cash cow' companies will be the most likely targets of LBOs. We can find many examples that fit the theory, including RJR Nabisco. The theory says that the gains in market value generated by LBOs are just the present value of the future cash flows that would otherwise have been frittered away.[61]

We do not endorse the free cash flow theory as an exclusive explanation for LBOs. We have mentioned several other plausible reasons, and we suspect that most LBOs are driven by a mixture of motives. Nor do we say that all LBOs are positive. On the contrary, there are many mistakes, and even soundly motivated LBOs face substantial default risks. However, we do quarrel with those who portray LBOs and takeovers *simply* as finance barbarians breaking up the traditional strengths of established companies. In many cases LBOs have generated true gains.

In the next section we sum up the longer-run impact of all takeovers on the Australian economy. We warn you, however, that there are no neat answers. Our assessment has to be mixed and tentative.

# 33.8  Takeovers and the economy

## Takeover waves

Takeovers come in waves. Each episode tends to coincide with a period of buoyant share prices.[62] Between different waves, there may be substantial differences in the types of companies that merge and the ways they go about it.

We do not really understand why takeover activity is so volatile. If takeovers are prompted by economic motives, at least one of these motives must be 'here today and gone tomorrow',

---

60   S. Kaplan, 'The Effects of Management Buyouts on Operating Performance and Value', *Journal of Financial Economics*, **24**: 217–54 (October 1989).

61   The free cash flow theory's chief proponent is Michael Jensen. See 'The Eclipse of the Public Corporation', *Harvard Business Review*, **67**: 61–75 (1989); and 'The Agency Costs of Free Cash Flow, Corporate Finance and Takeovers', *American Economic Review*, **76**: 323–9 (May 1986).

62   There are exceptions. The peak year for takeovers during the 1980s was 1988. Perhaps bargain hunters were tempted by low prices following the 1987 crash, or perhaps it was a consequence of low interest rates.

and it must somehow be associated with high share prices. But most of the economic motives that we review in this chapter have little to do with the general level of the share market. It is not clear that many burst on the scene in the 1980s when takeovers were rife, and departed in the early 1990s when takeovers declined.

Some takeovers may result from mistakes in valuation on the part of the share market or the buyer. In other words, the buyer may believe that investors have underestimated the value of the target, or may hope that they *will* overestimate the value of the combined firm. But we see (with hindsight) that mistakes are made in bear markets as well as bull markets. Why do we not see just as many firms hunting for bargain acquisitions when the share market is low? It is possible that 'suckers are born every minute', but it is difficult to believe that they can be harvested only in bull markets.

Companies are not the only active buyers and sellers in a bull market. Investors also trade much more heavily after a rise in share prices. Again, nobody has a good explanation of why this should be the case. Perhaps the answer has nothing to do with economics. Perhaps takeover booms and share market trading are behavioural phenomena—human beings, like some animals, are more active when the weather is sunny. But perhaps hubris is not the only explanation. When the market is rising, there is usually a climate of economic optimism and businesses are investing to expand. As we discussed under motives for mergers, there may be advantages to expanding by acquisition. Given that demand to expand, and opportunities for synergies from economies of scale, are greater in growing markets, this may help explain why merger activity is positively related to the level of the share market.

In the 1980s many of the takeovers worldwide involved cash surpluses—defending them or acquiring them. There were mature companies, such as those in the oil industry, that found themselves with limited investment opportunities. Many of these companies used their cash surpluses to buy into new areas. But they were also the subject of bids that obliged them to distribute cash. The conglomerate mergers initiated by Australian entrepreneurs of the 1980s were often driven by a need to acquire cash-rich businesses in order to help service the mountain of debt that the building of these conglomerate empires had created.

There were some broader economic forces behind these activities. During the 1980s rapid changes in technology, deregulation, higher oil prices and higher real interest rates required painful adjustments by companies in the developed world. In many cases the takeover, or even the threat of falling prey to a corporate raider, provided the impetus that forced necessary change on reluctant management. In countries such as Japan and Germany, where hostile takeovers are rare, change has had to come from within. It appears to have come later, but not less painfully.

This takes us back to our discussion of corporate governance in Chapter 14. In Australia the takeover market provides an important control on management. There may be other ways to provide this control, but if we are to rely less on *external* control, then we need to ensure that *internal* controls are able to provide effective incentives.

After a quiet start to the decade, by the second half of the 1990s equity markets are booming again and takeover activity is again growing. It will be interesting to see how this new wave of takeovers develops.

# Price movements and wealth effects for shareholders

In takeovers, is it better for shareholders to sell than to buy? In general, it is better to sell. Figure 33.2 summarises the results of a study by Bishop, Dodd and Officer of over 1400 takeovers from 1972 to 1985.[63] The study tracked abnormal returns to shareholders. The returns were calculated monthly, running from three years before the bid was announced to two years after bid announcement.[64] An estimate of the normal return was then made and

---

63    S. Bishop, P. Dodd and R. R. Officer, *Australian Takeovers: The Evidence, 1972–1985*, The Centre for Independent Studies, Policy Monograph No. 12, 1987.

64    Note that the sample gets progressively smaller after the announcement as bids are successfully concluded and targets are delisted.

subtracted from the observed monthly return, leaving the abnormal return for each month. The abnormal monthly returns were then added together in cumulative fashion over time starting at month $-36$. The result of this calculation is labelled the cumulative abnormal return (CAR for short). You can see that selling shareholders received a healthy gain, of the order of an extra 20 per cent return from six months before to one month after the bid. Note also how much of this gain occurs before the announcement date. Is this insider trading, or just the efficient market doing its job in anticipating events? Probably some of both. We do know that the extent of the pre-bid price run-up is greater where there is press speculation about a bid.[65] So it seems that investors do anticipate the announcement of the acquisition and the good news it brings.

In contrast to the target's shareholders, the acquiring companies' shareholders gained much less from the bid. Most of their gains were obtained long before the bid took place. And after the bid the cumulative abnormal return is almost flat, which means that their abnormal returns post-bid were approximately zero.

Bishop et al.'s study is one of dozens undertaken in Australia and overseas on the gains to bidders and to targets in contests for corporate control.[66] These studies consistently find positive abnormal returns that average between 20 and 30 per cent for the shareholders of the targets about the time of the bid. The results for bidder's shareholders are mixed. They show little or no abnormal return about the time of the bid. In some studies the abnormal return is negative, although usually not statistically significant. On average it appears that investors expect acquiring companies to just about break even, or perhaps make a small extra return.[67]

Why do sellers earn higher returns? There are two reasons. First, buyers are typically larger than sellers. In many takeovers the buyer is so much larger that even substantial net benefits would not show up clearly in the buyer's share price. Suppose, for example, that company A buys company B, which is only one-tenth A's size. Suppose the dollar value of the net gain to the takeover is split equally between A and B. Each company's shareholders receive the same *dollar* profit, but B's receive 10 times A's *percentage* return.

The second, and more important, reason is the monopolistic position of the seller and competition among potential bidders. Once the first bidder puts the target company 'in play', one or more additional suitors often jump in, sometimes as white knights at the invitation of the target firm's management. Every time one suitor tops another's bid, more of the takeover gain slides towards the target. At the same time, the target firm's management may mount various legal and financial counterattacks, ensuring that capitulation, if and when it comes, is at the highest attainable price.

It is clear why the target's price rises when a bid is in play. It is less clear why it is regularly observed that the price stays up in the case of bids that fail. There are three common explanations. The first is the 'kick in the pants theory'. As in the case of Phillips Petroleum, the bid wakes up the incumbent management and they perform better. The second is the 'tell them the good news' theory. As part of the bid defence management release information that leads to a positive revaluation of the company. The third is the subsequent bid theory. Once a target has

[65] See M. Aitken and R. Czernkowski, 'Information Leakage Prior to Takeover Announcements: The Effect of Media Reports', *Accounting and Business Research*, 3–20 (1992).

[66] For a classic review of some of these studies see M. C. Jensen and R. S. Ruback, 'The Market for Corporate Control: The Scientific Evidence', *Journal of Financial Economics*, **11**: 5–50 (April 1983).

[67] The story may be a little more complex than this. Bishop et al. show that firms which had a takeover strategy (evidenced by making more than one takeover bid) had higher abnormal returns pre-bid than firms which only made a single bid. Perhaps this reflects the market anticipation of gains from the takeover and that firms making multiple bids were better at the takeover game.
  In a 95-firm subset of the bidder firms originally studied by Bishop et al. it was found that:

∎ Significant abnormal returns were earned around the issue of a substantial shareholder notice. This suggests that gains from a takeover were anticipated.

∎ Multiple bidding firms or raiders earned abnormal returns while most non-raiders made abnormal negative returns.

See R. Casey, P. Dodd and P. Dolan, 'Takeovers and Corporate Raiders: Empirical Evidence from Extended Event Studies', *Australian Journal of Management*, **12**: 201–20 (December 1987).

been in play and the bid has failed, the price stays up because the market expects a subsequent higher bid. All three explanations have some merit. We tend to favour the third as being an explanation that often applies. Research shows that in cases where a bid fails and there is no subsequent bid the abnormal returns are wiped out.[68]

We can now give you a recipe for forecasting whether a bid will succeed. Watch the target's share price. If it increases quickly, or gradually, towards the bid price, but *not* above it, then the bid is likely to succeed. If the share price goes above the bid price, then the bid is likely to fail unless the bidder revises the offer upwards.[69]

Of course, bidders and targets are not the only possible winners. Unsuccessful bidders often win too, by selling off their holdings in target companies at substantial profits. Such shares may be sold on the open market or sold back to the target company in a greenmail transaction. Other winners include investment bankers, lawyers and accountants, and in some cases arbitrageurs (or 'arbs'), who speculate on the likely success of takeover bids.[70]

'Speculate' has a negative ring, but it can be a useful social service. A takeover offer may present shareholders with a difficult decision. Should they accept, should they wait to see if someone else produces a better offer, or should they sell their shares in the market? This dilemma presents an opportunity for the arbitrageurs. In other words, they buy from the target's shareholders and take on the risk that the deal will not go through, and that there will be no subsequent bid.

Of course, arbitrageurs can make even more money if they learn about the offer *before* it is publicly announced. This is insider trading. This is also the point at which a legitimate and useful activity becomes an illegal and possibly harmful one.

## Do takeovers generate net benefits?

There are undoubtedly good acquisitions and bad acquisitions, but economists find it hard to agree on whether acquisitions are beneficial *on balance*. We do know that takeovers generate substantial gains to acquired firms' shareholders. If buyers at least break even and sellers make substantial gains, it seems that there are positive overall benefits to takeover. This is exactly what the third graph in Figure 33.2 shows. But not everybody is convinced.[71] Some believe that investors analysing takeovers pay too much attention to short-term earnings gains and do not notice that these gains are at the expense of long-term prospects.[72] Such critics often use accounting data to support their criticisms. There is a problem with this as we will see in a moment. But first let us consider the evidence.

Since we cannot observe how companies would have fared in the absence of a takeover, it is difficult to measure the effects on profitability. Ravenscroft and Scherer, who looked at a large sample of takeovers in the United States during the 1960s and early 1970s, argued that

---

68  See M. Bradley, A. Desai and E. H. Kim, 'The Rationale Behind Interfirm Tender Offers', *Journal of Financial Economics*, **11**: 183–206 (1983).

69  Of course, you cannot rely on this rule if there is no trading. This might be more of a problem than you think. Elaine Hutson and Graham Partington (*Share Prices, Takeover Outcomes, and the Volume of Trades*, Australasian Finance and Banking Conference, Sydney, 1994) provide evidence that supports the rule, but also show that thin trading is often present during the bid period. Particularly for successful bids, trading often stops completely in the last 30 days of the bid.

70  Strictly speaking, an arbitrageur refers to an investor who takes a fully hedged, that is, riskless, position. Arbitrageurs in takeover battles often take very large risks indeed. Their activities are sometimes known as 'risk arbitrage'.

71  For example, Jensen and Ruback, after an extensive review of empirical work, conclude that 'corporate takeovers generate positive gains' (op. cit., Footnote 66). Richard Roll reviews the same evidence and argues that 'takeover gains may have been overestimated if they exist at all' (op. cit., Footnote 17).

72  There have been a number of attempts to test whether investors are myopic. For example, McConnell and Muscarella examined the reaction of share prices to announcements of capital expenditure plans. If investors were interested in short-term earnings, which are generally depressed by major capital expenditure programs, then these announcements should depress share prices. But they found that increases in capital spending were associated with *increases* in share prices and reductions were associated with *falls*. Similarly, Jarrell, Lehn and Marr found that announcements of expanded R&D spending prompted a *rise* in the share price. See J. McConnell and C. Muscarella, 'Corporate Capital Expenditure Decisions and the Market Value of the Firm', *Journal of Financial Economics*, **14**: 399–422 (July 1985); and G. Jarrell, K. Lehn and W. Marr, *Institutional Ownership, Tender Offers and Long-Term Investments*, The Office of the Chief Economist, Securities and Exchange Commission, April 1985.

**figure 33.2**
Cumulative abnormal returns about the time of a takeover announcement (returns are measured monthly)—target abnormal returns mostly came about the time of the bid; bidder abnormal returns mostly came well before the bid. Because bidders are so much bigger than targets, the cumulative abnormal return for bidders and targets combined show the returns to a value weighted portfolio.

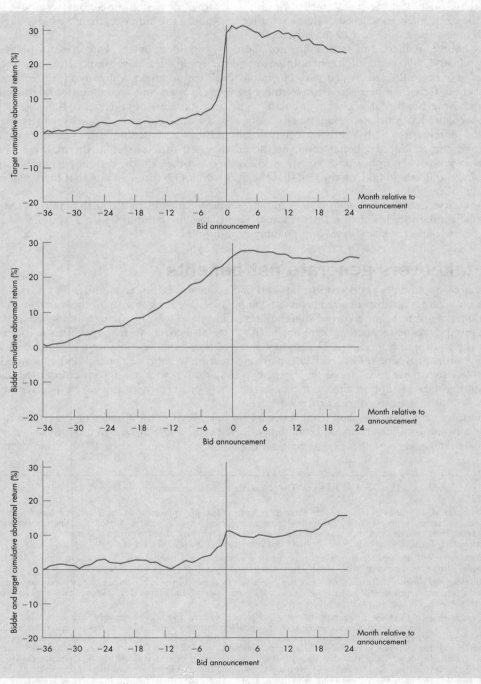

*Source*: S. Bishop, P. Dodd and R. R. Officer, op. cit., Footnote 63.

productivity declined in the years following takeover,[73] while a much smaller Australian study by McDougall and Round found that takeovers did not significantly improve profit performance.[74]

More recent studies of takeover activity in the United States suggest that takeovers do seem to improve real productivity. For example, Paul Healy, Krishna Palepu and Richard Ruback examined 50 large takeovers between 1979 and 1983 and found an average increase in the companies' pre-tax returns of 2.4 percentage points.[75] They argue that this gain came from generating a higher level of sales from the same assets. There was no evidence that the companies were mortgaging their long-term future by cutting back on long-term investments; expenditures on capital equipment and research and development tracked the industry average.

We suggest you do not place too much weight on the results of studies based on accounting data. First, there is the difficult problem of establishing a control or benchmark for performance. What would profitability have been if there had been no takeover? Second, the method of accounting for takeovers may result in depressed earnings, in the initial years at least. Under the Australian method of accounting for takeovers, the purchase method, there will be a write-up of assets that will increase book values, and the amortisation of goodwill that will depress earnings. It would be no surprise therefore to see that the accounting return on investment goes down, even if there is no real change in operating performance. Third, the effects of the takeover will extend over time and will emerge at different rates for different firms. Finally, methods of accounting differ substantially across companies. These latter two effects make it difficult to aggregate results across firms without the risk of bias.

If you are concerned with public policy towards takeovers, you do not want to look at only their impact on the shareholders of the companies concerned. For instance, we have already seen that in the case of RJR Nabisco some part of the shareholders' gain was at the expense of the bondholders and the government (through the enlarged interest tax shield). The acquirer's shareholders may also gain at the expense of the target firm's employees, who in some cases are laid off or are forced to take pay cuts after takeovers. As we noted in the Advance Bank–St George merger, it was suggested that a thousand jobs would go. Andrei Shleifer and Lawrence Summers argue that such activities may involve a loss of trust between employer and employee which can spread through the economic system.[76]

Some people worry that the takeover wave of the 1980s has led to excessive debt levels which not only left some Australian companies ill-equipped to survive the last recession, but which also may have contributed to its severity. In addition, many banks and financial institutions supplied debt to finance acquisitions. Defaults on these debts created solvency problems for some of the newer and smaller merchant banks and badly affected the profitability of some of the larger trading banks.

Perhaps the most important effect of acquisitions is felt by the managers of companies that are *not* taken over. For example, managers of our once largest company BHP could not feel safe from challenge. Perhaps the threat of takeover spurs the whole of corporate Australia to try harder. Unfortunately, we do not know whether on balance the threat of takeover makes more for active days or sleepless nights.

---

73  See D. J. Ravenscroft and F. M. Scherer, 'Takeovers and Managerial Performance', in J. C. Coffee, Jr, L. Lowenstein and S. Rose-Ackerman (eds.), *Knights, Raiders and Targets: The Impact of the Hostile Takeover*, Oxford University Press, New York, 1988.

74  See F. M. McDougall and D. K. Round, 'The Determinants and Effects of Corporate Takeovers in Australia, 1970–1981', in *The Effects of Mergers and Takeovers in Australia*, Australian Institute of Management (Victoria) and National Companies and Securities Commission, 1986.

75  See P. Healy, K. Palepu and R. Ruback, Does Corporate Performance Improve after Takeovers?, NBER Working Paper No. 3348, 1990. The study examined the pre-tax returns of the merged companies relative to industry averages. A study by Lichtenberg and Siegel comes to similar conclusions. Before takeover, acquired companies had lower levels of productivity than other firms in their industries, but by seven years after the control change, two-thirds of the productivity gap had been eliminated. See F. Lichtenberg and D. Siegel, 'The Effect of Control Changes on the Productivity of US Manufacturing Plants', *Journal of Applied Corporate Finance*, 2: 60–7 (Summer 1989).

76  See A. Shleifer and L. H. Summers, 'Breach of Trust in Corporate Takeovers', in A. J. Auerbach (ed.), *Corporate Takeovers: Causes and Consequences*, University of Chicago Press, Chicago, 1988. There is no doubt that some takeovers involve substantial redundancies. However, Lichtenberg and Siegel, op. cit., Footnote 75, found no evidence that *on average* ownership changes lead to layoffs or wage cuts.

But takeover activity is also very costly. For example, in the RJR Nabisco buy-out, the total fees paid to the investment banks, lawyers and accountants amounted to over $1 billion. Firms may spend a lot of money on defending themselves and on greenmail. Not to mention the amount of time management spend on defences rather than running their business.

Even if the gains to the community exceed the costs, one wonders whether the same benefits could not be achieved more cheaply than by acquisition. Perhaps the problem lies in the way in which many corporations reward and penalise their managers. Michael Jensen and Kevin Murphy calculated that in the 250 largest American corporations, a $1000 change in corporate value corresponds to a change of just 6.7 cents in the chief executives' salary and bonus over two years.[77] Perhaps many of the gains from takeover could be captured by linking management compensation more directly to performance.

## 33.9 Summary

A takeover generates an economic gain if the two firms are worth more together than apart. Suppose that firms A and B merge to form a new entity, AB. Then the gain from the takeover is

$$\text{Gain} = PV_{AB} - (PV_A + PV_B)$$

Gains from takeovers may reflect synergies of various sorts. Suggested sources of expected gains include economies of scale, economies of vertical integration, improved efficiency, fuller use of tax shields, the combination of complementary resources, quick and perhaps cheap expansion, or redeployment of surplus funds. We do not know how common these benefits are, but they do make economic sense. Sometimes takeovers are undertaken to reduce the costs of borrowing, diversify risks or play the bootstrap game. These motives are dubious.

You should go ahead with the takeover if the gain exceeds the premium. The premium that the buyer pays for the selling firm, over its value as a separate entity, determines how much of the gain from the takeover is captured by the target's shareholders. It is easy to estimate when the takeover is financed by cash. In that case,

$$\text{Premium} = \text{cash} - PV_B$$

When payment is in the form of shares, the premium naturally depends on what those shares are worth after the takeover is complete. If the takeover is a success, B's shareholders will share the takeover gains.

The mechanics of buying a firm are much more complex than those of buying a machine. You have to make sure that the purchase is unlikely to be judged anti-competitive by the Australian Competition and Consumer Commission. You have a choice of procedures you might follow in acquiring control of the target. For example, you could undertake a merger by scheme of arrangement; or initiate a takeover using either a Part A or Part C bid; or you might buy the individual assets of the seller. There are also other details to consider including tax matters and accounting for the acquisition.

Takeovers are sometimes amicably negotiated between the management and directors of the two companies; but if the seller is reluctant, the would-be buyer can decide to make a hostile takeover bid. We sketched some of the defensive tactics used in takeover battles.

---

[77]  See M. C. Jensen and K. J. Murphy, 'CEO Incentives—It's Not How Much You Pay, But How', *Harvard Business Review*, 68: 138–49 (May–June 1990).

We also observed that when the target firm loses, its shareholders typically win: Selling shareholders earn abnormal returns, averaging between 20 and 30 per cent in takeovers. The bidding firm's shareholders roughly break even. The typical takeover generates positive net benefits to investors, but competition among bidders, plus active defence by target managements, pushes most of the gains towards selling shareholders.

The threat of hostile takeover can stimulate corporate restructuring, which may involve additional borrowing, selling or spinning off businesses, and distributing more cash to shareholders. In a management buy-out (MBO) or leveraged buy-out (LBO), all public shares are repurchased and the company 'goes private'.

LBOs and other debt-financed takeovers are driven by a mixture of motives, including the value of interest tax shields; the transfer of value from lenders, who sometimes see the market values of their securities fall as the borrowing firm piles up more debt; and the opportunity to create better incentives for managers and employees, who have a greater personal financial stake in the company but must work harder to service debt. In addition, some takeovers are designed to force firms with cash surpluses to distribute cash rather than ploughing it back. Investors fear such companies would channel free cash flow into negative NPV investments.

Takeovers seem to generate net economic gains, but they are also costly. Merchant banks, lawyers, arbitrageurs, corporate raiders and greenmailers thrived during the 1980s takeover boom. Many companies were left with heavy debt burdens and had to sell assets in order to stay solvent. There were many casualties and conglomerate empires that had been quickly built up collapsed even more quickly. By the end of 1990 the takeover market had subsided and the corporate jousting field was strangely quiet. The takeover wave of the 1980s was over, and investors and managers began to think about the size, shape and timing of the next one. It was not long coming; by 1995 another takeover wave was beginning.

## FURTHER READING

The approach to analysing takeovers presented in this chapter is based on:

    S. C. Myers, 'A Framework for Evaluating Takeovers', in S. C. Myers (ed.), *Modern Developments in Financial Management*, Frederick A. Praeger, New York, 1976.

Jensen and Ruback review the extensive empirical work on takeovers. The same issue of the *Journal of Financial Economics* also contains a collection of some of the more important empirical studies:

    M. C. Jensen and R. S. Ruback, 'The Market for Corporate Control: The Scientific Evidence', *Journal of Financial Economics*, **11**: 5–50 (April 1983).

A comprehensive Australian study is:

    S. Bishop, P. Dodd and R. R. Officer, *Australian Takeovers: the Evidence, 1972–1985*, The Centre for Independent Studies, 1987.

One useful book on takeovers is:

    J. F. Weston, K. S. Chung and S. E. Hoag, *Takeovers, Restructuring and Corporate Control*, Prentice-Hall, Englewood Cliffs, N.J., 1990.

A concise and informative book on the legal framework for takeovers in Australia is:

    Rodd Levy, *Takeovers, Law and Strategy*, The Law Book Company, Sydney, 1996.

A useful database on Australian takeovers is maintained by *Corporate Adviser*.

Kaplan provides evidence on the performance of a sample of LBOs undertaken in the 1980s. Jensen, the chief proponent of the free cash flow theory of takeovers, provides a spirited and controversial defence of LBOs:

    S. Kaplan, 'The Effects of Management Buyouts on Operating Performance and Value', *Journal of Financial Economics*, **24**: 217–54 (October 1989).

    M. C. Jensen, 'The Eclipse of the Public Corporation', *Harvard Business Review*, **67**: 61–74 (September–October 1989).

Finally, here is a classic bedtime read which is both entertaining and an informative case study:

> B. Burrough and J. Helyar, *Barbarians at the Gate: The Fall of RJR Nabisco*, Harper & Row, New York, 1990.

# QUIZ

**1.** Are the following hypothetical takeovers horizontal, vertical or conglomerate?
 a. NAB acquires Westpac.
 b. Westpac acquires Coles Myer.
 c. Coles Myer acquires Nestlé.
 d. Nestlé acquires NAB.

**2.** Velcro Saddles is contemplating the acquisition of Pogo Ski Sticks, Inc. The values of the two companies as separate entities are $20 million and $10 million, respectively. Velcro Saddles estimates that by combining the two companies, it will reduce marketing and administrative costs by $500 000 per year in perpetuity. Velcro Saddles can either pay $14 million cash for Pogo or offer Pogo a 50 per cent holding in Velcro Saddles. If the opportunity cost of capital is 10 per cent,
 a. What is the gain from takeover?
 b. What is the premium for the cash offer?
 c. What is the premium for the share alternative?
 d. What is the NPV of the acquisition under the cash offer?
 e. What is its NPV under the share offer?

**3.** Which of the following statements is *not* true:
 a. The transactions costs of the bidder are usually tax deductible.
 b. The cost of defence by the target is usually tax deductible.
 c. The consideration for the bid is not tax deductible.
 d. The interest costs on borrowings to finance the bid are usually tax deductible.

**4.** True or false?
 a. Sellers almost always gain in takeovers.
 b. Buyers almost always gain in takeovers.
 c. Firms that do unusually well tend to be acquisition targets.
 d. Takeover activity in Australia varies dramatically from year to year.
 e. On average, takeovers produce substantial economic gains.
 f. On market bids require the approval of the selling firm's management.
 g. If a takeover can be treated as a pooling of interest rather than a purchase, reported earnings are usually increased.
 h. The premium paid in a takeover is always independent of the economic gain produced by the takeover.

**5.** Which of the following motives for takeovers make economic sense?
 a. Merging to achieve economies of scale.
 b. Merging to reduce risk by diversification.
 c. Merging to redeploy cash generated by a firm with ample profits but limited growth opportunities.
 d. Merging to make fuller use of tax-loss carry-forwards.
 e. Merging just to increase earnings per share.

**6.** Connect each term to its correct definition or description.
  a. LBO
  b. Poison pill
  c. Takeover scheme
  d. Greenmail
  e. Golden parachute

  f. Proxy fight

(A) Payment to target firm's managers who leave after a takeover.
(B) Attempt to gain control of a firm by winning the votes of its shareholders.
(C) Offer to buy shares directly from shareholders.
(D) Target company buys out shareholders threatening takeover; repurchase price exceeds market price.
(E) Rights that shareholders in the target can exercise in the event of a bid, allowing them to acquire additional securities at a bargain price.
(F) Company or business bought out by private investors, largely debt-financed.

**7.** True or false?
  a. One of the first tasks of an LBO's financial manager is to pay down debt.
  b. Shareholders of bidding companies are more likely to make abnormal returns when the takeover is financed with shares than in cash-financed deals.
  c. Takeovers are regulated by the ASIC and other agencies of the federal government.
  d. Takeover targets are usually bigger than bidders.
  e. Corporate raiders seem to earn higher abnormal returns than other bidders.

## QUESTIONS AND PROBLEMS

**1.** Examine several and preferably recent takeover bids. Describe the events that took place and suggest the principal motives for merging in each case. (Although it is not a recent takeover, the bid for BHP, the defence and its consequences makes a very interesting story; more recently, the history of St George Bank's takeover bids also provides an interesting saga.)

**2.** Examine a recent takeover in which at least part of the payment made to the seller was in the form of shares. Use share market prices to obtain an estimate of the gain from the takeover and the cost of the takeover.

**3.** The Muck and Slurry takeover has fallen through (see Section 33.3). But World Enterprises is determined to report earnings per share of $2.67. It therefore acquires the Wheelrim and Axle Company. You are given the following facts:

|  | World Enterprises | Wheelrim and Axle | Merged firm |
|---|---|---|---|
| Earnings per share | $2.00 | $2.50 | $2.67 |
| Price per share | $40.00 | $25.00 | ? |
| Price-earnings ratio | 20 | 10 | ? |
| Number of shares | 100 000 | 200 000 | ? |
| Total earnings | $200 000 | $500 000 | ? |
| Total market value | $4 000 000 | $5 000 000 | ? |

Once again, there are no gains from merging. In exchange for Wheelrim and Axle shares, World Enterprises issues just enough of its own shares to ensure its $2.67 earnings per share objective.
  a. Complete the above table for the merged firm.

b. How many shares of World Enterprises are exchanged for each share of Wheelrim and Axle?

c. What is the premium paid in the takeover by World Enterprises?

d. What is the change in the total market value of those World Enterprises shares that were outstanding before the takeover?

**4.** Explain the distinction between a creeping bid and an on market bid.

**5.** Can you identify any companies which you think would be takeover targets? If you can, explain your choice.

**6.** As treasurer of Leisure Products Ltd you are investigating the possible acquisition of Plastitoys. You have the following basic data:

|  | Leisure Products | Plastitoys |
|---|---|---|
| Earnings per share | $5.00 | $1.50 |
| Dividend per share | $3.00 | $0.80 |
| Number of shares | 1 000 000 | 600 000 |
| Share price | $90.00 | $20.00 |

You estimate that investors currently expect a steady growth of about 6 per cent in Plastitoys' earnings and dividends. Under new management this growth rate would be increased to 8 per cent per year, without any additional capital investment required.

a. What is the gain from the acquisition?

b. What is the premium paid for the acquisition if Leisure Products pays $25 in cash for each share of Plastitoys?

c. What is the premium paid for the acquisition if Leisure Products offers one share of Leisure Products for every three shares of Plastitoys?

d. How would the premium for the cash offer and the share offer alter if the expected growth rate of Plastitoys were not changed by the takeover?

**7.** Look again at Table 33.2. Suppose that B Company's fixed assets are re-examined after the merger and are found to be worth $1.3 million instead of $0.9 million. How would this affect AB Company's balance sheet under pooling and under purchase accounting? How would the value of AB Company change?

**8.** Do you have any rational explanation for the great fluctuations in aggregate takeover activity and the apparent relationship between takeover activity and share prices?

**9.** What was the common theme in the Phillips Petroleum restructuring and the RJR Nabisco LBO? Why was financial leverage a necessary part of both deals?

**10.** Explain why the fall in the value of a target's debt caused by a leveraged takeover represents a gain to the *equity* investors. (*Hint*: See Section 18.3.)

**11.** Read *Barbarians at the Gate* (see Further Reading). Does this story support Michael Jensen's free cash flow theory of takeovers?

**12.** What costs, dangers and inequities did the boom of the 1980s debt-financed conglomerate takeovers create? Would you support new legislation designed to restrict such transactions in the new millennium? Can you think of other ways companies could realise the benefits of these transactions without financing at very high debt ratios?

**13.** What policy towards takeovers would you wish to follow if you were:
   a.  Head of the Australian Competition and Consumer Protection Commission?
   b.  Head of the Foreign Investment Review Board?

**14.** The Advance Bank had been a part of the continuing takeovers of regional banks in the Australian Banking Industry, and had also managed to create a 'shark-repellent' that did not breach ASX listing requirements. During the latter part of 1995 there arose the prospect of an attractive bid for Advance by the St George Bank. The dilemma for the Advance board was whether to support the bid or continue its own strategy which might have included further acquisitions. It is possible that only by buying other banks would Advance maintain the market share and financial clout necessary to continuing success in a competitive industry. On the other hand, a takeover bid for Advance offered the prospect of significant gains for its shareholders.
   a.  Are shareholders generally better off as sellers rather than buyers in corporate acquisitions? Why?
   b.  Was Advance in a good bargaining position in the event of any bid?
   c.  Under what conditions would a policy of further acquisitions have made sense for Advance and its shareholders?

**15.** In December 1995 NatWest, one of the largest British banks, sold its American retail banking operations Fleet Financial for about US$3.5 billion. The price was much less than industry observers had expected, but NatWest's share price nevertheless increased sharply. 'The central explanation [for the share price rise] was found in strong hints in NatWest's announcement that it would not rush out immediately and spend the sale money on some ill-judged and overpriced acquisition.'[78] NatWest also announced that it was considering re-purchasing shares.

Explain how adherents of the free cash flow hypothesis would interpret this episode.

**16.** Examine a recent hostile acquisition and discuss the tactics employed by both the predator and target companies. Do you think the management of the target company was trying to defeat the bid or secure the highest price for its shareholders? How did each announcement by the protagonist affect their share prices?

**17.** In Italy the first firm to bid for a target is allowed to revise its offer, but subsequent bidders may only enter one bid that they are not allowed to revise. What do you think are the reasons for this rule? Should it be introduced in Australia?

---

[78]  George Graham, 'NatWest Bids Farewell to an Albatross', *Financial Times*, 23–24 December 1995, p. 2.

# chapter 34

# INTERNATIONAL FINANCIAL MANAGEMENT

So far we have talked principally about doing business domestically. But many companies have substantial overseas interests. Of course, your financial objectives when it comes to international financial management are still the same. You want to buy assets that are worth more than they cost, and you want to pay for them by issuing liabilities that are worth less than the money raised. It is when you come to apply these criteria to your international business that you come up against some additional problems.

The unique feature of international financial management is that you need to deal with more than one currency. We will therefore look at how foreign exchange markets operate, why exchange rates change, and what you can do to protect yourself against exchange risks.

The financial manager must also remember that interest rates differ from country to country. For example, in 1994 the rate of interest was about 2.5 per cent in Japan, 10 000 per cent in Brazil and increased from 4.75 to 9.25 per cent in Australia. We are going to discuss the reasons for these differences in interest rates, along with some of the implications for financing overseas operations. Issues to consider include: Should the parent company provide the money? Should it try to finance the operation locally? Or should it treat the world as its oyster and borrow wherever interest rates are lowest?

We will also discuss how international companies decide on capital investments. How do they choose the discount rate? And how does the financing method affect the choice of project? You will find that the basic principles of capital budgeting are the same but there are a few pitfalls to look out for.

## **34.1** The foreign exchange market

The foreign exchange market has no central marketplace. Business is conducted by telephone, computer link or fax, and the principal dealers are the larger retail and investment banks and the central banks around the world. Any corporation that wants to buy or sell currency usually does so through a bank.[1]

Turnover in the foreign exchange markets is huge. In London, nearly $200 billion of currency changes hands each day. Volume in both New York and Tokyo is well over $100 billion per day. The Australian dollar regularly trades in volumes over $50 billion per day. A survey in April 1998 by the Reserve Bank of Australia[2] found that volume averaged US$47 billion per day, with the A$/US$ currency pairing accounting for 54 per cent of all transactions. The survey also found that spot transactions accounted for 42 per cent of all transactions; 53 per cent of all transactions were between Australian foreign exchange dealers and overseas banks; and 34 per cent were between Australian dealers.

Most foreign exchange transactions are for the purpose of facilitating payment and receipts for international trade and for capital transactions involving the investment and borrowing of funds. For example, an Australian company that imports goods from the United States will need to sell Australian dollars and buy US dollars in order to pay for the purchase. An Australian company exporting to the United States receives US dollars, which it sells in exchange for Australian dollars. Both firms make use of the foreign exchange market. Hence, whether your firm or its competitors deal in foreign exchange, it is important that we familiarise ourselves with exchange rates, spot transactions and forward transactions.

An exchange rate represents the value of one currency in terms of another. Therefore, all exchange rate quotations involve two currencies. The currency being priced is often referred to as the commodity currency and the other currency is known as the terms currency.[3] Most world currencies are quoted with the US dollar as the commodity currency. Hence, most exchange rates are quoted as the number of units of a domestic currency needed to buy one US dollar. This is also known as a direct quote. A quote such as US$1 = A$1.2492, or US$/A$, is a direct quote as it uses the US dollar as its base or commodity rate. Using direct quotations, the amount of the domestic currency changes as the exchange rate changes. However, the Australian dollar is usually quoted against the US dollar in terms of how many US dollars you can buy with one unit of the Australian dollar. When the foreign currency is quoted in terms of the domestic currency this is known as an indirect quotation. For example, the Australian dollar is quoted as A$1 = US$0.8005, or A$/US$. Here, the amount of the foreign currency changes as the exchange rate changes and the Australian dollar is the base or commodity rate. Other currencies that quote their currency using the direct quotation method include the British pound sterling, the Irish punt, the New Zealand dollar and the European Union currency, the ECU.[4]

Most countries have their own exchange rate, and some have interesting names for their exchange rates, for example, Gibraltar (G Pounds), Mauritius (M Rupee), Iceland (Krona), Indonesia (Rupiah) and Bolivia (Boliviano).

---

1   In Australia, all financial institutions that deal in foreign exchange must be licensed by the Reserve Bank of Australia as authorised foreign exchange dealers. As at April 1998, there were 66 authorised dealers.

2   See Reserve Bank of Australia media release, 'Survey of Foreign Exchange and OTC Derivatives Turnover', No. 98–12, 29 September 1998.

3   In the exchange rate quotation A$1 = US$0.8000, the commodity being priced is the Australian dollar. The exchange rate is quoted such that one unit of the Australian dollar is expressed as 0.8000 units of US dollars. The Australian dollar is the commodity currency and the US dollar is the terms currency. If the exchange rate is US$1 = A$1.2500, then the US dollar is the commodity currency and the Australia dollar is the terms currency. Most world currencies are quoted with the US dollar as the commodity currency.

4   The ECU is a basket of currencies of European Union (EU) countries.

# Spot rates

Table 34.1 reproduces a table of mid-rate quotation exchange rates of major trading countries from the *Financial Review*. The table shows the price of currency for immediate or **spot** delivery. **Spot rates** involve deals agreed today with settlement in two working days. All rates in Table 34.1 are quoted with the Australian dollar as the base or commodity currency. For example, A$1 is equivalent to US$0.6504; or, more concisely, A$/US$0.6504.[5] If A$1 buys US$0.6504, then US$1 must buy 1/0.6504 = A$1.5375. Thus, the reciprocal of the indirect quotation, $A/US$0.6504, gives the direct quotation US$/A$1.5375.

**table 34.1**

Spot exchange rates, 11 August 1999

| Country | Currency | Currency symbol | Rate |
|---|---|---|---|
| United States | US dollar | US$ | 0.6504 |
| Japan | Yen | ¥ | 74.5200 |
| United Kingdom | Sterling | £Stg | 0.4026 |
| European Union | European Currency Unit | Euro | 0.6071 |
| Germany | Deutschmark | DM | 1.1915 |
| New Zealand | NZ dollar | NZ$ | 1.2318 |

*Source*: Adapted from the *Financial Review*, 12 August 1999.

In practice in the foreign exchange market, exchange rates are quoted from the dealer's perspective with bid and offer rates. For indirect quotations, the bid rate represents the rate at which the dealer will buy Australian dollars (A$) by selling US dollars (US$), while the offer rate represents the rate at which the dealer will sell Australian dollars for the purpose of buying US dollars.[6] The difference between the rates is known as the 'bid-offer spread' or 'the spread' and represents the gross profit to the bank undertaking the transactions. Heavily traded currencies such as $A/US$, US$/yen, US$/DM and £Stg/US$ usually trade at very narrow spreads. In the less frequently traded and retail markets for traveller's cheques and notes for overseas travellers, the spread between bid and offer widens quite substantially. For example, if the exchange rate is 0.7870/0.7875, there is a spread of five basis points, or 'pips'. The quoting bank is willing to buy Australian dollars (and sell US dollars) at a rate of A$/US$0.7870 and to sell Australian dollars (and buy US dollars) at a rate of A$/US$0.7875.

Consider the roles of the dealer and the corporate client on both the bid and offer sides of a quote:

| | Bid | Offer |
|---|---|---|
| Dealer | Buy A$ Sell US$ | Sell A$ Buy US$ |
| Company | Sell A$ Buy US$ | Buy A$ Sell US$ |

5   One Australian dollar will buy (sell) at a rate equivalent to 0.6504 US dollars.

6   In direct quotes, the buy quote represents the price at which the bank will buy US dollars, and the sell quote represents the price at which the bank will sell US dollars.

Assume a client wishes to sell Australian dollars and buy US$1 million. The bank is willing to act as a counterparty and will therefore buy Australian dollars and sell US$1 million. The amount of Australian dollars bought by the bank is equal to:

$$\frac{1\,000\,000}{0.7870} = \text{A\$1\,270\,648.03.}$$

Assume a client wishes to buy Australian dollars and sell US$1 million. The bank is willing to act as counterparty and will therefore sell Australian dollars and buy US$1 million. The amount of Australian dollars sold by the bank is equal to:

$$\frac{1\,000\,000}{0.7875} = \text{A\$1\,269\,841.27.}$$

The difference between the two transactions represents the bank's gross profit:[7]

$$1\,270\,648.03 \ - \ 1\,269\,841.27 \ = \ \text{A\$806.76.}$$

The term *immediate delivery* is a relative one, for a spot currency is usually purchased for delivery in two days time.[8] For example, suppose that you need US$500 000 to pay for imports from the United States. On Monday you telephone your bank in Melbourne and agree to purchase US$500 000 at A$/US$0.7870. The bank does not hand you a wad of American banknotes over the counter. Instead, it instructs its American correspondent bank to transfer US$500 000 on Wednesday to the account of the American supplier. The bank debits your account by 500 000/0.7870 = A$635 324 either on the Monday or, if you are a low risk, regular customer, on the Wednesday.

Not all transactions will be to exporters or importers wanting to transact in US dollars. From time to time you may need to buy or sell other currencies. When this occurs you will be confronted with the dilemma that some currencies may be quoted as direct quotes to the US dollar, while others may be quoted as indirect quotes. For example, let us assume you are about to leave for that long-awaited holiday to France. You are keen to buy 5000 French francs (Ffranc) to spend in the Paris cafés and to buy gifts at the Eiffel Tower and Notre Dame. To calculate the cost of the Ffranc5000 in Australian dollars (A$/Ffranc) you will need the following exchange rates:[9]

$$\frac{\text{A\$}}{\text{US\$}}$$

and

$$\frac{\text{S\$}}{\text{Ffranc}}$$

The problem confronting us is that the A$/Ffranc is a *cross exchange rate*. Cross rates involve the rate of exchange derived from two other exchange rates, provided both currencies are quoted in terms of a common rate. So, in our example above, both the Australian dollar and French francs are quoted in relation to US dollars. It is therefore possible to calculate an A$/Ffranc cross rate.

To calculate the cross rate we must first identify whether the component rates are direct or indirect rates. Then, as shown in Table 34.2, which summarises the appropriate procedures for

---

[7]  This is only an illustrative example from the retail foreign exchange market. Most transactions involve buying or selling US dollars in million dollar lots. Furthermore, as the liquidity of the market increases, the spread will narrow significantly. It is not uncommon for the spread to be as small as five pips in the interbank market.

[8]  It is also possible to negotiate settlement for today, where settlement is today, and for tomorrow, where settlement will be tomorrow. Each of these methods will result in a less attractive exchange rate from the dealer.

[9]  For the purpose of this demonstration, in the following example we will just look at the calculations for a single rate; normally a bid offer rate will be quoted.

calculating cross rates, we must make a decision as to whether we should multiply or divide the rates to identify the cross rate.[10]

Let us assume that the A$/US$ is currently trading at A$1 = US$0.6533 and that the French franc is trading at US$1 = 6.1105 or Ffranc6.1105. We have already established that the A$/US$ is an indirect quotation. The US$/Ffranc exchange rate is a direct exchange rate with the US dollar as the base or commodity currency. Using Table 34.2 it is obvious that we should multiply the two exchange rates to calculate the cross exchange rate. Hence

$$\frac{A\$}{US\$} \times \frac{US\$}{Ffranc} = \frac{A\$}{Ffranc}$$

$$0.6533 \times 6.1105 = 3.9920$$

Hence, A$1 = 3.9920 French francs. So to purchase 5000 French francs at the rate of A$1 = Ffranc3.9920 you need to sell the following amount of A$:

$$\frac{5000}{3.9920} = \$1252.51$$

Let us assume you also want to purchase 500 pounds sterling (£Stg) and the current rate is £Stg/US$1.6731 (an indirect quote). We can see from Table 34.2 that we need to divide the A$/US$ and £Stg/US$ rates to achieve the A$/£Stg rate:

$$\frac{A\$/US\$}{£Stg/US\$} = \frac{A\$}{£Stg}$$

$$\frac{0.6533}{1.6731} = 0.3905$$

Hence, to purchase 500 pounds sterling at the rate of A$1 = £Stg0.3905 you will need to sell the following amount of Australian dollars:

$$\frac{500}{0.3905} = \$1280.41$$

Table 34.2 summarises the appropriate procedures for calculating cross rates.

**table 34.2**

Cross-rate calculations

| Exchange rate 1 | Exchange rate 2 | Divide or multiply the rates |
| --- | --- | --- |
| Direct | Direct | Divide |
| Indirect | Indirect | Divide |
| Direct | Indirect | Multiply |
| Indirect | Direct | Multiply |

# Forward rates

In addition to the spot exchange market, there is also a forward market for foreign exchange. In the forward market you buy and sell currency for future delivery—usually in monthly intervals from one to six months time, or up to 12 months forward. If you know that you are going

---

10  Several other alternatives exist here, such as to set all exchange rates as direct quotes and then multiply the rates, or alternatively, to set all rates except the A$/US$ rate as direct rates and divide the rates. These approaches, while simpler than the method discussed in the text above, add a further step to the calculation process.

to pay out or receive foreign currency at some future date, you can hedge yourself against loss by buying or selling forward. Thus, if you need 100 000 francs in six months, you can enter into a six-month forward contract now. The *forward rate* on this contract is the price you agree to pay in six months time when the 100 000 francs are delivered, regardless of the market spot rate at that time.

Table 34.3 shows the forward exchange rate quotations for the A\$/US\$ exchange rate from the *Financial Review*. The table highlights that forward rates are a function of the current spot exchange rate and a forward margin.[11] If the forward margin is quoted as 'ascending' between bid and offer quotes, the forward price will be higher than the current spot rate and the forward margin is called a forward premium. Hence, if you were buying US dollars in the future you would get more US dollars per Australian dollar than if you were buying them in the spot market. While this may be good for an importer, it does not seem to be very useful for exporters. However, in the same way as the currency may be trading at a forward premium, it can also trade at a forward discount. If the forward margin is quoted as 'declining' between bid and offer quotes, the forward price will be lower than the current spot rate and the forward margin. This is called a forward discount. In Table 34.3 the forward margins are ascending. For example, the one-month offer forward margin is higher than the one-month bid forward margin. This indicates that the forward rates should all be higher than the current spot rates and are therefore trading at a forward premium.

**table 34.3**

Forward exchange rates (A\$), 11 August 1999

|  | **Bid** | **Offer** | **Difference (Pips)** |
|---|---|---|---|
| Forward margins |  |  |  |
| 1 month | 2 | 3 | +1 |
| 2 months | 5 | 7 | +2 |
| 3 months | 10 | 11 | +1 |
| 6 months | 24 | 26 | +2 |
| 12 months | 42 | 44 | +2 |
| Spot rate | 0.6500 | 0.6505 | 5 |
| Forward rates |  |  |  |
| 1 month | 0.6502 | 0.6508 | 6 |
| 2 months | 0.6505 | 0.6512 | 7 |
| 3 months | 0.6510 | 0.6516 | 6 |
| 6 months | 0.6524 | 0.6531 | 7 |
| 12 months | 0.6542 | 0.6549 | 7 |

*Source*: Adapted from the *Financial Review*, 12 August 1999.

---

[11]   This can be expressed as forward margin = forward rate – spot rate. Using this formula, if the forward margin is positive, the forward rate is at a premium to the spot. If the forward margin is negative, the forward rate is at a discount to the spot.

From Table 34.3 it is also obvious that the difference in the bid offer spread of the forward rate is equal to the sum of the bid offer spread of the spot rate plus the bid offer spread of the relevant forward margins.[12]

In assessing as to whether the forward rate is at a premium or a discount to the spot rate it is useful to consider the relationship between the interest rates in the two countries. As we will see shortly, forward rates reflect the difference in interest rates between countries. The higher interest rate currency will be at a forward discount against the lower interest rate currency. In contrast, the lower interest rate currency will be at a forward premium to the higher interest rate currency.

If you look again at Table 34.3, you can see that the bank's six-month forward rate to buy Australian dollars (i.e. sell US dollars) is quoted as A$/US$0.6524. If the bank buys Australian dollars for delivery in six months time, they get less Australian dollars for their US dollars than if they buy them in the spot market now.

A forward purchase or sale is a made-to-measure transaction between you and the bank. It can be for any currency, any amount and any delivery day. You could buy, say, 99 999 Vietnamese dông or Haitian gourdes for a year and 10 days forward, as long as you can find a bank ready to deal. Most forward transactions are for six months or less, but banks are prepared to enter into agreements to buy and sell the major currencies for several years forward.

Forward and spot trades are often undertaken at the same time as part of the same transaction. This is known as swap trade. For example, a company might need to use Japanese yen for one month. In this sell/buy swap the company would buy the yen spot by selling Australian dollars and simultaneously sell the yen and buy Australian dollars forward. Alternatively, the company might buy Australian dollars spot using US dollar receipts, and simultaneously sell Australian dollars in a forward contract. This is known as a buy/sell swap. In April 1998, swap transactions accounted for US$24.5 billion of the average daily foreign exchange market activity in the Australian market. Of this amount, almost 90 per cent is transacted by Australian authorised dealers and overseas banks—only a very small percentage of Australian companies outside the finance sector use swap transactions.[13]

There is also an organised market for currency for future delivery known as the currency futures market.[14] Futures contracts are highly standardised—they exist only for the main currencies, and they are for specified amounts and for a limited choice of delivery dates. The advantage of this standardisation is that there is a liquid market in currency futures. Huge numbers of contracts are bought and sold daily on the futures exchanges.[15]

When you buy a forward or a futures contract, you are committed to taking delivery of the currency. As an alternative, you can take out an option to buy or sell currency in the future at a price that is fixed today. Made-to-measure currency options can be bought from the major banks, and standardised options are traded on the options exchanges.[16]

Alternatively, you can agree with the bank that you will buy foreign currency in the future at the prevailing spot rate, *but subject to a maximum and minimum price*. If the value of the foreign currency rises sharply, you buy at the agreed upper limit; if it falls sharply, you buy at the lower limit.[17]

---

12  For a more detailed discussion of forward rates see S. Anthony, *Foreign Exchange Practice*, The Law Book Company, Sydney, 1989.

13  For a detailed discussion of swap transactions see Allen et al., *Foreign Exchange Management*, Allen & Unwin, Sydney, 1990. Be sure not to confuse swaps with currency and interest rate swaps, which are discussed in Chapter 25.

14  Currency futures involving the A$/$US are currently only traded at the Philadelphia Futures Exchange. In the 1980s a US dollar contract was traded at the Sydney Futures Exchange, but this contract was eventually removed due to a lack of liquidity.

15  See Chapter 25 for further discussion of the difference between forward and futures contracts.

16  Some investment banks have also made one-off issues of currency warrants (i.e. long-term options to buy currency).

17  This contract is equivalent to buying forward currency, buying a put option on the currency with an exercise price equal to the lower limit, and selling a call with an exercise price equal to the upper limit. Here is a chance to test your knowledge of options by checking this out with a position diagram. See Sections 20.1 and 20.2 if you need to review the topic.

## 34.2 Some basic relationships

### A little background about the Australian dollar

From December 1931 until December 1971 the Australian pound, and subsequently the Australian dollar,[18] was fixed against the pound sterling. Until 1971, all Australian foreign exchange dealings were denominated in sterling or were quoted against sterling with the banks acting as agents for the Reserve Bank of Australia, which fixed the exchange rates. In the period between 1971 and 1983 the Australian dollar's value was still fixed and determined by the Reserve Bank of Australia, but following the Smithsonian Agreement in 1971 the currency was quoted relative to the US dollar.

As noted by Manuell,[19] the period from 1971 to 1983 was one of uncertainty. Between 1971 and 1974 the Australian dollar was fixed against the US dollar; between 1974 and 1976 it was pegged to a trade weighted (fixed) exchange rate linked to a basket of currencies; and subsequently between 1976 and 1983 using a flexible (or managed float) peg mechanism it was linked to the trade weighted index, and involved smaller and more frequent changes in the exchange rate. The 1970s and early 1980s were dominated in Australia by high inflation, balance of payments deficits and capital outflows reducing domestic liquidity. These macro-economic variables were difficult to manage using fixed exchange rates determined by the Reserve Bank of Australia. Furthermore, the trade weighted index (TWI) became increasingly volatile during the flexible peg period due to increased central bank intervention and larger and more frequent capital flows between countries.

In December 1983 the Australian government floated the Australian dollar and allowed banks to quote their own exchange rates rather than having them determined by the Reserve Bank on a daily basis. The rates were allowed to reflect the demand and supply for the currency. Figure 34.1 shows a plot of the A$/US$ exchange rate during the floating period from 1984 to 1998. As can be seen from the plot, the exchange rate was very volatile during 1985 and later in 1997. The 1985 period reflected a perceived crisis in Australia's balance of payments due to a 'blow-out' in the current account and a decline in market sentiment. The more recent volatility was during the Asian economic crisis in late 1997. At other times the Australian dollar has been less volatile, but has still changed frequently.

**figure 34.1**

A$/US$ exchange rate, 1984–98.

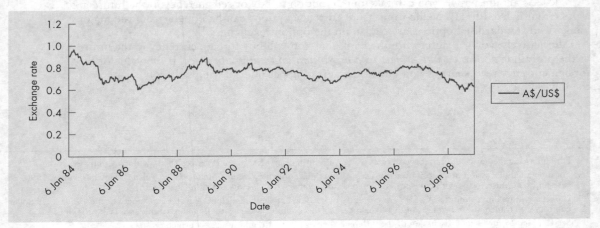

18  Decimal currency and the Australian dollar were introduced on 14 February 1966.

19  For a detailed discussion of the history of the Australian dollar during the fixed period to December 1983 see G. Manuell, *Floating Down Under: Foreign Exchange in Australia*, The Law Book Company, Sydney, 1986.

# Factors directly affecting the exchange rate

Analysis of variations in the exchange rate have revealed that the primary factors affecting the exchange rate include interest rates, prices of goods and services (expected inflation), unexpected components of economic and political news reports, and central bank intervention. We will have more to say about these issues shortly. But the Australian dollar is also linked to world commodity markets, due to our high level of resources. Hence, the long-term stability of our currency is not only linked to interest rates and expected inflation, but also to our competitiveness in global markets for our goods and services, which is usually reflected in the performance of our current account.

# Why is the current account so important in Australia?

The balance of payments is made up of two primary components—the current account, which reflects the inflows and outflows of goods and services from the Australian economy, and the capital account, which reflects the monetary flows. The demand for foreign exchange reflects the demand and supply of goods and services. If a country imports more than it exports, then there will not be a high demand for the overseas currencies relative to the domestic currency to pay for the imports. This will cause overseas currencies from where the imports originate to appreciate, making their goods more expensive relative to those in domestic economies. The appreciation or strengthening in other currencies will eventually cause a decline in demand for their goods relative to domestic goods and the current account balance will return to equilibrium. Well, that is the theory. The reality is somewhat different. Certainly, the current account is responsive to changes in each country's competitiveness, but changes in competitiveness do not occur instantaneously—they may require significant structural changes in the economy.[20] In the interim, and in the presence of global hedge funds treating foreign exchange as yet another avenue to make speculative profits, currency flows directly affect the exchange rate. Since the current account cannot adjust quickly to changes in competitiveness, any such adjustments must occur via the capital account in the form of currency flows between countries, which has an immediate impact on exchange rates.

Despite the richness of our domestic resource supply, most world commodity markets have prices that reflect the demand and supply for the resources. As substitutes or other sources of supply are developed, the demand for some Australian commodities will decrease as overseas countries turn to cheaper alternative suppliers.

# Asset market models of the exchange rate

You cannot develop a consistent international financial policy until you understand the reasons for differences in exchange rates and interest rates between world economies. Therefore, let us consider the following four problems:

- *Problem 1* Why is the Australian dollar rate of interest ($r_A$) different from, say, the US dollar rate of interest ($r_{US}$)?
- *Problem 2* Why is the forward rate of exchange ($f_{A\$/US\$}$) different from the spot rate ($s_{A\$/US\$}$)?
- *Problem 3* What determines next year's expected spot rate of exchange between Australian dollars and US dollars [$E(s_{A\$/US\$})$]?
- *Problem 4* What is the relationship between the inflation rate in Australia ($i_A$) and the US inflation rate ($i_{US}$)?

Suppose that individuals were not worried about risk and that there were no barriers or transaction costs to international trade. In that case, the spot exchange rates, forward

---

20  We hope we are not starting to sound like politicians, but certainly there is some support for the argument that increased competitiveness and access to foreign markets can impact on the current account balance.

exchanges rates, interest rates and inflation rates would stand in the following simple relationship to one another.

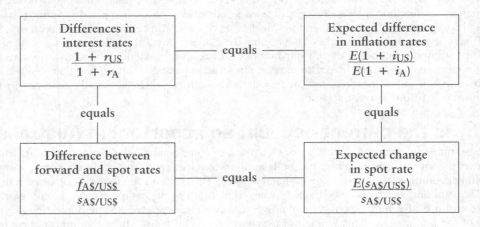

Why should this be so?

# Interest rates and exchange rates

You have $1 million to invest for one year. Is it better to make an Australian dollar loan or a US dollar loan? Let us work out a numerical example. Assume the Australian one-year interest rate is 7 per cent and the US dollar rate is 5.30 per cent.

- *Australian dollar loan*: The rate of interest on a one-year dollar deposit is 7.00 per cent. Therefore, at the end of the year you get $1\ 000\ 000 \times 1.07000 = \$1\ 070\ 000$.
- *US dollar loan*: The current rate of exchange is US$0.7930. For A$1 million, you can buy $1 \times 0.7930 = $ US$0.7930 million. The rate of interest on a one-year US deposit is 5.30 per cent. Therefore, at the end of the year you get $793\ 000 \times 1.0530 = $ US$835 029. Of course, you do not know what the exchange rate is going to be in one year's time. But that does not matter. You can fix today the price at which you will sell your US dollars. The one-year forward rate is US$0.7804. Therefore, by selling forward, you can make sure that you will get $835\ 029/0.7804 = $ A$1 070 000[21] at the end of the year.

Let us consider diagrammatically how we have achieved this.

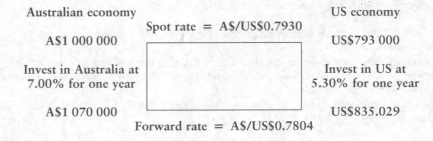

---

When you make the US dollars loan at 5.30 per cent, you lose because you get a lower interest rate in the United States. But you gain later because you sell US dollars forward (buy Australian dollars) at a higher (lower) price than you have to pay for them today.[22]

The interest rate differential is

$$\frac{1 + r_{US}}{1 + r_A}$$

And the differential between the forward and spot exchange rates is

$$\frac{f_{A\$/US\$}}{s_{\$A/\$US}}$$

**Interest-rate parity** theory says that the interest-rate differential must equal the differential between the forward and spot exchange rates.

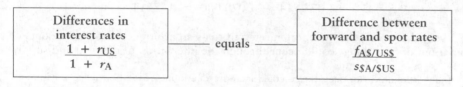

In our example,

$$\frac{1.0530}{1.0700} = \frac{0.7804}{0.7930}$$

It is therefore obvious that if we know the current spot exchange rate and the interest rates in both the foreign and domestic country it is possible to calculate the forward exchange rate. A general formula is

$$f_{A\$/US\$} = \frac{s_{US\$}(1 + r_{US})}{(1 + r_A)}$$

Substituting, we get

$$f_{A\$/US\$} = \frac{0.7930(1 + 0.0530)}{(1 + 0.07)}$$

$$= 0.7804$$

Our formula uses annual interest rates, but not all forward transactions are for periods of one year. So, we need an adjustment for when the time to maturity is less than one year. We also need an adjustment because money market interest rates in the United States are calculated based on a 360-day year, while Australian rates are based on a 365-day year. The adjusted formula thus becomes

$$f_{A\$/US\$} = \frac{s_{A\$/US\$}(1 + r_{US} \times d/360)}{(1 + r_A \times d/365)}$$

where $d$ is the number of days for the forward contract.

The above deal is often referred to as covered interest arbitrage. The two investments offer almost exactly the same rate of return. They have to—they are both risk-free. If the domestic

---

22   This result is consistent with our earlier discussion of forward rates and their relationships to interest rates in the domestic and foreign countries.

interest rate were different from the 'covered' foreign rate, you would have a money machine. If the forward rates, or the interest rates in either Australia or the United States, were not quoted such that the relationship fell into equilibrium, arbitrageurs would generate arbitrage profits by trading until such time as demand and supply for the interest rates and the forward rate caused the currency to return to equilibrium.

For example, assume that the US dollar interest rate is 6 per cent rather than 5.30 per cent. The return for Australian dollar investors would still be 7.00 per cent resulting in A$1 070 000. By buying US dollars, investing the funds for 12 months in the United States at 6 per cent and selling the US dollars forward (US$840 580), a trader can generate an Australian dollar cash flow of A$1 077 114.

How can the arbitrageurs take advantage here? They could borrow the funds in Australia at 7 per cent and invest them in the United States for 12 months. After 12 months this would generate a profit of:

$$1\ 077\ 114\ -\ 1\ 070\ 000\ =\ A\$7114$$

In a very short period of time, often referred to as an arbitrage window, any one, or some combination, of four things could occur through the interaction of demand and supply:

▮ The Australian dollar interest rate could increase due to increased borrowing pressure.
▮ The US dollar interest rate could decrease due to the increased supply of funds for investment.
▮ The spot rate A$/US$ could depreciate due to increased demand for US dollars.
▮ The forward rate A$/US$ could appreciate due to increased demand for Australian dollars in the forward market.

## The forward premium and changes in spot rates

Now let us think how the forward premium is related to changes in spot rates of exchange. If people did not care about risk, the forward rate of exchange would depend solely on what people expected the spot rate to be. For example, if the one-year forward rate on US dollars is US$0.7784/A$, in an efficient market traders expect the spot rate in one-year's time also to be US$0.7784/A$. If they expect it to be higher than this, no one would be willing to sell US dollars forward.

Therefore, the *expectations theory* of exchange rates tells us that the percentage difference between the forward rate and today's spot rate is equal to the expected change in the spot rate:

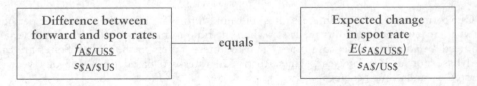

Of course, this assumes that traders do not care about risk. If they do care, the forward rate can be either higher or lower than the expected spot rate. For example, suppose that you have contracted to receive US$100 million in six months time. You can wait until you receive the money before you change it into Australian dollars, but this leaves you open to the risk that the price of US dollars may fall over the next six months. Your alternative is to *sell* the US dollars forward. In this case, you are fixing today the price at which you will sell the US dollars. Since you avoid risk by selling US dollars forward, you may be willing to do so even if the forward price of US dollars is a little *lower* than the expected spot price.

Other companies may be in the opposite position. They may have contracted to pay out US dollars in six months time. They can wait until the end of the six months and then buy US dollars, but this leaves them open to risk that the price of US dollars may fall. It is safer for these companies to fix the price today by *buying* US dollars forward. These companies may therefore be willing to buy forward even if the forward price of US dollars is a little *higher* than the expected spot price.

Thus, some companies find it safer to *sell* US dollars forward (buy Australian dollars), while others find it safer to *buy* US dollars forward (sell Australian dollars). If the first group predominates, the forward price of US dollars is likely to be less than the expected spot price. If the second group predominates, the forward price is likely to be greater than the expected spot price.

# Changes in the exchange rate and inflation rates

Now we come to the third side of our quadrilateral—the relationship between changes in the spot exchange rate and inflation rates. Suppose that you notice that silver can be bought in Sydney for A$6.70 a troy ounce and sold in Zurich for 8.00 Swiss francs. You think you may be onto a good thing. You decide to buy silver for A$6.70 in Sydney and put it on the first aeroplane to Zurich, where you sell it for SFr8.00. Then you exchange your SFr8 at the rate of 1A$ = SFr0.9554 and receive A$8.37. You have made a gross profit of A$1.67 an ounce. Of course, you have to pay transportation, insurance costs and bank fees out of this, but there should still be something left over for you. This great money machine is a form of arbitrage.

However, money machines do not exist for long. As others notice the disparity between the price of silver in Zurich and the price in Sydney, the price of silver will be forced down in Zurich and up in Sydney until the profit opportunity disappears. Arbitrage ensures that the dollar price of silver is about the same in the two countries.

Of course, silver is a standard and easily transportable commodity, but to some degree you might expect that the same forces would be acting to equalise the domestic and foreign prices of other goods. Those goods that can be bought more cheaply abroad will be imported, and that will force down the price of the domestic product. Similarly, those goods that can be bought more cheaply in Australia will be exported, and that will force down the price of the foreign product.

This is often called the *law of one price* or in a more general sense *purchasing-power parity*.[23] Just as the price of goods in a Safeways supermarket must be roughly the same as the price of goods in a Coles supermarket, so the price of goods in the United States when converted into Australian dollars must be roughly the same as the price in Australia.[24]

The law of one price implies that any differences in the rate of inflation will be offset by a change in the exchange rate. For example, if inflation is 4.50 per cent in Australia and 2.84 per cent in the United States, then in order to equalise the price of goods in the two countries, the price of the Australian dollar must fall by (1.0284)/(1.0450) − 1, or about 1.5885 per cent. Therefore, the law of one price suggests that in order to estimate changes in the spot rate of exchange, you need to estimate differences in inflation rates:[25]

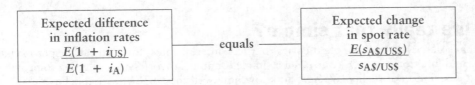

| Expected difference in inflation rates $\dfrac{E(1 + i_{US})}{E(1 + i_A)}$ | equals | Expected change in spot rate $\dfrac{E(s_{A\$/US\$})}{s_{A\$/US\$}}$ |
|---|---|---|

---

23　Economists tend to use the phrase *law of one price* when they are talking about the price of a single good. The notion that the price level of goods in general must be the same in the two countries is called *purchasing-power parity*.

24　Remember this is a theoretical concept—try purchasing the same trolley of goods at several stores and, as you know, they will not cost the same even if the stores are located in the same suburb.

25　We are suggesting here that the *expected* difference in the inflation rate equals the *expected* change in the exchange rate. Notice, however, that the law of one price also implies that the *actual* difference in the inflation rate always equals the *actual* change in the exchange rate.

In our example,[26] the expected difference in inflation rates is equal to the expected change in spot rates:

$$\frac{1.0284}{1.0450} = \frac{0.7804}{0.7930}$$

## Interest rates and inflation rates

Now for the fourth leg! Just as water always flows downhill, so capital always flows where returns are greatest. In equilibrium, the expected *real* return on capital is the same in different countries.

But bonds do not promise a fixed *real* return: they promise a fixed *money* payment. Therefore, we have to think about how the money rate of interest in each country is related to the real rate of interest. One answer to this has been provided by Irving Fisher, who argued that the money rate of interest will reflect the expected inflation.[27] In this case Australia and the United States will both offer the same expected *real* rate of interest, and the difference in money rates will be equal to the expected difference in inflation rates:

| Difference in interest rates $\dfrac{1 + r_{US}}{1 + r_A}$ | equals | Expected difference in inflation rates $\dfrac{E(1 + i_{US})}{E(1 + i_A)}$ |
| --- | --- | --- |

In other words, capital market equilibrium requires that *real* interest rates be the same in any two countries. In the United States, the real interest rate is about 2.4 per cent:

$$r_{US}(\text{real}) = \frac{1 + r_{US}}{E(1 + i_{US})} - 1 = \frac{1.0530}{1.0284} - 1 = 0.024$$

and ditto for Australia:

$$r_A(\text{real}) = \frac{1 + r_A}{E(1 + i_A)} - 1 = \frac{1.0700}{1.0450} - 1 = 0.024$$

Alternatively, this relationship can be demonstrated as follows. The difference in interest rates is equal to the expected difference in inflation rates

$$\frac{1.0530}{1.07} = \frac{1.0284}{1.0450}$$

## Is life really that simple?

We have described four simple theories that link interest rates, forward rates, spot exchange rates and inflation rates. Of course, such simple economic theories are not going to provide an exact description of reality. We need to know how well they predict actual behaviour.

1.  *Interest-rate parity theory.* Interest-rate parity theory says that the Australian rate of interest covered for exchange rate risk should be the same as the US dollar rate. Dealers often set

---

[26] A small rounding error is present, whereby expected difference in inflation rates = 0.984115, whereas expected change in spot rates = 0.984071, a difference of 0.000044.

[27] We discussed the Fisher effect in Chapter 23.

the forward price of currencies by looking at the difference between the interest rates on euro products. The eurocurrency market is an international market that is mostly free of government regulation or tax. Since money can be moved easily between different eurocurrency deposits, interest-rate parity almost always holds.[28]

The relationship does not hold so exactly for the domestic money markets. In these cases taxes and government regulations sometimes prevent the citizens of one country from switching out of domestic bank deposits and covering their exchange risk in the forward market.

2. *The expectations theory of forward rates.* The expectations theory of forward rates does not imply that managers are perfect forecasters. Sometimes the *actual* future spot rate will jump above previous forward rates. Sometimes it will fall below. But if the theory is correct, we should find that, *on average*, the forward rate is equal to the future spot rate. The theory passes this simple test with flying colours.[29] That is important news for the financial manager; it means that a company that always covers its foreign exchange commitments does not have to pay any extra for this insurance.

Although *on average* the forward rate is equal to the future spot rate, it does seem to provide an exaggerated estimate of the likely change in the spot rate. Therefore, when the forward rate appears to predict a sharp rise in the spot rate, the actual rise generally turns out to be less. And when the forward rate appears to predict a sharp decline in the spot rate, the actual decline is also likely to be less.

This result is *not* consistent with the expectations hypothesis. Instead, it looks as if sometimes companies are prepared to give up a little return in order to buy forward currency and at other times they are prepared to give up return in order to sell forward currency.[30]

We should also warn you that the forward rate does not usually tell you very much about the future spot rate. This does not mean that the forward rate is a poor measure of managers' expectations; it just means that exchange rates are very tough to predict. Many banks and consultants produce forecasts of future exchange rates. But Richard Levich found that more often than not the forward rate provided a more accurate forecast than the currency advisory services.[31]

3. *The law of one price.* What about the third side of our quadrilateral—the law of one price? No one who has compared prices in foreign stores with prices at home really believes that the law of one price holds exactly. Look at the first column of Table 34.4, which shows the price of a Big Mac in different countries in April 1999.

Notice, for example, that in April 1999 5.90 Swiss francs buys as many Big Macs as 2.65 Australian dollars. You could say that the Big Mac or *real* exchange rate was SFr5.90 = A$2.65 or, equivalently, SFr2.2264 per Australian dollar, or A$/SFr2.2264. This is the exchange rate you would expect to see if the law of one price held for Big Macs. But the opening exchange rate in April 1999 was A$/SFr0.9394, which meant the SFr5.90 burgers were equal to A$6.31. At this rate, Big Macs were almost 2.4 times as expensive in Lucerne as in Perth.

This suggests a possible way a few bucks could have been made. You could have bought a few takeaway burgers in (say) Perth for $2.65 and arranged for them to be resold in Lucerne where the price was SFr 5.90 (equivalent to A$6.31). This would result

---

28  See, for example, T. Agmon and S. Bronfield, 'The International Mobility of Short-Term Covered Arbitrage Capital', *Journal of Business Finance and Accounting*, 2: 269–78 (Summer 1975); and J. A. Frenkel and R. M. Levich, 'Transactions Costs and Interest Arbitrage: Tranquil Versus Turbulent Periods', *Journal of Political Economy*, 85: 1209–25 (November–December 1977).

29  For some evidence on the average difference between the forward rate and subsequent spot rate see B. Cornell, 'Spot Rates, Forward Rates, and Market Efficiency', *Journal of Financial Economics*, 5: 55–65 (1977).

30  For evidence that forward exchange rates contain risk premia that are sometimes positive and sometimes negative see, for example, E. F. Fama, 'Forward and Spot Exchange Rates', *Journal of Monetary Economics*, 14: 319–38 (1984).

31  See R. M. Levich, 'How to Compare Chance with Forecasting Expertise', *Euromoney*, 12: 61–78 (August 1981).

in a gain of $3.66 for each burger. So why didn't you take advantage of this? The answer, of course, is that the gain would not cover the costs.[32] These include, among others, costs associated with transportation, marketing, convenience, preserving product quality, taxation and regulatory compliance regarding the transfer of food.

On the other hand, there is clearly some relationship between inflation and changes in exchange rates. For example, between 1989 and 1994 prices in Brazil rose about a million times. Or, to put it another way, you could say that the purchasing power of money in Brazil declined by about 99.99 per cent relative to other countries. If exchange rates had not adjusted, Brazilian exporters would have found it impossible to sell their goods. But, of course, exchange rates did adjust. In fact, the value of the Brazilian currency also declined by more than 99.99 per cent relative to the US dollar and by slightly less to the Australian dollar.

Brazil is an extreme case, but in Figure 34.2 we have plotted the relative change in purchasing power for a sample of countries against the change in the exchange rate. Brazil is tucked in the bottom left-hand corner; Australia is closer to the top.

**figure 34.2** _____
A decline in a currency's purchasing power and a decline in the exchange rate usually go hand in hand. In this figure, each point represents the experience of a different country between 1989 and 1994. The vertical axis shows the change in value of a foreign currency relative to the average. The horizontal axis shows the change in the currency's purchasing power relative to the average.

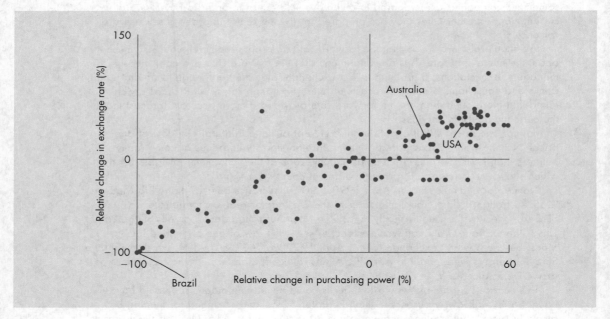

Strictly speaking, the law of one price implies that the differential inflation rate is always identical to the change in the exchange rate. But we do not need to go as far as that. We should be content if the *expected* difference in the inflation rate equals the *expected* change in the spot rate. That is all we wrote on the third side of our quadrilateral. In order to test this, Richard Roll looked at the exchange rates of

---

[32] And would the Swiss really want to buy 'stale' burgers? We think both McDonald's and the Swiss have a strong opinion about this.

**table 34.4**

Big Mac exchange rates, April 1999

| | Price in local currency | Exchange rate (currency/US$) | Local price converted to US$ | Local price converted to A$ |
|---|---|---|---|---|
| Australia | A$2.65 | 1.59 | 1.66 | 2.65 |
| Canada | C$2.99 | 1.51 | 1.98 | 3.15 |
| China | Yuan 9.90 | 8.28 | 1.20 | 1.91 |
| Denmark | DKr24.75 | 6.91 | 3.58 | 5.69 |
| France | FFr8.50 | 6.10 | 2.87 | 4.56 |
| Germany | DM4.95 | 1.82 | 2.72 | 4.32 |
| Hong Kong | HK$10.20 | 7.75 | 1.32 | 2.10 |
| Italy | L4500 | 1799 | 2.50 | 3.98 |
| Japan | ¥294 | 120 | 2.44 | 3.88 |
| Netherlands | F15.45 | 2.05 | 2.66 | 4.23 |
| New Zealand | NZ$3.40 | 1.87 | 1.82 | 2.90 |
| Poland | Zloty 5.50 | 3.98 | 1.38 | 2.19 |
| Spain | Pts 375 | 155 | 2.43 | 3.86 |
| Sweden | SKr24.00 | 8.32 | 2.88 | 4.58 |
| Switzerland | SFr5.90 | 1.48 | 3.97 | 6.31 |
| United Kingdom | £1.90 | 0.62 | 3.07 | 4.88 |
| United States | US$2.43 | — | 2.43 | 3.86 |

Source: The Economist, April 1999. © The Economist.

23 countries between 1957 and 1976.[33] He found that, on average, today's exchange rate provided the best estimate of the inflation-adjusted exchange rate. In other words, your estimate of the inflation differential is also your best estimate of the change in the exchange rate.

4. *Capital market equilibrium.* Finally, we come to the relationship between interest rates in different countries. Do we have a single world capital market with the same *real* rate of interest in all countries? Can we even extend the notion and think of a single world market for risk capital, so that the real opportunity cost of capital for risky investments is the same in all countries? It is an attractive idea. Unfortunately, the evidence is scant.

Since governments cannot directly control interest rates in the international eurocurrency markets, we might expect that in these markets, differences between the expected real rates of interest would be small. Governments have more control over their domestic rates of interest, at least in the short run. Therefore, it is possible for a country to have a real rate of interest in the domestic market that is below the real rate in other countries. But it is not easy to maintain this position indefinitely. Individuals and companies are capable of great ingenuity in transferring their cash from countries with low real rates of interest to those with high real rates of interest.

---

33 R. Roll, 'Violations of the "Law of One Price" and their Implications for Differentially Denominated Assets', in M. Sarnat and G. Szego (eds.), *International Finance and Trade*, Ballinger Press, Cambridge, Mass., 1979.

We cannot show the relationship between interest rates and *expected* inflation, but in Figure 34.3 we have plotted the average interest rate in each of 22 countries against the inflation that subsequently occurred. You can see that, in general, the countries with the highest interest rates also had the highest inflation rates. There were much smaller differences between the real rates of interest than between the nominal (or money) rates.

**figure 34.3** _____
Countries with the highest interest rates generally have the highest inflation rates. In this diagram each point represents the experience of a different country.

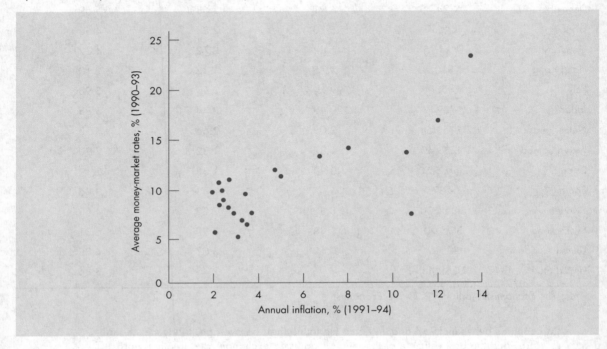

## 34.3 Insuring against currency risks

Although as we have seen in Figure 34.1 exchange rates do vary over time, such changes are usually gradual and small. From time to time, such as in 1985 and again in 1997 in Australia, the changes can be both sudden and large. Hence, any firm engaging in business where its competitors or its own operations are affected by foreign exchange rate changes potentially has a foreign exposure. This exposure is usually discussed in terms of either transaction, economic or translation exposures.

**Transaction exposure** relates to the degree that future cash transactions (when the company buys or sells goods or services) are affected by exchange rate fluctuations. The degree to which the present value of the company's future cash flows can be influenced is known as **economic exposure**. Domestic currency cash inflows include local sales (relative to foreign competitors in the same market), exports denominated in the domestic or foreign currencies and interest received from foreign investments. Cash outflows affected by changes in exchange rates include payments for imports in foreign currencies and interest paid on foreign funds borrowed. Finally, **translation exposure** relates to the exposure caused at the time of consolidating the financial statements of the company due to the size, number and location of foreign subsidiaries, the currencies in which each subsidiary operates and the accounting methods used to perform the consolidation.[34]

# To hedge, or not to hedge?

To illustrate how firms cope with foreign exchange risk, we will look at an example of a typical company in Australia, Outback PreFab, and walk through its foreign exchange problems.

## example: Outback Pre-Fab

Outback PreFab has a small but profitable export business in selling prefabricated housing in Southeast Asia. Contracts involve substantial delays in payment, but since the company has had a policy of always invoicing in Australia dollars, it is fully protected against changes in exchange rates. More recently, the export department has become unhappy with this practice and believes that it is causing the company to lose valuable orders to Japanese and German firms that are willing to quote in the customer's own currency or in US dollars.

The finance manager sympathises with these arguments, but she is worried about how the firm should price long-term export contracts when payment is to be made in foreign currency. If the value of the currency declines before payment is made, the company may make a large loss. The finance manager wants to take currency risk into account when these contracts are priced, but management also want to give the sales force as much freedom of action as possible.

Notice that the company can insure itself against this currency risk by selling the foreign currency forward.[35] This means that it is possible to separate the problem of negotiating individual contracts from that of managing the company's foreign exchange exposure. The sales force can allow for currency risk by pricing on the basis of the forward exchange rate, and the financial manager can decide whether the company *ought* to insure.

What is the cost of this insurance? You will sometimes hear managers say that it is equal to the difference between the forward rate and *today's* spot rate. That is wrong. If Outback does not insure, it will receive the spot rate at the time that the customer pays for the steel. Therefore, the cost of insurance is the difference between the forward rate and the expected spot rate when payment is received.

Insure or speculate? We generally vote for insurance. First, it makes life simpler for the firm and allows it to concentrate on its main business.[36] Second, it does not cost much. (In fact, the cost is zero if the forward rate equals the expected spot rate, as the expectations theory of forward rates implies.) Third, the foreign exchange market seems reasonably efficient, at least for the major currencies. Speculation should be a zero NPV game unless financial managers have information superior to the pros who make the market.

---

34  For a very detailed discussion of transaction, economic and translation exposures see J. Madura, *International Financial Management*, 3rd ed., West Publishing Company, St Paul, Minn., 1992.

35  Of course, if you do not know the exact payment date, you cannot be sure of the appropriate delivery date for the forward contract. Banks are prepared to deal in forward contracts that allow the company some choice of when to deliver, but these are not common.

36  It also relieves shareholders of worrying about the foreign exchange exposure they may have acquired by purchasing the firm's shares.

Is there any other way that Outback can protect itself against exchange loss? Of course. It can borrow foreign currency against its receivables, sell the foreign currency spot, and invest the proceeds in Australia. Interest-rate parity theory tells us that in free markets the difference between selling forward and selling spot should be exactly equal to the difference between the interest that you have to pay overseas and the interest that you can earn at home. However, in countries where capital markets are highly regulated, it may be cheaper to arrange foreign borrowing rather than forward cover.[37]

It is not always so simple to hedge exports against currency fluctuations. Suppose, for example, Outback has tendered for a large export order. It will not know for several weeks whether it has been successful in getting the order. If it sells the foreign currency forward and does not get the order, it stands to lose from a rise in the value of the foreign currency. If it does not sell the currency and *does* get the order, it stands to lose from a fall in the value of the foreign currency. When faced with this dilemma, many financial managers limit their downside risk by buying an option to sell the foreign currency at a specified price. That way they know the most they can lose is the cost of the option.[38]

Our discussion of Outback's export business illustrates three practical implications of our simple theories about forward rates. First, Outback can use forward rates to tell it how to allow for exchange risk in contract pricing. Second, the expectations theory suggests that insurance against exchange risk is usually worth having. Third, interest-rate parity theory is a reminder that the company can insure either by selling forward or by borrowing foreign currency and selling spot.

Perhaps we should add a fourth implication. The cost of forward cover is not the difference between the forward rate and *today's* spot rate; it is the difference between the forward rate and the expected spot rate when the forward contract matures. There is a corollary to this. You do not make money simply by buying currencies that go up in value and selling those that go down. If investors anticipate the change in the exchange rate, then it will be reflected in the interest-rate differential; therefore, what you gain on the currency you will lose in terms of interest income. You make money from currency speculation only if you can predict whether the exchange rate will change by more or less than the interest-rate differential. In other words, you must be able to predict whether the exchange rate will change by more or less than the forward premium or discount.

# 34.4 International investment decisions

Outback PreFab's export business has risen to the point at which it is worth establishing a subsidiary in Vietnam to hold inventories of steel. Outback's decision to invest overseas should be based on the same criteria as the decision to invest in Australia—that is, the company must identify the incremental cash flows, discount them at a rate that reflects the opportunity cost of capital, and accept all projects with a positive NPV.

---

[37]    Sometimes governments attempt to prevent currency speculation by limiting the amount that companies can sell forward.

[38]    It is even possible to buy options on options. In this case, Outback could pay a small sum for an option now that would allow it to buy another option when it hears the results of its tender.

Here are two ways that Outback could calculate the net present value of its Vietnamese venture:

■  *Method 1*  Outback could follow the practice of many multinational companies and do all its capital budgeting calculations in the home currency. In this case it must first estimate the Vietnamese dông cash flows from its Vietnamese operation and convert these into Australian dollars at the projected exchange rate. These dollar cash flows can then be discounted at the dollar cost of capital to give the investment's net present value in dollars.
■  *Method 2*  In order to avoid making forecasts of the exchange rate, Outback could simply calculate the project's net present value entirely in terms of Vietnamese dông. Outback could then covert this figure into Australian dollars at the current exchange rate.

Each method has three steps, but the orders of Steps 2 and 3 are different.

|        | Method 1                                                  | Method 2                                                    |
|--------|-----------------------------------------------------------|-------------------------------------------------------------|
| Step 1 | Estimate future cash flow in Vietnamese dông              | Estimate future cash flow in Vietnamese dông                |
| Step 2 | Convert to Australian dollars (at forecasted exchange rates) | Calculate present value (use Vietnamese dông discount rate) |
| Step 3 | Calculate present value (use Australian dollar discount rate) | Convert to dollars (use spot rate)                          |

Suppose Outback uses Method 1. Where do the exchange rate forecasts come from? It would be foolish for Outback to accept a poor project just because management is particularly optimistic about the dông—if Outback wishes to speculate in this way, it can simply buy dông forward. Equally, it would be foolish for Outback to reject a good project just because it is pessimistic about the prospects for the dông. The company would do much better to go ahead with the project and sell dông forward. In that way, it would get the best of both worlds.

Thus, as long as a company can alter its exchange exposure, its international capital expenditure decisions should *not* depend on whether the manager feels that a currency is wrongly valued. Instead of using its own exchange rate forecasts, Outback should base its capital investment decision on the foreign exchange market's consensus forecasts. To measure this consensus forecast, Outback can make use of the simple relationships described earlier in the chapter. If investors are on their financial toes, the expected movement in the exchange rate is equal to the difference between the interest rates in the two countries.

If Outback uses either of our two methods, its investment decision is also going to be heavily influenced by its assumption about the Vietnamese inflation rate. Although Outback's financial manager may well have her own views about Vietnamese inflation, it would again be foolish to let these views influence the investment decision. After all, there are more efficient ways to speculate on the inflation rate than by building (or not building) a steel distribution depot.[39]

Does it matter which of our two methods Outback PreFab uses to appraise its investment? It does if Outback employs its own forecasts of the exchange rate and inflation rate. However, as long as Outback assumes our simple parity relationships between interest rates, exchange rates and inflation, the two methods will give the same answer.

---

[39]  There is a general point here that is not confined to international investment. Whenever you face an investment that appears to have a positive NPV, decide what it is that you are betting on and then think whether there is a more direct way to place the bet. For example, if a copper mine looks profitable only because you are unusually optimistic about the price of copper, then maybe you would be better to buy copper futures rather than open a copper mine.

## example

We will illustrate with a simple example. Suppose Outback's Vietnamese facility is expected to generate the following cash flows in Vietnamese dông:

|  | Year | | | | |
|---|---|---|---|---|---|
|  | 1 | 2 | 3 | 4 | 5 |
| Cash flow, millions of dông | 400 | 450 | 510 | 575 | 650 |

How much is this cash flow worth today if Outback PreFab wants a 16 per cent Australian *dollar* return from its investment in Vietnam?

Outback's financial manager looks in the newspaper and finds that the nominal risk-free interest rate is 6.09 per cent in Australia ($r_A = 0.0609$) and is advised that the nominal risk-free rate in Vietnam is 9.18 per cent ($r_V = 0.0918$). She sees right away that if real risk-free rates of interest are expected to be the same in the two countries, at 3.00 per cent, then the consensus forecast of the expected Vietnamese inflation rate ($i_V$) must be approximately 3 percentage points higher than the inflation rate in Australia ($i_A$). For example, if the expected rate of inflation in Australia is 3 per cent, then the real rate of interest and the expected Vietnamese inflation rate are calculated as follows:

$$1 + \textbf{Nominal interest rate} = 1 + \textbf{Real interest rate} \times$$
$$1 + \textbf{Expected inflation rate}$$

| In dollars | $1.0609 = 1.03 \times 1.03$ |
|---|---|
| In dông | $1.0918 = 1.03 \times 1.06$ |

The financial manager therefore checks that the dông cash flow forecasts are consistent with this inflation rate.

Suppose the current spot rate is 11 020 dông to the Australian dollar. Since the nominal interest rate in Vietnam is 309 basis points, or approximately 2.91 per cent, higher than in Australia, the implied forward rate on the dông must rise by 2.91 per cent a year relative to the spot rate:

$$\textbf{Forward exchange rate for year } t = \textbf{spot rate} \times \frac{(1 + r_V)^t}{(1 + r_A)t}$$

For example,

$$\textbf{Forward exchange rate for year 1} = 11\ 020 \times \frac{1.0918}{1.0609}$$

$$= 11\ 020 \times 1.0291$$
$$= 11\ 341 \text{ dông per A\$}$$

By assuming that interest rates will remain constant into the future, the financial manager can use these forward exchange rates to produce a forecast of the cash flows in *dollars*:

|                    |        |        | Year   |        |        |
|--------------------|--------|--------|--------|--------|--------|
|                    | 1      | 2      | 3      | 4      | 5      |
| Cash flow, dông    | 400    | 450    | 510    | 575    | 650    |
| Forward rate       | 11 341 | 11 671 | 12 011 | 12 361 | 12 721 |
| Cash flow, dollars | 35 270 | 38 557 | 42 461 | 46 517 | 51 097 |

Now she uses Method 1 and discounts these *dollar* cash flows at the *dollar* cost of capital (we will assume this equals 9.75 per cent):

$$PV = \frac{35\,270}{(1 + 0.0975)^1} + \frac{38\,557}{(1 + 0.0975)^2} + \frac{42\,461}{(1 + 0.0975)^3}$$
$$+ \frac{46\,517}{(1 + 0.0975)^4} + \frac{51\,097}{(1 + 0.0975)^5}$$

$$PV = 32\,137 + 32\,011 + 32\,120 + 32\,062 + 32\,090$$
$$PV = A\$160\,420$$

Notice that she discounted at 9.75 per cent, not the domestic interest rate of 6.09 per cent. The cash flow is risky, so a risk-adjusted rate (assumed to be 9.75 per cent) is appropriate.

Just as a check, the financial manager tries Method 2. Since the dông interest rate is greater than the Australian dollar rate, the risk-adjusted discount rate must also be correspondingly greater:[40]

**1 + Risk-adjusted discount rate = 1 + Nominal risk-free interest rate**
**× 1 + Risk premium**

| | | |
|---|---|---|
| In dollars | 1.0975 = 1.0609 × 1.0345 |
| In dông | 1.1295 = 1.0918 × 1.0345 |

To use Method 2, the manager discounts the dông cash flow by the dông discount rate:

$$PV = \frac{400m}{(1 + 0.1295)^1} + \frac{450m}{(1 + 0.1295)^2} + \frac{510m}{(1 + 0.1295)^3} + \frac{575m}{(1 + 0.1295)^4}$$
$$+ \frac{650m}{(1 + 0.1295)^5}$$

$$PV = 354\,139\,000 + 352\,728\,087 + 353\,925\,187 + 353\,283\,133$$
$$+ 353\,575\,513$$
$$PV = 1\,767\,650\,920 \text{ dông}$$

---

[40] Here is a point that can cause confusion: We *multiply* (1 + nominal interest rate) by (1 + risk premium) in these calculations. In the CAPM we *added* the risk premium to the risk-free rate. Why the difference? Think of it this way: If the inflation rate in Australia is 3 per cent, then the *real* cost of capital on a risky investment is 1.0975/1.03 − 1 = 0.065534, or 6.55 per cent. If the real cost of capital is also 0.0655 in Vietnam and the Vietnamese inflation rate is 6 per cent, then the nominal cost of capital in Vietnam must be 1.06 × 1.065534 = 0.129466, or 12.95 per cent.

Now convert to Australian dollars at the spot rate, A$/d11 020:

$$PV = \frac{1\ 767\ 650\ 920}{11\ 020}$$

$$= 160\ 403.89 \text{ or A\$160 404}$$

If the discount rate of 12.9466 per cent had been applied, the PV of the dông would have been 1 767 828 400 dông, which would have equalled A$160 420. Therefore, after we account for all the rounding errors in the calculations it is quite obvious that the PVs from both methods are equivalent.

## 34.5 The cost of capital for foreign investment

Now we need to think more carefully about the risk of overseas investment and the reward that investors require for taking this risk. Unfortunately, these are issues on which few economists can agree.[41]

Remember that the risk of an investment cannot be considered in isolation; it depends on the securities that the investor holds in his or her portfolio. For example, at one extreme, we can imagine a single world capital market in which investors from each country hold well-diversified international portfolios. In that case, Outback PreFab could measure the risk of its Vietnamese venture by the project's beta relative to the *world* market portfolio. Since Outback would face exactly the same risk on its Vietnamese project as a local Vietnamese steel company, it would need to earn exactly the same return.

At the other extreme, we can imagine a world in which capital markets are completely segmented, so that Australian shareholders hold only Australian shares and Vietnamese investors hold only Vietnamese shares. In these circumstances, Outback and the Vietnamese company do not face the same risk. Outback could measure the project's risk by its beta relative to the Australian market, whereas the Vietnamese company would want to measure it by its beta relative to the Vietnamese market. An investment in the Vietnamese steel industry would appear to be a relatively low-risk project to Outback's shareholders who hold only Australian shares, whereas it might seem a relatively high-risk project to a Vietnamese company whose shareholders are already highly exposed to the fortunes of the Vietnamese market. In this case, Outback would be satisfied with a lower return on the project than the Vietnamese company would demand.

Here, in summary, are these two scenarios:

| A single world capital market | Completely segmented capital markets |
| --- | --- |
| Individuals invest internationally | Individuals invest domestically |
| Risk measured relative to world market index | Risk measured relative to domestic index |
| No further gains from international diversification | Large gains from international diversification |
| Outback's Vietnamese subsidiary has same cost of capital as local Vietnamese company | Outback's Vietnamese subsidiary has lower cost of capital than local Vietnamese company |

---

41  Why not? One fundamental reason is that economists have never been able to agree on what makes one country different from another. Is it just that they have different currencies? Or is it that their citizens have different tastes? Or is it that they are subject to different regulations and taxes? The answer affects the relationship between security prices in different countries. See, for example, F. L. A. Grauer, R. H. Litzenberger and R. E. Stehle, 'Sharing Rules and Equilibrium in an International Capital Market Under Uncertainty', *Journal of Financial Economics*, 3: 233–56 (June 1976); B. H. Solnik, 'An Equilibrium Model of the International Capital Market', *Journal of Economic Theory*, 8: 500–24 (1974); and F. Black, 'International Capital Market Equilibrium with Investment Barriers', *Journal of Financial Economics*, 1: 337–52 (December 1974).

The truth seems to lie closer to the scenario in the right-hand column. Australians are free to hold foreign shares but they generally invest only a small portion of their money overseas. This suggests that there are still unexploited opportunities for overseas investment to reduce risk through diversification. Therefore, investors may be willing to accept a somewhat *lower* return from international investment than they would from domestic investment.

No one knows quite why investors are so reluctant to buy foreign shares—maybe it is simply that there are extra costs in figuring out which shares to buy. Or perhaps investors are worried that a foreign government will expropriate their shares, restrict dividend payments or catch them by a change in tax law. However, the world is changing. Large Australian financial institutions have substantially increased their overseas investments, and literally dozens of mutual funds have been set up for individuals who want to invest abroad. For example, you can now buy funds that specialise in investment in smaller capital markets such as Chile, India, Thailand or Hungary.

If Australians incur extra costs when they invest in foreign shares, they must be prepared to earn a lower return on these shares than local investors. This suggests a standard for Australian corporations that are investing abroad. They need at least to match the return that Australian investors can earn on their own account. But if these investors are willing to pay a shade more for investing in overseas shares, they should be happy to see Australian corporations invest abroad even if they expect to earn a shade less than local companies.[42]

## Until recently why did Japan enjoy a lower cost of capital?

If there are costs in investing across national borders, then the cost of capital may not be identical in all countries. For example, you often hear people say that Japanese companies enjoy a lower cost of capital than their Australian and American rivals. This difference, it is argued, shows up in the lower earnings-price ratio of Japanese shares.[43]

This argument is two parts possible confusion and one part probable truth. What has the price-earnings ratio got to do with the cost of capital? Think back to Chapter 4 where we showed that this ratio, $EPS_1/P_0$, depends on the cost of equity capital, $r$, and the present value of growth opportunities, PVGO:

$$\frac{EPS_1}{P_0} = r\left(1 - \frac{PVGO}{P_0}\right)$$

Thus, a lower price-earnings ratio for Japanese shares could mean two things:[44]

1. PVGO is higher; that is, Japanese firms until 1997 had more growth opportunities.
2. $r$ is lower; that is, investors are satisfied with a lower expected return from Japanese companies.

Explanation 1 reminds us that a simple comparison of price-earnings ratios will not tell us whether Japan has the lower cost of capital. But how plausible is Explanation 2, that $r$ really is different in the two countries? Notice first that if the cost of capital in Japan is measured in yen and the cost in Australia is measured in Australian dollars, then the two figures are not

42   Cooper and Kaplanis have estimated the costs of foreign investments by asking how large the cost would need to be for the American holdings in foreign shares to make sense. A subsequent paper analyses implications for the cost of capital. See I. Cooper and E. Kaplanis, 'Costs to Crossborder Investment and International Equity Market Equilibrium', in J. Edwards et al. (eds.), *Recent Advances in Corporate Finance*, Cambridge University Press, Cambridge, 1986; and I. Cooper and E. Kaplanis, 'Home Bias in Equity Portfolios and The Cost of Capital for Multinational Firms', *Journal of Applied Corporate Finance*, 8: 95–102 (Fall 1995).

43   The argument that differences in earnings-price ratios indicate a lower cost of capital in Japan is put forward in R. N. McCauley and S. A. Zimmer, 'Explaining International Differences in the Cost of Capital', *Federal Reserve Bank of New York Quarterly Review*, 14: 7–28 (Summer 1989). (*Note*: McCauley and Zimmer adjust the ratios for differences in accounting practices.)

44   For a discussion of these possible explanations see K. R. French and J. M. Poterba, *Are Japanese Stock Prices Too High?*, Working Paper No. 547, Department of Economics, Massachusetts Institute of Technology, Cambridge, Mass., February 1990.

comparable.[45] For example, you would not say that a 25-centimetre high rabbit was taller than a 2-metre elephant. You are measuring their height in different units. In the same way, it makes no sense to compare an expected return in yen with a return in Australian dollars. The units are different.

But suppose that in each case you measure $r$ in *real* terms. Then you are comparing like with like,[46] and it does make sense to ask whether the *real* cost of capital may be lower in Japan.

Think about the cost of overseas investment. Japan has had substantial excess savings that could not be absorbed by Japanese industry and therefore had to be invested overseas. Japanese investors are not *compelled* to invest overseas. They need to be tempted to do so. If there are costs to buying foreign shares, then the relative price of Japanese shares must rise and the expected return must fall until Japanese investors are happy to hold foreign investments.

There is a general message here. If investors have large surpluses that must be invested overseas, or if they incur unusually large costs to get their money out, then the domestic cost of capital is likely to be forced down and it will no longer be the case that real returns will be the same in different countries.

## Avoiding fudge factors in international investment decisions

We certainly do not pretend that we can put a precise figure on the cost of capital for foreign investment. But you can see that we disagree with the frequent practice of automatically marking *up* the domestic cost of capital when foreign investment is considered. We suspect that managers mark up the required return for foreign investment to cover the risk of expropriation, foreign exchange restrictions or unfavourable tax changes. A fudge factor is added to the discount factor to cover these costs.

We think managers should leave the discount rate alone and reduce expected cash flows instead. For example, suppose that Outback PreFab is expected to earn 450 million dông in the first year *if no penalties are placed on the operations of foreign firms*. Suppose also that there is a 10 per cent chance that the Outback operation may be expropriated without compensation. The *expected* cash flow is not 450 million dông but $0.9 \times 450 = 405$ million dông.

The end result may be the same when you add a fudge factor to the discount rate. Nevertheless, adjusting cash flows brings management's assumptions about 'political risks' out in the open for scrutiny and sensitivity analysis.

## 34.6 Financing foreign operations

Outback PreFab can pay for its Vietnamese venture in three ways. It can export capital from Australia, it can borrow Vietnamese dông, or it can borrow wherever interest rates are lowest.

Notice that if the dông is devalued, other things being equal, the Vietnamese assets will be worth fewer Australian dollars than before. In this case, Outback could protect itself against exchange risk by borrowing dông. It would then have both a Vietnamese asset and an offsetting dông liability. If the dông is devalued, the Australian dollar value of the asset falls, but that is offset by the fact that Outback now needs fewer dollars to service its dông debt.

Unfortunately, other things are rarely equal, for the devaluation may be accompanied by changes in the dông value of Outback's assets. Remember that the law of one price states that

---

45  For example, it could be that investors in Australia foresee a high rate of inflation and a depreciating currency. In this case, they will demand high dollar returns to compensate.

46  We assume that the measured inflation rates used to calculate real returns are based on the same basket of goods. If the inflation rate in Japan reflects the price of sushi and the rate in the Australian reflects the price of meat pies, then our measure of real returns will not be comparable.

any change in the dông exchange rate will be exactly offset by a change in the relative price of Vietnamese goods. Of course, you know better than to take that theory literally, but it may not be too bad an approximation in the case of readily exportable goods such as steel inventory. In other words, even if the dông is devalued, Outback's steel inventory may largely hold its value in terms of dollars. Therefore, rather than finance the entire venture by dông debt, it may be safer to finance it with a mixture of dông and dollars.

Managers sometimes think of currency risk as arising only from delays in foreign currency payments. For example, a firm that invoices in foreign currency is at risk if overseas customers do not pay their bills immediately. These transaction exposures can be easily identified and hedged. But our discussion of Outback's financing choices suggests that firms need to think more broadly about risk and recognise the impact of a change in the exchange rate on the value of the entire business. This is an example of economic exposure.

During 1991 and 1992 the value of the deutschmark appreciated relative to that of other major currencies. As a result, Porsche and other German luxury-car manufacturers found it increasingly difficult to compete in Australia. Dealers that had a franchise to sell German luxury cars also took a bath. Thus, the German car producers and their dealers in Australia were exposed to exchange-rate changes even though they may have had no fixed obligations to pay or receive dollars. They had economic exposure as well as transaction exposure.[47]

### one final example

Suppose that your company sites a plant in Colombia to produce video recorders. The law of one price predicts that a high rate of inflation in Colombia will be offset by a change in the exchange rate. So the Australian dollar cash flows from the Colombian plant are not affected by the level of inflation in Colombia.

The problem occurs if the law of one price does not hold. For example, suppose that a relatively high rate of inflation in Colombia coincides with a rise in the value of the Colombia peso. In this case, there is a rise in the real value of the Colombian peso and, other things being equal, a rise in the plant's cash flows when measured in Australian dollars.

There are some other factors that you need to take into account. Because it is now more costly to manufacture in Colombia, the plant will find it less easy to compete in export markets and profit margins are likely to be cut. This will tend to reduce cash flows when measured in Australian dollars. You cannot determine how to hedge your exchange risk until you have decided whether on balance the firm gains or loses by a rise in the value of the Colombian peso.[48]

Instead of worrying about reducing risk, why doesn't Outback PreFab follow our third alternative and borrow wherever interest rates are lowest? For example, instead of borrowing in Vietnam or Australia, perhaps Outback should borrow in Switzerland, where the five-year bond rate is approximately 2.40 per cent. However, you must ask yourself why the Swiss rate

---

47  The German car producers could have hedged their exposure by borrowing dollars. As the deutschmark appreciated, their dollar income fell, but the cost of servicing dollar loans would also have fallen. However, we should repeat here a point that we made in Chapter 25: borrowing dollars would have reduced the risk for German car producers, but it should not have affected their decisions as to where to produce and sell cars.

48  Notice that it is the change in the *real* exchange rate that you would like to hedge against. In other words, the value of the Colombian venture would be equally affected by a rise in the exchange rate and by a rise in the Colombian inflation rate. Unfortunately, it is much easier to hedge against a change in the *nominal* exchange rate than against a change in the *real* rate.

is so low. Unless you know that the Swiss government is deliberately holding the rate down by restrictions on the export of capital, you should suspect that the real cost of capital is roughly the same in Switzerland as it is anywhere else. The nominal rate is low only because investors expect a low domestic rate of inflation and a strong currency. Therefore, the advantage of the low rate of interest is likely to be offset by the additional dollars required to buy the Swiss francs to pay off the loan.[49] In 1989, several Australian banks, which had induced their clients to borrow at low interest rates in Switzerland, found themselves sued by the same clients for not having warned them of the risk of a rise in the price of Swiss francs. Of course, borrowing in a particular capital market does not commit you to take on that particular currency risk. You can choose to finance in a particular market and then swap your debt into a different currency.

We think that it makes sense for a firm to establish a 'passive' or 'normal' financing strategy. But sometimes you may come across an opportunity that truly does make it cheaper to depart from your normal strategy and finance in one particular country. For example, here is a deal worked out by Massey-Ferguson, the Canadian farm equipment manufacturer, as described in a paper by Donald Lessard and Alan Shapiro:[50]

> *The key to Massey's strategy is to view the many foreign countries in which it has plants not only as markets, but also as potential sources of financing for exports to third countries. For example, in early 1978, Massey-Ferguson had the opportunity to ship 7200 tractors worth $53 million to Turkey, but was unwilling to assume the risk of currency inconvertibility. Turkey, at that time, already owed $2 billion to various foreign creditors and it was uncertain whether it would be able to come up with dollars to pay off its debts (especially since its reserves were at about zero).*
>
> *Massey solved this problem by manufacturing these tractors at its Brazilian subsidiary, 'Massey-Ferguson do Brazil', and selling them to Brazil's Interbras, the trading company arm of Petrobas, the Brazilian national oil corporation. Interbras in turn arranged to sell the tractors to Turkey and pay Massey in cruzieros. The cruziero financing for Interbras came from Cacex, the Banco de Brasil department that is in charge of foreign trade. Cacex underwrote all the political, commercial, and exchange risks as part of the Brazilian government's intense export promotion drive. Prior to choosing Brazil as a supply point, Massey made a point of shopping around to get the best export credit deal available.*

## Tax and the financing method

Outback PreFab's choice of initial financing may also depend on how it plans to use the profits of its Vietnamese subsidiary. In the early years the venture may well run a continuing deficit, but Outback hopes that it will generate a cash surplus eventually. You need to think about how you can best repatriate this surplus.

Broadly speaking, international affiliates make the following payments to the parent company:

- Dividends
- Interest payments and repayment of parent company loans
- Royalties for use of trade names and patents
- Management fees for central services
- Payments for goods supplied by the parent

---

[49]  For a further discussion of financing choices see D. R. Lessard and A. C. Shapiro, 'Guidelines for Global Financing Choices', *Midland Corporate Financial Journal*, **1**: 68–80 (Winter 1983).

[50]  The quote is from the working paper version of *Guidelines for Global Financing Choices*, MIT, Sloan School of Management, Cambridge, Mass., October 1982, p. 17.

The form of payment is important because it affects the taxes paid. Companies are generally subject to local taxes on their local earnings. Therefore Outback PreFab's Vietnamese subsidiary will pay corporate tax in Vietnam on all profits that it earns there. In addition, it is liable for Australian corporate tax on any dividends that are remitted to Australia.[51]

Many countries have a double-taxation agreement with Australia.[52] This means that the company can offset the payment of any local taxes against the Australian tax liability on the foreign dividends.[53] For example, suppose Outback PreFab's subsidiary pays Vietnamese income tax of 35 per cent on its profits, plus a withholding tax of 5 per cent on any dividends paid to Australia. The left-hand portion of Table 34.5 shows that Outback therefore is exempt from any additional tax on these dividends. The right-hand portion shows what would happen if the Vietnamese income tax rate were changed to 30 per cent. In this case, Outback could claim double tax relief only to the amount of taxes paid in Vietnam.

**table 34.5**

Calculation of Australian tax on dividends paid by Outback PreFab's Vietnamese subsidiary (figures in dollars).

|  | Vietnamese corporate tax | | |
|---|---|---|---|
|  | **40%** | **35%** | **30%** |
| **Profits before tax** | 100 | 100 | 100 |
| Vietnamese company tax | 40 | 35 | 30 |
| Withholding tax | 5 | 5 | 5 |
| **Net profits** | 55 | 60 | 65 |
| Australian company tax (assume 35%) | 35 | 35 | 35 |
| Less double-tax relief (maximum 35%) | 35 | 35 | 30 |
| Australian tax payable | 0 | 0 | 5 |
| **Available for dividend** | 55 | 60 | 60 |

If the subsidiary is operating in a high-tax country with a double-tax agreement, dividend payments are not subject to additional taxes in Australia. On the other hand, in such cases you may do better to arrange a loan from the parent to the subsidiary. The parent company must pay Australian tax on the interest, but the foreign subsidiary can deduct the interest before paying local tax. Another way to transfer income from high-tax areas to low-tax areas is to levy royalties or management fees on the subsidiary. Or it may be possible to change the transfer prices on sales of goods within the group. Needless to say, the tax and customs authorities are well aware of these incentives to minimise taxes and they will insist that all such intergroup payments be reasonable.

---

[51] If Outback's Vietnamese operation were a branch of the parent company rather than a subsidiary, the tax authorities in Australia would treat the income as part of the parent's income and tax it immediately rather than when it was remitted. That is usually a *disadvantage* when the foreign operation is showing profits but an *advantage* when it is making losses.

[52] Further details about double tax agreements and their application can be found in R. L. Hamilton and R. L. Deutsch, *Guidebook to Australian International Taxation*, Legal Books, Sydney, 1994.

[53] Australia's double tax agreement with Vietnam became effective on 1 July 1993.

## 34.7 Political risk

Think about what the political risk of a foreign investment really is. It is the threat that a foreign government will change the rules of the game—that is, break a promise or understanding—*after* the investment is made. Some managers think of political risks as an act of God, like a hurricane or earthquake. But the most successful multinational companies structure their business to reduce political risks.

Resource-based companies seem to attract particular attention when it comes to political risk—in part due to the geographical diversity of their operations and also due to the issues of environmental and resource extraction and to the appropriation of profits. Several recent examples involving Australian firms include the experiences of BHP and its subsidiary OK Tedi Mining Ltd at the copper and gold OK Tedi mine in Papua New Guinea, where a dispute arose with local landowners regarding environmental issues involving mine tailings and the OK Tedi River. CRA Ltd was also faced with the closure of its Bougainville mining operations following a dispute between locals and the Papua New Guinea government. Also, Anvil Mining's copper and silver mining activities in The Democratic Republic of Congo in Africa have been confronted with unstable economic and political regimes.[54]

Foreign governments are not likely to expropriate a local business if it cannot operate without the support of its parent. For example, the foreign subsidiaries of American computer manufacturers or pharmaceutical companies would have relatively little value if they were cut off from the know-how of their parents. Such operations are much less likely to be expropriated than, say, a mining operation that can be operated as a stand-alone venture.

We are not recommending that you turn your silver mine into a pharmaceutical company, but you may be able to plan overseas manufacturing operations to improve your bargaining position with foreign governments. For example, Ford has integrated its overseas operations so that the manufacture of components, subassemblies and complete cars is spread across plants in a number of countries. None of these plants would have much value on its own, and Ford can switch production between plants if the political climate in one country deteriorates.

Multinational corporations have also devised financing arrangements to help keep foreign governments honest. For example, suppose your firm is contemplating investing $500 million to reopen the San Tomé silver mine in Costaguana, with modern machinery, smelting equipment and shipping facilities. The Costaguanan government agrees to invest in roads and other infrastructure and to take 20 per cent of the silver produced by the mine in lieu of taxes. The agreement is to run for 25 years.

The project's NPV on these assumptions is quite attractive. But what happens if a new government comes to power five years from now and imposes a 50 per cent tax on 'any precious metals exported from the Republic of Costaguana'? Or changes the government's share of output from 20 to 50 per cent? Or simply takes over the mine 'with fair compensation to be determined in due course by the Minister of Natural Resources of the Republic of Costaguana'?

No contract can absolutely restrain a sovereign power. But you can arrange project financing to make these acts as painful as possible for the foreign government.[55] For example, you might set up the mine as a subsidiary corporation, which then borrows a large fraction of the required investment from a consortium of major international banks. If your firm guarantees the loan, make sure the guarantee stands only if the Costaguanan government honours its contract. The government will be reluctant to break the contract if that causes a default on the loans and undercuts the country's credit standing with the international banking system.

If possible, you should finance part of the project with a loan from the World Bank (or one of its affiliates). Include a *cross-default* clause, so that a default to any creditor automatically triggers default on the World Bank loan. Few governments have the guts to take on the World Bank.

---

54  Australian miners' experiences in Africa are discussed in T. Treadgold, 'Miners Shrug Off African Uncertainty', *Business Review Weekly*, 29 June 1998. Other experiences throughout the world are discussed in T. Treadgold, 'Foreign Follies', *Shares*, June 1997.

55  We discussed project financing in Chapter 24.

Here is another variation on the same theme. Arrange to borrow, say, $450 million through the Costaguanan Development Agency. In other words, the Development Agency borrows in international capital markets and re-lends to the San Tomé mine. Your firm agrees to stand behind the loan providing the government keeps *its* promises. If it does keep them, the loan is your liability. If not, the loan is *its* liability.

These arrangements do work. In the late 1960s Kennecott Copper financed a major expansion of a copper mine in Chile using arrangements like those we have just described. In 1970 a new government came to power, headed by Salvador Allende, who vowed to take over all foreign holdings in Chile giving 'ni un centavo' in exchange. Kennecott's mine was spared.

Political risk is not confined to the risk of expropriation. Multinational companies are always exposed to the criticism that they siphon funds out of countries in which they do business and, therefore, governments are tempted to limit their freedom to repatriate profits. This is most likely to happen when there is considerable uncertainty about the rate of exchange, which is usually when you would most like to get your money out.

Here again a little forethought can help. For example, there are often more onerous restrictions on the payment of dividends to the parent than on the payment of interest or principal on debt. So it may be better for the parent to put up part of the funds in the form of a loan. Royalty payments and management fees are less politically sensitive than dividends, particularly if they are levied equally on all foreign operations. A company can also, within limits, alter the price of goods that are bought or sold within the group, and it can require more or less prompt payment for such sales.

## 34.8 Interactions of investment and financing decisions

You cannot entirely divorce the value of an international project from the way that it is financed. For example, the taxes paid on Outback PreFab's Vietnamese venture depend on the form in which it remits profits to Australia. If it lends funds to the subsidiary rather than providing equity, the group will pay more tax in Australia and less in Vietnam.

Major international investments often have so many financing side effects that it is foolhardy to try to reduce the project analysis to one stream of cash flows and one adjusted discount rate. You need the adjusted-present-value (APV) rule, which we introduced in Chapter 19. Remember that APV is defined as:

1. 'base-case' project NPV, plus
2. the sum of the present values of the project's financing side effects.

The base-case NPV of an international project is usually calculated assuming all-equity-financing from the parent firm, and that all income is paid back as dividends at the first opportunity.

The next step is to value the financing side effects. If you finance the project in part by a loan from the parent rather than equity, you should calculate the value of any tax savings that result. And if the project also allows the firm *as a whole*[56] to borrow more on its own account, you should also calculate separately the value of any tax shields on this debt.

When you calculated your base-case net present value, you assumed that all funds were exported from Australia and all income was remitted as soon as possible. But you may do better to raise some of the money locally. Or you may already have surplus funds abroad that

---

56 Do not confuse a foreign subsidiary's debt with its contribution to the firm's *overall* debt capacity. For example, we spoke of borrowing 80 to 90 per cent of the $500 million cost of the San Tomé mine, but we did not assume the mine would support that debt. Instead, we assumed the firm could use relatively more of its overall borrowing capacity in Costaguana and less in Australia. It could finance the project by committing its debt capacity instead of cash.

you are not allowed to repatriate or that you do not wish to repatriate for tax reasons. Instead of remitting all income by the normal channels, you may be able to remit some income more profitably in the form of royalties or management fees, or you may prefer to retain the funds overseas for further expansion. Such benefits should also be valued separately.[57]

There are many other financing side effects. The subsidised financing provided to Massey-Ferguson by Brazil is one example. So make a complete list, value each side effect separately, and add up all the values to get APV.

## 34.9 Summary

The international financial manager has to cope with different currencies, interest rates and inflation rates and must be familiar with a variety of different capital markets and tax systems. The most we can hope to do in these pages it to whet your appetite.

To produce order out of chaos, the international financial manager needs some model of the relationship between exchange rates, interest rates and inflation rates. We described four very simple but useful theories.

Interest-rate parity theory states that the interest differential between two countries must be equal to the difference between the forward and spot exchange rates. In the international markets, arbitrage ensures that parity almost always holds. There are two ways to hedge against exchange risk—one is to take out forward cover, the other is to borrow or lend abroad. Interest-rate parity tells us that the cost of the two methods should be the same.

The expectations theory of exchange rates tells us that the forward rate equals the expected spot rate. If you believe the expectations theory, you will generally insure against exchange risks.

In its strict form, the law of one price states that $1 must have the same purchasing power in every country. That does not square very well with the facts, for differences in inflation rates are not perfectly related to changes in exchange rates. This means that there may be some genuine exchange risks in doing business overseas. On the other hand, the difference in the inflation rates is just as likely to be above as below the change in the exchange rate.

Finally, we saw that in an integrated world, capital market real rates of interest would have to be the same. In practice, government regulation and taxes can cause differences in real interest rates. But do not simply borrow where interest rates are lowest. Those countries are also likely to have the lowest inflation rates and the strongest currencies.

With these precepts in mind we looked at three common problems in international finance. First, we showed how you can use the forward markets or the loan markets to price and insure long-term export contracts.

Second, we considered the problem of international capital budgeting. We warned against making stupid investment decisions simply because you have a strong view about future exchange rates. And we showed that it makes no difference which currency you use for your calculations as long as you assume that prices, interest rates and exchange rates are linked by the simple theories that we described above. The main difficulty is to select the right discount rate. If there is a free market for capital, the discount rate for your project is the return that your shareholders expect from investing in foreign securities. This rate is difficult to measure, but we argued against just adding a premium for the 'extra risks' of overseas investment.

Finally, we looked at the problem of financing overseas subsidiaries. There are at least three issues that you should think about. Other things being equal, you would like to

---

[57] See, for example, D. Lessard, 'Evaluating Foreign Projects—An Adjusted Present Value Approach', in D. Lessard (ed.), *International Financial Management: Theory and Application*, 2nd ed., John Wiley, New York, 1986.

protect yourself against exchange risk: you may be able to do this by borrowing part of the money in the local currency. Second, you need to think about tax: for example, you can reduce tax by borrowing in high-tax countries and lending in low-tax countries. Third, you should consider whether you can structure the financing to reduce the risk that governments will change the rules of the game.

The incremental cash flow that the parent company receives from its overseas operations depends on the way that they are financed. Therefore, an adjusted-present-value approach is needed to analyse international investment proposals.

## FURTHER READING

There are a number of very useful textbooks in international finance. Here is a small selection.

D. K. Eiteman and A. I. Stonehill, *Multinational Business Finance*, 7th ed., Addison-Wesley, Reading, Mass., 1994.

I. H. Giddy, *Global Financial Markets*, D. C. Heath and Company, Lexington, Mass., 1994.

J. Madura, *International Financial Management*, West Publishing Company, St Paul, Minn., 1992.

R. Rodriguez and E. Carter, *International Financial Management*, 3rd ed., Prentice-Hall, Englewood Cliffs, N.J., 1984.

P. Sercu and R. Uppal, *International Financial Markets and the Firm*, South-Western College Publishing, Cincinnati, Ohio, 1995.

A. C. Shapiro, *Multinational Financial Management*, 3rd ed., Allyn & Bacon, Boston, 1989.

Australian books discussing the foreign exchange market include:

R. Allan, R. Elstone, G. Lock and T. Valentine, *Foreign Exchange Management*, Allen & Unwin, Sydney, 1990.

S. Anthony, *Foreign Exchange in Practice*, The Law Book Company, Sydney, 1990.

J. A. Batten, *International Finance in Australia: A Case Study Approach*, Butterworths, Sydney, 1993.

G. Manuell, *Floating Down Under: Foreign Exchange in Australia*, The Law Book Company, Sydney, 1986.

L. Wilson, 'Foreign Exchange', in R. Bruce, B. McKern, I. Pollard and M. Skully, *Handbook of Australian Corporate Finance*, 5th ed., Butterworths, Sydney, 1997.

Here are some general discussions of international investment and associated exchange risks:

B. Cornell and A. C. Shapiro, 'Managing Foreign Exchange Risks', *Midland Corporate Finance Journal*, 1: 16–31 (Fall 1983).

E. Flood and D. Lessard, 'On the Measurement of Operating Exposure to Exchange Rates: A Conceptual Approach', *Financial Management*, 15: 25–36 (Spring 1986).

D. R. Lessard, 'Global Competition and Corporate Finance in the 1990s', *Journal of Applied Corporate Finance*, 3: 59–72 (Winter 1991).

M. D. Levi and P. Sercu, 'Erroneous and Valid Reasons for Hedging Foreign Exchange Exposure', *Journal of Multinational Financial Management*, 1: 25–37 (1991).

J. J. Pringle, 'Managing Foreign Exchange Exposure', *Journal of Applied Corporate Finance*, 3: 73–82 (Winter 1991).

A. C. Shapiro, 'International Capital Budgeting', *Midland Corporate Finance Journal*, 1: 26–45 (Spring 1983).

And here is a sample of the articles on some of the relationships between interest rates, exchange rates and inflation rates:

Forward rates and spot rates

B. Cornell, 'Spot Rates, Forward Rates and Exchange Market Efficiency', *Journal of Financial Economics*, 5: 55–65 (1977).

E. F. Fama, 'Forward and Spot Exchange Rates', *Journal of Monetary Economics*, **14**: 319–38 (1984).

C. P. Wolff, 'Foreign Exchange Rates, Expected Spot Rates and Premia: A Signal Extraction Approach', *Journal of Finance*, **42**: 395–406 (June 1987).

Interest rate parity

K. Clinton, 'Transaction Costs and Covered Interest Advantage: Theory and Evidence', *Journal of Political Economy*, **96**: 358–70 (April 1988).

J. A. Frenkel and R. M. Levich, 'Covered Interest Arbitrage: Unexploited Profits?', *Journal of Political Economy*, **83**: 325–38 (April 1975).

Law of one price

N. Abuaf and P. Jorian, 'Purchasing Power Parity in the Long Run', *Journal of Finance*, **45**: 157–74 (March 1990).

M. Adler and B. Lehmann, 'Deviations from Purchasing Power Parity in the Long Run', *Journal of Finance*, **38**: 1471–87 (December 1983).

R. Roll, 'Violations of the "Law of One Price" and Their Implications for Differentially Denominated Assets', in M. Sarnat and G. Szego (eds.), *International Finance and Trade*, Ballinger Press, Cambridge, Mass., 1979.

International capital market equilibrium

F. Black, 'International Capital Market Equilibrium and Investment Barriers', *Journal of Financial Economics*, **1**: 337–52 (December 1974).

F. L. A. Grauer, R. H. Litzenberger and R. E. Stehle, 'Sharing Rules and Equilibrium in an International Capital Market Under Uncertainty', *Journal of Financial Economics*, **3**: 233–56 (June 1976).

B. H. Solnik, 'An Equilibrium Model of the International Capital Market', *Journal of Economic Theory*, **8**: 500–24 (1974).

R. M. Stultz, 'A Model of International Asset Price', *Journal of Financial Economics*, **9**: 383–406 (December 1981).

## QUIZ

**1.** Look at Tables 34.1 and 34.3:
   a. How many British pounds do you get for your Australian dollar?
   b. What is the three-month forward rate for the A$/US$?
   c. Is the dollar at a forward discount or premium on the US$?
   d. If the three-month interest rate on eurodollars is 8 per cent annually compounded, what do you think is the six-month euro-aussie interest rate?
   e. According to the expectations theory, what is the expected spot rate for the US dollar in six months time?
   f. According to the law of one price, what then is the expected difference in the rate of price inflation in Australia and the United States?

**2.** Define each of the following theories in a sentence or simple equation.
   a. Interest-rate parity theory.
   b. Expectations theory of forward rates.
   c. Law of one price.
   d. International capital market equilibrium (relationship of real and nominal interest rates in different countries).

**3.** The following table shows interest rates and exchange rates for the Australian dollar and French franc. The spot exchange rate is 7.05 francs per dollar. Complete the missing entries:

|                                                   | 3 months | 6 months | 1 year |
|---------------------------------------------------|----------|----------|--------|
| Eurodollar interest rate (annually compounded)    | 11.5%    | 12.25%   | ?      |
| Eurofranc interest rate (annually compounded)     | 19.5%    | ?        | 20%    |
| Forward francs per dollar                         | ?        | ?        | 7.5200 |
| Forward discount on franc, per cent per year      | ?        | −6.3%    | ?      |

4. An importer in Australia is due to take delivery of silk scarves from Italy in six months time. The price is fixed in lire. Which of the following transactions could eliminate the importer's exchange risk?
   a. Sell six-month call options on lire.
   b. Buy lire forward.
   c. Sell lire forward.
   d. Sell lire in the currency at the spot exchange rate.
   e. Borrow lire, buy dollars at the spot exchange rate.
   f. Sell lire at the spot exchange rate, lend dollars.

5. A firm in Australia is due to receive payment on one million deutschmarks in eight years time. It would like to protect itself against a decline in the value of the deutschmark, but finds it difficult to get forward cover for such a long period. Is there any other way in which it can protect itself?

6. Which of the following items do you need if you do all your capital budgeting calculations in your own currency?
   a. Forecasts of future exchange rates.
   b. Forecasts of the foreign inflation rate.
   c. Forecasts of the domestic inflation rate.
   d. Foreign interest rates.
   e. Domestic interest rates.
      Which of the above items do you need if you do all your capital budgeting calculations in the foreign currency?

7. Company A has two overseas subsidiaries in countries X and Y. Australia has a 35 per cent rate of corporate tax, X has a 60 per cent rate and Y a 40 per cent rate. Both X and Y have a double-tax agreement with Australia. Suppose that the company earns $100 pre-tax in both countries.
   a. What taxes would be paid in Australia and overseas if it remitted all net income in the form of dividends?
   b. What taxes would be paid if it remitted all net income in the form of interest?

## QUESTIONS AND PROBLEMS

1. Look at the Australian dollar foreign exchange table in a recent issue of the *Financial Review*.
   a. How many Australian dollars are worth one New Zealand dollar today?
   b. How many New Zealand dollars are worth one Australian dollar today?
   c. Suppose that you arrange today to buy US dollars in 180 days. How many Australian dollars could you buy for each US dollar?
   d. If forward rates simply reflect market expectations, what is the likely spot exchange rate for buying Australian dollars in 90 days time?

**2.** Table 34.3 shows the 12-month forward rate on the US dollar.
   a. Is the Australian dollar at a forward discount or a premium on the US dollar?
   b. Calculate the forward margin.
   c. If you have no other information about the two currencies, what is your best guess about the spot rate on the mark six months hence?
   d. Suppose that you expect to receive 100 000 US dollars in six months time. How many Australian dollars is this likely to be worth?

**3.** Look at Table 34.3. If the three-month interest rate on eurodollars (US) is 8.063 per cent, what do you think is the three-month euro-aussie interest rate? Explain what would happen if the rate were substantially above your figure.

**4.** Look at a recent issue of the *Financial Review*. How many Swiss francs can you buy with one Australian dollar? How many deutschmarks can you buy? What rate do you think a German bank would quote for buying or selling Swiss francs? Explain what would happen if it quoted a rate that was substantially above your figure.

**5.** What do our four basic relationships imply about the relationship between two countries' interest rates and the expected change in the exchange rate? Explain why you would or would not expect them to be related.

**6.** Ms Rosetta Stone, the treasurer of International Reprints Ltd, has noticed that the interest rate in Germany is below the rates in most other countries. She is therefore suggesting that the company should make an issue of deutschmark bonds. What considerations ought she first to take into account?

**7.** What considerations should an Australian company take into account when deciding how to finance its overseas subsidiaries?

**8.** An Australian firm is evaluating an investment in Germany. The project costs 12 million deutschmarks and it is expected to produce an income of three million deutschmarks a year in real terms for each of the next six years. The expected inflation rate in Germany is 6 per cent a year and the firm estimates that an appropriate discount rate for the project would be about 8 per cent above the risk-free rate of interest. Calculate the net present value of the project in dollars using each of the two methods described in this chapter. Exchange rates are given in Table 34.1. Assume the risk-free interest rate is about 9 per cent in Germany and 7 per cent in Australia.

**9.** An Australian firm is evaluating an investment in New Zealand. The project costs NZ$2 million and it is expected to produce an income of NZ$300 000 a year in real terms for each of the next 10 years. The expected inflation rate in New Zealand is 6 per cent a year, and the firm estimates that an appropriate discount rate for the project would be about 8 per cent above the risk-free rate of interest. Calculate the net present value of the project in dollars using each of the two methods described in this chapter. Exchange rates are given in Table 34.1. Assume the interest rate is about 9 per cent in New Zealand and 6.5 per cent in Australia.

**10.** 'The decline in the value of the dollar has made chemical producers in the United States attractive targets for takeover by European companies.' Discuss.

**11.** Suppose you are a corporate treasurer at Qantas. How is company value likely to be affected by exchange rate changes? What policies would you adopt to reduce exchange rate risk?

**12.** Suppose that you do use your own views about inflation and exchange rates when valuing an overseas investment proposal. Specifically, suppose that you believe that inflation will be 2 per cent in Vietnam and 5 per cent in Australia, but that the exchange rate will remain unchanged. Recalculate the NPV of the Outback PreFab project using both of our methods. Each NPV implies a different financing strategy. What are they?

**13.** Companies may be affected by changes in the nominal exchange rate or in the real exchange rate. Explain how this can occur. Which risks are easiest to hedge against?

**14.** A Holden dealer in Australia may be exposed to a devaluation in the yen if this leads to a cut in the price of Japanese cars. Suppose that the dealer estimates that a 1 per cent decline in the value of the yen would result in a permanent decline of 5 per cent in the dealer's profits. How should she hedge against this risk, and how should she calculate the size of the hedge position?

**15.** You have bid for a possible export order that would provide a cash inflow of one million deutschmarks in six months time. The spot exchange rate is A$/DM1.8 and the six-month forward rate is A$/DM1.7. There are two sources of uncertainty: (1) the deutschmark could appreciate or depreciate, and (2) you may or may not receive the export order. Illustrate in each case the profits or losses that you would make if:
 a. You sell one million deutschmarks forward.
 b. You buy a six-month put option on deutschmarks with an exercise price of A$/DM1.7.

**16.** On 18 August 1999, an Australian investor bought 1000 shares in a Greek company at a price of 500 drachmas a share. A year later she sold the shares for 550 drachmas each. The shares did not pay any dividend. The spot rate on 18 August 1999 was A$/dr200.
 a. How many dollars did she invest?
 b. If the exchange rate at the end of the year was A$/dr220, what was the investor's total return in drachmas? In Australian dollars?
 c. Do you think that the investor has made an exchange-rate profit or loss? Explain.

**17.** If investors recognise the impact of inflation and exchange-rate changes on a firm's cash flows, changes in exchange rates should be reflected in share prices. How would the share price of each of the following Swiss companies be affected by an unanticipated appreciation in the Swiss franc of 10 per cent, only 2 per cent of which could be justified by comparing Swiss inflation to that in the rest of the world?
 a. *SwissAir*: More than two-thirds of its employees are Swiss. Most revenues come from international fares set in US dollars.
 b. *Nestlé*: Fewer than 5 per cent of its employees are Swiss. Most revenues are derived from sales of consumer goods in a wide range of countries with competition from local producers.
 c. *Union Bank of Switzerland*: Most employees are Swiss. All non-Swiss franc monetary positions are fully hedged.

**18.** Suppose that Australian investors invest largely in Australia and are content to hold only a very small proportion of their portfolios in foreign shares. Suppose also that the average beta of German shares when measured against the portfolios of Australian investors is 0.7. The Australian interest rate is 5 per cent, and the expected risk premium on the Australian market is 8 per cent.

a.  What is the expected return on the average Australian share?

b.  What is the expected return to an Australian investor from the average German share?

c.  What is the cost of capital for an Australian firm investing in a German project that has about the same risk (beta relative to the portfolio of Australian investors) as the average German share?

**19.** Table 34.6 shows the foreign exchange rate for the Australian dollar, and for both Australian and US inflation rates from 1980 to 1993. Using this data, plot the nominal and real exchange rates. Which has been the more stable?

**table 34.6**

Comparative data for Australia and the United States, 1980–93

|  | Foreign exchange rate, A$/US$ | Inflation rate* | |
|---|---|---|---|
|  |  | **Australia** | **United States** |
| 1980 | 0.8776 | 100 | 100.0 |
| 1981 | 0.8701 | 110 | 110.4 |
| 1982 | 0.9829 | 122 | 117.1 |
| 1983 | 1.1082 | 134 | 120.9 |
| 1984 | 1.1369 | 140 | 126.1 |
| 1985 | 1.4269 | 149 | 130.5 |
| 1986 | 1.4905 | 162 | 133.1 |
| 1987 | 1.4267 | 176 | 137.9 |
| 1988 | 1.2752 | 189 | 141.2 |
| 1989 | 1.2618 | 203 | 146.7 |
| 1990 | 1.2799 | 218 | 151.7 |
| 1991 | 1.2835 | 225 | 156.4 |
| 1992 | 1.3600 | 227 | 159.3 |
| 1993 | 1.4704 | 231 | 162.2 |

\* Consumer price index: 1980 = 100.

**20.** Look again at Table 34.6. George and Bruce each have an equal share in a trust fund that provides them with an income of US$100 000 a year. George lives in Seattle, but Bruce emigrated to Sydney in 1980. What has happened to George's *real* income since 1980? What was Bruce's income in 1980 in Australian dollars? What was it in 1993? What has happened to Bruce's *real* income?

**21.** In 1992 a litre of Scotch cost $38.00 in Cairns, $22.84 in New York, $S69 in Singapore and 3240 roubles in Moscow.

a. If the law of one price held, what was the exchange rate between US dollars and Singapore dollars? Between US dollars and roubles?

b. Assume that in 1992 the actual exchange rates in 1992 were $A1.3605 = US$1, $S1.63 = US$1, and 250 roubles = US$1. Where would you prefer to buy your Scotch?

**22.** Table 34.7 shows the annual interest rate (annually compounded) and exchange rates against the Australian dollar for different currencies. Are there any arbitrage opportunities? If so, how could you secure a positive cash flow today, while zeroing out all future cash flows?

**table 34.7**
Interest rates and exchange rates

| | Interest rate (%) | Spot exchange rate* | 1-year forward exchange rate* |
|---|---|---|---|
| Australian (dollar) | 5.0 | — | — |
| Costaguana (pulga) | 23.0 | 10 000 | 11 942 |
| Westonia (ruple) | 5.0 | 2.6 | 2.65 |
| Gloccamorra (pint) | 8.0 | 17.1 | 18.2 |
| Anglosaxophonia (wasp) | 4.1 | 2.3 | 2.28 |

* Number of units of foreign currency that can be exchanged for $1.

**23.** 'Although recent currency turmoil will not in itself trigger deals, it will undoubtedly give the mergers and acquisitions market further impetus. The decline of the dollar has made US assets especially cheap for companies in Germany and Switzerland' (*Financial Times*, 18 April 1995). Discuss.

**24.** Alpha Ltd has a plant in Hamburg that imports components from Australia, assembles them and then sells the finished product in Germany. Omega Ltd is at the opposite extreme. It also has a plant in Hamburg, but it buys its raw materials in Germany and exports its output back to Australia.

How is each firm likely to be affected by a fall in the value of the deutschmark? How could each firm hedge itself against exchange risk?

**25.** In September 1995 interest rates were 8.50 per cent in Australia and 10.6 per cent in Italy. The spot exchange rate was A$/L1400. Suppose that one year later interest rates were 8 per cent in both countries, while the value of the lira had fallen to A$/L1600.

a. Floria Tosca from Rome invested in an Italian two-year zero coupon bond in September 1995 and sold it in September 1996. What was her return?

b. Benjamin Pinkerton from Sydney also invested in the Italian two-year bond in September 1995 and sold it in September 1996. What was his return *in Australian dollars*?

c. Suppose that Mr Pinkerton had correctly forecasted the price at which he sold his bond and that he hedged his investment against currency risk. How could he have done so? What would have been his return in dollars?

# part 11

# CONCLUSIONS

# chapter 35

# CONCLUSION: WHAT WE DO AND DO NOT KNOW ABOUT FINANCE

I t is time to sign off. Let us finish by thinking about some of the things that we do and do not know about finance.

## 35.1 What we do know: the seven most important ideas in finance

What would you say if you were asked to name the seven most important ideas in finance? Here is our list.

### 1. Net present value

When you wish to know the value of a used car, you look at prices in the second-hand car yards or the newspapers. Similarly, when you wish to know the value of a future cash flow, you look at prices quoted in the capital markets, where claims to future cash flows are traded (remember, those highly paid investment bankers are just second-hand cash flow dealers). If you can buy cash flows for your shareholders at a cheaper price than they would have to pay in the capital market, you have increased the value of their investment.

This is the simple idea behind *net present value* (NPV). When we calculate a project's NPV, we are asking whether the project is worth more than it costs. We are estimating its value by calculating what its cash flows would be worth if a claim on them were offered separately to investors and traded in the capital markets.

That is why we calculate NPV by discounting future cash flows at the opportunity cost of capital—that is, at the expected rate of return offered by securities having the same degree of risk as the project. In well-functioning capital markets, all equivalent-risk assets are priced to offer the same expected return. By discounting at the opportunity cost of capital, we calculate the price at which investors in the project could expect to earn that rate of return.

Like most good ideas, the net present value rule is 'obvious when you think about it'. But notice what an important idea it is. The NPV rule allows thousands of shareholders, who may have vastly different levels of wealth and attitudes towards risk, to participate in the same enterprise and to delegate its operation to a professional manager. They give the manager one simple instruction: 'Maximise present value.'

## 2. The capital asset pricing model

Some people say that modern finance is all about the *capital asset pricing model* (CAPM). That is nonsense. If the capital asset pricing model had never been invented, our advice to financial managers would be essentially the same. The attraction of the model is that it gives us a manageable way of thinking about the required return on a risky investment.

Again, it is an attractively simple idea. There are two kinds of risks—risks that you can diversify away and those that you cannot. You can measure the *non-diversifiable*, or *market*, risk of an investment by the extent to which the value of the investment is affected by a change in the *aggregate* value of all the assets in the economy. This is called the *beta* of the investment. The only risks that people care about are the ones that they cannot get rid of— the non-diversifiable ones. This is why the required return on an asset increases in line with its beta.

Many people are worried by some of the rather strong assumptions behind the capital asset pricing model, or they are concerned about the difficulties of estimating a project's beta. They are right to be worried about these things. In 10 or 20 years time we will probably have much better theories than we do now. But we will be extremely surprised if those future theories do not still insist on the crucial distinction between diversifiable and non-diversifiable risks—and that, after all, is the main idea underlying the capital asset pricing model.

## 3. Efficient capital markets

The third fundamental idea is that security prices accurately reflect available information and respond rapidly to new information as soon as it becomes available. This *efficient-market theory* comes in three flavours, corresponding to different definitions of 'available information'. The weak form (or random-walk theory) says that prices reflect all the information in past prices. The semistrong form says that prices reflect all publicly available information, and the strong form holds that prices reflect all acquirable information.

Do not misunderstand the efficient-market idea. It does not say that there are no taxes or costs; it does not say that there are not some clever people and some stupid ones. It merely implies that competition in capital markets is very tough—there are no money machines, and security prices reflect the true underlying values of assets.

## 4. Value additivity and the law of conservation of value

The principle of *value additivity* states that the value of the whole is equal to the sum of the values of the parts. It is sometimes called the *law of the conservation of value*.

When we appraise a project that produces a succession of cash flows, we always assume that values add up. In other words, we assume:

$$PV(\text{project}) = PV(C_1) + PV(C_2) + \ldots + PV(C_t)$$

$$= \frac{C_1}{1 + r} + \frac{C_2}{(1 + r)^2} + \ldots + \frac{C_t}{(1 + r)^t} + \ldots$$

We similarly assume that the sum of the present values of projects A and B equals the present value of a composite project AB.[1] But value additivity also means that you cannot increase value by putting two whole companies together unless you thereby increase the total cash flow. In other words, there are no benefits to mergers solely for diversification.

# 5. Capital structure theory

If the law of the conservation of value works when you add up cash flows, it must also work when you subtract them.[2] Therefore, financing decisions that simply divide up operating cash flows do not increase overall firm value. This is the basic idea behind Modigliani and Miller's famous proposition I: in perfect markets, changes in capital structure do not affect value. As long as the *total* cash flow generated by the firm's assets is unchanged by capital structure, value is independent of capital structure. The value of the whole pie does not depend on how it is sliced.

Of course, MM's proposition is not *the answer*, but it does tell us where to look for reasons why capital structure decisions matter. Taxes are one possibility. Debt provides a corporate interest tax shield. This tax shield may more than compensate for any extra personal tax that the investor has to pay on debt interest and the cost of lost imputation credits. Also, high debt levels may spur managers to work harder and to run a tighter ship. But debt has its drawbacks if it leads to costly financial distress.

# 6. Option theory

In everyday conversation we often use the word *option* as synonymous with *choice* or *alternative*; thus, we speak of someone as 'having a number of options'. In finance, *option* refers specifically to the opportunity to trade in the future on terms that are fixed today. Smart managers know that it is often worth paying today for the option to buy or sell an asset tomorrow.

If options are so important, the financial manager needs to know how to value them. Finance experts always knew the relevant variables—the exercise price and the exercise date of the option, the risk of the underlying asset and the rate of interest. But it was Black and Scholes who first showed how these can be put together in a usable formula.

The Black–Scholes formula was developed for simple call options and does not directly apply to the more complicated options often encountered in corporate finance. But Black and Scholes' most basic ideas—for example, the risk-neutral valuation method implied by their formula—work even where the formula does not. Valuing the real options described in Chapter 21 may require extra number crunching but no extra concepts.

# 7. Agency theory

A modern corporation is a team effort involving a number of players, such as managers, employees, shareholders and bondholders. The members of this corporate team are bound together by a series of formal and informal contracts to ensure that they pull together.

---

[1]  That is, if

$$PV(A) = PV[C_1(A)] + PV[C_2(A)] + \ldots + PV[C_t(A)] + \ldots$$

$$PV(B) = PV[C_1(B)] + PV[C_2(B)] + \ldots + PV[C_t(B)] + \ldots$$

And if for each period $t$, $C_t(AB) = C_t(A) + C_t(B)$, then

$$PV(AB) = PV(A) + PV(B)$$

[2]  If you *start* with the cash flow $C_t(AB)$ and split it into two pieces, $C_t(A)$ and $C_t(B)$, then total value is unchanged. That is, $PV[C_t(A)] + PV[C_t(B)] = PV[C_t(AB)]$. See Footnote 1.

For a long time, economists used to assume without question that all players acted for the common good, but in the last 20 years economists have had a lot more to say about the possible conflicts of interest and how companies try to overcome such conflicts. These ideas are collectively known as *agency theory*.

We devoted at least one chapter of this book to each of the other important ideas in finance. We did not allocate a chapter to agency theory, but the theory has helped us think more clearly about several questions, including:

▌ How can an entrepreneur persuade venture capital investors to join in his or her enterprise?
▌ What are the reasons for all the fine print in bond agreements?
▌ Why might a bank sometimes be unwilling to lend a firm more money at any price?
▌ Are LBOs simply attempts to 'rip off' the other players, or do they add value by increasing management's incentives to work hard?

Are these seven ideas exciting theories or plain common sense? Call them what you will, they are basic to the financial manager's job. If by reading this book you really understand these ideas and know how to apply them, you have learned a great deal.

## 35.2 What we do not know: 10 unsolved problems in finance

Since the unknown is never exhausted, the list of what we do not know about finance could go on forever. But, following our third law (see Chapter 28), we will list and briefly discuss 10 unsolved problems that seem ripe for productive research.

### 1. How are major financial decisions made?

Arnold Sametz commented in 1964 that 'we know very little about how the great non-routine financial decisions are made'.[3] That is no less true today. We know quite a bit about asset values, but we do not know very much about the decisions that give rise to these values. What is the process that causes one company to make a major investment and another to reject it? Why does one company decide to issue debt and another to issue equity? If we knew why companies made particular decisions, we would be better able to help improve those decisions.

Our ignorance is largest when it come to major *strategic* decisions. In Section 28.1 we described strategic planning as 'capital budgeting on a grand scale'. Strategic planning attempts to identify the lines of business in which the firm has the greatest long-run opportunities and to develop a plan for achieving success in those businesses. But it is hard to calculate the NPV of major strategic decisions. Think, for example, of a firm that makes a major commitment to the design and manufacture of computer memories. It is really embarking on a long-term effort which will require capital outlays over many years. It cannot identify all those future projects, much less evaluate their NPVs. Instead, it decides to go ahead because the computer memory business is growing rapidly, because firms already in that business are doing well and because it has intangible assets—special technology, perhaps—which it thinks will give it a leg up on the competition.

Strategic planning is a 'top-down' approach to capital budgeting: you choose the businesses you want to be in and make the capital outlays necessary for success. It is perfectly sensible and natural for firms to look at capital investments that way *in addition to* looking at

---

3   A. W. Sametz, 'Trends in the Volume and Composition of Equity Finance', *Journal of Finance*, **19**: 450–69 (September 1964), see p. 469.

them 'bottom-up'. The trouble is that we understand the bottom-up part of the capital budgeting process better than the top-down part.

Top-down and bottom-up should not be competing approaches to capital budgeting. They should be two aspects of a single integrated procedure. Not all firms integrate the two approaches successfully. No doubt some firms do so, but we do not really know how.

In Sections 21.1 and 28.1 we suggested that option pricing theory might help unravel some of the mysteries of strategic planning. We will have to wait and see whether it does.

## 2. What determines project risk and present value?

A good capital investment is one that has a positive NPV. We have talked at some length about how to calculate NPV, but we have given you very little guidance about how to find positive NPV projects, except to say in Section 11.2 that projects have positive NPVs when the firm can earn economic rents. But why do some companies earn economic rents while others in the same industry do not? Are the rents merely windfall gains, or can they be anticipated and planned for? What is their source, and how long do they persist before competition destroys them? Very little is known about any of these important questions.

Here is a related question: Why are some real assets risky and others relatively safe? In Section 9.4 we suggested a few reasons for differences in project betas—differences in operating leverage, for example, or in the extent to which a project's cash flows respond to the performance of the national economy. These are useful clues, but we have as yet no general procedure for estimating project betas. Assessing project risk is therefore still largely a seat-of-the-pants matter.

## 3. Risk and return—what have we missed?

In 1848 John Stuart Mill wrote, 'Happily there is nothing in the laws of value which remains for the present or any future writer to clear up; the theory is complete.' Economists today are not so sure about that. For example, the capital asset pricing model is an enormous step towards understanding the effect of risk on the value of an asset, but there are many puzzles left, some statistical and some theoretical.

The statistical problems arise because the capital asset pricing model is hard to prove or disprove conclusively. It appears that average returns from low-beta stocks are too high (that is, higher than the capital asset pricing model predicts) and that those from high-beta stocks are too low; but this could be a problem with the way the tests are conducted and not with the model itself.[4]

Meanwhile, scholars toil on the theoretical front. We discussed some of their work in Section 8.4. But just for fun here is another example: Suppose that you love fine wine. It may make sense for you to buy shares in a grand chateau, even if doing so soaks up a large fraction of your personal wealth and leaves you with a relatively undiversified portfolio. However, you are *hedged* against a rise in the price of fine wine: your hobby will cost you more in a bull market for wine, but your stake in the chateau will make you correspondingly richer. Thus, you are holding a relatively undiversified portfolio for a good reason. We would not expect you to demand a premium for bearing that portfolio's undiversifiable risk.

In general, if two people have different tastes, it may make sense for them to hold different portfolios. You may hedge your consumption needs with an investment in wine making, whereas somebody else may do better to invest in either Pizza Hut or McDonald's. The capital asset pricing model is not rich enough to deal with such a world. It assumes that all investors have similar tastes: the 'hedging motive' does not enter, and therefore they hold the same portfolio of risky assets.

---

4   See R. Roll, 'A Critique of the Asset Pricing Theory's Tests: Part 1: On Past and Potential Testability of the Theory', *Journal of Financial Economics*, 4: 129–76 (March 1977); and for a critique of Roll's critique see D. Mayers and E. M. Rice, 'Measuring Portfolio Performance and the Empirical Content of Asset Pricing Models', *Journal of Financial Economics*, 7: 3–28 (March 1979).

Merton has extended the capital asset pricing model to accommodate the hedging motive.[5] If enough investors are attempting to hedge against the same thing, the model implies a more complicated risk-return relationship. However, it is not yet clear who is hedging against what, and so the model remains difficult to test.

So the capital asset pricing model survives not from a lack of competition but from a surfeit. There are too many plausible alternative risk measures, and so far no consensus exists on the right course to plot if we abandon beta.

In the meantime, we must recognise the capital asset pricing model for what it is: an incomplete but extremely useful way of linking risk and return. Recognise too that the model's most basic message, that diversifiable risk does not matter, is accepted by nearly everyone.

## 4. How important are the exceptions to the efficient-market theory?

The efficient-market theory is strong, but no theory is perfect—there must be exceptions. What are the exceptions and how well does the evidence stand up?

We noted some apparent exceptions in Section 13.2. For example, we saw that the shares of small companies appear to have yielded higher average returns than those of larger companies with comparable betas. Thus, whatever your target portfolio beta, you can apparently generate superior average returns by investing in small companies.

Now, this could mean one of several things:

**1.** The share market is inefficient and consistently underprices the shares of small firms.
**2.** The difference between the share market performances of small and large firms is just a coincidence. (The more researchers study share performance, the more strange coincidences they are likely to find.)
**3.** Firm size happens to be correlated with variable $x$, that mysterious second risk variable that investors may rationally take into account in pricing shares.

In searching for an explanation of the small-firm phenomenon, researchers have uncovered other puzzles. For example, almost all the extra return on small-company shares has occurred in January. So the mystery deepens. Does the turn-of-the-year effect provide a clue to the explanation of the small-company effect, or is it just a false trail? Sorting out what is really going on in these cases will take considerable work and thought.

If shares were fairly priced, there would be no easy ways to make superior profits. That is why most tests of market efficiency have analysed whether there are simple rules that produce superior investment performance. Unfortunately, the converse does *not* hold: share prices could deviate substantially from fair value, and yet it could be difficult to make superior profits.

For example, suppose that the price of Coles Myer shares is always one-half of their fair value. As long as Coles Myer is *consistently* underpriced, the percentage capital gain is the same as it would be if the shares always sold at a fair price. Of course, if Coles Myer shares are underpriced, you get correspondingly more future dividends for your money, but for low-yield shares that does not make much difference to your total return. So, while the bulk of the evidence shows that it is difficult to earn abnormally high returns, we should be cautious about assuming that shares are *necessarily* fairly priced.

## 5. Is management an off-balance-sheet liability?

Closed-end funds are firms whose only asset is a portfolio of common shares. One might think that if you knew the value of these common shares, you would also know the value of the firm.

---

5    See R. Merton, 'An Intertemporal Capital Asset Pricing Model', *Econometrica*, **41**: 867–87 (1973).

However, this is not the case. The shares of the closed-end fund often sell for substantially less than the value of the fund's portfolio.[6]

All this might not matter much except that it could be just the tip of the iceberg. For example, real estate shares appear to sell for less than the market values of the firms' net assets. In the late 1970s and early 1980s the market values of many large oil companies were less than the market values of their oil reserves. Analysts joked that you could buy oil cheaper on Wall Street than in west Texas.

All these are special cases in which it was possible to compare the market value of the whole firm with the values of its separate assets. But perhaps if we could observe the values of other firms' separate parts, we might find that the value of the whole was often less than the sum of the values of the parts.

We do not understand why closed-end investment companies or any of the other firms sell at a discount on the market values of their assets. One explanation is that the value added by the firm's management is less than the cost of the management. That is why we suggest that management may be an off-balance-sheet liability. For example, the discount of oil company shares from oil-in-the-ground value can be explained if investors expected the profits from oil production to be frittered away in negative NPV investments and bureaucratic excess. The present value of growth opportunities (PVGO) was negative!

Another possibility is that the companies' reports do not provide all the information required to accurately calculate the market values of the individual assets. There might, for example, be hidden liabilities other than management, such as unrealised capital gains taxes.

Whenever firms calculate the net present value of a project, they implicitly assume that the value of the whole project is simply the sum of the values of all the years' cash flows. We referred to this earlier as the law of the conservation of value. If we cannot rely on that law, the tip of the iceberg could turn out to be a hot potato.

## 6. How can we explain the success of new securities and new markets?

In the last 20 years companies and the securities exchanges have created an enormous number of new securities—options, futures, options on futures; zero coupon bonds; bonds with currency options ... the list is endless. In some cases it is easy to explain the success of new markets or securities—perhaps they allow investors to insure themselves against new risks or they result from a change in tax or regulation. Sometimes a market develops because of a change in the costs of issuing or trading different securities. But there are many successful innovations that cannot be explained so easily. Why do investment bankers continue to invent, and successfully sell, complex new securities that outstrip our ability to value them? The truth is we do not understand why some innovations in markets succeed and others never get off the ground.

## 7. How can we resolve the dividend controversy?

We spent all of Chapter 16 on dividend policy without being able to resolve the dividend controversy. Many people believe dividends are good; others believe they are bad; and still others believe they are irrelevant. If pressed, we stand somewhere in the middle, but we cannot be dogmatic about it.

We do not mean to disparage existing research; rather, we say that more is in order. Whether future research will change anybody's mind is another matter. In 1979 Joel Stern wrote an article for the editorial page of *The Wall Street Journal* arguing for low dividends

---

[6]   There are relatively few closed-end funds. Most mutual funds are *open-end*. This means that they stand ready to buy or sell additional shares at a price equal to the fund's net asset value per share. Therefore, the share price of an open-end fund always equals net asset value.

and citing statistical tests in support of his position.[7] The article attracted several strongly worded responses, including one from a manager who wrote, 'While Mr Stern is gamboling from pinnacle to pinnacle in the upper realms of the theoretical, those of us in financial management are down below slogging through the foothills of reality.'[8]

## 8. What risks should a firm take?

Financial managers end up managing risk. For example:

- When a firm expands production, managers often reduce the cost of failure by building in the option to alter the product mix or to bail out of the project altogether.
- By reducing the firm's borrowing, managers can spread operating risk over a larger equity base.
- Most businesses take out insurance against a variety of specific hazards.
- Managers often use futures or other derivatives to protect against adverse movements in equity prices, commodity prices, interest rates and exchange rates.

All these actions reduce risk. But less risk cannot always be better. The point of risk management is not to reduce risk but to add value. We wish we could give general guidance on what bets the firm should place and what the *appropriate* level of risk is.

In practice, risk management decisions interact in complicated ways. For example, firms that are hedged against commodity price fluctuations may be able to afford more debt than those that are not hedged. Hedging can make sense if it allows the firm to take greater advantage of interest tax shields, provided the costs of hedging are sufficiently low.

How can a company set a risk management strategy that adds up to a sensible whole?

## 9. What is the value of liquidity?

Unlike bank bills, cash pays no interest. On the other hand, cash provides more liquidity than bank bills. People who hold cash must believe that this additional liquidity offsets the loss of interest. In equilibrium, the marginal value of the additional liquidity must equal the interest rate on these bills.

Now what can we say about corporate holdings of cash? It is wrong to ignore the liquidity gain and to say that the cost of holding cash is the lost interest. This would imply that cash always has a *negative* NPV. It is equally foolish to say that, because the marginal value of liquidity is equal to the loss of interest, it does not matter how much cash a firm holds. This would imply that cash always has a *zero* NPV.

We know that the marginal value of cash to a holder declines with the size of the cash holding, but we do not really understand how to value the liquidity service of cash. In our chapters on working capital management we largely finessed the problem by presenting models that are really too simple[9] or by speaking vaguely of the need to ensure an 'adequate' liquidity reserve. We cannot successfully tackle the problem of working capital management until we have a theory of liquidity.

The problem is that liquidity is a matter of degree. A bank bill is less liquid than cash, but it is still a highly liquid security because it can be sold and turned into cash easily and almost instantaneously.[10] Corporate bonds are less liquid than semigovernment bonds; trucks are less

---

[7]    Joel Stern, 'The Dividend Question', *The Wall Street Journal*, 16 July 1979, p. 13.

[8]    *The Wall Street Journal*, 20 August 1979, p. 16. The letter was from A. J. Sandblute, senior vice-president of Minnesota Light and Power Company.

[9]    For example, models based only on the transaction costs of switching between cash and interest-bearing assets. See Section 31.1.

[10]    That is, you can realise the asset's true economic value in a quick sale. Liquidity means that you do not have to accept a discount from true value if you want to sell the asset quickly.

liquid than corporate bonds; specialised machinery is less liquid than trucks; and so on. But even specialised machinery can be turned into cash if you are willing to accept some delay and cost of sale. The broad question is therefore not 'How much cash should the firm hold?', but 'How should it divide its total investment between relatively liquid and relatively illiquid assets?'—holding other things constant, of course. That question is hard to answer. Obviously, every firm must be able to raise cash on short notice, but we have no good theory of how much cash is enough or how readily the firm should be able to raise it. To complicate matters further, we note that cash can be raised on short notice by borrowing, or selling other securities, as well as by selling assets. The financial manager with a $1 million unused line of credit may sleep just as soundly as one whose firm holds $1 million in marketable securities.

## 10. How can we explain merger waves?

In the late 1960s, at the first peak of the post-war merger movement, Joel Segall noted, 'There is no single hypothesis which is both plausible and general and which shows promise of explaining the current merger movement. If so, it is correct to say that there is nothing known about mergers; there are no useful generalisations.'[11] As we discussed in Chapter 33, there are many plausible reasons why two firms might wish to merge. If you single out a *particular* merger, it is usually possible to think up a reason why that merger could make sense. But that leaves us with a special hypothesis for each merger. What we need is a *general* hypothesis to explain merger waves. For example, everybody seemed to be merging in the mid-1980s and again in the mid-1990s and yet few mergers occurred around 1990. Why?

We can think of other instances of apparent financial fashions. For example, from time to time there are hot new-issue periods when there seems to be an insatiable supply of speculative new issues and an equally insatiable demand for them. We need better theories to help explain these 'bubbles' of financial activity.

## 35.3 A final word

That concludes our list of unsolved problems. We have given you the 10 uppermost in our minds. If there are others that you find more interesting and challenging, by all means construct your own list and start thinking about it.

It will take years for our 10 problems to be finally solved and replaced with a fresh list. In the meantime, we invite you to go on to further study of what we *already* know about finance. We also invite you to apply what you have learned from reading this book.

---

11   J. Segall, 'Merging for Fun and Profit', *Industrial Management Review*, 9: 17–30 (Winter 1968).

# appendixes

# APPENDIX TABLE 1

Discount factors: Present value of $1 to be received after $t$ years $= 1/(1 + r)^t$

**Interest rate per year**

| Number of years | 1% | 2% | 3% | 4% | 5% | 6% | 7% | 8% | 9% | 10% | 11% | 12% | 13% | 14% | 15% |
|---|---|---|---|---|---|---|---|---|---|---|---|---|---|---|---|
| 1 | .990 | .980 | .971 | .962 | .952 | .943 | .935 | .926 | .917 | .909 | .901 | .893 | .885 | .877 | .870 |
| 2 | .980 | .961 | .943 | .925 | .907 | .890 | .873 | .857 | .842 | .826 | .812 | .791 | .783 | .769 | .756 |
| 3 | .971 | .942 | .915 | .889 | .864 | .840 | .816 | .794 | .772 | .751 | .731 | .712 | .693 | .675 | .658 |
| 4 | .961 | .924 | .888 | .855 | .823 | .792 | .763 | .735 | .708 | .683 | .659 | .636 | .613 | .592 | .572 |
| 5 | .951 | .906 | .863 | .822 | .784 | .747 | .713 | .681 | .650 | .621 | .593 | .567 | .543 | .519 | .497 |
| 6 | .942 | .888 | .837 | .790 | .746 | .705 | .666 | .630 | .596 | .564 | .535 | .507 | .480 | .456 | .432 |
| 7 | .933 | .871 | .813 | .760 | .711 | .665 | .623 | .583 | .547 | .513 | .482 | .452 | .425 | .400 | .376 |
| 8 | .923 | .853 | .789 | .731 | .677 | .627 | .582 | .540 | .502 | .467 | .434 | .404 | .376 | .351 | .327 |
| 9 | .914 | .837 | .766 | .703 | .645 | .592 | .544 | .500 | .460 | .424 | .391 | .361 | .333 | .308 | .284 |
| 10 | .905 | .820 | .744 | .676 | .614 | .558 | .508 | .463 | .422 | .386 | .352 | .322 | .295 | .270 | .247 |
| 11 | .896 | .804 | .722 | .650 | .585 | .527 | .475 | .429 | .388 | .350 | .317 | .287 | .261 | .237 | .215 |
| 12 | .887 | .788 | .701 | .625 | .557 | .497 | .444 | .397 | .356 | .319 | .286 | .257 | .231 | .208 | .187 |
| 13 | .879 | .773 | .681 | .601 | .530 | .469 | .415 | .368 | .326 | .290 | .258 | .229 | .204 | .182 | .163 |
| 14 | .870 | .758 | .661 | .577 | .505 | .442 | .388 | .340 | .299 | .263 | .232 | .205 | .181 | .160 | .141 |
| 15 | .861 | .743 | .642 | .555 | .481 | .417 | .362 | .315 | .275 | .239 | .209 | .183 | .160 | .140 | .123 |
| 16 | .853 | .728 | .623 | .534 | .458 | .394 | .339 | .292 | .252 | .218 | .188 | .163 | .141 | .123 | .107 |
| 17 | .844 | .714 | .605 | .513 | .436 | .371 | .317 | .270 | .231 | .198 | .170 | .146 | .125 | .108 | .093 |
| 18 | .836 | .700 | .587 | .494 | .416 | .350 | .296 | .250 | .212 | .180 | .153 | .130 | .111 | .095 | .081 |
| 19 | .828 | .686 | .570 | .475 | .396 | .331 | .277 | .232 | .194 | .164 | .138 | .116 | .098 | .083 | .070 |
| 20 | .820 | .673 | .554 | .456 | .377 | .312 | .258 | .215 | .178 | .149 | .124 | .104 | .087 | .073 | .061 |
| 25 | .780 | .610 | .478 | .375 | .295 | .233 | .184 | .146 | .116 | .092 | .074 | .059 | .047 | .038 | .030 |
| 30 | .742 | .552 | .412 | .308 | .231 | .174 | .131 | .099 | .075 | .057 | .044 | .033 | .026 | .020 | .015 |

**Interest rate per year**

| Number of years | 16% | 17% | 18% | 19% | 20% | 21% | 22% | 23% | 24% | 25% | 26% | 27% | 28% | 29% | 30% |
|---|---|---|---|---|---|---|---|---|---|---|---|---|---|---|---|
| 1 | .862 | .855 | .847 | .840 | .833 | .826 | .820 | .813 | .806 | .800 | .794 | .787 | .781 | .775 | .769 |
| 2 | .743 | .731 | .718 | .706 | .694 | .683 | .672 | .661 | .650 | .640 | .630 | .620 | .610 | .601 | .592 |
| 3 | .641 | .624 | .609 | .593 | .579 | .564 | .551 | .537 | .524 | .512 | .500 | .488 | .477 | .466 | .455 |
| 4 | .552 | .534 | .516 | .499 | .482 | .467 | .451 | .437 | .423 | .410 | .397 | .384 | .373 | .361 | .350 |
| 5 | .476 | .456 | .437 | .419 | .402 | .386 | .370 | .355 | .341 | .328 | .315 | .303 | .291 | .280 | .269 |
| 6 | .410 | .390 | .370 | .352 | .335 | .319 | .303 | .289 | .275 | .262 | .250 | .238 | .227 | .217 | .207 |
| 7 | .354 | .333 | .314 | .296 | .279 | .263 | .249 | .235 | .222 | .210 | .198 | .188 | .178 | .168 | .159 |
| 8 | .305 | .285 | .266 | .249 | .233 | .218 | .204 | .191 | .179 | .168 | .157 | .148 | .139 | .130 | .123 |
| 9 | .263 | .243 | .225 | .209 | .194 | .180 | .167 | .155 | .144 | .134 | .125 | .116 | .108 | .101 | .094 |
| 10 | .227 | .208 | .191 | .176 | .162 | .149 | .137 | .126 | .116 | .107 | .099 | .092 | .085 | .078 | .073 |
| 11 | .195 | .178 | .162 | .148 | .135 | .123 | .112 | .103 | .094 | .086 | .079 | .072 | .066 | .061 | .056 |
| 12 | .168 | .152 | .137 | .124 | .112 | .102 | .092 | .083 | .076 | .069 | .062 | .057 | .052 | .047 | .043 |
| 13 | .145 | .130 | .116 | .104 | .093 | .084 | .075 | .068 | .061 | .055 | .050 | .045 | .040 | .037 | .033 |
| 14 | .125 | .111 | .099 | .088 | .078 | .069 | .062 | .055 | .049 | .044 | .039 | .035 | .032 | .028 | .025 |
| 15 | .108 | .095 | .084 | .074 | .065 | .057 | .051 | .045 | .040 | .035 | .031 | .028 | .025 | .022 | .020 |
| 16 | .093 | .081 | .071 | .062 | .054 | .047 | .042 | .036 | .032 | .028 | .025 | .022 | .019 | .017 | .015 |
| 17 | .080 | .069 | .060 | .052 | .045 | .039 | .034 | .030 | .026 | .023 | .020 | .017 | .015 | .013 | .012 |
| 18 | .069 | .059 | .051 | .044 | .038 | .032 | .028 | .024 | .021 | .018 | .016 | .014 | .012 | .010 | .009 |
| 19 | .060 | .051 | .043 | .037 | .031 | .027 | .023 | .020 | .017 | .014 | .012 | .011 | .009 | .008 | .007 |
| 20 | .051 | .043 | .037 | .031 | .026 | .022 | .019 | .016 | .014 | .012 | .010 | .008 | .007 | .006 | .005 |
| 25 | .024 | .020 | .016 | .013 | .010 | .009 | .007 | .006 | .005 | .004 | .003 | .003 | .002 | .002 | .001 |
| 30 | .012 | .009 | .007 | .005 | .004 | .003 | .003 | .002 | .002 | .001 | .001 | .001 | .001 | .000 | .000 |

*E.g.:* If the interest rate is 10 per cent per year, the present value of $1 received at year 5 is $0.621.

## APPENDIX TABLE 2

Future value of $1 after $t$ years $= (1 + r)^t$

| Number of years | \multicolumn{15}{c}{Interest rate per year} |
|---|---|---|---|---|---|---|---|---|---|---|---|---|---|---|---|
| | 1% | 2% | 3% | 4% | 5% | 6% | 7% | 8% | 9% | 10% | 11% | 12% | 13% | 14% | 15% |
| 1 | 1.010 | 1.020 | 1.030 | 1.040 | 1.050 | 1.060 | 1.070 | 1.080 | 1.090 | 1.100 | 1.110 | 1.120 | 1.130 | 1.140 | 1.150 |
| 2 | 1.020 | 1.040 | 1.061 | 1.082 | 1.102 | 1.124 | 1.145 | 1.166 | 1.188 | 1.210 | 1.232 | 1.254 | 1.277 | 1.300 | 1.323 |
| 3 | 1.030 | 1.061 | 1.093 | 1.125 | 1.158 | 1.191 | 1.225 | 1.260 | 1.295 | 1.331 | 1.368 | 1.405 | 1.443 | 1.482 | 1.521 |
| 4 | 1.041 | 1.082 | 1.126 | 1.170 | 1.216 | 1.262 | 1.311 | 1.360 | 1.412 | 1.464 | 1.518 | 1.574 | 1.630 | 1.689 | 1.749 |
| 5 | 1.051 | 1.104 | 1.159 | 1.217 | 1.276 | 1.338 | 1.403 | 1.469 | 1.539 | 1.611 | 1.685 | 1.762 | 1.842 | 1.925 | 2.011 |
| 6 | 1.062 | 1.126 | 1.194 | 1.265 | 1.340 | 1.419 | 1.501 | 1.587 | 1.677 | 1.772 | 1.870 | 1.974 | 2.082 | 2.195 | 2.313 |
| 7 | 1.072 | 1.149 | 1.230 | 1.316 | 1.407 | 1.504 | 1.606 | 1.714 | 1.828 | 1.949 | 2.076 | 2.211 | 2.353 | 2.502 | 2.660 |
| 8 | 1.083 | 1.172 | 1.267 | 1.369 | 1.477 | 1.594 | 1.718 | 1.851 | 1.993 | 2.144 | 2.305 | 2.476 | 2.658 | 2.853 | 3.059 |
| 9 | 1.094 | 1.195 | 1.305 | 1.423 | 1.551 | 1.689 | 1.838 | 1.999 | 2.172 | 2.358 | 2.558 | 2.773 | 3.004 | 3.252 | 3.518 |
| 10 | 1.105 | 1.219 | 1.344 | 1.480 | 1.629 | 1.791 | 1.967 | 2.159 | 2.367 | 2.594 | 2.839 | 3.106 | 3.395 | 3.707 | 4.046 |
| 11 | 1.116 | 1.243 | 1.384 | 1.539 | 1.710 | 1.898 | 2.105 | 2.332 | 2.580 | 2.853 | 3.152 | 3.479 | 3.836 | 4.226 | 4.652 |
| 12 | 1.127 | 1.268 | 1.426 | 1.601 | 1.796 | 2.012 | 2.252 | 2.518 | 2.813 | 3.138 | 3.498 | 3.896 | 4.335 | 4.818 | 5.350 |
| 13 | 1.138 | 1.294 | 1.469 | 1.665 | 1.886 | 2.133 | 2.410 | 2.720 | 3.066 | 3.452 | 3.883 | 4.363 | 4.898 | 5.492 | 6.153 |
| 14 | 1.149 | 1.319 | 1.513 | 1.732 | 1.980 | 2.261 | 2.579 | 2.937 | 3.342 | 3.797 | 4.310 | 4.887 | 5.535 | 6.261 | 7.076 |
| 15 | 1.161 | 1.346 | 1.558 | 1.801 | 2.079 | 2.397 | 2.759 | 3.172 | 3.642 | 4.177 | 4.785 | 5.474 | 6.254 | 7.138 | 8.137 |
| 16 | 1.173 | 1.373 | 1.605 | 1.873 | 2.183 | 2.540 | 2.952 | 3.426 | 3.970 | 4.595 | 5.311 | 6.130 | 7.067 | 8.137 | 9.358 |
| 17 | 1.184 | 1.400 | 1.653 | 1.948 | 2.292 | 2.693 | 3.159 | 3.700 | 4.328 | 5.054 | 5.895 | 6.866 | 7.986 | 9.276 | 10.76 |
| 18 | 1.196 | 1.428 | 1.702 | 2.026 | 2.407 | 2.854 | 3.380 | 3.996 | 4.717 | 5.560 | 6.544 | 7.690 | 9.024 | 10.58 | 12.38 |
| 19 | 1.208 | 1.457 | 1.754 | 2.107 | 2.527 | 3.026 | 3.617 | 4.316 | 5.142 | 6.116 | 7.263 | 8.613 | 10.20 | 12.06 | 14.23 |
| 20 | 1.220 | 1.486 | 1.806 | 2.191 | 2.653 | 3.207 | 3.870 | 4.661 | 5.604 | 6.727 | 8.062 | 9.646 | 11.52 | 13.74 | 16.37 |
| 25 | 1.282 | 1.641 | 2.094 | 2.666 | 3.386 | 4.292 | 5.427 | 6.848 | 8.623 | 10.83 | 13.59 | 17.00 | 21.23 | 26.46 | 32.92 |
| 30 | 1.348 | 1.811 | 2.427 | 3.243 | 4.322 | 5.743 | 7.612 | 10.06 | 13.27 | 17.45 | 22.89 | 29.96 | 39.12 | 50.95 | 66.21 |

| | | | | | | Interest rate per year | | | | | | | | |
|---|---|---|---|---|---|---|---|---|---|---|---|---|---|---|
| Number of years | 16% | 17% | 18% | 19% | 20% | 21% | 22% | 23% | 24% | 25% | 26% | 27% | 28% | 29% | 30% |
| 1 | 1.160 | 1.170 | 1.180 | 1.190 | 1.200 | 1.210 | 1.220 | 1.230 | 1.240 | 1.250 | 1.260 | 1.270 | 1.280 | 1.290 | 1.300 |
| 2 | 1.346 | 1.369 | 1.392 | 1.416 | 1.440 | 1.464 | 1.488 | 1.513 | 1.538 | 1.563 | 1.588 | 1.613 | 1.638 | 1.664 | 1.690 |
| 3 | 1.561 | 1.602 | 1.643 | 1.685 | 1.728 | 1.772 | 1.816 | 1.861 | 1.907 | 1.953 | 2.000 | 2.048 | 2.097 | 2.147 | 2.197 |
| 4 | 1.811 | 1.874 | 1.939 | 2.005 | 2.074 | 2.144 | 2.215 | 2.289 | 2.364 | 2.441 | 2.520 | 2.601 | 2.684 | 2.769 | 2.856 |
| 5 | 2.100 | 2.192 | 2.288 | 2.386 | 2.488 | 2.594 | 2.703 | 2.815 | 2.932 | 3.052 | 3.176 | 3.304 | 3.436 | 3.572 | 3.713 |
| 6 | 2.436 | 2.565 | 2.700 | 2.840 | 2.986 | 3.138 | 3.297 | 3.463 | 3.635 | 3.815 | 4.002 | 4.196 | 4.398 | 4.608 | 4.827 |
| 7 | 2.826 | 3.001 | 3.185 | 3.379 | 3.583 | 3.797 | 4.023 | 4.259 | 4.508 | 4.768 | 5.042 | 5.329 | 5.629 | 5.945 | 6.275 |
| 8 | 3.278 | 3.511 | 3.759 | 4.021 | 4.300 | 4.595 | 4.908 | 5.239 | 5.590 | 5.960 | 6.353 | 6.768 | 7.206 | 7.669 | 8.157 |
| 9 | 3.803 | 4.108 | 4.435 | 4.785 | 5.160 | 5.560 | 5.987 | 6.444 | 6.931 | 7.451 | 8.005 | 8.595 | 9.223 | 9.893 | 10.60 |
| 10 | 4.411 | 4.807 | 5.234 | 5.695 | 6.192 | 6.728 | 7.305 | 7.926 | 8.594 | 9.313 | 10.09 | 10.92 | 11.81 | 12.76 | 13.79 |
| 11 | 5.117 | 5.624 | 6.176 | 6.777 | 7.430 | 8.140 | 8.912 | 9.749 | 10.66 | 11.64 | 12.71 | 13.86 | 15.11 | 16.46 | 17.92 |
| 12 | 5.936 | 6.580 | 7.288 | 8.064 | 8.916 | 9.850 | 10.87 | 11.99 | 13.21 | 14.55 | 16.01 | 17.61 | 19.34 | 21.24 | 23.30 |
| 13 | 6.886 | 7.699 | 8.599 | 9.596 | 10.70 | 11.92 | 13.26 | 14.75 | 16.39 | 18.19 | 20.18 | 22.36 | 24.76 | 27.39 | 30.29 |
| 14 | 7.988 | 9.007 | 10.15 | 11.42 | 12.84 | 14.42 | 16.18 | 18.14 | 20.32 | 22.74 | 25.42 | 28.40 | 31.69 | 35.34 | 39.37 |
| 15 | 9.266 | 10.54 | 11.97 | 13.59 | 15.41 | 17.45 | 19.74 | 22.31 | 25.20 | 28.42 | 32.03 | 36.06 | 40.56 | 45.59 | 51.19 |
| 16 | 10.75 | 12.33 | 14.13 | 16.17 | 18.49 | 21.11 | 24.09 | 27.45 | 31.24 | 35.53 | 40.36 | 45.80 | 51.92 | 58.81 | 66.54 |
| 17 | 12.47 | 14.43 | 16.67 | 19.24 | 22.19 | 25.55 | 29.38 | 33.76 | 38.74 | 44.41 | 50.85 | 58.17 | 66.46 | 75.86 | 86.50 |
| 18 | 14.46 | 16.88 | 19.67 | 22.90 | 26.62 | 30.91 | 35.85 | 41.52 | 48.04 | 55.51 | 64.07 | 73.87 | 85.07 | 97.86 | 112.5 |
| 19 | 16.78 | 19.75 | 23.21 | 27.25 | 31.95 | 37.40 | 43.74 | 51.07 | 59.57 | 69.39 | 80.73 | 93.81 | 108.9 | 126.2 | 146.2 |
| 20 | 19.46 | 23.11 | 27.39 | 32.43 | 38.34 | 45.26 | 53.36 | 62.82 | 73.86 | 86.74 | 101.7 | 119.1 | 139.4 | 162.9 | 190.0 |
| 25 | 40.87 | 50.66 | 62.67 | 77.39 | 95.40 | 117.4 | 144.2 | 176.9 | 216.5 | 264.7 | 323.0 | 393.6 | 478.9 | 581.8 | 705.6 |
| 30 | 85.85 | 111.1 | 143.4 | 184.7 | 237.4 | 304.5 | 389.8 | 497.9 | 634.8 | 807.8 | 1026 | 1301 | 1646 | 2078 | 2620 |

*E.g.*: If the interest rate is 10 per cent per year, the investment of $1 today will be worth $1.611 at year 5.

# APPENDIX TABLE 3

Annuity table. Present value of $1 per year for each of $t$ years $= 1/r - 1/[r(1+r)^t]$

**Interest rate per year**

| Number of years | 1% | 2% | 3% | 4% | 5% | 6% | 7% | 8% | 9% | 10% | 11% | 12% | 13% | 14% | 15% |
|---|---|---|---|---|---|---|---|---|---|---|---|---|---|---|---|
| 1 | .990 | .980 | .971 | .962 | .952 | .943 | .935 | .926 | .917 | .909 | .901 | .893 | .885 | .877 | .870 |
| 2 | 1.970 | 1.942 | 1.913 | 1.886 | 1.859 | 1.833 | 1.808 | 1.783 | 1.759 | 1.736 | 1.713 | 1.690 | 1.668 | 1.647 | 1.626 |
| 3 | 2.941 | 2.884 | 2.829 | 2.775 | 2.723 | 2.673 | 2.624 | 2.577 | 2.531 | 2.487 | 2.444 | 2.402 | 2.361 | 2.322 | 2.283 |
| 4 | 3.902 | 3.808 | 3.717 | 3.630 | 3.546 | 3.465 | 3.387 | 3.312 | 3.240 | 3.170 | 3.102 | 3.037 | 2.974 | 2.914 | 2.855 |
| 5 | 4.853 | 4.713 | 4.580 | 4.452 | 4.329 | 4.212 | 4.100 | 3.993 | 3.890 | 3.791 | 3.696 | 3.605 | 3.517 | 3.433 | 3.352 |
| 6 | 5.795 | 5.601 | 5.417 | 5.242 | 5.076 | 4.917 | 4.767 | 4.623 | 4.486 | 4.355 | 4.231 | 4.111 | 3.998 | 3.889 | 3.784 |
| 7 | 6.728 | 6.472 | 6.230 | 6.002 | 5.786 | 5.582 | 5.389 | 5.206 | 5.033 | 4.868 | 4.712 | 4.564 | 4.423 | 4.288 | 4.160 |
| 8 | 7.652 | 7.325 | 7.020 | 6.733 | 6.463 | 6.210 | 5.971 | 5.747 | 5.535 | 5.335 | 5.146 | 4.968 | 4.799 | 4.639 | 4.487 |
| 9 | 8.566 | 8.162 | 7.786 | 7.435 | 7.108 | 6.802 | 6.515 | 6.247 | 5.995 | 5.759 | 5.537 | 5.328 | 5.132 | 4.946 | 4.772 |
| 10 | 9.471 | 8.983 | 8.530 | 8.111 | 7.722 | 7.360 | 7.024 | 6.710 | 6.418 | 6.145 | 5.889 | 5.650 | 5.426 | 5.216 | 5.019 |
| 11 | 10.37 | 9.787 | 9.253 | 8.760 | 8.306 | 7.887 | 7.499 | 7.139 | 6.805 | 6.495 | 6.207 | 5.938 | 5.687 | 5.453 | 5.234 |
| 12 | 11.26 | 10.58 | 9.954 | 9.385 | 8.863 | 8.384 | 7.943 | 7.536 | 7.161 | 6.814 | 6.492 | 6.194 | 5.918 | 5.660 | 5.421 |
| 13 | 12.13 | 11.35 | 10.63 | 9.986 | 9.394 | 8.853 | 8.358 | 7.904 | 7.487 | 7.103 | 6.750 | 6.424 | 6.122 | 5.842 | 5.583 |
| 14 | 13.00 | 12.11 | 11.30 | 10.56 | 9.899 | 9.295 | 8.745 | 8.244 | 7.786 | 7.367 | 6.982 | 6.628 | 6.302 | 6.002 | 5.724 |
| 15 | 13.87 | 12.85 | 11.94 | 11.12 | 10.38 | 9.712 | 9.108 | 8.559 | 8.061 | 7.606 | 7.191 | 6.811 | 6.462 | 6.142 | 5.847 |
| 16 | 14.72 | 13.58 | 12.56 | 11.65 | 10.84 | 10.11 | 9.447 | 8.851 | 8.313 | 7.824 | 7.379 | 6.974 | 6.604 | 6.265 | 5.954 |
| 17 | 15.56 | 14.29 | 13.17 | 12.17 | 11.27 | 10.48 | 9.763 | 9.122 | 8.544 | 8.022 | 7.549 | 7.120 | 6.729 | 6.373 | 6.047 |
| 18 | 16.40 | 14.99 | 13.75 | 12.66 | 11.69 | 10.83 | 10.06 | 9.372 | 8.756 | 8.201 | 7.702 | 7.250 | 6.840 | 6.467 | 6.128 |
| 19 | 17.23 | 15.68 | 14.32 | 13.13 | 12.09 | 11.16 | 10.34 | 9.604 | 8.950 | 8.365 | 7.839 | 7.366 | 6.938 | 6.550 | 6.198 |
| 20 | 18.05 | 16.35 | 14.88 | 13.59 | 12.46 | 11.47 | 10.59 | 9.818 | 9.129 | 8.514 | 7.963 | 7.469 | 7.025 | 6.623 | 6.259 |
| 25 | 22.02 | 19.52 | 17.41 | 15.62 | 14.09 | 12.78 | 11.65 | 10.67 | 9.823 | 9.077 | 8.422 | 7.843 | 7.330 | 6.873 | 6.464 |
| 30 | 25.81 | 22.40 | 19.60 | 17.29 | 15.37 | 13.76 | 12.41 | 11.26 | 10.27 | 9.427 | 8.694 | 8.055 | 7.496 | 7.003 | 6.566 |

## Interest rate per year

| Number of years | 16% | 17% | 18% | 19% | 20% | 21% | 22% | 23% | 24% | 25% | 26% | 27% | 28% | 29% | 30% |
|---|---|---|---|---|---|---|---|---|---|---|---|---|---|---|---|
| 1 | .862 | .855 | .847 | .840 | .833 | .826 | .820 | .813 | .806 | .800 | .794 | .787 | .781 | .775 | .769 |
| 2 | 1.605 | 1.585 | 1.566 | 1.547 | 1.528 | 1.509 | 1.492 | 1.474 | 1.457 | 1.440 | 1.424 | 1.407 | 1.392 | 1.376 | 1.361 |
| 3 | 2.246 | 2.210 | 2.174 | 2.140 | 2.106 | 2.074 | 2.042 | 2.011 | 1.981 | 1.952 | 1.923 | 1.896 | 1.868 | 1.842 | 1.816 |
| 4 | 2.798 | 2.743 | 2.690 | 2.639 | 2.589 | 2.540 | 2.494 | 2.448 | 2.404 | 2.362 | 2.320 | 2.280 | 2.241 | 2.203 | 2.166 |
| 5 | 3.274 | 3.199 | 3.127 | 3.058 | 2.991 | 2.926 | 2.864 | 2.803 | 2.745 | 2.689 | 2.635 | 2.583 | 2.532 | 2.483 | 2.436 |
| 6 | 3.685 | 3.589 | 3.498 | 3.410 | 3.326 | 3.245 | 3.167 | 3.092 | 3.020 | 2.951 | 2.885 | 2.821 | 2.759 | 2.700 | 2.643 |
| 7 | 4.039 | 3.922 | 3.812 | 3.706 | 3.605 | 3.508 | 3.416 | 3.327 | 3.242 | 3.161 | 3.083 | 3.009 | 2.937 | 2.868 | 2.802 |
| 8 | 4.344 | 4.207 | 4.078 | 3.954 | 3.837 | 3.726 | 3.619 | 3.518 | 3.421 | 3.329 | 3.241 | 3.156 | 3.076 | 2.999 | 2.925 |
| 9 | 4.607 | 4.451 | 4.303 | 4.163 | 4.031 | 3.905 | 3.786 | 3.673 | 3.566 | 3.463 | 3.366 | 3.273 | 3.184 | 3.100 | 3.019 |
| 10 | 4.833 | 4.659 | 4.494 | 4.339 | 4.192 | 4.054 | 3.923 | 3.799 | 3.682 | 3.571 | 3.465 | 3.364 | 3.269 | 3.178 | 3.092 |
| 11 | 5.029 | 4.836 | 4.656 | 4.486 | 4.327 | 4.177 | 4.035 | 3.902 | 3.776 | 3.656 | 3.543 | 3.437 | 3.335 | 3.239 | 3.147 |
| 12 | 5.197 | 4.988 | 4.793 | 4.611 | 4.439 | 4.278 | 4.127 | 3.985 | 3.851 | 3.725 | 3.606 | 3.493 | 3.387 | 3.286 | 3.190 |
| 13 | 5.342 | 5.118 | 4.910 | 4.715 | 4.533 | 4.362 | 4.203 | 4.053 | 3.912 | 3.780 | 3.656 | 3.538 | 3.427 | 3.322 | 3.223 |
| 14 | 5.468 | 5.229 | 5.008 | 4.802 | 4.611 | 4.432 | 4.265 | 4.108 | 3.962 | 3.824 | 3.695 | 3.573 | 3.459 | 3.351 | 3.249 |
| 15 | 5.575 | 5.324 | 5.092 | 4.876 | 4.675 | 4.489 | 4.315 | 4.153 | 4.001 | 3.859 | 3.726 | 3.601 | 3.483 | 3.373 | 3.268 |
| 16 | 5.668 | 5.405 | 5.162 | 4.938 | 4.730 | 4.536 | 4.357 | 4.189 | 4.033 | 3.887 | 3.751 | 3.623 | 3.503 | 3.390 | 3.283 |
| 17 | 5.749 | 5.475 | 5.222 | 4.990 | 4.775 | 4.576 | 4.391 | 4.219 | 4.059 | 3.910 | 3.771 | 3.640 | 3.518 | 3.403 | 3.295 |
| 18 | 5.818 | 5.534 | 5.273 | 5.033 | 4.812 | 4.608 | 4.419 | 4.243 | 4.080 | 3.928 | 3.786 | 3.654 | 3.529 | 3.413 | 3.304 |
| 19 | 5.877 | 5.584 | 5.316 | 5.070 | 4.843 | 4.635 | 4.442 | 4.263 | 4.097 | 3.942 | 3.799 | 3.664 | 3.539 | 3.421 | 3.311 |
| 20 | 5.929 | 5.628 | 5.353 | 5.101 | 4.870 | 4.657 | 4.460 | 4.279 | 4.110 | 3.954 | 3.808 | 3.673 | 3.546 | 3.427 | 3.316 |
| 25 | 6.097 | 5.766 | 5.467 | 5.195 | 4.948 | 4.721 | 4.514 | 4.323 | 4.147 | 3.985 | 3.834 | 3.694 | 3.564 | 3.442 | 3.329 |
| 30 | 6.177 | 5.829 | 5.517 | 5.235 | 4.979 | 4.746 | 4.534 | 4.339 | 4.160 | 3.995 | 3.842 | 3.701 | 3.569 | 3.447 | 3.332 |

*E.g.:* If the interest rate is 10 per cent per year, the present value of $1 received in each of the next 5 years is $3.791.

# APPENDIX TABLE 4

Values of $e^{rt}$: Future value of $1 invested at a continuously compounded rate $r$ for $t$ years

| rt | .00 | .01 | .02 | .03 | .04 | .05 | .06 | .07 | .08 | .09 |
|----|------|------|------|------|------|------|------|------|------|------|
| .00 | 1.000 | 1.010 | 1.020 | 1.030 | 1.041 | 1.051 | 1.062 | 1.073 | 1.083 | 1.094 |
| .10 | 1.105 | 1.116 | 1.127 | 1.139 | 1.150 | 1.162 | 1.174 | 1.185 | 1.197 | 1.209 |
| .20 | 1.221 | 1.234 | 1.246 | 1.259 | 1.271 | 1.284 | 1.297 | 1.310 | 1.323 | 1.336 |
| .30 | 1.350 | 1.363 | 1.377 | 1.391 | 1.405 | 1.419 | 1.433 | 1.448 | 1.462 | 1.477 |
| .40 | 1.492 | 1.507 | 1.522 | 1.537 | 1.553 | 1.568 | 1.584 | 1.600 | 1.616 | 1.632 |
| .50 | 1.649 | 1.665 | 1.682 | 1.699 | 1.716 | 1.733 | 1.751 | 1.768 | 1.786 | 1.804 |
| .60 | 1.822 | 1.840 | 1.859 | 1.878 | 1.896 | 1.916 | 1.935 | 1.954 | 1.974 | 1.994 |
| .70 | 2.014 | 2.034 | 2.054 | 2.075 | 2.096 | 2.117 | 2.138 | 2.160 | 2.181 | 2.203 |
| .80 | 2.226 | 2.248 | 2.271 | 2.293 | 2.316 | 2.340 | 2.363 | 2.387 | 2.411 | 2.435 |
| .90 | 2.460 | 2.484 | 2.509 | 2.535 | 2.560 | 2.586 | 2.612 | 2.638 | 2.664 | 2.691 |
| 1.00 | 2.718 | 2.746 | 2.773 | 2.801 | 2.829 | 2.858 | 2.886 | 2.915 | 2.945 | 2.974 |
| 1.10 | 3.004 | 3.034 | 3.065 | 3.096 | 3.127 | 3.158 | 3.190 | 3.222 | 3.254 | 3.287 |
| 1.20 | 3.320 | 3.353 | 3.387 | 3.421 | 3.456 | 3.490 | 3.525 | 3.561 | 3.597 | 3.633 |
| 1.30 | 3.669 | 3.706 | 3.743 | 3.781 | 3.819 | 3.857 | 3.896 | 3.935 | 3.975 | 4.015 |
| 1.40 | 4.055 | 4.096 | 4.137 | 4.179 | 4.221 | 4.263 | 4.306 | 4.349 | 4.393 | 4.437 |
| 1.50 | 4.482 | 4.527 | 4.572 | 4.618 | 4.665 | 4.711 | 4.759 | 4.807 | 4.855 | 4.904 |
| 1.60 | 4.953 | 5.003 | 5.053 | 5.104 | 5.155 | 5.207 | 5.259 | 5.312 | 5.366 | 5.419 |
| 1.70 | 5.474 | 5.529 | 5.585 | 5.641 | 5.697 | 5.755 | 5.812 | 5.871 | 5.930 | 5.989 |
| 1.80 | 6.050 | 6.110 | 6.172 | 6.234 | 6.297 | 6.360 | 6.424 | 6.488 | 6.553 | 6.619 |
| 1.90 | 6.686 | 6.753 | 6.821 | 6.890 | 6.959 | 7.029 | 7.099 | 7.171 | 7.243 | 7.316 |

| rt | .00 | .01 | .02 | .03 | .04 | .05 | .06 | .07 | .08 | .09 |
|---|---|---|---|---|---|---|---|---|---|---|
| 2.00 | 7.389 | 7.463 | 7.538 | 7.614 | 7.691 | 7.768 | 7.846 | 7.925 | 8.004 | 8.085 |
| 2.10 | 8.166 | 8.248 | 8.331 | 8.415 | 8.499 | 8.585 | 8.671 | 8.758 | 8.846 | 8.935 |
| 2.20 | 9.025 | 9.116 | 9.207 | 9.300 | 9.393 | 9.488 | 9.583 | 9.679 | 9.777 | 9.875 |
| 2.30 | 9.974 | 10.07 | 10.18 | 10.28 | 10.38 | 10.49 | 10.59 | 10.70 | 10.80 | 10.91 |
| 2.40 | 11.02 | 11.13 | 11.25 | 11.36 | 11.47 | 11.59 | 11.70 | 11.82 | 11.94 | 12.06 |
| 2.50 | 12.18 | 12.30 | 12.43 | 12.55 | 12.68 | 12.81 | 12.94 | 13.07 | 13.20 | 13.33 |
| 2.60 | 13.46 | 13.60 | 13.74 | 13.87 | 14.01 | 14.15 | 14.30 | 14.44 | 14.59 | 14.73 |
| 2.70 | 14.88 | 15.03 | 15.18 | 15.33 | 15.49 | 15.64 | 15.80 | 15.96 | 16.12 | 16.28 |
| 2.80 | 16.44 | 16.61 | 16.78 | 16.95 | 17.12 | 17.29 | 17.46 | 17.64 | 17.81 | 17.99 |
| 2.90 | 18.17 | 18.36 | 18.54 | 18.73 | 18.92 | 19.11 | 19.30 | 19.49 | 19.69 | 19.89 |
| 3.00 | 20.09 | 20.29 | 20.49 | 20.70 | 20.91 | 21.12 | 21.33 | 21.54 | 21.76 | 21.98 |
| 3.10 | 22.20 | 22.42 | 22.65 | 22.87 | 23.10 | 23.34 | 23.57 | 23.81 | 24.05 | 24.29 |
| 3.20 | 24.53 | 24.78 | 25.03 | 25.28 | 25.53 | 25.79 | 26.05 | 26.31 | 26.58 | 26.84 |
| 3.30 | 27.11 | 27.39 | 27.66 | 27.94 | 28.22 | 28.50 | 28.79 | 29.08 | 29.37 | 29.67 |
| 3.40 | 29.96 | 30.27 | 30.57 | 30.88 | 31.19 | 31.50 | 31.82 | 32.14 | 32.46 | 32.79 |
| 3.50 | 33.12 | 33.45 | 33.78 | 34.12 | 34.47 | 34.81 | 35.16 | 35.52 | 35.87 | 36.23 |
| 3.60 | 36.60 | 36.97 | 37.34 | 37.71 | 38.09 | 38.47 | 38.86 | 39.25 | 39.65 | 40.04 |
| 3.70 | 40.45 | 40.85 | 41.26 | 41.68 | 42.10 | 42.52 | 42.95 | 43.38 | 43.82 | 44.26 |
| 3.80 | 44.70 | 45.15 | 45.60 | 46.06 | 46.53 | 46.99 | 47.47 | 47.94 | 48.42 | 48.91 |
| 3.90 | 49.40 | 49.90 | 50.40 | 50.91 | 51.42 | 51.94 | 52.46 | 52.98 | 53.52 | 54.05 |

*E.g.*: If the continuously compounded interest rate is 10 per cent per year, the investment of $1 today will be worth $1.105 at year 1 and $1.221 at year 2.

# APPENDIX TABLE 5

Present value of $1 per year received in a continuous stream for each of $t$ years (discounted at an annually compounded rate $r$) $= \{1 - 1/[1 + r]^t\}/\{\ln[1 + r]\}$

| Number of years | Interest rate per year | | | | | | | | | | | | | | |
|---|---|---|---|---|---|---|---|---|---|---|---|---|---|---|---|
| | 1% | 2% | 3% | 4% | 5% | 6% | 7% | 8% | 9% | 10% | 11% | 12% | 13% | 14% | 15% |
| 1 | .995 | .990 | .985 | .981 | .976 | .971 | .967 | .962 | .958 | .954 | .950 | .945 | .941 | .937 | .933 |
| 2 | 1.980 | 1.961 | 1.942 | 1.924 | 1.906 | 1.888 | 1.871 | 1.854 | 1.837 | 1.821 | 1.805 | 1.790 | 1.774 | 1.759 | 1.745 |
| 3 | 2.956 | 2.913 | 2.871 | 2.830 | 2.791 | 2.752 | 2.715 | 2.679 | 2.644 | 2.609 | 2.576 | 2.543 | 2.512 | 2.481 | 2.450 |
| 4 | 3.922 | 3.846 | 3.773 | 3.702 | 3.634 | 3.568 | 3.504 | 3.443 | 3.383 | 3.326 | 3.270 | 3.216 | 3.164 | 3.113 | 3.064 |
| 5 | 4.878 | 4.760 | 4.648 | 4.540 | 4.437 | 4.337 | 4.242 | 4.150 | 4.062 | 3.977 | 3.896 | 3.817 | 3.741 | 3.668 | 3.598 |
| 6 | 5.825 | 5.657 | 5.498 | 5.346 | 5.202 | 5.063 | 4.931 | 4.805 | 4.685 | 4.570 | 4.459 | 4.353 | 4.252 | 4.155 | 4.062 |
| 7 | 6.762 | 6.536 | 6.323 | 6.121 | 5.930 | 5.748 | 5.576 | 5.412 | 5.256 | 5.108 | 4.967 | 4.832 | 4.704 | 4.582 | 4.465 |
| 8 | 7.690 | 7.398 | 7.124 | 6.867 | 6.623 | 6.394 | 6.178 | 5.974 | 5.780 | 5.597 | 5.424 | 5.260 | 5.104 | 4.956 | 4.816 |
| 9 | 8.609 | 8.243 | 7.902 | 7.583 | 7.284 | 7.004 | 6.741 | 6.494 | 6.261 | 6.042 | 5.836 | 5.642 | 5.458 | 5.285 | 5.121 |
| 10 | 9.519 | 9.072 | 8.657 | 8.272 | 7.913 | 7.579 | 7.267 | 6.975 | 6.702 | 6.447 | 6.208 | 5.983 | 5.772 | 5.573 | 5.386 |
| 11 | 10.42 | 9.884 | 9.391 | 8.935 | 8.512 | 8.121 | 7.758 | 7.421 | 7.107 | 6.815 | 6.542 | 6.287 | 6.049 | 5.826 | 5.617 |
| 12 | 11.31 | 10.68 | 10.10 | 9.572 | 9.083 | 8.633 | 8.218 | 7.834 | 7.478 | 7.149 | 6.843 | 6.559 | 6.294 | 6.048 | 5.818 |
| 13 | 12.19 | 11.46 | 10.79 | 10.18 | 9.627 | 9.116 | 8.647 | 8.216 | 7.819 | 7.453 | 7.115 | 6.802 | 6.512 | 6.242 | 5.992 |
| 14 | 13.07 | 12.23 | 11.46 | 10.77 | 10.14 | 9.571 | 9.048 | 8.570 | 8.131 | 7.729 | 7.359 | 7.018 | 6.704 | 6.413 | 6.144 |
| 15 | 13.93 | 12.98 | 12.12 | 11.34 | 10.64 | 10.00 | 9.423 | 8.897 | 8.418 | 7.980 | 7.579 | 7.212 | 6.874 | 6.563 | 6.276 |
| 16 | 14.79 | 13.71 | 12.75 | 11.88 | 11.11 | 10.41 | 9.774 | 9.201 | 8.681 | 8.209 | 7.778 | 7.385 | 7.024 | 6.694 | 6.390 |
| 17 | 15.64 | 14.43 | 13.36 | 12.41 | 11.55 | 10.79 | 10.10 | 9.482 | 8.923 | 8.416 | 7.957 | 7.539 | 7.158 | 6.809 | 6.490 |
| 18 | 16.48 | 15.14 | 13.96 | 12.91 | 11.98 | 11.15 | 10.41 | 9.742 | 9.144 | 8.605 | 8.118 | 7.676 | 7.275 | 6.910 | 6.577 |
| 19 | 17.31 | 15.83 | 14.54 | 13.39 | 12.39 | 11.49 | 10.69 | 9.983 | 9.347 | 8.777 | 8.263 | 7.799 | 7.380 | 6.999 | 6.652 |
| 20 | 18.14 | 16.51 | 15.10 | 13.86 | 12.77 | 11.81 | 10.96 | 10.21 | 9.533 | 8.932 | 8.394 | 7.909 | 7.472 | 7.077 | 6.718 |
| 25 | 22.13 | 19.72 | 17.67 | 15.93 | 14.44 | 13.16 | 12.06 | 11.10 | 10.26 | 9.524 | 8.877 | 8.305 | 7.797 | 7.344 | 6.938 |
| 30 | 25.94 | 22.62 | 19.89 | 17.64 | 15.75 | 14.17 | 12.84 | 11.70 | 10.73 | 9.891 | 9.164 | 8.529 | 7.973 | 7.482 | 7.047 |

## Interest rate per year

| Number of years | 16% | 17% | 18% | 19% | 20% | 21% | 22% | 23% | 24% | 25% | 26% | 27% | 28% | 29% | 30% |
|---|---|---|---|---|---|---|---|---|---|---|---|---|---|---|---|
| 1 | .929 | .925 | .922 | .918 | .914 | .910 | .907 | .903 | .900 | .896 | .893 | .889 | .886 | .883 | .880 |
| 2 | 1.730 | 1.716 | 1.703 | 1.689 | 1.676 | 1.663 | 1.650 | 1.638 | 1.625 | 1.613 | 1.601 | 1.590 | 1.578 | 1.567 | 1.556 |
| 3 | 2.421 | 2.392 | 2.365 | 2.337 | 2.311 | 2.285 | 2.259 | 2.235 | 2.211 | 2.187 | 2.164 | 2.141 | 2.119 | 2.098 | 2.077 |
| 4 | 3.016 | 2.970 | 2.925 | 2.882 | 2.840 | 2.799 | 2.759 | 2.720 | 2.682 | 2.646 | 2.610 | 2.576 | 2.542 | 2.509 | 2.477 |
| 5 | 3.530 | 3.464 | 3.401 | 3.340 | 3.281 | 3.223 | 3.168 | 3.115 | 3.063 | 3.013 | 2.964 | 2.917 | 2.872 | 2.828 | 2.785 |
| 6 | 3.972 | 3.886 | 3.804 | 3.724 | 3.648 | 3.574 | 3.504 | 3.436 | 3.370 | 3.307 | 3.246 | 3.187 | 3.130 | 3.075 | 3.022 |
| 7 | 4.354 | 4.247 | 4.145 | 4.048 | 3.954 | 3.865 | 3.779 | 3.696 | 3.617 | 3.542 | 3.469 | 3.399 | 3.331 | 3.266 | 3.204 |
| 8 | 4.682 | 4.555 | 4.434 | 4.319 | 4.209 | 4.104 | 4.004 | 3.909 | 3.817 | 3.730 | 3.646 | 3.566 | 3.489 | 3.415 | 3.344 |
| 9 | 4.966 | 4.819 | 4.680 | 4.547 | 4.422 | 4.302 | 4.189 | 4.081 | 3.978 | 3.880 | 3.786 | 3.697 | 3.612 | 3.530 | 3.452 |
| 10 | 5.210 | 5.044 | 4.887 | 4.739 | 4.599 | 4.466 | 4.340 | 4.221 | 4.108 | 4.000 | 3.898 | 3.801 | 3.708 | 3.619 | 3.535 |
| 11 | 5.421 | 5.237 | 5.063 | 4.900 | 4.747 | 4.602 | 4.465 | 4.335 | 4.213 | 4.096 | 3.986 | 3.882 | 3.783 | 3.689 | 3.599 |
| 12 | 5.603 | 5.401 | 5.213 | 5.036 | 4.870 | 4.713 | 4.566 | 4.428 | 4.297 | 4.173 | 4.057 | 3.946 | 3.841 | 3.742 | 3.648 |
| 13 | 5.759 | 5.542 | 5.339 | 5.150 | 4.972 | 4.806 | 4.650 | 4.503 | 4.365 | 4.235 | 4.112 | 3.997 | 3.887 | 3.784 | 3.686 |
| 14 | 5.894 | 5.662 | 5.446 | 5.245 | 5.058 | 4.882 | 4.718 | 4.564 | 4.420 | 4.284 | 4.157 | 4.036 | 3.923 | 3.816 | 3.715 |
| 15 | 6.010 | 5.765 | 5.537 | 5.326 | 5.129 | 4.945 | 4.774 | 4.614 | 4.464 | 4.324 | 4.192 | 4.068 | 3.951 | 3.841 | 3.737 |
| 16 | 6.111 | 5.853 | 5.614 | 5.393 | 5.188 | 4.998 | 4.820 | 4.655 | 4.500 | 4.355 | 4.220 | 4.092 | 3.973 | 3.860 | 3.754 |
| 17 | 6.197 | 5.928 | 5.679 | 5.450 | 5.238 | 5.041 | 4.858 | 4.687 | 4.529 | 4.381 | 4.242 | 4.112 | 3.990 | 3.875 | 3.767 |
| 18 | 6.272 | 5.992 | 5.735 | 5.498 | 5.279 | 5.076 | 4.889 | 4.714 | 4.552 | 4.401 | 4.259 | 4.127 | 4.003 | 3.887 | 3.778 |
| 19 | 6.336 | 6.047 | 5.781 | 5.538 | 5.313 | 5.106 | 4.914 | 4.736 | 4.571 | 4.417 | 4.273 | 4.139 | 4.014 | 3.896 | 3.785 |
| 20 | 6.391 | 6.094 | 5.821 | 5.571 | 5.342 | 5.130 | 4.935 | 4.754 | 4.586 | 4.430 | 4.284 | 4.149 | 4.022 | 3.903 | 3.791 |
| 25 | 6.573 | 6.244 | 5.945 | 5.674 | 5.427 | 5.201 | 4.994 | 4.803 | 4.627 | 4.464 | 4.314 | 4.173 | 4.042 | 3.920 | 3.806 |
| 30 | 6.659 | 6.312 | 6.000 | 5.718 | 5.462 | 5.229 | 5.016 | 4.821 | 4.641 | 4.476 | 4.323 | 4.181 | 4.048 | 3.925 | 3.810 |

E.g.: If the interest rate is 10 per cent per year, a continuous cash flow of $1 a year for each of 5 years is worth $3.977. A continuous flow of $1 in year 5 only is worth $3.977 − $3.326 = $0.651.

# APPENDIX TABLE 6

Call option values, per cent of share price

*Standard deviation times square root of time* (left axis)

| | Share price divided by PV (exercise price) | | | | | | | | | | | | | | | | | | |
|---|---|---|---|---|---|---|---|---|---|---|---|---|---|---|---|---|---|---|---|
| | .40 | .45 | .50 | .55 | .60 | .65 | .70 | .75 | .80 | .82 | .84 | .86 | .88 | .90 | .92 | .94 | .96 | .98 | 1.00 |
| .05 | .0 | .0 | .0 | .0 | .0 | .0 | .0 | .0 | .0 | .0 | .0 | .0 | .0 | .0 | .1 | .3 | .6 | 1.2 | 2.0 |
| .10 | .0 | .0 | .0 | .0 | .0 | .0 | .0 | .0 | .0 | .1 | .2 | .3 | .5 | .8 | 1.2 | 1.7 | 2.3 | 3.1 | 4.0 |
| .15 | .0 | .0 | .0 | .0 | .0 | .0 | .1 | .2 | .5 | .7 | 1.0 | 1.3 | 1.7 | 2.2 | 2.8 | 3.5 | 4.2 | 5.1 | 6.0 |
| .20 | .0 | .0 | .0 | .0 | .0 | .1 | .4 | .8 | 1.5 | 1.9 | 2.3 | 2.8 | 3.4 | 4.0 | 4.7 | 5.4 | 6.2 | 7.1 | 8.0 |
| .25 | .0 | .0 | .0 | .1 | .2 | .5 | 1.0 | 1.8 | 2.8 | 3.3 | 3.9 | 4.5 | 5.2 | 5.9 | 6.6 | 7.4 | 8.2 | 9.1 | 9.9 |
| .30 | .0 | .1 | .1 | .3 | .7 | 1.2 | 2.0 | 3.1 | 4.4 | 5.0 | 5.7 | 6.3 | 7.0 | 7.8 | 8.6 | 9.4 | 10.2 | 11.1 | 11.9 |
| .35 | .1 | .2 | .4 | .8 | 1.4 | 2.3 | 3.3 | 4.6 | 6.2 | 6.8 | 7.5 | 8.2 | 9.0 | 9.8 | 10.6 | 11.4 | 12.2 | 13.0 | 13.9 |
| .40 | .2 | .5 | .9 | 1.6 | 2.4 | 3.5 | 4.8 | 6.3 | 8.0 | 8.7 | 9.4 | 10.2 | 11.0 | 11.7 | 12.5 | 13.4 | 14.2 | 15.0 | 15.9 |
| .45 | .5 | 1.0 | 1.7 | 2.6 | 3.7 | 5.0 | 6.5 | 8.1 | 9.9 | 10.6 | 11.4 | 12.2 | 12.9 | 13.7 | 14.5 | 15.3 | 16.2 | 17.0 | 17.8 |
| .50 | 1.0 | 1.7 | 2.6 | 3.7 | 5.1 | 6.6 | 8.2 | 10.0 | 11.8 | 12.6 | 13.4 | 14.2 | 14.9 | 15.7 | 16.5 | 17.3 | 18.1 | 18.9 | 19.7 |
| .55 | 1.7 | 2.6 | 3.8 | 5.1 | 6.6 | 8.3 | 10.0 | 11.9 | 13.8 | 14.6 | 15.4 | 16.1 | 16.9 | 17.7 | 18.5 | 19.3 | 20.1 | 20.9 | 21.7 |
| .60 | 2.5 | 3.7 | 5.1 | 6.6 | 8.3 | 10.1 | 11.9 | 13.8 | 15.8 | 16.6 | 17.4 | 18.1 | 18.9 | 19.7 | 20.5 | 21.3 | 22.0 | 22.8 | 23.6 |
| .65 | 3.6 | 4.9 | 6.5 | 8.2 | 10.0 | 11.9 | 13.8 | 15.8 | 17.8 | 18.6 | 19.3 | 20.1 | 20.9 | 21.7 | 22.5 | 23.2 | 24.0 | 24.7 | 25.5 |
| .70 | 4.7 | 6.3 | 8.1 | 9.9 | 11.9 | 13.8 | 15.8 | 17.8 | 19.8 | 20.6 | 21.3 | 22.1 | 22.9 | 23.6 | 24.4 | 25.2 | 25.9 | 26.6 | 27.4 |
| .75 | 6.1 | 7.9 | 9.8 | 11.7 | 13.7 | 15.8 | 17.8 | 19.8 | 21.8 | 22.5 | 23.3 | 24.1 | 24.8 | 25.6 | 26.3 | 27.1 | 27.8 | 28.5 | 29.2 |
| .80 | 7.5 | 9.5 | 11.5 | 13.6 | 15.7 | 17.7 | 19.8 | 21.8 | 23.7 | 24.5 | 25.3 | 26.0 | 26.8 | 27.5 | 28.3 | 29.0 | 29.7 | 30.4 | 31.1 |
| .85 | 9.1 | 11.2 | 13.3 | 15.5 | 17.6 | 19.7 | 21.8 | 23.8 | 25.7 | 26.5 | 27.2 | 28.0 | 28.7 | 29.4 | 30.2 | 30.9 | 31.6 | 32.2 | 32.9 |
| .90 | 10.7 | 13.0 | 15.2 | 17.4 | 19.6 | 21.7 | 23.8 | 25.8 | 27.7 | 28.4 | 29.2 | 29.9 | 30.6 | 31.3 | 32.0 | 32.7 | 33.4 | 34.1 | 34.7 |
| .95 | 12.5 | 14.8 | 17.1 | 19.4 | 21.6 | 23.7 | 25.7 | 27.7 | 29.6 | 30.4 | 31.1 | 31.8 | 32.5 | 33.2 | 33.9 | 34.6 | 35.2 | 35.9 | 36.5 |
| 1.00 | 14.3 | 16.7 | 19.1 | 21.4 | 23.6 | 25.7 | 27.7 | 29.7 | 31.6 | 32.3 | 33.0 | 33.7 | 34.4 | 35.1 | 35.7 | 36.4 | 37.0 | 37.7 | 38.3 |
| 1.05 | 16.1 | 18.6 | 21.0 | 23.3 | 25.6 | 27.7 | 29.7 | 31.6 | 33.5 | 34.2 | 34.9 | 35.6 | 36.2 | 36.9 | 37.6 | 38.2 | 38.8 | 39.4 | 40.0 |
| 1.10 | 18.0 | 20.6 | 23.0 | 25.3 | 27.5 | 29.6 | 31.6 | 33.5 | 35.4 | 36.1 | 36.7 | 37.4 | 38.1 | 38.7 | 39.3 | 40.0 | 40.6 | 41.2 | 41.8 |
| 1.15 | 20.0 | 22.5 | 25.0 | 27.3 | 29.5 | 31.6 | 33.6 | 35.4 | 37.2 | 37.9 | 38.6 | 39.2 | 39.9 | 40.5 | 41.1 | 41.7 | 42.3 | 42.9 | 43.5 |
| 1.20 | 21.9 | 24.5 | 27.0 | 29.3 | 31.5 | 33.6 | 35.5 | 37.3 | 39.1 | 39.7 | 40.4 | 41.0 | 41.7 | 42.3 | 42.9 | 43.5 | 44.0 | 44.6 | 45.1 |
| 1.25 | 23.9 | 26.5 | 29.0 | 31.3 | 33.5 | 35.5 | 37.4 | 39.2 | 40.9 | 41.5 | 42.2 | 42.8 | 43.4 | 44.0 | 44.6 | 45.2 | 45.7 | 46.3 | 46.8 |
| 1.30 | 25.9 | 28.5 | 31.0 | 33.3 | 35.4 | 37.4 | 39.3 | 41.0 | 42.7 | 43.3 | 43.9 | 44.5 | 45.1 | 45.7 | 46.3 | 46.8 | 47.4 | 47.9 | 48.4 |
| 1.35 | 27.9 | 30.5 | 33.0 | 35.2 | 37.3 | 39.3 | 41.1 | 42.8 | 44.4 | 45.1 | 45.7 | 46.3 | 46.8 | 47.4 | 47.9 | 48.5 | 49.0 | 49.5 | 50.0 |
| 1.40 | 29.9 | 32.5 | 34.9 | 37.1 | 39.2 | 41.1 | 42.9 | 44.6 | 46.2 | 46.8 | 47.4 | 47.9 | 48.5 | 49.0 | 49.6 | 50.1 | 50.6 | 51.1 | 51.6 |
| 1.45 | 31.9 | 34.5 | 36.9 | 39.1 | 41.1 | 43.0 | 44.7 | 46.4 | 47.9 | 48.5 | 49.0 | 49.6 | 50.1 | 50.7 | 51.2 | 51.7 | 52.2 | 52.7 | 53.2 |
| 1.50 | 33.8 | 36.4 | 38.8 | 40.9 | 42.9 | 44.8 | 46.5 | 48.1 | 49.6 | 50.1 | 50.7 | 51.2 | 51.8 | 52.3 | 52.8 | 53.3 | 53.7 | 54.2 | 54.7 |
| 1.55 | 35.8 | 38.4 | 40.7 | 42.8 | 44.8 | 46.6 | 48.2 | 49.8 | 51.2 | 51.8 | 52.3 | 52.8 | 53.3 | 53.8 | 54.3 | 54.8 | 55.3 | 55.7 | 56.2 |
| 1.60 | 37.8 | 40.3 | 42.6 | 44.6 | 46.5 | 48.3 | 49.9 | 51.4 | 52.8 | 53.4 | 53.9 | 54.4 | 54.9 | 55.4 | 55.9 | 56.3 | 56.8 | 57.2 | 57.6 |
| 1.65 | 39.7 | 42.2 | 44.4 | 46.4 | 48.3 | 50.0 | 51.6 | 53.1 | 54.4 | 54.9 | 55.4 | 55.9 | 56.4 | 56.9 | 57.3 | 57.8 | 58.2 | 58.6 | 59.1 |
| 1.70 | 41.6 | 44.0 | 46.2 | 48.2 | 50.0 | 51.7 | 53.2 | 54.7 | 56.0 | 56.5 | 57.0 | 57.5 | 57.9 | 58.4 | 58.8 | 59.2 | 59.7 | 60.1 | 60.5 |
| 1.75 | 43.5 | 45.9 | 48.0 | 50.0 | 51.7 | 53.4 | 54.8 | 56.2 | 57.5 | 58.0 | 58.5 | 58.9 | 59.4 | 59.8 | 60.2 | 60.7 | 61.1 | 61.5 | 61.8 |
| 2.00 | 52.5 | 54.6 | 56.5 | 58.2 | 59.7 | 61.1 | 62.4 | 63.6 | 64.6 | 65.0 | 65.4 | 65.8 | 66.2 | 66.6 | 66.9 | 67.3 | 67.6 | 67.9 | 68.3 |
| 2.25 | 60.7 | 62.5 | 64.1 | 65.6 | 66.8 | 68.0 | 69.1 | 70.0 | 70.9 | 71.3 | 71.6 | 71.9 | 72.2 | 72.5 | 72.8 | 73.1 | 73.4 | 73.7 | 73.9 |
| 2.50 | 67.9 | 69.4 | 70.8 | 72.0 | 73.1 | 74.0 | 74.9 | 75.7 | 76.4 | 76.7 | 77.0 | 77.2 | 77.5 | 77.7 | 78.0 | 78.2 | 78.4 | 78.7 | 78.9 |
| 2.75 | 74.2 | 75.4 | 76.6 | 77.5 | 78.4 | 79.2 | 79.9 | 80.5 | 81.1 | 81.4 | 81.6 | 81.8 | 82.0 | 82.2 | 82.4 | 82.6 | 82.7 | 82.9 | 83.1 |
| 3.00 | 79.5 | 80.5 | 81.4 | 82.2 | 82.9 | 83.5 | 84.1 | 84.6 | 85.1 | 85.3 | 85.4 | 85.6 | 85.8 | 85.9 | 86.1 | 86.2 | 86.4 | 86.5 | 86.6 |
| 3.50 | 87.6 | 88.3 | 88.8 | 89.3 | 89.7 | 90.1 | 90.5 | 90.8 | 91.1 | 91.2 | 91.3 | 91.4 | 91.5 | 91.6 | 91.6 | 91.7 | 91.8 | 91.9 | 92.0 |
| 4.00 | 92.9 | 93.3 | 93.6 | 93.9 | 94.2 | 94.4 | 94.6 | 94.8 | 94.9 | 95.0 | 95.0 | 95.1 | 95.2 | 95.2 | 95.3 | 95.3 | 95.4 | 95.4 | 95.4 |
| 4.50 | 96.2 | 96.4 | 96.6 | 96.7 | 96.9 | 97.0 | 97.1 | 97.2 | 97.3 | 97.3 | 97.3 | 97.4 | 97.4 | 97.4 | 97.5 | 97.5 | 97.5 | 97.5 | 97.6 |
| 5.00 | 98.1 | 98.2 | 98.3 | 98.3 | 98.4 | 98.5 | 98.5 | 98.6 | 98.6 | 98.6 | 98.6 | 98.7 | 98.7 | 98.7 | 98.7 | 98.7 | 98.7 | 98.7 | 98.8 |

*Note: Based on Black–Scholes model. To obtain corresponding European put values, add present value of exercise price and subtract share price.*

| Share price divided by PV (exercise price) | | | | | | | | | | | | | | | | | | | Standard deviation times square root of time |
|---|---|---|---|---|---|---|---|---|---|---|---|---|---|---|---|---|---|---|---|
| 1.02 | 1.04 | 1.06 | 1.08 | 1.10 | 1.12 | 1.14 | 1.16 | 1.18 | 1.20 | 1.25 | 1.30 | 1.35 | 1.40 | 1.45 | 1.50 | 1.75 | 2.00 | 2.50 | |
| 3.1 | 4.5 | 6.0 | 7.5 | 9.1 | 10.7 | 12.3 | 13.8 | 15.3 | 16.7 | 20.0 | 23.1 | 25.9 | 28.6 | 31.0 | 33.3 | 42.9 | 50.0 | 60.0 | .05 |
| 5.0 | 6.1 | 7.3 | 8.6 | 10.0 | 11.3 | 12.7 | 14.1 | 15.4 | 16.8 | 20.0 | 23.1 | 25.9 | 28.6 | 31.0 | 33.3 | 42.9 | 50.0 | 60.0 | .10 |
| 7.0 | 8.0 | 9.1 | 10.2 | 11.4 | 12.6 | 13.8 | 15.0 | 16.2 | 17.4 | 20.4 | 23.3 | 26.0 | 28.6 | 31.1 | 33.3 | 42.9 | 50.0 | 60.0 | .15 |
| 8.9 | 9.9 | 10.9 | 11.9 | 13.0 | 14.1 | 15.2 | 16.3 | 17.4 | 18.5 | 21.2 | 23.9 | 26.4 | 28.9 | 31.2 | 33.5 | 42.9 | 50.0 | 60.0 | .20 |
| 10.9 | 11.8 | 12.8 | 13.7 | 14.7 | 15.7 | 16.7 | 17.7 | 18.7 | 19.8 | 22.3 | 24.7 | 27.1 | 29.4 | 31.7 | 33.8 | 42.9 | 50.0 | 60.0 | .25 |
| 12.8 | 13.7 | 14.6 | 15.6 | 16.5 | 17.4 | 18.4 | 19.3 | 20.3 | 21.2 | 23.5 | 25.8 | 28.1 | 30.2 | 32.3 | 34.3 | 43.1 | 50.1 | 60.0 | .30 |
| 14.8 | 15.6 | 16.5 | 17.4 | 18.3 | 19.2 | 20.1 | 21.0 | 21.9 | 22.7 | 24.9 | 27.1 | 29.2 | 31.2 | 33.2 | 35.1 | 43.5 | 50.2 | 60.0 | .35 |
| 16.7 | 17.5 | 18.4 | 19.2 | 20.1 | 20.9 | 21.8 | 22.6 | 23.5 | 24.3 | 26.4 | 28.4 | 30.4 | 32.3 | 34.2 | 36.0 | 44.0 | 50.5 | 60.1 | .40 |
| 18.6 | 19.4 | 20.3 | 21.1 | 21.9 | 22.7 | 23.5 | 24.3 | 25.1 | 25.9 | 27.9 | 29.8 | 31.7 | 33.5 | 35.3 | 37.0 | 44.6 | 50.8 | 60.2 | .45 |
| 20.5 | 21.3 | 22.1 | 22.9 | 23.7 | 24.5 | 25.3 | 26.1 | 26.8 | 27.6 | 29.5 | 31.3 | 33.1 | 34.8 | 36.4 | 38.1 | 45.3 | 51.3 | 60.4 | .50 |
| 22.4 | 23.2 | 24.0 | 24.8 | 25.5 | 26.3 | 27.0 | 27.8 | 28.5 | 29.2 | 31.0 | 32.8 | 34.5 | 36.1 | 37.7 | 39.2 | 46.1 | 51.9 | 60.7 | .55 |
| 24.3 | 25.1 | 25.8 | 26.6 | 27.3 | 28.1 | 28.8 | 29.5 | 30.2 | 30.9 | 32.6 | 34.3 | 35.9 | 37.5 | 39.0 | 40.4 | 47.0 | 52.5 | 61.0 | .60 |
| 26.2 | 27.0 | 27.7 | 28.4 | 29.1 | 29.8 | 30.5 | 31.2 | 31.9 | 32.6 | 34.2 | 35.8 | 37.4 | 38.9 | 40.3 | 41.7 | 48.0 | 53.3 | 61.4 | .65 |
| 28.1 | 28.8 | 29.5 | 30.2 | 30.9 | 31.6 | 32.3 | 32.9 | 33.6 | 34.2 | 35.8 | 37.3 | 38.8 | 40.3 | 41.6 | 43.0 | 49.0 | 54.0 | 61.9 | .70 |
| 29.9 | 30.6 | 31.3 | 32.0 | 32.7 | 33.3 | 34.0 | 34.6 | 35.3 | 35.9 | 37.4 | 38.9 | 40.3 | 41.7 | 43.0 | 44.3 | 50.0 | 54.9 | 62.4 | .75 |
| 31.8 | 32.4 | 33.1 | 33.8 | 34.4 | 35.1 | 35.7 | 36.3 | 36.9 | 37.5 | 39.0 | 40.4 | 41.8 | 43.1 | 44.4 | 45.6 | 51.1 | 55.8 | 63.0 | .80 |
| 33.6 | 34.2 | 34.9 | 35.5 | 36.2 | 36.8 | 37.4 | 38.0 | 38.6 | 39.2 | 40.6 | 41.9 | 43.3 | 44.5 | 45.8 | 46.9 | 52.2 | 56.7 | 63.6 | .85 |
| 35.4 | 36.0 | 36.6 | 37.3 | 37.9 | 38.5 | 39.1 | 39.6 | 40.2 | 40.8 | 42.1 | 43.5 | 44.7 | 46.0 | 47.1 | 48.3 | 53.3 | 57.6 | 64.3 | .90 |
| 37.2 | 37.8 | 38.4 | 39.0 | 39.6 | 40.1 | 40.7 | 41.3 | 41.8 | 42.4 | 43.7 | 45.0 | 46.2 | 47.4 | 48.5 | 49.6 | 54.5 | 58.6 | 65.0 | .95 |
| 38.9 | 39.5 | 40.1 | 40.7 | 41.2 | 41.8 | 42.4 | 42.9 | 43.4 | 44.0 | 45.2 | 46.5 | 47.6 | 48.8 | 49.9 | 50.9 | 55.6 | 59.5 | 65.7 | 1.00 |
| 40.6 | 41.2 | 41.8 | 42.4 | 42.9 | 43.5 | 44.0 | 44.5 | 45.0 | 45.5 | 46.8 | 48.0 | 49.1 | 50.2 | 51.2 | 52.2 | 56.7 | 60.5 | 66.5 | 1.05 |
| 42.3 | 42.9 | 43.5 | 44.0 | 44.5 | 45.1 | 45.6 | 46.1 | 46.6 | 47.1 | 48.3 | 49.4 | 50.5 | 51.6 | 52.6 | 53.5 | 57.9 | 61.5 | 67.2 | 1.10 |
| 44.0 | 44.6 | 45.1 | 45.6 | 46.2 | 46.7 | 47.2 | 47.7 | 48.2 | 48.6 | 49.8 | 50.9 | 51.9 | 52.9 | 53.9 | 54.9 | 59.0 | 62.5 | 68.0 | 1.15 |
| 45.7 | 46.2 | 46.7 | 47.3 | 47.8 | 48.3 | 48.7 | 49.2 | 49.7 | 50.1 | 51.3 | 52.3 | 53.3 | 54.3 | 55.2 | 56.1 | 60.2 | 63.5 | 68.8 | 1.20 |
| 47.3 | 47.8 | 48.4 | 48.8 | 49.3 | 49.8 | 50.3 | 50.7 | 51.2 | 51.6 | 52.7 | 53.7 | 54.7 | 55.7 | 56.6 | 57.4 | 61.3 | 64.5 | 69.6 | 1.25 |
| 48.9 | 49.4 | 49.9 | 50.4 | 50.9 | 51.3 | 51.8 | 52.2 | 52.7 | 53.1 | 54.1 | 55.1 | 56.1 | 57.0 | 57.9 | 58.7 | 62.4 | 65.5 | 70.4 | 1.30 |
| 50.5 | 51.0 | 51.5 | 52.0 | 52.4 | 52.9 | 53.3 | 53.7 | 54.1 | 54.6 | 55.6 | 56.5 | 57.4 | 58.3 | 59.1 | 59.9 | 63.5 | 66.5 | 71.1 | 1.35 |
| 52.1 | 52.6 | 53.0 | 53.5 | 53.9 | 54.3 | 54.8 | 55.2 | 55.6 | 56.0 | 56.9 | 57.9 | 58.7 | 59.6 | 60.4 | 61.2 | 64.6 | 67.5 | 71.9 | 1.40 |
| 53.6 | 54.1 | 54.5 | 55.0 | 55.4 | 55.8 | 56.2 | 56.6 | 57.0 | 57.4 | 58.3 | 59.2 | 60.0 | 60.9 | 61.6 | 62.4 | 65.7 | 68.4 | 72.7 | 1.45 |
| 55.1 | 55.6 | 56.0 | 56.4 | 56.8 | 57.2 | 57.6 | 58.0 | 58.4 | 58.8 | 59.7 | 60.5 | 61.3 | 62.1 | 62.9 | 63.6 | 66.8 | 69.4 | 73.5 | 1.50 |
| 56.6 | 57.0 | 57.4 | 57.8 | 58.2 | 58.6 | 59.0 | 59.4 | 59.7 | 60.1 | 61.0 | 61.8 | 62.6 | 63.3 | 64.1 | 64.7 | 67.8 | 70.3 | 74.3 | 1.55 |
| 58.0 | 58.5 | 58.9 | 59.2 | 59.6 | 60.0 | 60.4 | 60.7 | 61.1 | 61.4 | 62.3 | 63.1 | 63.8 | 64.5 | 65.2 | 65.9 | 68.8 | 71.3 | 75.1 | 1.60 |
| 59.5 | 59.9 | 60.2 | 60.6 | 61.0 | 61.4 | 61.7 | 62.1 | 62.4 | 62.7 | 63.5 | 64.3 | 65.0 | 65.7 | 66.4 | 67.0 | 69.9 | 72.2 | 75.9 | 1.65 |
| 60.9 | 61.2 | 61.6 | 62.0 | 62.3 | 62.7 | 63.0 | 63.4 | 63.7 | 64.0 | 64.8 | 65.5 | 66.2 | 66.9 | 67.5 | 68.2 | 70.9 | 73.1 | 76.6 | 1.70 |
| 62.2 | 62.6 | 62.9 | 63.3 | 63.6 | 64.0 | 64.3 | 64.6 | 64.9 | 65.3 | 66.0 | 66.7 | 67.4 | 68.0 | 68.7 | 69.2 | 71.9 | 74.0 | 77.4 | 1.75 |
| 68.6 | 68.9 | 69.2 | 69.5 | 69.8 | 70.0 | 70.3 | 70.6 | 70.8 | 71.1 | 71.7 | 72.3 | 72.9 | 73.4 | 73.9 | 74.4 | 76.5 | 78.3 | 81.0 | 2.00 |
| 74.2 | 74.4 | 74.7 | 74.9 | 75.2 | 75.4 | 75.6 | 75.8 | 76.0 | 76.3 | 76.8 | 77.2 | 77.7 | 78.1 | 78.5 | 78.9 | 80.6 | 82.1 | 84.3 | 2.25 |
| 79.1 | 79.3 | 79.5 | 79.7 | 79.9 | 80.0 | 80.2 | 80.4 | 80.6 | 80.7 | 81.1 | 81.5 | 81.9 | 82.2 | 82.6 | 82.9 | 84.3 | 85.4 | 87.2 | 2.50 |
| 83.3 | 83.4 | 83.6 | 83.7 | 83.9 | 84.0 | 84.2 | 84.3 | 84.4 | 84.6 | 84.9 | 85.2 | 85.5 | 85.8 | 86.0 | 86.3 | 87.4 | 88.3 | 89.7 | 2.75 |
| 86.8 | 86.9 | 87.0 | 87.1 | 87.3 | 87.4 | 87.5 | 87.6 | 87.7 | 87.8 | 88.1 | 88.3 | 88.5 | 88.8 | 89.0 | 89.2 | 90.0 | 90.7 | 91.8 | 3.00 |
| 92.1 | 92.1 | 92.2 | 92.3 | 92.4 | 92.4 | 92.5 | 92.6 | 92.6 | 92.7 | 92.8 | 93.0 | 93.1 | 93.3 | 93.4 | 93.5 | 94.0 | 94.4 | 95.1 | 3.50 |
| 95.5 | 95.5 | 95.6 | 95.6 | 95.7 | 95.7 | 95.7 | 95.8 | 95.8 | 95.8 | 95.9 | 96.0 | 96.1 | 96.2 | 96.2 | 96.3 | 96.6 | 96.8 | 97.2 | 4.00 |
| 97.6 | 97.6 | 97.6 | 97.6 | 97.7 | 97.7 | 97.7 | 97.7 | 97.8 | 97.8 | 97.8 | 97.9 | 97.9 | 97.9 | 98.0 | 98.0 | 98.2 | 98.3 | 98.5 | 4.50 |
| 98.8 | 98.8 | 98.8 | 98.8 | 98.8 | 98.8 | 98.8 | 98.8 | 98.9 | 98.9 | 98.9 | 98.9 | 98.9 | 99.0 | 99.0 | 99.0 | 99.1 | 99.1 | 99.2 | 5.00 |

# APPENDIX TABLE 7

Hedge ratios for call options, per cent of share price

| | Share price divided by PV (exercise price) | | | | | | | | | | | | | | | | | | |
|---|---|---|---|---|---|---|---|---|---|---|---|---|---|---|---|---|---|---|---|
| | .40 | .45 | .50 | .55 | .60 | .65 | .70 | .75 | .80 | .82 | .84 | .86 | .88 | .90 | .92 | .94 | .96 | .98 | 1.00 |
| .05 | .0 | .0 | .0 | .0 | .0 | .0 | .0 | .0 | .0 | .0 | .0 | .1 | .6 | 1.9 | 5.0 | 11.3 | 21.4 | 35.2 | 51.0 |
| .10 | .0 | .0 | .0 | .0 | .0 | .0 | .0 | .2 | 1.5 | 2.7 | 4.5 | 7.2 | 11.0 | 15.8 | 21.7 | 28.5 | 36.0 | 44.0 | 52.0 |
| .15 | .0 | .0 | .0 | .0 | .0 | .3 | 1.1 | 3.3 | 7.9 | 10.6 | 13.8 | 17.6 | 21.9 | 26.5 | 31.5 | 36.8 | 42.2 | 47.6 | 53.0 |
| .20 | .0 | .0 | .0 | .2 | .7 | 2.0 | 4.6 | 9.0 | 15.5 | 18.6 | 22.0 | 25.7 | 29.5 | 33.5 | 37.6 | 41.7 | 45.9 | 50.0 | 54.0 |
| .25 | .0 | .1 | .4 | 1.2 | 2.8 | 5.5 | 9.7 | 15.3 | 22.1 | 25.2 | 28.4 | 31.6 | 35.0 | 38.3 | 41.7 | 45.1 | 48.5 | 51.8 | 55.0 |
| .30 | .2 | .6 | 1.5 | 3.3 | 6.0 | 9.9 | 14.9 | 20.9 | 27.6 | 30.4 | 33.3 | 36.2 | 39.1 | 42.0 | 44.9 | 47.8 | 50.6 | 53.3 | 56.0 |
| .35 | .7 | 1.8 | 3.6 | 6.3 | 9.9 | 14.6 | 19.9 | 25.9 | 32.2 | 34.8 | 37.3 | 39.9 | 42.5 | 45.0 | 47.5 | 49.9 | 52.3 | 54.7 | 56.9 |
| .40 | 1.8 | 3.6 | 6.3 | 9.8 | 14.1 | 19.0 | 24.5 | 30.2 | 36.0 | 38.4 | 40.7 | 43.0 | 45.2 | 47.5 | 49.7 | 51.8 | 53.9 | 55.9 | 57.9 |
| .45 | 3.5 | 6.1 | 9.4 | 13.5 | 18.1 | 23.2 | 28.5 | 33.9 | 39.3 | 41.4 | 43.5 | 45.6 | 47.6 | 49.6 | 51.6 | 53.5 | 55.3 | 57.1 | 58.9 |
| .50 | 5.7 | 8.9 | 12.8 | 17.2 | 22.0 | 27.0 | 32.2 | 37.2 | 42.2 | 44.2 | 46.1 | 47.9 | 49.8 | 51.6 | 53.3 | 55.0 | 56.7 | 58.3 | 59.9 |
| .55 | 8.2 | 12.0 | 16.2 | 20.8 | 25.7 | 30.6 | 35.4 | 40.2 | 44.8 | 46.6 | 48.3 | 50.0 | 51.7 | 53.3 | 54.9 | 56.5 | 58.0 | 59.4 | 60.8 |
| .60 | 11.0 | 15.1 | 19.6 | 24.3 | 29.1 | 33.8 | 38.4 | 42.9 | 47.1 | 48.8 | 50.4 | 51.9 | 53.5 | 55.0 | 56.4 | 57.8 | 59.2 | 60.5 | 61.8 |
| .65 | 13.9 | 18.3 | 22.9 | 27.6 | 32.2 | 36.8 | 41.1 | 45.3 | 49.3 | 50.8 | 52.3 | 53.7 | 55.1 | 56.5 | 57.8 | 59.1 | 60.3 | 61.6 | 62.7 |
| .70 | 16.9 | 21.5 | 26.1 | 30.7 | 35.2 | 39.5 | 43.7 | 47.6 | 51.2 | 52.7 | 54.0 | 55.4 | 56.6 | 57.9 | 59.1 | 60.3 | 61.5 | 62.6 | 63.7 |
| .75 | 19.9 | 24.5 | 29.1 | 33.6 | 38.0 | 42.1 | 46.0 | 49.7 | 53.1 | 54.4 | 55.7 | 56.9 | 58.1 | 59.3 | 60.4 | 61.5 | 62.6 | 63.6 | 64.6 |
| .80 | 22.8 | 27.5 | 32.0 | 36.4 | 40.6 | 44.5 | 48.2 | 51.6 | 54.8 | 56.0 | 57.2 | 58.4 | 59.5 | 60.6 | 61.6 | 62.7 | 63.6 | 64.6 | 65.5 |
| .85 | 25.7 | 30.3 | 34.8 | 39.0 | 43.0 | 46.7 | 50.2 | 53.4 | 56.5 | 57.6 | 58.7 | 59.8 | 60.8 | 61.8 | 62.8 | 63.8 | 64.7 | 65.6 | 66.5 |
| .90 | 28.5 | 33.1 | 37.4 | 41.5 | 45.3 | 48.9 | 52.1 | 55.2 | 58.0 | 59.1 | 60.1 | 61.1 | 62.1 | 63.0 | 64.0 | 64.8 | 65.7 | 66.6 | 67.4 |
| .95 | 31.2 | 35.7 | 40.0 | 43.9 | 47.5 | 50.9 | 54.0 | 56.8 | 59.5 | 60.5 | 61.5 | 62.4 | 63.3 | 64.2 | 65.1 | 65.9 | 66.7 | 67.5 | 68.3 |
| 1.00 | 33.9 | 38.3 | 42.3 | 46.1 | 49.6 | 52.8 | 55.7 | 58.4 | 60.9 | 61.9 | 62.8 | 63.7 | 64.5 | 65.3 | 66.2 | 66.9 | 67.7 | 68.4 | 69.1 |
| 1.05 | 36.4 | 40.7 | 44.6 | 48.2 | 51.5 | 54.6 | 57.4 | 59.9 | 62.3 | 63.2 | 64.0 | 64.9 | 65.7 | 66.4 | 67.2 | 67.9 | 68.7 | 69.3 | 70.0 |
| 1.10 | 38.9 | 43.0 | 46.8 | 50.3 | 53.4 | 56.3 | 58.9 | 61.4 | 63.6 | 64.4 | 65.2 | 66.0 | 66.8 | 67.5 | 68.2 | 68.9 | 69.6 | 70.3 | 70.9 |
| 1.15 | 41.2 | 45.2 | 48.9 | 52.2 | 55.2 | 57.9 | 60.4 | 62.7 | 64.8 | 65.6 | 66.4 | 67.1 | 67.9 | 68.6 | 69.2 | 69.9 | 70.5 | 71.1 | 71.7 |
| 1.20 | 43.5 | 47.4 | 50.9 | 54.1 | 56.9 | 59.5 | 61.9 | 64.1 | 66.1 | 66.8 | 67.5 | 68.2 | 68.9 | 69.6 | 70.2 | 70.8 | 71.4 | 72.0 | 72.6 |
| 1.25 | 45.7 | 49.4 | 52.8 | 55.8 | 58.6 | 61.0 | 63.3 | 65.4 | 67.2 | 67.9 | 68.6 | 69.3 | 69.9 | 70.6 | 71.2 | 71.8 | 72.3 | 72.9 | 73.4 |
| 1.30 | 47.8 | 51.4 | 54.6 | 57.5 | 60.1 | 62.5 | 64.6 | 66.6 | 68.4 | 69.1 | 69.7 | 70.3 | 70.9 | 71.5 | 72.1 | 72.7 | 73.2 | 73.7 | 74.2 |
| 1.35 | 49.9 | 53.3 | 56.4 | 59.2 | 61.7 | 63.9 | 65.9 | 67.8 | 69.5 | 70.1 | 70.7 | 71.3 | 71.9 | 72.5 | 73.0 | 73.5 | 74.0 | 74.5 | 75.0 |
| 1.40 | 51.8 | 55.2 | 58.1 | 60.8 | 63.1 | 65.3 | 67.2 | 69.0 | 70.6 | 71.2 | 71.8 | 72.3 | 72.9 | 73.4 | 73.9 | 74.4 | 74.9 | 75.4 | 75.8 |
| 1.45 | 53.7 | 56.9 | 59.8 | 62.3 | 64.5 | 66.6 | 68.4 | 70.1 | 71.6 | 72.2 | 72.7 | 73.3 | 73.8 | 74.3 | 74.8 | 75.2 | 75.7 | 76.1 | 76.6 |
| 1.50 | 55.5 | 58.6 | 61.3 | 63.7 | 65.9 | 67.8 | 69.6 | 71.2 | 72.6 | 73.2 | 73.7 | 74.2 | 74.7 | 75.2 | 75.6 | 76.1 | 76.5 | 76.9 | 77.3 |
| 1.55 | 57.3 | 60.3 | 62.8 | 65.1 | 67.2 | 69.0 | 70.7 | 72.2 | 73.6 | 74.1 | 74.6 | 75.1 | 75.6 | 76.0 | 76.5 | 76.9 | 77.3 | 77.7 | 78.1 |
| 1.60 | 59.0 | 61.8 | 64.3 | 66.5 | 68.5 | 70.2 | 71.8 | 73.2 | 74.6 | 75.0 | 75.5 | 76.0 | 76.4 | 76.9 | 77.3 | 77.7 | 78.1 | 78.4 | 78.8 |
| 1.65 | 60.6 | 63.3 | 65.7 | 67.8 | 69.7 | 71.4 | 72.9 | 74.2 | 75.5 | 76.0 | 76.4 | 76.8 | 77.3 | 77.7 | 78.1 | 78.5 | 78.8 | 79.2 | 79.5 |
| 1.70 | 62.2 | 64.8 | 67.1 | 69.1 | 70.9 | 72.5 | 73.9 | 75.2 | 76.4 | 76.8 | 77.3 | 77.7 | 78.1 | 78.5 | 78.8 | 79.2 | 79.6 | 79.9 | 80.2 |
| 1.75 | 63.7 | 66.2 | 68.4 | 70.3 | 72.0 | 73.5 | 74.9 | 76.1 | 77.3 | 77.7 | 78.1 | 78.5 | 78.9 | 79.2 | 79.6 | 79.9 | 80.3 | 80.6 | 80.9 |
| 2.00 | 70.6 | 72.6 | 74.3 | 75.8 | 77.2 | 78.4 | 79.4 | 80.4 | 81.3 | 81.6 | 81.9 | 82.2 | 82.5 | 82.8 | 83.1 | 83.4 | 83.6 | 83.9 | 84.1 |
| 2.25 | 76.4 | 77.9 | 79.3 | 80.5 | 81.5 | 82.5 | 83.3 | 84.1 | 84.8 | 85.0 | 85.3 | 85.5 | 85.7 | 86.0 | 86.2 | 86.4 | 86.6 | 86.8 | 87.0 |
| 2.50 | 81.2 | 82.4 | 83.5 | 84.4 | 85.2 | 85.9 | 86.6 | 87.2 | 87.7 | 87.9 | 88.1 | 88.3 | 88.5 | 88.6 | 88.8 | 89.0 | 89.1 | 89.3 | 89.4 |
| 2.75 | 85.1 | 86.1 | 86.9 | 87.6 | 88.3 | 88.8 | 89.3 | 89.8 | 90.2 | 90.4 | 90.5 | 90.7 | 90.8 | 90.9 | 91.1 | 91.2 | 91.3 | 91.4 | 91.5 |
| 3.00 | 88.4 | 89.1 | 89.8 | 90.3 | 90.8 | 91.3 | 91.6 | 92.0 | 92.3 | 92.4 | 92.5 | 92.6 | 92.7 | 92.9 | 93.0 | 93.0 | 93.1 | 93.2 | 93.3 |
| 3.50 | 93.2 | 93.6 | 94.0 | 94.3 | 94.6 | 94.8 | 95.0 | 95.2 | 95.4 | 95.5 | 95.5 | 95.6 | 95.7 | 95.7 | 95.8 | 95.8 | 95.9 | 95.9 | 96.0 |
| 4.00 | 96.2 | 96.4 | 96.6 | 96.8 | 96.9 | 97.1 | 97.2 | 97.3 | 97.4 | 97.4 | 97.5 | 97.5 | 97.5 | 97.6 | 97.6 | 97.6 | 97.7 | 97.7 | 97.7 |
| 4.50 | 98.0 | 98.1 | 98.2 | 98.3 | 98.4 | 98.4 | 98.5 | 98.6 | 98.6 | 98.6 | 98.6 | 98.7 | 98.7 | 98.7 | 98.7 | 98.7 | 98.7 | 98.8 | 98.8 |
| 5.00 | 99.0 | 99.0 | 99.1 | 99.1 | 99.2 | 99.2 | 99.2 | 99.3 | 99.3 | 99.3 | 99.3 | 99.3 | 99.3 | 99.3 | 99.3 | 99.4 | 99.4 | 99.4 | 99.4 |

*Standard deviation times square root of time* (row axis label)

Note: *Based on Black–Scholes model. Subtract 1.0 to obtain corresponding hedge ratios for European puts.*

| | | | | | Share price divided by PV (exercise price) | | | | | | | | | | | | | | |
|---|---|---|---|---|---|---|---|---|---|---|---|---|---|---|---|---|---|---|---|
| 1.02 | 1.04 | 1.06 | 1.08 | 1.10 | 1.12 | 1.14 | 1.16 | 1.18 | 1.20 | 1.25 | 1.30 | 1.35 | 1.40 | 1.45 | 1.50 | 1.75 | 2.00 | 2.50 | |
| 66.3 | 79.1 | 88.3 | 94.1 | 97.3 | 98.9 | 99.6 | 99.9 | 100. | 100. | 100. | 100. | 100. | 100. | 100. | 100. | 100. | 100. | 100. | .05 |
| 59.8 | 67.1 | 73.7 | 79.4 | 84.2 | 88.2 | 91.3 | 93.8 | 95.6 | 96.9 | 98.9 | 99.6 | 99.9 | 100. | 100. | 100. | 100. | 100. | | .10 |
| 58.2 | 63.2 | 67.8 | 72.2 | 76.1 | 79.7 | 82.9 | 85.6 | 88.1 | 90.2 | 94.1 | 96.6 | 98.1 | 99.0 | 99.5 | 99.7 | 100. | 100. | 100. | .15 |
| 57.9 | 61.6 | 65.2 | 68.6 | 71.8 | 74.8 | 77.5 | 80.0 | 82.3 | 84.4 | 88.8 | 92.1 | 94.5 | 96.3 | 97.5 | 98.3 | 99.8 | 100. | 100. | .20 |
| 58.1 | 61.1 | 64.0 | 66.7 | 69.4 | 71.8 | 74.2 | 76.4 | 78.4 | 80.4 | 84.6 | 88.0 | 90.7 | 92.9 | 94.6 | 96.0 | 99.1 | 99.8 | 100. | .25 |
| 58.6 | 61.1 | 63.5 | 65.8 | 68.0 | 70.1 | 72.1 | 74.0 | 75.9 | 77.6 | 81.4 | 84.7 | 87.5 | 89.8 | 91.8 | 93.3 | 97.8 | 99.3 | 99.9 | .30 |
| 59.2 | 61.3 | 63.4 | 65.4 | 67.3 | 69.1 | 70.9 | 72.5 | 74.1 | 75.7 | 79.2 | 82.2 | 84.9 | 87.2 | 89.2 | 90.9 | 96.2 | 98.4 | 99.7 | .35 |
| 59.9 | 61.7 | 63.5 | 65.3 | 66.9 | 68.6 | 70.1 | 71.6 | 73.0 | 74.4 | 77.6 | 80.4 | 82.9 | 85.1 | 87.1 | 88.8 | 94.5 | 97.3 | 99.4 | .40 |
| 60.6 | 62.3 | 63.9 | 65.4 | 66.9 | 68.3 | 69.7 | 71.0 | 72.3 | 73.6 | 76.5 | 79.0 | 81.4 | 83.5 | 85.3 | 87.0 | 92.9 | 96.1 | 98.8 | .45 |
| 61.4 | 62.9 | 64.3 | 65.7 | 67.0 | 68.3 | 69.6 | 70.8 | 71.9 | 73.1 | 75.7 | 78.1 | 80.2 | 82.2 | 84.0 | 85.6 | 91.5 | 94.9 | 98.1 | .50 |
| 62.2 | 63.5 | 64.8 | 66.1 | 67.3 | 68.5 | 69.6 | 70.7 | 71.8 | 72.8 | 75.2 | 77.4 | 79.4 | 81.2 | 82.9 | 84.4 | 90.2 | 93.8 | 97.4 | .55 |
| 63.0 | 64.3 | 65.4 | 66.6 | 67.7 | 68.8 | 69.8 | 70.8 | 71.8 | 72.7 | 74.9 | 77.0 | 78.8 | 80.5 | 82.1 | 83.5 | 89.1 | 92.7 | 96.6 | .60 |
| 63.9 | 65.0 | 66.1 | 67.1 | 68.1 | 69.1 | 70.1 | 71.0 | 71.9 | 72.8 | 74.8 | 76.7 | 78.4 | 80.0 | 81.5 | 82.9 | 88.2 | 91.8 | 95.9 | .65 |
| 64.7 | 65.8 | 66.8 | 67.7 | 68.7 | 69.6 | 70.4 | 71.3 | 72.1 | 72.9 | 74.8 | 76.6 | 78.2 | 79.7 | 81.1 | 82.4 | 87.5 | 91.0 | 95.1 | .70 |
| 65.6 | 66.5 | 67.5 | 68.4 | 69.2 | 70.1 | 70.9 | 71.7 | 72.4 | 73.2 | 74.9 | 76.6 | 78.1 | 79.5 | 80.8 | 82.0 | 86.9 | 90.3 | 94.5 | .75 |
| 66.4 | 67.3 | 68.2 | 69.0 | 69.8 | 70.6 | 71.4 | 72.1 | 72.8 | 73.5 | 75.1 | 76.7 | 78.1 | 79.4 | 80.6 | 81.8 | 86.4 | 89.7 | 93.9 | .80 |
| 67.3 | 68.1 | 68.9 | 69.7 | 70.4 | 71.2 | 71.9 | 72.6 | 73.2 | 73.9 | 75.4 | 76.8 | 78.2 | 79.4 | 80.6 | 81.6 | 86.1 | 89.3 | 93.4 | .85 |
| 68.2 | 68.9 | 69.7 | 70.4 | 71.1 | 71.8 | 72.4 | 73.1 | 73.7 | 74.3 | 75.7 | 77.1 | 78.3 | 79.5 | 80.6 | 81.6 | 85.8 | 88.9 | 92.9 | .90 |
| 69.0 | 69.7 | 70.4 | 71.1 | 71.7 | 72.4 | 73.0 | 73.6 | 74.2 | 74.8 | 76.1 | 77.4 | 78.5 | 79.6 | 80.7 | 81.6 | 85.6 | 88.6 | 92.5 | .95 |
| 69.8 | 70.5 | 71.2 | 71.8 | 72.4 | 73.0 | 73.6 | 74.2 | 74.7 | 75.2 | 76.5 | 77.7 | 78.8 | 79.9 | 80.8 | 81.7 | 85.5 | 88.4 | 92.2 | 1.00 |
| 70.7 | 71.3 | 71.9 | 72.5 | 73.1 | 73.7 | 74.2 | 74.7 | 75.3 | 75.8 | 77.0 | 78.1 | 79.1 | 80.1 | 81.0 | 81.9 | 85.5 | 88.2 | 91.9 | 1.05 |
| 71.5 | 72.1 | 72.7 | 73.2 | 73.8 | 74.3 | 74.8 | 75.3 | 75.8 | 76.3 | 77.4 | 78.5 | 79.5 | 80.4 | 81.3 | 82.1 | 85.5 | 88.1 | 91.7 | 1.10 |
| 72.3 | 72.9 | 73.4 | 74.0 | 74.5 | 75.0 | 75.5 | 75.9 | 76.4 | 76.8 | 77.9 | 78.9 | 79.8 | 80.7 | 81.5 | 82.3 | 85.6 | 88.1 | 91.5 | 1.15 |
| 73.1 | 73.7 | 74.2 | 74.7 | 75.2 | 75.6 | 76.1 | 76.5 | 77.0 | 77.4 | 78.4 | 79.4 | 80.2 | 81.1 | 81.8 | 82.6 | 85.7 | 88.1 | 91.4 | 1.20 |
| 73.9 | 74.4 | 74.9 | 75.4 | 75.8 | 76.3 | 76.7 | 77.1 | 77.6 | 78.0 | 78.9 | 79.8 | 80.7 | 81.4 | 82.2 | 82.9 | 85.8 | 88.1 | 91.3 | 1.25 |
| 74.7 | 75.2 | 75.6 | 76.1 | 76.5 | 76.9 | 77.4 | 77.8 | 78.2 | 78.5 | 79.4 | 80.3 | 81.1 | 81.8 | 82.5 | 83.2 | 86.0 | 88.2 | 91.2 | 1.30 |
| 75.5 | 75.9 | 76.4 | 76.8 | 77.2 | 77.6 | 78.0 | 78.4 | 78.7 | 79.1 | 80.0 | 80.8 | 81.5 | 82.2 | 82.9 | 83.5 | 86.2 | 88.3 | 91.2 | 1.35 |
| 76.2 | 76.7 | 77.1 | 77.5 | 77.9 | 78.3 | 78.6 | 79.0 | 79.3 | 79.7 | 80.5 | 81.3 | 82.0 | 82.6 | 83.3 | 83.9 | 86.4 | 88.4 | 91.3 | 1.40 |
| 77.0 | 77.4 | 77.8 | 78.2 | 78.5 | 78.9 | 79.3 | 79.6 | 79.9 | 80.3 | 81.0 | 81.8 | 82.4 | 83.1 | 83.7 | 84.2 | 86.7 | 88.6 | 91.3 | 1.45 |
| 77.7 | 78.1 | 78.5 | 78.9 | 79.2 | 79.5 | 79.9 | 80.2 | 80.5 | 80.8 | 81.6 | 82.2 | 82.9 | 83.5 | 84.1 | 84.6 | 86.9 | 88.7 | 91.3 | 1.50 |
| 78.5 | 78.8 | 79.2 | 79.5 | 79.9 | 80.2 | 80.5 | 80.8 | 81.1 | 81.4 | 82.1 | 82.7 | 83.4 | 83.9 | 84.5 | 85.0 | 87.2 | 88.9 | 91.4 | 1.55 |
| 79.2 | 79.5 | 79.9 | 80.2 | 80.5 | 80.8 | 81.1 | 81.4 | 81.7 | 82.0 | 82.6 | 83.2 | 83.8 | 84.4 | 84.9 | 85.4 | 87.5 | 89.1 | 91.5 | 1.60 |
| 79.9 | 80.2 | 80.5 | 80.8 | 81.1 | 81.4 | 81.7 | 82.0 | 82.3 | 82.5 | 83.2 | 83.7 | 84.3 | 84.8 | 85.3 | 85.8 | 87.8 | 89.3 | 91.6 | 1.65 |
| 80.6 | 80.9 | 81.2 | 81.5 | 81.8 | 82.0 | 82.3 | 82.6 | 82.8 | 83.1 | 83.7 | 84.2 | 84.8 | 85.3 | 85.7 | 86.2 | 88.1 | 89.6 | 91.8 | 1.70 |
| 81.2 | 81.5 | 81.8 | 82.1 | 82.4 | 82.6 | 82.9 | 83.1 | 83.4 | 83.6 | 84.2 | 84.7 | 85.2 | 85.7 | 86.2 | 86.6 | 88.4 | 89.8 | 91.9 | 1.75 |
| 84.4 | 84.6 | 84.8 | 85.0 | 85.3 | 85.5 | 85.7 | 85.9 | 86.1 | 86.2 | 86.7 | 87.1 | 87.5 | 87.9 | 88.2 | 88.5 | 90.0 | 91.1 | 92.8 | 2.00 |
| 87.2 | 87.3 | 87.5 | 87.7 | 87.8 | 88.0 | 88.2 | 88.3 | 88.5 | 88.6 | 89.0 | 89.3 | 89.6 | 89.9 | 90.1 | 90.4 | 91.5 | 92.4 | 93.7 | 2.25 |
| 89.6 | 89.7 | 89.9 | 90.0 | 90.1 | 90.2 | 90.4 | 90.5 | 90.6 | 90.7 | 91.0 | 91.2 | 91.5 | 91.7 | 91.9 | 92.1 | 93.0 | 93.7 | 94.7 | 2.50 |
| 91.7 | 91.8 | 91.9 | 92.0 | 92.1 | 92.2 | 92.3 | 92.3 | 92.4 | 92.5 | 92.7 | 92.9 | 93.1 | 93.3 | 93.4 | 93.6 | 94.3 | 94.8 | 95.6 | 2.75 |
| 93.4 | 93.5 | 93.6 | 93.6 | 93.7 | 93.8 | 93.9 | 93.9 | 94.0 | 94.1 | 94.2 | 94.4 | 94.5 | 94.7 | 94.8 | 94.9 | 95.4 | 95.8 | 96.4 | 3.00 |
| 96.0 | 96.1 | 96.1 | 96.2 | 96.2 | 96.3 | 96.3 | 96.3 | 96.4 | 96.4 | 96.5 | 96.6 | 96.7 | 96.8 | 96.8 | 96.9 | 97.2 | 97.4 | 97.8 | 3.50 |
| 97.8 | 97.8 | 97.8 | 97.8 | 97.9 | 97.9 | 97.9 | 97.9 | 97.9 | 98.0 | 98.0 | 98.1 | 98.1 | 98.1 | 98.2 | 98.2 | 98.4 | 98.5 | 98.7 | 4.00 |
| 98.8 | 98.8 | 98.8 | 98.8 | 98.8 | 98.9 | 98.9 | 98.9 | 98.9 | 98.9 | 98.9 | 99.0 | 99.0 | 99.0 | 99.0 | 99.0 | 99.1 | 99.2 | 99.3 | 4.50 |
| 99.4 | 99.4 | 99.4 | 99.4 | 99.4 | 99.4 | 99.4 | 99.4 | 99.4 | 99.4 | 99.5 | 99.5 | 99.5 | 99.5 | 99.5 | 99.5 | 99.5 | 99.6 | 99.6 | 5.00 |

Standard deviation times square root of time

# glossary

**Accelerated depreciation**   Any depreciation method that produces larger deductions for depreciation in the early years of a project's life, e.g. *depreciation, sum-of-the-years-digits depreciation*.

**Accounts payable** (*payables*, *trade debt*)   Money owed to suppliers.

**Accounts receivable** (*receivables*, *trade credit*)   Money owed by customers.

**Accrued interest**   Interest that has been earned but not yet paid.

**Acid-test ratio**   *Quick ratio*.

**Adjusted present value** (*APV*)   *Net present value* of an asset if it were to be financed solely by equity, plus the present value of any financing side effects.

**Adverse selection**   A situation in which a pricing policy causes only the least desirable customers to do business, e.g. a rise in insurance prices that leads only the worst risks to buy insurance.

**Ageing schedule**   Record of the length of time that *accounts receivable* have been outstanding.

**Agency theory**   Theory concerning the relationship between a principal, e.g. a shareholder, and an agent of the principal, e.g. the company's manager.

**All-or-none underwriting**   The security issue is cancelled if the *underwriter* is unable to resell the entire issue.

**American option**   Option that can be exercised any time before the final exercise date (cf. *European option*).

**Amortisation**   (1) Repayment of a loan by instalments, (2) allowance for *depreciation*.

**Annuity**   Investment that produces a level stream of cash flows for a limited number of periods.

**Anticipation**   Arrangements whereby customers who pay before the final date may be entitled to deduct a normal rate of interest.

**Appropriation request**   Formal request for funds for a capital investment project.

**APT**   Arbitrage pricing theory.

**APV**   *Adjusted present value*.

**Arbitrage**   Purchase of one security and simultaneous sale of another to give a risk-free profit.

**'Arbitrage' or 'risk arbitrage'**   Often used loosely to describe the taking of offsetting positions in related securities, e.g. at the time of a takeover bid.

**ASIC**   Australian Securities and Investment Commission.

**ASX**   Australian Stock Exchange.

**Authorised share capital**   Maximum number of shares that a company can issue, as specified in the firm's articles of incorporation.

**Balloon payment**   Large final payment (e.g. when a loan is repaid in instalments).

**Bank acceptance**   A bank endorses (adds its name) to a *bill*

*of exchange*, thereby guaranteeing payment of the bill. A fee is usually charged for this service.

**Basis point**   0.01 per cent.

**Basis risk**   Residual risk that results when the two sides of a hedge do not move exactly together.

**Bearer security**   Security for which primary evidence of ownership is possession of the certificate (cf. *registered security*).

**Bear market**   Widespread decline in security prices (cf. *bull market*).

**Benefit-cost ratio**   *Profitability index*.

**Best-efforts underwriting**   *Underwriters* do not commit themselves to selling a security issue, but promise only to use best efforts.

**Beta** ($\beta$)   Measure of *market risk*.

**Bill of exchange**   General term for a document demanding payment.

**Bill of lading**   Document establishing ownership of goods in transit.

**Blue-chip company**   Large and creditworthy company.

**Bond**   Long-term debt.

**Bonus share plans**   These plans offer shareholders the choice of bonus shares in lieu of a cash *dividend*.

**Book rate of return**   Accounting profit divided by accounting book value.

**Break-even analysis**   Analysis of the level of sales at which a project would just break even.

**Bridging loan**   Short-term loan to provide temporary financing until more permanent financing is arranged.

**Bull-bear bonds**   *Bonds* whose principal repayment is linked to the price of another security. The bonds are issued in two tranches: In the first, the repayment increases with the price of the other security; in the second, the repayment decreases with the price of the other security.

**Bulldog bond**   *Foreign bond* issue made in London.

**Bullet payment**   Single final payment, e.g. of a loan (in contrast to payment in instalments).

**Bull FRN**   *Reverse FRN*.

**Bull market**   Widespread rise in security prices (cf. *bear market*).

**Business plan**   A formal plan of the activities of the business detailing how the business will achieve its goals. The plan is usually supported by a set of projected financial statements.

**Call option**   *Option* to buy an asset at a specified *exercise price* on or before a specified exercise date (cf. *put option*).

**Call premium**   (1) Difference between the price at which a company can call its *bonds* and their *face value*; (2) price of an option.

**Cap**   An upper limit on the interest rate on a *floating-rate note*.

**Capital budget**  List of planned investment projects, usually prepared annually.

**Capital budgeting decision**  The decision about how much money (in total) to spend on capital projects and which particular projects to invest in.

**Capital lease**  *Financial lease.*

**Capital market**  Financial market (particularly the market for long-term securities).

**Capital market line**  The equation of the line that shows the relation between the required return and risk for *efficient portfolios.*

**Capital rationing**  Shortage of funds that forces a company to choose between projects.

**Capital structure**  Mix of different securities issued by a firm.

**Capitalisation**  Long-term debt, plus *preference shares,* plus *net worth.*

**CAPM**  Capital asset pricing model.

**Cash budget**  Forecast of sources and uses of cash.

**Cash and carry**  Purchase of a security and the simultaneous sale of a *future,* with the balance being financed with a loan or *repo.*

**Cash concentration**  A method of cash management where local company branches collect payments and then remit surplus cash balances to headquarters.

**Cash-deficiency arrangement**  Arrangement whereby a project's shareholders agree to provide the operating company with sufficient net working capital.

**CD**  *Certificate of deposit.*

**CEDEL**  A centralised clearing system for eurobonds. Also *Euroclear.*

**Certificate of deposit (*CD*)**  A certificate providing evidence of a bank time deposit.

**Chief financial officer (CFO)**  The head of the company's financial management.

**Clientele effect**  The adjustment of companies' financial policies to meet the requirements of shareholder clienteles so that no unsatisfied clienteles remain. Under these circumstances, no financial policy will command a valuation premium.

**Closed-end mortgage**  Mortgage against which no additional debt may be issued (cf. *open-end mortgage*).

**Collar**  An upper and lower limit on the interest rate on a *floating-rate note.*

**Collateral**  Assets that are given as security for a loan.

**Commercial draft** (*bill of exchange*)  Demand for payment.

**Commercial paper**  Unsecured *notes* issued by companies and maturing within 12 months.

**Compound interest**  Reinvestment of each interest payment on money invested, to earn more interest (cf. *simple interest*).

**Conditional sales**  Sales in which ownership does not pass to the buyer until payment is completed.

**Conglomerate merger**  Merger between companies in unrelated lines of business.

**Consideration**  The payment made for acquisition of an asset.

**Consol**  Name of a perpetual bond issued by the British government. Sometimes used as a general term for *perpetuity.*

**Contingent project**  Project that cannot be undertaken unless another project is also undertaken.

**Continuous compounding**  Interest compounded continuously rather than at fixed intervals.

**Convenience yield**  The return available from holding and therefore being able to use a real asset, as opposed to holding a futures contract on that asset.

**Conversion price**  *Par value* of a *convertible security* divided by the number of shares into which it may be exchanged.

**Convertible security**  *Bond* or *preference shares* that may be converted into another security at the holder's option.

**Corporate treasurer**  The manager primarily responsible for cash management, arranging the firm's financing, overseeing the firm's investment decisions and managing financial risks.

**Correlation coefficient**  Measure of the closeness of the relationship between two variables.

**Cost of capital**  *Opportunity cost of capital.*

**Cost company arrangement**  Arrangement whereby the shareholders of a project receive output free of charge but agree to pay all operating and financing charges of the project.

**Coupon**  (1) Specifically, a coupon attached to the certificate of a bearer bond that must be surrendered to collect interest payment. (2) More generally, interest payment on debt.

**Covariance**  Measure of the co-movement between two variables.

**Covenant**  Clause in a loan agreement.

**Credit scoring**  A procedure for assigning scores to companies on the basis of the risk of default.

**Cum-dividend**  *With dividend.*

**Cum-rights**  *With rights.*

**Cumulative preference share**  Shares that take priority over ordinary shares in regard to dividend payments. Dividends may not be paid on the ordinary shares until all past *dividends* on the *preference shares* have been paid.

**Cumulative voting**  A shareholder may cast all his or her votes for one candidate for the board of directors (cf. *majority voting*).

**Current asset**  Asset that normally will be turned into cash within a year.

Current liability    Liability that normally will be repaid within a year.

Current ratio    *Current assets* divided by *current liabilities*—a measure of liquidity.

DCF    *Discounted cash flow.*

Debenture    Secured *bond* in Australia; unsecured *bond* in the United States.

Debt defeasance    A borrower removes debt from its balance sheet by setting up a trust to hold for the lender's benefit securities with a present value equal to the debt.

Decision tree    Method of representing alternative sequential decisions and the possible outcomes from these decisions.

Defeasance    Borrower sets aside cash or *bonds* sufficient to service the borrower's debt. Both the borrower's debt and the offsetting cash or bonds are removed from the balance sheet.

Delta    *Hedge ratio.*

Depreciation    (1) Reduction in the book or market value of an asset. (2) Portion of an investment that can be deducted from taxable income.

Derivative    A financial asset that derives its value from another asset (cf. *forward cover, futures contract, option, swap*).

Development capital    Capital invested in a business as a form of *venture capital* when the business has a proven track record of operation, established markets, positive cash flow and is in need of the capital to reach its full potential.

Dilution    Diminution in the proportion of income to which each share is entitled.

Diminishing value basis    *Depreciation* calculated by applying a fixed percentage (say 20 per cent) each year to the depreciated book value of the asset.

Direct lease    *Lease* in which the *lessor* purchases new equipment from the manufacturer and leases it to the *lessee* (cf. *sale and lease-back*).

Discount bond    Debt sold for less than its *principal* value. If a discount bond pays no interest, it is called a 'pure' discount bond.

Discount factor    *Present value* of $1 received at a stated future date.

Discount rate    Rate used to calculate the *present value* of future cash flows.

Discounted cash flow (DCF)    Future cash flows multiplied by *discount factors* to obtain *present value*.

Disintermediation    Withdrawal of funds from a financial institution in order to invest them directly (cf. *intermediation*).

Dividend    Payment by a company to its shareholders.

Dividend decision    The decision about how much cash should be distributed to shareholders.

Dividend yield    Annual *dividend* divided by share price.

Dollar-weighted rate of return    *Internal rate of return* (cf. *time-weighted rate of return*).

Double-tax agreement    Agreement between two countries that taxes paid abroad can be offset against domestic taxes levied on foreign dividends.

Drop lock    An arrangement whereby the interest rate on a *floating-rate note* or *preference share* becomes fixed if it falls to a specified level.

Dual-currency bond    *Bond* with interest paid in one currency and *principal* paid in another.

Duration    The average time to an asset's *discounted cash flows*.

EBIT    Earnings before interest and taxes.

Economic depreciation    The change in the market value (*present value*) of an asset.

Economic income    Cash flow plus change in *present value*.

Economic rents    Profits in excess of the competitive level.

Economies of scale    Reductions in relative costs as the company gets bigger.

ECU    *European currency unit* or 'euro'.

Efficient capital market    See *efficient market*.

Efficient market    Market in which security prices reflect information instantaneously.

Efficient portfolio    Portfolio that offers the lowest risk (standard deviation) for its *expected return* and the highest expected return for its level of risk.

EPS    Earnings per share.

Equity    (1) Ordinary shares and *preference shares*. Often used to refer to ordinary shares only. (2) *Net worth*.

Equivalent annual cash flow    *Annuity* with the same *net present value* as the company's proposed investment.

Eurobond    *Bond* that is marketed internationally.

Euroclear    A centralised clearing system for *eurobonds*. Also *CEDEL*.

Eurodollar deposit    Dollar deposit with a bank outside the United States.

European currency unit (*ECU*)    A basket of different European currencies.

European option    Option that can be exercised only on the final exercise date (cf. *American option*).

Exchange of assets    Acquisition of another company by purchase of its assets in exchange for cash or shares.

Exchange of shares    Acquisition of another company where payment is made in the shares of the bidding company.

Exchange offers    Offers by a company, to its investors, to exchange one security for another. For example, an offer to shareholders to exchange shares for debt.

Ex-dividend    Purchase of shares in which the buyer is not entitled to the *dividend* (cf. *with dividend, cum-dividend*).

**Exercise price** (*striking price*)  Price at which a *call option* or *put option* may be exercised.

**Expected return**  Average of possible returns weighted by their probabilities.

**Ex-rights**  Purchase of shares in which the buyer is not entitled to the rights to buy shares in the company's *rights issue* (cf. *with rights*, *cum-rights*, *rights on*).

**Extendible bond**  Bond whose maturity can be extended at the option of the lender (or issuer).

**External finance**  Finance that is not generated by the firm: new borrowing or an issue of shares (cf. *internal finance*).

**Extra dividend**  *Dividend* that may or may not be repeated (cf. *regular dividend*).

**Face value**  *Par value*.

**Factoring**  Arrangement whereby a financial institution buys a company's *accounts receivable* and collects the debt.

**Field warehouse**  Warehouse rented by a warehouse company on another firm's premises (cf. *public warehouse*).

**Financial assets**  Claims on *real assets*.

**Financial engineering**  Combining, or dividing, existing instruments to create new financial products.

**Financial lease** (*capital lease*, *full-payout lease*)  Long-term, non-cancellable *lease* (cf. *operating lease*).

**Financial leverage** (*gearing*)  Use of debt to increase the *expected return* on *equity*. Financial leverage is measured by the ratio of debt to debt plus equity (cf. *operating leverage*).

**Financing decision**  The decision about how money should be raised to finance the firm's investment in assets.

**Float**  This is a term with two meanings. First, it can mean the issue of securities to the public, usually when a company is first listed on a stock exchange. Second, it can mean the difference between a company's cash balance at the bank and the balance it would have if all outstanding cheques had been charged to the account.

**Floating-rate note** (*FRN*)  *Note* whose interest payment varies with the short-term interest rate.

**Floating-rate preference shares**  *Preference shares* paying dividends that vary with short-term interest rates.

**Floor planning**  Arrangement used to finance inventory. A finance company buys the inventory, which is then held in trust by the user.

**Foreign bond**  A bond issued on the domestic *capital market* of another country.

**Forex**  Foreign exchange.

**Forfaiting**  Purchase of promises to pay (e.g. *bills of exchange* or *promissory notes*) issued by importers.

**Forward cover**  Purchase or sale of forward foreign currency in order to offset a known future cash flow.

**Forward exchange rate**  Exchange rate fixed today for exchanging currency at some future date (cf. *spot exchange rate*).

**Forward interest rate**  Interest rate fixed today on a loan to be made at some future date (cf. *spot interest rate*).

**Forward rate agreement** (*FRA*)  Agreement to borrow or lend at a specified future date at an interest rate that is fixed today.

**FRA**  *Forward rate agreement*.

**Free cash flow**  Cash not required for operations or reinvestment.

**FRN**  *Floating-rate notes*.

**Full-payout lease**  *Financial lease*.

**Full-service lease** (*rental lease*)  *Lease* in which the *lessor* promises to maintain and insure the equipment (cf. *net lease*).

**Funded debt**  Debt maturing after more than one year (cf. *unfunded debt*).

**Future**  A contract to buy or sell a defined asset at some future date.

**Futures contract**  A contract to buy a commodity or security on a future date at a price that is fixed today. Unlike forward contracts, futures are generally traded on organised exchanges and are *marked-to-market* daily.

**Garnishment**  A procedure allowing debt to be paid off by deductions from the debtor's wages.

**Gearing**  *Financial leverage*.

**General cash offer**  A general public offer of seasoned equity, made in preference to a rights issue. Common in the United States but not in Australia.

**Golden parachute**  A large termination payment due to a company's management staff if they lose their jobs as a result of a merger.

**Greenmail**  A large block of shares held by an unfriendly company, which forces the target company to repurchase the shares at a substantial premium to prevent a takeover.

**Grey market**  Purchases and sales of eurobonds that occur before the issue price is finally set.

**Growth shares**  Shares of companies that have an opportunity to invest money to earn more than the *opportunity cost of capital* (cf. *income shares*).

**Harmless warrant**  *Warrant* that allows the user to purchase a *bond* only by surrendering an existing bond with similar terms.

**Heaven-and-hell bonds**  *Dual-currency bonds* whose principal repayment is in a currency different from the interest payments. The size of the principal repayment is partially increased if the value of the currency falls, and vice versa.

**Hedge ratio** (*delta*, *option delta*)  The number of shares to buy for each option sold in order to create a safe position. More generally, the number of units of an asset that should be bought to hedge one unit of a liability.

**Hedging**  Buying one security and selling another in order to reduce risk. A perfect hedge produces a riskless portfolio (cf. *long hedge*, *short hedge*).

**Holding company**   Company whose sole function is to hold shares in other companies or subsidiaries.

**Horizontal merger**   *Merger* between two companies that manufacture similar products (cf. *vertical merger, conglomerate merger*).

**Horizontal spread**   The simultaneous purchase and sale of two options that differ only in their exercise date (cf. *vertical spread*).

**Hurdle rate**   Minimum acceptable rate of return on a project.

**Immunisation**   The construction of an asset and a liability that are subject to offsetting changes in value.

**Income shares**   Shares held primarily for their dividend yield.

**Indexed bonds**   *Bonds* whose payments are linked to an index, e.g. a consumer price index.

**Information motivated**   Trades motivated by superior information about the value of a security.

**Initial public offering (*IPO*)**   A company's first public issue of ordinary shares.

**Intangible assets**   Non-material assets such as technical expertise, trademarks and patents (cf. *tangible assets*).

**Integer programming**   Variant of *linear programming* where the solution values must be integers.

**Interest cover**   *Times interest earned*.

**Interest rate parity**   Theory that the differential between the *forward exchange rate* and the *spot exchange rate* is equal to the differential between the foreign and domestic interest rates.

**Intermediation**   Investment through a financial institution (cf. *disintermediation*).

**Internal finance**   Finance generated within a firm by retained earnings and *depreciation* (cf. *external finance*).

**Internal rate of return (*IRR*)** (*dollar-weighted rate of return*) Discount rate at which investment has zero *net present value*.

**Interval measure**   The number of days that a firm can finance operations without additional cash income.

**In-the-money option**   An option that would be worth exercising if it expired immediately (cf. *out-of-the-money option*).

**Investment banker**   *Underwriter*.

**Investment decision**   The decision about which capital assets (projects) to invest in.

**Investment-grade bonds**   *Bonds* rated Baa or above according to Moody's ratings.

**IPO**   *Initial public offering.*

**IRR**   *Internal rate of return.*

**Junior debt**   *Subordinated debt.*

**Junk bonds**   Bonds that are below investment grade. For example, bonds that are less than BBB according to Standard and Poor's ratings.

**Lease**   Long-term rental agreement.

**Legal capital**   Value at which a company's shares are recorded in its books.

**Lessee**   User of a leased asset (cf. *lessor*).

**Lessor**   Owner of a leased asset (cf. *lessee*).

**Letter of credit**   Letter from a bank stating that it has established a credit in the company's favour.

**Leverage**   See *financial leverage, operating leverage.*

**Leveraged lease**   *Lease* in which the *lessor* finances part of the cost of the asset by an issue of debt secured by the asset and the lease payments.

**Liabilities, total liabilities**   Total value of financial claims on a firm's assets. Equals (1) total assets or (2) total assets minus *net worth*.

**LIBOR (London interbank offered rate)**   The interest rate at which major international banks in London lend to each other. (LIBID is the London interbank bid rate; LIMEAN is the mean of the bid and offered rate.)

**Lien**   Lender's claims on specified assets.

**Limited liability**   Limitation of a shareholder's losses to the amount invested.

**Linear programming (*LP*)**   Technique for finding the maximum value of some equation subject to stated linear constraints.

**Line of credit**   Agreement by a bank that a company may borrow at any time up to an established limit.

**Liquid assets**   Assets that are easily and cheaply turned into cash—notably cash itself and short-term securities.

**Liquidating dividend**   Dividend that represents a return of capital.

**Liquidity motivated**   Trades where the motivation for selling is to obtain cash and where the motivation for buying is to invest surplus cash.

**Liquidity premium**   (1) Additional return for investing in a security that cannot easily be turned into cash. (2) Difference between the *forward rate* and the expected *spot rate* of interest.

**Lockbox facility**   Customers send payments to a post office box. A bank collects and processes the payments and transfers funds to the company's account for a fee.

**Long hedge**   Entering a contract to hedge future increases in the spot price of an asset or commodity (cf. *short hedge*)

**Long-term debt**   Debt with a maturity greater than one year, or in some contexts, a maturity greater than five years.

**Lookback option**   A *call* (*put*) option whose *exercise price* is fixed in retrospect as the lowest (highest) price of the asset during the life of the option.

**LP**   *Linear programming.*

**Maintenance margin**   Minimum margin that must be maintained on a *futures contract*.

**Majority voting**   Voting system under which each director is voted on separately (cf. *cumulative voting*).

**Management buyout (MBO)**   A takeover of the company by its management buying out the other shareholders. Often, the takeover is debt financed.

**Margin**   Cash or securities set aside by an investor as evidence that he or she can honour a commitment.

**Marked-to-market**   An arrangement whereby the profits or losses on a *futures contract* are settled up each day.

**Market capitalisation rate**   *Expected return* on a security.

**Market microstructure**   The fine detail of the organisation of financial markets, and the behaviour of prices examined at very short intervals.

**Market risk** (*systematic risk*)   Risk that cannot be diversified away.

**Maturity factoring**   *Factoring* arrangement that provides collection and insurance of *accounts receivable*.

**MDA**   *Multiple discriminant analysis*.

**Mean reversion in beta**   The tendency over time for estimated values of *beta* to drift back towards the mean value of one.

**Mean variance efficient portfolios**   Portfolios that give the maximum return for a given level of risk, where risk is measured by variance of returns.

**Medium-term note (MTN)**   Debt with a typical maturity of one to 10 years that is offered regularly by a company using the same procedure as commercial paper.

**Merger**   Acquisition in which all assets and liabilities are absorbed by the buyer (cf. *exchange of assets*, *exchange of shares*). More generally, any combination of two companies.

**Mismatch bond**   *Floating-rate note* whose interest rate is reset at more frequent intervals than the rollover period (e.g. a note whose payments are set quarterly on the basis of the one-year interest rate).

**Money market**   Market for short-term safe investments.

**Monte Carlo simulation**   Method for calculating the probability distribution of possible outcomes, e.g. from a project.

**Moral hazard**   The risk that the existence of a contract will change the behaviour of one or both parties to the contract; e.g. an insured firm may take fewer fire precautions.

**Mortgage bond**   *Bond* secured against plant and equipment.

**MTN**   *Medium-term note*.

**Multiple-discriminant analysis (MDA)**   Statistical technique for distinguishing between two groups on the basis of their observed characteristics.

**Mutually exclusive projects**   Two projects that cannot both be undertaken.

**Naked option**   Option held on its own, i.e. not used to hedge a holding in the asset or other options.

**Negative pledge clause**   Clause under which the borrower agrees not to permit an exclusive *lien* on any of its assets.

**Net lease**   *Lease* in which the *lessee* promises to maintain and insure the equipment (cf. *full-service lease*).

**Net present value (NPV)**   A project's net contribution to wealth—*present value* minus initial investment.

**Net working capital**   *Current assets* minus *current liabilities*.

**Net worth**   Book value of a company's ordinary shares and retained earnings.

**NIF**   *Note issuance facility*.

**Nominal interest rate**   Interest rate expressed in money terms (cf. *real interest rate*).

**Non-refundable debt**   Debt that may not be called in order to replace it with another issue at a lower interest cost.

**Normal distribution**   Symmetric bell-shaped distribution that can be completely defined by its mean and *standard deviation*.

**Note**   A short-term debt security usually issued at a discount to its face value.

**Note issuance facility (NIF)**   In the eurocurrency market, a facility that guarantees the company the right to borrow from a group of banks up to some agreed maximum.

**NYSE**   New York Stock Exchange.

**Off-balance-sheet financing**   Financing that is not shown as a liability in a company's balance sheet.

**Old-line factoring**   *Factoring* arrangement that provides collection, insurance and finance for *accounts receivable*.

**Open account**   Arrangement whereby sales are made with no formal debt contract. The buyer signs a receipt, and the seller records the sale in the sales ledger.

**Open-end mortgage**   Mortgage against which additional debt may be issued (cf. *closed-end mortgage*).

**Operating lease**   Short-term, cancellable *lease* (cf. *financial lease*).

**Operating leverage**   Fixed operating costs, so called because they accentuate variations in profits (cf. *financial leverage*).

**Opportunity cost of capital** (*hurdle rate*, *cost of capital*)   *Expected return* that is forgone by investing in a project rather than in comparable financial securities.

**Option**   See *call option*, *put option*.

**Option delta**   *Hedge ratio*.

**Out-of-the-money option**   An option that would not be worth exercising if it matured immediately (cf. *in-the-money option*).

**Par value** (*face value*)   Value of security shown on certificate.

**Pass-through securities**   *Notes* or *bonds* backed by a package of assets (e.g. mortgage pass-throughs).

**Payables**   *Accounts payable*.

**Payback period**   Time taken for a project to recover its initial investment.

**Payout ratio**   *Dividend* as a proportion of earnings per share.

**Perpetuity**   A cash flow that continues forever. It has the same value every period, or grows at a constant rate.

**P/E (or price-earnings) ratio**   Share price divided by earnings per share.

**Poison pill**   An issue of securities that is convertible, in the event of a *merger*, into the shares of the acquiring firm or must be repurchased by the acquiring firm.

**Poison put**   A *covenant* allowing the *bond*holder to demand repayment in the event of a hostile merger.

**Pooling of interest**   Method of accounting for *mergers*. The consolidated balance sheet of the merged firm is obtained by combining the balance sheets of the separate firms.

**Post-audit**   Evaluation of an investment project after it has been undertaken.

**Pre-emptive right**   Ordinary shareholder's right to anything of value distributed by the company.

**Preference shares**   Shares that take priority over ordinary shares in regard to *dividends*. Dividends may not be paid on ordinary shares until the dividend is paid on all preference shares (cf. *cumulative preference shares*). The dividend rate on preferred is usually fixed at time of issue.

**Present value (PV)**   Discounted value of future cash flows.

**Present value of growth opportunities**   The value of the company that derives from the company's future investment opportunities.

**Price of risk**   The extra return investors require for each additional unit of risk that they bear.

**Primary market**   The market in which securities are first sold, where the issuer sells to investors.

**Prime rate**   Rate at which banks lend to their most favoured customers.

**Principal**   Amount of debt that must be repaid.

**Privileged subscription issue**   *Rights issue.*

**Profitability index** (*benefit-cost ratio*)   Ratio of a project's *present value* to the initial investment.

**Pro-forma**   Projected.

**Project finance**   Debt that is largely a claim against the cash flows from a particular project rather than against the firm as a whole.

**Projected-benefit cost method**   *Level cost method.*

**Promissory note**   Promise to pay.

**Prospectus**   Summary statement providing information on an issue of securities.

**Proxy vote**   Vote cast by one person on behalf of another.

**Put option**   Option to sell an asset at a specified *exercise price* on or before a specified exercise date (cf. *call option*).

**q ratio**   The ratio of the market value of an asset to its replacement cost.

**Quadratic programming**   Variant of *linear programming*, where the equations are quadratic rather than linear.

**Quick ratio** (*acid-test ratio*)   Measure of liquidity: (*current assets* – inventory) divided by *current liabilities*.

**Real assets**   *Tangible assets* and *intangible assets* used to carry on business (cf. *financial assets*).

**Real interest rate**   Interest rate expressed in terms of real goods, i.e. *nominal interest rate* adjusted for inflation.

**Real options**   Valuable future choices that arise when investing in real assets, e.g. the option to expand if things go well.

**Receivables**   *Accounts receivable.*

**Record date**   Date set by directors when making dividend payment. *Dividends* are sent to shareholders who are registered on the record date.

**Recourse**   Term describing a type of loan. If a loan is with recourse, the lender has a general claim against the parent company if the *collateral* is insufficient to repay the debt.

**Registered security**   A security where the record of ownership is maintained in a central registry.

**Regression analysis**   In statistics, a technique for finding the line of best fit.

**Regular dividend**   *Dividend* that the company expects to maintain in the future.

**Rental lease**   *Full-service lease.*

**Repo**   *Repurchase agreement.*

**Repurchase agreement** (*RP, repo*)   Purchase of Treasury securities from a securities dealer with an agreement that the dealer will repurchase them at a specified price.

**Required return**   The return investors require from a particular asset before they will invest in it.

**Residual risk**   *Unique risk.*

**Retained earnings**   Earnings not paid out as *dividends*.

**Return on equity** (*ROE*)   Usually, equity earnings as a proportion of the book value of equity.

**Return on investment** (*ROI*)   Generally, book income as a proportion of net book value or investment.

**Reverse FRN** (*bull FRN*)   *Floating-rate note* whose payments rise as the general level of interest rates falls, and vice versa.

**Revolving credit**   Legally assured *line of credit* with a bank.

**Revolving underwriting facility** (*RUF*)   Issuance facility for short-term euronotes.

**Rights issue** (*privileged subscription issue*)   Issue of securities that is offered to current shareholders (cf. *general cash offer*).

**Rights on**   A share sold with rights to a new issue still attached.

**Risk premium**   Expected additional return for making a risky investment rather than a safe one.

**ROE** *Return on equity.*

**ROI** *Return on investment.*

**RP** *Repurchase agreement.*

**R squared** ($R^2$) Square of the *correlation coefficient*—the proportion of the variability in one series that can be explained by the variability of one or more other series.

**Sale and lease-back** Sale of an existing asset to a financial institution that then leases it back to the user (cf. *direct lease*).

**Salvage value** Scrap value of plant and equipment.

**Samurai bond** A yen *bond* issued in Tokyo by a non-Japanese borrower (cf. *bulldog bond, Yankee bond*).

**Seasoned issue** Issue of a security for which there is an existing market (cf. *unseasoned issue*).

**Secondary market** Market in which one can buy or sell *seasoned issues* of securities.

**Secured debt** Debt that, in the event of default, has first claim on specified assets.

**Securitisation** Substituting tradable securities for privately negotiated instruments.

**Security market line** Line representing the relationship between *expected return* and *market risk*.

**Self-liquidating loan** Loan to finance *current assets*. The sale of the current assets provides the cash to repay the loan.

**Semi-strong form efficient market** Market in which security prices reflect all publicly available information (cf. *weak-form efficient market* and *strong-form efficient market*).

**Senior debt** Debt that, in the event of bankruptcy, must be repaid before *subordinated debt* receives any payment.

**Sensitivity analysis** Analysis of the effect on project profitability of possible changes in sales, costs, and so on.

**Shareholder clientele** A group of shareholders who hold shares in a particular firm because that firm's dividend policy suits them.

**Shogun bond** Dollar *bond* issued in Japan by a non-resident.

**Short hedge** Entering a contract to hedge future decreases in the spot price of an asset or commodity (cf. *long hedge*)

**Short sale** Sale of a security that the investor does not own.

**Sight draft** Demand for immediate payment (cf. *time draft*).

**Signal** Action that demonstrates an individual's unobservable characteristics (because it would be unduly costly for someone without those characteristics to take the action).

**Simple interest** Interest calculated only on the initial investment (cf. *compound interest*).

**Simulation** *Monte Carlo simulation.*

**Sinking fund** Fund that is established by a company to retire debt before maturity.

**Skewed distribution** Probability distribution in which an unequal number of observations lie below and above the mean.

**Special dividend** (*extra dividend*) Dividend that is unlikely to be repeated.

**Specific risk** *Unique risk.*

**Spot exchange rate** Exchange rate on currency for immediate delivery (cf. *forward exchange rate*).

**Spot interest rate** Interest rate fixed today on a loan that is made today (cf. *forward interest rate*).

**Spot price** The current price of an asset for immediate delivery of that asset.

**Share split** 'Free' issue of shares to existing shareholders.

**Shark-repellent** Change to the company's articles of association designed to repel potential bidders.

**Standard deviation** Square root of the *variance*—a measure of variability.

**Standard error** In statistics, a measure of the possible error in an estimate.

**Straddle** The combination of a *put option* and a *call option* with the same exercise price.

**Striking price** *Exercise price* of an *option*.

**Stripped bond** A *bond* that can be subdivided into a series of *zero coupon bonds*.

**Strong-form efficient market** Market in which security prices reflect instantaneously all information available to investors (cf. *weak-form efficient market* and *semi-strong form efficient market*).

**Subordinated debt** (*junior debt*) Debt over which *senior debt* takes priority. In the event of bankruptcy, subordinated debtholders receive payment only after senior debt is paid off in full.

**Sum-of-the-years-digits depreciation** Method of *accelerated depreciation*.

**Sunk costs** Costs that have been incurred and cannot be reversed.

**Sushi bond** A *eurobond* issued by a Japanese corporation.

**Swap** An arrangement whereby two companies lend to each other on different terms, e.g. in different currencies, or one at a fixed rate and the other at a floating rate.

**Synergy** The source of value where the combined value of a merged entity is greater than the sum of its parts.

**Systematic risk** *Market risk.*

**Takeover** One company obtains control of another company.

**Tangible assets** Physical assets such as plant, machinery and offices (cf. *intangible assets*).

**Tender offer** General offer made directly to a firm's shareholders to buy their shares.

**Tender panel** Panel of underwriting banks established to bid for *notes* issued under a *note issuance facility*.

**Term loans** Medium-term, privately placed loans, usually made by banks.

**Term structure of interest rates**   Relationship between interest rates on loans of different maturities (cf. *yield curve*).

**Time draft**   Demand for payment at a stated future date (cf. *sight draft*).

**Times interest earned** (*interest cover*)   Earnings before interest and tax, divided by interest payments.

**Time-weighted rate of return**   Rate of return that gives equal weight to each time period; used in investment performance measurement (cf. *dollar-weighted rate of return*).

**Trade acceptance**   Written demand that has been accepted by an industrial company to pay a given sum at a future date (cf. *bank acceptance*).

**Trade credit**   *Accounts receivable*.

**Trade debt**   *Accounts payable*.

**Treasury note**   Short-term discount debt maturing in less than one year, issued regularly by the government.

**Two-tier tax system** (synonymous with classical tax system)   A tax system where taxes are levied on both companies' income and investors' income from investing in those companies.

**Underpricing**   Issue of securities below their market value.

**Underwriter** (*investment banker*)   Firm that buys an issue of securities from a company and resells it to investors.

**Unfunded debt**   Debt maturing within one year (cf. *funded debt*).

**Unique risk** (*residual risk, specific risk, unsystematic risk*)   Risk that can be eliminated by diversification.

**Unseasoned issue**   Issue of a security for which there is no existing market (cf. *seasoned issue*).

**Unsystematic risk**   *Unique risk*.

**Value additivity**   Rule that the value of the whole must equal the sum of the values of the parts.

**Variance**   Mean squared deviation from the expected value—a measure of variability.

**Variation margin**   The daily gains or losses on a *futures contract* that are credited to the investor's margin account.

**Venture capital**   Capital to finance a new firm (cf. *development capital*).

**Vertical merger**   *Merger* between a supplier and its customer (cf. *horizontal merger*, *conglomerate merger*).

**Vertical spread**   The simultaneous purchase and sale of two options that differ only in their exercise price (cf. *horizontal spread*).

**Warehouse receipt**   Evidence that a firm owns goods stored in a warehouse.

**Warrant**   Long-term *call option* issued by a company.

**Weak-form efficient market**   Market in which security prices instantaneously reflect the information in the history of security prices. In such a market, security prices follow a random walk (cf. *semi-strong form efficient market* and *strong-form efficient market*).

**Weighted average cost of capital**   *Expected return* on a portfolio of all the firm's securities. Used as *hurdle rate* for capital investment.

**White knight**   A friendly potential acquirer sought out by a target company threatened by a less welcome suitor.

**With dividend** (*cum-dividend*)   Term describing a purchase of shares by which the buyer is entitled to the forthcoming *dividend* (cf. *ex-dividend*).

**With rights** (*cum-rights, rights on*)   Purchase of shares in which the buyer is entitled to the rights to buy shares in the company's *rights issue* (cf. *ex-rights*).

**Withholding tax**   Tax levied on *dividends* paid abroad.

**Working capital**   *Current assets* and *current liabilities*. The term is commonly used as synonymous with *net working capital*.

**Writer**   *Option* seller.

**Yankee bond**   An American dollar denominated bond issued in the United States by a non-American issuer.

**Yield curve**   *Term structure of interest rates*.

**Yield to maturity**   *Internal rate of return* on a *bond*.

**Zero coupon bond**   *Discount bond* making no *coupon* payments.

index

# SOME COMMONLY USED SYMBOLS

| | |
|---|---|
| APV | Adjusted present value |
| BV | Book value |
| $C_t$ | Cash flow at time $t$ |
| $CEQ_t$ | Certainty-equivalent cash flow at time $t$ |
| $DIV_t$ | Dividend payment at time $t$ |
| $D$ | Market value of firm's debt |
| $DEP_t$ | Depreciation in year $t$ |
| $DF_t$ | Discount factor for cash flow in period $t$ |
| $e$ | 2.718 (base for natural logarithms) |
| $E$ | Market value of firm's equity |
| $EPS_t$ | Earnings per share in year $t$ |
| EX | Exercise price of option |
| $f_t$ | Expected return on a one-period forward loan maturing at time $t$ |
| $f_{\$/£}$ | Forward rate of exchange between dollars and pounds |
| $g$ | Growth rate |
| $i_t$ | Expected inflation in year $t$ |
| IRR | Internal rate of return |
| $L_j$ | Project's contribution to firm's debt capacity as proportion of project value |
| $LCF_t$ | Lease's cash outflow in year $t$ |
| NPV | Net present value |
| $P_t$ | Price at time $t$ |
| PV | Present value |
| PVGO | Present value of growth opportunities |
| $r_t$ | Expected rate of return (or cost of capital) in period $t$. We omit the subscript where the expected return is identical in each period. Sometimes we use a *second* subscript to define the date at which the investment is made. Thus, $_{t-1}r_t$ is the (spot) rate of return on an investment made at $t-1$ and paying off at time $t$. |

| | |
|---|---|
| $\tilde{r}_t$ | Uncertain actual rate of return in period $t$ |
| $r_D$ | Rate of return on firm's debt |
| $r_E$ | Expected rate of return on firm's equity |
| $r_f$ | Risk-free interest rate |
| $r_m$ | Expected rate of return on the market portfolio |
| $r_\$$ | Dollar rate of interest |
| $r^*$ | Adjusted cost of capital |
| $s_{SFr/\$}$ | Spot rate of exchange between Swiss francs and dollars |
| $t$ | Time |
| $T_c$ | Rate of corporate income tax |
| $T_p$ | Rate of personal income tax |
| $V$ | Market value of firm: $V = D + E$ |
| $\beta$ | Beta: a measure of market risk |
| $\delta$ | Delta: hedge ratio |
| $\lambda$ | Lambda: market price of risk $= \dfrac{r_m - r_f}{\sigma_m^2}$ |
| $\rho_{12}$ | Rho: correlation coefficient between investments 1 and 2 |
| $\sigma$ | Sigma: standard deviation |
| $\sigma_{12}$ | Sigma: covariance of investment 1 with investment 2 |
| $\sigma^2$ | Sigma squared: variance |
| $\Sigma$ | Capital sigma: 'the sum of' |

# SOME USEFUL FORMULAS

*(The section number indicates the principal reference in the text.)*

**Perpetuity** (3.2)
The value of a perpetuity of $1 per year is:

$$PV = \frac{1}{r}$$

**Annuity** (3.2)
The value of annuity of $1 per period for $t$ years ($t$-year annuity factor) is:

$$PV = \frac{1}{r} - \frac{1}{r(1 + r)^t}$$

**A growing perpetuity** (the 'Gordon' model) (3.2)
If the initial cash flow is $1 at year 1 and if cash flows thereafter grow at a constant rate of $g$ in perpetuity,

$$PV = \frac{1}{r - g}$$

**Continuous compounding** (3.3)
If $r$ is the continuously compounded rate of interest, the present value of $1 received in year $t$ is:

$$PV = \frac{1}{e^{rt}}$$

**Equivalent annual cash flow or cost** (6.3)
If an asset has a life of $t$ years, the equivalent annual cash flow is:

$$\frac{PV(costs)}{t\text{-year annuity factor}}$$

**Measures of risk** (7.2 to 7.4)

Variance of returns $= \sigma^2$
$\qquad\qquad = $ expected value of $(\tilde{r} - r)^2$

Standard deviation of returns $= \sqrt{variance}$
$\qquad\qquad\qquad\qquad\quad = \sigma$

Covariance between returns of shares 1 and 2
$= \sigma_{12}$
$=$ expected value of $[(\tilde{r}_1 - r_1)(\tilde{r}_2 - r_2)]$

Correlation between returns of shares 1 and 2
$= \rho_{12} = \dfrac{\sigma_{12}}{\sigma_1 \sigma_2}$

Beta of share $i = \beta_i = \dfrac{\sigma_{im}}{\sigma_m^2}$

The variance of returns on a portfolio with proportion $x_i$ invested in share $i$ is:

$$\sum_{i=1}^{N}\sum_{j=1}^{N} x_i x_j \sigma_{ij}$$

**Capital asset pricing model** (8.3)
The expected risk premium on a risky investment is:

$$r - r_f = \beta(r_m - r_f)$$

**Capital asset pricing model (certainty-equivalent form)** (Chapter 9 appendix)
The present value of a one-period risky investment is:

$$PV = \frac{C_1 - \lambda Cov(\tilde{C}_1, \tilde{r}_m)}{1 + r_f}$$

where

$$\lambda = \frac{r_m - r_f}{\sigma_m^2}$$

**Adjusted cost of capital** (19.2 and 19.3)
If $r$ is the cost of capital under all-equity financing, the adjusted cost of capital is:

MM formula:

$$r^* = r(1 - T_C L)$$

Miles–Ezzell formula:

$$r^* = r - r_D T_C L \frac{1 + r}{1 + r_D}$$

Weighted average cost of capital formula:

$$r^* = r_D(1 - T_C)\frac{D}{V} + r_E \frac{E}{V}$$

**Relationship between the value of a call and a put** (20.2)
The relationship between the value of a European call and a European put is:

Value of call + present value of exercise price
$\qquad\qquad = $ value of put + share price

**Black–Scholes formula for value of a call (20.5)**

Present value of call option
$$= PN(d_1) - EXe^{-r_f t}N(d_2)$$

where $d_1 = \dfrac{\log (P/EX) + r_f t + \sigma^2 t/2}{\sigma\sqrt{t}}$

$d_2 = \dfrac{\log (P/EX) + r_f t - \sigma^2 t/2}{\sigma\sqrt{t}}$

$N(d)$ = cumulative normal probability density function

$EX$ = exercise price of option

$t$ = time to exercise date

$P$ = price of asset now

$\sigma^2$ = variance per period of (continuously compounded) rate of return on the asset

$r_f$ = (continuously compounded) risk-free rate of interest

**Inputs to binomial option valuation Model (21.2)**

Upside change $= u = e^{(\sigma\sqrt{h})} - 1$

Downside change $= d = e^{(-\sigma\sqrt{h})} - 1$

Probability of upside change in risk-neutral world $= p = \dfrac{r_f - d}{u - d}$

where $\sigma$ = standard deviation of price changes per period

$h$ = number of step jumps per period

**Value of a future (25.3)**

$$\frac{\text{Futures price}}{(1 + r_f)^t} = \begin{array}{c}\text{spot} \\ \text{price}\end{array} + PV\left(\begin{array}{c}\text{storage} \\ \text{costs}\end{array}\right)$$

$$- PV\left(\begin{array}{c}\text{convenience} \\ \text{yield}\end{array}\right)$$

**Value of lease (26.3)**

If $LCF_t$ is the lease's cash outflow in period $t$, the value of an $N$-period lease of an asset costing INV is:

$$INV - \sum_{t=0}^{N} \frac{LCF_t}{[1 + r(1 - T_c)]^t}$$

**Cash inventory models (31.1)**

Baumol model:

Optimum amount of securities sold

$$= \sqrt{\frac{2 \times \begin{array}{c}\text{annual cash} \\ \text{disbursements}\end{array} \times \begin{array}{c}\text{cost per sale} \\ \text{of securities}\end{array}}{\text{interest rate}}}$$

Miller–Orr model:

Spread between upper and lower cash balance limits

$$= 3\left(\frac{3}{4} \times \frac{\begin{array}{c}\text{transaction} \\ \text{cost}\end{array} \times \begin{array}{c}\text{variance of} \\ \text{cash flows}\end{array}}{\text{interest rate}}\right)^{1/3}$$

**Interest rate parity (34.2)**

$$\frac{1 + r_{SFr}}{1 + r_{\$}} = \frac{f_{SFr/\$}}{s_{SFr/\$}}$$